SELECTED ACRONYMS	MEANING
GF	General Fund
GFOA	Government Finance Officers Association
GLTL	General Long-Term Liability
ISF	Internal Service Fund
ITF	Investment Trust Fund
MD&A	Management's Discussion and Analysis
MFAP	Major Federal Assistance Program
MFBA	Measurement Focus and Basis of Accounting
NCGA	National Council on Governmental Accounting (succeeded by GASB)
NPO	Net Pension Obligation (in government chapters); Not-for-Profit Organization elsewhere
OFS	Other Financing Sources
OFU	Other Financing Uses
OMB	Office of Management and Budget (U.S.)
ONPO	Other Not-for-Profit Organization(s)
OPEB	Other Postemployment Benefits
PERS	Public Employee Retirement System
PF	Permanent Fund
PG	Primary Government
PPTF	Private-Purpose Trust Fund
PTF	Pension Trust Fund(s)
RAN	Revenue Anticipation Note
RL	Related Liabilities (in governmental fund accounting equation)
RSI	Required Supplementary Information
SAS	Statements on Auditing Standards (AICPA)
SEC	Securities and Exchange Commission (U.S.)
SFAS	Statement of Financial Accounting Standards
SFFAS	Statement of Federal Financial Accounting Standards
SGL	Standard General Ledger (Federal)
SLG	State and Local Government
SRF	Special Revenue Fund(s)
TAN	Tax Anticipation Note
VHWO	Voluntary Health & Welfare Organization

GOVERNMENTAL AND NONPROFIT ACCOUNTING

GOVERNMENTAL AND NONPROFIT ACCOUNTING

Theory and Practice

TENTH EDITION

Robert J. Freeman
Texas Tech University

Craig D. Shoulders
Western Carolina University

Gregory S. Allison
University of North Carolina
Chapel Hill

G. Robert Smith, Jr.
Middle Tennessee State University

PEARSON

Boston   Columbus   Indianapolis   New York   San Francisco   Upper Saddle River   Amsterdam
Cape Town   Dubai   London   Madrid   Milan   Munich   Paris   Montreal   Toronto   Delhi
Mexico City   São Paulo   Sydney   Hong Kong   Seoul   Singapore   Taipei   Tokyo

Editor in Chief: Donna Battista
Director, Editorial Services: Ashley Santora
Project Manager, Editorial: Christina Rumbaugh
Editorial Assistants: Jane Avery and Lauren Zanedis
Marketing Manager: Alison Haskins
Marketing Assistant: Kimberly Lovato
Managing Editor: Nancy Fenton
Senior Production Project Manager: Roberta Sherman
Manufacturing Buyer: Carol Melville
Interior Design: BookMasters, Inc.

Cover Design: Anthony Gemmellaro
Creative Director: Blair Brown
Cover Illustration/Photo: © Brad Pict/Fotolia; © Dennis MacDonald / Alamy
Composition: S4Carlisle Publishing Services
Full-Service Project Management: Lynn Steines, S4Carlisle Publishing Services
Printer/Binder: Edwards Brothers Malloy Hagerstown
Typeface: 10.5/12 Times Ten LT Std

Credits and acknowledgments borrowed from other sources and reproduced, with permission, in this textbook appear on appropriate page within text.

Library of Congress Cataloging-in-Publication Data

Governmental and nonprofit accounting : theory and practice / Robert J. Freeman ... [et al.].—10th ed.
   p. cm.
  Includes index.
  ISBN-13: 978-0-13-275126-1
  ISBN-10: 0-13-275126-7
  1. Municipal finance—United States—Accounting. 2. Local finance—United States—Accounting. 3. Finance, Public—United States—Accounting. 4. Fund accounting—United States. 5. Nonprofit organizations—United States—Accounting.
I. Freeman, Robert J.
  HJ9777.A3L95 2012
  657′.83500973—dc23

2012014529

10 9 8 7 6 5 4 3 2

www.pearsonhighered.com

ISBN-10: 0-13-275126-7
ISBN-13: 978-0-13-275126-1

"Honor your father and your mother" is an easy directive to follow when blessed with loving, dedicated, and self-sacrificing parents. Each of us received the blessing of being loved, taught, encouraged, and supported by such parents—loving, hardworking, honest, and devoted men and women: truly the salt of the earth. We are thankful to be able to honor their memories and that of "Mamma B"—Beverly Freeman's mom, who touched each of our lives in her special ways. It is with genuine pride in them and thankfulness for them that we lovingly dedicate this edition of our text in memory of our parents:

E. H. & Edna May Freeman
Andy and Billye Shoulders
Paul and Wilma Allison
Bob and Jean Smith
and to
Bertie Farley—"Mamma B"

Brief Contents

Contents

Preface

Governmental and Nonprofit Accounting: Theory and Practice, **10th edition,** continues its tradition as a comprehensive, practice-relevant, up-to-date textbook covering state and local government, federal government, and not-for-profit organization accounting, financial reporting, and auditing. Changes in the 10th edition further enhance students' ability to maximize their knowledge and understanding at the lowest possible "cost." The Governmental Accounting Standards Board (GASB) adoption of four new standards impacting all state and local government financial statements and the Government Accountability Office's issuance of revised generally accepted government auditing standards (GAGAS) required the timely development of the 10th edition in keeping with our philosophy that what students learn in the accounting classroom should correlate highly with what they must understand and apply on the CPA examination and as professional accountants.

EYES OF THE LEARNER MOTIVATED CHANGES

Changes made specifically to allow students to master content more efficiently were identified by continuing to examine the text "through the eyes of the learner" and include:

- Chapter 10, "Enterprise Funds"—Content was reorganized so students are introduced to Enterprise Fund concepts, entries, and financial statements in a simple context. Then, additional complexities, including the use of restricted asset accounting and refundings, are added; and a more advanced set of financial statements for Enterprise Funds is presented.
- Chapter 14, "Financial Reporting: Deriving Government-Wide Financial Statements and Required Reconciliations"—The chapter is shortened, and the two-worksheet approach to deriving government-wide financial statements is discussed in terms of converting the governmental funds financial statement equation to the corresponding government-wide financial statement equation. Then the approach is illustrated using this construct for explanation and without journal entries.
- Chapter 16, "Non-SLG Not-for-Profit Organizations"—The accounting and reporting for restricted contributions, restricted investment income, and related net assets released from restrictions are illustrated more simply to permit quicker and more complete comprehension.

GAAP AND GAGAS DRIVEN CHANGES

All four of the key new GASB Statements will be in effect by the time students who use this text graduate. These statements contain guidance relevant to 13 of the 15 chapters on state and local government accounting as well as the chapters on health care accounting and college and university accounting. The statements are:

- *Statement No. 61,* "The Financial Reporting Entity: Omnibus, an amendment of GASB Statements No. 14 and No. 34," which makes the most significant changes in the criteria for determining a government's reporting entity and in the criteria for blending component units since *Statement No. 14* became effective in 1993.
- *Statement No. 62,* "Codification of Accounting and Financial Reporting Guidance Contained in Pre-November 30, 1989 FASB and AICPA Pronouncements"
- *Statement No. 63,* "Reporting Deferred Outflows of Resources, Deferred Inflows of Resources, and Net Position"
- *Statement No. 65,* "Reporting Items Previously Recognized as Assets and Liabilities"

Together with GASB *Statement No. 54,* which we incorporated in the revised 9th edition of the text, these statements constitute the most significant and pervasive changes in government financial reporting since the implementation of the new reporting model established in GASB *Statement No. 34.*

Changes required by these statements include the following:

- Chapter 2, "State and Local Government Accounting and Financial Reporting Model: The Foundation," is revised to include the definitions and discussion of two new financial statement elements—deferred outflows of resources and deferred inflows of resources. These new elements are included in the accounting equations for the three fund categories and in the financial statement formats illustrated in the chapter.

- Chapter 3, "The General Fund and Special Revenue Funds," points out the most common examples of deferred items in these fund types and incorporates the new elements in discussing the basic accounting and reporting requirements.

- Chapter 4, "Budgeting, Budgetary Accounting, and Budgetary Reporting," includes deferred inflows in the Harvey City Comprehensive Case that begins in the end of chapter material.

- Chapter 5, "Revenue Accounting—Governmental Funds," distinguishes liabilities for unearned revenues from deferred inflows of resources and illustrates accounting and reporting for the most common deferred inflows of resources in governmental funds—revenues deferred because they are not available and taxes collected in advance.

- Chapter 7, "Capital Projects Funds," continues to illustrate the presentation of deferred inflows of resources in governmental funds and discusses the GASB *Statement No. 65* requirement to not capitalize most bond issue costs—even in the government-wide financial statements.

- Chapter 8, "Debt Service Funds," contains the most extensive examples of the presentation of deferred inflows of resources in governmental funds, including deferred inflows related to special assessment projects. The chapter also introduces refunding transactions, which will be the source of a common deferred ouflow/deferred inflow item presented in the government-wide financial statements.

- Chapter 9, "General Capital Assets; General Long-Term Liabilities; Permanent Funds: Introduction to Interfund-GCA-GLTL Accounting," illustrates the new treatment of bond issue costs and is updated as necessary for the provisions of GASB *Statement No. 62*.

- Chapter 10, "Enterprise Funds," includes the new statement of net position and illustrates accounting for deferred outflows and deferred inflows from refunding transactions in a flows of economic resources context. The impact of *Statements Nos. 63 and 65* on the computation and presentation of net position categories also is discussed and illustrated here. The chapter is updated as necessary for *Statement No. 62*.

- Chapter 11, "Internal Service Funds," continues the presentation of the statement of net position for proprietary funds as required by *Statements Nos. 63 and 65*.

- Chapter 12, "Trust and Agency (Fiduciary) Funds: Summary of Interfund-GCA-GLTL Accounting," illustrates the presentation of the new statement of net position in the context of trust funds.

- Chapter 13, "Financial Reporting: The Basic Financial Statements and Required Supplementary Information," discusses and illustrates the government-wide statement of net position—including presentation of deferred outflows of resources and deferred inflows of resources in that statement—as well as in the various fund financial statements. The effect of deferred outflows and deferred inflows on the quantitative tests for major funds also is explained.

- Chapter 14, "Financial Reporting: Deriving Government-Wide Financial Statements and Required Reconciliations," illustrates the required conversion of certain deferred outflow/inflow items and their impact on the reconciliation of total fund balance of governmental funds to governmental activities total net position.

- Chapter 15, "Financial Reporting: The Comprehensive Annual Financial Report and the Financial Reporting Entity," incorporates the new reporting entity definition criteria adopted in *Statement No. 61* as well as the new criteria for blending.

- Chapters 4 to 15 contain revisions in the continuous Harvey City case—which is designed to be completed using Excel spreadsheets—to modify it according to the relevant changes in GASB *Statements Nos. 62, 63, and 65*.

- Chapter 17, "Accounting for Colleges and Universities," has been revised to incorporate the new statement of net position for governmental colleges and universities.

- Chapter 18, "Accounting for Health Care Organizations," has been updated for *Statements Nos. 62, 63, and 65* for government hospitals and for various modifications to FASB standards that affect not-for-profit hospitals.

Changes were also required in Chapters 19 and 20.

- Chapter 19, "Federal Government Accounting," required only minimal updating.
- Chapter 20, "Auditing Governments and Not-for-Profit Organizations," has been rewritten to reflect the recently approved revision of the GAO's "Yellow Book"—i.e., generally accepted **government** auditing standards—as well as certain changes in single audits and the latest AICPA auditing standards and reports.

In addition:

- End-of-chapter questions, exercises, and problems in each of these chapters were revised to be consistent with the GASB *Statement No. 54* changes.
- New end-of-chapter questions, exercises, and problems were added that address selected requirements of new standards.

CUSTOMIZATION FRIENDLY DESIGN

As in the past, the text design allows professors to tailor their courses to their students' needs and priorities. Therefore, the breadth of topics is wider than is covered in the typical government and not-for-profit accounting course. Chapters that tend to be among the ones omitted are constructed to permit their omission without harming the flow of a course.

LEARNING FRIENDLY

The 10th edition also continues to incorporate the building block approach to the learning process consistent with the following philosophy:

- Mastering governmental and not-for-profit accounting concepts, principles, and practices involves progressing through many different phases of knowledge and understanding.
- Learning efficiency and effectiveness requires this progression to follow a logical sequence.
- Logical sequencing keeps the next concept to be learned accessible from the base provided by the concepts learned already. (Students learn more in less time when taken through the right steps.)
- Efficiently achieving more advanced levels of learning and knowledge requires attaining any prerequisite knowledge first.
- Having this base of prior knowledge and understanding facilitates learning the new information and ideas.

This approach should guide both the ordering of chapters and the sequencing of material within a chapter. The learning process should take full advantage of the business accounting background the learner likely brings into the course.

OTHER POINTS OF DISTINCTION

Other key features of the text, in addition to the learner orientation, flow from our teaching philosophies and goals, including:

- Integrating the *computerized Harvey City Case* throughout Chapters 4 to 15 to simulate the experience of accounting and reporting for a small city
- Providing a second simpler comprehensive case for those who may not be able to devote adequate time to the Harvey City case
- Correlation with professional practice, enhanced by:
    - Using a practice-relevant, conversion worksheet approach to develop government-wide financial statement data
    - Integrating practice examples for teaching purposes throughout the state and local government accounting, reporting, and auditing chapters
    - Incorporating case problems developed from actual state and local government financial reports in the end-of-chapter materials

INSTRUCTOR SUPPLEMENTS

Supplements for the tenth edition of *Governmental and Nonprofit Accounting* are available for download by instructors only at Pearson's Instructor Resource center at www.pearsonhighered.com/IRC. Resources include a comprehensive case covering a small government, an Instructor's Manual, Solutions Manual, Excel solution templates for the Harvey City Comprehensive Case and for selected problems, Test Item File, and a PowerPoint presentation.

ACKNOWLEDGMENTS

We are grateful for the excellent input provided by numerous individuals that led to improvements in the 9th edition of the text. In addition to those who have made suggestions via personal discussions and correspondence, others responded to our surveys soliciting feedback and suggestions. Still others reviewed all or part of the 9th edition of the text and provided helpful recommendations. We thank Dwayne McSwain of Appalachian State University for his roles in the development of the 10th edition.

A few individuals have made significant contributions to several editions of this text. We offer special thanks to:

David R. Bean, GASB Director of Research and Technical Activities, and the GASB staff members

Mary K. Foelster, AICPA, Director of the Governmental Audit Quality Center

Stephen Gauthier, Government Finance Officers Association, Director, Technical Services

We appreciate the support and professional commitment of the development, marketing, production, and editorial staff at Pearson. We particularly appreciate the efforts of Donna Battista, Editor-in-Chief; Christina Rumbaugh, Editorial Project Manager; Roberta Sherman, Senior Production Project Manager; and Alison Haskins, Marketing Manager. Lynn Steines at S4Carlisle, who worked graciously with our schedule issues, made the task of reviewing page proofs as pleasant and efficient as possible both through her positive and accommodating spirit and the high quality of her, and her staff's, performance.

MOST IMPORTANTLY

Finally, we can never adequately express our love and appreciation to our wives, Beverly Freeman, Susan Allison, and Betsy Smith. Their contributions to all that we do—including the revision of this text—are essential. They encouraged, supported, and advised us as we labored over this revision and took care of many responsibilities that were rightfully ours to enable us to have the time and the energy to complete this task. Clearly, their help and support multiply what we are able to accomplish. Indeed, these incredible ladies are full partners in all that we do.

About the Authors

ROBERT J. FREEMAN

Robert J. Freeman, Ph.D., CPA, is the Distinguished Professor of Accounting Emeritus at Texas Tech University. He served on the Governmental Accounting Standards Board from 1990 to 2000 and on its predecessor, the National Council on Governmental Accounting, from 1974 to 1980. Dr. Freeman has received the Enduring Lifetime Contributions Award from the American Accounting Association Government and Nonprofit Section, the Louisiana Tech University Tower Medallion Award, and the AICPA Elijah Watt Sells Silver Medal Award.

Prior to joining the Texas Tech faculty, he was on the faculties of The University of Alabama and Louisiana Tech University, and served as national director of State and Local Government Activities at Arthur Young & Company.

Dr. Freeman has contributed numerous articles to professional journals, including *The Journal of Accountancy, Accounting Horizons, The Government Accountants Journal, Government Finance Review, The International Journal of Governmental Auditing,* and *The Journal of Public Budgeting, Accounting & Financial Management.* He has served on the editorial boards of *The Journal of Accountancy, Research in Governmental Accounting, The Journal of Accounting and Public Policy,* and *The Journal of Public Budgeting, Accounting & Financial Management.*

CRAIG D. SHOULDERS

Craig D. Shoulders, Ph.D., joined the accounting faculty of Western Carolina University in July 2012. Previously, Dr. Shoulders served on the accounting faculties at the University of North Carolina at Pembroke for 8 years and at Virginia Tech for more than 22 years.

Dr. Shoulders has received the Cornelius E. Tierney/Ernst & Young Research Award from the Association of Government Accountants and has been recognized twice by the AICPA as an Outstanding Discussion Leader. He teaches continuing education courses and seminars on governmental accounting and auditing across the country and is a past president of the Roanoke Area Chapter of the Virginia Society of CPAs. Dr. Shoulders has conducted research for the GASB on the financial reporting entity and has served on task forces on other projects.

Dr. Shoulders coauthors several continuing education courses and the government and not-for-profit sections of the ExamMatrix CPA Review. His articles have appeared in such journals as *Issues in Accounting Education, The Journal of Accountancy, Government Finance Review,* and the *Journal of Government Financial Management.* He received his bachelor's degree from Campbellsville University, his master's degree from the University of Missouri-Columbia, and his Ph.D. from Texas Tech University.

GREGORY S. ALLISON

Gregory S. Allison, CPA, is an Assistant Director and Senior Lecturer in Public Finance and Government with the University of North Carolina School of Government, where he was named the Albert and Gladys Hall Coates Term Lecturer for Teaching Excellence for the term 2002–2004. Mr. Allison has been on the faculty of the UNC School of Government since 1997.

Prior to joining the UNC faculty in Chapel Hill, Mr. Allison was an Assistant Director with the Government Finance Officers Association (GFOA) of the United States and Canada in Chicago. In this capacity, Mr. Allison assisted in administering the GFOA's Certificate of Achievement for Excellence in Financial Reporting program and Popular Annual Financial Reporting program. He led national training seminars in Introductory, Intermediate, and Advanced Governmental Accounting and Financial Reporting and authored two GFOA publications, *A Preparer's Guide to Note Disclosures* and *Accounting Issues and Practices: A Guide for Smaller Governments*. Mr. Allison began his governmental career as an auditor of governmental and not-for-profit clients with Deloitte Haskins and Sells. He then served as Finance Director of the City of Morganton, NC, for five years prior to joining the GFOA.

Mr. Allison regularly contributes articles to professional journals and publications, serves on GASB and GFOA task forces, and conducts national seminars. He was awarded the Outstanding Conference Speaker Award in both 2000 and 2001 and the Outstanding Chapter Speaker Award in both 2005 and 2006 by the North Carolina Association of Certified Public Accountants (NCACPA). He was named NCACPA's Outstanding Member in Government in 2000–2001. He is a member of the American Institute of Certified Public Accountants (AICPA), the NCACPA, the GFOA, the North Carolina GFOA, and the North Carolina Local Government Investment Association. He serves on the Board of Directors of the NCACPA and is past chair of its Governmental Accounting and Auditing Committee. Mr. Allison earned his bachelor of arts degree in accounting from North Carolina State University in 1984.

G. ROBERT SMITH, JR.

G. Robert Smith, Jr., Ph.D, CPA, CGFM, is an Associate Professor, and the Chair, in the Department of Accounting at Middle Tennessee State University. Prior to coming to MTSU, Dr. Smith was on the faculty of Auburn University, and he served in the United States Army for more than 13 years as a Finance Officer, Comptroller, and accounting instructor.

Dr. Smith, known as "Smitty," is a popular speaker and discussion leader at professional conferences and in continuing professional education seminars and courses throughout the country. He has written articles for several professional accounting publications and authored or coauthored four continuing professional education courses for the AICPA: *Governmental Accounting and Reporting: Putting It All Together; GASB No. 34 Implementation: From Here to There*; *GASB No. 34 Auditing: The Home of the Brave* (cowritten with Paul Zucconi); and *Extra Strength GASB No. 34.*

Dr. Smith has participated on Governmental Accounting Standards Board task forces for the *Implementation Guides* for GASB Statement Nos. 31 and 34 and served on the *Comprehensive Q&A* task force for 2006–2008. He was the President of the Government and Nonprofit Section of the American Accounting Association (AAA) for 2006–2007, and he was the AAA representative to the Governmental Accounting Standards Advisory Council from 2006–2011.

Dr. Smith received a bachelor of science degree from The University of Tennessee at Martin, his master of accountancy degree from The University of Tennessee at Knoxville, and his Ph.D. from Texas Tech University. His professional affiliations include the American Institute of Certified Public Accountants, the Tennessee Society of Certified Public Accountants, Government Finance Officers Association (national and Tennessee), Association of Government Accountants, and the American Accounting Association.

CHAPTER 1

Governmental and Nonprofit Accounting

Environment and Characteristics

LEARNING OBJECTIVES

After studying this chapter, you should be able to:

- Describe the key unique characteristics of government and nonprofit (G&NP) organizations.

- Discuss the major types of G&NP organizations and their importance in our economy.

- Discuss the similarities and differences between profit-seeking and G&NP organizations.

- Understand the key distinguishing characteristics, concepts, and objectives of G&NP accounting and financial reporting.

- Identify and discuss the users and uses of government financial statement information.

- Determine whether an entity is a government or a nongovernment organization for financial reporting purposes, and whether the Governmental Accounting Standards Board (GASB) or the Financial Accounting Standards Board (FASB) is the primary standards-setting body for a specific G&NP organization.

- Identify the authoritative sources of financial reporting standards for various types of G&NP organizations and the level of authority (hierarchy) of various pronouncements and guides.

Accounting and financial reporting for governments and nonprofit (G&NP) organizations, as well as G&NP auditing, are based on distinctive concepts, standards, and procedures that accommodate their environments and the needs of their financial report users. This book focuses on the most important of these concepts, standards, and procedures applicable to (1) state and local governments, including counties, cities, and school districts, as well as townships, villages, other special districts, and public authorities; (2) the federal government; and (3) nonprofit and governmental universities, hospitals, voluntary health and welfare organizations, and other nonprofit (or not-for-profit) organizations. Financial management and accountability considerations peculiar to G&NP organizations are emphasized throughout, and auditing G&NP organizations is discussed in the final chapter.

This chapter begins by introducing the characteristics and types of G&NP organizations and the objectives and nature of G&NP accounting and financial reporting. It concludes with discussions and illustrations of how to distinguish government and nongovernment organizations; the various authoritative sources of G&NP accounting principles and reporting standards, including their relative authoritativeness; and an introduction to the state and local government (SLG) accounting and financial reporting environment, concepts, objectives, and distinctive features, including funds, legally enacted budgets and appropriations, and budgetary control.

CHARACTERISTICS AND TYPES OF G&NP ORGANIZATIONS

Governments and other nonprofit organizations are unique in the following ways:

- They do not attempt to earn a profit—and most are exempt from income taxes—so typical business accounting, including income tax accounting, usually is not appropriate.

- They are owned collectively by their constituents; because ownership is not evidenced by equity shares that can be sold or traded, residents who are dissatisfied with their government must await a change in its elected governing body or move elsewhere.

- Those contributing financial resources to the organizations do not necessarily receive a direct or proportionate share of their services. For example, homeowners pay property taxes to finance public schools even if they do not have children in school.

- Their major policy decisions, and perhaps some operating decisions, typically are made by majority vote of an elected or appointed governing body (e.g., a state legislature, a city council, or a hospital board of directors) whose members serve part time, receive modest or no compensation, and have diverse backgrounds, philosophies, capabilities, and interests.

- Decisions usually must be made "in the sunshine"—in meetings open to the public, including the news media—and most have "open records" laws that make their accounting and other records open to the public.

A G&NP organization exists because a community or society decides to provide certain goods or services to its group as a whole. Often these goods or services are provided regardless of whether costs incurred will be recovered through charges for the goods or services or whether those paying for the goods or services are those benefiting from them. Indeed, many G&NP services could not be provided profitably through private enterprise. In addition, the community or society may consider these services so vital to the public well-being that they should be supervised by its elected or appointed representatives.

The major types of government and nonprofit organizations may be classified as:

1. **Governmental:** federal, state, county, municipal, township, village, and other local governmental authorities and special districts

2. **Educational:** kindergartens, elementary, and secondary schools; vocational and technical schools; and colleges and universities

3. **Health and welfare:** hospitals, nursing homes, child protection agencies, the American Red Cross, and United Service Organizations (USO)

4. **Religious:** Young Men's Christian Association (YMCA), Young Women's Christian Association (YWCA), Salvation Army, and other church-related organizations

5. **Charitable:** United Way, Community Chest, and similar fund-raising agencies; related charitable agencies; and other charitable organizations

6. **Foundations:** private trusts and corporations organized for educational, religious, or charitable purposes

This general classification scheme has much overlap among the classifications. Many charitable organizations are operated by churches, for example, and governments are deeply involved in education, health, and welfare activities.

G&NP Sector Significance Governments and other nonprofit organizations have experienced dramatic growth in recent years and are major economic, political, and social forces in our society. Indeed, the G&NP sector now accounts for more than one-third of all expenditures in the U.S. economy. The total value of financial and human resources devoted to this sector is gigantic, both absolutely and relatively.

Sound financial management—including thoughtful budgeting, proper accounting, meaningful financial reporting, and timely audits by qualified auditors—is at least as important in the G&NP sector as in the private business sector. Furthermore, because of the scope and diversity of its activities, proper management of the financial affairs of a city or town, for example, may be far more complex than that of a private business with comparable assets or annual expenditures.

As the size and complexity of governments and nonprofit organizations have increased in recent years, so have the number of career employment opportunities in this sector for college graduates majoring in accounting (and other disciplines). Likewise, the number of governmental and nonprofit organization auditing and consulting engagements with independent public accounting firms has increased significantly. Accordingly, a significant portion of the Uniform Certified Public Accountant (CPA) Examination is on G&NP accounting, financial reporting, and auditing concepts, principles, and procedures.

The G&NP Environment

G&NP organizations are similar in many ways to profit-seeking enterprises. For example:

1. They are integral parts of the same economic system and use financial, capital, and human resources to accomplish their purposes.
2. Both must acquire and convert scarce resources into their respective goods or services.
3. Both must have viable information systems, including excellent accounting systems to assure that managers, governing bodies, and others receive relevant and timely information for planning, directing, controlling, and evaluating the sources, uses, and balances of their scarce resources.
4. Cost analysis and other control and evaluation techniques are essential to ensure that resources are utilized economically, effectively, and efficiently.
5. In some cases, both produce similar products. For example, both governments and private enterprises may own and operate transportation systems, sanitation services, and electric utilities.

On the other hand, significant differences distinguish profit-seeking organizations from G&NP organizations. Broad generalizations about such a diversified group as G&NP organizations are difficult, but the major differences include (1) organizational objectives, (2) sources of financial resources, and (3) methods of evaluating performance and operating results.

Organizational Objectives

Expectation of income or gain is the principal factor that motivates investors to provide resources to profit-seeking enterprises. To the contrary:

- The objective of most governmental and nonprofit organizations is to provide as much service each year as their financial and other resources permit.
- G&NP organizations typically operate on a year-to-year basis—that is, each year they raise as many financial resources as necessary and expend them in serving their constituencies.
- They may seek to increase the amount of resources made available to them each year—and most do—but the purpose is to enable the organizations to provide more or better services, not to increase their wealth.

In sum, whereas private businesses seek to increase their wealth for the benefit of their owners, G&NP organizations seek to expend their available financial resources for the benefit of their constituencies. *Financial management in the G&NP environment thus typically focuses on acquiring and using financial resources—on sources and uses of expendable financial resources, budget status, and cash flow—rather than on net income.* Even G&NP entities whose external financial reports do not require primary emphasis on acquisition and use of financial resources emphasize this information for internal reporting and management decision-making purposes.

Sources of Financial Resources

The sources of financial resources differ between business and G&NP organizations, as well as among G&NP organizations. In the absence of a net income objective, *no distinction generally is made between invested capital and revenue of G&NP organizations. A dollar is a financial resource whether acquired through donations, user charges, sales of assets, loans, or some other manner.*

The typical nondebt sources of financial resources for business enterprises are investments by owners and sales of goods or services to customers. These sources of financing are usually not the primary sources of G&NP organizations' financial resources. Instead, G&NP organizations primarily rely on the following sources:

- Governments have the unique power to force involuntary financial resource contributions through taxation—of property, sales, and income—and all levels of government rely heavily on this power. Grants and shared revenues from other governments are also important state and local government revenue sources, as are charges for services provided.
- Religious groups and charitable organizations usually rely heavily on donations, although they may have other revenue sources.
- Some colleges and universities rely heavily on donations and income from trust funds; others depend primarily on state appropriations, federal and state grants, and/or tuition and fee charges for support.
- Hospitals and other health care organizations generally charge their clientele, although many do not admit patients solely on the basis of ability to pay. Indeed, many G&NP hospitals serve numerous charity patients and/or have large amounts of uncollectible accounts, and some hospitals rely heavily on gifts, federal and state grants, and bequests.

Other, more subtle differences in sources of G&NP organizations' financial resources as compared with profit-seeking businesses include these:

- Many services or goods provided by these organizations, such as police and fire protection, are monopolistic. Thus, an open market for objectively appraising or evaluating their value does not exist.
- User charges usually are based on the cost of the services provided rather than on supply-and-demand-related pricing policies.
- Charges levied for goods or services often cover only part of the costs incurred to provide them; for example, tuition generally covers only a fraction of the cost of operating state colleges or universities, and token charges (or no charges) may be made to a hospital's indigent patients.

Evaluating Performance and Operating Results

Profit-seeking enterprises usually will modify or withdraw unprofitable goods or services offered to the consuming public. The direct relationship between the financial resources each consumer provides and the goods or services a consumer receives from each enterprise essentially dictates the type and quality of goods and services each profit-seeking enterprise will provide. Firms with inept or unresponsive management will be unprofitable and ultimately will be forced out of business. Therefore, the profit motive and profit measurement constitute an automatic allocation and regulating device in the free enterprise segment of our economy.

This profit test/regulator device is not present in the usual G&NP situation. Because governments have the power to tax and lack market competition for most of the services they provide, governments generally continue to operate even if they are ineffective or inefficient. Because government services are unique or are provided without charge or at a token charge, consumers have no "dollar vote" to cast.

Evaluating the performance and operating results of most G&NP organizations is extremely difficult because:

1. No open market supply-and-demand test occurs to evaluate the value of the services they provide.

2. The relationship, if any, between the resource contributors and the recipients of the services is remote and indirect.

3. G&NP organizations are not profit oriented in the usual sense and are not expected to operate profitably; thus, the profit test is neither a valid performance indicator nor an automatic regulating device.

4. Governments can force financial resource contributions through taxation.

Accordingly, G&NP organizations must employ measures and controls of operating results other than net income to ensure that their resources are used appropriately and to prevent inefficient or ineffective G&NP organizations from operating indefinitely. *Governments and nonprofit organizations, particularly governments, are therefore subject to more stringent legal, regulatory, and other controls than are private businesses.*

All facets of a G&NP organization's operations—especially of SLGs—may be affected by legal or quasi-legal requirements (1) imposed externally, such as by federal or state statute, grant regulations, or judicial decrees, or (2) imposed internally or by mutual agreement, such as by charter, bylaw, ordinance, trust agreement, donor stipulation, or contract. Furthermore, the need to ensure compliance with such extensive legal and contractual requirements often necessitates more stringent operational and administrative controls than in private enterprise. Aspects of G&NP organizations' operations that may be regulated or otherwise controlled include:

1. **Organization structure:** form; composition of governing board; number and duties of its personnel; lines of authority and responsibility; policies concerning which officials or employees are to be elected, appointed, or hired

2. **Personnel policies and procedures:** who will appoint or hire personnel; tenure of personnel; policies and procedures upon termination; compensation levels; promotion policies; types and amounts of compensation increments

3. **Sources of financial resources:** types and maximum amounts of taxes, licenses, fines, or fees a government may levy; procedure for setting user charges; tuition rates; debt limits; purposes for which debt may be incurred; allowable methods for soliciting charitable contributions

4. **Uses of financial resources:** purposes for which resources may be used, including the legal restriction of certain resources only for specific purposes; purchasing procedures to be followed; budgeting methods, forms, or procedures

5. **Accounting:** any or all phases of the accounting system; for example, chart of accounts, bases of accounting, forms, and procedures

6. **Financial reporting:** type and frequency of financial reports; report format and content; report recipients

7. **Auditing:** frequency of audit; who is to perform the audit; scope and type of audit; time and place for filing the audit report; who is to receive or have access to the audit report

Finally, managers of G&NP organizations may have limited discretion compared with managers of businesses. The role and emphasis of G&NP financial accounting and reporting thus are correspondingly altered as compared with the profit-seeking business environment.

OBJECTIVES OF G&NP ACCOUNTING AND FINANCIAL REPORTING

Financial Accounting Standards Board (FASB) *Statement of Financial Accounting Concepts No. 4* (SFAC 4), "Objectives of Financial Reporting by Nonbusiness Organizations," addresses the objectives of **general purpose external financial reporting** by *nonbusiness (nonprofit)* organizations. SFAC 4 notes that:

- The *objectives* stem primarily from the needs of *external* users who generally cannot prescribe the information they want from an organization.

- *In addition* to information provided by general purpose *external* financial reporting, *managers* and . . . *governing bodies* need a great deal of *internal accounting information* to carry out their responsibilities in planning and controlling activities.[1]

The financial reporting *objectives* set forth in SFAC 4 state that financial reporting by nonbusiness organizations should provide information that is *useful* to present and potential resource providers and other users in:

- *Making rational decisions* about the allocation of resources to those organizations.
- *Assessing* the *services* that a nonbusiness organization provides *and its ability to continue* to provide those services.
- *Assessing how managers* of a nonbusiness organization have *discharged their stewardship* responsibilities and other aspects of their performance.

In addition, nonbusiness organization financial reporting should include explanations and interpretations to help users understand the financial information provided.[2]

Note that these broad objectives statements relate to *all* organizations and *nonbusiness* organizations, respectively. The objectives of *state and local government* accounting and financial reporting are discussed later in this chapter.

AUTHORITATIVE SOURCES OF G&NP ACCOUNTING PRINCIPLES AND REPORTING STANDARDS

G&NP accounting and reporting concepts, principles, and standards evolved separately from those for business enterprises. Beginning in the 1930s, unique principles and standards evolved separately for each of the several major types of G&NP organizations.

- The National Council on Governmental Accounting (NCGA) and several similar predecessor committees led the development of accounting concepts, principles, and standards for state and local governments until the Governmental Accounting Standards Board (GASB) was created in 1984.
- The American Hospital Association and the Healthcare Financial Management Association fostered the development of accounting principles and standards for hospitals and other health care institutions.
- The American Council on Education and the National Association of College and University Business Officers led the development of those for colleges and universities.
- Committees of the American Institute of Certified Public Accountants (AICPA) set forth accounting principles and standards for nonprofit organizations in AICPA audit

---

[1]Financial Accounting Standards Board, *Statement of Financial Accounting Concepts No. 4,* "Objectives of Financial Reporting by Nonbusiness Organizations" (Stamford, CT: FASB, December 1980), p. xii. Emphasis added.

[2]Ibid., pp. xiii–xiv.

and accounting guides until the FASB began issuing guidance for nongovernmental, non-profit organizations in 1993.

- The Comptroller General of the United States led the federal government accounting standards effort until the Federal Accounting Standards Advisory Board (FASAB) was established in 1990.

In addition, each G&NP field has its own journals, newsletters, and professional societies.

Both the Financial Accounting Standards Board (FASB) and the Governmental Accounting Standards Board (GASB) are overseen by the Financial Accounting Foundation (FAF), which is responsible to ensure that they are adequately financed. The FAF, which is comprised of prominent government and private sector leaders, also appoints new members to the FASB and the GASB.

The FAF

The FASB has seven full-time members and over 60 staff members. Although not limited by its original charter or rules of procedure to setting business accounting standards, the FASB devoted its early efforts almost exclusively to business accounting concepts and standards, deferring the decision on what role, if any, it would play in the G&NP standards area.

The FASB

In 1979, the FASB (1) agreed to exercise responsibility for all specialized accounting and reporting principles and practices set forth in AICPA statements of position, accounting guides, and audit guides *except* those dealing with state and local governments (*FASB Statement No. 32*). Subsequently, the FASB rescinded *FASB Statement No. 32* and issued standards for *non*governmental organizations—including *non*governmental not-for-profit organization accounting and financial reporting (discussed in Chapter 16).

The FASB deferred action concerning state and local government standards during this period because discussions were under way among representatives of interested organizations, including the NCGA and the AICPA, about the appropriate structure for setting governmental accounting standards. At issue was whether state and local government accounting standards should continue to be established by the NCGA or should be set by the FASB or perhaps a new standards-setting body. These discussions led to formation of the Governmental Accounting Standards Board in 1984.

The FAF created the Governmental Accounting Standards Board (GASB) in 1984 in a "brother-sister" relationship with the Financial Accounting Standards Board (FASB). The jurisdiction agreement states that:

FASB-GASB Jurisdictions

- The **GASB** is responsible for establishing accounting and financial reporting standards for activities and transactions of **state and local governments**, including government nonprofit organizations.
- The FASB is responsible for establishing accounting and financial reporting standards for all other organizations—including nongovernment nonprofit organizations.

Whether an organization is or is not a "*government*" is a critical determination that dictates whether it must follow GASB or FASB standards and guidance.

Most state and local governments—including states, counties, municipalities, townships, and school districts—clearly are "governments" subject to the GASB's jurisdiction. But it may be difficult to determine whether some not-for-profit and

"Government" Defined

other organizations are governmental or nongovernmental. Accordingly, the GASB and FASB jointly developed a definition of government.

- This definition, summarized in Illustration 1-1, is published in AICPA audit and accounting guides to assist practitioners in determining whether organizations are governmental or nongovernmental and thus are under GASB jurisdiction or FASB jurisdiction.
- Many nonprofit organizations are established by governments and are governments under this definition.

The practitioner must determine whether a specific organization is "government" or "nongovernment" using the FASB-GASB definition to apply the generally accepted accounting principles (GAAP) hierarchy guidance correctly.

ILLUSTRATION 1-1   Definition of State and Local Government Entities

Governmental organizations include [1] public corporations[1] and bodies corporate and politic, and [2] other organizations *if* they have one or more of the following characteristics:

- The popular election of officers or appointment (or approval) of a controlling majority of the members of the organization's governing body by officials of one or more state or local governments.
- The potential for unilateral dissolution by a government with the net assets reverting to a government.
- The power to enact and enforce a tax levy.
- The ability to issue directly (rather than through a state or municipal authority) debt that pays interest exempt from federal taxation.[2]

[1]*Black's Law Dictionary* defines a public corporation as "an instrumentality of the state, founded and owned in the public interest, supported by public funds and governed by those deriving their authority from the state."

[2]However, organizations possessing only that ability (to issue tax-exempt debt) and none of the other governmental characteristics may rebut the presumption that they are governmental if their determination is supported by compelling, relevant evidence.

Source: Adapted from "FASB and GASB Define 'Government,'" *Journal of Accountancy,* July 1996, pp. 16–17. This definition is cited in pertinent AICPA audit and accounting guides.

1-1 IN PRACTICE

Not-for-Profit (Nonprofit) Organizations May Be Governments

1. Several states have established health care, drug abuse, professional licensing, economic development, and other agencies as 501(c)(3) not-for-profit (nonprofit) corporations.
2. Cities and counties also have established industrial development, economic development, civic center, convention center, sports complex, and other activities and facilities as 501(c)(3) corporations.
3. A professional (AAA) baseball team, the Columbus (Ohio) Clippers, is a less commonly encountered type of not-for-profit organization.
4. Finally, many public television stations are legally established as not-for-profit or nonprofit corporations by states, state colleges and universities, or other governments.

Although all of these organizations are established as not-for-profit or nonprofit corporations legally, the GASB requires a "substance over form" approach to financial reporting. Thus, organizations such as these are "government not-for-profit or nonprofit organizations" and are under GASB jurisdiction for GAAP reporting.

The GASB succeeded the NCGA in 1984 (see Appendix 1-1) as the body authorized to establish accounting standards for state and local governments. (See Illustration 1-2.) The GASB, FASB, and FAF offices are in the same building in Norwalk, Connecticut. Again, the GASB is responsible for establishing financial reporting standards for activities and transactions of **state and local governments**; the **FASB** sets reporting standards for **all other organizations**, including *non*governmental, nonprofit organizations.

The GASB has seven members. The chairman serves full time, whereas the other six members serve part time. The Board is assisted by a full-time professional staff of approximately 12 persons, led by the director of research, and meets in open session for two to three days about every six weeks. The GASB mission— including its mission statement, an overview of how its mission is accomplished, and its due process—is summarized in Illustration 1-3.

GASB activities center around its agenda topics and projects. It may issue nonauthoritative invitations to comment, discussion memorandums, and preliminary views publications to obtain viewpoints of practitioners and others before issuing exposure drafts and, finally, an authoritative pronouncement. Its authoritative pronouncements are issued as Statements, Interpretations, Technical Bulletins, and Implementation Guides. The GASB issues *The GASB Report* newsletter each month to inform interested persons of its activities and also issues Concepts Statements, research studies, and other nonauthoritative publications from time to time.

GASB *Statement No. 1,* "Authoritative Status of NCGA Pronouncements and AICPA Industry Audit Guide," issued in 1984, provided a transition from the old standards-setting arrangements to the current one. *Statement No. 1* recognized the then-effective NCGA pronouncements and certain accounting and reporting guidance in the then-effective AICPA state and local government audit guide as authoritative, stating that they are "continued in force until altered, amended, supplemented, revoked, or superseded by a subsequent GASB pronouncement."[3] These NCGA and AICPA pronouncements—now recognized as

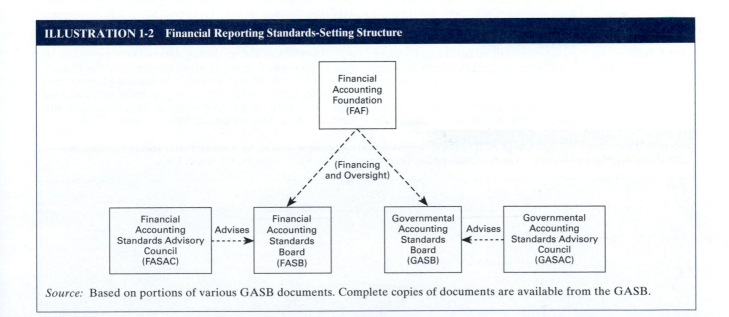

ILLUSTRATION 1-2   Financial Reporting Standards-Setting Structure

Source: Based on portions of various GASB documents. Complete copies of documents are available from the GASB.

---

[3]Governmental Accounting Standards Board, *Statement No. 1,* "Authoritative Status of NCGA Pronouncements and AICPA Industry Audit Guide" (GASB, July 1984).

ILLUSTRATION 1-3   Facts About GASB

What Is the GASB?

The Governmental Accounting Standards Board (GASB) is the independent organization that establishes and improves standards of accounting and financial reporting for U.S. state and local governments. Established in 1984 by agreement of the Financial Accounting Foundation (FAF) and 10 national associations of state and local government officials, the GASB is recognized by governments, the accounting industry, and the capital markets as the official source of generally accepted accounting principles (GAAP) for state and local governments.

Accounting and financial reporting standards designed for the government environment are essential because governments are fundamentally different from for-profit businesses. Furthermore, the information needs of the users of government financial statements are different from the needs of the users of private company financial statements. The GASB members and staff understand the unique characteristics of governments and the environment in which they operate.

The GASB is not a government entity; instead, it is an operating component of the FAF, which is a private sector not-for-profit entity. Funding for the GASB comes in part from sales of its own publications and in part from state and local governments and the municipal bond community. Its standards are not federal laws or regulations, and the organization does not have enforcement authority. Compliance with GASB's standards, however, is enforced through the laws of some individual states and through the audit process, when auditors render opinions on the fairness of financial statement presentations in conformity with GAAP.

Why Is the GASB's Work Important?

The GASB, in keeping with its mission, issues standards and other communications that result in decision-useful information for users of government financial reports, including, for example, owners of municipal bonds, members of citizen groups, legislators and legislative staff, and oversight bodies. Those standards also help government officials demonstrate to their constituents their accountability and stewardship over public resources. Additionally, the GASB works to educate the public, including financial statement preparers, auditors, and users, about its standards and the information those standards require governments to present in their financial reports.

In order to encourage broad public participation in the standards-setting process, GASB standards are issued only after completion of extensive and rigorous due process activities, which are discussed [below].

How Does the GASB Set Standards?

Before issuing its standards, the GASB follows the due process activities described in its published Rules of Procedure. The GASB's stringent due process activities are designed to encourage broad public participation in the standards-setting process. These activities promote timely, thorough, and open study of financial accounting and reporting issues by the preparers, auditors, and users of financial reports.

For many of the issues it addresses, the GASB

- Appoints an advisory task force of outside experts.
- Studies existing literature on the subject and conducts or commissions additional research if necessary.
- Publishes a discussion document for public comment setting forth the issues or concerns being addressed and possible solutions.
- Broadly distributes an Exposure Draft of a proposed standard for public comment.
- Conducts public hearings and forums on its due process documents.

Significant steps in the process are announced publicly. The GASB's meetings are open for public observation, and a public record is maintained. The GASB also is advised by the Governmental Accounting Standards Advisory Council (GASAC), a 30-member group appointed by the FAF Trustees that represents a wide range of the GASB's constituents.

Transcripts of public hearings, letters of comment and position papers, research reports, and other relevant materials on projects leading to issuance of pronouncements become part of the Board's public record and are available for inspection. To encourage public comment, discussion documents and Exposure Drafts are distributed by means of the Internet. Single printed copies are available without charge during the comment period to all who request them. Final pronouncements are distributed when published through GASB subscription plans or may be purchased separately by placing an order at the GASB Web site, http://www.gasb.org, or by contacting the GASB's Order Department at 800-748-0659.

GASB pronouncements—were integrated into its authoritative *Codification of Governmental Accounting and Financial Reporting Standards* in 1985.[4]

The GASB *Codification* is revised annually to incorporate subsequent GASB pronouncements, as is its companion *Original Pronouncements* volume, which contains the complete text of all GASB and NCGA pronouncements. The GASB also issues a *Comprehensive Implementation Guide (CIG)* annually to provide guidance on the implementation and application of a number of GASB standards. All of the GASB and predecessor literature is also available through its Governmental Accounting Research System (GARS), a readily accessible personal computer disk search and retrieval system that is revised semiannually. (The GASB maintains an informative Web site at http://www.gasb.org.)

Day-to-day accounting and interim reporting by G&NP organizations is often based on cash receipts, disbursements, and balances or assuring compliance with the organization's budget. But their annual financial statements must meet the GASB's uniform national standards if they are to comply with generally accepted accounting principles (GAAP) and thus be "presented fairly in conformity with generally accepted accounting principles."

GAAP Hierarchies

The AICPA established *parallel* but *distinct* GAAP hierarchies to assist practitioners in determining (1) which authoritative financial reporting standards or other guidance should be considered in determining what constitutes GAAP and (2) their relative status or ranking.

Both the GASB and the FASB recently adopted hierarchies that superseded the previous AICPA-established hierarchies. The FASB subsequently replaced its hierarchy with its Accounting Standards Codification. The guidance is summarized, for both government and nongovernment organizations, in Illustration 1-4.

The GAAP hierarchy indicates the relative authoritativeness of the various standards pronouncements and other literature on financial accounting and reporting principles and procedures. For governments, level (a) pronouncements are the most authoritative, followed by the pronouncements and other guidance at levels (b), (c), and (d), respectively. All other accounting literature is commonly referred to as "level e" and is nonauthoritative. However, this nonauthoritative literature may be relevant guidance if none is available at the higher levels of the hierarchy.

This text focuses initially on state and local governments and the "GASB Jurisdiction" hierarchy referred to as the "SLG GAAP hierarchy." The GAAP hierarchies for nongovernmental, nonprofit organizations and the federal government are discussed in later chapters.

Several points are particularly significant for the SLG GAAP hierarchy:

1. Its guidance applies only to state and local government organizations; non-SLGs follow the "FASB Jurisdiction" GAAP hierarchy in Illustration 1-4.

2. GASB Statements and Interpretations are the highest-ranking authoritative pronouncements for SLGs, followed by certain AICPA guidance that has been cleared by the GASB and certain GASB staff guidance.

3. FASB guidance either has been incorporated in GASB pronouncements or is *not* authoritative.

---

[4]Governmental Accounting Standards Board and Governmental Accounting Research Foundation of the Government Finance Officers Association, *Codification of Governmental Accounting and Financial Reporting Standards as of November 1, 1984* (Norwalk, CT: GASB, 1985).

ILLUSTRATION 1-4   GAAP Hierarchy—State and Local Government Accounting and Financial Reporting

GAAP Hierarchy Summary
SLG vs. Non-SLG

GASB Jurisdiction	FASB Jurisdiction
State and Local Governments (SLG)	**Nongovernment Entities (Non-SLG)**

Authoritative

(a) GASB Statements of Financial Accounting Standards and Interpretations (and authoritative pronouncements of its predecessor body, the NCGA). These are incorporated in the *Codification of Governmental Accounting and Financial Reporting Standards*.

(b) GASB Technical Bulletins, *and if* specifically *made applicable* to state and local governments by the AICPA *and cleared by* the *GASB:* AICPA Industry Audit and Accounting Guides and AICPA Statements of Position

(c) AICPA AcSEC Practice Bulletins—if specifically made applicable to state and local governmental entities, cleared by the GASB, and issued after March 15, 1992—as well as consensus positions of the GASB Emerging Issues Task Force* organized by the GASB that attempts to reach consensus positions on accounting issues applicable to state and local governmental entities

(d) GASB Implementation Guides (Q&As) issued by the GASB staff, as well as widely recognized and prevalent industry practices

Nonauthoritative

Application of guidance from other levels by analogy to issues not directly addressed in the higher level guidance and other accounting literature—including GASB Concepts Statements; pronouncements in categories (b) and (c) of the hierarchy for *governmental* entities *and* in categories (a) through (d) of the hierarchy for *non*governmental entities when *not* specifically *made applicable* to state and local governments *or not cleared by* the *GASB;* APB Statements; FASB Concepts Statements; the FASB Accounting Standards Codification; AICPA Issues Papers; International Accounting Standards Board and International Federation of Accountants pronouncements**; pronouncements of other professional associations or regulatory agencies; AICPA *Technical Practice Aids;* and accounting textbooks, handbooks, and articles

Authoritative

FASB Accounting Standards Codification

Nonauthoritative

Other accounting literature, including AICPA Issues Papers; International Accounting Standards Board and International Federation of Accountants pronouncements; pronouncements of other professional associations or regulatory agencies; AICPA *Technical Practice Aids;* and accounting textbooks, handbooks, and articles

*The GASB has *not* organized such a group.

**The International Public Sector Accounting Standards Board (IPSASB) of the International Federation of Accountants issues International Public Sector Accounting Standards. These standards are not GAAP for any U.S. government and thus are not covered in this text. To learn more about the IPSASB, its standards, and its current projects, visit its Web site (http://www.ifac.org/PublicSector/).

Source: Adapted from GASB Statement 55, "The Hierarchy of Generally Accepted Accounting Principles for State and Local Governments," and the FASB Accounting Standards Codification.

CONCEPTS AND OBJECTIVES OF SLG ACCOUNTING AND FINANCIAL REPORTING

The earlier discussions of the G&NP organization environment, concepts and objectives of G&NP accounting and financial reporting, and characteristics of G&NP accounting deal with G&NP organizations generally. This section builds on those discussions and considers similar factors from the state and local government perspective, as set forth in GASB *Concepts Statement No. 1,* "Objectives of Financial Reporting." The primary purposes of this section are to

- Help the reader understand the principal features of SLGs that have influenced the development of SLG accounting and financial reporting objectives, concepts, principles, and standards—particularly features that differ from those of business enterprises.
- Provide background necessary for the reader to understand and apply the GASB's basic principles, which are discussed in the next chapter.

The environment of SLG accounting and reporting is considered first, followed by a discussion of the users and uses of SLG financial reports. A summary of the objectives of SLG external financial reporting in GASB *Concepts Statement No. 1* concludes this section.[5]

One unique aspect of the SLG environment is that governments may be involved in both governmental-type and business-type activities.

- **Governmental-type (or governmental) activities** include fire and police protection, the courts, street and traffic control, health and welfare, executive and legislative offices, and other "general governmental" activities.
- **Business-type activities** include public utilities (e.g., electricity, water) and other activities for which user fees are charged and that are operated similarly to private businesses.

The environments of governmental-type and business-type activities may differ, even within one government, as may financial statement user information needs. Thus, the SLG environment, financial statement users, and user information needs are discussed first for governmental-type activities; then they are compared with those of business-type activities.

The governmental-type activity environment is unique in several respects. These aspects include the distinctive SLG:

Governmental-Type Activities

- Purpose
- Sources of financial resources
- Financial resource allocation mechanisms
- Accountabilities
- Reporting issues and problems

Purpose

As noted earlier, a government's primary reason for existence—particularly for its governmental-type activities—differs from that of business enterprises. Whereas the key objective of businesses is to earn a profit, the primary goal of governmental-type (also known as governmental or general government) activities is to provide goods or services, often without regard to the *individual recipient's* ability to pay for them.

Absence of the profit motive in governmental-type activities underlies several other differences between governments and businesses. As noted earlier, the basic performance evaluation measure in business—net income—does *not* apply to governmental-type activities. Moreover, most governments do *not* obtain significant financial resources for governmental-type activities from service charges to individual recipients in proportion to the services received.

---

[5]This section is drawn, with permission, primarily from GASB *Concepts Statement No. 1,* "Objectives of Financial Reporting," which is reproduced in Governmental Accounting Standards Board, *Codification of Governmental Accounting and Financial Reporting Standards as of June 30, 2011* (Norwalk, CT: GASB, 2011), Appendix B. Hereafter cited as GASB *Codification.*

Because proportionate service charges are not a key source of general government financial resources:

- Financial resources provided by one person or group may be used to finance services for another person or group, and
- Government goods and services are not automatically allocated to individual users who are willing and able to pay.

Thus, the market supply and demand allocation mechanism does not function as it does for business.

Sources of Financial Resources

Because significant revenues from sales of services are not available to finance governmental-type activities, governments must raise financial resources from other sources. Two primary examples of these revenue sources are taxes and intergovernmental grants and subsidies.

Taxation The power to tax is unique to governments and most governmental-type SLG services—such as police and fire protection, elementary and secondary education, and streets and highways—are financed primarily by tax revenues. Indeed, even when SLGs charge fees for general government services, they often must be subsidized with tax revenues (e.g., many public health clinics).

The power to tax causes taxpayers to be *involuntary* financial resource providers. Individual taxpayers cannot refuse to pay taxes if they think the government is using the resources improperly, or pay a lesser amount if they do not use as many of the government's services as do others. Rather, the amount of taxes a taxpayer must pay is based on the value of the taxpayer's real and/or personal property (property taxes), the amount of income earned (income taxes), retail purchases (sales taxes), and so forth—not on the amount or value of services received. Taxation is thus a _nonexchange_ transaction or event that eliminates any direct association between

1. The amount and quality of the services a constituent receives from the government, and
2. The amount the constituent pays to the government.

Many governments also have other powers similar to taxation, such as levying license and permit fees, fines, and other charges. This ability of governments to exact resources from individuals, businesses, and others by taxation and similar levies—without an arm's-length exchange transaction—means that the types, levels, and quality of services a government provides are not automatically dictated or regulated by what its constituents are willing to pay for the services. *This absence of the market resource allocation mechanism makes it difficult to measure the success of a governmental unit solely in financial terms.*

Intergovernmental Revenues Grants and subsidies from higher level governments are another significant source of SLG revenues. For many SLGs, intergovernmental revenues approach or exceed the amount of the SLG's own tax revenues in many fiscal years. The federal government provides several hundred billion dollars of revenues to SLGs every year, and states provide additional financial resources to local governments. Most intergovernmental revenues are not provided as a direct result of services received by the resource provider but are to help finance certain services for the recipient's constituency.

Financial Resource Allocation Mechanisms

General government financial resource allocations are derived from processes clearly different from business enterprises. Indeed, absent a direct relationship between the financial resources provided by an individual taxpayer and the services provided to that individual taxpayer, it is impossible for resource allocations to be made in the same manner as for business enterprises. Rather, for the most part, the nature of the U.S. system of governance, including various restrictions on financial resource use and the budget process, determines how the allocations are made.

Restrictions on Resource Use   One primary mechanism used for allocating general government resources to various uses is for restrictions to be placed on financial resource use by the resource providers or their representatives. One level of restriction requires that certain resources be used for a particular purpose or program. Such restrictions arise from

- Intergovernmental grantors requiring that the resources provided be used for a particular purpose.
- Taxes and similar resources being levied for a specific purpose, such as for roads, education, or debt service.
- Debt proceeds being restricted to a specific purpose.

These numerous restrictions are the primary reason for the use of *funds* and *nonfund accounts*—to account for financial resources segregated according to the purpose(s) for which they may or must be used and any related capital assets and long-term liabilities, respectively. The GASB recognizes the importance of the governmental fund structure and the fund accounting control mechanism in the SLG environment, observing that *funds and fund accounting controls*

- Complement the budgetary process and annual budget in ensuring that a government uses its financial resources in compliance with both external restrictions and the annual budget.
- Facilitate fulfilling the SLG's accountability to its constituency, grantors, and others.

The Budget   Taxes and other revenues are allocated to various uses by placing even more detailed *budgetary restrictions* on their use. Theoretically, taxpayers could meet and decide as a group how to allocate the resources to various uses. However, in our representative form of government, citizens have delegated that power to public officials through the election process. In addition, a system of checks and balances over the potential abuse of power is provided by the separation of powers among the executive, legislative, and judicial branches of government.

These more detailed restrictions are thus placed on the use of financial resources by elected officials through the budget process—a key element of the decision-making processes in government. The budget is adopted into *law* and essentially becomes a contract between the executive branch, the legislative branch, and the citizenry. In most jurisdictions, significant changes in this budget contract should be made only through a process similar to the budget process itself. In the budget process,

- The executive branch typically prepares a proposed budget and submits appropriation requests to the legislative branch.
- The legislative branch has the power to approve those requests, thus authorizing the executive branch to make expenditures within the limits of the appropriations and any laws that may affect programs covered by those appropriations.
- The executive branch is accountable to the legislative branch for operating within those appropriations and laws, and both branches are accountable to the citizenry.

The annual budgetary process and budget are extremely important in the SLG governmental-type activities environment. The budget is an expression of public policy and intent. It is also a financial plan that indicates the proposed expenditures for the year and the means of financing them. Moreover, an **adopted budget** has the force of law. It both

- *Authorizes* amounts to be expended for various specified purposes, *and*
- *Limits* the amount that may be expended for each of those purposes.

Budgetary limitations generally cannot be exceeded without due process.

Thus, the budget is both a form of control and a basis for evaluating performance in a budgetary context. Accordingly, a government must demonstrate its ***budgetary accountability***, which entails reporting whether revenues were obtained and expended as anticipated and whether authorized expenditure limitations (appropriations) were exceeded.

Establishing the budget—determining the types and amounts of taxes and other revenues to be exacted from the citizenry and how those resources will be used—is one of the most important functions that elected representatives perform. Indeed, the citizenry's perception of a representative's budgetary performance is a significant factor in voting decisions. Hence, the budget process is a vital part of the political process.

Accountabilities

The numerous environmental features discussed earlier result in distinct SLG accountabilities, which are unique both in terms of (1) to whom SLGs and their officials are accountable and (2) the focuses of their accountability.

To Whom Accountable The need for accountability exists between (1) SLGs and their constituencies, (2) SLGs and other governments, and (3) the SLG's own legislative and executive bodies.

1. SLGs are accountable to their constituencies for various reasons. Elected officials are empowered by citizens to act on their behalf and are evaluated by voters in part on their fiscal and budgetary performance, as well as on the perceived efficiency and effectiveness with which the SLG is operated. Thus, SLG officials must demonstrate to citizens that revenues or bond proceeds approved for specific purposes were in fact used for those purposes.

2. The SLG's accountability to other governments arises in part because senior levels of government often have some oversight authority over lower levels of government; it also arises when other governments provide grants or other intergovernmental subsidies to the SLG.

3. Accountability between each SLG's legislative and executive bodies focuses on demonstrating that the fund restrictions and budget contract have been complied with and that resources have been used efficiently and effectively.

Accountability Focuses The financial reports for governmental-type activities focus on two types of accountability: *fiscal accountability* and *operational accountability*.

- **Fiscal accountability** is a government's responsibility to demonstrate its compliance with public decisions about the raising and spending of public monies in the short term.[6] This accountability encompasses:
  - The use of financial resources from various revenue sources or bond issues in accordance with any restrictions on their use.
  - Compliance with fund and budget restrictions.
- **Operational accountability** is a government's responsibility to demonstrate the extent to which it has met its operating objectives and whether it can continue to meet its objectives in the foreseeable future.[7] This accountability results in a government providing:
  - A measure of the economic costs of providing services (operating costs).
  - An assessment of whether a government is raising sufficient revenues each period to cover the cost of providing services (operating results).
  - An assessment of whether services are being provided economically and efficiently.

---

[6]Governmental Accounting Standards Board, *Statement No. 34,* "Basic Financial Statements—and Management's Discussion and Analysis—for State and Local Governments" (Norwalk, CT: GASB, June 1999), par. 203.
[7]Ibid.

Reporting Issues and Problems

The characteristics of the SLG general government environment also create issues and problems that must be dealt with in SLG financial reporting and/or auditing, including

1. The need to demonstrate compliance with restrictions on the use of financial resources.
2. The need for appropriate budgetary reporting.
3. The impact of restrictions on the use of financial resources (such as from intergovernmental grants) on revenue recognition.
4. The difficulty of measuring and reporting the efficiency and effectiveness of SLGs in providing services.
5. The opportunity to hide or disguise the use or availability of financial resources for various purposes by (a) improperly reporting transactions between the various SLG funds and (b) developing an inappropriate fund structure.
6. The lack of comparability that can result between financial reports of two similarly designated governments that perform different functions (which is common in SLGs).
7. The existence of taxation and debt limits.
8. The impact on materiality and reporting judgments caused by (a) overexpenditure of appropriations being a violation of law and (b) failure to follow compliance requirements related to intergovernmental revenues, possibly requiring forfeiture of such revenues or loss of future revenues.

Furthermore, financial reporting for governments must be responsive to the temptations that result because the budget process is a vital part of the political process. Elected representatives serve for relatively short terms, and officials may be tempted to employ practices that permit a budget to be technically in balance even without true budgetary equilibrium.

Accordingly, to appropriately reflect the degree of budgetary equilibrium, the GASB notes that financial reporting should indicate the extent to which

- Current operations were financed by nonrecurring revenues or by incurring long-term liabilities.
- Certain essential costs, such as normal maintenance of government capital assets, have been deferred to future periods.

The GASB provides a more thorough discussion of the reasons for the unique characteristics of state and local governmental financial reporting in a White Paper that is posted at its Web site (http://www.gasb.org). The White Paper is entitled, "Why Governmental Accounting and Financial Reporting Is—and Should Be—Different."

Financial Report Users

The GASB has identified the primary groups of users of external financial reports of SLGs.[8] The user groups are:

1. **The citizenry:** those to whom the government is primarily accountable, including citizens (taxpayers, voters, service recipients), the media, advocate groups, and public finance researchers
2. **Legislative and oversight bodies:** those who directly represent the citizens, including members of state legislatures, county commissions, city councils, boards of trustees and school boards, and executive branch officials with oversight responsibility over other levels of government
3. **Investors and creditors:** those who lend or participate in the lending process, including individual and institutional investors and creditors, municipal security underwriters, bond rating agencies, bond insurers, and financial institutions

The needs of intergovernmental grantors and other users are considered by the GASB to be encompassed within those of these three primary user groups.

---

[8]GASB *Codification*, Appendix B, pars. 30–31.

Internal executive branch managers usually have ready access to the SLG's financial information through internal reports and are not considered primary users of external financial reports. However, if they are without adequate access, a fourth primary user group is:

4. **Government administrators:** internal executive branch managers who do not have ready access to the government's internal information

Financial Report Uses

The GASB notes that financial reporting should provide information useful in making economic and political decisions and in assessing accountability by[9]

1. Comparing actual financial results with the legally adopted budget.
2. Assessing financial condition and results of operations.
3. Assisting in determining compliance with finance-related laws, rules, and regulations.
4. Assisting in evaluating efficiency and effectiveness.

Business-Type Activities

In contrast to SLG governmental-type activities, a government's business-type activities

- Provide the same types of services as private sector businesses.
- Involve exchange relationships—that is, the consumer is charged a fee for services received, and there is a direct relationship between the services provided and the fee charged the consumer.
- Are often separate, legally constituted, self-sufficient organizations—though some resemble governmental-type activities because they are regularly subsidized by the SLG or are operated as departments of the SLG.

The GASB contrasts the general government environmental factors discussed earlier with those for SLG business-type activities.[10] The GASB discusses the differences in terms of the relationship between services received and resources provided by the consumer, revenue-producing assets, similarly designated activities and their potential for comparison, the nature of the political process, and budgets and fund accounting.

The Relationship Between Services Received and Resources Provided by the Consumer

Business-type activities often involve a direct relationship between the charge and the service. In that relationship, termed an "exchange relationship," a user fee is charged for a specific service provided, for example, a toll for use of a road, a charge for water, or a fare to ride the bus.

This exchange relationship in a business-type setting causes users of financial reports to focus on measuring the costs (or financial resource outflows, or both) of providing the service, the revenues obtained from the service, and the difference between the two. The difference is particularly important because it may affect future user charges.

Measurement of both the cost of services and financial resource outflows is useful. Whether one is more important than the other depends on various factors, including the way in which user charges are calculated and whether subsidies are provided by the general government.

Revenue-Producing Capital Assets

Most capital assets of business-type activities are revenue producing. Therefore, the incentive for business-type activities to defer needed maintenance may not be as great as that for governmental-type activities.

---

[9]Ibid., Appendix B, par. 32.
[10]Ibid., Appendix B, pars. 43–50.

Similarly Designated Activities and Potential for Comparison

The business-type activities of a government often perform only a single function. If the function is supplying water, for example, the problems, procedures, and cost elements of obtaining, treating, and delivering it are similar, regardless of whether the function is performed by a private sector business, a public authority, an Enterprise Fund, or an activity financed by the government's General Fund. As a result, there is normally a greater potential for comparability among business-type activities that are performing similar functions than among governmental-type activities, which vary from government to government.

The Nature of the Political Process

Some government business-type activities are designed to be insulated from the political process. They are not part of the general government budgetary process, they have a direct relationship between fees and services rendered, and they are separate, legally constituted agencies. In some instances, however, this insulation from the political process has less substance than appearances suggest. Indeed, especially in subsidized activities, rate setting—even by independent boards—is political in nature. For example, charging mass transit users sufficient fares to pay all costs of the system may be politically or economically undesirable, so subsidies are provided from general tax revenues or grants from other jurisdictions. If operating or capital subsidies are provided, the influences of the political process are often as significant as in governmental-type activities.

Budgets and Fund Accounting

Business-type organizations often perform a single function, so multiple-fund accounting is not as common as it is in governmental-type activities. The typical business-type activity is operated as a government department during the year, and budgets and budgetary controls are *internal* management processes and tools. Some lack the force of law, but most business-type activity budgets are legally enacted and have the force of law.

Users and Uses of Financial Reports

Several similarities and differences between the users and uses of financial reports on the SLG's business-type activities, compared with reports covering its governmental-type activities, are noted in GASB *Concepts Statement No. 1*:[11]

- The users and uses of governmental financial reports typically are essentially the same regardless of whether the activity is business-type or governmental-type. However, the users and uses of financial reports for business-type activities may differ, depending on whether the activity reports separately or as part of a broader general government.

- The uses of financial reports of business-type activities generally differ only in *emphasis* from the uses of financial reports of governmental-type activities. Users of separate financial reports of business-type activities are concerned primarily with the financial condition and results of operations for that activity; they are often not concerned with comparing actual results with budgeted amounts.

- Investors and creditors are concerned primarily with whether the business-type activity is generating, and will continue to generate, sufficient cash to meet debt service requirements. In addition, many investors and creditors are as concerned with compliance with bond provisions by business-type activities as they are about compliance by governmental-type activities.

- Citizen groups and consumers may use information on results of operations primarily to assess the reasonableness of user charges.

---

[11]Ibid., Appendix B, pars. 51–55, adapted.

- Legislative and oversight officials and executive branch officials review financial reports of business-type activities from the perspectives of the reasonableness of both the cash flow and the user charge.

- Legislative and oversight officials also use financial reports to assess the potential need to subsidize a business-type activity with general governmental revenues or the potential to subsidize the general government with business-type activity resources.

- Both citizen groups and legislative and oversight officials need information about effectiveness, economy, and efficiency, particularly because that information has an effect on user charges.

- All user groups may be concerned with the relationship between the financial position and operating results of the business-type activity and that of the government as a whole—particularly if the business-type activity is subsidized by, or subsidizes, the general government.

Financial Reporting Objectives

Financial reporting objectives set forth what SLG financial statements should accomplish. GASB *Concepts Statement No. 1,* "Objectives of Financial Reporting," does not establish GAAP standards. Rather, it describes concepts that the GASB uses as a framework for evaluating present standards and practices and for establishing financial reporting standards in the future.

The GASB notes that its financial reporting objectives are intended to describe broadly the nature of information needed to meet the needs of users of SLG external financial reports, giving consideration to the SLG environment. Briefly stated, the GASB concluded that accountability is the "cornerstone"—the paramount objective—of government financial reporting and that interperiod equity is a significant part of accountability. Moreover, the GASB concluded that governmental financial reporting should provide information to assist users in (1) assessing accountability and (2) making economic, social, and political decisions. Accordingly, SLG financial reporting should provide:

1. A means of demonstrating the SLG's accountability that enables users to assess that accountability. Specifically, the information provided should

   a. Permit users to determine whether current-year revenues were sufficient to pay for the current year's services and/or whether future-years' citizens must assume burdens for services previously provided.

   b. Demonstrate the SLG's budgetary accountability and compliance with other finance-related legal and contractual requirements.

   c. Assist users in assessing the SLG's service efforts, costs, and accomplishments.

2. Information necessary to evaluate the SLG's operating results for the period, including information

   a. About the sources and uses of financial resources.

   b. On how the SLG financed its activities and met its cash requirements.

   c. Necessary to determine whether the SLG's financial condition improved or deteriorated during the year.

3. Information necessary to assess the level of SLG services and its ability to continue to finance its activities and meet its obligations, including

   a. Information about the SLG's financial position and condition.

   b. Information about the SLG's physical and other nonfinancial resources having useful lives that extend beyond the current year, including information that can be used to assess their service potential.

   c. Disclosure of (1) legal and contractual restrictions on the use of resources and (2) risks of potential loss of resources.[12]

---

[12]Ibid., Appendix B, pars. 77–79.

CHARACTERISTICS OF SLG ACCOUNTING AND FINANCIAL REPORTING

Some SLG activities, such as utilities and public transportation, are similar to those of some profit-seeking enterprises. In such cases the accounting roughly parallels that of their privately owned counterparts. In most of their operations, however, governments and nonprofit organizations are not concerned with profit measurement. (Even those SLG entities that account for revenues, expenses, and income may not seek to maximize profits, but only to ensure continuity and/or improvement of service.) Operations established primarily to generate profits—such as lotteries—are the exception in government.

Accounting is a service function and must continually evolve to meet the information demands in a given environment. In the SLG environment, decisions concerning financial resource acquisition and allocation, managerial direction and control of financial resource utilization, and custodianship of financial and other resources have traditionally been framed in terms of social and political objectives and constraints rather than profitability. Legal and administrative constraints have served as society's methods of directing its SLG institutions in achieving those objectives. Thus, SLG accounting and reporting have a strong emphasis on control of and accountability for *expendable* financial resources. The two most important types of legal and administrative control provisions affecting accounting in this environment are (1) the use of **funds** and (2) the distinctive role of the **budget**.

Fund Accounting

Using financial resources in accordance with stipulations inherent in their receipt and reporting on this compliance to others are essential custodianship obligations. Recall that:

- Many financial resources provided to SLG organizations are restricted; that is, their use is limited to specified purposes or activities. For example, a county may receive donations for a building addition; a city may borrow money to construct a sewage treatment plant; a school district may receive a federal grant for research. Such **external restrictions** create significant accountability.

- Governing bodies and management may also constrain certain financial resources to use for specific purposes. For example, the governing body or management may wish to accumulate resources for equipment replacement or facility enlargement. Because such constraints are internal plans and may be changed by the governing body or management, some require only **internal** accountability.

SLG organizations establish funds to control restricted and designated resources and to both ensure and demonstrate compliance with legal and administrative requirements. **Funds** are separate fiscal and accounting entities and include both cash and noncash resources—segregated according to the purposes or activities for which they are to be used—as well as related liabilities.

Two basic categories of fund accounting entities are used by SLGs:

1. **Governmental (expendable) funds:** To account for the financial assets, related liabilities, changes in net assets, and balances that may be expended in its nonbusiness-type activities (e.g., for fire and police protection).

2. **Proprietary (nonexpendable) funds:** To account for the revenues, expenses, assets, liabilities, and net position of its business-type activities (e.g., utilities, cafeterias, or transportation systems).[13]

The fund concept involves an accounting segregation—not necessarily the physical separation—of assets and liabilities; however, fund assets are often physically

---

[13]In addition to assets and liabilities, governments report deferred outflows and deferred inflows of resources—which are discussed in later chapters. Net position is the title the GASB requires to refer to the residual balance of proprietary fund (and government-wide) assets and deferred outflows less liabilities and deferred inflows. Net position also is used to refer to the corresponding amounts in the government-wide statement of net position.

segregated as well, for example, through separate checking accounts for the cash of different funds.

Use of the term "*fund*" in G&NP situations should be sharply distinguished from its use in private enterprise.

- A fund of a commercial enterprise, such as a bond sinking fund, is simply a portion of its assets that has been restricted to specific uses, not a separate and distinct accounting entity. Revenues and expenses related to such funds are part of enterprise operations; that is, fund revenue and expense accounts appear side by side in the general ledger with other enterprise revenue and expense accounts.

- **A fund in the G&NP accounting sense is a self-contained accounting entity with its own asset, liability, revenue, expenditure or expense, and fund balance or net position accounts**—and with its own ledger(s). (See Illustration 1-5.)

- A complete set of financial statements may be prepared for each fund of an SLG organization, as well as for the organization as a whole.

Budgets and Appropriations

The creation of a governmental (expendable) fund ordinarily does not carry with it the authority to expend its resources. SLG expenditures may be made only within the authority of appropriations—which are authorizations to make expenditures for specified purposes—or similar authorizations by the governing body.

A **fixed-dollar budget** is commonly prepared for each governmental (expendable) fund. That is, the organization's chief executive (or perhaps each department head) asks the governing body for permission to incur a specified ("fixed") amount of expenditures—for salaries, equipment, supplies, and so on—during the budget period to carry out the department's mission. This budget is the vehicle normally used to make and communicate financial resource allocation decisions

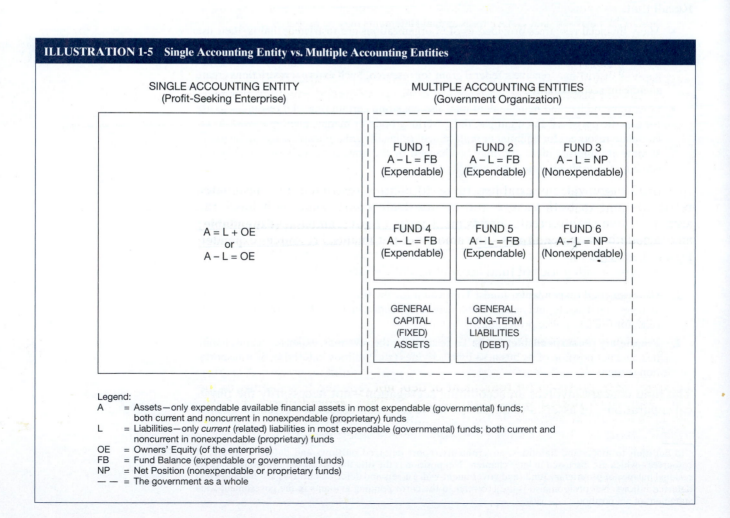

ILLUSTRATION 1-5   Single Accounting Entity vs. Multiple Accounting Entities

SINGLE ACCOUNTING ENTITY
(Profit-Seeking Enterprise)

MULTIPLE ACCOUNTING ENTITIES
(Government Organization)

$A = L + OE$
or
$A - L = OE$

FUND 1	FUND 2	FUND 3
$A - L = FB$	$A - L = FB$	$A - L = NP$
(Expendable)	(Expendable)	(Nonexpendable)

FUND 4	FUND 5	FUND 6
$A - L = FB$	$A - L = FB$	$A - L = NP$
(Expendable)	(Expendable)	(Nonexpendable)

GENERAL CAPITAL (FIXED) ASSETS

GENERAL LONG-TERM LIABILITIES (DEBT)

Legend:
A = Assets—only expendable available financial assets in most expendable (governmental) funds; both current and noncurrent in nonexpendable (proprietary) funds
L = Liabilities—only *current* (related) liabilities in most expendable (governmental) funds; both current and noncurrent in nonexpendable (proprietary) funds
OE = Owners' Equity (of the enterprise)
FB = Fund Balance (expendable or governmental funds)
NP = Net Position (nonexpendable or proprietary funds)
— — = The government as a whole

establishing the types and quantities of goods and services to be provided during the budget period.

When approved by the governing body, the budgetary expenditure estimates become binding **appropriations**, which both *authorize* expenditures for specified purposes and *limit* the amounts that can be expended for each specified purpose. Appropriations must indicate the fund from which the expenditure may be made and specify the purposes, the maximum amount, and the period of time for which the expenditure authority is granted. A department or activity may be financed from several funds. In such cases at least one appropriation must be made from each supporting fund to provide the requisite expenditure authority.

To ensure control and demonstrate budgetary compliance, most governments establish **budgetary accounts** within governmental fund ledgers. This technique permits managers to determine their remaining expenditure authority at any time during the period.

Fixed-dollar budgeting of governmental and/or proprietary funds often gives rise to a unique dual basis of accounting and reporting for G&NP organizations. This is because (1) GAAP prescribe specific standards for the measurement of revenues, expenditures, expenses, and other amounts reported in financial statements that "present fairly in conformity with GAAP"; but (2) for *budgetary* purposes, SLG governing boards may estimate revenues and authorize expenditures on a variety of non-GAAP bases—on the cash basis, for example.

Where the budgetary basis differs from the GAAP basis:

1. The accounts are maintained on the budgetary basis during the year to effect budgetary control through the accounts, so that interim and annual budgetary statements may be prepared on the budgetary basis.

2. Adjustments are made at year end—to convert the budgetary basis data in the accounts to the GAAP basis—so that GAAP basis annual statements may be prepared.

3. The differences between the budgetary basis and the GAAP basis statements are explained and reconciled in the annual financial report of the governmental organization.

Budgetary accounting and reporting are distinctive characteristics of SLG organizations, and are discussed and illustrated at numerous points throughout this text.

A key focus of most SLG accounting and reporting is expendable financial resources, accounted for in governmental fund entities and allocated by the budget and appropriation process.

Other Distinguishing Characteristics

The cost measurement focus of **proprietary (nonexpendable)** fund accounting and of entity-wide financial reports of G&NP organizations, like that of business accounting, is **expenses**—the cost of **assets and services consumed** during the period. In contrast, the cost measurement focus of **governmental (expendable)** fund accounting is **expenditures**—the amount of net **financial resources expended** during the period for:

- **Current operations** (e.g., salaries, utilities)
- **Capital outlay** (acquiring capital assets)
- **Long-term debt principal retirement and interest**

Expenditures thus *decrease* net expendable available financial assets.

More specifically, the term *expenditures* has been defined as "the cost of goods delivered or services rendered, whether paid or unpaid, including current operating costs, provision for retirement of debt not reported as a liability of the fund from which retired, and capital outlays."[14] Thus, *expenditures*—the term that is significant in expendable fund accounting—should not be confused with *expenses* as defined for accounting for profit-seeking enterprises.

---

[14] Adapted from National Committee on Governmental Accounting, *Governmental Accounting, Auditing, and Financial Reporting* (Chicago: Municipal Finance Officers Association of the United States and Canada, 1968), p. 160.

Capital assets that are not proprietary or trust fund assets are not appropriable financial resources. Thus, they are listed and accounted for separately from the governmental fund accounting entities in a ***nonfund*** accounting entity. Similarly, unmatured long-term liabilities that are not liabilities of a particular proprietary or fiduciary fund (but of the government as a whole) are listed in a separate nonfund accounting entity. Accordingly, the cost of acquiring a capital asset is considered an ***expenditure*** (use of expendable net financial resources) in the period in which it occurs, as is the retirement of a maturing long-term liability, because both reduce the net financial assets of a governmental fund.

Commercial Accounting Comparison

Though commercial-type accounting and financial reporting are employed where SLG organizations are engaged in commercial-type activities (e.g., electric utilities), accounting and reporting for other SLG endeavors have evolved largely in view of these key differences from profit-seeking enterprises:

1. **Objectives:** acquiring resources and expending them in a legal and appropriate manner, as opposed to seeking to increase, or even maintain, capital

2. **Control:** substitution of statutory, fund, and budgetary controls in the absence of the supply and demand and profit regulator/control devices inherent in profit-seeking endeavors

These factors—objectives and control—underlie the major differences between commercial and SLG accounting. The primary consideration in the SLG environment is on **compliance and accountability**, and SLG accounting, reporting, and auditing have developed principally as tools of compliance control and accountability demonstration.

Concluding Comments

There continue to be several sources of authoritative pronouncements concerning G&NP accounting and financial reporting and several distinct subsets of GAAP applicable to the various types of G&NP organizations. This text is based on the most authoritative pronouncements relevant to each of the organizations discussed. Sources of authoritative support are cited throughout the text.

Accounting is often referred to as the "language" of business. It is also the "language" of government and nonprofit organizations. Whereas most terms and their meanings are the same in both, each has some of its own terms and occasionally uses a term with a different connotation than the other. Accordingly, new terms and the occasional use of a familiar term in an unfamiliar way should be noted carefully in reviewing this and later chapters.

State and local government budgeting, accounting, and financial reporting concepts, principles, standards, and procedures are discussed and illustrated in the next several chapters. Federal government accounting and reporting—and that for public sector and nonprofit hospitals, colleges and universities, and other nonprofit organizations—are discussed in later chapters, as is auditing in the G&NP organization environment.

This first chapter is designed to help you begin the transition from business to nonbusiness accounting and financial reporting. As you study and restudy this chapter, note particularly the different environmental factors, concepts, objectives, and terms (e.g., *expenditures, fund balance, and net position*) as well as the abbreviations and acronyms peculiar to G&NP accounting and financial reporting.

The next several chapters focus on SLG accounting principles, budgeting, accounting, and financial reporting. You may find it useful to refer to this chapter as you study these and later chapters.

APPENDIX 1-1

Evolution of Accounting Principles and Standards—Prior to the GASB

Although the origin of the profession of accountancy is sometimes traced to ancient governments, modern municipal accounting developed in the twentieth century—its beginning inseparably woven within the municipal reform movement near the turn of the century. About that time, attention was focused on the scandalous practices in the financial administration of many cities; the National Municipal League suggested uniform municipal reporting formats, and the U.S. Census Bureau encouraged more uniformity in city accounts and reports.

INITIAL EVOLUTION (1900–1933)

A flurry of change in municipal accounting and reporting practices occurred during the first decade of the twentieth century. In 1901, the firm of Haskins and Sells, Certified Public Accountants, investigated the affairs of the city of Chicago at the request of the Merchants' Club. Subsequently, the firm installed a completely new system of accounting for that city. The cities of Newton, Massachusetts, and Baltimore, Maryland, published annual reports during 1901 and 1902 along lines suggested by the National Municipal League, and the states of New York and Massachusetts passed legislation in the areas of uniform accounting and reporting in 1904 and 1906, respectively. Many other examples of progress took place during this period as other cities and states followed suit.

During this era Herman A. Metz was elected Comptroller of New York City on a "business man for the head of the city's business office" slogan. At that time an estimated one-fourth of New York's $80 million personal services budget was being lost through collusion, idleness, or inefficiency, and city departments commonly issued bonds to finance current operating expenditures.

Although Metz was said to have been an outstanding comptroller, his most important contribution was the formation of the Bureau of Municipal Research. One of its purposes was "to promote the adoption of scientific methods of accounting [for] and of reporting the details of municipal business."[15]

The *Handbook of Municipal Accounting,* commonly referred to as "The Metz Fund Handbook," was called "the most significant contribution of the 1910 decade [because] it brought together for the first time many of the basic characteristics and requirements of municipal accounting and outlined methods of appropriate treatment."[16] Similarly, the bureau's publications were the "first organized materials that could be called a treatise in Municipal Accounting."[17] Pamphlets, articles, and a few textbooks appeared as others became more interested in the subject. Municipal leagues were formed in various states and, as Newton expressed it, "We soon began a very serious development of the specialized field of Municipal Accounting."[18]

Interest waned during the 1920s and early 1930s. In a study of Illinois cities during 1931 and 1932, W. E. Karrenbrock found that few had accounting systems adequate to segregate transactions of different activities. None had budgetary accounts coordinated within the regular accounting system.[19]

---

[15]Bureau of Municipal Research, *Making a Municipal Budget: Functional Accounts and Operative Statistics for the Department of Greater New York* (New York: BMR, 1907), 5.

[16]Lloyd Morey, "Trends in Governmental Accounting," *Accounting Review,* 23 (July 1948), 224.

[17]W. K. Newton, "New Developments and Simplified Approaches to Municipal Accounting," *Accounting Review,* 29 (October 1954), 656.

[18]Ibid.

[19]R. P. Hackett, "Recent Developments in Governmental and Institutional Accounting," *Accounting Review,* 8 (June 1933), 122.

Writing in 1933, R. P. Hackett observed:

> The first fact that we are confronted with when searching for recent developments, or any developments, in governmental accounting, particularly that of municipal governments, is the marked absence of any general improvement. . . . it must be admitted that there is very little development in the actual practice of governmental and institutional accounting.[20]

NATIONAL COMMITTEES ON MUNICIPAL AND GOVERNMENTAL ACCOUNTING (1934–1974)

The National Committee on Municipal Accounting was organized in 1934, under the auspices of the Municipal Finance Officers Association, to bring together representatives of various groups concerned with municipal accounting and to put into effect sound principles of accounting, budgeting, and reporting. Its membership included representatives of the American Association of University Instructors in Accounting; the American Institute of Accountants; the American Municipal Association; the American Society of Certified Public Accountants; the International City Managers' Association; the Municipal Finance Officers Association; the National Association of Cost Accountants; the National Association of State Auditors, Controllers, and Treasurers; the National Municipal League; and the Bureau of the Census.[21] Each group represented also had a subcommittee on municipal accounting within its own ranks.

At its organizational meeting, the Committee tentatively adopted certain "principles" of municipal accounting and reporting and began an extensive municipal accounting research program. The Committee's formation was hailed as "the first effort on a national scale to establish principles and standards for municipal accounting and actively promote their use."[22] It was the major event in municipal accounting until that time. Indeed, the Committee's principles were officially recognized by the American Institute of Accountants, predecessor of the American Institute of Certified Public Accountants (AICPA).[23]

Numerous publications defining proper or improved municipal accounting and financial administration practices were issued by the Committee and the Municipal Finance Officers Association (MFOA) in the 1930s and 1940s. In 1948, Morey stated,

> There is no longer any doubt as to what constitutes good accounting, reporting, and auditing for public bodies. The work of the National Committee on Municipal Accounting in particular, in establishing standards and models in these subjects, provides an authority to which officials, accountants, and public may turn with confidence.[24]

In 1951, the Committee, by then known as the National Committee on Governmental Accounting, issued *Municipal Accounting and Auditing.*[25] This book combined and revised the major publications of the Committee and became the basis for the major textbooks in the area, as well as for many state laws and guides relating to municipal accounting, auditing, and reporting. This "bible of municipal accounting," as it came to be called, was succeeded in 1968 by *Governmental Accounting, Auditing, and Financial Reporting* (GAAFR 68), often referred to as the "blue book."[26]

---

[20]Ibid., 122, 127.

[21]Carl H. Chatters, "Municipal Accounting Progresses," *Certified Public Accountant,* 14 (February 1934), 101.

[22]Ibid.

[23]American Institute of Accountants, *Audits of Governmental Bodies and Accounts of Governmental Bodies* (New York: AIA, 1934 and 1935).

[24]Morey, "Trends in Governmental Accounting," 231.

[25]Published by the Municipal Finance Officers Association (Chicago, 1951).

[26]Published by the Municipal Finance Officers Association (Chicago, 1968), hereafter cited as GAAFR (68).

In 1974, the AICPA issued an audit guide, *Audits of State and Local Governmental Units* (ASLGU), to assist its members in the conduct of governmental audits.[27] ASLGU recognized GAAFR as authoritative and stated that, except as modified in ASLGU, the principles in GAAFR constituted generally accepted accounting principles.

The National Committee on Governmental Accounting was not a staff-supported, permanent body that met regularly. Rather, a new committee was formed of appointees of various government agencies, public administration groups, and accounting organizations whenever deemed necessary—historically about every 10 years—and served in an advisory and review capacity for revisions proposed by its members and consultants.

NATIONAL COUNCIL ON GOVERNMENTAL ACCOUNTING (1974–1984)

The National Council on Governmental Accounting (NCGA) succeeded the National Committee on Governmental Accounting in 1974. The MFOA—now the Government Finance Officers Association (GFOA)—established the NCGA as an ongoing body to reconcile the differences between GAAFR and ASLGU and continually evaluate and develop state and local government accounting principles.

The Council consisted of 21 members who served four-year terms on a part-time, voluntary basis and met for about two days, two to four times each year. The NCGA maintained close liaison with the Financial Accounting Standards Board (FASB), the AICPA, and other organizations concerned with state and local government accounting and financial reporting standards.

The NCGA's major agenda project, called the GAAFR Restatement Project, was to develop a statement described as "a modest revision to update, clarify, amplify, and reorder GAAFR." An important related objective was to incorporate pertinent aspects of ASLGU and reconcile any significant differences between GAAFR and ASLGU.

NCGA *Statement 1,* "Governmental Accounting and Financial Reporting Principles," commonly known as the GAAFR Restatement Principles, was issued in 1979. The GAAFR-ASLGU differences had been reconciled during the principles restatement. Accordingly, the AICPA issued a statement of position in 1980 (*SOP 80–2*),[28] amending ASLGU to incorporate NCGA *Statement 1* by reference and provide additional guidance to auditors of state and local government financial statements.

The NCGA issued seven Statements, eleven Interpretations, and one Concepts Statement during its 1974–1984 tenure. Its early years coincided with a turbulent period marked by the fiscal emergency of New York City and by similar financial problems, including debt defaults, in several other major cities and school districts. These crises led to demands that the NCGA issue additional accounting standards. But the NCGA's efforts to provide timely guidance were hampered by the fact that its members served part time, at no pay, and had limited staff support. Thus, leaders of the accounting profession, including members of the NCGA, sought to devise an improved approach to setting accounting standards applicable to state and local governments. Their efforts led to the creation of the Governmental Accounting Standards Board (GASB) in 1984 to succeed the NCGA, as discussed earlier in this chapter.

---

[27]Committee on Governmental Accounting and Auditing, American Institute of Certified Public Accountants, *Audits of State and Local Governmental Units* (New York: AICPA, 1974).

[28]Audit Standards Division, American Institute of Certified Public Accountants, Inc., *Statement of Position 80–2,* "Accounting and Financial Reporting by Governmental Units" (New York: AICPA, June 30, 1980).

Questions

Q1-1 Discuss (a) the similarities in accounting for profit-seeking and G&NP organizations, and (b) the unique aspects of accounting for G&NP organizations designed to help ensure compliance with budgeted spending limits.

Q1-2 (a) Define *fund* as used in government organizations. (b) Contrast that definition with the same term as used in a profit-seeking organization. (c) Does the creation of a fund constitute authority to spend or obligate its resources? Explain.

Q1-3 Distinguish between governmental (expendable) funds and proprietary (nonexpendable) funds.

Q1-4 Contrast the terms *expense* and *expenditure*.

Q1-5 It was noted in this chapter that most of the differences between commercial accounting and accounting for G&NP organizations result from differences in (a) organizational objectives, (b) sources of financial resources, and (c) methods of evaluating performance and operating results. Explain.

Q1-6 Discuss the roles of the GASB and the FASB in standards setting for G&NP organizations.

Q1-7 The revenues of profit-seeking organizations are based on user charges. Users may be charged for various services provided by G&NP organizations as well. However, the nature and purpose of user charges of G&NP organizations and those of profit-seeking organizations often differ. Explain.

Q1-8 Different sets of accounting and reporting concepts, principles, and standards have evolved for state and local governments, nonprofit organizations, and business enterprises. Given the differences between and among them, how can they all be considered "generally accepted accounting principles"?

Q1-9 (a) What is the purpose of the GASB GAAP hierarchy guidelines? (b) How would an accountant or auditor use the hierarchy if the guidance given in a GASB statement and an AICPA audit and accounting guide regarding the proper accounting treatment of a state government transaction or event conflict?

Q1-10 How can one determine whether a specific not-for-profit organization should follow GASB guidance? FASB guidance?

Exercises

E1-1 (Multiple Choice) Identify the best answer for each of the following:
1. The body with primary accounting standards-setting authority for state and local governments is the
   a. American Institute of Certified Public Accountants.
   b. Financial Accounting Standards Board.
   c. Government Finance Officers Association.
   d. Governmental Accounting Standards Board.
   e. U.S. Government Accountability Office.
2. The body with primary accounting standards-setting authority for colleges and universities is the
   a. National Association of College and University Business Officers.
   b. Financial Accounting Standards Board.
   c. Governmental Accounting Standards Board.
   d. Governmental Accounting Standards Board for governmental colleges and universities and the Financial Accounting Standards Board for all other colleges and universities.
   e. U.S. Department of Education.
3. A governmental (expendable) fund accounting entity
   a. is often useful in accounting for general government activities but is optional (expendable).
   b. includes only financial assets and related liabilities and depreciable (expendable) capital assets. Nondepreciable capital assets are not reported in governmental funds.
   c. includes financial assets and related liabilities.
   d. has its operating activities measured and reported in terms of revenues and expenses, but the timing of expense recognition differs from that in similar business organizations.

4. In which of the following situations would the amounts of expense and expenditure for the period differ?
   a. An entity uses and is billed for utilities but has paid only half of the amount billed at year end.
   b. An entity purchases equipment for cash. The purchase occurred on the last day of the fiscal year.
   c. Salaries and wages incurred and paid during the period were $100,000. Additional salaries and wages accrued at year end were $4,000.
   d. The amount of expense and expenditure to be recognized differs in more than one of these situations.

5. Legally adopted budgets of governmental funds are
   a. fixed-dollar budgets, which establish expenditure limits that are not to be exceeded.
   b. fixed budgets that cannot be modified during the budget year.
   c. flexible budgets in which the expenditure limits are automatically modified to reflect larger than budgeted levels of various services.
   d. always adopted using the same basis of accounting required by GAAP.

6. Which of the following statements is *false*? A fund
   a. is an entity for which financial statements can be prepared.
   b. has a self-encompassing, self-balancing accounting equation.
   c. is used to account for a subset of an organization's resources that is to be used for a specific purpose or to achieve a particular objective.
   d. is an accounting entity that is used for one year only. Each year a new set of funds must be established.

7. Which of the following pronouncements provides the most authoritative guidance applicable to financial reporting for state and local governments?
   a. FASB Accounting Standards Codification
   b. Statements of Position of the AICPA that have been "cleared" by the GASB
   c. GASB Technical Bulletins
   d. The AICPA government audit guide
   e. GASB Interpretations.

8. One unique characteristic of most government and nonprofit organizations is that
   a. a primary source of financing is sales of services and goods to customers.
   b. their constituency automatically dictates what the government's or nonprofit organization's resources are (to be) used to accomplish.
   c. there is no direct relationship between the amount of goods or services that most resource providers receive and the amount of resources provided by each individual.
   d. these entities sometimes have restrictions placed on what their resources may be used for, whereas such restrictions cannot be placed on business resources.

9. Organizations that are considered to be nonprofit include all of the following except:
   a. churches.
   b. the Boy Scouts and Girl Scouts.
   c. Semi-professional baseball team
   d. state CPA societies.

10. Which of the following statements is true?
    a. Governmental and nonprofit organizations never operate with a profit motive.
    b. Businesses have scarce resources that must be allocated to different uses; governments and nonprofits are able to command sufficient resources to avoid the need for such allocations.
    c. Typically, governmental and nonprofit organizations have more restricted resources than do business entities.
    d. Nonprofit organizations never use fund accounting.

E1-2 (Expenditures vs. Expenses) Family Services, a small social service nonprofit agency, began operations on January 1, 20X1, with $40,000 cash and $150,000 worth of equipment, on which $60,000 was owed on a note to City Bank. The equipment was expected to have a remaining useful life of 15 years with no salvage value. During its first year of operations, ending December 31, 20X1, Family Services paid or accrued the following:
   1. Salaries and other personnel costs, $100,000.
   2. Rent and utilities, $24,000.
   3. Debt service—interest, $5,500, and payment on long-term note principal, $10,000.
   4. Capital outlay—additional equipment purchased January 3, $30,000, expected to last 6 years and have a $6,000 salvage value.
   5. Other current operating items paid with cash, $4,500.

There were no prepayals or unrecorded accruals at December 31, 20X1, and no additional debt was incurred during the year.

Compute for the Family Services agency, for the year ended December 31, 20X1, its total (a) expenses and (b) expenditures.

Required

Problems

P1-1 (Statement of Revenues and Expenditures—Worksheet) Hatcher Township prepares its annual General Fund budget on the cash basis and maintains its accounting records on the cash basis during the year. At the end of Hatcher Township's 20X9 calendar year, you determine the following:

General Fund	Budget (Cash) Basis		Accruals	
	Budget	Actual	1/1/X9	12/31/X9
Revenues:				
Taxes	$600,000	$595,000	$ —	$ 6,000
Licenses	200,000	206,000	—	—
Intergovernmental	100,000	110,000	9,000	1,000
Other	50,000	45,000	5,000	—
	950,000	956,000	14,000	7,000
Expenditures:				
Salaries	700,000	704,000	17,000	11,000
Utilities	80,000	85,000	—	—
Supplies	70,000	64,000	—	7,000
Equipment	60,000	58,000	2,000	12,000
Other	30,000	31,000	—	—
	940,000	942,000	$19,000	$30,000
Excess of Revenues Over (Under) Expenditures	$ 10,000	$ 14,000		

Required

(1) Prepare a worksheet to derive a GAAP basis (including accruals) statement of revenues and expenditures for the Hatcher Township General Fund for the 20X9 fiscal year.

(2) Could the readers of the budgetary basis and GAAP basis statements get different impressions of the 20X9 operating results of the Hatcher Township General Fund? Explain.

P1-2 (SLG GAAP Hierarchy) Mark O. Sleuth, a recent accounting graduate, has been assigned to research several local governmental accounting and financial reporting issues. For each issue, rank the sources of guidance according to the governmental GAAP hierarchy.

1. Issue 1: The AICPA state and local government (SLG) Audit and Accounting Guide, a GASB Technical Bulletin, a leading governmental accounting textbook, a GASB Interpretation, and a section of the FASB Accounting Standards Codification.
2. Issue 2: A leading governmental accounting textbook, a GASB Implementation Guide, an article in a leading auditing journal, and a speech by a leading governmental accounting professor.
3. Issue 3: The AICPA SLG Audit and Accounting Guide, a GASB Statement, a journal article that summarizes current practice on the issue in the United States, notes from a telephone conversation on the issue with the GASB director of research, and a FASB Interpretation.
4. Issue 4: An AICPA Statement of Position (cleared by the GASB), an article by the managing partner of an international public accounting firm, a GASB Technical Bulletin, and the FASB Accounting Standards Codification.
5. Issue 5: The GASB Comprehensive Implementation Guide, the AICPA SLG Audit and Accounting Guide, four articles from the *Journal of Accountancy,* and a leading governmental accounting textbook.

P1-3 (Internet Research Problem) Locate the homepages for the following organizations and prepare a brief critique (one to three pages, perhaps with attachments) of the contents of each site:

1. Governmental Accounting Standards Board.
2. Financial Accounting Standards Board.
3. American Institute of Certified Public Accountants.
4. Government Finance Officers Association.
5. Association of Government Accountants.
6. National Association of State Auditors, Comptrollers, and Treasurers.
7. National Association of College and University Business Officers.
8. Association of School Business Officials International.

P1-4 (Internet Research Problem) Locate the GASB White Paper, "Why Governmental Accounting and Financial Reporting Is—and Should Be—Different," on the Governmental Accounting Standards Board Web site. Prepare a brief summary and critical analysis of the White Paper.

CHAPTER 2

State and Local Government Accounting and Financial Reporting Model

The Foundation

LEARNING OBJECTIVES

After studying this chapter, you should be able to:

- Visualize and discuss the major overall aspects of the GASB state and local government financial reporting model, including the *dual perspective* of government-wide and fund financial statements.

- Define *fund*, identify and explain the three broad *categories* of funds—governmental, proprietary, and fiduciary—and identify the specific *types* of funds in each fund category.

- Identify the *measurement focus* and *basis* of accounting used for each category of funds and the financial statements required for funds of each category.

- Analyze the effects of transactions on the proprietary fund and governmental fund categories and on the General Capital Assets and General Long-Term Liabilities accounts.

- Discuss typical budgetary accounting and reporting requirements.

- Understand the specific types of funds in each fund category and the different uses of each fund type in each category.

- Explain the financial reporting requirements for a government's basic financial statements and its comprehensive annual financial report.

State and local government is truly "big business." The 50 states and 89,000 local governments within the United States employ more than 19 million persons—more than seven times the federal government civilian employment—and spend more than $2.6 trillion annually. Although the federal government accounts for over half of all government expenditures, state and local governments spend more for nondefense purposes than does the federal government. Furthermore, state and local government revenues, expenditures, debt, and employment—both total and per capita—have been increasing in recent years. Today the state government often is the largest industry within a state, and city hall often houses the biggest business in a town.

The types and numbers of local governments are shown in Illustration 2-1. However, the extent of local government jurisdictional overlap is not obvious from that listing. It is common for a given geographic area to be served by a municipality, a school district, a county, and one or more special districts. In fact, many metropolitan areas have 100 or more separate and distinct local government units.

ILLUSTRATION 2-1 Types of Local Governments	
Counties	3,033
Municipalities	19,492
Townships	16,519
School districts	13,051
Special districts	37,381
Total	89,476

Source: 2007 Census of Governments.

State and local governments (SLGs) have increased both the types and levels of goods and services provided to their citizens in recent years, and many governments are among the most complex and diversified organizations in existence. No doubt their scope and complexity—as well as their relative importance in our economy and society—will continue to grow as our society becomes increasingly urban and governments at all levels attempt to meet the demands of their constituencies for more and better goods and services.

The concepts and objectives of SLG financial reporting discussed and illustrated in Chapter 1 provide the background needed to understand the basic principles of governmental accounting and financial reporting. Standards of SLG accounting and financial reporting discussed in this chapter, including discussions and illustrations of transaction analysis and fund accounting, provide the foundation for understanding SLG accounting and financial reporting.

OVERVIEW OF THE GASB FINANCIAL REPORTING MODEL

The SLG financial reporting model is based primarily on GASB *Statement No. 34*, "Basic Financial Statements—and Management's Discussion and Analysis—for State and Local Governments,"[1] as amended. The ***basic financial statements*** of this model are summarized in Illustration 2-2.

The financial reporting model has been called a *"dual perspective"* model because it requires reporting *both*:

- **Fund Financial Statements**—*detailed* presentations of *fund* net position or fund balance, operating results, and (for proprietary funds) cash flows.
- **Government-wide Financial Statements**—*condensed consolidating overview* presentations of the SLG's net position and activities.

Observe in Illustration 2-2 that:

- the ***notes*** to the financial statements typically are notes to ***both*** the *fund* and *government-wide* **basic** financial statements, and
- the ***fund financial statements and government-wide financial statements*** are considered to be one set of financial statements and thus are ***linked*** by reconciliations (explanations) of their differences.

SLGs do *not* maintain separate fund and government-wide *accounts*. Rather:

- SLG accounting systems are designed to provide ***fund*** budget, grant, and other compliance controls as well as data from which ***fund*** financial statements are prepared.
- The ***government-wide*** statements typically are ***derived*** from the fund financial statements using ***worksheet*** adjustments that are ***not*** posted to the accounts.

---

[1]Governmental Accounting Standards Board (1999).

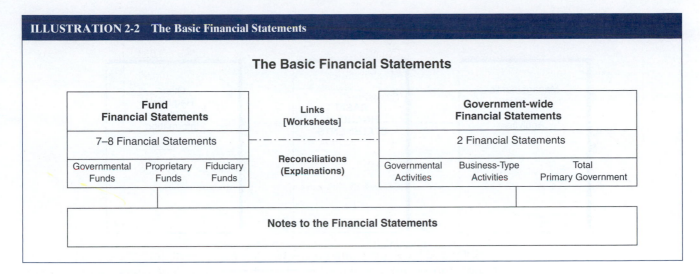

ILLUSTRATION 2-2   The Basic Financial Statements

The minimum requirements for external government financial reports that comply with generally accepted accounting principles (GAAP) are demonstrated in Illustration 2-3. Note in this illustration that:

1. The *shaded* arrow indicates that the *fund* financial statement data are ***adjusted*** to derive the data for the *government-wide* financial statements.

2. The fund financial statements, government-wide financial statements, and notes to the financial statements collectively comprise the ***"basic"* financial statements**.

3. The *light* arrow indicates that
   - the *government-wide* financial statements are highly summarized,
   - the *fund* financial statements are more detailed than the government-wide statements, and
   - the *notes* are more detailed than the fund financial statements.

4. The basic financial statements must be ***accompanied*** by certain "required supplementary information" (**RSI**) to meet the minimum requirements for a **general purpose external financial report**. RSI includes:
   - **Management's Discussion and Analysis (MD&A)**—a brief analysis and discussion by the SLG's management of its financial statements, its schedules, other specified analyses, and any known event or situation that is expected to affect the SLG in the near future.
   - **Other Required Supplementary Information (RSI)**—such as actuarial information related to the SLG's defined benefit pension plan and other postemployment benefit plans.

Note that *neither* the MD&A *nor* other RSI are integral parts of the basic financial statements. Rather, as noted earlier, they are required to "accompany" the basic financial statements.

These summary overviews of the GASB financial reporting model (summarized in Illustrations 2-2 and 2-3) are refined and expanded later in this chapter. The basic financial statements and the comprehensive annual financial report are discussed and illustrated in detail in Chapters 13 and 15, respectively.

THE FUNDAMENTAL FEATURES OF THE SLG ACCOUNTING AND FINANCIAL REPORTING MODEL

The GASB notes in introducing its *Codification of Governmental Accounting and Financial Reporting Standards* that governmental accounting entails many of the same basic concepts, conventions, and characteristics as business accounting. However, as stated in Chapter 1, the basic objectives of business and government

ILLUSTRATION 2-3 **Minimum Requirements for the General Purpose External Financial Report**

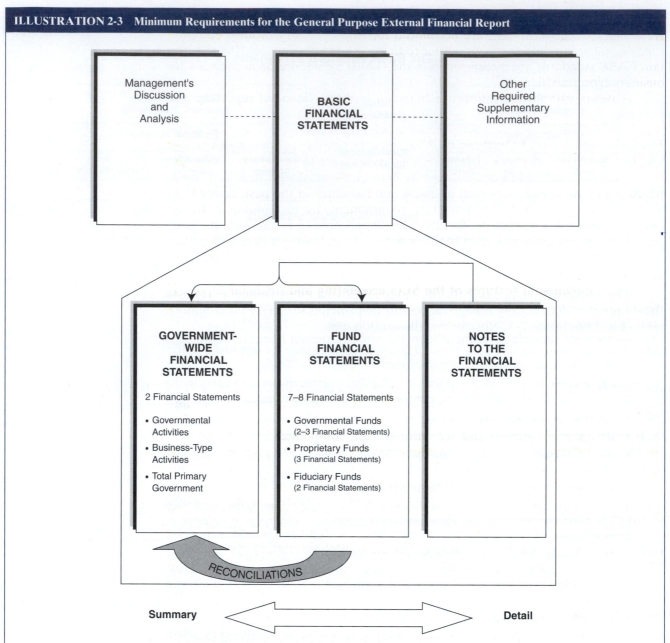

Source: Adapted from Governmental Accounting Standards Board, Continuing Professional Education, "The New Financial Reporting Model—A Review of GASB Statement 34, *Basic Financial Statements—and Management's Discussion and Analysis—for State and Local Governments*" (Norwalk, CT: GASB, 2000).

differ. Not surprisingly, the manner in which we report on each type of entity's progress toward its objectives also differs.

Consequently, the fundamental accounting and financial reporting principles for government entail many notable differences from those principles that apply to business activities. Many of the characteristics of governmental accounting and much of the GASB's guidance relate to the use of multiple fund accounting entities to account for and report on a state or local government. Most other features and GASB authoritative guidance are associated with the general government activities and transactions.

The GASB traditionally has focused its attention primarily on *general government* activities and transactions that are accounted for in governmental (expendable) funds. The public enterprise and other business-type activities of state and local governments are accounted for in proprietary (nonexpendable) funds using accounting methods similar to those used for businesses. Indeed, certain FASB standards are incorporated in the GASB's guidance on accounting for business-type activities.

A newly established difference between business financial reporting and government financial reporting is the inclusion of two additional financial statement elements in government balance sheets. GASB Statement No. 63, "Financial Reporting of Deferred Outflows of Resources, Deferred Inflows of Resources, and Net Position," requires government balance sheets to include separate sections to report deferred outflows and deferred inflows. These deferred items, which would have been reported as assets and liabilities in the past, result from changes in net assets that do not meet the requirements for recognition in the operating statements and that the GASB deems applicable to future periods. Only specific items designated by the GASB as deferred outflows and deferred inflows may be reported in these balance sheet classifications. We will address these items as they arise in the text.

The fundamental features of the SLG accounting and financial reporting model are divided into the following sections for ease of discussion: (1) GAAP and legal compliance, (2) fund accounting, (3) fund categories, (4) types of funds, (5) comparative financial statement formats, and (6) annual financial reporting.

GAAP and Legal Compliance

As discussed in Chapter 1, governments operate in a different environment than businesses. Governments must comply with the many *finance-related legal and contractual requirements, regulations, restrictions, and agreements* that affect their financial management and accounting. Such compliance must be demonstrable and be reported on regularly. Governments should also prepare financial statements in conformity with GAAP, which provide uniform minimum national standards of and guidelines for annual financial reporting to groups and persons outside the government. Therefore, a government's accounting system must be designed to maintain and provide information to accomplish multiple purposes.

Business accounting systems must provide data both for GAAP reporting and for income tax reporting. Similarly, governmental accounting systems must provide data both for external reporting in conformity with GAAP and for controlling and reporting on finance-related legal compliance matters.

GAAP Reporting

GAAP-based financial statements are necessary to ensure proper external financial reporting and a reasonable degree of comparability among the annual financial statements of governments across the nation. GAAP reporting

- Ensures that the annual financial reports of all state and local governments—regardless of their legal provisions and customs—contain the *same* types of financial statements and disclosures for the *same* categories and types of funds and activities and are based on the *same* measurement and classification criteria.
- Requires "*full*" disclosure, thus mandating far more note disclosures, in particular, than under the FASB "*adequate*" disclosure requirements.

Even though significant aspects of GAAP are intended to demonstrate compliance with legal and contractual requirements, many compliance reporting requirements are more extensive than those mandated by GAAP.

Compliance

Determining and reporting on compliance with *finance-related legal and contractual provisions* may be relatively simple or quite complex. In some instances, the only finance-related legal compliance provision is that the government prepare both its annual operating budget and its financial statements in conformity with GAAP. In such cases, legal compliance provisions and GAAP do not conflict, and the accounting system may be established on a GAAP basis.

In other instances, certain finance-related legal provisions conflict with GAAP. The most common conflict occurs when a government's annual operating budget is prepared on a basis significantly different from the GAAP basis. For example:

- A school district may budget on the *cash basis*, under which revenues are not recorded until cash is received and expenditures are not recognized until cash is disbursed.

- A city may budget on a cash basis but also consider *encumbrances*—the estimated cost of goods or services ordered but not yet received—to be expenditures for budgetary purposes. Note that encumbrances do not represent expenditures or liabilities under GAAP.

Finance-related compliance conflicts also occur if federal or state grantor agencies require a local government to keep its grant accounting records on a non-GAAP basis.

Many governments budget on a non-GAAP basis. Therefore, it is important to identify a government's *budgetary basis*. If the budgetary basis differs significantly from the GAAP basis, a government must (1) maintain budgetary accounting control during the year on the budgetary basis while also accumulating the additional data needed for GAAP reporting, (2) clearly distinguish its budgetary basis from the GAAP basis, and (3) prepare financial statements or schedules on both bases and explain and reconcile the differences between the budgetary basis and GAAP basis amounts.

Providing data for both legal compliance and GAAP reports does *not* require maintaining two accounting systems. Rather, just as the data for the government-wide financial statements are derived by adjusting the fund financial statement data, the accounts will be kept on the budgetary basis, and the system will also provide the additional data needed to adjust the accounts to the GAAP basis at year end.

The emphasis on budgeting, budgetary control, and budgetary accountability is unique to the governmental environment, and budgetary topics are discussed at several points in this book. Budgeting, budgetary accounting control, and budgetary reporting are considered in depth in Chapter 4 and in the chapters that deal with funds for which budgeting, budgetary control, and budgetary accountability are particularly important. The presentation of budgetary comparison statements or schedules for certain governmental funds in a government's annual financial reports is explained in detail in Chapter 13.

Fund Accounting

Fund accounting is the most distinctive feature of governmental accounting. Governmental accounting systems are designed, organized, and operated on a fund basis. The use of fund accounting allows governments both to maintain proper accounting controls over restricted and designated resources and to demonstrate compliance with finance-related legal and contractual provisions. For example, a local government often receives resources from a state government that are restricted for a particular use. By accounting for these resources in a fund, the local government can demonstrate that it complied with the restrictions placed on the resources. Understanding the fund structure, model, and interrelationships among funds is essential to mastering governmental accounting and financial reporting.

A **fund** is an independent accounting entity with a self-balancing set of accounts. In broad terms, a single fund accounting entity is somewhat like a business accounting entity:

- Each business accounting entity has a self-balancing set of accounts sufficient to capture all the reported attributes for the entire business and all its transactions.

- Likewise, each fund of a government has a self-balancing set of accounts sufficient to capture all the reported attributes of the portion of a government's activities and resources that are accounted for in each particular fund.

A *key difference* is that *one* accounting entity is used to account for all the activities and resources of a business, whereas *each fund* accounting *entity* is used to account for only a certain **subset** of a government's activities and resources.

Likewise, each business accounting entity has its own journals, its own ledger, its own trial balance, and its own financial statements. Similarly, for each fund of a government, there are separate journals and a separate ledger and trial balance; and separate financial statements are prepared and presented.

From an accounting and financial management viewpoint, a governmental unit is a combination of several distinctly different fiscal and accounting entities, each having a separate set of accounts and functioning independently of the other funds and nonfund accounts (see Illustration 2-4).

Fund Categories

Four distinct categories of accounting entities—three categories of funds and the nonfund accounts—are employed in governmental accounting. A few points from the discussion of the state and local government environment should help explain the categories of funds and the general capital assets (GCA) and general long-term liabilities (GLTL) nonfund accounts, and the nature of these accounting entities.

First, recall that a general purpose unit of government has a dual nature. Some of its activities are **general government** in nature; others are **business-type**

ILLUSTRATION 2-4   Accounting Entities of State and Local Governments

THE STATE OR LOCAL GOVERNMENT UNIT

The "General Government" Accounting Entities

Permanent Funds
Debt Service Funds
Capital Projects Funds
Special Revenue Funds
The General Fund
GOVERNMENTAL FUNDS

General Capital Assets and General Long-Term Liabilities
NONFUND ACCOUNTS

Internal Service Funds
Enterprise Funds
PROPRIETARY FUNDS

Agency Funds
Investment Trust Funds
Private-Purpose Trust Funds
Pension Trust Funds
FIDUCIARY FUNDS

Legend:
— Categories of funds and nonfund accounts
— Types of funds and nonfund accounts

Notes:
1. Each fund accounting entity is an independent accounting entity with a separate self-balancing set of accounts. (State and local governments do not have a single central accounting entity.)
2. Financial statements may be prepared for each fund (individual fund statements), for all nonmajor funds of each category or for all funds of each type (combining statements), and for the government reporting entity (major fund and government-wide financial statements).

activities. Next, recall that general government activities typically have unique sources of financial resources such as taxes and grants.

- Both decisions about allocating these resources to various purposes and control of **general government activities** focus heavily on sources and uses of *expendable financial* resources.
- The **business-type activities** may be controlled and evaluated much like their business counterparts. Many of the information needs of financial report users about these activities are similar to their needs for information about similar businesses.

Consistent with these key points, two broad *categories* of funds and the nonfund GCA and GLTL accounts are used to account for state and local government activities and resources (other than those held in a fiduciary capacity):

- *General government* activities and resources are accounted for in *governmental* funds and the nonfund GCA and GLTL accounts.
- *Business-type* activities are accounted for in *proprietary* funds.

Proprietary Funds

Although governmental funds are used to account for the majority of activities for most governments, the accounting for proprietary funds is more familiar to most accounting students because of its similarity to accounting for businesses. Proprietary funds are used to account for a government's continuing business-type organizations and activities. For example, municipalities often use a proprietary fund to account for the activities of a water utility—activities related to the sale and distribution of water to residents and businesses. All assets, liabilities, equities, revenues, expenses, and transactions pertaining to these business-type organizations and activities are accounted for through proprietary funds. Two new financial statement elements—deferred outflows and deferred inflows—are reported as well. Proprietary fund accounting measures net position, changes in net position, and cash flows.

Except for modifications related to reporting some balance sheet items as deferred outflows and deferred inflows, the basic proprietary fund accounting equation is similar to the familiar business accounting equation. The proprietary fund accounting equation is:

$$\text{Assets} + \text{Deferred Outflows} - \text{Liabilities} - \text{Deferred Inflows} = \text{Net Position}$$

Alternatively, the assets and liabilities in the equation may be divided into their components, resulting in this proprietary fund accounting equation that will be used in subsequent discussions:

$$\left(\begin{array}{c} \text{Current Assets} \\ + \\ \text{Noncurrent (including Capital) Assets} \\ + \\ \text{Deferred Outflows} \end{array} - \begin{array}{c} \text{Current Liabilities} \\ + \\ \text{Long-Term Liabilities} \\ + \\ \text{Deferred Inflows} \end{array} = \begin{array}{c} \text{Net} \\ \text{Position} \end{array} \right)$$

This variation of the basic proprietary fund accounting equation will be helpful later when comparing accounting for proprietary funds and governmental funds.

The GASB specifies different methods of applying the accrual concept. These different methods are referred to as the **measurement focus (MF)** and **basis of accounting (BA)**—or, together, as the **MFBA**. Elementary and intermediate business accounting textbooks generally do not refer to the MFBA used for business accounting. If they did, the business accounting MFBA would be the **economic resources** measurement focus and **accrual** basis of accounting. The business MFBA also are used to recognize assets, liabilities, revenues, and expenses in proprietary funds.

The **measurement focus** generally refers to the types of transactions, events, or elements that are reported in financial statements. An **economic resources** measurement focus results in financial statement recognition of *all* assets, both *current* and *noncurrent*, and *all* liabilities, both *current* and *long-term*, as well as all related deferred outflows and deferred inflows. Revenues and *expenses* that are recognized in proprietary fund operating statements generally represent changes in the net assets related to the reporting period.

The definitions of *current assets* and *current liabilities*—and most of the generally accepted accounting principles applicable to proprietary funds—are the same as those applicable to similar businesses. Like businesses, capital assets and long-term liabilities of proprietary funds are recognized in proprietary fund financial statements. Most capital assets (called fixed assets and intangible assets in business) generally should be *depreciated* (*amortized*) over their estimated useful lives. Certain capital assets, such as land and land improvements, are inexhaustible and should *not* be depreciated.

Governmental Funds

Governmental funds generally are used to account for the **sources, uses, and balances** of a government's **general government financial resources** and any related deferred outflows and deferred inflows. In their simplest form, governmental funds are merely segregations of general government **net financial assets** according to the purpose(s) for which they may be used.

- **Financial** assets are assigned to the several governmental funds according to the purposes for which they may (or must) be expended.

- **Related** liabilities—those general government liabilities (except unmatured general long-term liabilities) payable from governmental funds—are accounted for in the governmental fund from which the expenditures giving rise to the related liabilities were made, and thus from which they are to be paid.

- The *difference* between governmental fund *financial assets* plus *deferred outflows* less *related liabilities* less *deferred inflows* is known as the **fund balance**.

In sum, the accounting equation of a simple governmental fund is:

$$\begin{bmatrix} \text{Financial Assets} \\ \text{(FA)} \\ + \\ \text{Deferred Outflows} \end{bmatrix} - \begin{bmatrix} \text{Related Liabilities} \\ \text{(RL)} \\ + \\ \text{Deferred Inflows} \end{bmatrix} = \begin{matrix} \text{Fund Balance} \\ \text{(FB)} \end{matrix}$$

In *governmental funds*, these terms are used as follows:

- **Financial Assets (FA)** refers primarily to cash, investments, and receivables.[2]
- **Related Liabilities (RL)** refers primarily to general government liabilities that are related to the current year and are normally paid from available expendable financial assets.
- **Fund Balance (FB)** refers to the *net* position of the fund—the *difference* between its financial assets (FA) plus deferred outflows (DO) and its related liabilities (RL) and deferred inflows (DI).

The major difference between the proprietary fund and the governmental fund accounting equations is that the governmental fund accounting equation does *not* include either capital assets used in general government activities or unmatured long-term liabilities incurred for those activities. Therefore, one can conclude correctly that *governmental fund accounting and financial reporting focus on financial resources that are available for spending in the relatively near future.*

The accounting equations for proprietary funds and governmental funds differ because their MFBA differ. Governmental funds use the **current financial resources** measurement focus and **modified accrual** basis to recognize assets, liabilities (as well as deferred outflows and deferred inflows related to those assets and liabilities), revenues, and expenditures. Financial assets and related liabilities are accounted for through governmental funds primarily because these funds focus on sources, uses, and balances of financial resources available for spending. Revenues and *expenditures* that are recognized in governmental fund operating

---

[2]Inventories (e.g., of supplies) and prepayals (e.g., for part of next year's insurance premiums) may be reported as governmental fund assets.

statements generally represent current-period changes in these financial assets and related liabilities. *Revenues* and *expenditures* in governmental funds do *not* have the same meaning as *revenues* and *expenses* in proprietary funds. In governmental funds, revenues and expenditures generally are related to the receipt and use of available financial resources, respectively:

1. **Revenues** must be (1) *earned during or levied for* the period, (2) *objectively measurable*, and (3) "**available**"—*collected* within the period or soon enough thereafter to pay liabilities incurred for expenditures of the period. Otherwise, they must be reported either as unearned revenues or as *deferred* revenues. Revenues are recognized only when all three criteria, including the availability criterion, are met. (Thus, revenues may be recognized later in governmental funds than in proprietary funds.)

2. **Expenditures** (not expenses)—for current operations, capital outlay, and debt service—are recognized (1) when operating or capital outlay liabilities to be paid currently from governmental funds are incurred, and (2) when general government debt service (principal and interest) payments on long-term liabilities are due.

The distinction between *expenditures* and *expenses* is extremely important in governmental accounting. **Expenses**—recognized in proprietary fund, trust fund, and government-wide financial statements—are costs *expired* during a period, including depreciation and other allocations, as in business accounting.

Expenditures—recognized in governmental fund financial statements—are generally net financial assets *expended* during a period for current operations, capital outlay, long-term debt principal retirement, and interest. With the exception of long-term debt principal retirement, *expenditures* typically reflect the net financial assets *expended* to *acquire* goods or services, whereas *expenses* reflect the cost of goods or services *used*. This important distinction is explained further in Illustration 2-5.

In sum, the *modified accrual basis* is used to account for the inflows, outflows, and balances of net *expendable* financial assets and related deferred amounts of governmental funds. The term *accrual basis* refers to accounting for revenues earned, expenses incurred, and other changes in net position in proprietary fund, trust fund, and government-wide financial statements. The application of the modified accrual and accrual bases is discussed and illustrated throughout this text.

ILLUSTRATION 2-5 Expenditures vs. Expenses

Expenditures (Net Financial Resources Expended)		Expenses (Costs Expired)	
Operating:	Salaries	**Operating:**	Salaries
	Utilities, etc.		Utilities, etc.
Capital:	Capital Outlay	**Capital:**	Depreciation
Debt Service:	Interest	**Debt Service:**	Interest
	Long-Term Liability Principal Retirement		

Observations

1. **Operating.** Operating expenses and expenditures often are identical but *may differ* somewhat because of accrual or allocation differences in expense and expenditure measurement standards.

2. **Capital.** The entire cost of capital assets acquired during the period is accounted for as a *capital outlay expenditure*, whereas a portion of all exhaustible capital asset costs incurred to date is allocated to each period as *depreciation expense*. Depreciation expense is not a use of governmental fund net financial resources and thus is not recorded as an expenditure.

3. **Debt Service.** Interest is both an expenditure and an expense, though not necessarily of the same amount. Long-term debt principal retirement is an *expenditure* but *not* an *expense*.

Deferred Outflows and Deferred Inflows—Discussion Approach

In the previous section, our discussion of the accounting equations and financial statement elements adhered strictly to the GASB's model. From this point we will modify our approach. Most governments have relatively few types of deferred outflows and deferred inflows. Indeed, in governmental funds the most common examples of deferred inflows are:

- taxes collected in advance of the period for which they are levied or levied in the current period to finance the next period(s) and
- amounts related to deferral of revenue recognition because of the "availability" criterion—i.e., because cash was not collected soon enough after year end.

Deferred outflows are not common in governmental funds of most SLGs.

Deferred outflows and deferred inflows result from delaying operating statement recognition of certain changes in the net amount of assets less liabilities. The GASB requires these changes to be classified as deferred outflows instead of assets (or as deferred inflows instead of liabilities) when the GASB views the change as related to future periods.

Deferred outflows are reported similarly to assets, and changes in deferred outflows affect the operating statement in essentially the same way as changes in assets. Likewise, deferred inflows are reported similarly to liabilities, and changes in deferred inflows affect the operating statement in essentially the same manner as changes in liabilities.

Specific deferred outflows and deferred inflows are discussed as they arise in the text. We will avoid making the discussion cumbersome and confusing by referring to them each time assets and liabilities are mentioned.

Nonfund Accounts

As previously mentioned, capital assets used in general government activities (*general capital assets*) and ***unmatured*** long-term liabilities incurred for those activities (*general long-term liabilities*) are ***not*** accounted for in governmental funds or recognized in governmental fund financial statements. The GASB provides several reasons for ***not*** including general capital assets in governmental fund financial statements:

General capital assets do *not* represent *financial resources* available for expenditure, *but* are items for which *financial resources* have been *used* and for which accountability should be maintained.

- They are *not* assets of any *fund* but of the governmental unit as an instrumentality.
- Their inclusion in the financial statements of a governmental fund would increase the fund balance, which could *mislead* users of the fund balance sheet.
- The *primary purposes* for *governmental fund* accounting are to reflect its revenues and expenditures—the sources and uses of its financial resources—and its assets, the related liabilities, and the *net financial resources available for subsequent appropriation and expenditure*.[3]

The GASB rationale for ***not*** reporting general long-term liabilities in governmental fund financial statements complements the reasons given for ***not*** reporting general capital assets:

The **general long-term liabilities** of a state or local government are secured by the general credit and revenue-raising powers of the government rather than by the assets acquired or specific fund resources. Further, just as general capital assets do not represent financial resources available for appropriation and expenditure, the *unmatured* principal of general long-term liabilities does *not* require *current appropriation and expenditure* of governmental fund financial resources. To include it as a governmental fund liability would be *misleading and dysfunctional* to the current period management control (for example, budgeting) and accountability functions.[4]

---

[3]GASB *Codification*, sections 1400 and 1500.104, as adapted and with emphasis added.

[4]Ibid., section 1500.104, as adapted and with emphasis added.

Although general capital assets and unmatured general long-term liabilities do not fit in the governmental fund accounting equation and are not recognized under the governmental fund MFBA, significant amounts of these capital assets and long-term liabilities are used in governmental activities. *Accountability for these general capital assets and unmatured general long-term liabilities is maintained in separate nonfund accounts.*

The GASB does *not* specify how to maintain the nonfund accounts for general capital assets (GCA) and general long-term liabilities (GLTL). Thus, one set of nonfund accounts can be maintained for GCA and another set of nonfund accounts can be maintained for unmatured GLTL. We illustrate a single set of nonfund accounts that combine the GCA and unmatured GLTL accounts. The accounting equation for the combined **General Capital Assets and General Long-Term Liabilities Nonfund Accounts** is:

$$\begin{array}{ccccc} \text{General Capital} & & \text{Unmatured General} & & \\ \text{Assets} & - & \text{Long-Term Liabilities} & = & \text{Net Position} \\ \text{(GCA)} & & \text{(GLTL)} & & \text{(NP)} \end{array}$$

The governmental funds and the nonfund accounts are used to account for "*general government*" activities, whereas the *proprietary* funds and fiduciary funds are used to account for government organizations and relationships that are similar to those in the private sector.

 Only those assets, liabilities, deferred outflows, deferred inflows, transactions, and events that clearly relate specifically to the proprietary funds and fiduciary funds are recorded in those fund categories.

 All other assets, liabilities, deferred outflows, deferred inflows, transactions, and events are recorded in governmental funds and nonfund accounts.

Given the governmental fund accounting equation, the *operating results* of governmental funds are necessarily measured in terms of sources, uses, and balances of net financial resources rather than net income. Because the nonfund accounts do not account for sources, uses, and balances of net financial assets—but for general government capital assets and unmatured long-term liabilities—changes in the nonfund accounts do *not* directly affect the operating results of the governmental funds.

Fiduciary Funds

Fiduciary funds, the third category of funds, are used to account for assets held by a government in a trustee or agency capacity for the *benefit* of *others*, whether for individuals, private organizations, or other governmental units. Fiduciary funds are not used to report assets held for the benefit of a government's own programs or activities.

Fiduciary funds have the same MFBA as proprietary funds—the economic resources measurement focus and the accrual basis of accounting (except for the recognition of certain liabilities of defined benefit pension plans and certain postemployment health care plans). Capital assets of *fiduciary funds* and long-term liabilities directly related to and expected to be paid from fiduciary funds should be reported in the fiduciary fund financial statements.

Transaction Analysis Understanding the nature and interrelationships of governmental funds, nonfund accounts, and proprietary funds is critical to understanding governmental accounting. Thus, it is useful at this point to examine fund accounting at a practical level. Illustrations 2-6 and 2-7 show the accounting for 10 transactions listed below. (To simplify the illustration and maximize its benefits, deferred outflows and deferred inflows are not illustrated here.)

1. Purchased a capital asset with cash, $8,000.
2. Issued $1,000,000 of bonds at par and received cash to finance construction of a building.

ILLUSTRATION 2-6   Analysis of Transactions for Business-Type Activities

Proprietary Funds*

	CA	+	NCA	−	CL	−	LTL	=	NP
1.	($8,000)		$8,000						
2.	1,000,000						$1,000,000		
3.	1,000,000				$1,000,000				
4.			300,000		300,000				
5.	7,000		(9,000)						($2,000)
6.	(18,000)								(18,000)
7.	(80,000)						(50,000)		(30,000)
8.	(1,030,000)				(1,000,000)				(30,000)
9.			3,000		3,000				
10.			(20,000)						(20,000)

Detailed Analysis of Transactions

1. Purchased a capital asset with cash, $8,000.
   - $8,000 of cash is used (reducing CA) to purchase a capital asset (increasing NCA).
   - Because CA decreased and NCA increased by $8,000, NP is unaffected.
   - This transaction does not affect the proprietary fund operating statement.
2. Issued $1,000,000 of bonds at par and received cash to finance construction of a building.
   - $1,000,000 of cash is received (increasing CA).
   - The bonds issued increase LTL.
   - Because both CA and LTL increase by $1,000,000, NP is unaffected.
   - This transaction does not affect the proprietary fund operating statement.
3. Issued a $1,000,000, six-month note to provide temporary financing.
   - $1,000,000 of cash is received (increasing CA) from issuing the short-term note (increasing CL).
   - Because both CA and CL increase by $1,000,000, NP is unaffected.
   - This transaction does not affect the proprietary fund operating statement.
4. Received a bill from the contractor for $300,000 for construction costs on the building.
   - NCA (construction-in-progress) increase by $300,000.
   - CL (contracts payable) increase by $300,000.
   - Because both NCA and CL increase by $300,000, NP is unaffected.
   - This transaction does not affect the proprietary fund operating statement.
5. Sold a capital asset for $7,000 cash; its depreciated cost (book value) was $9,000.
   - Cash received from the sale increases CA by $7,000.
   - NCA (capital assets) decrease by $9,000.
   - Because CA increase by $7,000 and NCA decrease by $9,000, NP decreases by $2,000.
   - A $2,000 loss is reported in the proprietary fund operating statement.

Legend

CA   Current Assets
CL   Current Liabilities
LTL   Long-Term Liabilities
NCA   Noncurrent Assets (including capital assets)
NP   Net Position

*No deferred outflows or deferred inflows were affected by the transactions.

---

3. Issued a $1,000,000, six-month note to provide temporary financing.
4. Received a bill from the contractor for $300,000 for construction costs on the building.
5. Sold a capital asset for $7,000 cash; its depreciated cost was $9,000.
6. Paid employees for monthly salaries, $18,000.
7. $50,000 of the building bonds and $30,000 of interest matured and were paid.
8. The six-month note matured and was paid along with $30,000 of interest.
9. Purchased capital assets on short-term credit for $3,000.
10. Depreciation expense of $20,000 is recorded on a capital asset.

Illustrations 2-6 and 2-7 highlight the differences between accounting for proprietary funds and for governmental funds by showing how each of these transactions would be accounted for in a proprietary fund and in a governmental fund (and in

ILLUSTRATION 2-7 Analysis of Transactions for General Government Activities

| | Governmental Funds* | | | | General Capital Assets and General Long-Term Liabilities Accounts | | | |
	FA	–	RL	=	FB	GCA	–	GLTL	=	NP
1.	($8,000)				($8,000)	$8,000				$8,000
2.	1,000,000				1,000,000			$1,000,000		(1,000,000)
3.	1,000,000		$1,000,000							
4.			300,000		(300,000)	300,000				300,000
5.	7,000				7,000	(9,000)				(9,000)
6.	(18,000)				(18,000)					
7.	(80,000)				(80,000)			(50,000)		50,000
8.	(1,030,000)		(1,000,000)		(30,000)					
9.			3,000		(3,000)	3,000				3,000
10.						(20,000)				(20,000)

Detailed Analysis of Transactions

1. Purchased a capital asset with cash, $8,000.
   - $8,000 of cash is used (reducing FA) to purchase a capital asset.
   - The capital asset acquired does not "fit" in the governmental fund accounting equation because capital assets are not FA.
   - Because FA decrease and RL do not change, FB decreases by $8,000.
   - This decrease in FB will be reported as an expenditure in the governmental fund operating statement.
   - The capital asset is added to the GCA accounts, and NP is increased.
2. Issued $1,000,000 of bonds at par and received cash to finance construction of a building.
   - $1,000,000 of cash is received from issuing the bonds (increasing FA).
   - Because FA increase by $1,000,000 and RL do not change, FB increases by $1,000,000.
   - This increase in FB from issuing the bonds will be reported in the governmental fund operating statement. (Proceeds from issuing bonds are not revenues in governmental funds and are reported as "Other Financing Sources," which will be discussed later in this chapter.)
   - The bonds payable are long-term liabilities and thus do not "fit" in the governmental fund accounting equation because unmatured long-term liabilities are not governmental fund liabilities.
   - The bonds payable are added to the GLTL accounts, and NP decreases.
3. Issued a $1,000,000 six-month note to provide temporary financing.
   - $1,000,000 of cash is received (increasing FA) from issuing the note (increasing RL).
   - Because both FA and RL increase by $1,000,000, FB is unaffected.
   - This transaction does not affect the governmental fund operating statement.
   - No nonfund accounts are affected.
4. Received a bill from the contractor for $300,000 for construction costs on the building.
   - RL (accounts payable) increase by $300,000.
   - Because RL increase and FA do not change, FB decreases by $300,000.
   - This decrease in FB will be reported as an expenditure in the governmental fund operating statement.
   - Construction-in-progress (GCA) does not "fit" in the governmental fund accounting equation because GCA are not FA.
   - Construction-in-progress is added to GCA, and NP increases.
5. Sold a capital asset for $7,000 cash; its depreciated cost (book value) was $9,000.
   - FA (cash) increase by $7,000.
   - Because FA increase and RL do not change, FB increases by $7,000.
   - The increase in FB from the sale of the capital asset will be reported in the governmental fund operating statement. (Proceeds from selling general capital assets are not revenues in governmental funds and are reported as "Other Financing Sources," which will be discussed later in this chapter.)
   - The sale of a capital asset reduces GCA and NP by $9,000.

*No deferred outflows or deferred inflows were affected by the transactions.

Legend

FA	Financial Assets
FB	Fund Balance
GCA	General Capital Assets
GLTL	General Long-Term Liabilities
NP	Net Position
RL	Related Liabilities

the nonfund accounts, if applicable). Illustration 2-6 shows how each transaction affects the accounting equation of a proprietary fund. This accounting should be familiar because it is similar to the accounting used by businesses. Several of the transactions (1, 4, 5, 9, and 10) involve capital assets—commonly referred to as fixed assets by businesses—which are accounted for in the noncurrent assets column of Illustration 2-6.

Illustration 2-7 shows how the accounting equations of governmental funds and of nonfund accounts would be affected by the 10 transactions. The first nine transactions result in changes to financial assets or related liabilities and affect the governmental funds accounting equation. Transaction 6 illustrates the similar accounting that often occurs in proprietary funds for operating expenses and in governmental funds for operating expenditures. Several of the transactions (1, 2, 4, 5, 7, 9, and 10) involve general capital assets or general long-term liabilities, which are accounted for in nonfund accounts. The final transaction (10) affects the nonfund accounts but does not result in changes to current financial resources (i.e., financial assets or related liabilities) and therefore does not affect the governmental funds accounting equation.

We discuss the first five transactions in Illustrations 2-6 and 2-7 to help ensure that you understand transaction analysis. Review the others on your own to solidify your understanding of the model. If you understand the transaction analyses presented in these illustrations, you are beginning to understand the basics of governmental accounting. Moreover, you are well on your way to understanding the general government accounting methods discussed in Chapters 3 to 9.

Types of Funds

Illustrations 2-6 and 2-7 demonstrate the accounting for 10 transactions as if they had occurred within the proprietary fund category and the governmental fund category, respectively. In practice, governments do not account for transactions using only the three broad fund categories—proprietary funds, governmental funds, and fiduciary funds. Instead, accounting for a government's activities occurs in one or more of the 11 specific *types of funds* within the 3 fund categories and in the nonfund accounts, if applicable. The GASB has established two types of proprietary funds, five types of governmental funds, and four types of fiduciary funds.

Types of Proprietary Funds

The primary distinction between the two types of proprietary funds is based on their predominant "customers." Typically,

- the general public (as well as businesses and other entities beyond the government's own departments or agencies) is the predominant customer for **Enterprise Funds**, and
- other departments or agencies of the government are the predominant customers for **Internal Service Funds**.

1. **Enterprise Funds** are permitted to be used to account for any activity for which user fees charged for goods and services provided to external customers (outside the government) are a principal revenue source. Activities are required to be reported in Enterprise Funds if certain criteria are met. (These criteria are described in Chapter 10.)
    - Many municipal governments and special districts operate utilities that are accounted for in Enterprise Funds. Cities often operate water treatment and sanitary sewage facilities for which they charge a fee to customers. The operations of these facilities typically are accounted for in a "Water and Sewer" Enterprise Fund.
    - In addition, the activities of government-owned electric and gas utilities, solid waste landfills, and major airports commonly are accounted for in Enterprise Funds.
    - Various other activities may be accounted for in Enterprise Funds, including mass transit systems, civic centers, toll roads, and state lotteries. The City of Madison, Wisconsin, for example, accounts for the activities associated with its four municipal-owned golf courses in an Enterprise Fund.

    Accounting and financial reporting for Enterprise Funds are discussed in Chapter 10.

2. **Internal Service Funds** may be used to account for any activity of a fund, department, or agency that provides goods or services primarily to other funds, departments, or agencies of the governmental unit, or to other governmental units, on a *cost-reimbursement* basis.

   - A city, for example, may maintain all of its vehicles using a central garage. The garage bills the police, fire, and sanitation departments for the cost of maintaining their vehicles. The city accounts for the activities of the central garage in an Internal Service Fund.

   - A county may use an Internal Service Fund to account for the activities of a central duplicating and printing department that serves various county departments.

   - Other common activities that may be accounted for in Internal Service Funds include central stores, health care and other self-insurance activities, and computer services departments.

   Accounting and financial reporting for Internal Service Funds are discussed in Chapter 11.

Types of Governmental Funds

Governmental funds are distinguished from one another by the *purpose* for which the financial resources accounted for in each fund may be or must be used. The distinctions between the governmental funds are highlighted in Illustration 2-8. The governmental fund category includes five fund types.

1. **The General Fund** is used "to account for and report all financial resources not accounted for and reported in another fund."[5]

   - All governments with general government activities will have *one* General Fund.

   - For most governments, the majority of their general government activities and the largest number and dollar amount of their transactions are reported in the General Fund.

   - General government activities commonly reported in the General Fund include police protection, fire protection, general administration, street maintenance, and public park maintenance.

ILLUSTRATION 2-8 Governmental Fund Types: Classification and Typical Types of Expenditures

I. Classification

Purposes for Which General Government Financial Resources May or Must Be Used	Governmental Fund Type
Available for general SLG uses	General Fund (GF)
Specific operating purposes or activities	Special Revenue Fund (SRF)
Acquiring major general government capital facilities	Capital Projects Fund (CPF)
Payment of general long-term debt principal and interest	Debt Service Fund (DSF)
Various—as per trust or other agreement	Permanent Fund (PF)

II. Typical Types of Expenditures	GF	SRFs	CPFs	DSFs	PFs
Operating (e.g., salaries, rent, utilities)	XXX	XXX			X
Capital outlay	X	X	XXX		X
Debt service	X	X	X	XXX	X

Legend

XXX = Most expenditures are of this type.
   X = May have some expenditures of this type, usually minor.

---

[5]Governmental Accounting Standards Board, Statement No. 54, "Fund Balance Reporting and Governmental Fund Type Definitions" (GASB, February 2009), para. 29.

Governments use other types of governmental funds to assure compliance with specific legal or contractual requirements or to maintain adequate control and accountability over financial resources.

2. **Special Revenue Funds** are established "to account for and report the proceeds of specific *revenue sources* that are restricted or committed to expenditure for specified purposes other than debt service or capital projects."[6]

   - Many state governments charge a sales tax on gasoline that only can be used by the state to construct or maintain roads. The proceeds from this sales tax are recorded as revenues (increasing fund balance) in a Special Revenue Fund. Expenditures for road repairs reduce the fund balance in the Special Revenue Fund. The remaining amount in fund balance at year end is available to be used for road construction or maintenance in future periods.

   - Governments often account for *grant proceeds* that are restricted for a specific purpose in a Special Revenue Fund. For example, the Los Angeles Unified School District accounts for its food services program in a Cafeteria Special Revenue Fund because the program is financed primarily through federal and state subsidies that can only be used for the District's food services.

   Accounting and financial reporting for the General Fund and Special Revenue Funds are discussed in Chapters 3 to 6.

3. **Capital Projects Funds** are established "to account for and report financial resources that are restricted, committed, or assigned to expenditure for capital outlays, including the acquisition or construction of capital facilities and other capital assets."[7]

   - Governments purchase many smaller general capital assets—for example, police cars and office equipment—that typically are accounted for in the General Fund.

   - Capital outlays for major general government facilities and other projects financed from general obligation bond proceeds must be reported using a Capital Projects Fund.

   - Most governments use Capital Projects Funds to maintain accounting controls over resources that are *restricted* for a particular capital asset purpose.

   Accounting and financial reporting for Capital Projects Funds are discussed in Chapter 7.

4. **Debt Service Funds** are established "to account for and report financial resources that are restricted, committed, or assigned to expenditure for principal and interest."[8] Only accumulation of resources associated with general government long-term liabilities that are recorded in the GLTL accounts are accounted for in Debt Service Funds.

   - Some governments are legally required by bond covenants to accumulate resources in a Debt Service Fund to repay general long-term debt principal and interest.

   - Many other governments voluntarily accumulate amounts to repay the principal and interest on general long-term debt. These governments use Debt Service Funds to maintain accountability over resources that are to be used to repay debt.

   Accounting and financial reporting for Debt Service Funds are discussed in Chapter 8.

5. **Permanent Funds** are established to account for "resources that are legally restricted to the extent that only earnings, and not principal, may be used for purposes that support the reporting government's programs—that is, for the benefit of the government or its citizenry."[9]

   - Permanent Funds[10] are classified as governmental funds even though they may not be expendable funds like other governmental funds.

   - Therefore, much of the discussions and illustrations of governmental funds does not apply to Permanent Funds.

   Permanent funds are discussed at the end of Chapter 9.

---

[6]Ibid., para. 30, emphasis added.

[7]Ibid., para. 33.

[8]Ibid., para. 34.

[9]Ibid., para. 35.

[10]This was a matter of expediency. The GASB decided *not* to establish a separate Permanent Fund Category.

Identifying Governmental Fund Types in Transaction Analysis

Each of the proprietary fund transactions analyzed in Illustration 2-6 could have been recorded and reported in a single Enterprise Fund or a single Internal Service Fund, if appropriate. No single general government accounting entity could be used to account for each of those transactions if they were for general government activities, however. Illustration 2-9 identifies the governmental fund type that likely would be used to account for each of the first nine transactions in Illustration 2-7. In reviewing this illustration, the following should be noted:

- The purchases of capital assets in transactions 1 and 9 are accounted for in the General Fund because they do not result from a *major* general government capital project. However, such purchases also could be made through a Capital Projects Fund.

- The *construction* of more costly capital assets like the building in transaction 4 should always be accounted for in a Capital Projects Fund.

- The cash received from the issuance of bonds to finance the construction of a building (transaction 2) is accounted for in a Capital Projects Fund, whereas the cash received from the issuance of a *six-month* note to finance general government operations (transaction 3) is accounted for in the General Fund.

- The sale of general capital assets (transaction 5) typically is accounted for in the General Fund, unless use of the proceeds is restricted.

- The cash paid to employees for monthly salaries in transaction 6 likely would be accounted for in the General Fund or a Special Revenue Fund. A government, for example, could pay a school teacher of gifted students from its general unrestricted revenues or from a state grant that was restricted for salaries of gifted students' teachers. In the former case, the salary payment is accounted for in the General Fund, but in the latter case, the salary payment is accounted for in a Special Revenue Fund.

- The payment of principal and interest on the *long-term* building bonds (transaction 7) is accounted for in the Debt Service Fund, whereas the payment of principal and interest on the *short-term* note (transaction 8) is accounted for in the General Fund.

Types of Fiduciary Funds

Fiduciary funds include Trust Funds and Agency Funds. Trust Funds are established to account for resources held and administered by a reporting government when it is acting in a fiduciary capacity for beneficiaries outside the government—individuals,

---

ILLUSTRATION 2-9   Identification of Governmental Fund Type Affected

General Government Transaction	Governmental Fund Type
1. Purchased a capital asset with cash, $8,000.	General*
2. Issued $1,000,000 of bonds at par and received cash to finance construction of a building.	Capital Projects
3. Issued a $1,000,000, six-month note to provide temporary financing.	General*
4. Received a bill from the contractor for $300,000 for construction costs on the building.	Capital Projects
5. Sold a capital asset for $7,000 cash; its depreciated cost was $9,000.	General*
6. Paid cash to employees for monthly salaries, $18,000.	General*
7. $50,000 in building bonds and $30,000 interest matured and were paid.	Debt Service
8. The six-month note matured and was paid, along with $30,000 in interest.	General*
9. Purchased capital assets on short-term credit for $3,000.	General*

*Assumes that these transactions were for General Fund departments or agencies.

2-1 IN PRACTICE

Governmental Fund Accounting for the Dallas Cowboys Football Stadium

The voters of the City of Arlington, Texas, agreed to construct and finance much of a new football stadium for the Dallas Cowboys football team. The City of Arlington agreed to pay half the cost of the stadium up to $325 million. Upon completion, the stadium will be owned by the City and leased to the Dallas Cowboys for a minimum of 30 years.

The analyses of several City of Arlington transactions related to this project are presented here.

1. The city issued $297.9 million of 30-year Dallas Cowboys Complex Special Tax Revenue Serial Bonds for the construction of the stadium.

2. The City of Arlington paid $144.5 million cash for construction expenditures.

3. The City of Arlington paid $12.1 million in interest on its special tax revenue serial bonds from the City's Debt Service Fund.

4. Future Transaction—This analysis shows the accounting that will occur next year when the City repays $4.9 million in principal on the serial bonds along with $12.3 million in interest. Note that no expenditures related to these payments were accrued at the end of the first year.

Analysis of Transactions

Stadium Venue Capital Projects Fund				General Capital Assets and General Long-Term Liabilities Accounts			
FA	– RL	=	FB	GCA	– GLTL	=	NP
1. $297,900,000			$297,900,000		$297,900,000		($297,900,000)
2. ($144,500,000)			($144,500,000)	$144,500,000			$144,500,000

Debt Service Fund							
FA	– RL	=	FB				
3. ($ 12,100,000)			($ 12,100,000)				
4. ($ 17,200,000)			($ 17,200,000)		($ 4,900,000)		$4,900,000

Legend			
	FA = Financial Assets	GLTL = General Long-Term Liabilities	
	FB = Fund Balance	NP = Net Position	
	GCA = General Capital Assets	RL = Related Liabilities	

private organizations, or other governments. Agency Funds are established to account for resources that a government holds as a custodian for others. Trust Funds typically are distinguished from Agency Funds by the existence of a trust agreement that affects the degree of management involvement and the length of time the resources are held. The three types of Trust Funds and Agency Funds are defined here.

1. **Pension (and other employee benefit) Trust Funds** are established to account for "resources that are required to be held in trust for the members and beneficiaries of defined benefit pension plans, defined contribution plans, other postemployment benefit plans, or other employee benefit plans."[11] The California Public Employees' Retirement System (CalPERS), for example, has established multiple trusts to manage and account for the pension and health care benefits for California's approximately 1.5 million public employees, retirees, and their beneficiaries.

2. **Investment Trust Funds** are established to account for the external portion of investment pools held by the sponsoring government.[12] Most operate like a money market fund. For example, the State of Wisconsin established the Local Government Pooled Investment Fund to account for monies that local governments voluntarily send to the state to manage and to invest for the local governments' benefit.

3. **Private-Purpose Trust Funds**—such as a fund used to report escheat property—are established to account for *all other* trust arrangements under which principal and/or income benefit individuals or groups outside the government.

---

[11]GASB Codification, section 1300.111.

[12]Ibid., section 1300.112.

4. **Agency Funds** are established to account for resources held by a government in a ***purely custodial*** capacity for others. Agency Funds typically involve only the receipt, temporary investment, and remittance of fiduciary resources to individuals, private organizations, or other governments.[13] Agency Fund assets and liabilities are always equal.

   - The most common example of a significant Agency Fund occurs when one government, say a county, bills and collects the property taxes for the cities, school districts, and other taxing agencies within the county.

   - Another common application of Agency Funds occurs in public high schools. A high school's administrative personnel may maintain a bank account that holds the monies of all student organizations. The monies are held in an agency capacity for the student organizations.

   Accounting and financial reporting for Trust and Agency Funds are discussed in Chapter 12.

Summary of Types of Funds

As noted earlier, fund accounting evolved because significant portions of a government's financial resources may be restricted to use for a specific purpose(s).

- Restrictions may stem from grantor or donor stipulations, state or local government laws and regulations, contractual agreements, actions by the legislature or council, or other sources.

- The three fund *categories* vary primarily in accordance with (1) whether the resources of the fund may be expended (governmental funds) or are to be maintained largely on a self-sustaining basis (proprietary funds), and (2) whether the resources are available for the government's use or are held for the benefit of others.

Furthermore, the various *types* of governmental funds differ primarily according to the purposes for which their assets may be expended: (1) general operating (unrestricted), or (2) special purpose or project, such as for certain services or for capital outlay or debt service.

The types of fund and nonfund accounting entities recommended by the GASB are summarized in Illustration 2-10. Note:

- the *purposes* of each fund type and the nonfund accounts, and

- that a state or local government will have only *one* General Fund and *one* set of General Capital Assets and General Long-Term Liabilities accounts, but may have one, none, several, or many of the other types of funds.

Most general governments use many different funds to manage and demonstrate accountability for their resources. Selecting the number of funds that a government needs requires professional judgment:

- SLGs should maintain the funds needed to meet legal and contractual requirements and to facilitate sound financial management.

- Governments should exercise care in establishing new funds—and should discontinue funds that are no longer needed—because unnecessary funds can cause undue accounting system complexity and inefficient financial administration.

Also, recognize that the fund type to be used typically is determined by the purpose(s) for which resources may be used, not by the source of the financial resources. This was shown in Illustration 2-8.

Comparative Financial Statement Formats

A review of some of the important elements of proprietary and governmental fund financial statements will help highlight some principles of governmental accounting that have not yet been discussed. These financial statements are discussed in detail in later chapters.

---

[13]Ibid., section 1300.102 and sections 1300.104–114, adapted.

ILLUSTRATION 2-10   State and Local Government Funds, Nonfund Accounts, Accounting Equations, and Statements

The General Government Funds and Nonfund Accounts

The Governmental Funds	The Proprietary Funds
General (GF)	Enterprise (EF)
Special Revenue (SRF)	Internal Service (ISF)
Capital Projects (CPF) $FA - RL = FB*$	$CA + NCA = CL + LTL + NP*$
Debt Service (DSF)	
Permanent** (PF)	

Governmental Fund Statements	Proprietary Fund Statements
Balance Sheet	Statement of Net Position
Statement of Revenues, Expenditures, and Changes in Fund Balances	Statement of Revenues, Expenses, and Changes in Fund Net Position
If GF or major SRF budgeted annually, a Budgetary Comparison Statement or Schedule—such as a:	Statement of Cash Flows
Statement (Schedule) of Revenues, Expenditures, and Changes in Fund Balances—Budget and Actual—Budgetary Basis	

The General Capital Assets (GCA) and General Long-Term Liabilities (GLTL) Accounts	The Fiduciary Funds
$GCA - GLTL = NP$	Agency (AF) Assets = Liabilities
	Private-Purpose Trust (PPTF)
	Investment Trust (ITF) $CA + NCA =$
	Pension Trust (PTF) $CL + LTL + NP*$

Fiduciary Fund Statements

Note: Balances and changes therein are reported in the government-wide financial statements or disclosed in the notes to the Basic Financial Statements.

Statement of Fiduciary Net Position

Statement of Changes in Fiduciary Fund Net Position

Legend
FA = Financial Assets	CL = Current Liabilities
RL = Related Liabilities	DI = Deferred Inflows
FB = Fund Balance	DO = Deferred Outflows
GCA = General Capital Assets	LTL = Long-Term Liabilities
GLTL = General Long-Term Liabilities	NCA = Noncurrent Assets
CA = Current Assets	NP = Net Position

*Recall that each of these accounting equations and the balance sheets and statements of net position of each fund include deferred outflows and deferred inflows as well.

**PFs may have long-term investments and other NCA.

As previously discussed, a **fund** is an independent accounting entity with a self-balancing set of accounts similar to the self-balancing accounts of a business accounting entity. Somewhat similar to corporate transactions between a parent company and multiple subsidiaries, governments have transactions that involve multiple funds. Broadly, transactions between funds are referred to as **interfund activity**. Four types of interfund activities—interfund loans, interfund services provided and used, interfund reimbursements, and interfund transfers—are commonly encountered in state and local governments. These interfund activities are discussed in detail in Chapter 3, but interfund loans and interfund transfers are introduced now because they are reported as separate line items in the fund financial statements.

- **Interfund loans**—amounts provided by one fund to another *with a requirement* for *repayment*. Interfund loans are the only type of interfund transaction that initially affects only balance sheet accounts. Because interfund loans are expected to be repaid, a loan is reported as a receivable (asset) in the lending fund and as a payable (liability) in the debtor fund.
- **Interfund transfers**—flows of assets (such as cash or goods) from one fund to another without equivalent flows of assets in return *and* without a requirement for repayment.

    - In *governmental* funds, transfers should be reported as *other [nonexpenditure] financing uses* in the funds making transfers and as *other [nonrevenue] financing sources* in the funds receiving transfers.

    - In *proprietary* funds, transfers should be reported immediately before the increase or decrease in net assets.

Operating Statements

The reporting effects of interfund transfers are shown in Illustration 2-11, which presents comparative, side-by-side operating statement formats for a proprietary fund and a governmental fund. Two classifications of *increases* in fund balance—revenues and *other* (nonrevenue) *financing sources*—are presented in governmental fund operating statements. Likewise, two categories of fund balance *decreases* are presented in those statements—expenditures and *other* (nonexpenditure) *financing uses*. In studying Illustration 2-11, note (1) the distinct operating statement formats for governmental funds and for proprietary funds and the differences between these formats, (2) the reporting of interfund transfers in both operating statements, and (3) the presentation of GLTL issue proceeds in the governmental fund operating statement.

Reporting **other financing sources** and **other financing uses** is unique to governmental fund financial statements. The GASB requires that (1) interfund transfers and (2) certain transactions that affect *both* a financial asset or related liability in a governmental fund *and* a general capital asset or general long-term liability should be reported as other financing sources or other financing uses. For example, proceeds of general long-term liability debt issues—possibly proceeds of general obligation bonds that are to be expended through a Capital Projects Fund—are reported in the "Other [*Non*revenue] Financing Sources" section of the operating statement of the recipient governmental fund. (Note that this applies *only* to GLTL proceeds, *not* to proprietary and fiduciary fund long-term debt.)

Balance Sheets

Illustration 2-12 presents comparative, side-by-side balance sheet formats for a proprietary fund and a governmental fund. It highlights how the different measurement focuses and bases of accounting used by proprietary funds and governmental funds affect their balance sheets. By comparing the proprietary fund statement of net position to the governmental fund balance sheet, you will note that only proprietary funds report noncurrent assets and noncurrent liabilities. As previously discussed:

- The **economic resources measurement focus** used for proprietary *funds* results in reporting both *current* and *noncurrent assets* and both *current* and *noncurrent* (or long-term) *liabilities*.

- The **current financial resources measurement focus** used for *governmental funds* results in reporting *only financial assets and related liabilities* in the governmental fund balance sheet. Capital assets and unmatured long-term liabilities are not reported in governmental fund balance sheets.

- The statements of net position for proprietary funds and balance sheets for governmental funds report **interfund loans**. In Illustration 2-12, both the proprietary fund and the governmental fund show a "Due to other funds" account as liabilities. If either of the funds had been owed money from another fund, "Due from other funds" would be reported as part of its assets; a noncurrent interfund receivable is indicated by the term "Advance to other funds."

ILLUSTRATION 2-11   Operating Statement Formats

Proprietary Fund			Governmental Fund		
Statement of Revenues, Expenses, and Changes in Fund Net Position For the Year Ended June 30, 20X8 (in thousands)			Statement of Revenues, Expenditures, and Changes in Fund Balance For the Year Ended June 30, 20X8 (in thousands)		
Operating Revenues:			**Revenues:**		
Sales of goods		$1,200	Taxes		$1,260
Billings for services		600	Licenses and permits		20
Other		40	Intergovernmental		480
Total		1,840	Charges for services		30
			Miscellaneous		20
			Total		1,810
Operating Expenses:					
Operations		1,440	**Expenditures:**		
Depreciation		280	Operating		1,260
Other		20	Capital outlay		200
Total		1,740	Debt service		
Operating Income (Loss)		100	Long-term debt principal	$260	
			Interest	40	300
			Total		1,760
Nonoperating Revenues (Expenses):			**Excess (Deficiency) of Revenues over Expenditures**		50
Interest revenue	$ 6				
Interest expense	(22)				
Other	2	(14)			
Income (loss) Before Contributions, Special and Extraordinary Items, and Transfers		86	**Other Financing Sources (Uses):**		
			Transfer from (to) other funds	18	
Capital Contributions		6	Long-term debt issues	110	128
Special and Extraordinary Items:			**Special and Extraordinary Items:**		
Special item	4		Special item	8	
Extraordinary item	(84)	(80)	Extraordinary item	(24)	(16)
Transfer from (to) other funds		3			
			Net Change in Fund Balance:		162
Increase (Decrease) in Net Position:		15	Fund Balance—Beginning of Period		300
Net Position—Beginning of Period		556	Fund Balance—End of Period		$ 462
Net Position—End of Period		$ 571			

Notes:
Both (1) classification of governmental fund revenues and (2) classification of expenditures by function, program, and other categories are discussed and illustrated in Chapters 3 to 6. Governmental fund expenditures are classified by character in this example.

- A major difference in the proprietary fund statement of net position and the governmental fund balance sheet is found in the "equity" section.

  - The **proprietary fund** statement of net position ends with a "**Net Position**" section whereas the governmental fund balance sheet ends with a "**Fund Balance**" section.
  - Apart from the difference in the titles for the sections, the *line items* reported within the "Net Position" section are different from the line items reported within the "Fund Balance" section.
  - The meaning of the line items within each of the sections will be discussed thoroughly in later chapters.

ILLUSTRATION 2-12   Balance Sheet Formats

Proprietary Fund			Governmental Fund	
Statement of Net Position **June 30, 20X8** **(in thousands)**			**Balance Sheet** **June 30, 20X8** **(in thousands)**	
Assets			**Assets**	
Current Assets:			Cash	$230
Cash		$ 220	Receivables, net	280
Receivables, net		200	Inventory	38
Inventory		48	Total assets	$548
Total current assets		$ 468		
Noncurrent assets:				
Capital assets:				
Land		240		
Buildings and equipment	$3,650			
Less accumulated depreciation	(660)	2,990		
Total noncurrent assets		3,230		
Total assets		$3,698		

Proprietary Fund			Governmental Fund	
Liabilities, Deferred Inflows, **and Net Position**			**Liabilities, Deferred Inflows,** **and Fund Balance**	
Current liabilities:			Liabilities:	
Accounts payable		$ 28	Accounts payable	$ 24
Due to other funds		10	Due to other funds	20
Current portion of bonds payable		280	Total liabilities	44
Total current liabilities		318	Deferred inflows:	
Noncurrent liabilities:			Deferred revenues	42
Compensated absences		20	Total liabilities and deferred inflows:	86
Bonds payable		2,800	**Fund Balance**	
Total noncurrent liabilities		2,820	Nonspendable	38
Total liabilities		3,138	Restricted	70
Net Position			Committed	35
Net investment in capital assets		260	Assigned	95
Restricted for debt service		20	Unassigned	224
Unrestricted		280		
Total net position		560	Total fund balance	462
Total liabilities and net position		$3,698	Total liabilities and fund balance	$548

Note:
The proprietary fund statement was prepared using a balance sheet format, which reports a separate line item for "Total liabilities, deferred inflows and net assets." The GASB recommends, and many governments use, the "Assets − Liabilities = Net Position" format, which ends with a double-underlined "Total net position" as the final line of the statement. Neither deferred outflows nor deferred revenues are illustrated in the proprietary fund statement.

The recommended annual financial report of a state or local government is the **comprehensive annual financial report**, or **CAFR**. The CAFR contains three sections: (1) Introductory, (2) Financial, and (3) Statistical. The Financial section, which typically begins with the auditor's report, includes the MD&A (which is required supplementary information or RSI); Basic Financial Statements, including the related notes; and any other RSI. The **Basic Financial Statements** are summarized in Illustration 2-13. The **Financial Section** of the **CAFR** is diagrammed in Illustration 2-14.

Annual Financial Reporting

A CAFR, which often spans 150 to 200 pages, is required to include the following information:

1. **Introductory section**—includes a letter of transmittal, table of contents, and other introductory content.

2. **Financial section**—includes

    a. **Management's Discussion and Analysis (MD&A)**—a structured, objective, "required supplementary information (RSI)" narrative report by management that summarizes analytically the key events that occurred during the year and the status of the SLG at year end.

    b. **Basic Financial Statements (BFS)**—which include

        (1) Government-wide Financial Statements

            (a) Statement of Net Position

            (b) Statement of Activities

        (2) Fund Financial Statements

            (a) Governmental Funds Financial Statements

                - Balance Sheet

                - Statement of Revenues, Expenditures, and Changes in Fund Balances

                - Statement of Revenues, Expenditures, and Changes in Fund Balances: Budget and Actual (either as a basic financial statement or as RSI)

ILLUSTRATION 2-13 Composition of the Basic Financial Statements			
Basic Financial Statements* *(Consist of Two Categories of Statements)*	**Government-wide Financial Statements** *(One Set)*	Government-wide Statement of Net Position	
		Government-wide Statement of Activities	
	Fund Financial Statements *(Three Sets)*	*Governmental Funds Financial Statements*	Governmental Funds Balance Sheet
			Governmental Funds Statement of Revenues, Expenditures, and Changes in Fund Balances
			General Fund and Major Special Revenue Funds Statement of Revenues, Expenditures, and Changes in Fund Balances—Budget and Actual
		Proprietary Funds Financial Statements	Proprietary Funds Statement of Net Position
			Proprietary Funds Statement of Revenues, Expenses, and Changes in Fund Net Position
			Proprietary Funds Statement of Cash Flows
		Fiduciary Funds Financial Statements	Fiduciary Funds Statement of Fiduciary Net Position
			Fiduciary Funds Statement of Changes in Fiduciary Net Position
*The notes are an integral part of the financial statements.			

ILLUSTRATION 2-14 Basic Financial Statements and Accompanying Information

INDEPENDENT AUDITOR'S REPORT
(Precedes MD&A)

MANAGEMENT'S DISCUSSION AND ANALYSIS (MD&A)
Required Supplementary Information (RSI)

FUND
Financial Statements

Governmental Funds
(Modified Accrual)

- Balance Sheet
- Statement of Revenues, Expenditures, and Changes in Fund Balances
- Statement of Revenues, Expenditures, and Changes in Fund Balances—Budget and Actual (or RSI Schedule)

Proprietary Funds
(Accrual)

- Statement of Net Position
- Statement of Revenues, Expenses, and Changes in Fund Net Position
- Statement of Cash Flows (Direct Method)

Fiduciary Funds (Accrual)

- Statement of Net Position
- Statement of Changes in Net Position

RECONCILIATION
Summary of Consolidating Worksheet Adjustments

GOVERNMENT-WIDE
Financial Statements
(Accrual)

- Statement of Net Position
- Statement of Activities

NOTES
To the Financial Statements

Other Required Supplementary Information (RSI)

———— = Basic Financial Statements

    (b) Proprietary Funds Financial Statements
- Statement of Net Position
- Statement of Revenues, Expenses, and Changes in Fund Net Position
- Statement of Cash Flows

    (c) Fiduciary Funds Financial Statements
- Statement of Fiduciary Net Position
- Statement of Changes in Fiduciary Net Position

  (3) Notes to the Financial Statements

 c. RSI other than MD&A—including information the GASB requires on pension and other postemployment benefit plans, infrastructure condition, and risk management.

3. Statistical section—which includes statistical tables and information related to a government's financial trends, revenue capacity, debt capacity, demographic and economic information, and operating information.

Each of the basic financial statements is explained and illustrated in Chapter 13. Financial reporting is covered comprehensively in Chapters 13 through 15.

Individual and Combining Statements

A unique feature of state and local government financial reporting is that two types of fund financial statements and schedules—of statements of financial position, operating statements, and other statements and schedules—are used: (1) individual fund and (2) combining.

1. **Individual fund statements and schedules**, as the name implies, present status or operating data for a single fund, often in detail and/or with budget-to-actual or current year to prior year comparative data.

2. **Combining fund statements and schedules** present individual fund data for multiple funds in adjacent columns. A combining financial statement may include a column for (a) each of the individual funds of a fund type (e.g., all Special Revenue Funds or all Internal Service Funds), an "all funds" total, and perhaps a current year to prior year comparative total; (b) each individual nonmajor governmental (or Enterprise) fund and one for the sum of all nonmajor governmental (or Enterprise) funds; and (c) each individual nonmajor fund of a specific fund category or type.

Illustration 2-15 distinguishes individual fund statements and combining fund-type statements. Each of these types of statements is illustrated in the following chapters.

ILLUSTRATION 2-15   Individual Fund vs. Combining Financial Statements

Individual Fund Financial Statements

Special Revenue Fund A	
Revenues	$500
Expenditures	400
Excess of Revenues over Expenditures	100
Other Financing Sources (Uses)	
Other Financing Sources	80
Other Financing Uses	(240)
Net Other Financing Sources (Uses)	(160)
Net Change in Fund Balance	(60)
Fund Balance, Beginning	110
Fund Balance, Ending	$ 50

Special Revenue Fund B	
Revenues	$300
Expenditures	290
Excess of Revenues over Expenditures	10
Other Financing Sources (Uses)	
Other Financing Sources	60
Other Financing Uses	(40)
Net Other Financing Sources (Uses)	20
Net Change in Fund Balance	30
Fund Balance, Beginning	200
Fund Balance, Ending	$230

Combining Financial Statement

Special Revenue Funds

	Fund A	Fund B	Total
Revenues	$500	$300	$800
Expenditures	400	290	690
Excess of Revenues over Expenditures	100	10	110
Other Financing Sources (Uses)			
Other Financing Sources	80	60	140
Other Financing Uses	(240)	(40)	(280)
Net Other Financing Sources (Uses)	(160)	20	(140)
Net Change in Fund Balances	(60)	30	(30)
Fund Balances, Beginning	110	200	310
Fund Balances, Ending	$ 50	$230	$280

Financial Reporting Entity and Component Units

A government's **reporting entity** may include several separate legal entities—for example, the city itself, a city water and sewer utility authority, and the city airport authority. If so, the financial statements of both the city and all of its component units (the utility and the airport) are included in the city CAFR and BFS. The data for some component units are "blended" with those of the primary government funds, whereas data for most component units are "discretely presented" in a separate column(s) of the SLG's financial statements.

It also may be necessary to prepare separate, detailed financial statements for some or all of the component units of the city financial reporting entity. For example, when component unit revenue bonds such as water and sewer revenue bonds are outstanding, creditors often want detailed financial statements for the component unit. Defining the reporting entity and presenting financial statements for state and local governments with "complex" reporting entities that include component units are discussed and illustrated in Chapter 15. The basic financial statements (BFS) and the comprehensive annual financial report (CAFR) are discussed and illustrated in Chapters 13, 14, and 15. Most discussions and examples before Chapter 15 assume a reporting entity that does not include discretely presented component units.

Government-wide Financial Statements

As previously discussed, most governments' accounting systems are structured around funds. This chapter and the next several chapters emphasize fund reporting because it is critical to understand the details of fund accounting in order to understand governmental accounting and financial reporting.

Deriving and reporting government-wide financial statements are fiscal year-end financial reporting events. Whereas governments integrate fund accounts into their general ledger, government-wide information usually is not integrated into the general ledger in practice, but is derived using worksheets. Financial statement preparers use the accounts and balances of governmental and proprietary fund financial statements—as well as nonfund accounts for general capital assets and general long-term liabilities—as a starting point to derive the information that is reported in the government-wide financial statements. Chapter 14 describes the process of deriving government-wide financial statements.

Government-wide financial statements are prepared using the same MFBA used for proprietary funds—the **economic resources** measurement focus and the **accrual** basis of accounting. Similar to the accounting for business enterprises, revenues, expenses, gains, and losses as well as the related assets and liabilities that result from exchange and exchange-like transactions are recognized when the exchange takes place. Revenues, expenses, assets, deferred outflows, liabilities, and deferred inflows resulting from nonexchange transactions are recognized in accordance with GASB *Statement 33*, "Nonexchange Transactions," as amended.

Concluding Comments

Orienting oneself to state and local government accounting and reporting requires particular attention to fund categories and types, measurement focuses, budgetary control and accountability, and terminology. New and unique terms should be noted carefully. Familiar terminology also deserves analysis, because it may be used with either usual or unique connotations. Definitions of pertinent terms may be found in most chapters.

Adapting to a situation that involves many accounting entities requires both concentration and practice. The nature, role, and distinguishing characteristics of each of the categories and types of funds and nonfund accounts recommended by the GASB must be understood thoroughly. Each is discussed in depth in later chapters.

A peculiarity of the multiple-entity approach of fund accounting is that a single transaction may require entries in more than one accounting entity. For example, the purchase of a *general* capital asset necessitates entries to record both the expenditure in a governmental fund and the asset in the General Capital Assets accounts. Furthermore, one must both accept and adapt to virtual personification of the fund accounting entities and the definitions of *revenues*, *expenditures*, and *expenses* in a fund accounting context—as well as of two unique new financial statement elements, deferred outflows of resources and deferred inflows of resources. The nuances of governmental fund accounting will be discussed in detail beginning in Chapter 3.

Finally, as this chapter begins to show, government financial reporting must address numerous issues that differ from those in the business environment. As a result, different financial statements, financial statement elements, and reports have evolved for governments. This evolution was continued when the GASB issued *Statement No. 34,* "Basic Financial Statements—and Management's Discussion and Analysis—for State and Local Governments," in 1999 and *Statement No. 63,* "Financial Reporting for Deferred Outflows of Resources, Deferred Inflows of Resources, and Net Position," in 2011. Among other changes, *Statement No. 34* requires governments to include in their basic financial statements two government-wide, revenue- and expense-based financial statements in addition to as many as eight fund-based financial statements. *Statement No. 63* requires governments to report two new financial statement elements in their statements of financial position.

Questions

Q2-1 Governmental accounting systems are different from business accounting systems. Why?

Q2-2 Funds used in state and local government accounting and financial reporting are classified into three categories: (1) governmental funds, (2) proprietary funds, and (3) fiduciary funds. What measurement focus is used for each of these three categories, and what types of assets and liabilities are reported for each measurement focus?

Q2-3 Revenues and expenditures are reported in governmental funds, and revenues and expenses are reported in proprietary funds. How do *revenues* and *expenditures* in governmental funds differ from *revenues* and *expenses* in proprietary funds?

Q2-4 Why are a municipality's general capital assets and general long-term liabilities accounted for through nonfund accounts rather than within one of its governmental funds, such as the General Fund?

Q2-5 In what funds and nonfund accounts are (a) capital assets and (b) long-term liabilities accounted for?

Q2-6 Under what circumstances should a government use a Special Revenue Fund? A Capital Projects Fund? A Debt Service Fund?

Q2-7 Identify the fund types that are classified as proprietary funds. Which financial statements are required to be presented for these types of funds?

Q2-8 Identify the fund types that are classified as governmental funds. Which financial statements are required to be presented for these types of funds?

Q2-9 Identify the fund types that are classified as fiduciary funds. Which financial statements are required to be presented for these types of funds?

Q2-10 A state or local government may employ only one of certain fund or nonfund accounting entities but one, none, or many of other types. Of which accounting entities would you expect a government to have only one? One, none, or many?

Q2-11 Define interfund loans and interfund transfers, and explain how each is accounted for and reported by a municipality.

Q2-12 Distinguish between the basic financial statements of a government and its comprehensive annual financial report.

Q2-13 What measurement focus and basis of accounting is used to prepare government-wide financial statements?

Q2-14 What is the accounting equation for a governmental fund, including all possible financial statement elements?

Q2-15 What is the accounting equation for a proprietary fund, including all possible financial statement elements?

Q2-16 What are deferred outflows and deferred inflows? How are they reported?

Q2-17 (Research Question) How are the "major" funds of a state or local government determined?

Exercises

E2-1 (Multiple Choice) Identify the best answer for each of the following:

1. Which of the following is characteristic of governmental fund accounting and financial reporting?
   a. The inclusion of only financial assets and related liabilities.
   b. The inclusion of all financial and capital assets, as well as all related debt.
   c. The inclusion of all financial assets, as well as any capital assets and related debt that are related to General Fund functions.
   d. Depreciation is reported in all governmental funds that use capital assets.

2. Financial assets include
   a. capital assets that can be sold.
   b. cash, investments, and receivables.
   c. only cash and other governmental fund assets that have been converted to cash during the current year or early enough in the next year to pay the current year's liabilities.
   d. only cash and other governmental resources that have been converted to cash by the end of the current reporting period.

3. All of the following are considered governmental funds *except*
   a. a Special Revenue Fund.
   b. a Capital Projects Fund.
   c. a Permanent Fund.
   d. an Internal Service Fund.

4. Each of the following is a fiduciary fund *except*
   a. a Permanent Fund.
   b. an Investment Trust Fund.
   c. an Agency Fund.
   d. a Private-Purpose Trust Fund.

5. Which of the following definitions best describes the term *related liabilities*?
   a. Related liabilities are any fund liabilities that are either current or long-term in nature.
   b. Related liabilities refer primarily to general government liabilities that are related to the current year and are normally paid from available expendable financial assets.
   c. Related liabilities refer to governmental fund short-term and long-term liabilities that are either paid from available financial resources or transfers from other funds.
   d. Related liabilities are liabilities that are reported in the general long-term liabilities nonfund accounts.

6. Which of the following transactions would typically *not* be reported in a county's General Fund?
   a. The purchase of 10 new public safety vehicles.
   b. The annual lease payment for the copiers in the county courthouse.
   c. The collection of property taxes that are past due from previous years.
   d. General property taxes a county collects on behalf of municipalities located within the county.

7. The transactions associated with a Community Development Block Grant that must be used to finance rehabilitation of privately owned housing in an economically depressed neighborhood of the city typically would be reported in which of the following funds and/or nonfund accounts?
   a. The General Fund only.
   b. The General Fund and the General Capital Assets accounts.
   c. A Special Revenue Fund only.
   d. A Capital Projects Fund only.

8. The city of Hannah has established a trust to provide resources to offset the costs of maintenance of the city-owned cemetery. The majority of the resources of this trust will be cemetery plot sales and donations from families of those buried in the cemetery. The trust corpus is nonexpendable in nature. Transactions associated with this trust activity would most likely be accounted for in
   a. the General Fund.
   b. a Special Revenue Fund.
   c. a Private-Purpose Trust Fund.
   d. a Permanent Fund.

9. A transaction in which a municipal electric utility paid $150,000 out of its earnings for new equipment requires accounting recognition in
    a. an Enterprise Fund.
    b. the General Fund.
    c. the General Fund and the General Capital Assets and General Long-Term Liabilities accounts.
    d. an Enterprise Fund and the General Capital Assets and General Long-Term Liabilities accounts.

10. The activities of a municipal employee retirement plan that is financed by equal employer and employee contributions should be accounted for in
    a. an Agency Fund.
    b. an Internal Service Fund.
    c. a Special Revenue Fund.
    d. a Trust Fund.

E2-2 (Multiple Choice) Identify the best answer for each of the following:

1. The operations of a municipal government's public library receiving the majority of its support from property taxes levied solely for that purpose should be accounted for in
    a. the General Fund.
    b. a Special Revenue Fund.
    c. an Enterprise Fund.
    d. an Internal Service Fund.

2. The proceeds of a federal grant made to assist in financing the future construction of an adult training center should be recorded in
    a. the General Fund.
    b. a Special Revenue Fund.
    c. a Capital Projects Fund.
    d. a Permanent Fund.

3. The receipts from a special tax levy to retire and pay interest on general obligation bonds issued to finance the construction of a new city hall should be recorded in a
    a. Debt Service Fund.
    b. Capital Projects Fund.
    c. Revolving Interest Fund.
    d. Special Revenue Fund.

4. The operations of a municipal swimming pool with debt secured solely by charges to users should be accounted for in
    a. a Special Revenue Fund.
    b. the General Fund.
    c. an Internal Service Fund.
    d. an Enterprise Fund.

5. The monthly remittance to an insurance company of the lump sum of hospital-surgical insurance premiums collected as payroll deductions from employees should be recorded in
    a. the General Fund.
    b. an Agency Fund.
    c. a Special Revenue Fund.
    d. an Internal Service Fund.

6. A municipality's issuance of general obligation serial bonds to finance the construction of a fire station requires accounting recognition in the
    a. General Fund.
    b. Capital Projects and General Funds.
    c. Capital Projects Fund and the General Capital Assets and General Long-Term Liabilities accounts.
    d. General Fund and the General Capital Assets and General Long-Term Liabilities accounts.

7. Expenditures of $200,000 were made during the year on the fire station in the previous question. This transaction requires accounting recognition in the
    a. General Fund.
    b. Capital Projects Fund.
    c. Capital Projects Fund and the General Capital Assets and General Long-Term Liabilities accounts.
    d. General Capital Assets and General Long-Term Liabilities accounts.

8. The activities of a central motor pool that provides and services vehicles for the official use of municipal employees from several city departments and charges them a fee to recover costs incurred should be accounted for in
    a. an Agency Fund.
    b. the General Fund.
    c. an Internal Service Fund.
    d. a Special Revenue Fund.

9. A city collects property taxes on behalf of the local sanitary, park, and school districts and periodically remits collections to these units. This activity should be accounted for in
   a. an Agency Fund.
   b. the General Fund.
   c. an Internal Service Fund.
   d. a Special Revenue Fund.

10. A transaction in which a municipal electric utility issues bonds (to be repaid from its own operations) requires accounting recognition in
    a. the General Fund.
    b. a Debt Service Fund.
    c. an Enterprise Fund.
    d. an Enterprise Fund, a Debt Service Fund, and the General Capital Assets and General Long-Term Liabilities accounts.

(AICPA, adapted)

E2-3 (Fund and Nonfund Accounts Identification) Indicate the fund or nonfund accounts that should be used to account for each of the following:

1. Tax revenues restricted for road maintenance.
2. Resources restricted for construction of a new government office building.
3. Typical water and sewer departments.
4. Unrestricted tax revenues.
5. School buildings.
6. Bonds payable issued in a prior year for general government purposes.
7. The portion of general government bonds payable that matures in the next fiscal year.
8. Cash and investments of a bond sinking fund established to service general government long-term debt.
9. Capital assets of a government department that sells services to the public as the primary ongoing source of financing for its operations.
10. Long-term note for the government's central motor pool that "rents" vehicles to other departments and agencies of the government at a rate that reimburses its costs.

E2-4 (Fund Identification) The following are names of funds encountered in governmental reports and the purposes for which these funds have been established. Indicate the corresponding fund type recommended by the Governmental Accounting Standards Board. For example, the School Fund in (a) would be a Special Revenue Fund.

a. School Fund (to account for special taxes levied by a county to finance the operation of schools).
b. Bond Redemption Fund (to account for taxes and other revenues to be used in retiring bonds).
c. Bridge Construction Fund (to account for the proceeds from the sale of bonds).
d. Park Fund (to account for special taxes levied to finance the operation of parks).
e. Interdepartmental Printing Shop Fund (to account for revenues received from departments for printing done for them by the interdepartmental printing shop).
f. City Bus Line Fund (to account for revenues received from the public for transportation services).
g. Money Collected for the State Fund (to account for money collected as agent for the state).
h. Operating Fund (to account for unrestricted revenues not related to any other fund).
i. Electric Fund (to account for revenues received from the sale of electricity to the public).
j. Federal Fund (to account for federal construction grant proceeds).
k. Bond Redemption Fund (to account for cash and investments that are to be used to repay outstanding bonds).
l. School Endowment Fund (to account for contributions that cannot be expended but are to be invested to generate earnings to be used for special school programs).
m. Bond Proceeds Fund (to account for proceeds of bonds issued to finance street construction).
n. Employees' Pension and Relief Fund (to provide retirement and disability benefits to employees).

E2-5 (Expenditures) Which of the following should be reported as expenditures in governmental funds?

a. Salaries.
b. Interest on short-term debt.
c. Purchase of equipment.
d. Long-term liability principal retirement.
e. Depreciation.
f. Short-term liability principal retirement.

E2-6 (Statement of Revenues, Expenditures, and Changes in Fund Balance) Prepare a skeleton statement of revenues, expenditures, and changes in fund balances using the headings in Illustration 2-11 (e.g., Revenues, Expenditures, and Excess (Deficiency) of Revenues over Expenditures) that shows where (or if) each of the following items should be reported in that statement. Include all appropriate subtotals.

    a. Proceeds from issuing bonds.
    b. Transfer to another fund.
    c. Revenues.
    d. Salary expenditures.
    e. Extraordinary loss.
    f. Expenditures for operations.
    g. Expenditures for purchases of equipment.
    h. Expenditures for principal retirement of long-term liabilities.
    i. Expenditures for interest.
    j. Depreciation expense.
    k. Special items.

E2-7 (Statement of Revenues, Expenses, and Changes in Fund Net Position) Prepare a skeleton statement of revenues, expenses, and changes in fund net position using the headings in Illustration 2-11 (e.g., Operating Revenues, Operating Expenses, and Operating Income) that shows where (or if) each of the following items should be reported in that statement. Include all appropriate subtotals.

    a. Proceeds from issuing bonds.
    b. Transfer to another fund. (*Hint*: Include an appropriately titled line for this item in the statement.)
    c. Sales revenues.
    d. Salary expenses.
    e. Extraordinary loss.
    f. Expenditures for purchases of equipment.
    g. Expenditures for principal retirement of long-term liabilities.
    h. Interest expense.
    i. Depreciation expense.
    j. Special items.
    k. Investment income.

E2-8 (Governmental Fund Balance Sheet) Prepare a skeleton balance sheet for a governmental fund using the headings in Illustration 2-12 (i.e., Assets, Liabilities, Fund Balance) that shows where (or if) each of the following items should be reported in that statement. Include all appropriate subtotals.

    a. Cash.
    b. Unrestricted net position.
    c. Nonspendable fund balance.
    d. Due from other funds.
    e. Land.
    f. Bonds payable.
    g. Inventory.
    h. Current portion of bonds payable (maturing in 9 months).
    i. Unassigned fund balance.
    j. Accounts payable.
    k. Buildings and equipment.

E2-9 (Proprietary Fund Statement of Net Position) Prepare a skeleton statement of net position for a proprietary fund using the headings in Illustration 2-12 (i.e., Current Assets, Capital Assets, Current Liabilities) that shows where (or if) each of the following items should be reported in that statement. Include all appropriate subtotals.

    a. Cash.
    b. Unrestricted net position.
    c. Nonspendable fund balance.
    d. Due from other funds.
    e. Land.
    f. Bonds payable.
    g. Inventory.
    h. Current portion of bonds payable (maturing in 9 months).
    i. Unassigned fund balance.
    j. Accounts payable.
    k. Buildings and equipment.

E2-10 (Transaction Analysis—Proprietary vs. Governmental Model)

    1. Analyze the following transactions, assuming that a business-type activity was involved. (*Hint:* Use the proprietary funds accounting equation and the analysis format in Illustration 2-6.)
    2. Analyze the following transactions, assuming that a general government activity was involved. (*Hint:* Use the accounting equations for governmental funds and the nonfund accounts and the analysis format in Illustration 2-7.)

a. Salaries of $5,100 were incurred and paid during the year. Another $200 for salaries was incurred but not paid as of year end.
b. Charges for services rendered were billed (and received early the next fiscal year), $3,000.
c. Borrowed $2,000 on a 1-year, 10%, interest-bearing note, due 3 months after year end.
d. Principal ($2,000) and interest ($200) on the 1-year note were paid when due.
e. Received a $200 transfer from another fund.
f. Issued 10-year, 10% bonds payable for par of $1,000.
g. Annual interest on the bonds ($100) was paid when due—at year end.
h. Repaid the principal amount of a 5-year note, $800.
i. Purchased a computer with a 3-year useful life for cash, $900.
j. Straight-line depreciation of the computer is calculated to be $280 per year. The estimated residual value of the computer is $60.
k. The computer is sold at the end of its useful life for $35. Original cost was $900.

Problems

P2-1 (Transaction Analysis)
a. Analyze the effects of each of the following transactions on each of the funds and/or the nonfund accounts of the City of Nancy. Identify the fund that typically would be used to record the transaction.
b. Indicate how each transaction would be reported in the operating statement for each fund affected.

Example: Cash received for licenses during 20X1, $8,000.

Answer:

		Governmental Funds				General Capital Assets and General Long-Term Liabilities Accounts			
No.	Fund	FA	−	RL	=	FB	GCA	−	GLTL	=	NP
E.	GF	$8,000				$8,000			

Revenues of $8,000 are reported in the General Fund statement of revenues, expenditures, and changes in fund balance.
1. Salaries and wages for firefighters and police officers incurred but not paid, $75,000.
2. The city borrowed $9,000,000 to finance construction of a new city executive office building by issuing bonds at par.
3. The city paid $5,000,000 to the office building contractor for work performed during the fiscal year.
4. The city purchased several notebook computers by issuing a $60,000, 6%, 6-month note to the vendor. The note is due March 1 of the next fiscal year, which is the calendar year. (The note is considered a fund liability.)
5. General Fund resources of $8,000,000 were paid to a newly established Airport Enterprise Fund to provide initial start-up capital.
6. A $3,000,000 personal injury lawsuit has been filed against the city. The controller determines that it is probable that a judgment in that amount will be made in the future but does not expect to have to pay the judgment for another 3 years. The incident relates to general government activities.
7. The city repaid one-half ($10,000,000) of general obligation bonds that had been issued several years before to finance construction of a school building. Interest of $1,000,000 matured and was paid.
8. The city sold general capital assets with an original cost of $50,000 and a $1,000 book value for $1,500. There are no restrictions on the use of the money.

P2-2 (Transaction Analysis)
a. Analyze the effects of the following transactions on the accounting equations of the various funds and nonfund accounts of a state or local government. (For any borrowing transactions, reflect any necessary year-end interest accruals in your responses.)
b. Indicate how each transaction would be reported in the operating statement for each fund affected. Be sure to identify the fund and the operating statement.
1. A government incurred and paid salaries for general government employees, $500,000.
2. A government purchased a truck for $38,000 cash for the use of a general government department that is financed from restricted taxes that can be used only to support the department's programs.

3. A government issued $5,000,000 of 6%, 10-year bonds to help finance expansion of a facility used by one of its public utility operations. The bonds were issued at par 3 months before year end and pay interest annually.
4. A government issued a 9-month, 10% note payable for $50,000. The note was issued 6 months before the end of the fiscal year to provide financing for various programs that are financed primarily from general tax revenues.
5. A government issued general obligation bonds at par, $15 million, to finance construction of a new school building. The bonds bear interest at 8%, payable annually, and were dated and issued 6 months before the end of the year.
6. The government purchased land for the site of the school, $185,000.
7. The government incurred and paid construction costs on the school building, which was completed during the year, $14,715,000.
8. The government's governing body ordered that the unused school bond proceeds be set aside for paying principal and interest on the bonds, and those resources were set aside in the appropriate fund.
9. General tax revenues, $1,500,000, were paid to the fund to be used to pay principal and interest on the school bonds.
10. The first annual interest payment on the school bonds came due and was paid.
11. The 9-month note (from item 4) was repaid with interest when due.
12. The government-owned public utility sold services to the public on account, $1 million; no uncollectibles are expected.
13. The government-owned public utility sold services to other departments of the government, $110,000. The other departments have paid all but $10,000.
14. The government sold a police department computer for $4,000. Its original cost (3 years earlier) was $15,000. At the time of purchase the computer was expected to be used for 4 years and have a $7,000 residual value.
15. The government paid $100,000 principal and $10,000 interest on a long-term note when due, at mid-year.

P2-3 (Transaction Analysis) Analyze each of the following transactions and events. (1) Indicate all of the effects of each transaction on each of the funds and the nonfund accounts of a local government. Be sure to indicate the fund(s) affected. Include analysis of **any year-end adjustments** that are required. Assume that December 31 is the end of the fiscal year. (2) Indicate how each of the transactions, events, or related adjustments should be reported in the operating statement of each fund affected by each transaction.
1. The government issued $4,000,000 of 6%, 10-year bonds at 100 on July 15, 20X3. Interest is payable semiannually on January 15 and July 15 of each year. The bonds were issued to finance construction of a major addition to the government's primary office building.
2. The government was billed $2,800,000 during the year by the courthouse addition contractor for work performed on the courthouse during the year. The government paid $2,200,000 to the contractor.
3. On July 29, 20X3, the government paid $120,000 from the General Fund to the fund from which the courthouse bonds principal and interest are to be repaid.
4. The government repaid a 5-year, $300,000 note payable and interest on August 15, 20X3. The note was repaid directly from the General Fund. The payment included $15,000 of interest.
5. The government issued $14,000,000 of 6%, 10-year bonds at 100 on September 30, 20X3. Interest is payable semiannually on March 31 and September 30 of each year. The bonds were issued to finance construction of a major addition to the government's water plant. The water and sewer department is one of the government's business-type operations, not a general government operation.

P2-4 (Transaction Analysis) (1) Analyze the effects of each of the following transactions on each of the funds and nonfund accounts of the City of Timbuktu. (2) Indicate how each transaction would be reported in the operating statement for each fund affected.
1. Salaries and wages paid to general government employees from unrestricted resources during the year totaled $3,000,000. Salaries and wages payable at the beginning of the year totaled $50,000 and at year-end amounted to $32,000.
2. The city issued $10,000,000 of 10-year, 8% bonds at the beginning of the year. Interest is due semiannually at the beginning of each year and at mid-year. The bonds were issued at par to provide for the construction of a new police and fire facility.
3. Indicate any accruals required at the end of the year that the bonds were issued.
4. Construction costs totaling $5,000,000 were paid during the year related to the police and fire facility. A bill from the contractor requiring an additional payment of $346,500 was received before year end but was not paid by year end.
5. In the beginning of year 2, the city paid the bond interest due and retired $1,000,000 of bonds. Before the payments were made, an adequate amount of General Fund resources was paid to the fund from which the bond payments were made to provide for those payments. (Analyze both transactions.)

6. The city has potential claims and judgments against it that total $17,000,000. Of these claims, it is probable that $7,000,000 will be the total amount of the judgments against the government. Of the $7,000,000, none is due and payable at the end of the year. In addition, $500,000 of claims and judgments were paid for general government activities during the fiscal year.
7. The city sold land that had cost $500,000. The fair value of the land at the sale date was estimated to be $1,800,000, but the city sold it for $1,500,000.
8. The city sold equipment that cost $80,000 and had a remaining book value of $20,000 for $15,000. There are no restrictions on the use of the sale proceeds.

P2-5 (Modified Accrual Basis vs. Accrual Basis) On February 1, 20X3, Mobiline County acquired the following assets of Mobiline Transit, Inc., a privately owned bus line in financial difficulty, with the intent of establishing a county bus service for its residents:

Assets	Amount Paid by County
Land	$ 50,000
Garage and office building...........	80,000
Inventory of tires and parts	15,000
Shop equipment....................	15,000
Buses...........................	140,000
Total paid—February 1, 20X3	$300,000

Additional Information

1. The purchase was financed through the issue of 6% general obligation notes payable, scheduled to mature in amounts of $30,000 each February 1 for 10 years. Interest is payable annually each February 1.
2. Bus line revenues and expenditures are initially being accounted for through the General Fund. The capital assets acquired and the notes payable were recorded in the General Capital Assets and General Long-Term Liabilities accounts.
3. The buses had remaining useful lives of 5 years and the buildings and shop equipment had remaining useful lives of 10 years when acquired.
4. As of its fiscal year end (October 31, 20X3), the County had $3,000 of tires and parts on hand. Also, as of October 31, 20X3, the County was owed $1,000 by a local nonprofit agency for a special charter that was provided on October 20, 20X3.
5. The county's finance officer attempted to prepare an operating statement for the bus line's operations as of October 31, 20X3, using the information accounted for within the General Fund, as follows:

Mobiline County Bus Line
Operating Statement
For the Nine-Month Period Ending October 31, 20X3

Revenues:		
Passenger fares—routine route service	$77,000	
Special charter fees...............................	3,000	$80,000
Expenditures:		
Salaries (superintendent, drivers, mechanics)..........	52,000	
Fuel and lubrication	12,000	
Tires and parts....................................	1,000	
Contracted repairs and maintenance	8,000	
Miscellaneous	1,000	74,000
Net profit.......................................		$ 6,000

Required

a. Briefly analyze the propriety of Mobiline County using the General Fund to account for the operations of the bus service. How would the bus line's operations reflect a different "bottom line" if the activity were being accounted for in an Enterprise Fund?
b. Prepare an accrual basis operating statement of revenues and expenses for Mobiline County Bus Line for the 9-month period ending October 31, 20X3.

P2-6 (Entries Using Different Bases of Accounting)
a. Record each of the following transactions on (1) the cash basis, (2) the modified accrual basis, and (3) the accrual basis.

January	1	Billed customers $4,000 for services rendered.
	3	Purchased $500 of supplies on account.
	5	Purchased a truck costing $30,000 (to be paid for on February 3).
	11	Collected $2,000 from customers on account.
	15	Recorded accrued wages to date, $3,000.
	17	Paid for supplies.
	21	Paid wages.
February	3	Paid for the truck.
	5	$200 of supplies have been used.
	6	Depreciation on the truck for the month was $500.

Solution Format

		Cash Basis		Modified Accrual Basis		Accrual Basis	
Date	Accounts	Dr.	Cr.	Dr.	Cr.	Dr.	Cr.

b. Explain the similarities and differences between the modified accrual and accrual bases of accounting.

Cases

C2-1 (State of California—Fund Identification) The following list includes 13 funds of the State of California. Based on the description from the state's Comprehensive Annual Financial Report, indicate which type of fund each one is.

1. The **Cigarette and Tobacco Tax Fund** accounts for a surtax on cigarette and tobacco products that is used for various health programs.
2. The **Department of Technology Services Fund** accounts for charges for technology services performed for various state departments by the Department of Technology Services.
3. The **Economic Recovery Bond Sinking Fund** accounts for General Fund transfers, proceeds from sale of surplus property, and the 0.25% sales and use tax revenue collected for the payment of principal, interest, and other related costs of the Economic Recovery Bonds.
4. The **Electric Power Fund** accounts for the acquisition and resale of electric power to retail end-use customers.
5. The **Higher Education Construction Fund** accounts for bond proceeds used to construct facilities for state colleges and universities.
6. The **Natural Resources Acquisition and Enhancement Fund** accounts for bond proceeds and various revenues that are used to acquire or improve state parks, beaches, and other recreational areas.
7. The **Prison Construction Fund** accounts for bond proceeds that are used to construct state prisons.
8. The **Prison Industries Fund** accounts for charges for goods produced by inmates in state prisons that are sold to state departments and other governmental entities.
9. The **Receipting and Disbursing Fund** accounts for the collection and disbursement of revenues and receipts on behalf of local governments. This fund also accounts for receipts from numerous state funds, typically for the purpose of writing a single warrant when the warrant is funded by multiple funding sources.
10. The **Service Revolving Fund** accounts for charges for printing and procurement services rendered by the Department of General Services for state departments and other public entities.
11. The **State Lottery Fund** accounts for the sale of California State Lottery tickets and the Lottery's payments for education.
12. The **State Teachers' Retirement Fund** accounts for the employee, employer, and primary government contributions of the cost-sharing multiple-employer retirement plan that provides pension benefits to teachers and certain other employees of the California public school system.
13. The **Transportation Safety Fund** accounts for automobile registration fees and other revenues that are used for transportation safety programs.

(Based on a recent Comprehensive Annual Financial Report of the State of California.)

C2-2 (Humble Independent School District Transaction Analysis)

a. Analyze the effects of the following transactions on the accounting equations of the various funds and nonfund accounts of the Humble (Texas) Independent School District. (Reflect any necessary year-end interest accruals in your responses.)

b. Indicate how the school district should report each transaction in the operating statement for each fund affected. Be sure to identify the fund and the operating statement.

1. Salaries paid to teachers and other instructional staff during the year ended 20X6 totaled $67,000,000. Salaries payable increased $1,240,000 during the fiscal year.

2. Property taxes of $135,000,000 were levied by the school district for the fiscal year: $1,890,000 of the levy is expected to be uncollectible; $130,500,000 of the 20X6 levy was collected by the end of the fiscal year. There were no collections of 20X6 or earlier years' taxes during the first 60 days of the next fiscal year.

3. The school district issued $121,750,000 of construction bonds in 20X6 to provide the financing for general government capital projects.

4. The school district was billed $81,218,000 by contractors for work performed on the district's capital projects. All but $12,400,000 was paid by year end.

5. The school district incurred and paid maintenance costs of $17,600,000 during the year.

6. The school district incurred expenditures for regional day school programs and private residential placements for the deaf and hearing-impaired. These costs were paid from monies received from federal grants restricted to finance such programs. The total costs incurred and the grant collections from the federal government were $690,000.

7. The school district transferred $6,077,000 of General Fund resources to the fund used to service the district's general obligation bonds.

8. Bond principal of $1,400,000 and interest of $6,000,000 were paid on general government bonds.

(Based on a recent Comprehensive Annual Financial Report of the Humble Independent School District, Humble, Texas.)

CHAPTER 3

The General Fund and Special Revenue Funds

LEARNING OBJECTIVES

After studying this chapter, you should be able to:

- Discuss the differences and similarities between the General Fund and Special Revenue Funds.

- Explain the measurement focus and basis of accounting used for these funds.

- Analyze fact situations and prepare journal entries to record most common General Fund and Special Revenue Fund transactions and events, including interfund activity.

- Prepare adjusting and closing entries for the General Fund and Special Revenue Funds.

- Define and identify special items and extraordinary items.

- Understand the five fund balance reporting classifications.

- Prepare General Fund and Special Revenue Fund GAAP-based financial statements.

The General Fund and Special Revenue Funds are used to finance and account for most general government activities of states and local governments. General government activities include police protection, fire protection, central administration, street maintenance, and the general operating activities of independent school districts and nonproprietary special districts. The General Fund and Special Revenue Funds are discussed together because their accounting and reporting are identical.

- *The General Fund* is used to account for and report *all* financial resources *not* accounted for or reported in another fund. The General Fund is established at the inception of a government and exists throughout the government's life.

- *Special Revenue Funds* are established to account for general government financial resources that are raised from specific *revenue sources* that are *restricted or committed* to expenditure for specific purposes other than debt service or capital outlay.

As a rule, most of the financial resources of both types of funds are expended and replenished on an annual basis.

Some governments have only a few Special Revenue Funds, others have a relatively large number. The City of Corona, California, uses individual Special Revenue Funds to account for revenues from certain fines, which must be used for traffic safety; an apportionment of California's gas tax that must be used for the city's highways and streets; a half-cent local option sales tax for streets and roads; asset seizures and forfeitures resulting from police and court actions; development fees to be used to offset the burden resulting from new developments; and tax increment monies set aside to provide housing assistance to low and moderate income families. The inflows of restricted or committed resources into a Special Revenue Fund should comprise a substantial portion of all inflows into the fund. When a substantial portion of the expected inflows are not from restricted or committed revenue sources, the fund is terminated, and its remaining resources typically are transferred to the General Fund.

Most financial resources of the General Fund and Special Revenue Funds are expended for current operating purposes (e.g., salaries and supplies) rather than for capital outlay or debt service. Significant amounts to be expended for capital outlay or debt service from these funds usually are *transferred* to Capital Projects Funds and Debt Service Funds, respectively. The financial resources are then expended through those funds. However, routine capital outlay expenditures (e.g., for vehicles and equipment) and some debt service expenditures (e.g., for capital leases) generally are made directly from the General Fund and Special Revenue Funds.

Measurement Focus   Because of the recurring nature of their revenues and expenditures and the necessity of meeting current expenditures from the currently expendable (appropriable) net financial resources, accounting principles for the General Fund and Special Revenue Funds are based on the flows and balances of currently expendable financial resources rather than the income determination concept of business accounting.[1] Consistent with this measurement focus, recall that the General Fund and Special Revenue Funds are essentially *net* financial assets entities.

The basic accounting equation for each is

Financial Assets (FA)		Deferred Outflows (DO)		Related Liabilities (RL)		Deferred Inflows (DI)		Fund Balance (FB)
	+		−		−		=	

In this context, **Fund Balance** means ***Net Financial Assets,***[2] that is, *fund* Financial Assets (FA)—cash, investments, receivables, and other financial assets—*less* any *fund* Related Liabilities (RL) and Deferred Inflows. (Most governmental funds do not have deferred outflows.)

Accordingly, purchasing capital assets with the financial assets of these funds and the maturing of long-term liabilities to be repaid from them *decrease* their fund balance.

- Expenditures for capital assets thus have the same effect in governmental funds as expenditures for wages and salaries because capital assets are not financial resources; therefore they are *not* capitalized in the General Fund or Special Revenue Funds but in the General Capital Assets accounts.

- Similarly, if *maturing* general obligation bonds of the government—which are carried as liabilities in the General Long-Term Liabilities accounts prior to maturity—are paid from the General Fund or Special Revenue Funds, the expenditure *decreases* the fund balance in the same manner as expenditures for salaries and wages. The bond liability is removed from the General Long-Term Liabilities accounts.

Under the flows and balances of current financial resources concept, the General Fund or Special Revenue Fund year-end balance sheet presents the financial assets on hand, any related fund liabilities, and the fund balance. Furthermore, if some of the General Fund's net resources are *not* currently available for expenditure, such as occurs when a three-year interfund loan has been made from the General Fund to another fund, this is typically indicated by *reporting* a portion

---

[1]Note that this definition of *"current"* differs from the definition used in business accounting and proprietary fund accounting. In these latter contexts, *current* refers to assets that are to be consumed or converted to cash, and liabilities that should be paid, in the *next* (following) fiscal year.

[2]Technically, fund balance is net financial assets ± deferred outflows and deferred inflows. For most governments the only deferred items in the General or Special Revenue Funds result from deferral of revenue recognition because (1) the availability criterion discussed in Chapter 5 is not met—the revenues are not collected soon enough after year end, (2) property taxes or similar taxes were collected in advance of being imposed, or (3) the time period in which the resources can be used is the next year or later.

of the total fund balance as nonspendable fund balance (as discussed later in the chapter).

Purposes and Assumptions of This Chapter

This chapter discusses and illustrates the *basic* accounting procedures and financial statements for the General Fund and Special Revenue Funds. As discussed in Chapter 2, the budget, budgetary accountability, and budgetary reporting are essential components of managing and controlling the departments and activities accounted for in the General Fund and Special Revenue Funds. However, to facilitate your learning GAAP-based accounting and reporting, we delay discussing and illustrating budgetary accounting and reporting until Chapter 4. Therefore, except where stated otherwise, the discussions and illustrations in this chapter:

- Do not address budgetary accounting, reporting, and control issues.
- Assume the accounts are maintained on the modified accrual basis during the year.

Uniform CPA Examination questions also usually assume the accounts are maintained on the GAAP basis, although that is not typical in practice.

The discussions and illustrations in this chapter focus on demonstrating *one way* to account for and report a transaction or event properly—typically the manner most likely to appear in solutions to CPA exam questions and problems—even though there may be acceptable alternatives.[3]

To enhance illustrative clarity, small numerical dollar amounts are used in the illustrative journal entries, trial balances, and financial statements. Likewise, only a few Revenues Subsidiary Ledger accounts (by broad revenue source category) and a few Expenditures Subsidiary Ledger accounts (by function) are used. In practice, government departments maintain accounts in detail. Expenditures are classified not only by function or program but also by several other classifications, including departments and object classes, such as salaries, materials and supplies, and insurance. Thus, the public safety function is an aggregation of the expenditures of the public safety departments, such as Police Department, Fire Department, Jails and Corrections, and Emergency Medical Services. Hundreds or even thousands of subsidiary ledger accounts may be needed in practice.

Because accounting and financial reporting for the General Fund and Special Revenue Funds are identical, this chapter deals primarily with the General Fund, with only occasional reference to Special Revenue Funds. The principles, procedures, and illustrations are equally applicable to Special Revenue Funds, however.

GENERAL FUND ACCOUNTING—ILLUSTRATIVE EXAMPLE

To illustrate the essential aspects of General Fund and Special Revenue Fund accounting, assume that a *new* local governmental unit, a city we will call A Governmental Unit, was founded late in 20X0. A Governmental Unit uses revenues and expenditures subsidiary ledgers to maintain revenue source and expenditure classification detail. The trial balance of its General Fund at January 1, 20X1, appears in Illustration 3-1.

Entries During 20X1

The General Fund transactions, events, and related entries of A Governmental Unit for 20X1—except for budget-related and budgetary-accounting-related entries presented in Chapter 4—are discussed and illustrated in the following sections. The illustration concludes with the General Fund financial statements, except for the budgetary comparison statement included in Chapter 4.

---

[3]Some of the alternatives are discussed and illustrated in Appendix 3-3 and in other chapters.

ILLUSTRATION 3-1   General Ledger Trial Balance—Beginning of 20X1

A Governmental Unit
General Fund
General Ledger Trial Balance
January 1, 20X1

	Debit	Credit
Cash	$14,000	
Accounts Receivable	12,000	
Vouchers [Accounts] Payable		$15,000
Fund Balance		11,000
	$26,000	$26,000

Property Tax Levy

Property taxes usually are a major revenue source of local governments. For example, property taxes of the City of Charleston, South Carolina, were about 45% of total General Fund revenues for a recent fiscal year. Property taxes receivable accrue when they are formally *levied* by the legislative body of the city.

1. Assume that A Governmental Unit's property tax levy for 20X1 is $200,000, of which $3,000 is expected to be uncollectible. Assuming the taxes are both legally expendable for the year and available—i.e., expected to be collected during the year or soon thereafter—the following entry is made when the taxes are levied:

(1) Taxes Receivable—Current	$200,000	
Allowance for Uncollectible Current Taxes		$ 3,000
Revenues		197,000
To record levy of property taxes.		

Revenues Ledger:

Taxes	$197,000

If $5,000 of these 20X1 taxes receivable were not expected to be collected soon enough to be considered "available" to pay for 20X1 expenditures or related liabilities, Deferred Revenues would be credited $5,000 and Revenues would be credited $192,000. The deferred revenues would be reported as deferred inflows in the 20X1 balance sheet and recognized as revenues when they become "available," as will be discussed in more detail in Chapter 5.

The Allowance for Uncollectible Current Taxes amount is the portion of the 20X1 tax levy not expected to be collected. The allowance account is used at this time because the government does not know which specific tax bills will not be collected. Property taxes may be reduced upon appeal, for example, or the property may be sold for less than the taxes and related charges in a foreclosure sale. As specific amounts are determined to be uncollectible, they are written off by debiting the Allowance for Uncollectible Current Taxes account and crediting Taxes Receivable.

Observe in entry 1 that only the *net* expected tax collections are credited to Revenues. This ***net revenue*** approach, which is *used for proprietary fund and government-wide reporting as well as for governmental funds,* differs from business accounting.

- In business accounting, the gross receivable ($200,000) is credited to revenues at the time of the sale. At the end of the accounting cycle, the estimated uncollectible amounts

($3,000) are debited to expense. Note, however, that the entity does not collect $200,000, then pay out $3,000 for uncollectible accounts. Instead, there is an inflow of current financial resources ($197,000) and no outflow.

- Governmental funds account for outflows of net current financial resources—*expenditures*—rather than expenses; and the amount of taxes levied that is uncollectible does not constitute an expenditure. Furthermore, uncollectible taxes will *never* meet the modified accrual "available" revenue recognition criteria. The net revenue approach is required for proprietary fund reporting and government-wide reporting presumably to be consistent with the governmental fund treatment.

Other Revenues Billed or Accrued

2. Assume that A Governmental Unit bills service charge revenues of $36,000 during 20X1, that $1,000 of these revenues are expected to be uncollectible, and the remainder are expected to be collected currently. As these revenues are billed or accrue, the following entries are made:

(2) Accounts Receivable	$36,000	
Allowance for Uncollectible Accounts Receivable		$ 1,000
Revenues		35,000
To record accrual of revenues and related allowance		
for estimated losses.		
<u>Revenues Ledger:</u>		
Charges for Services		$35,000

These service charge revenues might be charges for court costs and fees, inspection fees, or parking fees, for example, and are both objectively measurable and available. Revenues that do *not* accrue, or are *not* deemed *sufficiently measurable* to be accrued in the accounts prior to collection, are debited to Cash and credited to Revenues when collected. Also, note that the "net revenue" approach is used with *all* revenues, not just tax revenues.

Orders and Contracts

3. Orders were placed for materials and equipment estimated to cost $30,000 for the functions indicated here:

Materials and Equipment Ordered:	**Estimated Cost**
General Government	$ 2,000
Public Safety	8,000
Highways and Streets	10,000
Other	4,000
Capital Outlay	6,000
	$30,000

(3) **No entry is required in the GAAP-based accounts.**

No expenditures or liabilities are incurred until the vendor has performed by delivering the materials and equipment ordered. GAAP-based financial reporting thus does not require recording unfilled orders placed or unperformed contracts signed. However, as illustrated in Chapter 4, governments do record governmental fund orders and contracts (called encumbrances) for budgetary control purposes. Further, governments must disclose encumbrances outstanding at year end. Also, as discussed later in this chapter, encumbrances may affect fund balance reporting classifications on the balance sheet.

4. The materials and equipment ordered were received. The actual cost was only $29,900.

(4) Expenditures	$29,900	
Vouchers Payable		$29,900
To record expenditures.		

Expenditures Ledger:

General Government	$ 1,700
Public Safety	8,000
Highways and Streets	10,100
Other	4,000
Capital Outlay	6,100
	$29,900

As stated earlier, the illustrative Expenditures Subsidiary Ledger accounts are maintained by function for A Governmental Unit. The function or program classification indicates the broad purpose for which an expenditure is incurred. More detailed expenditure accounts are maintained in practice. (The entry required to record encumbrances for budgetary control purposes is illustrated in Chapter 4, page 129.)

Finally, recall from Chapter 2 that the purchase of equipment also affects the General Capital Assets and General Long-Term Liabilities (GCA-GLTL) accounts. The equipment would be accounted for in the GCA-GLTL accounts, resulting in the following changes in the GCA-GLTL accounting equation:

$$GCA \text{ (Equipment)} - GLTL = \text{Net Position}$$
$$+\$6,100 \qquad\qquad +\$6,100$$

Salary Expenditures

Salaries, wages, and fringe benefits typically comprise about 75% of city General Fund expenditures and approximately 85% of school district General Fund expenditures. Governments thus must exercise effective controls over payroll and related costs. These controls, discussed in Chapter 6, typically differ from the controls exercised over nonsalary expenditures.

5. If the payroll at the end of a pay period were $40,000, the entry to record the payroll upon approval would be:

(5) Expenditures	$40,000	
Vouchers Payable		$40,000
To record approval of payroll.		

Expenditures Ledger:

General Government	$ 5,000
Public Safety	16,000
Highways and Streets	13,000
Health and Sanitation	4,000
Other	2,000
	$40,000

Interfund Activity

Transactions between a government's funds are common. Interfund activity is classified into four types—two types of nonreciprocal activities and two types of reciprocal activities. The *nonreciprocal* transactions, interfund reimbursements and interfund transfers, are illustrated in transactions 6 through 9. The *reciprocal* transactions, interfund services provided and used and interfund loans, are illustrated in transactions 10 through 12.

Interfund Reimbursements Interfund reimbursements are nonreciprocal transactions in which a government determines that an expenditure or expense

- Initially recorded in the current year in one fund
- Should be accounted for and reported as an expenditure or expense of a different fund.

Some governments use interfund reimbursement transactions to allocate costs incurred for the benefit of multiple departments financed from various funds. In such cases, the expenditures incurred for the goods or services, such as telephone charges or inventory costs, are initially recorded in one fund, usually the General Fund, and then allocated to other funds based on usage of the goods or services. Interfund reimbursement transactions also may occur because a government has inadvertently recorded an expenditure or expense in the wrong fund in the current year.

Accounting for interfund reimbursements requires:

- *Removing* the expenditure or expense from the accounts of the fund in which it was initially recorded and
- *Recording* the expenditure or expense in the reimbursing fund(s).

Either cash will be paid from the reimbursing fund to the reimbursed fund at this point or an interfund payable and receivable will be established in the respective funds. Reimbursements are not distinguished in the operating statements of the funds involved. The amounts initially recorded as expenditures in governmental funds or as expenses in proprietary funds are simply reduced or increased by the amount of the interfund reimbursement.

Transaction 6 is an example of an interfund reimbursement. Note when you review the General Fund operating statement of A Governmental Unit that the effects of this transaction are not separately identified.

6. A government accountant or auditor determined that General Fund expenditures of $1,500 should have been recorded as expenditures of a Special Revenue Fund.

(6) Due from Special Revenue Fund	$1,500	
Expenditures		$1,500
To record reimbursement due from Special Revenue Fund for expenditure recorded initially in the General Fund.		
Expenditures Ledger:		
General Government		$1,500

This **reimbursement** transaction would have the following effect on the specific Special Revenue Fund's accounting equation:

$$\text{Financial Assets} - \text{Related Liabilities} = \text{Fund Balance}$$
$$+\$1,500 \qquad\qquad -\$1,500 \text{ (Expenditures)}$$

Interfund Transfers Interfund transfers normally involve moving assets (e.g., cash and inventory) accounted for in one fund to another fund without a reciprocal flow of resources or services in return. Further, transfers involve neither a requirement nor a reasonable expectation of subsequent repayment. (If repayment is expected, the transaction is an interfund loan.)

Interfund transfers also result when departments financed by one fund, such as a water department Enterprise Fund, provide services to departments or agencies financed through other funds *without charging* for those services. The Enterprise Fund is required to report water fee revenues at its standard rates and an equal transfer out because the user department was not required to pay for the services. Expenditures—and an equal transfer in—based on the standard water rates must be reported in the General Fund.

Common examples of interfund transfers include:

- General Fund resources transferred to a Debt Service Fund to provide for principal and interest payments on bonds or other general long-term liabilities (as in transaction 7)
- General (or Special Revenue) Fund resources transferred to a Capital Projects Fund to provide part of the financing of a general government capital project
- Special Revenue Fund resources transferred to the General Fund to finance General Fund expenditures for the purpose to which the SRF resources are restricted (as in transaction 8)
- General Fund resources transferred to a proprietary fund to provide initial permanent financing (or financing for expansion) for a proprietary activity (as in transaction 9)
- Residual net assets of a Capital Projects Fund or Debt Service Fund transferred to another fund upon, respectively, completion of a capital project and settlement of related billings or full repayment of a general long-term liability serviced through a Debt Service Fund
- Enterprise Fund resources transferred from an Enterprise Fund activity with profitable operations (such as state lotteries, Indian casinos, and some government-owned public utilities) to the General Fund or other funds to subsidize their operations

Recall from Chapter 2 that fund balance increases or decreases resulting from interfund transfers must be distinguished clearly from revenues and expenditures in the operating statements of governmental funds. Likewise, transfers are distinguished from revenues and expenses in financial statements of proprietary funds and fiduciary funds.

This distinctive reporting is accomplished in governmental funds by reporting interfund transfers in a special classification of changes in fund balance in the Statement of Revenues, Expenditures, and Changes in Fund Balance. This special classification is called **other financing sources and uses**. The interfund transfers recorded in the next three transactions are clearly separated from revenues and expenditures in the Statement of Revenues, Expenditures, and Changes in Fund Balance for A Governmental Unit presented later in Illustration 3-7.

Interfund transfers are the most common item reported in this special section of the governmental fund operating statement, but several other *nonrevenue* increases and *nonexpenditure* decreases in fund balance resulting from transactions with external entities also are reported as **other financing sources (uses)**. These external transactions include the proceeds of issuing general long-term bonds payable and similar obligations and the proceeds received from the sale of general capital assets. Transactions 7 through 9 provide examples of interfund transfers.

7. $5,000 was authorized and paid to a Debt Service Fund to provide for principal and interest payments and for fiscal agent fees.

(7) Transfer to Debt Service Fund.............................	$5,000	
Cash...		$5,000
To record transfer to Debt Service Fund to meet debt service and fiscal charges.		

Note that interfund transfers must be reported separately from Revenues and Expenditures, and that this transfer affects the *Debt Service Fund* as follows:

Financial Assets − Related Liabilities = Fund Balance

+$5,000   +$5,000 (Other Financing Source)

8. The governing board ordered $10,000 to be transferred from a Special Revenue Fund to the General Fund; the cash will be disbursed and received later.

(8) Due from Special Revenue Fund $10,000
     Transfer from Special Revenue Fund $10,000
    To record interfund transfer from Special Revenue Fund
      ordered by governing board.

The impact of this transfer on the *Special Revenue Fund* accounting equation is:

Financial Assets − Related Liabilities = Fund Balance

+$10,000   −$10,000 (Other Financing Uses)

9. General Fund cash of $6,000 was paid to a new Enterprise Fund to provide capital for the Enterprise Fund.

(9) Transfer to Enterprise Fund....................... $ 6,000
    Cash .... $ 6,000
    To record transfer to provide capital to a new
      Enterprise Fund.

    Note that some interfund transfers occur between two governmental funds, some occur between two proprietary funds, and some occur between a governmental fund and a proprietary fund. Governmental fund interfund transfers must be reported separately from revenues and expenditures—as Other Financing Sources (Uses). Likewise, *proprietary fund interfund transfers* are reported separately from proprietary fund revenues and expenses—as the last item before the net change in net assets. This transfer affects the *Enterprise Fund* accounting equation as follows:

Assets − Liabilities = Net Position

+$6,000   +$6,000 (Transfer In)

Interfund Services The GASB defines interfund services provided and used transactions (hereafter "interfund services") as "sales and purchases of goods and services between funds for a price approximating their external market value." Thus, interfund services transactions are essentially "arm's-length" sales of goods and services between departments reported in or financed by two different funds.

    State and local governments account for and report interfund services transactions almost exactly as they would if the

- "Seller" fund sold goods or services to an external entity (i.e., as revenues).
- "Buyer" fund purchased the same goods or services from an external entity (i.e., as expenditures or expenses).

    Many interfund services transactions result from Internal Service Fund departments (e.g., central stores, central communication or data processing services, and central motor pools or garages) providing goods or services to the other departments or agencies of a government. Many others are from Enterprise Fund departments, such as a government's water and sewer department or its gas or electric department, providing (selling) their services to the government's other departments and agencies. Likewise, certain general government departments, such as inspection departments, may charge fees to other departments for certain services provided.

    The only required distinction in reporting interfund services transactions in governmental funds compared to sales and purchases from external entities is that unpaid balances from these transactions are reported as interfund receivables and payables, not as accounts receivable and accounts payable. Revenues and expenditures or expenses from interfund services transactions usually are *not* required to be *reported distinctively* in the operating statements of either governmental funds or proprietary funds to differentiate them from sales to or purchases from external entities.[4]

Transaction 10 is an example of an interfund services transaction.

10. Supplies were purchased from the Stores Internal Service Fund for the following functions: General Government, $4,000; Public Safety, $6,000; Highways and Streets, $10,000; Health and Sanitation, $7,000; and Other, $3,000.

(10) Expenditures	$30,000	
Due to Internal Service Fund		$30,000
To record supplies provided by an Internal Service Fund.		

Expenditures Ledger:

General Government	$ 4,000
Public Safety	6,000
Highways and Streets	10,000
Health and Sanitation	7,000
Other	3,000
	$30,000

This **interfund services** transaction would have the following impact on the *Stores Internal Service Fund* accounting equation:

$$\text{Assets} - \text{Liabilities} = \text{Net Position}$$

$$+\$30,000 \qquad\qquad +\$30,000 \text{ (Revenues)}$$

Interfund Loans Interfund loans are the final category of interfund transactions. Interfund loans involve loaning the resources (typically cash) of one fund to another fund with a requirement and expectation of repayment. These loans do not change the total fund balance of any fund. Rather, each fund has either an asset or a liability. Thus, the lender fund reports an interfund *receivable,* and the borrower fund reports an interfund *payable*.

Some governments are able to use short-term interfund loans like the one illustrated in transactions 11 and 12 to alleviate short-term cash needs in certain funds without external borrowings. Longer-term financing needs are sometimes met with long-term interfund loans. (Long-term interfund loans are illustrated later in the chapter.)

11. A $1,250 (90-day) loan was made from the General Fund to a Special Revenue Fund to provide temporary financing for expenditures to be reimbursed by a federal grant.

(11) Due from Special Revenue Fund	$ 1,250	
Cash		$ 1,250
To record short-term interfund loan to a Special Revenue Fund.		

The loan affects the *Special Revenue Fund* accounting equation as follows:

$$\text{Financial Assets} - \text{Related Liabilities} = \text{Fund Balance}$$

$$+\$1,250 \qquad\qquad +\$1,250$$

12. The $1,250 loan to the Special Revenue Fund was collected after that fund received a portion of the grant monies from the federal government.

(12) Cash	$ 1,250	
Due from Special Revenue Fund		$ 1,250
To record repayment of short-term interfund loan.		

---

[4]Internal Service Funds account for services provided to other funds (i.e., interfund sales) separately, however, and often report them separate from external sales.

The impact of the repayment on the Special Revenue Fund accounting equation is:

$$\text{Financial Assets} - \text{Related Liabilities} = \text{Fund Balance}$$

$$-\$1{,}250 \qquad\qquad -\$1{,}250$$

In transaction 11 a **fund** asset is recorded in the General Fund, and its Cash is decreased. At the same time a **fund** liability, Due to General Fund, is recorded in the Special Revenue Fund, and its Cash is increased. Neither the fund balance of the General Fund nor of the Special Revenue Fund is affected by the interfund borrowing in transaction 11 or by its repayment in transaction 12.

Note: A government may have more than one fund of each fund type except the General Fund. To simplify our illustrative example and reinforce fund type names, we use "fund type" accounts such as "Due to Internal Service Fund" and "Due from Special Revenue Fund." In practice the interfund receivable and payable accounts resulting from various interfund transactions include the names of specific funds—such as "Due to Stores Internal Service Fund"—or specific fund numbers—such as "Due from Special Revenue Fund #8" and "Due to Capital Projects Fund #5."

Short-Term External Borrowings

Governments sometimes have short-term cash needs that necessitate short-term *borrowings from external entities* such as banks. Short-term external borrowings and repayments of the principal of short-term borrowings do not change fund balance. A fund liability is recorded in the borrower fund, and its fund balance is affected only by interest incurred (whether paid or accrued) on short-term external borrowings. Transaction 13 illustrates an *external short-term borrowing*, and transaction 14 illustrates its *partial repayment with interest*.

13. The government borrowed $20,000 on a short-term note from a local bank to alleviate a General Fund cash shortage.

(13) Cash	$20,000	
Short-Term Notes Payable		$20,000
To record short-term borrowing from bank.		

14. $5,000 of principal and $600 of interest were paid from the General Fund on the short-term note payable.

(14) Short-Term Notes Payable	$ 5,000	
Expenditures	600	
Cash		$ 5,600
To record payment of the interest to date and part of the short-term note principal.		
Expenditures Ledger:		
Debt Service [Interest]	$ 600	

Note that the General Capital Assets and General Long-Term Liabilities accounts are *not* affected because the note payable was a short-term *fund* liability.

Extraordinary and Special Items

State and local governments may occasionally need to report extraordinary items and special items.

- **Extraordinary Items**—a term used in both the FASB and GASB standards—are transactions or events that are *not* within the control of management and are *both* (1) unusual in nature and (2) infrequent in occurrence.
- **Special Items**—as defined in GASB *Statement No. 34* (paras. 55 and 56)—are (1) *within* the control of management *and* (2) *either* unusual *or* infrequent.[5]

---

[5]GASB *Codification*, section 2200.141.

Earthquake damages and the crash of an organization's airplane would usually be extraordinary items. Special items might include a significant sale of part or all of city-owned beach property to help finance the current budget.

In practice, special items often are referred to as "one-shot" revenues or other financing sources because they help finance operations for a single year but are not a continuing source of financing. The GASB created the special item classification to highlight these transactions in a government's financial statements to avoid misleading statement users about the government's sustainable level of revenues.

Transaction 15 illustrates accounting for a *special item,* and transaction 16 illustrates accounting for an *extraordinary item* in the General Fund of A Governmental Unit.

15. A Governmental Unit's management decided to sell to developers, for $8,000, a section of beach property that was one of the city's general capital assets. The city's carrying value for the property was $2,000.

(15) Cash	$8,000	
Special Item—Proceeds from Sale of Beach Property		$8,000
To record the proceeds from the sale of a portion of the city-owned beach property.		

Capital asset sale proceeds are reported as other financing sources unless they meet the special item criteria. In either event, the GCA-GLTL effects are:

$$GCA\ (Land) - GLTL = Net\ Position$$
$$-\$2,000 \qquad\qquad -\$2,000$$

16. A new computer purchased for the accounting department for $6,000 was destroyed by a flash flood. (The city never had a flash flood before and does not expect to have another.) The city received $5,750 from the city's insurer to cover the cost of replacing the computer ($6,000) less the $250 deductible under the policy. The transaction was not under management's control and is deemed both unusual in nature and infrequent in occurrence.

(16) Cash	$5,750	
Extraordinary Item—Insurance Recovery Proceeds		$5,750
To record the insurance recovery proceeds from computer destruction.		

Recall from Chapter 2 that extraordinary items and special items are reported in a separate section of the Statement of Revenues, Expenditures, and Changes in Fund Balance. Also, the new computer is removed from the GCA-GLTL accounts as follows:

$$GCA\ (Equipment) - GLTL = Net\ Position$$
$$-\$6,000 \qquad\qquad -\$6,000$$

Other Transactions and Events

Additional entries that illustrate the operation of the General Fund of A Governmental Unit follow. Recall that entries are made in the Revenues Ledger or Expenditures Ledger *only* when the General Ledger entries affect the Revenues or Expenditures accounts. Revenues and expenditures detail is captured in these subsidiary ledgers. *The cumulative balance of each subsidiary ledger should always equal the balance of the related general ledger control account.*

17. Taxes receivable of $160,000 and accounts receivable of $15,000 were collected.

(17)	Cash	$175,000	
	Taxes Receivable—Current		$160,000
	Accounts Receivable		15,000
	To record collection of taxes receivable and accounts receivable.		

18. and 19. Current taxes receivable (entry 18) and the related allowance (entry 19) were reclassified as delinquent after the due date.

(18)	Taxes Receivable—Delinquent	$ 40,000	
	Taxes Receivable—Current		$ 40,000
	To record reclassification of past due taxes.		
	[Total levy of $200,000 (transaction 1) less collections of current taxes of $160,000 (transaction 17).]		
(19)	Allowance for Uncollectible Current Taxes	$ 3,000	
	Allowance for Uncollectible Delinquent Taxes		$ 3,000
	To record reclassification of allowance for estimated losses on taxes.		

When appropriate authorization is provided to write off taxes receivable, the entry will be to debit the allowance account and credit the receivable account. Write-offs of accounts receivable (entry 28) are identical.

20. Revenues that have not been accrued previously were collected as follows: taxes (other than property taxes), $58,000; licenses and permits, $68,000; intergovernmental revenues, $52,500; charges for services, $6,000; fines and forfeits, $19,000; and other revenues, $1,500.

(20)	Cash	$205,000	
	Revenues		$205,000
	To record receipt of revenues not previously accrued.		
	Revenues Ledger:		
	Taxes		$ 58,000
	Licenses and Permits		68,000
	Intergovernmental		52,500
	Charges for Services		6,000
	Fines and Forfeits		19,000
	Other		1,500
			$205,000

21. Purchase orders were issued for the following functions and amounts: Public Safety, $7,000, and Health and Sanitation, $13,000.

(21) As explained for transaction 3, no entry is required in the GAAP-based accounts until goods or services are received. But encumbrances of appropriations (authorizations for expenditure adopted in the budget) for unfilled orders and uncompleted contracts are recorded for budgetary control purposes as illustrated in Chapter 4.

22. $20,000 of delinquent taxes receivable and related interest and penalties (not previously accrued) of $200 were collected.

(22) Cash	$ 20,200	
Taxes Receivable—Delinquent		$ 20,000
Revenues		200

To record collection of delinquent taxes receivable and
of interest and penalties not accrued previously.

<u>Revenues Ledger:</u>

Other [Interest and Penalties]		$ 200

23. $10,000 of temporary investments were purchased.

(23) Investments	$ 10,000	
Cash		$ 10,000

To record temporary investment of cash.

Note: Investment accounting and reporting under GASB
Statement Nos. 31 and *40* are discussed and illustrated in
Chapter 5 and in later chapters.

24. Expenditures were vouchered for payment for the following functions: General Government, $30,000; Public Safety, $112,000; Highways and Streets, $90,000; Health and Sanitation, $35,400; Other, $9,600; and Capital Outlay (Equipment), $23,000.

(24) Expenditures	$300,000	
Vouchers Payable		$300,000

To record unencumbered expenditures.

<u>Expenditures Ledger:</u>

General Government	$ 30,000
Public Safety	112,000
Highways and Streets	90,000
Health and Sanitation	35,400
Other	9,600
Capital Outlay [Equipment]	23,000
	$300,000

The capital outlay expenditures ($23,000) increase the General Capital Assets accounts.

$$\text{GCA (Equipment)} - \text{GLTL} = \text{Net Position}$$
$$+\$23,000 \qquad\qquad +\$23,000$$

25. Vouchers payable were paid, $360,000.

(25) Vouchers Payable	$360,000	
Cash		$360,000

To record payment of vouchers.

26. $22,500 was paid from the General Fund on the balance owed to the Stores Internal Service Fund.

(26) Due to Internal Service Fund	$ 22,500	
Cash		$ 22,500

To record partial payment of amount due the Stores
Fund.

This transaction also results in a corresponding increase in Cash and decrease in Due from General Fund in the Stores Internal Service Fund.

27. $13,000 was collected on accounts receivable.

(27) Cash..	$13,000	
Accounts Receivable..............................		$13,000
To record collections of accounts receivable.		

28. An account receivable balance of $400 was determined to be uncollectible.

(28) Allowance for Uncollectible Accounts Receivable........	$ 400	
Accounts Receivable		$ 400
To record write-off of accounts receivable determined to be uncollectible.		

29. The audit disclosed that a 20X0 expenditure and liability, $300, had not been recorded at December 31, 20X0.

(29) Correction of Prior Year Error	$ 300	
Vouchers Payable		$ 300
To record correction of prior year (20X0) error.		

Note that, like transaction 17, transactions 25 through 27 are simply payments of liabilities or collections of receivables. Transactions 18 and 19 reclassify taxes receivable and the related allowance as past due, and transaction 28 is a write-off of receivables. Accounting for these transactions is not unique to governmental fund accounting.

Governments should review their accounts at year end to determine whether any adjusting entries are needed to properly reflect fund operating results and financial position. **Year-End Adjustments**

- *Revenue Adjustments.* Among the types of revenues that might be accrued in adjusting entries are interest on investments and delinquent taxes, unbilled charges for services, and unrestricted intergovernmental grants that have been earned and are available but have not been billed by year end.
- *Expenditure Adjustments.* Expenditures that might require accrual entries include interest on short-term debt and accrued payroll.

To illustrate year-end adjusting entries, assume that A Governmental Unit had no significant payroll accruals but that two revenue accruals—both related to "available revenues"—and one expenditure accrual are in order:

A1. Interest and penalties on taxes of $550, of which $50 is expected to be uncollectible, had accrued at year end.

(A1) Interest and Penalties Receivable on Taxes	$ 550	
Allowance for Uncollectible Interest and Penalties		$ 50
Revenues		500
To record interest and penalties accrued on delinquent taxes and to provide for estimated losses.		
Revenues Ledger:		
Other [Interest and Penalties]		$ 500

A2. Accrued interest on investments at year end was $400.

(A2) Accrued Interest Receivable........................	$400	
Revenues.......................................		$400
To record interest accrued on investments.		
Revenues Ledger:		
Other [Interest and Penalties]		$400

A3. Accrued interest on the short-term note payable at year end was $250.

(A3) Expenditures.....................................	$250	
Accrued Interest Payable		$250
To record interest accrued on short-term notes payable.		
Expenditures Ledger:		
Debt Service—Interest	$250	

This illustrative example assumes that all taxes, interest and penalties, accounts, and other receivables were collected "soon enough after year end" to be "available" to finance 20X1 expenditures, and the cash received is not restricted but can be used to pay the General Fund payables at year end. When this assumption is *not* valid, one or more adjusting entries are required to *reduce* reported Revenues and *increase* a Deferred Revenues account(s).

Preclosing Trial Balances

Illustration 3-2 presents the *preclosing* trial balance of the *General Ledger* accounts after the preceding illustrative journal entries are posted. Illustration 3-3 presents the *preclosing* trial balances of the *Revenues Subsidiary Ledger* and *Expenditures Subsidiary Ledger*. (These trial balances are the basis for the financial statements presented later in the chapter.)

Illustrative Example Worksheets

Appendix 3-1 includes the following for the General Fund of A Governmental Unit for the year ended December 31, 20X1:

1. Illustration 3-11—General Ledger Worksheet
2. Illustration 3-12—Revenues Subsidiary Ledger (Preclosing)
3. Illustration 3-13—Expenditures Subsidiary Ledger (Preclosing)

These summary worksheets are useful both in initial study and in review of this chapter.

20X1 Closing Entries

At the end of the fiscal year, entries are made to close the accounts. The closing process summarizes the results of operations in the Fund Balance account. More specifically, the purposes of closing entries are to:

1. **Close the operating accounts** in the **General Ledger** so they will begin the next year with zero balances—ready to record that year's operations—and **update the Fund Balance account** to its actual end-of-year balance.
2. **Close the Revenues Subsidiary Ledger and Expenditures Subsidiary Ledger accounts** so they are ready to record the next year's detailed operating data.

These purposes may be accomplished by differing sequences of entries. The simplest approach—a single compound entry closing all operating accounts simultaneously—is used here.

ILLUSTRATION 3-2   Preclosing Trial Balance—General Ledger—End of 20X1

A Governmental Unit
General Fund
Preclosing Trial Balance
General Ledger
December 31, 20X1

	Debit	Credit
Cash	$ 51,850	
Investments	10,000	
Accrued Interest Receivable	400	
Taxes Receivable—Delinquent	20,000	
Allowance for Uncollectible Delinquent Taxes		$ 3,000
Interest and Penalties Receivable on Taxes	550	
Allowance for Uncollectible Interest and Penalties		50
Accounts Receivable	19,600	
Allowance for Uncollectible Accounts Receivable		600
Due from Special Revenue Fund	11,500	
Vouchers Payable		25,200
Notes Payable		15,000
Accrued Interest Payable		250
Due to Internal Service Fund		7,500
Fund Balance		11,000
Revenues		438,100
Special Item—Proceeds from Sale of Beach Property		8,000
Extraordinary Item—Insurance Recovery Proceeds		5,750
Expenditures	399,250	
Transfer to Debt Service Fund	5,000	
Transfer from Special Revenue Fund		10,000
Transfer to Enterprise Fund	6,000	
Correction of Prior Year Error	300	
	$524,450	$524,450

General Ledger Closing Entry

The compound General Fund general ledger closing entry for A Governmental
Unit at December 31, 20X1, is:

(C)	Revenues	$438,100	
	Transfer from Special Revenue Fund	10,000	
	Special Item—Proceeds from Sale of Beach Property	8,000	
	Extraordinary Item—Insurance Recovery Proceeds	5,750	
	Fund Balance		$ 51,300
	Expenditures		399,250
	Transfer to Debt Service Fund		5,000
	Transfer to Enterprise Fund		6,000
	Correction of Prior Year Error		300
	To close the general ledger accounts.		

51,850-550

Subsidiary Ledger Closing Entries

The accounts in the Revenues Subsidiary Ledger and the Expenditures Subsidiary
Ledger are closed by simply debiting the credit balances and crediting the debit

---

ILLUSTRATION 3-3 Preclosing Trial Balances—Revenues and Expenditures
Subsidiary Ledgers—End of 20X1

A Governmental Unit
General Fund
Preclosing Trial Balances
Revenues and Expenditures Subsidiary Ledgers
December 31, 20X1

Revenues Subsidiary Ledger

Taxes	$255,000
Licenses and Permits	68,000
Intergovernmental	52,500
Charges for Services	41,000
Fines and Forfeits	19,000
Other	2,600
	$438,100

Expenditures Subsidiary Ledger

General Government	$ 39,200
Public Safety	142,000
Highways and Streets	123,100
Health and Sanitation	46,400
Other	18,600
Capital Outlay	29,100
Debt Service	850
	$399,250

---

balances, thus bringing all accounts to a zero balance. This task may be done automatically in computerized systems or manually by observing the preclosing account balances (see Illustrations 3-3, 3-12, and 3-13):

(C) **Revenues Ledger:**

Taxes	$255,000
Licenses and Permits	68,000
Intergovernmental	52,500
Charges for Services	41,000
Fines and Forfeits	19,000
Other	2,600
	$438,100

(C) **Expenditures Ledger:**

General Government	$ 39,200
Public Safety	142,000
Highways and Streets	123,100
Health and Sanitation	46,400
Other	18,600
Capital Outlay	29,100
Debt Service	850
	$399,250

ILLUSTRATION 3-4   Postclosing Trial Balance—General Ledger—End of 20X1

A Governmental Unit
General Fund
Postclosing Trial Balance
General Ledger
December 31, 20X1

	Debit	Credit
Cash	$ 51,850	
Investments	10,000	
Accrued Interest Receivable...........................	400	
Taxes Receivable—Delinquent........................	20,000	
Allowance for Uncollectible Delinquent Taxes		$ 3,000
Interest and Penalties Receivable on Taxes	550	
Allowance for Uncollectible Interest and Penalties		50
Accounts Receivable	19,600	
Allowance for Uncollectible Accounts Receivable		600
Due from Special Revenue Fund......................	11,500	
Vouchers Payable..		25,200
Short-Term Notes Payable............................		15,000
Accrued Interest Payable		250
Due to Internal Service Fund.........................		7,500
Fund Balance		62,300
	$113,900	$113,900

(11,000 + 51,300)

The *postclosing* trial balance of the General Fund is presented in Illustration 3-4.

Postclosing Trial Balance

BALANCE SHEETS

The essential character of the General Fund should be kept in mind as balance sheets and balance sheet accounts are discussed. Though the General Fund presumably will exist as long as the governmental unit exists, its operational focus is year to year. Each year the problem of financing a new year's operations with financial resources on hand and the new year's revenues and other financing resource inflows (e.g., transfers) is the central concern of those managing the finances of the fund. The balance sheet is prepared to provide information that assists in addressing this problem. Although some governments prepare interim balance sheets, only year-end balance sheets are required by GAAP.

Interim balance sheets may be prepared monthly, quarterly, or when needed for internal use, bond issues, or other purposes. SLGs rarely issue audited interim balance sheets. Accordingly, the GASB provides balance sheet standards and guidance only for year-end balance sheets.

Interim Balance Sheet

The balance sheet of the General Fund of A Governmental Unit at December 31, 20X1 (Illustration 3-5), is based on the postclosing trial balance at that date. The statement is largely self-explanatory, but comments on some of the accounts should help clarify its characteristics. The comments deal with (1) the reporting of Fund Balance, (2) interfund receivables and payables, and (3) the exclusion of general capital assets and unmatured general long-term liabilities. If a governmental fund

Year-End Balance Sheet

ILLUSTRATION 3-5 Balance Sheet—End of 20X1

A Governmental Unit
General Fund
Balance Sheet
December 31, 20X1

Assets

Cash		$ 51,850
Investments		10,000
Accrued interest receivable		400
Taxes receivable—delinquent	$20,000	
Less: Allowance for uncollectible delinquent taxes	3,000	17,000
Interest and penalties receivable on taxes	550	
Less: Allowance for uncollectible interest and penalties	50	500
Accounts receivable	19,600	
Less: Allowance for uncollectible accounts	600	19,000
Due from Special Revenue Fund		11,500
Total Assets		$110,250

Liabilities and Fund Balance

Liabilities:

Vouchers payable	$25,200	
Short-term notes payable	15,000	
Accrued interest payable	250	
Due to Internal Service Fund	7,500	$ 47,950
Fund Balance:		
Assigned	20,000	
Unassigned	42,300	62,300
Total Liabilities and Fund Balance		$110,250

---

has deferred outflows and deferred inflows, the deferred outflows are reported in a separate section following assets and the deferred inflows following liabilities.

Fund Balance One form of the governmental fund *accounting equation*, which is reflected in the balance sheet, is:

$$\underset{\text{(FA)}}{\underset{\text{Assets}}{\text{Financial}}} + \underset{\text{(DO)}}{\underset{\text{Outflows}}{\text{Deferred}}} = \underset{\text{(RL)}}{\underset{\text{Liabilities}}{\text{Related}}} + \underset{\text{(DI)}}{\underset{\text{Inflows}}{\text{Deferred}}} + \underset{\text{(FB)}}{\underset{\text{Balance}}{\text{Fund}}}$$

Governmental funds do *not* contain accounts for general capital assets (because they are not financial assets) or for unmatured general long-term liabilities (because their retirement will not require expenditure of existing expendable financial assets).

The General Fund (and Special Revenue Funds) also is a *current* fund in that it is officially budgeted and appropriated for *annually*. Thus, its fiscal operations are concerned with the *current-year* revenues and other financing sources, the *current-year* expenditures and other uses of financial resources, the *current-year* increases or decreases in total fund balances, and both the total fund balance and various subclassifications of fund balances at the end of the *current* year.

GASB *Statement No. 34* emphasizes reporting **total** fund balances and *changes* in **total** fund balances of governmental funds. Fund balance must be presented using the five fund balance classifications shown in Illustration 3-5. More detailed subclassifications also must be reported either on the governmental fund balance sheet or in the notes to the financial statements. Two of these detailed fund balance classifications are shown in Illustration 3-5. All five required fund balance classifications, including these, are discussed in the next section.

The GASB requires a hierarchical presentation of fund balance based on how difficult it is for the government to modify constraints on the specific uses for which its resources may be expended. Some constraints on the use of resources, such as external restrictions, cannot be modified or removed by the government. Modifying other constraints requires (1) reversal of its formal actions by the governing body—for commitments—or (2) decisions by a designated government official or committee that the government no longer intends to limit expenditure of the resources to the previously specified purpose(s)—for assignments. Many general government financial resources are available for general use and are not constrained to expenditure for a specific purpose.

Unassigned Fund Balance is the amount of governmental fund net assets (+ deferred outflows − deferred inflows) with no constraints on their use. Four other fund balance classifications indicate different levels of constraint on use of the remaining net assets of a governmental fund. The four classifications, in order of most binding constraints to least binding constraints, are:

- Nonspendable Fund Balance
- Restricted Fund Balance
- Committed Fund Balance
- Assigned Fund Balance

The basic distinctions between these four fund balance classifications are outlined in Illustration 3-6.

ILLUSTRATION 3-6 **Fund Balance Classifications**				
FUND BALANCE CLASSIFICATIONS TO DISCLOSE CONSTRAINTS ON USE BASIC INFORMATION				
Constraint	**Nonspendable**	**Restricted**	**Committed**	**Assigned**
Source of constraint	Nature of assets or unavailability for use because of legal or contractual requirements to maintain a certain principal amount	• External donor or grantors • Counterparties to contracts • The government's governing body • A senior government	A government's governing body—defined as its highest level decision-making body (including both the legislative body and the chief executive where approval by both is required for legislation)	A government's governing body or its designees—a committee or individuals to whom the governing body delegates its assignment authority
Nature of constraint	Not in spendable form—may result from: • Inventory and prepaid items in any governmental fund • Some long-term receivables and property held for resale in the *General Fund* only Legally required to be maintained intact—i.e., the nonexpendable corpus in Permanent Funds	• Provisions in donor or grantor agreements, debt agreements, or other contracts • Provisions in the constitution or enabling legislation—of either the government or a senior level of government—authorizing the revenue source	Provisions adopted by the governing body's formal action (e.g., ordinance or resolution) (The formal action, if any, through which this body commits resources to particular uses is determined by its own policy.)	Explicit indication of the government's intent to limit the use of resources to a purpose more narrow than the general purposes of the government
Modification of constraint requires	Not applicable	• Agreement of donor/grantor or counterparty • Legislation—for resources restricted by enabling legislation	Reversal of its formal action by the governing body	Decision of individual or committee with assignment authority (or by the governing body)
Reflected in	May be in any governmental fund	May be in any governmental fund	May be in any governmental fund	May be in any governmental fund

Nonspendable Fund Balance

Nonspendable fund balance of any governmental fund should reflect amounts held in inventories and prepaid assets. In the General Fund, it also includes fund balance related to long-term receivables (and property acquired for resale) that do *not* have restrictions, commitments, or assignments of the eventual proceeds. (In other funds these proceeds always are either restricted, committed, or assigned.) The portion of nonspendable fund balance representing such assets is classified as "***not in spendable form.***"

Nonspendable fund balance also reflects the nonexpendable corpus of Permanent Funds. This portion of nonspendable fund balance is classified as "legally or contractually required to be maintained intact."[6]

Note that nonspendable fund balance is reported for amounts equal to inventory and prepaid assets even if their use is restricted, committed, or assigned. Long-term receivables and property acquired for resale with restrictions, commitments, or assignments must be reflected in those other fund balance classifications. Therefore, as noted above, these assets can be reflected in nonspendable fund balance only in the General Fund but can be reflected in the other categories in any governmental fund. You may recall that nonspendable fund balance was reported in the balance sheet presented in Illustration 2-12, page 54. This occurred because the assets of the fund included inventory. Nonspendable fund balance will never be negative.

Restricted Fund Balance

Restricted fund balance equals assets restricted—by external parties, constitutional provisions, or enabling legislation[7]—for expenditure for a specific purpose less liabilities and deferred inflows related to those restricted assets. This category *cannot* have a *negative* balance. Major restricted purposes must either be displayed in the balance sheet or in the notes to the financial statements. The same display alternatives apply to committed and to assigned fund balance.

Committed Fund Balance

Committed fund balance equals assets committed for a purpose less liabilities and deferred inflows related to those committed assets. In addition to amounts committed via the process described in Illustration 3-6, committed fund balance is reported as a result of a government's:

- Outstanding orders or contracts (known as encumbrances outstanding) that both (1) otherwise would reduce unassigned fund balance when filled or completed and (2) were approved using the same formal action required by the commitment policy.

- Intent to use existing resources (held at the end of one year) to make scheduled payments in the next year on general long-term liabilities of the government. Potential examples include scheduled payments under capital leases or court settlements.

Committed fund balance *never* has a negative balance.

Assigned Fund Balance

Assigned fund balance equals assets assigned for a purpose less liabilities and deferred inflows related to those assigned assets. However, *assigned* fund balance can include two other amounts as well:

1. Encumbrances outstanding *not* related to already restricted, committed, or assigned fund balance—i.e., that would otherwise be reported in unassigned fund balance. (The assigned fund balance reported in the balance sheet of A Governmental Unit in

---

[6]Reporting resources that benefit the government's programs and are also legally or contractually required to be maintained intact in a fund other than a Permanent Fund is highly unusual.

[7]Enabling legislation is defined in GASB *Statement No. 54* as the legislation that "authorizes the government to assess, levy, charge, or otherwise mandate payment of resources (from external resource providers) and includes a legally enforceable requirement that those resources be used only for the specific purposes stipulated in the legislation."

Illustration 3-5 results from this situation.) Encumbrances can result in assignment of fund balance only in the General Fund.

2. Amounts to reflect the budgeted use of ending fund balance to finance an excess of appropriations over budgeted inflows in the next year's budget.

Assigned fund balance *cannot be negative,* and assignments *cannot* result in a *negative unassigned* fund balance. Except in the General Fund, assigned fund balance is used to report any positive fund balance residual (in excess of the amounts reported in the nonspendable, restricted, and committed classifications). Any resources above amounts that are nonspendable, restricted, or committed are presumed to be assigned in these *other* governmental funds. (In the General Fund, the assignment must be more narrow than the general purposes of the government. This would be true by definition in the other governmental funds.)

Unassigned Fund Balance

In the General Fund, unassigned fund balance is the *positive or negative* residual amount of fund balance in excess of the other fund balance classifications. Unassigned fund balance is used *only* to report *negative* amounts in the *other* governmental funds. Recognize that total fund balance will be positive, but unassigned fund balance will be negative if the sum of nonspendable fund balance, restricted fund balance, and committed fund balance exceed the total fund balance of a fund. However, assigned fund balance of a fund must be eliminated before reporting negative unassigned fund balance in the fund.[8]

Order of Fund Balance Reduction for Expenditures

When a government has resources that are restricted, committed, and assigned to the same specific purpose and/or also has unassigned resources, the GASB requires a government to establish a policy indicating whether restricted resources are considered to be the first expended for that purpose, which is the typical policy. The GASB also encourages governments to establish a policy specifying the order of expenditure of unrestricted resources for a given purpose. In the absence of such a policy, the GASB requires that unrestricted fund balance be reduced in the order of committed fund balance, assigned fund balance, and finally unassigned fund balance. The same logic should apply to purchases of inventory and prepaid items for purposes for which there are resources that are restricted, committed, or assigned.

Fund Balance Reporting Classifications Are Determined at Year End

Governments are not likely to attempt to maintain formal fund balance accounts for each of the fund balance reporting classifications because governments do not utilize the classifications for budgetary control purposes. The amounts to be reported for each classification will be determined by analysis when preparing the financial statements. For this reason, the journal entries in the chapter use a single total fund balance account. Governments will only maintain fund balance classifications in their accounts during the year if they are useful for budgetary control and budgetary reporting purposes. The traditional classification approach used for budgetary purposes is illustrated in the next chapter.

---

[8]Some governments set aside a portion of their resources in case (1) emergency or other unexpected needs arise or (2) budgeted revenues are not realized. These may be referred to as stabilization arrangements, reserves for contingencies, emergencies, or natural disasters, or various other names. Regardless of what they are called, most stabilization arrangement amounts must be reported as part of unassigned fund balance. They are disclosed in the notes to the financial statements but can only be included in restricted fund balance or committed fund balance if the government establishes nonroutine and specific criteria for when the resources may be used. "To be used only for emergencies or natural disasters" is not considered specific enough to meet the criteria. Stabilization amounts are never reported in assigned fund balance.

Fund Balance Reporting Illustrated

To illustrate the presentation of fund balance in a General Fund with $800,000 total fund balance, assume the following:

- Total fund assets of $900,000 include inventory of $12,000 and assets restricted for drug enforcement of $50,000.
- Total fund liabilities of $100,000 include $6,000 of liabilities to be paid from restricted assets and $2,000 of accounts payable related to inventory.
- A newly established commitment of $7,500 for health education and prevention related to flu viruses was adopted by the governing body in accordance with its commitments policy.
- Encumbrances are outstanding at year end for orders of $3,000 for materials and supplies not associated with restricted, committed, or assigned resources.
- Encumbrances are outstanding at year end for $1,500 for drug-enforcement-related contracts that will be financed from restricted assets when completed.

In this situation the fund balance section of the General Fund balance sheet appears as follows:

Fund Balance:	
Nonspendable	$ 12,000
Restricted for drug enforcement ($50,000 − $6,000)	44,000
Committed for H1N1 education and prevention	7,500
Assigned	3,000
Unassigned	733,500
Total fund balance	$800,000

Note in reviewing this example that the nonspendable fund balance resulting from the inventory of materials and supplies is not reduced by the related accounts payable. Consumable inventory results in nonspendable fund balance without regard to any other facts. Further, note that encumbrances of otherwise unassigned fund balance are presented as assigned fund balance of $3,000, but the encumbrances related to restricted resources do not change the presentation of fund balance. The GASB's logic is that encumbrances related to restricted, committed, or assigned amounts do not create more binding constraints on resource use than the constraints already in force. Encumbrances outstanding are disclosed in the notes to the financial statements.

Interfund Receivables and Payables

The Due from Special Revenue Fund account in the balance sheet in Illustration 3-5 points out a significant terminology distinction that warrants further discussion. The illustrative example entries earlier in the chapter recorded interfund receivables and payables resulting from interfund short-term loans, reimbursements, transfers, and services provided and used transactions in Due from (Fund) and Due to (Fund) accounts. However, as mentioned earlier in the chapter, some governments make long-term loans between funds as well.

Two issues arise when there are long-term interfund receivables and payables. First, the terms *due to (fund)* and *due from (fund)* should be used only to describe currently receivable and currently payable interfund balances. During the year, *currently* means collectible or payable within **this** year or soon thereafter. Although not required by the GASB, any *noncurrent* interfund receivable or payable should be recorded as *advance* to (fund) or *advance* from (fund). Furthermore, a General Fund *advance* to another fund results in reporting a corresponding amount of nonspendable fund balance (unless collections of the advance are restricted, committed, or assigned to a specific use, which is unusual in the General Fund).

Capital Assets and Long-Term Liabilities

As discussed and illustrated throughout this chapter, some General Fund expenditures are to acquire capital assets, which are *not* included in the General Fund balance sheet. For example, $6,100 of the total expenditures of $29,900, shown in entry (4) on page 74, was for equipment. General government capital assets are capitalized in separate *nonfund* General Capital Assets *accounts* rather than as assets of the General Fund.

Similarly, even if general obligation long-term liabilities (such as bonds) are ultimately payable from the General Fund, and even if they were issued to eliminate a deficit in the General Fund, *unmatured* general obligation long-term liabilities are *not* recorded as liabilities of the General Fund but in separate *nonfund* General Long-Term Liabilities *accounts* (see Chapter 9). The only long-term liabilities included in the General Fund are (1) interfund advances from other funds and (2) any general long-term liabilities that have *matured* and are payable from the financial resources of the General Fund (an unusual occurrence, except for capital leases, because matured bonds and other long-term debts typically are repaid from a Debt Service Fund).[9]

As noted earlier:

- Capital assets are *excluded* from the General Fund balance sheet because they are *not* financial assets with which the government may finance its current activities or pay its liabilities. These assets are not acquired for resale but for the purpose of rendering services over a relatively long period of time.

- Bonds and other long-term general government liabilities are *not* included as part of the liabilities of the General Fund because the existing financial resources of the fund are not expected to be used for their payment. The governmental unit's future taxes and other revenues will ultimately provide financial resources to pay them.

STATEMENT OF REVENUES, EXPENDITURES, AND CHANGES IN FUND BALANCES

The second major General Fund and Special Revenue Fund financial statement—the Statement of Revenues, Expenditures, and Changes in Fund Balances—presents the revenues, expenditures, and other increases and decreases in *total* fund balance during a year (or other time period) and reconciles the beginning and ending fund balances. It is prepared on the modified accrual basis, regardless of the basis of the budget, and is the *GAAP-based operating statement*.

The GASB *prescribes* the following *format*[10] for the *GAAP-based operating statement*:

	Revenues (detailed)
−	Expenditures (detailed)
	Excess (Deficiency) of revenues over (under) expenditures
±	Other financing sources (uses), including transfers (detailed)
±	Special and extraordinary items (detailed)
	Net change in fund balances
+	Fund balance—beginning of period
	Fund balance—end of period

The Statement of Revenues, Expenditures, and Changes in Fund Balances presented here (see Illustration 3-7) includes only the items that changed the *total* fund balance and its beginning and ending balances.

Observe also in Illustration 3-7 that:

1. The *beginning* fund balance is first presented "as previously reported," followed by the error correction and the restated amount.

2. Transfers between funds are reported separately from revenues and expenditures—as Other Financing Sources (Uses). No other fund balance changes from interfund transactions—neither the reimbursement in transaction 6 nor the interfund services transaction in transaction 10—are separately distinguishable in this statement.

---

[9]Taxes designated for debt service are usually treated as revenues of a Debt Service Fund and do not affect the General Fund. In specific cases, however, the taxes may be collected through the General Fund and used to service debt directly from the General Fund.

[10]Adapted from GASB *Codification*, section 2200.159.

3. The special item and the extraordinary item are reported in a final section between Other Financing Sources (Uses) and the net change in fund balance.

4. The statement explains the *changes* in *total* fund balances during the period.

Restatements Occasionally, a governmental fund Statement of Revenues, Expenditures, and Changes in Fund Balance for an accounting period must report a restatement of the beginning fund balance because of an error correction or the change to a

---

ILLUSTRATION 3-7 **Statement of Revenues, Expenditures, and Changes in Fund Balance—For 20X1**

A Governmental Unit
General Fund
**Statement of Revenues, Expenditures,
and Changes in [Total] Fund Balance**
For the 20X1 Fiscal Year

Revenues		
Taxes	$255,000	
Licenses and permits	68,000	
Intergovernmental	52,500	
Charges for services	41,000	
Fines and forfeits	19,000	
Other	2,600	
Total Revenues		$438,100
Expenditures		
Current:		
General government	39,200	
Public safety	142,000	
Highways and streets	123,100	
Health and sanitation	46,400	
Other	18,600	
Capital Outlay	29,100	
Debt Service (interest)	850	
Total Expenditures		399,250
Excess of Revenues over Expenditures		38,850
Other Financing Sources (Uses)		
Transfer from Special Revenue Fund	10,000	
Transfer to Debt Service Fund	(5,000)	
Transfer to Enterprise Fund	(6,000)	(1,000)
Special and Extraordinary Items		
Special Item—Proceeds of Sale of Beach Property	8,000	
Extraordinary Item—Insurance Recovery Proceeds	5,750	13,750
Net Change in Fund Balance		51,600
Fund Balance—January 1, 20X1—As Restated		
As previously reported	11,000	
Correction of prior year error	(300)	10,700
Fund Balance—December 31, 20X1		$ 62,300

preferable accounting principle. The restatement may be reported in either of two ways:

- The *beginning* fund balance in the statement can be noted as being "*as previously reported*," followed by the restatement amount and a restated beginning fund balance, as in Illustration 3-7:

$$\pm \frac{\text{Fund balance, beginning of period, as previously reported}}{\text{Restatements (e.g., correction of prior period errors)}}$$
$$\text{Fund balance, beginning of period, as restated}$$

- Alternatively, *only* the *restated* beginning fund balance may be presented in the statement, noted as being "*as restated*," with reference made to the explanation of the restatement contained in the *notes* to the financial statements:

  Fund balance, beginning of period, as restated (Note X)

  Note X would contain the information presented on the face of the statement in Illustration 3-7.

In *comparative* financial statements or schedules for two or more periods (1) the *cumulative effect of accounting changes* or error corrections on fund balance for periods prior to the *earliest* period reported should be reported as a *restatement of the beginning* fund balance of that period, and (2) the data reported for *later periods* should be *restated* to reflect the changed accounting principle or error correction.

Notice again the reporting of the special item and the extraordinary item in Illustration 3-7. Recall that extraordinary items must be **material** and **both** unusual in nature *and* infrequent in occurrence. Their timing and occurrence normally are *not* influenced by management. Special items, on the other hand, are significant transactions that are **both** (1) under the control of management, **and** (2) *either* unusual in nature *or* infrequent in occurrence.

Extraordinary Items and Special Items

GASB *Statement No. 34* (par. 89) states that extraordinary and special items should be reported separately *after* "other financing sources and uses."

- If both special items and extraordinary items are present in the same fiscal year, they should be reported separately within a "special and extraordinary items" caption.
- *Significant* transactions or events that are *either* unusual or infrequent, but not both, and are *not* within the control of management are not special items. These transactions should be (1) *separately identified within the appropriate revenue or expenditure category* in the Statement of Revenues, Expenditures, and Changes in Fund Balances or (2) *disclosed* in the *notes* to the financial statements.

CLASSIFICATION OF EXPENDITURES

A Governmental Unit reports its General Fund expenditures by function. The function or program classification is the *minimum* amount of *detail* permitted in the basic financial statements. Individual fund financial statements often present more detailed expenditure classifications, such as by department or agency. While A Governmental Unit maintained its expenditure accounts only by function in the Expenditures Ledger, extensive expenditure classification detail is maintained in practice. A government's expenditures are classified in several ways to serve several managerial purposes as well as financial reporting purposes. As observed in the GASB *Codification*,

Multiple classification of governmental fund expenditure data is important from both internal and external management control and accountability standpoints. It facilitates the aggregation and analysis of data in different ways for different purposes and in manners that cross fund and organizational lines, for internal evaluation, external reporting, and intergovernmental comparison purposes. The major accounting classifications of expenditures are by *fund, function (or program), organization unit, activity, character, and object class.*[11]

Because appropriations are made in terms of specified funds, the basic classification of expenditures is by fund. Recognize, however, that

- Expenditures of the General Fund and each Special Revenue Fund are incurred for one or more **functions** financed in part or in whole by that fund.
- Expenditures for each function or program are incurred by one or more departments or agencies (**organizational units**) and/or subunits of those departments or agencies.
- Each department or subunit performs one or more activities to accomplish its objectives, necessitating classification by **activity** (i.e., line of work performed).
- The expenditures of each department and activity will be for one or more types of expenditures called **object classes** (type of article purchased or service obtained).
- These object classes are logically grouped according to their **character** (the period or periods benefited—i.e., current operating, capital outlay, and debt service—or as intergovernmental).

To produce all the required information, the expenditures of a fund are also classified by function or program, activity, organization unit, character, and object class as depicted in Illustration 3-8. To capture this detail, governments must maintain a much more extensive Expenditures Ledger than illustrated for A Governmental Unit. Governments need this detail to serve managerial needs even if expenditures are reported only by function or department for GAAP purposes.

The GASB *Codification* does not contain a detailed chart of expenditure accounts for state and local governments. However, the National Committee on Governmental Accounting, the predecessor of the National Council on Governmental Accounting and the GASB, prepared a standard classification of accounts, including expenditure accounts. Although no longer required to be used, that classification of accounts is updated by the Government Finance Officers Association (GFOA) in *Governmental Accounting, Auditing and Financial Reporting,*[12] and is used widely in practice. Moreover, many states have agencies that prescribe the accounts to be used by other state agencies and local governments in their jurisdiction.

The budgeting, accounting, and reporting systems of a government *should be based on the same structure of accounts*.

- Some state and local governments have accounting systems and charts of accounts that classify every expenditure transaction by fund, function or program, organization unit, activity, character, and object class.
- Others use systems and charts of accounts that record expenditure data only in certain essential classifications—such as by fund, organization unit, and object class—and compile these data at year end to derive data for the other expenditure classifications.

Appendix 3-2 discusses and illustrates governmental fund expenditure classification by (1) function or program, (2) organization unit, (3) activity, (4) character, and (5) object class.

---

[11]Ibid., Sec. 1800.116.

[12]Stephen J. Gauthier, *Governmental Accounting, Auditing and Financial Reporting* (Chicago: GFOA, 2012), "Appendix E: Illustrative Accounts, Classifications, and Descriptions," 933–984.

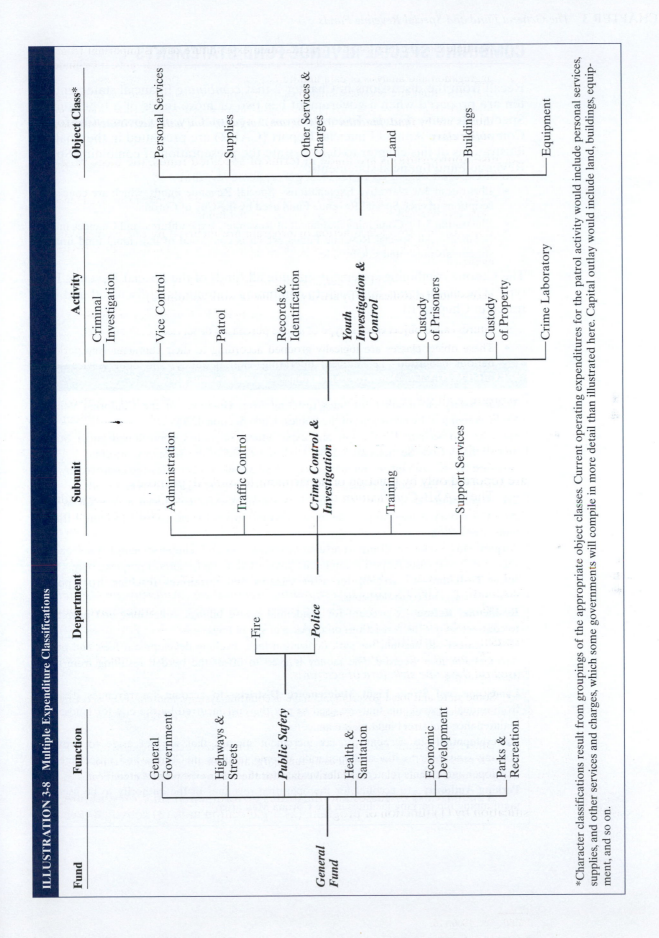

ILLUSTRATION 3-8 Multiple Expenditure Classifications

Fund	Function	Department	Subunit	Activity	Object Class*
General Fund	General Government				
	Highways & Streets				
	Public Safety	Fire			
		Police	Administration	Criminal Investigation	Personal Services
			Traffic Control	Vice Control	Supplies
			Crime Control & Investigation	Patrol	
				Records & Identification	Other Services & Charges
			Training	Youth Investigation & Control	Land
			Support Services	Custody of Prisoners	Buildings
	Health & Sanitation			Custody of Property	
	Economic Development			Crime Laboratory	Equipment
	Parks & Recreation				

*Character classifications result from groupings of the appropriate object classes. Current operating expenditures for the patrol activity would include personal services, supplies, and other services and charges, which some governments will compile in more detail than illustrated here. Capital outlay would include land, buildings, equipment, and so on.

97

COMBINING SPECIAL REVENUE FUND STATEMENTS

Recall from the discussions in Chapter 2 that *combining* financial statements often are prepared when a government has two or more funds of a type, such as Special Revenue Funds. Excerpts from a recent City of Corona, California, Comprehensive Annual Financial Report (CAFR) are presented in the final two illustrations of this chapter to demonstrate the presentation of combining Special Revenue Fund financial statements:

- Illustration 3-9: Narrative Explanations—Special Revenue Funds, which are concise descriptions of each Special Revenue Fund used by the City of Corona.
- Illustration 3-10: Combining Statement of Revenues, Expenditures, and Changes in Fund Balances—All Special Revenue Funds, which is composed of individual fund financial statements presented side by side.

The Corona combining statements include all funds of the Special Revenue Fund type. The *major funds* approach to combining statements is discussed and illustrated in Chapter 13.

ILLUSTRATION 3-9　Narrative Explanations—Special Revenue Funds

Traffic Safety—to account for fines resulting from violations of the California Vehicle Code as required by provisions of the Vehicle Code Section 42200.

Gas Tax—to account for receipts and expenditures of money apportioned under Street and Highway Code Sections 2105, 2106, 2107, and 2107.5 of the State of California.

Measure A—to account for money generated by a half-percent sales tax approved by the voters in 1989. This money is used to maintain and construct local streets and roads.

Trip Reduction—to account for allocations made by AB2766 known as the Clean Air Act. The money is used to provide means and incentives for ridesharing to reduce traffic and air pollution.

Airport—to account for all airport revenues, expenditures, and reimbursements to the General Fund for airport costs. Airport revenues are committed to use for airport purposes only.

Asset Forfeiture—to account for asset seizures and forfeitures resulting from police investigations and court decisions.

Residential Refuse—to account for residential refuse billings, collections, and payments to contractors per the restrictions on the uses of the billings.

Development—to account for park dedication fees, dwelling development fees, and other development fees received. The money is used to offset the burden resulting from new developments.

Landscape and Street Light Maintenance Districts—to account for revenues derived from annual assessments that are used to pay the cost incurred by the city for landscape maintenance and street light maintenance.

Redevelopment—to account for tax increment monies that are set aside to provide housing assistance to low and moderate income families in Corona and miscellaneous developer agreements related to sales tax generated in a specific project area.

Parking Authority—to account for the operating revenues of the authority to be used in maintaining the parking facilities in the Corona Mall area.

ILLUSTRATION 3-10 Combining Statement of Revenues, Expenditures, and Changes in Fund Balances—All Special Revenue Funds

City of Corona

Combining Statement of Revenues, Expenditures and Changes in Fund Balances—All Special Revenue Funds—Year Ended June 30, 20X0

	Traffic Safety	Gas Tax	Measure A	Trip Reduction	Airport	Asset Forfeiture	Residential Refuse	Development	Landscape & Street Light Maintenance Districts	Redevelopment	Parking Authority	Totals
Revenue:												
Property Taxes	$ —	$ —	$ —	$ —	$ —	$ —	$ —	$ —	$ —	$1,825,838	$ —	$ 1,825,838
Other Taxes	—	—								675,606	116,031	791,637
Licenses, Fees, and Permits					71,114			6,252,836				6,323,950
Fines, Penalties, and Forfeitures	1,106,618				825	92,398						1,199,841
Special Assessments									4,585,345			4,585,345
Investment Earnings	2,618	168,469	141,313	1,795	982	9,784	35,710	1,177,533	274,204	173,037	879	1,986,324
Intergovernmental Revenues		3,388,798	4,010,312	129,404	130,955		28,706	27,208	770,610			8,485,993
Current Services							4,616,217		48,166			4,664,383
Payments in Lieu of Services								1,232,640				1,232,640
Other Revenues		12,379	127,071	355	136,253		201	777,177	41,836	1,293,059	200	2,388,531
Total Revenues	1,109,236	3,569,646	4,278,696	131,554	340,129	102,182	4,680,834	9,467,394	5,720,161	3,967,540	117,110	33,484,482
Expenditures:												
Current:												
Public Works		438,557	288,382	138,957	248,508		4,604,511	173,067	1,288,578			7,180,560
Parks & Recreation									2,171,742			2,171,742
Police						140,806						140,806
Community Development										37,527	118,961	156,488
Capital Outlay		1,638,699	1,724,222		127,063			10,111,293	71,176	2,521,674		16,194,127
Debt Service:												
Principal Retirement			310,511						37,819			348,330
Interest and Fiscal Charges			207,521						8,240	27,115		242,876
Total Expenditures	—	2,077,256	2,530,636	138,957	375,571	140,806	4,604,511	10,284,360	3,577,555	2,586,316	118,961	26,434,929
Excess of Revenues Over (Under) Expenditures	1,109,236	1,492,390	1,748,060	(7,403)	(35,442)	(38,624)	76,323	(816,966)	2,142,606	1,381,224	(1,851)	7,049,553
Other Financing Sources (Uses):												
Transfers In		580	597	7		33	137	507,439	1,232	610		510,635
Transfers Out	(946,788)	(902,077)			(7,849)		(114,026)	(620,176)		(242,113)		(2,833,029)
Total Other Financing Sources (Uses)	(946,788)	(901,497)	597	7	(7,849)	33	(113,889)	(112,737)	1,232	(241,503)	—	(2,322,394)
Net Change in Fund Balances	162,448	590,893	1,748,657	(7,396)	(43,291)	(38,591)	(37,566)	(929,703)	2,143,838	1,139,721	(1,851)	4,727,159
Fund Balances, Beginning of Year	1,813	2,664,964	1,466,961	76,384	(330,522)	152,583	335,295	21,667,426	4,413,658	8,579,870	60,402	39,088,834
Fund Balances, End of Year	$ 164,261	$3,255,857	$3,215,618	$ 68,988	$(373,813)	$113,992	$ 297,729	$20,737,723	$6,557,496	$9,719,591	$ 58,551	$43,815,993

Concluding Comments

The General Fund and Special Revenue Funds typically account for significant portions of the financial resources of state and local government units. Thus, a thorough understanding of General Fund and Special Revenue Fund accounting is important to governmental accountants, auditors, systems specialists, and users of financial statements.

Moreover, accounting and reporting for most other governmental funds (e.g., Capital Projects and Debt Service) closely parallel that for the General Fund and Special Revenue Funds and can be understood largely by analogy. Thus, a firm foundation in General Fund and Special Revenue Fund accounting and reporting is essential for both students and practitioners.

This chapter discusses and illustrates the basic accounting and reporting procedures for the General Fund and Special Revenue Funds—which also apply to most other governmental funds—and necessarily includes several simplifying assumptions. In particular:

- The accounts were maintained on a GAAP basis during the year.
- Where alternative methods of accounting for certain transactions and events are acceptable, only one acceptable method has been discussed and illustrated in this "basics" chapter.

The examples in this chapter illustrate the "General Ledger–Subsidiary Ledger" approach to governmental fund accounting. The numbered illustrative entries in the chapter are posted to a General Ledger worksheet (Illustration 3-11), a Revenues Subsidiary Ledger (Illustration 3-12), and an Expenditures Subsidiary Ledger (Illustration 3-13) in Appendix 3-1.

The chapters that follow build on this chapter. Chapter 4 introduces and illustrates governmental fund budgetary accounting and reporting, and Chapters 5 and 6 refine and expand the basic discussions in this chapter on revenue accounting and expenditure accounting, respectively. Chapter 5 also contains additional discussion of governmental fund deferred outflows and deferred inflows. Then the other governmental funds are considered.

APPENDIX 3-1

General Ledger Worksheet and Subsidiary Ledgers

As noted in the chapter, this appendix presents, for the General Fund of A Governmental Unit, for the year ended December 31, 20X1,

- Illustration 3-11—General Ledger Worksheet
- Illustration 3-12—Revenues Subsidiary Ledger (Preclosing)
- Illustration 3-13—Expenditures Subsidiary Ledger (Preclosing)

APPENDIX 3-2

Classification of Expenditures

The GASB *Codification* states that governmental fund expenditures should be classified by (1) function or program, (2) organization unit, (3) activity, (4) character, and (5) object class, as well as by fund. Each of these expenditure classifications is discussed and illustrated here.

CLASSIFICATION BY FUNCTION OR PROGRAM

According to the GASB *Codification,*

> Function or program classification provides information on the **overall purposes** or **objectives** of expenditures. **Functions** group related activities that are aimed at accomplishing a major service or regulatory responsibility. **Programs** group activities, operations, or organizational units that are directed to the attainment of specific purposes or objectives.[13]

A government may choose between function and program classifications. Some governments are organized and budgeted by functions, whereas others are organized and budgeted by programs, so this option permits governments to use the corresponding functional or program classification in accounting and financial reporting.

Many governmental units provide services that are also provided by other governmental units. For example, typical city, county, and state governments all provide for public safety. If they all select the accounts necessary to record their expenditures for public safety from a standard classification, a total figure may be accumulated for a state or for the nation as a whole. Furthermore, it makes possible comparisons of expenditure data between and among cities and counties of comparable size that have similar problems. Thus, the functional classification provides the basic structure for the classification of expenditures in the basic financial statements (BFS).

Illustration 3-14 presents a condensed standard classification of expenditures by function. Observe the relationship between the broad functional classifications and the more detailed functional classifications. Both are used for illustrative purposes in budgets and journal entries in the text, with the caveat that more detailed department or other organization unit and object class accounts would be used in practice.

Note also that the more detailed functional classifications summarize the organizational structure of many governments. Many governments may have several departments within at least some of the functions, but many smaller governments have only one department, at most, in each function. For example, in many smaller governments, the police department is the police protection function. Thus, *many governmental budgets, accounting systems, and charts of accounts are classified by departments or other organization units, rather than by functions,* and the function or functional data are derived by aggregating the expenditure data by organizational unit.

CLASSIFICATION BY ORGANIZATION UNIT

The GASB *Codification* states that:

> Classification of expenditures by **organization unit** is essential to responsibility accounting. This classification corresponds with the governmental unit's **organization structure**.[14]

Sound budgetary control requires authority and responsibility for the activities of the government to be assigned in a definite fashion to its officials and employees. Assignment of appropriations and related expenditures to organization units is essential if department heads are to be held responsible for planning their activities and for controlling those activities that are authorized by the legislative body through the appropriations process. Classifying expenditures by

---

[13]GASB *Codification* sec. 1800.117. (Emphasis added.)

[14]Ibid., sec. 1800.118. (Emphasis added.)

ILLUSTRATION 3-11 General Ledger Worksheet—General Fund

General Ledger Worksheet—A Governmental Unit—General Fund—For the Year Ended December 31, 20X1

Accounts	Beginning Balances (BB) and Transactions				Preclosing Trial Balance		Closing Entries		Postclosing Trial Balance	
	Debit	#	Credit	#	Debit	Credit	Debit	Credit	Debit	Credit
Cash	$ 14,000	(BB)	$ 5,000	(7)	$ 51,850				$ 51,850	
	1,250	(12)	6,000	(9)						
	20,000	(13)	1,250	(11)						
	8,000	(15)	5,600	(14)						
	5,750	(16)	10,000	(23)						
	175,000	(17)	360,000	(25)						
	205,000	(20)	22,500	(26)						
	20,200	(22)								
	13,000	(27)								
Investments	10,000	(23)			10,000				10,000	
Accrued Interest Receivable	400	(A2)			400				400	
Taxes Receivable—Current	200,000	(1)	160,000	(17)						
			40,000	(18)						
Allowance for Uncollectible Current Taxes	3,000	(19)	3,000	(1)						
Taxes Receivable—Delinquent	40,000	(18)	20,000	(22)	20,000				20,000	
Allowance for Uncollectible Delinquent Taxes			3,000	(19)		$ 3,000				$ 3,000
Interest and Penalties Receivable on Taxes	550	(A1)			550				550	
Allowance for Uncollectible Interest and Penalties			50	(A1)		50				50
Accounts Receivable	12,000	(BB)	15,000	(17)	19,600				19,600	
	36,000	(2)	13,000	(27)						
			400	(28)						
Allowance for Uncollectible Accounts Receivable	400	(28)	1,000	(2)		600				600
Due from Special Revenue Fund	1,500	(6)	1,250	(12)	11,500				11,500	
	10,000	(8)								
	1,250	(11)								
Vouchers Payable	360,000	(25)	15,000	(BB)						
			29,900	(4)						
			40,000	(5)						

ILLUSTRATION 3-11 General Ledger Worksheet—General Fund (continued)

Accounts	Beginning Balances (BB) and Transactions — Debit	#	Beginning Balances (BB) and Transactions — Credit	#	Preclosing Trial Balance — Debit	Preclosing Trial Balance — Credit	Closing Entries — Debit	Closing Entries — Credit	Postclosing Trial Balance — Debit	Postclosing Trial Balance — Credit
			300,000 300	(24) (29)		25,200				25,200
Short-Term Notes Payable	5,000	(14)	20,000	(13)		15,000				15,000
Accrued Interest Payable			250	(A3)		250				250
Due to Internal Service Fund	22,500	(26)	30,000	(10)		7,500				7,500
Fund Balance			11,000	(BB)		11,000		51,300		62,300
Revenues			197,000 35,000 205,000 200 500 400	(1) (2) (20) (22) (A1) (A2)		438,100	438,100			
Special Item—Proceeds from Sale of Beach Property			8,000	(15)		8,000	8,000			
Extraordinary Item—Insurance Recovery Proceeds			5,750	(16)		5,750	5,750			
Expenditures	29,900 40,000 30,000 600 300,000 250	(4) (5) (10) (14) (24) (A3)	1,500	(6)	399,250			399,250		
Transfer to Debt Service Fund	5,000	(7)			5,000			5,000		
Transfer from Special Revenue Fund			10,000	(8)		10,000	10,000			
Transfer to Enterprise Fund	6,000	(9)			6,000			6,000		
Correction of Prior Year Error	300	(29)			300			300		
	$1,576,850		**$1,576,850**		**$524,450**	**$524,450**	**$461,850**	**$461,850**	**$113,900**	**$113,900**

ILLUSTRATION 3-12 Revenues Subsidiary Ledger—General Fund

A Governmental Unit
General Fund
Revenues Ledger: Preclosing
For the Year Ended December 31, 20X1

Taxes	$197,000	(1)
	58,000	(20)
Totals/Balance	255,000	
Licenses and Permits	68,000	(20)
Totals/Balance	68,000	
Intergovernmental	52,500	(20)
Totals/Balance	52,500	
Charges for Services	35,000	(2)
	6,000	(20)
Totals/Balance	41,000	
Fines and Forfeits	19,000	(20)
Totals/Balance	19,000	
Other	1,500	(20)
	200	(21)
	500	(A1)
	400	(A2)
Totals/Balance	2,600	

---

organization unit is, therefore, important because it provides the means for controlling expenditures and for definitively allocating and evaluating expenditure responsibility. Stated differently, *classifying expenditures by organizational unit is a prerequisite to effective responsibility accounting* and to ensuring and evaluating proper stewardship of public funds.

There is no standard classification of expenditure accounts by organization unit. Rather, this expenditure classification should correspond with how the government is organized into departments or other units and subunits. Thus, in a government in which the police, fire, and jail are separate departments—organizationally and budgetarily—this department structure would be the basis for expenditure classification by organization unit. But if in another government the jail is organized as an integral part of the police department, the jail would be budgeted and accounted for as a subunit of the police department.

CLASSIFICATION BY ACTIVITY

An **activity** is a specific line of work performed by a governmental unit as part of one of its functions or programs. Ordinarily, several activities are required to fulfill a function or program.

ILLUSTRATION 3-13 Expenditures Subsidiary Ledger—General Fund

A Governmental Unit
General Fund
Expenditures Ledger: Preclosing
For the Year Ended December 31, 20X1

General Government		
	$ 1,700	(4)
	5,000	(5)
	(1,500)	(6)
	4,000	(10)
	30,000	(24)
Totals/Balance	39,200	

Public Safety		
	8,000	(4)
	16,000	(5)
	6,000	(10)
	112,000	(24)
Totals/Balance	142,000	

Highways and Streets		
	10,100	(4)
	13,000	(5)
	10,000	(10)
	90,000	(24)
Totals/Balance	123,100	

Health and Sanitation		
	4,000	(5)
	7,000	(10)
	35,400	(24)
Totals/Balance	46,400	

Other		
	4,000	(4)
	2,000	(5)
	3,000	(10)
	9,600	(24)
Totals/Balance	18,600	

Capital Outlay		
	6,100	(4)
	23,000	(24)
Totals/Balance	29,100	

Debt Service		
	600	(14)
	250	(A3)
Totals/Balance	850	

A minimum requirement is that responsibility for an activity should be assigned to only one organization unit. Those units that cover more than one activity should have their budgeting, accounting, reporting, and administration arranged so that assignments or allocations of costs can be made by activity. Organization by

ILLUSTRATION 3-14 **Expenditure Classification by Functions**

Broad Functions or Functional Classifications		Functions	
Code*	Title	Code*	Title
1000–1999	General Government	1000	Legislative Branch
		1100	Executive Branch
		1200	Judicial Branch
		1300	Elections
		1400	Financial Administration
		1500	Other
2000–2999	Public Safety	2000	Police Protection
		2100	Fire Protection
		2200	Correction
		2300	Protective Inspection
3000–4999	Public Works	3000	Highways and Streets
		4000	Sanitation
5000–6999	Health and Welfare	5000	Health
		6000	Welfare
7000–7999	Education (Schools)		
8000–9999	Culture and Recreation	8000	Libraries
		9000	Parks
10000–14999	Conservation of Natural Resources	10000	Water Resources
		11000	Agricultural Resources
		12000	Mineral Resources
		13000	Fish and Game Resources
		14000	Other Natural Resources
15000–15999	Urban Redevelopment and Housing		
16000–16999	Economic Development and Assistance		
17000–17999	Economic Opportunity		
18000–19999	Debt Service	18000	Interest
		19000	Principal
		19500	Paying Agent's Fees
20000–20999	Intergovernmental		
21000–21999	Miscellaneous		

*Code numbers are illustrative only.

activity is highly desirable because it facilitates precise assignment of authority and responsibility and because it simplifies accounting for and controlling activities.

The typical classifications of **activities** (and illustrative account codes) for the police protection function are:

2000 Police Protection Function
2010 Police Administration
2020 Crime Control and Investigation
2021 Criminal Investigation

2022 Vice Control
2023 Patrol
2024 Records and Identification
2025 Youth Investigation and Control
2026 Custody of Prisoners
2027 Custody of Property
2028 Crime Laboratory
2030 Traffic Control
    2031 Motor Vehicle Inspection and Regulation
2040 Police Training
2050 Support Services
    2051 Communications Services
    2052 Automotive Services
    2053 Ambulance Services
    2054 Medical Services
    2055 Special Detail Services
    2056 Police Stations and Buildings

Expenditure data classified by activity are not required to be presented in published financial statements but are intended primarily for managerial use. The GASB *Codification* observes that:

> Activity classification is particularly significant because it **facilitates evaluation of the economy and efficiency** of operations by providing data for calculating expenditures per unit of activity. That is, the expenditure requirements of performing a given unit of work can be determined by classifying expenditures by activities and providing for performance measurement where such techniques are practicable. These expenditure data, in turn, can be used in preparing future budgets and in setting standards against which future expenditure levels can be evaluated.[15]

In addition, activity expenditure data is useful when expense data need to be derived for managerial decision-making purposes. Activity expenditure data provide a convenient **starting point for calculating total and/or unit expenses of activities** for decisions such as "make or buy" or "do or contract out." Current operating expenditures (total expenditures less those for capital outlay and debt service) may be adjusted by depreciation and amortization data to determine activity expense.

Many services traditionally provided by state and local governments are being outsourced or privatized—that is, contracted for from private firms or even relocated to the private sector. Thus, although not required for external financial reporting, expenditure data classified by activity may be particularly important for internal uses.

Classifying expenditures by activity is essential to secure cost (expenditure basis) data for budget preparation and managerial control. Unit cost accounting (expenditure or expense basis) is possible only if (1) expenditures are classified by activities and (2) statistics concerning units of output are accumulated. Even if unit costs are not computed, the costs (expenditure and/or expense bases) of an activity should be compared with the benefits expected from it as a basis for deciding whether the scope of the activity should be increased, decreased, or left unchanged. Accumulating cost data by activities also permits comparing such costs between governmental units and accumulating cost data by function or program.

This discussion of activity classification also illustrates the need to distinguish the expenditure and expense measurement concepts, both conceptually and in practice, and to use appropriate terminology. Too often, the term *expense* is used (e.g., operating expense) when the measurement being described is *expenditures*. Using these terms improperly or interchangeably, as if they were synonymous, causes confusion and should be avoided.

---

[15]Ibid., sec. 1800.119. (Emphasis added.)

CLASSIFICATION BY CHARACTER

The **character** classification, which has been used in earlier illustrative examples, identifies expenditures by the **period benefited** or as intergovernmental. The three main character classifications are current operating, capital outlay, and debt service. The fourth category, intergovernmental, is needed for governments that transfer resources to other governments, as when states transfer shared revenues to local governments.

Current operating expenditures are those expenditures expected to benefit primarily the current period, such as for salaries and utilities. **Capital outlay expenditures** are those expenditures expected to benefit not only the current period but also future periods. Purchases of desks, vehicles, and buildings are examples of capital outlays. **Debt service** expenditures are for *mature* long-term debt principal, interest, and related debt service charges. Payments made from the General Fund or Special Revenue Funds to Debt Service Funds for these purposes are transfers that ultimately will finance Debt Service Fund expenditures, perhaps many years hence. Though debt service expenditures are sometimes said to be expenditures that are made for past benefits, when debt proceeds were used to acquire capital outlay items, the expenditures may benefit past, present, and future periods.

Just as expenditure data by function or program can be derived by summarizing departmental (organization unit) expenditure data, data by character can be derived by aggregating data by object classes (discussed next). Thus, some accounting systems and charts of accounts do not provide for expenditure classification by character but obtain it by rolling up the expenditure data classified by object classes.

CLASSIFICATION BY OBJECT CLASSES

The **object class (object-of-expenditure)** classification groups expenditures according to the type of article purchased or service obtained. The following is a standard classification of object classes related to the character classification as indicated:

Character	Object Class
01–03* Current Operating	01 Personal Services 02 Supplies 03 Other Services and Charges
04–07 Capital Outlay	04 Land 05 Buildings 06 Improvements Other Than Buildings 07 Machinery and Equipment
08–10 Debt Service	08 Debt Principal 09 Interest 10 Debt Service Charges
11 Intergovernmental	11 Intergovernmental

*Code numbers are illustrative only.

The preceding object classes under "Current Operating" are major classifications. A small municipality, or a small organization unit in a larger municipality, might find that "Personal Services," "Supplies," and "Other Services and Charges" provide enough detail for administrative and reporting purposes. In most cases, however, each of these classifications would be subdivided into more detailed classifications. Personal Services could be subdivided into salaries, wages, employer contributions to the retirement system, insurance, sick leave, termination pay, and the like. Supplies may be detailed in whatever way proves useful—at a minimum, as office supplies, operating supplies, and repair and maintenance supplies. Other Services and Charges include such costs as professional services, communications, transportation, advertising, printing, and binding. In certain circumstances, the administration will find it useful to further subdivide some or all of the foregoing into even greater detail. For example, it might be useful to divide communications into such categories as telephone, internet, and postage.

The main object classes ordinarily provide sufficient detail for the basic financial statements and other summarized reports to the public, including the budgetary comparison statement or schedule. Classification by the main object classes may also provide sufficient detail to demonstrate budgetary compliance. The level of detail needed for budgetary reporting depends, however, on the detail in which the appropriations by the legislative body are considered binding on the executive branch. If budgetary compliance is at a more detailed level, then a budgetary compliance statement or schedule must be presented at the more detailed level, and the accounts must be classified at the more detailed level.

APPENDIX 3-3

Alternative Account Structure and Entries

Many governments no longer use the traditional General Ledger–Subsidiary Ledger account structure and entry approach illustrated in this chapter. Modern computerized systems facilitate the use of detailed General Ledger accounts in lieu of the General Ledger control accounts supported by detailed subsidiary ledgers. To familiarize readers with this approach—which is preferred by some practitioners and professors and may be useful on the Uniform CPA Examination—entries using the detailed General Ledger accounts approach are presented here for transactions 4 and 20. This approach is also used in selected later chapters.

(4)	Expenditures—General Government............	$ 1,700	
	Expenditures—Public Safety..................	8,000	
	Expenditures—Highways and Streets	10,100	
	Expenditures—Other.........................	4,000	
	Expenditures—Capital Outlay	6,100	
	Vouchers Payable		$29,900
	To record expenditures.		
(20)	Cash......................................	$205,000	
	Revenues—Taxes		$58,000
	Revenues—Licenses and Permits		68,000
	Revenues—Intergovernmental................		52,500
	Revenues—Charges for Services		6,000
	Revenues—Fines and Forfeits................		19,000
	Revenues—Other		1,500
	To record receipt of revenues not previously accrued.		

Questions

Q3-1 Explain the differences between the General Fund and Special Revenue Funds. How do accounting and reporting requirements for these two types of funds differ?

Q3-2 What characteristics of expenditures distinguish them from expenses in the financial accounting sense?

Q3-3 How does the purchase of a capital asset affect the General Fund financial statements?

Q3-4 Although the illustrative examples in this chapter use only a few Revenues Subsidiary Ledger and Expenditures Subsidiary Ledger accounts, a state or local government probably will use hundreds or even thousands of such accounts in practice. Why?

Q3-5 Explain what is meant by General Ledger control over the Revenues Subsidiary Ledger and the Expenditures Subsidiary Ledger.

Q3-6 List and explain the five fund balance reporting classifications required by the GASB.

Q3-7 Explain the net revenue approach to revenue recognition employed in General Fund and Special Revenue Fund (and other governmental fund) accounting and reporting, including why it is used.

Q3-8 Explain why proceeds from long-term borrowings for General Fund purposes from external lenders are reported as Other Financing Sources but proceeds from similar short-term borrowings are not.

Q3-9 Explain why some outstanding orders of the General Fund require assigned fund balance to be reported and others do not.

Q3-10 Explain why special items are sometimes referred to as "one-shot" revenues. Why are they not reported with other revenues? Review 10 governments' General Fund financial statements from the Internet or other sources. Do they report special items? If so, identify the government and explain the nature and amount of each special item.

Q3-11 Why are nonrevenue financing sources and nonexpenditure uses of financial resources distinguished from governmental fund revenues and expenditures?

Q3-12 The terms *advance to (from) other funds* and *due from (to) other funds* have distinct meanings in governmental fund accounting and financial reporting. Explain.

Q3-13 Define the following interfund transaction terms and explain how each is accounted for and reported by a municipality: (a) interfund reimbursement, (b) interfund loan, (c) interfund services provided and used, and (d) interfund transfer.

Q3-14 What are the most likely circumstances to cause deferred inflows to be reported in a governmental fund?

Q3-15 (Appendix 3-2) Distinguish between and among the four character-of-expenditures classifications.

Q3-16 (Appendix 3-2) The clerk of the City of Wilmaton is revising the city accounting system so that she can report expenditures by function, organization unit, activity, character, and object class, as well as by fund. Her assistant is perturbed because he considers all these classifications unnecessary and states, "It will take five extra sets of books to record expenditures this way. Every expenditure will have to be recorded six times!" Explain to the assistant (a) the purpose of each expenditure classification and (b) how to implement the multiple classification scheme without multiplying the work required to record expenditures.

Exercises

E3-1 (Multiple Choice) Identify the best answer for each of the following:
1. Which of the following is a characteristic of a Special Revenue Fund that *differentiates* it from a General Fund?
   a. A Special Revenue Fund is required to be budgeted on a multi-year basis.
   b. A Special Revenue Fund is established only if a revenue source is restricted or committed to expenditure for a specific purpose other than debt service and capital outlay.
   c. A governmental entity may only have one Special Revenue Fund.
   d. A Special Revenue Fund uses the total economic resources measurement focus.
2. The *net revenue* approach can be best described as
   a. being consistent with the reporting of revenues in the private sector.
   b. evidenced by the recognition of bad debt expense for revenues earned but deemed uncollectible by a governmental fund.
   c. the reporting of a reduction of revenue for those revenues deemed to be uncollectible.
   d. the approach used to account for uncollectible revenues in both governmental and proprietary funds.

3. Assume that Nathan County has levied its current year taxes and all revenue recognition criteria for property taxes have been met. The amount levied was $775,000, of which 2% is deemed to be uncollectible (based on historical experience). Which of the following entries would be made in the General Fund?

a. Taxes Receivable—Current $775,000

    Tax Revenues.. $775,000

b. Taxes Receivable—Current $759,500

    Tax Revenues.. $759,500

c. Taxes Receivable—Current $775,000

    Allowance for Uncollectible Taxes .... $ 15,500

    Tax Revenues..   759,500

d. Taxes Receivable—Current $775,000

    Bad Debt Expenditures 15,500

    Allowance for Uncollectible Taxes .... $ 15,500

    Tax Revenues..   775,000

4. Refer to the previous question. What amount of tax revenues should be recorded in the Revenues Subsidiary Ledger for the transaction?

a. $744,310.

b. $759,500.

c. $775,000.

d. $0—revenues should only be recorded in the Revenues Subsidiary Ledger when the cash is actually received.

5. Assume the following transactions that affected the General Fund and the Special Revenue Fund took place during the year. (a) $50,000 was borrowed from the General Fund for the Special Revenue Fund. The interfund loan will be repaid in equal installments over 10 years, starting next fiscal year. (b) It was discovered that $5,500 of expenditures that were supposed to have been charged to the General Fund were charged to the Special Revenue Fund in error. The error was corrected. (c) The General Fund transferred $8,000 to the Special Revenue Fund during the year. What is the *net effect* of these transactions or events on total fund balance in the General Fund and Special Revenue Fund, respectively?

a. General Fund fund balance increased $13,500; the Special Revenue Fund fund balance decreased $13,500.

b. General Fund fund balance decreased $63,500; the Special Revenue Fund fund balance increased $63,500.

c. General Fund fund balance decreased $13,500; the Special Revenue Fund fund balance increased $13,500.

d. General Fund fund balance decreased $36,500; the Special Revenue Fund fund balance increased $36,500.

6. Which of the following statements is *true* concerning assigned fund balance?

a. Assigned fund balance reflects a government's intent to use resources for a specific purpose.

b. Assigned fund balance cannot be negative unless necessary to avoid having a deficit in unassigned fund balance.

c. Reporting assigned fund balance is optional.

d. Items a, b, and c are all true.

7. The GAAP-based statements that are required to be presented for the General Fund are:

a. Balance Sheet and Statement of Revenues, Expenditures, and Changes in Fund Balances.

b. Balance Sheet; Statement of Revenues, Expenditures, and Changes in Fund Balances; and Budget Comparison Statement of Revenues, Expenses, and Changes in Fund Balances.

c. Balance Sheet only.

d. GAAP leave it to management discretion.

E3-2 (Multiple Choice) Identify the best answer to each question.

1. A city levies property taxes of $500,000 for its General Fund for a year and expects to collect all except the estimated uncollectible amount of $5,500 by year end. To reflect this information, the city should record General Fund revenues of

a. $500,000 and General Fund expenses of $5,500.

b. $500,000 and General Fund expenditures of $5,500.

c. $500,000 and no General Fund expenses or expenditures.

d. $494,500 and no General Fund expenses or expenditures.

2. At year end a school district purchases instructional equipment costing $100,000 by issuing a short-term note to be repaid from General Fund resources. This transaction should be reflected in the General Fund as

a. expenditures of $100,000 and a $100,000 liability.

b. expenditures of $100,000 and a $100,000 other financing source from the issuance of the note.

   c. a capital asset of $100,000 and a liability of $100,000.

   d. expenditures of $100,000 and revenues of $100,000 from issuance of the note.

3. A state borrowed $10,000,000 on a nine-month, 9% note payable to provide temporary financing for the General Fund. At year end, the note has been outstanding for six months. The state should report General Fund interest expenditures and interest payable on the short-term note in its financial statements of

   a. $0; the interest will be recognized when it matures.

   b. $450,000.

   c. $450,000 unless the state does not expect to be able to pay the interest when it matures.

   d. $675,000.

4. Charges for services rendered by a county's General Fund departments totaled $500,000, of which $5,500 is expected to be uncollectible. The county expects to collect $494,500 by year-end. To reflect this information, the county should record General Fund revenues of

   a. $500,000 and General Fund expenses of $5,500.

   b. $500,000 and General Fund expenditures of $5,500.

   c. $500,000 and no General Fund expenses or expenditures.

   d. $494,500 and no General Fund expenses or expenditures.

5. If the Warren County General Fund has a long-term receivable from another county fund (and the use of the proceeds when collected is not restricted, committed, or assigned), the receivable will be reported as

   a. an advance from other funds with an equivalent amount of nonspendable fund balance.

   b. an advance to other funds with an equivalent amount of nonspendable fund balance.

   c. an advance to other funds and will be used in computing unassigned fund balance.

   d. due from other funds with an equivalent amount of committed fund balance.

6. In the Statement of Revenues, Expenditures, and Changes in Fund Balances, transfers must be reported

   a. in a separate section immediately following revenues.

   b. in a section immediately following the excess of revenues over (under) expenditures.

   c. either a or b is permissible.

   d. immediately following the beginning fund balance.

7. The minimum expenditure classifications required in the basic financial statements for governmental funds are

   a. fund and function or program.

   b. fund, character, and function or program.

   c. fund, character, and department.

   d. fund, character, department, and line item.

E3-3 (Multiple Choice—Fund Balance Classification)

1. Which fund balance category is affected by having inventory and prepaid items at year-end?

   a. Assigned fund balance

   b. Committed fund balance

   c. Nonspendable fund balance

   d. Unassigned fund balance

2. Which fund balance category may be increased by encumbrances outstanding?

   a. Assigned fund balance

   b. Nonspendable fund balance

   c. Restricted fund balance

   d. Unassigned fund balance

3. The fund balance category that requires formal action of the highest level decision-making body of a government is

   a. assigned fund balance.

   b. committed fund balance.

   c. nonspendable fund balance.

   d. restricted fund balance.

4. The GAAP fund balance classifications are described as reflecting a hierarchy of constraints on resource use. From the most constrained to the least constrained, what is the order of the hierarchy?

   a. Unassigned, Assigned, Committed, Restricted, Nonspendable

   b. Restricted, Committed, Assigned, Unassigned, Nonspendable

   c. Nonspendable, Restricted, Committed, Assigned, Unassigned

   d. Restricted, Nonspendable, Committed, Assigned, Unassigned

5. The fund balance category that can have either a positive or a negative balance is

   a. assigned fund balance.

   b. committed fund balance.

   c. nonspendable fund balance.

   d. unassigned fund balance.

6. The fund balance category used to reflect a positive residual of assets less liabilities in any fund other than the General Fund is
   a. assigned fund balance.
   b. committed fund balance.
   c. nonspendable fund balance.
   d. restricted fund balance.

E3-4 (Multiple Choice—Fund Balance Classification)

1. The fund balance category that must be zero if unassigned fund balance of the same fund is a deficit is
   a. assigned fund balance.
   b. committed fund balance.
   c. nonspendable fund balance.
   d. All of the above must be zero if unassigned fund balance is negative.

2. Enabling legislation requiring that resources be expended only for a specific purpose result in which category of fund balance being present?
   a. Assigned fund balance
   b. Committed fund balance
   c. Nonspendable fund balance
   d. Restricted fund balance

3. Actions of the finance director may result in which category of fund balance being reported?
   a. Assigned fund balance
   b. Committed fund balance
   c. Nonspendable fund balance
   d. Restricted fund balance

4. If a government adopts a policy stating that it spends restricted resources before unrestricted resources but does not have a spend-down policy to indicate the category of fund balance reduced first by expenditures for which resources reflected in various fund balance categories are available, the presumed spend-down order is
   a. Restricted, Assigned, Committed, Unassigned.
   b. Restricted, Committed, Assigned, Unassigned.
   c. Committed, Restricted, Assigned, Unassigned.
   d. Restricted, Committed, Unassigned, Assigned.

5. Which of the following is not reflected as an assignment of fund balance?
   a. Encumbrance of otherwise unassigned fund balance.
   b. The budgeted use of a portion of unassigned fund balance to cover a budgeted excess of expenditures over revenues in the next fiscal year.
   c. Intent of the government to use a portion of unrestricted, uncommitted fund balance for expenditure for a specific program or project as indicated by the properly authorized official or committee.
   d. To indicate that a certain amount of resources will be held indefinitely to provide a safeguard against possible future revenue shortfalls or significant, unanticipated future expenditures.

E3-5 (Property Taxes) Record the following transactions in the General Ledger accounts of the Coleman County General Fund:

1. Coleman County levied its 20X7 property taxes on January 1, 20X7. The total tax levy was $80,000,000; 2% is expected to be uncollectible.
2. Coleman collected $55,000,000 of property taxes before the due date. The remaining taxes are past due.
3. Interest and penalties of $2,500,000 were assessed on the past due taxes; 6% is expected to be uncollectible.
4. Coleman County collected $20,000,000 of delinquent taxes and $2,000,000 of interest and penalties. At the end of 20X7, Coleman estimates that it will collect $3,000,000 of the delinquent taxes and $300,000 of the previously accrued interest and penalties in the first 60 days of 20X8. What amount of deferred inflows should the county report at December 31, 20X7, as a result of the above transactions?

E3-6 (Expenditure Accounting Entries) Record the following transactions of the General Fund of Kinlaw County in its General Ledger. Also, use transaction analysis to show any effects on the GCA-GLTL accounts.

1. Payroll was approved and paid, $630,000.
2. Materials and supplies were purchased for the Fire Department on account, $13,200.
3. Recreational equipment was purchased on account for $77,850.
4. The General Fund was billed $700 by the Electric Utility Enterprise Fund for electricity for the month.
5. Payments were approved and made for the recreational equipment and the electricity, $78,550.
6. Accrued, unpaid payroll at year-end amounted to $2,700.

E3-7 (Statement of Revenues, Expenditures, and Changes in Fund Balances) Prepare, in good form, the 20X9 GAAP-based Statement of Revenues, Expenditures, and Changes in Fund Balance for the General Fund of Hicks Township, based on the following information:

Property tax revenues	$13,000,000
Licenses and permits	800,000
Intergovernmental grants	2,500,000
Short-term note proceeds	775,000
General capital asset sale proceeds (Equal to book value less 10%)	523,000
Receipt of residual cash from terminated Debt Service Fund #1	90,000
Amount paid to Debt Service Fund #2 to cover principal and interest payments	100,000
General government expenditures	800,000
Education expenditures	10,250,000
Public safety expenditures	3,000,000
Highways and streets expenditures	2,460,000
Health and sanitation expenditures	920,000
Capital assets purchased	1,200,000
Retirement of principal of long-term note	300,000
Interest payment on long-term note	30,000
Interest expenditures on short-term note	68,000
Fund Balance, January 1, 20X9	4,750,000

E3-8 (Fund Balance Classification) Your firm is auditing the financial statements of the City of Mensah's Point for the year ended December 31, 20X4. You have been assigned to review a fund balance schedule to see if you can identify any likely errors in the fund balance section of the governmental funds balance sheet. The fund balance section, as prepared by the finance staff of the city, is presented below.

	General Fund	Streets Special Revenue Fund	Courthouse Capital Projects Fund	Other Governmental Funds	Total
Fund Balances:					
Nonspendable					
Inventory	$ 330	$ 800	$ 500	$ 200	$ 1,830
Prepaid items	80				80
Long-term receivables	600	200		75	875
Restricted for:					
Street maintenance		1,400			1,400
Courthouse expansion			3,200		3,200
Debt service reserve				600	600
Housing and Community Development				550	550
Committed for:					
Economic development	400			900	1,300
Contingencies	700				700
Parks				300	300
Assigned for:					
Development				220	220
City facility projects	300				300
Budget stabilization	1,500				1,500
Focused enhancement initiatives		1,000			1,000
Other purposes	100			250	350
Unassigned	2,200	(800)			1,400
Total fund balance	$6,210	$2,600	$3,700	$3,095	$15,605

a. Identify any apparent misclassifications of fund balance and explain the basis for your *Required* opinion that the amounts are misclassified.

b. Draft a corrected fund balance schedule. State any assumptions made other than those you explained in a.

Problems

P3-1 (Interfund Transactions and Errors) (a) Prepare general journal entries to record the following transactions in the General Ledger of the General Fund or a Special Revenue Fund, as appropriate. (b) Explain how these transactions and events are reported in the General Fund or Special Revenue Fund Statement of Revenues, Expenditures, and Changes in Fund Balance.

1. $100,000 of General Fund cash was contributed to establish a new Internal Service Fund.
2. A truck—acquired two years ago with General Fund revenues for $19,000—with a fair value of $10,000 was contributed to a department financed by an Enterprise Fund. (Record the contribution of the asset to the Enterprise Fund—not the purchase.)
3. The Sanitation Department, accounted for in the General Fund, billed the Municipal Airport, accounted for in an Enterprise Fund, $800 for garbage collection.
4. General Fund cash of $50,000—to be repaid in 90 days—was provided to enable construction to begin on a new courthouse before a bond issue was sold.
5. A $9,000,000 bond issue to finance construction of a major addition to the civic center was sold at par. The civic center is accounted for as part of general government activities.
6. General Fund disbursements during May included a contribution of $35,000 to a Capital Projects Fund to help finance a major capital project.
7. After retirement of the related debt, the balance of the net assets (all cash) of a Debt Service Fund, $8,500, was transferred to the General Fund.
8. General Fund cash of $70,000 was loaned to an Enterprise Fund from resources that have been assigned to a specific future purpose. The loan is to be repaid in three years.
9. An accounting error made during the preceding accounting period caused the General Fund cash balance at the beginning of the current year to be understated by $6,500.
10. Another accounting error was discovered: Expenditures of $4,000, properly chargeable to a Capital Projects Fund, were inadvertently charged to a Special Revenue Fund during the current year.

P3-2 (General Fund—Typical Transactions) Prepare all general journal entries required in the General Fund of Washington County for each of the following transactions. Also, use transaction analysis to show any effects on the GCA-GLTL accounts.

1. The county levied property taxes of $5,000,000. Two percent are expected to prove uncollectible. The rest of the taxes are expected to be collected by year end or soon enough thereafter to be considered available at year end.
2. The county collected $4,300,000 of the taxes receivable before the due date and the balance of taxes became delinquent.
3. The county collected another $540,000 of the taxes receivable by the end of the fiscal year.
4. The county paid salaries and wages of $3,500,000 to General Fund employees during the year. Accrued salaries at the beginning of the year were $180,000, and accrued salaries at year end were $200,000.
5. $800,000 was loaned from the county General Fund (from resources available for general purposes) to the Washington County Inland Port Authority Enterprise Fund. The loan is to be repaid in three years.
6. The county purchased materials and supplies for various General Fund departments. The actual cost of $398,000 was vouchered.
7. The county purchased road maintenance equipment at an actual cost of $40,000, which was vouchered.
8. The county contributed $500,000 of General Fund money to a CPF to provide partial financing for construction of its recently approved sports center. The balance of the cost will be financed by grants and borrowings.
9. The county borrowed $100,000 for General Fund purposes on a six-month, 6% note. The note was issued two months before year end. Prepare any required year-end adjustments as well as recording the original transaction.

P3-3 (Various General Fund Transactions) Prepare the general journal entries required for the following transactions of the Farmer County General Fund during 20X6. Also, use transaction analysis to show any effects on the GCA-GLTL accounts.

1. Levied property taxes, $9,000,000 (with uncollectible taxes estimated at $50,000).
2. Taxes collected before the due date totaled $7,500,000 of current taxes and $320,000 of 20X5 and other prior year taxes.
3. Purchased supplies on account for $110,000.
4. Purchased equipment costing $198,659, which was vouchered.
5. Issued a nine-month, 10% note to Jones National Bank on September 30, 20X6, to raise $300,000 to provide for a temporary cash shortfall in the General Fund.
6. Loaned $90,000 from resources available for general purposes to the Self-Insurance Internal Service Fund. Repayment is required in four years.
7. Paid salaries of $5,800,000 during 20X6. Accrued salaries at the end of the year totaled $100,000, while at the beginning of the year they were $75,000.
8. Contributed $82,000 of General Fund resources to help cover the cost of the new water distribution lines installed by the county's Water Department, which provides services for a fee that is intended to recover the costs of providing the services.
9. Received $5,000 from the Economic Development Special Revenue Fund because General Fund resources had been used to pay a bill of the Economic Development Fund earlier in the year. General Fund expenditures were recorded when the bill was paid.
10. Paid $1,750 to the Central Printing Internal Service Fund for printing services used by the general administration of the county.
11. Record any necessary accruals at December 31, 20X6.

P3-4 (Debt-Related Transactions) Prepare the general journal entries to record the following transactions of the Quinones County General Fund:

1. Quinones County borrowed $1,000,000 by issuing six-month tax anticipation notes bearing interest at 6%. The notes are to be repaid from property tax collections during the fiscal year.
2. The county repaid the tax anticipation notes, with $30,000 interest, at the due date.
3. The county received a new patrol car two months before the end of the fiscal year. It cost $35,000. The county paid $5,000 upon receipt and signed a 9% short-term note payable for the balance.
4. The county services one of its general obligation serial bond issues directly from the General Fund (a Debt Service Fund is not used). The annual principal and interest payment, which is due two months before year end, was paid. The principal payment was $200,000 and the interest was $120,000. (Next year's interest payment will be $108,000.)
5. Record all appropriate interest accruals.

P3-5 (Closing Entries and Financial Statements) The preclosing trial balance of a Special Revenue Fund of Mesa County at the end of its 20X7 fiscal year is:

General Ledger:	**Debit**	**Credit**
Cash...............................	$ 45,000	
Taxes Receivable—Delinquent	70,000	
Allowance for Uncollectible Delinquent Taxes		$ 10,000
Due from General Fund	16,000	
Advance to Enterprise Fund...........	25,000	
Accrued Receivables..................	9,000	
Vouchers Payable....................		21,000
Due to Internal Service Fund...........		4,000
Accrued Payables....................		6,000
Fund Balance		107,000
Revenues..........................		798,000
Expenditures.......................	789,000	
Transfer to Debt Service Fund..........	15,000	
Transfer from Capital Projects Fund		35,000
Correction of Prior Year Error.........	12,000	
	$981,000	$981,000

Revenues Ledger:

Taxes	$550,000
Intergovernmental	150,000
Charges for Services	80,000
Other	18,000
	$798,000

Expenditures Ledger:

General Government	$330,000
Parks and Recreation	200,000
Social Services	250,000
Other	9,000
	$789,000

The Advance to Enterprise Fund plus another $15,000 of the fund's net assets are related to resources set aside for the purposes of the Special Revenue Fund at the discretion of the county's management. The remainder comes from revenues restricted for the specific purpose for which the fund was established.

a. Prepare the entry or entries to close the General Ledger and subsidiary ledger accounts at the end of the 20X7 fiscal year. ***Required***
b. Based on the preclosing trial balance, prepare the following, in good form, for the Mesa County Special Revenue Fund:
   1. A balance sheet at the end of the 20X7 fiscal year.
   2. A statement of revenues, expenditures, and changes in fund balances for the 20X7 fiscal year.

P3-6 (Statement of Revenues, Expenditures, and Changes in Fund Balance) Prepare a Statement of Revenues, Expenditures, and Changes in Fund Balance for the year ended June 30, 20X8, for the General Fund of Powers Village, given the following information:

Fund balance, July 1, 20X7	$ 3,300,800
Property tax revenues	10,000,000
Licenses and fees revenues	1,400,000
Grant revenues	700,000
General government expenditures	1,900,000
Public safety expenditures	3,000,000
Highway and streets expenditures	3,200,000
Judicial expenditures	1,800,000
Purchases of equipment	1,700,000
Proceeds from issuance of short-term notes	750,000
Payments to retire long-term notes	900,000
Interest payments	120,000
Accrued interest on short-term notes	40,000
Accrued interest on long-term notes	50,000
Transfer to Debt Service Fund to provide for principal and interest payments on bonded debt	380,000
Transfer to establish a new Central Stores Fund	1,000,000
Encumbrances (Orders) outstanding at June 30, 20X8, were for:	
Equipment	72,000
General government purposes	144,000
Highway and streets purposes	134,500

P3-7 (Statement of Revenues, Expenditures, and Changes in Fund Balance) Using the following information, prepare the Statement of Revenues, Expenditures, and Changes in Fund Balance for the City of Nancy General Fund for the fiscal year ended December 31, 20X7.
1. Fund Balance, January 1, 20X7, was $225,000.
2. Revenues for 20X7 totaled $2,500,000, including

Property taxes	$1,800,000
Licenses and permits	190,000
Intergovernmental revenues	310,000
Proceeds from short-term note	50,000
Other	150,000

Other revenues include $40,000 received from a Capital Projects Fund upon completion of the project and termination of the fund and a $65,000 routine annual transfer from the city's Water Enterprise Fund.

3. Expenditures for 20X7 totaled $2,600,000, including

General government	$ 800,000
Public safety	1,000,000
Highways and streets	600,000
Health and sanitation.	150,000
Other	50,000

P3-8 (Fund Balance Reporting) The General Fund of Dilligan County, Virginia, has total fund balance of $17,000,000 at June 30, 20X0, the end of its fiscal year. Additional information is provided below.

1. The county has restricted General Fund assets that have been provided by local donors for the upkeep and improvement of the Professor Lake and Skipper Recreation Area in Lakatos Island Village, the largest community in the county. The net balance of these donated resources at June 30 was $300,000, including $20,000 of materials purchased for the restricted purposes.
2. Additional General Fund inventory of $65,000 on hand at June 30 is available for any General Fund purpose.
3. Encumbrances outstanding at year end were as follows:
   - Related to restricted resources—$32,000
   - Related to committed resources—$70,000
   - Related to assigned resources—$600,000
   - Related to resources not restricted, committed, or assigned—$1,000,000
4. Prepaid insurance in the General Fund was $18,000.
5. A long-term advance made from unassigned resources of the Dilligan County General Fund to its Desert Isle Golf Course Enterprise Fund of $150,000 was outstanding at June 30.
6. Assignment authority was delegated by the commissioners to County Chief Financial Officer Rich Howell. Mr. Howell has assigned a total of $3,200,000 to three specific purposes—$1,000,000 for prisoner rehabilitation programs, $800,000 for adult literacy programs in the community, and $1,400,000 for the future replacement of the county's computer information system.
7. Long-term investments of unassigned resources at June 30 were $400,000.
8. The county commissioners took formal action to commit $750,000 for a major economic development campaign. $100,000 of accounts payable were related to the economic development efforts as of June 30, 20X0.

Required Prepare the fund balance section of the General Fund balance sheet of Dilligan County as of June 30, 20X0.

P3-9 (Internet Research) Obtain copies of the General Fund and Special Revenue Funds financial statements from a state or local government, the Internet, your professor, a library, or elsewhere.

Required
a. Study the General Fund financial statements and compare them with those discussed and illustrated in this chapter, noting the following:
   1. Similarities.
   2. Differences.
   3. Other matters that come to your attention, such as formats and accounts not discussed in the text.
b. Study the Special Revenue Fund financial statements, noting the following:
   1. The nature and purpose of each fund.
   2. The similarities, differences, and other matters, as in requirement (a).
c. Prepare a brief report on requirements (a) and (b).
d. If the General Fund fund balance classifications in the government's report differ from those discussed in the chapter, determine—as best possible using information in the statements and the notes—how fund balance should be reported using the GASB *Statement No. 54* fund balance classifications discussed in the chapter.

Cases

C3-1 (Journal Entries and Financial Statements—Clark County, Nevada, Road Fund) The State of Nevada levies a tax on motor fuel purchased in the state. The state distributes the portion of the tax collected in each county to that county the month after the taxes are collected. The portion of this shared revenue that each county receives may only be used for road and street maintenance or construction. Clark County, Nevada, uses a Road Special Revenue Fund to account for its share of the motor fuel tax received from the state.

The transactions of the Clark County Road Fund for the fiscal year ended June 30, 20X6, are listed here. Assume that all revenues of the fund are susceptible to accrual in the fiscal year that they become receivable. (All amounts are in thousands of dollars.)

1. Motor fuel taxes collected in Clark County during the fiscal year totaled $23,858. All of the county's distributions from the state were collected before the end of the fiscal year *except* the distribution for the June 30, 20X6, motor fuel taxes. This distribution, $4,000, has been determined and will be received during July 20X6.
2. Interest collected on investments totaled $959 during the year, including $95 of interest receivable accrued on June 30, 20X5.
3. The County collected $751 of charges to several hotel developers for work performed during the fiscal year.
4. Salaries, wages, and employee benefit costs for the year totaled $12,100 for the year. $395 of these costs had not been paid as of June 30.
5. Capitalizable road construction costs totaled $7,527. Maintenance services on the roads and streets totaled $6,566. $1,000 remained unpaid as of June 30, 20X6.
6. The General Fund transferred $757 in cash to the Road Fund during the year.
7. Interest receivable accrued at June 30, 20X6, was $111.

In addition to these transactions, the following information is known about the fund:

- Total cash and investments at the end of the fiscal year totaled $13,819.
- Accounts receivable as of June 30, 20X6, were $778.
- Vouchers payable balances, including that from transaction 5, as of June 30, 20X6, were $1,812.
- Fund balance at the *beginning* of the fiscal year was $16,353.
- Outstanding encumbrances at the end of the fiscal year were $1,167. All encumbrances relate to items that will be financed from the road tax.
- All but $600 of ending fund balance is derived from the road tax.

1. Prepare journal entries to record the activities of the Clark County Road Fund for the   ***Required*** fiscal year.
2. Prepare a statement of revenues, expenditures, and changes in fund balance as of June 30, 20X6, for the Clark County Road Fund.
3. Prepare a balance sheet as of June 30, 20X6, for the Clark County Road Fund.

This case was based on the information in a recent Comprehensive Annual Financial Report for Clark County, Nevada.

C3-2 (Financial Statement Preparation—City of Savannah, Georgia) Presented on the following page is the Preclosing Trial Balance for the City of Savannah, Georgia's General Fund as of December 31, 20X6 (with amounts in thousands). Assume the following:

- Outstanding encumbrances as of December 31, 20X6, all related to activities financed from resources available for general purposes, are $1,157.
- Receivables are reported at net amounts on the balance sheet.

City of Savannah, Georgia
General Fund
Preclosing Trial Balance
December 31, 20X6
(in thousands)

	Debit	Credit
Cash and investments......................	$ 59,800	
Restricted cash and investments..............	3,467	
Taxes receivable	14,849	
Allowance for uncollectible accounts		$ 707
Due from other funds......................	2,671	
Intergovernmental receivables	40	
Prepaid items.............................	4	
Accounts payable		3,260
Accrued liabilities.........................		1,896
Due to other funds........................		42,813
Escrow deposits payable		3,467
Deferred revenue		8,778
Fund balance.............................		18,072
Property tax revenue		65,163
Sales tax revenue		47,082
Business tax revenue		7,691
Penalties/interest on delinquent taxes		746
Licenses/permits revenue		1,442
Inspection fees		2,941
Intergovernmental revenues.................		2,438
Charges for services		22,745
Fines and forfeitures.......................		3,854
Investment income		2,691
Miscellaneous revenue......................		1,082
General administration expenditures..........	2,394	
Management and financial services expenditures	7,994	
Facilities maintenance	20,923	
Police expenditures........................	52,370	
Court expenditures........................	1,934	
Fire expenditures	19,378	
Leisure services expenditures	12,877	
Social and cultural expenditures..............	2,034	
Economic development expenditures	5,349	
Other governmental services.................	14,103	
Transfers in		5,562
Transfers out	22,243	
Totals	$242,430	$242,430

Required Prepare the City of Savannah, Georgia, Balance Sheet at December 31, 20X6, and its 20X6 Statement of Revenues, Expenditures and Changes in Fund Balances. The City has taken the formal action required to commit $500 to economic development activities.

This case was based on the information in a recent Comprehensive Annual Financial Report for the City of Savannah, Georgia.

Budgeting, Budgetary Accounting, and Budgetary Reporting

LEARNING OBJECTIVES

After studying this chapter, you should be able to:

- Understand basic budgetary accounting and reporting concepts, requirements, and practices.

- Explain the role of the budget in governmental fund planning, budgetary control, budgetary accounting, and budgetary reporting.

- Understand commonly used budgeting terminology, approaches, and recommended practices.

- Understand the concept of budgetary control points.

- Discuss the basic procedures involved in preparing and adopting a budget.

- Understand the differences between "Budgetary Fund Balance" and "GAAP Fund Balance."

The General Fund and Special Revenue Fund accounting and reporting discussions and illustrations in Chapter 3 deferred the discussion and illustration of the following topics to this chapter:

- The role of the budget in raising and allocating financial resources for government use.

- The magnitude of the role of the budget in government decision making, operations, and performance evaluation.

- The manner in which the accounting system is used to enable, monitor, and report compliance with a government's budget and other important aspects of governmental fund budgeting, budgetary accounting, and budgetary reporting.

Chapter 4 builds on the discussions and illustrations in Chapter 3 to address these important issues. The discussions and illustrations in this chapter:

- Present an overview of government budgeting.

- Explain how governments use the accounting system to establish and report budgetary accountability.

- Use the illustrative transactions and entries of the General Fund of A Governmental Unit in Chapter 3 to demonstrate the modifications to those accounting entries and the accounting system needed to monitor actual results compared to the budget.

- Explain and demonstrate the key features of budgetary reporting using the illustrative data for A Governmental Unit's General Fund.

THE GOVERNMENT BUDGETARY PERSPECTIVE

Even the highest-level government officials cannot expend government resources without properly established budgetary authority. The pervasive importance of the budget in government is aptly demonstrated by the following requirement in the U.S. Constitution:

> No Money shall be drawn from the Treasury, but in Consequence of Appropriations made by Law; and a regular Statement and Account of the Receipts and Expenditures of all public Money shall be published from time to time.[1]

You may recall from history or political science classes that, as recently as the 1995–1996 fiscal year, all except essential functions of the federal government were shut down for three weeks because the Congress and President Clinton could not pass a federal budget or a temporary spending bill. Hundreds of thousands of federal employees either were furloughed or worked without pay (though were later paid retroactively for the three-week period).

Provisions like those in the federal constitution also exist for state and local governments (SLGs). Indeed, even as this chapter is being written, at least one state is no doubt operating under a temporary spending bill passed by the state legislature and signed by the governor after the legislature could not reach a budget compromise by the end of the fiscal year. Without passage of this temporary bill, the state government would essentially be closed down until a budget for the current fiscal year is adopted. At the same time, 25,000 state employees of one northeastern state were temporarily furloughed without pay because a budget impasse between the governor and the legislature caused closure of all "nonessential" state offices.

Budgetary accountability is of paramount importance in governments. Budget provisions in government constitutions and laws are designed to ensure that government revenues and expenditures are properly planned, authorized, controlled, evaluated, and reported to the citizenry, legislature, and creditors. These requirements are especially important because governments (1) are the only organizations in our society with the power to levy taxes; (2) provide services that are crucial to our well-being, such as police and fire protection, elementary and secondary education, and the courts; and (3) function in a delicate legislative-executive-judicial "checks and balances" environment.

Budgeting is the process of allocating scarce resources among unlimited demands, and a legally enacted **budget** is an official dollars-and-cents plan of operation for a specific period of time. At a minimum, such a plan should contain information about the types and amounts of authorized expenditures, the purposes for which they are to be made, and the planned means of financing them.

Approved budgets are *management plans* in both businesses and governments, but legally enacted budgets are also *laws* in governments. Thus, budgets typically play a far greater role in planning, controlling, and evaluating government operations than in businesses. **Appropriations** are legal authorizations to incur expenditures for various purposes that also limit legal authorization for incurring expenditures for specific purposes. Like other laws, violations of budget laws are subject to penalties. Government officials responsible for overexpenditure of appropriations—legally approved levels of expenditures—are subject to penalties ranging from dismissal to financial responsibility for the overexpenditure to imprisonment, depending on the jurisdiction and severity of the violation.

Given the importance of the budget in government, government officials must have timely, useful, up-to-date information on how actual operations during the year compare to the budget. This information is needed to assist government officials:

- Avoid unintentional overexpenditure of appropriation authority.
- Determine whether revenues are achieving budgeted levels.
- Know if they must deal with an unexpected shortage of resources.

---

[1]U.S. Constitution, Article I, Section 9—Limits on Congress

Expenditure authorizations in the budget are based in part on estimates of revenues to be raised during the budget year. If these revenues do not materialize, the government typically must reduce its appropriations and expenditures to avoid a deficit at year end. The sooner such revenue shortages are recognized, the more flexibility the government has to make changes to appropriations, and thus budgeted expenditures.

The GASB recognizes the importance of the budget process in its basic principles. These principles require that:

- An annual budget(s) be adopted by every governmental unit.
- The accounting system provide the basis for appropriate budgetary control.
- Budgetary comparison statements or schedules be presented as basic financial statements or required supplementary information (RSI) for
  1. The General Fund, and
  2. Each major Special Revenue Fund that has a legally adopted annual budget.

BUDGETARY ACCOUNTING AND REPORTING

To facilitate timely budgetary control monitoring throughout the year, governments are encouraged to incorporate the legally adopted annual budget into their accounts. This practice

- Permits the accounting system to provide automatic, ongoing information about the amount of expenditures and available expenditure authority for each type of expenditure authorized by the budget.
- Accumulates comparisons of budgeted and actual revenues and other financial resource inflows and outflows.

To illustrate how budgetary accounts are incorporated into a government's accounting system using subsidiary ledgers, assume that the annual operating budget adopted for the General Fund of A Governmental Unit for the fiscal year beginning January 1, 20X1—the government's first full year of operation—is summarized in Illustration 4-1. Note that, for illustrative purposes, the General Fund budget assumes the following:

1. The annual budget is adopted on the modified accrual (GAAP) basis, which results in *no* budgetary-GAAP basis differences.
2. Appropriations are made for operating expenditures by function and for capital outlay and debt service expenditures to be made directly from the General Fund.
3. The budget does *not* include appropriations for interfund transfers—though it might—but *assumes* that any interfund transfers will be *separately authorized* by the governing body. It also does not include special items or extraordinary items.

To maintain and demonstrate budgetary accountability:

Budgetary Accounting and Control

1. The accounts should be maintained during the year on the *budgetary basis,* which in this example is the modified accrual basis (i.e., the same as GAAP).
2. Encumbrances are recorded to track the estimated cost to complete encumbered transactions. The purpose is to facilitate proper and effective control of expenditures against appropriations and avoid overexpenditure of those appropriations. Encumbrances are offset by a balancing account we title Encumbrances Outstanding but many governments refer to as Reserve for Encumbrances. These accounts are used for budgetary control purposes, are closed at year end, and are not reported in the GAAP financial statements.
3. Accounts should be established in the Revenues Subsidiary Ledger and Expenditures Subsidiary Ledger at the level of detail (at least) of the adopted budget.
4. Any interfund transfers or other fund balance changes in the example should be recorded in appropriately titled General Ledger accounts, but should *not* be recorded in subsidiary ledger accounts because only revenues and expenditures are subject to formal budgetary accounting control procedures.

ILLUSTRATION 4-1 Annual Operating Budget for 20X1

A Governmental Unit
General Fund Annual Operating Budget
For 20X1 Fiscal Year
[Budgetary Basis Is the Modified Accrual (GAAP) Basis]

<u>Estimated Revenues:</u>

Taxes	$250,000
Licenses and permits	70,000
Intergovernmental	46,000
Charges for services	40,000
Fines and forfeits	20,000
Other	1,000
	427,000

<u>Appropriations:</u>

Current operating	
General government	40,000
Public safety	150,000
Highways and streets	114,000
Health and sanitation	60,000
Other	28,000
Total current operating expenditures	392,000
Capital outlay	30,000
Debt service	1,000
	423,000
Excess of Estimated Revenues over Appropriations	$ 4,000

Notes:

1. The enacted budget appropriates operating expenditures by function but includes separate appropriations for capital outlay and debt service expenditures of this fund. (Major capital outlay and debt service expenditures typically are financed through Capital Projects Funds and Debt Service Funds.)
2. The governmental unit may (and will) separately authorize interfund transfers during the year and, if appropriate, revise this original budget.
3. Because the budgetary basis is the modified accrual (GAAP) basis in this example, there are no differences between the budgetary basis and the GAAP basis.

The accounts must be maintained at the most detailed level that might be needed for *any* purpose because properly classified detailed information can always be aggregated, but aggregated data cannot be disaggregated. If the accounts are not maintained on the budgetary basis or if the subsidiary ledger accounts do not provide sufficient detail, incorporating the budget into the accounts will not be useful.

Budgetary Entry—General Ledger

The operation of the General Fund of A Governmental Unit begins with the official legal *adoption* of the budget. To facilitate monitoring actual operating results compared with the legally adopted budget, A Governmental Unit will record the ***estimated revenues*** and ***appropriations*** (authorized and estimated expenditures) in its General Ledger accounts as shown in entry B. The legally adopted appropriations and revenue estimates—which are now laws—require the following *general ledger* **budgetary entry**:

(B) **ESTIMATED REVENUES**	$427,000	
APPROPRIATIONS		$423,000
BUDGETARY FUND BALANCE		4,000
To record appropriations and revenue estimates.		

Note the use of Budgetary Fund Balance in this entry. Adopting the budget does not affect actual fund balance. Some governments use a Budgetary Fund Balance account to **record the budgeted increase or decrease in fund balance** for the year.

When budget revisions are made, their effect is recorded in this account as well so that its balance always equals the budgeted change in total fund balance for the year. At year end, the initial entry—adjusted for the effects of any budget revisions—is reversed. This action closes the budgetary accounts for the year and has no effect on amounts to be reported in the GAAP-based financial statements.

Other governments prefer to record the budgeted increase or decrease in the (actual) Fund Balance account. They prefer for the balance of the Fund Balance account to be carried at its targeted year end balance instead of at its beginning balance. Carrying the Fund Balance account at its *planned* end-of-year balance focuses attention during the year on the "target" *ending* fund balance ("where we want to be") rather than on the beginning-of-period fund balance ("where we *used* to be"). Under either approach the effects of recording the budget are reversed in the closing process at year end and do not affect the balances reported in the GAAP-based financial statements.

The budgetary entry alone will not enable a government accounting system to monitor revenues compared to budgeted revenues or expenditures incurred against appropriations. For A Governmental Unit to monitor its revenues effectively and ensure that it does not overexpend appropriations **requires more detailed information**. As presented in the previous chapter, revenue and expenditure *subsidiary ledgers* provide one approach to capturing this detail.

Revenues Ledger

A Governmental Unit's Revenues and Expenditures Subsidiary Ledgers must be modified from those used in the previous chapter in order to monitor the city's actual performance against its budget. *Each subsidiary ledger must be modified to add the detailed budget information.* For instance, the Revenues Subsidiary Ledger in Chapter 3 operated like any typical subsidiary ledger.

- It was controlled by a single general ledger account, Revenues.
- It captured only *actual* revenues.
- It was designed for the total of all the balances of the accounts in the Revenues Ledger always to equal the balance of the General Ledger Revenues control account.

For the Revenues Ledger to be used effectively for budgetary control, each of the six subsidiary ledger accounts *must include (1) the legally adopted budgeted amount* of the specific type of revenues recorded in each subsidiary ledger account *and (2) the actual amount* of revenues. The balance of each account will no longer reflect the amount of actual revenues to date—as in Chapter 3—but the *difference* between the budgeted revenues to date and the actual revenues to date. For example, the Taxes account in the Revenues Ledger would appear as follows:

	Taxes		
	Dr.	(Cr.)	Dr. (Cr.)
Date	Estimated Revenues	Revenues	Balance

If budgeted tax revenues were $400,000 and the actual tax revenues were $232,000, the balance of the Taxes account in the Revenues Subsidiary Ledger would be $168,000, the excess of the budgeted amount of tax revenues over the actual amount to date. Each of the other Revenues Ledger accounts would be modified in the same manner.

The sum of the balances of the various revenue subsidiary ledger accounts obviously will no longer equal the balance of the General Ledger Revenues control account. Now, two General Ledger accounts—Estimated Revenues and Revenues—are required to control the Revenues Ledger. **The sum of the balances** of the various Revenues Ledger accounts must equal the *difference* between the Estimated Revenues account and the Revenues account in the General Ledger.

Expenditures Ledger

The Expenditures Ledger requires somewhat more extensive modification than the Revenues Ledger to provide the information needed to avoid inadvertent overexpenditure of appropriations authority. Each of the seven Expenditures Ledger accounts, such as General Government, must be expanded from a single column account—used to keep up with only the actual amount of expenditures of that classification and controlled by the single General Ledger account—to a "4-column" account in which the following information is recorded for each Expenditures Ledger account:

- Appropriations
- Expenditures
- Encumbrances
- Unencumbered Balance (Appropriations less Expenditures less Encumbrances)

For example, the General Government account in the Expenditures Ledger of A Governmental Unit is not a single-column account that captures only actual expenditures. Instead, to serve the budgetary control function, it is expanded to include Appropriations and Encumbrances and appears as follows:

General Government

Date	Dr. (Cr.) Encumbrances	Dr. Expenditures	(Cr.) Appropriations	Dr. (Cr.) Unencumbered Balance

If the General Government appropriations for the fiscal year were $50,000, expenditures were incurred to date of $20,000, and $2,500 of encumbrances were outstanding for general government, the balance in the General Government account in the Expenditures Subsidiary Ledger would be $27,500. Each of the other Expenditures Ledger accounts is modified similarly.

The reason for recording encumbrances (the estimated cost of unfilled orders and unperformed contracts) to facilitate budgetary control is illustrated best with a brief example. Assume that a government's appropriations included total appropriations of $1,000 for supplies for the Jails and Corrections unit within the Police Department. Further, assume that expenditures to date against that appropriation (for supplies received) are $920. If the corresponding Expenditures Ledger account captures only appropriations and expenditures, the balance is $80.

To evaluate a purchase order requisition for $60 of Jails and Corrections supplies, the responsible official needs more information than is captured in the Expenditures account to determine whether sufficient unused appropriation authority remains to permit approval of the order. The official must know whether previously approved orders for Jails and Corrections supplies are still unfilled. For instance, assume an order for $50 of Jails and Corrections supplies is unfilled at the time that the $60 purchase order requisition is being considered. If the new order is approved without knowledge and consideration of the outstanding order, receipt of both orders will result in inadvertent overexpenditure of the Jails and Corrections supplies appropriation.

Adding Encumbrances to the Expenditures Ledger account avoids this problem. The first order for $50 will be recorded in the Jails and Corrections supplies account as Encumbrances. The balance of the account is the unencumbered balance of $30, not the unexpended balance of $80. The account balance immediately informs the official that insufficient appropriation authority remains to permit approval of the full requisition. The appropriate officials might reject or reduce the order or, alternatively, seek additional appropriation authority, but they would not unknowingly approve the order.

The balance of each Expenditures Ledger account is equal to Appropriations less Expenditures less Encumbrances—the unencumbered, unexpended appropriation balance for that expenditures classification. Therefore, for A Governmental

Unit, <mark>the sum of the balances of the seven Expenditures Ledger accounts will not equal the Expenditures Control account balance. The sum of those balances should now equal the **difference** between the General Ledger Appropriations control account and the General Ledger Expenditures and Encumbrances control accounts.</mark>

Let's revisit the entry recording the General Fund budget using these modified subsidiary ledgers. The budgetary entries, including both the General Ledger and subsidiary ledger entries, are:

Recording the Budget— General Ledger and Subsidiary Ledger

(B) **ESTIMATED REVENUES**	$427,000	
APPROPRIATIONS		$423,000
BUDGETARY FUND BALANCE		4,000

To record appropriations and revenue estimates.

Revenues Ledger (Estimated Revenues):

Taxes	$250,000
Licenses and Permits	70,000
Intergovernmental	46,000
Charges for Services	40,000
Fines and Forfeits	20,000
Other	1,000
	$427,000

Expenditures Ledger (Appropriations):

General Government	$ 40,000
Public Safety	150,000
Highways and Streets	114,000
Health and Sanitation	60,000
Other	28,000
Capital Outlay	30,000
Debt Service	1,000
	$423,000

Note that the General Ledger budgetary entry causes the Budgetary Fund Balance account to be stated at the **planned** $4,000 increase in total fund balance. This is how the Estimated Revenues and Appropriations budgetary accounts *traditionally* have been incorporated into the General Ledger and subsidiary ledgers to effect budgetary control during the period. Note also that the subsidiary ledger entries must indicate both the subsidiary ledger affected and the column of the subsidiary ledger account that is affected.

Entry B *compounds* two possible separate General Ledger budgetary entries:

(B1) ESTIMATED REVENUES	$427,000	
BUDGETARY FUND BALANCE		$427,000

To record estimated revenues and the *expected* fund balance *increase* to result during the period.

(B2) BUDGETARY FUND BALANCE	$423,000	
APPROPRIATIONS		$423,000

To record appropriations and the *expected* fund balance *decrease* to result during the period.

<mark>The *budgetary* accounts do *not* affect the *actual* asset, deferred outflow, liability, deferred inflow, revenue, or expenditure General Ledger accounts. **In fact, all changes in *actual* assets, deferred outflows, liabilities, deferred inflows, revenues, and expenditures were recorded and reported in the illustrative transactions, entries, and statements presented in Chapter 3.**</mark>

Budget Revisions

Budgets are usually prepared several months before the beginning of the year to which they apply, based on the best information available at that time. Although preliminary estimates are often revised prior to formal adoption of the budget, revisions may also be appropriate after the budget has been adopted. For example, the government may find it is not going to receive a sizable grant it had expected during the budget year, or it may be granted a significantly different amount than planned.

Appropriations may be revised during the year for a variety of reasons. Increases in revenues over those estimated—whether from regular sources or because of unanticipated special grants—may either permit or require additional expenditures that must be authorized by appropriations. Or, conversely, declines in revenues as compared with the original expectations may necessitate that appropriations be reduced to avoid having insufficient year-end fund balance or a fund balance deficit.

Appropriations revisions may also arise because of utility cost increases, damage to streets caused by unusually cold or wet weather, unanticipated costs of patrolling and cleaning up the town after the hometown university won the national football championship, or for an infinite variety of other reasons. Appropriations increases are not necessarily bad, of course, nor are appropriations decreases necessarily good.

The continuing process of reviewing budgeted and actual revenues and comparing appropriations, expenditures, and encumbrances—and revising the budget as needed in view of changing circumstances—is considered good financial management. Thus, as noted earlier, an annual budget that may have been enacted well before the beginning of the current year should not be considered unchangeable but should be continually reviewed and appropriately revised throughout the year.

It is important to understand that revisions of appropriations typically are subject to more legal constraints than are revisions of revenue estimates. Because appropriations are legally established authority to spend that are created following specific guidelines, which typically include public notice and public hearings, changes in appropriations often require similar steps. This process can make appropriations revisions cumbersome and are a key reason why many governments adopt appropriations at broad expenditure classification levels such as function or department instead of at the detailed objects of expenditure level.

If the revenue estimate is increased during the period, the increase would be debited to Estimated Revenues and credited to Budgetary Fund Balance— indicating an increase in the planned change in fund balance. An estimated revenues decrease would be recorded by debiting the expected decrease to Budgetary Fund Balance—indicating a decrease in the planned change in fund balance—and crediting Estimated Revenues. Similarly, if additional appropriations are made during the year, Budgetary Fund Balance would be debited and Appropriations credited for the increase as in Entry B2 on page 127. The opposite would be true should appropriations be decreased.

To illustrate recording the adoption of budget revisions, assume that during the year the governing body increased the official estimate of intergovernmental revenues by $4,000 and also increased the total appropriations by $3,000, thus increasing the anticipated change in Fund Balance estimate by $1,000. Further assume that the total appropriations increase of $3,000 consists of an increase of $6,000 in the highways and streets appropriation and a decrease of $3,000 in the appropriation for "other" expenditures. The General Ledger and subsidiary ledger entries to record these budget revisions are:

(B3) ESTIMATED REVENUES	$4,000	
APPROPRIATIONS	3,000	
APPROPRIATIONS.		$6,000
BUDGETARY FUND BALANCE		1,000
To record budget revisions.		
Revenues Ledger (Estimated Revenues):		
Intergovernmental.	$4,000	
Expenditures Ledger (Appropriations):		
Highways and Streets		$6,000
Other.	$3,000	

Note that *neither* the Estimated Revenues and Appropriations accounts *nor* the budgetary entry affect the actual Fund Balance. At *year end*—having effected budgetary control during the year—the budgetary entry (as revised) is *reversed* in the closing entries.

Encumbrances and Related Expenditures

Several types of expenditures, such as purchases of materials and supplies and contractual services, involve making a purchase commitment to a vendor in the form of a purchase order or contract prior to incurring actual expenditures. To establish budgetary control over such expenditures, a record of the *estimated expenditures in process* (i.e., *encumbrances*) usually is maintained through the use of an Encumbrances account. Encumbrances are *recorded*—in total in the General Ledger and in detail in the Expenditures Ledger—*when purchase orders are issued or contracts are signed* for goods and services.

Recall that A Governmental Unit, in transaction 3 in Chapter 3, placed orders for materials and equipment estimated to cost $30,000. In Chapter 3, no entry was required for GAAP purposes. However, to provide for budgetary control, the following entry is recorded at the time the orders are placed:

(3) **ENCUMBRANCES**	$30,000	
ENCUMBRANCES OUTSTANDING		$30,000
To record encumbering appropriations.		
Expenditures Ledger (Encumbrances):		
General Government	$ 2,000	
Public Safety	8,000	
Highways and Streets	10,000	
Other	4,000	
Capital Outlay	6,000	
	$30,000	

Comparing appropriations with the *sum* of expenditures and encumbrances shows the amount of uncommitted (unencumbered) appropriations available for expenditure. When the actual expenditure occurs, the entry setting up the encumbrances (estimated expenditures in progress) is reversed and the actual expenditure is recorded. Consequently, entry 4 from Chapter 3 would include an entry reversing the Encumbrances as well as the same GAAP entry made in Chapter 3.

Note that use of encumbrances accounting is equally necessary for budgetary control regardless of whether the resources from which the ultimate expenditure is to be paid are restricted, committed, assigned, or unassigned from a GAAP viewpoint. In all cases, appropriations are required as legal authority to expend resources, and management must not overexpend the appropriation authority.

In transaction 4, A Governmental Unit received the materials and equipment ordered in transaction 3 at an actual cost of only $29,900. The entries to (1) remove the encumbrances and (2) record the actual expenditures are:

(4a) **ENCUMBRANCES OUTSTANDING**	$30,000	
ENCUMBRANCES		$30,000
To reverse the encumbering entry.		
Expenditures Ledger (Encumbrances):		
General Government	$ 2,000	
Public Safety	8,000	
Highways and Streets	10,000	
Other	4,000	
Capital Outlay	6,000	
	$30,000	

(4b) Expenditures...	$29,900	
Vouchers Payable		$29,900
To record expenditures.		

Expenditures Ledger (Expenditures):

General Government...............................	$ 1,700
Public Safety	8,000
Highways and Streets..............................	10,100
Other	4,000
Capital Outlay......................................	6,100
	$29,900

Entry 4b is identical to entry 4 in Chapter 3. Recall that the subsidiary ledger entries must specify the subsidiary ledger affected and the column of the subsidiary ledger affected as well as the account that is affected. Finally, recognize that entries 4a and 4b accomplish two things:

1. Entry 4a—While the order was outstanding, the *net* unencumbered balances of the Appropriations, Expenditures, and Encumbrances accounts in the General Ledger were temporarily reduced. Likewise, the unencumbered balance of each affected account in the Expenditures Subsidiary Ledger was temporarily reduced—while the order was outstanding—by the estimated amount of the expenditures in progress, i.e., the encumbrance. This effect is now eliminated in entry 4a because the order has arrived and the actual expenditures amount is known and can be recorded.

2. Entry 4b—Now that the actual expenditures amount is known and the entry setting up the *encumbrances* has been *reversed*, the *actual* expenditures are recorded.

The General Ledger effects of these entries are as follows:

	After Entry B	After Entry 3	After Entries 4a and 4b
Appropriations..................	$423,000	$423,000	$423,000
Less: Expenditures...............	—	—	29,900
Unexpended Balance	423,000	423,000	393,100
Less: Encumbrances	—	30,000	—
Unencumbered Balance	$423,000	$393,000	$393,100

Note from entries 4a and 4b that encumbrances are *estimates* of subsequent expenditures and that the resulting *actual* expenditures may be more than, less than, or equal to the encumbrances. In this case the Public Safety and Other expenditures were exactly as planned—perhaps the result of a price quotation or bid on a purchase order. But the General Government order cost less than anticipated, perhaps because of a price decline or because part of the order was cancelled. On the other hand, the Highways and Streets and Capital Outlay expenditures were more than originally estimated, possibly because of freight, delivery, or other costs that were not anticipated or because of an approved change in specifications after the purchase order was issued. In any case, the accounting upon receipt of encumbered goods or services is simply: *Reverse the encumbrance entry and record the actual expenditure.*

Encumbrance accounting is required for one other transaction of A Governmental Unit. In transaction 21 in Chapter 3, purchase orders were issued for the following functions and amounts: Public Safety, $7,000, and Health and Sanitation, $13,000.

(21) ENCUMBRANCES	$20,000	
ENCUMBRANCES OUTSTANDING............		$20,000
To record reduction of appropriation available for expenditure by estimated cost of purchase orders issued.		

Expenditures Ledger (Encumbrances):

Public Safety	$ 7,000
Health and Sanitation	13,000
	$20,000

This order was not received by year-end. Thus, as shown in Illustration 4-2, the only entries that must be added or modified to maintain budgetary accountability during the fiscal year for A Governmental Unit are:

- The budgetary entry to record adoption (and revisions) of the budget
- Entries recording encumbrances for orders placed or contracts approved
- Entries to reduce encumbrances upon receipt of goods ordered or contractual services

The year-end entry to close the accounts will be modified as well.

Illustration 4-2 also highlights the fact that Revenues Ledger entries and Expenditures Ledger entries are not required for most transactions. Subsidiary ledger entries are required *only* for entries that affect one of the corresponding General Ledger *control* accounts—Estimated Revenues, Revenues, Appropriations, Expenditures, or Encumbrances.

ILLUSTRATION 4-2	Effects of Budgetary Accounting on Entries for Various Transactions			
Ch. 3 Trans. No.	**Transaction Description**	**Differences From Chapter 3 (If Any)**	**Revenues Ledger Affected?**	**Expenditures Ledger Affected?**
	Adopted budget (omitted in Chapter 3)	Record budget	Yes	Yes
1	Levied property taxes		Yes	
2	Billed service charges		Yes	
3	Placed purchase order	Record encumbrances		Yes
4	Received order	Reverse encumbrances		Yes
		(Record expenditures as in Chapter 3)		Yes
5	Approved payroll			Yes
6	Interfund reimbursement			Yes
7	Interfund transfer in			
8	Interfund transfer in			
9	Interfund transfer out			
10	Acquired interfund services			Yes
11	Made interfund loan			
12	Collected interfund loan			
13	Short-term external borrowing			
14	Repaid part of short-term loan and paid interest			Yes (Interest)
15	Special item			
16	Extraordinary item			
17	Collected receivables			
18	Reclassified taxes receivable as delinquent			
19	Reclassified allowance for uncollectible taxes			
20	Collected revenues not accrued previously		Yes	
21	Placed purchase order	Record encumbrances		Yes
22	Collected receivables and interest and penalties revenues		Yes	
23	Purchased investments			
24	Vouchered unencumbered expenditures			Yes
25	Paid vouchers payable			
26	Paid interfund liability			
27	Collected accounts receivable			
28	Wrote-off accounts receivable			
29	Corrected prior year error			

Revenues and Expenditures Ledgers Incorporating Budgetary Accounts

The budgetary accounting entries affect the subsidiary ledgers of A Governmental Unit and its Preclosing Trial Balances. The revised ledgers and the revised preclosing subsidiary ledger trial balances are presented in the following four illustrations:

- Illustration 4-3 presents the Revenues Ledger after incorporating Estimated Revenues and posting both the budgetary entries illustrated in this chapter and the entries recording actual revenues from Chapter 3.
- Illustration 4-4 presents the Expenditures Ledger after incorporating both Appropriations and Encumbrances and posting both the budgetary entries illustrated in this chapter and the entries recording actual expenditures from Chapter 3.
- Illustration 4-5 presents the preclosing trial balance of the general ledger of the General Fund of A Governmental Unit after incorporating the budgetary entries as well as the entries from Chapter 3. The differences from the preclosing trial balance in Chapter 3 (Illustration 3-2) are highlighted in bold.
- Illustration 4-6 presents the preclosing trial balances of the Revenues Ledger and the Expenditures Ledger after incorporating the budgetary entries as well as the Chapter 3 and Chapter 4 entries for both actual revenues and actual expenditures.

ILLUSTRATION 4-3 Revenues Subsidiary Ledger—General Fund

A Governmental Unit
General Fund
For the Year Ended December 31, 20X1: Preclosing
Revenues Ledger

	Dr. Estimated Revenues	Cr. Revenues	Dr. (Cr.) Balance
Taxes	$250,000 (B)		$250,000
		$197,000 (1)	53,000
		58,000 (20)	(5,000)
Totals/Balance	250,000	255,000	(5,000)
Licenses and Permits	70,000 (B)		70,000
		68,000 (20)	2,000
Totals/Balance	70,000	68,000	2,000
Intergovernmental	46,000 (B)		46,000
	4,000 (B3)		50,000
		52,500 (20)	(2,500)
Totals/Balance	50,000	52,500	(2,500)
Charges for Services	40,000 (B)		40,000
		35,000 (2)	5,000
		6,000 (20)	(1,000)
Totals/Balance	40,000	41,000	(1,000)
Fines and Forfeits	20,000 (B)		20,000
		19,000 (20)	1,000
Totals/Balance	20,000	19,000	1,000
Other	1,000 (B)		1,000
		1,500 (20)	(500)
		200 (22)	(700)
		500 (A1)	(1,200)
		400 (A2)	(1,600)
Totals/Balance	1,000	2,600	(1,600)

ILLUSTRATION 4-4   Expenditures Subsidiary Ledger—General Fund

A Governmental Unit
General Fund
For the Year Ended December 31, 20X1: Preclosing
Expenditures Ledger

	Dr. Encumbrances	Dr. Expenditures	Cr. Appropriations	Cr. (Dr.) Unencumbered Balance
General Government			$40,000 (B)	$40,000
	$2,000 (3)			38,000
	(2,000) (4a)	$1,700 (4b)		38,300
		5,000 (5)		33,300
		(1,500) (6)		34,800
		4,000 (10)		30,800
		30,000 (24)		800
Totals/Balance	—	39,200	40,000	800
Public Safety			150,000 (B)	150,000
	8,000 (3)			142,000
	(8,000) (4a)	8,000 (4b)		142,000
		16,000 (5)		126,000
	7,000 (21)			119,000
		6,000 (10)		113,000
		112,000 (24)		1,000
Totals/Balance	7,000	142,000	150,000	1,000
Highways and Streets			114,000 (B)	114,000
			6,000 (B3)	120,000
	10,000 (3)			110,000
	(10,000) (4a)	10,100 (4b)		109,900
		13,000 (5)		96,900
		10,000 (10)		86,900
		90,000 (24)		(3,100)
Totals/Balance	—	123,100	120,000	(3,100)
Health and Sanitation			60,000 (B)	60,000
		4,000 (5)		56,000
	13,000 (21)			43,000
		7,000 (10)		36,000
		35,400 (24)		600
Totals/Balance	13,000	46,400	60,000	600
Other			28,000 (B)	28,000
			(3,000) (B3)	25,000
	4,000 (3)			21,000
	(4,000) (4a)	4,000 (4b)		21,000
		2,000 (5)		19,000
		3,000 (10)		16,000
		9,600 (24)		6,400
Totals/Balance	—	18,600	25,000	6,400
Capital Outlay			30,000 (B)	30,000
	6,000 (3)			24,000
	(6,000) (4a)	6,100 (4b)		23,900
		23,000 (24)		900
Totals/Balance	—	29,100	30,000	900
Debt Service			1,000 (B)	1,000
		600 (14)		400
		250 (A3)		150
Totals/Balance	—	850	1,000	150

ILLUSTRATION 4-5 Preclosing Trial Balance—General Ledger—End of 20X1

A Governmental Unit
General Fund
Preclosing Trial Balance General Ledger
December 31, 20X1

	Debit	Credit
Cash	$ 51,850	
Investments	10,000	
Accrued Interest Receivable	400	
Taxes Receivable—Delinquent	20,000	
Allowance for Uncollectible Delinquent Taxes		$ 3,000
Interest and Penalties Receivable on Taxes	550	
Allowance for Uncollectible Interest and Penalties		50
Accounts Receivable	19,600	
Allowance for Uncollectible Accounts Receivable		600
Due from Special Revenue Fund	11,500	
Vouchers Payable		25,200
Notes Payable		15,000
Accrued Interest Payable		250
Due to Internal Service Fund		7,500
Fund Balance		11,000
BUDGETARY FUND BALANCE		**5,000**
ESTIMATED REVENUES	**431,000**	
Revenues		438,100
Special Item—Proceeds from Sale of Beach Property		8,000
Extraordinary Item—Insurance Recovery Proceeds		5,750
APPROPRIATIONS		**426,000**
Expenditures	399,250	
ENCUMBRANCES	**20,000**	
ENCUMBRANCES OUTSTANDING		**20,000**
Transfer to Debt Service Fund	5,000	
Transfer from Special Revenue Fund		10,000
Transfer to Enterprise Fund	6,000	
Correction of Prior Year Error	300	
	$975,450	$975,450

The revised General Ledger trial balance has five differences from the preclosing trial balance (without budgetary accounts) in Illustration 3-2. The differences are all budgetary accounts. Specifically, the following five accounts and balances are included:

- ESTIMATED REVENUES, $431,000
- APPROPRIATIONS, $426,000
- BUDGETARY FUND BALANCE, $5,000
- ENCUMBRANCES, $20,000
- ENCUMBRANCES OUTSTANDING, $20,000

General Ledger Closing Entries

The General Ledger closing entry in Chapter 3 does not need to change when using budgetary accounts. All that is required is to add the closing of the Estimated

ILLUSTRATION 4-6 Preclosing Trial Balances—Revenues and Expenditures Subsidiary Ledgers—End of 20X1

A Governmental Unit
General Fund
Preclosing Trial Balances
Revenues and Expenditures Subsidiary Ledgers
December 31, 20X1

Revenues Subsidiary Ledger	Debit	Credit
Taxes		$ 5,000
Licenses and Permits	$2,000	
Intergovernmental		2,500
Charges for Services		1,000
Fines and Forfeits	1,000	
Other		1,600
	$3,000	$10,100

Proof: $10,100 – $3,000 = $ 7,100

Compare to General

Ledger control accounts:

Revenues	$438,100	
Estimated Revenues	431,000	
Difference	$ 7,100	

Expenditures Subsidiary Ledger

	Debit	Credit
General Government		$ 800
Public Safety		1,000
Highways and Streets	$3,100	
Health and Sanitation		600
Other		6,400
Capital Outlay		900
Debt Service		150
	$3,100	$ 9,850

Proof: $ 9,850 – $3,100 = $ 6,750

Compare to General

Ledger control accounts:

Appropriations		$426,000	
Expenditures	$399,250		
Encumbrances	20,000	419,250	
Difference		$ 6,750	

Revenues, Appropriations, Encumbrances, and Encumbrances Outstanding accounts to the Budgetary Fund Balance account as a separate entry.

The General Ledger closing entries would be:

(C1) BUDGETARY FUND BALANCE	$ 5,000	
APPROPRIATIONS	426,000	
ENCUMBRANCES OUTSTANDING	20,000	
ESTIMATED REVENUES		$431,000
ENCUMBRANCES		20,000
To close the budgetary accounts.		

(C2) Revenues...................................	$438,100	
Transfer from Special Revenue Fund....................	10,000	
Special Item—Proceeds from Sale of Beach Property........	8,000	
Extraordinary Item—Insurance Recovery Proceeds.........	5,750	
Fund Balance...................................		$ 51,300
Expenditures...................................		399,250
Transfer to Debt Service Fund.....................		5,000
Transfer to Enterprise Fund.......................		6,000
Correction of Prior Year Error.....................		300
To close the general ledger nonbudgetary accounts.		

Entry C2 is the same closing entry made in Chapter 3.

This illustration assumes that only revenues and expenditures are subject to formal budgetary accounting control procedures, which is often the case because the governing board directly controls interfund transfers. Alternatively, budgetary accounts such as Estimated Transfers In and Estimated Transfers Out could have been used and would be closed at this time. Accounting procedures where interfund transfers and debt issue proceeds are subject to formal budgetary accounting control are considered in later chapters.

Subsidiary Ledger Closing Entries

The accounts in the Revenues Ledger and the Expenditures Ledger are closed by simply debiting the credit balances and crediting the debit balances, thus bringing all accounts to a zero balance. The accounts may be closed automatically in computerized systems or manually by observing the preclosing account balances (see Illustrations 4-3, 4-4, and 4-6). The entries to close the subsidiary ledgers of A Governmental Unit are:

(C) **Revenues Ledger (Balance):**

Taxes.....................................	$ 5,000	
Licenses and Permits.........................		$2,000
Intergovernmental............................	2,500	
Charges for Services.........................	1,000	
Fines and Forfeits...........................		1,000
Other.....................................	1,600	
	$ 10,100	$3,000

Proof: $10,100 – $3,000 =	$ 7,100	
Compare to General		
Ledger control accounts:		
Revenues..............................	$438,100	
Estimated Revenues.....................	431,000	
Difference.............................	$ 7,100	

(C) **Expenditures Ledger (Balance):**

General Government..........................	$ 800	
Public Safety...............................	1,000	
Highways and Streets.........................		$3,100
Health and Sanitation........................	600	
Other.....................................	6,400	
Capital Outlay..............................	900	
Debt Service...............................	150	
	$ 9,850	$3,100

Proof: $9,850 – $3,100 =	$ 6,750	
Compare to General		
Ledger control accounts:		
Appropriations...........		$426,000
Expenditures...........	$399,250	
Encumbrances..........	20,000	419,250
Difference..............		$ 6,750

Because A Governmental Unit's budget was adopted at a function level for illustrative purposes, only a few accounts had to be maintained in its Expenditures Ledger to provide for budgetary accountability and control at a level commensurate with the legal constraint of not overexpending appropriations. Although many governments legally adopt appropriations only at an aggregated level such as function or department, many others adopt appropriations at the detailed object class level discussed in Chapter 3. The Expenditures Ledger for these latter governments would need an account for each appropriation item in order to be used to monitor compliance with the legal budget and to provide the basis for reporting on that budgetary compliance.

Level of Detail in Subsidiary Ledgers

Even governments that adopt appropriations using broad classifications such as functions or departments, like A Governmental Unit, should maintain detailed Expenditures Ledger accounts. Governments should maintain their records at the most detailed level that they might ever need for any reason. Aggregating detailed amounts to determine the amounts of more aggregate classifications is relatively simple, but disaggregation ranges from difficult to impracticable. Although not technically necessary to demonstrate budgetary compliance at the legal budgetary control points, it is important to recognize that:

- The level of detail in which a government adopts its appropriations acts or ordinances establishes the level at which executive branch accountability to the legislative branch is legally enforceable. This is the legislative-to-executive branch "budgetary control points" level of detail.
- Governments that establish highly aggregated legislative-to-executive branch budgetary control points by adopting appropriations at an aggregated level, such as function or program or perhaps department, still prepare a budget document that includes detailed objects of expenditure amounts that support and justify the broad appropriation amounts.
- The detailed budget amounts within a legally adopted appropriation category, such as General Government, are used to manage the operation during the year. The broader budgetary control point level of detail does not provide an effective internal management tool to ensure that the government functions substantially as planned.
- The city manager or other chief executive may want to control appropriations at a level more detailed than the official budgetary control points. In this case, the unofficial, detailed components of each appropriation are called *allocations*. The portion of the appropriation allocated to each object of expenditure accounted for in each detailed Expenditures Ledger account will be treated as if it were a legally adopted appropriation in accounting for and controlling that particular expenditure item internally, though the budgetary results are required to be reported publicly only at the budgetary control point level of detail, at a minimum.

In summary, even if a government adopts appropriations at a broad level, its Expenditures Ledger likely will have the same accounts and operate in the same fashion that would have been required if it had legally adopted appropriations at the object of expenditure detail reflected in its budget document. The difference is that if a government's legally adopted budget is on a detailed object of expenditure basis, the government or its manager cannot shift appropriation authority from one activity to another or from one department to another—even within the same function—without formally adopting budget revisions.

BUDGETARY REPORTING OVERVIEW

GAAP-based financial reporting for governmental funds was discussed and demonstrated in Chapter 3 using the information from the A Governmental Unit illustration. Budgetary accounting and reporting do not change the GAAP-based financial statements—the Balance Sheet and the Statement of Revenues, Expenditures, and Changes in Fund Balance—discussed in that chapter. However, the unique importance of budgeting, budgetary control, and budgetary accountability in the state and local government environment necessitates preparation of both *interim* (e.g., monthly) and annual budgetary statements or schedules. Interim budgetary reports are widely used to help governing bodies monitor, evaluate, and manage a government's operations during a fiscal year. The GASB requires *annual* budgetary reporting for the General Fund and each major Special Revenue Fund either as basic financial statements (BFS) or as required supplementary information (RSI). Governments that publish comprehensive annual financial reports (CAFRs) also must include budgetary reports for each of the other governmental funds with legally adopted annual budgets.

The Budgetary Basis

Recall from previous discussions that a government does not have to use the GAAP basis for budgeting purposes. Instead, absent state legal or regulatory requirements, the governing body can *choose* the basis on which its annual budget is prepared, adopted, controlled, and reported upon. Accordingly, some governments budget their governmental funds on the modified accrual (GAAP) basis, and others budget revenues and expenditures on the cash basis. That is, for budgetary accounting and reporting purposes they do not recognize revenues and expenditures until the related cash is received or disbursed, respectively. In any event, *governments maintain their accounts on the budgetary basis during the year—for budgetary control and for interim and annual budgetary reporting purposes—then adjust the accounts to the GAAP basis at year end for annual GAAP-based reporting purposes.*

Furthermore, some governments consider *encumbrances* outstanding at year end to be the equivalent of *expenditures* for *budgetary* purposes, and they compare the sum of expenditures and encumbrances with appropriations. This approach is known as the **encumbrances method**. Other governments consider encumbrance accounting to be only an *internal* budgetary control technique to avoid incurring expenditures in excess of appropriations. Because these governments do not consider encumbrances to be equivalent to expenditures for budgetary reporting purposes, they (1) compare budgetary basis expenditures (only) with appropriations and report the unexpended (not unencumbered) appropriation balances, and (2) disclose encumbrances outstanding in the notes to the financial statements.

Because of the variation of budgetary bases in practice, the need for effective budgetary control, and GAAP requirements related to budgetary reporting, the governmental accountant and auditor must

- Carefully identify the budgetary basis used by each state or local government, particularly for its General Fund and its major annually budgeted Special Revenue Funds.
- Ensure that the budgetary basis is appropriately used in budgetary accounting and reporting and that the differences between the budgetary basis and the GAAP basis are adequately explained and reconciled in government financial reports.

Interim Budgetary Statements

Monthly or quarterly interim budgetary statements typically are prepared directly from the Revenues and Expenditures Subsidiary Ledger accounts demonstrated in Illustrations 4-3 and 4-4. Because the GASB has *not* set standards for interim financial statements, interim budgetary reports may contain whatever statements, schedules, and other information management deems appropriate.

Interim Revenues Statements

Interim revenues statements typically include, as a minimum, data from the Revenues Subsidiary Ledger accounts (Illustration 4-3) on

1. The revenues recognized to date
2. The estimated revenues for the year

In addition, interim statements typically include the difference between the two.

Furthermore, percentage data are frequently presented, such as the percentage of the estimated annual revenues realized to date, by revenue category and in total, and the percentage of each revenue source and total revenues that had been realized at this time last year. For example, a monthly budgetary revenues statement might present, for each revenue source and in total, the following:

		Percent of Budget Realized to Date	
Revenues Year to Date	Estimated Revenues for the Year	Current Year	Prior Year

In addition, management analyses and commentary accompanying the interim revenue statement should describe any significant factors affecting revenues to date or apt to affect the revenues in the upcoming months and for the year. Indeed, evaluations of budgetary reports are often the basis on which the governing body revises the estimated revenues budget and/or revises appropriations during the year.

Interim Expenditures Statements

Interim expenditures statements typically include, as a minimum, data drawn from the Expenditures Subsidiary Ledger accounts (Illustration 4-4) at the interim statement date on

1. Appropriations for the year
2. Expenditures to date
3. Encumbrances outstanding at the interim date
4. The unencumbered balance of each appropriation

For example, a monthly budgetary expenditures statement might present the following for each appropriation and in total:

Year to Date				
Expenditures	Encumbrances	Total	Annual Appropriations	Unencumbered Balance

Some governments *allot* appropriations to specific months or quarters to improve budgetary control and as part of a cash flow management plan. When an allotment system is used, only appropriations allotted to the current and previous time periods provide valid expenditure authority. Two General Ledger accounts, Unallotted Appropriations and Allotments, are maintained to account for the two portions of appropriations. Expenditures cannot be made against unallotted appropriations. The Expenditures Subsidiary Ledger is used to record allotments to date, not total appropriations, for each detailed expenditure account, and the Allotments account replaces Appropriations as a control account for the subsidiary ledger.

In interim reports, governments using monthly allotments controls would include data for the allotment period, and those budgeting on the encumbrances method may present only the expenditures and encumbrances total. Further, as in interim revenues budgetary reporting, interim expenditure budgetary statements

1. May contain year-to-date and/or prior year comparative percentage data.
2. Should contain management commentary on any significant factors affecting expenditures and encumbrances to date or apt to affect total expenditures for the year or encumbrances outstanding at year end.
3. Often serve as the basis for governing body revisions of appropriations during the year.

Interim Revenues and Expenditures Statements

Although interim budgetary statements for revenues and expenditures may be presented separately, they are often presented in the same statement. This type of interim budgetary comparison statement is presented in Illustration 4-7, using

ILLUSTRATION 4-7   Interim Budgetary Comparison Statement

INTERIM BUDGETARY COMPARISON STATEMENT
(Budgetary Basis)
A Governmental Unit
General Fund
At End of (Month), 20X1

	Actual (To Date)	Revised Annual Budget	Unrealized/ Unexpended	Percent (%) Actual to Date to Total 20X1	20X0
Revenues					
Taxes	$152,750	$250,000	$ 97,250	61.1	66.0
Licenses and permits	26,250	70,000	43,750	37.5	31.0
Intergovernmental	28,550	50,000	21,450	57.1	60.7
Charges for services	20,000	40,000	20,000	50.0	45.4
Fines and forfeits	8,000	20,000	12,000	40.0	35.6
Other	350	1,000	650	35.0	33.3
	235,900	431,000	195,100	54.7	49.7
Expenditures					
General government	19,200	40,000	20,800	48.0	51.3
Public safety	78,000	150,000	72,000	52.0	48.0
Highways and streets	42,000	120,000	78,000	35.0	55.0
Health and sanitation	36,000	60,000	24,000	60.0	51.4
Other	13,350	25,000	11,650	53.4	41.6
Capital outlay	6,000	30,000	24,000	20.0	41.8
Debt service	600	1,000	400	60.0	80.4
	195,150	426,000	$230,850	45.8	46.0
Excess of Revenues over (under)					
Expenditures and Encumbrances.	$ 40,750	$ 5,000			

Notes:
1. This statement may also contain beginning fund balance and anticipated ending fund balance amounts.
2. The numbers presented in the "Actual to Date" column in this illustrative statement are *assumed*. The revised budget numbers are those used in the budgetary accounting illustration for A Governmental Unit.
3. If encumbrances are viewed as equivalent to expenditures for budgetary purposes, both expenditures and encumbrances are presented in this statement. The total of expenditures and encumbrances may be presented, or expenditures and encumbrances may be presented separately, as well as in total.

the budget information from A Governmental Unit and *assumed* numbers for the interim amounts of actual revenues and expenditures. Further, the budgetary comparison data may be summarized by broad category in the budgetary comparison statement, which may be supported by separate, more detailed revenues and expenditures budgetary schedules.

BUDGET COMPARISON SCHEDULE OR STATEMENT OF REVENUES, EXPENDITURES, AND CHANGES IN FUND BALANCE—BUDGET AND ACTUAL

The General Fund balance sheet and statement of revenues, expenditures, and changes in fund balance of A Governmental Unit are not changed as a result of budgetary accounting. A third statement or schedule required for the General Fund and certain Special Revenue Funds with legally adopted annual budgets compares budgeted and actual operating results. The budgetary comparison statement or schedule is *unique* in that the reporting government *may choose* to present it *either* as (1) a *basic financial statement* (*audited*) or (2) *required supplementary information* (*unaudited*) following the notes to the financial statements.

Because of the importance of the budget and the budget process in government accountability and decision making, *we strongly recommend that the budgetary comparison be presented as a basic financial statement.* But, again, the government may choose the RSI alternative.

The Statement of Revenues, Expenditures, and Changes in Fund Balance—*Budget and Actual*—is prepared on the *budgetary basis,* which often differs from GAAP. Thus it is often called the "budgetary comparison statement" or simply the "budgetary statement."

Whereas the GAAP-based operating statement must comply with GAAP standards and guidelines, *the budgetary-basis operating statement must demonstrate budgetary accountability in terms of the government's own methods of budgeting, including its budgetary basis.* The budgetary operating statement may be presented in *either* (1) the *format* for the *GAAP* operating statement, the Statement of Revenues, Expenditures, and Changes in Fund Balances, *or* (2) in the *format* in which the *budget was adopted.* However, regardless of basis or format, it usually has columns headed

Budget		Actual	Variance Over
Original	Final		(Under)

The "Budget" columns should contain *both* the budget data as originally adopted and revised budget data. The *original budget* is the first complete, legally enacted budget; the *final budget* is the original adopted budget adjusted for all budget amendments adopted throughout the fiscal year. This final budget sometimes differs significantly from the originally adopted budget.

The Variance column is *optional* but typically is presented. When presented, the *variance* is based on comparing the *actual* amounts with those in the *final* revised budget. Headings other than *Variance—Favorable (Unfavorable),* such as *Actual (Over) Under Budget,* may be used to describe the Variance column.

If the legally adopted budget is prepared on a basis consistent with GAAP, the *actual* data in this statement will correspond with the data presented in the GAAP-based Statement of Revenues, Expenditures, and Changes in Fund Balance (Illustration 3-7). However, *if the budget is prepared on a basis other than GAAP*—for example, on the cash receipts and disbursements basis or the encumbrances basis—*both* the *budget data and the actual data* should be presented on the *budgetary* basis. Using the budgetary basis results in an accurate budgetary comparison and a meaningful variance—favorable (unfavorable) comparison.

If the budgetary statement is prepared on a basis other than GAAP, the notes to the financial statements (or to the RSI) should (1) explain the non-GAAP budgetary basis employed, and (2) reconcile the budgetary amounts with the GAAP amounts. Alternatively, the budgetary basis may be explained in the notes and the reconciliation of the budgetary-basis and the GAAP-basis data included in the Statement of Revenues, Expenditures, and Changes in Fund Balance—Budget and Actual, as illustrated later for A Governmental Unit.

Budgetary Comparison Statement Illustrated—Budgetary Basis *Same* as GAAP

A Statement of Revenues, Expenditures, and Changes in Fund Balance—Budget and Actual—for the General Fund of A Governmental Unit for the 20X1 fiscal year is presented in Illustration 4-8. *This illustrative example assumes that the budget is prepared on the GAAP basis.* Therefore, the budgetary operating statement in Illustration 4-8 is prepared on the GAAP basis, which in this case is also the budgetary basis. Note the following in studying Illustration 4-8:

- The title of the statement includes the term *budget and actual* and indicates the budgetary basis on which the statement is prepared.
- Both the original and revised budget data are presented (in adjacent columns) in the budgetary comparison statement.

ILLUSTRATION 4-8 Statement of Revenues, Expenditures, and Changes in Fund Balance—Budget and Actual—For 20X1 (Budgetary Comparison Statement)

A Governmental Unit
General Fund
Statement of Revenues, Expenditures, and Changes in Fund Balance—Budget and Actual
(Budgetary Basis Is Modified Accrual Basis)
For the 20X1 Fiscal Year

	Original Budget	Revised Budget (Note 1)	Actual	Variance—Favorable (Unfavorable)
Revenues				
Taxes.............................	$250,000	$250,000	$255,000	$ 5,000
Licenses and permits.................	70,000	70,000	68,000	(2,000)
Intergovernmental...................	46,000	50,000	52,500	2,500
Charges for services	40,000	40,000	41,000	1,000
Fines and forfeits...................	20,000	20,000	19,000	(1,000)
Other.............................	1,000	1,000	2,600	1,600
Total Revenues	427,000	431,000	438,100	7,100
Expenditures (Note 2)				
Current operating				
General government...............	40,000	40,000	39,200	800
Public safety.....................	150,000	150,000	142,000	8,000
Highways and streets	114,000	120,000	123,100	(3,100)
Health and sanitation	60,000	60,000	46,400	13,600
Other............................	28,000	25,000	18,600	6,400
Total Current Operating Expenditures.................	392,000	395,000	369,300	25,700
Capital outlay.......................	30,000	30,000	29,100	900
Debt service	1,000	1,000	850	150
Total Expenditures	423,000	426,000	399,250	26,750
Excess of Revenues over Expenditures	4,000	5,000	38,850	33,850
Other Financing Sources (Uses)				
Transfer from Special Revenue Fund...	—	10,000	10,000	—
Transfer to Debt Service Fund	—	(5,000)	(5,000)	—
Transfer to Enterprise Fund	—	(6,000)	(6,000)	—
	—	(1,000)	(1,000)	—
Special and Extraordinary Items				
Special Item—Proceeds from Sale of Beach Property............	—	—	8,000	8,000
Extraordinary Item—Insurance Recovery Proceeds	—	—	5,750	5,750
	—	—	13,750	13,750
Net Change in Fund Balance	4,000	4,000	51,600	47,600
Fund Balance—January 1— As Restated (Note X)	11,000	11,000	10,700	(300)
Fund Balance—December 31	$ 15,000	$ 15,000	$ 62,300	$47,300

Notes:

1. In this example, the governing body both revised its original revenue estimates and appropriations (entry B3) and authorized interfund transfers that were not included in the original budget.
2. Because this illustrative example assumes that the budget is prepared and adopted on the modified accrual (GAAP) basis, only expenditures are reported (encumbrances are excluded).

- Encumbrances are not reported (only expenditures) because encumbrances are not considered equivalent to expenditures on the modified accrual basis.

- Although the interfund transfers were not included in the fiscal budget, they were separately authorized, and these legally authorized amounts are included in the final budget.

- The special item and extraordinary item (as would be expected) were not included in the budget.

- Both the net changes in fund balance and the ending fund balance reported in the "Actual" column of this budgetary statement equal the corresponding amounts reported in the GAAP-based statement in Illustration 3-7. No reconciliation is needed in this case because there are no differences to reconcile. Likewise, noting that the budgetary basis is the modified accrual basis (or noting that it is the GAAP basis) is sufficient to communicate the essence of the budgetary basis of accounting to statement readers when the budget is adopted on the GAAP basis.

Budgetary reporting is simplified in many ways if a government budgets using the modified accrual basis. In reality, few governments do so. Even in states where GAAP budgets are required by law or regulation, few budgets are found that apply all aspects of modified accrual accounting. Most budgetary bases used have a limited number of variations from GAAP. Many other governments prepare budgets on other bases of accounting, such as the cash basis, that vary widely from GAAP.

Budgetary Comparison Statement Illustrated— Budgetary Basis *Differs* from GAAP

As noted earlier, when the budgetary basis of accounting differs from GAAP, the budgetary comparison statement must be presented using the budgetary basis of accounting for both the budget information and the actual information reported. Further, the budgetary basis of accounting must be explained clearly and the government must present a reconciliation between the actual data reported in the budgetary statement and the amounts reported in the GAAP financial statements. This reconciliation may explain either (1) the differences between the net *changes* in fund balance reported in the two statements or (2) the differences between the *ending* fund balance presented in the GAAP operating statement and the ending budgetary fund balance reported in the budgetary comparison statement.

The following illustration (4-9) is based on the A Governmental Unit transactions *except* it assumes that the city adopted its budget on the cash basis. On the cash basis, revenues and expenditures would be recognized as cash is received or paid. The city's cash basis revenues—both in total and by source—are derived directly from the illustrative entries in Chapter 3; only the *total* cash basis expenditures come directly from those entries. The *functional detail* is based on *assumed* distributions of the cash payments for expenditures to different functions.

Note that:

- The title of the statement indicates that it is prepared on the budgetary basis, in this case the cash basis.

- Encumbrances are not reported (only expenditures) because encumbrances are not considered equivalent to expenditures for budgetary or other purposes on the cash basis.

- As in the previous illustration, the interfund transfers were authorized independent of the fiscal budget, so only "Revised Budget" amounts are presented for interfund transfers. Likewise, the special item and extraordinary item were not budgeted.

- Both the net changes in fund balance and the ending fund balance reported in the "Actual" column of this budgetary statement *differ from* the corresponding amounts reported in the GAAP-based statement in Illustration 3-7. The government is required to reconcile one of these amounts to the corresponding amount on the GAAP-based Statement of Revenues, Expenditures, and Changes in Fund Balance (Illustration 3-7). The reconciliation may be presented either at the bottom of the budgetary comparison statement or in the notes to the financial statements.

Illustration 4-10 explains the budgetary basis of accounting that A Governmental Unit used and presents the reconciliation of its budgetary fund balance (cash basis) and its GAAP fund balance.

ILLUSTRATION 4-9   Statement of Revenues, Expenditures, and Changes in Fund Balance— Budget and Actual—For 20X1—Cash Basis Budget Adopted

A Governmental Unit
General Fund
Statement of Revenues, Expenditures, and Changes in Fund Balance—Budget and Actual
(Budgetary Basis Is Cash Basis)
For the 20X1 Fiscal Year

	Original Budget	Revised Budget (Note 1)	Actual	Variance— Favorable (Unfavorable)
Revenues				
Taxes	$250,000	$250,000	$238,000	$(12,000)
Licenses and permits	70,000	70,000	68,000	(2,000)
Intergovernmental	46,000	50,000	52,500	2,500
Charges for services	40,000	40,000	34,000	(6,000)
Fines and forfeits	20,000	20,000	19,000	(1,000)
Other	1,000	1,000	1,700	700
Total Revenues	427,000	431,000	413,200	(17,800)
Expenditures (Note 2)				
Current operating				
General government	40,000	40,000	38,550	1,450
Public safety	150,000	150,000	140,900	9,100
Highways and streets	114,000	120,000	120,950	(950)
Health and sanitation	60,000	60,000	34,900	25,100
Other	28,000	25,000	18,100	6,900
Total Current Operating Expenditures	392,000	395,000	353,400	41,600
Capital outlay	30,000	30,000	29,100	900
Debt service	1,000	1,000	600	400
Total Expenditures	423,000	426,000	383,100	42,900
Excess of Revenues over Expenditures	4,000	5,000	30,100	25,100
Other Financing Sources (Uses)				
Transfer to Debt Service Fund	—	(5,000)	(5,000)	—
Transfer to Enterprise Fund	—	(6,000)	(6,000)	—
	—	(11,000)	(11,000)	—
Special and Extraordinary Items				
Special Item—Proceeds from Sale of Beach Property	—	—	8,000	8,000
Extraordinary Item— Insurance Recovery Proceeds	—	—	5,750	5,750
	—	—	13,750	13,750
Net Change in Fund Balance	4,000	(6,000)	32,850	38,850
Fund Balance—January 1— As Restated (Note X)	14,000	14,000	14,000	—
Fund Balance—December 31	$ 18,000	$ 8,000	$ 46,850	$ 38,850

Notes:

1. In this example the governing body both (1) revised its original revenue estimates and appropriations and (2) authorized interfund transfers that were not included in the original budget.
2. Because this illustrative example assumes that the budget is adopted on the cash basis, revenues and other financing sources are reported only when collected. Likewise, expenditures and other uses of financial resources are reported only when paid. (The distributions of expenditures to functions on the cash basis is assumed correct for illustrative purposes.)

ILLUSTRATION 4-10	Budgetary Basis and Reconciliation of Budgetary Fund Balance to GAAP Fund Balance General Fund	
Budgetary Fund Balance, December 31, 20X1 (Illustration 4-9)		$46,850
Add: Accrued revenues not included in budgetary fund balance		48,400
Deduct: Accrued expenditures not included in budgetary fund balance		(32,950)
		15,450
GAAP Fund Balance, December 31, 20X1 (Illustration 3-7)		$62,300

Budgetary Basis of Accounting:
A Governmental Unit adopts its budget using the cash basis of accounting. Revenues are recognized when cash is received, and expenditures are recognized when cash is disbursed. As is common in practice, investments are not considered expenditures and short-term borrowings are not considered revenues or other financing sources under the budgetary basis.

ENTRIES DURING 20X2

The only additional step needed to maintain budgetary accountability for the General Fund of A Governmental Unit in 20X2 relates to encumbrances outstanding at the end of 20X1 and the related expenditures made in 20X2. The first entry of 20X2 is to *reverse* the 20X1 entry that closed Encumbrances and Encumbrances Outstanding.

ENCUMBRANCES	$20,000	
ENCUMBRANCES OUTSTANDING		$20,000

To reestablish the encumbrances carried over from 20X1 to facilitate budgetary control for 20X2.

Expenditures Ledger (Encumbrances):

Public Safety	$ 7,000
Health and Sanitation	13,000
	$20,000

When the goods or services ordered in 20X1 are received in 20X2, the usual entries are made to *reverse the encumbrances and record the actual expenditures*. The expenditures are charged against the 20X2 appropriations. Assuming that the goods or services actually cost $21,000, the entry to record their receipt is:

ENCUMBRANCES OUTSTANDING	$20,000	
Expenditures	21,000	
ENCUMBRANCES		$20,000
Vouchers Payable		21,000

To record expenditures for goods and services and to reverse the related encumbrance entry.

Expenditures Ledger (Encumbrances):

Public Safety	$ 7,000
Health and Sanitation	13,000
	$20,000

Expenditures Ledger (Expenditures):

Public Safety	$ 7,400
Health and Sanitation	13,600
	$21,000

If the government wanted to account separately for the goods or services received during 20X2 that were ordered in 20X1, it could use separate General Ledger and/or Expenditures Subsidiary Ledger accounts classified by the year in which the appropriations were made. Furthermore, some of the year-end 20X1 adjusting entries may be reversed at the beginning of 20X2 to facilitate the 20X2 GAAP accounting process and routine.

BUDGETARY PLANNING, CONTROL, AND EVALUATION

The adoption of a budget implies that decisions have been made—on the basis of a planning process—about how the government is to reach its objectives. The accounting system then helps the administrators (1) control the activities authorized to finance and carry out the plans and (2) prepare the statements that permit comparison of actual operations with the budget and evaluation of variances. The first part of this chapter focused on explaining and illustrating how the accounting system is used to accomplish budgetary accountability and reporting. Little attention has been given to the development of the budget or to other aspects of the three key budgetary phases and functions: **planning, control,** and **evaluation**. Each phase is crucial.

Planning The prominence of the budgetary process in government is a natural outgrowth of its environment. **Planning** is a special concern here because, as noted previously:

1. The type, quantity, and quality of governmental goods and services provided are not normally evaluated and adjusted through the open market mechanism.

2. These goods and services (e.g., education, police and fire protection, and sanitation) are often among the most critical to the public interest.

3. The immense scope and diversity of modern government activities make comprehensive, thoughtful, and systematic planning a prerequisite to orderly decision making.

4. Government planning and decision making is generally a joint process involving its citizen "owners," either individually or in groups, their elected representatives in the legislative branch, and members of the executive branch.

The legislative-executive division of powers, the so-called checks and balances, is operative in all states and in most local governments. In these and in most manager-council forms of organization, *"the executive proposes, the legislature disposes"*; that is, the executive is responsible for drafting tentative budgetary plans, but final budgetary plans and revenue- and expenditure-related authorizations are made by the legislative body—often after public hearings in which interested citizens or groups are invited to participate.

Control Budgets are also widely used **control** devices in governments. Budgets facilitate both (1) legislative branch control over the executive branch and (2) chief executive control over subordinate executive agencies or departments. As observed earlier, when a budget is enacted by the legislative branch, the expenditure estimates become **appropriations**—both **authorizations** to expend and expenditure **limitations** on the executive branch.

Appropriations may be enacted in broad terms or in minute detail. When appropriations are enacted in broad terms, the legislature exercises policy-level control and the executive is given much managerial discretion. But when appropriations are enacted in minute detail, the chief executive has almost no discretion and is restricted to carrying out specific, detailed orders from the legislature. Similarly, the chief executive may restrict subordinates by granting agency or departmental expenditure authority in more detailed or specific categories (**allocations**) than those approved by the legislature. Likewise, either the chief executive or the legislature may ration expenditure authority to subordinate agencies or departments in terms of monthly or quarterly expenditure ceilings, referred to as **allotments**. Thus, as discussed in the first part of this chapter, the accounting system must provide information that enables (1) agencies or departments to keep their expenditures within limitations imposed by the chief executive and demonstrate compliance with those limitations, and (2) the chief executive to keep the expenditures of the government within limitations imposed by the legislative branch and demonstrate such compliance.

Recall from earlier discussions that monitoring actual revenues compared to budgeted amounts is critical. Management must institute controls to ensure revenue collections. Specific individuals should be responsible for monitoring actual versus budgeted revenues and alerting management to material variations from expected levels of revenues as early as possible. Similarly, various officials must be responsible for enforcing taxes, licenses, fines and forfeits, and numerous other revenue sources.

Evaluation

The budgetary authority extended to one branch or level of government by another becomes a standard for **evaluating** legal and administrative compliance or noncompliance. The financial reports that compare the budgeted and actual revenue and expenditure amounts for the period (see Illustrations 4-7, 4-8, and 4-9) serve as a basis for evaluating the extent of compliance with standards established by the various "dollar stewardship" accountability relationships in this environment.

BASIC BUDGETARY TERMINOLOGY

Although the operating budget of each year stands alone from a legal standpoint, *budgeting is a continuous process*. Budget officials are engaged each year in

- Ensuring that the *prior* year's budgetary reports are properly prepared and audited.
- Administering the *current* year budget.
- Preparing the budget for the *next* year(s).

Indeed, the budget for any year goes through five phases: (1) preparation; (2) legislative enactment; (3) administration, including internal audit; (4) reporting; and (5) postaudit.

State and local governments typically prepare several types of financial plans that may be referred to as "budgets." For purposes of this discussion, budgets may be classified as:

1. Capital or current
2. Tentative or enacted
3. General or special
4. Fixed or flexible
5. Executive or legislative

Capital vs. Current Budgets

Sound fiscal management requires continual planning for several periods into the future. Most governments provide certain services continuously, or at least for several years; acquire buildings, land, and other major capital assets that must be scheduled and financed (such as by issuing bonds); and must pay long-term debt service commitments. Some SLGs prepare comprehensive multiyear plans that include all current operations, capital outlay, and debt service. Other long-term budgetary plans include *only* the *capital outlay* plans for the organization. This type plan generally covers two to six years and is referred to as a *capital program*.

Each year the current segment of the capital program becomes the *capital budget* in the *current budget.* The current budget also includes the operating budget, which includes the proposed expenditures for current operations and debt service, as well as estimates of all expendable financial resources expected to be available during the current period.

The typical interrelationships of a capital program, capital budget, and current budget are shown in Illustration 4-11; an *actual* summary of the impact of the capital program on the annual operating budgets is presented in Illustration 4-12. The remainder of this chapter is concerned primarily with *current or operating* budgets.

Tentative vs. Enacted Budgets

The key distinction among budgets is their legal status. Various types of documents may be called "budgets" prior to approval by the legislative body. Such *tentative budgets* should be distinguished from the final, *legally enacted budget.* For example, *capital programs* are plans, not executive branch requests, and are subject to change.

Similarly, a *department* budget request may be called a "budget," but it may be changed several times by the department head or budget officials before being included in the chief executive's final proposed budget, which is presented to the legislature. The legislature may make additional changes before the budget is approved and legally enacted. *Enactment of an appropriation bill by the legislative branch is the legal basis of its control over the executive branch.* Only the legislature may revise the terms or conditions of this *final,* legally enacted *budget,* which is the basis for executive branch accountability to the legislature.

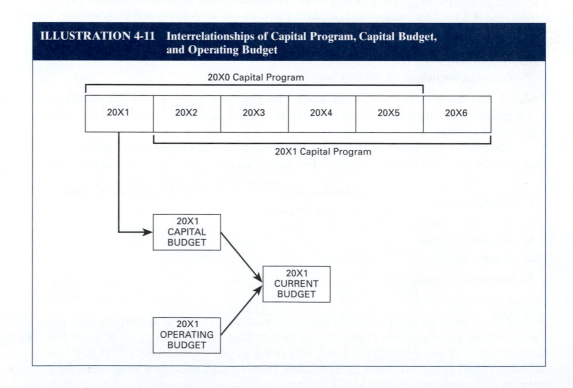

ILLUSTRATION 4-11   Interrelationships of Capital Program, Capital Budget, and Operating Budget

20X0 Capital Program

| 20X1 | 20X2 | 20X3 | 20X4 | 20X5 | 20X6 |

20X1 Capital Program

20X1 CAPITAL BUDGET

20X1 CURRENT BUDGET

20X1 OPERATING BUDGET

ILLUSTRATION 4-12   Five-Year Capital Improvement Program: Summary of Impact on the Operating Budget ($000)

Service Area/Department	Year 1 FY 20X4	Year 2 FY 20X5	Year 3 FY 20X6	Year 4 FY 20X7	Year 5 FY 20X8	Five-Year Total
Neighborhood Services						
Fire	$ 969.2	$ 4,728.8	$ 4,693.9	$ 6,574.0	$ 6,721.6	$ 23,687.5
Library	—	1,205.0	1,242.2	1,278.0	1,316.4	5,041.6
Parks and Recreation	143.0	3,077.5	3,702.1	3,702.7	3,704.3	14,329.6
Police	—	—	—	—	88.0	88.0
	1,112.2	9,011.3	9,638.2	11,554.7	11,830.3	43,146.7
Environment and Development						
Transportation	—	1,491.0	1,535.7	1,581.9	1,629.3	6,237.9
Tucson Water	9,979.9	10,471.1	10,873.3	11,283.1	11,760.8	54,368.2
Environmental Management	890.0	1,140.0	1,170.0	1,200.0	1,230.0	5,630.0
	10,869.9	13,102.1	13,579.0	14,065.0	14,620.1	66,236.1
Nondepartmental						
General	170.0	351.0	395.7	407.6	419.8	1,744.1
	170.0	351.0	395.7	407.6	419.8	1,744.1
Total	$12,152.1	$22,464.4	$23,612.9	$26,027.3	$26,870.2	$111,126.9
Source of Funds Summary						
General Purpose Funds						
General Fund	$ 2,172.2	$ 9,297.3	$ 9,927.5	$11,849.1	$12,127.5	$ 45,373.6
Library Fund: General Fund Transfer	—	602.5	621.1	639.0	658.2	2,520.8
Mass Transit Fund: General Fund Transfer	—	1,434.1	1,477.1	1,521.4	1,567.1	5,999.7
	2,172.2	11,333.9	12,025.7	14,009.5	14,352.8	53,894.1
Grants and Contributions						
Highway User Revenue Fund	—	56.9	58.6	60.5	62.2	238.2
Library Fund: Pima County Contribution	—	602.5	621.1	639.0	658.2	2,520.8
	—	659.4	679.7	699.5	720.4	2,759.0
Enterprise Funds						
Tucson Water Revenue and Operations Fund	9,979.9	10,471.1	10,873.3	11,283.1	11,760.8	54,368.2
	9,979.9	10,471.1	10,873.3	11,283.1	11,760.8	54,368.2
Other Local Funds						
General Fund: TEAM Fees and Charges	—	—	34.2	35.2	36.2	105.6
	—	—	34.2	35.2	36.2	105.6
Total	$12,152.1	$22,464.4	$23,612.9	$26,027.3	$26,870.2	$111,126.9

Source: A recent City of Tucson, Arizona, capital program.

General vs. Special Budgets

The budgets of general government activities—commonly financed through the General Fund, Special Revenue Funds, and Debt Service Funds—are referred to as *general budgets.* A budget prepared for any other fund is referred to as a *special budget.* Special budgets are commonly enacted for Capital Projects Funds, as well as for Internal Service Funds and Enterprise Funds. Legally adopted budgets and appropriations are not usually required for fiduciary funds.

Fixed vs. Flexible Budgets

Fixed budgets are those in which appropriations are for specific (fixed) dollar amounts of expenditures or expenses. These appropriated amounts may not be exceeded because of changes in demand for governmental goods or services. On the other hand, expenditures or expenses authorized by *flexible budgets* are *fixed per unit* of goods or services but are *variable in total* according to demand for the goods or services.

Fixed budgets are relatively simple to prepare and administer and are more easily understood than flexible budgets. Also, fixed budgets lend themselves to the desire of strong legislatures to limit (control) the discretion of the chief executive. Finally, fixed budgets are readily adaptable to integrating budgetary control techniques into accounting systems and are consistent with the intent of allocating a fixed amount of financial resources among various departments or programs. Governmental fund budgets are almost invariably fixed expenditure budgets, as was true for A Governmental Unit's budget (Illustration 4-1).

Flexible budgets are more realistic when changes in the quantities of goods or services provided directly affect resource availability and expenditure or expense requirements and when formal budgetary control (in the account structure) is not deemed essential. Flexible budgets—of either expenses or expenditures—are appropriate for some Enterprise Funds and Internal Service Funds, but are not widely used.

Executive vs. Legislative Budgets

Budgets are also sometimes categorized by the *preparer*. As noted earlier, budget preparation is usually considered an executive function, though the legislature may revise the budget prior to approval. In some instances, however, the legislative branch prepares the budget, possibly subject to executive veto; in other instances, the budget may originate with a joint legislative-executive committee (possibly with citizen representatives) or with a committee composed solely of citizens or constituents. Such budgets are frequently referred to by such terms as *executive* budget, *legislative* budget, *joint* budget, and *committee* budget, respectively.

BUDGETARY APPROACHES AND EMPHASES

A government's budgetary system should be designed to fit its environmental factors—some of which may be unique—and should provide a budgetary planning, control, and evaluation balance that is appropriate to its circumstances. Thus, do *not* expect to find two governments with identical budgetary approaches and procedures.

The proposed budget provides information to decision makers and indicates the decisions made by the executive branch. Top officials in the executive branch develop policy guidelines for departmental supervisors to use to support departmental budget requests. The chief executive, with the assistance of the budgetary staff, decides what information and budget requests will go to the legislative body. The ultimate example of the use of the budget to indicate the decisions made by the legislative branch is the enacted appropriations bill, a law.

The proposed and enacted governmental fund budgets are important internal management and compliance assurance tools. Accordingly this chapter focuses next on governmental fund budget preparation, including the traditional expenditure budgeting approach, legislative consideration and action with regard to a proposed budget, and budget execution.

BUDGET PREPARATION

A substantial part of most government *budgeting* textbooks is devoted to designing, planning, and implementing appropriate budget preparation procedures. In addition, many SLGs have developed extensive and detailed manuals on budget preparation procedures. Our budget preparation discussions are not comparably exhaustive and detailed but summarize the usual executive budget preparation process from the perspective of the governmental accountant and auditor.

Overview

Sound financial planning requires that budget preparation begin in time for the budget to be adopted before the beginning of the budget period. To ensure that adequate time will be allowed, a budget calendar, listing each step in the budgetary process and the time allowed for its completion, should be prepared. Budget preparation begins with several preliminary estimates, then proceeds in a manner similar to that shown in Illustration 4-13.

Preliminary Estimates

The budget officer and chief executive typically begin preliminary work on the budget for the upcoming year before the steps indicated in the budget cycle are begun in order to:

- Make preliminary estimates of the overall budgetary outlook and parameters—such as the overall levels of expected revenues and appropriations that might be made, including the probable ranges of overall revenues and appropriations increases and decreases.
- Inform department heads and others involved in the budgeting process of the plausible ranges of appropriation requests, the chief executive's priorities for the upcoming year, and related matters.

The preliminary estimates of the ideal levels of appropriations and expenditures during the upcoming year almost always exceed the financial resources estimated to be available. Thus, *budgeting has been described as "the process of allocating scarce resources to unlimited demands."*

The **basic formula** for **budget** decision makers is:

Estimated fund balance, beginning of budget year.............	$ X
Add: Estimated revenues and other financing sources (e.g., transfers from other funds), budget year	Y
Total appropriable resources, budget year...................	$ X + Y
Deduct: Estimated expenditures (appropriations) and other uses of financial resources (e.g., transfers to other funds), budget year...	Z
Estimated fund balance, end of year.....................	$X + Y – Z

After estimating the fund balance to be available at the beginning of the upcoming budget year, the budget officer must obtain preliminary estimates of

1. The revenues expected from all revenue sources at current rates of taxes, fees, and other charges.
2. Any other sources of appropriable resources (e.g., transfers from other funds).
3. The fund balance needed at the end of the upcoming budget year for carryover to the next year.

The budget officer and the chief executive then compare these estimates with revenues, expenditures, and interfund transfers of prior years and integrate their knowledge of changes in demands on the government and its programs. Such analyses should provide an indication of the adequacy of estimated financial resources to finance the needed expenditures.

Preparing the Budget

Once the preliminary estimates have been evaluated, budget preparation proceeds as indicated in Illustration 4-13:

1. **Expenditures Requested.** Most expenditure requests originate at the departmental level, but *nondepartmental* expenditure requirements (such as for debt service) also must be considered in developing the total expenditure needs included in the *Expenditures Summary.*

2. **Estimates of Appropriable Financial Resources.** Both departmental and nondepartmental revenues must be estimated—and both *estimated beginning* fund balance and *required ending* fund balance must be considered—in arriving at the *Summary of Available Balances and Projected Revenues.*

3. **The Executive Budget.** This budget is a **compromise** between (a) the expenditure authority requested and (b) the expendable financial resources estimated to be available to finance the expenditure requests.

The chief executive and department heads typically interact frequently during the budget preparation process. For example,

- The chief executive may revise the preliminary parameters and ranges of plausible departmental appropriation requests—for example, that appropriations will only be increased up to 3%—and indicate his or her budget priorities.

- The department heads usually confer informally with the budget officer or chief executive during the budget preparation process, possibly seeking exceptions to the overall budget guidelines for certain activities or to persuade the chief executive to place special priority on certain programs.

- After reviewing the departmental appropriation requests, the budget officer or chief executive may confer with department heads to revise these requests in preparing the final executive budget.

ILLUSTRATION 4-13   Traditional Information Flows—Budget Preparation

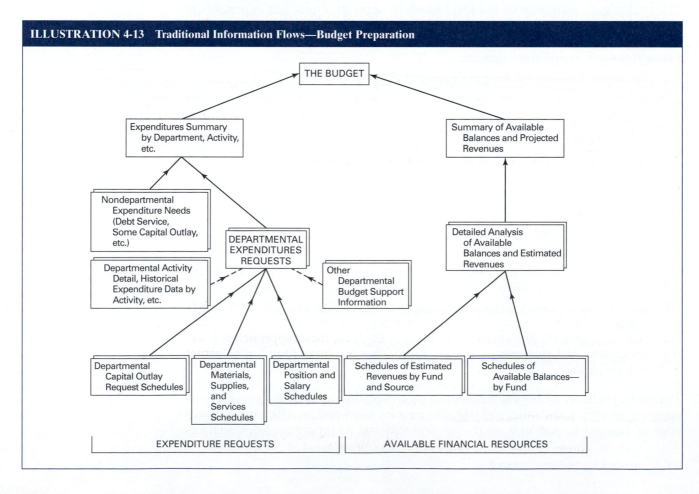

Each revenue source is analyzed in detail—in terms of past amounts, trends, factors apt to affect it next year, and expected level in the upcoming year—in preparing the proposed budget. Because most revenues relate to the government as a whole (e.g., property taxes, sales taxes, and interest), the budget officer makes most revenue estimates. However, the various departments often estimate the revenues that relate to specific departments, such as inspections, permits, and charges for services.

Revenue Estimates and Requests

To *simplify* the earlier illustrations, we assumed that A Governmental Unit's budget is presented, approved, controlled, accounted for, and reported in six broad *revenue source categories:*

- Taxes
- Licenses and Permits
- Intergovernmental
- Charges for Services
- Fines and Forfeits
- Other

As noted previously, revenues typically are controlled, accounted for, and reported on in more detail in practice. Indeed, many governments have hundreds of revenue-related accounts.

Each departmental expenditure category is similarly analyzed in detail—in terms of past amounts, trends, factors apt to affect it next year, and its necessary level in the upcoming year—in preparing the budget. This is a major, time-consuming task because governments often have hundreds or even thousands of expenditure-related accounts. As noted earlier, much interaction may occur between and among the department heads, budget officer, and chief executive in determining the appropriation proposals for the upcoming year.

Expenditure Estimates and Requests

Several general approaches to governmental budgeting have marked differences in their emphasis on planning, control, and evaluation. The approaches differ in their suitability for planning, control, and evaluation. The principal groups that exercise control are executive branch officials and the legislature. However, citizens, creditors, officials of higher-level governments, and other groups often have control powers that indirectly affect the budgetary planning, control, and evaluation process.

Expenditure Budgeting Approaches

The most common approaches to expenditure budgeting may be characterized as:

1. Object-of-expenditure
2. Performance
3. Program and planning-programming-budgeting (PPB)
4. Zero-base budgeting (ZBB)

The *object-of-expenditure* approach is emphasized here because it is used widely and underlies the other approaches. Budget nomenclature is not standardized, each approach may be implemented to varying degrees, these approaches overlap significantly, and elements of all four approaches are often found in an actual budget. One should always look to the *substance* of a budgetary approach rather than to the terminology used. For example, an object-of-expenditure budget may be referred to publicly as a performance, program, or zero-base budget because these have been considered the more modern approaches in recent years. However, regardless of the approach used to develop a budget, appropriations or allocations of appropriations at the object-of-expenditure level of detail are essential for sound budgetary control.

The Object-of-Expenditure Approach

The **object-of-expenditure** approach to expenditure budgeting, often referred to as the line-item object-of-expenditure approach or the **traditional approach**, has an *expenditure control* orientation. The object-of-expenditure approach became popular as the basis for legislative control over the executive branch, and it continues to be widely used, though elements of newer approaches are often added.

Essential Elements of the Approach Simply described, in the object-of-expenditure method:

1. Subordinate agencies submit *detailed* budget requests to the chief executive in terms of the *types* of expenditures to be made. These requests include the number of people to be hired in each specified position and salary level and the specific goods or services to be purchased during the upcoming period.

2. The chief executive compiles and modifies the agency budget requests and submits an overall request for the organization to the legislature in the same object-of-expenditure terms.

3. The legislature makes *line-item* appropriations, possibly after revising the requests, along *object-of-expenditure* lines. Performance or program data may be included in the budget document to supplement or support the object-of-expenditure requests.

The basic elements of this approach are shown in Illustration 4-14.

ILLUSTRATION 4-14   Simplified Object-of-Expenditure Budget
(Classified by Organizational Unit and Object-of-Expenditure)

Mayor's Office

Police Department

Salaries and Wages:	Rate		
1—Chief	$137,000	$137,000	
2—Captains	69,500	139,000	
3—Sergeants	47,000	141,000	
22—Patrol officers	28,000	616,000	
3—Radio operators	20,000	60,000	
10—School guards (part-time)	8,800	88,000	$1,181,000
Supplies:			
Stationery and other office supplies		12,200	
Janitorial supplies		31,100	
Gasoline and oil		43,000	
Uniforms		22,200	
Other		5,500	114,000
Other Services and Charges:			
Telephone		11,400	
Out-of-town travel		21,800	
Towing and storage		11,600	
Utilities		23,000	
Other		9,200	77,000
Capital Outlay:			
2—Motorcycles (net)		16,600	
2—Patrol cars (net)		54,400	71,000
Total Police Department			$1,443,000

Fire Department

Total Expenditures Budget			$9,801,720

Control Points As discussed briefly earlier in this chapter, various degrees of appropriation control that a legislature might exercise through object-of-expenditure budgets may be illustrated by identifying the possible **budgetary control points** in the example in Illustration 4-14. A great degree of legislative control will be typified if appropriations are stated in terms of the most detailed level. For example:

- The police department appropriations might be in *detailed line-item* object-of-expenditure listings of one chief, $137,000; two captains, $139,000; and so on.

- Alternatively, a lesser amount of control results if appropriations are stated in terms of object *classes*—that is, Salaries and Wages, $1,181,000; Supplies, $114,000; Other Services and Charges, $77,000; and Capital Outlay, $71,000. In this case, the detailed line-item objects listed indicate the types of goods and services to be secured, but the executive branch has discretion over determining an appropriate mix as long as these expenditure category subtotals are not exceeded.

- An even greater degree of executive discretion is permitted when its appropriations are stated in a lump sum at the *departmental level,* for example, police department, $1,443,000. Even though all of the supporting details would have been developed during the budget process and probably would have been presented to the legislature, only departmental totals would be legally binding on the executive branch in such a situation.

In any event, *the accounting system must capture data in sufficient detail to permit budgetary control and accountability at the legislative-to-executive budgetary control points.*

Furthermore, recall that the chief executive may refine the level of legislative control—and make departmental *allotments* and/or *allocations*—to achieve the desired degree of fiscal control over subordinates. In such cases, the *accounting system must accumulate data in sufficient detail to permit budgetary control and accountability at the chief executive–department head budgetary control points.*

Other Estimates and Requests

The budget officer and chief executive might also include other proposed sources and uses of financial resources, such as interfund transfers. To *simplify* earlier illustrations, we *assumed that interfund transfers are not included in the annual operating budget but are separately authorized, nonbudgeted sources and uses of expendable financial resources.* In practice, many governments include expected transfers in their budgets.

The Budget Document

Given these simplifying assumptions, assume also that the budget proposed (and subsequently approved) for a governmental fund (e.g., the General Fund) of A Governmental Unit for the 20X2 fiscal year is that presented in Illustration 4-15.

LEGISLATIVE CONSIDERATION AND ACTION

After receiving the proposed budget document, the legislative body must **adopt** an **official** budget. A state legislature or the council or commissioners of a large city usually turn the proposed budget over to a committee. The committee makes investigations, calls on department heads and the chief executive for justifications of their requests, and conducts public hearings. The committee then makes its recommendations to the legislature. In smaller municipalities, the council or board of supervisors may act as a committee of the whole to consider the budget.

After completing the budget hearings and investigations, the legislative body *adopts* the budget, as revised. *The appropriations detail adopted in the act*

ILLUSTRATION 4-15   Annual Operating Budget

Annual Operating Budget
A Governmental Unit
Governmental Fund
20X2 Fiscal Year

Estimated Revenues

Taxes	$ 900,000
Licenses and permits	400,000
Intergovernmental	350,000
Charges for services	50,000
Fines and forfeits	100,000
Other	200,000
	2,000,000

Appropriations

General government	250,000
Public safety	575,000
Highways and streets	500,000
Health and sanitation	375,000
Culture and recreation	200,000
Other	50,000
	1,950,000
Excess of Estimated Revenues over Appropriations	50,000
Estimated Fund Balance—Beginning of 20X2	450,000
Estimated Fund Balance—End of 20X2	$ 500,000

Note:

In practice, the estimated revenue and revenue accounts would be established in more detailed source categories, and the appropriation and expenditure accounts would be established by department and object-of-expenditure categories.

determines the flexibility granted to the executive branch by the legislative body and the budgetary control points.

- Lump-sum appropriations may be made for functions or activities or, more likely, for departments or other organization units.
- Many legislative bodies insist on fairly detailed object-of-expenditure data in the executive budget, and appropriations may be made in comparable detail.

Legislative approval of appropriations *authorizes expenditures.* It is also necessary to provide the means of financing them. Some revenues (e.g., interest on investments) will accrue to the governmental unit without any legal action on its part. Other revenues will come as a result of legal action taken in the past. Examples of these are licenses and fees, income taxes, and sales taxes, the rates for which continue until the legislative body changes them. A third type of revenue—for example, the general property tax—usually requires new legal action each year. Accordingly, as soon as the legislative body has passed the appropriations ordinance or act, it proceeds to levy general property taxes.

BUDGET EXECUTION

Just as the budget approved by the legislative body expresses in financial terms the government's planned activities, the process of budget execution includes every operating decision and transaction made during the budget period. Accounting records each transaction and the results of the transactions, and permits their summarization, reporting, and comparison with plans (the approved budget). Therefore, *the following chapters that describe the accounting and reporting for the governmental funds are all related to budget execution.*

The legally adopted revenue estimates and appropriations are such a controlling influence in government that, contrary to business practice, *the budget is recorded as an integral part of the accounting system.* Among other benefits, this practice helps governments avoid inadvertent overexpenditure of appropriations. In the general ledger, as well as in the subsidiary ledgers for revenues and expenditures, legally adopted *budgeted* amounts are recorded and can be directly compared with their *actual* counterparts during the year and at year end. Similarly, accountability for budget *compliance* is reported in the financial statements and schedules together with the appropriate GAAP-basis information.

Concluding Comments

Budgeting, budgetary accounting, and budgetary reporting are uniquely important features of the governmental fund accounting and financial reporting environment. Indeed, governmental fund accounting is sometimes referred to as budgetary accounting, and budgeting, budgetary accounting, and budgetary reporting have been recurring topics on the Uniform CPA Examination.

Accordingly, much of this chapter is devoted to explaining and illustrating how the legally adopted budget is incorporated into the accounts to permit monitoring the actual results compared to the enacted budget using the accounting system. Preparation and use of budgetary reports and budgetary reporting requirements are discussed and illustrated, and the chapter concludes with discussions of budgetary terminology, the most common budgetary approach, and preparation of the annual operating budget. In sum, the chapter builds on the coverage of GAAP-based accounting and reporting to complete coverage of the basics of accounting and financial reporting for General and Special Revenue Funds.

The next two chapters build on the foundation established in Chapters 3 and 4. Chapter 5 addresses revenue accounting for governmental funds in more detail. Chapter 6 covers major expenditure accounting issues for governmental funds.

Questions

Q4-1 Governmental budgeting and budgetary control are deemed so important by the GASB that it devotes an entire principle to the subject. Why?

Q4-2 Distinguish between the following types of budgets: (a) capital and current, (b) tentative and enacted, (c) general and special, (d) fixed and flexible, and (e) executive and legislative.

Q4-3 Budgeting is a continuous process. Explain.

Q4-4 What are budgetary control points? How do they affect budgetary accounting and reporting?

Q4-5 Why are encumbrances not considered expenditures under the modified accrual (GAAP) basis of governmental fund accounting?

Q4-6 Why might a local government not prepare and adopt its General Fund annual operating budget on the modified accrual (GAAP) basis?

Q4-7 Revenue estimates and appropriations enacted are standards against which performance is subsequently measured. What implications can be drawn at year end if variances from these standards occur? If no variances occur?

Q4-8 In business accounting, a single general ledger account—such as Cash, Accounts Receivable, Investments, or Accounts Payable—typically controls the related subsidiary ledger accounts. Explain how in governmental fund accounting the general ledger accounts control (a) the Revenues Subsidiary Ledger accounts and (b) the Expenditures Subsidiary Ledger accounts.

Q4-9 Illustrations 4-3 and 4-4 show Revenues Subsidiary Ledger accounts classified by major revenue source category and Expenditures Subsidiary Ledger accounts classified by function. Could more detailed subsidiary ledger accounts be necessary in practice? Explain.

Q4-10 An *interim* budgetary comparison statement for a governmental fund is found in Illustration 4-7. (a) Should this statement be prepared on the unit's budgetary basis or on the GAAP basis? Why? (b) Why are interim budgetary comparison statements important to effective management control and legislative oversight?

Q4-11 Explain how the budgetary fund balance account is used. What effect does recording the budget have on the GAAP-based financial statements? How is Budgetary Fund Balance reported in the General Fund Balance Sheet?

Q4-12 Annual budgetary comparison statements for A Governmental Unit's General Fund are shown in Illustrations 4-8 and 4-9. (a) Why do the reported variances differ between these two statements? (b) Why does the GASB require governments to include both original and revised budget data in a budgetary comparison statement?

Q4-13 Explain the purpose, nature, and effect of the entry re-establishing encumbrances in the accounts at the beginning of a new year.

Exercises

E4-1 (Multiple Choice) Identify the best answer for each of the following:
1. *General* budgets are most common for which of the following funds?
   a. General Fund.
   b. Capital Projects Fund.
   c. Permanent Fund.
   d. Internal Service Fund.
2. *Special* budgets are best defined as budgets
   a. that include special items.
   b. prepared for any fund other than the General, Special Revenue, and Debt Service Funds.
   c. that are always multiyear in nature.
   d. for proprietary funds.
3. Which of the following statements about capital budgets is *true*?
   a. Most capital program budgets cover only General Fund capital outlay for the next year.
   b. The current segment of a capital program is typically included as the capital outlay of the current annual budget.
   c. Governments typically have one year capital plans for governmental funds but multiyear plans for proprietary funds.
   d. Capital budgets include proposed expenditures for operations and debt service as well as for capital outlay.
4. Which of the following statements is *false*?
   a. Generally Accepted Accounting Principles (GAAP) dictate the basis of budgeting for all governmental funds.
   b. Budgets of different governments may have different budgetary control points.
   c. A good budget process incorporates a long-term perspective, even if the budget is adopted annually.
   d. Allocations are executive branch subdivisions of an appropriation to more detailed expenditure classifications.
5. Which of the following statements is *true*?
   a. Encumbrances are equivalent to expenditures, and encumbrances outstanding at the end of a year should be reported as liabilities.
   b. No expenditure can be reported without first being encumbered.
   c. Encumbrances are recorded at the estimated cost of goods ordered or services contracted for. The subsequent amount recognized as expenditures upon receipt of the goods or services must equal the encumbered amount.
   d. Encumbrances are recorded at the estimated cost of goods ordered or services contracted for. The subsequent amount recognized as expenditures upon receipt of the goods or services equals the actual cost.

E4-2 (Multiple Choice—Budgetary Accounting and Reporting) Identify the best answer for each of the following:
1. Appropriation requests for the General Fund are commonly approved, controlled, accounted for, and reported in each of the following expenditure categories except:
   a. Function or program.
   b. Organizational unit.
   c. Fund.
   d. Object of expenditure.

2. Which of the following statements would be *true* concerning budgetary integration?
   a. The integration of budgetary accounts into the general ledger does not affect the asset and liability accounts.
   b. Estimated revenue control accounts are often used to record actual revenues during the year.
   c. Budgetary integration is the integration of both capital budget and operating budget data.
   d. Budgetary integration affects the amount reported as assigned fund balance.

3. The budgetary basis of accounting is
   a. determined by a governmental entity's governing body or by law or regulation.
   b. dictated by GAAP.
   c. the same for all governmental entities.
   d. always the cash basis.

4. Which of the following GAAP requirements for budgetary reporting is true?
   a. Original and final budget amounts are required for the General Fund only.
   b. Original and final budget amounts are required for the General Fund and major Special Revenue Funds only.
   c. Original and final budget *variance* amounts are required only for those funds that adopt an annual budget.
   d. Final budget amounts only are required for all governmental and proprietary funds.

5. The following GAAP requirements for budgetary reporting are true *except*
   a. budgetary comparisons for the General Fund and major Special Revenue Funds *must* include expenditure data that is at least as detailed as the appropriations detail legally adopted in the budget.
   b. budgetary comparisons for the General Fund and major Special Revenue Funds *must* be reported as required supplementary information (RSI).
   c. the budgetary basis of accounting may be the cash basis.
   d. governmental entities may report required budgetary information as part of the basic financial statements.

E4-3

1. Which of the following transactions requires entries recording encumbrances in an Expenditures Subsidiary Ledger?
   a. Legal adoption of the General Fund budget.
   b. Purchase of equipment on account.
   c. Accrual of salaries and wages.
   d. Order of supplies.

2. Which of the following items does a government with a modified accrual and encumbrances basis budget report differently in its budgetary basis statement of revenues, expenditures, and changes in fund balances—budget and actual—than in its GAAP-based statement of revenues, expenditures, and changes in total fund balances?
   a. Personal services expenditures.
   b. Encumbrances outstanding.
   c. Interfund reimbursements.
   d. Proceeds of general long-term debt issuances.

3. The budget data presented in a school district General Fund statement of revenues, expenditures, and changes in fund balances—budget and actual—are to be
   a. the original, legally adopted budget.
   b. the final revised budget, as amended.
   c. both the original, legally adopted budget and the final revised budget, as amended.
   d. presented on the modified accrual basis of accounting even if the budget is adopted on the cash basis.

4. Allotments are best defined as
   a. legislative appropriations subdivided into more detailed expenditure categories by the executive branch.
   b. legislative appropriations subdivided by time periods.
   c. operating grants that must be used for a specific purpose.
   d. a budgeting tool that must be used in conjunction with the purchases method of inventory accounting.

E4-4 (Budgetary accounts) Indicate which of the following transactions require entries to accounts used only for budgetary control purposes, even if other accounts also are involved.

1. Adopted the budget—estimated revenues of $5,000,000 and appropriations of $4,900,000.
2. Levied property taxes of $3,500,000. One percent has been uncollectible historically.
3. Paid salaries of $2,700,000.
4. Hired a new director of public works at an agreed salary of $60,000.

5. Ordered materials and supplies expected to cost $103,000.
6. Amended the appropriation for public works to increase it by $10,000.
7. Received half of the materials and supplies order at an actual cost of $51,500.

E4-5 (Budgetary and other entries—General Ledger) Prepare the general journal entries required for the transactions in **E4-4**. Assuming a beginning total fund balance of $1,000,000, what would the total fund balance be after taking into consideration the effects of these transactions?

E4-6 (Budgetary Entries—General Ledger) The city of Cherokee Hill adopted its fiscal year 20X8 General Fund budget, using the modified accrual basis of accounting, on January 1, 20X8. Budgeted revenues were $17 million; budgeted expenditures were $16,500,000.

- August 5, 20X8, the Cherokee Hill city council adopted a motion by Mayor Clyde Fisher to increase the police department appropriation by $200,000. All other budgeted items remained unchanged.
- September 1, the city council revised the estimate of sales tax revenues upward by $60,000.

Required
a. Record the budgetary events in the General Fund general ledger accounts.
b. Close the General Fund accounts (both budgetary and actual events). Assume the actual transaction entries were recorded properly. In addition to the foregoing events, assume the following information:

- Actual revenues for the year totaled $17,300,000.
- Expenditures for the year totaled $16,600,000.
- Transfers to Debt Service Funds totaled $800,000.
- Encumbrances of $80,000 were outstanding at year-end.

c. Assuming a beginning total fund balance of $3,000,000, what is the postclosing, total fund balance to be reported in the GAAP financial statements for the city of Cherokee Hill?

E4-7 (General Ledger–Subsidiary Ledgers Relationship, Closing Entries, Budgetary Statement) The City Council of the City of Eastover adopted the following budget for its General Fund for 20X8. The budget was not revised during the fiscal year. The budgetary basis was modified accrual.

City of Eastover
General Fund
Budget
For Fiscal Year 20X8

Estimated Revenues		
Taxes......................................	$3,500,000	
Interest and penalties.......................	96,000	
Licenses and permits	240,000	
Fines and forfeitures........................	75,000	
Intergovernmental grants	1,300,000	
Investment income..........................	85,000	
Total estimated revenues................		$5,296,000
Appropriations		
General government	$ 560,000	
Public safety	1,900,000	
Highways and streets	1,090,000	
Health and sanitation......................	500,000	
Economic development.....................	500,000	
Public housing............................	370,000	
Parks and recreation.......................	330,000	
Total appropriations......................		5,250,000
Budgeted excess of revenues		
over appropriations		$ 46,000

[Handwritten margin notes:]

4-6
Budget
Est. Rev 17mil   16.5mil
  Approp
Budg FB   500K
Budg FB 200K   300K
  Approp

Est. Revenue 60K 60K
  Budg FB

est Rev | Approp
7mil | 16.5mil
60K	200K
17.06mil	16.7mil 16.7m

B FB
200K | 500K
     | 60K
360K | 360K

Actual

Rev 17.3m
Exp   16.6m
Transfers 800K
Encum   80K
Fund balance 180M

The preclosing trial balances of the Revenues and Expenditures Subsidiary Ledgers at the end of fiscal year 20X8 are:

City of Eastover
General Fund
Preclosing Trial Balances
Revenues and Expenditures Subsidiary Ledgers
September 30, 20X8

	Debit	Credit
Revenues Subsidiary Ledger		
Taxes..	$ 30,000	
Interest and penalties.................................		5,000
Licenses and permits	20,000	
Fines and forfeitures...............................		13,000
Intergovernmental grants		500,000
Investment income................................	5,000	
Totals	$ 55,000	$518,000
Expenditures Subsidiary Ledger		
General government	$ 200	
Public safety		$ 500
Highways and streets		1,000
Health and sanitation.............................	1,000	
Economic development...........................		1,800
Public housing....................................		1,800
Parks and recreation.............................	330	
Totals	$ 1,530	$ 5,100

The only encumbrances outstanding at year end were for $75,000 of unperformed contracts for the Health and Sanitation function. The beginning total fund balance was $312,000.

a. Prepare closing entries for both the General Ledger accounts and the subsidiary ledgers of the City of Eastover General Fund. (*Hint:* You will have to derive the General Ledger balances of some accounts.)

b. Prepare the Statement of Revenues, Expenditures, and Changes in Fund Balance—Budget and Actual for the General Fund of the City of Eastover for fiscal year 20X8.

E4-8 (General Ledger Entries) Record the following transactions in the General Ledger accounts of the General Fund of the Keffer Independent School District.

1. Ordered textbooks with an estimated cost of $80,000.
2. Ordered laboratory supplies with an estimated cost of $25,000.
3. Signed a contract with Victory Transportation Services for athletic team transportation. The estimated total cost of the services was $7,000.
4. Hired a new clerk and approved a salary of $18,000 per year.
5. The textbooks were received at an actual cost of $80,400. The invoice was approved for payment.
6. Approximately half of the laboratory supplies were received and vouchered at an actual cost of $12,000. (Estimated cost was $12,400.)
7. Actual transportation costs billed to Keffer School District by Victory Transportation Services were $8,000.

E4-9 (Encumbrances) Record the following transactions in the General Fund general ledger accounts. (Analyze the effects of the transactions on all other funds and nonfund accounts.)

1. Martinsville ordered supplies for its General Fund departments at an estimated cost of $300,000.
2. Martinsville ordered equipment for its General Fund departments at an estimated cost of $490,250.
3. Martinsville received half the supplies ordered. The actual cost of $151,000 was paid.
4. Martinsville received the equipment it had ordered. The actual cost was $490,250.

Problems

P4-1 (Operating Budget Preparation) The finance director of the Bethandy Independent School District is making preliminary estimates of the budget outlook for the General Fund for the 20X8 fiscal year. These estimates will permit the superintendent to advise the department heads properly when budget instructions and forms are distributed. She has assembled the following information:

	Estimated 20X7	Expected Change— 20X8
1. **Revenues**		
Property taxes....................................	$2,000,000	+6%
State aid..	1,000,000	+3%
Federal grants..................................	500,000	−$40,000
Other...	300,000	+$10,000
	$3,800,000	
2. **Expenditures**		
Salaries and wages..............................	$2,700,000	?
Utilities..	400,000	+4%
Maintenance....................................	300,000	+$24,000
Capital outlay..................................	200,000	−$15,000
Debt service....................................	100,000	+$20,000
Other...	50,000	+$ 5,000
	$3,750,000	

3. Fund balance at the end of 20X7 is expected to be $1,600,000; at least $1,500,000 must be available at the end of 20X8 for carryover to help finance 20X9 operations.

Required

a. Prepare a draft operating budget for the Bethandy Independent School District for the 20X8 fiscal year, including 20X7 comparative data and expected change computations. Assume that 20X8 appropriations are to equal 20X8 estimated revenues.

b. What total salaries and wages amount and average percentage increase or decrease are implied in the draft operating budget prepared in part (a)? What are the maximum salary and wages amount and percentage increase that seem to be feasible in 20X8?

P4-2 (Budgetary and Other Entries—General and Subsidiary Ledgers) The Murphy County Commissioners adopted the following General Fund budget for the 20X8 fiscal year:

Murphy County
General Fund
Budget—20X8

Estimated Revenues:	
Taxes..	$ 8,000,000
Licenses and Permits.......................................	800,000
Intergovernmental..	2,000,000
Charges for Services	200,000
Fines and Forfeits	400,000
Other..	600,000
	12,000,000
Appropriations:	
General Government	1,000,000
Public Safety	4,000,000
Highways and Streets	5,000,000
Health and Sanitation......................................	900,000
Culture and Recreation	400,000
Other..	600,000
	11,900,000
Excess of Estimated Revenues over Appropriations....................	100,000
Fund Balance—Beginning...................................	1,400,000
Fund Balance—Ending (Anticipated).............................	$ 1,500,000

The following events occurred during 20X8:

1. Purchase orders issued and contracts let were expected to cost:

General Government...	$ 300,000
Public Safety	1,200,000
Highways and Streets..	2,500,000
Health and Sanitation	500,000
Culture and Recreation	300,000
Other	200,000
	$5,000,000

2. The commissioners reviewed the budget during the year and (a) revised the estimate of Intergovernmental Revenues to $1,500,000 and reduced the Public Safety and Highways and Streets appropriations by $225,000 each to partially compensate for the anticipated decline in intergovernmental revenues, and (b) increased the Health and Sanitation appropriation by $70,000 because of costs incurred in connection with an unusual outbreak of Tasmanian flu.

3. Revenues (actual) for 20X8 were

Taxes...	$ 8,150,000
Licenses and Permits............................	785,000
Intergovernmental...............................	1,520,000
Charges for Services	210,000
Fines and Forfeits	395,000
Other...	500,000
	$11,560,000

4. Goods and services under purchase orders and contracts were received:

	Estimated Cost	Actual Cost
General Government..............	$ 280,000	$ 278,000
Public Safety....................	900,000	910,000
Highways and Streets.............	2,500,000	2,500,000
Health and Sanitation	440,000	440,000
Culture and Recreation...........	300,000	295,000
Other	180,000	181,000
	$4,600,000	$4,604,000

The remaining orders are still outstanding.

5. Other expenditures incurred were

General Government	$ 700,000
Public Safety	2,560,000
Highways and Streets	2,271,000
Health and Sanitation..........................	485,000
Culture and Recreation	45,000
Other..	391,000
	$6,452,000

1. Set up general ledger T-accounts and also revenues and expenditures subsidiary ledgers like those in Illustrations 4-3 and 4-4. ***Required***
2. Record the Murphy County 20X8 General Fund budget in the general ledger and subsidiary ledger accounts, keying these entries "B" (for budget). Then record the numbered transactions and events, keying these entries by those numbers.

P4-3 (Budgetary Comparison Statement) This problem is based on the information about the Murphy County General Fund budgeted and actual transactions and events described in Problem 4-2.

1. Prepare a budgetary comparison statement for the General Fund of Murphy County for the 20X8 fiscal year. The statement should present revenues (by source category), expenditures ***Required***

and encumbrances (by function), and the excess of revenues over (under) expenditures and encumbrances. Use these column headings:

Original Budget
Revised Budget
Actual
Variance—Favorable (Unfavorable)

Assume that no encumbrances were outstanding at the beginning of 20X8.

2. Because encumbrances do not constitute expenditures, some governmental fund budgetary comparison statements omit data on encumbrances. (a) If no encumbrances were outstanding at the beginning of 20X8, what effects would omission of encumbrances data have on the Murphy County General Fund budgetary comparison statement for the 20X8 fiscal year? (b) In what circumstances would including or excluding encumbrances data mislead users of a governmental fund budgetary comparison statement?

P4-4 (GL and SL Entries) Prepare the journal entries (budgetary and actual) to record the following transactions and events in the General Ledger, Revenues Ledger, and Expenditures Ledger of a local government General Fund. Identify whether the entry is for the General Ledger or for the subsidiary ledgers. Also, note whether the General Ledger entries are budgetary or actual in nature.

1. The annual budget was adopted, using the modified accrual basis of accounting, as follows:

Estimated Revenues:

Property taxes	$400,000
Sales taxes	200,000
Charges for services	100,000
Other	50,000
	$750,000

Appropriations:

General administration	$ 80,000
Police	310,000
Fire	320,000
Other	30,000
	$740,000

2. Property taxes of $408,000 were levied, of which $7,000 are expected to be uncollectible.
3. Purchase orders and contracts were approved for goods and services expected to cost:

Police	$ 50,000
Fire	90,000
	$140,000

4. Most of the goods and services ordered were received.

	Encumbered For	Actual Cost
Police	$ 40,000	$ 41,000
Fire	70,000	68,500
	$110,000	$109,500

5. The budget was revised during the year to decrease the sales tax revenue estimate by $5,000 and increase the police appropriation by $7,000.
6. Interfund transfers were ordered as follows:

From the General Fund

To provide for principal and interest payments on GLTL	$30,000
To establish a new data processing Internal Service Fund	50,000
	$80,000

To the General Fund

Balance of Capital Projects Fund terminated upon project completion	$60,000
Routine annual transfer from a Special Revenue Fund	25,000
	$85,000

All of the transfers were paid or received except that from the Special Revenue Fund, which will be paid soon.

7. It was discovered that $2,000 of supplies charged to Police in transaction 4 should be charged to Parks, which is financed through a Special Revenue Fund.

P4-5 (GL and SL Entries) Prepare in proper form the journal entries (budgetary and actual) to record the following transactions and events in the General Ledger, Revenues Ledger, and Expenditures Ledger of a Special Revenue Fund of a local independent school district. Identify whether each General Ledger entry is budgetary or actual in nature.

1. The annual operating budget (GAAP basis) provides for

   Estimated Revenues:
State appropriation	$500,000
Property taxes	300,000
Other	100,000
	$900,000

   Appropriations:
Administration	$100,000
Instruction	750,000
Other	40,000
	$890,000

2. Purchase orders and contracts for goods and services were approved at estimated costs of

Administration	$15,000
Instruction	60,000
Other	20,000
	$95,000

3. Property taxes were levied, $320,000, of which $15,000 are estimated to be uncollectible.

4. Most of the goods and services ordered in transaction 2 arrived and the invoices were approved and vouchered for payment:

	Encumbered For	Actual Cost
Administration	$ 15,000	$14,800
Instruction	40,000	40,000
Other	20,000	20,300
	$ 75,000	$75,100

5. Cash receipts and year-end revenue accruals were

	Cash Receipts	Year-End Accrued Receivable
State appropriation	$460,000	$38,000
Current property taxes	290,000	—
Delinquent property taxes	15,000	—
Accrued revenue receivable (beginning)	30,000	—
Other	41,000	2,000
	$836,000	$40,000

6. Cash disbursements, including payment of payroll and other unencumbered expenditures, and year-end expenditure accruals were

	Cash Disbursements	Year-End Accrued Payables
Administration	$ 84,000	$ 1,000
Instruction	700,000	8,000
Other	20,000	—
Accrued expenditures payable (beginning)	30,000	—
	$834,000	$ 9,000

7. Interfund transfers were ordered (not yet paid) as follows: (a) $25,000 to the Debt Service Fund to be used to pay general long-term debt principal and interest, and (b) $40,000 from an Internal Service Fund that is being discontinued.
8. It was discovered that $1,500 charged to Instruction (in transaction 6) should be charged to Transportation, which is financed through the General Fund.

P4-6 (Research and Analysis) Obtain a recent state or local government annual operating budget from a library, your professor, the Internet, or elsewhere, and submit a brief report on this research assignment.

Required
1. Identify the government and describe the budget type (e.g., line item, program, performance).
2. On what basis of accounting was the budget adopted?
3. What are the budgetary control points?
4. Which aspects of the budget document(s) were similar to what you expected based on this chapter? Explain.
5. Which aspects of the budget document(s) were different from what you expected based on this chapter? Explain.

Cases

C4-1 (Budgetary Comparison Statement—Budgetary Basis Differs from GAAP—Town of Blacksburg, Virginia) Selected data for the Town of Blacksburg, Virginia, General Fund for the fiscal year ended June 30, 20X7, are presented in the following table. The town's budgetary basis is the modified accrual basis except that encumbrances are treated as budgetary expenditures when the encumbrance is established, not when the goods or services are received.

Town of Blacksburg, Virginia
General Fund
Selected Information
For the Year Ended June 30, 20X7

	Original Budget	Budget Revisions	Actual (GAAP)	Encumbrances Beginning	Ending
Revenues					
General property taxes	$ 3,622	$ —	$ 3,724		
Other local taxes	6,596	—	6,781		
Business license taxes	1,285	1	1,370		
Permits and fees.	840	(1)	880		
Intergovernmental.	4,422	13,225	8,223		
Charges for services.	1,866	—	1,944		
Fines and forfeitures	311	—	265		
Investment earnings	150	—	88		
Other.	532	—	574		
Total revenues	19,624	13,225	23,849		
Expenditures					
Legislative.	179	39	179	$ 40	$ 79
Executive	1,912	(49)	1,912	230	8
Legal	230	—	230	32	4
Judicial	11	—	11	4	3
Financial services.	1,249	37	1,249	90	96
Technology	378	2	378	25	26
Police.	5,240	(160)	5,241	340	54
Fire and rescue.	683	46	683	50	92
Public works.	4,008	863	4,008	95	952
Recreation	1,434	46	1,434	101	50
Planning and engineering.	1,373	504	1,373	3	264
Community development.	755	543	755	350	39
Contingency	42	(41)	42	42	—
Grants	5	—	5	—	5
Total expenditures	17,499	1,830	17,500	$1,402	$1,672
Excess of revenues over expenditures.	2,125	11,395	6,349		

	Original Budget	Budget Revisions	Actual (GAAP)
Other Financing Sources (Uses)			
Transfers in..................	$ —	$ 607	$ 607
Transfers out...............	(2,000)	(12,351)	(6,532)
Net change in fund balances....	125	(349)	424
Budgetary fund balance, July 1, 20X7...............	1,554	1,554	1,200
Budgetary fund balance, June 30, 20X8.............	$1,679	$1,205	$1,624

Prepare the Statement of Revenues, Expenditures, and Changes in Fund Balance—Budget and Actual for the General Fund of the Town of Blacksburg, Virginia, for the year ended June 30, 20X7.   ***Required***

(This case is based on a recent Comprehensive Annual Financial Report of the Town of Blacksburg, Virginia.)

C4-2 (Journal Entries—City of Ann Arbor, Michigan, Special Revenue Fund) (a) Prepare general ledger and subsidiary ledger entries to record the following transactions of the City of Ann Arbor, Michigan, Community Television Network Special Revenue Fund for the year ended June 30, 20X3. (b) Reconcile the general ledger and the subsidiary ledgers at year end. (c) Close the accounts.

1. The Ann Arbor City Council adopted the following budget on the modified accrual basis for the Community Television Network Special Revenue Fund:

<u>Estimated Revenues:</u>	
Licenses, permits, & registrations...................	$1,270,080
Charges for services.............................	36,000
Investment income..............................	7,375
	1,313,455
<u>Appropriations:</u>	
Personnel services	519,339
Payroll fringes/insurance........................	175,364
Other services..................................	194,541
Materials and supplies...........................	20,000
Other charges..................................	159,547
Capital outlay..................................	252,664
	1,321,455
Excess (Deficiency) of Estimated Revenues over Appropriations	($ 8,000)

2. The city collected cash for the network as follows:

Licenses, permits, & registrations...................	$1,388,335
Charges for services.............................	27,603
Investment income..............................	1,000
	$1,416,938

3. City Council revised the Community Television Network Special Revenue Fund appropriations for "Personnel services" and "Payroll fringes/insurance" upward by $40,000 and $15,000, respectively, as a result of hiring an additional employee and minor modifications to the employees' insurance benefits. Appropriations for "Materials and supplies" and "Capital outlay" were reduced by $3,000 and $60,000, respectively.
4. The payroll was approved and paid, $559,339.
5. Payroll fringe benefit and insurance costs of $190,000 were incurred during the year; $10,000 was not paid by year end.

6. The network ordered materials and supplies with an estimated cost of $17,000 and equipment expected to cost $192,664.
7. "Other services" of $194,000 and "Other charges" of $159,547 were incurred and paid.
8. The network received the materials and supplies ordered. The actual cost was $16,980. The network also received most of the equipment ordered, but orders for $50,000 of transmission equipment had not been received by year end. The actual cost of the equipment received was equal to the expected costs.

C4-3 (Budgetary Comparison Statement) Using the information from C4-2 and assuming that the beginning budgetary and GAAP fund balance is $1,952,667, prepare the Statement of Revenues, Expenditures, and Changes in Fund Balance—Budget and Actual for the year ended June 30, 20X3, for the Community Television Network Special Revenue Fund of the City of Ann Arbor, Michigan.

Harvey City Comprehensive Case

The Harvey City Comprehensive Case consists of the last problem in each chapter from Chapters 4 through 15. Completing this case essentially requires that you account for all the transactions of a moderately complex city for a year (dealing with summary transactions) and that you prepare the basic financial statements and a significant portion of the financial section of the comprehensive annual financial report (CAFR) for that city. If you complete all of the requirements for the Comprehensive Case, you will:

- ◆ Prepare journal entries and financial statements for one or more funds of each type for Harvey City, except Permanent Funds. Like most local governments, Harvey City does not have a Permanent Fund. (Chapters 3–8 and 10–12)

- ◆ Account for Harvey City's general capital assets and general long-term liabilities. (Chapter 9)

- ◆ Account for and report the vast majority of transactions that are either unique to governments or are handled in a unique manner by governments. (Chapters 3–12)

- ◆ Determine which of Harvey City's funds are *major* funds. (Chapter 13)

- ◆ Prepare a complete set of *fund* financial statements for Harvey City, including governmental fund financial statements, proprietary fund financial statements, and fiduciary fund financial statements. (Chapter 13)

- ◆ Prepare *worksheets* to derive Harvey City's government-wide financial statement data from its fund financial statement data. (Chapter 14)

- ◆ Prepare a complete set of *government-wide* financial statements for Harvey City, including both a government-wide statement of net assets and a government-wide statement of activities. (Chapter 14)

- ◆ Prepare *reconciliations* of Harvey City's fund financial statements and its government-wide financial statements. (Chapter 14)

- ◆ Prepare *combining* financial statements that articulate with Harvey City's presentations for nonmajor funds in its fund financial statements. (Chapter 15)

Except for the General Fund, the transactions and events affecting each individual fund of Harvey City are dealt with in the chapter on that fund type. Most General Fund transactions are presented in this chapter, but more advanced transactions of the General Fund are presented in Chapters 5 and 6—after the related topics have been covered.

HARVEY CITY SOLUTION APPROACH

Various approaches may be used to complete the Harvey City Comprehensive Case. We believe that the most efficient approach is to use electronic spreadsheets similar to the worksheet shown in the appendix to Chapter 3 in Illustration 3-11 on pages 102–103. The one difference we would suggest is that you use detailed revenue and expenditures accounts in the worksheet instead of using the control account–subsidiary ledger approach demonstrated in this chapter. The use of detailed general ledger accounts is illustrated in Appendix 3-3 and is used in several later chapters. You may want to see Illustration 7-3 for an example of a simple detailed general ledger worksheet.

Using a worksheet approach to solve the problem will be particularly helpful when you begin to prepare fund financial statements in Chapter 13 and a worksheet to derive government-wide financial statement data in Chapter 14. (Worksheet templates are available for the case.)

Again, other approaches—use of a general ledger and detailed subsidiary ledgers, for instance—are acceptable, if your professor prefers.

HARVEY CITY CHAPTER 4 REQUIREMENTS

a. Enter the beginning (January 1, 20X4) trial balance of the General Fund of Harvey City in a General Fund worksheet. (A different solution approach may be used if desired by your professor.) The worksheet (which is similar to Illustration 3-11) may be set up as follows:

1. The first column should be used for account titles.
2. Columns 2 and 3 should be the debit and credit columns, respectively, for the beginning trial balance of the General Fund.
3. Column 4 of the worksheet should be a reference column to tie the journal entry *debits* to the transaction number in this problem.
4. Columns 5 and 6 are the debit and credit columns in which the 20X4 transactions and events of the Harvey City General Fund are to be recorded. Add rows as necessary to provide sufficient room for all transactions. (The solution template should have the proper number of rows.)
5. Column 7 of the worksheet should be a reference column to tie the journal entry *credits* to the transaction number in this problem.
6. Columns 8 and 9 are for the preclosing trial balance of the Harvey City General Fund. They will be used in Chapter 6.
7. Columns 10 and 11 are to be used to close the nonbudgetary accounts of Harvey City. These columns also will contain all balances that are to be reported in the General Fund statement of revenues, expenditures, and changes in fund balances.
8. Columns 12 and 13 are to be used for the postclosing trial balance (balance sheet data). All asset, deferred outflow, liability, deferred inflow, and fund balance amounts should be entered here from the trial balance columns.
9. The differences between the closing entry columns and the balance sheet columns should be equal to each other and to the net change in fund balances of the General Fund. This amount should be entered in the smaller of the closing entry columns and the smaller of the balance sheet columns. (If the closing entry debit column is smaller, the balance sheet credit column should be smaller—and vice versa.)

b. Enter the effects of the following transactions and events in the appropriate columns of the worksheet. (Again, a different solution approach may be used if desired by your professor.)

HARVEY CITY GENERAL FUND TRIAL BALANCE

The trial balance of the General Fund of Harvey City at January 1, 20X4, was:

Harvey City
General Fund
Trial Balance
January 1, 20X4

	Debit	Credit
Cash	$1,000,000	
Investments	480,000	
Taxes Receivable—Delinquent	160,000	
Allowance for Uncollectible Delinquent Taxes		$ 20,000
Interest and Penalties Receivable	54,500	
Allowance for Uncollectible Interest and Penalties		17,500
Accrued Interest Receivable	2,000	
Inventory of Materials and Supplies	53,000	
Accrued Salaries Payable		50,000
Vouchers Payable		112,000
Deferred Revenues		100,000
Due to Internal Service Fund		8,000
Fund Balance		1,442,000
Totals	$1,749,500	$1,749,500

HARVEY CITY GENERAL FUND BUDGET

The General Fund budget for 20X4 was adopted by the city council. The city budgets on the modified accrual basis. Transfers are not budgeted. The adopted budget is presented here:

Estimated Revenues

Taxes	$1,500,000	
Interest and penalties	15,500	
Licenses and permits	122,000	
Fines and forfeitures	50,000	
Intergovernmental grants	300,000	
Investment income	45,000	
Total estimated revenues		$2,032,500
Appropriations		
General government	$ 260,000	
Public safety	868,000	
Highways and streets	290,000	
Health and sanitation	215,000	
Parks and recreation	330,000	
Total appropriations		1,963,000
Budgeted excess of revenues over appropriations		$ 69,500

HARVEY CITY GENERAL FUND TRANSACTIONS—20X4

1. Record the budget. (You may use a single Estimated Revenues account and a single Appropriations account.)
2. Reestablish the encumbrances of $19,000 that were closed at the end of last year.
3. The city levied its general property taxes for the year of $1,580,000. The city estimates that $30,000 of the taxes will prove uncollectible. Record the taxes assuming the city will collect the remaining balance later during the fiscal year.
4. The city collected $1,300,000 of property taxes before the due date for taxes. The remainder of the taxes receivable became delinquent.
5. The city received and vouchered the materials and supplies that were on order from the previous year. The actual cost equaled the estimated cost of these materials and supplies, $19,000. The city records expenditures for materials and supplies when they are consumed. A perpetual inventory system is used.
6. The city collected $200,000 when investments matured and also collected the following General Fund revenues during the year:

Fines and forfeitures	$ 48,480
Unrestricted grants from the state	346,200
Licenses and permits	122,460
Interest revenue from investments (including $2,000 accrued at the end of 20X3)	42,000
Total	$ 559,140

7. The city incurred and paid salary expenditures as follows:

Accrued salaries payable, January 1	$ 50,000
General government	180,000
Public safety	580,000
Highways and streets	175,000
Health and sanitation	150,000
Parks and recreation	220,000
Total	$1,355,000

8. The city ordered General Fund materials and supplies as follows:

General government.	$ 10,000
Public safety.	40,000
Highways and streets	75,000
Health and sanitation	40,000
Parks and recreation.	30,000
Total	$195,000

9. Billings were received from the Water and Sewer Enterprise Fund as follows:

General government.	$ 900
Public safety.	13,500
Highways and streets	3,300
Health and sanitation	2,900
Parks and recreation.	1,900
Total	$ 22,500

10. Equipment was ordered for the following functions:

General government.	$ 35,000
Public safety.	150,000
Highways and streets	25,300
Health and sanitation	8,900
Parks and recreation.	60,000
Total	$279,200

11. The equipment ordered was received (and vouchers approved) as follows:

	Estimated Cost	Actual Cost
General government.	$ 35,000	$ 35,000
Public safety.	134,000	135,000
Highways and streets	25,300	25,300
Health and sanitation	8,900	8,900
Parks and recreation.	60,000	60,000
Totals	$263,200	$264,200

12. Billings were received from the Central Communications Network Internal Service Fund for communications services used by general government agencies and departments as follows:

General government.	$ 18,000
Public safety.	15,000
Highways and streets	3,500
Health and sanitation	6,630
Parks and recreation.	13,940
Total	$ 57,070

13. $61,000 was paid on the amounts owed to the Central Communications Network Internal Service Fund.
14. Other unencumbered expenditures incurred during the year were vouchered as follows:

General government.	$ 11,420
Public safety.	41,280
Total	$ 52,700

15. $500,000 was loaned from the General Fund to the Addiction Prevention Special Revenue Fund to provide working capital for that fund. The loan is to be repaid within a year.

16. The General Fund transferred resources to other funds as follows:

Addiction Prevention Special Revenue Fund.........	$ 60,000
Parks and Recreation Capital Projects Fund.........	200,000
Bridge Capital Projects Fund	70,000
Refunding Debt Service Fund......................	729,965
Total...	$1,059,965

17. The General Fund received a transfer of $100,000 from the Water and Sewer Enterprise Fund.

18. Accrued salaries and wages for General Fund employees at December 31 were as follows:

General government.............................	$ 1,800
Public safety...................................	5,800
Highways and streets	1,750
Health and sanitation	1,500
Parks and recreation............................	2,200
Total...	$ 13,050

CHAPTER 5

Revenue Accounting— Governmental Funds

LEARNING OBJECTIVES

After studying this chapter, you should be able to:

- Determine when various types of governmental fund revenues should be recognized and reported.

- Identify the four categories of nonexchange transactions and when to recognize the related assets and revenues.

- Identify the most common deferred inflows of resources reported in governmental funds.

- Discuss and apply modified accrual revenue recognition criteria in both simple and complex situations.

- Understand accounting for the levy, collection, revenue recognition, and enforcement of property taxes and other taxes.

- Account for and report governmental fund investment income in accordance with GASB *Statements No. 31* and *40*.

- Distinguish and account for the various types of intergovernmental revenues, including pass-through grants and other grants, entitlements, shared revenues, and payments in lieu of taxes.

- Understand classification of and accounting for various other types of governmental fund revenues and other (nonrevenue) financing sources.

- Account for and report changes in revenue accounting principles and error corrections.

R evenue accounting in government parallels that for business enterprises in some respects. In both, revenues must be distinguished from nonrevenue resource inflows, and accounting guidelines have been established for the timing of revenue recognition. Proprietary fund revenue recognition is virtually identical to that in business accounting.

Significant differences and unique considerations are involved, however, particularly in revenue accounting for *governmental* (expendable) funds. This chapter focuses on these differences and special considerations:

1. The definition of revenue in the governmental fund environment, the revenue recognition criteria used, and the circumstances when delay of revenue recognition results in reporting deferred inflows instead of liabilities

2. Classification of revenue accounts

3. Accounting for revenue sources that are unique to governments, such as taxes, licenses and permits, and intergovernmental grants

4. Revenue-related changes in accounting principles

These discussions and illustrations focus on GAAP-based revenue accounting and reporting. Thus, as in Chapter 4, we assume that the SLG governmental fund budgetary basis is the governmental fund GAAP basis (modified accrual), except where noted otherwise, and that the governmental fund revenue accounts are maintained on (or near) the modified accrual basis during the year.

REVENUE DEFINITION AND RECOGNITION

Governmental fund *revenues* are increases in the net assets of a governmental fund that *either*

a. Result in a corresponding increase in the net assets of the governmental unit as a whole, *or*

b. Result from *exchange-like* interfund services provided and used transactions.

Revenues may be operationally defined in a governmental fund accounting context as *all* increases in fund net assets *except* those arising from interfund reimbursements, interfund transfers, sale (or compensation for loss) of capital assets, or long-term debt issues.

Governmental fund revenues may result from *exchange transactions* (or exchange-like interfund transactions) or from *nonexchange transactions*, and are recognized in accordance with the modified accrual revenue recognition criteria. If assets are recorded before meeting the criteria for recognizing revenues, the government must report either (1) a *liability for unearned revenues* or (2) a *deferred inflow (such as deferred revenues),* depending on the circumstances.

Governments have a wide variety of revenue sources. Some revenues, such as property taxes, are levied in known amounts prior to collection, and uncollectible amounts can usually be estimated with reasonable accuracy. Such revenues are recorded on the modified accrual basis, as are other revenues billed by the government.

The *modified* accrual basis of governmental fund revenue recognition takes into account the diverse government revenue sources and the varying degrees to which government revenues can be recorded on the accrual basis. Under the *modified* accrual basis, revenues are recognized *only* if they are *susceptible to accrual,* meaning they are objectively measurable *and both*:

a. Available—collected in the current period or soon enough thereafter (typically limited to a 60-day maximum) to be used to pay liabilities of the current period, *and*

b. Legally usable to finance current period expenditures.

Revenues are recognized in the earliest period that *both criteria* are met. Hence, revenues that become legally usable in 20X1 but are not collected until late in 20X3 are not recognized as revenues until 20X3. Likewise, revenues collected in 20X1 that do not become legally usable until 20X2 are not recognized as revenues until 20X2. If a government has a valid legal claim to resources that are not legally usable, a receivable and deferred revenues are recorded.

Illustration 5-1 demonstrates that revenues must be deferred and recognized in future years if they are

• Earned or legally usable but *not* collected before the end of the fiscal year (or soon enough thereafter to be used to pay the period's liabilities).

• Collected by the end of a year (or soon enough thereafter to be used to pay the period's liabilities) but *not* earned or legally usable for expenditure for that year (e.g., taxes or grants to finance a later year's activities).

Revenues are *legally usable* if the government's legal claim to the resources has been established by the end of the period and the resources were raised to finance the expenditures of the current or prior periods. A government's legal claim to revenues is established in different ways depending on the nature of the revenues:

• Performing services—i.e., earning revenues—establishes a government's claim to charges for services of general government departments.

• Levying a tax establishes a government's claim to taxes it assesses, such as property taxes.

• A business making a taxable sale establishes a taxing government's legal claim to sales taxes.

• Taxpayers earning taxable income establishes a taxing government's legal claim to income taxes.

ILLUSTRATION 5-1   Timing of Revenue Recognition

Legally Usable Beginning in	Collected in					
	20X1	**Early* 20X2**	**Later in 20X2**	**Early* 20X3**	**Later in 20X3**	**Early* 20X4**
20X1	*20X1 Revenues*	*20X1 Revenues*	20X2 Revenues	20X2 Revenues	20X3 Revenues	20X3 Revenues
20X2	20X2 Revenues	20X2 Revenues	*20X2 Revenues*	*20X2 Revenues*	20X3 Revenues	20X3 Revenues
20X3	20X3 Revenues	20X3 Revenues	20X3 Revenues	20X3 Revenues	*20X3 Revenues*	*20X3 Revenues*

*Early means soon enough to be used to pay the liabilities of the prior year. Early 20X2 should be interpreted as early enough to pay 20X1 liabilities.

You may understand the substance of modified accrual revenue recognition better if you recognize that "modified *accrual*" accounting might have been more accurately named "modified *cash*" accounting. Consider the constraints provided by the key revenue recognition requirements that revenues must be:

- Available—collected by the end of the period (or soon enough thereafter to be used to pay liabilities outstanding at the end of the period) *and*
- Legally usable for expenditure in the period.

The available criterion means that for revenues to be recognized they must be collected by the end of the fiscal year. The only exception is that amounts collected shortly after the end of the year—soon enough for the cash to be used to pay bills of the year just ended—may be recognized as revenues. Conceptually, the period ("soon enough") after year end during which revenues collected may be reported as revenues of the current year depends on how long after that year end the government has before it must pay the liabilities of the year. But, practically, the GASB standards say this period normally should not exceed 60 days.

The protection afforded by the legal usability requirement relates to the fact that a government raises many types of revenues (e.g., property taxes), primarily to finance a particular year's operations. The legal usability criterion prevents governments from recognizing these revenues in an earlier period, even if collected in the earlier period. Hence, property taxes levied in 20X0 to finance the 20X1 fiscal year cannot be reported as revenues in 20X0, even if substantial portions are collected in 20X0.

Essentially, we recognize as revenues of 20X1 amounts of cash that are collected in 20X1 or shortly thereafter that were raised for the primary purpose of financing expenditures incurred in 20X1 (and expected to be paid during 20X1 or shortly thereafter, as will be explained in Chapter 6). In short, revenue recognition varies from cash basis revenue recognition when the cash is

- Collected before the period the revenue was raised to finance (i.e., *not* legally usable).
- Collected from a legally usable revenue source after year end but soon enough to be used to pay the liabilities of the period.

When revenue recognition must be delayed to a future period, a government must report either a liability or a deferred inflow. Deferred inflows are reported when revenue recognition is delayed because the revenue is

- Not available—not collected by year end or soon enough thereafter.
- An imposed tax revenue levied (or otherwise imposed) to finance operations of a future year.
- Collected in advance, and there is no performance obligation to earn the revenue.

ILLUSTRATION 5-2 Modified Accrual Revenue Recognition Application

Case	Year 20X1	20X2	20X3	Treatment
A		• Legal Claim* • Legally Usable • Cash Collected		20X2—Revenues
B	Legal Claim	• Legally Usable • Cash Collected		20X2—Revenues
C	Cash Collected	• Legal Claim • Legally Usable		20X2—Revenues
D		• Legal Claim • Legally Usable	Cash Collected (during cutoff period of ≤ 60 days)	20X2—Revenues (and Receivables)
E		• Legal Claim • Legally Usable	Cash Collected (after cutoff period)	20X3—Revenues

*Legal claim means legal claim established in this period.

Notes:

1. Revenues typically are recognized when cash is collected (Cases A, B, E).
2. Exceptions:
   - Revenue recognition is *delayed* beyond cash collection if the purpose for raising the revenues is to finance a later period's expenditures (Case C). This is the application of the "legally usable" criterion.
   - Revenue is recognized *before* cash is collected only if collected early in the next period (Case D)—soon enough to be used to pay the current period's liabilities (for expenditures of the current period that are not paid by year end). This is the application of the "availability" criterion.

In other cases delaying revenue recognition beyond the time that cash is collected or a legal claim to resources is established results in reporting a liability—unearned revenues.

Illustration 5-2 summarizes the application of the modified accrual revenue recognition criteria and further highlights the points made in this discussion.

NONEXCHANGE TRANSACTIONS

Many of the most significant revenue sources in governmental funds result from nonexchange transactions. The GASB has identified four distinct types of nonexchange transactions, as outlined in Illustration 5-3. The illustration describes each category of nonexchange transactions and the conditions requiring recognition of receivables for these transactions, but does not specify when revenues are recognized.

Because modified accrual revenue recognition requires both legal usability and availability (collection at least by the end of a short cutoff period in the next year), governments often must report significant amounts of governmental fund assets and either *liabilities or deferred* inflows, such as deferred revenues, from nonexchange transactions prior to recognizing governmental fund revenues.

- Sometimes cash is collected from nonexchange transactions prior to meeting the governmental fund revenue recognition criteria.
- At other times, the receivable recognition criteria specified in Illustration 5-3 are met prior to meeting the governmental fund revenue recognition criteria.

The government must report either a liability for unearned revenues or a deferred inflow such as *deferred revenues* in these cases until the revenue recognition

ILLUSTRATION 5-3 Nonexchange Transactions—Types and Receivable Recognition

Type of Nonexchange Transaction	Characteristics	Receivables Recognized When (*Unless Cash Received Earlier*)
Derived Tax Revenues (e.g., income taxes, sales taxes, gas taxes)	Taxes assessed on exchange transactions of other (nongovernment) entities or individuals	Underlying exchange transaction occurs (e.g., when taxable sale is made, taxable income is earned, motor fuel is purchased) (*Note 1*)
Imposed Tax Revenues (e.g., property taxes, fines and forfeitures)	Tax or other levy assessed on a nongovernment entity for an act committed or omitted; act is not an exchange transaction	The government establishes a legally enforceable claim (*Note 1*)
Government-Mandated (e.g., state grant to local government to cover a portion of construction cost of mandated environmental facilities; federal grants distributed to states for a mandatory drug and alcohol abuse prevention program in the schools)	Provider is a senior level of government whose enabling legislation mandates implementation of a particular program by the recipient or subrecipient; certain eligibility requirements must be met	Eligibility requirements are met (*Notes 1 and 2*). Eligibility requirements may include: • Required characteristics of recipients specified by the provider (e.g., some revenue sources are only available for schools) • Time requirements specified by enabling legislation or by the provider requiring use in a certain period or beginning after a certain date • Recipient must incur allowable costs (as defined by the provider or enabling legislation) under a reimbursement (expenditure-driven) program
Voluntary (e.g., state reimbursement to schools of portion of secondary education technology costs incurred; state distribution of resources to cities and counties for street and road improvements)	Typically the grantee applies for the grant; certain eligibility requirements must be met	Eligibility requirements are met (*Notes 1 and 2*)

Notes:

1. Revenues are *not* recognized until the *modified accrual revenue recognition criteria—including the availability criterion—are met.* Also, any time requirements establishing that resources are not legally usable until a future period—such as the levy of taxes to finance activities of the next fiscal year—must be met to recognize revenues.
2. Eligibility requirements also include any actions on which grantee or donee provision of resources is contingent (e.g., raising matching funds).

Source: Portions of various GASB documents, copyright by the Governmental Accounting Standards Board, 401 Merritt, PO Box 5116, Norwalk, CT 06856-5116, are reproduced with permission. Complete copies of those documents are available from the GASB.

criteria are met. Revenues cannot be recognized until a government meets *both* (1) the asset recognition criteria or receives cash and (2) the revenue recognition criteria.

Note that *time requirements* (requiring use of resources during a certain period or after a certain date) may affect both asset recognition and revenue recognition. If only the availability (cash collection in time to recognize revenue in the period) criterion or a time requirement remains to meet the revenue recognition criteria, deferred inflows—typically deferred revenues—are reported in the balance sheet. The GASB considers the other eligibility requirements to represent a performance obligation that require reporting a liability for unearned revenues, not deferred inflows.

Purpose restrictions (limiting use of resources to a specific program or purpose) do not affect either asset recognition or revenue recognition except when they are part of an eligibility requirement for restricted grants. Purpose restrictions such as

ILLUSTRATION 5-4 Deferred Revenues: Unearned or Unavailable

Shelby County, Tennessee
Notes to Financial Statements
June 30, 20X2

Revenues that cannot be recognized until future periods include the following:

	General Fund	Debt Service Fund	Education Fund	Grants Fund	Capital Projects Fund	Totals
Unearned:						
Grant revenue	$ —	$ —	$ —	$8,253,730	$ —	$ 8,253,730
Other	8,101	307,166	—	—	59,112	374,379
Levied for Next Year or Not Available:						
Property Taxes receivable— levied to finance 20X2–20X3	171,627,500	70,021,980	278,731,600	—	—	520,381,080
Property Taxes receivable— levied for current or prior periods	11,099,043	4,522,416	18,037,087	—	—	33,658,546
Notes receivable	783,901	13,103,532	—	633,015	14,428,551	28,948,999
Due from Shelby County Health Care Corporation	—	5,441,563	—	—	—	5,441,563
Due from Agricenter	123,578	—	—	—	137,496	261,074
Due from Other Governments	492,627	—	—	—	—	492,627
	$184,134,750	$93,396,657	$296,768,687	$8,886,745	$14,625,159	$597,811,998

Source: Based on a recent Shelby County, Tennessee comprehensive annual financial report.

restrictions of a portion of a government's property taxes or sales taxes to a specific purpose should typically result in the resources being accounted for in a Special Revenue Fund but should not delay revenue recognition.

Taxes collected before the year for which they are levied or assessed are recorded initially as *deferred inflows*, a liability. Similarly, taxes levied or assessed in one year that will not be collected until a future year are recorded initially as receivables and deferred revenues—a deferred inflow—because only passage of time and collection of cash are required to meet the revenue recognition criteria. Amounts collected in advance for revenue sources such as restricted grants before expenditures are made that qualify under eligibility requirements other than time requirements are recorded as *unearned revenues*, a liability. The GASB considers the other eligibility requirements for recognition of grant revenues to be a performance obligations, which require liabilities to be reported instead of deferred inflows. The unearned amounts shown in Illustration 5-4 must be reported as liabilities. The other amounts are deferred inflows.

GOVERNMENTAL FUND AND PROPRIETARY FUND REVENUE RECOGNITION COMPARED

Revenue recognition for both nonexchange transactions and exchange transactions is summarized in Illustration 5-5. Note that Illustration 5-5 includes:

- A comparison of revenue recognition criteria under the
  - *Economic Resources* measurement focus and *accrual* basis applicable to *proprietary fund* and *government-wide* financial statements presented in accordance with GAAP.
  - *Current Financial Resources* measurement focus and *modified accrual* basis applicable to *governmental fund* financial statements prepared in conformity with GAAP.

ILLUSTRATION 5-5 Revenue Recognition: Accrual Basis vs. Modified Accrual Basis

Economic Resources
Measurement Focus—Accrual Basis
- **Proprietary Fund**
  Financial Statements
- **Government-Wide**
  Financial Statements

Revenues recognized when:
1. Earned or levied for the period (e.g., property taxes) and
2. Objectively measurable
Regardless of when collected.

Current Financial Resources
Measurement Focus—Modified Accrual Basis
- **Governmental Fund**
  Financial Statements

- *Revenues* recognized when:
  1. Earned or levied for the period, i.e., legally usable (e.g., property taxes levied for the period)
  2. Objectively measurable **and**
  3. *Available* to finance *this year's* expenditures
  "Available" means *collected*
  1. during this year, *or*
  2. *"Soon enough"* in next year to be used to pay for this year's expenditures (fund liabilities)
  "Soon enough" usually means within 60 days after the end of this year into next year.
- *Deferred Revenues* thus means either:
  1. Not Available or
  2. Time requirement not met (Not Legally Usable)
- Unearned Revenues means there is a performance obligation—as with restricted grants—which is a liability

Examples and Illustrative Entries

Property Taxes:
- *Levied* in and for THIS YEAR (20X1), all of which are expected to be collected eventually, $100,000
- *Collected* on THIS YEAR's (20X1) property tax levy:
  — During 20X1, $70,000
  — Within the first 60 days of 20X2, $5,000
  — After the first 60 days of 20X2, in 20X2 and later, $25,000

This Year—20X1

Proprietary Fund

Taxes Receivable—20X1	100,000	
Revenues—Taxes		100,000
Cash	70,000	
Taxes Receivable—20X1		70,000

Governmental Fund

Taxes Receivable—20X1	100,000	
Deferred Revenues—Taxes		100,000
Cash	70,000	
Taxes Receivable—20X1		70,000
Deferred Revenues—Taxes	75,000	
Revenues—Taxes		75,000

Next Year—20X2

Proprietary Fund

Cash	5,000	
Taxes Receivable—20X1		5,000
Cash	25,000	
Taxes Receivable—20X1		25,000

Governmental Fund

Cash	5,000	
Taxes Receivable—20X1		5,000
Cash	25,000	
Taxes Receivable—20X1		25,000
Deferred Revenues—Taxes	25,000	
Revenues—Taxes		25,000

- Examples and illustrative entries for
  - Simplified proprietary fund and governmental fund *property tax* levy and collections.
  - Revenue recognition **"This Year (20X1)"**—during which the property taxes were levied, some taxes were collected, and some uncollected taxes were "available" because they were collected within the first 60 days of the next year (20X2)—and **"Next Year (20X2)"** during which additional property taxes were collected.

Illustration 5-5 should be reviewed repeatedly as various revenue recognition topics are discussed and illustrated in this chapter and in later chapters.

CLASSIFICATION OF REVENUE ACCOUNTS

Revenues are classified by source in the accounts to provide information that management may use to:

1. Prepare and control the budget.
2. Control the assessment, billing, and collection of revenues.
3. Prepare financial statements and schedules for reporting to the public.
4. Prepare financial statistics.

The revenue accounts provide the basic data for revenue reports used for all of these purposes. Revenue classification for the General Fund, for other governmental funds, and for the governmental unit as a whole is discussed next.

General Fund Revenues

The following are typically the main revenue *source classes* for a city or county General Fund:

- Taxes (including property, sales, income, and other taxes; penalties and interest on delinquent taxes)
- Licenses and permits
- Intergovernmental (including grants, shared revenues, and payments by other governments in lieu of taxes)
- Charges for services (for general government activities), including interfund services provided
- Fines and forfeits
- Investment earnings
- Miscellaneous (including rents and royalties, escheats, and contributions and donations from private sources)

These preceding revenue classes are not account titles. Rather, they are broad revenue source categories for reporting purposes, just as Current Assets and Capital Assets are category groupings on the business balance sheet. For example, though we do so for illustrative purposes, no account would be set up for fines and forfeits. Instead, individual accounts would be provided for each type of revenue falling in that class, including court fines, library fines, and bail forfeits. The total revenues accrued or received from fines and forfeits would be the sum of the balances of these accounts.

Other Governmental Funds Revenues

The revenue classes described for the General Fund are also suitable for the other governmental funds of a governmental unit. For example, taxes may be a revenue source of Special Revenue Funds and Debt Service Funds, and interest earnings are likely to be a revenue source of all governmental funds. Clearly, no other governmental fund is likely to have as many different revenue sources as the General Fund.

This chapter is concerned with accounting for the principal revenue sources of the General Fund, Special Revenue Funds, and other governmental funds. Those types of revenues that are peculiar to another fund type are discussed in the chapter on that fund type.

TAXES

As noted earlier, taxes are forced contributions to a government to meet public needs. Typically, the amount of a tax bears no direct relationship to any benefit received by the taxpayer from the taxing unit.

The amount of any tax is computed by applying a rate or rates set by the governmental unit to a defined base, such as the value of property, amount of income, or number of units. From the standpoint of administration, taxes may be divided into two groups—those that are **taxpayer assessed** and those that are **levied**. For the levied group, the governmental unit establishes the amount of the tax base to which the rate or rates will be applied. The general property tax on real property and personal property is the primary example of this group. Income taxes and sales taxes, as well as taxes on gasoline, tobacco, alcoholic beverages, severance of natural resources, and inheritance, are taxpayer assessed (also called self-assessed). For these taxes, the taxpayer is expected to determine the amount of the tax base (such as taxable income or tons of coal mined), apply the proper rate or rates, and submit the payment with the return that shows the computation.

Taxpayer-Assessed Taxes

When taxpayers assess their own tax, verifying the amount of tax requires determining whether

1. The tax *base* has been properly reported by the taxpayer.
2. The proper *rates* have been applied accurately to the tax base to arrive at the total amount of the tax.

The first task is the most difficult. For example, verifying income taxes requires determining that all income that should have been reported has been reported. Furthermore, investigations should *not* be limited to those taxpayers who file returns. The governmental unit must also make certain that all taxpayers who should pay taxes have filed returns.

The GASB notes that revenues from taxpayer-assessed taxes, such as sales taxes and income taxes (net of estimated refunds), should be recognized in the accounting period in which they become "*susceptible to accrual*"—that is, when they become measurable and *both* available and legally usable to finance expenditures of the fiscal period.[1]

In practice, most taxpayer-assessed taxes are accounted for on a cash basis because the return and the remittance are ordinarily received at the same time. Furthermore, no objectively measurable basis on which to set up accruals may be available because the amount of tax is not known before the return is filed.

The GASB specifies that a government should accrue *sales taxes collected by merchants during a fiscal year, but held by the merchants or another government at year-end if the government is to receive the sales tax collections soon enough to use them to pay governmental fund liabilities incurred during the fiscal year.*[2] Being remitted "in time" to be used to pay liabilities for current operations is not defined by the GASB but is generally considered to mean collected by the government during the year or within not more than 60 days after year end. Finally, the GASB indicates that year-to-year comparability should be considered in determining whether to recognize sales taxes and other self-assessed revenues that are collected after year end.

Many states, cities, and counties with income taxes have continually improved their ability to reasonably estimate income tax revenues for the year and the related income tax receivables and refund liabilities. In some jurisdictions, income tax returns are filed at a specified time and the tax is paid currently in installments. In such cases, because the amount of the tax is known, the receivables are

---

[1]GASB *Codification*, sec. 1600.106.
[2]Ibid., sec. N50.127.

accrued and revenue (or deferred revenue, if not available) is reported as soon as the return is filed.

Some taxes require the attachment of stamps to an article to indicate that the tax has been paid. For example, liquor taxes and tobacco taxes are frequently paid through the purchase of stamps to be affixed to bottles or packages. In such cases the taxes are considered to be revenue as soon as the stamps are sold to the manufacturer, distributor, or dealer, even though the articles to which the stamps are affixed may not be sold for an indefinite period following the purchase of the tax stamps.

Property Taxes

Property taxes are ad valorem ("according to value") taxes in proportion to the assessed valuation of real or personal property. They typically are the most important imposed tax revenues of school districts, cities, counties, and other local governments. The procedure for administering general property taxes is as follows:

1. The assessed valuation of each piece of real property and of the taxable personal property of each taxpayer is determined by the local tax assessor based on appraisals and other information.
2. A local assessment review board hears complaints about assessments.
3. County and state boards of equalization assign equalized values to taxing districts.
4. The legislative body levies the total amount of taxes it needs, but not in excess of the amount permitted by law.
5. The tax levy is distributed among taxpayers on the basis of the assessed value of property owned by them.
6. Taxpayers are billed.
7. Tax collections are credited to taxpayers' accounts.
8. Tax collections are enforced by the imposition of penalties, interest, and the sale of property for taxes.

Each of these steps in general property tax administration is discussed briefly in the following sections.

Assessment of Property

Valuing property for taxation purposes is called *assessment*. Assessment of property for local taxes is usually performed by an elected or appointed official known as an **assessor**. The **assessed value** of each piece of real property and personal property of every taxpayer—based on appraisals and other information—is recorded in the assessment column of the tax roll. Not all real and personal property in the government's jurisdiction will be subject to real or personal property assessment and taxation. Properties owned by governments and religious organizations are usually exempt from such taxes and are referred to as *exempt* properties.

On the other hand, *several governmental units with overlapping jurisdictions—such as a state, county, city, and school district—may tax many of the same pieces of property*. One year, for instance, property owners in the City of Providence, Kentucky, were subject to real property taxes (per $100 of assessed value—also stated in mills, or tenths of a cent per dollar of valuation) levied by the four governments as follows:

Taxing Unit	Tax Rate per $100 Valuation	Tax Rate in Mills per $1 Valuation
Commonwealth of Kentucky	$0.128	1.28
Webster County	$0.325	3.25
City of Providence	$0.500	5.00
Providence Independent School District...	$0.379	3.79
Total	$1.332	13.32

In these situations, only one jurisdiction ordinarily has the assessment responsibility, and perhaps the billing and collection responsibilities. Accounting and reporting for such *centralized* tax assessment, billing, and collection are discussed in Chapter 12, "Trust and Agency (Fiduciary) Funds."

Review of Assessment

Individual property owners are notified of the assessments on their properties and are permitted to protest (appeal) the assessments to a local review board. This board may be composed of officials of the government, other residents of the governmental unit, or both. The board hears objections to assessments, weighs the evidence, and changes the assessments if deemed appropriate. Taxpayers may appeal the board action to the courts.

Equalization of Assessments

In most states, property assessments are made by a local government (city, county, school district), based on appraisals of taxable properties, or by a tax appraisal district. The taxes of the state and perhaps even the county are levied on the basis of assessments made by a number of different assessors. Each assessor may have different ideas about the valuations that should be assigned to property. The law usually requires the assessments to be *equalized* to a specific percentage of *fair market value* (often 100 percent). Lack of equalization or poor equalization causes widespread dissatisfaction with the property tax as a revenue source. Thus, both state and county equalization boards attempt to ensure that assessments are made equitably—at fair market value or at the same percentage of fair market value—among and within the counties.

Levying the Tax

Taxes are levied through the passage of a *tax levy* act or ordinance, usually passed at the time the appropriation act or ordinance is passed. The levy establishes a legally enforceable receivable and is ordinarily applicable to only one year.

Tax levies vary in detail and restrictiveness. Some governments levy taxes in one or two lump sums for unrestricted general government purposes or perhaps also for one or two broad specified purposes (e.g., schools). Other tax levies are detailed and restricted. A statute or charter may require certain taxes to be levied for specific identified purposes. In that event, the legislative body must indicate the amount levied for each purpose. Another effect of detailed tax levies that restrict specific portions of the total tax levy to specific purposes is to provide a basis for creating a Special Revenue Fund(s). For example, if a special levy is made for parks, a Special Revenue Fund for parks normally is established to ensure that the taxes collected are used only for parks.

Determining the Tax Rate The tax rate is determined by dividing the amount of taxes levied by the assessed valuation. Thus, if a government has an assessed valuation of $100,000,000 and its total tax levy is $2,500,000, the tax rate is 2.5 percent, or 25 **mills** per dollar ($0.025), of assessed value ($2,500,000 ÷ $100,000,000). (Many governments state the tax rate per $100 valuation rather than in mills: 25 mills are the same as $2.50 per $100 of assessed value.)

The total tax rate consists of the tax rate for general purposes and any special tax rates for specific purposes. For example, if we assume that the total levy of $2,500,000 consisted of $1,500,000 for general purposes, $100,000 for parks, $500,000 for schools, and $400,000 for debt service, the tax rates would be as follows:

Purpose	Rate (mills per dollar of assessed value)
General	15
Parks	1
Schools	5
Debt Service	4
	25

Maximum tax rates or percentage increases in tax rates are frequently prescribed for governmental units by the constitution, statutes, or charters. If the total property tax revenues the legislative body wants to result from the levy will require a rate higher than the maximum legal rate, the amount of the levy must be reduced to avoid exceeding the maximum rate. In some jurisdictions a higher tax rate can be approved by the local government body—say, a 4% rate increase rather than the 3% rate increase allowed by statute—but the citizenry can vote to "roll back" the tax rate if they disagree with the higher tax rate.

Determining the Amount Due from Each Taxpayer Multiplying the assessed value of a taxpayer's property by the tax rate determines the amount due from an individual taxpayer. For example, a taxpayer who owns real estate with an assessed value of $80,000 when the city tax rate is 25 mills per dollar of assessed value will owe taxes of $2,000 ($80,000 × 0.025).

Calculating property taxes due from a property owner is often complicated by various exemptions and abatements. Many jurisdictions have homestead exemptions under which homeowners are not taxed on, for example, the first $40,000 of the value of their home. Some jurisdictions also have property tax "freeze" provisions whereby the property taxes of disabled or older taxpayers are frozen at a specified dollar amount regardless of future increases in the fair value of their properties. Finally, business taxpayers may be granted property exemptions for several years in consideration of the firm relocating to a city or expanding its activities there.

Setting Up Taxes Receivable and Billing Taxpayers

As soon as the amount due from each taxpayer is determined, it is entered on the tax roll. The taxes receivable are then recorded in the accounts, and the taxes are billed to taxpayers.

The Tax Roll A tax roll is a record of the taxes levied against each piece of real property and against each owner of personal property. The tax roll

- Provides a record of each parcel of real or personal property—including its assessed value, taxes levied against the property, property tax collections, and balances owed with respect to the property.
- Serves as a subsidiary ledger, supporting the Taxes Receivable control accounts in the General Ledger.
- Shows any accrued interest and penalties on delinquent taxes.

Recording Taxes in the Accounts Some of the entries to record taxes in the accounts were introduced in Chapter 3. Recall that:

- When taxes are levied, the usual general ledger entry in each fund is to debit Taxes Receivable—Current and credit both Allowance for Uncollectible Current Taxes and Revenues. (If the tax is levied prior to the year to which it applies, a Deferred Revenues account is credited initially.)

- Taxes that become delinquent (and the related allowance) are *reclassified* by debiting Taxes Receivable—Delinquent and Allowance for Uncollectible Current Taxes and crediting Taxes Receivable—Current and Allowance for Uncollectible Delinquent Taxes. This entry *renames* the receivables and related allowance to indicate the delinquent (past due) status of the receivables.

Separate Taxes Receivable accounts should be set up for each type of tax, such as real property taxes, personal property taxes, and income taxes. Furthermore, each of these taxes should be recorded in a way that identifies the *amount applicable to each year.* One way to make this distinction is to set up control accounts for each kind of tax receivable by levy year.

Because the proportion of the total tax levy for each purpose may vary from year to year, each year's levy is identified by year so that the proper Taxes Receivable accounts may be credited and the cash collected may be allocated to the proper fund(s). For example, suppose that the property tax levy is $100,000, both for this year and for last year, but that the *amounts* and *percentages vary,* as follows:

| | This Year | | Last Year | |
| | Amount | Percentage | Amount | Percentage |
Fund	Levied	of Total	Levied	of Total
General Fund............	$ 46,700	46.7	$ 40,000	40.0
Parks Fund	13,300	13.3	13,300	13.3
School Fund	26,700	26.7	33,400	33.4
Debt Service Fund......	13,300	13.3	13,300	13.3
	$100,000	100.0	$100,000	100.0

The General Fund portion of the proceeds of this year's tax levy is found by multiplying the amount collected from the levy by 46.7%. Thus, if $10,000 of this year's taxes is collected, $4,670 is allocated to the General Fund ($10,000 × 46.7%). On the other hand, if $10,000 of last year's levy is collected, only $4,000 is allocated to the General Fund ($10,000 × 40%). Collections from other years' levies are allocated to the proper funds in the same manner.

Recording Tax Collections

Assume that the preceding $100,000 property tax levy was for 20Y0 and that the delinquent receivables and related allowance are:

Property Taxes Receivable—Delinquent:	
Levy of 20X9......................................	$30,000
20X8...	19,500
20X7...	10,500
20X6...	5,000
20X5 and prior	3,000
	68,000
Less: Allowance for Uncollectible Delinquent Taxes	10,000
	$58,000

As taxes are collected, the entry in the recipient fund is as follows:

Cash...	$90,000	
Taxes Receivable—Current.........................		$70,000
Taxes Receivable—Delinquent........................		20,000

To record collection of current and delinquent taxes in the following *assumed amounts*:

Year of Levy	Amount
20Y0..........................	$70,000
20X9..........................	10,000
20X8..........................	5,000
20X7..........................	3,000
20X6..........................	1,000
20X5..........................	500
20X4..........................	500
	$90,000

If deferred revenues have been recorded related to the receivables collected, an entry recognizing $90,000 of revenues and reducing deferred revenues also is required.

Collection of a Government's Taxes by Another Unit

Frequently, one governmental unit acts as *collecting agent* for other units. In that case, each governmental unit *certifies* its tax levy to the collecting unit, which in turn bills the taxpayers. The collecting unit accounts for these taxes in an Agency Fund (Chapter 12).

The accounting procedures outlined thus far for governments that collect their own taxes also apply to those that do not. Therefore,

- The collecting unit transmits a report indicating the amount collected for each year's levy of real property taxes and of personal property taxes.
- The recipient, on the basis of this report, distributes the proceeds among the various funds and credits the proper General Ledger accounts.

Governments that do *not* collect their own taxes typically do *not* prepare a tax roll or keep a record of the amounts paid or owed by individual taxpayers. Those records are kept for it by the collecting governmental unit.

Taxes Levied to Finance Next Year's Budget

In some governments, taxes are levied in one year to finance the next year's budget—and hence are *not* recognized as *revenue* in that year. Revenue recognition is *deferred* if *either* (1) the taxes were levied to finance the *next year's* operations, or (2) the taxes will *not* be *collected soon enough* in the next period for the resources to be available to finance current-year expenditures.[3] The entry to record the levy of taxes in either case is:

Taxes Receivable—Current.............................	$100,000	
Allowance for Uncollectible Current Taxes		$ 3,000
Deferred Revenues..................................		97,000
To record levy of taxes not available to finance current-period expenditures.		

Deferred revenues of $97,000 are reported as deferred inflows in the balance sheet at year end.

When the taxes receivable *become available* in the year for which they were levied (or later periods), the *deferred revenues* would be *reclassified* as *revenues*:

Deferred Revenues...................................	$ 97,000	
Revenues..		$97,000
To record the taxes levied last period becoming available.		
Revenues Ledger (Revenues):		
Taxes...		$97,000

---

[3]The GASB *Codification* (sec. P70.104) allows property taxes collected up to approximately 60 days after the end of the year for which they were levied to be considered "available" at year end, and thus recognized as revenue in the year preceding collection.

Deferred revenues for property taxes may also need to be recorded or adjusted in the year-end adjusting entry process. Whenever a government records the property tax levy under the assumption that the revenues *are* available—as in the illustrative example in Chapter 3—the related amounts in the preclosing trial balance (see Illustration 3-2) should be examined to determine whether significant amounts are *not* available at year end. The amount of the current property tax levy that has been recorded as revenues during the period but is *not* expected to be collected within about 60 days after year end should be reclassified as deferred revenues:

Revenues.................................	$12,000	
Deferred Revenues........................		$12,000
To adjust the accounts for property taxes that are not available at year end.		
Revenues Ledger (Revenues):		
Taxes....................................		$12,000

This adjusting entry is *reversed* at the beginning of the next year.

Some governments that recognize property tax revenues on the *cash basis* during the year use a similar deferred revenues accounting technique. They record the property tax levy as deferred revenues, then recognize revenues (and reduce deferred revenues) as property taxes are collected.

Taxes Collected in Advance

Sometimes a taxpayer will pay the subsequent year's taxes *before* the *tax* has been *levied*. Such tax collections are subsequent period revenue, not revenue of the period in which they are collected. The General Fund (or other governmental fund) entry is:

Cash.....................................	$ 2,500	
Taxes Collected in Advance................		$ 2,500
To record collection of taxes on next year's roll.		

The Taxes Collected in Advance account, which indicates that these taxes were *collected before* they were *levied*, is reported as deferred inflows in the balance sheet.

When the taxes are levied, the usual tax levy entry is made recording the Taxes Receivable—Current, the related allowance(s), and Revenues. These revenues include the revenues for the taxes collected in advance and then recorded as deferred inflows (Taxes Collected in Advance) in the preceding entry; $2,500 of the Taxes Receivable—Current are also related to these previously collected taxes. The following General Fund (or other governmental fund) entry eliminates these asset and liability amounts:

Taxes Collected in Advance..................	$ 2,500	
Taxes Receivable—Current................		$ 2,500
To record application of taxes collected in advance to reduce General Fund taxes receivable.		

Discounts on Taxes

Some governments allow discounts on taxes paid before a certain date. These discounts are considered **revenue deductions**, not expenditures. An Allowance for

Discounts on Taxes account should be established, and the tax revenues recognized should equal only the *net revenues*. For example, a tax levy of $300,000, including $9,000 expected to be uncollectible and $2,000 of discounts expected to be taken, would be recorded:

Taxes Receivable—Current	$300,000	
Allowance for Uncollectible Current Taxes		$ 9,000
Allowance for Discounts on Taxes		2,000
Revenues		289,000
To record levy of taxes, estimated uncollectible taxes, and estimated discounts to be taken.		
Revenues Ledger (Revenues):		
Taxes		$289,000

As taxes are collected and discounts are taken, the discounts are charged against the Allowance for Discounts on Taxes account. For example, tax collections of $150,000 and discounts taken of $1,500 are recorded as

Cash	$150,000	
Allowance for Discounts on Taxes	1,500	
Taxes Receivable—Current		$151,500
To record collection of taxes net of discounts.		

When the discount period expires, the following entry is made:

Allowance for Discounts on Taxes	$ 500	
Revenues		$ 500
To record increase in revenues for estimated discounts not taken.		
Revenues Ledger (Revenues):		
Taxes		$ 500

If discounts taken are *less* than estimated, as is the case illustrated here, the excess is credited (restored) to Revenues. But if discounts taken exceed the balance of the Allowance for Discounts on Taxes account, the excess is debited to Revenues.

Enforcing the Collection of Taxes

The laws of most jurisdictions prescribe a date after which unpaid taxes become delinquent and are subject to specified penalties and interest. Taxes, interest, and penalties in most states become a **lien** against property without any action by the governmental unit. After a specified period of time, the governmental unit can sell the property to satisfy its lien.[4]

The property owner is usually given the privilege of *redeeming* the property within a certain period of time. If the property is not redeemed by the specified date, the acquirer obtains title.

Typically, more than one governmental unit has liens against property that is being sold for delinquent taxes. Accordingly, the statutes often provide for a single

[4]In some states the state government pays the delinquent taxes and related amounts to the local governments, obtains their liens on the properties, and disposes of the properties at tax sales. In these states, the local governments would recognize revenues at this point if the criteria for sales of receivables established in GASB *Statement No. 48,* "Sales and Pledges of Receivables and Future Revenues and Intra-Entity Transfers of Assets and Future Revenues," are met.

governmental unit to attempt to collect the delinquent taxes and perform all the steps necessary to enforce the tax lien. Each taxing unit receives from the collecting unit its proportionate share of tax collections, net of collection costs.

Recording Interest and Penalties on Taxes   Some governmental units accrue interest and penalties on delinquent taxes, whereas others do not record them until they are collected. They should be accrued if material, of course, and added to the tax roll or other subsidiary record for the tax levy to which they apply. The entry to record the accrual of $15,000 of interest and penalties, of which $1,000 is estimated to be uncollectible, is:

Interest and Penalties Receivable—Delinquent Taxes	$15,000	
Allowance for Uncollectible Interest and Penalties.......		$ 1,000
Revenues		14,000

To record interest and penalties revenues on delinquent
  taxes net of the estimated uncollectible.

Revenues Ledger (Revenues):

Interest and Penalties	$14,000

If the available criterion is not met when interest and penalties receivable are accrued, Deferred Revenues would be credited (rather than Revenues) and reported as deferred inflows in the balance sheet. Revenue would be recognized when the receivable is collected.

Accounting for Tax Sales   After the legally specified period has passed without payment of taxes, penalties, and interest, some governments officially *reclassify* these assets to **tax liens receivable**:

Tax Liens Receivable	$28,000	
Taxes Receivable—Delinquent		$25,000
Interest and Penalties Receivable—Delinquent Taxes		3,000

To record conversion of delinquent taxes and of interest
  and penalties thereon to tax liens as follows:

Levy of	Taxes	Interest and Penalties	Total
20X8	$10,000	$1,000	$11,000
20X7	15,000	2,000	17,000
	$25,000	$3,000	$28,000

Subsidiary taxes receivable records (including penalties and interest) for each piece of property are credited at this time, and subsidiary records of the individual tax liens are established. In most cases the estimated net realizable value of the tax liens will be reflected in the amount of Deferred Revenues. Revenues associated with these receivables normally will not have been recognized at this point.

    Court costs and other costs incurred in converting property into tax liens and in selling the properties typically are recoverable from the taxpayer or sale of the taxpayer's property and should be added to the tax lien:

Tax Liens Receivable	$ 1,000	
Cash		$ 1,000

 To record court costs and other costs incurred in
  converting delinquent taxes, related interest,
  and penalties into tax liens.

When the assets are converted into tax liens, appropriate amounts of the related allowances for uncollectible tax-related accounts are reclassified to an Allowance for Uncollectible Tax Liens:

Allowance for Uncollectible Delinquent Taxes	$2,000	
Allowance for Uncollectible Interest and Penalties.	100	
Allowance for Uncollectible Tax Liens		$2,100

To reclassify the allowances for estimated uncollectible taxes, interest, and penalties on specific properties to the allowance for uncollectible tax liens (assumes a $26,900 value).

If the proceeds from the sale of a property equal the amount of the tax lien against it, there is simply a debit to Cash and a credit to Tax Liens Receivable. Revenues for the same amount[5] should normally be recognized at this point.

- If a property is sold for more than the amount of the liens, the excess is paid to the property owner and/or mortgage holder. The revenues are the same as previously indicated.
- If the cash received from the sale of a property is not sufficient to cover the tax liens, the difference is charged to Allowance for Uncollectible Tax Liens. Revenues equal to the cash collected are recognized (and Deferred Revenues is reduced).

If the governmental unit bids in (retains) properties at the time of the sale, it becomes (as is any other purchaser) subject to the redemption privilege of the property owners. As properties are redeemed, an entry is made debiting Cash and crediting Tax Liens Receivable.

If some of the properties are *not* redeemed and the government officials decide to keep them for government purposes—for example, for neighborhood parks—the Tax Liens Receivable accounts are removed from the funds in which they are carried through the following entry:

Expenditures.	$4,000	
Allowance for Uncollectible Tax Liens	2,000	
Tax Liens Receivable		$6,000
To record the expenditure for tax sale property retained.		
Expenditures Ledger (Expenditures):		
Capital Outlay	$4,000	

The debit to Expenditures is for the estimated *salable value* of the property, whereas the debit to Allowance for Uncollectible Tax Liens is the *difference* between the salable value of the property and the liens receivable against it. If the property's salable value is *more* than the receivable, only the amount of the receivable—the government's cost—is charged to Expenditures. Thus, the amount charged to Expenditures when a government retains bid-in property is the *lesser* of its salable value and the Tax Liens Receivable. An equal amount of revenues should be recorded as follows:

Deferred Revenues	$4,000	
Revenues.		$4,000
To record the revenue for tax sale property retained.		
Revenues Ledger (Revenues):		
Taxes		$4,000

---

[5]The amount of revenues would be reduced by costs of holding the sale that are not reported as expenditures because this portion of the amount collected reimburses those costs and is not collection of revenues.

The bid-in property retained usually becomes a general capital asset and is recorded (capitalized) in the General Capital Assets accounts at the *lower* of cost (i.e., the tax liens) or market value of the property (in this case, $4,000). The joint cost incurred should be allocated between the land and building in proportion to their relative fair values.

If several governments have liens on the same piece of property, the proceeds from its sale are distributed among the various units to satisfy their liens, and any remaining cash is turned over to the property owner. If the proceeds are not sufficient to cover all the liens, each governmental unit receives a proportionate share of the money realized, unless statutes specify another basis of distribution. Some alternative distribution requirements have caused financial stress for the government that acts as the collection agent. Nassau County, New York, for instance, guarantees the tax collections of several other units whose taxes it collects out of its own share of tax collections. Consequently, Nassau County retains tax collections that are only a small percentage of its levy. This is one reason this wealthy county was facing severe fiscal stress in 2012.

Property Tax Statements/ Schedules

Several types of property tax statements and schedules are usually prepared to provide adequate disclosure of the details of property taxes. These statements and schedules may be divided into two classes: (1) those related to the financial statements of the current period and (2) those showing data for other periods, as well as for this period.

Some property tax statements and schedules are prepared primarily for internal use. Others are included in either the financial section or the statistical section of the comprehensive annual financial report (CAFR) of a state or local government (see Chapter 15). The general property tax statements and schedules that are directly related to the financial statements of the current period belong in the financial section of the annual report, whereas those that show data for a number of periods are known as statistical schedules and appear in the statistical section.

LICENSES AND PERMITS

Governments have the right to permit, control, or forbid many activities of individuals and corporations. Governments issue licenses or permits to grant the privilege of performing acts that would otherwise be illegal. Licenses and permits revenues may be divided into business and nonbusiness categories. In the *business category* are alcoholic beverages, health care, corporations, public utilities, professional and occupational, and amusements licenses, among others. The *nonbusiness category* may include building permits and motor vehicle, motor vehicle operator, hunting and fishing, marriage, burial, and animal licenses.

The rates for licenses and permits are established by ordinance or statute. In contrast to property taxes, however, new rates need not be established each year. Instead, the legislative body adjusts the rates of particular licenses from time to time. Revenues from most licenses and permits are not recognized until cash is received. This is because the amount is not known until the licenses and permits are issued, and cash is collected upon their issuance.

Proper control over these revenues must ensure not only that the revenues actually collected are handled properly but also that all the revenues that should be collected are collected. In other words, the governmental unit must see that all those who should secure licenses or permits do so. For example, if a license is required to operate a motor vehicle, no vehicle should be operated without one. Of course, the governmental unit must also institute controls to ensure that the revenues actually collected are recorded, which is accomplished in part by using sequentially numbered licenses, permits, and similar documents.

INTERGOVERNMENTAL REVENUES

Intergovernmental revenues consist of grants and other financial assistance received from other governmental units. The GASB literature addresses intergovernmental grants, entitlements, and shared revenues as follows:

- **Government-mandated nonexchange transactions** occur when a government (including the federal government) at one level (1) *provides resources* to a government at another level and (2) *requires* the recipient to use them for a specific purpose(s) established in the provider's enabling legislation. In essence, the provider establishes *purpose restrictions* and also may establish *time requirements and other eligibility requirements.*

- **Voluntary nonexchange transactions** result from legislative or contractual agreements—other than exchanges—entered into *willingly* by two or more parties. Examples of voluntary nonexchange transactions include certain grants, certain entitlements, and donations by nongovernmental entities, including individuals (private donations). The provider may establish *purpose restrictions* and *eligibility requirements,* and may require the return of the resources if the purpose restrictions or other eligibility requirements are not met.[6]

Capital grants are *solely* for capital purposes; all other grants—including those for *both* capital and operating purposes—are **operating grants**. Federal or state grants for airport improvements, buses, subway systems, and wastewater treatment systems are examples of *capital grants*. Grants such as those for the operation of social welfare programs are *operating grants*.

The primary distinction between entitlements and shared revenues lies in the difference between the natures of the amounts being allocated by formula. *Entitlements* are portions of a fixed, appropriated amount of money—for example, a state revenue-sharing appropriation—that are allocated among eligible state or local governments by some formula, such as according to their relative populations. *Shared revenues,* on the other hand, are portions of a federal or state revenue source that varies in amount each month, quarter, or year—for example, gasoline, sales, liquor, and tobacco taxes. Shared revenues are also allocated among eligible state or local governments according to some formula, such as by the relative number of vehicles registered or by relative sales of the products or services taxed at the federal or state level. This distinction is often confused in practice and in political rhetoric. For example, federal and state revenue-sharing programs usually are actually entitlements, and state tax-sharing programs are often referred to as entitlements. State-collected, locally shared taxes should be identified in the Revenues Subsidiary Ledger according to the kind of tax being shared.

Payments in lieu of taxes from other governments—a significant intergovernmental revenue source of some local government public school systems—are *amounts paid to one government by another to reimburse the payee for revenues lost because the payer government does not pay taxes.* For example, the federal government does not pay sales taxes to local governments, and local governments do not pay state occupancy taxes. The maximum amount would usually be computed by determining the amount that the receiving government would have collected had the property of the paying government been subject to taxation.

Payments in lieu of taxes are particularly significant when the federal government makes payments in lieu of taxes to local governments and school districts near its major military bases. Presumably, the receiving government would record payments in lieu of taxes in the same fund(s) and manner as it records its tax revenues.

Twelve possible classifications of intergovernmental revenues result from listing the four kinds of intergovernmental revenue under federal, state, and local unit categories. For example, there would be federal grants, state grants, local grants, federal entitlements, and so on.

Intergovernmental Revenue Classifications

---

[6]Adapted from GASB *Codification*, sec. N50.104.

As previously indicated, grants are ordinarily made for a specified purpose(s). Entitlements and shared revenues may also be restricted as to use but frequently are not. Accordingly:

- *Restricted* grants, entitlements, and shared revenues—whether from federal, state, or local government sources—should be (1) recorded in the appropriate fund and (2) classified both by source and according to the function for which the grants are to be spent (e.g., general government, public safety, highways and streets, sanitation, and health).
- *Unrestricted* entitlements and shared revenues should be (1) recorded in the appropriate fund and (2) classified according to the *source* of the revenues. Similarly, intergovernmental payments in lieu of taxes are classified only by governmental source—federal, state, or local unit—because they are not ordinarily restricted as to use.

Intergovernmental Revenue Accounting

GASB's guidance on nonexchange transactions establishes financial reporting standards for intergovernmental grants and other financial assistance involving financial resources, nonfinancial resources, or both. This assistance includes entitlements, shared revenues, pass-through grants, and on-behalf payments for fringe benefits and salaries. This section of this text has the same "intergovernmental restricted" resource focus. Neither the GASB guidance nor this section applies to other resources such as contributed services or food stamps.[7]

Fund Identification

The purpose and requirements of each grant, entitlement, or shared revenue establish the proper fund(s) to use. Existing funds should be used when possible; it is not always necessary to establish a separate fund for each grant, entitlement, or shared revenue.

- Operating grants restricted to a specific general government program or activity usually are reported in Special Revenue Funds.
- Intergovernmental revenues received for the payment of principal and/or interest on general long-term debt should be accounted for in a debt service fund.
- Capital grants or shared revenues restricted for capital acquisitions or construction, other than those associated with enterprise and internal service funds, should be accounted for in a capital projects fund.
- Grants, entitlements, or shared revenues received or utilized for enterprise or internal service fund operations and/or capital assets should be accounted for in those fund types.[8]

It is possible, though not common, for a government to receive intergovernmental revenues that must be maintained intact indefinitely in a Permanent Fund or Private-Purpose Trust Fund.

Pass-Through Grants

The distinction between pass-through and other types of grants is important. A **pass-through** grant is where:

- The **primary recipient**, such as a state government, receives the grant—say, from the federal government to support special education programs.
- The primary recipient cannot spend the resources for its own purposes but must "pass through" the resources to a **secondary recipient**—say, a local government or public school district—which is referred to as the **subrecipient**.
- The subrecipient then spends the grant resources for the specified purposes—perhaps under both federal and state regulations and oversight—or may *pass through* some or all of the resources, if permitted, to its subrecipients or sub-subrecipients.

State governments, in particular, are primary recipients of significant pass-through grants for public education and other purposes.

[7]GASB *Codification*, sec. N50.101–103.
[8]Ibid., sec. 1300.104–114.

The GASB notes, with respect to pass-through grants:

> All *cash* pass-through grants received by a governmental entity (referred to as a recipient government) should be reported in its financial statements. As a general rule, *cash pass-through grants should be recognized as [intergovernmental] revenue and expenditures or expenses in the [governmental, proprietary, or trust] funds of the primary government and in the government-wide financial statements.* In those infrequent cases in which a recipient government serves *only* as a *cash conduit,* the grant should be reported in an agency fund. A recipient government serves only as a cash conduit if it merely transmits grantor-supplied moneys without having administrative or direct financial involvement in the program.[9]

Revenue Recognition

Regarding *governmental fund* revenue recognition for grants, entitlements, and shared revenues, the GASB *Codification* states:

- Revenues [earned or levied] from *nonexchange transactions* should be recognized "in the accounting period when they become available and measurable."

- Revenue resulting from *government-mandated nonexchange transactions [grants] and voluntary nonexchange transactions [grants]* should be recognized in the period when all applicable *eligibility requirements* have been *met* and the *resources* are *available.*[10]

Whereas *unrestricted* grants, entitlements, and shared revenues are recognized immediately as revenues of governmental funds if available, *restricted* grants, whether mandatory or voluntary nonexchange transactions, are *not recognized as revenue until all eligibility requirements are met and the resources are available* (i.e., collected).

In the usual case, a restricted grant must be expended for allowable costs for the specified purposes to meet the eligibility requirements. Thus, such grants are often referred to as **expenditure-driven grants**—because *grant revenue is recognized only when qualifying expenditures are incurred.* That is, grant revenue recognition is "driven" by grant-related expenditures being incurred.

If a *restricted* grant has been *awarded* to a government but has *neither* been *received nor earned* by the SLG making qualifying expenditures, the grant awarded is *not* reported in the financial statements, though it *may* be *disclosed* in the notes to the financial statements. This situation is essentially equivalent to an *unperformed* executory *contract.*

Grant Received Before Earned When revenues should not be recognized at the time the cash from the grant, entitlement, or shared revenue is received—as when a restricted cash grant has been received but is not yet earned—the following entry is appropriate:

Cash	$100,000	
Unearned Revenues		$100,000

To record receipt of grant, entitlement, or shared revenue
    prior to revenue being earned and recognized.

When an entitlement or shared revenue applicable to the next year is received currently, the credit should be to Deferred Revenues unless there is a performance obligation similar to that of a restricted grant. Deferred revenues are reported as deferred inflows.

---

[9]Ibid., sec. N50.128. (Emphasis added.) The GASB also notes that a recipient government has **administrative involvement** if, for example, it (a) monitors secondary recipients for compliance with program-specific requirements; (b) determines eligible secondary recipients or projects, even if using grantor-established criteria; or (c) has the ability to exercise discretion in how the funds are allocated. A recipient government has **direct financial involvement** if, for example, it finances some direct program costs because of a grantor-imposed matching requirement or is liable for disallowed costs.

[10]Ibid., sec. N50.126–127. (Emphasis added.) Note that the stipulation that "resources are available" means that the cash has been received by year end or soon enough thereafter to be used to pay the liabilities of the period.

When the conditions of the grant, entitlement, or shared revenue restrictions have been met, the revenue is recognized. For example, if we assume that any local matching requirements have been met and the only remaining requirement is that the resources must be expended for a specified purpose, the following entries are made for a 1:1 reimbursement grant upon incurring qualifying expenditures of $40,000:

(1) Expenditures....................................	$40,000	
Vouchers Payable...............................		$40,000
To record expenditures qualifying under restricted grant program.		
Expenditures Ledger (Expenditures):		
Grant (Specify type)	$40,000	
(2) Unearned Revenues	$40,000	
Revenues.....................................		$40,000
To record recognition of revenues concurrent with expenditures meeting grant restrictions.		
Revenues Ledger (Revenues):		
Intergovernmental		$40,000

A more detailed subsidiary ledger account title—such as Federal Grants or even one by grant name and number—would be used in practice. Broad account titles such as Intergovernmental are used only for illustrative purposes.

Grant Earned Before Received A state or local government may make qualifying expenditures under a grant and meet all other eligibility requirements before the grant cash is received. Although this may occur in many grant programs, some grants—known as **reimbursement grants**—specify that the government must first incur qualifying expenditures, then file for reimbursement under the grant program.

A government that makes an expenditure that qualifies for 1:1 reimbursement under an approved grant (and that receives the cash soon enough for resources to be considered available) should record both (1) the expenditure and (2) the corresponding grant revenue:

(1) Expenditures....................................	$75,000	
Vouchers Payable...............................		$75,000
To record expenditure that qualifies for reimbursement under approved grant.		
Expenditures Ledger (Expenditures):		
Grant X (Specify type)	$75,000	
(2) Due from Grantor	$75,000	
Revenues.....................................		$75,000
To record grant revenues earned and receivable under reimbursement grant.		
Revenues Ledger (Revenues):		
Intergovernmental—Grant X.......................		$75,000

Note that this entry assumes both (1) that the grant is a pure reimbursement grant—that is, the actual direct expenditures are reimbursed under the grant—and (2) that collection of the receivable is expected soon enough for the revenue to be considered available.

- If the reimbursement grant pays more or less than the direct expenditures incurred, the amount reimbursed is recorded as the grant receivable and revenue.
- If the grant receivable is not expected to be collected soon enough for the related revenue to be considered available, Deferred Revenues (not Revenues) is credited initially and reported as deferred inflows on the balance sheet. Revenue is recognized when the grant receivable becomes available.

The qualifying expenditure entry and the entry to accrue the related grant receivable and recognize grant revenue are not always made simultaneously in practice. For example, the total qualifying expenditures for several days, a month, or a quarter may be accumulated, then filed for reimbursement. Thus, controls should be established to ensure that all qualifying expenditures are properly filed for reimbursement and are indeed reimbursed. Furthermore, qualifying expenditure entries should be reviewed at year end to ensure that grant receivables have been properly accrued or are accrued in the year end adjusting entries and any related grant revenue is recognized.

Revenue recognition for grants, entitlements, and shared revenues restricted for proprietary fund purposes is discussed and illustrated in Chapters 10 and 11.

CHARGES FOR SERVICES

Revenues from charges for services consist of charges made by various general government departments for goods or services rendered by them to the public, other departments of the government, or other governments. Similarly, special assessments for current services are considered departmental charges for services revenues.

It is important to distinguish between revenues derived from departmental earnings and those from licenses and permits. Only those charges resulting directly from the activity of the department and made for the purpose of recovering part of the costs of the department are considered charges for current services. Some of these charges may involve the issuance of permits, but the revenues should be classed as charges for services, not as permits revenues.

Interfund Services vs. Reimbursements

It is also important to distinguish charges for services rendered by one department to other departments that constitute exchange-like interfund services transactions, from interfund reimbursements.

- **Exchange-like interfund services transactions** result in (1) revenues being recognized in the fund used to finance the *provider* department (i.e., seller) and (2) expenditures or expenses being recognized in the fund used to finance the department *receiving* the goods or services.

- **Interfund reimbursements** result in expenditures or expenses being recognized in the fund from which the department *receiving* the goods or services is financed but a reduction (recovery) of expenditures or expenses being recorded in the fund through which the *provider* department is financed.

An exchange-like interfund services transaction occurs when interdepartmental services (or goods) of the type routinely rendered to external parties are provided in the equivalent of an interdepartmental arm's-length transaction.

Charges for Services

Charges for services collected when services are rendered are recorded as revenues. If charges are not collected when services are rendered, revenues (or deferred revenues, if not available) should be recorded when billed or in year-end adjusting entries. The following entries illustrate some transactions that result in revenues being recorded as soon as they are earned:

Due from Other Governmental Units	$25,000	
Revenues		$25,000
To record earnings resulting from charges to other governmental units for patients in mental hospitals and for inmates in prisons.		
Revenues Ledger (Revenues):		
Hospital Fees		$10,000
Prison Fees		15,000
		$25,000

Accounts Receivable...............................	$20,000	
Revenues.......................................		$20,000

To record street lighting, street sprinkling, and trash collection charges made to property owners.

Revenues Ledger (Revenues):

Street Light Charges..............................	$ 5,000
Street Sanitation Charges..........................	8,000
Refuse Collection Fees............................	7,000
	$20,000

The following entry illustrates some of the transactions in which *revenues* typically are *recognized* only *as cash is collected* (rather than as billed or accrued):

Cash	$38,200	
Revenues.......................................		$38,200

To record receipt of cash representing charges for services.

Revenues Ledger (Revenues):

Sale of Maps and Publications	$ 4,200
Building Inspection Fees...........................	9,000
Plumbing Inspection Fees	5,000
Swimming Pool Inspection Fees	2,000
Golf Fees	7,000
Fees for Recording Legal Instruments	6,000
Animal Control and Shelter Fees	5,000
	$38,200

Finally, some government services may be provided in one period, billed to service recipients, and collected in a later period or periods. Thus, expenditures may be recognized before the related revenues are recognized. A common example is street maintenance or improvement programs financed by special assessments against benefited properties or citizens. Some assessments are essentially taxes; others are charges for services. *The following entries illustrate transactions in which governments render services and bill service recipients in one period but collect the charges (say, special assessments) and recognize revenues during one or more future periods.* (Subsidiary ledger entries are omitted.)

Mid-20X1: Assessment-financed services rendered; service recipients billed—charges payable in five annual installments, with 6% interest, beginning in mid-20X2:

Expenditures....................................	$100,000	
Vouchers Payable		$100,000

To record expenditures incurred.

Assessments Receivable—Deferred	$100,000	
Deferred Revenues		$100,000

To record levy of special assessments.

Mid-20X2: One-fifth of the deferred receivables came due and reminder notices were mailed.

Assessments Receivable—Current	$ 20,000	
Assessments Receivable—Deferred		$ 20,000

To record currently maturing special assessment receivables.

Deferred Revenues	$ 20,000	
Revenues—Special Assessments		$ 20,000

To recognize special assessment revenues.

| Interest Receivable on Special Assessments (6%) .... | $ 6,000 | |
| Revenues—Interest on Special Assessments .... | | $ 6,000 |

To record current interest billed on special assessments.

The special assessments are to mature and be collected during 20X2–20X6, with interest on the unpaid balances. This example is highly simplified, of course; for example, it assumes all receivables will be collected when due. More complex special assessment situations are addressed in Chapters 7 and 8.

As implied by the foregoing discussions and illustrations, the chart of accounts for charges for services should be based on the activity for which the charge is made. These activities can be classified according to the function of the government in which the activity is conducted. For example, under the general government function we would expect to find accounts such as these:

- Court costs, fees, and charges
- Recording of legal instruments
- Zoning and subdivision fees
- Plan-checking fees
- Sale of maps and publications
- Building inspection fees

FINES AND FORFEITS

Revenues from fines and forfeits are not usually an important source of a government's income. *Because they are not often susceptible to accrual prior to collection, these revenues are usually accounted for on a cash basis,* particularly by local governments. States may assess large corporate fines, say for violating pollution laws, which *are* susceptible to accrual when assessed.

Fines are penalties imposed for the commission of statutory offenses or for violation of lawful administrative rules. Fines and other penalties included in this section are primarily those imposed by the courts.

When courts accept cash bonds or fine payments, adequate cash receipt and related controls are essential. In any event, all activities of the court should be documented to provide an appropriate record of all cases brought before the court, the cash or property bond or bail related to each case, and the disposition of each case, including any bond or bail forfeitures ordered and fines levied.

Similar types of controls are essential when any police department, sheriff's office, or other law enforcement agency accepts cash for any reason. Effective cash and related controls, such as over traffic and parking tickets, are essential. Even small improprieties within courts and law enforcement agencies damage their credibility, public image, and effectiveness.

The money from cash bonds and bail is often first accounted for in an Agency Fund (Chapter 12). If forfeited, it must be disbursed as specified in applicable laws. Unless the law provides otherwise, forfeited bail money is paid from the Agency Fund to the General Fund, where it is recorded:

| Cash .... | $5,000 | |
| Revenues .... | | $5,000 |

To record receipt of money representing forfeited bail.

Revenues Ledger (Revenues):

| Fines and Forfeits .... | | $5,000 |

INVESTMENT EARNINGS

Short-term investment of cash available in excess of current needs is authorized by legislative bodies throughout the country. Indeed, many states have statewide depository and investment policies and procedures, and many state and local governments have highly sophisticated cash and investment management systems. Thus, in addition to interest on long-term investments of Debt Service Funds, for example, interest earned on short-term investments of idle cash is a substantial general revenue source in many municipalities. Interest receivable should be accrued as it is earned by the governmental unit and recognized as revenue if it will be received (or constructively received) during the period or soon enough thereafter to be considered available.

GASB *Statement No. 31* establishes fair value[11] standards for investments in

a. Participating interest-earning investment contracts.
b. External investment pools.
c. Open-end mutual funds.
d. Debt securities.
e. Equity securities, option contracts, stock warrants, and stock rights that have readily determinable fair values.

Two terms are particularly important to understanding GASB *Statement No. 31*:

- **Participating** investment contracts are investments whose value is affected by market (interest rate) changes because (1) they are negotiable or transferable, or (2) their redemption value considers market rates.
- **Fair value** is the amount at which a financial instrument could be exchanged in a current transaction between willing parties, other than in a forced or liquidation sale.

GASB *Statement No. 31* requires that:

1. Governmental entities report *many types* of investments at fair value in the balance sheet.
2. All investment income, *including changes in the fair value of investments*, usually should be reported as revenue in the operating statements.

However, *Statement No. 31 permits* governmental units to continue reporting *certain* investments at amortized cost, including lower of amortized cost or fair value, rather than at fair value. These *exempted* investments include:

- Nonparticipating interest-earning investment contracts.
- Money market investments and participating interest-earning investment contracts that have a remaining maturity *when purchased* of one year or less.[12]
- Equity securities, option contracts, stock warrants, and stock rights that do not have readily determinable fair values.

These *Statement No. 31* exceptions exempt significant amounts of the general government investments of many local governments from the fair value standards. These exemptions also may result in some of a governmental unit's investments being accounted for under the fair value approach and other investments being accounted for using the amortized cost method.

To illustrate the differences in amortized cost and fair value accounting for investments, consider these facts: A Governmental Unit made two, 2-year

---

[11]Governmental Accounting Standards Board, *Statement No. 31,* "Accounting and Financial Reporting for Certain Investments and for External Investment Pools" (GASB, March 1997).

[12]Ibid., par. 22. The terms *interest-earning investment contract* and *money market investment* are defined as:
- **Interest-earning investment contract.** A direct contract, other than a mortgage or other loan, that a government enters into as a creditor of a financial institution, broker-dealer, investment company, insurance company, or other financial services company and for which it receives, directly or indirectly, interest payments. Interest-earning investment contracts include time deposits with financial institutions (such as certificates of deposit), repurchase agreements, and guaranteed and bank investment contracts (GICs and BICs).
- **Money market investment**. A short-term, highly liquid debt instrument, including commercial paper, banker's acceptances, and U.S. Treasury and agency obligations.

$500,000 investments on July 1, 20X1, the beginning of its fiscal year, in 6% interest-earning contracts. Each investment was purchased at a discount of $4,000. The fair value of each investment at June 30, 20X2, was $497,000.

1. One investment, Investment A, is exempt from the fair value requirements of GASB *Statement No. 31* and will be accounted for on the **amortized cost method**.

2. The other investment, Investment B, is to be accounted for on the fair value method.

The governmental fund entries to record the investment acquisition and interest received are identical for Investments A and B:

Investment (Same for Investments A and B)

7/1/X1	Investments	$496,000	
	Cash		$496,000
	To record investments purchased.		

Interest Received (Same for Investments A and B)

6/30/X2	Cash	$ 30,000	
	Revenues—Interest		$ 30,000
	To record interest received.		

The *amortized cost* and *fair value* entries at June 30, 20X2, *differ:*

Amortized Cost (Investment A)

6/30/X2	Investments	$ 2,000	
	Revenues—Interest		$ 2,000
	To amortize unamortized investment discount.		

Investment income reported: $30,000 + $2,000 = $32,000

Fair Value (Investment B)

6/30/X2	Investments[13]	$ 1,000	
	Revenues—Increase in Fair Value of Investments ..		$ 1,000
	To record change in fair value of investments.		
	(Fair value of investments is $497,000.)		

Investment income reported: $30,000 + $1,000 = $31,000

These *entries* are *summarized* in Illustration 5-6.

ILLUSTRATION 5-6	Investment Accounting Methods—Interest-Bearing Debt Securities				
	Amortized Cost		**Fair Value**		
When Acquired	Investments $496,000		Investments $496,000		
	Cash	$496,000	Cash		$496,000
Interest Received	Cash .... $ 30,000		Cash .... $ 30,000		
	Revenues—Interest ...	$ 30,000	Revenues—Interest...		$ 30,000
Discount Amortized	Investments .... $ 2,000		No entry		
	Revenues—Interest ...	$ 2,000			
Change in Fair Value Recognized	No entry—unless apparently permanent decline in fair value		Investments .... $ 1,000		
			Revenues—Increase in Fair Value of Investments		$ 1,000
Investment Income Reported	$32,000		$31,000		

[13]Some governments maintain the Investments account at cost or amortized cost. These governments record the difference between the cost or amortized cost and fair value in a valuation allowance account.

Note that the fair value approach is affected by interest rate changes, whereas the amortized cost approach assumes that the interest rate was established when the investments were acquired. Note also that the **net** increase or decrease in fair value of investments is reported as **revenue** or a *deduction* from *net* revenue. A net loss would not be reported unless the decrease in investment fair value exceeds all interest and other investment revenue received and accrued, and it would be reported as *negative* revenue rather than as an expenditure.

GASB *Statement No. 31* includes illustrations of computing changes in fair values of investments—the difference between the fair value of investments at the beginning of the year and at the end of the year, taking into consideration investment purchases, sales, and redemptions—under both the specific identification method and the aggregate method. Both approaches are demonstrated in Illustration 5-7.

Finally, GASB *Statement No. 31 permits* governments to:

1. *Report investment income either in one summary amount, with details disclosed in the notes to the financial statements, or in detail,* such as:

Investment income	
Interest	$ 30,000
Net increase in the fair value of investments	1,000
Total investment income	$ 31,000

2. *Disclose the detailed amounts presented at 1 above and details of realized and unrealized investment gains and losses only in the notes to the financial statements.*

ILLUSTRATION 5-7 Investment Fair Value Changes Analysis Approaches

1. Fair Value Analysis of Investment Activity—Specific Identification Method

		Fair Value					
		A	B	C	D*	E	F**
Security	Cost	Beginning Fair Value 1/1/X1	Purchases	Sales	Subtotal	Ending Fair Value 12/31/X1	Changes in Fair Value
1	$100	$100	—	—	$100	$120	$20
2	520	540	—	—	540	510	(30)
3	200	240	—	$250	(10)	—	10
4	330	—	$330	—	330	315	(15)
		$880	$330	$250	$960	$945	($15)

2. Calculation of the Net Change in the Fair Value of Investments—Aggregate Method

Fair Value at December 31, 20X1	$ 945
Add: Proceeds of investments sold in 20X1	250
Less: Cost of investments purchased in 20X1	(330)
Less: Fair value at December 31, 20X0	(880)
Change in fair value of investments	($ 15)

*Column D = Columns A + B − Column C.
**Column F = Column E − Column D.

Source: GASB *Statement No. 31,* "Accounting and Financial Reporting for Certain Investments and for External Investment Pools" (GASB, March 1997), par. 78.

Government finance officers, accountants, and auditors should ensure that any state or local government regulations relating to short-term investments are observed, as well as those of the federal government with respect to **arbitrage** in the Internal Revenue Code (IRC) and related regulations. Briefly, the IRC provides that a state or local government **investing proceeds of a tax-exempt debt issue** (interest *exempt* from federal income taxes) in *non-tax-exempt* investments at rates higher than that being paid on the debt may have to rebate the excess interest earned to the U.S. Treasury. SLGs that do not comply may be assessed both a 50% penalty and interest on the unpaid arbitrage and penalty. Or they may have the tax-exempt status of their debt issues revoked. Although the immediate and direct impact of such revocation would adversely affect the investors in those debt securities rather than the government, the rating agencies consider it a covenant default. The government's reputation and credit rating would be damaged, and its future debt issues would probably be difficult to sell and would carry much higher interest rates than formerly. Furthermore, the U.S. Securities and Exchange Commission (SEC) requires disclosures of debt defaults, and GASB *Statement No. 40,* "Deposit and Investment Risk Disclosures," requires numerous disclosures about each government's investment activities in the notes to its financial statements.[14]

The recognition of changes in fair value introduces an additional concern for government officials who do not intend to sell some of these investments in the short term. Because fund balance is increased—even though cash has not been received and is not intended to be received from the immediate sale of the investments, some officials are concerned that the financial statements may be interpreted as meaning that the government has more currently available resources than is substantively the case.

MISCELLANEOUS REVENUES

The miscellaneous category includes sources of revenues such as rents and royalties, escheats, and contributions and donations from private sources. All of the revenues discussed in this chapter may be found in the General Fund and Special Revenue Funds; some of them may also appear in other funds. In addition, other funds may have sources of revenues that have not been described here but will be discussed in subsequent chapters. Most of the revenues in the miscellaneous category are self-explanatory, but a discussion of some of them may prove useful.

Escheats

The laws of most states specify that the net assets of deceased persons who died intestate (without a valid will) and with no known relatives revert to the state. Similarly, most state laws specify that amounts in inactive checking accounts (and perhaps other accounts) in banks revert to the state after a period of time, often seven years. Such laws result in what are referred to as **escheats** to the state. *The cash or equivalent values of financial resources (e.g., cash, stocks, and bonds) received by escheat—net of any amounts expected to be claimed by heirs—are recognized as revenues* by the recipient state.[15] Capital assets received by escheat and retained for use by the government should be recorded in the General Capital Assets accounts at their fair value when received by the state.

---

[14]GASB *Codification,* sec. C20, I50, and I60.

[15]Ibid., sec. E70.

Private Contributions Occasionally, a government will receive contributions or donations from private sources. Unrestricted contributions, which are rare, are recognized as General Fund revenues. Restricted donations (except those to be held in trust for others) usually are recognized as Special Revenue Fund, Capital Projects Fund, or Permanent Fund revenue, as appropriate to the operating or capital purpose; those in trust for others would be accounted for initially in a Private-Purpose Trust Fund, as discussed in Chapter 12.

SELECTED NONREVENUE FUND BALANCE INCREASES

Numerous nonrevenue increases in the fund balance of governmental funds have been referred to earlier in the text. Some, such as transfers, have been discussed and illustrated in detail. This section highlights three types of such transactions: capital asset sales/losses, internal "payments in lieu of taxes," and collateralized borrowings.

Capital Asset Sales/Losses Capital assets financed from General Fund and Special Revenue Fund resources are *not* governmental fund assets. Financial resources received from disposing of general capital assets *are* governmental fund assets, however, and net proceeds from the sale of and compensation for loss of general capital assets are reported as **other financing sources** of these funds. The GASB *requires* SLGs to report such sale and loss compensation proceeds as *nonrevenue other financing sources* because they result from converting general capital assets to financial assets—*not* from revenue transactions.

Ideally, general capital asset sale and loss compensation proceeds should be recorded in the fund that financed the acquisition of the asset that has been sold or destroyed. But identifying the source from which assets were financed may be difficult and in many instances the funds used to finance the purchase of assets are abolished before the assets are disposed of. Accordingly, the net proceeds from the sale and compensation for loss of general capital assets usually flow into the General Fund or a Special Revenue Fund, and thus are reported as *other (nonrevenue) financing sources* of that fund. Proceeds from the sale and compensation for loss of assets carried in Internal Service Funds, Enterprise Funds, and Trust Funds are ordinarily accounted for in those funds rather than in the General Fund.

Internal PILOTs Payments in lieu of taxes from other governments are a significant source of intergovernmental revenues for some governments, as discussed earlier. Some governments also refer to payments made to a government's General (or other) Fund by an enterprise of that government in lieu of property taxes or other taxes as payments in lieu of taxes (PILOTs).

It is important to understand the distinction between external PILOTs from other governments, which are intergovernmental revenues, and these "internal" PILOTs involving two funds of a government.

- Internal PILOTs almost always must be reported as interfund transfers.
- Internal PILOTs should only be reported as revenues **if** the amounts approximate the value of services provided.
- In such cases, it probably is a misnomer to refer to the transaction as a PILOT. Interfund PILOTs should rarely (if ever) be reported because transactions that meet the GASB's PILOT criteria are more properly termed "Interfund Services Provided or Used."

GASB *Statement No. 48,* "Sales and Pledges of Receivables and Future Revenues and Intra-Entity Transfers of Assets and Future Revenues," specifies criteria a government must meet to report transfers of receivables as a sale. If the criteria are met in a transaction involving governmental fund receivables, revenues equal to the proceeds of the sale of the receivables typically will be reported in the governmental fund operating statement. If the criteria are not met, the transaction is classified as a borrowing. Assuming that the liability is not a governmental fund liability, other financing sources equal to the proceeds from the transaction should be reported for the governmental fund.

Collateralized Borrowings

REVENUE REPORTING: GAAP VS. BUDGETARY

Both the managerial uses of budgetary accounts and interim reports and year-end budgetary and GAAP financial reporting were introduced in earlier chapters. Likewise, it has been noted that (1) any significant differences between the budgetary basis and the GAAP basis must be explained and (2) *non*-GAAP budgetary statements and schedules must be *reconciled* to the GAAP financial statements, as discussed and illustrated later.

Another important consideration is the differing levels of detail that may be required in GAAP and budgetary statements and schedules. Recall that

- **GAAP** statements must "*present fairly*" in accordance with GAAP, as in Illustration 5-8.
- **Budgetary** statements and schedules must *demonstrate compliance* at the executive-legislative "*budgetary control points*" level of detail, as in Illustration 5-9.

In this example:

1. The **GAAP-based operating statement** (Illustration 5-8) reports revenues using terminology similar to that illustrated in Chapters 3 and 4 and at about the same level of detail.
2. The **budgetary comparison schedule** (Illustration 5-9) reports revenues information summarized in Illustration 5-8 in much more detail in compliance with the legally enacted budget (and perhaps in response to requests by members of the governing body, investors, or analysts).

As noted in discussing revenue recognition, when assets are recognized or received in advance of meeting the revenue recognition criteria in a governmental fund, either a liability for unearned revenues or deferred inflows must be reported in the balance sheet. To illustrate the balance sheet reporting, assume the following for the General Fund of a school district at December 31, 20X1:

Balance Sheet Reporting Related to Unrecognized Revenues

Taxes receivable related to the 20X2 tax levy, net of estimated uncollectibles	$100,000
Taxes receivable on taxes levied for 20X1 or earlier, but not available	8,000
Due from state government for grant revenues earned, but not available	27,000
Cash received in advance from a federal grant for which spending-related eligibility requirements are not yet met	75,000

The amounts reported as liabilities and as deferred inflows in the school district's General Fund balance sheet at December 31, 20X1 are:

Liabilities:		
Unearned grant revenues		$ 75,000
Deferred Inflows:		
Deferred tax revenues	108,000	
Deferred grant revenues	27,000	135,000

ILLUSTRATION 5-8 General Fund GAAP Operating Statement

City of Lakewood, Colorado
General Fund
Statement of Revenues, Expenditures, and Changes in Fund Balance
Year Ended December 31, 20X3

Revenues

Taxes and Special Assessments	$49,585,301
Licenses and Permits	2,647,062
Intergovernmental	5,871,202
Charges for Services	6,190,503
Fines and Forfeitures	2,373,970
Miscellaneous	
Investment Income	329,672
Sale of Maps	899
Other	972,004
Total Revenues	67,970,613

Expenditures

Current	
General Government	18,719,299
Public Safety	33,283,467
Public Works	4,727,350
Culture and Recreation	6,086,603
Urban Development and Housing	3,282,751
Miscellaneous	2,610,755
Capital Outlay	
General Government	902,374
Public Safety	44,628
Public Works	386,684
Culture and Recreation	62,133
Urban Development and Housing	114,423
Total Expenditures	70,220,467
Excess (Deficiency) of Revenues	
Over Expenditures	(2,249,854)

Other Financing Sources (Uses)

Transfers In	1,730,000
Transfers Out	(3,987,976)
Total Other Financing Sources (Uses)	(2,257,976)
Net Change in Fund Balance	(4,507,830)
Fund Balance, Beginning of Year	13,358,993
Fund Balance, End of Year	$ 8,851,163

The accompanying notes are an integral part of the financial statements.

Source: Adapted from a recent City of Lakewood, Colorado, comprehensive annual financial report (CAFR).

Liabilities are reported when revenue recognition is delayed because a performance obligation is not met. Deferred inflows are reported when the revenue recognition delay occurs because of a time requirement or because the availability criterion has not been met.

ILLUSTRATION 5-9   Budgetary Comparison Schedule—Revenues

City of Lakewood, Colorado
General Fund
Budgetary Comparison Schedule
Year Ended December 31, 20X3

	Original Budget	Final Budget	Actual	Variance Favorable (Unfavorable)
REVENUES				
Taxes				
Property Tax	$ 7,054,745	$ 7,054,745	$ 6,896,935	$ (157,810)
Sales Tax	32,157,939	30,297,939	29,446,631	(851,308)
General Use Tax	1,973,547	1,973,547	1,562,996	(410,551)
Building Material Use Tax	1,980,604	1,980,604	1,486,018	(494,586)
Specific Ownership Tax	767,755	802,264	804,967	2,703
Motor Vehicle Use Tax	3,549,943	3,399,943	3,137,063	(262,880)
Cigarette Tax	600,000	519,689	474,636	(45,053)
Franchise Tax	5,647,362	5,847,362	5,776,055	(71,307)
Total Taxes	53,731,895	51,876,093	49,585,301	(2,290,792)
Licenses and Permits				
Building Permits	2,000,934	1,925,677	1,781,226	(144,451)
Contractor Licenses	215,000	215,000	260,795	45,795
Contractor Permits	297,788	445,045	427,930	(17,115)
Liquor Licenses	50,000	50,000	53,988	3,988
Sales Tax Licenses	13,246	7,300	12,466	5,166
Other	169,400	87,900	110,657	22,757
Total Licenses and Permits	2,746,368	2,730,922	2,647,062	(83,860)
Intergovernmental Revenues				
State Highway Users Tax	3,586,433	3,486,433	3,184,585	(301,848)
County Road and Bridge Fund	2,175,679	2,155,679	1,973,602	(182,077)
Motor Vehicle Registration	542,539	502,539	474,492	(28,047)
State Highway Department Signal Maintenance	226,807	226,807	238,523	11,716
Total Intergovernmental Revenues	6,531,458	6,371,458	5,871,202	(500,256)
Charges for Services				
Liquor Administration Service Fee	190,000	190,000	194,964	4,964
Zoning and Subdivision Fees	122,953	122,953	104,040	(18,913)
Culture and Recreation Fees	2,396,326	2,396,326	2,517,328	121,002
Other	4,934,029	4,205,967	3,374,171	(831,796)
Total Charges for Services	7,643,308	6,915,246	6,190,503	(724,743)
Fines and Forfeitures	2,517,896	2,667,896	2,373,970	(293,926)
Miscellaneous				
Investment Income	448,154	282,019	329,672	47,653
Sale of Maps	—	—	899	899
Other	968,396	887,511	972,004	84,493
Total Miscellaneous	1,416,550	1,169,530	1,302,575	133,045
TOTAL REVENUES	74,587,475	71,731,145	67,970,613	(3,760,532)

See the accompanying Independent Auditors' Report.

Source: Adapted from a recent City of Lakewood, Colorado, comprehensive annual financial report (CAFR).

CHANGES IN ACCOUNTING PRINCIPLES

Restatement of the beginning fund balance of a governmental fund to correct a prior year error was illustrated briefly in Chapter 3. Restatements may also be necessary to report the *cumulative effect of changes in accounting principles*. Three types of events that might cause a government to change its governmental fund revenue recognition principles are:

1. Management decides to change from one acceptable revenue recognition principle or policy to another acceptable, alternative revenue recognition principle or policy. (This practice is not common in governmental fund accounting.)

2. Changed circumstances require a change in the method of applying the acceptable principle in use. For example, a revenue source not previously deemed objectively measurable and/or available is now considered to be both objectively measurable and available at year-end. (This type of change is common in governmental fund accounting.)

3. The GASB or another recognized standards-setting body issues a new revenue recognition standard that requires a different revenue accounting policy than that presently used.

In any event, (1) changes in accounting principles are made *effective* at the *beginning* of the year in which the change occurs, the current year; (2) the *cumulative effect of the change*—computed by comparing the revenues recognized and effects on fund balance of the governmental fund under the old accounting policy, with the effects as if the new accounting policy had been in effect—are reported as a *restatement of the beginning fund balance* of the earliest year presented; (3) *revenues are reported under the new accounting policy* for each year presented; and (4) the *change* in accounting principle is *disclosed and explained in the notes* to the current year financial statements.

New GASB Standards

Most changes in governmental fund accounting principles occur because the GASB issues a new revenue recognition standard or revises an existing standard. If the new or revised revenue recognition standard requires a different revenue recognition policy than that presently being used in its governmental fund accounting, a state or local government must change its accounting policy to comply with the new or revised standard.

GASB statements and interpretations include an "Effective Date and Transition" section that specifies when and how the new standards are to be implemented. Furthermore, such GASB standards typically encourage (but do not require) early application—that is, implementation prior to the effective date specified.

Prospective Application

Occasionally, the transition instructions are that a new accounting policy is to be applied *prospectively*—that is, applied only to transactions occurring on or after the effective date or, if implemented earlier, the implementation date. For example, a revised standard might require that a type of transaction previously recognized as revenues must be reported as other financing sources in the future; or a new standard might specify that transactions previously reported as giving rise to gains and losses by some governments (e.g., advance refundings of GLTL) must be reported as other financing sources (uses) in the future, with no gain or loss recognized.

Changed standards that are implemented *prospectively* apply only to transactions and events occurring *on or after the implementation date*. They *do not require retroactive application* as if the new standard had been in effect earlier, and they *do not require restatement* of governmental fund assets, liabilities, and fund balance. Thus, new standards that are applied prospectively do not give rise to cumulative effect of changes in accounting principles restatements of beginning fund balance.

Retroactive Application

Most new and revised GASB standards are required to be implemented retroactively — that is, as if the new standard had been in effect earlier. Thus, they require that (1) assets, liabilities, and fund balance at the *beginning* of the year in which the new standard is implemented must be *restated as if the new standard had been applied earlier*, and (2) the *cumulative effect* of applying the changed accounting principle retroactively must be reported as a *restatement of the beginning fund balance* of that year. The logic and approach involved in implementing a new accounting principle are identical to those for *correcting errors* that require retroactive restatement.

ERROR CORRECTIONS

Locating and correcting errors is a significant role and activity of professional accountants and auditors. Error correction is discussed and illustrated in most standard intermediate accounting textbooks, and those sections should be reviewed as needed to supplement this and later chapters.

Correcting errors in SLG accounts and statements is usually easier than in business because SLGs:

- Are *not* subject to federal income tax, so there is *no* "income tax effect."
- Do *not* compute or report earnings per share.

If revenue-related errors are found, the correcting entry or entries depend on whether the accounts have been closed for the year in which the error occurred:

- **Accounts Open.** Understand the *incorrect* entry that was made, *compare* it to the entry that *should* have been made, and *correct* the revenue and related accounts.
- **Accounts Closed.** The initial approach is the same—understand the *incorrect* entry that was made, *compare* it to the entry that *should* have been made—except the correction will increase or decrease the *beginning* of the current year Fund Balance account to which the prior year revenues, expenditures, and other changes have been closed. (Recall that error corrections are reported as adjustments to beginning total fund balance in a governmental fund's statement of revenues, expenditures, and changes in fund balance as illustrated in Chapter 3.)

Concluding Comments

Proper revenue administration, including revenue accounting and reporting, has never been more important to state and local governments. During periods of rapid economic growth, some governments become lax on revenue administration, assuming that growth in revenues will compensate for any administrative shortcoming. Well-managed governments, however, place equal emphasis on excellent revenue administration and expenditure administration.

Several important revenue sources were discussed in this chapter, and additional types of revenue accounting entries were illustrated. Governmental fund revenue recognition standards require that revenue(s) be *both* measurable *and* available—*as well as* earned or levied—before being recognized. Applying these criteria in practice requires judgment, consistency in application, and disclosure of the major judgments made in the notes to the financial statements. Also, investment income and intergovernmental grant revenues are subject to special revenue recognition criteria. Furthermore, it is important to distinguish revenues from *non*revenue reimbursements, capital asset sale proceeds, bond issue proceeds, and transfers in.

Finally, revenues subsidiary ledger accounting, revenue budgetary revision entries, and entries to effect changes in revenue accounting principles and error corrections were discussed and illustrated. These procedures and the concepts and procedures discussed earlier are essential in practice and will be applied throughout subsequent chapters.

Questions

Q5-1 What is the meaning of the term *available* as used in governmental fund revenue recognition?

Q5-2 A revenue item must be objectively measurable, as well as available, to be accrued as governmental fund revenue. What is meant by the term *objectively measurable* in this context?

Q5-3 The term *deferred revenues* seems out of place in governmental fund accounting. It would seem that a government either has or does not have expendable financial resources as a result of a property tax, grant, or other revenue transaction. Furthermore, no similar concept, such as deferred working capital, is used in business accounting. Explain the use of the term *deferred revenues* in governmental fund accounting.

Q5-4 Governments often collect cash or must record receivables before revenues are to be recognized in a governmental fund. What determines whether a liability or a deferred inflow is reported in these various situations?

Q5-5 Modified accrual basis revenue recognition is often referred to as "near cash basis" revenue recognition. Explain why this statement probably is made. Do you agree? Explain.

Q5-6 (a) Should estimated uncollectible amounts of taxes be accounted for as direct deductions from revenues or as expenditures? Why? (b) Should discounts on taxes be accounted for as direct deductions from revenues or as expenditures? Why?

Q5-7 (a) What are expenditure-driven intergovernmental grants? (b) When and how are revenues from such grants recognized?

Q5-8 Distinguish between *unearned* revenues and *deferred* revenues as the terms are used in governmental fund accounting and financial reporting.

Q5-9 The controller of a school district had recorded the entire property tax levy, $20,000,000, as revenues when levied during the first month of the year. At year-end the auditor states that $3,000,000 must be reclassified as deferred revenues because that amount of the property tax levy will not be collected until more than 60 days into the next year or later. The controller objects, noting that the property tax receivables are as available as cash because the school district regularly uses them as the basis for borrowing on tax anticipation notes at local banks. Furthermore, the penalties and interest charged on delinquent taxes exceed the interest charges on the tax anticipation notes. With whom do you agree? Why? If deferred revenues must be reported, explain how they are reported.

Q5-10 During the course of your audit of a city, you noted an $800,000 payment to the General Fund from an Enterprise Fund. The payment was recorded in both funds as a payment in lieu of property taxes. (a) How should this payment be reported? (b) What would your answer be if the payment were from the county?

Q5-11 One county might properly account for its investments at fair value, whereas another county might properly account for its investments at amortized cost or the lower of amortized cost or fair value. Explain.

Exercises

E5-1 (Multiple Choice) Identify the best answer to each question:
1. Which of the following is least likely to be reported as governmental fund revenue?
   a. Taxes.
   b. Fines and forfeitures.
   c. Special assessments.
   d. Payments in lieu of taxes from a government's own Enterprise Funds.
2. Generally, General Fund sales tax revenues should be recognized by a local government in the period
   a. in which the local government receives the cash.
   b. that the underlying sale occurs, whether or not the local government receives the cash in that period.
   c. in which the state—which collects all sales taxes in the state—receives the cash from the collecting merchants.
   d. in which the state—which collects all sales taxes in the state—receives the cash from the collecting merchants if the local government collects the taxes from the state in that period or soon enough in the next period to be used as a resource for payment of liabilities incurred in the first period.

3. On *June 1, 20X4,* a school district levies the property taxes for its fiscal year that will end on June 30, 20X5. The total amount of the levy is $1,000,000, and 1% is expected to be uncollectible. Of the levy, $250,000 is collected in June 20X4 and another $500,000 is collected in July and August 20X4. What is the maximum amount of property tax revenue associated with the June 1, 20X4, levy that the school district might report as revenue in the fiscal year ending June 30, 20X4?
   a. $0
   b. $750,000
   c. $760,000
   d. $990,000

4. A city levied $2,000,000 of property taxes for its current fiscal year. The city collected $1,700,000 cash on its taxes receivable during the year and granted $72,000 in discounts to taxpayers who paid within the legally established discount period. It is expected that the city will collect another $88,000 on these taxes receivable during the first two months of the next fiscal year. One percent of the tax levy is expected to be uncollectible. What amount of governmental fund property tax revenues should the city report for the current fiscal year?
   a. $1,788,000
   b. $1,860,000
   c. $1,980,000
   d. $2,000,000

5. What would the answer be to number 4 *if* the city also collected $100,000 of the prior year's taxes during the first two months of the current fiscal year *and* another $53,000 of the prior year's taxes during the remainder of the current year?
   a. $1,788,000
   b. $1,860,000
   c. $1,941,000
   d. $1,980,000

6. A county received $3,000,000 from the state. Of that amount, $1,500,000 was received under an entitlement program and was not restricted as to use. The other $1,500,000 was received under a grant agreement that requires the funds to be used for specific health and welfare programs. The county accounts for the resources from both of these programs in a Special Revenue Fund. Expenditures of that fund that qualified under the grant agreement totaled $900,000 in the year that the grant and entitlement were received. What amount of revenues should the county recognize in that year with respect to the entitlement and the grant?
   a. $900,000
   b. $1,500,000
   c. $2,400,000
   d. $3,000,000

7. A Special Revenue Fund expenditure of $40,000 was initially paid from and recorded in the General Fund. The General Fund is now being reimbursed. The General Fund should report
   a. revenues of $40,000.
   b. other financing sources of $40,000.
   c. a $40,000 reduction in expenditures.
   d. other changes in fund balances of $40,000.

8. A state received an unrestricted gift of $80,000 of stocks and bonds from a private donor. The General Fund statement of revenues, expenditures, and changes in fund balance should report
   a. revenues of $80,000.
   b. other financing sources of $80,000.
   c. special items for all such gifts.
   d. extraordinary items for all such gifts.

9. A city has formalized tax liens of $50,000 against a property that is subject to delinquent taxes receivable. The estimated salable value of the property is $39,000. The remaining *total* balances in Property Taxes Receivable—Delinquent and the related allowance are $113,000 and $28,000, respectively. What amount should be reclassified from allowance for uncollectible delinquent taxes to allowance for uncollectible tax liens?
   a. $0
   b. $11,000
   c. $28,000
   d. $8,589

10. If the city in the previous question decides to keep the property for its own use, what amount of expenditures and revenues should be recognized?
   a. $0
   b. $39,000
   c. $50,000
   d. $85,000

E5-2 (Multiple Choice) Identify the best answer to each question:

1. Each of the following criteria is a factor when determining Special Revenue Fund *property tax* revenue recognition *except:*
   a. Whether the taxes collected were for future fiscal years' taxes.
   b. Whether the taxes were collected no later than 60 days following the fiscal year being reported.
   c. Whether the taxes collected were prior year taxes and were collected not later than 60 days after the beginning of the current year.
   d. Whether the property taxes receivable are current or delinquent.

2. Property taxes billed but not collected by the end of the fiscal period or within 60 days following the end of the fiscal period should be
   a. charged to bad debt expense.
   b. reported as deferred revenues, a deferred inflow.
   c. reported as unearned revenues, a liability.
   d. reported as revenues as long as the taxes are expected to be collected within the next year.

3. Wakefield Village levies $6,255,000 in property taxes at the beginning of its fiscal year. Two percent is deemed to be uncollectible. The proper general ledger journal entry that would be made when the taxes are levied would be
   a. debit Taxes Receivable $6,255,000; credit Tax Revenues $6,255,000.
   b. debit Taxes Receivable $6,255,000; credit Tax Revenues $6,129,900; credit Allowance for Uncollectible Taxes $125,100.
   c. debit Taxes Receivable $6,129,900; credit Tax Revenues $6,129,900.
   d. Either a or c—Taxes Receivable may be recorded at the levy amount or only at the net realizable value.

4. Which of the following statements reflects the proper accounting treatment for grant revenues?
   a. Unrestricted grants are recognized as revenue in governmental funds when cash is received and appropriate expenditures are incurred.
   b. Restricted grants are recognized as revenue in governmental funds when cash is received.
   c. Restricted grants are recognized as revenue in governmental funds as eligibility requirements *and* the availability criteria are met.
   d. All grants are recognized as revenues in the period awarded by the grantor—without regard to timing of expenditures or cash receipt.

5. Which of the following are governmental fund revenues that are typically recognized only as cash is collected?
   a. Speeding fines.
   b. Property taxes.
   c. Sales taxes.
   d. Sales of general capital assets.

6. GASB *Statement No. 31* requires
   a. all investment income, including increases or decreases in the fair value of all investments that are reported at fair value, to be reported as revenue in the operating statement.
   b. changes in the fair value of investments to be reported separately from interest and dividend income that has been earned.
   c. all investments to be adjusted to their fair value for reporting purposes.
   d. governmental entities to report changes in the fair value for investments only if the change is a reduction in the value of the investment portfolio overall.

7. Which of the following statements regarding the accounting and reporting requirements for governmental fund investments is *false*?
   a. Certain governmental fund investments may be reported at amortized cost rather than fair value.
   b. Many general government investments are exempt from fair value standards.
   c. Money market investments with *remaining* maturities of less than one year as of the end of the reporting period are exempt from fair value reporting standards.
   d. A change in the fair value of investments is reported in revenue, whether the change is an increase or a decrease.

8. If a government has an established legal claim associated with a revenue source, but has not collected any of the revenues, governmental fund revenues
   a. should be recognized.
   b. should be recognized if the resources also are legally usable.
   c. should be recognized at the point the revenues are collected.
   d. should be recognized when collected if they are also legally usable.

9. If a government has collected revenues for which it has a valid legal claim, governmental fund revenues
   a. may be reported in the current year if that is the government's policy.
   b. may only be reported in the current year if they are also legally usable for expenditure in that year.

c. may be reported in the current year if they become legally usable during the first 60 days (or fewer) of the next fiscal year.

d. should have been recognized in the previous fiscal year if collected in the first 60 days of the current fiscal year.

10. Which criteria are sufficient for grant revenues to be recognized in a government's General Fund?

a. Cash must be received by year end or within not more than 60 days (or shorter period specified by policy) after the end of the fiscal year.

b. Cash must be collected by year end.

c. The eligibility criteria for the grant must be met, and cash must be collected within not more than 60 days after the end of the fiscal year.

d. The eligibility criteria under the grant must be met, but the cash collection criterion does not apply because another government is involved—and is assumed creditworthy.

E5-3 (Investments) Aslan County purchased $3,000,000 of bonds as a General Fund investment on March 1, 20X7, for $3,060,000 plus four months accrued interest of $80,000. The bonds mature in four years and two months.

1. The county received the semiannual interest payment on the bonds ($120,000) on April 30, 20X7.

2. The county received the October 31 semiannual interest payment ($120,000).

3. On December 31, the end of Aslan's fiscal year, the fair value of its bond investment was $3,065,000 (excluding accrued interest).

(a) Record these transactions in the General Ledger accounts of the Aslan County General Fund.   *Required*

(b) Compute the investment income that should be reported for this investment.

E5-4 (Property Tax Allocation)

(a) The 20X7, 20X6, and 20X5 tax rates for the City of Yonker are:

	Rate per $100 of Assessed Value		
	20X7	*20X6*	*20X5*
General Fund	$1.00	$1.10	$1.20
Library Fund	.09	.09	.09
Municipal Bonds—Redemptions	.20	.18	.16
	$1.29	$1.37	$1.45

The total assessed value for 20X7 was $88,400,000.

Compute the amount of taxes levied for each fund for 20X7.

(b) Collections were made in 20X7 as follows:

20X7 levy	$1,000,000
20X6 levy	100,000
20X5 levy	50,000
	$1,150,000

Compute the amount of collections applicable to each fund for each year.

E5-5 (Investment Income)

a. Prepare the general journal entries to record the following transactions in the General Fund General Ledger of Alderman City:

1. Purchased investments in bonds at January 1, 20X6, for $350,000.

2. Received interest of $23,000 at December 31, 20X6.

3. Fair value of the bonds at December 31, 20X6, $360,000.

4. Received interest of $23,000 at December 31, 20X7.

5. Fair value of the bonds at December 31, 20X7, $345,000.

b. Show how Alderman City should report its investment income each year. The city reports the required detail in the financial statements, not in the notes.

E5-6 (Tax Liens) A county decided to keep land it bid in at its property tax sale to use for parks and recreation purposes. The redemption period has passed, and the county has a valid deed to the land. Taxes, interest, penalties, and sheriff's sale costs (of $150) applicable to the land total $15,000, and the land could have been sold for $12,000. The Tax Liens Receivable account in the General Fund has been charged to the Allowance for Uncollectible Tax Liens Receivable account, and the land has been capitalized (recorded) at $15,000 in the General Capital Assets accounts. (a) Do you agree with the recording of this transaction? (b) Would your answer differ if the land could be sold for $18,000?

E5-7 (Property Taxes) Prepare general journal entries to record the following transactions in Menefee City's General Ledger and make adjusting entries, if needed:

1. Menefee City levied property taxes of $12,000,000 for 20X6. The taxes were levied on January 1, 20X6. Menefee expects $80,000 to be uncollectible. Three-fourths of the taxes receivable are expected to be collected within the 2% discount period. Another $1,000,000 of taxes receivable should be collected before year-end but after the discount period. The balance of the collectible taxes is expected to be collected at a uniform rate over the first 10 months of 20X7.
2. Menefee collected $9,100,000 (before discounts) of its taxes receivable prior to the end of the discount period. The balance of the taxes receivable are past due.
3. Menefee wrote off taxes receivable of $30,000 as uncollectible.
4. Menefee collected another $900,000 of its taxes receivable after the discount period but before year-end.

E5-8 (Revenue Recognition) For each situation outlined in the following chart, explain how the year-end balance sheet and statement of revenues, expenditures, and changes in fund balances of a governmental fund would be affected in 20X5, 20X6, and 20X7.

	Year		
Case	20X5	20X6	20X7
A	Legal Claim Established	• Legally Usable • Cash Collected in first 60 days	
B	• Legal Claim Established • Legally Usable	Cash Collected in first 60 days	
C	• Legal Claim Established • Legally Usable	Cash Collected after first 60 days	
D	Cash Collected in last 60 days	• Legal Claim Established • Legally Usable	
E		• Legal Claim Established • Legally Usable	Cash Collected in first 60 days
F		• Legal Claim Established • Legally Usable	Cash Collected after first 60 days

E5-9 (Grant Revenues) The City and County of PreVatte received a state grant for revitalizing its downtown district. The grant of $18,000,000 requires the government to file for reimbursement after incurring qualifying expenditures. The state routinely reviews such requests and pays the grantees within 45 days. Record the following transactions of the City and County of PreVatte's Downtown Revitalization Special Revenue Fund. Ignore budgetary and subsidiary ledger entries.

1. Hired a director of downtown revitalization responsible for planning activities and projects designed to improve the downtown district. The approved salary was $87,500.
2. Paid $3,000,000 to various business owners as grants to assist them in refurbishing downtown buildings.
3. Paid the director's and other appropriate employees' salaries, $125,000.
4. Filed for reimbursement from the state at year end.

Problems

P5-1 (GL and SL Entries; SL Trial Balance) The City of Asher had the following transactions, among others, in 20X7:

1. The council estimated that revenues of $210,000 would be generated for the General Fund in 20X7. The sources and amounts of expected revenues are as follows:

Property taxes	$150,000
Parking meters	5,000
Business licenses	30,000
Amusement licenses	10,000
Charges for services.	8,000
Other revenues.	7,000
	$210,000

2. Property taxes of $152,000 were levied by the council; $2,000 of these taxes are expected to be uncollectible.

3. The council adopted a budget revision increasing the estimate of amusement licenses revenues by $2,000 and decreasing the estimate for business licenses revenues by $2,000.
4. The following collections were made by the city:

Property taxes................................	$140,000
Parking meters	5,500
Business licenses.............................	28,000
Amusement licenses...........................	9,500
Charges for services (not previously accrued)	9,000
Other revenues...............................	10,000
	$202,000

5. The resources of a discontinued Capital Projects Fund were transferred to the General Fund, $4,800.
6. Enterprise Fund cash of $5,000 was paid to the General Fund to subsidize its operations.

a. Prepare general journal entries and budgetary entries to record the transactions in the General Ledger and Revenues Subsidiary Ledger accounts.   **Required**
b. Prepare a trial balance of the Revenues Ledger after posting the general journal entries prepared in item (a). Show agreement with the control accounts.
c. Prepare the general journal entry(ies) to close the revenue accounts in the General Ledger and Revenues Ledger.

P5-2 (GL and SL Entries; Statement)
1. The following are the estimated revenues for a Special Revenue Fund of the city of Marcelle at January 1, 20X5:

Taxes...................................	$175,000
Interest and penalties	2,000
Fines and fees............................	700
Permits	300
Animal licenses	900
Rents...................................	500
Other licenses............................	3,500
Interest	1,000
	$183,900

2. The city records its transactions on a cash basis during the year and adjusts to the modified accrual basis at year end. At the end of January, the following SRF collections had been made.

Taxes...................................	$ 90,000
Interest and penalties	1,000
Fines and fees............................	50
Permits	140
Animal licenses	800
Rents...................................	45
Other licenses............................	2,000
	$ 94,035

3. An unanticipated grant-in-aid of $5,000 was received from the state on February 1.
4. SRF collections for the remaining 11 months were as follows:

Taxes...................................	$ 70,000
Interest and penalties	800
Fines and fees............................	400
Permits	30
Animal licenses	70
Rents...................................	455
Other licenses............................	300
Interest	900
	$ 72,955

5. Accrued SRF receivables at year-end were as follows:

Taxes	$ 20,000
Interest and penalties	300
Rents	10
Interest	50
	$ 20,360

Only half of the taxes and interest and penalties receivable is expected to be collected during the first 60 days of 20X6. All of the rent and interest receivable should be received in January 20X6.

Required

a. Prepare the General Ledger and subsidiary ledger entries to record the SRF estimated revenues, revenue collections, and revenue accruals.
b. Post to SRF General Ledger worksheet (or T-accounts) and to subsidiary revenue accounts.
c. Prepare SRF closing entries for both the General and Revenues Subsidiary Ledgers.
d. Post to the SRF General Ledger worksheet (or T-accounts) and to the subsidiary revenue accounts.
e. Prepare a SRF statement of estimated revenues compared with actual revenues (i.e., essentially the revenue portion of a budgetary comparison statement) for 20X5.

P5-3 (Revenue Recognition) In auditing the City of Pippa Passes General Fund, a staff member asks whether the following items should be reported as calendar year 20X4 revenues:
1. Property taxes—which are levied in December and due the following April 30
   a. Taxes for 20X4 levied in 20X3 and collected in April 20X4, $800,000
   b. Taxes for 20X5 levied in 20X4 and collected in May 20X5, $850,000
   c. Taxes for 20X3 levied in 20X2 and collected in January 20X4, $8,000
   d. Taxes for 20X4 levied in 20X3 and collected in January 20X5, $137,000
   e. Taxes for 20X5 levied and collected in 20X4, $22,000
   f. Taxes for 20X4 levied in 20X3, not expected to be collected until late 20X5 or 20X6, $12,000
2. Proceeds of a 6%, 10-year general obligation bond issued December 28, 20X4, $540,000
3. Sales taxes
   a. Returns filed (for 20X4 sales) and taxes collected in 20X4, $42,000
   b. Returns filed in 20X3 and taxes collected in June 20X4, $7,400
   c. Returns filed in 20X4 and taxes collected in the first week of 20X5, $6,200
4. Proceeds of a 10% note payable, dated November 1, 20X4, and due March 1, 20X5, $15,000
5. Grant awarded in 20X4—received in full in mid-20X4 (portion not used for designated purposes by 20X7 must be refunded)
   a. Total amount of award, $250,000
   b. Qualifying expenditures made in 20X4, $172,000
6. 20X4 payment from a Special Revenue Fund to finance street improvements, $12,000
7. Interest and penalties
   a. Accruing and collected during 20X4, $2,200
   b. Accruing, but not recorded in the accounts, during 20X0–X3 and collected in mid-20X4, $7,800
   c. Accruing during 20X4 and expected to be collected in early 20X5, $3,400
   d. Accruing during 20X4 and expected to be collected in 20X6 and later, $1,200

Required

a. What is your recommendation for each of the preceding items? (Indicate how each item not reported as 20X4 revenue should be reported.) Explain your recommendations using this format:

Item	Recommendation(s)	20X4 Revenues	Reason(s)

b. What total revenue amount should Pippa Passes report for 20X4?

P5-4 (Grants) The Sinking Creek School District was notified that the federal government has awarded it a $5,000,000 grant to finance a special program that the school had developed to teach math to a select group meeting specified criteria. Record the following transactions in a Special Revenue Fund General Ledger.

Situation A. Cash received in advance of incurring expenditures.
1. The school district received the grant in cash on January 22, 20X8.
2. The school purchased 10 computers and related software for use in the program, $75,000.
3. The school paid salaries for the three instructors who are assigned to the program, $112,000.
4. The school purchased materials for students for the program, $1,420,000.
5. December 31 is the end of the school's fiscal year. All of the foregoing expenditures qualify as expenditures payable from the grant resources.

Situation B. Cash received to reimburse expenditures after they are incurred.
1. Received a 1-year loan from the General Fund, $1,700,000.
2. The school purchased 10 computers and related software for use in the program, $75,000.
3. The school paid salaries for the three instructors who are assigned to the program, $112,000.
4. The school purchased materials for students for the program, $1,420,000.
5. The school filed for and received reimbursement of $1,300,000.
6. As of year-end, the school had filed for reimbursement for all but $30,000 of the expenditures. It will file for reimbursement for the remaining $30,000 of qualifying expenditures early in the next year. It should receive all amounts for which it has already filed within 45 days after year end. The remaining $30,000 probably will not be received until the end of the first quarter of the next year.

P5-5 (Error Correction, Change in Accounting Principle, and Adjusting Entries) The following transactions and events affected a Special Revenue Fund of Stem Independent School District during 20X4.
1. The chief accountant discovered that (a) the $20,000 proceeds of a sale of used educational equipment in 20X3 had been recorded as 20X4 revenues when received in early 20X4, and (b) $150,000 of property taxes receivable were not available at the end of 20X3 but were reported as revenues in 20X3.
2. Because of a change in the timing of the payments of the state minimum education program assistance grants to school districts, the related revenue recognition policy was changed. Substantial amounts of the state payments for the prior fiscal year were reported as deferred revenue at year end under the old policy, but most will now be considered available revenue. The comparative Deferred State Assistance account balances at the end of the current year and prior year under the old and new policies were determined to be:

Deferred State Assistance	Old Policy	New Policy
End of 20X3	$300,000	$ 75,000
End of 20X4	400,000	100,000

3. The auditor discovered the following errors:
   a. Special instruction fees of $8,000 paid for the hearing-impaired education program, properly chargeable to the 20X4 Education—Hearing-Impaired account in the General Fund, were charged to that account in this Special Revenue Fund.
   b. $130,000 of federal grant revenues were earned by incurring qualifying expenditures during 20X3, but no grant cash had been received and no revenues were recorded in 20X3. Furthermore, the federal grantor agency has not been billed for this payment.
   c. A transfer from the General Fund during 20X4, $85,000, was credited to the Revenues—Other account in this Special Revenue Fund.
   d. Interest revenue earned and received during 20X4, $15,000, was improperly recorded as Revenues—Other, whereas a separate Revenues—Interest account is maintained.
   e. A 20X4 payment in lieu of taxes by the federal government was erroneously credited to the Education—General and Administrative expenditures account, $50,000.
4. The following adjusting entries were determined to be necessary at the end of 20X4:
   a. State special education grants received during 20X4 and recorded as 20X4 revenues, $800,000, were only 75% earned by incurring qualifying expenditures during 20X4.
   b. The Stem Independent School District was notified that the state had collected $300,000 of sales taxes for its benefit and would remit them early in 20X5.

Prepare the journal entries to record these error corrections, changes in accounting principles, and adjustments in the General Ledger accounts only of the Special Revenue Fund of Stem Independent School District. ***Required***

P5-6 (Investments Fair Value Analysis) The fair values of the Bruni Independent School District (BISD) General Fund investments, all subject to the fair value provisions of GASB *Statement No. 31,* were:

	Fair Value	
Investment	7/1/20X3	6/30/20X4
A	$10,000	$ 4,000
B	5,000	29,000
C	20,000	—
D	—	15,000
E	—	40,000

During the 20X3–20X4 fiscal year, the BISD purchased and sold securities as follows:

Investment	Cost of Purchases	Sales Proceeds
A	$ —	$ 7,000
B	20,000	—
C	—	19,000
D	13,000	—
E	43,000	—

Required
(1) Compute the net change in the fair value of the BISD investment using (a) the specific identification method and (b) the aggregate method.
(2) Prepare the general journal entry required to record the net change in the fair value of the General Fund investment portfolio.

P5-7 (Research Problem) Obtain a copy of a recent comprehensive annual financial report (CAFR) of a state or local government from the government, the Internet, your professor, or a library.

Required
(1) *Letter of Transmittal.* Review the revenue-related discussions and presentations. What were the most significant general government revenue sources? Which general government revenues increased (decreased) significantly from the previous year?
(2) *Financial Statements.* Indicate the sources of general government revenues. Did any revenue sources differ from what you expected based on your study of Chapters 2–5? Explain.
(3) *Summary of Significant Accounting Policies (SOSAP).* Review the general government revenue-related SOSAP disclosures. Were any of these disclosures different from, or in addition to, those you expected based on your study of Chapters 2–5? Explain.
(4) *Statistical Section.* Review the general government revenue-related statistical presentations. Explain how these might be useful in evaluating the general government financial position and changes in financial position.

Cases

C5-1 (Investment Revenue—City of Phoenix, Arizona) The City of Phoenix, Arizona, has a variety of General Fund investments. The city had General Fund investments at July 1, 20X5, with a fair value of $29,269,000 and accrued interest receivable of $71,000. (a) Record the following transactions for the City of Phoenix, General Fund, assuming that fair value accounting applies to all General Fund investments. (b) Assuming that the investments are investments of unrestricted resources that have not been committed or assigned to a specific purpose, which GAAP fund balance classification will be affected by the investment income?

1. The city collected $21,000,000 as General Fund investments matured (including $1,000,000 of interest).
2. The city purchased $98,978,000 of investments for the General Fund.
3. The city collected interest on its General Fund investments of $19,157,000 during the fiscal year.
4. Accrued interest at June 30, 20X6, was $129,000.
5. The fair value of Phoenix's General Fund investments at June 30, 20X6, was $101,910,000.

(Based on a recent City of Phoenix, Arizona, Comprehensive Annual Financial Report.)

C5-2 (Property Taxes—City of Des Moines, Iowa) The City of Des Moines, Iowa, reported General Fund property taxes receivable (net of uncollectibles) of $49,015,040 on June 30, 20X5, and Deferred Revenues of $47,622,447.

a. Record the following transactions in the City of Des Moines General Fund.
   1. From July 1, 20X5, to August 29, 20X5, the city collected $3,800,000 of taxes, including $1,392,593 of taxes that had been levied for the 20X4–20X5 fiscal year. (The city uses a 60-day cutoff for recognizing governmental fund revenues.)
   2. Between August 30, 20X5, and March 15, 20X6, the city collected $36,000,000 of taxes receivable.
   3. On March 15, 20X6, the city levied taxes for 20X6–20X7 totaling $53,000,000, of which $2,000,000 is expected to be uncollectible.
   4. Between March 15, 20X6, and June 30, 20X6, the city collected $6,800,000 of taxes, including $1,800,000 of taxes levied for the next fiscal year. The city expects to collect another $1,500,000 of 20X5–20X6 taxes between July 1, 20X6, and August 29, 20X6.
b. Compute the amount of tax revenues that Des Moines should report for the fiscal year ended June 30, 20X6.
c. Compute the amount of deferred revenues (including taxes collected in advance) that the city should report at June 30, 20X6. Where should the deferred revenues be reported in the city's General Fund balance sheet?

(Based on a recent City of Des Moines, Iowa, Comprehensive Annual Financial Report.)

Harvey City Comprehensive Case

In this chapter we continue to record the 20X4 transactions of the General Fund of Harvey City. In addition, Harvey City has two Special Revenue Funds—the Addiction Prevention Special Revenue Fund and the Economic Development Special Revenue Fund. In this chapter, we will record the transactions of the Addiction Prevention Special Revenue Fund and prepare its financial statements. We will account for the Economic Development Special Revenue Fund in Chapter 6.

HARVEY CITY GENERAL FUND REQUIREMENTS

Using the worksheet you began in Chapter 4, enter the effects of the following additional 20X4 transactions and events of the Harvey City General Fund in the transactions columns of the worksheet. (A different solution approach may be used if desired by your professor.)

19. The city levied interest and penalties of $35,000 on the overdue taxes receivable. Interest and penalties of $5,600 are expected to prove uncollectible.
20. The city collected $216,000 of delinquent taxes receivable and $27,000 of interest and penalties receivable.
21. The city wrote off uncollectible taxes receivable of $23,000 and related interest and penalties of $4,800.
22. General government equipment with an original cost of $300,000 and accumulated depreciation of $187,000 was sold for $72,000, which was deposited in the General Fund.
23. The city formalized tax liens against properties that had claims against them for delinquent taxes of $12,000 and interest and penalties of $800. The estimated salable value of the properties was $14,000.
24. The following revenue-related information was available at year end:
    a. $144,000 of the December 31, 20X4, balance of delinquent taxes receivable and $34,400 of the December 31, 20X4, balance of interest and penalties receivable are *not* expected to be collected within the first 60 days of 20X5. (The January 1, 20X4, delinquent taxes receivable balance included $79,100 of taxes that were collected after the first 60 days of 20X4, and the January 1, 20X4, interest and penalties receivable balance included $20,900 of interest and penalties on taxes that were collected after the first 60 days of 20X4.) (*Hint:* Deferred Revenues must be adjusted.)
    b. Accrued interest receivable on investments at December 31, 20X4, totals $2,700.
    c. The fair value of General Fund investments at December 31, 20X4, is $800 more than their book value.

HARVEY CITY ADDICTION PREVENTION SPECIAL REVENUE FUND

The Addiction Prevention Special Revenue Fund was established in 20X4 to account for federal grants intended to help communities prevent and battle drug and alcohol addictions. Because this is the first year for this fund, there is no beginning trial balance for the Addiction Prevention Special Revenue Fund.

HARVEY CITY ADDICTION PREVENTION SPECIAL REVENUE FUND REQUIREMENTS

a. Prepare a worksheet for the Addiction Prevention Special Revenue Fund similar to the General Fund worksheet you created in Chapter 4. Enter the effects of the following transactions and events in the appropriate columns of the worksheet. (A different solution approach may be used if desired by your professor.)
b. Enter the preclosing trial balance in the appropriate worksheet columns.
c. Enter the preclosing trial balance amounts in the closing entry and postclosing trial balance (balance sheet data) columns, as appropriate.

d. Prepare the 20X4 Statement of Revenues, Expenditures, and Changes in Fund Balance for the Addiction Prevention Special Revenue Fund.

e. Prepare the 20X4 balance sheet for the Addiction Prevention Special Revenue Fund. (Assume that all but $60,000 of the resources of the fund at December 31, 20X4 are restricted.)

Transactions and Events—20X4

1. The city council adopted the budget for the Addiction Prevention Special Revenue Fund. The budget for the fund included estimated grant revenues of $530,000 and appropriations for public safety of $525,000.

2. The city was awarded a federal grant for drug addiction and enforcement programs. The grant requires the city to incur qualifying expenditures, then apply for reimbursement. The total amount of the grant award, which can be used anytime during the next 3 years, is $1,200,000—none of which is received at this time.

3. The city contracted for and received services costing $450,000 that qualify for reimbursement under the grant agreement. The expenditures, for the Public Safety function, were vouchered.

4. The Addiction Prevention Special Revenue Fund borrowed $500,000 from the General Fund on a short-term basis.

5. The city paid $430,000 of the vouchers payable.

6. The city applied for and received reimbursement of $450,000 from the federal grantor agency under the provisions of the grant agreement.

7. The city incurred and vouchered $75,000 of Public Safety expenditures for the Addiction Prevention program: $50,000 of the costs is reimbursable under the grant agreement. The city applied for reimbursement, which is expected early next year.

8. $250,000 of the loan from the General Fund was repaid.

9. A transfer of $60,000 was received from the General Fund.

10. The budgetary accounts were closed at year end. (Close the budgetary accounts in the transactions columns.)

CHAPTER 6

Expenditure Accounting—Governmental Funds

LEARNING OBJECTIVES

After studying this chapter, you should be able to:

- Define expenditures as used in governmental fund accounting and reporting.

- Understand and apply governmental fund expenditure recognition guidance.

- Account for personal services costs, materials and supplies (purchases and consumption methods), and prepayments in governmental funds.

- Account for typical debt service and capital outlay expenditures.

- Understand the accounting and reporting for capital leases, claims and judgments, compensated absences, and pension and other postemployment benefit expenditures in governmental funds.

- Account for and report changes in expenditure accounting principles and error corrections in governmental funds.

The annual operating budget prepared by the executive branch contains the activity and expenditure plans the chief executive wants to carry out during a fiscal year. The legislative branch reviews the plans; then, by providing appropriations, it enters into a "contract" with the executive branch for putting those plans into effect—or as much of the plans as it endorses. The executive branch is then charged with the responsibility of carrying out the contract in a legal and efficient manner.

The primary measurement focus of governmental funds is on *currently expendable* net financial assets and changes in *currently expendable* net financial assets. Therefore, activities financed through governmental funds are usually planned, authorized, controlled, and evaluated in terms of expenditures—the primary outflow measurement in governmental fund accounting. **Expenditures**, a different measurement concept than expenses, is a measure of *fund* liabilities incurred (or expendable fund financial resources used) during a period for operations, capital outlay, and debt service. **Expenses** indicate the measure of costs expired or consumed during a period.

This chapter focuses on *expenditure* accounting for governmental funds. Specifically, it addresses:

1. The definition of expenditures in the governmental fund accounting environment and the expenditure recognition criteria used;

2. Selected expenditure accounting controls and procedures; and

3. Several important expenditure accounting topics—including claims and judgments, compensated absences, unfunded and underfunded pension contributions, other postemployment benefits, and changes in expenditure accounting principles.

You may wish to review the expenditures classification discussion in Chapter 3 and in Appendix 3-2 as you study this chapter.

The discussions and illustrations in this chapter, like most of those in Chapters 3 to 5, are in the context of state and local governments (SLGs) with no significant differences between their budgetary basis and the GAAP basis for governmental funds. Also, except where noted otherwise, the accounts are maintained on (or near) the GAAP basis during the year.

EXPENDITURE DEFINITION AND RECOGNITION

As mentioned previously, *expenditures* may be *defined* for governmental fund accounting as *all decreases in fund net position—for current operations, capital outlay, or debt service—except those arising from transfers to other funds*. Only exchange-like interfund service transactions result in the recognition of fund expenditures that are not expenditures of the government as a whole.

The GASB *Codification* states that:

> The measurement focus of governmental fund accounting is upon *expenditures*—decreases in net financial resources—rather than expenses.[1]

The *Codification* observes that most expenditures and transfers out are objectively measurable and should be recorded when the related fund liability is incurred. Specifically, it provides that:

> Expenditures should be *recognized* in the accounting period in which the *fund liability* is *incurred*, if measurable, **except for unmatured principal and interest on general long-term liabilities**, which should be recognized **when due**.[2]

Illustration 6-1 summarizes the distinctions between:

- **Current Liabilities**, including the related **one year look-out** procedure, used in the *economic resources* measurement focus and *accrual* basis applicable to *proprietary fund* and *government-wide* financial statements presented in conformity with *GAAP*, and

- **Fund Liabilities**—used in the *current financial resources* measurement focus and *modified accrual* basis applicable to *governmental fund* financial statements presented in conformity with *GAAP*—including the relationship between fund liabilities and unmatured general government liabilities (General Long-Term Liabilities).

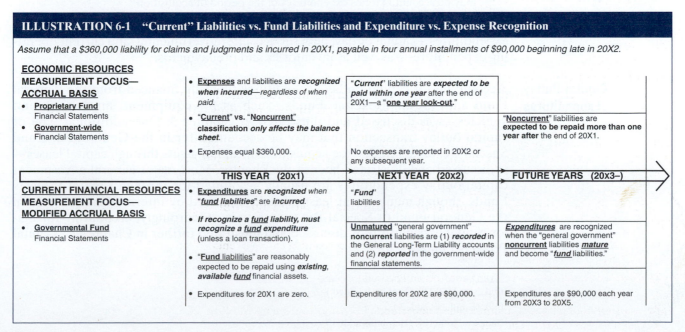

ILLUSTRATION 6-1   "Current" Liabilities vs. Fund Liabilities and Expenditure vs. Expense Recognition

Assume that a $360,000 liability for claims and judgments is incurred in 20X1, payable in four annual installments of $90,000 beginning late in 20X2.

ECONOMIC RESOURCES MEASUREMENT FOCUS— ACCRUAL BASIS • **Proprietary Fund** Financial Statements • **Government-wide** Financial Statements	• **Expenses** and liabilities are *recognized when incurred*—regardless of when paid. • **"Current"** vs. **"Noncurrent"** classification *only affects the balance sheet.* • Expenses equal $360,000.	*"Current"* liabilities are *expected to be paid within one year* after the end of 20X1—a **"one year look-out."** No expenses are reported in 20X2 or any subsequent year.	**"Noncurrent"** liabilities are **expected to be repaid more than one year after** the end of 20X1.
	THIS YEAR (20X1)	**NEXT YEAR (20X2)**	**FUTURE YEARS (20X3–)**
CURRENT FINANCIAL RESOURCES MEASUREMENT FOCUS— MODIFIED ACCRUAL BASIS • **Governmental Fund** Financial Statements	• **Expenditures** are *recognized* when "**fund liabilities**" are **incurred**. • *If recognize a fund liability, must recognize a fund expenditure* (unless a loan transaction). • "**Fund liabilities**" are reasonably expected to be repaid using *existing, available fund* financial assets.	*"Fund"* liabilities **Unmatured** "general government" **noncurrent** liabilities are (1) *recorded* in the General Long-Term Liability accounts and (2) *reported* in the government-wide financial statements.	**Expenditures** are recognized when the "general government" **noncurrent** liabilities *mature* and become "**fund**" liabilities.
	• Expenditures for 20X1 are zero.	Expenditures for 20X2 are $90,000.	Expenditures are $90,000 each year from 20X3 to 20X5.

---

[1]GASB *Codification*, sec. 1600.116.

[2]Ibid., sec. 1100.110a. (Emphasis added.)

Illustration 6-1 also summarizes—using a This Year (20X1), Next Year (20X2), and Future Years (20X3–) *timeline*—the *similarities and differences* between:

- **Expense** recognition—applicable to *proprietary fund* and *government-wide* financial statements presented in conformity with GAAP, and
- **Expenditure** recognition—applicable to *governmental fund* financial statements presented in conformity with GAAP.

Illustration 6-1 should be reviewed repeatedly as various topics are discussed and illustrated in this chapter and in later chapters.

The *Codification* also states that principal and interest expenditures on general long-term liabilities (GLTL) are usually *not* accrued at year end:

> The **major exception** to the general rule of **expenditure accrual** relates to **unmatured principal and interest** on **general obligation long-term liabilities**. . . . Financial resources usually are appropriated in other funds for transfer to a debt service fund in the period in which maturing liability principal and interest must be paid. *Such amounts thus are not . . . liabilities of the debt service fund as their settlement will not require expenditure of existing fund assets.*[3]

Thus, both GLTL principal retirement expenditures and related interest expenditures are usually recorded when they are due to be paid rather than being accrued at year-end. But the *Codification* sets forth circumstances in which SLGs are *permitted* to accrue GLTL debt service expenditures. The *Codification* states that:

> On the other hand, if [dedicated] debt service fund resources have been provided [paid to a DSF] during the current year for payment of principal and interest due early [no more than one month] in the following year, the expenditure and related liability *may* be recognized in the debt service fund [and the debt principal amount removed from the General Long-Term Liability accounts].[4]

Furthermore, the *Codification* provides two other expenditure recognition alternatives:

1. Inventory items (e.g., materials and supplies) may be considered expenditures either when purchased (**purchases method**) or when used (**consumption method**), but significant amounts of inventory should be reported in the balance sheet.

2. Expenditures for insurance and similar services extending over more than one accounting period [prepayments] need not be allocated between or among accounting periods, but may be accounted for as expenditures of the period of acquisition.[5]

The remainder of this section discusses the various broad types of expenditures—capital outlay, debt service, intergovernmental, and current operating expenditures—as well as inventories and prepayments.

Capital Outlay Expenditures

Accounting for capital outlay expenditures typically financed from the General Fund and Special Revenue Funds—such as for equipment, machinery, and vehicles—was discussed and illustrated in Chapter 3. One additional type of capital outlay transaction that may be accounted for in the General Fund and Special Revenue Funds—the acquisition of capital assets through capital leases—is discussed and illustrated later in this chapter. Most major general government capital outlay expenditures are usually accounted for through Capital Projects Funds, though many are at least partially financed by interfund transfers from the General Fund or Special Revenue Funds. Accordingly, accounting for major capital expenditures is discussed and illustrated further in Chapter 7, "Capital Projects Funds."

---

[3]Ibid., sec. 1500.111. (Emphasis added.)
[4]Ibid. (Emphasis added.)
[5]Ibid., sec. 1600.127. (Emphasis added.)

GLTL debt service expenditures are recognized "when due" mainly because most SLGs levy the related property taxes and budget debt service payments on a **when-due** basis. Thus, the appropriations for GLTL principal and interest expenditures equal the payments to be made during the year, regardless of any accruals at year end. Permitting governments to account and report for GAAP purposes on the basis on which the budget is prepared avoids a significant GAAP-budgetary difference that would have to be explained and reconciled in almost every governmental fund financial statement. Other practical and theoretical reasons also support use of this when-due approach.

Debt Service Expenditures

Most GLTL debt service is accounted for through Debt Service Funds. However:

1. Capital lease debt service may be accounted for in the General Fund and in Special Revenue Funds.

2. Financial resources may be transferred from the General Fund and Special Revenue Funds to finance debt service payments accounted for in Debt Service Funds.

Accordingly, accounting for capital lease debt service is discussed and illustrated in this chapter. Both when-due recognition of GLTL principal and interest expenditures and the alternative before-due recognition for payments due early in the following year are discussed and illustrated further in Chapter 8, "Debt Service Funds."

State governments, in particular, often incur intergovernmental expenditures under state revenue-sharing, grant, and other financial assistance programs to counties, cities, school districts, and other local governments. State gasoline taxes may be shared with cities and counties, for example, and program grants and other aid may be provided to school districts within the state. The intergovernmental expenditure classification signals that these state-level expenditures were not for goods and services at that level but were payments to local governments to finance local-level expenditures. Similarly, local governments that receive grants they pass through to other governmental entities report intergovernmental expenditures for the pass-through awards they make.

Intergovernmental Expenditures

All governmental fund expenditures other than those for capital outlay, debt service, or intergovernmental purposes are referred to as *current operating* expenditures or simply **current** expenditures or *operating* expenditures.

Current Operating Expenditures

Payroll and related personnel costs are the largest current operating expenditures of most state and local governments. Indeed, payroll and related costs often are 65%–75% of the General Fund and Special Revenue Fund expenditures of cities, counties, and other local governments and 75%–85% of public school system expenditures of these fund types. Accordingly, accounting procedures for personal services expenditures are discussed in this chapter.

The GASB permits inventories and prepayments to be charged as expenditures immediately because—from a cash or convertible-to-cash perspective—such items are not financial resources available for financing future expenditures. Also, many governments make appropriations in terms of the inventory to be acquired or insurance to be purchased during a fiscal year. Permitting them to report such items on the budgetary basis in the governmental fund Statement of Revenues, Expenditures, and Changes in Fund Balances avoids a potential conflict between budgetary accounting procedures and generally accepted accounting principles (GAAP) that would have to be explained and reconciled in the notes to the financial statements. Governmental fund inventory accounting procedures and prepayments are discussed and illustrated later in this chapter.

Inventories and Prepayments

Expenditure Recognition Summary

To summarize, governmental fund expenditures are recognized at one of three different points, depending upon the type of expenditure (see Illustration 6-2):

- When the asset or service is acquired
- When the asset or service is used
- When payment is due

Note that most expenditures are recognized either when assets or services are acquired—which typically is when a governmental fund incurs a liability—or when payment is due. However, governments are permitted to recognize expenditures for supplies, materials, and prepaid items either when purchased or when used. Also, note that for many common expenditures, acquisition and use occur concurrently. This typically is true for salaries, utilities, and contractual services, for instance.

The expenditure recognition exception requiring recognition of GLTL debt service expenditures when due at maturity has a broad impact. As discussed later, this exception determines the timing of recognition of several major types of expenditures, including:

- Claims and judgments
- Compensated absences
- Pensions
- Other postemployment benefits (OPEB) such as retiree health care benefits

As with modified accrual *revenue* accounting, modified accrual accounting for expenditures could have just as easily been called modified cash basis accounting for *expenditures*. Indeed, delaying recognition of many expenditures until the period they are due essentially results in recognizing these expenditures in the period that they are expected to be paid. Likewise, typical operating costs such as salaries are paid, for the most part, in the same period the liability is incurred. To the extent that this is true, this requirement is consistent with cash basis accounting. The requirement that salaries, equipment purchases, other capital outlay, and similar costs that normally are paid when, or shortly after, goods or services are received prevents GAAP recognition of expenditures from being affected by one of the common abuses of cash basis budgeting—delaying payment to avoid recognizing budgetary expenditures in the current period. In effect, modified accrual

---

ILLUSTRATION 6-2 Timing of Expenditure Recognition—Various Expenditures

Types of Expenditures Recognized When

Acquired	Used	Due
Salaries and wages*		Interest on GLTL
Utilities*		GLTL Principal Retirement
Contractual services*		
Capital outlay		Claims and judgments
Interest on fund liabilities		Compensated absences
Materials and supplies (Purchases Method)	Materials and supplies (Consumption Method)	Pensions
Insurance** (Purchases Method)	Insurance** (Consumption Method)	Other postemployment benefits
Rent** (Purchases Method)	Rent** (Consumption Method)	

*These services typically are acquired and used at the same point in time.

**If insurance, rent, or similar expenditures are prepaid, either the purchases method (expenditures recognized when purchased) or the consumption method (expenditures recognized when used) may be used. If there is no prepayment, the two methods yield the same result.

expenditure recognition generally requires expenditures to be recognized only if they are paid by year end (or shortly thereafter). "Shortly" means by the next payday or when normally due to vendors. The exceptions that allow prepaid items and materials and supplies to be recognized as expenditures when used arose because some governments budgeted these items on a consumption basis. Utilizing the exception would make the GAAP information for those governments consistent with the budgetary information with respect to prepaid items and materials and supplies.

EXPENDITURE ACCOUNTING CONTROLS

The accounting system is a powerful expenditures control tool. Though its obvious role is financial- and compliance-related, it may also be used to record and report quantitative data of all kinds. Indeed, the statistical data that must be accumulated to plan and control the operations of a government are best used in conjunction with financial data, and frequently the two kinds of data can be accumulated simultaneously. The accounting system also plays important *managerial* roles with respect to the following problems and controls:

- Misapplication of assets
- Illegal expenditures
  - Overspending of appropriations
  - Spending for illegal purposes
- Use of improper methods and procedures
- Unwise or inappropriate expenditures
- Allocation and allotment of appropriations

Most expenditure control principles are internal control principles. Thus, exhaustive discussions of these topics are not presented here.[6]

EXPENDITURE ACCOUNTING PROCEDURES

Expenditure control and accounting procedures differ significantly according to different management philosophies, styles, and approaches as well as the expenditure-related software or manual procedures utilized.

- Some chief finance officers (CFOs) prefer highly *centralized* expenditure control systems that provide for the CFO to approve all significant transactions.
- Other CFOs prefer highly *decentralized* expenditure control systems that delegate expenditure control authority, responsibility, and accountability to department heads.

Whether expenditure control is centralized or decentralized, most systems provide for some form of *preaudit* and require that encumbrances and expenditures be classified and coded in the expenditure control process.

Preaudit consists of approving transactions before they occur, as in the case of purchase order encumbrances, or before they are recorded, as in the case of expenditures. Preaudit of expenditures is designed to control the expenditure process, methods, and procedures, as well as to prevent illegal expenditures. The chief accounting officer is usually responsible for this function, although large departments may have accountants who perform some or all of the preaudit functions.

Most governmental units use some form of the *voucher system*, which requires all cash disbursements to be authorized by an approved voucher. Vouchers

---

[6]See Auditing Standards Board, American Institute of Certified Public Accountants, *Codification of Statements on Auditing Standards,* sec. 319, and related interpretations.

usually provide a space by each step in the approval and preaudit process for the persons responsible for each step to sign or initial—manually or using "electronic signatures"—after completing that step. These signature blocks are also an important part of the postaudit trail of transactions that is evaluated both in the study of internal controls and as transactions are tested in the **postaudit** process.

All governmental fund expenditures—whether current operating, capital outlay, debt service, or intergovernmental—should be properly controlled through the voucher and preaudit processes and included in the scope of the postaudit. Most accounting procedures for capital outlay and debt service expenditures are discussed in Chapters 7 and 8. This chapter focuses primarily on accounting for current operating expenditures for personal services, materials and supplies, and other services and charges.

Personal Services

The steps in accounting for personal services are (1) ensuring that the person is a bona fide employee, (2) determining rates of pay, (3) establishing the amounts earned by employees, (4) recording payments made to employees, and (5) charging the resultant expenditures to the proper accounts.

The personal services expenditures charged against the departmental appropriations properly include employee fringe benefit costs—such as employer payroll taxes, insurance costs, pension and other retirement benefit costs, and the costs of compensated absences such as vacation and sick leave time—as well as employee salaries and wages. However, many governments make separate appropriations for fringe benefit expenditures and charge the expenditures against these separate appropriations rather than as departmental expenditures. The use of separate fringe benefit appropriations and expenditure accounts is an accepted alternative in practice.

Pension Cost and OPEB Cost Expenditure Recognition

Most state and local governments contribute to a pension or retirement plan for the benefit of their employees. Some participate in statewide or other group plans, but others manage their own plans. Most governments also provide other postemployment benefits, such as retiree health care benefits, for their employees. Many governments have not advance funded these other postemployment benefits (OPEB) as they do their pension plans. Therefore, pay-as-you-go financing, which is not common for pension plans, is relatively commonplace for OPEB plans.

Transactions between a government and its self-managed pension or OPEB plans are considered *exchange-like interfund services* transactions. Therefore, properly determined pension or OPEB contributions are recognized as *expenditures*, not transfers, in the employer governmental funds. A few governments have no pension plans, or employee retirement benefits are budgeted on a *pay-as-you-go* cash basis. But most governments have or participate in either defined contribution or defined benefit pension plans.

Defined Contribution Plans The government *employer's obligation* under a defined contribution pension or OPEB plan is *limited to making the contributions required* to the plan. Retiree benefits are determined by the total contributions to the defined contribution plan on the retiree's behalf and by the plan's investment performance over time. Benefits are not guaranteed by the employer government. *Governments with defined contribution plans should charge the contractually required contribution amount, including current accruals at year end, to expenditures in the year it was earned by the general government employees.*[7] Most state and local governments make the required contributions to defined contribution plans

---

[7]GASB *Codification*, sec. P20.122.

when due. Any unpaid portion is *a fund liability*. Once the appropriate contribution is paid, these governments have no further liability under the defined contribution pension plan.

Defined Benefit Plans Most state and local government pension and retirement plans are defined benefit pension plans. Governments often have defined benefit OPEB plans as well. Indeed, it is not uncommon for these plans to be administered as part of a pension plan.

Under a defined benefit pension plan, the government *guarantees the employee-retiree a determinable pension benefit*, which is usually *based on a formula* such as:

1. Number of years service $\times$
2. Average compensation during the highest 3 to 5 years $\times$
3. A percentage, such as 1.5% to 2.5% $=$
4. Annual pension or retirement benefit

The annual benefit is divided by 12 to determine the monthly benefit.

Defined benefit OPEB plans often are designed to cover the health care costs of a government's qualifying retirees (and in some cases those of a spouse or other dependents). A portion of employee salaries is contributed to most government defined benefit pension plans, and retirees often must pay part of the retiree health care (or other) costs. The government is responsible for the remaining costs incurred to provide the specified level and types of benefits.

Defined benefit pension and OPEB plan contributions (advance funding) are necessarily based on numerous actuarial estimates. For pensions, such estimates include the number of years an employee will serve; levels of inflation and pay rates over time; employee turnover; retiree life spans and mortality rates; and plan funding, investment returns, and administrative costs. Furthermore, plan provisions may be changed in the future, or other events may occur that necessitate major revisions of actuarial estimates of the government employer's ultimate liabilities under the defined benefit pension plan. Thus, the amount that should properly be recognized as governmental fund expenditures and liabilities each year under defined benefit pension plans is difficult to estimate. OPEB cost estimates are subject to many of the same estimates and assumptions as well as one other major factor—the rate of health care cost inflation; as a result, the cost of these plans are even more difficult to estimate than are defined benefit pension plan costs.

GASB *Statement No. 27,* "Accounting for Pensions by State and Local Governmental Employers," provides extensive guidance, including specific actuarial parameters that must be met, for determining the employer's annual required contribution (ARC). The ARC is normally paid during the year, so it typically equals the annual pension expenditures. However, GASB *Statement No. 27* specifies that, consistent with the modified accrual basis, any *underpayment liability* should be reported as *General Long-Term Liabilities.*[8] These underpayment amounts will not be reported as current period expenditures.

GASB *Statement No. 45,* "Accounting and Financial Reporting by Employers for Postemployment Benefits Other Than Pensions," provides equivalent guidance for OPEB. However, many governments do not contribute the ARC to OPEB trust funds. The governmental fund OPEB expenditures recognized by these governments are often significantly lower than the ARC, and the governments accumulate significant general long-term liabilities from such underfunding.

Accounting for pension plan and OPEB contributions is discussed and illustrated later in this chapter. Pension and OPEB Trust Fund accounting and reporting are discussed and illustrated in Chapter 12.

---

[8]Ibid., sec. P20.113.

Materials and Supplies

The accounting procedures for materials and supplies may be divided into two parts: (1) accounting for purchases of materials and supplies and (2) accounting for use of materials and supplies.

Accounting for Purchases of Materials and Supplies

The details of purchasing procedures vary according to whether:

1. The materials and supplies are purchased directly by individual departments or through a central purchasing agency.
2. The materials and supplies are purchased for a central storeroom or directly for departments.

Nearly all city, county, and state governments, as well as the federal government, use varying degrees of central purchasing. Throughout this chapter, purchases are assumed to be made through a central agency. If a central storeroom is not used, all materials and supplies are delivered directly to the departments; and, even if a storeroom is used, many deliveries will be made directly to departments.

The purchasing procedure and the related accounting procedures consist of the following steps:

1. Preparing purchase requisitions and placing them with the purchasing agent
2. Securing prices or bids
3. Placing orders
4. Receiving the materials and supplies
5. Receiving the invoice and approving the liability
6. Paying the liability

Accounting for Use of Materials and Supplies

The law may determine how a government accounts for materials and supplies. Two different legal assumptions are common in practice:

1. The Expenditures account is to be charged with the amount of materials and supplies *consumed* (consumption method).
2. The Expenditures account is to be charged with the amount of materials and supplies *purchased* (purchases method).

Both alternatives are recognized as *acceptable* in the GASB *Codification. The expectation and historical practice was that* a state or local *government would select the alternative that corresponds with the inventory appropriations method in its annual operating budget, both to facilitate budgetary accounting and reporting during the year and to avoid budget-GAAP basis differences that must be explained and reconciled at year end.* The consumption method can be used with either a periodic or perpetual inventory system, whereas the purchases method is used only with the periodic inventory system.

Consumption Method

When stores accounting is on the *consumption* method, the inventory-related appropriations are provided on the basis of estimated usage and the Expenditures account is charged with actual usage. As noted earlier, inventory may be kept on the consumption method by using either a periodic or a perpetual system. Entries for both the perpetual and periodic systems using the consumption method are shown in Illustration 6-3.

Perpetual System The primary advantage of the perpetual system is that the government knows both (1) the inventory that should have been on hand at year end, and (2) by comparison with what actually is on hand, the amount of the inventory overage or shortage at year end. Under the periodic system, the government knows only what is on hand at year end and cannot distinguish what was used

ILLUSTRATION 6-3   Inventory Accounting Methods Overview (Amounts Are in $000s)

	Consumption Method		Purchases Method
	Perpetual System	**Periodic System**	**Periodic System**

When Purchased (*Numbers assumed.*)	Inventory of Supplies 850
	    Vouchers Payable 850
		Expenditures 850
		    Vouchers Payable 850
			Expenditures 850
			    Vouchers Payable 850

When Issued	Expenditures 774 Inventory of Supplies 774	No entry	No entry

End of Year	**No entry required— unless there is:**
	
	 • A shortage (increase expenditures and decrease inventory) or
	 • An overage (decrease expenditures and increase inventory)
		Inventory of Supplies 73
		    Expenditures 73
		
		 • To record increase in inventory during the year
		 • If inventory decreased, accounts would be reversed
			If inventory level increases:
			
			 Inventory of Supplies 73
			    OFS—Inventory
			      Increase* 73

	If inventory shortage:
	 Expenditures 3
	    Inventory of Supplies 3
			If inventory level decreases:
			 OFU—Inventory
			    Decrease* X
			 Inventory of Supplies X

Amounts Reported on the Operating Statement**	Expenditures of $777	Expenditures of $777	Expenditures of $850 and an Other Financing Source—Increase in inventory of $73. The net effect on the net change in fund balance in the statement is $777, the same as under the consumption method.

*OFS means Other Financing Sources; OFU means Other Financing Uses.

**Balance sheet reporting is the same for both the consumption and the purchases method. Inventory and an equal amount of nonspendable fund balance must be reported for the cost of materials and supplies on hand at year end.

from what was stolen, damaged, or improperly accounted for. Thus, as in business accounting, under the periodic inventory system what is termed *cost of goods sold* is in fact "cost of goods sold, stolen, or otherwise mysteriously disappeared or not accounted for properly."

Ideally, then, all governments (and other organizations) should use a perpetual inventory system. But whereas perpetual inventory systems provide better accounting control and information, they also add accounting system implementation and operating costs. Thus, accounting system decisions, like other decisions, must be evaluated from a cost-benefit perspective. The usual result is that (1) the perpetual inventory system is used to account for large amounts of supplies and other inventories that justify the accounting control costs involved from an asset management and/or expenditure accounting perspective, but (2) lesser amounts of inventory, inventories that do not lend themselves to perpetual systems (e.g., sand and gravel), and inventories that may be controlled otherwise (e.g., by department personnel) are accounted for on the periodic system—on either the consumption method or the purchases method.

Periodic System   Applying the consumption method using a periodic inventory system should yield essentially the same financial reporting results as the perpetual method. As noted earlier, a periodic system is less costly but does not provide the same level of inventory control.

Purchases Method

The *purchases* method is used when the *inventory-related appropriations authorize* inventory *purchases*. Its use is limited to the periodic system because it is not compatible with the perpetual inventory system. Under the purchases method, the Expenditures account is charged with inventory purchases during the year.

Note in Illustration 6-3 that the only difference between the entries for the purchases method and the consumption method using a periodic inventory system is the entry recording the change in inventory—a $73,000 increase in the illustration. The increase in the inventory account reduces expenditures under the consumption method but results in recording an other financing source under the purchases method. The total change in fund balance is the same under both methods (a decrease of $777,000). However, under the consumption method the net decrease is reported as Expenditures. Under the purchases method, the decrease is the net effect of reporting Expenditures of $850,000—for the cost of the supplies purchased—less an Other Financing Source of $73,000 for the increase in the inventory on hand.

The *Other Financing Sources—Inventory Increase* results from the fact that (1) GAAP *permits* the use of the *purchases* method *only* for *expenditure* accounting, and (2) any significant amounts of *inventory* must be *reported* in the governmental fund *balance sheet*.

Compared with the consumption method, the purchases method overstates Expenditures—in this case, by $73,000—so the Fund Balance account will be understated $73,000 after the Expenditures account is closed. Thus, the $73,000 credit to Other Financing Sources—Inventory Increase, which is closed at year end to Fund Balance, may be viewed as correcting for the understatement of Fund Balance caused by the Expenditures overstatement. Note that both the inventory of materials and supplies and the nonspendable fund balance reported in the balance sheet are identical under the two methods.

Other Services and Charges

When services are being acquired under *contract*, an entry is made *encumbering* appropriations for the amount of the *estimated ultimate* contractual expenditure liability at the time the contract is awarded. As services and the related invoices are received, the encumbering entries are reversed and the actual expenditures are recorded.

Whereas the accounting for most other services and charges is apparent from the discussions in this text, several specific types of other services and charges expenditures warrant at least brief mention. Two types are discussed here: prepayments and capital leases. Related topics—including interest on short-term governmental fund debt, claims and judgments, compensated absences, and pension and other postemployment benefits (OPEB) contribution underfunding—are discussed in the Adjusting Entries section later in this chapter.

Prepayments

Governments may prepay costs that benefit two or more accounting periods. For example, a two-year insurance policy may be purchased, or rental on a building may be paid for a year in advance at midyear. As in the case of inventories, governments are *permitted* to use **either** the **consumption** method **or** the **purchases** method in accounting for prepayments (prepayals).[9] Moreover, those using the purchases method are *not* required to report prepayments on the balance sheet. If prepayments are reported as assets, the accounting and financial reporting are identical to that for materials and supplies. Thus, if a two-year insurance policy

---

[9]Ibid., sec. 1600.127.

were purchased for $88,000 at the beginning of 20X1, the entries (omitting subsidiary ledger entries) would be as follows:

When Insurance Policy Purchased:

Expenditures..	$88,000	
Vouchers Payable		$88,000

To record payment for two-year insurance policy at beginning
  of 20X1.

End of 20X1:

(a) **Purchases Method**—No entry.

(b) **Consumption Method**—

Prepaid Insurance	$44,000	
Expenditures		$44,000

To record prepaid insurance

Under the consumption method, the General Fund balance sheet
  must include $44,000 of nonspendable fund balance related to the
  Prepaid Insurance. If a government using the purchases method
  reports this Prepaid Insurance as an asset, nonspendable fund
  balance must be reported on the balance sheet—and an other
  financing source or use must be reported on the operating
  statement for the change in the prepaid insurance balance during
  the year.

Beginning of 20X2:

(a) **Purchases Method**—No entry.

(b) **Consumption Method**—

Expenditures...	$44,000	
Prepaid Insurance		$44,000

To reverse the 20X1 adjusting entry and charge the
  applicable insurance cost to 20X2 expenditures.

Capital Leases and Certificates of Participation

Many governments lease assets—such as vehicles, computers, photocopy machines, other equipment, and buildings—rather than buy them. When such leases are ordinary rentals—for example, monthly rentals that may be canceled with little notice—the rents paid or accrued are usually recorded as rental expenditures. (Advance rental payments might be initially recorded as prepayments, as discussed earlier.) However, if the government is in substance buying the assets or is leasing them for most or all of their useful lives, GAAP require that the accounting for such capital leases reflect their substance instead of their legal form.

The GASB's lease accounting and reporting guidance are in GASB *Statement No. 62,* "Accounting and Financial Reporting Guidance Contained in Pre-November 30, 1989 FASB and AICPA Pronouncements." GASB *Statement No. 62* requires governments to classify leases following essentially the same guidance currently required for businesses. Reporting capital leases parallels FASB guidance as well *except* in the governmental funds.[10] The GASB *Codification* requires that:

- General capital assets (GCA) acquired in capital lease agreements should be capitalized in the GCA accounts at the inception of the lease at the present value of the future lease payments, calculated following guidance equivalent to that for businesses and a general long-term liability in the same amount (less any payment at inception) should be recorded in the GLTL accounts.

- When a general capital asset is acquired by capital lease, its acquisition should be reported in an appropriate governmental fund as both (1) a capital outlay *expenditure* and (2) an *other financing source*, as if long-term debt had been issued to finance the capital asset acquisition.[11]

---

[10]These requirements are discussed in intermediate accounting textbooks.

[11]GASB *Codification*, sec. L20.113.

- Capital lease proceeds need not be accounted for through a Capital Projects Fund, nor does capital lease debt service have to be accounted for through a Debt Service Fund, unless use of such funds is legally or contractually required.

Illustration 6-4 presents an overview of general government capital lease accounting. The General Capital Assets (GCA) and General Long-Term Liabilities (GLTL) entries are illustrated in Chapter 9. The key points here are the following:

1. Both a governmental fund *expenditure **and** an other financing source* must be recognized at the inception of the capital lease.

2. Neither use of a Capital Projects Fund at the inception of the capital lease nor use of a Debt Service Fund to service the capital lease debt is required unless legally or contractually required, which is rare.

3. Both the governmental fund expenditure and other financing source and the related debt service expenditure on the capital lease may be accounted for in the General Fund or perhaps a Special Revenue Fund.

To illustrate, assume that a general government department entered into a capital lease of equipment. The capitalizable cost of the equipment (per FASB *Statement No. 13*) is $900,000, and the government makes a $40,000 down payment at the inception of the lease. Regardless of the governmental fund in which the capital lease transaction and debt service are recorded, the governmental fund entries are:

Inception of Capital Lease:

Expenditures	$900,000	
Other Financing Sources—Capital Lease		$860,000
Cash...		40,000
To record capital lease expenditure and related other financing source.		

Expenditures Ledger (Expenditures):

Capital Outlay	$900,000

ILLUSTRATION 6-4   Capital Lease and Certificate of Participation Accounting Overview (Amounts are in $000s)

	General Fund (or other fund paying for capital lease)		General Capital Assets Accounts		General Long-Term Liabilities Accounts	
Inception of the lease	Expenditures—		Equipment under		Net Position	860
	Capital Outlay	900	Capital Lease	900	Capital Lease	
	OFS—Capital Lease	860	Net Position	900	Payable	860
	Cash	40				
	Expenditures recorded at *present value* of the minimum lease payments.		**Recorded at *present value* of the *minimum lease payments*.**		**Recorded at *present value* of the minimum lease *payments* less any initial payment.**	
Annual lease payment	Expenditures—Debt		None		Capital Leases	
	Service—Principal	13			Payable	13
	Expenditures—Debt				Net Position	13
	Service—Interest	5				
	Cash	18				
	Principal and interest amounts determined using the *effective interest* rate method.		**Depreciation expense will be recorded in the GCA accounts.**		**For principal amounts only.**	

Note that the effect of the entry at the inception of the capital lease on the fund balance of the governmental fund is equal to the $40,000 decrease in fund financial resources, which indicates the net effect of the $860,000 other financing source and the $900,000 expenditure. Also, $900,000 is the fair market value of the capital asset acquired.

The leased equipment and the related capital lease liability affect the GCA-GLTL accounts as follows:

$$GCA \quad - \quad GLTL \quad = \quad \text{Net Position (NP)}$$
$$+\$900,000 \qquad +\$860,000 \qquad\qquad +\$40,000$$

Now assume that the first monthly lease payment after inception is for $18,000, including $5,000 of interest.

First Debt Service Payment:

Expenditures......................................	$ 18,000	
Cash..		$ 18,000

To record capital lease debt service payment.

Expenditures Ledger (Expenditures):

Debt Service—Interest (Capital Lease)	$ 5,000
Debt Service—Principal (Capital Lease)	13,000
	$ 18,000

Note that the capital lease debt service payment must be allocated between interest expenditures and debt principal reduction based on the *effective interest rate* of the capital lease agreement. The effective interest amount for the first payment is computed by multiplying the effective interest rate for the lease by the carrying amount (book value) of the lease liability, initially $860,000, and dividing by 12. The capital lease liability principal reduction resulting from this first payment affects the GCA-GLTL accounts:

$$GCA \quad - \quad GLTL \quad = \quad NP$$
$$-\$13,000 \qquad +\$13,000$$

Several variations of the traditional capital lease have appeared recently. Certificates of participation (COPs), the most common variation, typically involve governments dealing with brokerage firms or banks rather than with product manufacturers—and receiving cash that is used to purchase the computers, vehicles, or other equipment. COPs are otherwise like traditional leases and are accounted for in the same manner.

Accounting for general government leases—both capital leases and operating leases—is illustrated further using transactions and information from the City and County of Denver, Colorado, in the In Practice example on the following page. Accounting for the inception of a major capital lease, the Wellington Webb Municipal Office Building, capital lease payments, and operating leases are included.

ADJUSTING ENTRIES

Most of the expenditure-related adjusting entries that may be required in a governmental fund at year end are similar to those covered in intermediate accounting courses. That is, the accountant must ensure that a proper year-end cutoff is made for expenditures for payrolls, utilities, and similar costs.

The *available* revenue recognition criterion does *not* apply to governmental fund *expenditure* accounting, and an expenditure-related liability payable beyond

6-1 IN PRACTICE

Government Lease Transactions

The City and County of Denver, Colorado, uses leasing—both capital and operating—extensively. A recent Comprehensive Annual Financial Report indicates that Denver has capitalized leases for a variety of general government properties and other assets, including:

- Wellington Webb Municipal Office Building
- Blair-Caldwell Research Library
- Buell Theatre
- 5440 Roslyn maintenance facility property
- Jail dorm facility
- Three fire stations
- Computer and safety equipment
- Production press

The net book value of Denver's general government leased assets exceeds $300 million.

In addition to the capital leases, Denver has significant operating leases. Accounting for a few of Denver's lease transactions is illustrated below.

In one recent year, Denver entered into a capital lease of the Wellington Webb Municipal Office Building. The present value of the minimum lease payments for this building lease was $52,103,000. The entry to record this transaction in the General Fund—assuming no initial payment was made by the city—would be:

Expenditures—Capital Outlay	$52,103,000	
Other Financing Sources—Capital Leases...............		$52,103,000
To record capital lease expenditure and related other financing source.		

The GCA-GLTL accounts entry (discussed in Chapter 9) would be:

Buildings Under Capital Lease	$52,103,000	
Liability for Capital Lease		$52,103,000
To record leased building and capital lease liability.		

In another recent year, Denver made capital lease payments of $30,672,000 that reduced the principal of its general government lease liabilities by $15,176,000. The entry to record this transaction in the General Fund would be:

Expenditures—Lease Principal Retirement.................	$15,176,000	
Expenditures—Interest.................................	15,496,000	
Cash...		$30,672,000
To record capital lease payments.		

The GCA-GLTL accounts entry (discussed in Chapter 9) would be:

Liability for Capital Lease	$15,176,000	
Net Position		$15,176,000
To record reduction of capital lease liability.		

Finally, in the same year Denver paid operating leases of $7,018,000 from its General Fund. The operating leases affect only the General Fund and should be recorded as follows:

Expenditures—Operating Leases	$ 7,018,000	
Cash...		$ 7,018,000
To record operating lease payments.		

Adapted from a recent Comprehensive Annual Financial Report of the City and County of Denver, Colorado.

60 days into the next year may be considered a governmental fund expenditure and liability. The governmental fund *expenditure* recognition criteria are not as clearly defined as the available *revenue* recognition criterion, but a general rule has evolved.

The general rule is that any expenditure and related liability applicable to a fund are recorded as a fund expenditure and liability unless the liability is an unmatured liability that is properly classified as a general long-term liability and thus is recorded in the GLTL accounts. In this regard the GASB *Codification* states that:

> **General long-term debt** is not limited to liabilities arising from debt issuances *per se,* but **may also include noncurrent [unmatured] liabilities on capital and operating leases, compensated absences, claims and judgments, pensions, special termination benefits, landfill closure and postclosure care, and other commitments** that are **not current [matured] liabilities properly recorded in governmental funds.**[12]

The *Codification* states that:

> **Governmental fund liabilities and expenditures** for claims and judgments, compensated absences, termination benefits, and landfill closure and postclosure care costs should be **recognized** to the extent the **liabilities** are **"normally expected to be liquidated with expendable available financial resources."** Governments . . . are normally expected to liquidate liabilities with expendable available financial resources to the extent that the liabilities **mature** (come due for payment) each period.[13]

The notion of "to be liquidated with expendable available financial resources" is not an issue in most routine adjusting entries made at year end. Such accrued expenditure liabilities as payroll, utilities, and similar costs are presumed to be payable from existing fund resources and are accrued. Rather, the *"to be liquidated with expendable available financial resources"* notion relates primarily to accruing expenditures for (1) debt service; (2) claims and judgments; (3) accrued vacation and sick leave, referred to as compensated absences; and (4) pension and OPEB plan contributions. Such expenditures and liabilities typically are recognized in the fund in the same period that they mature (are due for payment). These expenditures are the main topics of this section and are considered after a brief discussion of encumbrances.

Encumbrances

The encumbrances outstanding at year end should be reviewed both to assure that all encumbrances are recorded *and* because, as noted in the GASB *Codification*:

> If performance on an executory contract is complete, or virtually complete, an expenditure and liability should be recognized rather than an encumbrance.[14]

A failure to record completed contracts as governmental fund expenditures and liabilities (rather than encumbrances) may be unintentional. Invoices for the goods or services may not have arrived at the government's offices by year end, for example, and they are inadvertently recorded as expenditures in the next year. On the other hand, it may be intentional, as when recording expenditures for an encumbered order would cause departmental expenditures to exceed appropriations. These situations may occur when the budgetary basis is the modified accrual basis—on which encumbrances are not considered equivalent to expenditures and thus are not charged against appropriations—or when the budgetary basis includes encumbrances but the encumbrance recorded is significantly less than the actual expenditure incurred.

In any event, the encumbrances outstanding against a governmental fund at year end should be analyzed. If any are found to be expenditures misclassified as encumbrances, the adjusting entry (omitting subsidiary ledger entries) would be:

---

[12]GASB Codification, sec. 1500.103. (Emphasis added.)

[13]Ibid., sec. 1600.122. (Emphasis added.)

[14]Ibid., sec. 1700.128(c).

ENCUMBRANCES OUTSTANDING	$19,000	
Expenditures	20,000	
ENCUMBRANCES		$19,000
Accounts Payable (or Accrued Liabilities)		20,000

To record reclassifying encumbrances as expenditures
at year end.

Finally, with respect to actual encumbrances outstanding at year end, recall that they must be analyzed to determine which are related to unassigned fund balance and affect the amount reported as assigned or committed fund balance for GAAP purposes.

Debt Service   As noted earlier, debt service expenditures on *un*matured general long-term liabilities typically are *not* accrued at year end. *This approach is usually consistent with the "to be liquidated with expendable available financial resources" criterion* because the property tax rates of many state and local governments are set to provide the financial resources required for the GLTL debt service payments due each year. Thus, the financial resources available at the end of a year need not ordinarily be used for the following year's debt service payments because those resources will be provided by that year's tax levy.

   Governments are ***permitted***, *but not required*, to accrue GLTL debt service expenditures (principal and interest) *if two conditions are met:*

1. The debt service payment must be *due early* (not more than 30 days) in the *next* fiscal year.
2. Dedicated financial resources to pay the debt service payment due early in the next year must have been provided by the current year end to a *Debt Service Fund*.

   If a government opts to make the accrual, the full amount of the debt service payment due early in the next year must be accrued. Clearly, the SLG should adopt an appropriate debt service expenditure accounting policy and apply it consistently each year.

   It was noted earlier that state and local governments may borrow on **short-term** notes such as tax anticipation notes (TANs), revenue anticipation notes (RANs), and similar debt instruments such as bond anticipation notes (BANs). The GASB *Codification* states that TANs, RANs, and similar short-term debt instruments usually should be accounted for as **fund liabilities** of the governmental fund that receives the debt issue proceeds.[15] Also, the short-term notes and interest would usually be paid from that fund. Thus, whereas interest on *un*matured general long-term liabilities is ordinarily recorded when due rather than accrued at year end, interest on governmental fund (non-GLTL) short-term notes and other debts *is* accrued at year end:

Accrual of Interest on Short-Term Debt

Expenditures	$36,000	
Accrued Interest Payable		$36,000

To record interest accrued at year end on short-term notes
payable.

Expenditures Ledger (Expenditures):

Interest	$36,000

Various types of borrowings and related debt service are discussed and illustrated further in Chapters 7–9.

Claims and Judgments   Lawsuits and other claims for personal injury, property damage, employee compensation, or other reasons are frequently filed against states and local governments. Such claims include, but are by no means limited to, those arising from:

- Employment, such as worker compensation and unemployment claims
- Contractual actions, such as claims for delays or inadequate specifications

---

[15]Ibid., sec. B50.102.

- Actions of government personnel, such as claims for medical malpractice, damage to privately owned vehicles by government-owned vehicles, and improper police arrest
- Government properties, such as claims relating to personal injuries and property damage

Many claims filed against state and local governments are characterized by conditions that make it extremely difficult to reasonably estimate the ultimate liability, if any, that will result. These conditions include:

- *Unreasonably high claims.* Some claims may be filed in amounts far greater than those reasonably expected to be agreed to by the government and the claimant or awarded by a court.
- *Time between occurrence and filing.* The time permitted (e.g., by law) between the occurrence of an event giving rise to a claim and the actual filing of the claim may be lengthy. (An event leading to a claim may occur during a year, but the claim may not be filed by year end; thus, the government may not be aware of the claim at year end.)
- *Time between filing and settlement and payment.* Likewise, many months or even years may elapse between (1) the filing of the claim and its ultimate settlement, perhaps after court appeals, and (2) the settlement of the claim and its ultimate payment because adjudicated or agreed settlement amounts may be paid over a period of years after settlement.

On the other hand, the outcome of some claims may be readily estimable, such as when a court has entered a judgment that will not be appealed against the government, or the government has appropriate estimates by its attorneys and/or sufficient data about past settlements of similar claims to reasonably estimate the ultimate liabilities to result from such claims, either individually or by type of claim.

The GASB standards for claims and judgments are discussed and their application, including the effect of insurance recoveries, is illustrated in the following sections.

GASB Standards

Claims outstanding against a government are *contingencies,* regardless of whether the claims have been filed, are being negotiated or arbitrated, or have resulted in judgments for or against the government that will be appealed by either the claimant or the government. As in business accounting, the GASB *Codification* requires that contingencies—including the *liability* for claims and judgments (CJ) outstanding—be recognized in the accounts if information available prior to issuance of the financial statements indicates *both*:

1. It is probable that an asset has been impaired or a liability has been incurred, as of the date of the financial statements.
2. The amount of the loss can be reasonably estimated.

If these contingencies recognition criteria are *not* met, the claims and judgments outstanding would be *disclosed* in the notes to the government's financial statements but would not be recorded in the accounts or presented in the financial statements.

If the CJ recognition *criteria* are *met*, CJ expenditures and related liabilities are to be accounted for as follows:

- The amount calculated in accordance with the provisions of FASB *Statement No. 5* should be recognized as *expenditures and fund liabilities to the extent that the amounts are payable with expendable available financial resources.*[16]
- Any *remaining* accrued *liabilities* should be recorded in the *General Long-Term Liabilities* accounts.

---

[16]Ibid., sec. C50.124. (Emphasis added.)

Adjusting Entries—CJ

During the year a government will typically record the amounts paid or vouchered as payable for claims and judgments as expenditures. To illustrate CJ adjusting entries at year end, assume that CJ expenditures and fund liabilities are recorded in the General Fund, that no CJ fund liabilities were accrued at the end of the prior year (20X0), and that the following entry summarizes the CJ entries during 20X1:

During the Year (20X1)

Expenditures..	$300,000	
Cash or Vouchers Payable		$300,000

To record CJ expenditures paid or vouchered during 20X1.
   (None accrued at end of 20X0.)

Expenditures Ledger (Expenditures):

Claims and Judgments	$300,000

Assume also at the end of 20X1 that:

1. Claims and judgments totaling $900,000 are outstanding.

2. It is reasonably estimated that the ultimate CJ liabilities resulting, including legal fees, will be $200,000.

3. $50,000 of the $200,000 total unrecorded CJ liability is due at the end of 20X1 (and is scheduled to be paid early in 20X2).

Given these facts, this CJ adjusting entry would be made in the General Fund accounts at the end of 20X1:

End of Year (20X1)

Expenditures.......................................	$ 50,000	
Accrued Liabilities (CJ)............................		$ 50,000

To record additional 20X1 expenditures for CJ fund
   liabilities due at the end of 20X1.

Expenditures Ledger (Expenditures):

Claims and Judgments	$ 50,000

The impact on the GCA-GLTL accounts would be:

$$\text{GCA} \quad - \quad \text{GLTL} \quad = \quad \text{NP}$$
$$+\$150,000 \qquad -\$150,000$$

Additionally, all of the outstanding claims and judgments ($900,000)—except those for which the probability of loss is remote—would be disclosed in the notes to the 20X1 financial statements.

In sum, $350,000 of CJ expenditures would be reported in the General Fund for 20X1, and a $50,000 CJ liability would be reported in the General Fund at the end of 20X1; a $150,000 CJ unmatured liability would be added to the GLTL accounts; and all CJ contingencies, including those not recorded in the accounts, would be disclosed in the notes to the 20X1 financial statements.

Insurance, Self-Insurance, and No Insurance

The discussions of CJ liability estimation noted that the final *estimate* of *each* major CJ *liability* **and** *total* CJ liabilities should include legal and other related costs, as well as the settled or adjudicated claim amount, ***net*** *of any insurance or similar recoveries*. But the GASB also requires[17] that insurance recoveries be reported in

---

[17]Governmental Accounting Standards Board, *Statement No. 42*, "Accounting and Financial Reporting for Impairment of Capital Assets and for Insurance Recoveries," pars. 21 and 22.

governmental funds as "other financing sources" or, rarely, as extraordinary items. Thus, if a currently payable claim was settled in 20X1 for $250,000 but related insurance simultaneously reimbursed the government for $200,000, the governmental fund entry (omitting subsidiary ledger entries) would be:

During 20X1

Expenditures	$250,000	
Cash or Receivable from Insurance Company............	200,000	
Cash or Vouchers Payable..........................		$250,000
Other Financing Sources—Insurance Proceeds........		200,000

To record settlement of claim net of related insurance recovery.

The insurance company and the insured government may occasionally disagree on the amount of a CJ expenditure to be reimbursed, however, and thus the insurance recovery might not be reasonably estimable or its receipt might be delayed until a subsequent year.

Amount Estimable, but Settlement Delayed Suppose, for example, that the $200,000 insurance recovery in this example is reasonably estimable but will *not* be received until late in 20X2. Because the *available criterion* does *not* apply to *expenditure recognition*, the preceding entry would be made. If the insurance recovery receivable is a General Fund asset and not to be collected until 20X3, nonspendable fund balance would be reported at the end of 20X1 if the proceeds will be unassigned. If the insurance proceeds are restricted, committed, or assigned to a specific purpose, the fund balance will be reported in the corresponding category.[18]

Not Estimable in 20X1; Settled and Received in 20X2 On the other hand, suppose that (1) the insurance recovery amount was in dispute and was *not* reasonably estimable at the end of 20X1, but (2) was *agreed* to and received in 20X2, after the 20X1 financial statements were issued by the government. In this situation the entries would be:

During 20X1

Expenditures	$250,000	
Cash or Vouchers Payable..........................		$250,000

To record settlement of claim. (Insurance recovery not reasonably estimable.)

During 20X2

Receivable from Insurance Company...................	$200,000	
Other Financing Sources—Insurance Proceeds		$200,000

To record insurance recovery on 20X1 claim expenditures.

Self-Insured Plans Liability insurance premiums have increased rapidly in recent years, and some governments have been unable to obtain adequate levels of insurance for what they consider to be reasonable or affordable premiums. Thus, many state and local governments have instituted *self-insured* plans—alone or in pools with other governments—or are uninsured. Self-insurance plans are discussed and illustrated in Chapter 11, "Internal Service Funds."

Governments that are uninsured assume more CJ risk than those that are insured or self-insured. Accordingly, some governments may establish governmental

---

[18]Long-term General Fund receivables that are not offset by deferred revenues must be reflected in the amount of nonspendable fund balance if proceeds from ultimate collection are *not* either restricted, committed, or assigned.

fund *commitments or assignments* of fund balance to indicate that some net assets must be maintained in view of the uninsured CJ contingencies, and others obtain *umbrella* insurance *policies*—with large deductibles but covering large amounts above the deductibles—to insure partially against catastrophic CJ liabilities being incurred.

Compensated Absences

The accounting and reporting for compensated absences (CA), such as accumulated vacation and sick leave, parallel that for claims and judgments. Accordingly, the GASB standards require government employers to accrue a liability for future **vacation and similar compensated absences** that meet *both* of these conditions:

a. The employees' rights to receive compensation for future absences are attributable to *services* already *rendered.*

b. It is *probable* that the *employer* will *compensate* the *employees* for the benefits through paid time off or by some other means, such as cash payments at termination or retirement.[19]

Sick leave and similar payments during employees' working years are considered expenditures of the years during which the employees are ill. Thus, **sick leave and similar compensated absences** *are accrued only to the extent they are expected to be paid* when employees retire or otherwise terminate employment.

To determine whether an adjusting entry is required and, if so, the amount of the adjustment

1. The accumulated **vacation and similar CA liabilities** at year-end are *inventoried at current salary levels.*
   - *Only* the *hours or days* of *each employee's accumulated* CA time that *carry over* to the next year should be inventoried.
   - For example, an employee may have accumulated 36 days of vacation. But if only 24 days may be carried forward to the next year—that is, the other 12 days are lost if not taken currently—then only 24 days are inventoried.

2. **Sick leave** calculations can be made similarly—but must be *capped* at the amount expected to be *paid* upon employee *retirement or other termination.* (Alternatively, sick leave calculations may be based on overall estimates of expected termination payments.)

The estimated liabilities for compensated absences must include salary-related payments (e.g., payroll taxes and fringe benefits), as well as base compensation levels.

Adjusting Entries—CA

To illustrate CA accounting, we use the General Fund assumptions and amounts used in the claims and judgments (CJ) illustration earlier in this section. The General Fund CA entries—if reversing entries are not made and omitting subsidiary ledger entries—are as follows:

During the Year (20X1)

Expenditures..	$300,000	
Cash or Vouchers Payable		$300,000

To record CA expenditures paid or vouchered during 20X1.
(None were accrued at the end of 20X0.)

End of Year (20X1)

Expenditures..	$ 50,000	
Accrued Vacation and Sick Leave Payable		$ 50,000

To record additional 20X1 expenditures for
CA liabilities due at the end of 20X1.

---

[19]GASB *Codification*, sec. C60.104. (Emphasis added.)

The impact on the GCA-GLTL accounts would be the same as shown in the CJ example.

$$GCA \quad - \quad GLTL \quad = \quad NP$$
$$+\$150,000 \qquad -\$150,000$$

Rationale

The rationale of CA accounting and reporting is largely the same as that for CJ accounting and reporting. Only the measurement differs because of the differing natures of CJ and CA liabilities. Thus, the unmatured *CA liabilities recognized should be recorded in the GLTL accounts—not in a governmental fund—*and the notes to the financial statements should describe both the unit's vacation, sick leave, and other CA policies and the related CA accounting and reporting policies.

Pension/OPEB Plan Contributions

GASB *Statement No. 27,* "Accounting for Pensions by State and Local Governmental Employers," provides specific actuarial parameters and other guidance for computing employer pension expenditures and liabilities. GASB *Statement No. 27 requires* that state and local government employers:

- Use *acceptable actuarial methods* in computing employer contribution liabilities under most *defined benefit* pension plans, and
- *Enforce* statutory or contractual *requirements* for *defined contribution* pension plans.

The GASB requires that the pension contribution expenditures and liabilities related to defined benefit plans be recognized in the same manner as for claims and judgments and compensated absences (CJCA). Thus, if some of the *actuarially required* pension plan *contributions* for the year have *not* been paid or vouchered as payable at year end,

1. *The amount that would normally be liquidated with expendable available financial resources of a governmental fund* would be recorded as a *fund expenditure and liability,* and
2. *The remaining amount* would be recorded as a *liability* in the *GLTL accounts.*

Most statewide and other group plans require that participating employer governments pay the required contributions promptly to both defined contribution and defined benefit pension plans. However, some governments that manage their own single employer pension plans do not make the required contributions. This omission may occur regularly, as when the legislative body routinely fails to appropriate the actuarially required amount, or only occasionally during financial crises. In any event, the amounts involved may be large—in the millions or even billions of dollars—both currently and cumulatively.

Because the accounting and reporting for underfunded required pension contributions parallels that for CJCA, a brief example should suffice. If a government that (1) had no unfunded pension contribution liability at the beginning of the year, (2) had charged the pension contributions paid during the year to Expenditures, and (3) had an additional (unrecorded) unfunded actuarially required pension contribution of $800,000, of which $100,000 is considered a matured liability of the General Fund, the adjusting entry (omitting subsidiary ledger entries) in the General Fund at year end would be:

Expenditures	$100,000	
Liability—Pension Contribution		$100,000

To record additional expenditures for the matured portion
of the unfunded actuarially required pension contribution
at year end.

The remaining $700,000 would affect the GLTL accounts as shown here.

$$\begin{array}{ccccc} \text{GCA} & - & \text{GLTL} & = & \text{NP} \\ & & +\$700,000 & & -\$700,000 \end{array}$$

As with claims, judgments, and compensated absences, a government must determine the matured portion, if any, of its underfunded pension contributions in order to recognize the appropriate amount of pension expenditures for a governmental fund. Local governments frequently participate in *statewide* defined benefit retirement plans that require the local governments to contribute their shares of the **annual required contribution (ARC)** each period. In these cases, assuming the contribution required by the pension plan meets the GASB *Statement No. 27* parameters, the government will not have a current period unfunded pension liability. The expenditures recognized will equal the contribution, which equals the ARC. If part of the required contribution has not been paid, it is reported as a fund liability, not as a general long-term liability.

GASB *Statement No. 45*, "Accounting and Financial Reporting by Employers for Postemployment Benefits Other Than Pensions [OPEB]," requires that the government employer's expenditures and liabilities for OPEB extended to retirees and their families be computed, reported, and disclosed essentially as if these plans were pension plans. The most common types of OPEB are:

- Health care insurance
- Vision insurance
- Life insurance

Government employer OPEB expenditures and liabilities are particularly significant in cases where employees such as police officers, firefighters, and public school teachers and administrators can retire after 20 years of service—perhaps still in their 40s—and be covered by the OPEB health care insurance provisions until they become eligible for Medicare at age 65. In some cases employers pay all premiums and administrative costs; in other cases the employees pay a substantial part of the costs.

GASB *Statement No. 45* has a few terms and alternatives that differ from GASB *Statement No. 27,* primarily because OPEB costs and liabilities are more difficult to estimate than pension costs and liabilities. But, again, the underlying concepts, actuarial methods, financial reporting, and note disclosures closely parallel those of GASB *Statement No. 27.*

EXPENDITURE REPORTING: GAAP VS. BUDGETARY

Both the managerial uses of expenditure-related budgetary accounts and interim reports and year-end budgetary and GAAP financial reporting were introduced in earlier chapters. Likewise, earlier chapters have pointed out that (1) any significant differences between the budgetary basis and the GAAP basis must be explained in the notes to the financial statements and (2) *non*-GAAP budgetary statements and schedules must be *reconciled* to the GAAP financial statements, as discussed and illustrated later.

Another important consideration is the differing levels of detail that may be required in GAAP and budgetary statements and schedules. Recall that:

- **GAAP** statements must *"present fairly"* in accordance with GAAP, as is illustrated in Chapter 5 in Illustration 5-8.
- **Budgetary** statements and schedules must *demonstrate compliance* at the executive-legislative *"budgetary control points"* level of detail on the *budgetary basis*, as is illustrated for expenditures in Illustration 6-5.

ILLUSTRATION 6-5   Budgetary Comparison Schedule: Expenditures

City of Lakewood, Colorado
General Fund
Budgetary Comparison Schedule
Year Ended December 31, 20X3

EXPENDITURES	Original Budget	Final Budget	Actual	Variance Favorable (Unfavorable)
General Government				
Legislative				
Personnel Services	$ 213,514	$ 182,773	$ 183,215	($442)
Supplies and Services	222,145	231,445	220,368	11,077
Total Legislative	435,659	414,218	403,583	10,635
Judicial				
Personnel Services	1,597,686	1,581,986	1,534,736	47,250
Supplies and Services	125,288	137,375	135,668	1,707
Capital Outlay	20,322	—	3,250	(3,250)
Total Judicial	1,743,296	1,719,361	1,673,654	45,707
Executive				
Personnel Services	823,865	788,544	796,873	(8,329)
Supplies and Services	205,992	167,332	155,145	12,187
Total Executive	1,029,857	955,876	952,018	3,858
Administrative				
Personnel Services	3,762,486	3,719,900	3,359,092	360,808
Supplies and Services	1,843,674	1,828,465	1,664,068	164,397
Capital Outlay	(8,859)	(7,580)	12,305	(19,885)
Total Administrative	5,597,301	5,540,785	5,035,465	505,320
Other				
Personnel Services	4,964,601	4,764,929	4,701,071	63,858
Supplies and Services	5,984,878	6,092,759	5,969,063	123,696
Capital Outlay	2,627,984	1,255,926	886,819	369,107
Total Other	13,577,372	12,113,614	11,556,953	556,661
Total General Government	22,383,458	20,743,854	19,621,673	1,122,181
Public Safety				
Law Enforcement				
Personnel Services	28,851,787	28,445,306	27,720,311	724,995
Supplies and Services	3,040,737	2,699,043	2,496,841	202,202
Capital Outlay	211,467	80,929	44,628	36,301
Total Law Enforcement	32,103,991	31,225,278	30,261,780	963,498
Correction				
Personnel Services	514,509	500,338	487,194	13,144
Supplies and Services	12,799	10,259	7,689	2,570
Total Correction	527,308	510,597	494,883	15,714
Protective Inspection				
Personnel Services	1,696,360	1,637,449	1,650,885	(13,436)
Supplies and Services	193,590	193,590	150,337	43,253
Total Protective Inspection	1,889,950	1,831,039	1,801,222	29,817
Other Protection				
Personnel Services	588,481	593,603	555,529	38,074
Supplies and Services	205,724	338,948	216,609	122,339
Other Services and Charges	—	—	(1,928)	1,928
Total Other Protection	794,205	932,551	770,210	162,341
Total Public Safety	35,315,454	34,499,465	33,328,095	1,171,370

(*Continued*)

ILLUSTRATION 6-5 Budgetary Comparison Schedule: Expenditures (*Continued*)

	Original Budget	Final Budget	Actual	Variance Favorable (Unfavorable)
Public Works				
Highways and Streets				
Personnel Services	2,386,872	2,188,895	2,065,078	123,817
Supplies and Services	2,615,402	2,461,751	2,250,605	211,146
Capital Outlay	238,895	213,912	362,399	(148,487)
Total Highways and Streets	5,241,169	4,864,558	4,678,082	186,476
Sanitation				
Personnel Services	328,848	327,989	316,335	11,654
Supplies and Services	190,701	153,798	95,332	58,466
Capital Outlay	—	25,000	24,285	715
Total Sanitation	519,549	506,787	435,952	70,835
Total Public Works	5,760,718	5,371,345	5,114,034	257,311
Culture and Recreation				
Recreation				
Personnel Services	3,836,094	3,672,397	3,538,790	133,607
Supplies and Services	926,261	894,777	709,528	185,249
Total Recreation	4,762,355	4,567,174	4,248,318	318,856
Parks				
Personnel Services	928,629	904,687	908,036	(3,349)
Supplies and Services	1,060,591	977,336	992,382	(15,046)
Total Parks	1,989,220	1,882,023	1,900,418	(18,395)
Total Culture and Recreation	6,751,575	6,449,197	6,148,736	300,461
Urban Development and Housing				
Economic Development and Assistance				
Personnel Services	2,992,675	2,729,740	2,694,131	35,609
Supplies and Services	976,908	1,163,729	703,043	460,686
Total Urban Development and Housing	3,969,583	3,893,469	3,397,174	496,295
Miscellaneous				
Other Miscellaneous				
Personnel Services	323,363	218,402	236,364	(17,962)
Supplies and Services	2,202,390	2,464,139	2,374,391	89,748
Total Miscellaneous	2,525,753	2,682,541	2,610,755	71,786
Contingency	8,712,728	8,797,138	—	8,797,138
TOTAL EXPENDITURES	85,419,387	82,437,009	70,220,467	12,216,542
Excess (Deficiency) of Revenues Over Expenditures	(10,831,912)	(10,705,864)	(2,249,854)	8,456,010
OTHER FINANCING SOURCES (USES)				
Transfers In	5,238,618	1,730,000	1,730,000	—
Transfers Out	(7,660,454)	(4,383,126)	(3,987,976)	395,150
TOTAL OTHER FINANCING SOURCES (USES)	(2,421,836)	(2,653,126)	(2,257,976)	395,150
Net Change in Fund Balance	(13,253,748)	(13,358,990)	(4,507,830)	8,851,160
FUND BALANCE, Beginning of Year	13,253,748	13,358,990	13,358,993	3
FUND BALANCE, End of Year	$ —	$ —	$ 8,851,163	$ 8,851,163

See the accompanying Independent Auditor's Report.

Source: Adapted from a City of Lakewood, Colorado, comprehensive annual financial report.

In the Chapter 5 and 6 examples:

1. The **GAAP-based operating statement** (Illustration 5-8) reports expenditures using terminology similar to that illustrated in Chapters 3 and 4 and at about the same level of detail.

2. The **budgetary comparison schedule** (Illustration 6-5)—actually the Expenditures section of the budgetary comparison schedule presented in Illustration 5-9—reports expenditures by broad objects-of-expenditure within departments to demonstrate compliance with the legally enacted appropriations.

Finally, a variety of other expenditure-related schedules may be provided by the chief financial officer, perhaps at the request of the governing body, rating agencies, or investors. The General Fund **Schedule of Expenditures and Other Financing Uses by Department—Budget and Actual**, presented as Illustration 6-6, *reclassifies* the expenditures and other financing uses information presented by *function* in the budgetary comparison schedule and summarizes it by *department*.

CHANGES IN ACCOUNTING PRINCIPLES

Restatements may be required to report the cumulative effect of changes in accounting principles. Four types of events that might cause, or result from, a change in the expenditure recognition accounting principles of a governmental fund are:

- A type of expenditure not previously deemed to be objectively measurable, such as claims and judgments, may now be considered reasonably estimable.

- Management chooses to change from one acceptable alternative principle to another when there are acceptable alternative expenditure recognition principles, such as the purchases and consumption methods of inventory and prepayment expenditure recognition.

- Management chooses to change the method of applying an accounting principle where there are two or more acceptable methods of applying an accounting principle, such as the FIFO (first-in, first-out), LIFO (last-in, first-out), and average cost methods of inventory accounting on the consumption basis, using a periodic method.

- The GASB or another recognized standards-setting body issues a new expenditure recognition standard that requires a different expenditure accounting policy than presently used.

Two of these types of events and changes in accounting principles and the methods of applying principles are discussed briefly in this section.

Alternative Principles

To illustrate the implementation of changes between acceptable alternative principles, assume that a government that accounts for inventory using the consumption method decides to change from the first-in, first-out (FIFO) method to the average cost method of General Fund inventory accounting. The FIFO method inventory at the end of the prior year was $400,000; the average cost method valuation at that time was $300,000. The journal entry at the beginning of the current year to implement the change to the average method would be:

Cumulative Effect of Change in Accounting Principle	$100,000	
Inventory of Materials and Supplies		$100,000

To record fund balance restatement for change from FIFO to average.

ILLUSTRATION 6-6 Schedule of Expenditures and Other Financing Uses by Department

City of Lakewood, Colorado
General Fund
Schedule of Expenditures and Other Financing Uses by Department
Budget and Actual
Year Ended December 31, 20X3

EXPENDITURES	Original Budget	Final Budget	Actual	Variance Favorable (Unfavorable)
Mayor and City Council	$ 435,659	$ 414,218	$ 403,583	$ 10,635
City Manager's Office	1,422,116	1,326,205	1,300,586	25,619
City Attorney	817,483	793,383	806,558	(13,175)
City Clerk	608,133	556,964	490,650	66,314
Community Planning and Development	1,796,426	1,706,963	1,645,502	61,461
Community Resources	10,147,090	9,799,118	9,402,047	397,071
Employee Relations	4,121,555	4,172,748	3,798,847	373,901
Finance	2,685,003	2,554,266	2,519,795	34,471
Housing and Family Services	3,690,203	3,468,319	3,072,015	396,304
Information Technology	4,922,111	4,733,866	4,498,817	235,049
Municipal Court	2,270,604	2,232,013	2,168,537	63,476
Police Department	31,070,186	30,239,813	29,204,084	1,035,729
Public Works	11,409,355	10,963,898	10,652,151	311,747
Nondepartmental	3,389,451	2,756,813	257,295	2,499,518
Miscellaneous (Contingency)	6,634,012	6,718,422	—	6,718,422
Total Expenditures	85,419,387	82,437,009	70,220,467	12,216,542
OTHER FINANCING USES				
TRANSFERS (IN) OUT				
City Manager's Benefit Fund	8,979	62,495	—	62,495
Debt Service Fund	775,279	771,904	771,904	—
Equipment Replacement Fund	422,321	377,321	377,321	—
General Recreation Fund (Participation)	1,859,129	—	—	—
Heritage, Culture and The Arts Fund (Participation)	766,541	742,690	732,514	10,176
Housing and Family Services Fund (Participation)	1,649,489	—	—	—
Lakewood Reinvestment Authority Fund	100,000	350,000	29,634	320,366
Lakewood Public Building Authority	2,078,716	2,078,716	2,076,603	2,113
Transfers In	(5,238,618)	(1,730,000)	(1,730,000)	—
Total Uses	2,421,836	2,653,126	2,257,976	395,150
TOTAL EXPENDITURES AND USES	$87,841,223	$85,090,135	$72,478,443	$12,611,692

See the accompanying Independent Auditor's Report.

Source: A recent City of Lakewood, Colorado, comprehensive annual financial report (CAFR).

New GASB Standards   Changes in accounting principles may also occur if the GASB issues a new expenditure recognition standard or revises an existing standard. If the new or revised standard requires a different expenditure recognition principle than that presently being used in its governmental fund accounting, a state or local government must change its accounting policy to comply with the new or revised standard.

As noted in the discussion on revenue-related accounting changes in Chapter 5, the GASB and other standards-setting bodies' pronouncements specify when (at the latest) and how the new standards are to be implemented. If a new standard is required to be applied *prospectively*—that is, only to transactions and events occurring on or after the implementation date—the change will not have a cumulative effect on the beginning fund balance. For example, such a standard might specify that, from the implementation date forward, certain transactions that had previously been reported as expenditures must be reported as other financing uses.

Most new or revised standards require *retroactive* application, however. That is, the new expenditure recognition standard is to be implemented as if it had been applied in prior periods. Accordingly, the entry to implement new retroactive application expenditure recognition standards resembles a correction entry—as do those illustrated earlier in this section—except that the fund balance restatement is referred to as the cumulative effect of change(s) in accounting principles.

ERROR CORRECTION

As noted in Chapter 5, locating and correcting errors is a significant role and activity of professional accountants and auditors. Error correction is discussed and illustrated in most standard intermediate accounting textbooks, and those sections should be reviewed as needed to supplement the discussions and illustrations in this and later chapters.

Correcting errors in state and local government (SLG) accounts and statements is usually easier than in business because SLGs:

- Are *not* subject to federal income tax, so there is *no* "income tax effect."
- Do *not* compute or report earnings per share.

If expenditure-related errors are found, the correcting entry or entries depend on whether the accounts have been closed for the year in which the error occurred:

- **Accounts Open.** Understand the *incorrect* entry that was made, *compare* it to the entry that *should* have been made, and *correct* the revenue and related accounts.
- **Accounts Closed.** The initial approach is the same—understand the *incorrect* entry that was made, *compare* it to the entry that *should* have been made—except the correction will increase or decrease the *beginning* of the current year Unreserved Fund Balance account to which the prior year revenues, expenditures, and other changes have been closed.

As discussed and illustrated in earlier chapters, the restatement will be reported as an adjustment to beginning fund balance in the statement of revenues, expenditures, and changes in fund balance—or disclosed in the notes to the financial statements.

Concluding Comments

Several significant conceptual, standards, and procedural considerations are important in governmental fund expenditure accounting and reporting. Most are discussed at least briefly in this chapter and some are discussed in detail and illustrated.

The concept and definition of expenditures in a governmental fund context were considered initially and at several points throughout the chapter, as were related GASB standards. Brief discussions of expenditure accounting controls and procedures—over personal services, purchases of materials and supplies, and other services and charges—included discussions and illustrations of related matters such as the purchases and consumption methods of inventory and prepayment accounting and accounting for capital leases and certificates of participation. Other important expenditure accounting and reporting topics—including claims and judgments, compensated absences, unfunded pension contributions, debt service, and encumbrances—were discussed and illustrated in the section on adjusting entries. In addition, accounting for error corrections and changes in expenditure-related accounting principles was discussed and illustrated.

Questions

Q6-1 Distinguish between an expenditure in the governmental accounting sense and an expense in the commercial accounting sense.

Q6-2 When should General Fund expenditures be recognized? What are the major exceptions?

Q6-3 On January 2, 20X1, materials costing $100 were issued from perpetual inventory to the police department. What General Ledger journal entry or entries should be made?

Q6-4 A city entered into a capital lease of equipment for a General Fund department. An initial payment of $30,000 was required. The city recorded the payment as current operating expenditures for rent of $30,000. Discuss the propriety of the city's accounting for the lease.

Q6-5 Is a government's nonspendable fund balance in the General Fund affected by whether inventory is reported using the purchases method or the consumption method? By whether it used a periodic or perpetual inventory system? Explain.

Q6-6 (a) Whether a government uses the purchases method to report materials and supplies expenditures or the consumption method, the total fund balance and the net change in fund balance are the same. Explain why. (b) Explain how reporting in the statement of revenues, expenditures, and changes in fund balances differs, if at all, under the two methods. (c) Explain how the balance sheet differs, if at all, under the two methods.

Q6-7 Why would a school district consider changing certain expenditure recognition principles?

Q6-8 Why are adjusting entries often required in governmental funds at year end in accounting for claims and judgments?

Q6-9 Under what conditions is a government required or permitted to accrue debt service expenditures on general long-term liabilities?

Q6-10 A government uses the purchases method to account for both inventories and prepaid assets. Its General Fund balance sheet includes Inventory of Materials of $35,000 and Prepaid Insurance of $40,000. Which fund balance category should be reported on the balance sheet as a result of these assets? Does your answer differ if the government uses the consumption method?

Exercises

E6-1 (Case Discussions) Provide analysis for the following scenarios:
(a) The newly elected mayor of the town of Dewey, a well-respected businessman, is perplexed because the town's finance director has given him an interim financial statement that reports repayment of a 10-year note through the General Fund as an expenditure. The mayor is aware that several short-term notes were repaid during the interim period as well, and these are not reported as expenditures. "Two things puzzle me," says the mayor. "First, why should repayment of a note be reported as an expenditure? We decreased our assets and liabilities by equal amounts; therefore, the city's equity did not change. Second, if such a practice is appropriate, why is only part of the principal retirement reported as expenditures?" Respond to the mayor.
(b) An accountant for the Town of Don's Grove previously worked for the City of Victorville. Don's Grove records purchases of materials and supplies as expenditures and reports any change in the inventory of materials and supplies in its Statement of Revenues, Expenditures, and Changes in Fund Balance. The accountant recalls, however, that the City of Victorville recorded expenditures for materials and supplies when they were used, not when they were purchased. Also, Victorville did not report changes in inventory in its Statement of Revenues, Expenditures, and Changes in Fund Balance unless there were shortages or overages. The accountant asks his supervisors which way is correct. Respond.
(c) Why does the GASB require employers to recognize sick leave liabilities only to the extent they will be paid upon employee termination or retirement, but require vacation leave liabilities to be recognized as earned—regardless of whether the employees will receive paid time off or be paid for the leave upon retirement or other termination?

E6-2 (Multiple Choice) Identify the best answer for each of the following:
1. In governmental funds, expenditures should be recognized in the period in which a fund liability is incurred, though there are some exceptions to the general rule. Which of the following is *not* an exception to the expenditure accrual rule?
   a. Expenditures for inventory.
   b. Salaries and wages expenditures.
   c. Debt service expenditures.
   d. Prepayments for insurance premiums.
2. Which of the following is *not* a common type of governmental fund expenditure?
   a. Capital outlay.
   b. Debt service.

   c. Salaries and wages.

   d. Depreciation.

3. An Expenditures account in a General Fund should be charged for materials and supplies
   a. only as the materials and supplies are being consumed.
   b. only as the materials and supplies are purchased.
   c. only as the materials and supplies are distributed to departments or agencies.
   d. either as the materials and supplies are consumed or when they are purchased.

4. Both the periodic and perpetual inventory systems may be used with
   a. the consumption method.
   b. the purchases method.
   c. either the consumption or purchase methods.
   d. the purchases method if local laws require this method of accounting.

5. Which of the following statements is *true* concerning the accounting and financial reporting for capital leases in governmental funds?
   a. Both the leased asset and the current portion of the lease liability must be reported in the governmental fund balance sheet.
   b. When a governmental fund enters into a capital lease, the transaction should result in a capital outlay expenditure *and* an other financing source.
   c. Capital leases in governmental funds *do not* result in expenditures in either the current or future periods.
   d. The fund liability equals the present value of the minimum lease payments.

6. Assume a governmental entity enters into a capital lease for the purchase of seven new public safety vehicles. The present value of the future minimum lease payments is $224,750, and a down payment of $25,000 is made at the inception of the lease. The net effect on fund balance of the General Fund in the year of inception is
   a. a decrease of $25,000.
   b. a decrease of $224,750.
   c. a decrease of $199,750.
   d. an increase of $224,750.

7. A state pays salaries and wages of $118 million to General Fund employees during a year. Unpaid, accrued salaries were $3 million at the beginning of the year and $6 million at year end. General Fund salary expenditures should be reported for the year in the amount of
   a. $115 million.
   b. $118 million.
   c. $121 million.
   d. $124 million.

8. Which of the following events could require a restatement of the beginning fund balance of a governmental fund?
   a. Management changes the method of accounting for inventory to FIFO.
   b. A claim that was previously not reported due to uncertainties about its validity is now considered probable and reasonably estimable.
   c. The GASB issues new accounting and financial reporting guidance that must be implemented retroactively.
   d. Items a and c only.

E6-3 (Various Entries) Record the following transactions in General Ledger accounts of the General Fund of Fergieville.

1. Incurred salaries of $300,000, $280,000 of which was paid.
2. A long-term note ($400,000 face value) matured. The interest of $40,000 was paid but the principal was not.
3. Purchased computers with a cost of $45,000; $22,000 was paid; the balance is due and is expected to be paid at the end of the first quarter of the next fiscal year.
4. Purchased materials for cash, $19,000. Assume purchases method of accounting for inventory.
5. Received bill from the water and sewer department for services, $7,500; $4,000 was paid.
6. Ordered, but have not yet received, materials costing $70,000.
7. Paid required annual contribution to pension plan, $250,000.
8. Determined that the Capital Projects Fund should be reimbursed $3,000 for wages that should have been charged to General Fund departments but were paid from the Capital Projects Fund.
9. Repaid a six-month note (face value, $50,000) and interest on the note ($2,500).
10. Paid $75,000 to the Golf Course Enterprise Fund to cover its operating deficit for the year.

E6-4 (Capital Lease Entries) Record the following 20X8 transactions in the Town of Colin General Fund General Ledger.

1. The Town of Colin entered into a capital lease for firefighting equipment. The capitalizable cost of the equipment was $3,800,000, and the town made a 10% down payment at the inception of the lease. The effective interest rate implicit in the lease was 10%, compounded semiannually.
2. The town paid its first semiannual lease payment of $240,000.
3. The second semiannual lease payment of $240,000, due the last day of the town fiscal year, was paid.

E6-5 (Pension Entries) Assume that the actuarially required pension plan contribution for a county for its general government employees is $8,000,000. Compute the pension expenditures to be reported in each of the following situations:

1. The county contributed $5,000,000 to the pension plan. Its unfunded pension liability increased by $3,000,000 (all classified as unmatured).
2. The county contributed $4,500,000 to the pension plan. Its unfunded pension liability increased by $3,500,000 (all classified as unmatured).
3. The county contributed $4,200,000 to the pension plan. The matured portion of its unfunded pension liability increased $150,000.
4. The county contributed $9,000,000 to the pension plan. The matured portion of its unfunded pension liability decreased $200,000.

E6-6 (Purchases vs. Consumption Method) The City of Bettinger's Bend General Fund had a beginning inventory of materials and supplies of $86,000.

1. Materials and supplies costing $740,000 were ordered during the year.
2. The materials and supplies ordered were received; actual cost, $741,000.
3. According to the physical inventory, $90,000 of materials and supplies were on hand at year end.

Required
(a) Prepare general journal entries to record the foregoing information using the **purchases** method of accounting for inventories.
(b) Prepare general journal entries to record the foregoing information using the **consumption** method and assuming a perpetual inventory system is used.
(c) What amounts will be reported in the General Fund balance sheet related to inventory for GAAP reporting purposes under the purchases method? Under the consumption method?

Problems

P6-1 (Multiple Choice Problems and Computations) Identify the best answer for each of the following:

Questions 1, 2, 3, and 4 are based on the following scenario:

Laperla County entered into a capital lease on June 30, 20X8, for equipment to be used by General Fund departments. The capitalizable cost of the leased asset was $200,000. An initial payment of $20,000 was made at the inception of the lease. The first annual lease payment of $35,000 was due and paid on July 1, 20X9. Assume a 6% implicit rate of interest on the lease.

1. General Fund expenditures in the fiscal year ended December 31, 20X8, would be
   a. capital outlay expenditures of $20,000.
   b. capital outlay expenditures of $200,000.
   c. capital outlay expenditures of $200,000 and interest expenditures of $5,400.
   d. rent expenditures of $20,000 and no capital outlay or debt service expenditures.
2. Laperla County should report General Fund expenditures for the fiscal year ended December 31, 20X9, in the amount of
   a. rent expenditures of $35,000.
   b. interest expenditures of $35,000.
   c. principal retirement expenditures of $35,000.
   d. interest expenditures of $10,800 and principal retirement expenditures of $24,200.
3. The capital lease transaction will affect Laperla County's fund balance during the fiscal year ended December 31, 20X8, by
   a. an increase of $20,000.
   b. an increase of $180,000.
   c. a decrease of $180,000.
   d. a decrease of $20,000.
4. The capital lease transaction will affect Laperla County's fund balance during the fiscal year ended December 31, 20X9, by
   a. $0.
   b. a decrease of $10,800.
   c. a decrease of $35,000.
   d. an increase of $24,200.

The following information pertains to questions 5 and 6.

A school district Special Revenue Fund's beginning materials inventory was $100,000; its ending materials inventory was $120,000. Materials costing $400,000 were purchased for the fund during the year. Accounts payable for the fund's materials were $17,000 at the beginning of the year and $7,000 at year end.

5. The school district should report expenditures for materials in its Special Revenue Fund of:

If the School District Uses

	Purchases Method	Consumption Method
a.	$400,000	$400,000
b.	$400,000	$380,000
c.	$410,000	$380,000
d.	$400,000	$420,000

6. In the school district Special Revenue Fund statement of revenues, expenditures, and changes in fund balance, what amount(s) besides expenditures must be reported related to materials?

	Purchases Method	*Consumption Method*
a.	Nothing	Nothing
b.	Other financing source of $20,000	Other financing source of $20,000
c.	Nothing	Other financing source of $20,000
d.	Other financing source of $20,000	Nothing

7. Equipment purchased for county General Fund departments on a line of credit with a supplier cost $800,000 by year end; $200,000 had been paid, including $4,000 interest. The county expects to repay another $300,000, including $7,000 interest, during the first two months of the next fiscal year. The remaining balance is to be repaid by midyear. Capital outlay expenditures should be reported for the county General Fund in the amount of
   a. $800,000.
   b. $200,000.
   c. $489,000.
   d. $196,000.

8. How should the purchase of land for General Fund purposes by entering a three-year, $80,000, capital lease be reported in the General Fund statement of revenues, expenditures, and changes in fund balance?
   a. No effect.
   b. Expenditures of $80,000.
   c. Expenditures of $80,000 and other financing sources of $80,000.
   d. Other financing uses of $80,000 and other financing sources of $80,000.

9. Which of the following should be reported as expenditures in a county General Fund?
   (1) Reimbursement of a Special Revenue Fund for General Fund expenditures inadvertently paid for from and recorded in the Special Revenue Fund.
   (2) Water services received from the county Water Enterprise Fund.
   (3) Payment of the federal income tax withheld from employee paychecks to the federal government.
   (4) Payment to a Debt Service Fund to provide resources for principal and interest payments that matured and were paid during the year.
   a. (1) and (2)
   b. (2) only
   c. (3) and (4)
   d. (4) only

10. The Village of Nathan has 43 employees who work in departments accounted for in the General Fund. As of the beginning of the fiscal year, the compensated absences liability associated with those employees was $52,300. None of this liability was due and payable at the end of the prior year. During the year, employees earned an additional amount of leave valued at $46,700. The compensated absences liability for the General Fund employees as of the end of the year was $59,800, of which $4,000 was due and payable at year end. Assuming that General Fund payments for compensated absences during the year were $39,200, the General Fund would report expenditures for compensated absences for the fiscal year of
   a. $39,200.
   b. $43,200.
   c. $46,700.
   d. $54,200.

P6-2 (Capital Outlay; Inventory—Purchases Method) (a) Record the following transactions in the General Fund General Ledger of a school district that uses the purchases method to account for materials, supplies, and prepayments. Record both the budgetary and actual entries. Assume that materials and supplies costing $37,000 were on hand at the beginning of the year. (b) What amount of nonspendable fund balance should be reported at year end?

1. The school district ordered the following:

	Estimated Cost
School buses—2	$225,000
Supplies	112,000

2. The school received one of the buses at an actual cost of $120,000, which equaled the estimated amount.
3. The school received most of the supplies ordered (estimated cost, $95,000). The actual cost was $95,800.
4. The school paid $93,000 of the vouchers payable for the supplies.
5. At year end, the school had supplies on hand costing $22,000.

P6-3 (Capital Outlay; Inventory—Consumption Method) (a) Record the following transactions in the General Fund General Ledger of Benford Township using the consumption method (periodic inventory system) to account for materials, supplies, and prepayments. Record both the budgetary and actual entries. (b) Compute the amount of expenditures to be reported in the school district General Fund statement of revenues, expenditures, and changes in fund balance. (c) Compute the amount of nonspendable fund balance to be reported at year end. Materials and supplies costing $90,000 were on hand at the beginning of the year.

1. The town ordered the following:

	Estimated Cost
Garbage vehicles—4	$225,000
Supplies	312,000

2. The town received the garbage vehicles. The actual cost of $222,000 was vouchered for payment.
3. The town received most of the supplies ordered (estimated cost $302,000). The actual cost was $301,800.
4. The town paid $523,800 of vouchers payable.
5. At year-end, the town had supplies on hand costing $102,000.

P6-4 (Capital Asset Purchases and Leases)

1. Record the following 20X9 transactions in the Percy County General Fund General Ledger. Assume:
   - a. The county entered into a capital lease for police safety equipment. The capitalizable cost of the equipment was $2,500,000, and the county made a $500,000 down payment at the inception of the lease. The effective interest rate implicit in the lease was 5%, compounded semiannually.
   - b. The county paid its first semiannual lease payment of $180,000.
   - c. The second semiannual lease payment of $180,000, due the last day of the county's fiscal year, was paid.
   - d. The county purchased patrol cars costing $128,000. The county paid $40,000 down and signed a 5% note requiring semiannual payments of $30,812.
   - e. The county paid the first semiannual payment on the note, $30,812.
   - f. The second semiannual note payment of $30,812, due the last day of the county's fiscal year, was paid.
2. What amount of capital outlay expenditures should be reported for the county General Fund for 20X9?
3. What amount of debt service expenditures should be reported for the General Fund for 20X9?
4. If the second semiannual payments on the lease and on the note are due two months after year end, what amount of capital outlay expenditures should the county report for 20X9? What amount of debt service expenditures should be reported for 20X9?

P6-5 (Compensated Absences, Claims and Judgments, and Pensions)

1. A newly incorporated town incurred and paid compensated absences for vacation pay and sick leave of $40,000 during its first year of operation, 20X1.
2. At the end of 20X1, the town estimated that its total liability for compensated absences, none of which is payable from available expendable financial resources, was $75,000.
3. In 20X2, the town paid $130,000 for compensated absences for vacation pay and sick leave.

4. At the end of 20X2, the town estimated that its total liability for compensated absences was $160,000. Of the $160,000 liability for compensated absences, $5,000 was deemed to be payable from available expendable financial resources.
5. In 20X3, the town paid $210,000 for compensated absences for vacation pay and sick leave.
6. At the end of 20X3, the town estimated that its total liability for compensated absences was $140,000. None of the $140,000 liability for compensated absences was deemed to be payable from available expendable financial resources.

a. Prepare the journal entries required in the General Ledger of the town's General Fund to record the information in the preceding items.   *Required*
b. What amount of liabilities should be reported in the General Fund balance sheet for compensated absences for each of these years?
c. What amount of expenditures must the town report each year in the General Fund for compensated absences?
d. Calculate the amount of expenditures that would have been reported each year by the town if the payments and liabilities involved had been for claims and judgments instead of for compensated absences.
e. Assume that the above payments and liabilities are associated with payments to and liabilities payable to the town's defined benefit pension plan. Calculate the amount of General Fund pension expenditures for each year.

P6-6 (GL and SL Entries—Errors, Pensions, Changes, Leases, Claims and Judgments, Etc.) The following transactions and events relate to the General Fund of Antonio County for the 20X6 fiscal year.

1. Early in 20X6 it was discovered that at the end of 20X5 (a) the inventory of supplies was overstated by $30,000, and (b) interest payable of $11,000 on General Fund debt was not accrued.

2. Appropriations were revised as follows:

Increased Appropriations:	
Police Department—Supplies	$10,000
Streets Department—Equipment	50,000
Decreased Appropriations:	
Parks Department—Wages	20,000

3. The county entered a capital lease for equipment that could have been purchased for $850,000 (which is also the net present value of the lease) for the Roads and Bridges Department.
4. An equipment capital lease payment, $80,000 (including $45,000 interest), was made.
5. Antonio County changed its method of inventory accounting from the purchases method to the consumption method (perpetual system) at the beginning of 20X6. The inventory of supplies at the end of 20X5 was $150,000.
6. During the year it was found that (a) $12,000 charged to Fire Department—Contractual Services should have been charged to that account in the Police Department, and (b) $16,000 charged to Salaries and Wages in a Capital Projects Fund should have been charged to the Streets Department, which is financed from the General Fund.
7. At year end it was determined that the county had estimated liabilities (including legal fees and related costs) for unsettled claims and judgments of $400,000, of which $100,000 is due and payable and is considered a fund liability. The comparable estimated liability amounts (which had been properly recorded) at the end of 20X5 were $350,000 and $60,000, respectively. The 20X5 liability balances remain in the accounts at this time.
8. The year-end physical count of the inventory of supplies revealed that $25,000 of supplies had been stolen; $20,000 will be recovered from the insurance company that bonds employees.
9. Although the actuarially required defined benefit pension plan contribution for 20X6 was $600,000, Antonio County made contributions of only $200,000. The County Commission voted to appropriate an additional $100,000 in the 20X7 budget—to be paid early in 20X7 and applied to the 20X6 contribution deficiency—but made no provision for the remaining unfunded balance of the 20X6 contribution.

Prepare the journal entries to record these transactions and events in the General Ledger and   *Required*
Expenditures Subsidiary Ledger of the General Fund of Antonio County, assuming that the county's accountant does not make reversing entries at the beginning of each year for prior year-end adjusting entries.

P6-7 (General and Subsidiary Ledger Entries; Reconciliation)

The City of Beverly Heights General Fund had the following transactions, among others, in 20X7:

1. Appropriations were made as follows:

Personal Services	$111,400
Contractual Services	8,700
Materials and Supplies	8,500
New Patrol Cars	21,000
Other	12,000
	$161,600

2. General Fund cash, $2,000, was paid to a Debt Service Fund to provide for debt service.
3. A long-term note of $8,300, including interest of $1,300, and a short-term note of $2,500 (including $150 interest) came due. The Beverly Heights Council had not made appropriations for these items. The necessary action was taken, and the notes and interest were paid.
4. General Fund cash, $100,000, was paid to an Enterprise Fund to finance construction of a new auxiliary generator, and $50,000 was contributed to establish a central motor pool facility. The Enterprise Fund will repay the General Fund in 10 equal annual installments beginning January 1, 20X9.
5. The council increased the appropriation for personal services by $500.
6. Materials and supplies are accounted for on the purchases method. The beginning inventory was $200; $8,500 of materials and supplies were ordered during the year. A new patrol car costing $20,000 was also ordered.
7. The following expenditures were made by the city:

Personal Services	$111,700
Contractual Services	8,700
Materials and Supplies (Estimated to cost $7,600)	7,500
New Patrol Cars	21,200
Other	11,800
	$160,900

8. The new patrol cars were received. The balance of the materials order is expected early next year. The council passed amendments to its appropriations necessary to make the foregoing expenditures legal. The expenditures were paid.
9. Materials and supplies on hand at year end amounted to $1,000.

Required
  a. Prepare the general journal entries required to record the transactions in the General Ledger and in the Expenditures Ledger of the Beverly Heights General Fund. Assume that there were no outstanding encumbrances at the end of 20X6.
  b. Prepare a trial balance of the Expenditures Ledger and prove its agreement with the General Ledger control accounts.

P6-8 (Worksheets, Operating Statement)

Waynesville had the following General Fund trial balance on January 1, 20X1, after the reversing entry for the 20X0 encumbrances closing entry was made:

Cash	$ 7,000	
Taxes Receivable—Delinquent	48,000	
Allowance for Uncollectible Delinquent Taxes		$ 4,000
Due from Water Fund	500	
Vouchers Payable		11,000
Due to Taxpayers		1,000
ENCUMBRANCES	3,000	
Deferred Revenues		3,000
ENCUMBRANCES OUTSTANDING		3,000
Fund Balance		36,500
	$58,500	$58,500

The following information summarizes the transactions of the General Fund during 20X1:

1. The city council approved the following budget for 20X1:

Expenditures:

City Manager.	$20,000
Police Department	13,000
Fire Department	10,000
Streets and Roads	20,000
	$63,000

Revenues:

Property Taxes	$75,000
Fines and Fees.	5,000
Miscellaneous	5,000
	$85,000

2. The council levied property taxes of $75,000. It was estimated that $2,000 of the taxes would never be collected.

3. Cash collected during the year may be summarized as follows:

Prior years' levies	$45,000
20X1 levy	46,000
Fines and fees	4,000
Taxes written off in prior years.	500
Interest.	500
Service charges	2,000
	$98,000

4. With council approval, $5,000 was borrowed on a 90-day note.

5. Orders placed during the year were as follows:

City Manager.	$ 4,000
Police Department	3,000
Fire Department.	3,000
Streets and Roads.	5,000
	$15,000

6. Payrolls vouchered during the year were as follows:

City Manager.	$15,000
Police Department	7,000
Fire Department.	6,500
Streets and Roads.	14,000
	$42,500

7. Invoices vouchered during the year were as follows:

City Manager.	$ 4,500
Police Department	6,100
Fire Department.	3,000
Streets and Roads.	4,000
Repayment of note plus interest (see item 4)	5,200
	$22,800

The preceding invoices completed all orders except one, dated June 1, 20X1, for an attachment for a Streets and Roads road grader for $950.

8. Payments *to* other funds:

Fund	Purpose	Amount
Debt Service	Provide for payment of bond principal and interest	$ 8,000
Capital Projects	City contribution to construction of city park facilities	15,000
Water Fund	Water supply for Streets and Roads Department	1,500
		$24,500

9. Analysis of collections revealed that taxpayer A, to whom the city owed $1,000 on January 1, 20X1, for overpayment of taxes, had paid his tax for 20X1 minus $1,000.
10. The Streets and Roads Department rendered services in the amount of $250 to the Water Fund.
11. The city council made an additional appropriation in the amount of $5,000 (including $600 interest) for a long-term note maturity that was overlooked in preparing the budget.
12. The note matured and was vouchered.
13. Vouchers of $70,000 were paid.
14. Delinquent taxes of $500 were written off on the authority of the council.
15. Current taxes became delinquent, and the allowance for uncollectible delinquent taxes was reduced by $2,400.

Required a. Prepare a worksheet or worksheets summarizing the year's operations in such a way that the General Ledger closing entries and required statements may be easily prepared.

b. Prepare a Statement of Revenues, Expenditures, and Changes in Fund Balance for the General Fund of Waynesville for the year ended December 31, 20X1.

P6-9 (Internet Research and Analysis) Obtain a copy of a recent comprehensive annual financial report (CAFR) of a state or local government from the government, the Internet, your professor, or a library.

Required 1. **Letter of Transmittal.** Review the expenditure-related discussions and presentations. What were the most significant general government expenditure categories? Which general government expenditures increased (decreased) significantly from the previous year?

2. **Financial Statements.** Indicate the types of general government expenditures reported. Did any expenditure types differ from those you expected based on your study of Chapters 2–6? Explain.

3. **Summary of Significant Accounting Policies (SOSAP).** Review the general government expenditure-related (SOSAP) disclosures. Were any of these disclosures different from, or in addition to, those you expected based on your study of Chapters 2–6? Explain.

4. **Statistical Section.** Review the general government expenditure-related statistical presentations. Explain how these might be useful in evaluating the general government financial position and changes in financial position.

P6-10 (Research and Analysis) Obtain a copy of GASB *Statement No. 47*, "Accounting for Termination Benefits." Familiarize yourself with the accounting and financial reporting requirements, as well as the background of the statement and the rationale for the GASB's decisions.

Required 1. Prepare a brief summary defining "termination benefits" and describing how GASB *Statement No. 47* potentially affects the financial statements of state and local governments. How is financial reporting improved?

2. Briefly explain the difference between *involuntary* termination benefits and *voluntary* termination benefits. How do recognition requirements for termination benefits differ for statements prepared on an accrual basis compared to those prepared on a modified accrual basis?

3. Summarize the note disclosures that are required for employers that offer termination benefits.

Cases

C6-1 (Capital Leases and Certificates of Participation—State of Alaska) The State of Alaska general government transactions for the fiscal year ended June 30, 20X3, related to leases and certificates of participation are given here. Prepare the required General Fund General Ledger entries assuming that all lease payments for general government activities are made through the General Fund.

1. The state paid operating lease payments of $29,800,000.
2. The state entered into capital leases for equipment with a capitalizable cost of $8,628,000, making an initial payment of $500,000.

3. The state made payments of $21 million, including $6,600,000 of interest on its capital leases.
4. The state has lease purchase agreements funded through certificates of participation (COPs) for the purchase of buildings. Third-party leasing companies assigned their interest in the lease to underwriters, which issued certificates for the funding of these obligations. The COPs represent an ownership interest of the certificate holder in a lease purchase agreement. While the state is liable for lease payments to the underwriters, the state is not liable for payments to holders of the certificates. The state paid $13.2 million on the certificates of participation in 20X3, including $3.7 million of interest.

(Based on a recent State of Alaska Comprehensive Annual Financial Report.)

C6-2 (OPEB and Claims and Judgments—New York City) The City of New York, New York, reported the following liabilities, among others, at June 30 of the years indicated. The amounts in the table are stated in thousands of dollars.

	Year		
Liability for	*20X2*	*20X3*	*Scheduled Reduction by June 30, 20X4*
Judgments and claims........	$ 4,810,471	$ 5,018,908	$ 1,360,426
Vacation and sick leave......	2,593,691	2,840,213	247,937
Pensions...................	806,200	764,000	—
Other postemployment benefits (OPEB)..........	50,000,000	53,507,451	1,400,000

None of these liabilities were due and payable at the indicated dates. The amounts the city paid during the 20X2–20X3 fiscal year for each of these categories are presented in the following table.

20X2–20X3 Payments for	
Judgments and claims...	$ 516,801
Vacation and sick leave.......................................	247,937
Pensions..	4,015,000
Other postemployment benefits (OPEB)........................	2,182,871

a. Calculate the amount of General Fund expenditures that the City of New York must report for the fiscal year ended June 30, 20X3, assuming that all the amounts shown relate to General Fund departments and activities, for:
   1. Judgments and claims
   2. Vacation and sick leave
   3. Pensions
   4. OPEB
b. How would your answers differ if 10% of each of the liability balances presented in the first schedule were due and payable at the end of 20X2 and the end of 20X3, respectively?

Required

(Based on a recent City of New York, New York, Comprehensive Annual Financial Report.)

Harvey City Comprehensive Case

The remainder of the 20X4 transactions of the General Fund of Harvey City are included in this chapter. We will record these transactions and prepare the General Fund financial statements for 20X4. In addition, we will record the transactions of the Economic Development Special Revenue Fund and prepare its financial statements.

GENERAL FUND REQUIREMENTS

Additional 20X4 transactions and events for the Harvey City General Fund are presented next, and conclude the General Fund case from Chapters 4 and 5.

a. Using the worksheet you began in Chapter 4, enter the effects of the following additional 20X4 transactions and events of the Harvey City General Fund in the transactions column of the worksheet. (A different solution approach may be used if desired by your professor.)

b. Prepare the 20X4 statement of revenues, expenditures, and changes in fund balance for the Harvey City General Fund.

c. Prepare the 20X4 statement of revenues, expenditures, and changes in fund balance—budget and actual for the Harvey City General Fund.

d. Prepare the 20X4 balance sheet for the Harvey City General Fund. Assume that $100,000 of fund balance was assigned by the city manager, under authority delegated to her by city council, to be used to establish new park and recreation programs in the next year. Also, assume that the city has *budgeted* a $75,000 decrease of otherwise unassigned fund balance to provide for a budgeted excess of General Fund expenditures over revenues for *20X5*.

25. Materials and supplies ordered were received as follows:

	Estimated Cost	Actual Cost
General government	$ 10,000	$ 10,000
Public safety	32,000	32,500
Highways and streets	60,000	59,700
Health and sanitation	36,000	36,000
Parks and recreation	30,000	30,000
Totals	$168,000	$168,200

26. Materials and supplies were used by General Fund departments during the year as follows:

General government	$ 11,000
Public safety	35,000
Highways and streets	75,300
Health and sanitation	39,400
Parks and recreation	30,000
Total	$190,700

27. The city entered into a capital lease for parks and recreation equipment on December 31. The capitalizable cost of the equipment was $90,000, including a downpayment of $10,000.

28. A lawsuit has been filed against the city related to an accident that occurred during the fiscal year. A city employee is at fault. The city expects to settle the lawsuit by sometime late in the next fiscal year and considers it probable that the city will lose $62,000.

29. The city contributed $60,200 to the city Police and Fire Pension Trust Fund.

30. The General Fund received $250,000 from the Addiction Prevention Special Revenue Fund in partial repayment of the interfund loan.

31. The city paid vouchers payable of $500,000.

32. The budgetary accounts, including encumbrances, were closed at year end. (Close the budgetary accounts in the transactions columns.)

ECONOMIC DEVELOPMENT SPECIAL REVENUE FUND

The beginning trial balance of the Harvey City Economic Development Grants Special Revenue Fund and its 20X4 budget and transactions are presented next.

a. Prepare a worksheet for the Economic Development Special Revenue Fund similar to the General Fund worksheet you created in Chapter 4. Enter the effects of the following transactions and events in the appropriate columns of the worksheet. (A different solution approach may be used if desired by your professor.)

b. Prepare the preclosing trial balance in the appropriate worksheet columns.

c. Enter the preclosing trial balance amounts in the closing entry or postclosing trial balance (balance sheet data) columns, as appropriate.

d. Prepare the 20X4 statement of revenues, expenditures, and changes in fund balance for the Economic Development Special Revenue Fund.

e. Prepare the 20X4 balance sheet for the Economic Development Special Revenue Fund.

Economic Development Special Revenue Fund Requirements

The trial balance of the Economic Development Special Revenue Fund of Harvey City at January 1, 20X4, is presented here.

Economic Development Special Revenue Fund Beginning Trial Balance

Harvey City
Economic Development Special Revenue Fund
Trial Balance
January 1, 20X4

	Debit	Credit
Cash	$342,230	
Investments	125,000	
Accrued Salaries Payable		$ 450
Vouchers Payable		82,000
Fund Balance		384,780
Totals	$467,230	$467,230

The Economic Development Special Revenue Fund budget was adopted by the city council. The adopted budget included estimated operating grant revenues of $930,000 and estimated investment income of $40,000. Appropriations of $945,000 were adopted for economic development programs.

Economic Development Special Revenue Fund Budget

TRANSACTIONS AND EVENTS—20X4

1. Record the budget.
2. The city received a $1,500,000 economic development grant from the state's Department of Economic Development. The grant cash was received and is to be used in certain specified efforts to attract new businesses to the city and surrounding area.
3. The city purchased investments of $1,300,000. The grant requires that all investment income from the investment of the grant proceeds *must* be used for economic development.
4. The city received interest on its investments, $55,000.
5. The city incurred and vouchered $840,000 of economic development expenditures that qualify under the state grant program.
6. The city paid salaries of $75,000 to economic development personnel. The payment included $450 of accrued salaries payable from the prior year. The salaries expenditures qualify under the grant program.
7. The city sold investments costing $800,000 for $815,000.
8. The city paid $800,000 on vouchers payable for economic development.
9. The fair value of the investments of the Economic Development Special Revenue Fund at year end increased by $1,700. In addition, accrued interest on the investments at year end was $12,000.
10. Accrued salaries payable at year end totaled $200.
11. Grant revenues for the year were recorded (if not recorded earlier).
12. The budgetary accounts were closed at year end. (Close the budgetary accounts in the transactions columns.)

CHAPTER 7

Capital Projects Funds

LEARNING OBJECTIVES

After studying this chapter, you should be able to:

- Understand the nature and purposes of Capital Projects Funds (CPFs) and when CPFs are used.

- Understand the typical capital projects financing sources, the number of Capital Projects Funds required, and the life cycle of a Capital Projects Fund.

- Determine the costs that should be charged to a Capital Projects Fund.

- Understand typical budgeting and budgetary reporting issues of Capital Projects Funds.

- Understand Capital Projects Fund accounting for general long-term debt issuances, including accounting for bond proceeds (face amount, premiums and discounts, bond issuance costs) and bond anticipation notes.

- Make "detailed general ledger" journal entries to record typical Capital Projects Fund transactions and events.

- Understand what arbitrage is and its potential impact.

- Prepare Capital Projects Fund financial statements.

apital Projects Funds are established to account for financial resources that are to be used for capital outlay, especially those to be used to construct or otherwise acquire **major**, long-lived **general government capital facilities**, such as buildings, highways, storm water drainage systems, and bridges. Their principal purpose is to ensure and demonstrate the economical and legal expenditure of the dedicated financial resources, but they also serve as cost accounting mechanisms for major capital outlay projects. Capital Projects Funds *must be used to account for capital outlay financed from general obligation bond proceeds and whenever they are legally or contractually required*—even for nonmajor capital asset acquisitions or construction projects. Indeed, they *may* be used to account for *any* significant general government capital asset acquisition.

Not all general government capital asset acquisitions are financed through Capital Projects Funds.

- Routine capital asset purchases—for example, school buses and photocopy equipment— often may be financed from the General Fund or Special Revenue Funds.
- Capital leases are commonly reported in the General Fund.
- Acquisitions of *specific fund* capital assets are accounted for through the specific proprietary fund or Trust Fund.

Major general government capital projects usually must be financed at least partly with bond issues, and many are partly financed with intergovernmental grants. *Both bond covenants and grant agreements—as well as GAAP—often require that a Capital Projects Fund be used.* Furthermore, many state and local government finance officers prefer to account for most general government capital projects through Capital Projects Funds—even when their use is not required—to better control and account for each project and its related resources. That is, because the accounting systems of Capital Projects Funds are designed to control the expenditure of financial resources for major capital assets, some prefer to transfer resources from the General Fund and Special Revenue Funds to Capital Projects Funds rather than to account for capital expenditures through systems oriented to current operations.

Not all long-term debt issue proceeds are accounted for in Capital Projects Funds. The GASB standards recommend accounting for the proceeds of bonds and other long-term debt issues in the following funds:

- Proceeds that are to be used to acquire general government capital assets should be accounted for in a Capital Projects Fund.
- Proceeds of refunding issues should be accounted for in a Debt Service Fund.
- Proceeds of proprietary fund and Trust Fund issues should be accounted for in those funds because such liabilities are the primary responsibility of and will be serviced by the issuing funds.

GASB standards do not address debt issued for other purposes. But it seems appropriate for proceeds of debt issued to finance a fund deficit to be accounted for in the fund that has the deficit. Furthermore, the proceeds of debt issued to provide disaster relief, for example, might properly be accounted for in Capital Projects Funds or the General Fund, depending on the situation.

Both major and nonmajor capital projects, and other capital outlay, may be accounted for in Capital Projects Funds. Capital Projects Funds typically are used for major general government capital projects even if not legally or contractually required. Practice varies with respect to nonmajor projects and other significant capital outlay. What is major is subject to interpretation in practice, particularly relative to governments of varying sizes. A $10,000,000 street improvement program would be a major capital project in a small town, for example, but might be considered a nonmajor, routine activity of a state highway department. Thus, if no legal or contractual provisions require a Capital Projects Fund, the town would nonetheless use a Capital Projects Fund, whereas the state might account for the capital expenditure through the General Fund.

Furthermore, some capital projects, such as neighborhood street construction or improvement projects, are financed by **special assessments** levied against the properties improved. Special assessments are essentially a *special tax* imposed on those properties or taxpayers benefited by the capital improvement or service financed by the assessment:

- Special assessments for capital improvements are normally payable, along with related interest, over 5 to 10 years.
- Long-term debt typically is issued to finance construction of the improvements.
- The special assessment collections are used to service the debt.

The proceeds of long-term special assessment debt issued to finance general government capital improvement special assessment projects should be reported in the Capital Projects Fund financial statements. Any related debt service transactions and balances, including the special assessments receivable, typically should be reported in a Debt Service Fund.

This chapter begins with brief discussions of Capital Projects Fund (CPF) operations and accounting standards. These discussions are followed by a CPF illustrative case example. Finally, several other CPF operations, accounting, and reporting matters are considered at the conclusion of the chapter.

CAPITAL PROJECTS FUND OPERATIONS AND ACCOUNTING STANDARDS

In this section, we discuss Capital Projects Fund operations and accounting standards under the following topic headings:

1. Sources of Financial Resources
2. Number of Funds Required
3. Capital Projects Fund Life Cycle
4. The Budget
5. Interim Financing
6. Costs Charged to Projects
7. Intergovernmental Revenues
8. Bond Premiums, Discounts, and Issuance Costs

CPF Financial Resources

Typical sources of Capital Projects Fund financial resources are bond issues or other long-term general obligation debt issues, special assessment indebtedness, grants or shared revenues from other governments, transfers from other funds, and interest earned on temporary investments of project resources. The City of Chicago's Capital Projects Funds for a recent year had total bond proceeds of $121,000,000 and revenues of only $8,101,000. All but $820,000 of the revenues were investment income.

Capital Projects Fund revenues from intergovernmental grants should be recognized when all eligibility requirements are met and the resources are available, as discussed in Chapter 5. Interest on CPF investments should be recognized when earned and available unless fair value recognition is applicable. Transfers and long-term debt issue proceeds are reported in the Other Financing Sources section of the Capital Projects Fund statement of revenues, expenditures, and changes in fund balance.

Number of Funds

Separate Capital Projects Funds usually are established for each major project or debt issue. Separate funds are used because the nature of such projects varies widely. They typically involve significant amounts of financial resources, they are usually budgeted on an individual project or debt issue basis, and legal and contractual requirements differ significantly among projects. When debt issues or grants are involved, a major purpose of the Capital Projects Funds is to show that the proceeds were used only for authorized purposes and that unexpended balances or deficits have been handled in accordance with applicable contractual agreements or legal provisions. Thus, CPFs assist governments both to determine and demonstrate compliance with legal and contractual provisions and to provide both a project-related auditable entity(ies) and project audit trails.

A single Capital Projects Fund will suffice, however, when a single debt issue is used to finance several projects or a series of closely related projects is financed through a single grant or by internal transfers from the General Fund or Special Revenue Funds. Combining statements may be used to present data on financial operations or financial position when a government has more than one Capital Projects Fund in operation during a given year.

Some state and local governments properly use a single Capital Projects Fund accounting entity even when several restricted financing sources (e.g., bonds and grants) and several different capital projects are involved. This is accomplished through what is known as a "funds within a fund" or "subfund" approach, in which each capital project is accounted for as a separate *subfund* of the overall Capital Projects Fund.[1] This "funds within a fund" or "subfund"

---

[1] That is, the overall Capital Projects Fund is assigned a number in the governmental fund chart of accounts, say, 300, and each separate capital project is assigned a separate "300" number, such as 319 or 368. Thus, every subfund asset, deferred outflow, liability, deferred inflow, and fund balance—and every subfund revenue, expenditure, other financing source, and so on—is identified (coded) by subfund within the overall Capital Projects Fund.

approach should be used only when the substance of separate Capital Projects Fund accounting and control is achieved and the compliance reporting objectives of Capital Projects Funds are met.

Illustration 7-1 overviews the typical Capital Projects Fund "life cycle." In studying the illustration, note the following: **CPF Life Cycle**

- **Project Authorization and Duration.** Capital projects must be properly authorized by the legislative body; capital projects often last three to five years or more and extend over several fiscal years.
- **Capital Projects Fund(s).** The Capital Projects Fund(s) also is authorized by the legislative body, directly or indirectly, and extends over the life of the capital project.
- **Financing.** Capital projects typically are financed with bond issues or other long-term borrowings (the related liabilities are recorded in the General Long-Term Liabilities accounts), intergovernmental grants, interfund transfers, special assessments, interest income, and private donations.
- **Expenditures.** Project expenditures are typically all "capital" (or "capital outlay") expenditures, and the resulting assets are capitalized in the General Capital Assets accounts.
- **Termination of Capital Projects Fund(s).** CPFs are terminated when the project has been completed, the related CPF liabilities have been paid, any refunds due grantors for overpayment of their share of project costs have been paid, and any remaining CPF assets have been transferred to a CPF-related Debt Service Fund or to another fund (most likely the one from which the most financing was received).
- **Records Retention.** The CPF accounting records are retained for audit and to demonstrate the fiscal stewardship of the state or local government.

In extremely simple situations, as when purchasing existing facilities for a single payment, the life of the Capital Projects Fund may be brief and its entries uncomplicated:

1. Receipts of all financial resources will occur and revenues or other financing sources will be credited.
2. Expenditures will be recorded and paid.
3. The revenues, expenditures, and other fund balance change accounts will be closed.
4. Any remaining financial resources of the fund will be transferred to another fund (or disposed of in some other way as required by law or contract) and the fund will be closed.

ILLUSTRATION 7-1 Capital Projects Fund Life Cycle: An Overview

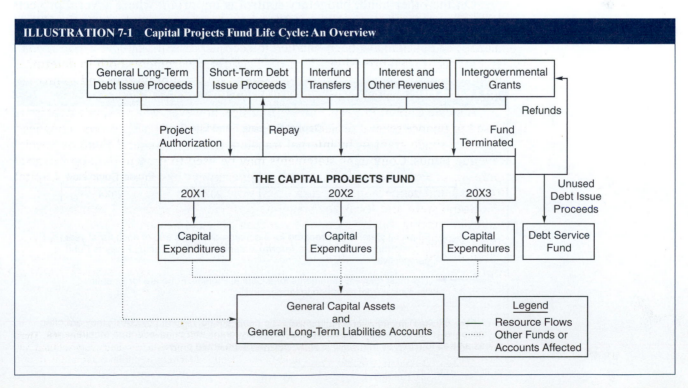

In most cases, however, a Capital Projects Fund is used to finance complex construction projects where the government acts as a general contractor, possibly using its own employees and equipment for part or all of the work. In this situation, accounting procedures are more complicated and closely resemble those of the General Fund.

In addition, as shown in Illustration 7-2, the capital project and related Capital Projects Fund extend over several fiscal years, and project construction typically does not begin precisely at the start of a fiscal year or end precisely at the end of a fiscal year. Thus, as discussed more fully later:

- Though not required by GAAP, the most relevant financial statement for a Capital Projects Fund is one that covers the *entire* project life cycle—from inception to completion of the project.
- Financial statements for fiscal years that end *within* the project life cycle are essentially *interim* financial statements that may be misleading from the perspective of the entire project life cycle.

Laws or contracts typically determine the disposition of any unused balance remaining in the Capital Projects Fund after completion of and payment for the project. As noted earlier, refunds to the grantors who participated in financing the project may be required. The city's portion usually is transferred to the Debt Service Fund that will service the debt incurred to finance the project. Any bond premium kept in the Capital Projects Fund in conformity with legal provisions or debt indenture requirements typically will be transferred to a Debt Service Fund when the Capital Projects Fund is closed.

The Budget   The projects financed through Capital Projects Funds usually are planned in the government's long-term capital budget. Appropriations for capital projects often are on a project basis, in which appropriations do not lapse at the end of each fiscal year. If annual reappropriations are made of project appropriations, they are considered to be allotments.

In some cases, adequate control is provided without the budgetary process, and detailed appropriations are not made. The entire CPF is viewed as appropriated for the project in such cases. Reasons for not budgeting capital projects in detail include (1) in some cases only one project is financed from a single fund, and (2) project cost control is provided by specifications, bids, inspections, and the like.

On the other hand, budgetary control is important where several projects are accounted for through a single CPF, when the government budgets the CPF in detail, when the government uses its own employees to construct a major capital

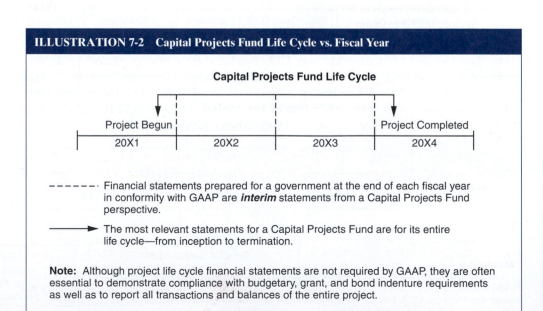

ILLUSTRATION 7-2   Capital Projects Fund Life Cycle vs. Fiscal Year

Capital Projects Fund Life Cycle

Project Begun			Project Completed
20X1	20X2	20X3	20X4

- - - - - · Financial statements prepared for a government at the end of each fiscal year in conformity with GAAP are ***interim*** statements from a Capital Projects Fund perspective.

⟶ The most relevant statements for a Capital Projects Fund are for its entire life cycle—from inception to termination.

Note: Although project life cycle financial statements are not required by GAAP, they are often essential to demonstrate compliance with budgetary, grant, and bond indenture requirements as well as to report all transactions and balances of the entire project.

asset, and when the CPF is budgeted annually. The *case illustration* in this chapter *assumes that the capital project is appropriated on a project basis and full budgetary control is desirable.*

Interim Financing

Cash may be borrowed short term, especially during the early stages of the CPF life cycle, to pay for project planning and start-up expenditures incurred before the bond issue proceeds or other CPF financial resources are received. Governments may use short-term financing to allow them to issue long-term debt close to the time that the bulk of the resources will be expended, to take advantage of anticipated improvements in bond market conditions, or to avoid delaying a project while technical details associated with a debt issuance are addressed. Such short-term borrowing may be from other funds of the governmental unit or bond anticipation notes (BANs), revenue anticipation notes (RANs), or other notes issued to local banks or other creditors. The short-term borrowing is ordinarily repaid when the bond issue proceeds or other CPF resources are received.

Most types of interim borrowing are considered CPF liabilities. Accordingly, CPF Cash is debited and Notes Payable or Due to General (or other) Fund is credited—*not* a debt proceeds Other Financing Source account—to record the short-term loan. The entries are reversed when the loan is repaid, and any interest (but not note principal) paid is recorded as Expenditures of the CPF. For example, if at midyear a government issued a one-year, $500,000, 6% bond anticipation note payable to provide temporary financing for a major general government capital project, and expended 90% of the proceeds on the project by year end, the following Capital Projects Fund *Detailed General Ledger* entries would be required:[2]

(a) Cash	$500,000	
Notes Payable		$500,000
To record issuance of the notes at par.		
(b) Expenditures—Capital Outlay	$450,000	
Cash or Payables		$450,000
To record expenditures incurred on the project.		
(c) **Expenditures—Debt Service**	$ 15,000	
Accrued Interest Payable		$ 15,000
To record *accrual of interest* on the *short-term* bond anticipation notes.		
(d) Fund Balance	$465,000	
Expenditures—Capital Outlay		$450,000
Expenditures—Debt Service		15,000
To close the CPF accounts at year end.		

Note that (1) the note payable is a CPF fund liability (so its proceeds do *not* increase fund balance and are *not* reported as "Other Financing Sources") and (2) this sequence of events results in a fund balance *deficit* in the Capital Projects Fund at *year end*. Also, the expenditures for capital outlay would be reflected in the GCA accounts by increasing GCA (Construction in Progress) and Net Position by $450,000.

An exception to the general rule of recording short-term loans as CPF liabilities is made for certain Bond Anticipation Notes (BANs). This exception, which results in reporting a fund balance increase from the BAN proceeds as an

---

[2]The examples in Chapters 3 through 6 used the traditional general ledger with detailed Revenues and Expenditures subsidiary ledgers, referred to as the *general ledger–subsidiary ledger approach*. This approach is used in practice and to help newcomers visualize the nuances of governmental fund accounting and financial reporting.

   Most accounting systems of larger governments are based on the "Detailed General Ledger" approach in which all accounts are in one detailed ledger or file. Because both approaches may be found in practice and on the Uniform CPA Examination, we illustrate the "Detailed General Ledger" approach in this and future chapters, beginning with the illustrative entries in this section.

Other Financing Source, is discussed and illustrated later in a section on bond anticipation notes.

Demand bonds are sometimes used for interim financing. Demand bonds have a "put," or demand provision that allows the bondholder to require bonds to be redeemed by the issuer at any time, with appropriate notice. Demand bonds may be issued because a government is not able to borrow at a cost-effective interest rate, if at all, using traditional bonds. Or, they may be callable, which permits the issuer to minimize any additional economic benefit to the purchaser. If demand bonds are secured by letters of credit that provide long-term financing in the event that bondholders demand payment, demand bonds are classified as long-term debt, not as fund debt. Accounting for demand bonds thus is essentially the same as accounting for bond anticipation notes.

Project Costs

All expenditures incurred to bring the capital facility to a state of readiness for its intended purpose are properly chargeable as CPF expenditures. Clearly, the direct cost of items such as land, buildings, materials, and labor are included. Also, the total project cost would include such related items as engineering and architect fees, transportation costs, damages occasioned by the project, and other costs associated with the endeavor. The treatment of overhead and interest warrants more in-depth consideration.

Overhead

General government overhead is rarely charged to the project unless it is reimbursable, such as under terms of the grant through which the project is financed. When costs such as overhead are reimbursable, the reimbursable amount is frequently stated in the grant or calculated in accordance with a predetermined formula, not derived from cost accounting or similar records.

This is not to say that no government overhead costs are charged to the project unless reimbursable. Overhead is charged to the project, for example, to the extent that such costs are included in charges for goods or services provided for the project through Internal Service Funds, and additional overhead costs caused by the project are properly charged to the CPF. Because of past abuses, however, and because intergovernmental grants are often intended only to *supplement* existing resources, charges for overhead may be specifically excluded from the project cost as defined by statute, grant or other contractual agreement, or administrative determination.

Interest

Interest expenditures on interim **short-term** CPF notes are usually paid from the fund and accounted for as expenditures in the CPF. But interest expenditures for bonds and other **long-term debt** issued to finance capital projects are typically financed and accounted for through a Debt Service Fund. Interest is not included in the cost of the asset constructed. Interest earned by investing CPF cash is recognized as CPF revenue. However, interest earned by investing bond issue proceeds may be transferred to the appropriate Debt Service Fund to help finance the related bond interest expenditures.

Both interest revenues and interest expenditures related to capital projects must be carefully planned, controlled, and accounted for in the Capital Projects Funds and Debt Service Funds. Although this is true from sound financial management and accountability perspectives generally, both interest expenditures and interest revenues amounts are used in determining whether the state or local government has complied with federal **arbitrage** provisions. These provisions require the *net interest earnings* from investing *tax-exempt* bond issue proceeds in *taxable* investments to be *remitted to the federal government*. Arbitrage provisions are discussed in more detail later in this chapter.

Because grants, shared revenues, and contributions from other governments are revenues, they are subject to the modified accrual basis for governmental funds. Thus, to be recognized as revenues, they must be both measurable and available. These two qualities are determined by the legal and contractual requirements of each case.

Intergovernmental Revenues

Both unrestricted grants received or receivable and those restricted to a specific purpose (but not to capital outlay) are usually recognized as assets and revenues of the General Fund or a Special Revenue Fund, as appropriate. Subsequently, they might be transferred to a Capital Projects Fund if authorized by the governing body. But *some intergovernmental grants and other contributions are restricted to capital project use*. Most such **capital grants** are **expenditure-driven**— that is, earned by the grantee's incurring of expenditures that qualify under the terms of the grant or other contribution agreement.

- If restricted capital grant financial resources are *received before* appropriate *expenditures* that meet all eligibility requirements have been made, both the assets and a liability are recognized in the CPF. Thereafter, revenue is recognized as appropriate expenditures are made.

- If *qualifying* expenditures are incurred *before* the grant resources are *received*, the grant receivable should be *accrued* and revenue should be *recognized*, assuming the receivable is available. (Deferred revenue, a deferred inflow, is reported if not available.)

- If an expenditure-driven grant has been *awarded* but *no* cash has been received and *not* all eligibility requirements have been met:

  1. *neither* the asset *nor* a liability is *reported* in the financial statements *but*

  2. the grant award and the related potential financial resources *may* be *disclosed* in the *notes* to the financial statements.

Governments are required to report the separate components—face amount, premium (or discount), and bond issue costs—of the net fund balance increase that results from issuing general government bonds.

Recording Bond Issues

- The *face amount* of the bonds is reported as an Other Financing Source.

- Any premium on a bond issuance must be reported as a separate Other Financing Source; any discount must be reported separately as an Other Financing Use.

- Bond issuance costs are reported as debt service expenditures.

Because interest on the bonds will typically be paid from a Debt Service Fund, the premium and any payment received for accrued interest are often transferred to that fund.

CAPITAL PROJECTS FUND—CASE ILLUSTRATION BEGUN, 20X1

To illustrate Capital Projects Fund accounting, assume that in 20X1 the governing body of A Governmental Unit decided to construct a bridge expected to cost $3,000,000. The bridge construction and related costs are to be financed as follows:

	Total	Percent
Federal grant	$1,200,000	40
State grant	600,000	20
Bond issue proceeds	900,000	30
Transfer from General Fund	300,000	10
	$3,000,000	100

The $600,000 state grant is a fixed sum irrevocably granted for the bridge project. It will revert to the state only if the bridge is not built. The federal grant is for 40% of the qualifying project expenditures, with a maximum grant limit of $1,200,000; any excess "unearned" grant cash received would be refunded to the federal government. Thus, the federal grant is an expenditure-driven grant, and federal grant revenues will be recognized accordingly.

The bridge is to be constructed by a private contracting firm, Bean Bridge Builders, Inc., doing business as Bean & Co., selected by sealed bids based on engineering specifications; the government's workforce will do related earthmoving and landscape work. The estimated costs of the bridge project are:

Bridge Structure:		
Bean & Co. contract..........................		$2,400,000
Earthmoving and Landscaping (Government Roads Department):		
Labor..	$ 300,000	
Machine time	200,000	
Fuel and materials	100,000	600,000
		$3,000,000

Bean & Co. has posted a performance bond guaranteeing the quality and timeliness of its work. In addition, 5% of the amounts payable to Bean & Co. under the contract will be retained as a further guarantee of the quality of the work. This retainage will be remitted upon final inspection of the bridge and its acceptance by the governing body of A Governmental Unit. The bridge construction will begin in 20X1 and should be completed in 20X2.

Budgetary Entry   The governing body adopted an ordinance officially authorizing the bridge capital project, including the estimated financing sources and appropriations outlined earlier. The budgetary entry to record the budgetary amounts is:

(B) ESTIMATED REVENUES—Federal Grant	$ 1,200,000	
ESTIMATED REVENUES—State Grant	600,000	
ESTIMATED OTHER FINANCING SOURCES—Bonds ...	900,000	
ESTIMATED OTHER FINANCING SOURCES—Transfer from General Fund	300,000	
APPROPRIATIONS—Bean & Co. Contract		$2,400,000
APPROPRIATIONS—Labor.......................		300,000
APPROPRIATIONS—Machine Time................		200,000
APPROPRIATIONS—Fuel and Materials		100,000
To record project budget.		

Note that budgetary control is to be achieved over all financing sources, not just revenues. The examples in earlier chapters assumed that a Revenues Ledger was used and that interfund transfers and long-term debt issues were separately authorized and, thus, were not included in the budget or budgetary accounts. This Revenues Ledger approach may also be used in Capital Projects Fund accounting. But, the *detailed* General Ledger account approach better fits the typical Capital Projects Fund financing situation.

Note also that the controller established detailed General Ledger Expenditures accounts. Because all appropriations, expenditures, and encumbrances relate to the same bridge project and only one government department is involved, the accounts are set up to control and account for the appropriations for the most significant bridge costs: (1) the Bean & Co. construction contract and (2) the government's labor, machine time, and fuel and materials related to the bridge, which are assumed to be charged directly to this CPF. The following Expenditures accounts would more appropriately be titled "Expenditures—Roads Department—Labor," and so on, but are shortened for illustrative purposes because only one department is involved. If several contracts and/or departments were involved, Appropriations, Expenditures, and Encumbrances accounts for each contract and for each government department participating in the project would be used.

The following entries—which are posted to the worksheet in Illustration 7-3— summarize the several Capital Projects Fund transactions and events that occurred during 20X1:

(1) The contract with Bean & Co. was signed and work began on the bridge.

ENCUMBRANCES—Bean & Co. Contract	$2,400,000	
ENCUMBRANCES OUTSTANDING		$2,400,000
To record signing of bridge contract.		

(2) The bonds were sold at a slight premium for $911,000; bond issue costs of $2,000 were incurred and paid.

Cash	$ 911,000	
Other Financing Sources—Bonds (Face amount)		$ 900,000
Other Financing Sources—Bond Premium		11,000
To record sale of bonds at a premium.		

Expenditures—Bond Issue Costs.	$ 2,000	
Cash		$ 2,000
To record payment of bond issue costs.		

Notes: (1) The GASB requires that (a) bond proceeds be recorded at *gross*—at face or par amount— and bond premium, discount, and issue costs be recorded *separately*, and (b) general long-term liabilities be reported *only* in the government-wide Statement of Net Position.

(2) Issue costs must be reported as expenditures. This treatment of bond issue costs was required both to accommodate the calculation of interest expense for government-wide reporting and to make "yield-burning" or other excessive bond cost situations apparent in the financial statements.

The face amount and premium also affect the GCA-GLTL accounts as follows:

$$\text{GCA} \quad - \quad \text{GLTL} \quad = \quad \text{NP}$$

GCA	−	GLTL	=	NP
		+$900,000		−$911,000
		(Bonds Payable Face Amount)		
		+$11,000		
		(Bond Premium)		

Note that GASB *Statement No. 65*, "Reporting Items Previously Recognized as Assets and Liabilities," permits only prepaid insurance included in bond issue costs to be reported as assets. All other bond issue costs must be expensed in the government-wide (and the proprietary and fiduciary fund) financial statements.

(3) Fuel and materials ordered during the year totaled $55,000.

ENCUMBRANCES—Fuel and Materials	$ 55,000	
ENCUMBRANCES OUTSTANDING		$ 55,000
To record encumbrances incurred.		

(4) The state grant was received. The governing body authorized a $130,000 transfer from the General Fund during 20X1, which was received.

Cash.	$ 730,000	
Revenues—State Grant		$ 600,000
Other Financing Sources—Transfer from		
General Fund.		130,000
To record receipt of state grant and partial General Fund transfer.		

(5) Invoices were received and vouchered for fuel and materials, $49,000 (encumbered at $48,000); machine time, $81,000; and the Bean & Co. contract, $1,000,000 (as encumbered).

(a) ENCUMBRANCES OUTSTANDING	$1,048,000	
ENCUMBRANCES—Fuel and Materials		$ 48,000
ENCUMBRANCES—Bean & Co. Contract		1,000,000
To reverse encumbrances.		

(b) Expenditures—Fuel and Materials .... $ 49,000
    Expenditures—Machine Time 81,000
    Expenditures—Bean & Co. Contract 1,000,000
    Contracts Payable—Retained Percentage $ 50,000
    Vouchers Payable............................. 1,080,000
    To record vouchering expenditures for payment and 5%
    retainage on Bean & Co. contract.

Note: General capital assets are capitalized in the GCA accounts—*not* in the CPFs. GASB requires them to be reported only in the *government-wide* financial statements. The effects on the GCA accounts are:

$$\text{GCA} \quad - \quad \text{GLTL} \quad = \quad \text{NP}$$

   +$1,130,000   +$1,130,000
   (Construction
   in Progress)

When the project is completed, the Construction in Progress will be reclassified as Bridges in the GCA-GLTL accounts.

(6) Cash disbursements during 20X1 were:

Vouchers Payable............................. $ 970,000
Investments.................................. 400,000
Payroll 140,000
                             $1,510,000

Vouchers Payable............................. $970,000
Investments.................................. 400,000
Expenditures—Labor 140,000
    Cash..................................... $1,510,000
To record vouchers and payroll paid.

The labor costs increase GCA as follows:

$$\text{GCA} \quad - \quad \text{GLTL} \quad = \quad \text{NP}$$

   +$140,000   +$140,000
   (Construction
   in Progress)

(7) Filed for federal grant reimbursement for 40% of the expenditures (transactions 5 and 6) incurred for the project during 20X1.

Due from Federal Government $508,000
    Revenues—Federal Grant $508,000
To record filing for federal grant reimbursement for
   qualifying expenditures.

Calculation: 0.4 ($1,130,000 + $140,000) = $508,000

(8) Unrestricted, accrued interest receivable on investments at year end was $18,000.

Accrued Interest Receivable .... $ 18,000
    Revenues—Interest......................... $ 18,000
To record accrued interest at year-end.

General Ledger Worksheet(s)   A detailed general ledger transactions and balances worksheet for the first year, 20X1, of the Bridge Project Capital Projects Fund is presented as Illustration 7-3. Note that the preceding illustrative entries B and 1–8 are posted to this worksheet

ILLUSTRATION 7-3   **Detailed General Ledger Worksheet—Capital Projects Fund**

A Governmental Unit
Capital Projects Fund (Bridge Project)
General Ledger Transactions and Balances Worksheet
For 20X1 (Project Incomplete)

Accounts	Worksheet Entries Debit	Worksheet Entries Credit	Preclosing Trial Balance Debit	Preclosing Trial Balance Credit
Cash	$ 911,000 (2)	$ 2,000 (2)		
	730,000 (4)	1,510,000 (6)	$ 129,000	
Investments	400,000 (6)		400,000	
Accrued Interest Receivable	18,000 (8)		18,000	
Due from Federal Government	508,000 (7)		508,000	
Vouchers Payable	970,000 (6)	1,080,000 (5b)		$ 110,000
Contracts Payable—Retained Percentage		50,000 (5b)		50,000
ESTIMATED REVENUES—Federal Grants	1,200,000 (B)		1,200,000	
ESTIMATED REVENUES—State Grant	600,000 (B)		600,000	
ESTIMATED OTHER FINANCING SOURCES—Bonds	900,000 (B)		900,000	
ESTIMATED OTHER FINANCING SOURCES—Transfer from General Fund	300,000 (B)		300,000	
APPROPRIATIONS—Bean & Co. Contract		2,400,000 (B)		2,400,000
APPROPRIATIONS—Labor		300,000 (B)		300,000
APPROPRIATIONS—Machine Time		200,000 (B)		200,000
APPROPRIATIONS—Fuel and Materials		100,000 (B)		100,000
Revenues—Federal Grant		508,000 (7)		508,000
Revenues—State Grant		600,000 (4)		600,000
Revenues—Interest		18,000 (8)		18,000
Other Financing Sources—Bonds (Face Amount)		900,000 (2)		900,000
Other Financing Sources—Bond Premium		11,000 (2)		11,000
Other Financing Sources—Transfers from General Fund		130,000 (4)		130,000
Expenditures—Bean & Co. Contract	1,000,000 (5b)		1,000,000	
Expenditures—Labor	140,000 (6)		140,000	
Expenditures—Machine Time	81,000 (5b)		81,000	
Expenditures—Fuel and Materials	49,000 (5b)		49,000	
Expenditures—Bond Issue Costs	2,000 (2)		2,000	
ENCUMBRANCES—Bean & Co. Contract	2,400,000 (1)	1,000,000 (5a)	1,400,000	
ENCUMBRANCES—Fuel and Materials	55,000 (3)	48,000 (5a)	7,000	
ENCUMBRANCES OUTSTANDING	1,048,000 (5a)	2,400,000 (1)		
		55,000 (3)		1,407,000
	$11,312,000	$11,312,000	$6,734,000	$6,734,000

and the resulting balances are entered in the Preclosing Trial Balance columns. (Illustration 7-4 begins with the preclosing trial balance, which is the last two columns of Illustration 7-3. In practice, both illustrations would be a single worksheet. They are separated here for ease of reading.)

Financial statements could be prepared from this preclosing trial balance. However, the addition of closing entries and postclosing trial balances columns—as in Illustration 7-4—facilitates financial statement preparation.

Preclosing Trial Balance   The preclosing trial balance of the bridge project Capital Projects Fund General Ledger accounts at the end of 20X1 appears in the first two columns of the worksheet in Illustration 7-4, which includes closing entries (operating statement) and postclosing trial balance (balance sheet) data. (Again, the worksheets in Illustrations 7-3 and 7-4 can be combined into a single worksheet.)

The worksheet accounts illustrated here differ from the preclosing trial balance for the General Fund example in Chapter 3 because detailed General Ledger accounts are used instead of summary General Ledger accounts and separate Revenues and Expenditures Subsidiary Ledgers.

Closing Entries   As shown in Illustration 7-2, the most relevant time frame in Capital Projects Fund accounting is its *life cycle*—the period between its inception and its termination after the project is completed. Appropriations are made on a project life basis in this example, as is often the case, and all budgetary compliance, project cost, and similar determinations are made when the project has been completed. Thus, *the end of a government's fiscal year within the Capital Projects Fund life cycle is an interim date that is not particularly significant from a CPF perspective.*

Financial statements must be prepared for state and local governments at the end of each year, however. Accordingly, Capital Projects Fund financial statements must be prepared at year end, even though they are *interim* statements from a Capital Projects Fund standpoint (Illustration 7-2). The Capital Projects Fund accounts need not be closed at the end of a government's fiscal year, however.

Accounts Not Closed

If the CPF accounts are not closed at fiscal year end, a worksheet giving effect to *pro forma* ("as if") closing entries is prepared. This type of worksheet, like the worksheet in Illustration 7-4, begins with the preclosing trial balance (columns 1 and 2), from which are derived the pro forma closing entries (columns 3 and 4) and the postclosing trial balance (columns 5 and 6).

*The pro forma closing entries are **not** journalized and posted to the accounts in this approach.* Rather, the information needed to prepare the Capital Projects Fund financial statements is obtained from the General Ledger closing entries (operating statement) and postclosing trial balance (balance sheet) *worksheet* columns.

Accounts Closed

If the accounts are closed, as assumed here, they may be closed using the approach illustrated in Chapter 4. Alternatively, they may be closed using a sequence of closing entries referred to as the "variance approach." In this approach, budgetary amounts are closed in one entry and actual amounts in another. The balancing debit or credit to Fund Balance in the latter entry reflects the net change in total fund balance for the fiscal year.

The closing entries (see Illustration 7-4) are

(C1) APPROPRIATIONS—Bean & Co. Contract.........	$2,400,000	
APPROPRIATIONS—Labor.....................	300,000	
APPROPRIATIONS—Machine Time..............	200,000	
APPROPRIATIONS—Fuel and Materials..........	100,000	
ENCUMBRANCES OUTSTANDING	1,407,000	
ESTIMATED REVENUES—Federal Grant.......		$1,200,000
ESTIMATED REVENUES—State Grant.........		600,000
ESTIMATED OTHER FINANCING SOURCES—Bonds............................		900,000
ESTIMATED OTHER FINANCING SOURCES—Transfer from General Fund		300,000
ENCUMBRANCES—Bean & Co. Contract		1,400,000
ENCUMBRANCES—Fuel and Materials		7,000
To close the budgetary accounts at year end.		

(C2) Revenues—Federal Grant..........................	$ 508,000	
Revenues—State Grant	600,000	
Revenues—Interest................................	18,000	
Other Financing Sources—Bonds (Face Amount)	900,000	
Other Financing Sources—Bond Premium	11,000	
Other Financing Sources—Transfer from General Fund ..	130,000	
Expenditures—Bean & Co. Contract................		$1,000,000
Expenditures—Labor............................		140,000
Expenditures—Machine Time.....................		81,000
Expenditures—Fuel and Materials.................		49,000
Expenditures—Bond Issue Costs		2,000
Fund Balance...................................		895,000

To close the actual revenue, expenditure, and other financing source accounts.

The $895,000 credit to fund balance in entry C2 equals the net change in fund balance for the year for the CPF.

Financial Statements

Two annual financial statements are required for a Capital Projects Fund: (1) a balance sheet (Illustration 7-5) and (2) a Statement of Revenues, Expenditures, and Changes in Fund Balance (Illustration 7-6). In addition, a budgetary comparison schedule may be legally or contractually required or requested by the governing body, rating agencies, or bondholders.

Balance Sheet

The balance sheet for the Capital Projects Fund at the end of 20X1 (Illustration 7-5) is like that presented for the General Fund. Recall, however, that outside the General Fund, Unassigned Fund Balance is used only to report a negative amount. Unassigned Fund Balance is negative when the sum of a fund's nonspendable, restricted, and committed fund balances exceed its total fund balance. Assigned fund balance is zero in a fund that reports negative unassigned fund balance. Only encumbrances of otherwise unassigned fund balance affect fund balance classification. There is no positive unassigned fund balance outside the General Fund. Consequently, encumbrances should not affect fund balance reporting in a CPF. Note that the encumbrances outstanding will be disclosed in the notes to the financial statements.

Operating Statement

The GAAP-basis operating statement for the Capital Projects Fund at the end of 20X1 is presented in Illustration 7-6. The format of this CPF Statement of Revenues, Expenditures, and Changes in Fund Balance is the same as that of the corresponding statement presented for the General Fund in Chapter 3.

   Note that the CPF operating statement in Illustration 7-6 presents an excess of expenditures over revenues of $146,000. Readers may interpret this negative excess—which may be many millions of dollars in practice—as being "bad," even though there is a positive net change in fund balance.

   The excess of expenditures over revenues arises primarily because Capital Projects Funds' key financing sources typically differ from those of the General Fund and Special Revenue Funds. Bond issue proceeds usually are major CPF financing sources, for example, whereas they are rarely used to finance General Fund operations except in times of financial distress. Likewise, significant amounts of transfers from other funds provide financing for some capital projects and other CPF capital outlay.

ILLUSTRATION 7-4 Worksheet—Preclosing General Ledger Trial Balance, Closing Entries, and Postclosing Trial Balance—End of 20X1 (Project Incomplete)

A Governmental Unit
Capital Projects Fund (Bridge Project)
Preclosing General Ledger Trial Balance, Closing Entries, and Postclosing Trial Balance Worksheet
End of 20X1 (Project Incomplete)

Accounts	Preclosing Trial Balance Dr.	Preclosing Trial Balance Cr.	Closing Entries (Actual or Worksheet Only) Dr.	Closing Entries (Actual or Worksheet Only) Cr.	Postclosing Balance Dr.	Postclosing Balance Cr.
Cash	$ 129,000				$ 129,000	
Investments	400,000				400,000	
Accrued Interest Receivable	18,000				18,000	
Due from Federal Government	508,000				508,000	
Vouchers Payable		$ 110,000				$ 110,000
Contracts Payable—Retained Percentage		50,000				50,000
ESTIMATED REVENUES—Federal Grant	1,200,000			$1,200,000 (C1)		
ESTIMATED REVENUES—State Grant	600,000			600,000 (C1)		
ESTIMATED OTHER FINANCING SOURCES—Bonds	900,000			900,000 (C1)		
ESTIMATED OTHER FINANCING SOURCES—Transfer from General Fund	300,000			300,000 (C1)		
APPROPRIATIONS—Bean & Co. Contract		2,400,000	$2,400,000 (C1)			
APPROPRIATIONS—Labor		300,000	300,000 (C1)			
APPROPRIATIONS—Machine Time ..		200,000	200,000 (C1)			
APPROPRIATIONS—Fuel and Materials		100,000	100,000 (C1)			
Revenues—Federal Grant		508,000	508,000 (C2)			
Revenues—State Grant		600,000	600,000 (C2)			
Revenues—Interest		18,000	18,000 (C2)			
Other Financing Sources—Bonds (Face Amount)		900,000	900,000 (C2)			
Other Financing Sources—Bond Premium		11,000	11,000 (C2)			
Other Financing Sources—Transfer from General Fund		130,000	130,000 (C2)			
Expenditures—Bean & Co. Contract	1,000,000			1,000,000 (C2)		
Expenditures—Labor	140,000			140,000 (C2)		
Expenditures—Machine Time	81,000			81,000 (C2)		
Expenditures—Fuel and Materials	49,000			49,000 (C2)		
Expenditures—Bond Issue Costs	2,000			2,000 (C2)		
ENCUMBRANCES—Bean & Co. Contract	1,400,000			1,400,000 (C1)		
ENCUMBRANCES—Fuel and Materials	7,000			7,000 (C1)		
ENCUMBRANCES OUTSTANDING		1,407,000	11,407,000 (C1)			
	$6,734,000	$6,734,000				
Fund Balance				895,000 (C2)	**12**	895,000
			$ 6,574,000	$6,574,000	$1,055,000	$1,055,000

ILLUSTRATION 7-5   Balance Sheet—End of 20X1 (Project Incomplete)

A Governmental Unit
Capital Projects Fund
(Bridge Project)
Balance Sheet
December 31, 20X1

Assets

Cash		$ 129,000
Investments		400,000
Accrued interest receivable		18,000
Due from federal government		508,000
		$1,055,000

Liabilities and Fund Balances

Liabilities		
Vouchers payable	$ 110,000	
Contracts payable—retained percentage	50,000	$ 160,000
Fund Balances:		
Restricted*		747,000
Assigned		148,000
		$1,055,000

*The fund balance classification presented assumes:

(1) restricted financial resources available for the project are assumed to be expended before other resources, and

(2) neither the resources from the transfer nor the interest are restricted or formally committed by the governing body to expenditure for the project.

ILLUSTRATION 7-6   Operating Statement for 20X1 Fiscal Year (Project Incomplete)

A Governmental Unit
Capital Projects Fund
(Bridge Project)
Statement of Revenues, Expenditures, and Changes in Fund Balance
For 20X1 Fiscal Year
(Project Incomplete)

Revenues:		
Federal grant	$ 508,000	
State grant	600,000	
Interest	18,000	$1,126,000
Expenditures:*		
Bean & Co. contract	1,000,000	
Labor	140,000	
Machine time	81,000	
Fuel and materials	49,000	
Bond issue costs	2,000	1,272,000
Excess of Revenues Over (Under) Expenditures		(146,000)
Other Financing Sources (Uses):		
Bonds (face amount)	900,000	
Bond premium	11,000	
Transfer from General Fund	130,000	1,041,000
Net Change in Fund Balance		895,000
Fund Balance—Beginning of 20X1		—
Fund Balance—End of 20X1		$ 895,000

*All are capital outlay expenditures, except the bond issue costs, and may be reported in practice as a single total capital outlay expenditures amount.

CAPITAL PROJECTS FUND—CASE ILLUSTRATION CONCLUDED, 20X2

Whether any preliminary entries are required at the beginning of 20X2—before recording the 20X2 transactions and events—depends on whether closing entries were made at the end of 20X1. Furthermore, if closing entries were made, the preliminary entries depend on whether reversing entries are used.

20X1 Accounts Closed

If the General Ledger accounts were closed at the end of 20X1, three entries are needed at the *beginning of 20X2:*

(B1) ESTIMATED REVENUES—Federal Grant	$ 692,000		
ESTIMATED OTHER FINANCING SOURCES—			
Transfer from General Fund.	170,000		
BUDGETARY FUND BALANCE	868,000		
APPROPRIATIONS—Bean & Co. Contract		$1,400,000	
APPROPRIATIONS—Labor		160,000	
APPROPRIATIONS—Machine Time		119,000	
APPROPRIATIONS—Fuel and Materials		51,000	

To record the budgeted revenues and other financing sources not received in 20X1 and the unexpended appropriations for the project.

(B2) ENCUMBRANCES—Bean & Co. Contract	$1,400,000		
ENCUMBRANCES—Fuel and Materials	7,000		
ENCUMBRANCES OUTSTANDING		$1,407,000	

To reestablish the encumbrances outstanding at the end of 20X1.

(R1) Revenues—Interest	$ 18,000		
Accrued Interest Receivable		$ 18,000	

To reverse the interest accrual entry made at the end of 20X1.

Note in analyzing these *beginning-of-20X2 entries* that:

- *Entry B1 reestablishes* the Estimated Revenues and Estimated Other Financing Sources budgetary accounts at the amount of project financial resources yet to be realized *and restores* the Appropriations account to its unexpended balance.
- *Entry B2 reestablishes* the encumbrances for the project.
- *Entry R1 reverses* the interest accrual entry made at the end of 20X1 to record the 20X1 interest revenues as a debit (deduction) to the 20X2 Revenues—Interest account. This permits all interest received or accrued during 20X2 to be credited to the Revenues—Interest account.

Note also that the entry recording the federal grant earned in 20X1 was not reversed because that receivable was recorded as billed. The Due from Federal Government account is presumably used to control the unpaid billings throughout the years the Capital Projects Fund exists. If some unbilled federal grant revenue had been accrued at the end of 20X1, however, that accrual entry would have been reversed at the beginning of 20X2.

Case Illustration Assumptions and Entries—20X2

The remaining General Ledger accounting for 20X2 transactions is essentially the same (except reversing entries), regardless of whether the General Ledger accounts were closed at the end of 20X1. But the temporary accounts will accumulate (1) total project data if they were not closed at the end of 20X1, or (2) if they were closed at the end of 20X1, either total project data or 20X2 data, depending on whether gross balances or net remaining balances of budgetary accounts are reestablished at the beginning of 20X2. Our example assumes that only net remaining balances of the budgetary accounts are reestablished.

To conclude the bridge project Capital Projects Fund illustration, assume that the following entries summarize the transactions and events that occurred during 20X2.

(1) Invoices were received and vouchered for fuel and materials, $43,000 (partially encumbered for $7,000); machine time, $108,000; and the Bean & Co. contract, $1,410,000 (encumbered for $1,400,000), including a $10,000 adjustment in the contract, approved by the governing body, for necessary work not anticipated in the contract specifications. No other encumbrances were incurred or outstanding.

    (a) ENCUMBRANCES OUTSTANDING.............. $1,407,000

        ENCUMBRANCES—Bean & Co. Contract....... $1,400,000

        ENCUMBRANCES—Fuel and Materials.........   7,000

    To reverse encumbrances outstanding.

    (b) Expenditures—Bean & Co. Contract $1,410,000

       Expenditures—Fuel and Materials   43,000

       Expenditures—Machine Time   108,000

          Contracts Payable—Retained Percentage......... $ 70,500

          Vouchers Payable   1,490,500

    To record expenditures incurred.

$$\begin{array}{ccccc} \text{GCA} & - & \text{GLTL} & = & \text{NP} \\ +\$1,561,000 & & & & +\$1,561,000 \\ \text{(Construction in} \\ \text{Progress)} \end{array}$$

(2) Cash receipts during 20X2 were from:

Federal grant..........................	$1,198,000
Investments (including interest)...........	430,000
Transfer from General Fund..............	170,000
	$1,798,000

Cash....................................	$1,798,000	
Due from Federal Government		$ 508,000
Revenues—Federal Grant		690,000
Investments...........................		400,000
Revenues—Interest		30,000
Other Financing Sources—Transfer		
from General Fund		170,000
To record cash receipts.		

(3) Cash disbursements made during 20X2 included:

Vouchers payable.....................	$1,600,500
Payroll	129,000
	$1,729,500

Vouchers Payable....................	$1,600,500	
Expenditures—Labor	129,000	
Cash..............................		$1,729,500
To record cash disbursements.		

$$\begin{array}{ccccc} \text{GCA} & - & \text{GLTL} & = & \text{NP} \\ +\$129,000 & & & & +\$129,000 \\ \text{(Construction} \\ \text{in Progress)} \end{array}$$

(4) Under terms of the federal grant: (a) the $10,000 additional payment to Bean & Co. is *not* an allowable cost, (b) only the *actual* costs for earthmoving and landscaping are allowable, and (c) the otherwise allowable costs must be reduced by the interest earned by investing project monies. Accordingly, $30,000 was recorded as payable to the federal government, pending final inspection of the completed bridge.

Revenues—Federal Grant	$ 30,000	
Due to Federal Government		$ 30,000
To record liability for unallowable federal		
grant costs previously reimbursed.		

Calculation:

Allowable costs and reimbursement—	
Bean & Co. Contract	$2,400,000
Labor	269,000
Machine Time	189,000
Fuel and Materials	92,000
	2,950,000
Less: Interest earned	30,000
Allowable costs	2,920,000
Federal grant share (40%)	.4
Reimbursement	1,168,000
Federal grant revenue recognized to date	1,198,000
Due to federal government	$ 30,000

(5) The new bridge was approved by the inspectors and accepted by the governing body, which ordered that (a) the retained percentage should be paid to the contractor, (b) the federal government should be repaid (transaction 4), and (c) the remaining CPF fund balance should be transferred to the related Debt Service Fund.

Contracts Payable—Retained Percentage	$ 120,500	
Due to Federal Government	30,000	
Other Financing Uses—Transfer to Debt Service Fund . .	47,000	
Cash		$ 197,500

To record payment of retained percentage, reimbursement to federal government, and transfer of remaining net assets.

(C1) The accounts were closed, and the bridge project Capital Projects Fund was terminated.

APPROPRIATIONS—Bean & Co. Contract	$ 1,400,000	
APPROPRIATIONS—Labor	160,000	
APPROPRIATIONS—Machine Time	119,000	
APPROPRIATIONS—Fuel and Materials	51,000	
BUDGETARY FUND BALANCE		$ 868,000
ESTIMATED REVENUES—Federal Grant		692,000
ESTIMATED OTHER FINANCING SOURCES—Transfer from General Fund		170,000
(C2) Revenues—Federal Grant	$ 660,000	
Revenues—Interest	12,000	
Other Financing Sources—Transfer from General Fund	170,000	
Fund Balance	895,000	
Expenditures—Bean & Co. Contract		1,410,000
Expenditures—Labor		129,000
Expenditures—Machine Time		108,000
Expenditures—Fuel and Materials		43,000
Other Financing Uses—Transfer to Debt Service Fund		47,000

To close the accounts.

The Construction in Progress account in the GCA-GLTL accounts must be reclassified as Bridges.

GCA	–	GLTL	=	NP
+$2,960,000				
(Bridges)				
−$2,960,000				
(Construction in Progress)				

General Ledger Worksheet The general ledger worksheet containing the 20X2 beginning balance (the 20X1 post-closing trial balance), the 20X2 budgetary, reversing, and transaction entries, the pre-closing trial balance, and the closing entries is presented as Illustration 7-7. For ease of comparison the accounts are arranged in the same order as in Illustration 7-4.

ILLUSTRATION 7-7 General Ledger Worksheet for 20X2

A Governmental Unit
Capital Projects Fund
(Bridge Project)
General Ledger Worksheet
For 20X2 (Project Complete)

Accounts	Beginning Trial Balance Dr.	Cr.	Budgetary, Reversing, and Transaction Entries (1–5)—20X2 Dr.	Cr.	Preclosing Trial Balance Dr.	Cr.	Closing Entries Dr.	Cr.
Cash	$ 129,000		1,798,000 (2)	1,729,500 (3)				
				197,500 (5)				
Investments	400,000			400,000 (2)				
Accrued Interest Receivable ...	18,000			18,000 (R1)				
Due from Federal Government ..	508,000			508,000 (2)				
Vouchers Payable		$ 110,000	1,600,500 (3)	1,490,500 (1b)				
Contracts Payable—Retained Percentage		50,000	120,500 (5)	70,500 (1b)				
ESTIMATED REVENUES— Federal Grant			692,000 (B1)		692,000			692,000 (C1)
ESTIMATED OTHER FINANCING SOURCES— Transfer from General Fund ...			170,000 (B1)		170,000			170,000 (C1)
APPROPRIATIONS— Bean & Co. Contract				1,400,000 (B1)		1,400,000	1,400,000 (C1)	
APPROPRIATIONS—Labor ..				160,000 (B1)		160,000	160,000 (C1)	
APPROPRIATIONS— Machine Time				119,000 (B1)		119,000	119,000 (C1)	
APPROPRIATIONS—Fuel and Materials				51,000 (B1)		51,000	51,000 (C1)	
Revenues—Federal Grant			30,000 (4)	690,000 (2)		660,000	660,000 (C2)	
Revenues—Interest			18,000 (R1)	30,000 (2)		12,000	12,000 (C2)	
Other Financing Sources— Transfer from General Fund .				170,000 (2)		170,000	170,000 (C2)	
Expenditures—Bean & Co. Contract			1,410,000 (1b)		1,410,000			1,410,000 (C2)
Expenditures—Labor			129,000 (3)		129,000			129,000 (C2)
Expenditures—Machine Time ..			108,000 (1b)		108,000			108,000 (C2)
Expenditures—Fuel and Materials			43,000 (1b)		43,000			43,000 (C2)
ENCUMBRANCES— Bean & Co. Contract			1,400,000 (B2)	1,400,000 (1a)				
ENCUMBRANCES—Fuel and Materials			7,000 (B2)	7,000 (1a)				
ENCUMBRANCES OUTSTANDING			1,407,000 (1a)	1,407,000 (B2)				
Fund Balance		895,000				895,000	895,000 (C2)	
	$1,055,000	$1,055,000						
BUDGETARY FUND BALANCE			868,000 (B1)		868,000			868,000 (C1)
Due to Federal Government ...			30,000 (5)	30,000 (4)				
Other Financing Uses—Transfer to Debt Service Fund			47,000 (5)		47,000			47,000 (C2)
			$9,878,000	$9,878,000	$3,467,000	$3,467,000	$3,467,000	$3,467,000

20X2 Financial Statements

Because the capital project is complete and the Capital Projects Fund has been terminated, no CPF balance sheet is prepared at the end of 20X2. The only statement required is a Statement of Revenues, Expenditures, and Changes in Fund Balance. Only the 20X2 operating statement is required to be presented in the government's annual financial report. But an operating statement for the *project* is prepared for *internal* use and may also be included in the annual financial report.

ILLUSTRATION 7-8 Operating Statement for the Project—20X1 and 20X2 Fiscal Years (Project Complete)

A Governmental Unit
Capital Projects Fund (Bridge Project)
Statement of Revenues, Expenditures, and Changes in Fund Balances
For the Project—20X1 and 20X2 Fiscal Years
(Project Complete)

	20X2	20X1	Total
Revenues:			
Federal grant......................	$ 660,000	$ 508,000	$ 1,168,000
State grant	—	600,000	600,000
Interest..............................	12,000	18,000	30,000
	672,000	1,126,000	1,798,000
Expenditures:			
Bean & Co. contract..................	1,410,000	1,000,000	2,410,000
Labor	129,000	140,000	269,000
Machine time........................	108,000	81,000	189,000
Fuel and materials	43,000	49,000	92,000
Bond issue costs		2,000	2,000
	1,690,000	1,272,000	2,962,000
Excess of Revenues Over (Under) Expenditures......................	(1,018,000)	(146,000)	(1,164,000)
Other Financing Sources (Uses):			
Bond issue (face amount)	—	900,000	900,000
Bond premium	—	11,000	11,000
Transfer from General Fund............	170,000	130,000	300,000
Transfer to Debt Service Fund	(47,000)	—	(47,000)
	123,000	1,041,000	1,164,000
Net Changes in Fund Balance	(895,000)	895,000	—
Fund Balance—Beginning	895,000	—	—
Fund Balance—End of Year..............	$ —	$ 895,000	$ —

Project Operating Statement

A Statement of Revenues, Expenditures, and Changes in Fund Balance for the 20X1–20X2 project period is presented as Illustration 7-8. Although only the data in the 20X2 column needs to be presented in the government's annual financial statements, this operating statement for the *total project* is obviously more useful than a single-year statement. Accordingly, some governments include it in the annual financial report.

Project Budgetary Comparison Statement

Although not required for external reporting, government accountants usually prepare a project budgetary comparison statement at the conclusion of a capital project. The CPF budgetary comparison statement is used primarily for *internal* purposes but may be required by project grantors and creditors and may also be included as a schedule in the annual financial report.

Note that:

- One "Original and Final Budget" column is sufficient when the *project* budget was *not* revised (as assumed here).
- A SLG may use its *own* budget format (as assumed here) or the GAAP operating statement format.

ILLUSTRATION 7-9 Budgetary Comparison Statement for the Project—20X1 and 20X2 Fiscal Years (Project Complete)

A Governmental Unit
Capital Projects Fund
(Bridge Project)
Statement of Revenues, Expenditures, and Changes in Fund Balance—Budget and Actual
For the Project—20X1 and 20X2 Fiscal Years
(Project Complete)

	Original and Final Budget	Actual	Variance—Favorable (Unfavorable)
Revenues:			
Federal grant	$1,200,000	$1,168,000	$ (32,000)
State grant	600,000	600,000	—
Interest	—	30,000	30,000
	1,800,000	1,798,000	(2,000)
Other Financing Sources:			
Bond issue (face amount)	900,000	900,000	—
Bond premium	—	11,000	11,000
Transfer from General Fund	300,000	300,000	—
	1,200,000	1,211,000	11,000
Total Revenues and Other Financing Sources	3,000,000	3,009,000	9,000
Expenditures:			
Bean & Co. contract	2,400,000	2,410,000	(10,000)
Labor	300,000	269,000	31,000
Machine time	200,000	189,000	11,000
Fuel and materials	100,000	92,000	8,000
Bond issue costs	—	2,000	(2,000)
	3,000,000	2,962,000	38,000
Excess of Revenues and Other Financing Sources Over (Under) Expenditures	—	47,000	47,000
Other Financing Uses:			
Transfer to Debt Service Fund	—	(47,000)	(47,000)
Fund Balance—Beginning of 20X1	—	—	—
Fund Balance—End of 20X2	$ —	$ —	$ —

Note: CPF budgetary comparison statements are *not* required by GAAP.

- The format used in Illustration 7-9 is a common budget comparison format that is consistent with the logic of a budget.

A Statement of Revenues, Expenditures, and Changes in Fund Balance—Budget and Actual for the bridge project Capital Projects Fund is presented in Illustration 7-9. Clearly, this *total project* budgetary comparison statement and the 20X1–20X2 operating statement for the project (as in Illustration 7-8) provide the data managers and others need to evaluate the fiscal and budgetary management of the capital project, determine the cost of the capital assets acquired, and understand the sources and uses of the Capital Projects Fund financial resources. Indeed, the data in Illustration 7-8 and 7-9 are sometimes included in a single CPF summary operating and budgetary comparison statement with columns headed as follows:

Actual		Total Project		Variance Favorable
20X1	20X2	Actual	Budget	(Unfavorable)

OTHER CAPITAL PROJECTS FUND OPERATIONS, ACCOUNTING, AND REPORTING MATTERS

Several other CPF operations, accounting, and reporting matters warrant at least brief attention as we conclude this chapter. These topics include (1) bond anticipation notes, (2) investment of idle cash, (3) disposing of fund balance or deficit, (4) reporting several projects financed through one fund, and (5) combining CPF financial statements.

Bond Anticipation Notes (BANs)

The accounting for CPF interim financing described previously is based on the "Bond, Tax, and Revenue Anticipation Notes" section of the GASB *Codification*. Bond anticipation notes (BANs) are sometimes issued to provide interim financing for Capital Projects Funds prior to the issuance of authorized bonds. BANs may be issued for two main reasons:

1. Even though the bonds have been authorized, the bond issue process (including the "official statement" disclosures, other legal procedures, bond ratings, bond insurance, etc.) may take several weeks or months, though CPF cash is required immediately.

2. If long-term bond interest rates are expected to decline in the months ahead, the bond issue may be purposefully delayed to take advantage of the lower long-term interest rates.

In any event, the BANs should be repaid from the bond issue proceeds.

Accounting for TANs, RANs, and most short-term BANs, as well as other short-term notes payable, was illustrated in the section on interim financing. However, even though all tax anticipation notes (TANs) and revenue anticipation notes (RANs)[3] must be treated as fund liabilities, short-term BANs are treated as *long-term* debt *if **both*** (1) the BANs are issued in relation to a bond issue that is legally authorized and definitely issuable, and (2) two specific GASB BAN refinancing criteria are met. The BAN refinancing criteria established by the GASB *Codification* requires BANs with short-term maturities to be reported as general long-term liabilities if:

> [1] all legal steps have been taken to refinance the bond anticipation notes and [2] the intent is supported by an ability to consummate refinancing the short-term note on a long-term basis.[4]

If BANs with long-term maturities are issued, they are reported as long-term liabilities as well. When BANs that qualify for long-term debt treatment are issued, BAN proceeds are reported as Other Financing Sources in the CPF, and the BAN liability is recorded in the General Long-Term Liabilities (GLTL) accounts (not the CPF). The logic underlying the treatment of qualifying BANs as GLTL is that they definitely will be repaid from the related bond issue proceeds, and thus their repayment will not require the use of existing CPF financial resources.

To illustrate the issuance and repayment of BANs, suppose that A Governmental Unit issued $500,000 of BANs in 20X1 prior to issuing the bonds. The notes were issued at the face amount to the XYZ Bank; no issue costs were incurred. As noted earlier, if the BANs meet the GASB *Codification* noncurrent criteria, the entry to record the BAN issue proceeds in the Capital Projects Fund would be:

Cash	$500,000	
Other Financing Sources—BANs (Face Amount)		$500,000
To record issuance of noncurrent BANs.		

Because they are noncurrent liability BANs, the related liability would be recorded in the GLTL accounts rather than in the CPF.

---

[3]GASB *Codification*, sec. B50.102.

[4]*Statement No. 62*, "Codification of Accounting and Financial Reporting Guidance Contained in Pre-November 30, 1989 FASB and AICPA Pronouncements" (Norwalk, CT: GASB, December 2010) para. 38.

$$GCA \quad - \quad \underset{\substack{+\$500,000 \\ \text{(BANs Payable)}}}{GLTL} \quad = \quad \underset{-\$500,000}{NP}$$

Other transactions will be recorded as illustrated.

If we assume that interest on the BANs ($30,000) was paid from the Capital Projects Fund rather than from a Debt Service Fund or the General Fund, the BAN retirement would be recorded in the Capital Projects Fund as follows:

Other Financing Uses—BAN Principal Retirement	$500,000	
Expenditures—Interest on BANs.	30,000	
Cash		$530,000
To record retirement of BANs.		

Also, the BAN liability would be removed from the GLTL accounts.

$$GCA \quad - \quad \underset{\substack{-\$500,000 \\ \text{(BANs Payable)}}}{GLTL} \quad = \quad \underset{+\$500,000}{NP}$$

(Alternatively, the BANs may have been retired through the General Fund, or $530,000 might have been transferred to a Debt Service Fund through which the BANs were retired.)

Investments and Arbitrage

Significant sums of cash commonly are involved in capital project fiscal management. Cash receipt, investment, and disbursement, therefore, warrant careful planning, timing, and control.

Prudent financial management typically requires that loan transactions not be closed (and interest charges begun) until the cash is needed. Some exceptions to this rule include when statutes require bonds to be issued before the project begins, when loan interest rates are expected to rise soon, or when investments yield the government more than enough to cover the related interest costs. Similarly, significant sums should not be permitted to remain on demand deposit, but should be invested until such time as they are to be disbursed.

State and local governments that issue tax-exempt bonds or other debt issues must carefully observe the federal government's **arbitrage** regulations. Generally, the Internal Revenue Service (IRS) arbitrage regulations require state and local governments that:

- issue *tax-exempt* debt securities (the interest on which is not subject to federal income tax) and *invest the tax-exempt debt proceeds in* **taxable** *investments*

- *to* **rebate** the arbitrage—*the excess interest earned*—to the federal government.

The arbitrage rules and regulations are complex—like much of the federal income tax code and regulations—and contain several exemptions and penalties, including loss of tax-exempt status. In any event, investment revenues should be reduced and arbitrage rebate liabilities should be established when calculations indicate that arbitrage liabilities have been incurred during a period and are re-estimated at each year end. Similarly, state and local governments that draw down federal grant money before it is expended for the grant project may owe interest to the federal government.

Remaining Fund Balance

Frequently, bond covenants, grant agreements, or the governing body specifies what shall be done with any remaining CPF fund balance, as assumed in the case illustration. When disposing of fund balance, it may be either necessary or appropriate to refund unused resources provided by intergovernmental grants or intragovernmental transfers.

In the absence of legal or contractual restrictions, the balance is usually transferred to the Debt Service Fund from which the bonds or other related debt will be retired. The rationale for such action is that the balance arose because project expenditure requirements were overestimated, with the result that a larger amount than necessary was borrowed.

Reporting Multiple Projects

Earlier in this chapter, it was noted that a single Capital Projects Fund may be used to account for several projects when only one debt issue or grant is involved or the projects are financed through internal transfers from other funds. For example, the capital project may consist of several general improvements, possibly financed through one general obligation bond issue.

It was also noted that several Capital Projects Funds may be accounted for on a "funds within a fund" or "subfund" approach within a single overall Capital Projects Fund accounting entity. Each project undertaken may be separately budgeted in such cases; and, in any event, each must be separately controlled and accounted for within the CPF accounts.

Separate project control and accounting within a single CPF is best done by using distinctively titled (and coded) Estimated Revenues, Estimated Other Financing Sources, Revenues, Other Financing Sources, Appropriations, Expenditures, and Encumbrances control accounts and a set of appropriately named and coded subsidiary ledger accounts. Accounting for this type of fund corresponds with procedures discussed previously.

Financial statements for such composite CPFs, where the subfunds are in substance a series of separate Capital Projects Funds, are often presented as a series of separate fund statements—individually and/or in combining statements—as if each were accounted for separately. Financial statements for a multiproject fund would thus show data for each project as if traditional CPFs were used.

Combining CPF Statements

To focus attention on capital projects activities as a whole and to reduce the number of separate statements required, a government's CPF financial statements often are presented in combining form. With adequate disclosure, such combining statements fulfill the requirement for separate statements for each fund. Combining totals should be shown with the details applicable to each fund either being presented in the statement itself or being incorporated by reference therein to a statement or schedule containing the separate fund details.

Combining CPF balance sheets and operating statements are presented in the formats illustrated earlier in this chapter, but the column headings might appear as follows:

Completed Projects		Incomplete Projects		Totals	
Bridge Fund	**Sewer System Fund**	**Civic Center Fund**	**General Improvements Fund**	**This Period**	**Last Period**

The distinction between completed and incomplete projects is made more often in combining statements prepared for *internal* use than in those published in the government's annual financial report. Combining CPF financial statements issued for *external* users often are similar to the combining CPF operating statement headings in a recent annual financial report of the City of Sioux City, Iowa.

Street Improvement	Storm Sewer Improvement	Special Improvement	Park Improvement	Miscellaneous Improvements	Total

Concluding Comments

Capital Projects Funds are used to account for a state or local government's major general government capital outlays for buildings, highways, storm sewer systems, bridges, and other capital assets. Accordingly, they often involve many millions of dollars of financial resource inflows and expenditures.

The main aspects of CPF financing, financial management, and accounting discussed in this chapter include sources of CPF resources, number of funds required, CPF life cycle, interim financing, budgeting CPFs, costs charged to projects, investment of idle cash, and disposing of the CPF fund balance or deficit upon its termination. In addition, a CPF case illustration and illustrative financial statements were presented.

Although this chapter illustrates the accounting and financial reporting for CPFs with general long-term bond proceeds, it does not address the repayment of that debt or the related interest and fiscal charges. Those topics are covered in Chapter 8, "Debt Service Funds."

Questions

Q7-1 When is a Capital Projects Fund used by a governmental entity? In what situations would a Capital Projects Fund *not* be used for reporting in accordance with generally accepted accounting principles (GAAP)? Explain.

Q7-2 Would it be possible for a governmental entity to use a Capital Projects Fund for budgetary accounting purposes but not for GAAP reporting purposes? Explain.

Q7-3 What is the life cycle of a Capital Projects Fund?

Q7-4 Why is each significant capital project usually financed and accounted for through a separate Capital Projects Fund?

Q7-5 In what situations could several capital projects properly be financed and accounted for through a single Capital Projects Fund?

Q7-6 What are the typical sources of financing for general government capital projects? How are these sources reported in the statement of revenues, expenditures, and changes in fund balance for a Capital Projects Fund?

Q7-7 When a city issues general obligation bonds with a face value of $10,000,000 for $10,500,000 and incurs $100,000 of bond issue costs to finance construction of a major general government capital asset, how is this presented in the Capital Projects Fund Statement of Revenues, Expenditures, and Changes in Fund Balance?

Q7-8 A state finance director is concerned that the draft financial statements prepared for the state's Capital Projects Funds present large (millions of dollars) excesses of expenditures over revenues even though all of the funds are well within their appropriations and none are expected to have deficit balances when the projects are completed. (a) Why are such excesses reported? (b) What do you suggest?

Q7-9 Under what circumstances should short-term bond anticipation notes be reported as general long-term liabilities?

Q7-10 What is meant by *arbitrage* as the term is used in this chapter? Why should governmental accountants and auditors be concerned about arbitrage?

Q7-11 Neither the capital assets acquired through a Capital Projects Fund nor the long-term debt issued to finance capital projects is normally accounted for in the CPF. Why? Where are such capital assets and long-term debt accounted for, and are there exceptions to this general rule?

Q7-12 What are demand bonds? In what circumstances is a government most likely to issue demand bonds? Are demand bonds reported as general long-term liabilities? Explain.

Exercises

E7-1 (Multiple Choice) Identify the best answer for each of the following:
1. Which of the following general government capital asset acquisitions would be the *least likely* to be accounted for in a Capital Projects Fund?
   a. Construction of a new fire station financed by a portion of a special tax levy (the tax levy is being accounted for in a Special Revenue Fund).
   b. Acquisition of new police vehicles through a capital lease arrangement.

   c. Construction of a new government center financed by the issuance of general obligation serial bonds.

   d. Expansion of a town's main thoroughfare from three to five lanes financed by a federal highway grant.

2. Budgets for Capital Projects Funds are
   a. often project-length, or multiyear, budgets.
   b. always required by GAAP.
   c. indirectly budgeted through an entity's General Fund.
   d. common for projects financed by proprietary funds.

3. Which of the following are sometimes reported as long-term liabilities even if they have short-term maturities?
   a. Bond anticipation notes.
   b. Grant anticipation notes.
   c. Tax anticipation notes.
   d. Revenue anticipation notes.

4. Wakefield Heights sold $6,000,000 of general obligation serial bonds at a 1.5% discount to finance the construction of a new recreation center. Bond issuance costs were 2% of the face amount of the bonds. The entry to record the sale of the bonds in a Capital Projects Fund would be

a.	Cash	$6,000,000	
	Other financing sources—bonds		$6,000,000
b.	Cash	5,910,000	
	Other financing uses—bond discount	90,000	
	Other financing sources—bonds		6,000,000
c.	Cash	5,910,000	
	Other financing sources—bonds		5,910,000
d.	Cash	5,790,000	
	Expenditures	120,000	
	Other financing uses—bond discount	90,000	
	Other financing sources—bonds		6,000,000

5. Which of the following statements regarding the required GAAP reporting for a Capital Projects Fund is *false*?
   a. A GAAP-basis balance sheet and a Statement of Revenues, Expenditures, and Changes in Fund Balance are required for Capital Projects Funds.
   b. The format of the Statement of Revenues, Expenditures, and Changes in Fund Balance for a Capital Projects Fund is the same as for a General Fund.
   c. A GAAP-basis operating statement is not required for a Capital Projects Fund if a multi-year budget has been adopted.
   d. It is not uncommon for a Capital Projects Fund operating statement to report an excess of expenditures over revenues during a project.

6. Common expenditures in a Capital Projects Fund include
   a. bond issue costs.
   b. payments to contractors.
   c. bond discounts.
   d. Items a and b only.

7. Bond anticipation notes may be reported as a general long-term liability in which of the following circumstances?
   a. It has been determined that there is a favorable market for issuing the bonds.
   b. The government intends to refinance the bond anticipation notes within the next fiscal period.
   c. The bond anticipation notes have an original maturity of more than one year.
   d. Bond anticipation notes, like other anticipation notes, must always be reported as a fund liability.

8. In practice, which of the following is *false* regarding the disposition of any remaining fund balance of a completed Capital Projects Fund?
   a. Frequently, a governing body will specify what shall be done with any remaining fund balance before the project even starts, subject to other legal or contractual requirements.
   b. It is not uncommon for the remaining fund balance to be transferred to a Debt Service Fund.

   c. Grantors may specify that remaining amounts will revert to them based upon their percentage of initial funding.

   d. Remaining fund balance is transferred to the General Fund regardless of its source.

E7-2

1. The revenue sources for a Capital Projects Fund include proceeds of a general obligation bond issuance and a capital grant from the State Highway Trust. Assuming there are no other revenue sources and expenditures have not exceeded such resources, the ending fund balance should be reported as
   a. nonspendable.
   b. restricted.
   c. committed.
   d. assigned.

2. If a state or local government uses a single Capital Projects Fund for several different capital projects, it is recommended that
   a. "subfunds" be used to differentiate the separate projects.
   b. project-length budgets *not* be used.
   c. enterprise fund-related projects be included as well.
   d. fund balance be classified as unassigned.

3. When grant resources are received *before* eligibility requirements other than time requirements are met, the recipient should report both
   a. an asset and a deferred inflow of resources.
   b. an asset and a revenue.
   c. an asset and a liability.
   d. neither an asset nor a liability.

4. Bonds are sold to finance the construction of a new public safety station. Bond proceeds equal to the face value of the bonds are reported in a Capital Projects Fund as
   a. a deferred inflow of resources.
   b. an other financing source.
   c. an other financing use.
   d. a revenue.

5. After restricted and committed levels of fund balance have been identified in a Capital Projects Fund that has no inventory or prepaid assets, the remaining positive amount of fund balance would automatically be classified as
   a. nonspendable.
   b. assigned.
   c. designated.
   d. unassigned.

6. Which of the following would *not* be reported on the balance sheet of a Capital Projects Fund?
   a. Bond anticipation note payable.
   b. Restricted fund balance.
   c. Nonspendable fund balance.
   d. Capital assets.

7. The City of Hope received an unrestricted grant in the General Fund. The City chose to transfer an amount equal to this unrestricted grant to the Capital Projects Fund. Assuming expenditures had not occurred by the end of the fiscal year, the transferred funds would be reported in the Capital Projects Fund as
   a. restricted fund balance.
   b. committed fund balance.
   c. assigned fund balance.
   d. unassigned fund balance.

8. Expenditures are made in a Capital Projects Fund from resources advanced from the General Fund. The Capital Projects Fund anticipates receiving bond proceeds that will be restricted to the purpose for which the expenditures were made. Assuming no other resources currently exist in the Capital Projects Fund, the fund balance will reflect
   a. a negative restricted fund balance.
   b. a positive restricted fund balance.
   c. a negative assigned fund balance.
   d. a negative unassigned fund balance.

9. A GAAP-based Statement of Revenues, Expenditures, and Changes in Fund Balance for a Capital Projects Fund includes each of the following categories *except*
   a. revenues.
   b. expenditures.
   c. nonoperating revenues and expenditures.
   d. other financing sources and use.

10. As capital assets are acquired or constructed in a Capital Projects Fund, they are reported as
   a. construction in progress *only* in the Capital Projects Fund financial statements.
   b. construction in progress in *both* the Capital Projects Fund and the government-wide financial statements.
   c. construction in progress *only* in the government-wide financial statements.
   d. capitalized and depreciable capital assets *only* in the Capital Projects Fund financial statements.

E7-3 (Bond Anticipation Notes) Record the following transactions (both budgetary and actual entries) in the General Ledger of a CPF of Santiago County. Reflect all required accruals.

1. The county issues $3,000,000 of 5%, 9-month bond anticipation notes at midyear to allow it to begin construction of a new library addition. The bond anticipation notes meet the criteria for treatment as long-term liabilities.
2. The county signs a contract for construction of the library addition for $3,000,000.
3. The contractor billed the county $2,000,000 for work completed by the end of the fiscal year.
4. The bonds, which have a par value of $10,000,000, were issued at 101, net of issue costs of $90,000.
5. The bond anticipation notes and interest were paid at maturity.

E7-4 (General Ledger Entries) The following transactions and events occurred in Lanesburg Township during 20X7:

1. The township assembly agreed that a new police and fire department building would be constructed at a cost not to exceed $1,500,000, on land owned by the township.
2. Cash with which to finance the project was received from the following sources:

Transfer from General Fund	$ 100,000
State-Federal grant	500,000
Bank of Lanesburg (long-term note)	900,000
	$1,500,000

The state–federal grant is for one-third of the project cost, not to exceed $500,000, and any unearned balance must be returned to the state.

3. Cash was disbursed for building costs from the Capital Projects Fund as follows:

Construction contract	$1,400,000
Architect fees	50,000
Engineering charges	20,000
	$1,470,000

4. The unearned portion of the grant was refunded to the state, the remaining cash was transferred to the General Fund, and the Capital Projects Fund was terminated.

Required Prepare general journal entries to record the foregoing facts in the Capital Projects Fund General Ledger; assume that budgetary accounts and subsidiary ledgers are not used.

E7-5 (Long-Term Debt Issuances) Swenson Township issued $5,000,000 of 10-year, 6% bonds on July 1, 20X8. Bond issue costs of $93,000 were incurred. The bonds were issued to finance a courthouse expansion.

Required Record the bond issue in the Capital Projects Fund under each of the following three assumptions:
(a) The bonds were issued at par.
(b) The bonds were issued at a 3% premium.
(c) The bonds were issued at a 2% discount.

E7-6 (Short Discussion and Analysis) Briefly discuss each of the following short case studies. Provide explanations for your analysis.
(a) The governing board of a city recently levied a gasoline tax "for the express purpose of financing the construction and operation of a civic center, servicing debt issued for construction and related capital outlay, or any combination of the three." The board instructed the comptroller to establish a Gasoline Tax Fund to account for the receipt, expenditure, and balances of the tax proceeds. What type fund(s) should be established?
(b) What problems might one encounter in attempting to determine the proper disposition of a Capital Projects Fund balance remaining after the project has been completed and all Capital Projects Fund liabilities have been paid?

(c) A government has been awarded a grant to finance a major general government capital project. At year-end, the government has not met the eligibility requirements for the $2 million capital grant, nor has it received any cash. How is the grant reported by the government?

(d) What are special assessments? What is unique about them, and how do they affect a Capital Projects Fund?

E7-7 (Statement of Revenues, Expenditures, and Changes in Fund Balance) Prepare a statement of revenues, expenditures, and changes in fund balance for the Ahmed Village Park Improvement Capital Projects Fund for 20X7, given the following information:

Fund balance, January 1, 20X7.	$2,000,000
Intergovernmental grant revenue.	850,000
Interest revenue	30,000
Increase in fair value of investments	3,000
Construction costs incurred under contract with Builtwell Co..	2,400,000
Architect fees	32,000
Engineering fees.	17,000
Bond proceeds (face amount was $1,000,000)	1,008,000
Bond issuance costs	5,000
Purchase of land	92,000
Repayment of bond anticipation notes treated as long-term debt:	
Principal.	600,000
Interest.	3,500
Transfer from General Fund.	250,000
Construction contracts outstanding at year end.	450,000

Problems

P7-1 (Multiple Choice Problems and Computations) Identify the best answer for each of the following:

Questions 1 through 3 are based on the following scenario:

Matthew County issued a six-month, 6%, $1,000,000 bond anticipation note on March 31, 20X5, to provide temporary financing for a major general government capital project. The issuance of long-term bonds had not yet received the legally required voter approval when the financial statements were issued, but most agree the voters will approve the referendum. However, in the event that the voters reject the long-term bond issue, the county has other sources it can use to finance the project.

1. Assuming the county has incurred $800,000 of construction costs on the project by the end of its fiscal year (June 30, 20X5), the fund balance of the Capital Projects Fund used to account for this project would be
   a. $185,000.
   b. $200,000.
   c. ($800,000).
   d. ($815,000).

2. Assume voter approval has in fact occurred as of the end of the fiscal year and all other legal requirements related to the bond issuance have been met. The county issued the bonds after the balance sheet date (June 30, 20X5), but before the financial statements were issued and soon enough to use the bond proceeds to repay the bond anticipation notes. As of June 30, 20X5, the county should report fund balance in this Capital Projects Fund of
   a. $185,000.
   b. $200,000.
   c. $800,000 deficit.
   d. $815,000 deficit.

3. The BANs were repaid when due from the proceeds of the bonds. The *expenditures* reported in the Capital Projects Fund for the repayment of the bond anticipation note principal and interest in the fiscal year ended June 30, 20X6, would be
   a. $0.
   b. $30,000.
   c. $1,000,000.
   d. $1,030,000.

Questions 4 and 5 are based on the following scenario:

Robeson County has a Capital Projects Fund for its courthouse renovations. The appropriation authority for the fund continues until the end of the project. The voters approved a bond issue for the specific purpose of financing courthouse renovations, and the county commissioners committed a revenue source specifically for that purpose. The commission's policy is that expenditures are presumed to be made first from bond proceeds, then from the committed revenue source. The fund has the following balances as of September 30, 20X8, its first fiscal year end:

Revenues	$1,500,000
Bond proceeds (face amount)	$5,000,000
Expenditures	$1,500,000
Encumbrances	$8,000,000
Appropriations	$9,500,000

4. Fund Balance should be reported as follows at September 30, 20X8:
   a. Restricted, $5,000,000.
   b. Assigned (by voters) $5,000,000.
   c. Restricted, $3,500,000 and Committed $1,500,000.
   d. Committed, $1,500,000 and Assigned, $3,500,000.
5. Assume that $1,500,000 of unassigned General Fund resources were transferred to the Capital Projects Fund from the General Fund to provide financing instead of the commission committing revenues specifically to the project. How should Fund Balance as of September 30, 20X8, be reported?
   a. Restricted, $5,000,000.
   b. Assigned (by voters) $5,000,000.
   c. Restricted, $3,500,000 and Assigned, $1,500,000.
   d. Restricted, $3,500,000 and Unassigned, $1,500,000.

Questions 6 through 9 are based on the following information:

The City of Cole is installing a lighting system in the Harvey Subdivision, which is considered to be a major general government capital project for the city. The system is being financed by levying $500,000 of special assessments on benefited property owners and transferring $750,000 (in the next year) from the General Fund. $100,000 of these assessments were due and collected during the current year. Also, as of the end of the fiscal year, the city had incurred expenditures of $750,000 on the project.

6. What amount of special assessment *revenues* should be reported in the Capital Projects Fund as of the end of the current year?
   a. $0—Special assessments should be accounted for in a Special Revenue Fund.
   b. $100,000.
   c. $500,000.
   d. $0—Special assessments should be accounted for as other financing sources, not revenues.
7. The effect of the preceding transactions on the net change in fund balance of the Capital Projects Fund for the fiscal year would be
   a. a decrease of $750,000.
   b. a decrease of $250,000.
   c. a decrease of $650,000.
   d. an increase of $500,000.
8. Assume that instead of levying the special assessments to finance a portion of the project, the city issued $500,000 of five-year, 6% notes payable six months before the end of the fiscal year. The net effect of the note issuance, as well as the incurred expenditures, on the net change in fund balance of the Capital Projects Fund for the fiscal year would be
   a. a decrease of $750,000 because the notes payable would be reported as a direct fund liability in the Capital Projects Fund.
   b. an increase of $500,000. The incurred expenditures would actually be reported as an increase to assets as the system will be a capitalized asset when it is completed.
   c. a decrease of $265,000. Expenditures as of the end of the fiscal year would include six months of accrued interest on the debt.
   d. a decrease of $250,000.

9. Assume that instead of levying the special assessments to finance a portion of the project, the city levies the special assessments to pay for the notes payable issued in Item 8. Of the $500,000 of special assessments levied, $100,000 is due and collected during the first year. What amount of special assessment revenues should be recognized in the Capital Projects Fund as of the end of the first fiscal year?
   a. $0. The special assessments should be reported in a Debt Service Fund.
   b. $0. Special assessments should be reported as other financing sources, not as revenues.
   c. $100,000.
   d. $500,000.
10. Luke County issued $20,000,000 par of capital improvement bonds for a general government project. The bonds were issued at a discount of 2% of par. The bond indenture requires that $500,000 of the proceeds be set aside for future debt service. These transactions should be reflected in the county's Capital Projects Fund as
   a. other financing sources—bond proceeds, $20,000,000.
   b. other financing sources—bond proceeds, $19,600,000.
   c. other financing sources—bond proceeds, $20,000,000; other financing uses—bond discount, $400,000; other financing uses—transfers out, $500,000.
   d. other financing sources—bond proceeds, $19,600,000; debt service expenditures—$500,000.

P7-2 (General Ledger Entries; Statements) The following transactions took place in the town of Burchette during 20X3:
   1. A bond issue of $12,000,000 was authorized for the construction of a library, and the estimated bond issue proceeds and related appropriations were recorded in the General Ledger accounts of a new Capital Projects Fund.
   2. The bonds were sold at a premium of $90,000.
   3. The cost of issuing the bonds, $80,000, was paid.
   4. An order was placed for materials estimated to cost $6,500,000.
   5. Salaries and wages of $500,000 were paid.
   6. The premium, net of bond issuance costs, was transferred to a Debt Service Fund.

The following transactions took place during 20X4:
   7. The materials were received; the actual cost was $6,585,000.
   8. Salaries and wages of $4,010,000 were paid.
   9. All outstanding bills were paid.
   10. The project was completed. The accounts were closed, and the remaining balance was transferred to a Debt Service Fund.

a. Prepare all journal entries (budgetary and actual), including closing entries, to record the Capital Projects Fund transactions for 20X3 and 20X4.   ***Required***
b. Prepare a Capital Projects Fund balance sheet as of December 31, 20X3.
c. Prepare a Capital Projects Fund Statement of Revenues, Expenditures, and Changes in Fund Balance for the project, including (1) the year ended December 31, 20X3, and (2) a separate budgetary combined comparison statement for the years ended December 31, 20X3 and 20X4.

P7-3 (GL Entries; Bond Anticipation Notes) Butler County issued $2,000,000 of 9-month, 9% bond anticipation notes to provide financing for construction of a county baseball stadium. This prevented delays in beginning the project, which had been approved at an estimated cost of $4,000,000. December 31 is the end of the county's fiscal year. The following transactions occurred during 20X8 and 20X9:
   1. The bond anticipation notes were issued at par on July 1, 20X8.
   2. The county signed a contract on July 1, 20X8, with the King of Swat Construction Company to build the stadium. The contract price was $4,000,000.
   3. The King of Swat Construction Company billed the county $1,800,000 during 20X8 for work completed on the project. The county paid the amount billed less a 5% retainage to be remitted upon final approval of the stadium.
   4. On February 20, 20X9, the county issued the baseball stadium bonds ($4,000,000 par) at a price of $4,180,000, net of $120,000 bond issue costs.
   5. The county repaid the bond anticipation notes and interest upon maturity from the bond proceeds.
   6. The King of Swat Construction Company billed Butler County $2,200,000 for work performed in 20X9 to complete the baseball stadium. The project was approved by the county, and the King of Swat Construction Company was paid in full. The remaining assets were transferred to the related Debt Service Fund.

a. Prepare the general journal (budgetary and actual) entries to record the preceding transactions for Butler County. Also, prepare 20X8 and 20X9 financial statements for the county's Baseball Stadium CPF. Assume that the bond anticipation notes do not qualify as long-term liabilities and that the proceeds of the note and of the bond are limited to use for costs directly related to construction of the baseball stadium.   ***Required***

b. Repeat the requirements in (a) under the assumption that the bond anticipation notes meet the criteria for being treated as general long-term liabilities.

P7-4 (GL and SL Entries; Trial Balances; Statements) The following transactions and events relate to the Harmer Independent School District High School Building Capital Projects Fund during 20X6.

1. The school board appropriated $9,000,000 to construct and landscape a new regional high school building to be financed as follows:

Bond issue proceeds	$6,000,000
Federal grant (for 20% of cost)	1,800,000
State grant	700,000
Transfer from General Fund	500,000
	$9,000,000

All of the financing sources are restricted to high school construction-related expenditures except the transfer from the General Fund that was from unassigned General Fund resources. Harmer's policy is to expend restricted resources before committed, assigned, or unassigned resources available for the same purpose. The appropriations made for the high school building were:

Structure	$5,000,000
Plumbing and heating	1,800,000
Electrical	1,300,000
Landscaping	700,000
Other	200,000
	$9,000,000

2. Contracts were let to private contractors:

Structure	$4,700,000
Plumbing and heating	1,825,000
Electrical	1,300,000
	$7,825,000

Thus, the plumbing and heating appropriation was increased $25,000, and the structure appropriation was decreased $300,000.

3. Cash receipts during 20X6 included:

Federal grant	$ 250,000
State grant	350,000
Bond issue proceeds (par $2,000,000)	2,020,000
Transfer from General Fund	100,000
	$2,720,000

The federal grant is for 20% of actual qualifying costs incurred (expenditure-driven) up to its $1,800,000 maximum, but the state grant is an outright contribution to the project. The remaining bonds authorized will be issued as needed, depending on market conditions; and the board authorized only part of the General Fund transfer but is expected to authorize the remainder during 20X7.

4. Invoices from contractors were received, approved, and vouchered for payment less a 5% retained percentage:

Structure	$2,000,000
Plumbing and heating	500,000
Electrical	700,000
Other (not encumbered)	50,000
	$3,250,000

5. The school board borrowed $150,000 for the project on a short-term note from First State Bank of Harmer.
6. Cash disbursements during 20X6 included

Vouchers Payable		$2,600,000
Payroll:		
Landscaping	$ 120,000	
Other	80,000	200,000
Machinery charges—Landscaping		50,000
		$2,850,000

7. The school board billed the federal government for the balance of its share of project costs incurred to date. Payment from the federal agency is expected early in 20X7.
8. Accrued interest payable on the note at year end was $4,000. Interest expenditures on this note are considered a project cost (other) but are not reimbursable under terms of the federal grant.

The following transactions and events relate to the Harmer Independent School District High School Building Capital Projects Fund during 20X7.
1. Cash receipts during 20X7 included:

Bond issue proceeds (par less $15,000 of bond issue costs)	$3,985,000
Federal grant	1,440,000
State grant	350,000
Transfer from General Fund	375,000
	$6,150,000

2. Final invoices from contractors were received, approved, and vouchered for payment minus a 5% retained percentage:

Structure................................	$2,750,000
Plumbing and heating....................	1,325,000
Electrical	600,000
Landscaping (not encumbered)............	400,000
	$5,075,000

3. Cash disbursements during 20X7 included:

Vouchers Payable		$5,308,750
Short-term note payable (including interest) .		160,000
Transfer of net bond issue premium to Debt Service Fund		5,000
Payroll:		
Landscaping	$ 75,000	
Other................................	62,000	137,000
Machinery charges—Landscaping		60,000
		$5,670,750

4. The federal government was billed for the balance of its share of qualifying project costs (excluding interest expenditures).
5. The school board received final payment on the federal grant as billed, except for $400 disallowed because of a $2,000 unallowable cost included in the billing.
6. The high school building was inspected, approved, and accepted by the school board. Accordingly, the retained percentages were paid to the contractors.
7. The remaining cash was transferred to the Debt Service Fund.
8. The High School Building Capital Projects Fund accounts were closed, and the fund was terminated.

Required a. Prepare the journal entries to record the 20X6 and 20X7 transactions and events in the General Ledger, Revenues Ledger, and Expenditures Ledger of the Harmer Independent School District High School Building Capital Projects Fund. (Detailed General Ledger accounts may be used instead of the subsidiary ledgers, if desired.)

b. Prepare a balance sheet for the Harmer Independent School District Capital Projects Fund as of the end of 20X6 and a Statement of Revenues, Expenditures, and Changes in Fund Balance for the 20X6 fiscal year.

c. Prepare a Statement of Revenues, Expenditures, and Changes in Fund Balance—Budget and Actual for the High School Building Capital Projects Fund for the 20X6–20X7 period. The columns of the statement should be headed:

Actual				Variance—
			Budget	Favorable
20X7	20X6	Total	(Revised)	(Unfavorable)

P7-5 (Fund Balance Reporting) Musselwhite Independent School District (ISD) began construction of a new building (for McCoin Middle School) during its 20X1 fiscal year, which ended April 30, 20X1. The plan for financing the construction of the facility was:

Financing Source	Restricted for Construction Costs	Committed for Construction, Furniture, and Equipment Costs
Bonds	$9,000,000	
Lamm County Grant	2,000,000	
Transfers of committed resources from General Fund		$1,500,000

During fiscal year **20X0–20X1:**

- The $2,000,000 restricted grant from the county was received and used to begin construction.
- The full amount of the grant was recognized as revenue.
- The bonds were issued, generating $9,000,000 of cash for the project late in the fiscal year. No General Fund money was transferred to the McCoin Middle School Capital Projects Fund in this fiscal year.
- Total construction costs incurred during 20X0–20X1 were $3,500,000.

Restricted Fund Balance of $7,500,000 was reported in the balance sheet of the McCoin Middle School CPF at April 30, 20X1.

During the **20X1–20X2 fiscal year:**

- The Musselwhite ISD transferred $1,500,000—committed by a resolution of the school board in accordance with its commitments policy—from the ISD's General Fund to its McCoin Middle School CPF. The cash was committed to construction costs and/or furniture and equipment purchases for the middle school.
- The district's finance director later transferred $300,000 of unrestricted, uncommitted cash from the General Fund to the CPF to finance landscaping of the school site and $50,000 to be used for purchases of furniture and equipment. The finance director was authorized by the board to determine the amount that the county could afford for these purposes in 20X1–20X2 and approve the transfer. The ISD expects the total cost of landscaping to exceed the amount transferred but cannot transfer more during 20X1–20X2 because of budget constraints.
- Construction was completed in April 20X2. Construction expenditures incurred during 20X1–20X2 to complete the middle school totaled $7,680,000 because of unexpected cost overruns.
- $1,000,000 of furniture and equipment was ordered and received. Encumbrances outstanding for orders placed for furniture and equipment, but not yet filled, totaled $552,000.

- Landscaping expenditures incurred were $158,000, but a contract was signed for $95,400 of additional landscaping work to be completed before the school opens in September 20X2.

$20,000 of the landscaping expenditures was for landscaping materials purchased by the ISD and is still on hand at April 30.

a. Prepare a schedule (or schedules) computing the balances that Musselwhite ISD should report in each category of fund balance in the balance sheet of its McCoin Middle School CPF. Musselwhite ISD's policy related to restricted assets is that restricted financial resources for a certain purpose are expended for the restricted purpose before unrestricted resources are expended. The board does not have a spend-down policy for unrestricted resources.
b. Prepare the fund balance section of the McCoin Middle School CPF balance sheet at April 30, 20X2.

Required

P7-6 (Research and Analysis) Obtain a copy of a recent comprehensive annual financial report (CAFR) of a state or local government from the government, the Internet, your instructor, or a library. You should supplement your responses with copies of relevant CAFR pages.

a. **Letter of Transmittal.** Review the capital projects–related discussions and presentations. Which were the most significant general government capital projects? Which planned capital projects (if any) were discussed?
b. **Management's Discussion and Analysis.** What discussions and analysis relate to general capital assets?
c. **Financial Statements.** What were the major types of Capital Projects Funds revenues, other financing sources, expenditures, and other financing uses? Were any reported that were not discussed in Chapter 7 or in earlier chapters? Discuss.
d. **Narrative Explanations.** Which individual Capital Projects Funds were reported? (Attach a photocopy of the narrative explanations.) Were any of these funds different from those you expected based on your study of Chapter 7? Explain.
e. **Combining and Individual Fund Statements.** Review the combining and individual fund statements for the Capital Projects Funds. What additional information is more apparent than in the basic financial statements?
f. **Statistical Section.** What information in the statistical section might be relevant in planning and financing future general government capital projects?

Required

Cases

C7-1. (CPF Journal Entries—Blue Earth County, Montana) Record the following transactions in the Building and Capital Purchases Capital Projects Fund of Blue Earth County, Montana, for the year ended December 31, 20X6.

1. Levied property taxes of $4,385,559 that are restricted for general government capital projects. Of the total amount, $150,000 is expected to be uncollectible.
2. Collected $4,135,559 before the due date for taxes. The balance of the property taxes became delinquent.
3. Issued $4,000,000 (face amount) of bonds at a premium of $33,479. Bond issue costs of $33,815 were paid.
4. Received the General Fund contribution to the building projects, $3,223,980.
5. Signed contracts on building projects totaling $9,500,000.
6. Incurred construction costs under contracts of $6,300,000.
7. Incurred and paid unencumbered construction costs of $70,242.
8. Paid contractors the amounts due less $393,060 retainage.
9. Billed grantor agencies $2,778,235 for costs reimbursable under grant awards.
10. Collected $2,000,385 from grantor agencies. Another $24,000 is expected to be collected within the first 60 days of 20X7.

(Based on a recent Comprehensive Annual Financial Report of Blue Earth County, Montana.)

C7-2. (CPF Statements—Montgomery County, Maryland) Using the Montgomery County, Maryland, preclosing trial balance at June 30, 20X9, presented here, prepare the county's Capital Projects Fund (a) statement of revenues, expenditures, and changes in fund balance for the year ended June 30, 20X9, and (b) balance sheet at June 30, 20X9.

Montgomery County, Maryland
Capital Projects Fund
Preclosing Trial Balance
June 30, 20X9

Accounts	Debit	Credit
Equity in Pooled Cash and Investments..	$103,671,506	
Cash with Fiscal Agents	4,320,358	
Accounts Receivable..................	572,175	
Notes Receivable....................	91,465	
Mortgages Receivable................	300,000	
Other Receivables...................	3,829	
Due from Other Governments	21,180,411	
Inventory of Supplies	828,573	
Prepaid Items.......................	1,335	
Accounts Payable		$ 12,308,083
Retainage Payable...................		6,080,192
Accrued Liabilities		643,718
Due to Other Funds		53,986,924
Due to Other Governments...........		20,801,660
Deferred Revenues		2,454,122
Fund Balance	37,114,464	
Taxes..............................		58,073,018
Intergovernmental Revenues..........		19,555,194
Charges for Services		787,887
Investment Income		2,323,949
Other Revenues.....................		777,212
Transfers In		59,491,660
Sale of Capital Assets		3,750
Bond Anticipation Note Proceeds.......		313,707,787
Capital Outlay	382,096,212	
Transfers Out.......................	814,828	
Totals...........................	$ 50,995,349	$ 50,995,349

The long-term receivables are assigned to specific projects when collected. Bond indentures require maintaining a reserve for legal debt restrictions. The required balance of this reserve in the fund at June 30, 20X9, is $4,211,706.

(Based on a recent Comprehensive Annual Financial Report of Montgomery County, Maryland.)

Harvey City Comprehensive Case

CAPITAL PROJECTS FUNDS

Harvey City has two Capital Projects Funds in 20X4. The Parks and Recreation Capital Projects Fund is created in 20X4. The Bridge Capital Projects Fund was established in 20X3, and the bridge is completed in 20X4.

REQUIREMENTS—PARKS AND RECREATION CAPITAL PROJECTS FUND

a. Prepare a worksheet for the Parks and Recreation Capital Projects Fund similar to the General Fund worksheet you created in Chapter 4. Enter the effects of the following transactions and events in the appropriate columns of the worksheet. (A different solution approach may be used if desired by your professor.)

b. Enter the preclosing trial balance in the appropriate worksheet columns.

c. Enter the preclosing trial balance amounts in the closing entry (operating statement data) and postclosing trial balance (balance sheet data) columns, as appropriate.

d. Prepare the 20X4 statement of revenues, expenditures, and changes in fund balance for the Parks and Recreation Capital Projects Fund.

e. Prepare the year-end 20X4 balance sheet for the Parks and Recreation Capital Projects Fund.

TRANSACTIONS AND EVENTS—20X4—PARKS AND RECREATION CAPITAL PROJECTS FUND

1. The city approved a major capital improvement project to construct a recreational facility. The project will be financed by a bond issue of $1,500,000, transfers from the General Fund of $500,000, and a contribution from the county of $300,000. Record the budget assuming these amounts, along with an equal appropriation for the project, were adopted for 20X4.
2. The city received the county's contribution of $300,000. These resources are required to be used for the construction project. (The grant is expenditure-driven. The city's policies indicate that resources restricted for a given purpose are considered expended prior to any unrestricted resources available for that purpose.)
3. The city transferred $200,000 from the General Fund to the Parks and Recreation Capital Projects Fund.
4. The city issued bonds with a face (par) value of $1,500,000 at a premium of $50,000 on January 1. Bond issue costs of $15,000 were incurred. Interest of 8% per year and $100,000 of principal are due each December 31.
5. The city signed a $2,190,000 contract for construction of the new recreational facility. The process to establish the contract qualifies as a commitment under the city's commitments policy.
6. The city purchased land as the site for the facility at a cost of $110,000. Payment was made for the land.
7. The contractor billed the city $1,200,000. The city paid all but a 5% retainage.
8. The outstanding encumbrances were closed. (Use the transactions columns for this entry.)
9. The budgetary accounts were closed at year end. Appropriations do not lapse at year end. (Close the budgetary accounts in the transactions columns.)

REQUIREMENTS—BRIDGE CAPITAL PROJECTS FUND

a. Prepare a worksheet for the Bridge Capital Projects Fund similar to the General Fund worksheet you created in Chapter 4. Enter the effects of the following transactions and events in the appropriate columns of the worksheet. (A different solution approach may be used if desired by your professor.)

b. Enter the preclosing trial balance in the appropriate worksheet columns.

c. Enter the preclosing trial balance amounts in the closing entry and postclosing trial balance (balance sheet data) columns, as appropriate.

d. Prepare the 20X4 statement of revenues, expenditures, and changes in fund balance for the Bridge Capital Projects Fund.

e. Prepare the 20X4 year-end balance sheet for the Bridge Capital Projects Fund.

BEGINNING 20X4 TRIAL BALANCE—BRIDGE CAPITAL PROJECTS FUND

The trial balance for the Bridge Capital Projects Fund at January 1, 20X4, is presented here:

Harvey City
Bridge Capital Projects Fund
Trial Balance
January 1, 20X4

	Debit	Credit
Cash	$ 155,000	
Investments	1,650,000	
Contracts Payable—Retained Percentage		$ 85,000
Fund Balance		1,720,000
Totals	$1,805,000	$1,805,000

All the resources of the fund at January 1, 20X4, are restricted to expenditure for the bridge project.

TRANSACTIONS AND EVENTS—20X4—BRIDGE CAPITAL PROJECTS FUND

1. Estimated revenues and other financing sources for 20X2 included budgeted investment income of $25,000 and a budgeted transfer from the General Fund of $55,000. Unexpended appropriations of $1,720,000 carried over from the prior year. (Record the budget.)
2. The city reestablished its encumbrances of $1,720,000 that were closed at the end of 20X3.
3. The contractor billed the city $1,800,000 for the costs to complete the bridge. The project received final approval. The total cost of $3,500,000 included costs of $1,700,000 incurred in 20X3.
4. The city sold the Capital Projects Fund investments for $1,660,000, a gain of $10,000.
5. The city transferred $70,000 from the General Fund to the Bridge Capital Projects Fund.
6. The city paid the contractor the balance due, $1,885,000, and the fund was terminated.
7. The budgetary accounts were closed at year end. (Close the budgetary accounts in the transactions columns.)

CHAPTER 8

Debt Service Funds

LEARNING OBJECTIVES

After studying this chapter, you should be able to:

- Understand the basic nature and purposes of Debt Service Funds and the types of liabilities serviced through Debt Service Funds.

- Understand when Debt Service Funds are required and when debt service on general long-term liabilities may be accounted for in other funds.

- Understand when expenditures for debt service on general long-term liabilities (GLTL) are recognized.

- Understand the conditions under which governments are permitted to accrue GLTL principal and interest expenditures before maturity.

- Record debt service transactions and prepare Debt Service Fund financial statements.

- Understand accounting and reporting for special assessment Debt Service Funds.

- Understand the basic accounting and reporting requirements for debt service on GLTL term bonds and deep discount debt.

- Understand, record, and report refundings of general long-term liabilities.

The purpose of Debt Service Funds (DSFs) is "to account for and report financial resources that are restricted, committed, or assigned to expenditure for principal and interest [on general long-term liabilities]."[1] Thus, only *general government* long-term liabilities that are recorded in the General Long-Term Liabilities accounts are serviced through Debt Service Funds.

Not all general long-term liabilities must be serviced through Debt Service Funds. The GASB *Codification* provides that "Debt Service Funds are *required* [only] *if* (1) they are legally mandated or (2) financial resources are being accumulated for principal and interest payments maturing in future years."[2]

Thus, capital lease liabilities and serial bond debt might properly be serviced directly from the General Fund or a Special Revenue Fund—rather than from a Debt Service Fund—if

- a Debt Service Fund is not required legally or contractually and
- debt service resources are not being accumulated beyond those needed currently.

Of course, such debt *can* be serviced through a Debt Service Fund. Indeed, many government accountants prefer to account for all general long-term debt service through one or more Debt Service Funds (1) so that all general long-term liabilities are serviced through the same fund type and (2) to enhance control over and accountability for debt service resources.

---

[1]GASB *Codification*, sec. 1300.104.
[2]Ibid.

The responsibility of providing for the retirement of long-term general obligation debt is ordinarily indicated by the terms of the debt indenture or other contract.

- The term *general obligation* debt indicates that the "full faith and credit" of the governmental unit has been pledged to the repayment of the debt.
- The term *revenue debt* indicates that a specific revenue source—such as special assessments, property taxes, or tolls—is dedicated to repayment of the debt.
- A *"double barrel"* debt is a *revenue* debt that "has general obligation backing"—that is, repayment is guaranteed by the full faith and credit of the issuing government.

Long-term liabilities of specific proprietary or fiduciary funds are *not* general long-term liabilities, even if they constitute "full faith and credit" debt, and they are normally serviced through those funds rather than the Debt Service Fund(s). For example, when general obligation bonds are issued for the benefit of a public enterprise, the enterprise frequently has primary responsibility for repayment of the bonds (Chapter 10). The same is true of Internal Service Fund debt (Chapter 11). Similarly, some Trust Funds (Chapter 12) may have long-term liabilities. In these situations the debt is a *specific fund liability*—not a general long-term liability—and is accounted for in and serviced through those Trust Funds.

This chapter includes discussions and illustrations of (1) the *general government* Debt Service Fund (DSF) environment, including its unique terminology, debt service financing, and expenditure recognition; (2) accounting and reporting for conventional serial bond DSFs and term bond DSFs; (3) accounting for and reporting debt service on general government special assessment debt—debt that is issued to finance special assessment capital improvements and is serviced by assessments levied against the owners of the properties benefited; and (4) general long-term liability refundings and the accounting and reporting for DSFs for such refundings. We begin with brief discussions of several important DSF environment, terminology, financing, and expenditure recognition matters.

DEBT SERVICE FUND ENVIRONMENT, FINANCING, AND EXPENDITURE RECOGNITION

Several features of state and local government (SLG) long-term liabilities and debt service should be noted at this point. Some are similar to the business environment, but others are unique to the SLG environment.

Long-Term Liabilities Four types of long-term liabilities are frequently incurred by state and local governments: bonds; notes; time warrants; and capital leases, lease-purchase agreements, certificates of participation, and installment purchase contracts.

A **bond** is a written promise to pay a specified principal sum at a specified future date, usually with interest at a specified rate. Bond issues are often for many millions of dollars because bonds are a major source of long-term financing of capital improvements of most governments. Bonds are usually issued in $1,000 and $5,000 denominations, with maturities scheduled over 15 to 25 years, and interest paid semiannually or annually.

1. **Term** *bonds* are those for which the entire principal amount is payable at a single, specified maturity date.
2. **Serial** *bonds,* by far the most widely used, provide for periodic maturities ranging up to the maximum period permitted by law in the respective states.

Specific arrangements of maturities vary widely. For example:

- *Regular* serial bonds are repayable in equal annual principal installments, with interest paid on the declining balance over the life of the issue.
- *Deferred* serial bonds defer the *beginning* of the principal *repayment* for several years into the future, after which equal annual principal installments are to be paid.

- *Other* serial bonds, such as where the indenture provides for *increasing* amounts of annual *principal* payments that are computed so that the total annual payment of interest and principal is constant over the life of the issue.

Notes, less formal documents than bonds, indicate an obligation to repay borrowed money with interest. The issuance of notes—some called certificates of obligation, commercial paper, and other non-bond debt—often does not require a vote of the citizenry.

- Notes typically have a single maturity date, as do term bonds, but their maturity usually ranges from as soon as 30 to 90 days to as long as 5 to 10 years after issuance.
- A single note usually evidences the borrowing transaction, whereas bonds are generally issued in $5,000 denominations.

General obligation notes with original maturities of a year or less traditionally have been classified as short-term debt (and reported as fund liabilities), while those issued for more than a year have been considered long-term debt. Notes payable and other debt securities that are classified as long-term debt are recorded in the General Long-Term Liabilities accounts and may be serviced through a Debt Service Fund.

Warrants are *promises* to pay and are used differently by different SLGs.

- **Notes.** Some SLGs issue multiyear *time warrants* that are, in substance, notes payable. Thus, a three-year time warrant is essentially the same as a three-year note payable.
- **Checks.** Many state and local governments issue warrants instead of checks. Warrants are *promises* to pay a payee, rather than *orders* to pay; thus, the SLG can order the bank to temporarily not pay some warrants if to do so would cause an overdraft. This option is particularly important if constitutional or statutory provisions prohibit overdrafts. The difference between warrants and checks is usually technical, rather than substantive, but can be important legally. Warrants to be paid more than one year after issue are recorded in the General Long-Term Liabilities accounts and may be serviced through a Debt Service Fund.

Capital leases, lease-purchase agreements, and installment purchase contracts have come into widespread use in the public sector. A variation of lease agreements that has grown more common recently is the "carving up" of leases into shares, called **certificates of participation**, which are sold to individual investors. When the substance of these transactions indicates that a general government purchase (or capital lease) and liability exist, they should be recorded as General Capital Assets and General Long-Term Liabilities.

Some bond and notes have abnormally low (even zero) stated interest rates and are issued or sold at significant *discounts* from face (par).

- Such **deep discount** debt requires little or no interest payments during its life.
- But the entire face or par amount, which includes a single *balloon* payment of compounded prior period interest, must be paid at maturity.

Most deep discount debt is issued in relatively small amounts in conjunction with serial debt issues, rather than as stand-alone issues. Indeed, issuance of stand-alone deep discount debt is often prohibited by state or local law.

Debt Service Funds for notes, warrants, and other types of general long-term debt are not discussed separately because the accounting for them is similar to that for DSFs for bonds. However, debt service for deep discount debt is discussed later in this chapter.

Fixed vs. Variable Rates

Municipal bonds issued by state and local governments have traditionally been *fixed rate* bonds. That is, the annual interest rate, say 6%, is determined upon issuance of the bonds and remains the same throughout the period the bonds are outstanding.

In recent years, some *variable rate* municipal bonds have been issued. In variable rate bond issues, the interest rate is set initially, say at 6%. But the interest rate changes periodically (is "re-set") while the bonds are outstanding—perhaps annually or semiannually—according to an agreed index such as a certain bank's prime rate or a specified federal security interest rate. Furthermore, some variable rate bonds have interest floor (minimum) and ceiling (maximum or cap) rates, which limit the range within which the interest rate can vary.

Government interest expenditure planning, budgeting, and appropriation obviously are simpler and more precise when fixed rate bonds are issued. However, initial interest rates are often lower on variable rate bonds—because the SLG bears some or all of the interest rate change risk—but might also be higher. Thus, it is extremely difficult to predict whether a SLG will obtain lower interest costs over the life of a fixed rate or a variable rate issue, all other factors being equal. Interest rate "swaps" and "caps" are outgrowths of variable rate debt issues. Governments can pay a fee to speculators to "swap" the variable rate for a fixed rate or to "cap" the maximum interest rate by agreeing to pay any amounts exceeding the limit.[3] The examples in this chapter assume fixed interest rate bonds for the sake of illustrative simplicity.

Debt Service Payments

Interest expenditure is an annual cost that is directly proportional to the principal amount of debt outstanding. Because a common debt service planning objective is to keep the drain on each year's resources relatively constant, the pattern of debt service payments for long-term debt is usually designed so that total annual debt service requirements will not fluctuate materially.

Regular fixed rate serial bonds meet the objective fairly well, and both serial bond issues and lease agreements may be structured to meet the objective extremely well, as do most term bonds. A term bond or deep discount debt security maturing 20 years in the future usually requires the government to accumulate the par amount due 20 years hence through annual contributions to a Debt Service Fund that, together with earnings on the invested contributions, will equal the par (face) amount.

Bonds and Fiscal Agents

Both serial bonds and term bonds may be either *registered* bonds or *bearer* bonds. All tax-exempt municipal bonds issued since the mid-1980s are *registered bonds*—that is, the bonds are registered in the name of the investor-creditor, whose name appears on the bond, and bond principal and interest payments are made by checks or electronic payments issued to each investor-creditor.

Bearer bonds, which are no longer issued as tax-exempt debt, are not registered but are presumed to belong to whoever has possession of them (the bearer). Each *bearer bond* has dated interest coupons attached, which the bearer clips and deposits at a bank; the bank processes it like a check. (The bond is deposited and processed similarly upon its maturity.) Thus, bearer bonds are sometimes referred to as "coupon" bonds, and investors in bearer bonds are often referred to as "coupon clippers."

A few SLGs perform all bond-related registration and debt service payment functions internally. That is, they register and reregister their bonds, prepare individual interest and principal payment checks, and prepare required annual reports of their debt service activities and payments to the federal and state governments. However, most SLGs retain a registration agent and/or a *paying agent* (fiscal agent) to perform such bond-related functions. A SLG that retains a bond registrar and paying agent—usually a large bank—sends its debt service checks (including a fiscal agent fee) to the fiscal agent. The *fiscal agent* prepares and processes the individual investor-creditor checks, registers and reregisters bonds as ownership changes, prepares and files the necessary federal and state reports on the SLG's debt service payments, and sends the SLG regular reports that summarize its activities on behalf of the SLG.

---

[3]Use of derivative financial instruments such as these has become common enough in state and local governments that the GASB has made accounting and reporting for derivatives a major technical agenda project.

Required DSF Reserves

Many SLG bond indentures require the SLGs to maintain a specified level of DSF fund balance that is restricted for debt service—referred to as *funded reserves*. A common provision is that assets in the amount of the highest year's principal and interest requirements of the bond issue must be maintained in the DSF. A certain dollar amount, say, $2,000,000, may also be specified; and in some agreements the SLG can accumulate the funded reserve amounts over 2 to 5 years. Such funded reserve amounts may typically be expended only for (1) debt service payments in the event the SLG encounters financial difficulty during the time the bonds are outstanding or (2) payment of the final year's debt service. Any amount remaining after the bonds are retired becomes available for general use by the SLG.

Required DSF reserves, or funded reserves, go by many names and are reported as **Restricted Fund Balance** because they are externally restricted by the bond indenture or other debt agreement. Examples include Fund Balance Restricted for Financial Exigencies, for Contingencies, or for Debt Service Assurance. (Note that amounts externally restricted for contingencies do not have to meet the stabilization arrangement criteria on conditions for use to be reported as restricted fund balance.) The assets may be held by the SLG or by the trustee for the bondholders, depending on the agreement. In any event, *their purpose is to give bondholders additional assurance that they will be paid promptly—even if the SLG encounters financial difficulty—and that the bonds will not be allowed to go into default*. Such important contractual agreements must be observed by SLG officials, and compliance with these agreements should be examined by the internal auditor and must be examined by the external auditor.

Existence of such funded reserves also dictates that a Debt Service Fund—not the General Fund or a Special Revenue Fund—must be used to account for debt service for the debt issue. A DSF is required when "financial resources are being accumulated for principal and interest payments maturing in future years."[4]

Bond Ratings

Several private firms, including Standard & Poor's, Moody's, and Fitch Rating, may be retained by bond and other debt issuers to *rate debt issues on the certainty of the payments of interest and principal by the debtor*. These credit ratings are signified by letters and/or numerals: AAA is typically the best rating.

Higher-rated bonds and other debt securities command lower interest rates—and thus cost borrowers less interest—than lower-rated securities. In addition, investors in lower-rated securities may demand that the debtor maintain large funded reserves to ensure timely debt service payments. Finally, securities that are *not* rated high enough to be considered *investment grade* ("junk bonds") may *not* be purchased or held by many banks, insurance companies, and other investor firms.

Bond Insurance

Several private firms, including MBIA Inc., Financial Guaranty Insurance Company (FGIC), and AMBAC Financial Group, issue *insurance policies* that *guarantee timely payment* of bond and other debt principal and interest payments to investors. Bond issuers must pay premiums for such insurance, of course, but their bonds or other debt instruments are usually rated AAA and can be issued at lower interest costs than otherwise. Moreover, investors may not insist on large funded reserves being established for insured bonds or other insured debt instruments.

Bond insurance has become popular in recent years because governments issuing debt can often save more interest costs and funded reserve costs than the insurance premiums they must pay. In addition, some governments would not be able to issue debt securities at a reasonable cost without insuring their bonds or other debt securities.

---

[4]GASB *Codification*, sec. 1300.104.

Sources of Financing

The money for repaying long-term debt may come from numerous sources with varying legal restrictions. The typical source is *property taxes*. A special tax rate may be assessed for a single bond issue, or a total annual rate may be used, with the proceeds prorated to several debt issues. Legislative bodies may earmark a tax for a specified purpose, with a provision that the proceeds may be used for current operating expenditures, for capital outlay, or to repay debt incurred to finance the specified purpose. In such cases, the proceeds of the tax would be accounted for in a Special Revenue Fund; the portion of the proceeds allocated to debt service would be transferred to a Debt Service Fund.

Some SLGs levy a *sales tax*—in addition to or instead of a property tax—to service some of their general long-term debt. Also, general government special assessment debt service is typically financed from *special assessments* levied on benefited properties and interest charged on the unpaid assessments.

Still another method of providing for debt service is required by bond indentures or other contracts that specify that the debt shall be repaid out of "the first revenues accruing to the treasury." Such agreements *require the government to contribute the necessary amounts to the Debt Service Fund from the General Fund;* the obligation has first claim on the assets of the General Fund.

When a term bond issue is to be repaid through a fund in which resources are being accumulated to retire the principal at maturity, the assets of the fund will be invested in income-producing securities. Similarly, some serial bond Debt Service Funds have investable resources. The income from these securities—net of any arbitrage—constitutes still another form of Debt Service Fund revenue.

Finally, maturing bonds may be *refunded;* that is, they may be retired by either (1) exchanging new bonds for old ones, or (2) selling a new bond issue and using the proceeds to retire an old issue. The new bond issue constitutes the financing source in refunding transactions.

DSF Investments

The financial resources of DSFs are invested until such time as they are needed to pay maturing debt service. State laws and/or bond indenture requirements often specify the types of DSF investments that may be made, and such provisions must be complied with and audited for compliance.

The federal arbitrage regulations, discussed earlier, may also influence the SLG's Debt Service Fund investments. Recall that these federal arbitrage regulations generally limit the yield the SLG may earn when investing the proceeds of tax-exempt debt issues—and usually require that any excess be paid (rebated) to the U.S. Treasury. In turn, the U.S. Treasury makes available to SLGs a special type of investment security—known as State and Local Government Series (SLGS)—which yield rates of return sufficiently low that DSF investment portfolio earnings are acceptable under federal arbitrage regulations.

Most SLG Debt Service Fund investments are in certificates of deposit, U.S. Treasury bills, SLGS (pronounced "slugs"), or other high-grade debt securities. Investments are initially accounted for at cost, including any investment-related fees. Thereafter, investments are accounted for at fair value, as discussed in Chapter 5, unless they are exempt from the provisions of GASB *Statement No. 31.*

DSF Expenditure Recognition

Debt service payments are made routinely for three types of debt-related expenditures:

1. Interest on long-term debt outstanding
2. Retirement of debt principal as it matures
3. Fiscal agent fees charged by a bank or other institution for preparing and processing debt service checks, registering and reregistering bonds, and related services

Assuming a fiscal agent is used, a SLG typically issues only one annual or semi-annual check—to its fiscal agent—for all debt service expenditures for each bond issue.

As discussed in detail early in Chapter 6, GLTL debt service expenditures are usually *not* accrued at year end but are recorded as expenditures *when due* (i.e., when they mature and are due and payable). Several practical and conceptual reasons are the *basis for the when-due recording:*

1. *Most SLGs budget and appropriate on the basis of how much debt service must be paid during the year,* either directly to bondholders or through fiscal agents. Permitting SLGs to report debt service expenditures when due avoids a potential budgetary basis–GAAP basis difference that otherwise would have to be reported, explained, and reconciled in the governmental fund financial statements and notes.

2. *Few government budgets separate the bond interest*—the main potentially accruable debt service component—*from the bond principal payments and related fiscal agent fees.* Rather, they view the total required payments as the debt service expenditures.

3. *Many governments transfer resources from the General Fund or Special Revenue Funds to the Debt Service Fund(s) when debt service payments are due.* Thus, to accrue interest expenditures and liabilities in the Debt Service Fund prior to the debt service due date could cause an artificial fund balance deficit to be reported in the Debt Service Fund.

Although most SLGs recognize debt service expenditures on the when-due approach, recall that the GASB *Codification* provides this **option**: *If dedicated DSF* financial resources have been *provided during the current year for payment* of principal and interest *due in the first month of the following year,* the debt service expenditure and related liability *may be recognized* at year end in the Debt Service Fund and the debt principal amount removed from the GLTL accounts.

- If resources are held in another fund (other than a DSF), no accrual is permitted.
- If nondedicated resources are held in a DSF at the discretion of management, no accrual is permitted.[5]

This option has arisen because many SLGs budget and appropriate in this manner. *Note that under this option the entire next debt service payment would be recorded as a current year expenditure and liability.*

A SLG can combine the when-due approach and "if due early next year" option by using the former for most issues and using the latter for those issues that meet its criteria. However, each SLG should adopt appropriate debt service expenditure recognition policies and apply them consistently so that 12 months of debt service expenditures are reported in each fiscal year. Further, if the criteria for accrual option are met but the expenditures are not accrued, fund balance committed for the upcoming payment must be reported unless the resources are restricted.

DEBT SERVICE FUND FOR A SERIAL BOND ISSUE: CASE ILLUSTRATION

To illustrate the operation of a Debt Service Fund for a serial bond issue, assume that A Governmental Unit issued $1,000,000 of 5% Flores Park Serial Bonds at par on January 1, 20X1, to finance the purchase and development of a park. The bond indenture requires annual payments of $100,000 to retire the principal and additional amounts for annual payments of interest. The debt service requirements (principal and interest) are to be financed by a property tax levied for that purpose.

---

[5]Ibid., sec. 1500.111–112.

The bond indenture requires that a $150,000 funded and invested reserve for fiscal exigencies be accumulated—$80,000 in 20X1 and $70,000 in 20X2. The purpose of the funded reserve is to provide added assurance of timely payments to bondholders. The governing body of A Governmental Unit agreed to transfer those amounts from the General Fund to the Flores Park Serial Bonds Debt Service Fund.

The Third State Bank was retained as the bond registrar and paying agent (fiscal agent) for the Flores Park serial bond issue. The 20X1 fiscal agent fee will be $10,000.

The governing body of A Governmental Unit adopted the following budget for the Flores Park Serial Bonds Debt Service Fund for 20X1:

Estimated Revenues and Transfers In:

Property taxes	$162,000
Investment income	6,000
Transfer from General Fund	80,000
	248,000

Appropriations:

Bond principal retirement	100,000
Interest on bonds	50,000
Fiscal agent fees	10,000
	160,000
Budgeted increase in fund balance	$ 88,000

Furthermore, it ordered that the $80,000 transferred from the General Fund be invested to fund the required reserve for fiscal exigencies.

Illustrative Entries The following journal entries record the 20X1 transactions and events affecting the Flores Park Serial Bonds Debt Service Fund. (The nature of the transactions being recorded and the amounts involved are clear from the journal entry explanations and the recorded amounts; therefore, transaction descriptions are not stated separately before each entry.)

Entries during 20X1

(1)	ESTIMATED REVENUES—Property Taxes	$162,000	
	ESTIMATED REVENUES—Investment Income	6,000	
	ESTIMATED TRANSFER FROM GENERAL FUND	80,000	
	APPROPRIATIONS—Bond Principal Retirement		$100,000
	APPROPRIATIONS—Interest on Bonds		50,000
	APPROPRIATIONS—Fiscal Agent Fees		10,000
	BUDGETARY FUND BALANCE		88,000
	To record adopted 20X1 budget.		
(2)	Cash	$ 80,000	
	Other Financing Sources—Transfer from General Fund		$ 80,000
	To record transfer received.		
(3)	Investments	$ 80,000	
	Cash		$ 80,000
	To record purchase of investments to establish funded reserve required by bond indenture. (Note that restricted fund balance must be reported for this reserve.)		
(4)	Taxes Receivable—Current	$165,000	
	Allowance for Uncollectible Current Taxes		$ 3,000
	Revenues—Property Taxes		162,000
	To record property tax levy of $165,000. (Estimated uncollectible taxes are $3,000.)		

(5)	Cash	$158,000	
	Taxes Receivable—Current		$158,000

To record property tax collections.

(6)	Cash	$ 4,000	
	Revenues—Investment Income		$ 4,000

To record receipt of interest on investments.

(7)	Expenditures—Bond Principal Retirement	$100,000	
	Expenditures—Interest on Bonds	50,000	
	Expenditures—Fiscal Agent Fees	10,000	
	Matured Bonds Payable		$100,000
	Matured Interest Payable		50,000
	Fiscal Agent Fees Payable		10,000

To record liability for first annual serial bond maturity.

The bond principal is removed from the GLTL accounts when it matures:

$$GCA \quad - \quad GLTL \quad = \quad NA$$
$$-\$100,000 \quad +\$100,000$$

(8)	Matured Bonds Payable	$100,000	
	Matured Interest Payable	50,000	
	Fiscal Agent Fees Payable	10,000	
	Cash		$160,000

To record payment of matured debt service liabilities.

Note: Many governments pay the debt service to the paying agent several days before or upon its maturity. Therefore, in practice *entries (7) and (8) often are compounded* into one expenditures and cash disbursement entry.

(9a)	Taxes Receivable—Delinquent	$ 7,000	
	Allowance for Uncollectible Current Taxes	3,000	
	Taxes Receivable—Current		$ 7,000
	Allowance for Uncollectible Delinquent Taxes		3,000

To reclassify taxes receivable and related allowance accounts from current to delinquent.

(9b)	Revenues—Property Taxes	$ 2,000	
	Deferred Property Tax Revenue		$ 2,000

To record deferred inflows for the portion of the current levy not expected to be collected within the first 60 days of the next fiscal year (i.e., not considered available).

(10)	Investments	$ 300	
	Accrued Interest Receivable	2,700	
	Revenues—Investment Income		$ 3,000

To record net increase in fair value of investments and accrued interest on investments at year end.

Closing Entries—End of 20X1

(C1)	APPROPRIATIONS—Bond Principal Retirement	$100,000	
	APPROPRIATIONS—Interest on Bonds	50,000	
	APPROPRIATIONS—Fiscal Agent Fees	10,000	
	BUDGETARY FUND BALANCE	88,000	
	ESTIMATED REVENUES—Property Taxes		$162,000
	ESTIMATED REVENUES—Investment Income		6,000
	ESTIMATED TRANSFER FROM GENERAL FUND		80,000

To reverse budgetary entry.

(C2)	Revenues—Property Taxes............................	$160,000	
	Revenues—Investment Income....................	7,000	
	Other Financing Sources—Transfer from		
	General Fund...............................	80,000	
	Expenditures—Bond Principal Retirement........		$100,000
	Expenditures—Interest on Bonds...............		50,000
	Expenditures—Fiscal Agent Fees...............		10,000
	Fund Balance.................................		87,000
	To close operating accounts.		

Note that a single Investment Income account is used in these illustrative entries rather than the separate Interest on Investments and Net Increase (Decrease) in Fair Value of Investments accounts illustrated in Chapter 5. Although the more detailed approach would be preferable in accounting for large interest-bearing security investment portfolios, both methods are acceptable.

Financial Statements   Like other governmental funds, the annual financial statements required for Debt Service Funds are:

- Balance Sheet
- Statement of Revenues, Expenditures, and Changes in Fund Balance (GAAP operating statement)

A Statement of Revenues, Expenditures, and Changes in Fund Balance—Budget and Actual (budgetary comparison statement) may be prepared for internal use and/or publication in the annual financial report, but is not required by GAAP.

The balance sheet at the end of 20X1 for the Flores Park Serial Bonds Debt Service Fund is presented in Illustration 8-1. Its Statement of Revenues, Expenditures, and Changes in Fund Balance is presented in Illustration 8-2.

ILLUSTRATION 8-1   Serial Bonds Debt Service Fund Balance Sheet

A Governmental Unit
Flores Park Serial Bonds Debt Service Fund
Balance Sheet
December 31, 20X1

Assets

Cash...		$ 2,000
Taxes receivable—delinquent........................	$ 7,000	
Less: Allowance for uncollectible delinquent taxes.......	3,000	4,000
Investments.....................................		80,300
Accrued interest receivable.........................		2,700
Total assets.................................		$89,000

Deferred Inflows of Resources and Fund Balance

Deferred Inflows of Resources:		
Deferred property tax revenues.....................		$ 2,000
Fund Balance*:		
Restricted.......................................	$80,000	
Assigned.......................................	7,000	87,000
Total deferred inflows of resources and fund balance...		$89,000

*The classification of fund balance presumes that the resources transferred in from the General Fund are restricted for fiscal exigencies by the bond indenture, but that investment earnings are not restricted. Restricted resources are presumed to be used first, if available.

ILLUSTRATION 8-2	Serial Bonds Debt Service Fund Operating Statement

A Governmental Unit
Flores Park Serial Bonds Debt Service Fund
Statement of Revenues, Expenditures, and Changes in Fund Balance
For the Year Ended December 31, 20X1

Revenues:	
Property taxes	$160,000
Investment income	7,000
	167,000
Expenditures:	
Bond principal retirement	100,000
Interest on bonds	50,000
Fiscal agent fees	10,000
	160,000
Excess of Revenues over Expenditures	7,000
Other Financing Sources:	
Transfer from General Fund	80,000
Net Change in Fund Balance	87,000
Fund Balance—January 1	—
Fund Balance—December 31	$ 87,000

SPECIAL ASSESSMENT DEBT SERVICE FUNDS

One unique type of Debt Service Fund, referred to as a Special Assessment Debt Service Fund, is used to account for servicing general long-term debt issued to finance special assessment capital improvement projects. As noted in previous chapters, *a special assessment is, in substance, a special property tax levied on properties or property owners benefited by a particular capital project,* such as for streets and sidewalk construction in a new subdivision. The projects are referred to as special assessment projects because of the underlying financing source—the special assessments—and range in size from relatively small projects to very large ones.

In the typical special assessment project, the benefited area is made a special assessment district, and the local government serves as the general contractor and financing agent for the project. As the *general contractor,* the government oversees the project, arranges for the necessary engineering studies, prepares specifications for the project, and so on. As the *financing agent,* the government:

- Provides interim financing for construction. The government may issue its own bonds or notes or issue special assessment bonds or notes, which it typically guarantees.

- Levies assessments against the properties or property owners benefited upon completion, inspection, and approval of the project. Each property owner is billed for a proportionate share of the project costs but is allowed to pay in installments over a period of 5–10 years. The government charges interest on the unpaid assessment receivable balances.

- Bills and collects the special assessments and related interest.

- Services the general long-term debt associated with the project, using the special assessment collections. If the government is responsible for part of the cost of the project, some general government cash may be transferred to the Special Assessment Capital Projects Fund for this purpose as well.

The primary uniqueness of a Special Assessment Debt Service Fund is that most of the receivables that are not yet due are noncurrent. Indeed, the key differences between special assessments and property taxes are that special assessments are (1) levied at one point in time for amounts that are payable over several years, and (2) levied only on a subset of properties in a government's jurisdiction. Given the similarities, revenue accounting for special assessments follows the same principles as property taxes. Revenue is recognized when it is measurable, levied for the period or an earlier period, and available—i.e., collected by year end or within the revenue recognition cutoff period (not more than 60 days) thereafter.

- The long-term special assessments receivable is offset by *deferred revenues*—a deferred inflows of resources account.
- Any portion of current or delinquent special assessments receivable that does not meet the revenue recognition criteria will result in additional *deferred revenues*—and less revenues—being reported for a period.

Debt Service Funds are not used to account for debt service on all special assessment indebtedness. Enterprise-related special assessment indebtedness may be accounted for entirely in the appropriate Enterprise Fund if the government chooses to do so. Also, *if the government is not obligated in any manner on special assessment revenue debt:*

- The debt is not viewed as debt of the government.
- No Debt Service Fund is used, because the debt is not an obligation of the government.
- An Agency Fund is used to reflect the government's fiduciary responsibility as the fiscal agent for the special assessment district.

In most cases, governments are obligated in some manner for the debt issued to finance special assessment projects for their constituency. Indeed, in describing the intended breadth of this criterion, the GASB notes that:

> . . . the phrase "obligated in some manner" . . . is intended to include all situations other than those in which (a) the government is prohibited (by constitution, charter, statute, ordinance, or contract) from assuming the debt in the event of default by the property owner or (b) the government is not legally liable for assuming the debt and makes no statement, or gives no indication, that it will, or may, honor the debt in the event of default.[6]

Note that when a general government special assessment project is financed with special assessment debt for which the government is not obligated in any manner, the construction costs are still reported in a Capital Projects Fund. Accounting for the costs through a CPF is required because the capital asset will become the property of the government when completed. The primary difference in the Capital Projects Fund reporting under these circumstances is that instead of reporting an other financing source for proceeds from issuance of the special assessment indebtedness, revenues are reported for "Contributions from property owners."

Illustrative Entries

To illustrate, assume that A Governmental Unit financed a general government special assessment capital project by issuing special assessment bonds backed by its full faith and credit. The city will contribute $260,000 to be used for the first principal and interest payment on the special assessment bonds. The remaining costs are to be recovered through special assessments levied against benefited properties.

The par value of the five-year, 6%, special assessment bonds was $1,000,000 and the bonds were issued at par on July 1, 20X0. Interest and one-fifth of the principal are due each June 30, beginning June 30, 20X1. The project was completed during 20X0 at the budgeted cost of $1,000,000.

The bond issuance and the construction phase of the project would be accounted for like any other major general government capital project—in a

---

[6]Ibid., sec. S40.115.

Capital Projects Fund. The capital assets constructed would be recorded in the General Capital Assets accounts, and the bonds payable would be recorded in the General Long-Term Liabilities accounts.

The following transactions are used to illustrate the accounting and reporting for the Special Assessment Debt Service Fund. *Budgetary entries are omitted* to focus on the entries for the actual transactions and events.

1. Special assessments of $800,000 were levied on benefited properties upon completion of the project on **December 31, 20X0**. One-fourth of the levy, along with 7.5% interest on the beginning uncollected balance, is due each of the next four years beginning December 31, 20X1.

Assessments Receivable—Noncurrent	$800,000	
Deferred Revenues—Assessments.		$800,000
To record levy of special assessments.		

Note that the Special Assessment DSF financial statements at December 31, 20X0, would consist only of a balance sheet reporting the accounts and amounts from the preceding entry. Recall that deferred revenues—recognized in governmental funds primarily when revenue recognition is delayed because revenues are not available or because of time requirements—are reported as deferred inflows of resources.

The following transactions occurred in 20X1:

2. $200,000 of special assessments became current in 20X1.

Assessments Receivable—Current.	$200,000	
Assessments Receivable—Noncurrent		$200,000
To reclassify deferred assessments that are due in 20X1.		

Deferred Revenues—Assessments.	$200,000	
Revenues—Assessments		$200,000
To recognize assessment revenues for current assessments.		

   Note that this entry assumes that the $200,000 is *available*—that is, will be collected by year end or within 60 days thereafter.

3. A $260,000 transfer is received from the General Fund.

Cash	$260,000	
Other Financing Sources—Transfer from		
General Fund		$260,000
To record receipt of General Fund transfer.		

4. The principal and interest on the special assessment bonds matured and were paid.

Expenditures—Principal Retirement.	$200,000	
Expenditures—Interest	60,000	
Cash.		$260,000
To record payment of debt service.		

   The principal retirement is reflected in the GLTL accounts as follows:

GCA	−	GLTL	=	NA
		−$200,000		+$200,000

5. Special assessment collections included $185,000 principal and $55,000 interest.

Cash	$240,000	
Assessments Receivable—Current.		$185,000
Revenues—Interest		55,000
To record collections during 20X1.		

6. The uncollected assessments receivable that were due in 20X1 were reclassified as delinquent, and the uncollected interest ($5,000) was accrued. It is expected that all amounts except $1,500 of interest will be collected within the first 60 days of 20X2.[7]

Assessments Receivable—Delinquent.....................	$ 15,000	
Accrued Interest Receivable...........................	5,000	
Assessments Receivable—Current.....................		$ 15,000
Revenues—Interest		3,500
Deferred Revenues—Interest.......................		1,500

To accrue interest receivable and reclassify assessment receivables.

Note that interest expenditures are not accrued because the debt is GLTL.

7. The accounts were closed.

Revenues—Assessments	$200,000	
Revenues—Interest	58,500	
Other Financing Sources—Transfer from General Fund......	260,000	
Expenditures—Principal Retirement....................		$200,000
Expenditures—Interest		60,000
Fund Balance.....................................		258,500

To close the accounts at the end of 20X1.

Illustrative Financial Statements

The balance sheet for the Special Assessment Bonds Debt Service Fund of A Governmental Unit at the end of 20X1 is presented in Illustration 8-3. The 20X1 Statement of Revenues, Expenditures, and Changes in Fund Balance is presented in Illustration 8-4. The balance sheet continues to be quite simple, as in the serial bond example, though it is complicated somewhat by the reporting of the special assessments receivable and deferred revenues. Note that only the assessments that meet the property tax revenue recognition criteria are reported as revenues in the operating statement.

ILLUSTRATION 8-3   Special Assessment Debt Service Fund Balance Sheet

A Governmental Unit
Special Assessment Bonds Debt Service Fund
Balance Sheet
December 31, 20X1

Assets

Cash	$240,000
Special assessments receivable—noncurrent.....................	600,000
Special assessments receivable—delinquent	15,000
Interest receivable on assessments	5,000
Total assets	$860,000

Deferred Inflows of Resources and Fund Balance

Deferred Inflows of Resources:	
Deferred assessment revenues	$600,000
Deferred interest revenues	1,500
Total deferred inflows of resources	601,500
Restricted fund balance	258,500
Total deferred inflows of resources and fund balance..........	$860,000

---

[7]Because governments generally do not issue their financial statements until 4 to 6 months after year end, the amount collected during this period will be known, not estimated, in practice.

ILLUSTRATION 8-4   Special Assessment Debt Service Fund Operating Statement

A Governmental Unit
Special Assessment Bonds Debt Service Fund
Statement of Revenues, Expenditures, and Changes in Fund Balance
For the Year Ended December 31, 20X1

Revenues:		
Special assessments	$200,000	
Interest	58,500	$258,500
Expenditures:		
Principal retirement	200,000	
Interest	60,000	260,000
Excess of Expenditures over Revenues		(1,500)
Other Financing Sources:		
Transfer from General Fund		260,000
Net Change in Fund Balance		258,500
Fund Balance—January 1		—
Fund Balance—December 31		$258,500

OTHER CONVENTIONAL DEBT SERVICE FUND CONSIDERATIONS

Several other accounting and reporting considerations should be noted or reviewed briefly at this point: (1) nonaccrual of interest payable, (2) the combining DSF balance sheet, and (3) the combining DSF operating statement.

Nonaccrual of Interest

Recall that the GASB *Codification* does *not permit*—much less require—*accrual* of the year-end balances of unmatured interest payable on conventional bonds or other general long-term debt *unless*

1. *dedicated* resources to pay the interest have been *received in* a *Debt Service Fund by year end, and*

2. the debt service payment is *due in the first month* of the next year.

If a fund is on a calendar-year basis and the annual interest on its bonds was paid as scheduled on October 31, 20X1, the government clearly would be obligated, as of December 31, 20X1, for the interest for the last two months of 20X1. On the other hand, the 20X1 tax levy and budget would typically provide for the payment of the interest expenditure falling due in the current year, and the following year's tax levy and budget would provide for payment of interest due in 20X2. Because the resources that will be used to pay the interest for the months of November and December 20X1 cannot be accrued as of December 31, 20X1, accruing that interest expenditure and liability could result in (1) an unwarranted deficit being reported in serial bond Debt Service Funds, and (2) an unwarranted fund balance deficiency being reported in term bond Debt Service Funds. Thus, interest payable at year end typically is not recorded in Debt Service Funds.

Combining Balance Sheet

Separate balance sheets are prepared for each of the Debt Service Funds of A Governmental Unit, as in Illustrations 8-1 and 8-3, and may be sent to bond trustees. But a government with two or more funds may present them in a combining balance sheet, as shown in Illustration 8-5.

Debt Service Fund balance sheets might include such additional assets as Cash with Fiscal Agents, Taxes Receivable—Current, Tax Liens Receivable, and Interest and Penalties Receivable on Taxes. In addition, the unamortized premiums and discounts on investments not reported at fair value may be presented

ILLUSTRATION 8-5 Debt Service Funds Combining Balance Sheet

A Governmental Unit
Debt Service Funds
Combining Balance Sheet
December 31, 20X1

	Flores Park Serial Bonds	Special Assessment Bonds	Total
Assets			
Cash.	$ 2,000	$240,000	$242,000
Special assessments receivable—noncurrent	—	600,000	600,000
Special assessments receivable—delinquent	—	15,000	15,000
Taxes receivable—delinquent (net of estimated uncollectible taxes)	4,000	—	4,000
Investments	80,300	—	80,300
Interest receivable on investments	2,700	—	2,700
Interest receivable on assessments	—	5,000	5,000
Total assets	$89,000	$860,000	$949,000
Deferred Inflows of Resources and Fund Balances			
Deferred Inflows of Resources:			
Deferred property tax revenues.	$ 2,000	$ —	$ 2,000
Deferred assessment revenues.	—	600,000	600,000
Deferred interest revenues.	—	1,500	1,500
Total deferred inflows of resources	2,000	601,500	603,500
Fund Balance:			
Restricted	80,000	258,500	338,500
Assigned	7,000	—	7,000
Total fund balances	87,000	258,500	345,500
Total deferred inflows of resources and fund balance	$89,000	$860,000	$949,000

separately in the combining balance sheet rather than the investments being reported at net amortized cost. Similarly, liability accounts such as Matured Bonds Payable and Matured Interest Payable may be used.

Combining Operating Statement

A Combining Statement of Revenues, Expenditures, and Changes in Fund Balances for the Debt Service Funds of A Governmental Unit is presented in Illustration 8-6.

Additional revenue accounts that might appear in the statement include Interest and Penalties on Property Taxes; Revenue from Other Agencies, such as shared taxes from more senior-level governments; and Gains or Losses on Sales of Investments. Also, additional transfers may have increased the fund balance during the period.

DEBT SERVICE FUND FOR A TERM BOND ISSUE

Although most recent bond issues have been serial issues, term debt issues are found occasionally in practice. Term bond issues differ from serial issues in that, whereas some serial bond principal matures each year (or most years)—and, thus, some serial bond principal is paid each year, together with interest on the remaining outstanding principal balance—the entire principal of a term bond issue matures at the end of the bond issue term, say, 20 years. *Thus, with term bond issues, (1) interest is paid on the entire principal (par or face) balance throughout the life of the issue, and (2) all of the principal is paid at the end of the bond issue term.*

ILLUSTRATION 8-6 Debt Service Funds Combining Operating Statement

A Governmental Unit
Debt Service Funds
Combining Statement of Revenues, Expenditures, and Changes in Fund Balances
For the Year Ended December 31, 20X1

	Flores Park Serial Bonds	Special Assessment Bonds	Total
Revenues:			
Property taxes	$160,000	$ —	$160,000
Special assessments	—	200,000	200,000
Investment income	7,000	—	7,000
Interest on assessments	—	58,500	58,500
	167,000	258,500	425,500
Expenditures:			
Bond principal retirement	100,000	200,000	300,000
Interest on bonds	50,000	60,000	110,000
Fiscal agent fees	10,000	—	10,000
	160,000	260,000	420,000
Excess of revenues over (under) expenditures	7,000	(1,500)	5,500
Other Financing Sources:			
Transfer from General Fund	80,000	260,000	340,000
Net Change in Fund Balances	87,000	258,500	345,500
Fund Balances—January 1	—	—	—
Fund Balances—December 31	$ 87,000	$258,500	$345,500

To ensure timely payment of term bond interest and principal (at maturity), most term bond issue indentures require the issuing government to establish a Debt Service Fund that provides for:

1. Accumulation of any required funded reserves.
2. Payment of interest (and fiscal agent charges) during each year the term bonds are outstanding.
3. Systematic accumulation of a sinking fund (savings subfund) within the Debt Service Fund that will be sufficient to retire the term bond principal upon its maturity at the end of the bond issue term.

Because of the sinking fund provision, term Debt Service Funds are often referred to as *sinking funds*.

Deep discount bonds differ from traditional term bonds in that neither principal nor interest payments are made during the term of the bonds, although in some cases a relatively minor portion of the effective interest is paid. Rather, the compound unpaid interest for the term of the bonds, as well as the principal, must be paid upon maturity of the deep discount bonds. Clearly, the debt service sinking fund for a deep discount debt issue must accumulate more financial resources than the traditional term DSF sinking fund. However, the sinking fund concept and approach are the same for both traditional term bonds and deep discount bonds. Deep discount debt accounting and financial reporting are discussed further later in this chapter.

The sinking fund assets and funded reserves may be held and invested by the issuing government or by a trustee for the bondholders, depending on terms of the bond issue indenture. In either event, the *sinking fund requirements must be computed at the origination of the issue, and both term bond and deep discount bond Debt Service Funds must be maintained in compliance with the bond indenture provisions throughout the life of the issue.* This makes the net position of the fund, up to the required balance, externally restricted.

SINKING FUND REQUIREMENTS

As noted earlier, term bonds are ordinarily repaid from a debt service sinking (savings) fund in which resources are accumulated over the life of the bonds by means of annual additions to the fund and by earnings on the fund assets. A schedule of sinking fund requirements (Illustration 8-7) has been prepared for the city hall bonds of A Governmental Unit. These are 9%, 20-year term bonds, $1,000,000 par, issued January 1, 20X0, to be repaid out of the first revenues accruing to the treasury. Recall that the latter terminology indicates that the source of financing for the Debt Service Fund for these bonds is the General Fund of A Governmental Unit.

The first payment to the sinking fund is scheduled for the end of year 1 (20X0). A similar payment will be made at the end of each succeeding year until, when the twentieth payment has been made, fund resources should total $1,000,000—the amount required to pay the term bond principal upon its maturity.

For illustrative purposes, an estimated earnings rate of 10% was used in developing Illustration 8-7. The amount of the required annual additions was determined by selecting from a table the amount of an ordinary annuity of $1 per period at 10% for 20 periods. As indicated in the schedule, the last addition is somewhat less than the preceding ones because of rounding errors. In any event, the final

---

ILLUSTRATION 8-7 Schedule of Sinking Fund Requirements

Schedule of Sinking Fund Requirements
$1,000,000, 20-Year Term Bond Issue
(Assuming an Annual Earnings Rate of 10%)

Year	(1) Required Annual Additions	(2) Required Fund Earnings (4PY) × 10%	(3) Required Fund Increases (1) + (2)	(4) Required Fund Balances (3) + (4PY)
1 (20X0)	$ 17,460		$ 17,460	$ 17,460
2 (20X1)	17,460	$ 1,746	19,206	36,666
3 (20X2)	17,460	3,667	21,127	57,793
4 (20X3)	17,460	5,779	23,239	81,032
5 (20X4)	17,460	8,103	25,563	106,595
6 (20X5)	17,460	10,660	28,120	134,715
7 (20X6)	17,460	13,472	30,932	165,647
8 (20X7)	17,460	16,565	34,025	199,672
9 (20X8)	17,460	19,967	37,427	237,099
10 (20X9)	17,460	23,710	41,170	278,269
11 (20Y0)	17,460	27,827	45,287	323,556
12 (20Y1)	17,460	32,356	49,816	373,372
13 (20Y2)	17,460	37,337	54,797	428,169
14 (20Y3)	17,460	42,817	60,277	488,446
15 (20Y4)	17,460	48,845	66,305	554,751
16 (20Y5)	17,460	55,475	72,935	627,686
17 (20Y6)	17,460	62,769	80,229	707,915
18 (20Y7)	17,460	70,792	88,252	796,167
19 (20Y8)	17,460	79,617	97,077	893,244
20 (20Y9)	17,432*	89,324	106,756	1,000,000
	$349,172	$650,828	$1,000,000	

*The last year's addition has to be only $17,432 because of rounding errors.
PY = Prior year-end required fund balance.

payment in 20Y9 will be in the amount that brings the sinking fund resources to the $1,000,000 required to retire the term bonds.

The schedule of sinking fund requirements provides the amounts of the budgetary requirements for the DSF for the duration of the fund, provided the accumulation process proceeds as planned or departs from the plan by immaterial amounts. *The required fund balance at the end of each year (as shown in Illustration 8-7) provides a standard against which the actual accumulation may be compared—and it may be a required minimum amount under the terms of the bond indenture.*

The primary uniqueness in reporting term debt service funds is the need to report restricted fund balance equal to the required balance of accumulated net assets at the end of each fiscal year. If the fund balance is less than that required by the bond indenture, this fact should be disclosed in the notes to the financial statements as it violates a contractual obligation. Failure to maintain the required fund balance may violate the bond issue covenants and—if not waived (permitted) by the bond trustee—could cause the bond issue to be in default and the entire principal balance to become due immediately. Thus, compliance with bond indenture provisions must be monitored closely by internal managers and auditors and examined by external auditors.

DEBT SERVICE FUNDS FOR DEEP DISCOUNT ISSUES

Although most state and local government bond and note issues are conventional serial or term issues, some issues are nonconventional deep discount bonds and notes. The pure deep discount issue—the *zero coupon bond*—has a 0% stated interest rate and provides that neither interest nor principal will be paid while the bond issue is outstanding. Rather, *both the principal and accumulated interest, compounded at the effective rate for the life of the bonds—typically ranging from 10 to 25 years—are paid in a lump-sum payment of the par (face) amount upon maturity of the zero coupon bonds.* Thus, zero coupon bonds are like term bonds except that the total compound interest for the term of the bond—as well as the principal—is included in the single balloon payment of the par (face) amount upon maturity of the bonds.

A variation of the pure zero coupon deep discount bond, the *low-interest bond,* may bear an interest rate of 1% to 2% when the market rate—the effective interest rate at which the bonds are issued (at a significant discount)—is 6% to 8%.

Both zero coupon bonds and low-interest bonds and notes are discounted from issuance until maturity at the effective interest rate by investors, so their issue proceeds are only a fraction of their par (face) value. The discount from par (face) thus represents the interest (or additional interest) on the bonds that will not be paid until their maturity.

Deep discount bonds and notes are generally defined as those issued with a stated (or face) interest rate less than 75% of the effective interest rate. Such deep discount debt issued as general long-term debt presents debt service accounting problems because either (1) fund liabilities are not incurred until the maturity of the debt, or (2) the fund liabilities incurred on low-interest debt are not a reasonable measure of the interest cost of such debt issues.

The GASB *Codification* does *not* contain special guidance on governmental fund accounting for deep discount bond and note issues. Thus, governments with deep discount debt *should recognize debt service expenditures and liabilities on such debt—for both interest and principal retirement—on the "when due" or "due early next year" approaches* discussed and illustrated earlier for conventional interest-bearing (at market rates) bonds and notes. The result is that most or all of the interest expenditures—as well as the principal retirement expenditures—are reported in the year the deep discount debt matures, perhaps 15 to 25 years after issuance of the debt instrument. The bond liability is reported in the government-wide balance sheet at the accreted amount—i.e., at the present value at the balance sheet date of the remaining payments (in the case of zero coupon bonds, the single payment of the face amount at maturity) discounted at the effective rate of interest at issuance.

REFUNDINGS

The term and serial Debt Service Fund examples presented earlier in the chapter are based on the following usual assumptions of conventional Debt Service Funds, that during the life of the debt issue:

1. Financial resources are accumulated in DSFs from non-GLTL sources—such as property taxes, special assessments, interest earned on investments, and interfund transfers.

2. DSF financial resources are expended to pay GLTL principal and interest at their scheduled maturities.

3. The payments or accruals of GLTL principal and interest from non-GLTL financial resources as they mature are reported in accounts such as Expenditures—Bond Principal Retirement to reflect the extinguishment of the GLTL principal, and Expenditures—Interest on Bonds.

But governments may issue *new* GLTLs to pay (or service) *old* GLTLs either at or prior to their maturity—thus effectively substituting the new GLTL issue for the old GLTL issue. Accordingly, such transactions—known as ***advance refundings***—are accounted for as *substitutions* of GLTL rather than as *extinguishments* of GLTL.

Reasons for Refundings   State and local governments may issue new debt to refund old debt for a variety of reasons, including:

1. **Lower effective interest rates.** The SLG may be able to issue new bonds or notes at interest rates sufficiently lower than those being paid on the old bonds or notes so that—even after paying the related refunding costs—it obtains lower net effective interest rates (and costs) and thus has an *economic gain* as a result of the advance refunding.

2. **Extend maturity dates.** When old debt principal matures soon, perhaps without adequate financial resources having been accumulated, the SLG may effectively extend the maturity date of the old debt by a refunding.

3. **Revise payment schedules.** If the total debt service requirements—including both interest and principal—of the old debt are not relatively stable for each future year, the SLG may effectively rearrange its debt service payment schedule by an advance refunding.

4. **Remove or modify restrictions.** Onerous restrictions of old debt indentures, covenants, or other agreements—such as those requiring large funded reserves or specifying that no (or limited) new debt may be incurred while the old debt is outstanding—may be removed or modified by issuing new advance refunding debt with different indenture provisions.

In sum, certain refundings are undertaken to obtain an economic advantage—such as lower net effective interest rates and interest costs—but other refundings are designed to obtain noneconomic advantages, to extend maturity dates, revise debt service payment schedules, and remove or modify debt-related restrictions.

Refundings Defined   The GASB states that:

> **Refundings** involve the issuance of new debt whose proceeds are used to repay previously issued ("old") debt. The new debt proceeds may be used to repay the old debt immediately (a ***current refunding***); or the new debt proceeds may be placed with an escrow agent and invested until they are used to pay principal and interest on an old debt at a future time (an ***advance refunding***).[8]

Both types of refundings are depicted in Illustration 8-8.

In some advance refundings, the SLG uses the proceeds of the new GLTL issue to retire the old GLTL issue directly within a few weeks or months. This may occur, for example, when the new GLTL is issued to refund an old term bond or deep discount note that matures soon but for which adequate resources have not been accumulated in a DSF sinking fund. These refundings are similar to *current refundings,* which are accounted for as new debt issuances and old debt retirements, as shown in Illustration 8-8 [A].

---

[8]Ibid., sec. D20.102. (Emphasis added.)

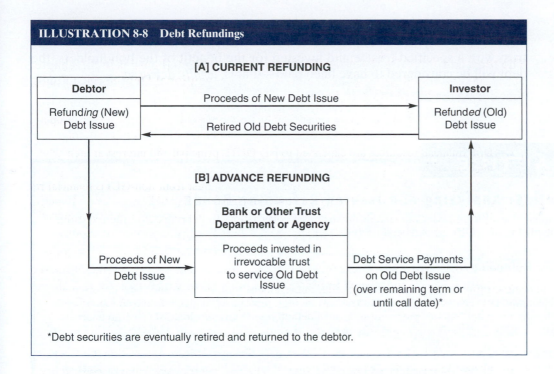

ILLUSTRATION 8-8   Debt Refundings

[A] CURRENT REFUNDING

Debtor		Investor
	Proceeds of New Debt Issue →	
Refund*ing* (New) Debt Issue	← Retired Old Debt Securities	Refund*ed* (Old) Debt Issue

[B] ADVANCE REFUNDING

Bank or Other Trust Department or Agency

Proceeds of New Debt Issue → Proceeds invested in irrevocable trust to service Old Debt Issue

Debt Service Payments on Old Debt Issue (over remaining term or until call date)*

*Debt securities are eventually retired and returned to the debtor.

Advance refundings (Illustration 8-8 [B]) do not result in immediate, direct retirement of the old GLTL issue, however. Rather, *in advance refunding transactions:*

1. The proceeds of the new GLTL issue are placed in *escrow—*in an *irrevocable trust—*with a bank or other financial institution trust department for the benefit of the old GLTL investors-creditors.

2. The proceeds are invested in appropriate securities that are acceptable under the terms of the old GLTL issue indenture, covenant, or other agreement and in compliance with applicable federal arbitrage and other regulations.

3. The invested proceeds and related earnings are used to pay interest and principal on the old debt—which remains outstanding—at the regularly scheduled maturities or, if the old debt is called for early redemption, until (and at) the call date.

Defeasance of Debt

The term *defeased* means "terminated" or "rendered null and void." *Debt that has been defeased is considered to be extinguished, is removed from the GLTL accounts, and is not reported in the SLG's balance sheet.*

In conventional serial and term Debt Service Funds, the debt is defeased by being paid off directly at its scheduled maturity. An expenditures account such as Expenditures—Debt Principal Retirement is recorded in the DSF, the liability is removed from the GLTL accounts, the debt instrument is marked "paid" and canceled, and the debt is no longer reported in the balance sheet.

In advance refundings it may not be possible or advantageous to actually pay off the old debt with the proceeds of the new substitute debt. Instead, the old debt may remain outstanding for much or all of its originally scheduled life and be serviced by the resources of an *irrevocable trust* financed (entirely or partly) by the proceeds of the new refunding debt issue. In such cases the old debt is considered to be extinguished—and is removed from the GLTL accounts and the SLG's balance sheet—if it is either *legally defeased* or *defeased in substance.* If defeasance is not achieved, both the old and the new debt—as well as the assets set aside for servicing the old debt—must be reported by the government.

Legal Defeasance

In law, a debt may be considered defeased—terminated and rendered null and void—by being legally defeased when the debtor fulfills the defeasance provisions of the debt indenture or other agreement. *Defeasance provisions of bond indentures* may specify, for example, that if a sufficient sum is placed in an irrevocable trust with a specified trustee and invested for the benefit of the bondholders, the debt will be considered to have been paid—that is, *legally defeased*.

8-1 IN PRACTICE

GFOA Best Practice: Analyzing and Issuing Refunding Bonds

Advance refundings can yield significant savings or significant costs to a government. In February 2011 the Executive Board of the Government Finance Officers Association (GFOA) approved a Best Practice report on refundings. Excerpts appear here.

Analyzing an Advance Refunding

Background. Bond refinancing ("refunding") is an important debt management tool for state and local government issuers. Refundings are commonly executed to achieve interest cost savings, remove or change burdensome bond covenants, or restructure the stream of debt service payments to avoid a default or, in extreme circumstances, an unacceptable tax or rate increase.

Recommendation. At the outset of evaluating each refunding, the Government Finance Officers Association (GFOA) encourages issuers to solicit the advice of their bond counsel and financial advisor in order to outline key legal and financial issues.

There are three key concepts that must be taken into consideration when evaluating a refunding candidate:

1. Financial and Policy Objectives
2. Financial Savings / Results
3. Bond Structure and Escrow Efficiency . . .

Financial Savings / Results—The GFOA recommends that issuers develop formal policy guidelines in their debt management policies to provide a financial framework for decision makers regarding the evaluation of refunding candidates. Formal policy guidelines

- offer a systematic approach for determining if a refunding is cost-effective,
- promote consistency with other financial goals and objectives,
- provide the justification for decisions on when to undertake a refunding,
- ensure that staff time is not consumed unnecessarily in evaluating refunding proposals,
- ensure that some minimum level of cost savings is achieved, and
- reduce the possibility that further savings could have been achieved by deferring the sale of refunding bonds to a later date.

If a refunding is undertaken to achieve cost savings, the issuer should evaluate

- issuance costs that will be incurred and the interest rate at which the refunding bonds can be issued,
- the maturity date of the refunded bonds,
- call date of the refunded bonds,
- call premium on the refunded bonds,
- structure and yield of the refunding escrow, and
- any transferred proceeds penalty.

One test often used by issuers to assess the appropriateness of a refunding is the requirement specifying the achievement of a minimum net present (NPV) value savings. A common threshold is that the savings (net of all issuance costs and any cash contribution to the refunding), as a percentage of the refunding bonds, should be at least 3–5 percent. This test can be applied to the entire issue or on a maturity-by-maturity basis. In addition, issuers may establish a minimum dollar threshold (e.g., $100,000 or $1 million NPV savings).

It is important to note that federal tax law typically permits an issuer to conduct one advance refunding over the life of a bond issue. As such, an issuer must take greater care (i.e., require a higher savings threshold) when evaluating an advance refunding candidate.

In certain circumstances, lower savings thresholds may be justified. For example, when the advance refunding is being conducted primarily for policy reasons (other than economic savings), interest rates are at historically low levels or the time remaining to maturity is limited, and as such, future opportunities to achieve greater savings are not likely to occur.

In-Substance Defeasance

Not all bond and note agreements contain defeasance provisions. Indeed, many agreements are silent; that is, they do not contain provisions that permit legal defeasance. The GASB has established highly restrictive and specific standards for in-substance defeasance.[9] If the conditions of these in-substance defeasance standards are met in an advance refunding or otherwise, the old debt is considered to be *defeased in substance*—for accounting and financial reporting purposes—even though a legal defeasance has not occurred. Accordingly, the old debt is removed from the GLTL accounts and from the SLG's balance sheet as in a legal defeasance.

Nondefeasance

Most advance refundings are carefully planned and conducted to result in either legal defeasance or in-substance defeasance of the old debt. However, in the event that the old debt is not defeased legally or in substance, (1) both the old debt and the new debt must be recorded in the GLTL accounts and reported as liabilities in the SLG's government-wide statement of net position, and (2) amounts deposited in escrow (trust) are reported as investments in a Debt Service Fund.

DEBT SERVICE FUNDS FOR REFUNDINGS

Debt Service Funds for refundings that result in retirement or defeasance of the old debt are usually simple and short-lived. Indeed, they may involve only two transaction entries—one for the receipt of the refunding bond proceeds and another for the payment to the escrow trustee—and, after a closing entry, be terminated.

The accounting for refunding DSFs also differs from that for conventional serial and term DSFs. In refunding DSFs, the defeasance of the old debt is not considered an extinguishment but a *substitution* of the new debt for the old debt. Thus, unlike the payment of bond principal in a conventional serial or term DSF, which is reported as Expenditures—Bond Principal Retirement, the defeasance of the old debt in a GLTL refunding is recorded as an Other Financing Use. In other words, *debt principal retirement or defeasance is accounted for as an expenditure only if the payment is not financed by financial resources raised by issuing new GLTL.* **Debt principal retirement or defeasance that is financed by issuing new GLTL is accounted for as an** Other Financing Use to signal that new debt has been substituted for old debt.

The relationship between the source(s) of financial resources for retirement or defeasance of general long-term liabilities and the reporting of the retirement or defeasance payment is illustrated in Illustration 8-9. Note in Illustration 8-9 that the only factor determining if amounts paid for debt retirements or defeasances are reported as other financing uses or as expenditures is whether the payments are financed with borrowed resources (refundings) or other (existing) resources.

To emphasize this point further, Illustration 8-10 shows how a government should report a $1,000,000 payment to retire or defease outstanding debt given several different scenarios. Note that only differences in the first two columns (the sources of the resources) result in changes in the division of the payment between Other Financing Uses and Expenditures.

Three types of refunding transactions are discussed and illustrated in this section. These transactions involve (1) retirement of the old issue (current refunding), (2) legal or in-substance defeasance of the old issue (advance refunding), and (3) use of both existing financial resources and new debt proceeds to effect an advance refunding.

---

[9]Ibid., sec. D20. To achieve defeasance paragraph D20.103 requires that (1) the debtor must irrevocably place cash or other assets with an escrow agent in a trust, (2) the sole use of the trust is to satisfy scheduled principal and interest, (3) the noncash assets are limited to monetary assets that are risk-free as to the amount, timing, and collection of interest and principal—and are denominated in the same currency as the debt. The maturities of the noncash monetary assets must match the scheduled maturities of principal and interest on the debt such that cash is always available for debt service payments when scheduled. For debt denominated in U.S. dollars, the list of acceptable investments of the trust are limited to certain U.S. government or U.S. government-backed securities.

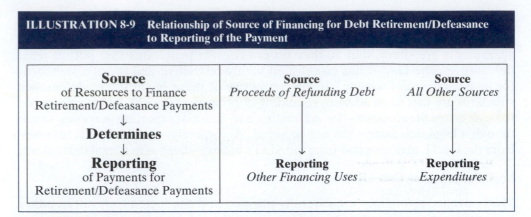

ILLUSTRATION 8-9 Relationship of Source of Financing for Debt Retirement/Defeasance to Reporting of the Payment

ILLUSTRATION 8-10 Classification of Debt Retirement and Defeasance as Other Financing Uses vs. Expenditures

Portion of Payment from		Carrying Amount of Debt Retired or Defeased in Substance	Amount Reported as	
Borrowed Resources	Other Resources		Other Financing Uses	Expenditures
$1,000,000	—	$1,000,000	*$1,000,000*	—
1,000,000	—	900,000	*1,000,000*	—
1,000,000	—	1,100,000	*1,000,000*	—
$ 800,000	*$ 200,000*	$1,000,000	*$ 800,000*	$ 200,000
800,000	200,000	900,000	*800,000*	200,000
800,000	200,000	1,100,000	*800,000*	200,000
$ 600,000	*$ 400,000*	$1,000,000	*$ 600,000*	$ 400,000
600,000	400,000	900,000	*600,000*	400,000
600,000	400,000	1,100,000	*600,000*	400,000
—	$1,000,000	$1,000,000	—	$1,000,000
—	1,000,000	900,000	—	1,000,000
—	1,000,000	1,100,000	—	1,000,000

Current Refunding A government may not have accumulated sufficient sinking fund resources to retire a term bond upon its impending maturity. Thus, it may issue new current refunding bonds (or notes) to pay the maturing term bond principal—effectively *refinancing* the term bond to extend its debt service over the life of the new refunding issue.

To illustrate, assume that a $2,000,000 term bond issue will mature soon. Assume also that the SLG has already paid the $55,000 interest due upon maturity of the term bonds and will refund the principal of the term bonds by issuing $2,000,000 of refunding bonds. If the new refunding bonds are issued at 101, bond issue costs of $15,000 are withheld by the bond underwriter, and the old term bonds are retired at par (face) before or upon maturity, the DSF General Ledger entries for these current refunding transactions are:

Issuance of Refunding Bonds:

Cash	$2,005,000	
Expenditures—Bond Issue Costs	15,000	
Other Financing Sources—**Refunding Bonds (Face)**		$2,000,000
Other Financing Sources—**Refunding Bond Premium**		20,000
To record issuance of advance refunding bonds.		

The refunding bonds payable and related premium must be recorded in the GCA-GLTL accounts to reflect the following:

GCA	−	GLTL	=	NP
		+$2,000,000		−$2,020,000
		(Refunding		
		Bonds Payable)		
		+$20,000		
		(Premium on		
		Refunding Bonds)		

Retirement of Old Bonds:
Other Financing Uses—Retirement of Refunded
    Term Bonds $2,000,000
  Cash $2,000,000
  To record payment of term bond principal before or upon
    its maturity.

The old term bond debt will be removed from the GLTL accounts as follows:

GCA	−	GLTL	=	NP
		−$2,000,000		+$2,000,000
		(Term Bonds Payable)		

When the $5,000 remaining fund balance has been disposed of—probably by transfer to the DSF for the new debt—the final closing entry will be made, and the term bond principal refunding DSF will be terminated.

To illustrate DSF accounting for the legal and in-substance defeasance of an old debt, assume the same facts as noted earlier except: **Advance Refunding**

1. The new advance refunding bonds ($2,000,000) were issued at a discount of $85,000, and $15,000 of bond issuance costs were withheld by the bond underwriter.

2. The old term bonds mature several years hence, and the amount necessary to be invested at this time to service them, $1,900,000, was placed in an escrow trust that was properly invested in accordance with the bond indenture defeasance provisions of the GASB's in-substance defeasance standards.

The DSF entries to record this legal or in-substance defeasance are:

Issuance of Refunding Bonds:
  Cash $1,900,000
  Other Financing Uses—Refunding Bond Discount   85,000
  Expenditures—Bond Issue Costs   15,000
    Other Financing Sources—Refunding Bonds (Face) . . $2,000,000
  To record issuance of advance refunding bonds.

The impact on the GCA-GLTL is:

GCA	−	GLTL	=	NP
		+$2,000,000		−$1,915,000
		(Refunding		
		Bonds Payable)		
		−$85,000		
		(Discount on		
		Refunding Bonds)		

Defeasance of Old Bonds:
Other Financing Uses—Payment to Refunded Bond
    Escrow Agent $1,900,000
  Cash $1,900,000
  To record payment to escrow agent to defease old bonds.

The impact on the GCA-GLTL accounts is the same as the previous example:

$$\begin{array}{ccccc} \text{GCA} & - & \text{GLTL} & = & \text{NP} \\ & & -\$2{,}000{,}000 & & +\$2{,}000{,}000 \\ & & \text{(Term Bonds Payable)} & & \end{array}$$

Note that the first entry is essentially the same in all cases. The second entry differs from the entry for a direct retirement, however, in that the amount expended to defease the debt is distinctly reported as *Other Financing Uses—Payment to Refunded Bond Escrow Agent*. That the amount paid to the escrow trustee is less than the par (face) of the old bonds indicates that the amount paid can be invested at an interest rate higher than the rate the SLG is paying on the old defeased issue. However, U.S. government arbitrage regulations limit the amount of arbitrage permissible in advance refunding investment portfolios.

The legal or in-substance defeasance of an old debt is considered to be a settlement that terminates the old debt. Thus, the old debt is removed from the GLTL accounts and the new refunding debt is recorded in the GLTL accounts. Furthermore, neither the assets nor the operations of the escrow trustee's investment portfolio are reported in the SLG's financial statements.

Debt and Nondebt Financing

As a final example, assume the same facts as the legal or in-substance defeasance example except:

1. The SLG has $600,000 of net assets in an existing DSF for the old debt.
2. The remaining $1,300,000 ($1,900,000 – $600,000) will be financed by (a) a $300,000 transfer to the DSF from the General Fund and (b) a $1,000,000 advance refunding bond issue that is sold to net par (face) after issuance cost of $10,000.

The advance refunding DSF entries in this situation are:

Transfer and Refunding Bond Issuance:		
Cash..	$1,300,000	
Expenditures—Bond Issuance Costs	10,000	
Other Financing Sources—Transfer from		$ 300,000
General Fund		
Other Financing Sources—Refunding Bonds (Face)		1,000,000
Other Financing Sources—Refunding Bond		10,000
Premium		
To record interfund transfer and issuance of refunding		
bonds.		

The changes in the GCA-GLTL accounts to reflect the bond issuance are like those for the earlier examples:

$$\begin{array}{ccccc} \text{GCA} & - & \text{GLTL} & = & \text{NP} \\ & & +\$1{,}000{,}000 & & -\$1{,}010{,}000 \\ & & \text{(Refunding} & & \\ & & \text{Bonds Payable)} & & \\ & & +\$10{,}000 & & \\ & & \text{(Premium on} & & \\ & & \text{Refunding Bonds)} & & \end{array}$$

Recall from earlier discussions and from Illustration 8-9 that the amount of borrowed resources used for the in-substance defeasance determines the amount of the payment that is reported as an Other Financing Use. Therefore, the bond defeasance is recorded as follows:

Defeasance of Old Bonds:

Expenditures—Payment to Refunded Bond Escrow Agent..	$ 900,000	
Other Financing Uses—Payment to Refunded Bond Escrow Agent..................................	1,000,000	
Cash..		$1,900,000
To record payment to escrow agent to defease bonds.		

The key point here is that payments from existing *nonborrowed* financial resources ($900,000 in this example) are accounted for as expenditures, whereas such payments from refunding debt issue proceeds ($1,000,000 in this example) are accounted for as other financing uses—*not* as expenditures. This applies to both current and advance refundings.

The GCA-GLTL changes are not affected by the sources of payments for the defeasance. Therefore, the changes in those accounts are the same as under the previous assumption, as shown here:

$$\text{GCA} \quad - \quad \underset{\substack{-\$2,000,000 \\ \text{(Term Bonds Payable)}}}{\text{GLTL}} \quad = \quad \underset{+\$2,000,000}{\text{NP}}$$

Like the DSFs illustrated earlier, this fund is short-lived. Because its function is accomplished and the fund has no remaining balance, the DSF accounts will now be closed and the fund terminated.

Reporting Refundings

The substitution aspect underlying the typical treatment of general government refunding transactions is reflected well in DSF operating statements. Indeed, note the equal amounts of advance refunding debt proceeds and other financing uses reported in the Streets and Highways DSF in the city of Phoenix, Arizona, Combining Statement of Revenues, Expenditures, and Changes in Fund Balances for its DSFs (Illustration 8-11).[10] Also, note the types of DSFs reported, the statement content and format, and the details presented in Illustration 8-11 and in Illustration 8-12, which shows the city of Garden Grove, California, DSF Combining Statement of Revenues, Expenditures, and Changes in Fund Balances.

Advance Refunding Disclosures

The GASB requires SLGs to make certain disclosures about their advance refundings in the notes to their financial statements. Most of these disclosures are made only in the year the advance refunding occurs, but one must be made each year as long as any old in-substance defeased debt remains outstanding.

The major GASB advance refunding **disclosure requirements** are:

In the Year of the Advance Refunding

A. **General Description.** The advance refunding transaction(s) should be described generally—for example, which debt issues were advance-refunded, what par (face) amounts were refunded, how the advance refundings were financed (e.g., refunding bonds only or some existing financial resources), which defeasances were legal defeasances and which were in-substance defeasance transactions, and which bank or other institution serves as the escrow agent's trustee.

---

[10]This equality occurs because all of the refunding debt proceeds—and perhaps some other nonborrowed amounts—were expended to effect the refunding. The equality does *not* imply that refundings are "equal amount" transactions. To the contrary, "good" refundings (new debt issued at a lower interest rate than that on the old debt) require more than the face amount of the old debt to be invested in the irrevocable trust. "Bad" refundings (new debt bears a higher interest rate than the old debt) can be done at less than the face amount.

City of Phoenix, Arizona
Debt Service Funds
Combining Statement of Revenues, Expenditures, and Changes in Fund Balances
For the Fiscal Year Ended June 30, 20X4
With Comparative Totals for the Fiscal Year Ended June 30, 20X3 (in $000s)

	General Obligation Secondary Property Tax	Streets and Highways	Public Housing	City Improvement	Special Assessment	Totals 20X4	20X3
Revenues							
Secondary Property Taxes	$ 51,902	$ —	$ —	$ —	$ —	$ 51,902	$ 56,078
Special Assessments	—	—	—	—	1,749	1,749	1,661
Interest on Assessments	—	—	—	—	1,182	1,182	916
Interest on Investments	7,679	2	42	44	56	7,823	4,086
Other	477	369	—	329	—	1,175	785
Total Revenues	60,058	371	42	373	2,987	63,831	63,526
Expenditures							
Debt Service							
Principal	21,047	10,965	485	3,503	1,901	37,901	31,535
Interest	26,503	19,620	381	8,997	1,169	56,670	55,065
Arbitrage Rebate and Fiscal Agent Fees	16	—	—	21	—	37	1,622
Total Expenditures	47,566	30,585	866	12,521	3,070	94,608	88,222
Excess (Deficiency) of Revenues over Expenditures	12,492	(30,214)	(824)	(12,148)	(83)	(30,777)	(24,696)
Other Sources (Uses)							
Transfers from Other Funds							
General Fund	380	—	—	1,987	—	2,367	1,503
Excise Tax	900	—	—	5,646	—	6,546	7,769
Highway Users	2,000	30,214	—	—	—	32,214	35,982
Public Housing Special Revenue	—	—	866	27	—	893	875
Sports Facilities	1,295	—	—	4,556	—	5,851	5,388
Capital Projects	—	—	—	518	7	525	1,637
Proceeds from Refunding Bonds (Face)	41,006	63,422	—	24,076	—	128,504	239,140
Transfers to Other Funds General Fund	—	—	—	—	(201)	(201)	(259)
Payments to Refunding Escrow Agent	(41,039)	(63,422)	—	(26,362)	—	(130,823)	(239,491)
Net Sources (Uses) of Financial Resources	4,542	30,214	866	10,448	(194)	45,876	52,544
Net Change in Fund Balances	17,034	—	42	(1,700)	(277)	15,099	27,848
FUND BALANCES, JULY 1							
As Previously Reported	96,711	—	1,424	1,825	1,991	101,951	74,103
Prior Period Adjustments	—	—	—	—	275	275	275
FUND BALANCES, JULY 1							
As Restated	96,711	—	1,424	1,825	2,266	102,226	74,378
FUND BALANCES, JUNE 30	$113,745	$ —	$1,466	$ 125	$1,989	$117,325	$102,226

The accompanying notes are an integral part of these financial statements.
Source: Adapted from a recent annual financial report of the City of Phoenix, Arizona.

ILLUSTRATION 8-12 **Combining Statement of Revenues, Expenditures, and Changes in Fund Balances— Debt Service Funds—City of Garden Grove**

CITY OF GARDEN GROVE
Debt Service Funds
Combining Statement of Revenues, Expenditures, and Changes in Fund Balances
Year Ended June 30, 20X4
With Comparative Totals for Year Ended June 30, 20X3

	Community Project	Buena-Clinton Project	Totals 20X4	Totals 20X3
Revenues				
Taxes	$ 8,329,996	$220,669	$ 8,550,665	$ 9,083,893
From use of money and property	200,447	—	200,447	74,718
From other agencies	42,580	33	42,613	38,337
Total revenues	8,573,023	220,702	8,793,725	9,196,948
Expenditures				
Bond issue costs	784,635	—	784,635	—
Principal retirement	—	—	—	1,400,000
Interest and fiscal charges	2,482,526	—	2,482,526	2,342,351
Total expenditures	3,267,161	—	3,267,161	3,742,351
Excess of revenues over expenditures	5,305,862	220,702	5,526,564	5,454,597
Other Financing Sources (Uses)				
Bond proceeds, net*	35,194,851	—	35,194,851	—
Payment to refunded bond escrow agent	(33,849,672)	—	(33,849,672)	—
Transfer to other funds	(5,534,224)	(257,387)	(5,791,611)	(5,431,319)
Total other financing sources (uses)	(4,189,045)	(257,387)	(4,446,432)	(5,431,319)
Net change in fund balances	1,116,817	(36,685)	1,080,132	23,278
Fund balances at beginning of year	3,827,919	38,677	3,866,596	3,843,318
Fund balances at end of year	$ 4,944,736	$ 1,992	$ 4,946,728	$ 3,866,596

*GASB *Statement No. 37* requires the face amount to be presented, with related premium, discount, and other details presented separately.

Source: Adapted from a recent annual financial report of the City of Garden Grove, California.

B. **Difference in Debt Service Requirements.** SLGs should disclose the *difference* between (1) the total of the remaining debt service requirements of the *old* defeased issue, and (2) the total debt service requirements of the *new* issue, adjusted for any additional cash received or paid. These totals and the difference are computed by using scheduled debt service amounts derived from the respective debt service requirement schedules—not present values—and indicate the overall cash flow consequences of the advance refundings *without regard to the time value of money or present values.*

C. **Economic Gain or Loss.** The *present value* of the net debt service savings or cost of the advance refunding transaction—referred to as the economic gain or loss—must also be disclosed. The economic gain or loss is the *difference between* (1) the present value of the *new* advance refunding debt issue debt service requirements, adjusted for any additional cash paid or received in the advance refunding transaction, and (2) the present value of the *old* defeased debt's debt service requirements. Both present values are calculated by using the net effective interest rate (considering premiums, discounts, issuance costs, etc.) of the new refunding issue.

As Long as In-Substance Defeased Debt Is Outstanding

D. **Amount of In-Substance Defeased Debt Outstanding.** Any debt defeased in substance in an advance refunding—as opposed to being retired or legally defeased—must be disclosed as long as it is outstanding. This requirement is because the SLG remains a guarantor of the debt, in effect, even though the possibility of its having to pay any of the debt is remote.

ILLUSTRATION 8-13 **Disclosure Notes Regarding Refundings and Debt Defeasance**

County of Charleston, South Carolina
Notes to Financial Statements
June 30, 20X6

Advance Refundings. On March 21, 20X6 the Charleston County Park and Recreation Commission issued $19,000,000 General Obligation Improvement and Refunding Bonds Series 20X6 A & B. Series A Bonds of $7,040,000 were issued for repair and maintenance projects identified within the Commission's Capital Improvement Program. Series B Bonds of $11,960,000 with an average interest rate of 3.819% were issued to advance refund $11,450,000 of outstanding 20X6 Series Bonds with a coupon rate of 5.065%. The net proceeds of $11,905,619 (after payment of $125,902 in underwriting discount and issuance costs) plus an additional $2,146 in additional funds were used to purchase US government securities. Those securities were deposited in an irrevocable trust with Wachovia Bank and Trust and later assigned to US Bank to provide for all future debt service payments on the 20X6 series bonds. As a result the 20X6 series bonds are considered to be defeased and a liability for these bonds has been removed from the business related activities of the statements.

The commission advance refunded the 20X6 series bonds to reduce its total debt service payments over the next eight years by $406,313 and to obtain an economic gain (difference between the present values of the debt service payments on the old and new debt) of $378,565.

Prior Year Defeasance of Debt. In prior years, the primary government defeased various outstanding debt issues by placing proceeds of new debt or other funds in an irrevocable trust to provide for all future debt service payments on the old debt. Accordingly, the trust accounts and the defeased debt are not included in these financial statements. At June 30, 20X6, the following debt issues outstanding are considered defeased:

	Governmental Activities	Business-type Activities
Primary government:		
General Obligation Bonds:		
Series 19W4	$17,825,000	
Series 19W9	20,045,000	
Series 20X1	18,200,000	
Total General Obligation Bonds	56,070,000	
Certificates of Participation:		
Series 19W5	37,304,936	$ 8,795,064
Total Certificates of Participation	37,304,936	8,795,064
Revenue Bonds:		
Solid Waste User Fee Revenue Bonds		
Series 19W4	—	12,430,000
Total Revenue Bonds	—	12,430,000
Total primary government	$93,374,936	$21,225,064

Source: "Disclosure Notes Regarding Refunding and Debt Defeasance" June 2006, from COUNTY OF CHARLESTON, SOUTH CAROLINA NOTES TO FINANCIAL STATEMENTS. Reprinted with permission. www.charlestoncounty.org

An excellent note disclosure related to both (1) a current period advance refunding and (2) prior year defeasance of debt (from a recent County of Charleston, South Carolina, CAFR) is presented as Illustration 8-13.

Concluding Comments

Most government bond issues in recent years have been serial issues; term bond issues have been less popular. Likewise, most SLG bond issues have been traditional fixed rate issues, though some have been variable rate issues and a few have been deep discount issues.

Some serial bonds have been serviced by annual transfers from the General Fund or a Special Revenue Fund to a Debt Service Fund even though no DSF assets are accumulated, and use of a Debt Service Fund is not required legally or by GAAP. In similar cases, some other governments record such debt service directly in the General Fund and Special Revenue Funds instead of making annual transfers to Debt Service Funds. On the other hand, the law or contractual agreements *usually require Debt Service Funds for bonds and other long-term debt,* and *GAAP require DSFs whenever significant amounts are accumulated for future debt service.* In addition, many finance officers prefer to control and account for all general government general obligation debt service through Debt Service Funds.

The use of various forms of lease arrangements, including certificates of participation, as well as certificates of obligation, commercial paper, and other debt that does not require a vote of the citizens, has increased significantly in recent years. Some finance officers prefer to centralize the control of and accounting for general long-term debt service in Debt Service Funds and use them to service most general long-term liabilities. Other finance officers prefer to control and account for as much of the general operations of government as possible through the General Fund and Special Revenue Funds and do not use Debt Service Funds to service any general long-term liabilities unless required to do so by law or contractual agreement. Thus, the use of Debt Service Funds for leases varies widely among state and local governmental units.

Finally, the issuance of nonconventional deep discount bonds and notes by state and local governments has increased in recent years, as have SLG refundings of outstanding long-term debt. Accordingly, the GASB has issued standards to ensure that deep discount debt issues, refundings, and other debt-related and debt service-related transactions of state and local governments are appropriately accounted for, reported, and disclosed in the notes to the financial statements.

Questions

Q8-1 Describe the purpose of Debt Service Funds. When do GAAP require the use of a Debt Service Fund? Why might a government use a Debt Service Fund if it is not required to do so?

Q8-2 What are the main sources of resources for a Debt Service Fund?

Q8-3 Distinguish (a) between fixed rate and variable rate debt issues and (b) between conventional serial bond and term bond issues and deep discount bond issues.

Q8-4 What criteria must be met for a government to have the option of accruing unmatured interest on some of its general obligation bonds?

Q8-5 Interest on its city hall bonds is paid from Allen City's Debt Service Fund on February 1 and August 1. Should interest payable be accrued at December 31, the end of the city's fiscal year? Why? Would your answer differ if the interest payment dates were July 15 and January 15?

Q8-6 Why might a governmental unit want to refund an outstanding bond issue (a) at maturity? (b) Prior to maturity?

Q8-7 (a) Bond sinking fund investment securities have risen in value. Should the appreciation in value be recorded in the accounts of the Debt Service Fund? (b) Would your answer be different if the securities had declined in value?

Q8-8 Some accountants believe that budgetary control of Debt Service Fund operations such as those illustrated in this chapter is unnecessary unless required by law. Others disagree. What is your opinion?

Q8-9 What is meant by *defeasance*? What conditions are necessary to achieve legal defeasance or in-substance defeasance?

Q8-10 Distinguish between a current refunding and an advance refunding.

Q8-11 When would bond interest or principal due soon in the next year be accrued as expenditures and liabilities of a Debt Service Fund? When would they not be accrued?

Q8-12 The town of Sinking Creek has a semiannual debt service payment of $1,300,000 (including $1,000,000 interest) due on January 3, 20X5. The finance director transferred $1,500,000 from the General Fund to the Debt Service Fund on December 15, 20X4, to provide for this payment and future payments. Mayor Arnold Mills asks you if Sinking Creek is either required or permitted to accrue the $1,000,000 of interest at December 31, 20X4, the end of its fiscal year. Respond.

Q8-13 What is "deep discount debt"? When should expenditures for debt service on zero coupon bonds be reported?

Q8-14 What disposition should be made of the balance remaining in a Debt Service Fund after the bonds mature and are paid?

Q8-15 Explain how refunding transactions are reported in the Statement of Revenues, Expenditures, and Changes in Fund Balances.

Q8-16 When are other financing uses reported for retirement of general long-term bonds payable? What factors(s) determine the amount of other financing uses reported?

Exercises

E8-1 (Multiple Choice) Identify the best answer for each of the following:
1. Which of the following is *not* a common type of general government long-term liability?
   a. Bonds.
   b. Contracts payable.
   c. Capital leases.
   d. Notes.
2. As a general rule, debt service expenditures in a Debt Service Fund are recognized
   a. when the debt service payment is due.
   b. when resources to be used for the repayment are made available to a Debt Service Fund.
   c. when due for principal repayments but on an accrual basis for interest.
   d. in accordance with the requirements of the original bond order that specifies the basis of expenditure recognition.
3. Which of the following financial statements are required for a Debt Service Fund?
   a. Balance Sheet only.
   b. Statement of Revenues, Expenditures, and Changes in Fund Balance only.
   c. Balance Sheet and Statement of Revenues, Expenditures, and Changes in Fund Balance.
   d. Balance Sheet; Statement of Revenues, Expenditures, and Changes in Fund Balance; and Statement of Cash Flows.
4. Which of the following statements about Special Assessment Debt Service Funds is *false*?
   a. Most of the receivables in a typical Special Assessment Debt Service Fund are noncurrent.
   b. Revenue accounting for special assessments follows the same principles as that for property taxes.
   c. Debt Service Funds must be used to service all debt issued for special assessment capital projects even if the government is not obligated in any manner for the debt.
   d. It is common for deferred revenues to be reported in a Special Assessment Debt Service Fund.
5. What are the characteristics of a term bond?
   a. Term bonds may not exceed 15 years.
   b. Principal and interest on the entire principal are paid throughout the life of the issue.
   c. No interest is paid during the life of the issue.
   d. Principal is paid at the end of the bond issue term.
6. Which of the following statements concerning debt refundings is *false*?
   a. Advance refundings do not result in immediate, direct retirement of existing long-term debt.
   b. Often, resources of an irrevocable trust are used to service old long-term debt, even though the liability has been removed from the financial statements of the issuing government.
   c. Both legal defeasance and in-substance defeasance may result in the removal of the old debt from the original issuer's balance sheet.
   d. Expenditures are reported in a legal defeasance and other financing uses are reported in an in-substance defeasance.
7. Nondefeasance, in a refunding transaction, would result in
   a. both the old debt and the new debt being recorded as liabilities by the issuing government, even if resources to service the old debt have been placed in an irrevocable trust.
   b. both the old debt and the new debt being recorded as liabilities by the issuing government, but only if resources to service the old debt have *not* been placed in an irrevocable trust.
   c. the reporting of only the old debt liability. The new debt liability would not be reported until the old debt is extinguished.
   d. a budgetary compliance violation in the Debt Service Fund.

8. In the year that any advance refunding occurs, which of the following disclosures is *not* required by GAAP?
   a. Difference in debt service requirements of the old defeased issue and new issue, adjusted for any additional cash paid or received.
   b. Difference between the *present value* of the new issue's debt service requirements and the old defeased issue's debt service requirements.
   c. Any clarification necessary concerning whether the defeasance was a legal defeasance or an in-substance defeasance.
   d. Identity of the escrow agent managing the irrevocable trust established to service the old defeased issue's debt service requirements.

E8-2

1. Taxes levied in the Debt Service Fund and due in the current fiscal year include $125,000 that is *not* expected to be collected within the first 60 days of the new fiscal year. As of the end of the current fiscal year, this amount would be reported as
   a. revenue.
   b. a liability.
   c. a deferred inflow of resources.
   d. an other financing source.

   Questions 2 through 5 are based on the following scenario:

   A governmental entity levied $1,000,000 in special assessments. The assessments are due and payable in equal installments at the beginning of each fiscal year for the next five years. Assume that all installments are collected in the year they are due.

2. At the time of the levy (which is 10 months before the first installment comes due in the middle of the next fiscal year), the Special Assessment Debt Service Fund would report *revenue* in the amount of
   a. $1,000,000.
   b. $800,000.
   c. $200,000.
   d. $0.
3. As of the end of the fiscal year in which the levy was made, the Special Assessment Debt Service Fund would report *deferred inflows of resources* in the amount of
   a. $1,000,000.
   b. $800,000.
   c. $200,000.
   d. $0.
4. As of the end of the fiscal year in which the first installment is due and collected, the Special Assessment Debt Service Fund would report *revenue* in the amount of
   a. $1,000,000.
   b. $800,000.
   c. $200,000.
   d. $0.
5. As of the end of the fiscal year in which the first installment is due, the Special Assessment Debt Service Fund would report $800,000 as
   a. revenues.
   b. liabilities.
   c. deferred inflows of resources.
   d. deferred outflows of resources.
6. The General Fund transferred $700,000 to a Debt Service Fund. The Debt Service Fund would report this transaction as
   a. an other financing source.
   b. a revenue.
   c. a deferred inflow of resources.
   d. contributed capital.

   Questions 7 through 9 are based on the following scenario:

   A government is making debt service payments of $200,000 every six months, beginning in fiscal year 20Y1, and continuing for 5 years. The government's General Fund transfers $200,000 in fiscal year 20Y0 to the Debt Service Fund. The transfer is made 10 days before the end of the fiscal year. However, the debt service payments that the transfer was made to finance are not due until 15 days into the new fiscal year (20Y1).

7. The minimum amount of debt service expenditures for 20Y0 that may be reported in the Debt Service Fund is
   a. $0.
   b. $200,000.
   c. $400,000.
   d. $2,000,000.

8. The government could opt to report debt service expenditures for 20Y0 of
   a. $183,333.
   (b.) $200,000.
   c. $400,000.
   d. $2,000,000.
9. Assuming that (1) the Debt Service Fund did *not* exercise the early recognition option and (2) the resources of the fund are not restricted, at least $200,000 of the fund balance as of the end of fiscal year 20Y0 should be classified as
   a. nonspendable.
   (b.) committed.
   c. assigned.
   d. unassigned.
10. If a Debt Service Fund issues bonds at a premium, the premium is reported on the operating statement as
   a. a revenue.
   b. a nonoperating revenue.
   (c.) an other financing source.
   d. an other financing use.

E8-3 (Use of Debt Service Fund) For which of the following would a government typically use a Debt Service Fund?
1. Repayment of term bonds issued to finance construction of a general government office building.
2. Amounts paid to settle long-term claims and judgments liabilities associated with general government operations.
3. Accumulation of resources to be used to repay zero coupon bonds issued to finance construction of a courtroom annex.
4. Payments required by general government capital leases.
5. Repayment of general government special assessment debt that the government does *not* guarantee and for which it is not obligated in any other manner.
6. Payment upon retirement to a general government employee of an amount reported as a long-term vacation pay liability in the General Long-Term Liabilities accounts.
7. Repayment of general obligation bonds issued for Enterprise Fund purposes. Enterprise Fund revenues are intended to be used to service the debt.
8. Repayment (from bond proceeds) of bond anticipation notes issued for a general government capital project.

E8-4 (Debt Refundings) For each of the cases summarized in the following chart, explain how the payments should be reported in a Debt Service Fund. Assume that the debt was retired at maturity in Cases A and B and that the debt was defeased in substance in Cases C to F.

Case	Portion of Payment from Refunding Bonds	Total Payment to Escrow Agent	Carrying Value of Retired or Defeased Debt
A	$13,000,000	$13,000,000	$13,000,000
B	$18,000,000	$20,000,000	$20,000,000
C	$16,000,000	$18,000,000	$18,500,000
D	$20,000,000	$20,000,000	$22,000,000
E	$ 5,000,000	$15,000,000	$16,000,000
F	$ 8,000,000	$12,000,000	$11,000,000

E8-5 (Advance Refunding) Record the following simple transactions in the Debt Service Fund of Ledford County.
1. The county issued $50,000,000 of refunding bonds at par to provide most of the financing to refund $60,000,000 of outstanding bonds.
2. The county transferred $5,000,000 from the General Fund to the fund from which the outstanding bonds are to be defeased.
3. The county paid $55,000,000 into an irrevocable trust established in a manner that defeased in substance the $60,000,000 of previously outstanding bonds.

E8-6 (Current Refunding) Barton Village has $7,000,000 of 10-year, 6% bonds maturing on March 15, 20X7. To repay the bonds and interest, the Village Council approved issuance of refunding bonds. Record the following:
1. The village issued $7,300,000 (face value) of refunding bonds at a premium of $180,000 and paid bond issue costs of $60,000.
2. The village paid principal ($7,000,000) and interest ($420,000) on the maturing bonds on March 15, 20X7.

E8-7 (Journal Entries—School District DSF) Guerrero Independent School District entered into the following transactions related to its McFadyen Elementary School Bonds DSF during the 20X9 fiscal year. Record the transactions in the General Ledger of the DSF.

1. Property taxes restricted for payment of principal and interest on the McFadyen Elementary School Bonds were levied and collected, $15,000,000.
2. The school district purchased investments costing $14,500,000 for the DSF.
3. The school district collected $7,000,000 from maturing investments.
4. Principal of $4,900,000 and interest of $2,400,000 came due on the bonds and were paid.
5. The school district received interest of $600,000 on the DSF investments.
6. The school district collected $7,000,000 from maturing investments.
7. Principal of $4,900,000 and interest of $2,160,000 came due on the bonds and were paid. The next payment of principal and interest (which will be $1,920,000) will mature on February 15 of the next fiscal year.
8. The fair value of the school district's investment declined by $175,000 during the year.

E8-8 (Operating Statement—School District DSF) The December 31, 20X1, preclosing trial balance of the St. Louey Independent School District DSF is presented on the next page. Prepare the Statement of Revenues, Expenditures, and Changes in Fund Balance for the DSF for the year ended December 31, 20X1.

St. Louey Independent School District
Debt Service Fund
Trial Balance
December 31, 20X1

	Debit	Credit
Cash and cash equivalents.	$ 2,351,161	
Investments.	42,955,866	
Property taxes receivable.	15,196,782	
Allowance for uncollectible taxes.		$ 500,000
Deferred revenues		14,592,002
Fund balance.		61,763,591
Revenues—Property taxes		14,981,675
Revenues—County appropriation		266,084
Revenues—State appropriation		1,478,157
Revenues—Investment income		582,300
Transfer from General Fund	500,000	
Expenditures—Interest on bonds	14,120,000	
Expenditures—Bond principal retirement	19,040,000	
Totals	$94,163,809	$94,163,809

Problems

P8-1 (Multiple Choice Problems and Computations) Identify the best answer for each of the following.

Questions 1 through 3 are based on the following scenario:

The city of Lora issued $5,000,000 of general government, general obligation, 8%, 20-year bonds at 103 on April 1, 20X7, to finance a major general government capital project. Interest is payable semiannually on each October 1 and April 1 during the term of the bonds. In addition, $250,000 of principal matures each April 1.

1. If Lora's fiscal year-end is December 31, what amount of debt service expenditures should be reported for this DSF for the 20X7 fiscal year?
   a. $0
   b. $200,000
   c. $300,000
   d. $400,000
2. If Lora's fiscal year-end is March 31 and Lora accumulates dedicated resources in the DSF by fiscal year end sufficient to pay the principal and interest due on April 1 of the subsequent fiscal year, what amount of debt service expenditures should Lora report for the fiscal year ended March 31, 20X8?
   a. $200,000
   b. $400,000
   c. $650,000
   d. $200,000 or $650,000, depending on whether the city opts to accrue the debt service

3. Assume the same information as in item 1, except that Lora has not made the October 1, 20X7, interest payment as of the fiscal year end. What amount of debt service expenditures should be reported for this DSF for the 20X7 fiscal year?
   a. $0
   b. $200,000
   c. $300,000
   d. $400,000

4. A county had borrowed $18,000,000 to finance construction of a general government capital project. The debt will be serviced from collections of a special assessment levy made for the project. The county levied the special assessments in 20X8. Ten percent of the assessments are due in 20X8. The 20X8 and early 20X9 collections on the assessments total $1,500,000. The amount of special assessments revenue that should be recognized in the county's Special Assessments DSF for 20X8 is
   a. $0. Special assessments are reported as other financing sources.
   b. $1,500,000.
   c. $1,800,000.
   d. $18,000,000.

Assume for Questions 5 through 9 that the state of Exuberance issued $10,000,000 of 5%, 20-year refunding bonds in 20X5 at par.

5. If the state used the proceeds to retire $10,000,000 of general long-term debt upon its maturity, the state should report
   a. revenues of $10,000,000 and expenditures of $10,000,000.
   b. other financing sources of $10,000,000 and expenditures of $10,000,000.
   c. revenues of $10,000,000 and other financing uses of $10,000,000.
   d. other financing sources of $10,000,000 and other financing uses of $10,000,000.

6. If the state placed the $10,000,000 in an irrevocable trust that is to be used to service an outstanding $9,000,000 general obligation bond issue and those bonds are deemed defeased in substance, the state should report
   a. expenditures of $9,000,000 and other financing uses of $1,000,000.
   b. expenditures of $10,000,000.
   c. expenditures of $1,000,000 and other financing uses of $9,000,000.
   d. other financing uses of $10,000,000.

7. If the state placed the $10,000,000 in an irrevocable trust as in item 6 but the transaction did not meet the defeasance in substance criteria, the state should report
   a. expenditures of $10,000,000.
   b. expenditures of $1,000,000 and other financing uses of $9,000,000.
   c. other financing uses of $10,000,000.
   d. no expenditures or other financing uses.

8. If the state placed $12,000,000 (the $10,000,000 from the advance refunding plus $2,000,000 from previously accumulated DSF resources) in the irrevocable trust in item 6 and the debt was deemed defeased in substance, the state should report
   a. expenditures of $9,000,000 and other financing uses of $3,000,000.
   b. expenditures of $3,000,000 and other financing uses of $9,000,000.
   c. expenditures of $2,000,000 and other financing uses of $10,000,000.
   d. other financing uses of $12,000,000.

9. If the state of Exuberance defeased its $9,000,000 debt in substance as in item 8 except that no advance refunding debt was issued, the state should report
   a. expenditures of $9,000,000 and other financing uses of $3,000,000.
   b. expenditures of $2,000,000 and other financing uses of $10,000,000.
   c. expenditures of $12,000,000.
   d. other financing uses of $12,000,000.

10. A government paid $3,500,000 to its fiscal agent on June 30, 20X6, to provide for principal ($2,000,000) and interest payments due on July 1, 20X6. The fiscal agent will make payments to bondholders on July 1. The payment to the fiscal agent does not constitute legal or in-substance defeasance of the principal and interest payments. If the government uses the option of accruing its principal and interest expenditures due early in the next year, which of the following assets and liabilities should be reported in the government's DSF balance sheet at June 30, 20X6?
    a. No assets or liabilities from the preceding information would be reported because the government has paid the fiscal agent.
    b. Cash with fiscal agent, $3,500,000.
    c. Cash with fiscal agent, $3,500,000.
       Matured bonds payable, $2,000,000.
       Matured interest payable, $1,500,000.
    d. Cash with fiscal agent, $3,500,000.
       Accrued interest payable, $1,500,000.

P8-2 (General Ledger Entries) Gotham City issued $500,000 of 8% regular serial bonds at par (no accrued interest) on January 2, 20X0, to finance a capital improvement project. Interest is payable semiannually on January 2 and July 2, and $50,000 of the principal matures each January 2 beginning in 20X1 and ending in 20Y0. Resources for servicing the debt will be made available through a special tax levy for this purpose and transfers as needed from a Special Revenue Fund. The required transfers typically will be made on January 1 and July 1, respectively. The DSF is not under formal budget control; the city's fiscal year begins October 1.

Prepare general journal entries to record the following transactions and events in the General Ledger of the DSF.
1. June 28, 20X0—The first installment of the special tax was received, $52,000.
2. June 29, 20X0—A Special Revenue Fund transfer of $38,000 was received.
3. July 2, 20X0—The semiannual interest payment on the bonds was made.
4. July 3, 20X0—The remaining cash ($70,000) was invested.
5. December 30, 20X0—The investments matured, and $73,000 cash was received.
6. January 2, 20X1—The semiannual interest payment and the bond payment were made.
7. January 2, *20Y0*—At the beginning of 20Y0, the DSF had accumulated $30,000 in investments (from transfers) and $25,000 in cash (from taxes). The investments were liquidated at face value, and the final interest and principal payment on the bonds was made.
8. January 3, 20Y0—The DSF purpose having been served, the council ordered the residual assets transferred to a Special Revenue Fund and the DSF terminated.

P8-3 (General Ledger Entries and Statements) Hatcher Village, which operates on the calendar year, issued a 5-year, 8%, $100,000 note to the Bank of Hatcher on January 5, 20X4. The proceeds of the note were recorded in a Capital Projects Fund. Interest and one-tenth of the principal are due semiannually, on January 5 and July 5, beginning July 5, 20X4. A DSF has been established to service this debt; financing will come from General Fund transfers and a small debt service tax approved several years ago. The net assets of the fund at year end are not restricted or committed.

a. Prepare the general journal entries (budgetary and actual) needed to record the following transactions and events. *Required*
b. Prepare a balance sheet at December 31, 20X4, and a Statement of Revenues, Expenditures, and Changes in Fund Balance for the year then ended for the DSF.

Transactions and Events
1. January 6—The DSF budget for 20X4 was adopted. The General Fund contribution was estimated at $10,000; the tax levy was expected to yield $18,000. The appropriations included the January 5, 20X5, debt service payment.
2. The taxes were levied and received, $20,000.
3. The July 5, 20X4, payment of principal and interest was made.
4. The General Fund contribution of $10,000 was received.
5. The residual balance of a discontinued Capital Projects Fund, $6,000, was transferred to the DSF.
6. The January 5, 20X5, payment was accrued.
7. Closing entries were prepared at December 31, 20X4.

P8-4 (Advance Refunding) The state of Artexva advance refunded $8,000,000 par of 20X2, 10% serial bonds by issuing $9,000,000 par of 20Y6, 6% serial bonds.

Prepare the entries required to record the following advance refunding transactions, which occurred during 20Y6, in the Artexva Advance Refunding Debt Service Fund. *Required*
1. The new $9,000,000, 6%, 20Y6 serial bonds were issued at 101 (no accrued interest) less $290,000 issuance costs, and the net proceeds were accounted for in a new advance refunding DSF.
2. The net proceeds of the 20Y6 serial bond issue were paid to the Second National Bank of Artexva as escrow agent of an irrevocable trust for the benefit of the holders of the 20X2, 10% serial bonds. That amount, $8,800,000, is sufficient under terms of the defeasance provisions in the 20X2, 10% serial bond covenant, as invested, to legally defease that issue.
3. The advance refunding DSF accounts were closed, and, its purpose having been served, the fund was discontinued.
4. Assume that the state of Artexva advance refunding bonds yielded only $7,800,000, net of $200,000 issuance costs; an additional $1,000,000 was transferred from the General Fund to the advance refunding DSF; and $8,800,000 was paid to the escrow agent. Prepare the entry necessary to record the payment to the escrow agent.
5. Assume the same facts as in number 4 except (1) the 20X2, 10% serial bonds matured soon after the 20Y6, 6% serial bonds were issued, and (2) the $8,800,000 payment was to retire the $8,000,000 of 20X2 serial bonds and to pay the $800,000 20Y6 interest on those bonds. Prepare the entry to record the bond principal and interest payment.

P8-5 (Detailed General Ledger or General Ledger–Subsidiary Ledger Entries; Statements) The Leslie Independent School District (LISD) services all of its long-term debt through a single Debt Service Fund. The LISD DSF balance sheet at December 31, 20X4, appeared as follows:

Leslie Independent School District
Debt Service Fund
Balance Sheet
December 31, 20X4
Assets

Cash		$220,000
Investments		670,000
Accrued interest receivable		10,000
		$900,000

Liabilities and Fund Balance

Liabilities:		
Matured interest payable.......................	$101,500	
Matured serial bonds payable....................	50,000	
Accrued fiscal agent fees payable................	1,005	$152,505
Fund Balance:		
Restricted....................................	665,285	
Assigned.....................................	82,210	747,495
		$900,000

The district's bond indenture required a fund balance reserve for term bond principal of $315,285 and a reserve for serial bond debt service assurance of $350,000 as of December 31, 20X4.

1. The LISD adopted the following DSF budget for its 20X5 calendar fiscal year:

Appropriations:

(1) <u>Serial bonds</u> (8%, $2,500,000 unmatured at 1/1/X5):

(a) 7/5/X5—Principal	$ 50,000	
Interest	100,000	
Fiscal agent fees......................	1,000	$151,000
(b) 1/5/X6—Principal	50,000	
Interest	98,000	
Fiscal agent fees......................	995	148,995
		299,995

The 1/5/X5 debt service payment was accrued at 12/31/X4 because dedicated resources were provided for that payment during 20X4.

(2) <u>Term bonds</u> (6%, $1,000,000 unmatured at 1/1/X5):

(a) 4/15/X5—Interest		30,000
(b) 10/15/X5—Interest		30,000
		60,000

The board also approved a $21,019 addition to the sinking fund Reserve for Term Bond Principal as required by the term bond indenture.

(3) <u>Capital lease</u> (7%, $400,000 book value at 1/1/X5):

Annual payment (including interest) due 3/25/X5......		38,986
Total Appropriations...........................		$398,981
Required Financing:		
Appropriations......................................		$398,981
Addition to term bond sinking fund...................		21,019
		$420,000

Authorized Financing Sources:

Estimated property tax revenues	$250,000
Estimated interest revenues	52,000
Authorized transfer from General Fund	118,000
	$420,000

2. All debt service payment transactions occurred during 20X5 as they were budgeted and scheduled. Investments were liquidated—in $1,000 blocks—the day before cash was required; the cash balance was never permitted to be less than $5,000.
3. The General Fund transfer was made on 2/12/X5 and was invested (at par); the sinking fund Reserve for Term Bond Principal was also adjusted on that date. The School Board committed amounts equal to the transfer for debt service. Amounts equal to the balance in the reserves are considered externally restricted regardless of the source of the resources.
4. Investment earnings during 20X5 were $54,000, including $15,000 of accrued interest receivable at 12/31/X5. The ending cash balance at 12/31/X5 was $13,509. (Record all investment earnings transactions and events at 12/31/X5.)
5. Property taxes for the year, all received on 5/8/X5, totaled $256,000. The tax revenues are restricted for debt service.

(a) Prepare the summary journal entries necessary to record these transactions and events in the detailed General Ledger accounts or in the General Ledger, Revenues Ledger, and Expenditures Ledger of the Leslie Independent School District during 20X5, including closing entries. Key the entries by date. ***Required***
(b) Prepare a balance sheet at 12/31/20X5 and a Statement of Revenues, Expenditures, and Changes in Fund Balances for the year then ended for the LISD Debt Service Fund.

P8-6 (Statement of Revenues, Expenditures, and Changes in Fund Balance) Prepare a Statement of Revenues, Expenditures, and Changes in Fund Balance for the Broadus County Courthouse Bonds Debt Service Fund for 20X6, given the following information:

Fund balance, January 1, 20X6	$1,500,000
Interest revenue	80,000
Decrease in fair value of investments	5,000
Bond principal retirement	5,000,000
Bond interest matured and paid	1,200,000
Fiscal agent fees	75,000
Property tax revenues	3,065,000
Transfer from General Fund	5,250,000

P.44

The next debt service payment is the semiannual interest payment that matures on March 31, 20X7. The county plans to meet that payment with dedicated resources already in the Debt Service Fund at December 31, 20X6.

P8-7 (Research) Define and briefly explain *crossover* as the term is used in bond refundings in the governmental environment. In your analysis, be sure to include a brief discussion of the following questions:
a. What types of situations give rise to a crossover refunding?
b. What are the financial statement effects of a crossover refunding?
c. Are there potential budgetary implications when a governmental entity has a crossover refunding?

P8-8 (Research and Analysis) Obtain a comprehensive annual financial report (CAFR) of a state or local government (SLG). Familiarize yourself with the financial statements and disclosures with respect to the SLG's Debt Service Funds.

a. How many DSFs are maintained by the SLG? What is the purpose of each DSF? (Attach a copy of the DSF narrative explanations.) ***Required***
b. Does this SLG employ a type of DSF you were not expecting based on the DSF coverage of this chapter? If so, explain.
c. Note the format and content of the DSF balance sheet. Are any format features or content different from those you expected? If so, explain.
d. Note the format and content of the DSF Statement of Revenues, Expenditures, and Changes in Fund Balance. Are any format features or content different from those you expected? If so, explain.
e. Attach a copy of the combining or individual fund DSF financial statements.

Cases

C8-1 (Operating Statement—Milwaukee, Wisconsin, DSF) The following information is taken from the trial balance of the General Obligation Debt Service Fund of the City of Milwaukee, Wisconsin, at December 31, 20X5. Prepare the Statement of Revenues, Expenditures, and Changes in Fund Balance for this Debt Service Fund for the year ended December 31, 20X5.

City of Milwaukee, Wisconsin
General Obligation Debt Service Fund
Partial Trial Balance
December 31, 20X5 (in $000s)

	Debit	*Credit*
Deferred revenues		$128,823
Fund balance		43,807
Property tax revenues		52,942
Other tax revenues		14,695
Investment revenues		3,418
Other revenues		8,214
Refunding bonds issued—face value		28,112
Refunding bonds issued—premium		12,209
Transfers in		31,930
Expenditures—debt principal retirement	$81,206	
Expenditures—interest	29,593	
Bond issue costs	750	
Payment to refunded bond escrow agent	39,571	

(Adapted from a recent Comprehensive Annual Financial Report of the City of Milwaukee, Wisconsin.)

C8-2 (Journal Entries and Statements—Hawaii County, Hawaii) The July 1, 20X5, trial balance for the Bond Redemption and Interest Debt Service Fund of the County of Hawaii, Hawaii, is presented here. The resources of the fund are committed to debt service.

County of Hawaii
Bond Redemption and Interest Debt Service Fund
Trial Balance
July 1, 20X5

	Debit	*Credit*
Cash and cash equivalents	$15,374,722	
Accrued interest payable		$ 332,964
Fund balance		15,041,758
Total	$15,374,722	$15,374,722

The County had the following transactions in its Bond Redemption DSF from July 1, 20X5, through June 30, 20X6.

1. Paid accrued interest when due, July 18, 20X5.
2. Received transfers of unassigned resources from the General Fund totaling $105,396,619.
3. Paid principal ($12,878,605) and interest ($9,776,065) on the bonds.
4. Purchased $7,300,000 of investments.
5. An interest payment of $320,521 is due and payable on July 18, 20X6.

Required a. Prepare the General Ledger general journal entries required to record the preceding transactions and information for the Bond Redemption and Interest DSF of the County of Hawaii for the fiscal year ended June 30, 20X6.

b. Prepare the required financial statements for this DSF for the 20X5–20X6 fiscal year.

Harvey City Comprehensive Case

DEBT SERVICE FUNDS

Harvey City has two Debt Service Funds in 20X4. The City Hall Bonds Debt Service Fund was established several years ago when bonds were issued to finance construction of a new city hall. Debt service on these bonds has been accomplished with transfers of unassigned General Fund resources in the past. State law requires all bonded debt service to be reported in a Debt Service Fund. Harvey City decided to refund the City Hall bonds in 20X4. The General Debt Service Fund is used to account for debt service on several small bond issues. It is financed by a combination of taxes restricted for debt service and General Fund transfers of unassigned resources.

REQUIREMENTS—CITY HALL BONDS DEBT SERVICE FUND

a. Prepare a worksheet for the City Hall Bonds Debt Service Fund similar to the General Fund worksheet you created in Chapter 4. Enter the effects of the following transactions and events in the appropriate columns of the worksheet. (A different solution approach may be used if desired by your professor.)

b. Enter the preclosing trial balance in the appropriate worksheet columns.

c. Enter the preclosing trial balance amounts in the closing entry (operating statement data) and postclosing trial balance (balance sheet data) columns, as appropriate.

d. Prepare the 20X4 Statement of Revenues, Expenditures, and Changes in Fund Balance for the City Hall Bonds Debt Service Fund.

e. Prepare the 20X4 year-end balance sheet for the City Hall Bonds Debt Service Fund.

TRANSACTIONS AND EVENTS—20X4—CITY HALL BONDS DEBT SERVICE FUND

1. The city issued $3,000,000 of city hall refunding bonds at par on July 1. The refunding bonds are 5-year bonds and pay interest semiannually each July 1 and January 1. The refunding bonds bear interest of 6% per year. The proceeds of the refunding bonds will provide part of the financing for an in-substance defeasance of $3,200,000 (face value) of *original* city hall bonds that were issued several years earlier. An unamortized premium of $180,000 is associated with the *original* city hall bonds, which mature in 8 years. The *original* city hall bonds bear interest of 8%, payable semiannually each June 30 and December 31.

2. The city transferred $729,965 from the General Fund to the City Hall Bonds Debt Service Fund to provide for payment of interest on the *original* city hall bonds and to help finance the refunding of those *original* city hall bonds.

3. The city paid the interest ($128,000) on the *original* city hall bonds when due on June 30.

4. The city paid $3,601,965 into an irrevocable trust to defease the *original* city hall bonds. The trust meets all the requirements for a defeasance in substance.

REQUIREMENTS—GENERAL DEBT SERVICE FUND

a. Prepare a worksheet for the General Debt Service Fund similar to the General Fund worksheet you created in Chapter 4. Enter the effects of the following transactions and events in the appropriate columns of the worksheet. (A different solution approach may be used if desired by your professor.)

b. Enter the preclosing trial balance in the appropriate worksheet columns.

c. Enter the preclosing trial balance amounts in the closing entry (operating statement data) and postclosing trial balance (balance sheet data) columns, as appropriate.

d. Prepare the 20X4 Statement of Revenues, Expenditures, and Changes in Fund Balance for the General Debt Service Fund.

e. Prepare the 20X4 year-end balance sheet for the General Debt Service Fund. (All resources of this fund, except from investment income, are restricted for debt service.)

BEGINNING 20X4 TRIAL BALANCE

The trial balance of the General Debt Service Fund at January 1, 20X4, is:

Harvey City
General Debt Service Fund
Trial Balance
January 1, 20X4

	Debit	Credit
Cash..	$ 171,350	
Investments...	1,237,000	
Taxes Receivable—Delinquent	52,000	
Allowance for Uncollectible Delinquent Taxes............		$ 5,800
Interest and Penalties Receivable	10,900	
Allowance for Uncollectible Interest and Penalties		3,500
Deferred Revenues		50,000
Fund Balance		1,411,950
Totals...	$1,471,250	$1,471,250

The fund balance is not restricted or committed.

TRANSACTIONS AND EVENTS—20X4—GENERAL DEBT SERVICE FUND

1. The city levied $300,000 of special property taxes that are restricted by statute and by bond indentures for the servicing of general obligation bonds. One percent (1%) of the taxes is expected to be uncollectible.
2. The city collected $246,800 of property taxes before the due date for taxes. The remainder of the taxes receivable became delinquent.
3. The city levied interest and penalties of $6,650 on the overdue taxes receivable. $1,370 of the interest and penalties is expected to prove uncollectible. The interest and penalties on taxes are restricted for debt service as well.
4. The city collected $41,040 of delinquent taxes and $5,130 of interest and penalties receivable.
5. The city wrote off uncollectible taxes receivable of $4,370 and related interest and penalties of $1,370.
6. Investments that cost $1,000,000 were sold for $1,050,000. Investment income is not restricted, but is retained in the fund to be used for debt service if needed.
7. The city paid interest of $800,000 on bonds payable and retired $500,000 of principal.
8. $45,050 of the December 31, 20X4, balance of delinquent taxes receivable and $6,950 of the December 31, 20X4, balance of interest and penalties receivable are not expected to be collected within the first 60 days of 20X5. (The January 1, 20X4, delinquent taxes receivable balance included $43,100 of taxes that were collected after the first 60 days of 20X4, and the January 1, 20X4, interest and penalties receivable balance included $6,900 of interest and penalties on taxes that were collected after the first 60 days of 20X4.) (*Hint:* Deferred revenues must be adjusted.)
9. The fair value of investments at year end was $254,000.

CHAPTER 9

General Capital Assets; General Long-Term Liabilities; Permanent Funds

Introduction to Interfund-GCA-GLTL Accounting

LEARNING OBJECTIVES

After studying this chapter, you should be able to:

- Understand how governments maintain the general capital assets (GCA) and general long-term liabilities (GLTL) information that governments need for managerial, accountability, and government-wide financial reporting purposes.

- Understand and account for the various types of transactions affecting general capital assets and general long-term liabilities.

- Understand the relationships between governmental funds and the general capital assets and general long-term liabilities accounts.

- Account for and report general infrastructure capital assets properly.

- Understand and apply the modified approach for accounting for infrastructure capital assets.

- Understand the financial reporting requirements for General Capital Assets and General Long-Term Liabilities.

- Understand the nature and use of Permanent Funds and how to account for and report Permanent Funds.

- Account for transactions that affect both governmental funds and the General Capital Assets and General Long-Term Liabilities accounts.

The governmental funds for which accounting principles have been presented thus far are separate, self-balancing entities that are used to account for sources, uses, and balances of expendable general government financial assets. In these governmental funds:

- Capital assets purchased have been reported as fund *expenditures* rather than as fund assets.
- Capital asset sale proceeds have been recorded as *other financing sources*.
- The proceeds of general long-term debt issues have been recorded as *other financing sources* (e.g., Capital Projects Funds).
- Retirement of such debt has been accounted for as *expenditures or other financing uses* (e.g., Debt Service Funds).

The general government capital assets acquired through governmental funds and the general government long-term liabilities are discussed and illustrated in this chapter.

We begin the chapter with discussions and illustrations of the *overall* accounting procedures for General Capital Assets and General Long-Term Liabilities. Then, we focus on the accounting procedures for general capital assets (GCA) and the roles and interrelationships of the General Capital Assets accounts and the funds from which the capital assets are financed. Finally, the accounting procedures for a government's general obligation long-term debt—and its other general long-term liabilities (GLTL)—and the relationship of that indebtedness to the governmental funds are discussed.

Upon completing the GCA-GLTL discussions, we discuss and illustrate accounting and financial reporting for Permanent Funds. Permanent Funds are not common in local governments. Furthermore, although they are classified as governmental funds, they differ significantly from the other governmental funds. Therefore, we deal with them separately in this chapter.

We conclude the chapter with a formal review and summary of accounting for interfund and interfund-GCA-GLTL transactions and relationships. Numerous illustrative journal entries are provided both to assure understanding of this chapter and to serve as a review of Chapters 1–8.

OVERVIEW OF GENERAL CAPITAL ASSETS AND GENERAL LONG-TERM LIABILITIES ACCOUNTING PROCEDURES

The GASB's authoritative guidance specifies how GCA and GLTL are ***reported*** in the ***government-wide*** financial statements but does *not* set forth GCA and GLTL *accounting procedures*. Consequently, one encounters various GCA and GLTL accounting approaches in practice. For example, some governments use a free-standing GCA accounting system that is separate from their free-standing GLTL accounting system. Some keep lists on electronic worksheets; a number maintain lists manually; still others use an integrated approach similar to that illustrated in this chapter.

Illustration 9-1 summarizes the integrated GCA-GLTL accounting system used here. This type of system accumulates most of the information needed for reporting the GCA and the GLTL in the government-wide financial statements, as well as for disclosing related information (e.g., the changes in GCA and GLTL) in the notes to the basic financial statements.

Although net position is not subclassified in Illustration 9-1, three net position classifications must be used in both proprietary fund *and* government-wide financial statements and are discussed in detail in Chapter 10. Briefly, these classifications are:

- *Net Investment in Capital Assets* is the carrying value of capital assets plus capital-asset-related deferred outflows of resources minus the balance of capital-asset-related borrowings and capital-asset-related deferred inflows.

- *Restricted Net Position* is the difference between restricted assets and all liabilities and deferred inflows of resources related to those assets.

- *Unrestricted Net Position* is the difference between the remaining assets and deferred outflows of resources less the remaining liabilities and deferred inflows of resources.

These net position amounts must be determined and reported for a SLG's *governmental activities* data, as well as for its *business-type activities* and proprietary funds. Recognize in studying Illustration 9-1 that most GCA-GLTL transactions will involve capital assets of governmental activities and the capital-asset-related debt of those activities. All of the GCA and the majority of the GLTL of most general purpose local governments affect the Net Investment in Capital Assets classification. However, we do not use the net position classifications in this chapter because in practice these amounts are computed at year end by classifying each asset, deferred outflow, liability, and deferred inflow account according to the net position

ILLUSTRATION 9-1 General Capital Assets and General Long-Term Liabilities Accounts

General Capital Assets*		−	General Long-Term Liabilities		=	Net Position**	
(1) Cost of GCA acquired			(5) GLTL retired	GLTL incurred (2)		(2) GLTL incurred	Cost of GCA acquired (1)
	Cost of GCA disposed of (4)					(3) Depreciation expense***	
						(4) Net carrying value of GCA disposed of**	GLTL retired (5)
Balance				Balance			Balance

Accumulated Depreciation

(4) Related to GCA disposed of	Depreciation expense (3)
Balance	

*Subsidiary ledgers or other records should record (a) General Capital Assets by type (e.g., land or buildings) and organizational unit, function, and/or activity and (b) General Long-Term Liabilities by type (e.g., bonds payable or notes payable).

**In the government-wide statement of net position, net position will be subclassified into three categories that are discussed in Chapters 10 and 13. Since the classification process is a year-end procedure, the subcategories are not maintained by most governments during the year.

***Separate *operating* or *activity* accounts—such as Depreciation Expense and Net Carrying Value of General Capital Assets Disposed of—may be used during the year and closed at year end to Net Investment in Capital Assets.

classification it affects. Some GLTL—primarily those related to when-due expenditures, such as claims and judgments, pensions, and OPEB—typically reduce Unrestricted Net Position or, in more limited instances, Restricted Net Position.

GENERAL CAPITAL ASSETS

Governments use many durable, long-term assets in their operations. *Capital assets* include land, improvements to land, easements, buildings, building improvements, vehicles, machinery, equipment, works of art and historical treasures, infrastructure, and all other tangible or intangible assets that (1) are used in operations, and (2) have useful lives extending beyond a single reporting period. Most possess physical substance, and all are expected to provide service for periods that extend beyond the year of acquisition. They are not physically consumed by their use, though their economic usefulness typically declines over their lifetimes. Their proper recording and control are necessary for efficient management and for financial reporting.

General Capital Assets Defined

A clear-cut distinction is maintained between accounting for *general* capital assets in the General Capital Assets (GCA) accounts and for capital assets of specific proprietary and fiduciary fund entities. The GASB *Codification* defines **general capital assets** as all capital assets *other than* those accounted for in proprietary funds or trust funds.[1] In some Trust Funds and in Internal Service Funds and Enterprise Funds, capital assets are accounted for in the same manner as for businesses.

The governmental funds are used to account for the sources, uses, and balances of expendable, general government net financial assets.

- Acquiring capital assets *uses* governmental fund net financial assets because the capital assets are *not* expendable financial assets.

- These assets belong to the organization as a whole, *not* to any specific fund.

[1]GASB *Codification*, sec. 1400.101.

Capital assets thus are *not* recorded as governmental fund assets. Rather, acquisition of capital assets is an *expenditure* of governmental fund resources. The capital assets are capitalized in the General Capital Assets accounts and reported in the government-wide financial statements.

Initial Valuation

A government may purchase or construct general capital assets (GCA) or it may acquire them by capital lease, gift, or escheat.

Cost

Most general capital assets should be recorded initially at cost. The cost principle used in state and local government accounting is essentially the same as that included in generally accepted accounting principles for businesses. *Cost* is generally defined as *the value of consideration given or consideration received, whichever is more clearly determinable.* Cost includes all normal and necessary outlays incurred to bring the asset into a state of readiness for its intended use.

The GASB *Codification* specifically states that general capital assets include those acquired, in substance, through noncancellable leases.[2] Furthermore, it contains extensive guidance on accounting for and reporting state and local government (SLG) capital leases.

Estimated Cost

In the past, many governments failed to maintain adequate records of capital assets. When these governments began reporting their capital assets in accordance with GAAP, records of the original cost of many of their capital assets were not available, and obtaining capital asset cost records in some cases was either impossible or prohibitively expensive. Both GAAP and widely accepted practice permitted recording the **estimated original cost** on the basis of available information. The GASB also permitted estimated costs to be used when governments retroactively implemented GASB *Statement No. 51,* "Accounting and Financial Reporting for Intangible Assets," for assets for which it was not practicable to determine the actual original historical cost. The basis of capital asset valuation, whether actual or estimated cost, should be disclosed in the financial statements.

Gifts, Foreclosures, Eminent Domain, and Escheat

Governments may acquire capital assets by gift (donation), as well as by purchase, construction, or capital lease. Capital assets acquired by gift are recorded at their fair value when given to the government.

In addition, governments acquire assets by three methods not customary for business enterprises: foreclosure, eminent domain, and escheat.

- In cases of **foreclosure**, the valuation should normally be the *lower* of (1) the amount due for taxes or special assessments, related penalties and interest, and applicable foreclosure costs, or (2) the appraised fair value of the property.

- **Eminent domain** is the power of government to seize private property for public use, compensation to the owner normally being determined through the courts. Property thus acquired is accounted for in the same manner as that acquired in a negotiated purchase.

- Acquisition by **escheat** occurs when title to property is vested in or reverts to the government because the rightful owner does not come forward to claim it or dies without known heirs. Capital assets obtained in this manner are accounted for in the same manner as gifts; that is, they are capitalized in the general capital assets accounts at estimated fair value when the government gains legal title.

---

[2]Ibid., sec. 1400.122.

The GASB has not specified a standard (uniform) classification of general capital assets accounts. However, many SLGs follow or adapt the recommendation of the Government Finance Officers Association (GFOA) that capital assets should be classified as (1) land, (2) buildings, (3) infrastructure, (4) machinery and equipment, or (5) construction in progress.

1. **Land.** The cost of land includes the amount paid for the land, costs incidental to the acquisition of land, and expenditures incurred in preparing the land for use (e.g., for storm water drainage and for water and sewer connection charges).

2. **Buildings or Buildings and Improvements.** This classification includes (a) relatively permanent structures used to house persons or property and (b) fixtures that are permanently attached to and made a part of buildings and that cannot be removed without cutting into walls, ceilings, or floors or otherwise damaging the building.

3. **Infrastructure.** This classification (defined later) includes certain long-lived improvements (other than buildings) that add value (including use value) to land. Examples of items in this category are bridges, sidewalks, streets, dams, and tunnels.

4. **Machinery and Equipment.** Examples are trucks, automobiles, pumps, desks, computers, and bookcases. Movable machinery and equipment must be accounted for with particular care.

5. **Construction in Progress.** Construction in progress includes the cost of construction work undertaken but incomplete at a balance sheet date. These costs are appropriately reclassified to one or more of the other classifications upon project completion.

The GFOA likely will add a sixth category now that GASB *Statement No. 51* requires most intangible assets to be reported like other capital assets, including amortizing limited life intangibles.

These general capital asset classifications are not all-inclusive. For example, a county public school system might report Library Books, and a city museum might include Museum Collections. The table shown in *9-1 In Practice* provides some sense of the significance of general capital assets of state governments compared to overall general government (or governmental activities) total assets. Likewise, it provides a basis for understanding the significance of state government *infrastructure* general capital assets compared to both (1) total *general* capital assets and (2) *general* government total assets.

Before establishing GCA property records, most SLGs establish a GCA capitalization policy. One aspect of a SLG's GCA capitalization policy is the dollar threshold (e.g., $500 or $5,000) at which to capitalize GCA for *external* financial reporting in conformity with GAAP. National organizations such as the GFOA offer GCA threshold and other advice, and state agencies may require or recommend GCA capitalization policies.

9-1 IN PRACTICE

		Governmental Activities	
State	Total Assets	Total General Capital Assets (Net)	Infrastructure Assets (Net)
Hawaii	$ 11.4 billion	$ 8.7 billion	$ 4.2 billion
Kentucky	$ 26.7 billion	$ 21.4 billion	$18.1 billion
New York	$111.0 billion	$ 77.4 billion	$65.3 billion
Nebraska	$ 12.0 billion	$ 7.8 billion	$ 6.9 billion
Texas	$136.2 billion	$101.3 billion	$ 57.5 billion

GAAP apply only to items that are material and significant for *external reporting purposes*. The SLG may establish additional GCA *internal* accounting policies and procedures—such as for firearms, cell phones, personal digital assistants, and notebook computers—based on control and legal compliance considerations.

Legal Compliance

Some state and local laws or regulations require every capital asset costing a certain amount—say $1,500, $500, or even $100—or more to be capitalized in the accounts. The wisdom of such laws may be questioned from materiality and cost-benefit perspectives—particularly when assets such as highways, right-of-ways, buildings, and building improvements are involved—but the SLG must comply with the laws. If in doubt about legal requirements, practitioners should seek appropriate legal advice—for example, from the SLG attorney, the state attorney general, or perhaps the state auditor.

Intangible Assets

As stated earlier, GASB *Statement No. 51* defines intangible assets and requires that they be reported as capital assets—following most of the same guidance that applies to other capital assets. The statement defines intangible assets as assets of a nonfinancial nature that lack physical substance and have initial useful lives extending beyond a single reporting period. Common intangible assets of governments include rights of way, easements, and water rights.

Statement No. 51 also requires governments to report internally created intangible assets, which is unique to government reporting. The conditions that must be met before a government begins capitalizing costs incurred for an internally generated capital asset are:

a. Determination of the specific objective of the project and the nature of the service capacity that is expected to be provided by the intangible asset upon the completion of the project

b. Demonstration of the technical or technological feasibility for completing the project so that the intangible asset will provide its expected service capacity

c. Demonstration of the current intention, ability, and presence of effort to complete or, in the case of a multiyear project, continue development of the intangible asset[3]

Costs incurred prior to meeting all these conditions must be expensed in the government-wide financial statements and/or proprietary fund and fiduciary fund financial statements.

The most common internally generated assets in typical state and local government entities are internally generated software such as financial reporting systems. These are considered internally generated whether they are developed by the government's own staff or by contractors. Purchased software that requires more than minimal effort to modify it to achieve the desired service capacity also is considered internally generated.

Intangible assets with indefinite lives are not amortized. All other intangible assets must be reported over their expected useful lives.

Reporting Works of Art and Historical Treasures

With one exception, governments should capitalize works of art, historical treasures, and similar assets at their historical cost or fair value at date of donation, whether they are held as individual items or in a collection. Governments are *not* required to capitalize a collection (or additions to that collection), whether

---

[3]GASB, *Statement No. 51,* "Accounting and Financial Reporting for Intangible Assets" (June 2007).

donated or purchased, *if* that collection—known as an *inexhaustible* collection— *meets all three* of the following *criteria:*

1. The collection is held for public exhibition, education, or research in furtherance of public service, rather than financial gain.
2. It is protected, kept unencumbered, cared for, and preserved.
3. It is subject to an organizational policy that requires the proceeds from sales of collection items to be used to acquire other items for collections.

Governments should continue to capitalize collections that were capitalized as of June 30, 1999, and should describe their noncapitalized collections and why they are not capitalized.

A government should recognize *revenues* in its *government-wide* Statement of Activities when it receives a donated collection. If the donated collection is capitalized, assets are recorded. When donated collection items are not capitalized, governments should report *program expenses equal to the revenues recognized.*

Capitalized collections or individual items that are *exhaustible*—such as exhibits whose useful lives are diminished by display, educational, or research applications—should be depreciated over their useful lives. Depreciation is not required for collections or individual items that are *inexhaustible.*[4]

Materiality and Control Considerations

In accounting and auditing, an item is considered *material* if *either* (1) its dollar magnitude is significant to the financial statements *or* (2) its nature is such that proper accounting is required regardless of its dollar magnitude. Thus, *both the relative dollar amount and its nature must be considered in determining its materiality.*

Materiality is important in GAAP accounting and reporting because, although items that are material must be accounted for and reported strictly in accordance with GAAP, those that are not material need not be. Thus, *within the confines of legal constraints, SLGs can set GCA accounting policies in a materiality context.*

General Capital Assets capitalization materiality judgments may thus be made in terms of the various classifications of GCA—Land, Buildings and Improvements, Infrastructure, Machinery and Equipment, and Construction in Progress—and different capitalization policies may be established for each GCA classification. But, again, the nature of the items, as well as their dollar magnitude, should be considered in establishing GCA capitalization policies.

Control considerations may dictate capitalizing certain types of GCA even if their cost is less than the legal or other materiality thresholds. Control issues are important reasons to capitalize certain types of movable machinery and equipment— such as personal computers, guns, and communication devices (e.g., two-way radios, cell phones, and pagers)—that may readily be converted to personal use, pawned, or sold. Even if the asset is not capitalized, control may be enhanced by painting it distinctively, by attaching a property identification tag, or by other physical control methods.

Property Records

After the GCA capitalization policies have been established and the cost or other valuation of a capital asset to be capitalized has been determined, it is recorded in an individual GCA property record. A separate record is established for each unit of property. (A unit of property is any item that can be readily identified and accounted for separately, but it may be a group of similar items, such as folding chairs.) These records of individual assets or groups of similar minor assets constitute the subsidiary accounts that support the GCA accounts in the general ledger and include information on each unit of property, such as the following:

1. Property system identification number
2. Serial number, vehicle identification number, and so on

---

[4]Ibid., sec. 1400.111.

3. Abbreviated description
4. Date of acquisition
5. Name and address of vendor
6. Payment voucher number
7. Fund and account from which purchased
8. Federal financing, if any
9. Cost or estimated cost
10. Estimated life, estimated salvage value, annual depreciation
11. Accumulated depreciation
12. Department, division, or unit charged with custody
13. Location
14. Date, method, and authorization of disposition

These subsidiary records must provide for classification in a number of ways:

- **General Ledger–Subsidiary Ledger Control.** They should permit a reconciliation of the detailed subsidiary ledger account amounts with the summary amounts in the Land, Buildings, and other control accounts in the general ledger.

- **Organizational Accountability.** The assets in use by the several organizational units of a government are the responsibility of the agencies, bureaus, departments, and so on. The system should permit identification of such assets by organizational unit for custodial control, cost finding, and accountability purposes.

- **Availability.** Assets not in use should be easily identifiable so that requests for assets may be filled from assets on hand and unnecessary purchases avoided.

- **Location.** Assets should be classifiable by location so that custodial control by physical inventory will be feasible.

Capital Assets Inventory

Land, buildings, infrastructure, and other *immovable* GCA need not be inventoried annually, though their records should be reviewed regularly for accuracy and completeness. However, a physical inventory of machinery, equipment, and other *movable* GCA should be taken on a regular basis for internal control, accounting, and accountability purposes. The physical count can then be compared with recorded descriptions and quantities. All differences between counts and records should be investigated. Missing assets must be removed from the accounts, and significant shortages should be disclosed in the statements or notes. Management should correct the weaknesses in internal control or accounting systems revealed by the shortages and related investigations.

Inventories of machinery, equipment, and other *movable* GCA may be taken annually or on a cycle approach throughout the year. The GCA property records, classified by organization unit responsible and location, are essential to such an inventory. The usual procedure is for the SLG finance officer to send a list of the machinery and equipment for which each department is responsible to that department, asking that the inventory be made and any discrepancies noted. After the department has conducted the inventory, which may be observed or reviewed by the SLG's internal auditors and/or external auditors, the department head and finance officer (or their representatives) determine whether any adjustments and corrective actions are necessary. Thereafter, the department head takes any needed corrective actions, and the finance officer adjusts the GCA records as necessary.

Additions, Betterments, and Renewals

The costs of additions, betterments, and renewals are additional costs of general capital assets. The costs may be incurred in one of the governmental funds, where the distinction between expenditures to be capitalized and those to be treated as repair or maintenance costs should be made. Because expenditures for both purposes must be authorized by appropriations, the distinction should first be made in the budget.

As noted earlier, the distinction between capital outlay and repair and maintenance expenditures is often difficult in practice. Moreover, it is *common to find in practice that (1) amounts that do not meet the GCA capitalization criteria are recorded as capital outlay expenditures in governmental funds, but (2) amounts that should be recorded as capital outlay expenditures in governmental funds and capitalized in the GCA accounts are misclassified*—usually unintentionally—as repairs and maintenance or as other operating expenditures (e.g., capital leases recorded as rentals) in the governmental funds. The first situation presents no problems—the GCA accountant need only select those capital outlay expenditures to be capitalized and perhaps prepare a reconciliation of the governmental fund capital outlay expenditures and those capitalized in the GCA accounts. But *the second situation may require extensive analysis and evaluation of the governmental fund operating expenditure accounts to determine additional amounts that should be capitalized in the GCA accounts.*

Additions to capital assets are not classified according to whether they are buildings, other improvements, or equipment until the additions are completed. As noted earlier, costs incurred are accumulated in the Construction in Progress account during the construction period and are reclassified by asset type after completion of the project.

Depreciation/ Accumulated Depreciation

Depreciation expense and accumulated depreciation of depreciable general government capital assets are recorded in the GCA accounts. The accumulated depreciation is reported in the governmental activities column of the *government-wide* Statement of Net Position and the related depreciation expense is reported in the governmental activities expenses column of the *government-wide* Statement of Activities. Depreciation expense is *not* an expenditure, so it is *not* recorded or reported in the governmental funds. Also, for *infrastructure* capital assets, governments are permitted to use a *modified approach* instead of reporting depreciation in the government-wide financial statements.

Modified Approach

The GASB permits governments to use a modified approach to account for infrastructure assets. The GASB *Codification* states that:

> *Infrastructure assets* are long-lived capital assets that normally are stationary in nature and normally can be preserved for a significantly greater number of years than most capital assets. Examples of infrastructure assets include roads, bridges, tunnels, drainage systems, water and sewer systems, dams, and lighting systems. Buildings, except those that are an ancillary part of a network of infrastructure assets, should not be considered infrastructure assets.[5]

In the "*modified* approach,"[6] *infrastructure assets* that are part of a network or subsystem of a network are *not* required to be depreciated and, additionally, most costs incurred to maintain or preserve the network are expensed *if* two requirements are met:

1. The government *manages* the eligible infrastructure assets by using an *asset management system* that has certain characteristics.
2. The government *documents* that the eligible infrastructure assets are *being preserved* approximately at or above a condition level established and disclosed by the government.

The asset management system must:

- Have an up-to-date inventory of eligible infrastructure assets,
- Perform condition assessments of the eligible infrastructure assets in a manner that can be replicated and summarize the results by using a measurement scale, and
- Estimate each year the annual amount to maintain and preserve the eligible infrastructure assets at the condition level established and disclosed by the government.

[5]Ibid., sec. 1400.103.
[6]Ibid., secs. 1400.105–108.

What constitutes "adequate documentary evidence" to meet the second requirement for using the modified approach requires professional judgment because asset management systems and condition assessment methods vary among governments. These factors may also vary within governments for different eligible infrastructure assets. However, governments should document that:

1. Complete *condition assessments* of eligible infrastructure assets are performed in a consistent manner *at least every three years*.

2. The results of the three most recent complete condition assessments provide reasonable assurance that the eligible infrastructure assets are being preserved approximately at or above the condition level established and disclosed by the government.

If the modified approach is used for eligible infrastructure assets, only those additions and improvements to eligible infrastructure assets that increase the capacity or efficiency of infrastructure assets—rather than extend the useful life of the assets—should be capitalized. *All other costs incurred to maintain or preserve these assets are expensed, but depreciation expense is not reported on them.* If these modified approach requirements are no longer met, the usual capitalization and depreciation requirements should be applied for *subsequent* reporting periods.

Illustration 9-2 summarizes the key financial reporting provisions discussed to this point. The next section illustrates the accounting for capital asset acquisitions of various types.

Updating GCA Accounts

Practice varies considerably for the updating of the General Capital Assets accounts. Computerized systems may be programmed to generate GCA entries continually, periodically, or at year end. In systems that are not fully automated, (1) some accountants prefer to update the GCA ledger whenever a relevant transaction occurs—which typically has been assumed in Uniform CPA Examination questions and problems; (2) others maintain a GCA journal that is posted to the GCA ledger periodically during the year or at year end; and (3) still others update the GCA ledger only at year end, perhaps based on worksheet analyses of fund capital outlay expenditures. Regardless of individual preference, there should be an established, workable system for updating the general capital assets control and subsidiary records at least annually prior to statement preparation.

ILLUSTRATION 9-2   General Capital Assets Reporting Summary

A. *Valuation* of GCA acquired via:

Purchase	Cost
Gift	Fair value when received
Eminent domain	Cost (established by court)
Escheat	Fair value when escheat occurs
Foreclosure	Lower of (1) government's claims against the property or (2) the property's fair value at foreclosure

B. Use of *estimated costs* — Permitted when:

(1) establishing initial GCA records and

(2) actual costs are not practicably determinable

C. Capitalization of *infrastructure* capital assets — Required

D. Reporting of *accumulated depreciation* — Required except for infrastructure reported under the modified approach

E. *Capitalization* of

Exhaustible collections	Required
Inexhaustible collections	Optional

Illustration 9-1 presents the accounting equation applicable to the General Capital Assets and General Long-Term Liabilities accounts. The following *trial balance* further illustrates the account relationships:

General Capital Assets and General Long-Term Liabilities Accounts
Trial Balance
(Date)

Land..	$ 700,000	
Buildings.....................................	3,000,000	
Streets and Other Infrastructure....................	5,100,000	
Machinery and Equipment........................	819,200	
Construction in Progress.........................	500,800	
Accumulated Depreciation—Buildings...............		$ 500,000
Accumulated Depreciation—Streets and Other Infrastructure.............................		1,000,000
Accumulated Depreciation—Machinery and Equipment..		200,000
Serial Bonds Payable............................		2,500,000
Premium on Serial Bonds........................		35,000
Estimated Claims and Judgments Liabilities...........		1,500,000
Capital Lease Liabilities..........................		1,150,000
Special Assessment Bonds with Governmental Commitment..................................		300,000
Net Position....................................		2,935,000
	$10,120,000	$10,120,000

The entries to record the capital expenditures in each governmental fund have already been given. To highlight the relationship between these funds and the General Capital Assets accounts, some of the fund general ledger entries will be repeated and the corresponding general ledger entries in the General Capital Assets and General Long-Term Liabilities accounts will be indicated. A series of Land, Machinery and Equipment, and similar capital asset subsidiary ledgers would also be used, of course, but these subsidiary ledgers are not unique to governmental accounting and are not illustrated here.

Assets Financed from the General Fund or Special Revenue Funds

To record the $6,100 of capital outlay expenditures for equipment in the General Fund illustrative example (entry 4, Chapter 3), the entry in the **General Fund** is:

Expenditures—Capital Outlay......................	$ 6,100	
Vouchers Payable		$ 6,100
To record purchase of equipment.		

A companion entry would be made in the **General Capital Assets accounts**:

Machinery and Equipment........................	$ 6,100	
Net Position....................................		$ 6,100
To record cost of capital assets financed from current revenues.		

General capital assets acquired by capital lease are recorded similarly. Recall that the **governmental fund** general ledger entry (Chapter 6, page 234) upon the inception of a capital lease was:

Expenditures—Capital Outlay......................	$ 900,000	
Other Financing Sources—Capital Lease		$ 860,000
Cash		40,000
To record capital lease expenditure and related other financing source.		

The companion entry in the **General Capital Assets accounts**—assuming the lease was for land and a building—would be:

Land—Under Capital Lease	$ 100,000	
Buildings—Under Capital Lease	800,000	
Capital Lease Liabilities		$ 860,000
Net Position		40,000

To record land and building acquired by capital lease.

Note that the capital assets are identified as "under capital lease" during the term of the lease. Then, if the government takes title to the capital assets, they are reclassified to the usual accounts (e.g., Land and Buildings).

Assets Financed Through Capital Projects Funds and Special Assessments

Whether construction expenditures accounts are closed at the end of each year or only when the bridge construction is completed, this **Capital Projects Fund** general ledger entry (Chapter 7) is made—in the accounts or in the year-end worksheets—at the end of the first year:

Revenues—Federal Grant	$ 508,000	
Revenues—State Grant	600,000	
Revenues—Interest	18,000	
Other Financing Sources—Bonds (Face Amount)	900,000	
Other Financing Sources—Bond Premium	11,000	
Other Financing Sources—Transfer from General Fund	130,000	
Expenditures—Bean & Co. Contract		$1,000,000
Expenditures—Labor		140,000
Expenditures—Machine Time		81,000
Expenditures—Fuel and Materials		49,000
Expenditures—Bond Issue Costs		2,000
Fund Balance		895,000

To close the actual revenues, other financing sources, and expenditures to date (project incomplete).

The following entry is required in the **General Capital Assets accounts**:

Construction in Progress	$1,270,000	
Net Position		$ 1,270,000

To record construction in progress ($1,000,000 + $140,000 + $81,000 + $49,000 = $1,270,000).

Note that the bond issue costs are expensed and are not part of the capital asset cost recorded. Note also that *encumbered* amounts, whether closed out at year end or not, are *not* capitalized; *only expended amounts are capitalized.*

When the project is completed, during the second year in our example, the general ledger "actual" accounts closing entry in the **Capital Projects Fund**—assuming the accounts are closed annually—is:

Revenues—Federal Grant	$ 660,000	
Revenues—Interest	12,000	
Other Financing Sources—Transfer from General Fund	170,000	
Fund Balance	895,000	
Expenditures—Bean & Co. Contract		$1,410,000
Expenditures—Labor		129,000
Expenditures—Machine Time		108,000
Expenditures—Fuel and Materials		43,000

To close the accounts (project completed).

In the **General Capital Assets accounts**, the entry is:

Streets and Other Infrastructure......................	$2,960,000	
Construction in Progress		$1,270,000
Net Position		1,690,000

To record the cost of completed bridge project ($1,270,000 +
$1,410,000 + $129,000 + $108,000 + $43,000 = $2,960,000)
and to close the Construction in Progress account.

As noted in Chapter 7, most special assessment projects are accounted for in
Capital Projects Funds. In any event, the procedure for recording general capital
assets acquired through special assessments parallels that illustrated for capital
projects.

Assets Acquired Through Foreclosure

We noted earlier that capital assets acquired through foreclosure should be recorded
at the *lower* of (1) fair value or (2) the amount of taxes or assessments, penalties, and
interest due on the property and costs of foreclosure and sale. To illustrate, assume
that land with an estimated value of $2,000 was acquired through foreclosure. At the
time of foreclosure, the following were due a Special Revenue Fund:

Taxes	$ 900
Penalties	100
Interest.......................................	75
Costs of foreclosure and sale.....................	25
	$1,100

Further assuming that these receivables had been reclassified as tax liens receivable prior to the decision to retain the property for the government's use, the following entry should be made in the **Special Revenue Fund**:

Expenditures—Capital Outlay	$ 1,100	
Tax Liens Receivable		$ 1,100

To record acquisition of land through foreclosure;
estimated fair value, $2,000.

The accompanying entry in the **General Capital Assets accounts** would be:

Land...	$ 1,100	
Net Position.....................................		$ 1,100

To record acquisition of land through foreclosure of tax lien.

Note that had the fair value of the property been less than charges against it, say
$800, the Special Revenue Fund expenditure would be recorded at $800, and $300
would be charged against the allowance for uncollectible taxes and interest (or tax
liens) receivable.

Assets Acquired through Gifts

No governmental fund assets are relinquished in acquiring property donated to
the government. Thus, general government capital assets acquired by gift are recorded directly in the General Capital Assets accounts. Donated property should
be recorded in the GCA accounts at estimated fair value at the time of donation:

Land...	$ 1,500	
Net Position.....................................		$ 1,500

To record land received by gift at estimated fair value.

Note also that $1,500 of capital contribution revenue will be reported in the *government-wide* Statement of Activities.

Recording Depreciation

Depreciation expense and accumulated depreciation on depreciable general capital assets are recorded in the General Capital Assets accounts and are *reported in the government-wide Statement of Activities*. In the accounting model illustrated here, depreciation expense might be recorded as follows:

Depreciation Expense (detailed by function)	$423,261	
Accumulated Depreciation (detailed by depreciable assets)		$423,261
To record depreciation expense and accumulated depreciation.		

The *Depreciation Expense* accounts would be *closed to* (and reduce) the *Net Position* account.

Sale, Replacement, or Retirement

General capital assets may be disposed of in sale, replacement, or retirement transactions with other governments, nongovernment organizations, and individuals. The accounting procedure upon **disposal** is:

1. **General Capital Assets accounts.** Remove the asset carrying value by debiting the related accumulated depreciation account(s) and crediting the asset account(s); reduce the Net Position account accordingly.

2. **Fund receiving proceeds of sale.** Record any salvage value, insurance proceeds, or other receipts as other financing sources in the accounts of the recipient governmental fund.

3. **Government-Wide Statement of Activities.** Report a gain or loss on disposal equal to the *difference* between items 1 and 2, as discussed in Chapter 13.

Sale

If a fire truck with a book value of $100,000 (cost, $800,000; accumulated depreciation, $700,000) is sold for $20,000, the following entries are made:

General Fund:		
Cash	$ 20,000	
Other Financing Sources—Sales of Equipment		$ 20,000
To record sale of fire truck.		
General Capital Assets accounts:		
Net Position	$100,000	
Accumulated Depreciation—Machinery and Equipment. . .	700,000	
Machinery and Equipment		$800,000
To record sale of fire truck with book value of $100,000.		

Note that an *$80,000 loss* on the sale of the fire truck is to be reported in the *government-wide* Statement of Activities. Records of such gains and losses should be maintained to facilitate preparing the government-wide financial statements.

Replacement (Trade-In)

If the fire truck is traded in on a new one costing $920,000 (fair value) and an allowance of $30,000 is made for the old truck, the transaction is recorded as follows:

General Fund:		
Expenditures—Capital Outlay	$890,000	
Cash		$890,000
To record purchase of fire truck costing $920,000, net of trade-in allowance of $30,000.		

General Capital Assets accounts:

Net Position......................................	$100,000	
Accumulated Depreciation—Machinery and Equipment...	700,000	
Machinery and Equipment		$800,000

To record disposal (trade-in) of old fire truck with book
value of $100,000.

Machinery and Equipment	$920,000	
Net Position...................................		$920,000

To record purchase of fire truck at a cost of $920,000.

Note that the book value of the old fire truck traded in should be removed from the GCA accounts, as in a sale, and the new fire truck should be recorded at its fair value in the GCA accounts. (One of the most common GCA accounting errors in practice is erroneous capitalization of the new capital asset at the amount of the "boot" given in an exchange—the amount of the governmental fund expenditure—rather than at its fair value.) Also, a $70,000 loss should be reported in the government-wide statement of activities for the difference between the book value of the old truck ($100,000) and its $30,000 fair value.

Retirement

The entries to record retirements may be more complicated than other capital asset sales because the cost of retirement, as well as the proceeds received from the sale of salvage, must be taken into account. For example, assume that a fire station with a cost of $750,000 and book value of $150,000 was torn down. The cost of tearing it down was $10,000, and $15,000 was realized from the sale of salvage. The entries to record these transactions are as follows:

General Capital Assets accounts:

Net Position.....................................	$150,000	
Accumulated Depreciation—Buildings.................	600,000	
Buildings		$750,000

To record retirement of fire station.

General Fund:

Expenditures—Other...............................	$ 10,000	
Cash		$ 10,000

To record cost of dismantling building—to be reimbursed
from sale of salvage.

Cash	$ 15,000	
Expenditures—Other.............................		$ 10,000
Other Financing Sources—Salvage Proceeds		5,000

To record sale of salvage.

Note that whereas the *salvage costs* are temporarily recorded as expenditures, those costs are *netted* against the gross salvage proceeds, and the *net* amount is reported as *Other Financing Sources—Salvage Proceeds*. Note also that a $145,000 loss on retirement of the fire station will be reported in the *government-wide* Statement of Activities.

Thus far we have assumed that the assets were sold or traded to private non-SLG organizations or persons. Sometimes property accounted for in a proprietary or similar Trust Fund is sold to a department financed through a governmental fund. Capital assets may also be transferred among agencies of the government.

Intragovernmental Transactions

Intragovernmental Sale

Assume that an enterprise (Enterprise Fund) sells equipment at book value to the public works department, which is financed from the General Fund. The following entries would be made:

Enterprise Fund:		
Due from General Fund...........................	$ 15,000	
Accumulated Depreciation—Equipment	1,000	
Equipment......................................		$ 16,000
To record sale of equipment to department of public works at net book value.		
General Fund:		
Expenditures—Capital Outlay	$ 15,000	
Due to Enterprise Fund...........................		$ 15,000
To record purchase of equipment from Enterprise Fund for department of public works.		
General Capital Assets accounts:		
Machinery and Equipment	$ 16,000	
Accumulated Depreciation—Equipment		$ 1,000
Net Position.....................................		15,000
To record purchase of equipment for public works department.		

If the sale were for more or less than book value, a transfer should be reported in the Enterprise Fund and in the General Fund for the difference between the book value of the capital asset and the amount exchanged for it. GASB *Statement No. 48* "Sales and Pledges of Receivables and Future Revenues and Intra-Entity Transfers of Assets and Future Revenues" (para. 15) prohibits treating the transaction the same as a sale to and purchase from an external entity and requires reporting transfers for the differential in the reporting entity financial statements. The machinery and equipment should be recorded at the book value of $15,000 in the GCA accounts regardless of the sales price.

Interagency sales of capital assets in exchange-like transactions appear to occur most often in state governments and in large local governments with rather autonomous departments and agencies. Capital assets may also be transferred and reclassified (rather than sold) between agencies.

Intragovernmental "Transfer"

Capital assets may be transferred (reassigned) both (1) between general government departments, financed by governmental funds, and (2) between general government departments and proprietary fund departments or agencies. The accounting procedures differ for each type of reassignment. Note that although reassignments are commonly referred to as transfers of capital assets, they involve only one fund—a proprietary fund—at most. Therefore, they are not interfund transfers and are not reported as transfers in the fund financial statements. As discussed below, some reassignments are reported as transfers in the government-wide statement of activities.

General Government Transfer When capital assets are reassigned from one general government department or agency to another general government department or agency, or even from one location to another, appropriate authorization should be issued by the proper authority. The authorization will be the basis for changes in the GCA subsidiary records—reassignments of departmental responsibility and/or location—to permit continuing control. *The GCA general ledger accounts will not be affected.*

Note that such GCA transfers are *not* interfund transfers. Rather, although they may be referred to informally as *transfers,* they are *reclassifications* within the GCA accounts.

Proprietary Fund–General Government Transfer Reassignments of capital assets between agencies financed by governmental funds and agencies financed by proprietary funds affect both the general ledger and the subsidiary property records of both the GCA accounts and the proprietary fund. They do not affect any governmental fund. These reassignments are recorded at net book value. Assuming that equipment with a fair value of $15,000 and net book value of $10,000 (cost of $30,000) is reassigned from the Water Fund to the fire, police, and public works departments—which are general government departments—the following entries are required:

Water (Enterprise) Fund:

Nonoperating Expenses—Transfer of Capital Assets	$10,000	
Accumulated Depreciation—Equipment	20,000	
Equipment.		$30,000

To record reassignment of equipment to general government
   departments as follows:

Department	Cost of Equipment	Accumulated Depreciation	Net Book Value
Police	$ 5,000	$ 3,000	$ 2,000
Fire	10,000	6,500	3,500
Public Works . . .	15,000	10,500	4,500
	$30,000	$20,000	$10,000

General Capital Assets accounts:

Machinery and Equipment	$30,000	
Accumulated Depreciation—Machinery and Equipment. . .		$20,000
Net Position.		10,000

To record receipt of equipment.

Note that this *"transfer" is reported in the Enterprise Fund as a nonoperating expense*—rather than as a transfer—because the transaction does not involve two funds and, therefore, cannot be an interfund transfer. In the *government-wide* financial statements, this transaction will be reclassified as and reported as a *transfer* between governmental activities and business-type activities.

General Government–Proprietary Fund Transfer Capital assets may also be transferred (reassigned) from the general government departments to proprietary fund departments or agencies. The GCA accounting required is to remove the capital asset accounts, as in any capital asset disposal. The capital assets are then recorded in the proprietary fund at their depreciated cost—as if they had been originally acquired for proprietary fund use. Furthermore, the amount is reported as capital contributions in the proprietary fund financial statements and as a *transfer* in the *government-wide* financial statements.

Capital asset ***impairment*** is ***defined*** in GASB *Statement No. 42*[7] as a:

    Impairment

- ***Significant*** [material]
- ***Unexpected*** [not normal, not ordinary]
- ***Decline*** in the ***service utility*** of a capital asset

---

[7]GASB *Statement No. 42,* "Accounting and Financial Reporting for Impairment of Capital Assets," November 2003, pars. 5–20.

This definition **excludes**:

1. events or changes in circumstances that, upon capital asset acquisition, might be expected to occur during the useful life of the asset,

2. capital assets accounted for on the modified approach, and

3. impairments caused by deferred maintenance.

The GASB does *not require* SLGs to actively search for potentially impaired capital assets, but presumes the potential impairment circumstances will be "prominent" and "readily observable."

Indicators of Impairment

A capital asset should be *tested* for impairment whenever prominent *unexpected* events or changes in circumstances indicate that the service utility of the capital asset has declined significantly [materially]. *Common indicators of impairment* include:

- **Evidence of physical damage**—such as a building damaged by fire or flood.
- **Change in legal or environmental factors**—such as a water treatment plant that cannot meet—and cannot be modified to meet—new water quality standards.
- **Technological development or evidence of obsolescence**—such as that related to diagnostic equipment that is rarely used because newer equipment is more accurate.
- **A change in the manner or expected duration of usage of a capital asset**—such as closure of a school prior to the end of its useful life.
- **Construction stoppage**—such as stoppage of construction of a building due to lack of funding.

Tests of Impairment

Any capital asset that presents *one or more indicators* of impairment should be *tested* by considering two factors:

1. The *magnitude* of the decline in service utility. The expenses, including depreciation, associated with the continued operation and maintenance of the capital asset, or the restoration costs, are significant [material] in relation to the current service utility. (*Management's action or inaction* may indicate that the operating expenses or restoration costs are too high.)

2. The *unexpected* nature of the decline in service utility. The restoration cost or other impairment circumstances are not part of the capital asset's normal life cycle.

Applying Impairment Standards

Both the *determination* of impairment and measurement(s) of the impairment, and the related *materiality* determinations, may be applied to either:

- *Individual components* of capital assets (e.g., a building roof or heating/cooling system),
- *Individual assets* (e.g., a building),
- *Groups of related assets* (e.g., multi-building county building complex), or
- *Infrastructure subsystems or systems.*

The GASB permits professional judgment to be used in determining the level at which GASB *Statement No. 42* is applied.

Impairment Measurement

The appropriate *measurement* of impairment depends on *both*

- The *nature* of the impairment, and
- Whether the impaired capital asset(s) *will continue to be used* by the SLG.

A capital asset that a government has decided to sell but is *continuing to use* until the sale occurs is not considered to exhibit a change in manner or expected duration of use. However, the accounting estimates of its remaining useful life *and salvage value* should be *reevaluated* for such capital assets and changed if appropriate. A capital asset that a government has decided to sell and is *not using* is considered to exhibit a change in manner or expected duration of use and should be evaluated for impairment.

Measurement—Assets Continue to Be Used

The *amount of impairment*—**the *portion of historical cost that should be written off*—should be measured by the following method that best reflects the *value-in-use* or *remaining service utility* of the impaired capital asset:

   a. **Restoration cost approach.** Under this approach—generally used for impairments resulting from *physical damage*—the amount of impairment is derived from the *estimated costs to restore* the *utility* of the capital asset. The restoration cost can be *converted* to *historical cost* either (1) by deflating the restoration cost using an appropriate cost index or (2) by applying a ratio of restoration cost over replacement cost to the carrying value of the capital asset.

   b. **Service units approach.** This approach—generally used for impairments resulting from *changes in legal or environmental factors or from technological development or obsolescence*—isolates the historical cost of the service utility of the capital asset that cannot be used due to the impairment event or change in circumstances. The amount of impairment is determined by evaluating the service provided by the capital asset—either maximum service units or total service units throughout the life of the capital asset—before and after the event or change in circumstances.

   c. **Deflated depreciated replacement cost approach.** This approach—generally used for impairments identified from a *change in the manner or duration of use*—replicates the historical cost of the service produced. The current cost for a capital asset to replace the current level of service is identified. The current cost is (1) depreciated to reflect the fact that the capital asset is not new and then is (2) deflated to convert it to historical cost dollars.

Measurement—Assets No Longer Used

Impaired capital assets that will not continue to be used by the SLG—and those impaired from construction stoppage—should be reported at the *lower of carrying value or fair value*.

Reporting Impairment Losses

How an impairment loss is reported depends on whether the impairment is temporary.

- **Temporary**—An impairment generally should be considered permanent, but evidence might demonstrate it is temporary. If so, no *impairment loss* would be reported.

- **Other Than Temporary**—Related expenditures would be reported in governmental funds. Most impairment losses should be reported as a program expense, special item, or extraordinary item, as appropriate, in the government-wide and proprietary fund financial statements.

The amount and financial statement classification of impairment losses should be disclosed in the notes if not otherwise apparent on the face of the financial statements.

GASB *Statement No. 42*[8] provides guidance for *all insurance recoveries:*   **Insurance Recoveries**

- In *governmental fund* financial statements, *restoration or replacement* of an impaired capital asset should be reported as a *separate* transaction *from* the associated *insurance*

---
[8]Ibid., pars. 21–22.

recovery, which is reported as an *other financing source* or *extraordinary item,* as appropriate.

- In both **governmental and business-type activities** in *government-wide* financial statements *and* in **proprietary fund** financial statements, *restoration or replacement* of an impaired capital asset should be reported as a *separate* transaction *from* the *impairment loss* and associated *insurance recovery.*
- The *impairment loss* should be reported *net* of the associated *insurance recovery* when the recovery and loss occur in the *same year.*
- **Insurance recoveries** reported in *subsequent* years should be reported in the government-wide financial statements and in proprietary fund financial statements as a *program revenue, nonoperating revenue, or extraordinary item,* as appropriate.
- **Insurance recoveries other than those related to impairment of capital assets**—such as for theft or embezzlement of cash or other monetary assets—should be accounted for as already described, as should recoveries from Internal Service Funds.
- **Recoveries received from the General Fund** should be accounted for as *reimbursements* to the extent of the impairment loss, if any, and be reported as *transfers* in the fund financial statements *for amounts in excess* of the impairment loss, if any.

Insurance recoveries should be *recognized* **only** when **realized** or **realizable**. For example:

1. If an insurer has *admitted or acknowledged* coverage, an insurance recovery would be realizable.
2. If the insurer has *denied* coverage, the insurance recovery generally would *not* be *realizable.*

If not otherwise apparent in the financial statements, the amount and financial statement classification of insurance recoveries should be disclosed.

Damage or Destruction

Damage or destruction of property is an example of capital asset impairment. Expenditures for repairs necessary to restore damaged property to its former condition are reported as current operating expenditures in the governmental fund from which the cost of repairs is financed. Insurance proceeds are reported as other financing sources. To illustrate, assume that the total book value of a police station (original cost, $1,500,000) is $800,000, that the station is destroyed by fire, and that the governmental unit collects insurance of $200,000. The following entries would be made in the GCA accounts and in the General Fund, respectively, to record these transactions:

General Capital Assets accounts:		
Net Position................................	$800,000	
Accumulated Depreciation—Buildings..................	700,000	
Buildings		$1,500,000
To record destruction of police station by fire.		
General Fund:		
Cash	$200,000	
Other Financing Sources—Insurance Proceeds		$ 200,000
To record receipt of proceeds of insurance policy on police station.		

Based on the restoration cost approach to measurement of impairments, a $600,000 loss (after deducting the insurance recovery proceeds) would be reported in the *government-wide* Statement of Activities. If the government intends to use some or all of the proceeds for replacements, a commitment or assignment could be established in the General Fund by the appropriate authority.

The GASB standards require that:

- General capital assets are reported in the *governmental activities* column of the *government-wide* Statement of Net Position.

- Detailed capital assets information—which distinguishes those assets associated with governmental activities from those associated with business-type activities—must be provided in the notes to the basic financial statements.

The notes should disclose GCA information by *major classes* of general capital assets, should separately disclose any GCA that are not being depreciated, and should include the following:

1. Beginning- and end-of-year balances (regardless of whether beginning-of-year balances are presented on the face of the government-wide financial statements), with accumulated depreciation presented separately from historical cost

2. Acquisitions of capital assets

3. Sales or other dispositions

4. Current period depreciation expense, with disclosure of the amounts charged to each of the functions in the Statement of Activities

Illustration 9-3 presents an example of the required note disclosure.

GENERAL LONG-TERM LIABILITIES

General long-term liabilities of a government are defined in the GASB *Codification* as *all* of its *unmatured* long-term debt *except* that of proprietary funds or Trust Funds.[9] General long-term liabilities (GLTL) thus include the *unmatured principal* of bonds, warrants, notes, capital leases, certificates of participation, underfunded pension and underfunded OPEB contributions, claims and judgments, compensated absences, landfill closure and postclosure care, and other forms of general government debt that are not a primary obligation of any fund. Unmatured long-term *special assessment debt* is included in GLTL *if* the government is *obligated in any manner* on the debt and it is not being serviced through a specific Enterprise Fund, as noted in Chapter 8. The GLTL data presented in "9-2 In Practice" demonstrate the magnitude of various types of GLTL of several governments. Note the significance of the Net Pension Obligation in several of these governments, while the Net OPEB Obligation was not presented because the reported amount is small or zero even though it is a very large obligation for many governments. The Net OPEB Obligation reported is small because the governments were only beginning to implement the OPEB standards prospectively in the fiscal year reported in these data.

Matured general obligation debt that has been recorded in and will be paid from a Debt Service Fund (DSF) is *excluded* from the GLTL definition, as are all debts to be paid by proprietary funds or Trust Funds. The excluded debt is not recorded in the General Long-Term Liabilities accounts, but if non-GLTL debt is guaranteed by the government, the government's contingent liability should be disclosed.

The same type of clear-cut distinction maintained between capital assets of specific funds and general capital assets is maintained between (1) *fund* long-term liabilities that are the primary responsibility of specific funds and (2) *general* long-term liabilities. *Unmatured* general long-term liabilities are recorded in the GLTL accounts, *not* in the fund used to account for the proceeds from their issuance (e.g., the Capital Projects Fund) or the fund from which they will eventually be paid (e.g., the Debt Service Fund).

Practice varies somewhat concerning the timing of the entries in the General Long-Term Liabilities accounts. As a general rule, (1) entries to record incurrence

---

[9]GASB *Codification*, sec. 1500.103.

of debt are made immediately upon its incurrence, though estimated liabilities may be recorded and adjusted at year end, and (2) entries to record debt maturity are prepared when the debt is due.

ILLUSTRATION 9-3   Illustrative Disclosure of Information About Capital Assets

Capital asset activity for the year ended December 31, 20X2, was as follows (in thousands):

	Primary Government			
	Beginning Balance	Increases	Decreases	Ending Balance
Governmental activities:				
Capital assets not being depreciated:[†]				
Land and improvements	$ 29,484	$ 2,020	$ (4,358)	$ 27,146
Construction in progress	2,915	13,220	(14,846)	1,289
Total capital assets not being depreciated	32,399	15,240	(19,204)	28,435
Other capital assets:				
Buildings and improvements	40,861	334	—	41,195
Equipment	32,110	1,544	(1,514)	32,140
Road network[†]	72,885	10,219	—	83,104
Bridge network[†]	18,775	4,627	—	23,402
Total other capital assets at historical cost	164,631	16,724	(1,514)	179,841
Less accumulated depreciation for:				
Buildings and improvements	(10,358)	(691)	—	(11,049)
Equipment	(9,247)	(2,676)	1,040	(10,883)
Road network[†]	(12,405)	(823)	—	(13,228)
Bridge network[†]	(2,896)	(197)	—	(3,093)
Total accumulated depreciation	(34,906)	(4,387)*	1,040	(38,253)
Other capital assets, net	129,725	12,337	(474)	141,588
Governmental activities capital assets, net	$162,124	$27,577	$(19,678)	$170,023

__Depreciation expense__ was charged to functions as follows:

Governmental activities:	
General government	$ 275
Public safety	330
Public works, which includes the depreciation of road and bridge networks[†]	1,315
Health and sanitation	625
Cemetery	29
Culture and recreation	65
Community development	40
In addition, depreciation on capital assets held by the City's internal service funds is charged to the various functions based on their usage of the assets.	1,708
Total governmental activities depreciation expense	$ 4,387

	Primary Government			
	Beginning Balance	Increases	Decreases	Ending Balance
Business-type activities:				
Capital assets not being depreciated:[†]				
Land and improvements	$ 3,691	$ 145	$ —	$ 3,836
Construction in progress	5,013	767	(3,208)	2,572
Total capital assets not being depreciated	8,704	912	(3,208)	6,408
Other capital assets:				
Distribution and collection systems	37,806	4,968	(829)	41,945
Buildings and equipment	121,357	2,827	(32)	124,152
Total other capital assets at historical cost	159,163	7,795	(861)	166,097
Less accumulated depreciation for:				
Distribution and collection systems	(8,483)	(897)	829	(8,551)
Buildings and equipment	(11,789)	(808)	32	(12,565)
Total accumulated depreciation	(20,272)	(1,705)*	861	(21,116)
Other capital assets, net	138,891	6,090	—	144,981
Business-type activities capital assets, net	$147,595	$7,002	$(3,208)	$151,389

***Depreciation expense** was charged to functions as follows:*

Business-type activities:

Water	$ 550
Sewer	613
Parking facilities	542
Total business-type activities depreciation expense	$1,705

[†]Capital assets that are not being depreciated are reported separately in this note. In addition, if this government used the modified approach for infrastructure assets, there would be no depreciation expense or accumulated depreciation for those assets.

Note: Disclosures similar to those above would be made for component units' balances and changes.

Source: GASB Comprehensive Implementation Guide (2011), Appendix 7-1, Illustration A, Note 1.

Portions of various GASB documents, copyright by the Governmental Accounting Standards Board, 401 Merritt, PO Box 5116, Norwalk, CT 06856-5116, are reproduced with permission. Complete copies of those documents are available from the GASB.

9-2 IN PRACTICE

	General Long-Term Liabilities					
Government	Bonds and Notes	Leases	Claims and Judgments	Compensated Absences	Pensions	Total GLTL
Illinois	$23.9 billion	$129 million	$190 million	$424 million	$14.5 billion	$39.1 billion
Kansas	$ 3 billion	$152 million	$ 68 million	$109 million		$ 3.3 billion
New Jersey	$14.5 billion	$ 17 billion		$519 million	$ 3 billion	$ 40 billion
Oklahoma	$ 1.5 billion	$ 2.3 million		$ 66 million	$ 1.9 million	$ 4.8 billion
Chicago, IL	$ 6.9 billion	$278 million	$527 million		$ 1.9 billion	$11.1 billion

CPF-DSF-GLTL To illustrate the relationship among Capital Projects Funds, Debt Service Funds, and the General Long-Term Liabilities accounts, recall the Flores Park bonds example in Chapter 8, pages 307–311. Upon issuance of the debt instruments in 20X1 at par, entries would have been made as follows:

Capital Projects Fund:		
Cash	$1,000,000	
Other Financing Sources—Bonds		$1,000,000
To record receipt of bond issue proceeds.		
General Long-Term Liabilities accounts:		
Net Position	$1,000,000	
Serial Bonds Payable		$1,000,000
To record issuance of serial bonds.		

Recall, also, that a Flores Park Serial Bonds Debt Service Fund was established to service this debt. When the 20X1 principal ($100,000) and interest ($50,000) payment on the Flores Park bonds became due along with $10,000 of fiscal agent fees, the following entries were required:

Debt Service Fund:		
Expenditures—Bond Principal Retirement	$ 100,000	
Expenditures—Interest on Bonds	50,000	
Expenditures—Fiscal Agent Fees	10,000	
Matured Bonds Payable		$ 100,000
Matured Interest Payable		50,000
Fiscal Agent Fees Payable		10,000
To record maturity of bonds and interest along with fiscal agent fees.		
General Long-Term Liabilities accounts:		
Serial Bonds Payable	$ 100,000	
Net Position		$ 100,000
To record serial bonds maturing and being recorded as a DSF liability.		

Similar entries would be made at least annually throughout the life of the Debt Service Fund and the debt issue.

Serial Debt Some serial Debt Service Funds closely parallel the Flores Park Serial Bonds Debt Service Fund example from Chapter 8 that was used in the previous section. Others are essentially flow-through vehicles through which current period principal and interest requirements and payments are accounted for. Many such funds have minimal (or zero) balances at year-end. For example, capital leases and long-term notes payable do not usually have funded reserve or other requirements in which amounts in excess of the annual debt service requirements must be accumulated in a Debt Service Fund. Furthermore, any related Debt Service Funds are often financed by interfund transfers in the amount of the annual debt service requirements. Hence, no excess resources are accumulated in the DSF in such cases.

In the case of regular serial bonds with *funded reserve* requirements—like the Flores Park serial bonds—an amount at least equal to the requirement(s) should be accumulated in the related DSF and reflected in restricted fund balance. When debt principal maturities are staggered over a period of years, the government may equalize its annual debt service provisions, thereby accumulating resources in low-requirement years for use during high-requirement years. When a significant excess of serial Debt Service Fund assets over current year principal and interest requirements exists, the serial bond Debt Service Fund becomes similar to a term bond Debt Service Fund and should be accounted for similarly. In this case, the amounts reported in fund balance may be classified as assigned or committed rather than restricted.

Recall from Chapter 8 that the GASB *Codification* (sec. S40) requires a government to report *unmatured* special assessment bonds, notes, or other debt in its GLTL accounts *if* the government is *even remotely contingently obligated in any manner on the debt*. Thus, whereas other contingent liabilities are disclosed in the notes to the financial statements—rather than reported as liabilities in the financial statements—the GASB requires a unique exception for special assessment indebtedness.

Special Assessment Debt

    Recognizing the unusual nature of this requirement, the GASB also specified that the special assessment liability should be distinguished from other GLTL. These liabilities must be reported as *Special Assessment Debt with Governmental Commitment.* Thus, issuance of $900,000 of special assessment bonds that are expected to be serviced by related special assessments—but on which a government is obligated in some manner—would be recorded in the **General Long-Term Liabilities accounts** as follows:

Net Position.	$900,000	
Special Assessment Bonds [or Debt] with Governmental		
Commitment		$900,000
To record issuance of special assessment debt on which the		
government is obligated in some manner.		

With this exception, the GLTL entries parallel those discussed earlier.

The GASB *Codification* definition of the modified accrual basis of governmental fund accounting states that a *fund expenditure is* recognized when a *fund liability* is incurred. The *Codification* also provides that *all unmatured noncurrent indebtedness except specific fund indebtedness is GLTL* and that GLTL "is not limited to liabilities arising from debt issuances *per se,* but may also include . . . other commitments that are not current liabilities properly recorded in governmental funds."[10]

Other Government Liabilities

    Furthermore, the *Codification* states—with regard to claims and judgments, compensated absences, and unfunded actuarially required pension plan contributions—that in governmental funds, liabilities usually are **not** considered **current** until they "are normally expected to be liquidated with expendable available financial resources."[11] Indeed, this criterion generally is met when these liabilities are due and payable. The *Codification* then provides direction for determining the liability for general government underfunded pension contributions, OPEB, claims and judgments, and compensated absences liabilities—and changes therein—and directs that (1) the amount of the liability that would normally be expected to be liquidated with available expendable financial resources should be recorded as a governmental fund expenditure and liability, and (2) the excess should be recorded in the GLTL accounts. GASB *Interpretation No. 6* specifies that *the amount normally liquidated with available expendable financial resources* is the amount that *matures* (becomes due) during the period. (We have referred to the related expenditures as when-due type expenditures.)

    Thus, GLTL may include numerous types of *unmatured general government liabilities,* such as claims and judgments; accumulated vacation, sick leave, and other compensated absences; landfill closure and postclosure care; and underfunded pension and OPEB contributions—as well as unmatured bonds, notes, and capital leases payable.

---

[10]Ibid. See also GASB, *Interpretation No. 6,* "Recognition and Measurement of Certain Liabilities and Expenditures in Governmental Fund Financial Statements" (March 2000); *Codification* secs. 1500–1600.

[11]GASB *Codification,* sec. 1500.108.

To illustrate, recall the claims and judgments (CJ) expenditures example from Chapter 6 (page 240). This example assumed the following key information:

20X1 Transaction/Information Summary	Amount
Total CJ liabilities at beginning of year	$ 0
Claims and judgments (CJ) paid during year	300,000
Total CJ liabilities outstanding at year-end	200,000
Portion of CJ liabilities considered current at year-end	50,000

The entries required to record the preceding information in the General Fund and in the General Long-Term Liabilities accounts are as follows:

General Fund:

Expenditures—Claims and Judgments	$300,000	
Cash		$300,000

To record payment of CJ expenditures.

General Fund:

Expenditures—Claims and Judgments	$ 50,000	
Accrued CJ Liabilities		$ 50,000

To record additional expenditures for current CJ liabilities that become due and are to be paid from existing fund assets.

General Long-Term Liabilities accounts:

Net Position	$150,000	
Accrued CJ Liabilities		$150,000

To record the increase in the long-term portion of CJ liabilities.

Note that 20X1 CJ *expenditures* reported in the General Fund are $350,000 ($300,000 + $50,000), but 20X1 CJ *expenses* reported in the government-wide Statement of Activities are $500,000 ($350,000 + $150,000).

As an additional example, recall the capital lease transactions discussed in Chapter 6, page 234. The General Fund entry to record the inception of the lease and the General Capital Assets accounts entry to record the leased asset are shown in this chapter on page 354.

Next, recall that the **General Fund** entry to record the first lease payment of $18,000 (including interest of $5,000) was:

Expenditures—Interest	$ 5,000	
Expenditures—Principal	13,000	
Cash		$ 18,000

To record capital lease debt service payment due and paid.

The companion entry in the **General Long-Term Liabilities** accounts would be:

Capital Lease Liability	$ 13,000	
Net Position		$ 13,000

To record reduction of outstanding capital lease liability.

Similar entries would be required to record each subsequent lease payment.

Interest-Related Adjustments

As noted earlier, *general long-term liabilities are reported only in the government-wide financial statements.* In these statements, the liabilities are reported at their present values (based on the effective interest rate at issuance), not at their face amounts. Likewise, interest expenses, not interest expenditures, are reported. Reporting interest expenses requires amortization of any debt premium or discount as well as amortization of related issue costs. (Interest payable will be adjusted for in worksheet adjustments illustrated in Chapter 14.)

Assuming that the premium on serial bonds from the GCA-GLTL accounts trial balance on page 353 are amortized on a straight-line basis over a remaining term of five years, the GLTL entry is:

Premium on Serial Bonds ($35,000/5 years)	$ 7,000	
Expenses—Interest		$ 7,000
To amortize bond premium.		

As with Depreciation Expense, the adjustment to interest expense is closed to Net Position at year end. Alternatively, some SLGs may record the net asset changes directly in the Net Position account. Finally, the effective interest method is preferred over the straight-line method, which was used here for illustrative simplicity.

Defaulted Bonds

The GASB *Codification* does not provide specific guidance for reporting when a government defaults on its *general* long-term debt, but it does provide guidance when proprietary fund or trust fund long-term debt on which the unit is contingently liable is in (or near) default:

> In the event that **fund liabilities** for which the unit is **contingently liable** are **in default—or** where for other reasons it appears probable that they will not be paid on a timely basis from the resources of these funds and **default is imminent**—these liabilities should be reported separately from other liabilities in the fund balance sheet.[12]

Furthermore, *all significant facts* concerning the government's contingent liability on the proprietary fund or trust fund debt in default, or which will soon be in default, should be *disclosed* in the notes to the financial statements. In the unlikely event of a *general* long-term debt default, the SLG should (1) *record* the *maturity and default* in a Debt Service Fund or the General Fund and (2) *remove* the *debt from* the *GLTL accounts*—since GLTL are, by definition, the *unmatured* principal of general government long-term debt. If it is not paid, the government should report "*Defaulted Bonds Payable*" in the DSF or General Fund to draw attention to the default. The government should also *disclose* the default in a note to the financial statements and/or in the government-wide Statement of Net Position.

In-Substance Defeasance

As discussed in Chapter 8, governments may set aside resources in an irrevocable trust to provide for future debt service requirements for a particular debt issue. When the conditions outlined in Chapter 8 are met, the debt is deemed to be defeased in substance. These liabilities should be removed from a government's GLTL accounts as if they have been retired. This treatment applies regardless of whether the defeasance was achieved by using advance refunding bond proceeds or other government financial resources. If long-term advance refunding bonds were issued, the liability for the refunding bonds would be recorded in the GLTL accounts.

Sometimes governments fail to meet all the technical requirements for defeasance in substance of general long-term debt that the government desires to defease. *If the in-substance defeasance criteria are not met,* the old debt cannot be removed from the GLTL accounts. Rather (1) the assets placed in trust would be accounted for as investments of the DSF servicing the old debt, and (2) any new advance refunding debt issued in such situations would also be recorded and reported in the GLTL accounts.

GLTL Records

A *file* should be established for each debt issue. The file should contain copies of, or references to, all pertinent correspondence, ordinances or resolutions, advertisements for the authorization referendum, advertisements or calls for bids, bond indentures or other agreements, debt service schedules, and the like.

---

[12]Ibid., sec. 1500.114. (Emphasis added.)

Subsidiary records should be established and maintained for each liability. The exact nature of each record will vary with the pertinent details of the debt, but typical information would include title and amount of the issue; nature of the debt; dates of issue, required interest payments, and maturity; denominations; nominal and effective interest rates; and issuance costs and premium or discount. Furthermore, if the issue is registered—as all recent debt issues now must be—provision must be made to record owners' names and addresses. The subsidiary record will support the liabilities recorded in the GLTL accounts, as well as the related debt service payments.

The debt instruments should be prenumbered and carefully controlled at all stages of their life cycle. Most government bonds issued before the mid-1980s are bearer instruments with interest coupons attached, which makes strict control essential.

As debt principal and interest are paid, whether by the government or through a fiscal agent, paid coupons and bonds should be marked "Paid" or "Canceled," reconciled with reports of payments, and retained at least until the records have been audited. Paid bonds and coupons are typically destroyed periodically, usually by cremation, with appropriate documentation of the destroyed bonds and coupons maintained.

GLTL Reporting and Disclosures

The general long-term liabilities are reported by type (e.g., bonds payable, notes payable) in the governmental activities column of the government-wide Statement of Net Position.

In addition to the GLTL reporting in the basic financial statements, the comprehensive annual financial report ordinarily includes a number of detailed schedules that are designed to provide additional (usually unaudited) financial data. One example is presented in Chapter 15, which discusses the Comprehensive Annual Financial Report.

Several *note disclosures* are required for both general long-term liabilities and for other long-term liabilities. Specifically, information presented about long-term liabilities should include the following:

1. Beginning- and end-of-year balances (regardless of whether prior-year data are presented on the face of the government-wide financial statements).
2. Increases and decreases (separately presented).
3. The portions of each item that are due within one year of the statement date.
4. Governmental funds that have typically been used to liquidate other long-term liabilities (such as compensated absences and pension liabilities) in prior years.

A long-term liabilities note disclosure example is presented as Illustration 9-4.

PERMANENT FUNDS

One governmental fund type—Permanent Funds—has not been discussed and illustrated yet. Recall from Chapter 2 that **Permanent Funds** are used to account for *resources held in trust by the government for the benefit of the government (or of its citizenry as a whole)*. One requirement is that the principal of the trust is to be maintained intact. Expendable trusts for which the government is the beneficiary are reported as Special Revenue Funds. Trusts to benefit private individuals, private organizations, or other governments are reported in Private-Purpose Trust Funds—whether expendable or nonexpendable. Private-Purpose Trust Funds are fiduciary funds and are discussed in Chapter 12.

We have not discussed and illustrated Permanent Funds primarily for two reasons. First, local governments are not likely to have many significant Permanent Funds. Indeed, the most common example we have found in local governments of an activity financed through Permanent Funds is perpetual care of cemeteries. Second, *Permanent Funds differ significantly in nature from the other governmental funds*. Because they do not logically fit the governmental fund model, covering

ILLUSTRATION 9-4 Illustrative Disclosure of Information About Long-Term Liabilities

Long-term liability activity for the year ended December 31, 20X2, was as follows (in thousands):

	Beginning Balance	Additions	Reductions	Ending Balance	Amount Due within One Year
GOVERNMENTAL ACTIVITIES					
Bonds and notes payable:					
General obligation debt	$32,670	$22,205	$(22,300)	$32,575	$2,729
Revenue bonds	14,485	15,840	(14,485)	15,840	1,040
Redevelopment agency bonds	14,965	18,000	(540)	32,425	1,300
Special assessment bonds	—	1,300	—	1,300	92
Equipment note	1,203	—	(954)	249	249
	63,323	57,345	(38,279)	82,389	5,410
Less deferred amount on refundings	—	(3,409)	341	(3,068)	—
Total bonds and notes payable	63,323	53,936	(37,938)	79,321	5,410
Other liabilities:					
Compensated absences	5,537	2,744	(2,939)	5,342	2,138
Claims and judgments	8,070	2,669	(2,864)	7,875	1,688
Total other liabilities	13,607	5,413	(5,803)	13,217	3,826
Governmental activities long-term liabilities	$76,930	$59,349	$(43,741)	$92,538	$9,236
BUSINESS-TYPE ACTIVITIES					
Bonds and notes payable:					
Water and sewer debt	$56,975	$ 3,600	$ (2,178)	$58,397	$3,944
Parking facilities debt	21,567	9,514	(8,895)	22,186	360
	78,542	13,114	(11,073)	80,583	4,304
Less deferred amount on refundings	(1,207)	(1,329)	254	(2,282)	—
Total bonds and notes payable	77,335	11,785	(10,819)	78,301	4,304
Compensated absences	572	1,286	(1,250)	608	122
Business-type activities long-term liabilities	$77,907	$13,071	$(12,069)	$78,909	$4,426

Source: Adapted from GASB Comprehensive Implementation Guide (2011), page 7-156.

these funds earlier may have made it more difficult to grasp the overall governmental fund nature, accounting, and reporting.

The GASB classified Permanent Funds as governmental funds as a matter of expediency. Among other things, the GASB's research indicated that the preponderance of nonexpendable trust Permanent Funds were for the benefit of governmental activities, not business-type activities. Permanent Funds were classified as governmental funds to simplify the reconciliation between government-wide and fund financial statements.

GASB *Statement No. 34* requires governments with general government activities to use **Permanent Funds** "to account for and report resources that are restricted to the extent that only earnings, and not principal, may be used for purposes that support the reporting government's programs, that is, for the benefit of the government or its citizenry."[13] Trust relationships that require the use of a Permanent Fund include:

1. Receiving a **gift or bequest** of real or personal property—for example, a citizen gives his investment portfolio to a municipality with the stipulation that (a) the principal is to be kept intact and (b) the earnings are to be used for certain purposes. Likewise, an apartment or office complex might be given to a SLG to be "operated and accounted for like

[13]Ibid., sec. 1300.108.

a business," with the income to be used for certain government purposes. (The earnings would usually be transferred to and expended through a Special Revenue Fund.)

2. Establishing an **employee loan fund** or entering into similar trust relationships. If the earnings must be retained to finance additional lending activities, both the principal and the earnings must be maintained intact. The principal could not be voluntarily reduced in this case, though bad debts, investment losses, and administrative costs might be chargeable to principal (corpus).

3. Entering **other trust agreements**—for example, to maintain cemeteries, landmark buildings, or other structures in perpetuity. In such cases the earnings are expendable only for maintenance, repairs, restorations, and/or operations.

Financial reporting for Permanent Funds is the same as that for other governmental funds. Both a balance sheet and a statement of revenues, expenditures, and changes in fund balances are required. The nonexpendable corpus of a Permanent Fund is classified as nonspendable fund balance. *If a Permanent Fund includes both nonexpendable principal amounts and expendable earnings, the expendable earnings typically are reflected in restricted fund balance. If the earnings are unrestricted, they should be reported as committed or assigned, as appropriate.*

The example in the following section illustrates the basic accounting principles that apply to Permanent Funds.

Transactions and Entries

1. Cash of $210,000 was received to establish a fund whose income is to be used to maintain the county's new Little League baseball field.

   (1) Permanent Fund

Cash..	$210,000	
Revenues—Donations...........................		$210,000

   To record establishment of a nonexpendable trust in a Permanent Fund.

2. Investments, par value $200,000, were purchased at par plus accrued interest of $400.

   (2) Permanent Fund

Investments....................................	$200,000	
Accrued Interest Receivable	400	
Cash..		$200,400

   To record purchase of investments.

3. A check for $3,000 was received for interest on the investments.

   (3) Permanent Fund

Cash..	$ 3,000	
Accrued Interest Receivable......................		$ 400
Interest Revenues...............................		2,600

   To record collection of interest on investments.

4. Securities with a carrying value of $3,042 were sold for $3,055 plus accrued (previously unrecorded) interest of $35.

   (4) Permanent Fund

Cash..	$ 3,090	
Investments....................................		$ 3,042
Interest Revenues...............................		35
Gain on Sale of Investments......................		13

   To record sale of investments at a gain of $13, and related interest income of $35.

   Note: In this example Permanent Fund investments are assumed to be exempt from the fair value provisions of GASB *Statement No. 31.*

5. Interest receivable, $2,600, was recorded.

   (5) Permanent Fund

Interest Receivable on Investments	$ 2,600	
Interest Revenues...............................		$ 2,600

   To record accrual of interest on investments.

6. Transfer of $5,000 of interest earnings to the General Fund to pay for maintenance costs for the ball field was approved.

(6) (a) Permanent Fund

Other Financing Uses—Transfer to General Fund	$ 5,000	
Cash		$ 5,000
To record transfer.		

(6) (b) General Fund

Cash	$ 5,000	
Other Financing Sources—Transfer from		
Permanent Fund		$ 5,000
To record transfer.		

7. Closing entries were prepared.

(7) Permanent Fund

Revenue—Donations	$210,000	
Interest Revenues	5,235	
Gain on Sale of Investments.	13	
Other Financing Uses—Transfer to General Fund		$ 5,000
Fund Balance—Nonspendable.		210,013
Fund Balance—Restricted		235
To close accounts.		

Note that this is one of the few situations in which it is expeditious to use the GAAP fund balance classifications for accounting purposes. The gain on sale of investments is added to the *nonspendable* fund balance either because it resulted from sale of investments of the original corpus of the trust or because the trust agreement specifies that gains and losses affect the trust principal and are not expendable. If the trust agreement or applicable laws specify that gains and losses are part of the expendable income from a trust, the net gains or losses affect the *expendable* (restricted, committed, or assigned) fund balance or must be transferred to another fund.

The Permanent Fund balance sheet for this fund is shown in Illustration 9-5. A statement of revenues, expenditures, and changes in fund balance also would be prepared for the Permanent Fund.

INTRODUCTION TO INTERFUND-GCA-GLTL ACCOUNTING

Thus far in this chapter we have indicated how the transactions in the various governmental funds affect the General Capital Assets and General Long-Term Liabilities accounts. The following entries illustrate interfund-GCA-GLTL

ILLUSTRATION 9-5   Permanent Fund Balance Sheet

A Governmental Unit
Permanent Fund
Balance Sheet
At End of Fiscal Year

Assets

Cash	$ 10,690
Investments	196,958
Interest receivable on investments	2,600
	$210,248

Liabilities and Fund Balance

Fund balance—nonspendable	$210,013
Fund balance—restricted	235
	$210,248

accounting when transactions in one fund affect another fund, the GCA, and/or the GLTL accounts. *To simplify these entries, "Other Financing Sources" is abbreviated "OFS" and "Other Financing Uses" is abbreviated "OFU."*

1. A $500,000 serial bond issue to finance capital improvements was issued at a $5,000 premium.

Capital Projects Fund:

Cash	$505,000	
OFS—Bonds (Face)		$500,000
OFS—Premium on Bonds		5,000
To record bond issue at a $5,000 premium.		

General Long-Term Liabilities accounts:

Net Position	$505,000	
Serial Bonds Payable		$500,000
Premium on Serial Bonds		5,000
To record liability for serial bond issue.		

2. The bond premium was transferred to the Debt Service Fund for either principal or interest payments on the serial bonds.

Capital Projects Fund:

OFU—Transfer to Debt Service Fund	$ 5,000	
Cash		$ 5,000
To record transfer of cash representing premium on bonds to the Debt Service Fund.		

Debt Service Fund:

Cash	$ 5,000	
OFS—Transfer from Capital Projects Fund		$ 5,000
To record receipt of cash representing premium on bonds.		

3. An $80,000 contribution was made from the General Fund to the Debt Service Fund: $30,000 for interest payments and $50,000 for serial bond principal payments.

General Fund:

OFU—Transfer to Debt Service Fund	$ 80,000	
Cash		$ 80,000
To record payment of contribution to Debt Service Fund.		

Debt Service Fund:

Cash	$ 80,000	
OFS—Transfer from General Fund		$ 80,000
To record receipt of contribution from General Fund.		

4. Capital Projects Fund capital outlay expenditures were made, $496,000, for improvements.

Capital Projects Fund:

Expenditures—Capital Outlay	$496,000	
Vouchers Payable		$496,000
To record capital improvement expenditures.		

General Capital Assets accounts:

Improvements Other Than Buildings	$496,000	
Net Position		$496,000
To record capital improvements made.		

5. The $4,000 remaining unused bond proceeds of a terminated Capital Projects Fund were transferred to the Debt Service Fund for use as needed.

Capital Projects Fund:

OFU—Transfer to Debt Service Fund...................	$ 4,000	
Cash		$ 4,000

To record transfer of balance of Capital Projects Fund
to Debt Service Fund.

Debt Service Fund:

Cash	$ 4,000	
OFS—Transfer from Capital Projects Fund		$ 4,000

To record receipt of Capital Projects Fund balance.

6. Maturing serial bonds ($50,000) and interest ($30,000) were paid from the Debt Service Fund.

Debt Service Fund:

Expenditures—Bond Principal........................	$ 50,000	
Expenditures—Interest on Bonds	30,000	
Cash		$ 80,000

To record payment of serial bond debt service.

General Long-Term Liabilities accounts:

Serial Bonds Payable	$ 50,000	
Net Position......................................		$ 50,000

To record retirement of serial bonds.

7. A General Fund department entered into a capital lease of equipment with a capitalizable cost of $250,000. A $25,000 down payment was made at the inception of the lease.

General Fund:

Expenditures Capital Outlay	$250,000	
OFS—Capital Lease...............................		$225,000
Cash		25,000

To record the inception of a capital lease and the initial
down payment.

General Long-Term Liabilities accounts:

Net Position......................................	$225,000	
Capital Lease Liabilities		$225,000

To record capital lease liabilities.

General Capital Assets accounts:

Equipment Under Capital Lease	$250,000	
Net Position......................................		$250,000

To record leased assets.

The last two entries may be *compounded* as follows:

**General Capital Assets and General Long-Term
Liabilities accounts:**

Equipment Under Capital Lease	$250,000	
Capital Lease Liabilities		$225,000
Net Position......................................		25,000

To record leased assets and capital lease liabilities.

8. Lease payments of $50,000, including $20,000 interest, were paid.

General Fund:

Expenditures—Capital Lease Principal..................	$ 30,000	
Expenditures—Interest on Capital Lease	20,000	
Cash		$ 50,000

To record periodic lease payments.

General Long-Term Liabilities accounts:

Capital Lease Liabilities	$ 30,000	
Net Position.......................................		$ 30,000

To record retirement of a portion of the capital lease liabilities.

9. The government accrued its liability to pay part ($100,000) of the cost of special assessment improvements being accounted for in a Capital Projects Fund from the General Fund.

General Fund:

OFU—Transfer to Capital Projects Fund	$100,000	
Due to Capital Projects Fund		$100,000

To record governmental unit's liability for contribution toward construction of special assessment improvements.

Capital Projects Fund:

Due from General Fund...............................	$100,000	
OFS—Transfer from General Fund		$100,000

To record amount due from General Fund for governmental unit's share of cost of project.

10. Inspection services were performed (**internal services**) by a department financed through the General Fund for a capital project.

General Fund:

Due from Capital Projects Fund........................	$ 8,000	
Revenues—Inspection Services		$ 8,000

To record revenues for inspection services rendered on capital projects.

Capital Projects Fund:

Expenditures—Capital Outlay	$ 8,000	
Due to General Fund................................		$ 8,000

To record cost of inspection services performed by a department financed through the General Fund.

General Capital Assets accounts:

Construction in Progress	$ 8,000	
Net Position.......................................		$ 8,000

To record inspection cost as capital asset cost.

11. Maintenance services (recorded earlier as CPF expenditures) were rendered by construction workers paid from a Capital Projects Fund for a department financed through the General Fund (**reimbursement**).

Capital Projects Fund:

Due from General Fund	$ 5,000	
Expenditures—Capital Outlay		$ 5,000

To record reduction of construction expenditures by cost of services rendered to Department X.

General Capital Assets accounts:

Net Position..	$ 5,000	
Construction in Progress		$ 5,000

To record reduction of construction cost by reimbursement. (This entry *assumes* that Capital Projects Fund expenditures were recorded previously in construction in progress. If not, the GCA entry is not required.)

General Fund:

Expenditures—Maintenance...........................	$ 5,000	
Due to Capital Projects Fund		$ 5,000

To record amount due to Capital Projects Fund for maintenance services rendered to Department X.

12. A short-term (e.g., 90-day) loan to be repaid during the current year was made from the General Fund to the Debt Service Fund.

General Fund:

Due from Debt Service Fund	$ 40,000	
Cash		$ 40,000

To record short-term loan to Debt Service Fund.

Debt Service Fund:

Cash	$ 40,000	
Due to General Fund		$ 40,000

To record short-term loan from General Fund.

13. A noncurrent loan (e.g., two-year advance) was made from the General Fund to a Capital Projects Fund.

General Fund:

Advance to Capital Projects Fund	$ 75,000	
Cash		$ 75,000

To record 2-year advance to Capital Projects Fund.

Recall that the fund balance related to such long-term interfund receivables of the General Fund will be reported as either nonspendable, restricted, committed, or assigned fund balance, depending on the constraint, if any, on use of the proceeds.

Capital Projects Fund:

Cash	$ 75,000	
Advance from General Fund.........................		$ 75,000

To record 2-year advance from General Fund.

14. A government sold computers used by its Department of Comptroller for $13,000. The computers originally cost $96,000 when purchased three years before and were expected to last four years. The sale proceeds are unrestricted.

General Fund:

Cash	$ 13,000	
OFS—General Capital Asset Sale Proceeds.............		$ 13,000

To record proceeds from sale of general capital assets.

General Capital Assets accounts:

Net Position..	$ 24,000	
Accumulated Depreciation—Equipment	72,000	
Equipment..		$ 96,000

To remove capital assets upon sale.

Note that a loss on capital asset disposal of $11,000 ($24,000 – $13,000) will be reported in the *government-wide* Statement of Activities.

15. Cash payments for vacation and sick leave totaled $400,000. The payable for current vacation and sick leave increased $20,000, to $45,000. The noncurrent portion of the payable decreased by $67,000.

General Fund:

Expenditures—Vacation and Sick Leave..................	$375,000	
Current Liability for Vacation and Sick Leave (Beginning) ..	25,000	
Cash		$400,000

To record payments of vacation and sick leave.

Expenditures—Vacation and Sick Leave..................	$ 45,000	
Current Liability for Vacation and Sick Leave (Ending)...		$ 45,000

To accrue the fund liability for vacation and sick leave.

General Long-Term Liabilities accounts:

Noncurrent Liability for Vacation and Sick Leave..........	$ 67,000	
Net Position.......................................		$ 67,000

To record the decrease in the noncurrent portion of the
vacation and sick leave liability.

Note that the General Fund vacation and sick leave *expenditure* is $420,000 ($375,000 + $45,000), but the vacation and sick leave *expense* reported in the government-wide Statement of Activities is $353,000 ($420,000 – $67,000). Also, this is one of several types of expenditures that must be recognized when due. Any one of the other types of when-due expenditures—claims and judgments, pensions, OPEB, and so on—could have been substituted for vacation and sick leave and would have been accounted for in the same way as illustrated here with vacation and sick leave.

Concluding Comments

These discussions and illustrations of general capital assets, general long-term liabilities, and interfund-GCA-GLTL accounting and reporting conclude the several *general government* accounting and reporting chapters of this text. This general government accounting model—the governmental funds and GCA and GLTL accounts—clearly constitutes the most distinctive aspect of state and local government accounting and financial reporting.

The remaining parts of the governmental accounting model—the proprietary funds and fiduciary funds—are discussed and illustrated in Chapters 10–12. As these additional funds are presented, typical interfund transactions and relationships of each type of fund with other funds are illustrated. Finally, a comprehensive summary of interfund and interfund-GCA-GLTL accounting is presented in Chapter 12.

Questions

Q9-1 Distinguish between fund capital assets and *general* capital assets.

Q9-2 What criteria must be met for an asset to be classified as a *capital* asset? A *general* capital asset?

Q9-3 Generally speaking, what is meant by the term *cost* when determining what costs should be assigned to a capital asset?

Q9-4 How are intangible assets reported? Are costs incurred to create or produce internally generated intangible assets expensed as in business? If not, under what circumstances are they capitalized?

Q9-5 Capital assets may be acquired through exercise of a government's power of *eminent domain* and by *escheat*. Distinguish between these terms.

Q9-6 What approach should be used to measure a capital asset impairment loss that results from physical damage to the capital asset?

Q9-7 Explain the *modified approach* to infrastructure accounting.

Q9-8 When is a capital asset considered to be impaired?

Q9-9 Explain why General Capital Assets and General Long-Term Liabilities are accounted for separately from the governmental funds.

Q9-10 What liabilities are accounted for through the General Long-Term Liabilities accounts? Which long-term liabilities are excluded?

Q9-11 On June 1, 20W3, a government issued $300,000 par value of 20-year term general obligation sinking fund bonds. Only $50,000 had been accumulated in the Debt Service (Sinking) Fund by the maturity date of May 30, 20Y4, the end of the unit's fiscal year. Also, it was not possible to retire the bonds using resources of other funds during that year. Should the matured bonds be reported in the General Fund or in the Debt Service Fund, or should they continue to be accounted for in the General Long-Term Liabilities accounts? Why?

Q9-12 Unmatured general government liabilities are recorded in the General Long-Term Liabilities accounts. Neither special assessment debt that is expected to be serviced by special assessments, but on which the government is obligated in some manner, nor underfunded pension contributions seem to fit this definition—yet both are recorded in the GLTL accounts. Why are they treated this way?

Q9-13 What are the elements of the note disclosures required for General Capital Assets and General Long-Term Liabilities?

Q9-14 What are some examples of when Permanent Funds would be reported by a governmental entity? How do Permanent Funds differ from other governmental funds? Do they have unique defining characteristics? Briefly explain.

Q9-15 Explain how General Capital Assets and General Long-Term Liabilities are reported in GAAP financial statements.

Exercises

E9-1 (Multiple Choice) Select the best response for each of the following questions.
1. Which of the following classifications of capital assets are often *not* capitalized?
   a. Land
   b. Inexhaustible art collections
   c. Construction in progress
   d. Buildings
2. Which of the following is *not* a criterion of an inexhaustible collection?
   a. Collection is held for public exhibition, education, or research.
   b. Collection is protected, cared for, and preserved.
   c. Collection is declared historical.
   d. Collection is subject to policies that require proceeds for collection sales to be used to procure other items for the collection.

Questions 3 through 6 are based on the following information:

The City of Panther Creek owns a tract of land that was donated three years ago.

The land was valued at $250,000 when it was received; however, the current market value of the tract is $300,000. In addition, the city recently purchased 10 new police cars at a combined cost of $400,000. Their estimated useful life is 5 years. Finally, the city constructed a warehouse at a cost of $150,000. The warehouse has an anticipated useful life of 15 years.

3. Assuming the above facts and also assuming that all of the assets, including the warehouse, are for General Fund departments, the amount of depreciation expense that would be reported in the General Fund at the end of year one would be
   a. $0.
   b. $90,000.
   c. $250,000.
   d. $340,000.
4. At what value should the land be capitalized in the General Fund?
   a. $0
   b. $50,000
   c. $250,000
   d. $300,000
5. The original capitalized value of the capital assets in the General Capital Asset accounts would be
   a. $0.
   b. $550,000.
   c. $800,000.
   d. $850,000.
6. Assume that land and the vehicles are used for the General Fund departments, but the warehouse was actually constructed for the city's Enterprise Fund. The recorded value of the capitalized assets in the General Capital Asset accounts in the year of acquisition would be
   a. $400,000.
   b. $650,000.
   c. $700,000.
   d. $800,000.

Questions 7 through 10 are based on the following information:

To finance a general government construction project Nathan Township issued $10,000,000 face value general obligation bonds for $9,900,000. The township also incurred issuance costs equal to 2% of the face value. A Debt Service Fund will be used to account for repayment of the debt.

7. The Debt Service Fund liability that should be reported by Nathan Township in the year of the debt issuance would be
   a. $0.
   b. $9,700,000.
   c. $9,900,000.
   d. $10,000,000.
8. At the date of issue the Township's General Long-Term Liability accounts would reflect total liabilities for bonds payable liability of
   a. $9,700,000.
   b. $9,900,000.
   c. $10,000,000.
   d. $10,100,000.
9. In the year of debt issuance, the Capital Projects Fund would report Other Financing Sources in the amount of
   a. $0.
   b. $9,700,000.
   c. $9,900,000.
   d. $10,000,000.
10. In the year of debt issuance, the township would report unamortized bond issue costs in its government-wide Statement of Net Position of
    a. $0.
    b. $100,000.
    c. $200,000.
    d. $300,000.

E9-2 (Multiple Choice) Identify the best answer for each of the following
1. Which of the following statements concerning the accounting and financial reporting for capital assets is *false*?
   a. Capitalization thresholds differ among governments and often within governments among classes of assets.
   b. All capital assets are reported as assets of the purchasing fund.
   c. Proprietary fund capital assets are reported as assets in both the fund financial statements and the government-wide financial statements.
   d. Governments may choose to use the modified approach in lieu of reporting depreciation for qualifying infrastructure assets.
2. Donated capital assets are valued by the recipient government at
   a. fair market value at the date of donation.
   b. the original cost of the donated asset per the donor's records.
   c. the net book value of the asset at the date of donation.
   d. the assessed valuation at the date of donation.
3. Assume that a building used by Carter County's police department is destroyed by a fire. It is then discovered that the building was not properly insured and that its current net book value was $170,000. The controller, Austin Miller, estimated that it will cost $350,000 to replace the building. The loss that would be reported in the General Fund for the reporting period in which the fire occurred would be
   a. $170,000 (current net book value).
   b. $350,000 (estimated replacement cost).
   c. $180,000 (the difference between the net book value and the estimated replacement cost).
   d. $0.
4. When a capital asset of a department reported in a proprietary fund is transferred to a general government department, the effect of the transaction is reported as
   a. a transfer in both the proprietary fund and a governmental fund.
   b. a nonoperating item in both the proprietary fund and a governmental fund.
   c. a nonoperating expense in the proprietary fund.
   d. a transfer out in the proprietary fund.
5. Which of the following is *never* reported as a general long-term liability?
   a. Capital leases
   b. Compensated absences
   c. Certificates of participation
   d. Advances from other funds
6. GAAP require all of the following note disclosures for capital assets *except:*
   a. current year depreciation expense by function.
   b. a differentiation between depreciable and nondepreciable assets.
   c. capital assets that will be fully depreciated within one year.
   d. increase in accumulated depreciation by class of asset.
7. Which of the following statements concerning the reporting of general long-term liabilities is *true*?
   a. General long-term liabilities are reported both in the governmental funds and the government-wide financial statements.
   b. General long-term liabilities are only reported in the government-wide financial statements.

c. General long-term liabilities are only reported in the governmental funds.

d. Advances from other funds that are being repaid over a 10-year period would be reported as a general long-term liability.

8. In which of the following scenarios would a general long-term liability be reported as a governmental fund liability?

a. The current portion of long-term debt should always be reported as a governmental fund liability.

b. Debt that has been defeased in substance.

c. Debt that is in default.

d. The current portion of refunding bonds.

E9-3 (Multiple Choice) Indicate the best answer for each of the following:

1. Joshua Village issued the following bonds during the year ended June 30, 20X5:

Revenue bonds to be repaid from admission fees collected by the Joshua Zoo Enterprise Fund	$ 200,000
General obligation bonds issued for the Joshua Water and Sewer Enterprise Fund, which will service the debt	300,000

How much of these bonds should be accounted for as Joshua's General Long-Term Liabilities?

a. $500,000

b. $200,000

c. $300,000

d. $0

2. The following assets are among those owned by the city of Heidi:

Apartment building (part of the principal of a Private Purpose Trust Fund)	$ 200,000
City hall	800,000
Three fire stations..................................	1,000,000
City streets and sidewalks	5,000,000

How much should be included in Heidi's General Capital Assets accounts?

a. $2,000,000

b. $1,800,000

c. $6,800,000

d. $7,000,000

3. Penn City's Capital Projects Fund incurred expenditures of $4,000,000 on a project in 20X0. $3,600,000 has been paid on these expenditures. Also, encumbrances outstanding on the project at December 31, 20X0, total $8,000,000. What amount should be recorded in Penn City's General Capital Assets accounts at December 31, 20X0, for this project?

a. $3,600,000

b. $4,000,000

c. $11,600,000

d. $12,000,000

4. Stephen Latzka donated a building to Elizabeth City in 20X3. His original cost of the property was $100,000. Accumulated depreciation at the date of the gift amounted to $60,000. Fair value at the date of the gift was $300,000. At what amount should Elizabeth City record this donated capital asset in its General Capital Assets accounts?

a. $300,000

b. $100,000

c. $40,000

d. $0

5. The following items were among Payne Township's General Fund expenditures during the year ended July 31, 20X3:

Computer for tax collector's office......................	$ 44,000
Equipment for Township Hall..........................	80,000

How much should be classified as capital assets in Payne's General Fund balance sheet at July 31, 20X3?

a. $124,000

b. $80,000

c. $44,000

d. $0

6. Other Financing Sources—Bonds is an account of A Governmental Unit that would most likely be included in the
   a. Enterprise Fund.
   b. Capital Projects Fund.
   c. Debt Service Fund.
   d. General Long-Term Liabilities accounts.
7. When equipment purchased from General Fund revenues was received, the appropriate journal entry was made in the General Capital Assets accounts. What account, if any, should have been debited in the General Fund?
   a. No journal entry should have been made in the General Fund.
   b. Equipment.
   c. Expenditures.
   d. Due from capital accounts.
8. Which of the following statements about accounting and financial reporting for impaired capital assets is *false*?
   a. Impairments deemed to be temporary are *not* reported as impairment losses.
   b. GAAP do not require governmental entities to actively search for potentially impaired capital assets.
   c. Construction stoppage is considered a common indicator of impairment.
   d. Impairment is defined as a material unexpected decline in the life of a capital asset.

E9-4 (GCA/GLTL Entries) Prepare the journal entries required *in the General Capital Assets and General Long-Term Liabilities accounts* of Percy County to record the following transactions. Indicate whether any gains and losses are to be reported in the government-wide financial statements.
1. Land was donated for use as the site of a bike and nature trail. The donor had acquired the land for $3,000 about 20 years earlier. Its estimated fair value when donated to the county was $40,000.
2. Computer equipment was ordered for General Fund departments. The estimated cost was $48,000.
3. The computer equipment was received by the county. The actual cost was $47,750. The county had paid $42,000 to the vendor by year end.
4. The county sold a (general government) dump truck that had cost $55,000. Accumulated depreciation on the truck was $50,000. The county sold the truck at auction for $3,300.
5. A storage building used by general government departments was destroyed by a tornado. The building, which cost $150,000, is expected to be rebuilt at a cost of $200,000. The building was 50% depreciated when destroyed. Construction has not begun on the new building.
6. The government leased a building under a capital lease agreement. The capitalizable cost was $1,200,000. The county made an initial down payment of $100,000.

E9-5 (GCA/GLTL Entries) Prepare the entries required in the *General Capital Assets and General Long-Term Liabilities accounts* for the following transactions.
1. A city leased fire trucks under a long-term capital lease agreement. The capitalizable cost of the trucks was $1,400,000. The city paid $200,000 at the inception of the lease and is to make annual lease payments of $350,000 per year.
2. The city made the first annual lease payment at the end of the first year of the lease. The $350,000 payment included $225,000 interest.
3. The city incurred claims and judgments associated with general government activities during the year. Claims of $450,000 were paid. The city expects another $1,200,000 of losses associated with unsettled claims. These claims are not expected to require payment for some time to come.

E9-6 (All Funds and GCA/GLTL Entries) Wildwood Township entered into the following transactions during 20X6:
1. The township authorized a bond issue of $5,000,000 par to finance construction of a fountain in the town square. The bonds were issued for $5,120,000. Bond issue costs of $30,000 were incurred and paid. The premium, less bond issue costs, was transferred to the fund from which the debt is to be serviced.
2. The township entered into a contract for construction of the fountain at an estimated cost of $4,850,000.
3. The town received and paid a $4,890,000 bill for the construction upon completion of and approval of the fountain.
4. The unused bond proceeds were set aside for debt service on the bonds. Accordingly, those resources were paid to the appropriate fund.

Required   Prepare the journal entries (budgetary and actual) required in the various accounts (both in the funds and in the General Capital Assets and General Long-Term Liabilities accounts) of Wildwood Township to record these transactions.

E9-7 (Refunding Entries) The City of Burton has $5,000,000 par value of general government, general obligation bonds payable outstanding. The city has decided to defease those bonds in substance. Record the following transactions in all the accounts (both in the funds and in the General Capital Assets and General Long-Term Liabilities accounts) of the City of Burton that are affected.

1. The city issued $3,000,000 of refunding bonds at par.
2. The city transferred $1,850,000 from its General Fund to its Debt Service Fund to provide the additional resources needed to defease the bonds in substance.
3. The city paid $4,850,000 into an irrevocable trust established at the First National Bank of Burton to defease the bonds in substance.

E9-8 (Short Case Study Analysis) Analyze each of the following scenarios. Provide a brief explanation of your analysis and answers to each one.

a. A governmental unit acquired land, buildings, other improvements, and certain equipment for a single lump-sum purchase price. How should the portion of the total cost attributable to various assets be determined?

b. A municipality was granted certain land for use as a playground. The property was appraised at $400,000 at the time of the grant. Subsequently, all land in the neighborhood rose in value by 30%. Should the increase be reflected in the GCA accounts? Why or why not?

c. An asset originally financed by Special Revenue Fund revenues and accounted for in the General Capital Assets accounts was sold. To which fund would you credit the proceeds and why?

d. Assume that the asset referred to in the preceding question was financed through special assessment bonds of the government. To which fund should the proceeds from the sale of this asset be credited? Briefly explain.

e. Near the end of 20X5, a city purchased an automobile at a cost of $15,000. The uninsured vehicle was wrecked during 20X6 (the vehicle's accumulated depreciation at the time of the wreck was $2,000) and sold for salvage for $1,000. If the automobile were purchased from General Fund resources and the salvage proceeds were also recorded there, what entries would be made in 20X5 and 20X6 to reflect these facts? What amount would be reported in the government-wide Statement of Activities?

Problems

P9-1 (GCA Entries) Prepare general journal entries to record the effects *on the General Capital Assets accounts* of the following transactions. The transactions are independent of each other unless otherwise noted. Assume straight-line depreciation.

1. A government leased computers with a capitalizable cost of $150,000, including $30,000 paid at the inception of the lease agreement. The lease is properly classified as a capital lease, and the computers are for the use of the government's finance and accounting division.

2. A government foreclosed on land against which it had tax liens amounting to $20,000. The estimated salable value of the land is $18,500. The government decided to use the land as the site for a new baseball park.

3. Construction costs billed during the year on a new addition to city hall totaled $8,000,000. $7,600,000 was paid to the contractors. Encumbrances of $10,000,000 related to the project were outstanding at year end. General revenues of $3,000,000 were transferred to the City Hall Addition Capital Projects Fund; the remainder of the construction costs are being financed from bond proceeds.

4. In the next year, the city hall addition in item 3 was completed at an additional cost of $9,800,000. The building was inspected and approved, but $2,000,000 of the construction costs have not been paid.

5. General government equipment with an original cost of $300,000 (estimated salvage: zero) was sold three-fourths through its useful life for $65,000.

6. A bridge was destroyed by a tornado. Its original cost was $92,000. Its useful life was only half over, and it is estimated that it will cost $250,000 to replace the bridge.

7. A dump truck originally purchased for and used by a city Enterprise Fund has been transferred to the streets and roads department—a general government department. The truck originally cost $80,000 and is halfway through its estimated useful life. Its residual value is $18,000. The fair value of the dump truck at the date of the transfer to the streets and roads department is $52,000.

8. Computers with an original cost of $40,000 and estimated residual value of $5,000 were transferred from General Fund departments to the municipal golf course, which is accounted for in an Enterprise Fund. The transfer occurred at the end of the original estimated useful life of the computers.

P9-2 (GLTL Entries) Prepare general journal entries to record the effects *on the General Long-Term Liabilities accounts* of the following transactions. The transactions are independent of one another unless otherwise noted.

1. Bond anticipation notes that meet the criteria for noncurrent treatment were issued to provide financing for a general government capital project. The notes were issued at their face (par) value of $5,000,000.
2. Special assessment bonds guaranteed by the government matured and were paid during the year: $50,000 principal and $30,000 interest were paid.
3. Principal and interest on the County Courthouse Serial Bonds matured during the year. The maturing interest ($200,000) was paid from the related Debt Service Fund, but the maturing principal ($75,000) had not been paid by year end. General Fund revenues were transferred to cover the interest payments.
4. General Fund expenditures accounts included a Rent Expenditures account with a balance of $200,000. Further investigation of the account indicated that the balance resulted from the payment of $40,000 on operating leases and $160,000 of lease payments on a capital lease (of which $90,000 was for imputed interest).
5. The total general government underfunded pension liability at the beginning of the fiscal year was $14,000,000. Of this amount, $1,500,000 was considered a fund liability. The total general government underfunded pension liability at the end of the fiscal year was $14,500,000. Of this amount, $2,500,000 was considered due and payable at year end.
6. Advance refunding bonds ($10,000,000 par) were issued at 100. The proceeds of the refunding and $2,000,000 of previously accumulated Debt Service Fund resources were set aside in an irrevocable trust to defease in substance $11,500,000 of School Bonds.
7. Assume the same information as in item 6, except that the School Bonds are not defeased in substance as a result of the transaction described.

P9-3 (Interfund-GCA-GLTL Entries) Prepare all journal entries (budgetary and actual) required in all funds and the GCA and GLTL accounts to record the following transactions and events:

1. A state issued $50,000,000 of 4%, 20-year term bonds at 105 to provide financing for construction of a new state legislative office building. The premium, which is to be used for debt service, was transferred to the appropriate fund. Bond issue costs of $75,000 were paid directly from the General Fund. The bonds were issued on April 1, 20X1, and annual interest is due each March 31.
2. The state signed contracts for $55,000,000 for construction of the building. Costs incurred for construction of the office building during 20X1 amounted to $18,000,000 and all but 10% was paid.
3. Annual interest of $2,000,000 was paid on the bonds on March 31, 20X2.
4. General Fund resources, $5,000,000, were transferred to the Legislative Office Building Capital Projects Fund during 20X2 for use on the project.
5. The project was completed. Expenditures in 20X2 totaled $36,500,000, and all fund liabilities were paid. The remaining resources, to be used for debt service, were paid to the appropriate fund.
6. $3,300,000 was transferred from the General Fund to service the bonds in 20X3.
7. Interest of $2,000,000 was paid on March 31, 20X3.
8. The bonds were retired on March 31 of 20Z1. Funds totaling $46,000,000 had been accumulated previously in the Debt Service Fund to retire the bonds; the remainder needed to retire the bonds and make the last $2,000,000 interest payment was transferred from the General Fund in 20Z1.

P9-4 (Interfund-GCA-GLTL Entries) Prepare all journal entries (budgetary and actual) required in all funds and the GCA-GLTL accounts to record the following transactions and events:

1. The county sold old equipment—original cost $800,000, accumulated depreciation $600,000—for $127,000. The equipment was included in the General Capital Assets accounts. The sale proceeds are not restricted.
2. The county leased equipment for use by departments financed through the General Fund under a capital lease. The capitalizable cost was $780,000; an initial payment of $100,000 was made.
3. The county ordered new patrol cars estimated to cost $100,000.
4. The county received the patrol cars along with an invoice for $101,200.
5. Land with a fair value of $90,000 was donated to the county. The donor had paid $37,000 for the land when he acquired it four years ago.
6. Bonds of $2,000,000 were issued at par for Enterprise Fund purposes. The bonds are to be repaid from the revenues of the Enterprise Fund. However, they are backed by the full faith and credit of the county; if the bonds cannot be repaid from the Enterprise Fund, general revenues must be used to repay them.

P9-5 (Interfund-GCA-GLTL Entries) The following transactions and events (among others) affected the state of Texva during 20X6.

1. It was discovered that in 20X5, $440,000 of expenditures properly chargeable to Highway Patrol—Salaries and Wages in the General Fund had been inadvertently charged to the

Highway Department—Salaries and Wages account in Special Revenue Fund #4. The amount was repaid during 20X6.

2. The Health Department, which is financed from Special Revenue Fund #2, entered a capital lease for equipment with a capitalizable cost of $600,000. (The capital lease has a 6% effective interest rate and $100,000 was paid upon entering the lease.)

3. Special Revenue Fund #4 was reimbursed for $700,000 of 20X6 salaries and wages for Highway Department employees working on a bridge construction project, which is financed by serial bonds and accounted for in Capital Projects Fund #7.

4. The first annual $100,000 payment on the Health Department equipment capital lease (transaction 2) was made, and $60,000 accumulated depreciation was recorded.

5. A 3-year advance was made from unassigned resources of the General Fund to Debt Service Fund #12, $500,000.

6. Serial bonds, $4,000,000, were issued at 96 to finance a construction project being financed from Capital Projects Fund #7.

7. After its accounts were closed for 20X6, the $375,000 net assets (cash) of term bond Debt Service Fund #1 were transferred to establish Debt Service Fund #14 to service the serial bonds issued at transaction 6, and Debt Service Fund #1 was abolished.

8. Health Department land and buildings—originally purchased through Special Revenue Fund #2 for $50,000 and $450,000, respectively—were sold for $12,000,000, and the proceeds were recorded in Special Revenue Fund #2. Accumulated depreciation of $300,000 had been recorded on the buildings.

9. Although the actuarially required payment from the General Fund to the state pension plan was $15,000,000, only $6,000,000 was paid during 20X6. The 20X7 appropriation bill enacted recently provides for another $2,000,000 payment on the 20X6 contribution—which normally would have been paid from assets on hand at the end of 20X6 and was considered due and payable at that time. The $2,000,000 payment was provided for by continuing the 20X6 appropriations for that purpose, but it is uncertain when the remaining $7,000,000 will be paid.

Required

Prepare the journal entries to record these transactions and events in the general ledgers of the various governmental funds and GCA-GLTL accounts of the state of Texva. Assume that an appropriate series of Revenues, Expenditures, General Capital Assets, and General Long-Term Liabilities accounts is used in each general ledger.

P9-6 (Interfund-GCA-GLTL Error Correction Entries) You have been engaged by the Town of Rego to examine its June 30, 20X8, balance sheet. You are the first CPA to be engaged by the town and find that acceptable methods of municipal accounting have not been employed. The town clerk stated that the books had not been closed and presented the following preclosing trial balance of the General Fund as of June 30, 20X8:

	Debit	Credit
Cash	$150,000	
Taxes Receivable—Current	59,200	
Allowance for Uncollectible Current Taxes		$ 18,000
Taxes Receivable—Delinquent	8,000	
Allowance for Uncollectible Delinquent Taxes		10,200
Estimated Revenues	310,000	
Appropriations		348,000
Donated Land	27,000	
Building Addition	50,000	
Serial Bonds Paid	16,000	
Expenditures	280,000	
Special Assessment Bonds Payable		100,000
Revenues		354,000
Accounts Payable		26,000
Fund Balance		44,000
	$900,200	$900,200

Additional Information:

1. The estimated losses of $18,000 for current taxes receivable were determined to be a reasonable estimate. Current taxes become delinquent on June 30 of each year.

2. Included in the Revenues account is a $27,000 credit representing the value of land donated by the state as a grant-in-aid for construction of a municipal park.

3. The Building Addition account balance is the cost of an addition to the town hall building. This addition was constructed and completed in June 20X8. The payment was recorded in the General Fund as authorized.

4. The Serial Bonds Paid account reflects the annual retirement of general obligation bonds issued to finance construction of the town hall. Interest payments of $7,000 for this bond issue are included in Expenditures.
5. Operating supplies ordered in the prior fiscal year ($8,800) were received, recorded, and consumed in July 20X7. (Encumbered appropriations lapse one year after the end of the fiscal year for which they are made.)
6. Outstanding purchase orders at June 30, 20X8, for operating supplies totaled $2,100. These purchase orders were not recorded in the accounts. The purchase will be completed using financial resources available for general purposes.
7. The special assessment bonds are guaranteed by the town of Rego and were sold in June 20X8 to finance a street-paving project. No contracts have been signed for this project and no expenditures have been made.
8. The balance in the Revenues account includes credits for $20,000 for a note issued to a bank to obtain cash in anticipation of tax collections. The note was still outstanding at June 30, 20X8.
9. The fund balance account has been adjusted for the difference between Estimated Revenues and Appropriations.

Required
a. Prepare the formal adjusting and closing journal entries (budgetary and actual) for the General Fund for the fiscal year ended June 30, 20X8.
b. The foregoing information disclosed by your examination was recorded only in the General Fund even though other funds or accounts were involved. Prepare the formal adjusting journal entries for any other funds or GCA-GLTL accounts involved.

(AICPA, adapted)

P9-7 (Interfund-GCA-GLTL Entries) Prepare all entries that a state or local government should make to record the following transactions and events.

1. A $2,500,000 term bond issue to finance construction of a new bridge was issued at a $35,000 premium. $10,000 of bond issue costs were paid from the proceeds.
2. The bond premium, less the bond issue costs, was transferred to the Debt Service Fund for the term bonds.
3. A $400,000 contribution was paid from the General Fund to the Debt Service Fund: $150,000 for interest payments and $250,000 to provide for future principal payments.
4. Bridge construction expenditures were vouchered, $2,480,000, for improvements.
5. The remaining unused bond proceeds of the Bridge Capital Projects Fund were transferred to the Debt Service Fund for use as needed.
6. Maturing long-term notes payable ($50,000) and interest ($30,000) were paid from a Debt Service Fund.
7. The Police Department entered into a capital lease of equipment with a capitalizable cost of $1,250,000. A $125,000 down payment was made at the inception of the lease.
8. Lease payments of $250,000, including $100,000 interest, were paid.
9. The government pays retiree health care benefits on a pay-as-you-go basis. Payments for the year totaled $400,000. The actuarially required contribution computed in accordance with the parameters required by GAAP was $3,200,000.
10. Inspection services were performed (internal services) by a department financed through the General Fund for a capital project and billed to the project, $3,000.
11. Maintenance services of $1,800 (recorded earlier as CPF expenditures) were rendered by construction workers paid from a Capital Projects Fund for a department financed through the General Fund. (Record the recognition of this correction prior to payment.)
12. A 6-month loan of $400,000 to be repaid during the current year was made from the General Fund to the Debt Service Fund.
13. A 2-year loan of $2,000,000 was made from the General Fund to a Capital Projects Fund.
14. A government sold police vehicles for $65,000. The vehicles originally cost $480,000 when purchased and are 80% depreciated. The sale proceeds are unrestricted.
15. Cash payments for claims totaled $2,000,000. The fund liability for claims and judgments increased $100,000, to $225,000. The noncurrent portion of the payable decreased by $335,000.

P9-8 (Research and Analysis) Obtain a recent comprehensive annual financial report (CAFR) from a state or local government, and note its presentations and disclosures with respect to general capital assets (GCA) and general long-term liabilities (GLTL).

Required
1. **Table of Contents.** What indications of GCA and GLTL presentations and disclosures are evident from the CAFR table of contents? (Attach a copy of the table of contents.)
2. **Basic Financial Statements (BFS).** Describe the GCA and GLTL information presented in the BFS—including the categories of GCA and GLTL, the relative aggregation or disaggregation of the GCA and GLTL information, and the other significant matters that come to your attention as you review the BFS. (Attach copies of the BFS that include GCA and/or GLTL presentations.)

Notes. Describe the GCA and GLTL information presented in the notes to the BFS—including the type of information, the relative aggregation or disaggregation of the information, and other matters coming to your attention as you review the notes. (Attach copies of the GCA and GLTL note presentations and disclosures.)

4. **Combining and Individual Fund and GCA-GLTL Financial Statements and Schedules.** Describe the GCA and GLTL information presented in the combining and individual fund financial statements and in other statements or schedules that are not part of the BFS—including whether the CAFR has separate sections (perhaps tabbed) for GCA and GLTL information, the nature of the presentations and disclosures, and other matters coming to your attention during your review. (Attach copies of the more significant GCA and GLTL presentations and disclosures in this CAFR section.)

P9-9 (Research and Analysis) Review the GASB's latest publications or pronouncements on pollution remediation.

1. Summarize the GASB's definition of *pollution remediation obligations*.   *Required*
2. Describe the potential effects of identified pollution remediation obligations on the financial statements of SLGs. Specifically, what effects would such obligations have on an entity's liabilities? On its capitalized assets?
3. What are the *obligating events* that give rise to potential obligations?
4. When are liabilities and expenditures and/or expenses associated with pollution remediation potentially accrued?

Cases

C9-1 (Interfund-GCA-GLTL Transactions—State of Delaware) Record the following transactions of the State of Delaware general government activities for the year ended June 30, 20X6. (Amounts are stated in thousands of dollars.) Make all required entries.

1. On September 1, 20X5, the state issued $132,000 (face amount) of 20-year bonds at a premium of $4,850 to finance construction of school buildings (owned by the state) across the state. Bond issue costs of $343 were paid from the proceeds.
2. The state signed construction contracts totaling $168,000.
3. The state incurred construction costs of $120,000 on the school buildings. These costs included the costs incurred on buildings completed during the year, $100,000. The remaining costs, $20,000, were incurred on projects still in progress at year end.
4. The state paid general government bond principal of $113,781 and interest of $49,037 during fiscal year 20X6.
5. The state depreciates its buildings over 40 years and takes a full year's depreciation in the year that a capital asset is placed in service.
6. Profits in the amount of $230,000 were transferred to the General Fund from the Lottery Enterprise Fund during the year.
7. The following capital assets were purchased with General Fund resources: Land, $22,241; Vehicles, $7,670; and Equipment, $4,981. Vehicles are depreciated using a five-year useful life, and other equipment is depreciated using a four-year life.
8. The beginning balance of general government claims and judgments liabilities (all long-term) was $126,499. Claims and judgments incurred during the year totaled $562,441. Actual claim payments during the year were $556,089. None of the unpaid claims and judgments at June 30, 20X6, are due and payable.
9. The state's annual pension cost for the fiscal year based on an acceptable actuarial computation, with appropriate adjustments for interest on the state's Net Pension Obligation and adjustments to the actuarially required contribution is $24,623. The state contributed $20,655 to the pension trust fund during the year. None of the underpayment is due and payable at June 30, 20X6.

(Adapted from a recent Comprehensive Annual Financial Report of the State of Delaware.)

C9-2 (Interfund-GCA-GLTL Transactions—Greene County, Ohio) Record the following transactions of the Greene County, Ohio, general government activities for the year ended December 31, 20X7. Make all required entries.

1. The county uses the modified approach to report roads and bridges, which are reported as infrastructure in governmental activities in the government-wide financial statements. The county spent $2,349,688 in the fiscal year to maintain its roads and bridges at an acceptable level.
2. The county sold general government equipment during 20X7 for $54,538. The cost of the equipment was $800,000 and the related accumulated depreciation was $534,598.

3. Depreciable assets at January 1 included:
   - Buildings, structures, and improvements of $35,036,945 being depreciated over 40 years.
   - Capitalized leases of equipment of $46,896 being depreciated over 2 years.
   - Equipment, furniture and fixtures of $9,409,251 being depreciated over 12 years.
4. Greene County paid interest of $745,034 and principal of $425,000 on its general obligation bonds.
5. The county participates in the Ohio Public Employees Retirement System (OPERS). The county contributed $4,941,519 to OPERS during 20X7 for its employees, which was the actuarially required amount.
6. The county transferred the following amounts from the General Fund to other funds:
   - Health and Human Services Special Revenue Fund, $508,122.
   - Capital Projects Fund, $2,299.
   - Water and Sewer Enterprise Fund, $192,505.
   - Internal Service Fund, $2,782.

Harvey City Comprehensive Case

GENERAL CAPITAL ASSETS AND GENERAL LONG-TERM LIABILITIES

The general government capital assets and general government long-term liabilities of Harvey City are accounted for in general capital assets and general long-term liabilities accounts, as illustrated in this chapter. General capital assets and general long-term liabilities are not reported in Harvey City's fund financial statements. Rather, this information will be used in deriving the government-wide financial statement data in Chapter 14.

REQUIREMENTS—GENERAL CAPITAL ASSETS AND GENERAL LONG-TERM LIABILITIES

a. Prepare a worksheet for the General Capital Assets and General Long-Term Liabilities accounts similar to the General Fund worksheet you created in Chapter 4. Enter the effects of the following transactions in the appropriate columns of the worksheet. (A different solution approach may be used if desired by your professor.)

b. Enter the ending trial balance in the appropriate worksheet columns.

BEGINNING 20X4 TRIAL BALANCE

The January 1, 20X4, trial balance for the General Capital Assets and General Long-Term Liabilities accounts is presented below:

Harvey City
General Capital Assets and General Long-Term Liabilities Accounts
Trial Balance
January 1, 20X4

	Debit	Credit
Land	$ 800,000	
Buildings	5,300,000	
Accumulated Depreciation—Buildings		$ 2,200,000
Machinery and Equipment	1,750,000	
Accumulated Depreciation—Machinery and Equipment		550,000
Infrastructure (Streets, roads, and bridges)	13,000,000	
Accumulated Depreciation—Infrastructure		6,000,000
Construction in Progress	1,700,000	
Bonds Payable		9,000,000
Premium on Bonds Payable		180,000
Long-Term Claims and Judgments Payable		700,000
Long-Term Compensated Absences Payable		220,000
Net Position		3,700,000
Totals	$22,550,000	$22,550,000

TRANSACTIONS AND EVENTS—20X4

Numerous transactions of Harvey City's various governmental funds also involved general capital assets and general long-term liabilities. Those transactions are repeated as follows. (The number assigned to each transaction indicates the chapter in which the transaction appeared and the transaction number assigned to it in that chapter.)

General Fund Transactions

4-10. Equipment was ordered for the following functions:

General government	$ 35,000
Public safety	150,000
Highways and streets	25,300
Health and sanitation	8,900
Parks and recreation	60,000
Total	$279,200

4-11. The equipment ordered was received as follows:

	Estimated Cost	Actual Cost
General government	$ 35,000	$ 35,000
Public safety	134,000	135,000
Highways and streets	25,300	25,300
Health and sanitation	8,900	8,900
Parks and recreation	60,000	60,000
Total	$263,200	$264,200

5-22. General government equipment with an original cost of $300,000 and accumulated depreciation of $187,000 was sold for $72,000, which was deposited in the General Fund.

6-27. The city entered into a capital lease for parks and recreation equipment on December 31. The capitalizable cost of the equipment was $90,000, including a down payment of $10,000.

6-28. A lawsuit has been filed against the city related to an accident that occurred during the fiscal year. A city employee is at fault. The city expects to settle the lawsuit sometime late in the next fiscal year and considers it probable that the city will lose $62,000.

Parks and Recreation Capital Projects Fund Transactions

7-4. The city issued bonds with a face (par) value of $1,500,000 at a premium of $50,000 on January 1. Bond issue costs of $15,000 were incurred. Interest of 8% per year and $100,000 of principal are due each December 31.

7-5. The city signed a $2,190,000 contract for construction of the new recreational facility.

7-6. The city purchased land as the site for the facility at a cost of $110,000. Payment was made for the land.

7-7. The contractor billed the city $1,200,000. The city paid all but a 5% retainage.

Bridge Capital Projects Fund Transactions

7-3. The contractor billed the city $1,800,000 for the costs to complete the bridge. The project received final approval. The total cost of $3,500,000 included costs of $1,700,000 incurred in 20X3.

City Hall Refunding Bonds Debt Service Fund Transactions

8-1. The city issued $3,000,000 of city hall refunding bonds at par on July 1. The refunding bonds are 5-year bonds and pay interest semiannually each July 1 and January 1. The refunding bonds bear interest of 6% per year. The proceeds of the refunding bonds will provide part of the financing for an in-substance defeasance of $3,200,000 (face value) of *original* city hall bonds that were issued several years ago. At January 1, 20X4, an unamortized premium of $180,000 is associated with the *original* city hall bonds, which mature in eight years. The *original* city hall bonds bear interest of 8%, payable semiannually each June 30 and December 31.

8-4. The city paid $3,601,965 into an irrevocable trust to defease the *original* city hall bonds and met all the requirements for a defeasance in substance. (Record six months premium amortization of $11,250 before recording the payment.)

General Debt Service Fund Transactions

8-7. The city paid interest of $800,000 on bonds payable and retired $500,000 of principal.

1. Depreciation by function of general capital assets for 20X4 for each type of asset is presented in the following chart:

Function	Buildings	Machinery	Infrastructure
General government	$ 40,000	$ 18,000	
Public safety	100,000	60,000	
Highways and streets	50,000	97,000	$520,000
Health and sanitation	35,000	30,000	
Parks and recreation	20,000	17,000	
Economic development	5,000	3,000	
Totals	$250,000	$225,000	$520,000

2. The Long-Term Compensated Absences Payable increased by $20,000 during the year. All of this liability increase was associated with health and sanitation workers.
3. Amortization of bond premiums amounted to $14,580 during the year, including amortization of $11,250 of the premium on the *original* city hall bonds before they were defeased. The accrued interest payable on bonds at the end of 20X4 was $580,000. The January 1, 20X4, balance of accrued interest payable on bonds was $480,000.
4. Close the interest-related expenses to net position.

CHAPTER 10

Enterprise Funds

LEARNING OBJECTIVES

After studying this chapter, you should be able to:

- Determine what activities should be reported using Enterprise Funds.

- Understand the proprietary fund accounting principles.

- Understand proprietary fund reporting for intergovernmental grant revenues and debt refundings.

- Journalize typical proprietary fund transactions.

- Understand the formats and classifications of the proprietary fund financial statements.

- Understand and compute the three components of proprietary fund net position.

- Prepare the proprietary fund financial statements.

A s discussed in Chapter 2, governments finance and account for some activities in a manner similar to private business entities. Such activities are accounted for in proprietary funds. Proprietary funds include Enterprise Funds, covered in this chapter, and Internal Service Funds, covered in Chapter 11. Most activities reported as business-type activities in the government-wide financial statements are accounted for and reported as Enterprise Funds.

Because Enterprise Funds and Internal Service Funds are both proprietary funds, many of their accounting and reporting requirements are identical. The first section of this chapter highlights several proprietary fund accounting and reporting principles and practices that are common to all proprietary funds—both Enterprise Funds and Internal Service Funds. The remainder of the chapter extends the discussion of several of these principles and practices while focusing on Enterprise Funds.

COMMON CHARACTERISTICS AND PRINCIPLES OF PROPRIETARY FUNDS

As discussed in Chapter 2, accounting and reporting for proprietary funds is similar to that for similar privately owned businesses. Revenues and expenses are accounted for using the flow of economic resources measurement focus and accrual basis of accounting. Features common to all proprietary funds include the accounting equation, the applicable authoritative literature and accounting principles, and the required financial statements.

Accounting Equation   The proprietary fund accounting equation is:

$$\begin{bmatrix} \text{Current} \\ \text{Assets} \end{bmatrix} + \begin{matrix}\text{Capital}\\\text{Assets}\end{matrix} + \begin{matrix}\text{Other}\\\text{Noncurrent}\\\text{Assets}\end{matrix} + \begin{matrix}\text{Deferred}\\\text{Outflows}\\\text{of Resources}\end{matrix} - \begin{bmatrix}\text{Current}\\\text{Liabilities}\end{bmatrix} + \begin{matrix}\text{Long-Term}\\\text{Liabilities}\end{matrix} - \begin{matrix}\text{Deferred}\\\text{Inflows}\\\text{of Resources}\end{matrix} = \begin{matrix}\text{Net}\\\text{Position}\end{matrix}$$

Note that capital assets and long-term liabilities related to proprietary activities are accounted for in the proprietary fund, as are depreciation and amortization and expense amounts affected by changes in long-term liabilities.[1]

Particularly in Enterprise Funds, the pertinent accounting principles or standards typically are similar to those used in accounting for privately owned enterprises. Indeed, one of the most recent GASB standards—*Statement No. 62,* "Codification of Accounting and Financial Reporting Guidance Contained in Pre-November 30, 1989 FASB and AICPA Pronouncements"—establishes how the pertinent pronouncements of the FASB and its predecessor bodies, through Statement of Financial Accounting *Standards No. 102,* apply to proprietary funds and to government-wide financial statements. (Selected portions of those standards also apply to governmental funds.) Further, many municipally owned utilities are required by supervisory commissions to follow the same accounting guidance as privately owned utilities of the same class.

Accounting Principles

Fixed budgets (like governmental fund budgets) are sometimes used to establish budgetary control of proprietary activities. In some cases, these budgets and the related budgetary control processes are internal management tools that lack the force of law. Whether or not the budget has the force of law, an enterprise activity with a fixed budget typically is *accounted* for on the *budgetary* basis during the year and the accounts are *adjusted*—typically using worksheets—to proprietary fund GAAP at year end to facilitate preparing GAAP-based annual financial statements.

Likewise, prescribed accounting procedures for entities such as utilities may differ from GAAP. *Accounting* requirements that differ from GAAP may require the utility to use *prescribed* non-GAAP *accounts* during the year. In such cases, as for fixed budgets, the non-GAAP accounting information must be *adjusted* to the GAAP basis at year end—typically using worksheets—if the utility is to present financial statements in conformity with GAAP.

Legal or contractual reporting requirements that differ from GAAP usually are met in supplemental schedules presented in the Comprehensive Annual Financial Report or by issuing special purpose reports.

Whereas most proprietary fund transactions and events are accounted for and reported in virtually the same way as for a business, there are significant differences as well. These differences include reporting uncollectible accounts as reductions of revenues, accounting for pensions and other postemployment benefits, accounting for debt refundings, and accounting for interest capitalization on construction projects that are financed at least in part by tax-exempt debt or restricted grants. The most noteworthy differences are substantive differences in the financial statements presented for proprietary funds.

The required proprietary fund financial statements have both significant similarities to and major differences from the financial statements of businesses. The same financial statements are required for all proprietary funds, both Enterprise Funds and Internal Service Funds. The three required financial statements for these fund types are the:

Financial Statements

- Statement of fund net position
- Statement of revenues, expenses, and changes in fund net position
- Statement of cash flows

Each of these financial statements will be discussed in detail in the discussion of the illustrative Enterprise Fund presented in this chapter. First, the Enterprise Fund definition and a few common enterprise fund transactions and issues are discussed.

---

[1]Interest expense will include amortization of premiums and discounts, changes in accrued interest payable, and so on. Changes in long-term liabilities for claims and judgements, compensated absences, and other similar items will affect the expenses reported for those items.

ENTERPRISE FUNDS DEFINED

Enterprise Funds are established to account for activities of a government that *provide goods or services primarily to the public* at large *on a consumer charge basis.* Most business-type activities of a government are accounted for and reported in Enterprise Funds. Enterprise Funds should be distinguished from Internal Service Funds, which account for activities that provide the majority of their goods or services to other departments of the governmental unit, and from general government activities that charge the public for incidental services, such as libraries and museums.

The GASB defines Enterprise Funds as follows:

[1] Enterprise funds **may** be used to report any activity for which a fee is charged to external users for goods or services. [2] Activities are **required** to be reported as enterprise funds **if** any one of the following criteria is met. [3] Governments should apply each of these criteria in the context of the activity's principal revenue sources.

  a. The activity is financed with debt that is secured *solely* by a pledge of the net revenues from fees and charges of the activity. Debt that is secured by a pledge of net revenues from fees and charges and the full faith and credit of a related primary government or component unit—even if that government is not expected to make any payments—is *not* payable solely from fees and charges of the activity. (Some debt may be secured, in part, by a portion of its own proceeds but should be considered as payable "solely" from the revenues of the activity.)

  b. Laws or regulations require that the activity's costs of providing services, including capital costs (such as depreciation or debt service), be recovered with fees and charges, rather than with taxes or similar revenues.

  c. The pricing policies of the activity establish fees and charges designed to recover its costs, including capital costs (such as depreciation or debt service).[2]

This definition *permits* an activity to be reported in an Enterprise Fund if two conditions are met. The activity must

  1. Provide goods or services to outside entities or individuals (typically the general public) *and*

  2. Charge fees to external users for its goods or services.

Note several key factors in the conditions that *require* an activity to be accounted for as an Enterprise Fund. *First,* to meet the first criterion, it is not enough that net revenues from user charges for an activity are pledged as security for the activity's debt. Those user charges must be the *only* security for the debt in order for Enterprise Fund accounting to be required. *Second,* in the last two criteria, note that if the activity's prices are set to cover *either* depreciation expense *or* debt service (on the related capital assets), an Enterprise Fund is required. The charges do not necessarily have to be established so that they cover depreciation. *Finally,* note that there does not have to be a law or regulation requiring such a pricing strategy. If a government has a *policy* of pricing the services to recover all costs, including capital costs, Enterprise Fund accounting is required. Indeed, the policy need not be a written policy. If a government's practice is to price services for an activity at a level that recovers all costs, including capital costs, a policy is presumed to exist.

The most common examples of government activities or organizations that *often* are *required* to be reported in Enterprise Funds are *public sector* utilities and similar activities, including:

  • Water and sewer departments
  • Electric utilities
  • Gas utilities

---

[2]GASB, *Statement No. 34,* par. 67. (Emphasis added.)

- Sanitary sewer operations
- Garbage and other solid waste collection and disposal services
- Off-street parking lots and garages
- Solid waste landfills
- Airports

Not all governments are required to report all of these activities as Enterprise Funds, because these activities will not meet the criteria for some governments. Governments are permitted to report these activities in an Enterprise Fund, however, as long as external users are charged for the services provided. Similarly, some governments will be required to account for certain other activities as Enterprise Funds, whereas most governments will not.

The logic for allowing activities to be reported in Enterprise Funds even when their use is not required includes the following:

1. This option enables a government to use an Enterprise Fund consistently for an activity that sometimes meets the conditions for required use of Enterprise Fund reporting but at other times does not.

2. An activity that never meets the requirements for Enterprise Fund reporting—as is true with some transit systems and civic centers—is permitted to be reported in a manner that indicates full cost and is more comparable to reporting of similar nongovernment activities.

3. Whereas most governments operate certain activities (e.g., public water systems) in a manner that meets the conditions for required use of Enterprise Fund reporting, others do not. The option to report any activity for which external users are charged a fee for goods or services as an Enterprise Fund allows the latter governments to report their water departments, for instance, in a manner comparable with other governments and consistent with the norm.

Common examples of activities sometimes accounted for in Enterprise Funds under the option criterion are:

- Mass transit operations
- Civic centers
- Toll highways and bridges
- Public housing
- Public school food services

State and local governments engage in a seemingly unlimited variety of businesses. In addition to the preceding examples, other government activities commonly financed through Enterprise Funds include public docks and wharves, hospitals, nursing homes and other health care facilities, airports, lotteries, liquor wholesaling and retailing operations, swimming pools, and golf courses.

Most enterprise activities are administered through a department of a general purpose government. Others are administered by a separate board or commission under the jurisdiction of a general purpose government. Still others are operated by an independent special district or authority not under a general purpose government's jurisdiction.

A separate fund usually should be established for each government enterprise. Also, all transactions or events relating to a specific enterprise should be recorded in the appropriate Enterprise Fund records. However, closely related activities, such as water and sewer utilities, are sometimes merged because of their complementary nature or because joint revenue bonds are used in financing such operations.

EF ACCOUNTING ILLUSTRATED

Services of the type generally referred to as public utilities are among the most common enterprise activities undertaken by local governments. Such activities invariably involve significant amounts of assets, liabilities, revenues, and expenses and are seldom considered in contemporary undergraduate accounting courses. For these reasons, we have chosen an electric utility to illustrate Enterprise Fund accounting procedures. The utility is assumed to be nonregulated. (Regulated utilities are subject to special accounting and reporting requirements not discussed here.) The example is presented in several phases.

In the first stage of the illustration, after reviewing a few basic issues, we will present journal entries for a number of common Enterprise Fund transactions and assume that the illustrative utility has no restricted assets. Next, a preclosing trial balance and financial statements are presented based upon the illustrative transactions. Proprietary fund financial statements are discussed in detail in this stage. Once this is completed, restricted asset accounting, interest capitalization, and long-term debt refundings are discussed, and additional transactions are presented for the illustrative utility for the same fiscal year. Finally, a new set of financial statements incorporating the effects of the additional transactions is presented.

Before presenting the illustrative transactions, four topics are reviewed. First, we discuss Enterprise Fund budgetary issues. The illustration assumes that transactions are recorded on a GAAP basis without regard to budgetary control issues to focus attention on the GAAP requirements and the similarity of business accounting and Enterprise Fund accounting. Next, proprietary fund accounting and reporting for interfund activity and for intergovernmental grants are discussed to facilitate understanding the recording and reporting of those transactions in the example. Finally, the effects restricted gifts and grants and tax-exempt financing on the computation of interest capitalized as part of the cost of a capital asset are discussed.

Budgeting and Appropriations

Careful planning and realistic budgeting are prerequisites to sound Enterprise Fund management. *Flexible budgets* may be adopted as guides to action and means of managerial control, as in business enterprises. However, most governments are required to adopt *fixed budgets* because of legal requirements or because the executive or legislative body desires to control some (e.g., capital outlay) or all expenditures. In these cases, the Enterprise Fund accounts are maintained on the budgetary basis during the year, then converted to GAAP at year end.

Interfund Activity

Transactions between funds were discussed in Chapter 2 and have been illustrated extensively for governmental funds. Most transactions between the enterprise and other government departments should be accounted for in the same manner as "outsider" transactions—that is, as *interfund services provided and used* (i.e., interfund service transactions). Therefore, goods or services provided by an Enterprise Fund department or activity to other departments of the government should be billed at regular, predetermined rates and reported as operating revenues.

Revenues are recognized at standard rates even if the enterprise provides "free" goods or services to other departments. In this case, a transfer out equal to the standard charges for the "free" goods or services must be reported. This reporting clearly signals the fact that the enterprise is subsidizing the operations of these other departments by providing "free" services. Likewise, all goods or services provided to the enterprise by other government departments should be billed to it on the same basis that other users are charged. Failure to do so distorts the operating and position statements of all funds involved.

Interfund transfers are the last item reported before the changes in net position in the statement of revenues, expenses, and changes in fund net position. *Reimbursements* are reflected in this statement by increasing or decreasing appropriate expenses for the effects of any reimbursement transactions. *Interfund loans* are reported only in the statement of net position.

Intergovernmental Grants

The GASB *Codification* provides general guidelines for all proprietary funds for reporting grants, entitlements, and shared revenues. Grants are much more likely to be received for activities accounted for in Enterprise Funds than in Internal

Service Funds. Restricted intergovernmental grants are classified as either *capital grants* or *operating grants*. *Capital* grants are intergovernmental grants that must be used *solely* for construction, acquisition, or improvement of capital assets. All other intergovernmental grants are *operating* grants.

The usual criteria for recognizing grants apply to the timing of recognition of both operating and capital grants. Therefore, grant revenue is recognized when all eligibility requirements are fulfilled. As discussed in Chapter 5, one of the *key eligibility requirements* typically is that *qualifying costs* have been incurred.

- If grant cash is received before the recognition criteria are met, *unearned revenues* (i.e., liabilities) are reported in the proprietary fund.
- When the recognition criteria are met for an *operating* grant, *nonoperating* revenues are reported.
- *Capital* grant revenues are reported as "capital contributions" immediately following the subtotal for "Income before other revenues, expenses, and transfers."

Reporting of cash flows from grants is discussed later.

Interest Capitalization

State and local governments may issue both taxable and tax-exempt bonds and other debt securities to finance Enterprise Fund capital assets. Capitalization of interest cost on *taxable* debt follows the same guidance as for commercial entities.

When feasible, SLGs will finance their major construction activities with *tax-exempt* debt and/or grants that are restricted for construction of a capital facility. *Interest capitalization differs significantly* when these sources of financing are used:

- No *interest cost* should be *capitalized* on asset costs financed by *restricted* gifts or grants.
- Interest capitalization associated with tax-exempt debt is *computed differently* from that associated with taxable debt.
  1. The interest *capitalization period* begins when *tax-exempt debt restricted* for construction of a qualifying asset is *issued* instead of when construction begins.
  2. The *interest cost capitalized* is *computed* as *all* interest costs of the borrowing during the capitalization period *minus* any investment *earnings* on temporary investment of the debt proceeds during that period.

Establishment of Fund and Acquisition of Plant

The Enterprise Fund example begins with the acquisition of an existing, nonregulated electric utility by A Governmental Unit. The acquisition of a utility may be financed from various sources, including the sale of bonds to be retired from utility earnings, contributions or grants from the governmental unit, intergovernmental grants, intergovernmental or intragovernmental loans, and contributions from subdivision developers and prospective customers.

Assume that the acquisition of the utility plant is financed by a General Fund contribution.

1. The entry to record the receipt of a contribution of $400,000 and to establish the fund at the end of 20X1 is:

(1) Cash	$400,000	
Transfer from General Fund		$400,000
To record governmental unit's contribution for acquisition of utility.		

2. The net position of an existing private electricity generation and distribution plant are acquired by the government at the end of 20X1. The government paid $280,000. This amount equals the fair value of the assets acquired less the fair value of the liabilities assumed.

The entry to record the acquisition of the plant and the assumption of the liabilities (assume that all the amounts in the entries are the correct fair values) is:

(2) Land	$ 50,000	
Buildings	90,000	
Improvements Other Than Buildings	480,000	
Machinery and Equipment	110,000	
Accounts Receivable	62,000	
Inventory of Materials and Supplies	10,000	
Allowance for Uncollectible Accounts		$ 12,000
Bonds Payable		400,000
Long-Term Liability for Compensated Absences		100,000
Vouchers Payable		10,000
Due to ABC Electric Company		280,000

To record the acquisition of the assets and liabilities of the ABC Electric Company.

3. Payment of the amount due to ABC Electric Company is recorded as follows:

| (3) Due to ABC Electric Company | $280,000 | |
| Cash | | $280,000 |

To record payment to ABC Electric Company.

4. At the end of 20X1, the transfer account would be closed with the following entry:

| (4) Transfer from General Fund | $400,000 | |
| Net Position | | $400,000 |

To close transfer from General Fund.

Accounting for Routine Operating Transactions

The following transactions and entries illustrate the operation of an Enterprise Fund for a utility. These transactions occur in 20X2, the first year of operations.

For simplicity, all operating revenues are credited to an Operating Revenues control account. Likewise, all expenses are charged to either an Operating Expenses or a Nonoperating Expenses control account. (A detailed operating expense statement is provided later in the chapter in Illustration 10-9.)

Transactions and Entries—During 20X2

5. Materials costing $59,000 were received.

| (5) Inventory of Materials and Supplies | $ 59,000 | |
| Vouchers Payable | | $ 59,000 |

To record purchase of materials (consumption method *required*).

6. Revenues billed during the year totaled $300,000.

| (6) Accounts Receivable | $300,000 | |
| Operating Revenues | | $300,000 |

To record operating revenue.

7. Equipment costing $50,500 was purchased on account.

| (7) Machinery and Equipment | $ 50,500 | |
| Vouchers Payable | | $ 50,500 |

To record purchase of equipment.

8. Rental due on equipment rented to the State Public Works Department totaled $7,000.

| (8) Due from State Public Works Department | $ 7,000 | |
| Nonoperating Revenues—Equipment Rental | | $ 7,000 |

To record rental of equipment to State Public Works Department.

9. Collections on accounts receivable were $290,000. Interest received totaled $1,000.

(9) Cash	$291,000	
Accounts Receivable		$290,000
Nonoperating Revenues—Interest		1,000

    To record collection of accounts receivable and
    interest revenues.

10. A bill was received from an Internal Service Fund for services used, $12,800.

| (10) Operating Expenses .... | $ 12,800 | |
| Due to Internal Service Fund .... | | $ 12,800 |

    To record cost of services purchased from Internal
    Service Fund.

11. Bond principal ($50,000) and interest ($20,000) were paid.

(11) Bonds Payable	$ 50,000	
Nonoperating Expenses—Interest	20,000	
Cash		$ 70,000

    To record debt service payment.

12. Other cash payments were made during the year for:

Salaries and wages.....................	$127,200
Telephone and Internet services	500
Fire insurance premiums (2-year policy) ...	1,000
Utilities.............................	10,500
Vouchers payable (including $30,000 on the equipment from Transaction 7)	70,000
	$209,200

(12) Operating Expenses	$139,200	
Vouchers Payable	70,000	
Cash		$209,200

    To record payments of various expenses and
    liabilities.

    (Prepaid insurance, $600, is recorded in an adjusting entry later in the example.)

13. $10,000 was paid from the Enterprise Fund to the General Fund to subsidize General Fund operations.

| (13) Transfer to General Fund .... | $ 10,000 | |
| Cash .... | | $ 10,000 |

    To record payment of transfer to General Fund.

14. A subdivision developer donated a subdivision electricity system (fair value $30,000) to the utility.

| (14) Improvements Other Than Buildings .... | $ 30,000 | |
| Capital Contributions from Subdividers .... | | $ 30,000 |

    To record donation of subdivision distribution
    lines to the utility.

15. The utility received a one-time unrestricted operating grant of $100,000 from a federal utility commission.

| (15) Cash .... | $100,000 | |
| Nonoperating Revenues—Intergovernmental Grants .... | | $100,000 |

    To record the receipt of federal utility commission
    grant.

As reflected in the journal entries, all changes in net position are reported as revenues, expenses, gains, or losses, as specified by the all-inclusive approach that the GASB requires in the statement of revenues, expenses, and changes in fund net position. Note, too, that operating revenues and operating expenses are carefully distinguished from nonoperating revenues and expenses and from revenues from capital contributions.

The *distinction* between *operating* and *nonoperating* revenues and expenses is *significant*.

- If significant nonoperating revenues, capital contributions, or transfers are needed to cover operating expenses, the full cost of services provided is not being charged to users of Enterprise Fund services.

- This situation implies that the activity may not be able to sustain itself in the future without rate increases if (1) the nonoperating revenues, capital contributions, or transfers are reduced significantly, or (2) the demand for the department's (underpriced) services increases significantly.

Finally, note and review the other key differences between governmental fund and proprietary fund accounting. They include the required use of the consumption method of inventory accounting [entry (5)] in proprietary funds, reporting capital assets and noncurrent liabilities in proprietary funds [entries (2) and (7)], and accounting for expenses (rather than expenditures) in proprietary funds.

Adjusting Entries—End of 20X2

16. Necessary adjusting entries at the end of 20X2 were based on the following data.

a. Accrued salaries and wages

payable	$ 4,500
Accrued interest payable	2,000
Accrued utilities payable	7,500
Accrued long-term compensated absences (increase)	1,500
b. Prepaid insurance	600
c. Ending inventory of materials and supplies	30,000
d. Estimated losses on accounts receivable	1,500
e. Depreciation:	
Buildings	5,000
Improvements other than buildings	15,000
Machinery and equipment	16,000
f. Unbilled receivables	21,000
Accrued interest receivable	200

(16) (a) Operating Expenses	$13,500	
Nonoperating Expenses—Interest	2,000	
Accrued Salaries and Wages Payable		$ 4,500
Accrued Interest Payable		2,000
Accrued Utilities Payable		7,500
Liability for Compensated Absences (Long-Term)		1,500
To record accrued expenses.		
(b) Prepaid Insurance	$ 600	
Operating Expenses		$ 600
To record unexpired insurance.		
(c) Operating Expenses	$39,000	
Inventory of Materials and Supplies		$39,000
To record operating expenses for materials used during year. ($10,000 + $59,000 − $30,000)		
(d) Operating Revenues	$ 1,500	
Allowance for Uncollectible Accounts		$ 1,500
To record estimated losses on accounts receivable.		

(e) Operating Expenses	$36,000	
Accumulated Depreciation—Buildings		$ 5,000
Accumulated Depreciation—Improvements Other Than Buildings		15,000
Accumulated Depreciation—Machinery and Equipment		16,000
To record depreciation expense for fiscal year.		
(f) Unbilled Accounts Receivable	$21,000	
Accrued Interest Receivable	200	
Operating Revenues		$ 21,000
Nonoperating Revenues—Interest		200
To record unbilled receivables and revenues and accrued interest receivable on customer accounts at year end.		

Pay particular attention to entry 16(d)—the adjusting entry for uncollectible accounts. Governments report all revenues—whether in governmental fund, proprietary fund, or government-wide financial statements—*net* of uncollectible accounts. In other words, the provision for bad debts reduces the amount of revenues reported instead of being reported as an expense. Therefore, entry 16(d) reduces operating revenues for the estimated loss from uncollectible accounts instead of recording operating expenses.

Unbilled Receivables

For ease of illustration, most of the required adjusting entries were included in the various phases of the example. Most of the adjusting entries required are similar to those common in commercial accounting; and, as in commercial accounting, those of an accrual nature would typically be reversed at the beginning of the subsequent period. The adjusting entry for unbilled receivables may be less familiar to the reader. Accurately determining the revenue earned during a year requires significant amounts of unbilled receivables to be accrued at year end, particularly if the amount of such receivables varies materially from year to year.

Accounting for Extraordinary and Special Items

As was noted and defined in Chapter 3, governments occasionally need to report extraordinary items and/or special items. The accounting and financial reporting for these items in Enterprise Funds is similar to that in the governmental funds. Specifically, extraordinary items and special items are reported separately *after* nonoperating revenues (expenses). A special item is presented here to illustrate proprietary fund reporting of this operating statement classification that is unique to governments. It would have been recorded when it occurred, prior to the adjustment entries.

Transactions and Entries—During 20X2

17. The Electric Fund sold land with a book value of $25,000 for $150,000 in a transaction that meets the special item criteria.

(41) Cash	$150,000	
Land		$ 25,000
Special Item—Gain on Sale of Land		125,000
To record the sale of land.		

An adjusted, preclosing trial balance incorporating the effects of the 17 transactions recorded thus far for the Electric Enterprise Fund of A Governmental Unit is presented as Illustration 10-1. The required financial statements for an Enterprise Fund will be discussed, and examples of each will be presented for the Electric Fund. Recall that the required financial statements include:

Preclosing Trial Balance and Financial Statements—Basic Example

- Statement of Net Position
- Statement of Revenues, Expenses, and Changes in Net Position
- Statement of Cash Flows

ILLUSTRATION 10-1   Preclosing Trial Balance—Basic Example

A Governmental Unit
Electric (Enterprise) Fund
Preclosing (Adjusted) Trial Balance
December 31, 20X2

Cash	$ 371,800	
Accounts Receivable	72,000	
Allowance for Uncollectible Accounts		$ 13,500
Unbilled Accounts Receivable	21,000	
Accrued Interest Receivable	200	
Due from State Public Works Department	7,000	
Inventory of Materials and Supplies	30,000	
Prepaid Insurance	600	
Land	25,000	
Buildings	90,000	
Accumulated Depreciation—Buildings		5,000
Improvements Other Than Buildings	510,000	
Accumulated Depreciation—Improvements Other Than Buildings		15,000
Machinery and Equipment	160,500	
Accumulated Depreciation—Machinery and Equipment		16,000
Vouchers Payable		49,500
Due to Internal Service Fund		12,800
Accrued Salaries and Wages Payable		4,500
Accrued Interest Payable		2,000
Accrued Utilities Payable		7,500
Bonds Payable		350,000
Liability for Compensated Absences (Long-Term)		101,500
Net Assets		400,000
Operating Revenues		319,500
Operating Expenses	239,900	
Nonoperating Revenues—Intergovernmental Grants		100,000
Nonoperating Revenues—Equipment Rental		7,000
Nonoperating Revenues—Interest		1,200
Nonoperating Expenses—Interest	22,000	
Capital Contributions from Subdividers		30,000
Special Item—Gain on Sale of Land		125,000
Transfer to General Fund	10,000	
Total	$1,560,000	$1,560,000

Statement of Fund Net Position

The proprietary fund statement of net position (or statement of fund net position) is much like the balance sheet of a business entity. Capital assets, intangible assets, and similar accounts that are not included in governmental fund balance sheets are reported in the proprietary fund statement of net position. Reporting such assets in this statement is consistent with the application of the business accounting model to proprietary funds. Likewise, long-term liabilities issued for the purposes of and payable from the resources of a proprietary fund are reported in the statement of net position of that proprietary fund. The GASB prefers the statement to be presented in the net position format with five distinct sections (assets + deferred outflows of resources − liabilities − deferred inflows of resources = net position). However, the balance sheet format (assets + deferred outflows of resources = liabilities + deferred inflows of resources + net position). Illustration 10-2, the Statement of Net Position of the Electric Enterprise Fund, is presented in the net position format. However, this fund does not have deferred outflows or deferred inflows; therefore, those financial statement elements do not appear in the illustration. Note the similarity of the asset and liability classifications to those of business entities.

    The principal differences between the statement of net position of a proprietary fund and the typical business entity balance sheet are the inclusion of the two additional financial statement elements—deferred outflows of resources and deferred inflows of resources and the presentation of equity (or net position). Proprietary fund net position is classified into three categories:

ILLUSTRATION 10-2 Statement of Net Position

A Governmental Unit
Electric Enterprise Fund
Statement of Net Position
December 31, 20X2

ASSETS

Current Assets:

Cash	$ 371,800
Accounts receivable (less allowance for doubtful accounts of $13,500)	58,500
Unbilled accounts receivable	21,000
Accrued interest receivable	200
Due from State Public Works Department	7,000
Inventory of materials and supplies	30,000
Prepaid insurance	600
Total Current Assets	489,100

Capital Assets:

Land	25,000
Buildings (less accumulated depreciation of $5,000)	85,000
Improvements other than buildings (less accumulated depreciation of $15,000)	495,000
Machinery and Equipment (less accumulated depreciation of $16,000)	144,500
Total Capital Assets	749,500
Total Assets	$1,238,600

LIABILITIES

Current Liabilities:

Vouchers payable	$ 49,500
Due to Internal Service Fund	12,800
Accrued salaries and wages payable	4,500
Accrued interest payable	2,000
Accrued utilities payable	7,500
Total Current Liabilities	76,300

Long-Term Liabilities:

Bonds payable	350,000
Liability for compensated absences	101,500
Total Long-Term Liabilities	451,500
Total Liabilities	527,800

NET POSITION

Net investment in capital assets	379,000
Unrestricted	331,800
Total Net Position	$ 710,800

1. Net Investment in capital assets
2. Restricted net position
3. Unrestricted net position

Corporate businesses distinguish equity primarily between contributed capital and retained earnings. These classifications are *not permitted* in government financial statements.

Net Investment in Capital Assets Net investment in capital assets is the net position component that indicates the fund's net investment in capital assets. This component equals the:

- Fund's capital assets
- *Plus,* capital-asset-related deferred outflows of resources
- *Less,* accumulated depreciation

- *Less,* capital-asset-related deferred inflows of resources
- *Less,* capital-asset-related borrowings (debt) of the fund

Capital-asset-related borrowings (debt) include the *outstanding balances* of any current or noncurrent bonds, mortgages, notes, or other borrowings attributable to the acquisition, construction, or improvement of capital assets. The most likely example of deferred outflows or deferred inflows that will affect this classification of net position is deferred amounts from refunding transactions, which are discussed later.

However, this component excludes any *unexpended* proceeds of debt issued for capital asset purposes or of capital-asset-related deferred inflows of resources. The *unexpended* portion of the capital borrowings (or deferred inflows) is deducted from the restricted net position component to offset the unexpended proceeds, which ordinarily are reported in the restricted net position component. The Net Investment in Capital Assets reported for the Electric Fund in its Statement of Net position shown in Illustration 10-2 is $379,000 (capital assets, net, equal to $749,500 less bonds payable and vouchers payable for capital assets).

Restricted Net Position Restricted net position is the net position component that indicates the amount of *restricted assets* of a proprietary fund in excess of *liabilities* related to those restricted assets. Assets are considered *restricted only if the constraints* placed on the use of the assets *are narrower than the general limits of the activity.* Accordingly, an Airport Enterprise Fund does *not* report revenues restricted to use by the airport (for any airport purpose) as restricted net position. As with governmental fund resources, restrictions may be imposed:

1. Externally by creditors (such as through debt covenants), grantors, contributors, or laws or regulations of other governments,
2. By constitutional provisions, or
3. By enabling legislation that (a) authorizes the government to assess, levy, charge, or otherwise mandate payment of resources externally and (b) places a legally enforceable purpose restriction on those resources.[3]

As discussed in the previous section, unexpended proceeds of capital-asset-related borrowings or of capital-asset-related deferred inflows of resources ordinarily are included in this net position component. An equal amount of the related capital debt or deferred inflow is deducted to offset these proceeds. This situation is the only time a capital borrowing is deducted in computing the amounts of either restricted net position or unrestricted net position.

Five points about restricted net position are important.

1. The restriction on asset usage must be more limited than the scope of activities accounted for in the particular entity being reported—in this case a specific Enterprise Fund or Internal Service Fund. Surprisingly, the GASB Implementation Guide requires that such amounts also must be reported as unrestricted net assets in the government-wide statements, even though the restriction is substantive when multiple enterprise activities are aggregated into business-type activities in the government-wide financial statements.
2. Neither the restricted net position component in total nor the portion that is restricted for any specific purpose, such as for debt service, can ever be negative. If liabilities and deferred inflows to be deducted from restricted assets exceed the amount of assets restricted for that purpose, zero is reported in restricted net position and the amount of liabilities in excess of restricted assets is deducted from unrestricted net position.
3. Although it is rare with enterprise activities, some assets (e.g., those of a permanent endowment) are required to be retained in perpetuity. These assets are nonexpendable. If an enterprise has assets restricted in this way, the restricted net position must be presented in two subcomponents—expendable and nonexpendable.
4. The restricted net position component does *not* necessarily equal the difference between the restricted assets and the liabilities payable from the restricted assets reported in the proprietary fund's statement of net position because

---

[3]GASB *Statement No. 46,* "Net Assets Restricted by Enabling Legislation" (December 2004).

- Some assets restricted for a short-term purpose may be reported as current assets, not as restricted assets.
- Some capital-asset-related borrowings may be included in liabilities payable from restricted assets. These capital-asset-related liabilities must be deducted in computing Net Investment in Capital Assets, not in computing Restricted Net Position.

5. Deferred outflows of resources do not affect restricted net position.

Note that the Electric Enterprise Fund does not have restricted assets or restricted net position in this basic example. The example will be extended to include both restricted asset accounting and reporting and debt refundings in the next phase of the illustration of the Electric Enterprise Fund of A Governmental Unit.

Unrestricted Net Position Unrestricted net position is the balance of the remainder of the fund's assets and deferred outflows less its remaining liabilities and deferred inflows. It represents the portion of net position that does *not* meet the definition of "restricted" or "net investment in capital assets."

Management is *permitted* to establish designations of *unrestricted* net position to indicate that the government does not intend to use them for general operations of the proprietary fund. Designations of proprietary fund net position are rare in practice and are disclosed in the notes to the financial statements, not presented in the financial statements themselves.

Net Position Components Computed at Year End As with the GAAP fund balance classifications for governmental funds, governments are *not* apt to maintain the balances of the three net position classifications in their accounts. None of the individual net position classifications, nor the changes therein, articulates with the changes reported in the statement of revenues, expenses, and changes in fund net position. Various transactions affect the balances of the individual net position components but do not affect the total net position and are not revenues, expenses, gains, losses, or transfers. For instance, using unrestricted resources either to purchase a capital asset or to retire capital-asset-related liabilities increases the Net Investment in Capital Assets and decreases the Restricted Net Position. These transactions significantly change the composition of net position but do not affect the statement of revenues, expenses, and changes in fund net position. Therefore, many changes in the three components of net position are not captured in temporary accounts during the year. As a result, the proper year-end balances of each net position component must be computed from the asset and liability balances at year end. The computation of each category is summarized in Illustration 10-3.

ILLUSTRATION 10-3   Calculation of Net Position Components

Net Investment in Capital Assets	Restricted Net Position**	Unrestricted Net Position
+ Capital Assets (All)	+ Assets restricted to a particular purpose*	+ All other assets
− Accumulated Depreciation	− Noncapital liabilities related to the restricted assets	− All other liabilities
− Capital borrowings (if proceeds have been expended)*	− Capital debt equal to unexpended proceeds of capital debt included in restricted assets	
+ Related Deferred Outflows of Resources		+ All other deferred outflows
− Related Deferred Inflows	− Deferred inflows related to restricted assets	− All other deferred inflows

*Capital debt (i.e., capital-asset-related debt), whether current or long-term, is borrowings incurred to finance construction, acquisition, or improvement of capital assets. If the proceeds have not been expended, the financial resources are included in computing Restricted Net Position. An equal amount of the capital debt must be deducted from the Restricted Net Position category to offset the unexpended financial resources.

**Restrictions may be imposed by (1) external parties through contracts, grant agreements, laws and regulations of other governments, and so on, or (2) a government's own constitutional provisions or enabling legislation passed to raise the revenues.

The balances reported for each net asset category in Illustration 10-2 are computed as follows:

Net Investment in Capital Assets:

Total capital assets, net of accumulated depreciation		$749,500
Less: Bonds payable	$ 350,000	
Vouchers payable (for equipment)	20,500	370,500
Net investment in capital assets		$379,000

Unrestricted Net Assets:

Total assets	$1,238,600	
Less capital assets, net	(749,500)	$489,100
Less:		
Total liabilities	$ 527,800	
Less: Bonds payable	(350,000)	177,800
Unrestricted net assets		$311,300

Statement of Revenues, Expenses, and Changes in Fund Net Position

As discussed in Chapter 2, the proprietary fund operating statement is the statement of revenues, expenses, and changes in fund net position. As can be seen in the Statement of Revenues, Expenses, and Changes in Fund Net Position of the Electric Fund in Illustration 10-4, the statement has numerous similarities to a business income statement. Its initial sections closely resemble a business income statement, and extraordinary items are reported in virtually the same manner as in a business income statement. However, the proprietary fund operating statement also differs in major ways from a business income statement. Key *differences* include the following:

1. Governments use an *all-inclusive* approach. All changes in total net position of a proprietary fund are considered revenues, expenses, gains, or losses in proprietary fund reporting. No fundamental distinction is made between contributed capital transactions and income transactions.

2. Estimated bad debts are deducted in computing the amount of revenues to report, as in governmental funds, and no expense for bad debts or similar amounts is reported. The GASB *requires* the *net* revenue approach to enhance comparability between the governmental and business-type activities data in the *government-wide* Statement of Activities. The availability criterion for revenue recognition in governmental funds does *not* apply in proprietary funds.

3. Net income is *not* reported in proprietary fund financial statements. Although the statement of revenues, expenses, and changes in fund net position closely resembles a business income statement prior to presentation of the "Income before other revenues, expenses, and transfers" subtotal, some of the items reported thereafter are not considered income items in business reporting. The GASB decided to use this "changes in total net position (fund equity)" presentation and not distinguish earned equity from contributed amounts.

4. Certain reporting elements such as special items and transfers, shown in Illustration 10-4, are *unique* to government reporting. These items are not reported in business financial statements.

5. Governments may use the *modified approach* discussed in Chapter 9 to report expenses for infrastructure capital assets.

Finally, the GASB acknowledges that the distinction between operating and non-operating revenues and expenses is, to a point, a matter of judgment. Governments should establish, and consistently apply, a policy that defines "operating" activities for each of their proprietary activities. Furthermore, the GASB expects reasonable consistency between the transactions that are reported as operating revenues and expenses in the statement of revenues, expenses, and changes in fund net position and those classified as cash flows from operating activities in the proprietary fund statement of cash flows, which is discussed next.

ILLUSTRATION 10-4 Operating Statement

A Governmental Unit
Electric Enterprise Fund
Statement of Revenues, Expenses, and Changes in Fund Net Position*
For the Year Ended December 31, 20X2

Operating Revenues:

Residential sales (net of uncollectible amounts of $xx)	$153,700
Commercial sales (net of uncollectible amounts of $xx)	91,300
Industrial sales (net of uncollectible amounts of $xx)	62,500
Public street lighting	12,000
Total Operating Revenues	319,500

Operating Expenses:

Production	137,400
Distribution	49,200
Accounting and collection	13,800
Sales promotion	1,000
Administrative and general	38,500
Total Operating Expenses	239,900

Operating Income	79,600

Nonoperating Revenues (Expenses):

Intergovernmental grants	100,000
Equipment rental	7,000
Investment income	1,200
Interest expense	(22,000)
Net Nonoperating Revenues (Expenses)	86,200

Income before Other Revenues, Expenses, and Transfers	165,800
Capital contributions from subdividers	30,000
Special item—Gain on sale of land	125,000
Transfer to General Fund	(10,000)
Change in Net Position	310,800
Net position, January 1, 20X2	400,000
Net position, December 31, 20X2	$710,800

*The operating revenue and operating expense classification detail is assumed—it was not provided in the transactions.

Statement of Cash Flows

The statement of cash flows for proprietary funds serves essentially the same purposes as the business statement of cash flows. However, cash flows resulting from similar or identical transactions and events are often required to be classified differently in proprietary fund cash flow statements than in business cash flow statements. Instead of the three classifications of cash flows used in business cash flow statements (operating, financing, and investing), the GASB requires four cash flow categories. Observe in the Statement of Cash Flows for the Electric Enterprise Fund in Illustration 10-5 that those four categories are:

1. Cash flows from operating activities
2. Cash flows from noncapital financing activities
3. Cash flows from capital and related financing activities
4. Cash flows from investing activities

Moreover, GASB standards require that SLG cash flow statements report *all* cash flows and balances—*both restricted and unrestricted* cash and cash equivalents.

ILLUSTRATION 10-5 Statement of Cash Flows

A Governmental Unit
Electric Enterprise Fund
Statement of Cash Flows
For the Year Ended December 31, 20X2

Cash Flows from Operating Activities:

Cash received from customers	$290,000
Cash paid to suppliers of goods and services	(41,500)
Cash paid to employees	(127,200)
Cash paid for utilities	(10,500)
Net cash provided by operating activities	110,800

Cash Flows from Noncapital Financing Activities:

Cash received from intergovernmental operating grant	100,000
Cash paid for interfund transfers	(10,000)
Net cash flows from noncapital financing activities	90,000

Cash Flows from Capital and Related Financing Activities:

Cash received from sale of land	150,000
Cash paid for retirement of bonds	(50,000)
Cash paid for interest	(20,000)
Cash paid for equipment	(30,000)
Net cash flows from capital and related financing activities	50,000

Cash Flows from Investing Activities:

Cash received from interest	1,000
Net cash flows from investing activities	1,000
Net increase (decrease) in cash	251,800
Cash, January 1, 20X2*	120,000
Cash, December 31, 20X2*	$371,800

Reconciliation of operating income to net cash flows from operating activities:

Operating income	$ 79,600
Adjustments to reconcile operating income to cash flows from operating activities:	
Depreciation	36,000
Increase in vouchers payable (associated with operating activities)	19,000
Increase in interfund payable	12,800
Increase in salaries and wages payable	6,000
Increase in utilities payable	7,500
Increase in accounts receivable	(29,500)
Increase in inventories	(20,000)
Increase in prepaid insurance	(600)
Net adjustments	31,200
Net cash provided by operating activities	$110,800

Noncash Financing and Investing Activities:

Subdivision electricity system donation (transaction 14)	$ 30,000

*Includes both unrestricted and restricted cash.

Cash Flows from Operating Activities The classification of proprietary fund *cash flows from operating activities* differs from that of business cash flows from operating activities. The primary difference is that cash flows from operating activities for proprietary funds generally *incorporates only the cash effects of transactions and events that enter into **operating income*** rather than *net income.* Consequently, the cash effects associated with nonoperating revenues and expenses, such as interest revenue and interest expense, are not included in cash flows from operating activities. The GASB *Codification* states that:

> Operating activities generally result from providing services and producing and delivering goods, and include all transactions and other events that are not defined as capital and related financing, noncapital financing, or investing activities.[4]

The *Codification* further states that the **direct method** of presenting cash flows from operating activities is **required.** Unlike businesses, governments are not permitted to use the indirect (reconciliation) method. In addition, certain operating cash flows—such as payments to suppliers and to employees—must be reported as separate line items (Illustration 10-6), and a reconciliation of operating income and cash flows from operating activities must be presented either at the bottom of the cash flow statement or as a separate schedule. The reconciliation is the equivalent of the indirect method presentation of cash flows from operating activities.

Cash Flows from Noncapital Financing Activities and Cash Flows from Capital and Related Financing Activities *"Noncapital" financing activities and "capital and related" financing activities are distinguished by whether the cash flow is clearly attributable to the financing of capital asset acquisition, construction, or improvement.*

ILLUSTRATION 10-6   Cash Flow Classifications Summary

Cash Flows from Operating Activities

- Cash received from sales of goods or services
- Cash paid for materials used in providing services or manufacturing goods for resale
- Cash paid to suppliers for other goods or services
- Cash paid to employees for services
- Cash received or paid resulting from interfund services transactions
- Cash received from other funds for reimbursement of operating transactions
- Cash payments for taxes
- Cash received or paid from grants for specific activities that are part of grantor government's operating activities
- Other cash flows that are not properly reported in the other classifications

Cash Flows from Noncapital Financing Activities

- Cash received from issuing (or paid to repay) borrowings not clearly attributable to capital assets
- Cash paid for interest on those borrowings
- Cash received from operating grants not included in operating activities
- Cash paid for grants or subsidies to other governments that are not included in operating activities

- Cash paid (1) for transfers out and (2) for interfund reimbursements not included in operating activities
- Cash received from transfers from other funds that are not clearly made for capital asset purposes

Cash Flows from Capital and Related Financing Activities

- Cash received from issuing (or paid to repay) borrowings clearly attributable to capital assets
- Cash paid for interest on those borrowings
- Cash received from capital grants
- Cash paid or received from *acquisition or disposal of capital assets*
- Cash received from transfers from other funds for the specific purpose of financing capital assets
- Cash received from special assessments or taxes levied to finance capital assets

Cash Flows from Investing Activities

- Cash paid or received for the acquisition or disposal of investments in debt or equity securities
- Cash paid or received from loans made to others
- Cash received from interest and dividends

Note: This illustration is not intended to be comprehensive. Many transactions and situations are beyond the scope of this text.

---

[4]GASB *Codification,* sec. 2450.113.

Cash flows from issuing (or repaying) debt, interest payments, interfund *transfers from* other funds, and certain other transactions are classified as *capital* and related financing activities *if clearly attributable to capital asset financing*. *Otherwise,* they are classified as *noncapital* financing activities. For example,

- Cash received from issuing bonds for the explicit purpose of financing construction of a capital asset is reported as cash flows from capital and related financing activities.
- Cash payments of interest or principal on those bonds will also be classified as capital and related financing activities.
- The cash effects of issuing or servicing all other debt issuances (not clearly related to capital asset financing) are reported as noncapital financing activities, as are all cash payments for *transfers to* other funds.

One striking difference from the business cash flow statement classifications is that *cash payments to acquire capital assets* are reported as *capital* and related financing activities, *not* as *investing* activities. Likewise, cash received from the sale or disposal of capital assets is reported as capital and related financing activities.

Cash Flows from Investing Activities Investing activities include:

- Making or disposing of investments in debt or equity instruments.
- Making and collecting most loans.
- The related interest and dividends received.

As noted earlier, *purchases and sales of capital assets are not reported as investing activities* in government cash flow statements. Indeed, the government cash flow classifications center on distinguishing capital-asset-related cash flows from noncapital-asset-related cash flows, whereas the business cash flow classifications focus on distinguishing financing cash flows and investing cash flows.

As in business cash flow statements, the GASB requires disclosure of information about significant *noncash financing and investing activities* such as contributions of water or sewer lines in a newly developed subdivision to a city enterprise fund. This information is presented in a schedule either on the face of the statement or in a separate, accompanying schedule.

Illustration 10-6 summarizes the common classifications of the typical cash flows of proprietary funds. Illustration 10-5 presents a number of these cash flows in the Statement of Cash Flows for the Electric Fund of A Governmental Unit.

EF ACCOUNTING—EXTENDED ILLUSTRATION

The basic illustration for the Electric Enterprise Fund effectively demonstrates the similarity of proprietary fund accounting and financial reporting. It also illustrates many of the unique features of proprietary fund financial statements. To illustrate additional features of Enterprise Fund accounting and financial reporting, we now assume that the Electric Enterprise Fund engaged in numerous transactions in 20X2 that were not considered in the basic illustration. The additional transactions involve refunding bonds payable and accounting for various types of restrictions placed on assets.

Discussing long-term debt refundings not only provides a basis to understand proprietary fund accounting and reporting for this common transaction but also permits the presentation of deferred outlows (inflows) of resources to be illustrated in the Electric Enterprise Fund Statement of Net Position. This statement is presented at the conclusion of the extended version of the illustrative enterprise activity example. Accounting for restricted assets is important because it is a common issue that governments face in accounting and reporting for Enterprise Funds. Reporting restricted assets also is illustrated in the statement of net position presented after the additional illustrative transactions and entries.

Extension of the Electric Enterprise Fund illustration proceeds as follow:

- Accounting and financial reporting for long-term debt refundings of proprietary funds
- Illustrative Electric Enterprise Fund refunding transactions and entries
- Restricted asset accounting in proprietary funds
- Illustrative Electric Enterprise Fund restricted asset transactions and entries
- Presentation of Electric Enterprise Fund extended example preclosing trial balance and financial statements

Long-Term Debt Refundings

Refundings of general long-term liabilities were discussed and illustrated in Chapter 8. Refundings of proprietary fund long-term debt are reported differently from those of both general government activities and business entities. A key difference from business reporting is that businesses report a difference between the carrying amount of retired debt and the amount paid to retire it as an *extinguishment* gain or loss in the period that the debt is retired—regardless of whether a refunding is involved. This gain or loss treatment is also required for government proprietary activity early retirements of debt that do *not* involve a refunding.

To illustrate the *early retirement* of proprietary fund debt with **no** *refunding* involved, assume that:

- A county Airport Enterprise Fund paid $1,985,000 of existing resources to repay a $1,935,000 bond issue.
- The bond issue had been outstanding for several years prior to its call date, December 31, 20X4.
- The call premium was $50,000.
- The scheduled maturity of the old bonds was in five years—December 31, 20X9.
- The unamortized bond discount on the old debt at the call date was $35,000.

The entry to record this **nonrefunding** transaction on December 31, 20X4, which is also the fiscal year end, is:

Bonds Payable	$1,935,000	
Loss on Early Extinguishment of Debt	85,000	
Unamortized Discount on Bonds Payable		$ 35,000
Cash		1,985,000
To record early retirement of bonds payable		

When **refunding** *proceeds* are used to retire or defease proprietary fund debt prior to its scheduled maturity date, however, the *refunding* debt issue is viewed as a *continuation* of the original debt issue. Thus,

- The *difference* between the acquisition price and the carrying value of the debt is deferred. The deferred amount is reported as a deferred outflow of resources if it is a debit amount and as a deferred inflow of resources if it is a credit amount. Deferred amounts from refunding transactions are among the most common examples of deferred outflows and deferred inflows reported in proprietary fund and government-wide financial statements. Note that the deferred amount is *not* reported as a *gain or loss* as it is in the previous entry.
- The *deferred amount* must be *amortized* as a component of *interest expense* over the *shorter* of the remaining term of the old debt or the term of the refunding issue. The *amortization method* must be *systematic and rational*—the effective interest method, the straight-line method, and other systematic and rational methods are permitted.

To illustrate accounting for a **refunding**, assume that the previous bond retirement was financed with the proceeds of refunding bonds. Assume that the county issued $2,000,000 of 4%, 10-year Airport Refunding Bonds on December 31, 20X4, to finance retirement of the old bonds. The refunding bonds were issued at par, and $15,000 of bond issue costs were incurred and paid from the bond proceeds.

The entries to record these *refunding* transactions on December 31, 20X4, which is also the fiscal year end, are:

Cash	$1,985,000	
Expenses—Bond Issue Costs (New bonds)	15,000	
Refunding Bonds Payable (New bonds)		$2,000,000
To record *issuance* of refunding bonds at par, net of issue costs.		
Bonds Payable (Old bonds)	$1,935,000	
Deferred Interest Expense Adjustment—		
Refunding Bonds	85,000	
Unamortized Discount on Bonds Payable (Old bonds)		$ 35,000
Cash		1,985,000
To record *retirement* of refunded bonds payable.		

No gain or loss from the retirement of debt is reported in the Airport Enterprise Fund Statement of Revenues, Expenses, and Changes in Fund Net Position for 20X4. The liability for the refunding bonds payable would be reported net of the unamortized Deferred Interest Expense Adjustment—Refunding Bonds, at $1,915,000 ($2,000,000 minus $85,000).

In this example the term of the refunding bonds is longer than the remaining life of the old bonds. Therefore, the amortization period for the deferred amount on the refunding is the remaining term of the old bonds, five years.

1. If the county uses the straight-line method to amortize the deferred amount on refunding, it will simply add one-fifth of the original amount of the deferred interest expense adjustment to interest expense for each of the next five years, 20X5 through 20X9.

2. Therefore, the interest expense reported on the refunding bonds in the first of those years would be $97,000. This amount is the cash interest of $80,000 ($2,000,000 × .04 × 1) plus the amortization of the deferred interest expense adjustment, $17,000.

The *interest expense and deferred interest expense adjustment amortization* would be recorded as follows:

Interest Expense	$ 80,000	
Cash		$ 80,000
To record *payment* of *interest* on *refunding* bonds.		
Interest Expense	.$ 17,000	
Deferred Interest Expense Adjustment—		
Refunding Bonds		$ 17,000
To record *amortization* of *deferred amount* on refunding.		

The carrying value of the bonds will be increased each year by the amortization. The amount reported for the refunding bonds payable in the December 31, 20X5, statement of net position, for instance, would be $1,932,000 ($2,000,000 − $85,000 + $17,000).

If a refunding results in a Deferred Interest Expense Adjustment credit, the effect on interest expense and the carrying value of the liability would be opposite from that illustrated previously. The unamortized deferred amount would increase the carrying value reported for the refunding bonds payable in the statement of net position. Amortization of the deferred amount would reduce interest expense.

Refunding Transactions for Extended Example

To illustrate further the accounting and reporting for refunding transactions and the presention of deferred outflows and deferred inflows of resources in proprietary fund financial statements, assume that the Electric Enterprise Fund had the following refunding transactions on December 31, 20X2.

18. Refunding bonds with a face amount of $370,000 were issued at par.

(18) Cash	$370,000	
Refunding Bonds Payable.		$370,000
To record issuance of refunding bonds.		

19. Paid $370,000 to an irrevocable to defease in substance $350,000 of outstanding bonds.

(18) Bonds Payable	$350,000	
Deferred Interest Expense Adjustment—		
Refunding Bonds.	20,000	
Cash		$370,000
To record in-substance defeasance of bonds.		

Accounting for Restricted Asset Accounts

Enterprise activities may involve restricted asset transactions or relationships that, if encountered in a general government situation, would require the use of several separate and distinct fund entities. Thus, utilities may require customers to post deposits (Trust or Agency), may acquire or construct major capital facilities (Capital Projects), or may have funded reserves or other debt-related resources (Debt Service). In some cases, certain enterprise-related intrafund "funds" are required to be established under terms of bond indentures or other contractual agreements.

The term *funds* usually is interpreted in this instance in the usual commercial accounting connotation of *restricted assets*. Thus, Enterprise Funds may contain several "funds within a fund." Restricted asset and liability accounts are distinctively titled to establish "funds" within the Enterprise Fund. In this way, a single fund serves the purpose of several separate fund entities. Some governments choose to maintain restricted net position accounts equal to the net difference between the portion of restricted assets available for each specific restricted purpose and the liabilities payable from those restricted assets. We do so in the extension of the Electric Enterprise Fund illustration that follows.

Recall that the amount reported as Restricted Net Position in an Enterprise Fund's statement of net position does not always equal the difference between the restricted assets and the liabilities and deferred inflows of resources related to those restricted assets. This inequality occurs when a portion of a government's liabilities payable from restricted assets is capital debt. Construction-related payables and the maturing portion of capital debt payable from resources restricted to service that debt are examples. This capital debt is deducted in computing the Enterprise Fund's Net Investment in Capital Assets, instead of being deducted in determining its Restricted Net Position. Before studying the procedures that follow, note how the Trial Balance (Illustration 10-7) and the Statement of Net Position (Illustration 10-8) at the conclusion of this example separate those intrafund "funds" from the unrestricted assets and other liabilities and equities.

The types of restricted asset situations encountered in practice vary widely. They range from simple customer deposits "funds" to complex series of "funds" required under terms of bond indentures, through legislative decree, or for administrative purposes. Several common restricted asset situations are used here to illustrate intrafund restricted asset accounting, sometimes referred to as secondary accounts, in Enterprise Fund accounting.

The following illustrations use distinctively titled asset and liability accounts for each "fund." The appropriate *restricted net position accounts are adjusted only at period end.* "Fund" revenues and expenses are recorded in the Electric (Enterprise) Fund revenue and expense control accounts. Any "fund" detail needed is assumed to be maintained in subsidiary records. If needed, special purpose reports are issued for these restricted subfunds to satisfy legal or contractual reporting requirements.

Restricted Asset Transactions and Relationships for Extended Example

Several common examples of "funds within a fund" accounting are illustrated for the Electric Enterprise Fund to extend the earlier illustrative Enterprise Fund example.

Customer Deposits Trust or Agency Subfund A utility usually requires its customers to post deposits as a partial protection against bad debt losses. The utility typically pays interest on the deposits. The following transactions and entries illustrate the key aspects of accounting for customer deposits. Note that not all accounts affected by these transactions are subfund accounts. **The subfund accounts are in boldface** type to emphasize the effects of the transactions on the subfund.

Transactions and Entries—During 20X2

20. Deposits of $11,000 were received.

(20) **Customer Deposits—Cash**	$11,000	
Customer Deposits—Deposits Payable		$11,000
To record receipt of customer deposits.		

21. Deposits of $10,000 were invested.

(21) **Customer Deposits—Investments**	$10,000	
Customer Deposits—Cash		$10,000
To record investment of customer deposits.		

22. Interest receivable accrued on customer deposit investments, but not received, totaled $200.

(22) **Customer Deposits—Accrued Interest Receivable** . .	$ 200	
Nonoperating Revenues—Interest		$ 200
To record interest revenues.		

23. Interest accrued on customer deposits payable at year end, $150.

(23) Nonoperating Expenses—Interest	$ 150	
Customer Deposits—Accrued Interest Payable . .		$ 150
To record interest expense.		

24. A customer's deposit was declared forfeited for nonpayment of his account.

(24) (a) **Customer Deposits—Deposits Payable**	$ 12	
Customer Deposits—Accrued Interest Payable . .	2	
Allowance for Uncollectible Accounts	8	
Accounts Receivable		$ 22
To record forfeiture of customer's deposit, offset against overdue receivable, and write-off of the uncollectible balance.		
(b) Cash.	$ 14	
Customer Deposits—Cash		$ 14
To reclassify forfeited customer deposit cash to unrestricted cash.		

Note that entry 24(b) reclassifies the forfeited customer deposits as unrestricted cash. The customer no longer has a valid claim against the assets—as reflected in entry 24(a); therefore, use of the assets is no longer restricted.

25. A customer moving to another town requested that her service be disconnected. Her final bill was offset against her deposit, and the balance was remitted to her.

(25) (a) **Customer Deposits—Deposits Payable**	$ 15	
Customer Deposits—Accrued Interest Payable . .	3	
Accounts Receivable		$ 10
Customer Deposits—Cash		8
To record offsetting of final bill against deposit account and remittance of the balance.		
(b) Cash.	$ 10	
Customer Deposits—Cash		$ 10
To reclassify customer deposit cash applied to final bill as unrestricted cash.		

Adjusting Entries—End of 20X2

26. The fair value of the subfund investments at year end was $10,100.

(26) **Customer Deposits—Investments** .... $ 100
    **Nonoperating Revenues—Net Increase
      (Decrease) in Fair Value of Investments** ...... $ 100
    To adjust investments to fair value.

27. The appropriate restricted net position account was adjusted at period end to equal the net assets of the fund.

(27) **Net Position**. .... $ 150
    **Net Position Restricted for Earnings on
      Customer Deposits** .... $ 150
    To indicate that net position of the Customer
    Deposits subfund is restricted for customer
    deposit interest requirements.

Entry 27 assumes that subfund revenues are restricted for paying interest on deposits. Under these conditions, some accountants prefer to use distinctively titled subfund revenue and expense accounts to facilitate preparation of this entry. If the revenues from the restricted assets are unrestricted, no Restricted Net Position balances would be established and the Customer Deposits subfund would be an Agency subfund rather than a Trust subfund.

Construction Financed by Bond Issue (Capital Projects Fund Subfund)
Accounting for Enterprise Fund construction financed through the sale of bonds is not unlike that for private construction. Both the authorization of the bond issue and appropriations, if any, are usually recorded in memorandum form rather than formally within the accounts. However, Enterprise Fund bond indentures may require accounting for proceeds of the bond issue in a Capital Projects Fund (CPF) and/or accounting for resources required to be set aside for debt service in a Debt Service Fund (DSF). The "funds within a fund" approach illustrated here usually satisfies these legal or contractual requirements.

The following transactions and entries illustrate appropriate procedures in the typical case.

Transactions and Entries—During 20X2

28. Bonds ($200,000 par) were sold at a premium of $2,000 to provide financing for expanding and modernizing the utility's distribution system. The premium cash was restricted for debt service.

(28) **Construction—Cash** $200,000
    Debt Service—Cash 2,000
      Unamortized Premium on Bonds .... $ 2,000
      Bonds Payable 200,000
    To record sale of bonds at a premium.

29. A contract was entered into with Smith & Company to construct part of the project at a cost of $100,000.

(29) No entry is necessary to record the contract; a narrative memorandum entry may be made.

30. Materials costing $41,000 were purchased by the utility and delivered to the construction site.

(30) Construction Work in Progress. .... $ 41,000
    Construction—Vouchers Payable .... $ 41,000
    To record cost of construction materials.

31. A bill for $30,000 was received from Smith & Company.

(31) Construction Work in Progress. .... $ 30,000
    Construction—Contracts Payable .... $ 30,000
    To record receipt of bill from Smith & Company
    for part of cost of contract.

32. The amount due Smith & Company and the bill for materials were paid.

(32) **Construction—Vouchers Payable**	$ 41,000	
Construction—Contracts Payable	30,000	
Construction—Cash		$ 71,000

To record payment of amount now due on contract
and of bill for materials.

33. Construction labor and supervisory expenses of $56,000 were paid.

(33) Construction Work in Progress.................	$ 56,000	
Construction—Cash		$ 56,000

To record cost of labor and supervisory expenses.

34. Smith & Company completed its part of the construction project and submitted its bill for $70,000. The completed project was found to be satisfactory.

(34) (a) Construction Work in Progress...............	$ 70,000	
Construction—Contracts Payable		$ 70,000

To record receipt of bill from Smith & Company
to cover remaining cost of contract.

(b) Improvements Other Than Buildings	$ 197,000	
Construction Work in Progress		$197,000

To close Construction Work in Progress
account and to record the cost of
completed improvements.

35. Smith & Company was paid in full, and the remaining bond cash was transferred to the Enterprise debt service "fund."

(35) **Construction—Contracts Payable**	$ 70,000	
Debt Service—Cash	3,000	
Construction—Cash		$ 73,000

To record final payment to contractor and transfer
of unused bond proceeds to Debt Service "fund."

Entry 35 assumes that the bond indenture requires unused bond proceeds to be used for debt service on the bonds.

Debt Service and Related Accounts A variety of intrafund "funds" related to bond issues may be required (in addition to a construction or Capital Projects "fund") under terms found in contemporary bond indentures. Among the most usual of these are the following:

1. **Term Bond Principal Sinking Fund.** Often referred to merely as a "sinking" fund, its purpose is to accumulate specified amounts of assets, and earnings thereon, for the eventual retirement of term bond principal. These funds usually apply to older issues because most recent issues are serial bonds rather than term bonds.

2. **Serial Bond Debt Service Fund.** This type of intrafund fund may be referred to as an Interest and Redemption, Interest and Sinking, or Bond and Interest fund. It is often required to ensure timely payment of serial bond interest and principal. A common indenture provision is that one-sixth of the next semiannual interest payment, plus one-twelfth of the next annual principal payment, must be deposited monthly into a "fund" of this type.

3. **Principal and Interest Reserve Fund.** Often referred to simply as a Reserve fund, these intrafund "funds" are often required to give bondholders an additional cushion or safety margin. "Funds" of this sort usually must be accumulated to a specific sum immediately or within the first 60 months after bonds are issued. The "fund" resources are used (a) to pay matured bonds and interest if the resources in the Debt Service "fund" prove inadequate, or (b) if not required earlier to cover deficiencies, to retire the final bond principal and interest maturities.

4. **Contingencies Fund.** This intrafund "fund," sometimes referred to as the Emergency Repair or Operating Reserve fund, affords bondholders even more security by providing

for potential emergency expenditures or for operating asset renewal or replacement. Thus, bondholders receive additional assurance (a) that the operating facilities will not be permitted to deteriorate in order to meet bond principal and interest requirements and (b) that the utility will not be forced into receivership because of such unforeseen expenditure requirements. Like the Principal and Interest Reserve "fund," the Contingencies "fund" is usually required to be accumulated in a specific amount early in the life of the bond issue.

To illustrate the operation and accounting for debt-service-related "funds" within an Enterprise Fund, assume that Debt Service, Principal and Interest Reserve, and Contingencies "funds," as described previously, are required by an enterprise bond indenture. A total of $5,000 has already been classified as Debt Service—Cash (Construction "fund" transactions 28 and 35) as a result of a bond issue premium ($2,000) and unused bond issue proceeds ($3,000). The following transactions illustrate typical activities related to these restricted asset accounts.

Transactions and Entries—During 20X2

36. Per debt covenant requirements, the Debt Service "fund" was increased by $25,000 and $10,000 was added both to the Principal and Interest Reserve "fund" and to the Contingencies "fund."

(36) **Debt Service—Cash**	$25,000	
Principal and Interest Reserve—Cash	10,000	
Contingencies—Cash	10,000	
Cash		$45,000

To record amounts restricted and set aside for these "funds."

37. Interest on bonds, $15,000, was paid.

(37) Nonoperating Expenses—Interest	$15,000	
Debt Service—Cash		$15,000

To record payment of bond interest.

38. A $7,000 unforeseen emergency repair expense to be paid from the Contingencies "fund" was incurred.

(38) Operating Expenses	$ 7,000	
Contingencies—Vouchers Payable		$ 7,000

To record liability for emergency repair expense.

39. Principal and Interest Reserve "fund" cash, $9,000, was invested.

(39) **Principal and Interest Reserve—Investments**	$ 9,000	
Principal and Interest Reserve—Cash		$ 9,000

To record investment of fund cash.

40. Interest of $430 was earned on the investment; $300 was collected.

(40) **Principal and Interest Reserve—Cash**	$ 300	
Principal and Interest Reserve—Accrued Interest Receivable	130	
Nonoperating Revenues—Interest		$ 430

To record interest earned and received.

Adjusting Entries—End of 20X2

41. Bond interest payable had accrued at year end, $6,000; premium of $300 was amortized.

(41) Nonoperating Expenses—Interest	$ 5,700	
Unamortized Premium on Bonds	300	
Debt Service—Accrued Bond Interest Payable		$ 6,000

To record bond interest accrued and amortization of bond premium.

42. The investments of the Principal and Interest Reserve "funds" are participating, interest-earning investment contracts that are subject to fair value accounting requirements. The fair value of the investments increased by $20 during the year.

(42) **Principal and Interest Reserve—Investments**	$ 20	
Nonoperating Revenues—Net Increase (Decrease) in Fair Value of Investments		$ 20

To record increase in fair value of investments.

43. The appropriate restricted net position accounts were adjusted at year end to equal the net position of the funds.

(43) Net Position...................................	$ 22,450	
Net Position Restricted for Bond Debt Service...		$ 9,000
Net Position Restricted for Bond Principal and Interest Payments Guarantee...........		10,450
Net Position Restricted for Contingencies.......		3,000

To adjust restricted net position accounts at year end.

The restricted net position accounts constitute the balancing accounts of the self-balancing "funds within a fund." As noted previously, *these amounts are not necessarily the restricted net position balances that must be reported in the statement of net position.* Maintaining the restricted net position accounts makes the "funds" self-balancing.

Preclosing Trial Balance—Extended Example

An adjusted, preclosing trial balance for the Electric (Enterprise) Fund extended example, based on all the numbered illustrative journal entries in this chapter, appears as Illustration 10-7. To emphasize the "funds within a fund" approach common to Enterprise Fund accounting, this trial balance has been modified from the usual trial balance format. It is divided into two major sections, entitled "General Accounts" and "Restricted Accounts," respectively, and subtotals are included to indicate the self-balancing nature of many Enterprise Fund intrafund "funds." Recall that not all intrafund restricted accounts must be self-balancing. Thus, had we not assumed in our example that the net position of the Customer Deposits "fund" were restricted to guarantee future interest liabilities to customers, (1) no Net Position Restricted for Earnings on Customer Deposits would be needed, and (2) this "fund" would not be self-balancing.

Closing Entries

As observed earlier, any reasonable closing entry combination that brings the temporary accounts to a zero balance and updates the Net Position accounts is acceptable. The compound closing entry approach is demonstrated here:

(44) Operating Revenues............................	$319,500	
Nonoperating Revenues—Intergovernmental Grant	100,000	
Nonoperating Revenues—Equipment Rental	7,000	
Nonoperating Revenues—Interest	1,830	
Nonoperating Revenues—Net Increase (Decrease) in Fair Value of Investments	120	
Capital Contributions from Subdividers	30,000	
Special Item—Gain on Sale of Land	125,000	
Operating Expenses		$246,900
Nonoperating Expenses—Interest		42,850
Transfer to General Fund.......................		10,000
Net Position		283,700

To close the temporary accounts.

ILLUSTRATION 10-7 **Preclosing Trial Balance—Extended Example**

A Governmental Unit
Electric (Enterprise) Fund
Preclosing (Adjusted) Trial Balance
December 31, 20X2

General Accounts:

Cash	$ 326,824	
Accounts Receivable	71,968	
Allowance for Uncollectible Accounts		$ 13,492
Unbilled Accounts Receivable	21,000	
Accrued Interest Receivable	200	
Due from State Public Works Department	7,000	
Inventory of Materials and Supplies	30,000	
Prepaid Insurance	600	
Land	25,000	
Buildings	90,000	
Accumulated Depreciation—Buildings		5,000
Improvements Other Than Buildings	707,000	
Accumulated Depreciation—Improvements Other Than Buildings		15,000
Machinery and Equipment	160,500	
Accumulated Depreciation—Machinery and Equipment		16,000
Vouchers Payable		49,500
Due to Internal Service Fund		12,800
Accrued Salaries and Wages Payable		4,500
Accrued Interest Payable		2,000
Accrued Utilities Payable		7,500
Bonds Payable		200,000
Unamortized Premium on Bonds		1,700
Refunding Bonds Payable		370,000
Deferred Interest Expense Adjustment—Refunding Bonds	20,000	
Liability for Compensated Absences (Long-Term)		101,500
Net Position		377,400
Operating Revenues		319,500
Operating Expenses	246,900	
Nonoperating Revenues—Intergovernmental Grants		100,000
Nonoperating Revenues—Equipment Rental		7,000
Nonoperating Revenues—Interest		1,830
Nonoperating Revenues—Net Increase (Decrease) in Fair Value of Investments		120
Nonoperating Expenses—Interest	42,850	
Capital Contributions from Subdividers		30,000
Special Item—Gain on Sale of Land		125,000
Transfer to General Fund	10,000	
Subtotal	1,759,842	1,759,842

Restricted or Secondary Accounts:

Customer Deposits "Fund"	Customer Deposits—Cash	968	
	Customer Deposits—Investments	10,100	
	Customer Deposits—Accrued Interest Receivable	200	
	Customer Deposits—Deposits Payable		10,973
	Customer Deposits—Interest Payable		145
	Net Position Restricted for Earnings on Customer Deposits		150
	Subtotal	11,268	11,268
Debt Service "Fund"	Debt Service—Cash	15,000	
	Debt Service—Accrued Interest Payable		6,000
	Net Position Restricted for Bond Debt Service		9,000
	Subtotal	15,000	15,000
Principal And Interest "Fund"	Principal and Interest Reserve—Cash	1,300	
	Principal and Interest Reserve—Investments	9,020	
	Principal and Interest Reserve—Accrued Interest Receivable	130	
	Net Position Restricted for Bond Principal and Interest Payments Guarantee		10,450
	Subtotal	10,450	10,450
Contingencies "Fund"	Contingencies—Cash	10,000	
	Contingencies—Vouchers Payable		7,000
	Net Position Restricted for Contingencies		3,000
	Subtotal	10,000	10,000
	Total	$1,806,560	$1,806,560

Enterprise Fund Reporting—Extended Example

The three required financial statements for the Electric Enterprise Fund of A Governmental Unit are revised for the effects of the additional transactions included in the extended example. In addition to an Enterprise Fund's financial statements, supplemental schedules may be used to present the details of any aspects of the principal statements that need additional explanation. Typical schedules of this type are for budgeted versus actual operating expenses and for capital assets and depreciation, including changes therein. Schedules describing aspects of intrafund restricted accounts may also be desirable or required. For example, contractual requirements may dictate a statement of net assets restricted for bond debt service. Schedules detailing changes in the cash and investment accounts of other intrafund restricted asset accounts may be useful as well. Also, schedules demonstrating compliance with pertinent legal requirements may be needed.

Statement of Net Position

The statement of net position for the Electric (Enterprise) Fund extended example appears in Illustration 10-8. The primary differences between this statement of net position and the more basic example in Illustration 10-2 are (1) the inclusion of restricted assets and liabilities related to restricted assets, (2) inclusion of the resulting restricted net position classification in the net position section, and (3) the inclusion of the deferred outflows of resources financial statement element required to report the deferred refunding amount. Deferred inflows were not included in the illustration. The statement in Illustration 10-8 is presented in the balance sheet format; that is, assets and deferred outflows of resources are totaled together, then liabilities and net position are totaled together. The net position format, in which liabilities and deferred inflows are deducted from assets and deferred outflows to arrive at net position, was shown in Illustration 10-2.

Notice the asset categorization among current assets, restricted assets, and plant and equipment in the Statement of Net Position in Illustration 10-8, as well as the parallel division of liabilities into current liabilities, liabilities payable from restricted assets, and long-term liabilities. Such categorization permits ready comparisons and analyses across the statement of net position. The use of distinctively titled restricted asset and liability accounts distinguishes the restricted subfund assets and liabilities from unrestricted amounts. Use of these subfunds does not affect revenues, expenses, changes in net position, or total net position. Although the Restricted Net Position reported in this example equals the difference between restricted assets and liabilities payable from restricted assets, recall that these amounts are not equal if some of the liabilities payable from restricted assets are capital debt.

Statement of Revenues, Expenses, and Changes in Fund Net Position

The Statement of Revenues, Expenses, and Changes in Fund Net Position for the extended example in Illustration 10-9 has only minor differences in some amounts reported compared to the same statement for the basic example in Illustration 10-4. No additional items are reported related to the additional transactions. Note that in addition to being reported annually, this statement should also be prepared on an interim basis as necessary. The statement for the Electric Fund shown in Illustration 10-9 is prepared in the format specified in GASB *Statement No. 34* (as is Illustration 10-4). Operating revenues and expenses and nonoperating revenues and expenses are distinguished in the statement. In this example, operating revenues are presented in detail because relatively few revenue sources were assumed. However, operating expenses are reported in summary form and supported by a Detailed Statement of Operating Expenses (Illustration 10-10). Had there been many significant types of operating revenues, these, too, might have been reported in summary and supported

ILLUSTRATION 10-8   Statement of Net Position—Extended Example

A Governmental Unit
Electric Enterprise Fund
Statement of Net Position
December 31, 20X2

Assets and Deferred Outflows of Resources		Liabilities and Net Position	
Current Assets:		**Current Liabilities:**	
Cash	$ 326,824	Vouchers payable	$ 49,500
Accounts receivable (less allowance for		Due to Internal Service Fund	12,800
doubtful accounts of $13,492)	58,476	Accrued salaries and wages payable	4,500
Unbilled accounts receivable	21,000	Accrued interest payable	2,000
Accrued interest receivable	200	Accrued utilities payable	7,500
Due from State Public Works Department	7,000	Total Current Liabilities (Payable from	
Inventory of materials and supplies	30,000	Current Assets)	76,300
Prepaid insurance	600		
Total Current Assets	444,100	**Liabilities Payable from Restricted Assets:**	
		Customer deposits:	
Noncurrent Assets:		Deposits payable	10,973
Restricted Assets:		Interest payable	145
Customer deposits:			11,118
Cash	968		
Investments	10,100	*Debt service:*	
Accrued interest receivable	200	Accrued bond interest payable	6,000
	11,268	*Contingencies:*	
Debt service:		Vouchers payable	7,000
Cash	15,000	Total Liabilities Payable from	
		Restricted Assets	24,118
Principal and interest reserve:			
Cash	1,300	**Long-Term Liabilities:**	
Investments	9,020	Bonds payable	200,000
Accrued interest receivable	130	Refunding bonds payable	370,000
	10,450	Unamortized premium on bonds	1,700
Contingencies:		Liability for compensated absences	101,500
Cash	10,000	Total Long-Term Liabilities	673,200
Total Restricted Assets	46,718	Total Liabilities	773,618
Property, Plant, and Equipment:		**Net Position:**	
Land	25,000	Net investment in capital assets*	374,300
Buildings (less accumulated depreciation		Restricted*	22,600
of $5,000)	85,000	Unrestricted*	286,800
Improvements other than buildings (less		Total Net Position	683,700
accumulated depreciation of $15,000)	692,000	Total Liabilities and Net Position	$1,457,318
Machinery and Equipment (less accum-			
ulated depreciation of $16,000)	144,500		
Total Property, Plant, and Equipment	946,500		
Total Assets	1,437,318		

Deferred Outflows of Resources

Deferred Refunding Amount	20,000
Total Assets and Deferred Outflows	$1,457,318

---

*Computations of Net Position Components

Net Investment in Capital Assets:		Restricted Net Position:		Unrestricted Net Position:	
Total Property, Plant,		Total Restricted		All other assets and	
and Equipment	$ 946,500	Assets	$ 46,718	deferred outflows	
Plus:		Less:		(includes only current	
Deferred refunding amount	20,000	Liabilities Payable		assets in this	
Less:		From Restricted		example)	$ 444,100
Vouchers payable (for		Assets (all non-		Less:	
equipment)	(20,500)	capital)	(24,118)	All other liabilities	
Bonds Payable (plus		Total	$ 22,600	($773,618 – $20,500 –	
unamortized premium)	(571,700)			$571,700 – $24,118)..	(157,300)
Total	$ 374,300			Total	$ 286,800

ILLUSTRATION 10-9 Operating Statement—Extended Example

A Governmental Unit
Electric Enterprise Fund
Statement of Revenues, Expenses, and Changes in Fund Net Position
For the Year Ended December 31, 20X2

Operating Revenues:

Residential sales (net of uncollectible amounts of $xx)	$153,700
Commercial sales (net of uncollectible amounts of $xx)	91,300
Industrial sales (net of uncollectible amounts of $xx)	62,500
Public street lighting	12,000
Total Operating Revenues	319,500

Operating Expenses:

Production	144,400
Distribution	49,200
Accounting and collection	13,800
Sales promotion	1,000
Administrative and general	38,500
Total Operating Expenses	246,900
Operating Income	72,600

Nonoperating Revenues (Expenses):

Intergovernmental grants	100,000
Equipment rental	7,000
Investment income	1,950
Interest expense	(42,850)
Net Nonoperating Revenues (Expenses)	66,100
Income before Other Revenues, Expenses, and Transfers	138,700
Capital contributions from subdividers	30,000
Special item—Gain on sale of land	125,000
Transfer to General Fund	(10,000)
Change in Net Position	283,700
Net position, January 1, 20X2	400,000
Net position, December 31, 20X2	$683,700

by a detailed schedule. Notice that as in the prior example, capital contribution revenues and transfers, as well as the special item, are reported below the nonoperating revenues and expenses. If the Electric (Enterprise) Fund had extraordinary gains (losses), they would be reported as the last item(s) before transfers. It should be noted that if a special item and extraordinary gain (loss) occur in the same fiscal year, the special item would be reported immediately *before* the extraordinary gain (loss). Transfers are reported immediately before the change in net position.

Statement of Cash Flows

The Statement of Cash Flows for the extended example in Illustration 10-11 includes several specific line items not found in the statement for the basic example in Illustration 10-5. Note in particular the cash flows related to customer deposits, the bond issuance and defeasance in substance, and the cash flows for the construction project. The statement of cash flows was discussed in depth at the

ILLUSTRATION 10-10 Detailed Operating Expenses Statement

A Governmental Unit
Electric Enterprise Fund
Detailed Statement* of Operating Expenses
For the Fiscal Year Ended December 31, 20X2

Production Expenses:

Electric generating:

Supervision	$ 8,000	
Station labor	15,000	
Fuel	54,000	
Water	4,000	
Depreciation	20,000	
Supplies and other	8,400	$109,400

Maintenance of plant and equipment:

Supervision	4,000	
Maintenance of structures and improvements	8,000	
Maintenance of boiler plant equipment	10,000	
Maintenance of generating and electric plant equipment	10,000	
Depreciation	1,000	33,000
Power purchased		2,000
Total production expenses		144,400

Distribution Expenses:

Supervision	2,500	
Services on consumers' premises	4,500	
Street lighting and signal system	4,000	
Overhead system	18,200	
Depreciation	13,000	
Maintenance and servicing of mobile equipment	3,000	
Utility storeroom expenses	4,000	
Total distribution expenses		49,200

Accounting and Collection Expenses:

Customers' contracts and orders	2,500	
Meter reading	3,500	
Collecting offices	1,000	
Delinquent accounts—collection expense	2,300	
Customers' billing and accounting	4,000	
Depreciation	500	
Total accounting and collection expenses		13,800

Sales Promotion Expenses 1,000

Administrative and General Expenses:

Salaries of executives	8,000	
Other general office salaries	3,500	
General office supplies and expenses	400	
Insurance	2,000	
Employees' benefit expenses	1,500	
Pension fund contributions	2,800	
Utilities	18,000	
Depreciation	1,500	
Miscellaneous general expenses	800	
Total administrative and general expenses		38,500
Total operating expenses		$246,900

*The detailed amounts in this statement cannot be derived from the example in the chapter.
They have been assumed for illustrative purposes only.

ILLUSTRATION 10-11 Statement of Cash Flows—Extended Example

A Governmental Unit
Electric Enterprise Fund
Statement of Cash Flows
For the Year Ended December 31, 20X2

Cash Flows from Operating Activities:

Cash received from customers	$301,000
Cash paid to suppliers of goods and services	(41,500)
Cash paid to employees	(127,200)
Cash paid for utilities	(10,500)
Cash deposits refunded to customers	(5)
Net cash provided by operating activities	121,795

Cash Flows from Noncapital Financing Activities:

Cash received from intergovernmental operating grant	100,000
Cash paid for interfund transfers	(10,000)
Cash paid for interest on customer deposits	(3)
Net cash flows from noncapital financing activities	89,997

Cash Flows from Capital and Related Financing Activities:

Cash received from issuing bonds	202,000
Cash received from issuing refunding bonds	370,000
Cash received from sale of land	150,000
Cash paid to trust to defease bonds	(370,000)
Cash paid for retirement of bonds	(50,000)
Cash paid for interest	(35,000)
Cash paid for equipment	(30,000)
Cash paid for construction of capital assets	(197,000)
Net cash flows from capital and related financing activities	40,000

Cash Flows from Investing Activities:

Cash paid for investments	(19,000)
Cash received from interest	1,300
Net cash flows from investing activities	(17,700)
Net increase (decrease) in cash	234,092
Cash, January 1*	120,000
Cash, December 31*	$354,092

Reconciliation of operating income to net cash flows from operating activities:

Operating income	$ 72,600
Adjustments to reconcile operating income to cash flows from operating activities:	
Depreciation	36,000
Increase in vouchers payable (associated with operating activities)	26,000
Increase in interfund payable	12,800
Increase in salaries and wages payable	6,000
Increase in utilities payable	7,500
Increase in customer deposits payable	10,973
Increase in accounts receivable (adjusted for noncash decrease from offset against customer deposits interest payable—transaction 21)	(29,478)
Increase in inventories	(20,000)
Increase in prepaid insurance	(600)
Net adjustments	49,195
Net cash provided by operating activities	$121,795

Noncash Financing and Investing Activities:

Subdivision electricity system donation (transaction 14)	$ 30,000

*Includes both unrestricted and restricted cash.

beginning of this chapter in the context of the basic example. For review purposes, note the following in Illustration 10-11:

- The statement has four classifications of cash flows as required by GASB *Statement No. 9.*
- Cash paid for interest is *not* an operating activity, as it is in business cash flow statements. Cash paid for interest associated with long-term debt issued clearly and specifically for capital asset acquisition, construction, or improvement is reported as cash flows from capital and related financing activities. Cash paid for interest on all other indebtedness is classified as cash flows from noncapital financing activities.
- Cash paid for capital asset acquisition, construction, or improvement and cash received from selling capital assets are classified as capital and related financing activities, not as investing activities.
- As is typical in a government cash flow statement, the only activities resulting in investing cash flows are buying and selling investments and receipt of earnings on investments.
- Cash includes not only unrestricted cash balances but also the fund's restricted cash balances.

COMBINING ENTERPRISE FUND FINANCIAL STATEMENTS

Combining financial statements reporting either all funds or all nonmajor funds of a fund type may also be presented for internal purposes or to report on the fund type in external financial reports. The combining nonmajor Enterprise Fund financial statements in a recent Commonwealth of Virginia comprehensive annual financial report are preceded by this narrative explanation.

The Enterprise Funds account for operations that are financed and operated in a manner similar to private business enterprises. It is the intent that the cost of providing such goods or services will be recovered through user charges.

Department of Alcoholic Beverage Control—operates facilities for the distribution and sale of distilled spirits and wine.

Risk Management—accounts for pooled resources received and used by the Department of the Treasury for financing local government insurance programs. This includes Local Entities Bond Insurance, Public Officials Insurance and Law Enforcement Insurance.

Local Choice Health Care—administers a health care plan for the employees of participating local governments.

Virginia Industries for the Blind—manufactures products for sale to governments, certain private organizations, and the general public.

Consolidated Laboratory—provides water testing services and a newborn screening program.

eVA Procurement System—accounts for the statewide electronic procurement system.

Department of Environmental Quality—accounts for the Title V program that offers services to the general public.

Wireless E-911 Service Board—assists in the establishment of wireless E-911 service in Virginia localities.

Virginia Museum of Fine Arts—accounts for gift shop and food service activities.

Science Museum of Virginia—accounts for gift shop activities.

Behavioral Health Local Funds—account for the canteen store and work activity programs.[5]

The Commonwealth of Virginia combining financial statements for its nonmajor Enterprise Funds are reproduced in part as follows:

- Illustration 10-12, Combining Statement of Net Position
- Illustration 10-13, Combining Statement of Revenues, Expenses, and Changes in Fund Net Position
- Illustration 10-14, Combining Statement of Cash Flows

If a government has more than one *nonmajor* Enterprise Fund, combining nonmajor Enterprise Fund financial statements are required in its Comprehensive

---

ILLUSTRATION 10-12   Combining Statement of Net Position—Nonmajor Enterprise Funds

Commonwealth of Virginia
All Enterprise Funds
Combining Statement of Net Position
June 30, 20X1

ASSETS	Department of Alcoholic Beverage Control	Risk Management	Local Choice Health Care	Behavioral Health Local Funds	Total
Current Assets:					
Cash and Cash Equivalents	$ 2,326	$ 28,374	$106,557	$ 480	$ 187,272
Investments	101	—	—	1	102
Receivables, Net	4,078	1	19,741	—	33,940
Due From Other Funds	—	—	—	—	860
Inventory	46,870	—	—	—	51,815
Prepaid Items	2,011	1	—	—	2,014
Other Assets	160	—	—	—	169
Total Current Assets	55,546	28,376	126,298	481	276,172
Noncurrent Assets:					
Nondepreciable Capital Assets	1,828	—	—		6,290
Depreciable Capital Assets, Net	9,199	—	—	—	16,913
Total Noncurrent Assets	11,027	—	—	—	23,203
Total Assets	66,573	28,376	126,298	481	299,375
LIABILITIES					
Current Liabilities:					
Accounts Payable	17,414	192	4,724	—	26,357
Amounts Due to Other Governments	—	—	—	—	5,399
Due to Other Funds	10,825	12	—	—	12,436
Due to External Parties (Fiduciary Funds) . . .	802	24	—	—	1,041
Interfund Payable	29,468	—	—	—	29,468
Unearned Revenue	104	585	—	—	1,917
Obligations Under Securities Lending Program	431	—	—	—	431
Other Liabilities	—	—	—	179	302
Claims Payable Due Within One Year	—	5,930	18,656	—	24,586
Long-term Liabilities Due Within One Year . .	2,750	21	—	—	3,740
Total Current Liabilities	61,794	6,764	23,380	179	105,677
Noncurrent Liabilities:					
Claims Payable Due in More Than One Year	—	12,625	—		12,625
Long-term Liabilities Due in More Than One Year	27,695	272	—	—	35,566
Total Noncurrent Liabilities	27,695	12,897	—	—	48,191
Total Liabilities	89,489	19,661	23,380	179	153,868
Net Position:					
Net Investment in Capital Assets	11,027	—	—	—	23,203
Unrestricted	(33,943)	8,715	102,918	302	122,304
Total Net Position (Deficit)	$ (22,916)	$ 8,715	$ 102,918	$ 302	$ 145,507

Source: Adapted from COMPREHENSIVE ANNUAL FINANCIAL REPORT (CAFR) VIRGINIA, 2011. Changes to the CAFR represent the author's projections and are not provided or endorsed by the Virginia DOA. To view the original Virginia CAFR, please visit: http://www.doa.virginia.gov/Financial_Reporting/CAFR/2011/2011_CAFR.cfm. Copyright © 2011 by the State of Virginia, Department of Accounts. Reprinted with permission.

ILLUSTRATION 10-13 Combining Statement of Revenues, Expenses, and Changes in Fund Net Position—Nonmajor Enterprise Funds

Commonwealth of Virginia
All Enterprise Funds
Combining Statement of Revenues,
Expenses, and Changes in Fund Net Position
For the Fiscal Year Ended June 30, 20X1

	Department of Alcoholic Beverage Control	Risk Management	Local Choice Health Care	Behavioral Health Local Funds	Total
Operating Revenues:					
Charges for Sales and Services	$ 581,018	$ 4,131	246,731	$ 478	$ 956,302
Other	17,521	—	—	—	17,528
Total Operating Revenues	598,539	4,131	246,731	478	973,830
Operating Expenses:					
Cost of Sales and Services	340,017	—	—	446	343,334
Prizes and Claims		7,081	213,695	—	220,776
Personal Services	84,680	606	—	—	109,701
Contractual Services	24,181	565	15,850	—	56,544
Supplies and Materials	2,852	4	—	—	24,953
Depreciation	3,176	—	—	—	3,627
Rent, Insurance, and Other Related Charges	23,849	51	—	—	27,986
Non-recurring Cost Estimate Payments to Providers		—	—	—	37,044
Other	2,050	53	—	—	2,416
Total Operating Expenses	480,805	8,360	229,545	446	826,381
Operating Income (Loss)	117,734	(4,229)	17,186	32	147,449
Nonoperating Revenues (Expenses):					
Interest, Dividends, Rents, and Other Investment Income	197	—	—	—	197
Other	9,018	—	—	—	8,975
Total Nonoperating Revenues (Expenses)	9,215	—	—	—	9,172
Income (Loss) Before Transfers	126,949	(4,229)	17,186	32	156,621
Transfers In	1,039	—	—	—	3,512
Transfers Out	(134,295)	(81)	—	(5)	150,127)
Change in Net Position	(6,307)	(4,310)	17,186	27	10,006
Total Net Position (Deficit), July 1, as restated	(16,609)	13,025	85,732	275	135,501
Total Net Position (Deficit), June 30	$ (22,916)	$ 8,715	$ 102,918	$ 302	$ 145,507

Source: Adapted from COMPREHENSIVE ANNUAL FINANCIAL REPORT (CAFR) VIRGINIA, 2011. Changes to the CAFR represent the author's projections and are not provided or endorsed by the Virginia DOA. To view the original Virginia CAFR, please visit: http://www.doa.virginia.gov/Financial_Reporting/CAFR/2011/2011_CAFR.cfm. Copyright © 2011 by the State of Virginia, Department of Accounts. Reprinted with permission.

Annual Financial Report. These statements must have, at a minimum, a column for each nonmajor Enterprise Fund and a total column for all nonmajor Enterprise Funds. (Identification of major funds is explained in Chapter 13.) Individual fund statements may also be presented if additional detail, individual fund comparative data, or other additional information is deemed appropriate.

The total column for all nonmajor Enterprise Funds from the combining statements is included in the appropriate proprietary fund financial statements that are part of the basic financial statements. Also, segment information on individual Enterprise Funds, or on an individual activity reported as part of an Enterprise Fund, is typically required in the notes to the basic financial statements, as discussed in Chapter 13.

ILLUSTRATION 10-14   Combining Statement of Cash Flows—Nonmajor Enterprise Funds

Commonwealth of Virginia
All Enterprise Funds
Combining Statement of Cash Flows
For the Fiscal Year Ended June 30, 20X1

	Department of Alcoholic Beverage Control	Risk Management	Local Choice Health Care	Behavioral Health Local Funds	Total
Cash Flows from Operating Activities:					
Receipts for Sales and Services	$ 593,091	$ 4,186	$ 247,090	$ 478	$ 960,177
Internal Activity-Receipts from Other Funds	—	—	—	—	7,993
Internal Activity-Payments to Other Funds	—	—	—	—	(2,297)
Payments to Suppliers for Goods and Services	(369,235)	—	—	(446)	(397,278)
Payments for Contractual Services	(24,181)	(469)	(15,787)	—	(56,273)
Payments for Prizes, Claims, and Loss Control	—	(3,699)	(216,452)	—	(220,151)
Payments to Employees	(79,460)	(744)	—	—	(102,552)
Payments to Providers for Non-recurring Cost Estimates . .	—	—	—	—	(42,384)
Other Operating Revenue	5,107	—	—	—	5,107
Other Operating Expense	—	—	—	—	(283)
Net Cash Provided by (Used for) Operating Activities . .	125,322	(726)	14,851	32	152,059
Cash Flows from Noncapital Financing Activities:					
Transfers In From Other Funds	1,039	—	—	(5)	3,512
Transfers Out to Other Funds	(295,551)	(76)	—	—	(311,358)
Other Noncapital Financing Receipt Activities	203,806	—	—	—	203,806
Other Noncapital Financing Disbursement Activities	(32,722)	—	—	—	(33,082)
Net Cash Provided by (Used for) Noncapital Financing Activities	(123,428)	(76)		(5)	(137,122)
Cash Flows from Capital and Related Financing Activities:					
Acquisition of Capital Assets	(1,825)	—	—	—	(4,672)
Payment of Principal and Interest on Bonds and Notes	(189)	—	—	—	(189)
Other Capital and Related Financing Disbursement Activities	—	—	—	—	(100)
Net Cash Provided By (Used for) Capital and Related Financing Activities.	(2,014)	—	—	—	(4,961)
Net Increase (Decrease) in Cash and Cash Equivalents	(120)	(802)	14,851	27	9,976
Cash and Cash Equivalents, July 1	2,276	29,176	91,706	453	177,135
Cash and Cash Equivalents, June 30	$ 2,156	$ 28,374	$ 106,557	$ 480	$ 187,111
Reconciliation of Cash and Cash Equivalents					
Per the Statement of Net Assets:					
Cash and Cash Equivalents	$ 2,326	$ 28,374	$ 106,557	$ 480	$ 187,272
Cash and Travel Advances	160	—	—		
Less:				—	169
Securities Lending Cash Equivalents	(330)	—	—	—	(330)
Cash and Cash Equivalents per the Statement of Cash Flows . .	$ 2,156	$ 28,374	$ 106,557	$ 480	$ 187,111

Source: Adapted from COMPREHENSIVE ANNUAL FINANCIAL REPORT (CAFR) VIRGINIA, 2011. Changes to the CAFR represent the author's projections and are not provided or endorsed by the Virginia DOA. To view the original Virginia CAFR, please visit: http://www.doa.virginia.gov/Financial_Reporting/CAFR/2011/2011_CAFR.cfm. Copyright © 2011 by the State of Virginia, Department of Accounts. Reprinted with permission.

Concluding Comments

Enterprise Funds are used to account for activities in which governments sell goods and services to external users. Some of these activities are required to be reported as Enterprise Funds; others are reported as Enterprise Funds at the discretion of the government. For the most part, the same activities reported in Enterprise Funds comprise the business-type activities reported in the government-wide financial statements. The Enterprise Fund accounting equation is similar to the business accounting equation. Likewise, accounting and reporting for Enterprise Funds parallels that of businesses in many major respects.

Key common accounting and reporting requirements of proprietary funds— the accounting equation, the applicable principles, and the financial statements— were discussed in the beginning of the chapter. Several unique aspects of Enterprise Fund accounting were discussed and illustrated in the remainder of the chapter. Most notable were (1) the reporting of net position; (2) reporting deferred outflows of resources and deferred inflows of resources; (3) the extensive use of restricted asset accounting, using a "funds within a fund" approach, found in many SLG enterprise activities; (4) accounting for and reporting intergovernmental grants; and (5) accounting for refundings of Enterprise Fund debt. The chapter dealt primarily with principles applicable to a broad spectrum of Enterprise Fund activities, as opposed to industry specific applications such as Enterprise Fund accounting for municipal solid waste landfills, which is covered in GASB *Statement No. 18.*

This chapter sets the foundation for the relatively easy understanding of Chapter 11 on Internal Service Funds, the other proprietary fund type. Chapter 12's discussion of fiduciary funds concludes the coverage of specific fund types and also contains a summary review of interfund (or multifund) accounting.

Questions

Q10-1 Under what circumstances is an Enterprise Fund required to be used? When is its use permitted but not required?

Q10-2 The garbage collection and disposal services of a local government might be accounted for through the General Fund, a Special Revenue Fund, or an Enterprise Fund. Indicate the circumstances in which each of these fund types might be appropriate.

Q10-3 What is the accounting equation for a proprietary fund? What are the three components of net position? Explain the nature of each component.

Q10-4 How should a government determine the appropriate balance to report for each of the three components of net position of an Enterprise Fund?

Q10-5 What are the required financial statements for a proprietary fund?

Q10-6 An asset costing $10,000 was reclassified from the General Capital Assets accounts of a governmental unit to one of the governmental unit's enterprise activities. What effect would this reclassification have on the General Fund and the Enterprise Fund, respectively?

Q10-7 The City of Cherokee Hills is adjacent to a freeway leading to a nearby metropolitan area and has grown rapidly from a small village to a city of 75,000. Its population is expected to double every 10 years in the foreseeable future. The city has owned and operated the local electricity generation and distribution system since its inception many years ago and has never charged itself for electricity consumption. The newly employed comptroller of Cherokee Hills seeks your advice in this regard. What is your response?

Q10-8 Having been told repeatedly during his many years of service that depreciation was charged "in order to provide for the replacement of capital assets," a member of a government's electric utility (Enterprise Fund) board of directors was visibly upset upon being advised by the controller that it would be necessary for the utility to go deeply in debt "in order to replace some of our capital assets." "How can it be true," he asks, "that we have operated profitably each year, have an $850,000 Net Position balance and total Accumulated Depreciation account balances of $6,000,000, have never made transfers to the General Fund, and yet have cash and investments totaling only $100,000?" What is your response?

Q10-9 Virgie Township is retiring Enterprise Fund bonds before their maturity date. How does the difference between the amount paid to retire the debt and the carrying value of the debt affect interest expense reported in future years if Virgie does not borrow to accomplish the early retirement? How does it affect the statement of net position? If Virgie does retire the old debt with new debt proceeds, how is future years' interest expense affected by the difference between the payment and the carrying value? How does it affect the statement of net position?

Q10-10 Explain any differences in the accounting for bond premiums or discounts related to general obligation construction bonds and to enterprise revenue bonds.

Q10-11 A government transfers equipment with a book value of $600,000 from its General Capital Assets accounts to an Enterprise Fund. How is this transaction reported in the Enterprise Fund statement of revenues, expenses, and changes in fund net position?

Q10-12 How is a deferred interest expense adjustment reported in the statement of net position of an Enterprise Fund? If a government has Refunding Bonds Payable of $5 million with an associated premium of $200,000 and an associated deferred interest expense adjustment of $30,000 (debit balance), what amount of liabilities should be reported in the statement of net position?

Q10-13 Which net position classifications may be affected by deferred inflows of resources? By deferred outflows of resources?

Q10-14 What are the major classifications of cash flows that must be presented for a proprietary fund? Distinguish among them and give at least two examples of each classification.

Q10-15 What are the key differences between the cash flow statement requirements for Enterprise Funds and those for business enterprises?

Q10-16 When are cash flows from transfers *from* an Enterprise Fund to other funds reported as capital and related financing activities in the Enterprise Fund statement of cash flows?

Q10-17 What determines whether cash received from a borrowing is reported as cash flows from noncapital financing activities or from capital and related financing activities?

Exercises

E10-1 (Multiple Choice) Identify the best answer for each of the following:
1. Which of the following statements about accounting principles used in Enterprise Funds is *false*?
   a. Management may choose whether or not to apply recent FASB standards if they do not conflict with GASB standards.
   b. An Enterprise Fund's statement of cash flows is prepared in the same format as a statement of cash flows for a private-sector entity.
   c. Enterprise Funds may adopt budgets on a basis of accounting contrary to GAAP.
   d. GAAP does not require Enterprise Funds to legally adopt budgets.
2. Which of the following activities would be least likely to be operated as and accounted for in an Enterprise Fund?
   a. Town planning department
   b. Sports stadium
   c. Parking garage
   d. Mass transit authority
3. The City of Philaburg arranged for a 10-year, $40 million loan to finance construction of a toll bridge over the Tradewater River. If the toll bridge is accounted for as an Enterprise Fund activity and a certain portion of the tolls collected is required to be set aside for maintaining the bridge, these resources should be accounted for in
   a. a Debt Service Fund.
   b. the General Fund.
   c. the Toll Bridge Enterprise Fund.
   d. a Capital Projects Fund.
4. The fund equity of an Enterprise Fund could include any of the following *except*
   a. net investment in capital assets.
   b. fund balance.
   c. restricted net position.
   d. unrestricted net position.
5. The City of Silerville operates a water authority that sells water to city residents. Each new customer is required to pay a $75 deposit at the time of hookup. The deposit cannot be spent, but is returned with interest if the customer maintains a satisfactory payment record for two years. The city should record these deposits
   a. in a Private-Purpose Trust Fund.
   b. as restricted cash and a liability payable from restricted assets in the Water Fund.
   c. as unrestricted cash and a long-term liability in the Water Fund.
   d. as unrestricted cash and a liability payable from restricted assets in the General Fund.

6. Enterprise Fund transfers are reported in an Enterprise Fund's operating statement as
   a. nonoperating revenues.
   b. other financing sources.
   c. special items.
   d. the last items before the change in net position.
7. Enterprise Fund transfers are reported in an Enterprise Fund's operating statement for
   a. "free" services provided to other departments.
   b. capital assets transferred in from other governments without compensation.
   c. interfund loans that are not to be repaid from available expendable financial resources.
   d. Reassignments of capital assets to general government agencies.
8. Depreciation expense on all of an Enterprise Fund's capital assets must be reported as expenses in the fund's operating statement. However, expenditures to maintain certain capital assets may be expensed in lieu of reporting depreciation. These capital assets include
   a. infrastructure capital assets donated to the government.
   b. infrastructure capital assets that meet specific criteria.
   c. only infrastructure capital assets constructed or acquired prior to July 1, 1980.
   d. buildings.
9. Enterprise Fund resources of $3,000,000 are paid yearly to the General Fund. If these payments are payments in lieu of taxes (not payments for services), they should be recorded in the Enterprise Fund as
   a. expenses.
   b. other financing uses.
   c. reductions of revenues.
   d. transfers out.
10. Combining Enterprise Fund statements in the CAFR are required to include at a minimum:
    a. each individual Enterprise Fund.
    b. each individual major Enterprise Fund.
    c. each individual nonmajor Enterprise Fund.
    d. each individual Enterprise Fund used to account for activities that are required to be reported in Enterprise Funds.

E10-2 (Net Position Components) Using the format at the end of this exercise, indicate the impact that each of the following transactions has on the total net position of a proprietary fund and on each net position component. Also, indicate whether the transaction is reported in the statement of revenues, expenses, and changes in fund net position of a proprietary fund. A sample transaction is analyzed for you.

Sample Transaction: Purchase of equipment costing $5,000 with unrestricted cash.
1. Sold building with a book value of $150,000 for $225,000 (proceeds *not* restricted).
2. Land costing $500,000 was purchased by issuing a five-year, 8% note payable for $450,000. The balance was paid from cash restricted for an expansion project.
3. Depreciation expense for the year was $200,000.
4. Interest expense of $36,000 on the note in transaction 2 was paid from unrestricted resources.
5. Bonds payable of $200,000 were repaid from restricted resources, along with $50,000 of interest. The bonds were issued several years earlier to finance capital asset construction.
6. A capital grant of $500,000 was received, but no qualifying costs have been incurred.
7. $300,000 of the restricted capital grant from transaction 6 was expended for its intended purpose.
8. Sales revenues amounted to $1,000,000.
9. Interest revenues restricted to the use of the Enterprise Fund, $40,000, were received.
10. The cost of materials and supplies used for the year was $75,000.

			Net Position		
Transaction Number	Affect Operating Statement?	Unrestricted	Restricted	Net Investment in Capital Assets	Total
Sample	No	$(5,000)	—	+$5,000	—

E10-3 (Refunding) Prepare the journal entries needed in an Enterprise Fund to record the following transactions. Include any *adjusting entries* required.
1. Issued refunding bonds at par, $8,000,000. The bonds bear interest at 8% payable annually and mature in 5 years. (Ignore bond issue costs.)
2. Paid the $8,000,000 into an irrevocable trust to defease in substance the previously outstanding bonds payable of the Enterprise Fund. These old bonds have a par value of $7,200,000 and an unamortized discount of $100,000. The old bonds are scheduled to mature in six years.
3. The annual interest payment on the new bonds was made at year end when due.

E10-4 (Grants) A government's Enterprise Fund received two intergovernmental grants in cash. The specifics of the grants and the ensuing transactions were as follows:
(a) The grants totaled $4,000,000—$3,000,000 was restricted for capital purposes and $1,000,000 was solely for operations.
(b) The government incurred and paid construction costs of $1,200,000, payable from the capital grant, and operating costs of $300,000, payable from the operating grant. Also, the government acquired and paid for $50,000 of equipment (which was deemed to be a qualifying use of the operating grant).

Required
1. Record the preceding transactions in the Enterprise Fund's general ledger.
2. What amount of operating revenues should be reported by the Enterprise Fund, based on the information given?
3. What amount of nonoperating revenues should be reported by the Enterprise Fund, based on the information given?
4. What amounts should be reported as cash flows from noncapital financing activities?
5. What amounts should be reported as cash flows from capital and related financing activities?
6. What amounts should be reported as cash flows from investing activities?

E10-5 (Cash Flow Statement) Indicate the classification in which each of the following would be reported in a government proprietary fund cash flow statement. Use the following letters for each classification to respond:
(a) Cash flows from operating activities
(b) Cash flows from noncapital financing activities
(c) Cash flows from capital and related financing activities
(d) Cash flows from investing activities
(e) None of the above
1. Cash paid to purchase investments with resources restricted for capital asset construction.
2. Cash received from the sale of equipment.
3. Cash paid for salaries.
4. Cash received from interest on investments that are restricted for servicing bonds that were issued to finance construction of a building.
5. Cash paid for interest on refunding bonds that were issued for repayment of bonds that were originally issued to finance purchase of major pieces of equipment.
6. Cash transfer paid to General Fund. (The General Fund budget requires these funds to be used to help finance acquisition of a fire truck.)
7. Cash received from operating grants.
8. Cash received from a transfer from the General Fund to finance expansion of the physical plant.
9. Cash received from capital grants.
10. Cash paid for interest on a short-term note issued to fulfill a temporary need for operating funds.

E10-6 (Grant Accounting)
(a) Prepare journal entries, including adjusting entries when needed, to record the following transactions in a government's Enterprise Fund:
1. Received cash for a grant of $3,000,000, which was restricted to constructing a production facility.
2. Expended half of the grant funds for the construction of the building for which the grant was received.
(b) Prepare journal entries, including adjusting entries when needed, to record the following transactions affecting a government's Enterprise Fund:
1. Received cash for a grant of $3,000,000, which was restricted to paying the salaries of air-quality monitors.
2. Expended half of the grant funds for the salary payments for which the grant was received.

E10-7 (Operating Statement) Explain or illustrate how the following items should be reported in an Enterprise Fund's statement of revenues, expenses, and changes in fund net position:
1. Depreciation on capital grant–financed capital assets.
2. Depreciation on infrastructure assets.
3. Transfers from other funds.
4. Cash proceeds of short-term note issuances.
5. Retirement of bonds payable of the fund.
6. Routine annual transfers from other funds.
7. Gain on sale of capital assets.
8. "Loss" on advance refunding of bonds.
9. Restricted grants received that can be used for operations or for capital asset acquisition— assume 30% was expended during the year to acquire capital assets, 30% to cover operating expenses, and 40% has not been expended.
10. Entering into a capital lease with a capitalizable cost of $4,000,000 on the last day of the year—assume an initial payment on that day of $1,000,000.

E10-8 (Operating Statement Preparation) Using the information provided here for the Airport Enterprise Fund of the City of Demere, prepare a statement of revenues, expenses, and changes in fund net position for 20X3.

Charges for services	$3,500,000
Salaries expense	1,000,000
Contractual services used	1,100,000
Supplies used	200,000
Depreciation	1,500,000
Interest received	120,000
Increase in fair value of investments	23,000
Loss on sale of capital assets	4,000
Transfers from the General Fund	222,000
Capital assets donated for Enterprise Fund use	500,000
Interest expense	450,000
Amortization of deferred interest expense adjustment (credit balance)	25,000
Expenditures that qualify (100% reimbursable) under capital grant	1,300,000
Net Position, January 1, 20X3	3,827,000

Problems

P10-1 (Multiple Choice) Identify the best answer for each of the following:

Questions 1 through 4 are based on the following scenario:

On January 1, 20X7, Clyde County issued $100 million of 5%, 20-year bonds at 102. Interest is payable semiannually. The proceeds were restricted for the construction of a new county water purification plant for its Water Enterprise Fund.

1. The bond issuance should be reflected in the Water Fund Statement of Revenues, Expenses, and Changes in Fund Net Position as
   a. revenues of $102 million.
   b. other financing sources of $102 million.
   c. revenues of $100 million.
   d. The transaction does not affect this statement.
2. What effect will the bond premium amortization have on interest expense in 20X7, assuming straight-line amortization is used where appropriate?
   a. No effect.
   b. Increase interest expense by $100,000.
   c. Decrease interest expense by $100,000.
   d. Decrease interest expense and increase transfers from Debt Service Funds by $2,000,000.
3. Assume that at the fiscal year end the capital project had not yet begun; thus the debt proceeds were still unspent. What classifications of net position would be affected by this fact?
   a. Net investment in capital assets would be reduced because no capital assets have been added to offset the new capital-related debt.
   b. Restricted net position would include the unspent cash as well as the outstanding liability.
   c. Unrestricted net position would reflect an increase due to the cash received from the debt issuance, but net investment in capital assets would decrease by the amount of unspent debt proceeds.
   d. None—net position classifications are not affected by the issuance of long-term debt.
4. How would the Enterprise Fund's statement of cash flows be affected by the debt issuance?
   a. Cash flows from operating activities would increase.
   b. Cash flows from noncapital financing activities would increase because bond proceeds have not yet been spent for capital purposes.
   c. Cash flows from capital financing activities would increase.
   d. Cash flows from investing activities would increase.

Questions 5 through 7 are based on the following scenario:

The town of Brittainville has two Enterprise Funds—one for its water and wastewater operations and another for its cable television operation. The Water and Wastewater

Enterprise Fund issued $11,000,000 of 6%, 15-year refunding bonds at par during the year. It also received a $175,000 federal grant to expand water and wastewater lines to economically depressed residential neighborhoods. The Cable Enterprise Fund made its annual payment of $1,000,000 to the General Fund to subsidize operations. It also was the recipient of a Federal Communications Commission unrestricted grant of $100,000.

5. How would the receipt of the grants be reported on the statement of cash flows for the Water and Wastewater Enterprise Fund and the Cable Enterprise Fund, respectively?
   a. Cash flows from capital and related financing activities for the Water and Wastewater Enterprise Fund and cash flows from noncapital financing activities for the Cable Enterprise Fund.
   b. Assuming the Cable Enterprise Fund chose to use the proceeds of its grant for capital needs, both funds would reflect the grant receipt in cash flows from capital and related financing activities.
   c. Cash flows from capital and related financing activities for the Water and Wastewater Enterprise Fund and cash flows from operating activities for the Cable Enterprise Fund.
   d. Both funds would report the grant receipt as cash flows from operating activities.
6. How will the interfund payment be reported on the Cable Enterprise Fund's operating statement?
   a. Transfer out of $1,000,000.
   b. Operating expense of $1,000,000.
   c. Nonoperating expense of $1,000,000.
   d. Capital contribution out of $1,000,000.
7. How would the changes in net position amount be affected in the Water and Wastewater Enterprise Fund by the transactions listed?
   a. Changes in net position would not be affected by the debt issuance; the grant would increase changes in net position.
   b. Changes in net position would be decreased by any costs associated with issuing the refunding bonds; the grant would increase changes in net position.
   c. Both the refunding transaction and the grant would not affect the changes in net position.
   d. Changes in net position would not be affected by either transaction.

Questions 8 through 10 are based on the following facts about an Enterprise Fund for a utility operation:

Outstanding bonds issued for capital improvements	$ 10,500,000
Transfer to General Fund (occurs annually)	500,000
Charges for services earned in the current year	14,600,750
Unspent capital bond issue proceeds	4,000,000
Salaries and wages expense for the current year	9,600,000
Interest earnings on all investments	600,000
Fair market value of water lines donated by a local developer	1,000,000
Net book value of all other existing capital assets	7,310,500

8. Net investment in capital assets would be
   a. $7,310,500.
   b. $8,310,500.
   c. $4,310,500.
   d. $1,810,500.
9. Cash flows for noncapital financing activities would *decrease*
   a. $0.
   b. $10,100,000.
   c. $9,500,000.
   d. $500,000.
10. The operating statement of the Enterprise Fund would *not* be directly affected by
   a. the amount of unspent bond proceeds at the end of the year.
   b. the donation by the local developer.
   c. the transfer to the General Fund.
   d. Interest earnings on investments.

P10-2 (Operating Statement) Using the following information, prepare the Statement of Revenues, Expenses, and Changes in Fund Net Position for the town of Robinson Water and Sewer Enterprise Fund for the year ended June 30, 20X6.

Charges for water services rendered................................	$ 1,800,000
Charges for sewer services rendered.............................	2,000,000
Interest income	50,000
Increase in fair value of investments............................	12,000
Proceeds of bond issuance	13,000,000
Salaries and wages...	400,000
Contractual services (purchased)	2,600,000
Depreciation on infrastructure capital assets.....................	100,000
Depreciation on capital assets contributed by subdividers	75,000
Depreciation on other capital assets............................	80,000
Capital grants received (all grant conditions met)	1,500,000
Operating grants received (half expended for operations; half for capital asset purchases; all grant conditions met)	250,000
Gain on sale of equipment.....................................	13,000
Deferred interest expense adjustment (debit), beginning of year.....	100,000
Transfer to General Fund......................................	127,000
Transfer from Special Revenue Fund	500,000
Interest on short-term note payable	5,000
Repayment of short-term note payable	75,000
Interest on bonds payable......................................	95,000
Net Position, July 1, 20X5.....................................	22,000,000

Water and sewer service claims and judgments paid during the year totaled $100,000. The liability (half of which is long-term) for these claims and judgments increased by $10,000 during the year. The refunded bonds have a 5-year remaining term, and the term of the new bonds is 10 years.

P10-3 (Worksheet and Statements) The City of Lynn operates its municipal airport. The trial balance of the Airport Fund as of January 1, 20X0, was as follows:

Cash..	$ 37,000	
Accounts Receivable	50,000	
Allowance for Uncollectible Accounts		$ 2,000
Land	200,000	
Structures and Improvements	700,000	
Accumulated Depreciation—Structures and Improvements		50,000
Equipment	250,000	
Accumulated Depreciation—Equipment		90,000
Vouchers Payable		48,000
Bonds Payable.................................		800,000
Net Position		247,000
	$1,237,000	$1,237,000

The following transactions took place during the year:
1. Revenues collected in cash: aviation revenues, $340,500; concession revenues, $90,000; revenues from airport management, $30,000; revenues from sales of petroleum products, $10,500.
2. Expenses (all paid in cash with the exception of $24,000, which remained unpaid at December 31) were operating, $222,000; maintenance, $75,000; general and administrative, $73,000.
3. Bad debts written off during the year, $1,900.
4. The vouchers payable outstanding on January 1, 20X0, were paid.
5. Bond principal paid during the year, $50,000, along with interest of $40,000.
6. The remaining accounts receivable outstanding on January 1, 20X0, were collected.
7. Accounts receivable on December 31, 20X0, amounted to $30,000, all applicable to aviation revenues, of which $1,400 is estimated to be uncollectible.
8. Accrued interest payable at year end, $3,000.

9. Depreciation charges:

Structures and Improvements	$14,000
Equipment	21,000

Required a. Prepare a worksheet to reflect the beginning trial balance, the transactions and adjustments during 20X0, the revenues and expenses of the year (or closing entries), and the ending statement of net position data.

b. Compute the beginning and ending balances of each of the three net position components.

c. Prepare a statement of net position for the Airport Fund as of December 31, 20X0.

d. Prepare a statement of revenues, expenses, and changes in fund net position for the Airport Fund for the fiscal year ended December 31, 20X0.

P10-4 (Cash Flow Statement)

(a) Using the letters provided, indicate how each of the items should be reported in an Enterprise Fund statement of cash flows for Kauffman County.

1.	Cash received from sales to public	$ 3,000,000
2.	Cash received from sales to other departments	500,000
3.	Cash paid to employees	700,000
4.	Cash paid to suppliers	1,200,000
5.	Cash paid in lieu of taxes (not based on services provided)	50,000
6.	Cash received from operating grants	1,000,000
7.	Cash paid for equipment	1,500,000
8.	Cash received from sale of equipment (gain of $10,000)	100,000
9.	Cash received from short-term borrowing for working capital . .	25,000
10.	Cash received from sale of unrestricted investments to finance upcoming equipment purchases	80,000
11.	Cash received from capital grants	14,000,000
12.	Cash paid for interest on bonds issued to finance plant expansion	600,000
13.	Capital assets donated by developers.	5,000,000
14.	Purchase of investments from cash restricted for retirement of capital bonds	100,000
15.	Cash paid in discretionary transfer to General Fund to finance general capital asset purchases	75,000
16.	Interest received on unrestricted investments	44,000
17.	Interest received on investments restricted for capital asset purchases (The interest is restricted.)	79,000
18.	Cash received from sale of bonds to construct new plant	15,000,000
19.	Unrestricted cash, beginning of year	3,300,000
20.	Restricted cash, beginning of year	1,200,000

A = Cash flows from operating activities
B = Cash flows from noncapital financing activities
C = Cash flows from capital and related financing activities
D = Cash flows from investing activities
E = Significant noncash financing and investing activities
F = Other (Explain.)

(b) Using the information in (a), prepare the statement of cash flows for this Kauffman County Enterprise Fund. (A reconciliation of operating income is not required because sufficient data are not provided.) Assume 20X5 is the year.

P10-5 (Worksheet and Statements) The City of Clifton provides electric energy for its citizens through an operating department. All transactions of the Electric Department are recorded in a self-sustaining fund supported by revenues from the sales of energy. Plant expansion is financed by the issuance of bonds that are repaid out of revenues. All cash of the Electric Department is held by the city treasurer. Receipts from customers and others are deposited in the treasurer's account. Disbursements are made by drawing warrants on the treasurer.

The following is the postclosing trial balance of the department as of June 30, 20X7:

Cash and Investments with City Treasurer	$ 2,250,000	
Due from Customers.............................	2,120,000	
Other Current Assets	130,000	
Construction in Progress.........................	500,000	
Land	5,000,000	
Electric Plant	50,000,000*	
Accumulated Depreciation—Electric Plant		$10,000,000
Accounts Payable and Accrued Liabilities		3,270,000
5% Electric Revenue Bonds Payable		20,000,000
Net Position		26,730,000
	$60,000,000	$60,000,000

* The plant is being depreciated on the basis of a 50-year composite life.

During the year ended June 30, 20X8, the department had the following transactions:
1. Sales of electric energy, $10,700,000.
2. Purchases of fuel and operating supplies, $2,950,000.
3. Construction expenditures relating to miscellaneous system improvements in progress (financed from operations), $750,000.
4. Fuel consumed, $2,790,000.
5. Miscellaneous plant additions and improvements constructed and placed in service at midyear, $1,000,000.
6. Wages and salaries paid, $4,280,000.
7. Sale at par on December 31, 20X7, of 20-year, 5% Electric Revenue Bonds, dated January 1, 20X8, with interest payable semiannually, $5,000,000.
8. Expenditures out of bond proceeds for construction of Clifton Steam Plant Unit No. 1, $2,800,000.
9. Operating materials and supplies consumed, $150,000.
10. Payments received from customers, $10,500,000.
11. Expenditures out of bond proceeds for construction of Clifton Steam Plant Unit No. 2, $2,200,000.
12. Warrants drawn on city treasurer in settlement of accounts payable, $3,045,000.
13. The Clifton Steam Plant was placed in service June 30, 20X8.
14. Interest on bonds paid during the year, $500,000.

a. Prepare a worksheet for the Electric Department Fund showing: *Required*
  1. The statement of net position amounts at June 30, 20X7.
  2. The transactions for the year and closing entries. (Note: Formal journal entries are not required and interest capitalization may be ignored.)
  3. The statement of net position amounts at June 30, 20X8.
b. Compute the correct June 30, 20X7, and June 30, 20X8, balances for each component of net position.
c. Prepare a Statement of Cash Flows for the Electric Department Fund for the year ended June 30, 20X8.

P10-6 (Various Entries) Prepare journal entries, including adjusting entries needed, to record the following transactions for the Pickens County Transit Authority. Assume the fiscal year ends on April 30.
1. Issued refunding bonds at par, $10,000,000. The interest rate is 10%, payable annually. Bonds mature in 10 years. Bond issue costs were $200,000.
2. Retired old debt with refunding proceeds of $9,800,000.
   - Bonds payable outstanding (old), $9,300,000.
   - Unamortized premium on outstanding bonds, $300,000.
   - Remaining term of old debt, four years.
3. Annual interest payment ($1,000,000) on new bonds was made at the due date, which is year end.
4. On April 30, 20X2, the Transit Authority leased 10 buses under a six-year, noncancellable capital lease. The capitalizable cost of the buses was $680,000, and an $80,000 down payment was made. The county does not receive title to the leased buses at the end of the lease term.
5. Lease payments made during the fiscal year ended April 30, 20X3, totaled $130,262, including interest of $37,932.
6. The county estimates its probable losses from claims and judgments against the Transit Authority for events occurring in 20X2–20X3 at $227,000. However, only $85,000 of this amount is a current liability.

P10-7 (Restricted Asset Accounting) McKenzie's Point issued $1,200,000 of 6%, 10-year serial bonds at par on July 1, 20X4. Interest is due semiannually on January 1 and July 1 each year, and one-tenth of the principal is due each July 1. The bond indenture requires that the proceeds be accounted for in a separate fund and used to construct an addition to the maintenance building for the municipal airport, which is accounted for in an Enterprise Fund. Furthermore, the bond agreement requires McKenzie's Point to set aside airport revenues of $20,000 per month plus one-sixth of the next interest payment each month in a separate fund for debt service from which debt service payments are to be made. The following also occurred during 20X4:

> July 2—The city signed a contract with Keith Construction for construction of the addition, $1,200,000.
>
> July 31—The city set aside the required amount to provide for debt service.
>
> August 29—The city received a bill from Keith Construction for $1,200,000 upon completion of the addition. After inspection and approval, the bill was paid.
>
> August 31, September 30, October 31, November 30, and December 31—On each of these dates the city set aside the required amounts to provide for debt service.

Required Assuming August 31 is the end of the fiscal year of McKenzie's Point, prepare the general journal entries, including adjusting and closing entries, for the preceding transactions. Ignore interest capitalization.

P10-8 (Essay—Financial Reporting) Explain how each of the following should be reported in the financial statements of an Enterprise Fund. If assumptions are necessary, state them clearly.
1. Capital grant received in cash, but not earned, $500,000
2. Capital grant earned, but not collected until 90 days after year end, $1,200,000
3. Estimated uncollectible accounts related to current year sales, $75,000
4. Deferred interest expense adjustment credit balance of $300,000 at year end
5. Amortization of deferred interest expense adjustment credit balance, $50,000
6. Reassignment at year end of a general capital asset (cost, $1,000,000 and accumulated depreciation, $350,000) as an Enterprise Fund capital asset
7. Operating grant earned and collected during the year, $89,000
8. Accrued interest on Enterprise Fund long-term bonds payable, $100,000
9. Free services provided to General Fund departments, $65,000
10. Charges for services provided to other Enterprise Funds, $20,000

Cases

C10-1 (Financial Statement Classifications—Anchorage, Alaska) The Municipality of Anchorage, Alaska, reports three enterprise funds: the Electric Utility Fund, the Water Utility Fund, and the Wastewater Utility Fund. The following accounts and amounts are reported on the financial statements of the Electric Utility Fund as of December 31, 20X6:

Statement of Net Position

1. Cash	$ 37,482,310
2. Inventories	13,964,133
3. Advances to other funds	3,688,437
4. Capital assets, net	333,322,546
5. Accounts payable and retainages	18,763,885
6. Revenue bonds payable	175,017,807
7. Unfunded pension obligation	618,092
8. Net investment in capital assets	108,993,625

Statement of Revenues, Expenses, and Changes in Fund Net Position

9. Charges for services	$114,413,016
10. Salaries, supplies, and miscellaneous expenses	56,647,540
11. Depreciation expense	24,385,773
12. Transfers out	(5,964,169)
13. Investment income	5,106,764
14. Interest expense	13,310,236
15. Amortization of deferred refunding charges	390,784

Statement of Cash Flows

16. Transfers to other funds	$ 5,964,169
17. Principal payments on capital-related long-term obligations	21,225,000

18. Receipts from customers and users	137,768,092	
19. Capital purchases with notes payable	5,236,376	
20. Payments to employees with notes payable	18,076,957	
21. Interest payments on long-term obligations	12,297,847	
22. Proceeds from maturities of investments	6,217,570	
23. Contributed capital assets	396,540	
24. Investment income received	4,278,603	

1. For the statement of net position, identify how each of the accounts would most likely be **Required** classified, using the following classifications:
   a. Current assets
   b. Noncurrent assets
   c. Deferred outflows of resources
   d. Current liabilities
   e. Noncurrent liabilities
   f. Deferred inflows of resources
   g. Net position
2. For the statement of revenues, expenses, and changes in fund net position, identify how each of the reported amounts would be classified, using the following classifications:
   a. Operating revenues
   b. Operating expenses
   c. Nonoperating revenues
   d. Nonoperating expenses
   e. Other categorizations
3. For the statement of cash flows, identify how each cash flow amount should be classified, using the following classifications:
   a. Cash flows from operating activities
   b. Cash flows from noncapital financing activities
   c. Cash flows from capital financing activities
   d. Noncash investing, capital, and financing activities

(Adapted from a recent Comprehensive Annual Financial Report for the Municipality of Anchorage, Alaska.)

C10-2 (Financial Statement Preparation—DuPage County, Illinois) DuPage County, Illinois, has a Convalescent Center that is reported as an Enterprise Fund. The following represents the pre-closing trial balance for the Convalescent Center as of the fiscal year ended November 30, 20X6:

DuPage County, Illinois
Convalescent Center Enterprise Fund
Preclosing Trial Balance
November 30, 20X6

	Dr.	Cr.
Cash	$ 231,752	
Accounts receivable, net	5,465,885	
Due from other funds	24,333	
Inventory	373,372	
Capital assets—land and improvements	784,360	
Capital assets—buildings and improvements	28,005,704	
Capital assets—vehicles	265,583	
Capital assets—equipment	4,544,660	
Capital assets—construction in progress	101,629	
Accumulated depreciation		$22,493,255
Accounts payable		1,440,009
Accrued payroll		1,431,020
Due to other funds		200,000
Capital lease obligation		34,986
Accrued vacation		985,759
Net position		14,155,260
Patient revenue		24,949,646
Investment income		9,333

Intergovernmental grants		694,852
Transfers in		2,700,000
Capital contributions		4,362,635
Personnel services	22,974,937	
Supplies used	4,912,013	
Contractual services	4,475,447	
Depreciation expense	1,292,015	
Interest expense	3,249	
Loss of disposal of assets	1,816	
Totals	$73,456,755	$73,456,755

Required   In addition, assume that the capital lease obligation is all long-term and that it is the only liability related to capital assets. Further, assume that the center has no restricted assets or liabilities.

Prepare the DuPage County Convalescent Center Statement of Net Position as of November 30, 20X6, and its Statement of Revenues, Expenses, and Changes in Fund Net Position for the year ending November 30, 20X6.

(Adapted from a recent Comprehensive Annual Financial Report for DuPage County, Illinois.)

Harvey City Comprehensive Case

ENTERPRISE FUND

Harvey City's Water and Sewer Enterprise Fund is used to account for the city's Water and Sewer Department. This department serves city residents and also provides services to the city's own departments and agencies. City policy is that the charges for water and sewer services should be set at rates sufficient to recover the full cost of providing the services.

REQUIREMENTS

a. Prepare a worksheet for the Water and Sewer Enterprise Fund similar to the General Fund worksheet you created in Chapter 4. Enter the effects of the following transactions and events in the appropriate columns of the worksheet. (A different solution approach may be used if desired by your professor.)

b. Enter the preclosing trial balance in the appropriate worksheet columns.

c. Enter the preclosing trial balance amounts in the closing entry (operating statement data) and postclosing trial balance (statement of net position data) columns, as appropriate.

d. Prepare the 20X4 statement of revenues, expenses, and changes in fund net position for the Water and Sewer Enterprise Fund.

e. Prepare the year-end 20X4 statement of net position for the Water and Sewer Enterprise Fund.

f. Prepare the 20X4 statement of cash flows for the Water and Sewer Enterprise Fund.

BEGINNING 20X4 TRIAL BALANCE

The January 1, 20X4, trial balance for the Water and Sewer Enterprise Fund of Harvey City is presented here:

Harvey City
Water and Sewer Enterprise Fund
Trial Balance
January 1, 20X4

	Debit	Credit
Cash	$ 175,000	
Accounts Receivable	45,000	
Allowance for Uncollectible Accounts		$ 1,100
Inventory of Materials and Supplies	27,000	
Customer Deposits—Cash	30,000	
Land	17,000	
Buildings	1,200,000	
Accumulated Depreciation—Buildings		300,000
Machinery and Equipment	2,000,000	
Accumulated Depreciation—Machinery and Equipment		1,000,000
Water and Sewer Lines	4,500,000	
Accumulated Depreciation—Water and Sewer Lines		3,250,000
Vouchers Payable		68,000
Accrued Interest Payable		500
Customer Deposits Payable		30,000
Bonds Payable		800,000
Long-Term Claims and Judgments Payable		25,000
Net Position		2,519,400
Totals	$7,994,000	$7,994,000

TRANSACTIONS AND EVENTS—20X4

1. Water sales for 20X4 totaled $530,000 and sewer charges amounted to $320,000; $5,160 of receivables for water sales and $3,015 of receivables for sewer sales are expected to prove uncollectible. The charges included $22,500 billed to the General Fund.
2. The department collected $815,000 of accounts receivable during the year.
3. The department wrote off accounts receivable totaling $6,400 during the year.
4. New deposits of $4,500 were collected from new customers during the year.
5. Payroll of $190,000 was paid, and an additional $12,000 was contributed to the statewide retirement system.
6. The department purchased investments for $120,000.
7. The Water and Sewer Department was billed $33,000 by the Central Communications Network Internal Services Fund for services used; $30,000 was paid at this time.
8. Investment income of $8,000 was received during the year, with no accrued interest at year end, and the fair value of the investments at year end approximately equaled their cost.
9. The department purchased materials and supplies costing $89,900, and a voucher payable in that amount was approved.
10. Materials and supplies costing $88,700 were used by the Water and Sewer Department during 20X4.
11. The city paid interest, $40,000 (including $500 accrued interest payable at the beginning of the year) and principal, $80,000, on the outstanding bonds of the Water and Sewer Department.
12. Vouchers payable of $82,000 were paid.
13. Depreciation for the year was:

    On equipment—$150,000

    On buildings—$40,000

    On lines—$110,000

14. Cash of $100,000 was transferred from the Water and Sewer Fund to the General Fund.
15. Salaries and wages payable of $10,000 was accrued at year end.
16. Accrued interest on the Water and Sewer Fund bonds at December 31, 20X4, was $450.

CHAPTER 11

Internal Service Funds

LEARNING OBJECTIVES

After studying this chapter, you should be able to:

- Understand the nature and usage of Internal Service Funds.

- Understand the accounting principles that apply to Internal Service Funds.

- Understand the pricing policies and methods that are used in Internal Service Funds.

- Prepare basic journal entries for various types of Internal Service Funds.

- Prepare Internal Service Fund financial statements, including combining statements.

- Understand the unique aspects of accounting for self-insurance Internal Service Funds.

- Understand and discuss the problems associated with having significant accumulated increases or decreases in total net position of an Internal Service Fund.

Internal Service Funds are established to finance, administer, and account for departments or agencies of a government whose exclusive or nearly exclusive purpose is to provide goods and services (e.g., printing services) to the government's other departments on a **cost-reimbursement** basis. (The break-even objective has caused such funds to be referred to as "working capital" or "revolving" funds in many jurisdictions.)

Internal Service Fund departments may provide a limited portion of their services to other governments in some instances. If providing services to other governments (or to other external customers) is the primary purpose of the department, however, an Enterprise Fund should be used, not an Internal Service Fund. As discussed in Chapter 10, Enterprise Funds are used to account for and finance the provision of goods or services for compensation primarily to the general public and to outside entities rather than to other departments of the government.

Internal Service Funds are *internal intermediary* fiscal and accounting entities through which some of the expenditures of other departments are made. They are used (1) to attain greater economy, efficiency, and effectiveness in the acquisition and distribution of common goods or services used by several or all departments within the organization and (2) to facilitate an equitable sharing of costs among the various departments served and, hence, among the funds of the organization. They also may be used to provide interim financing for capital projects.

The type and complexity of activities accounted for through Internal Service Funds vary widely in practice. Among the simpler types are those used (1) to distribute common or joint costs—such as the cost of telephone, radio, or other communication facilities—among departments; (2) to acquire, distribute, and allocate costs of selected items of inventory, such as office supplies or gasoline; or (3) to provide temporary loans to other funds. More complex activities accounted for through Internal Service Funds include motor pools; data-processing activities; duplicating and printing facilities; repair shops and garages; cement and asphalt plants; purchasing, warehousing, and distribution services; and insurance and other risk management services.

OVERVIEW OF ACCOUNTING PRINCIPLES

As explained in Chapter 10, Internal Service Funds are **proprietary** (nonexpendable) funds. Because their accounting and reporting are essentially the same as for an Enterprise Fund, the *economic resources measurement focus and accrual basis of accounting* are used. Also, both the related capital assets—which normally are replaced from Internal Service Fund resources—and any long-term liabilities to be serviced through the fund are recorded as "fund" assets and liabilities in the Internal Service Fund. Depreciation expense is recorded, and both operating income and the change in net position are computed. Again, the flow of economic resources measurement focus and accrual basis of proprietary funds is used. Therefore, most transactions and events are accounted for and reported just as for business enterprises. Leases, for example, are classified and reported in virtually the same way as in business accounting. Pension costs and other postemployment benefit costs and related liabilities are not accounted for in the same manner as for businesses, however. Instead, pension costs and other postemployment benefit costs and liabilities are reported in accordance with GASB *Statement No. 27* and GASB *Statement No. 45,* respectively, as discussed in Chapter 12.

The application of generally accepted business accounting principles is consistent with the funds' typical objectives:

1. The usual policy requires break-even pricing and the maintenance of the invested capital. (As mentioned earlier, Internal Service Funds are sometimes referred to as revolving funds because the fund resources are used to provide goods or services and are subsequently replenished by charges to other funds; then those resources are used to provide goods and services; and so on.) Information on revenues and expenses is essential to fulfilling this policy.

2. Full costing provides appropriate information for determining equitable charges to the departments that use the services of the Internal Service Fund.

Before illustrating Internal Service Fund accounting and reporting, we discuss several issues that affect these funds. In addition to the creation of and initial financing for Internal Service Funds, we consider Internal Service Fund pricing policies and methods, the role of the budget in Internal Service Funds, and Internal Service Fund financial statements.

Initial Establishment Ordinarily, an Internal Service Fund is created by constitutional, charter, or legislative action. However, in some instances, the chief executive is empowered to create an Internal Service Fund. Capital to finance Internal Service Fund activities may come from various sources. Examples include appropriations from the General Fund, the issue of general obligation bonds or other debt instruments, transfers or loans from other funds, or contributions from another government. Capital may also be provided by contributing all, or excessive, inventories of materials and supplies that a fund's future "clients" (a governmental unit's departments) may have on hand at a specified time. Likewise, general capital assets may be reclassified for use in Internal Service Fund operations as Internal Service Fund assets. The sources of capital used to finance a specific Internal Service Fund depend to some extent on whether the Internal Service Fund is being established to account for a new activity or for an activity previously accounted for in other funds.

If the General Fund provides permanent capital ($50,000) for the Internal Service Fund, the following entries are made in the respective funds:

General Fund

Transfer to Internal Service Fund	$ 50,000	
Cash		$ 50,000
To record capital provided to Internal Service Fund.		

Internal Service Fund

Cash	$ 50,000	
Transfer from General Fund		$ 50,000
To record receipt of capital from General Fund.		

Transfers from other funds should be closed to the Internal Service Fund net position account.

Transfers must be distinguished from interfund loans. If the Internal Service Fund must ultimately repay the General Fund, the following entries would replace the preceding entries to record the interfund loan:

General Fund

Advance to Internal Service Fund	$ 50,000	
Cash		$ 50,000
To record advance to Internal Service Fund.		

Internal Service Fund

Cash	$ 50,000	
Advance from General Fund		$ 50,000
To record advance from General Fund.		

Recall that the terms *advance to* and *advance from* are typically used to indicate intermediate- and long-term receivables and payables. *Due to* and *due from* connote short-term relationships.

If general obligation bonds ($100,000) intended to be repaid from the Internal Service Fund are issued at par to finance an Internal Service Fund, the following entry is made:

Internal Service Fund

Cash	$100,000	
Bonds Payable		$100,000
To record bond issue.		

In this case the contingent "general government" liability for the bonds need only be disclosed in the notes to the financial statements. If the bonds were not intended to be repaid from the Internal Service Fund and receipt of the bond proceeds were recorded in the General Fund, the following entries would be made:

General Fund

Cash	$100,000	
Other Financing Sources—Bonds		$100,000
To record issuance of bonds.		
Transfer to Internal Service Fund	$100,000	
Due to Internal Service Fund		$100,000
To record transfer of bond proceeds to Internal Service Fund.		

General Long-Term Liabilities accounts

Net Position	$100,000	
Bonds Payable		$100,000
To record issuance of bonds to finance Internal Service Fund but to be repaid from general revenues.		

Internal Service Fund

Due from General Fund	$100,000	
Transfer from General Fund		$100,000

To record transfer from General Fund.

Sometimes an Internal Service Fund is established to account for an activity previously financed and accounted for through the governmental funds. In such cases, inventories or general capital assets are often contributed to the Internal Service Fund. If equipment with a five-year estimated useful life that was acquired for $30,000 two years prior to creation of an Internal Service Fund is contributed to the Internal Service Fund, the following entries are required:

General Capital Assets accounts

Net Position	$ 18,000	
Accumulated Depreciation—Equipment	12,000	
Equipment		$ 30,000

To record reclassification of equipment to Internal Service Fund.

Internal Service Fund

Equipment	$ 30,000	
Accumulated Depreciation—Equipment		$ 12,000
Revenues—Capital Contributions		18,000

To record capital assets reclassified from General Capital Assets accounts.

Note that the equipment is recorded at its original cost less the accumulated depreciation to date (as discussed in Chapter 9). Also, no entry is required in the General Fund because General Fund resources are not involved in the transaction. Finally, note that the reclassification of the capital asset is treated as capital contributions revenues in the Internal Service Fund. General capital asset transfers or reclassifications cannot be reported as transfers in the fund financial statements because the transaction does not involve two funds. As explained in Chapter 14, in the government-wide financial statements, this transaction will be eliminated if the Internal Service Fund activity is combined with governmental activities. It will be reclassified and reported as a transfer between governmental activities and business-type activities if the Internal Service Fund activity is part of business-type activities.

Pricing Policies The preceding pricing policy discussions assumed that the prices charged by the Internal Service Fund would be based on (historical) cost. Most authorities agree that cost is the proper pricing basis. Internal Service Fund activities that are very modest in scope, have no full-time personnel, and do not incur other significant costs sometimes base charges to user departments on direct costs. This approach might be used, for example, when:

1. Limited group purchasing and warehousing is done only occasionally or as a small part of the overall purchasing operation.

2. The Internal Service Fund is essentially a flow-through or clearance device for common costs, such as two-way radio facility rentals.

More commonly, however, Internal Service Fund activities involve substantial amounts of personnel, space, materials, and other overhead costs that are recovered through billing user departments for more than the direct cost of the goods or services provided.

The Internal Service Fund usually has a "captive" clientele. In most governments, the departments may not use another source of supply if a service or material is available through an Internal Service Fund. The lack of outside competition can lead to inefficiencies. Therefore, the economy, efficiency, and effectiveness of

Internal Service Fund activities should be monitored closely under such circumstances. Without such precautions, the convenience of having an "in-house" supplier may result in significantly higher costs than otherwise necessary.

Being the sole source of a particular good or service also permits Internal Service Fund prices to be set at levels that will produce profit or loss. In some cases, Internal Service Fund net position has been built up through substantial annual profits. The increase in net position was paid for, of course, by the funds that financed the expenditures used to buy Internal Service Fund services or supplies. In a few instances, the accumulated unrestricted net position of an Internal Service Fund even provided the basis for a cash "dividend" that was transferred to the General Fund. To the extent that Internal Service Fund revenues were derived from departments financed by the General Fund, the profit thus transferred merely had the effect of offsetting excessive charges to it previously. But, if departments or activities financed through other funds patronized the Internal Service Fund, the effect of overcharging was to transfer resources from these other funds to the General Fund.

Overcharging user departments sometimes results in diverting restricted resources to other purposes. This use of Internal Service Fund charges cannot be condoned. Such a practice erodes confidence in the organization's administrators and in the accounting system. It also constitutes indirect fraud at best, and at worst results in illegal use of intergovernmental grant, trust, or other restricted resources. Excessive charges for Internal Service Fund goods or services to federally (or state) financed programs are properly disallowed for reimbursement. The government also risks being penalized by having to repay the grantor government and not receiving such financial assistance in the future.

The pricing method used by an Internal Service Fund is usually based on estimates of total costs and total consumption of goods or services. From these two estimates, a rate is developed and applied to each purchase. Assume that the cost of materials to be issued by a Stores Fund during the coming year was expected to be $300,000 and that other costs of fund operation were estimated at $12,000. Goods would be priced to departments at $1.04 for every $1.00 of direct cost of materials issued. Similarly, rental rates for automotive equipment may be based on time or mileage, or both. If a truck was expected to be driven 12,000 miles during the year at a total cost of $3,600, the departments would be charged $0.30 per mile.

The alternative to using predetermined rates is to charge the departments on the basis of actual costs determined at the end of each month, quarter, or year. Though this method is sometimes used for uncomplicated Internal Service Funds, a predetermined charge rate is generally used for more complex operations. This practice is preferable because (1) some Internal Service Fund expenses may not be determinable until the end of the month (or later), whereas it may be desirable to bill departments promptly so that they know how much expense or expenditure is charged to their jobs and activities at any time, and (2) charges based on actual monthly costs are likely to spread the burden inequitably among departments. For example, assume that the costs of extensive equipment repairs made in June are included in the charges to the departments using the equipment during that month. In this situation, those departments that used the equipment in June would be billed for costs more properly allocated to several months or years. The departments that used the equipment in previous or succeeding months would not bear their fair share of these costs. Furthermore, even if one department used the equipment throughout the year, charges based on actual monthly costs would often result in an inequitable distribution of costs among jobs and activities carried on by the department.

Internal Service Fund expenses, including overhead, should be recorded in appropriately titled expense accounts. Internal Service Fund charges for the goods or services provided are credited to a revenue account such as *Billings to Departments* or *Intragovernmental Sales,* and corresponding receivables from (due from) other funds or other governments are recorded.

Pricing Methods

Relation to Budget

The level of activity of an Internal Service Fund depends upon the demand of the user departments for its services. Therefore, Internal Service Fund appropriations might not be made, and formal budgetary control might not be employed in Internal Service Fund accounts. These controls might not be used because the Internal Service activity must be able to respond to service demands, not constrained by inflexible appropriation levels, and the appropriations to the various user departments place an indirect budgetary ceiling on the Internal Service Fund activities.

Ideally, sound management requires the use of flexible budgetary techniques in planning and conducting major Internal Service Fund activities. Although the budget developed with these techniques may be formally approved, the expense element is not considered to be appropriated. Budgetary control is exercised as in a business. The expenses incurred are compared with estimated expenses at the level of activity actually achieved.

Laws or custom in many cases prohibit the incurrence of obligations against or disbursement of cash from Internal Service Funds without appropriation authority. In these cases—and whenever management wants budgetary control over the Internal Service Fund—it is necessary to record not only those transactions that affect the actual position and operations of the fund (i.e., those transactions that affect the actual revenues, expenses, assets, deferred outflows, liabilities, deferred inflows, and net position) but also those relating to appropriations, expenditures, and encumbrances. Because budgetary accounting has been illustrated in previous chapters, the examples that follow illustrate the accounting for proprietary accounts only. Budgetary accounting for proprietary funds is typically accomplished by using self-balancing budgetary accounts in which the budgetary effects of transactions are recorded. Accounting for the proprietary accounts is not affected by the budgetary accounting entries in this approach.

Financial Statements

The required Internal Service Fund financial statements parallel those for Enterprise Funds. The three required financial statements for Internal Service Funds are the:

- Statement of Net Position
- Statement of Revenues, Expenses, and Changes in Fund Net Position
- Statement of Cash Flows

Each of these statements was discussed and illustrated in Chapter 10. Internal Service Fund statements are included in the illustrations later in this chapter.

In government-wide financial statements, the Internal Service Funds are included in either governmental activities or in business-type activities, depending on whether the predominant customers are (1) departments included in governmental activities or (2) Enterprise Fund departments. Reporting Internal Service Fund activities is discussed and illustrated further in Chapters 13 to 15.

INTERNAL SERVICE FUND ACCOUNTING ILLUSTRATED

Three illustrations of Internal Service Fund activities, accounting, and reporting make up this section. The fund activities illustrated are a central automotive equipment operation, a Stores Fund, and a Self-Insurance Fund. Only general ledger entries are illustrated in the examples. Subsidiary ledgers and cost accounting systems are maintained for Internal Service Funds but are not illustrated because they should be identical to those for similar business operations.

Automotive Equipment Unit

Assume that a Central Automotive Equipment Fund has been created and that some of the needed assets have been acquired. The Internal Service Fund statement of net position prior to operations is presented in Illustration 11-1. Fund resources will be used to buy automobiles, trucks, tractors, and the like. The use of each machine and the cost of operation on a per-mile or per-hour basis will be estimated. Records of actual costs will be kept for comparison with the estimates

ILLUSTRATION 11-1   Beginning Statement of Net Position

A Governmental Unit
Central Automotive Equipment (Internal Service) Fund
Statement of Net Position
(Date)

Assets

Current Assets:		
Cash		$ 75,000
Capital Assets:		
Land	$10,000	
Buildings	40,000	
Machinery and equipment	10,000	60,000
		$135,000

Net Position

Net investment in capital assets	$ 60,000
Unrestricted	75,000
	$135,000

and for making estimates for coming years. Such records are also useful in evaluating the efficiency of management and economy of operation of various types and brands of equipment.

The following transactions and entries illustrate how a typical Internal Service Fund equipment activity operates. Note that in this case every transaction is recorded substantially the same as it would have been for a business enterprise.

Transactions and Entries

1. Purchased equipment by paying $25,000 cash and issuing a two-year, 6% note for $15,000 on October 1.

(1) Machinery and Equipment	$40,000	
Notes Payable.		$15,000
Cash		25,000
To record purchase of equipment.		

Note that the long-term note is recorded and reported in the Internal Service Fund, as is the equipment.

2. Materials and supplies purchased on credit, $10,000.

(2) Inventory of Materials and Supplies	$10,000	
Vouchers Payable.		$10,000
To record purchase of materials and supplies.		

3. Salaries and wages paid, $19,000, distributed as follows:

Mechanics' Wages.	$ 9,000
Indirect Labor	3,000
Superintendent's Salary	3,500
Office Salaries	3,500
	$19,000

(3) Expenses—Mechanics' Wages	$ 9,000	
Expenses—Indirect Labor	3,000	
Expenses—Superintendent's Salary	3,500	
Expenses—Office Salaries	3,500	
Cash.		$19,000
To record salaries and wages expenses.		

4. Heat, light, and power paid, $2,000.

(4) Expenses—Heat, Light, and Power	$ 2,000	
Cash..		$ 2,000
To record heat, light, and power expenses.		

5. Depreciation:

Buildings	$ 2,400
Machinery and Equipment	9,200
	$11,600

(5) Expenses—Depreciation—Buildings	$ 2,400	
Expenses—Depreciation—Machinery and Equipment	9,200	
Accumulated Depreciation—Buildings		$ 2,400
Accumulated Depreciation—Machinery and Equipment		9,200
To record depreciation expense.		

6. Total billings to departments for services rendered, $42,800, of which $30,000 is billed to the General Fund and $12,800 is billed to the Enterprise Fund.

(6) Due from General Fund.........................	$30,000	
Due from Enterprise Fund......................	12,800	
Revenues—Billings to Departments..............		$42,800
To record billings to departments.		

This transaction is an *interfund services* transaction. Expenditures will be charged in the General Fund, and expense accounts will be charged in the Enterprise Fund. In both cases, the credit will be Due to Central Automotive Equipment (Internal Service) Fund.

The "Billings to Departments" revenues account is often used by governments for Internal Service Fund charges to user departments. Some accountants consider the title to be more descriptive than "Sales." Others consider titles such as "Sales" to connote the inclusion of a "profit" element in the charges, which should not be true with IS Fund charges. Still other accountants prefer to use the account title "Sales" (such as "Intragovernmental Sales").

7. Vouchers payable paid, $7,500.

(7) Vouchers Payable	$ 7,500	
Cash		$ 7,500
To record payment of vouchers payable.		

8. Cash collected from the General Fund, $29,000, and from the Enterprise Fund, $10,000.

(8) Cash...	$39,000	
Due from General Fund		$29,000
Due from Enterprise Fund.....................		10,000
To record collections on interfund receivables.		

9. Office maintenance expenses paid, $200.

(9) Expenses—Office Maintenance	$ 200	
Cash		$ 200
To record miscellaneous office expenses.		

10. Materials and supplies issued during the period, $7,000.

(10) Expenses—Cost of Materials and Supplies Used	$ 7,000	
Inventory of Materials and Supplies..............		$ 7,000
To record cost of materials and supplies used.		

11. Accrued salaries and wages, $1,000, distributed as follows:

Mechanics' Wages	$500
Indirect Labor	150
Superintendent's Salary	175
Office Salaries	175

Also, interest was accrued on notes payable, $400.

(11) Expenses—Interest	$ 400	
Expenses—Mechanics' Wages	500	
Expenses—Indirect Labor	150	
Expenses—Superintendent's Salary	175	
Expenses—Office Salaries	175	
Accrued Interest Payable		$ 400
Accrued Salaries and Wages Payable		1,000

To record accrued salaries, wages, and interest.

After these entries have been posted, the trial balance of the accounts of the ISF will appear as follows:

A Governmental Unit
Central Automotive Equipment (Internal Service) Fund
Preclosing Trial Balance
(Date)

	Dr.	Cr.
Cash	$ 60,300	
Due from General Fund	1,000	
Due from Enterprise Fund	2,800	
Inventory of Materials and Supplies	3,000	
Land..	10,000	
Buildings	40,000	
Accumulated Depreciation—Buildings		$ 2,400
Machinery and Equipment	50,000	
Accumulated Depreciation—Machinery and Equipment ...		9,200
Vouchers Payable		2,500
Accrued Salaries and Wages Payable		1,000
Accrued Interest Payable		400
Notes Payable [Capital-related]		15,000
Net Position		135,000
Revenues—Billings to Departments		42,800
Expenses—Cost of Materials and Supplies Used	7,000	
Expenses—Mechanics' Wages	9,500	
Expenses—Indirect Labor	3,150	
Expenses—Superintendent's Salary	3,675	
Expenses—Depreciation—Buildings	2,400	
Expenses—Depreciation—Machinery and Equipment	9,200	
Expenses—Heat, Light, and Power	2,000	
Expenses—Office Salaries	3,675	
Expenses—Office Maintenance	200	
Expenses—Interest	400	
	$208,300	$208,300

The closing entries for the Central Automotive Equipment Fund are on the next page. Closing entries may be made in a variety of methods. Some accountants prefer to make one compound entry that closes all revenue and expense accounts directly to net position. Any reasonable closing entry or combination of entries is acceptable if it (1) updates the Net Position account to its period end balance, and (2) brings the temporary proprietary accounts to zero balances so that they are ready for use during the next period.

Closing Entries

(C1) Revenues—Billings to Departments................	$42,800	
Expenses—Cost of Materials and Supplies Used....		$7,000
Expenses—Mechanics' Wages...................		9,500
Expenses—Indirect Labor......................		3,150
Expenses—Superintendent's Salary..............		3,675
Expenses—Depreciation—Buildings.............		2,400
Expenses—Depreciation—Machinery and Equipment...................................		9,200
Expenses—Heat, Light, and Power		2,000
Expenses—Office Salaries......................		3,675
Expenses—Office Maintenance		200
Expenses—Interest............................		400
Change in Net Position........................		1,600
To close revenue and expense accounts and determine the change in net position for the period.		
(C2) Change in Net Position	$ 1,600	
Net Position		$1,600
To close change in net position to Net Position.		

Illustrations 11-2, 11-3, and 11-4 present the Statement of Net Position; the Statement of Revenues, Expenses, and Changes in Fund Net Position; and the Statement of Cash Flows for the illustrative Central Automotive Equipment Fund. Note that the capital assets of the fund and the related accumulated depreciation accounts appear in the statement of net position. Because departments are billed for overhead charges, including depreciation, part of the money received from departments represents depreciation charges. An amount equal to depreciation charges may be debited to a separate cash account (set up in a separate "fund") to ensure its availability to replace assets; or it may be included in the fund's other unrestricted cash and used for various purposes, pending the replacement of the assets. In any event, the resources are *not* restricted unless enabling legislation, external grants or contracts, or similar items establish restrictions. In the present case, it is assumed that no segregation is made.

Long-term liabilities incurred for Internal Service Fund purposes are reported in the fund's statement of net position if the resources of the fund are to be used to service and retire the debt. Certain types of long-term debt, such as capital lease obligations and the long-term portion of the liability for compensated absences, will typically be repaid from Internal Service Fund resources. Others may be intended to be paid out of general taxation or other sources, such as enterprise earnings in the case of Internal Service Funds that are furnishing services to a utility department. In such cases, the liability should be accounted for in the General Long-Term Liabilities accounts or in an Enterprise Fund, whichever is appropriate in the circumstances.

Central Stores Fund Many departments and agencies of a government often use similar or identical materials and supplies. In some governments, each department or agency is responsible for acquiring and maintaining a sufficient inventory of the needed materials and supplies. However, many other governments centralize their purchasing and warehousing operations and operate them as an Internal Service Fund activity to enhance economy, efficiency, and control in these activities. In these governments, the materials and supplies are purchased and stored by the personnel in the central stores operation. Then, the central stores department eventually distributes them to user departments when requisitioned by those departments. Departmental billings are usually based on direct inventory cost plus an overhead factor. To simplify the discussion, it is again assumed that appropriations are not required for Internal Service Fund expenditures.

ILLUSTRATION 11-2 Ending Statement of Net Position

A Governmental Unit
Central Automotive Equipment (Internal Service) Fund
Statement of Net Position
At Close of Fiscal Year (Date)

Assets

Current Assets:

Cash	$60,300	
Due from General Fund	1,000	
Due from Enterprise Fund	2,800	
Inventory of materials and supplies	3,000	$ 67,100

Capital Assets:

Land		10,000	
Buildings	$40,000		
Less: Accumulated depreciation	2,400	37,600	
Machinery and equipment	50,000		
Less: Accumulated depreciation	9,200	40,800	88,400
Total Assets			$155,500

Liabilities

Current Liabilities:

Vouchers payable	$ 2,500	
Accrued salaries and wages payable	1,000	
Accrued interest payable	400	$ 3,900

Long-Term Liabilities:

Notes payable		15,000
Total Liabilities		18,900

Net Position:

Net investment in capital assets*		73,400
Unrestricted**		63,200
Total Net Position		$136,600

*Book value of capital assets ($88,400) minus capital-related debt ($15,000) equals $73,400.

**Total assets ($155,500) minus total liabilities ($18,900) minus Net investment in capital assets ($73,400).

Inventory Acquisition

The first step in the accounting process occurs when an invoice for supplies of inventory items ($20,000) is received and approved for payment. At that time, an entry is made to record the purchase and to set up the liability. The entry is as follows:

Inventory of Materials and Supplies	$20,000	
Vouchers Payable		$20,000
To record the purchase of materials and supplies.		

Note that a Purchases account is not used. The purchases are recorded directly in an Inventory of Materials and Supplies account because perpetual inventory records usually should be kept for a central storeroom operation.

Perpetual Inventory Procedures

Materials or supplies purchased for central storerooms are not charged against departmental appropriations until the materials or supplies are withdrawn from the storeroom. One procedure in withdrawing materials and charging appropriations is as follows: When a department needs materials, it prepares a stores requisition and presents it to the storekeeper. The storekeeper issues the items called for on the requisition and has the employee receiving them sign one copy of the requisition.

ILLUSTRATION 11-3 Operating Statement

A Governmental Unit
Central Automotive Equipment (Internal Service) Fund
Statement of Revenues, Expenses, and Changes in Fund Net Position
For (Period)

Operating Revenues:		
Billings to departments		$ 42,800
Operating Expenses:		
Cost of materials and supplies used	$ 7,000	
Other operating costs:		
Mechanics' wages	9,500	
Indirect labor	3,150	
Superintendent's salary	3,675	
Depreciation—building	2,400	
Depreciation—machinery and equipment	9,200	
Heat, light, and power	2,000	
Office salaries	3,675	
Office maintenance	200	
Total other operating costs	33,800	
Total operating expenses		40,800
Operating Income		2,000
Nonoperating Expenses:		
Interest expense		(400)
Change in net position		1,600
Net position, beginning of the period		135,000
Net position, end of the period		$136,600

ILLUSTRATION 11-4 Statement of Cash Flows

A Governmental Unit
Central Automotive Equipment (Internal Service) Fund
Statement of Cash Flows
For (Period)

Cash Flows from Operating Activities:		
Cash received from user departments	$39,000	
Cash paid to suppliers for goods and services	(9,700)	
Cash paid to employees	(19,000)	
Net cash provided by operating activities		$10,300
Cash Flows from Capital and Related Financing Activities:		
Acquisition of equipment		(25,000)
Net decrease in cash		(14,700)
Cash and cash equivalents at beginning of year		75,000
Cash and cash equivalents at end of year		$60,300*
Reconciliation of Operating Income to Net Cash Provided		
by Operating Activities:		
Operating income		$ 2,000
Adjustments to reconcile operating income to net cash provided		
by operating activities:		
Depreciation	$11,600	
Increase in vouchers payable	2,500	
Increase in accrued salaries and wages payable	1,000	
Increase in billings receivable	(3,800)	
Increase in inventories	(3,000)	
Total adjustments		8,300
Net cash provided by operating activities		$10,300

*A schedule describing the fund's noncash financing, capital, and investing activities would also be presented in the government's financial report.

The storekeeper retains this copy as evidence that the materials have been withdrawn and as the basis for posting the individual stock records to reduce the amount shown to be on hand. Subsequently, individual items on the requisition are priced, and the total cost of materials withdrawn on that requisition is computed. Sometimes requisitions are priced before they are filled. When practicable, this procedure ensures that the cost of materials requisitioned does not exceed a department's unencumbered appropriation.

Billing Rates

In the perpetual inventory record, the unit cost should include the purchase price plus transportation costs. To keep the Internal Service Fund capital intact, overhead costs must also be recovered. Overhead costs include, for example, the salary of the purchasing agent, wages of storekeepers, and amounts expended for heat, light, and power. As noted earlier, these expenses are usually allocated to each requisition based on a predetermined percentage of the cost of the materials withdrawn. The percentage is determined by dividing the estimated total stores overhead expenses for the year by the total estimated costs of materials to be issued. Assume that total estimated stores overhead expenses for the forthcoming year are $20,000 and that the estimated cost of the materials to be withdrawn during the period is $500,000. The overhead rate applicable to materials issued is 4% ($20,000 ÷ $500,000). The overhead charge upon the issue of materials that cost the Stores Fund $2,600 is $104 (4% of $2,600).

Inventory Issued

Once the requisition is priced, the department that is withdrawing the materials is billed. The entry to record the issue and billing is:

Due from General Fund	$2,704	
Cost of Materials and Supplies Issued	2,600	
Billings to Departments		$2,704
Inventory of Materials and Supplies		2,600
To record the billing and cost of materials issued to Department of Public Works on Requisition 1405.		

Note that the General Fund is billed for both the cost of the materials and a portion of the estimated overhead expenses ($2,600 + $104).

Overhead Expenses

Entries to record actual overhead expenses in the Internal Service Fund are made at the time the expenses are incurred rather than when materials are issued. For example, at the time that storekeepers' salaries ($1,000) are approved for payment, the following entry is made:

Salaries and Wages Expenses	$1,000	
Vouchers Payable		$1,000
To record storekeepers' salaries.		

Physical Inventory

In the system of accounting for materials described here, the inventory of materials and supplies on hand is available from the records at any time. To ensure that the recorded balances of materials and supplies are actually on hand, a physical inventory should be taken at least annually. Usually the actual amount on hand will be smaller than the amount shown by the records. The shortage may result from such things as shrinkage, breakage, theft, or improper recording. The records must be adjusted to equal the actual physical count by making entries on each perpetual inventory record affected. The Inventory of Materials and Supplies account in the general ledger must also be adjusted, of course. If the physical count indicates $2,000 less inventory than shown on the records, the entry is as follows:

Inventory Losses....................................	$2,000	
Inventory of Materials and Supplies		$2,000
To record inventory losses as revealed by actual physical count.		

Inventory losses must be recovered to keep the Internal Service Fund capital intact. Hence, such losses should be included when estimating the overhead expenses of the central storeroom and establishing the overhead rate to be charged.

Closing Entries

Closing entries for the Stores Fund would parallel those illustrated earlier for the Central Automotive Equipment Fund. Similarly, a Statement of Net Position; Statement of Revenues, Expenses, and Changes in Fund Net Position; and Statement of Cash Flows like those in Illustrations 11-2 to 11-4 should be prepared at least annually.

Entries in Other Funds

Thus far we have discussed the entries to be made in the Internal Service Fund. Corresponding entries are, of course, made for the departments receiving the materials. In the case of a public works department financed from the General Fund, the entry is as follows:

General Fund

Expenditures—Materials...........................	$2,704	
Due to Internal Service Fund		$2,704
To record receipt of materials by the Department of Public Works and liability to Internal Service Fund.		

Self-Insurance Fund

State and local governments sometimes find insurance coverage for some types of risks to be overly expensive or unavailable. Partly as a result, some governments "self-insure" part or all of their properties, potential liabilities for claims and judgments, and other risks. Often a government that self-insures part (or all) of its risks also centralizes its risk financing activities. The government then establishes a program designed to provide for potential losses—other than those covered by outside insurers—from its own resources. The amount of resources to be set aside should be actuarially determined to help ensure that it will cover actual losses. Also, if the government is partially insured by third-party insurers, insurance premiums will have to be paid to outside insurers for such coverage.

Other governments do not centralize their risk financing activities. These governments account for claims and judgments associated with general government activities in the various governmental fund(s) and General Capital Assets and General Long-Term Liabilities accounts in accordance with the guidance illustrated in Chapters 6 and 9.

Governments that centralize their risk financing activities should most often use either the General Fund or an Internal Service Fund to account for those activities.[1] If the General Fund is used, all covered claims and judgments are recorded as General Fund expenditures when they are paid or are due—and any remainder is recorded in the General Long-Term Liabilities accounts. Amounts charged to other (user) funds are

---

[1]Prior to issuance of GASB *Statement No. 66*, "Technical Corrections—2012—an amendment of GASB Statements No. 10 and No. 62," in March 2012 only an Internal Service Fund or the General Fund could be used to report centralized risk financing activities. *Statement No. 66* removed that restriction primarily because some governments have taxes restricted for a specific risk financing activity. In such cases, use of a Special Revenue Fund is an appropriate alternative to report the centralized risk financing activity.

11-1 IN PRACTICE

Practice Examples: Internal Service Funds

Some governments use Internal Service Funds liberally. Others avoid using them at all. The Internal Service Funds described in this City of Juneau, Alaska, narrative explanation from its Comprehensive Annual Financial Report are examples of commonly used Internal Service Funds.

Internal Service Funds are used to account for the financing of goods or services provided by one department or agency to other departments or agencies of a governmental unit, or to other governmental units, on a cost-reimbursement basis.

Central Equipment Service Fund—To provide for the maintenance, repair, and purchase of vehicles and electronics for City and Borough services. Revenues are from rental charges from user departments within the City and Borough. Expenses include labor, materials, supplies, and services. Replacement of equipment is part of the rental rate of the equipment.

Self-Insurance Fund—To provide for the cost of administering the City and Borough's Risk Management Program. This program provides coverage for the various risks of loss from legal liabilities, property damage, and workers' compensation claims. The program also provides coverage for medical, dental, and vision claims, and term life coverage. Charges for services are based on estimates of the amounts needed to pay prior and current year claims in addition to the cost of the excess and special insurance policy premiums.

---

recorded as reductions of General Fund expenditures (as reimbursements—not as revenues). The In Practice box above describes the Self-Insurance Fund of Juneau, Alaska. Use of Self-Insurance Internal Service Funds is illustrated next.

Use of Self-Insurance Internal Service Funds

In practice, self-insurance plans are often established by charging the various departments and agencies of the government for their share of the cost of the self-insurance coverage. Some governments use actuarially determined rates or the amount that an insurance policy would have cost. Other governments base the cost on other techniques that do not ensure as appropriate an allocation of self-insurance costs, either over time or among departments, as do actuarially based costing methods.

Governments that use an Internal Service Fund to account for centralized risk financing activities are required to:

- Recognize all claims and judgments liabilities and expenses in the Internal Service Fund.

- Charge the other funds amounts that are reasonable and equitable—preferably actuarially based—so that Self-Insurance Internal Service Fund revenues and expenses are approximately equal. In addition, charges may include a reasonable provision for expected future catastrophic losses. The amount of net position associated with the provision for catastrophic losses should be disclosed in the notes.

- Any net position resulting from incremental charges made to provide for expected future catastrophic losses should be disclosed in the notes as *designations* for future catastrophe losses (designations of net position should never be on the face of the statement of net position).

- Determine whether payments to the Self-Insurance Internal Service Fund that differ from the required amounts are in substance interfund transfers or loans.

Accounting for Self-Insurance Internal Service Funds

Accounting for Self-Insurance Internal Service Funds primarily involves three aspects. The first is accounting for the revenues from billings to departments for the actuarially determined contributions or premiums to be paid to the fund. The second is accounting for investment of the fund's resources. The final aspect is accounting for the recognition and settlement of claims and judgments against the fund for self-insured losses.

Accounting for Internal Service Fund investments presents no unique problems. The other two primary aspects of accounting for Self-Insurance Internal Service Funds are discussed in the following paragraphs.

11-2 IN PRACTICE

Practice Example: Self-Insurance Note Disclosure

The following is an excerpt from the note disclosures in a recent Comprehensive Annual Financial Report for the City of Berkeley, California. GASB *Statement No. 10*, "Accounting and Financial Reporting for Risk Financing and Related Insurance Issues," encourages (but does not require) governmental entities to use an Internal Service Fund to account for self-insurance activities. This sample note disclosure describes the City of Berkeley's use of an Internal Service Fund for this purpose.

2. Workers' Compensation

The City of Berkeley is self-insured for workers' compensation. Payments are made to the Workers' Compensation Self-Insurance Internal Service Fund by transfers from all City funds. Funds are available to pay claims and administrative costs of the program.

At June 30, 20X6, $1,466,175 and $18,137,000 have been accrued for public liability and workers' compensation claims, respectively.

These accruals represent estimates of amounts to ultimately be paid for reported claims and upon past experience, recent claim settlement trends, and other information. It is the City's practice to obtain an actuarial study on an annual basis. Although the amount of actual losses incurred through June 30, 20X6, are dependent on future developments, based on information from the administrators and others involved with the administration of the programs, the City's management believes that the aggregate accrual is adequate to cover such losses.

Changes in the balance of claim liabilities during the fiscal year for all self-insurance are as follows:

	Balance 07/01/X4	Incurred Claims	Claims Paid	Balance 07/01/X5	Incurred Claims	Claims Paid	Balance 06/30/X6
Public Liability	$ 1,523,353	$ 726,766	$ 623,811	$ 1,626,308	$ 681,374	$ 841,507	$ 1,466,175
Workers' Compensation	$19,509,000	$6,043,548	$5,042,548	$20,510,000	$2,214,823	$4,587,823	$18,137,000
Total	$21,032,353	$6,770,314	$5,666,359	$22,136,308	$2,896,197	$5,429,330	$19,603,175

There were no significant reductions in insurance coverage from the prior year in public liability, and there were no settlements exceeding the limits of the City's excess coverage for the past three years.

Revenues Amounts paid to or accrued by Self-Insurance Internal Service Funds based on actuarial or other acceptable estimates should be reported as revenues. Amounts paid to the Self-Insurance Internal Service Funds that differ from these charges should be evaluated carefully to determine the substance of the transaction or event. For instance, overpayments in one year may be in-substance prepaid assets of subsequent years' "premiums"—if the intent is to reduce or eliminate the need for a particular department or agency to contribute to the fund in the next year. In such cases, these overpayments should be treated as Internal Service Fund unearned revenues and as prepaid assets in the payer fund(s).

In other cases, overpayments are made to the Self-Insurance Fund from one or more other funds with no intention of payments being reduced or avoided in subsequent years. Rather, these payments might be interfund loans or advances. Or they might be made to provide a net position balance from which losses in excess of those provided for through departmental billings can be financed temporarily until made up through increased charges to insured departments or agencies in subsequent years. In the latter case, transfers should be recorded for the overpayment received.

Expenses Claims and judgments for covered losses should be recorded as expenses in the Self-Insurance Internal Service Fund—not in the insured funds. ISF expenses should be recognized when *both* of the following conditions are met:

1. Information prior to the issuance of the financial statements indicates that it is probable that an asset was impaired or a liability incurred at the date of the financial statements.
2. The amount of the loss can be reasonably estimated.

Illustrative Transactions and Entries

These principles are illustrated in the following transactions and entries for a newly established Self-Insurance Internal Service Fund of A Governmental Unit.

Transactions and Entries

1. General Fund resources of $500,000 were transferred to establish a Self-Insurance Internal Service Fund. The Internal Service Fund is (a) to acquire insurance from third-party insurers, where available at reasonable cost, and (b) to self-insure other risks.

    General Fund

(1a) Transfer to Internal Service Fund	$500,000	
Cash		$500,000
To record contribution of resources to establish a Self-Insurance Fund.		

    Internal Service Fund

(1b) Cash	$500,000	
Transfer from General Fund		$500,000
To record contribution from General Fund.		

2. Actuarially determined charges of $80,000 to the General Fund and $20,000 to the Enterprise Fund were billed for insurance or self-insurance.

    General Fund

(2a) Expenditures	$ 80,000	
Due to Self-Insurance Internal Service Fund . .		$ 80,000
To record billings for insurance coverage and self-insurance for General Fund departments.		

    Enterprise Fund

(2b) Expenses	$ 20,000	
Due to Self-Insurance Internal Service Fund . .		$ 20,000
To record billings for insurance coverage and self-insurance for the enterprise activity.		

    Internal Service Fund

(2c) Due from General Fund	$ 80,000	
Due from Enterprise Fund	20,000	
Revenues—Billings to Departments (or Premiums)		$100,000
To record revenues from billings to departments "insured" through the Internal Service Fund.		

3. Three-fourths of the amounts due from the other funds were collected.

    General Fund

(3a) Due to Self-Insurance Internal Service Fund	$ 60,000	
Cash		$ 60,000
To record payment of interfund payable.		

    Enterprise Fund

(3b) Due to Self-Insurance Internal Service Fund . . .	$ 15,000	
Cash		$ 15,000
To record payment of interfund payable.		

    Internal Service Fund

(3c) Cash	$ 75,000	
Due from General Fund		$ 60,000
Due from Enterprise Fund		15,000
To record collection of interfund receivables.		

Note again that if more than the actuarially determined amount had been paid to the Internal Service Fund, only the actuarially required amounts would be recorded as expenditures or expenses in the "insured" funds and as revenues in the

Self-Insurance Internal Service Fund. Any additional payments should be treated as discussed previously. Underpayments should be recorded as interfund payables/receivables—as in this example—if they are to be settled in some definite time frame. Otherwise, underpayments are reported as interfund transfers out of the Internal Service Fund.

4. Investments were purchased for $460,000.

Internal Service Fund

(4) Investments..............................	$460,000	
Cash....................................		$460,000
To record purchase of investments.		

5. Premiums paid to third-party insurers were $8,000, of which $500 was for coverage for the next fiscal year.

Internal Service Fund

(5) Expenses—Insurance Premiums	$ 7,500	
Prepaid Insurance	500	
Cash....................................		$ 8,000
To record payment of insurance premiums.		

6. Payments in settlement of claims and judgments incurred during the year amounted to $22,000, net of insurance recovery.

Internal Service Fund

(6) Expenses—Claims and Judgments.............	$ 22,000	
Cash....................................		$ 22,000
To record settlement of claims and judgments.		

7. The accrued liability for probable losses for claims and judgments is estimated to total $70,000 at year end, net of expected insurance recovery. (The accrued liability was zero at the beginning of the year.) Administrative expenses paid totaled $3,800. Half of the liabilities for claims and judgments are expected to be settled in the next fiscal year and the remainder in subsequent periods.

Internal Service Fund

(7) Expenses—Claims and Judgments.............	$ 70,000	
Expenses—Administrative...................	3,800	
Liability for Claims and Judgments— Current		$ 35,000
Liability for Claims and Judgments— Long-Term		35,000
Cash....................................		3,800
To adjust the accrued liabilities for claims and judgments to their year-end balances and record administrative expenses incurred.		

Note that recognition of the expenses for claims and judgments is not affected by whether the liability is current or long term.

8. Interest on investments of $27,600 was accrued at year end.

Internal Service Fund

(8) Accrued Interest Receivable..................	$ 27,600	
Revenues—Interest.......................		$ 27,600
To record accrual of interest.		

9. The fair value of the investments increased $1,200 during the year.

Internal Service Fund

(9) Investments...............................	$ 1,200	
Revenues—Net Increase (Decrease) in Fair Value of Investments......................		$ 1,200
To adjust investments to fair value.		

10. The Self-Insurance Internal Service Fund accounts were closed.

Internal Service Fund

(10) Revenues—Billings to Departments............	$100,000	
Revenues—Interest........................	27,600	
Revenues—Net Increase (Decrease) in Fair Value of Investments	1,200	
Transfer from General Fund	500,000	
Expenses—Insurance Premiums............		$ 7,500
Expenses—Claims and Judgments		92,000
Expenses—Administrative.................		3,800
Net Position		525,500
To close the accounts.		

The financial statements required for the Self-Insurance Internal Service Fund are a Statement of Net Position; a Statement of Revenues, Expenses, and Changes in Fund Net Position; and a Statement of Cash Flows. These statements would be similar to those in Illustrations 11-2 to 11-4 for the Central Automotive Repair Internal Service Fund.

DISPOSITION OF INCREASE OR DECREASE IN NET POSITION

Because charges to departments must be based on estimates, an Internal Service Fund usually has some change in net position at the end of a year. The change in net position may be disposed of in one of the following ways:

1. It may be charged or credited to the billed departments in accordance with their usage. If the intent is for the fund to break even, this procedure is theoretically the correct one.

2. The amount may be closed to Net Position with the intent of adjusting the following year's billings to eliminate the change in the balance. This procedure is a practical substitute for the first.

3. The amount may be closed to and left in Net Position without subsequent adjustment of billing rates—on the theory that the fund will have both "profitable" and "loss" years, but will break even over a period of several years.

In the absence of specific instructions, the change in net position should be closed to Net Position. No refunds, supplemental billings, or transfers should be made in the absence of specific authorization or instructions in this regard.

DISSOLUTION OF AN INTERNAL SERVICE FUND

An Internal Service Fund is dissolved when the services provided through it are no longer needed or a preferable method of providing the services is found. The net current assets of a dissolved fund are usually transferred to the funds from which the capital was originally secured. However, if capital was generated by incurring general obligation long-term debt, the net current assets are usually transferred to the Debt Service Fund that will retire the debt.

Capital assets are usually transferred to departments financed from the funds that contributed the capital or to the departments that can best use them. Unless they are transferred to one of the governmental unit's other proprietary funds, the assets are recorded in the General Capital Assets accounts. If transferred to an enterprise, they are recorded in the Enterprise Fund.

COMBINING INTERNAL SERVICE FUND FINANCIAL STATEMENTS

Internal Service Funds are reported only by fund type in the basic financial statements. Combining financial statements are presented in the CAFR for Internal Service Funds by governments having more than one Internal Service Fund.

ILLUSTRATION 11-5   Combining Statement of Net Position

Arlington County, Virginia
Internal Service Funds
Combining Statement of Net Position
June 30, 20X1
(With Summarized Comparative Totals for 20X0)

			Totals	
	Automotive Equipment	Printing	June 30, 20X1	June 30, 20X0
ASSETS				
CURRENT ASSETS:				
Equity in pooled cash and investments	$10,813,055	$ 4,275	$10,817,330	$ 8,627,792
Accounts receivable	1,650,085	2,004	1,652,089	2,628,793
Inventories	704,706	20,418	725,124	779,551
Total Current Assets	13,167,846	26,697	13,194,543	12,036,136
CAPITAL ASSETS:				
Equipment and other capital assets	56,525,607	—	56,525,607	51,981,340
Less accumulated depreciation	(28,564,145)	—	(28,564,145)	(25,975,218)
Net Capital Assets	27,961,462	—	27,961,462	26,006,122
Total Assets	$41,129,308	$ 26,697	$41,156,005	$38,042,258
LIABILITIES AND NET POSITION				
CURRENT LIABILITIES:				
Vouchers payable	$ 1,114,186	$ 93,828	$ 1,208,014	$ 357,167
Compensated absences	41,936	9,399	51,335	52,034
Obligations under capital lease	629,956	—	629,956	607,208
Due to other funds	—	—	—	127,720
Accounts payable	—	—	—	24,955
Total Current Liabilities	1,786,078	103,227	1,889,305	1,169,084
LONG-TERM LIABILITIES:				
Compensated absences	377,422	84,592	462,014	468,302
Obligations under capital lease	2,213,157	—	2,213,157	2,843,113
Total Long-Term Liabilities	2,590,579	84,592	2,675,171	3,311,415
Total Liabilities	4,376,657	187,819	4,564,476	4,480,499
Net Position:				
Net investment in capital assets	25,118,349	—	25,118,349	22,555,801
Unrestricted	11,634,302	(161,122)	11,473,180	11,005,958
Total Net Position	36,752,651	(161,122)	36,591,529	33,561,759
Total Liabilities and Net Position	$41,129,308	$ 26,697	$41,156,005	$38,042,258

The notes to the financial statements are an integral part of this statement.

Source: Derived from a recent comprehensive annual financial report of Arlington County, Virginia.

Individual fund statements for less complex Internal Service Funds may not be necessary. Sufficient individual fund detail may be provided in the individual fund columns of the combining statements and any schedules accompanying them. The total columns of the combining statements are included in the Internal Service Funds column of the proprietary fund financial statements that are part of the required Basic Financial Statements.

The combining Internal Service Fund statements included in a recent Comprehensive Annual Financial Report for Arlington County, Virginia, are presented in Illustrations 11-5, 11-6, and 11-7.

ILLUSTRATION 11-6 Combining Statement of Revenues, Expenses, and Changes in Fund Net Position

Arlington County, Virginia
Internal Service Funds
Combining Statement of Revenues, Expenses, and Changes in Fund Net Position
For the Year Ended June 30, 20X1
(With Summarized Comparative Totals for 20X0)

	Automotive Equipment	Printing	Totals June 30, 20X1	Totals June 30, 20X0
OPERATING REVENUES				
Charges for services	$20,158,821	$2,039,281	$22,198,102	$19,772,548
OPERATING EXPENSES				
Cost of store issuances	4,735,480	406,561	5,142,041	5,141,140
Personnel services	3,593,712	536,950	4,130,662	4,166,381
Fringe benefits	1,391,738	186,095	1,577,833	1,487,537
Material and supplies	136,509	186,850	323,359	347,091
Utilities	211,481	5,722	217,203	261,843
Operating equipment	35,478	—	35,478	11,161
Outside services	2,224,800	931,500	3,156,300	2,296,649
Depreciation	4,372,782	—	4,372,782	4,536,583
Total Operating Expenses	16,701,980	2,253,678	18,955,658	18,248,385
Operating Income (Loss)	3,456,841	(214,397)	3,242,444	1,524,163
NONOPERATING REVENUES (EXPENSES)				
Interest payment on capital lease	(121,616)	—	(121,616)	(115,033)
Gain/(Loss)on disposal of assets	(168,757)	—	(168,757)	261,789
Total Nonoperating Revenues (Expenses)	(290,373)	—	(290,373)	146,756
Income Before Transfers	3,166,468	(214,397)	2,952,071	1,670,919
TRANSFERS IN (OUT)				
Transfers in	—	207,699	207,699	467,785
Transfers out	(130,000)	—	(130,000)	(130,000)
Total Operating Transfers	(130,000)	207,699	77,699	337,785
Change in Net Position	3,036,468	(6,698)	3,029,770	2,008,704
Net Position, beginning of year	33,716,183	(154,424)	33,561,759	31,553,055
Net Position, end of year	$36,752,651	($161,122)	$36,591,529	$33,561,759

The notes to the financial statements are an integral part of this statement.

Source: Derived from a recent comprehensive annual financial report of Arlington County, Virginia.

ILLUSTRATION 11-7   Combining Statement of Cash Flows

Arlington County, Virginia
Internal Service Funds
Combining Statement of Cash Flows
For the Year Ended June 30, 20X1
(With Summarized Comparative Totals for 20X0)

			Totals	
	Automotive Equipment	**Printing**	**June 30, 20X1**	**June 30, 20X0**
CASH FLOWS FROM OPERATING ACTIVITIES				
Cash received from customers	$21,015,874	$2,037,277	$23,053,151	($ 2,373,925)
Cash received from interfund charges	121,656	—	121,656	19,542,695
Cash paid to suppliers	(6,595,923)	(1,398,139)	(7,994,062)	(8,053,161)
Cash paid to employees	(5,000,640)	(714,842)	(5,715,482)	(5,621,110)
Net cash provided (used) by operating activities	9,540,967	(75,704)	9,465,263	3,494,499
CASH FLOWS FROM NONCAPITAL FINANCING ACTIVITIES				
Payment of temporary loan	—	(127,720)	(127,720)	(94,207)
Temporary loan from general fund	—	—	—	127,720
Operating transfers in	—	207,699	207,699	467,785
Operating transfers out	(130,000)	—	(130,000)	(130,000)
Net cash provided by noncapital financing activities	(130,000)	79,979	(50,021)	371,298
CASH FLOWS FROM CAPITAL AND RELATED FINANCING ACTIVITIES				
Proceeds from capital lease	—	—	—	2,258,274
Principal payment on capital lease	(607,208)	—	(607,208)	(928,720)
Payment of interest on capital lease	(121,616)	—	(121,616)	(115,033)
Purchases of equipment	(6,810,338)	—	(6,810,338)	(8,553,103)
Removal Clearing	(6,783)	—	(6,783)	(10,652)
Proceeds from sale of equipment	320,241	—	320,241	1,146,808
Net cash used by capital and related financing activities	(7,225,704)	—	(7,225,704)	(6,202,426)
Net increase (decrease) in cash and cash equivalents	2,185,263	4,275	2,189,538	(2,336,629)
Cash and cash equivalents at beginning of year	8,627,792	—	8,627,792	10,964,421
Cash and cash equivalents at end of period	$10,813,055	$ 4,275	$10,817,330	$ 8,627,792
Reconciliation of operating income to net cash provided (used) by operating activities				
Operating income (loss)	$ 3,456,841	($ 214,397)	$ 3,242,444	$ 1,524,163
Adjustments to reconcile operating income to net cash provided (used) by operating activities:				
Depreciation	4,372,782	—	4,372,782	4,536,583
Increase (Decrease) in OPEB liability	—	—	—	—
(Increase) Decrease in accounts receivable	978,709	(2,004)	976,705	(2,603,777)
(Increase) Decrease in inventories	(45,258)	99,685	54,427	188,953
Increase (Decrease) in vouchers payable	793,083	32,809	825,892	(239,493)
Increase (Decrease) in compensated absences	(15,190)	8,203	(6,987)	32,808
Increase (Decrease) in prepaid	—	—	—	55,262
Net cash provided by (used) operating activities	$ 9,540,967	($ 75,704)	$ 9,465,263	$ 3,494,499

Supplemental Disclosure of Noncash Capital and Related Financing Activities:
The Printing Fund purchased assets in 20X3 under a capital lease agreement for $49,406.

The notes to the financial statements are an integral part of this statement.

Source: Derived from a recent comprehensive annual financial report of Arlington County, Virginia.

Concluding Comments

Internal Service Funds are used to account for departments or agencies of a state or local government that provide goods or services to its other departments or agencies or to other governments on a *cost-reimbursement* basis. Such activities are intended to be *self-sustaining*. Therefore, income determination and capital maintenance are important aspects of accounting and financial reporting for such funds. Accordingly, the accounting and reporting principles that apply are the same as those for Enterprise Funds, and the same financial statements are prepared.

Although use of an Internal Service Fund is never required by GAAP, activities commonly managed and accounted for through Internal Service Funds include communications, data processing, printing and duplication, motor pools and maintenance services, central purchasing and stores operations, and self-insurance programs. Such activities often involve millions of dollars of government resources, as indicated in the Arlington County, Virginia, financial statements presented in Illustrations 11-5 through 11-7.

Appropriately classifying activities that should be reported in Internal Service Funds rather than in the governmental funds and General Capital Assets and General Long-Term Liabilities accounts is essential. Significantly different accounting and reporting principles apply, and different financial statements are prepared under the two approaches. Indeed, misclassifying an Internal Service Fund activity as a general government operation—or vice versa—would result in reporting its assets, liabilities, and equities in several governmental funds, using the wrong basis of accounting, and presenting the wrong fund financial statements.

Questions

Q11-1 What advantages would a government unit expect from the use of an Internal Service Fund to account for the acquisition, storage, and provision of supplies for the various departments?

Q11-2 What major benefits should accrue from accurate cost data being maintained for activities accounted for through the Internal Service Fund?

Q11-3 Why are Internal Service Funds sometimes not subject to fixed budgetary control?

Q11-4 Internal Service Funds are required to be reported by fund type in the basic financial statements. Discuss the significance of this requirement. Compare and contrast the financial reporting required in the basic financial statements and the supplemental statements and schedules.

Q11-5 In what ways might the original capital required to establish an Internal Service Fund be acquired?

Q11-6 Under what circumstances would the *direct* cost of the goods or services provided (with no additions to acquisition cost for such items as depreciation or overhead) be the appropriate basis for Internal Service Fund reimbursement? Explain.

Q11-7 An Internal Service Fund established by a county is intended to operate on a break-even basis. How might a government dispose of increases or decreases in net position remaining at year end?

Q11-8 Accounting for an Internal Service Fund that is controlled by a fixed budget may be referred to as double accounting. Why?

Q11-9 An Internal Service Fund was established 10 years ago through the sale of 20-year bonds. What disposition should be made of the assets of the fund if it is dissolved?

Q11-10 In general, what approaches may a government use to establish the charges that a Self-Insurance Internal Service Fund should levy on user funds?

Q11-11 What funds may a government use to account for centralized risk financing activities?

Q11-12 Internal Service Fund net position is sometimes increased over time as a result of charges for services being established at a level that exceeds the costs of providing the services. Why does this practice occur? What concerns should governments have about the practice?

Q11-13 When should combining Internal Service Fund financial statements be presented in a Comprehensive Annual Financial Report? Where should they be presented?

Q11-14 What financial statements must a government present for an Internal Service Fund?

Exercises

E11-1 (Multiple Choice) Identify the best answer for each of the following:

1. Which of the following activities is *not* commonly accounted for in an Internal Service Fund?
   a. Self-insurance
   b. Central garage
   c. Landfill operations
   d. Warehouse facility

2. GAAP *require* the use of an Internal Service Fund for which of the following activities?
   a. Self-insurance
   b. Central garage
   c. Warehouse facility
   d. No specific type of activity is required to be reported as an Internal Service Fund.

3. Internal Service Funds are required to be reported in the proprietary fund financial statements
   a. by major fund.
   b. by fund type.
   c. as governmental funds.
   d. as either governmental or proprietary funds, depending on the nature of the Internal Service Fund operation.

4. GAAP require which of the following statements to be prepared for an Internal Service Fund?
   a. Statement of net position
   b. Statement of budgetary compliance
   c. Statement of cash flows
   d. Items a and c

5. In the government-wide financial statements, activities of an Internal Service Fund are
   a. always reported as governmental activities.
   b. always reported as business-type activities.
   c. reported either as governmental activities or business-type activities, depending on the fund's primary customer base.
   d. eliminated and do not affect the statements.

6. Which of the following equity classifications is *not* reported for an Internal Service Fund?
   a. Net investment in capital assets
   b. Restricted net position
   c. Retained earnings
   d. Unrestricted net position

7. Which method of cash flow reporting is used to report operating activities?
   a. Indirect method
   b. Direct method
   c. Either the indirect or direct method, depending on the method chosen for the government's Enterprise Funds
   d. Cash flow reporting is optional for Internal Service Funds.

8. Which of the following accounts would *not* typically be reported on the operating statement of an Internal Service Fund?
   a. Salaries and wages expense
   b. Supplies expense
   c. Capital outlay expense
   d. Maintenance expense

9. Which of the following transactions would *not* be allowed in an Internal Service Fund?
   a. The purchase of capital items
   b. Borrowing from another fund
   c. Transfers from other funds
   d. Negative accumulated, net changes in net position on an ongoing basis over time

10. What method of accounting does GAAP require for inventories in an Internal Service Fund?
    a. Consumption method
    b. Purchases method
    c. Acquisition method
    d. LIFO inventory costing

E11-2 (Multiple Choice) Identify the best answer for each of the following:

1. Which of the following statements about Internal Service Fund liabilities is *false*?
   a. Internal Service Funds may report both current and long-term liabilities.
   b. Internal Service Funds may not issue bonds for financing purposes.

c. Internal Service Funds may report contingent liabilities.
d. Due to Other Funds would be reported as a current liability.

2. Initial financing for Internal Service Fund activities may be obtained from
   a. advances from another fund.
   b. transfers from other funds.
   c. transfer of related materials held by governmental departments.
   d. all of the above.

3. The Yourtown Motor Pool Fund estimates that the cost of operating and maintaining its fleet of 20 vehicles during 20X8 will be $150,000. On the basis of past experience, each vehicle can be expected to be used 150 days during the year and can be expected to be driven 3,000 miles during the year. The other costs of operating the fund are estimated at $15,000 for the year. The price that the Motor Pool Fund should charge other Yourtown government departments for use of a motor pool vehicle is
   a. $50 per day.
   b. $50 per day plus $0.25 per mile.
   c. $2.50 per mile.
   d. $2.75 per mile.

4. Transfers are always reported in an Internal Service Fund operating statement as
   a. revenues.
   b. other financing sources.
   c. the last item before changes in net position.
   d. special items.

5. If a computer previously recorded in the General Capital Assets accounts is contributed to a department accounted for in an Internal Service Fund, the computer will be recorded in the Internal Service Fund accounts
   a. at the original cost recorded in the General Capital Assets accounts.
   b. at the historical cost, less the related accumulated depreciation on the contribution date.
   c. at the computer's fair market value on the contribution date.
   d. at the computer's replacement cost on the contribution date.

6. The charge by an Internal Service Fund department to other departments for a service should include
   a. the direct cost to the fund of providing the service.
   b. the direct cost to the fund of providing the service, plus a proportionate share of the fund's variable overhead costs.
   c. the direct cost to the fund of providing the service, plus a proportionate share of the fund's total overhead costs.
   d. the direct cost to the fund of providing the service, plus a proportionate share of the fund's variable overhead costs, plus a reasonable cushion for contingencies and capital growth.

7. The activity level of an Internal Service Fund is normally controlled by
   a. the appropriations made by its controlling legislative body.
   b. the flexible budget enacted by its controlling legislative body.
   c. the formal budget enacted by its controlling legislative body.
   d. the needs of the various governmental departments using its services.

8. The actuarially based charges to the General Fund from a Self-Insurance Internal Service Fund should be reported in the Internal Service Fund as
   a. transfers.
   b. revenues.
   c. deferred inflows of resources until collected.
   d. deferred revenues until claims and judgments are incurred.

9. Loans to an Internal Service Fund from another fund are reported in the Internal Service Fund cash flow statement as
   a. cash flows from operating activities.
   b. cash flows from noncapital financing activities.
   c. cash flows from capital and related financing activities.
   d. cash flows from capital and related financing activities or as cash flows from noncapital financing activities depending on the purpose of the loan.

10. Transfers from an Internal Service Fund to another fund are reported in the Internal Service Fund cash flow statement as
    a. cash flows from operating activities.
    b. cash flows from noncapital financing activities.
    c. cash flows from capital and related financing activities.
    d. cash flows from investing activities.

E11-3 (Entries) Prepare journal entries to record the following transactions of an Internal Service Fund:
1. Paid salaries of $10,000. Additional salaries accrued but not paid totaled $300.
2. Purchased equipment costing $50,000 by issuing a three-year, 10%, $45,000 note and making a down payment of $5,000.

3. Billed users for services, $100,000; $90,000 was collected during the year; $10,000 is expected to be collected during the second quarter of the next fiscal year.
4. Incurred a probable loss from claims and judgments of $25,000. Nothing is expected to be paid for at least two years, however.
5. Ordered supplies with an estimated cost of $80,000.
6. Received half of the supplies at an actual cost of $41,000. A voucher was prepared and paid.
7. Supplies that cost $25,000 were used.
8. Depreciation for the year was $16,000 on equipment and $25,000 on buildings.
9. The first interest payment on the $45,000 note (item 2) is not due until the end of the first quarter of the next fiscal year. Prepare any required adjusting entry.
10. Sold equipment with an original cost of $28,000 for $10,000. Accumulated depreciation on the equipment was $21,000 at the date of the sale.

Problems

P11-1 (Cash Flow Statement Classifications) Use the letter beside the appropriate cash flow statement classification to indicate the section of the cash flow statement in which each of the following transactions of an Internal Service Fund should be reported.
   a. Cash flows from operating activities.
   b. Cash flows from noncapital financing activities.
   c. Cash flows from capital and related financing activities.
   d. Cash flows from investing activities.
   e. Either b or c, additional information required. Explain.
   f. None of the above. Explain.
      1. Cash purchase of equipment
      2. Transfer received from the General Fund
      3. Payment of accounts payable created by the acquisition of supplies on credit
      4. A cash contribution by the General Fund for the purpose of financing half the cost of new equipment
      5. Payment of capital lease payments
      6. Cash received from the collection of billings to other departments
      7. Cash paid for investments in bonds of other governments
      8. Transfer to another fund
      9. Cash received from borrowing on a short-term basis for operations
     10. Interest paid on the short-term borrowing

P11-2 (Self-Insurance Fund Entries)
1. Christie County established a self-insurance program in 20X8 by transferring $2 million of General Fund resources to an Internal Service Fund that is to be used to account for the county's self-insurance program.
2. An actuarial study indicated that to provide the appropriate loss reserve for the county's self-insurance program for risks self-insured for various departments, $75,000 should be charged to the General Fund for the year and $15,000 to the various Enterprise Funds of the county. The $75,000 General Fund payment was made to the Self-Insurance Fund, and $30,500 was paid from the Enterprise Funds to cover the estimated cost chargeable to those funds for the next fiscal year as well as the current year's cost.
3. Administrative expenses payable from the Internal Service Fund totaled $3,600.
4. Claims filed against the county during the year were settled for $42,000 (paid).
5. The county attorney estimated that it is probable that the county will incur additional losses from current year incidents, giving rise to claims and judgments of $36,000. Of those claims, $22,000 probably will be settled and paid within 30 to 60 days after the end of the year; the remainder most likely will not be finally settled for at least two to three years. In addition, it is reasonably likely that other claims for events occurring during 20X8 will result in additional losses of $4,200.

Required   a. Prepare the journal entries required in 20X8 for the Christie County Self-Insurance Fund.
   b. Prepare the Internal Service Fund journal entries that would have been required in transactions 4 and 5 if (1) there were no Self-Insurance Internal Service Fund—and thus transactions 1, 2, and 3 had not occurred, and (2) all of the claims relate to the Central Printing Internal Service Fund.

P11-3 (Entries and Trial Balance) The city of Morristown operates a printing shop through an Internal Service Fund to provide printing services for all departments. The Central Printing Fund was established by a contribution of $30,000 from the General Fund on January 1, 20X5, at which time the equipment was purchased. The postclosing trial balance on June 30, 20X8, was as follows:

	Debit	Credit
Cash	$ 35,000	
Due from General Fund	2,000	
Accounts Receivable	1,500	
Supplies Inventory	3,000	
Equipment	25,000	
Accumulated Depreciation—Equipment		$ 8,750
Accounts Payable		4,750
Advance from General Fund		20,000
Net Position		33,000
	$ 66,500	$ 66,500

The following transactions occurred during fiscal year 20X9:
1. The publicity bureau, financed by the General Fund, ordered 30,000 multicolor travel brochures printed at a cost of $1.20 each. The brochures were delivered.
2. Supplies were purchased on account for $13,000.
3. Employee salaries were $30,000. One-sixth of this amount was withheld for taxes and is to be paid to the city's Tax Fund; the employees were paid.
4. Taxes withheld were remitted to the Tax Fund.
5. Utility charges for the year, billed by the Enterprise Fund, were $2,200.
6. Supplies used during the year cost $10,050.
7. Other billings during the period were Electric Enterprise Fund, $300; Special Revenue Fund, $4,750.
8. The inventory of supplies at year end was $5,900.
9. Collections from other funds on account during the year ended June 30, 20X9, were General Fund, $35,000; Special Revenue Fund, $4,000; and Enterprise Fund, $300.
10. Printing press number 3 was repaired by the central repair shop, operated from the Maintenance Fund. A statement for $75 was received but has not been paid.
11. The accounts receivable at June 30, 20X8, were collected in full.
12. Printing shop accounts payable of $14,950 were paid.
13. Depreciation expense was recorded, $2,500.

a. Journalize all transactions and adjustments required in the Central Printing Fund accounts. *Required*
b. Prepare closing entries for the Central Printing Fund accounts as of June 30, 20X9.
c. Prepare a postclosing trial balance for the Central Printing Fund as of June 30, 20X9.
d. Prepare a schedule computing the amounts to be reported for each of the three net position components in the statement of net position at June 30, 20X9.

P11-4 (Transaction and Closing Entries) The city of Merlot operates a central garage through an Internal Service Fund to provide garage space and repairs for all city-owned and -operated vehicles. The Central Garage Fund was established by a contribution of $500,000 from the General Fund on July 1, 20X7, at which time the building was acquired. The postclosing trial balance at June 30, 20X9, was as follows:

	Debit	Credit
Cash	$150,000	
Due from General Fund	20,000	
Inventory of Materials and Supplies	80,000	
Land	60,000	
Building	200,000	
Accumulated Depreciation—Building		$ 10,000
Machinery and Equipment	56,000	
Accumulated Depreciation—Machinery and Equipment		12,000
Vouchers Payable		38,000
Net Position		506,000
	$566,000	$566,000

The following information applies to the fiscal year ended June 30, 20Y0:
1. Materials and supplies were purchased on account for $74,000.
2. The inventory of materials and supplies at June 30, 20Y0, was $58,000, which agreed with the physical count taken.

3. Salaries and wages paid to employees totaled $230,000, including related costs.
4. A billing from the Enterprise Fund for utility charges totaling $30,000 was received and paid.
5. Depreciation of the building was recorded in the amount of $5,000. Depreciation of the machinery and equipment was $8,000.
6. Billings to other departments for services rendered to them were as follows:

General Fund	$262,000
Water and Sewer Fund	84,000
Special Revenue Fund	32,000

7. Unpaid interfund receivable balances at June 30, 20Y0, were as follows:

General Fund	$ 6,000
Special Revenue Fund	16,000

8. Vouchers payable at June 30, 20Y0, were $14,000.

Required a. For the period July 1, 20X9, through June 30, 20Y0, prepare journal entries to record all of the transactions in the Central Garage Fund accounts.
b. Prepare closing entries for the Central Garage Fund at June 30, 20Y0. (AICPA, adapted)

P11-5 (Worksheet) The trial balance for the Metro School District Repair Shop at January 1, 20X6, was as follows:

	Debit	*Credit*
Cash	$ 30,000	
Due from Other Funds	40,000	
Inventory	10,000	
Building	35,000	
Equipment	100,000	
Accumulated Depreciation—Building		$ 12,000
Accumulated Depreciation—Equipment		30,000
Vouchers Payable		35,000
Net Position		138,000
	$215,000	$215,000

The Repair Shop Fund had the following transactions during 20X6:

1. Materials purchased on account, $20,000.
2. Materials used, $7,000.
3. Payroll paid, $12,000.
4. Utilities paid, $3,500.
5. Billings to departments for repair services, $29,500.
6. Collections from departments, $27,900.
7. Equipment acquired under a capital lease; capitalizable cost, $8,000, and initial payment, $300.
8. Subsequent lease payments, $1,000, including $100 interest.
9. Depreciation on:

Buildings	$ 2,000
Equipment	4,000
	$ 6,000

10. Payments on vouchers payable (for materials), $30,000.

Required (a) Prepare a worksheet for the Metro School District Repair Shop Fund for 20X6 with columns for the beginning trial balance, transactions and adjustments, adjusted trial balance, closing entries (operating statement), and year-end statement of net position.

(b) Prepare a schedule computing the amounts to be reported for each of the three components of net position in the statement of net position of the Metro School District Repair Shop Fund at December 31, 20X6.

P11-6 (Statement of Cash Flows) From the information in P11-5, prepare the statement of cash flows (direct method) for the Metro School District Repair Shop Internal Service Fund for the year ended December 31, 20X6. (Omit reconciliation and schedules.)

Cases

C11-1 (Financial Statement Classifications—County of San Luis Obispo, California) The County of San Luis Obispo, California, maintains a Garage Internal Service Fund. The following account captions appear on the County's preclosing trial balance as of June 30, 20X6:

	Accounts	Amount
1.	Inventory	$ 48,000
2.	Charges for current services	4,630,000
3.	Depreciation expense	1,128,000
4.	Accounts payable	144,000
5.	Unrestricted net position	2,774,000
6.	Accrued payroll	37,000
7.	Capital assets, net of accumulated depreciation	3,656,000
8.	Net investment in capital assets	3,943,000
9.	Salaries and benefits expense	1,011,000
10.	Interest income	85,000
11.	Cash and cash equivalents	2,978,000
12.	Transfers out	26,000
13.	Deferred refunding amount (credit)	47,000

Required

1. Using the key below, identify where each of the preceding accounts and amounts would appear on the Internal Service Fund's financial statements.
   A. Statement of Net Position – Current Assets
   B. Statement of Net Position – Noncurrent Assets
   C. Statement of Net Position – Deferred Outflows of Resources
   D. Statement of Net Position – Current Liabilities
   E. Statement of Net Position – Noncurrent Liabilities
   F. Statement of Net Position – Deferred Inflows of Resources
   G. Statement of Net Position – Net Position
   H. Statement of Revenues, Expenses, and Changes in Fund Net Position – Operating Revenues
   I. Statement of Revenues, Expenses, and Changes in Fund Net Position – Operating Expenses
   J. Statement of Revenues, Expenses, and Changes in Fund Net Position – Nonoperating Revenues (Expenses)
   K. Statement of Revenues, Expenses, and Changes in Fund Net Position – Other Categorizations

2. The Garage Fund is one of four Internal Service Funds reported by the County of San Luis Obispo. Where in the Comprehensive Annual Financial Report should the individual financial information for the Garage Fund be reported and why?

(Based on a recent Comprehensive Annual Financial Report for the County of San Luis Obispo, California.)

C11-2 (Internal Service Funds Financial Reporting—City of Great Falls, Montana) The City of Great Falls, Montana, reports four Internal Service Funds: a Central Communications Fund, a Health and Benefit Fund, an Information Technology Fund, and a Central Garage Fund.

Required

1. Discuss how these Internal Service Funds will be reported in (a) the fund financial statements and (b) the combining financial statements.
2. Identify the financial statements that would be required for the Internal Service Funds.
3. Describe the classifications of net position that would potentially be reported in each fund.

(Based on a recent Comprehensive Annual Financial Report for the City of Great Falls, Montana.)

Harvey City Comprehensive Case

CENTRAL COMMUNICATIONS NETWORK INTERNAL SERVICE FUND

Harvey City uses an Internal Service Fund to account for its Central Communications Network. This centralized department provides information system and telephone services to all city departments and agencies. The user departments and agencies are charged for services used. The Central Communications Network is required to establish reimbursement rates that approximately equal the costs incurred by the agency to provide network services.

REQUIREMENTS

a. Prepare a worksheet for the Central Communications Network Internal Service Fund similar to the General Fund worksheet you created in Chapter 4. Enter the effects of the following transactions and events in the appropriate columns of the worksheet. (A different solution approach may be used if desired by your professor.)

b. Enter the preclosing trial balance in the appropriate worksheet columns.

c. Enter the preclosing trial balance amounts in the closing entry (operating statement data) and postclosing trial balance (statement of net position data) columns, as appropriate.

d. Prepare the 20X4 statement of revenues, expenses, and changes in fund net position for the Central Communications Network Internal Service Fund.

e. Prepare the 20X4 year-end statement of net position for the Central Communications Network Internal Service Fund.

f. Prepare the 20X4 statement of cash flows for the Central Communications Network Internal Service Fund.

BEGINNING 20X4 TRIAL BALANCE

The January 1, 20X4, trial balance for the Central Communications Network Internal Service Fund of Harvey City is presented here:

Harvey City
Central Communications Network Internal Service Fund
Trial Balance
January 1, 20X4

	Debit	*Credit*
Cash	$ 57,000	
Due from General Fund	8,000	
Inventory of Materials and Supplies	5,800	
Machinery and Equipment	850,000	
Accumulated Depreciation—Machinery and Equipment		$145,000
Vouchers Payable		3,800
Net Position		772,000
Totals	$920,800	$920,800

TRANSACTIONS AND EVENTS—20X4

1. Billings to departments for communications network services during 20X4 were as follows:

General Fund departments	$57,070
Water and Sewer Department....................	33,000
Total	$90,070

2. The department collected $61,000 from the General Fund and $30,000 from the Enterprise Fund.
3. Payroll of $60,000 was paid, and $3,000 was contributed to the statewide retirement system.
4. The department purchased materials and supplies costing $14,000 and a voucher was approved.
5. Materials and supplies costing $17,700 were used by the Central Communications Network during 20X4.
6. Vouchers payable of $15,000 were paid.
7. Depreciation for the year was $8,370.
8. Salaries and wages of $1,000 were accrued at the end of the year.

CHAPTER 12

Trust and Agency (Fiduciary) Funds

Summary of Interfund-GCA-GLTL Accounting

LEARNING OBJECTIVES

After studying this chapter, you should be able to:

- Understand and discuss the circumstances in which fiduciary funds are used to report assets held by governments in fiduciary relationships.

- Define and distinguish among the four types of fiduciary funds.

- Prepare basic journal entries for fiduciary funds.

- Prepare Agency Fund financial statements.

- Prepare Trust Fund financial statements.

- Account for common transactions that affect more than one fund and/or general capital assets and general long-term liabilities.

Governments often hold significant financial resources in a fiduciary capacity as a trustee, custodian, or agent. Some of these resources are held for the benefit of the government or its programs. Examples include resources donated as an endowment to provide investment income to finance a government program—perhaps a research program or maintenance of a recreational area—well into the future. Other resources are held for the benefit of others—individuals, other governments, or private organizations. Examples of the latter include:

- Government pension plans, the assets of which are held for the benefit of individual pension plan participants and beneficiaries.

- External investment pools, the assets of which are held for and invested for the benefit of the various governments that participate in the pool.

- Endowments that finance college scholarships for residents of the city or county.

- Taxes, insurance premiums, and dues withheld from employees' pay, which are to be transmitted to other governments, businesses, or not-for-profit organizations.

- Taxes collected as a collection agent for other governments.

Not all fiduciary relationships require the use of a fiduciary fund for accounting and reporting. Some fiduciary responsibilities of a government—such as the responsibility to employees who participate in multi-employer health care plans or retirement plans administered by other governments (e.g., the state)—are not reported in a government's financial statements because the government does not manage the assets and is not accountable for them. Assets held in a trust or agency relationship for the benefit of the government's own programs are accounted for in other funds. If such resources are available for expenditure for a specific government program or purpose, they are reported in a Special Revenue Fund. If the resources must be maintained and invested, with only the earnings available for expenditure for a government program or purpose, the resources are accounted for in a Permanent Fund, as discussed and illustrated in Chapter 9. Some enterprise activity fiduciary relationships are accounted for and reported in the Enterprise Funds, as discussed in Chapter 10.

Fiduciary funds are used to account for many of the more significant amounts of *resources that a government receives and holds in a trust or agency capacity for the benefit of others*. Trust Funds are used if the government is acting in the capacity of a trustee. Agency Funds are used to account for assets received and held by a government in an agency relationship for the benefit of others. However, most agency relationships, such as for amounts withheld from payroll, are permitted to be reported in the governmental fund or proprietary fund used to account for the activity that created the agency relationship instead of in an Agency Fund. In limited circumstances, an Agency Fund is required by a GASB standard or by law.

The government acts in a **fiduciary** capacity in all trust or agency relationships. Typically, the government is managing assets that belong to another agency or individual, and how the assets must be handled and used is directed by that agency or individual. The difference between trust and agency relationships is often one of degree. **Trust Funds** may be subject to complex administrative and financial provisions set forth in trust agreements, may exist for long periods of time, and may involve investment or other management of trust assets. Thus, Trust Fund management and accounting are often complex. **Agency Funds**, on the other hand, are primarily clearance devices for cash collected for others, held briefly, and then disbursed to authorized recipients. The essential equation for Agency Funds is that assets equal liabilities.

After explaining the accountability focus of fiduciary funds, this chapter discusses and illustrates accounting and reporting for Agency Funds. Each type of Trust Fund reported by governments is then discussed, as is the appropriate use of combining financial statements of fiduciary funds. The chapter concludes with a review of transactions that affect more than one governmental fund and/or the general capital assets and long-term liabilities accounts.

THE ACCOUNTABILITY FOCUS

General Fund and Special Revenue Fund accounting focuses primarily on operating budget compliance during a specified fiscal year. Capital Projects Fund accounting generally focuses mainly on the project, rather than on a specific year, and on the capital program or capital budget. *The accountability focus in Trust and Agency Fund accounting is on the government's fulfillment of its fiduciary responsibilities during a specified period and on its remaining fiduciary responsibilities at the end of the period.*

Trust Fund accounting must ensure that the money or other resources are handled in accordance with the terms of the trust agreement and/or applicable trust laws. The accounting for Agency Funds must ensure proper handling of collections and prompt payments to those for whom they are collected. The net amount of resources in a Trust Fund is usually indicated in a "Net Position Restricted for . . ." account. This account reflects the government's accountability as trustee for the use and disposition of the resources in its care. The accountability concept of Agency Funds is the liability concept, and even in Trust Funds there is an obligation for the government to use fund resources to discharge the assigned function. Violating trust terms could result in litigation, civil penalties, or even forfeiture of fund resources.

Essentially, the assets accounted for in fiduciary funds are not government assets. They are assets held by the government for the benefit of others. Trust and Agency Funds' existence, size, and operations are *not* important factors in judging the ability of a government to fulfill its missions or the adequacy of its resources. Hence, a government's accountability for its fiduciary responsibilities is satisfied by reporting on those responsibilities in its fiduciary fund financial statements. Fiduciary funds are *not* reported in the government-wide financial statements, as will be discussed in Chapter 13.

AGENCY FUNDS

For **internal management and accounting** purposes, Agency Funds are *conduit,* or *clearinghouse,* funds established to **account for assets (usually cash) received for and paid to other** *funds,* **individuals, or organizations**. The assets thus received are usually held only briefly; investment or other fiscal management complexities are rarely involved, except in situations such as that of the Tax Agency and Special Assessment Agency Funds illustrated later in this chapter. *For* **external financial reporting**, *however, the GASB permits only assets held for the benefit of others to be reported as Agency Fund assets (or Trust Fund assets).* Therefore, for management and accountability purposes, a county that collects taxes for itself and for other governments will use a Tax Agency Fund to account for all of the taxes it is responsible to collect—both its own and those of other governments. However, the county's portion of the taxes receivable will *not* be *reported* as assets of the Tax Agency Fund in the county's *external* financial statements. These receivables must be reported (only) in the funds to which the collections are to be disbursed from the Agency Fund.

The GASB *Codification* mandates use of an Agency Fund for only a limited number of situations. An Agency Fund is required to account for "pure" pass-through grants that the primary recipient government must transfer to, or spend on behalf of, other governments (or other entities), called *subrecipients.* In a "pure" pass-through grant, the primary recipient serves only as a "cash conduit" between the grantor agency and the subrecipient. *The primary recipient is a cash conduit if it has no administrative or direct financial involvement in the grant program.* The government should record the receipt and disbursement of a pure pass-through grant in an Agency Fund rather than as revenues and expenditures. Other pass-through grants are reported by a primary recipient as intergovernmental revenues (reflecting its role as a grantee) and as expenditures or expenses (reflecting its role as a grantor) in governmental funds or in proprietary funds, as appropriate in the circumstances. The GASB also requires use of an Agency Fund to account for and report the debt service transactions for projects financed with special assessment debt for which the government is not obligated in any manner.

As noted earlier, not all agency relationships arising in the conduct of a government's business require an Agency Fund. For example, payroll deductions for such items as insurance premiums and income tax withholdings create agency responsibilities that are often accounted for (as liabilities) in the fund used to pay the payroll. On the other hand, if payrolls are paid from several funds, it may be more convenient to pay withheld amounts to an Agency Fund initially. Using an Agency Fund permits forwarding a single check and remittance report to the recipient. As a general rule, Agency Funds should be used whenever the volume of agency transactions, the magnitude of the sums involved, and/or the management and accounting capabilities of government personnel make it either unwieldy or unwise to account for agency responsibilities through other funds.

Though agency relationships are commonly viewed as arising between the government and individuals or organizations external to it, recall that each government fund is a distinct fiscal and accounting entity. **Intragovernmental Agency Funds** are used to alleviate some of the awkwardness caused by using numerous fund accounting entities in governments. These *internal* Agency Funds are also used to establish clear-cut audit trails, where a single transaction affects several funds. Thus, although a special-imprest[1] bank account will often suffice, some governments establish an Agency Fund, in which (1) receipts must be allocated among several funds or (2) a single expenditure is financed through several funds. In the first case, a single check may be deposited in an Agency Fund and separate checks payable to the various funds drawn against it. In the latter, checks drawn against several funds are placed in an Agency Fund and a single check is drawn against it in payment for the total expenditure. Judgment is required to decide whether an Agency Fund is useful in such cases. A special imprest checking account may serve the government's needs adequately and avoid unneeded additional record keeping.

Many governments use Intragovernmental Agency Funds to maintain accountability for intergovernmental revenues in two other situations:

1. A government may receive a **grant, entitlement, or shared revenue that is permitted to be used, at the government's discretion, for programs or projects financed through more than one fund**. The government may choose to maintain accountability for the resources initially in an Agency Fund. Once the government decides the programs or projects to which to allocate the resources, they are removed from the Agency Fund and recorded in the governmental and/or proprietary fund(s) used to finance these programs or projects. *These resources are not reported in Agency Fund financial statements.*

2. A government may receive a **grant, entitlement, or shared revenue that must be accounted for in a prescribed way that differs from GAAP** for purposes of reporting to the grantor government. The recipient government may account for the resources initially in an Agency Fund. The transactions are accounted for in the Agency Fund using "memoranda" accounts that accumulate data for the prescribed special purpose reports *but are not reported in the GAAP financial statements*; instead, they are reported in the fund(s) financed as revenues and as expenditures or expenses, as appropriate, in conformity with GAAP.

Whether the agency relationship is external or internal, the *accounting* is the same, although *only assets held for the benefit of others are reported in the GAAP financial statements as Agency Fund assets*. The accounting in situations discussed thus far is not complicated. Agency Fund entries such as the following are prepared upon receipt and disbursement of cash or other assets:

Cash (or other assets)	$100,000	
Due to individual (or fund or organization)		$100,000
To record receipt of assets.		
Due to individual (or fund or organization)	$100,000	
Cash (or other assets)		$100,000
To record payment of assets.		

Note that **all Agency Fund assets are owed** to some person or organization. The **government has no equity** in the Agency Fund's assets. Marion County, Indiana's Agency Funds are described in 12-1 In Practice.

The Agency Funds cited in the preceding examples require little management action or expertise. Other Agency Funds, such as Tax Agency Funds, may involve significant management responsibilities and more complex accounting procedures.

---

[1]An imprest bank account is one to which deposits are made periodically in an amount equal to the sum of the checks written thereon. When all checks written have cleared, the bank account balance will equal a predetermined amount, often zero. Imprest bank accounts are often used to enhance cash control and/or to facilitate bank-to-book reconciliations.

12-1 IN PRACTICE

Practice Examples: Agency Funds

Most fiduciary obligations accounted for in an Agency Fund could be accounted for within a governmental fund or proprietary fund under current GAAP. Some governments use agency funds and others do not. The following are excerpts of the descriptions of the Agency Funds of Marion County, Indiana, which uses Agency Funds extensively.

Agency Funds are used to account for transactions related to assets of others held in their behalf by the County.

GROSS INCOME TAX—Established to account for gross income taxes collected by the County Treasurer to be remitted to the State of Indiana.

EXCISE TAX REFUNDS—Established to refund monies to taxpayers where an error or overpayment has occurred in the payment of excise tax.

PROPERTY TAX REFUNDS—Established to refund monies to taxpayers where an error has occurred in the payment assessment of property tax.

STATE TAXES—Established to account for inheritance taxes, forfeiture of bonds, and fines paid in all courts, which are collected by the County and remitted to the State of Indiana.

TAX SALE SURPLUS—Established to account for funds received over and above delinquent taxes received from property sold in a tax sale.

STATE PUBLIC SAFETY FEES—Established to account for various fees collected by the Courts and then remitted to the State. These include domestic violence fees, judicial fees, infraction judgments, state prosecutor fees, state docket fees, judicial salary fees, and victims of violent crimes fees.

TREASURER'S SURPLUS—Established to account for overpayment of taxes or misapplication of tax payments received.

TRUST CLEARANCE—Established as an escrow fund for assets held for disadvantaged children under the care of the Division of Family and Children. Authorization for receipts and disbursements is made through the Division of Family and Children by order of the Circuit Court.

COURT COSTS TO MUNICIPALITIES—Established to account for the portion of court costs collected and subsequently disbursed to various municipalities within Marion County.

TREASURER'S TAX COLLECTION—Established to account for advancement and final distribution of taxes collected by the County Treasurer for all taxing units within the County.

PAYROLL—Established to account for the receipt of the gross payroll transfers from all County funds having personal services expenditures and the subsequent disbursements of net payroll checks and withholdings.

JUVENILE COURT, PROBATION, CLERK OF CIRCUIT COURT, SHERIFF—Represent various custodial and fiduciary bank accounts maintained by the designated department in the course of normal operations.

Often several entities levy taxes on properties within a state, county, or other geographic area. One of the taxing governments typically bills and collects all the taxes levied on the properties in that jurisdiction. This practice avoids duplicating assessment and collection efforts and facilitates enforcement of equitable and economical tax laws. The billing and collecting unit is an agent for the other taxing units and establishes an Agency Fund such as the Tax Agency Fund described here. In the usual case, the several taxing bodies (e.g., the state, county, and school district) certify the amounts or rates of taxes to be levied for them. The billing and collecting unit then levies the total tax, including its own, against specific properties and proceeds to collect the tax. It normally makes pro rata payments of collections to the various taxing bodies during the year, often quarterly. Finally, it charges a collection or service fee to the other units.

Tax Agency Funds are used to account for all taxes a government is responsible to collect—both its own taxes and taxes for other governments. However, *only taxes receivable held for other governments are reported in the Tax Agency Fund GAAP-based financial statements.* The following example illustrates the general approach to Tax Agency Fund accounting. Though not illustrated here, detailed records of levies and collections for each property taxed, by year of levy, are required. Collections from each year's levy are distributed among the taxing bodies in the ratio of each unit's levy to the total levy of that year.

To illustrate Tax Agency Fund accounting, assume that City A serves as the property tax collecting agent for several governmental units. The city charges the other units a collection fee equal to 2% of the taxes collected for them. City A's levies and those of the other units for 20X2 and 20X3 are as follows:

	20X3		20X2	
	Amount Levied	**Percentage of Total**	**Amount Levied**	**Percentage of Total**
City A*	$100,000	25.0	$ 91,200	24.0
School District B	200,000	50.0	188,100	49.5
Park District X	50,000	12.5	49,400	13.0
Sanitary District Y	50,000	12.5	51,300	13.5
	$400,000	100.0	$380,000	100.0

*Although these taxes are the taxes of the collecting governmental unit, they are accounted for during the year in the same manner as if they were being collected for it by another unit, except no collection fees are charged on those collections.

The accounts and balances in the Tax Agency Fund trial balance at December 31, 20X2, consist of Taxes Receivable for Taxing Units of $75,000 and Due to Taxing Units of $75,000. These amounts are from the 20X2 levy. Transactions and entries illustrated for the General Fund of City A are similar to those of the other recipient governmental units.

Transactions and Entries

1. The 20X3 levies are placed on the tax roll and recorded on the books.

(1)(a) City A—Tax Agency Fund

Taxes Receivable for Taxing Units	$400,000	
Due to Taxing Units.......................		$400,000

To record 20X3 taxes placed on the tax roll.
Due to Taxing Units Ledger (Uncollected):

City A	$100,000
School District B	200,000
Park District X...............................	50,000
Sanitary District Y...........................	50,000
	$400,000

(1)(b) City A—General Fund

Taxes Receivable—Current	$100,000	
Allowance for Uncollectible Current Taxes....		$ 1,000
Revenues—Taxes.........................		99,000

To record the 20X3 tax levy, assuming 1% estimated uncollectible.

Taxes Receivable for Taxing Units may be classified into two accounts, Current and Delinquent, if desired. The distinction would be apparent in the subsidiary records, however, because (1) taxes are levied by year, and (2) a separate ledger account or column would be provided for each year's levy against each property. Appropriate subsidiary records for Taxes Receivable for Taxing Units by taxpayer would be maintained.

2. Taxes of $300,000 and interest and penalties (not previously accrued) of $15,000 are collected. Collections should be identified by type, year, and governmental unit to enable distributions in accordance with the original levies. (This detail is not provided here, so **assume the following amounts are correct.**)

(2) City A — Tax Agency Fund

Cash...................................	$315,000	
Taxes Receivable for Taxing Units............		$ 300,000
Due to Taxing Units......................		15,000

To record collections of taxes and interest and
  penalties.

Due to Taxing Units Ledger (Uncollected):

City A.....................................	$ 74,250
School District B...........................	149,625
Park District X.............................	37,875
Sanitary District Y.........................	38,250
	$300,000

Due to Taxing Units Ledger (**Collected**):

City A.....................................	$ 77,850
School District B...........................	157,050
Park District X.............................	39,825
Sanitary District Y.........................	40,275
	$315,000*

*Note that this amount includes collections of previously recorded taxes receivable for taxing units
($300,000) and the previously unrecorded interest and penalties that were collected ($15,000).

The balances in the **Collected** subsidiary ledger accounts are currently payable
to the taxing units. The **Uncollected** balances ($175,000 after these collections)
reflect amounts not yet required to be paid to the taxing units because they have
not been collected.

3. The collections (transaction 2) are paid from the Tax Agency Fund to the respective governmental units, except for a 2% collection charge levied upon the **other** governments.

(3) City A — Tax Agency Fund

Due to Taxing Units.......................	$315,000	
Cash....................................		$310,257
Due to General Fund		4,743

To record payment of amounts collected, less a 2%
  collection charge for taxes collected for other
  governmental units.

Due to Taxing Units Ledger (**Collected**):

City A.....................................	$ 77,850
School District B...........................	157,050
Park District X.............................	39,825
Sanitary District Y.........................	40,275
	$315,000

(3)(a) City A — General Fund

Cash....................................	$ 77,850	
Taxes Receivable — Current		$ 56,250
Taxes Receivable — Delinquent		18,000
Revenues — Interest and Penalties............		3,600

To record receipt of collections of taxes and interest
  and penalties from Tax Agency Fund.

Note that interest and penalties receivable would be credited instead of revenues if the
interest and penalties were previously accrued.

(3)(b) City A — General Fund

Due from Tax Agency Fund	$ 4,743	
Revenues — Tax Collection Fees		$ 4,743

To record revenues for tax collection fees charged.

The collection fee and the amounts paid to the other governments were calculated as follows:

	Collections	2% Collection Fee	Net
City A	$ 77,850	$ —	$ 77,850
School District B	157,050	3,141	153,909
Park District X.........	39,825	796	39,029
Sanitary District Y......	40,275	806	39,469
	$315,000	$4,743	$310,257

Preparing the tax roll, accounting for taxes, and handling the collections involve considerable costs, and the collecting unit usually charges for these services. The charges are legitimate financial expenditures of the various taxing units and are provided for in their budgets. The usual practice, illustrated earlier, is for the collecting unit to retain a portion of the taxes and interest and penalties collected. To illustrate further, School District B makes the following entry to record receipts from the Tax Agency Fund:

(3) School District B—General Fund

Cash...	$153,909	
Expenditures—Tax Collection Fees	3,141	
Taxes Receivable—Current		$112,500
Taxes Receivable—Delinquent		37,125
Revenues—Interest and Penalties................		7,425

To record receipt of amounts collected by City A less collection charge of 2%.

Note again that revenues from interest and penalties are recognized in this entry because they were not accrued previously.

The December 31, 20X3, Trial Balance of the Tax Agency Fund of City A is presented in Illustration 12-1. The account balances include cash of $4,743 and taxes receivable of $43,750, which are assets of the city—not held for the benefit of others. These amounts and the related liability balances are not reported in the GAAP-based Statement of Net Position of the Tax Agency Fund of City A, shown in Illustration 12-2. Rather, the cash and the city's portion of taxes receivable are reported as General Fund assets.

The December 31, 20X3, Statement of Net Position of the Tax Agency Fund of City A is presented in Illustration 12-2. A Statement of Changes in Assets and Liabilities for the Tax Agency Fund is presented in Illustration 12-3. Note that this statement does not report operating results but simply reports, in summary form, the changes in each of the fund's assets and liabilities. This reporting reflects that Agency Funds have no "operations." The Statement of Changes in Agency Fund Assets and Liabilities is not part of the basic financial statements, but a Combining

---

ILLUSTRATION 12-1 Agency Fund Trial Balance

City A
Tax Agency Fund
Trial Balance
December 31, 20X3

Cash	$ 4,743	
Taxes Receivable for Taxing Units	175,000	
Due to General Fund		$ 4,743
Due to Taxing Units (for uncollected taxes)		175,000
	$179,743	$179,743

ILLUSTRATION 12-2   Agency Fund Statement of Net Position

City A
Tax Agency Fund
Statement of Net Position
December 31, 20X3

Assets

Taxes receivable for taxing units $131,250

Liabilities

Due to taxing units (for uncollected taxes) $131,250

Statement of Changes in Agency Fund Assets and Liabilities—presenting each fund separately and the fund type totals—should be included in a government's Comprehensive Annual Financial Report. An example of this combining statement is presented in Illustration 12-11 near the end of this chapter.

Special Assessment Agency Funds

As discussed in Chapters 7 and 8, most special assessment projects—and any related debt and debt service—are accounted for and reported essentially like other capital projects, long-term debt, and related debt service. The same is not true, however, for special assessment capital improvements financed by issuing *special assessment debt* for which the government is *not obligated in any manner.*

In these cases, the government merely acts as an agent for the property owners and would not honor the debt if default occurred. Therefore, the debt is not reported in the government's financial statements. The construction or acquisition of the capital assets is reported in a Capital Projects Fund (or Enterprise Fund, if appropriate), because the government is acquiring a capital asset. However, the proceeds from the special assessment debt should *not* be called "Other Financing Sources—Bonds" because the government is not incurring debt. Rather, the GASB requires reporting a revenue account such as "Contributions from Property Owners." Further, the capital assets constructed or acquired will be reported in the General Capital Assets accounts (or an Enterprise Fund if for Enterprise Fund use).

Even when the government is not obligated in any manner for special assessment debt, the government usually acts as a debt service agent for the special assessment district. In this capacity, the government (1) collects the special assessments levied for the project and (2) pays the debt service for the property owners

---

ILLUSTRATION 12-3   Agency Fund Statement of Changes in Assets and Liabilities

City A
Tax Agency Fund
Statement of Changes in Assets and Liabilities
For the Year Ended December 31, 20X3

	Balances, January 1, 20X3	Additions	Deductions	Balances, December 31, 20X3
Assets				
Cash	$ —	$237,150	$237,150	$ —
Taxes receivable for taxing units	57,000	300,000	225,750	131,250
Total assets	$57,000	$537,150	$462,900	$131,250
Liabilities				
Due to taxing units for uncollected taxes	$57,000	$311,400	$237,150	$131,250
Total liabilities	$57,000	$311,400	$237,150	$131,250

from collections of these receivables (and, perhaps, any remaining construction phase assets). The government has a fiduciary responsibility to collect the special assessments and to remit the collections to the bondholders when debt service payments come due. Again, however, if collections do not cover required debt service payments, the government is not obligated to pay the difference and probably does not intend to do so. Thus, the government is acting purely in an agency capacity for the debt service transactions, and these transactions are accounted for in an Agency Fund.

TRUST FUNDS

The GASB classifies Trust Funds, for financial reporting purposes, as Pension (and Other Employee Benefit) Trust Funds, Investment Trust Funds, and Private-Purpose Trust Funds. The *flow of economic resources measurement focus and accrual basis of accounting* are required for reporting each type of Trust Fund. Trust Fund reporting is oriented toward providing accountability for the sources, uses, and balances of resources held in trust for others. The three types of Trust Funds and the accounting and reporting for each are fundamentally the same. Pension (and Other Employee Benefit) Trust Funds and Investment Trust Funds are simply Trust Funds used to account for specific types of common, major trust relationships of governments. Special disclosures are also required for these trusts. Private-Purpose Trust Funds are used to account for all other types of trust responsibilities (with external beneficiaries) of governments. The three types of Trust Funds are described as follows:

- **Pension** (and Other Employee Benefit) **Trust Funds** should be used to report resources that are required to be held in trust for benefits for the members and beneficiaries of defined benefit pension plans, defined contribution plans, other postemployment benefit plans, or other employee benefit plans.
- **Investment Trust Funds** should be used to report the external portion of investment pools reported by the sponsoring government, as required by GASB *Statement No. 31*.
- **Private-Purpose Trust Funds** should be used to report all other trust arrangements under which principal and income benefit individuals, private organizations, or other governments.

Financial statements for Trust Funds are relatively straightforward regardless of the type of Trust Fund. A Statement of Net Position and a Statement of Changes in Net Position are required. The Statement of Net Position reports the assets of the trusts, followed by the liabilities. The difference between the assets and liabilities is presented next as the Net Position Restricted for (purpose). The Statement of Changes in Net Position reports all additions to trust net position, followed by all deductions in trust net position. These sections are followed by the net change in net position, then the beginning and ending net position balances. These statements are illustrated for both Private-Purpose Trust Funds and for Pension Trust Funds in the following sections. The statements for an Investment Trust Fund would be similar.

An exhaustive treatment of trust law and accounting is beyond the scope of this text. Rather, some common types of Trust Funds found in state and local governments are briefly considered and illustrated here. Determining appropriate systems and procedures in specific cases may require a search of the more technical accounting, legal, and insurance literature or the assistance of specialists within one or more of these fields.

Private-Purpose Trusts

Private-Purpose Trust Funds are used to report all trust arrangements of a government *except* those related to:

- Pension (or other employee benefit) plans. Pension plans are reported in Pension Trust Funds.
- External investment pools. These are reported in Investment Trust Funds.

- Trusts that benefit general government programs. These trust relationships are reported in the appropriate governmental fund—typically a Special Revenue Fund or a Permanent Fund.
- Specific proprietary activities' fiduciary responsibilities. These are reported on a funds-within-a-fund basis in the proprietary fund, as discussed and illustrated in Chapter 10.

Private-Purpose Trust Funds may be either expendable or nonexpendable. A Private-Purpose Trust is *expendable* if the principal of the trust gift, as well as the earnings, is expendable for benefits. A *nonexpendable* private-purpose trust, of which endowments are the most common, is one for which either (1) the principal must be maintained intact and only the earnings are expendable or (2) neither the principal nor the earnings are expendable (such as loan funds).

Private-purpose trusts with expendable earnings but nonexpendable principal may be reported in one fund—with the expendable and nonexpendable net position distinguished. Alternatively, a government may establish two funds—one to account for the nonexpendable principal and to determine the expendable earnings and one to account for the expenditure of the expendable earnings. In the following example of a private-purpose trust that results from an endowment provided by a citizen to generate income required to be used to benefit the efforts of a local, not-for-profit organization, we illustrate Private-Purpose Trust Fund accounting and reporting by *using a single fund to account for a trust with both nonexpendable and expendable resources*.

Transactions and Entries

1. Cash of $210,000 was received by A Governmental Unit to establish a fund whose income is to be used to reimburse a local, not-for-profit museum for preservation and maintenance of an historic home located in the government's jurisdiction. The principal of the donations is to be maintained intact. Gains and losses from sales of investments are to be added to or deducted from principal, as required by state law.

Cash.	$210,000	
Additions—Nonexpendable Donations		$210,000

To record establishment of endowment.

2. Investments, par value $200,000, were purchased at a premium of $3,000, plus accrued interest of $400.

Investments	$203,000	
Accrued Interest Receivable	400	
Cash.		$203,400

To record purchase of investments.

3. A check for $3,000 was received for interest on the investments.

Cash.	$ 3,000	
Accrued Interest Receivable		$ 400
Additions—Interest Revenues.		2,600

To record collection of interest on investments.

4. Securities with a carrying value of $3,042 were sold for $3,055 plus accrued (previously unrecorded) interest of $35.

Cash.	$ 3,090	
Investments		$ 3,042
Additions—Interest Revenues.		35
Additions—Gain on Sale of Investments		13

To record sale of investments at a gain of $13, and related interest income of $35.

5. Interest receivable, $2,400, was recorded.

Interest Receivable on Investments	$ 2,400	
Additions—Interest Revenues.		$ 2,400

To record interest accrued on investments.

Recall from Chapter 5 that premium amortization is *not* required if accounting for investments at fair value.

6. The fair value of the investments increased by $25.

Investments	$ 25	
Additions—Increase in Fair Value of Investments		$ 25

To record increase in investment fair value.

7. A Governmental Unit paid $2,000 to the not-for-profit organization to reimburse preservation and maintenance costs incurred by the organization. The not-for-profit organization submitted $15 of invoices for reimbursement that A Governmental Unit has approved but has not yet paid.

Deductions—Preservation and Maintenance Costs	$ 2,015	
Cash.		$ 2,000
Vouchers Payable.		15

To record reimbursement of preservation and maintenance costs.

8. Closing entries were prepared.

Additions—Nonexpendable Donations	$210,000	
Additions—Interest Revenues.	5,035	
Additions—Gain on Sale of Investments	13	
Additions—Increase in Fair Value of Investments	25	
Deductions—Preservation and Maintenance Costs		$ 2,015
Net Position—Restricted for Endowment— Nonexpendable		210,038
Net Position—Restricted for Historical Preservation—Expendable.		3,020

To close accounts.

The gain on sale of investments is added to the nonexpendable principal of the trust because the trust agreement specifies that gains and losses, both realized and unrealized, affect the trust principal and are not expendable. If the trust agreement or applicable laws specify that gains and losses are part of the expendable income from a trust, the net gains or losses affect the amount of expendable net position.

The Statement of Net Position and the Statement of Changes in Net Position for this Private-Purpose Trust Fund are presented in Illustrations 12-4 and 12-5. As noted earlier, the statements are relatively simple presentations, reporting on fiduciary accountability for the trust assets. If endowments are in the form of operating assets, accounting for the trust is more complex because of the issues involved in properly determining the amount of expendable income. The financial statements remain relatively simple, however, as demonstrated later in the chapter in the statements for a defined benefit pension plan.

Investment Trusts

When a government pools (and commingles) its resources primarily for investment purposes with those of one or more other legally separate entities that are not part of its reporting entity, it has established an external investment pool. *External investment pool managers receive resources from participants, invest the resources to earn a return, typically maintain records at fair value, identify the portion of net position to which each participant is entitled, and disburse resources to*

ILLUSTRATION 12-4 Statement of Net Position

A Governmental Unit
Historical Society Private-Purpose Trust Fund
Statement of Net Position
At End of Fiscal Year

Assets:

Cash	$ 10,690
Investments	199,983
Interest receivable on investments	2,400
Total assets	213,073

Liabilities:

Accounts payable	15

Net Position:

Restricted for endowment—nonexpendable	210,038
Restricted for preservation and maintenance costs—expendable	3,020
Total net position	$213,058

ILLUSTRATION 12-5 Statement of Changes in Net Position

A Governmental Unit
Historical Society Private-Purpose Trust Fund
Statement of Changes in Net Position
For Fiscal Year

Additions:

Contributions	$210,000
Investment earnings:	
Interest earnings	5,035
Net increase in fair value of investments	38
Total investment earnings	5,073
Total additions	215,073

Deductions:

Reimbursement of preservation and maintenance costs	2,015
Change in net position	213,058
Net position, beginning	—
Net position, ending	$213,058

---

participants when withdrawals are made. The portion of the assets held for other entities is required to be reported in an *Investment Trust Fund*. Significant amounts of assets are managed in many investment trust funds. The net position of Florida's investment trust funds reported in its 2010 financial statements was almost $7 billion. The primary additions to such funds are new contributions and investment income (including changes in fair value of investments). The primary deductions are withdrawals and investment expenses incurred. The financial statements of an Investment Trust Fund are the same as for a Private-Purpose Trust Fund and so are not illustrated here.

Pension Trusts Pension Trust Funds (PTFs) are the largest Trust Funds of many governments. They are growing rapidly, and the cost to governments of contributions to them is significant. Their ability to pay pensions on schedule is vitally important to individual retirees, to workforce morale, and to the SLG's solvency.

Many types of retirement plans exist within governments. Both state and local governments may have retirement plans, though in some states employees of all governmental units of a certain type (e.g., municipalities) or all employees within certain functional fields (e.g., teachers, police, and firefighters) are included in a plan within a statewide retirement system. In some cases, these plans are integrated with federal social security benefits; in others, employees are not covered under that program. The administrative mechanisms established also differ widely. Some retirement plans are managed and accounted for by the finance department or some other executive agency of the government. In other cases, an independent board, or even a separate corporation, is charged with retirement system management and accountability. These entities are often referred to as public employee retirement systems (PERS).

In addition to pension benefits, many governments also provide other postemployment benefits (OPEB), such as postemployment health care and life insurance. Postemployment *health care* benefits—the most common OPEB—may be provided either through the government's pension plan or through a separate plan. But the GASB defines postemployment benefits such as life insurance as OPEB *only* if provided separately from a pension plan. The following discussion of pension plans is equally applicable to OPEB plans.

Plans are classified according to whether they are for (1) the employees of only one unit of government, **single-employer plans**, or (2) the employees of more than one employer government, **multiple-employer plans**. The GASB further categorizes multiple-employer plans as either *agent* PERS or *cost-sharing* PERS based on the extent to which the interests and risks of the various employer governments are integrated. Plans that are aggregations of **single-employer PERS**, with pooled administrative and investment functions, are referred to as **agent PERS**. Each entity participating in an **agent** PERS receives a separate actuarial valuation to determine its required periodic contribution. **Cost-sharing** PERS [plans] are essentially one large pension plan with cost-sharing arrangements. All risks and costs, including benefits costs, are shared proportionately by the participating entities. Only one actuarial valuation is performed for the PERS as a whole. Likewise, the same contribution rate applies to each participating entity.[2]

Of far more consequence to sound public finance policy and to the public interest generally is the disparate array of financial management practices relating to retirement systems. Government plans are not subject to the federal ERISA (Employee Retirement Income Security Act) regulations on vesting, funding, and the like, though various PERISA (Public Employee Retirement Income Security Act) and similar bills have been proposed in Congress in years past. Some governments are on a *pay-as-you-go* basis—pension payments are paid from current revenues. In such cases, pensioners must depend on the adequacy of current revenues and compete with other demands for appropriations and other uncertainties of the budget process. At the other extreme, some governments have *overfunded* retirement systems. Most government pension plans fall between these extremes and are actuarially sound. (It is more common for other postemployment benefits than for pension benefits to be provided on a pay-as-you-go basis.)

Accounting and reporting for pension **plans** and PTFs must be **distinguished from** accounting and reporting for the pension costs and liabilities of **employer funds and the general long-term liability accounts of the employer government(s)**. However, accounting and reporting for pension plans are the primary focus of the discussion of pensions in this chapter, though accounting and reporting requirements for the employer governments are outlined briefly. Also, the discussion here assumes that the pension plans are **defined benefit plans**, in which the amounts of benefits to be paid under the plan are specified, rather than **defined contribution plans**, which specify a level of contributions to be made but do not guarantee a specific level of benefits.

---

[2]GASB *Codification*, secs. Pe5.511, 522, and 565.

Accounting Standards

In 1994, the GASB completed a long-term project on pensions and issued three statements: *Statement No. 25,* "Financial Reporting for Defined Benefit Pension Plans and Note Disclosures for Defined Contribution Plans"; *Statement No. 26,* "Financial Reporting for Postemployment Healthcare Plans Administered by Defined Benefit Pension Plans"; and *Statement No. 27,* "Accounting for Pensions by State and Local Governmental Employers." These pronouncements superseded all previous government pension standards. In 2007 the GASB issued *Statement No. 50,* "Pension Disclosures—an Amendment of GASB *Statements No. 25 and No. 27.*"

The GASB expects to issue new statements on accounting and reporting for pension plans and on employer accounting for pensions soon. The guidance will not become effective until fiscal years ending June 30, 2013, or later. The statements will require fundamental changes in reporting for pension plans and in employer government reporting of pension expense and pension liabilities.

In 2004, the GASB issued two statements on other postemployment benefits: *Statement No. 43,* "Financial Reporting for Postemployment Benefit Plans Other Than Pension Plans," and *Statement No. 45,* "Accounting and Financial Reporting by Employers for Postemployment Benefits Other Than Pensions." These statements superseded the prior guidance on other postemployment benefits, including GASB *Statement No. 26.* Once the new pension accounting guidance is adopted, the GASB is expected to issue statements adopting substantially the same guidance for other postemployment benefits.

The primary accounting and reporting requirements of *Statement No. 25* and *Statement No. 43* are as follows:

- Plan assets and liabilities (primarily short-term liabilities) are presented in a **Statement of Plan Net Position**. Additions and deductions to plan net position are presented in a **Statement of Changes in Plan Net Position**.
- **The Statement of Changes in Plan Net Position** categorizes changes as *additions* and *deductions* rather than as revenues, expenses, gains, or losses.
- **Investments** (excluding insurance contracts) are reported **at fair value**. Fixed income securities are *not* amortized.
- Capital assets used in plan operations are reported at historical cost and depreciated.
- **Actuarial information** is not reported in the basic financial statements or the notes to the financial statements. These data are **reported as required supplementary information**.
- **Parameters** (e.g., acceptable actuarial assumptions) are **established** for actuarially determined information.
- A standardized pension benefit obligation measurement is *not* required—several different actuarial cost methods are acceptable under the parameters.

Actuarial information is reported in two schedules included in required supplementary information—a Schedule of Funding Progress and a Schedule of Employer Contributions. Actuarial information is not reported in the Statement of Plan Net Position or in the Statement of Changes in Plan Net Position. Because accounting and reporting requirements for other postemployment benefits are largely the same as for pensions and pension plans, only Pension Trust Fund accounting and reporting are illustrated in the next section.

Although the standards indicate that the flow of economic resources measurement focus and accrual basis of accounting are used for Trust Funds, the deductions and liabilities of Pension Trust Funds and OPEB Trust Funds are measured, in substance, using an approach more consistent with the modified accrual basis used for governmental funds. Even though additions and assets are recognized using the flow of economic resources measurement focus and basis of accounting, you will see in the financial statements presented later that the key liability and

12-2 IN PRACTICE

Defined Benefit Pension Trust Funds: Statement Information vs. Schedule of Funding Progress

Government/Retirement Plan	Date	Net Position Restricted for Benefits	Unfunded Accrued Actuarial Liability*
California Public Employee Retirement System (CalPERS)	6/30/10	$203.4 billion	$ 49.1 billion
State Teachers' Retirement System of Ohio	6/30/11	63.1 billion	40.7 billion
North Dakota Teachers' Fund for Retirement	6/30/11	1.7 billion	927 million
City of Seattle Pension Trust Funds	12/31/10	1.8 billion	947 million
Louisville (KY)/Jefferson County Retirement Plans for Policemen and Firemen	6/30/10	13.9 million	29.8 million

*Based on most recent actuarial valuation data and taken from the schedule of funding progress.

related cost of a pension plan or OPEB plan (i.e., the liability for benefits that the government is obligated to pay in future years) is not reported in the statement of net position, but in the actuarial schedule of funding progress. Likewise, deductions are not reported for additional costs incurred to provide future benefits. Liabilities and deductions for these costs are recognized only when due. Actuarial information is presented only in the actuarial schedules.

In practice, the difference in information about defined benefit pension plans presented in the financial statements and that presented in the required supplementary information is significant. In Practice 12-2 provides a table that demonstrates how the statement of net position reports the amount of net position available to provide for future benefit payments, not whether that amount is adequate. Financial statement users must depend on the required supplementary information (schedule of funding progress) to determine the adequacy of those assets. Each of the defined benefit plans reported in the table has significant net position, but none is fully funded. Other pension plans might have fewer dollars of net position, yet be overfunded.

Retirement Fund Example

To illustrate the accounting for a pension plan—whether it is a single-employer, agent, or cost-sharing plan—assume that a fund is already in operation and its beginning trial balance appears as in Illustration 12-6. Assume also that (1) the plan is financed by employer contributions, employee contributions, and investment earnings and (2) the equities of employees resigning or dying prior to retirement are returned to them or to their estates, but employer contributions on their behalf remain in the fund. The nature and purposes of most of the accounts in the beginning trial balance will become evident in the course of the illustration. The Net Position—Restricted for Pension Benefits account is the residual balance of the pension plan assets and deferred outflows of resources minus its liabilities and deferred inflows of resources.

ILLUSTRATION 12-6 Pension Trust Fund Trial Balance

A Governmental Unit
Pension Trust Fund
Trial Balance
At Beginning of Fiscal Year (Date)

	Debit	Credit
Cash	$ 56,000	
Due from General Fund	8,000	
Interest Receivable	3,000	
Investments	985,000	
Due to Resigned Employees		$ 3,000
Annuities Payable		2,800
Net Position—Restricted for Pension Benefits		1,046,200
	$1,052,000	$1,052,000

The following transactions and events occurred during the year and would be recorded in the **Pension Trust Fund** as indicated:

Transactions and Entries

1. Employer ($50,000) and employee ($125,000) contributions were accrued in the General Fund.

(1) Due from General Fund	$175,000	
Additions—Employee Contributions		$125,000
Additions—Employer Contributions.		50,000
To record employee and employer contributions due from the General Fund.		

Although the employer contribution would be budgeted in the fund through which payrolls are paid, the plan in this example is not under formal budgetary accounting control. The levels of its activity are determined by such factors as levels of employment in the government and the changes in status of participants in the system.

2. A check for $170,000 was received from the General Fund.

(2) Cash	$170,000	
Due from General Fund		$170,000
To record receipt of contributions from the General Fund.		

3. Accrued interest of $45,000 on investments was recorded.

(3) Interest Receivable..........................	$ 45,000	
Additions—Interest Income		$ 45,000
To record accrued interest receivable on investments.		

4. Interest receivable of $40,000 was collected.

(4) Cash	$ 40,000	
Interest Receivable........................		$ 40,000
To record receipt of interest receivable.		

5. Three nonvested employees resigned and one died prior to retirement. The accumulated balances of their contributions totaled $16,000 and $9,000, respectively.

(5) Deductions—Payments to Deceased Employees' Estates	$ 9,000	
Deductions—Payments to Resigned Employees ..	16,000	
Due to Deceased Employees' Estates		$ 9,000

Due to Resigned Employees...............		16,000

To record amounts due upon employee resignations and the death of one employee prior to retirement.

6. Checks were mailed to two of the resigned employees ($13,000) and to the estate of the deceased employee ($9,000).

(6) Due to Deceased Employees' Estates...........	$ 9,000	
Due to Resigned Employees	13,000	
Cash		$ 22,000

To record payments to former employees and to the estate of a deceased employee.

7. Annuities payable of $24,000 were accrued.

(7) **Deductions—Annuity Payments**	$ 24,000	
Annuities Payable.........................		$ 24,000

To record accrual of liability for annuities payable.

8. Annuities payable were paid except for that owed to one retiree who has moved and has no known mailing address.

(8) Annuities Payable.........................	$ 23,000	
Cash		$ 23,000

To record payment of annuities.

9. Additional investments were made for $150,000 less a discount of $7,000.

(9) Investments	$ 143,000	
Cash		$143,000

To record investments.

10. At year end the following adjusting entry was made because the fair value of the fund's investments had decreased by $20,000 during the year.

(10) Deductions—Net Increase (Decrease) in Fair Value of Investments	$ 20,000	
Investments...............................		$ 20,000

To record the decrease in the fair value of the investments of the fund.

All PTF net position additions and deductions are closed to Net Position—Restricted for Pension Benefits.

The closing entry for the illustrative Pension Trust Fund is as follows:

Closing Entries

(C1) Additions—Employee Contributions	$125,000	
Additions—Employer Contributions............	50,000	
Additions—Interest	45,000	
Deductions—Net Increase (Decrease) in Fair Value of Investments.................		$ 20,000
Deductions—Payments to Deceased Employees' Estates......................		9,000
Deductions—Payments to Resigned Employees		16,000
Deductions—Annuity Benefits...............		24,000
Net Position—Restricted for Pension Benefits ..		151,000

To close the accounts.

The postclosing trial balance for the illustrative Pension Trust Fund is presented in Illustration 12-7. Illustrations 12-8 and 12-9 display the plan's basic financial statements.

Most of the data presented in the Schedule of Funding Progress and the Schedule of Employer Contributions are *not* derived from the accounting system but are provided by the actuary. Examples of these schedules for our illustrative

ILLUSTRATION 12-7   Pension Trust Fund Postclosing Trial Balance

A Governmental Unit
Pension Trust Fund
Postclosing Trial Balance
At Close of Fiscal Year (Date)

Cash	$ 78,000	
Due from General Fund	13,000	
Interest Receivable	8,000	
Investments	1,108,000	
Due to Resigned Employees		$ 6,000
Annuities Payable		3,800
Net Position—Restricted for Pension Benefits		1,197,200
	$1,207,000	$1,207,000

ILLUSTRATION 12-8   Statement of Plan Net Position

A Governmental Unit
Pension Trust Fund
Statement of Plan Net Position
As of Fiscal Year (Date)

Assets:

Cash		$ 78,000
Receivables:		
Employer	$ 13,000	
Interest	8,000	
Total Receivables		21,000
Investments at Fair Value:		
U.S. Government Obligations	325,300	
Municipal Bonds	220,300	
Stocks	562,400	
Total Investments		1,108,000
Total Assets		1,207,000
Liabilities:		
Refunds Payable		6,000
Annuities Payable		3,800
Total Liabilities		9,800
Net Position—Restricted for Pension Benefits		
(See Schedule of Funding Progress)		$1,197,200

PTF are in Illustration 12-10. The data are assumed, but note the dramatic difference between that reported in the financial statements and that in the actuarial schedules. Even actuarially underfunded pension plans typically have significant Net Position—Restricted for Pension Benefits because the liability for future benefits is not included in determining net position.

Employer Government/Employer Fund Reporting

GASB *Statement No. 27* requires governments to measure their annual pension costs, or APC. The APC is measured differently by employer governments that participate in cost-sharing defined benefit plans than by those participating in

---

ILLUSTRATION 12-9 Statement of Changes in Plan Net Position

A Governmental Unit
Pension Trust Fund
Statement of Changes in Plan Net Position
For the Fiscal Year Ended (Date)

Additions:		
Contributions:		
Employee	$125,000	
Employer	50,000	
Total Contributions		$ 175,000
Investment Income:		
Interest	45,000	
Net Decrease in Fair Value of Investments	(20,000)	
Total Investment Income		25,000
Total Additions		200,000
Deductions:		
Benefits	24,000	
Refunds	25,000	
Total Deductions		49,000
Net Increase for the Year		151,000
Net Position—Restricted for Pension Benefits:		
Beginning of Year		1,046,200
End of Year		$1,197,200

---

single-employer or agent plans. The APC for an employer government involved in a cost-sharing plan is simply the contractually required contribution to the plan. For employers that have single-employer plans or that participate in agent plans, the APC is:

- Measured as the employer's *actuarially determined* annual required contribution (ARC).
- Adjusted for interest on any beginning net pension obligation (NPO) balance (the net pension obligation is the cumulative difference between the APC and the employer's contributions to the plan).
- An adjustment to the annual required contribution to eliminate any actuarial amortization resulting from past contribution deficiencies or past excess contributions.

Statement No. 27 also requires that the annual required contribution for governments participating in single-employer or agent plans be measured by using the same parameters, or guidelines, as required for pension plan accounting and reporting by *Statement No. 25*.

Parameters are established for such things as actuarial assumptions, actuarial cost methods that may be used, and length of amortization periods. A government's annual pension cost (APC) must be computed in a manner that meets these *Statement No. 27* parameters if it is to be used as the basis for reporting the government's *employer* pension liability, expenditure, and expense in accordance with GAAP. This statement applies to both governmental and proprietary funds.

Employer fund/employer government accounting and reporting are addressed in GASB *Statement No. 27*. As discussed in Chapter 6:

1. Governmental fund employers must report as expenditures the portion of the annual pension cost that has been or will be funded with expendable available financial resources of the fund, i.e., the amount that is due and payable for the fiscal year.

2. If a portion of the annual pension cost of governmental fund employers is not payable from expendable available financial resources, the unfunded portion is accounted for as

ILLUSTRATION 12-10   Required Supplementary Information

A Governmental Unit
Pension Trust Fund
Schedule of Funding Progress
(in thousands)
December 31, 20X1

Actuarial Valuation Date	Actuarial Value of Assets (a)	Actuarial Accrued Liability (AAL) Entry Age (b)	Unfunded AAL (UAAL) (b − a)	Funded Ratio (a/b)	Covered Payroll (c)	UAAL as a Percentage of Covered Payroll [(b − a)/c]
12/31/W6	$ 990	$1,233	$243	80.3%	$433	56.1%
12/31/W7	1,025	1,173	148	87.4	396	37.4
12/31/W8	1,175	1,373	198	85.6	419	47.3
12/31/W9	1,200	1,370	170	87.6	408	41.7
12/31/X0	1,280	1,421	141	90.1	406	34.7
12/31/X1*	1,300	1,448	148	89.8	401	36.9

Schedule of Employer Contributions
(in thousands)

Employer Contributions

Year Ended June 30	Annual Required Contribution	Percentage Contributed
20W6	$46	100%
20W7	40	100
20W8	42	100
20W9	41	100
20X0	42	100
20X1*	44	100

*Assume that 20X1 is the current year.

an unfunded pension liability, called the net pension obligation, in the General Long-Term Liabilities accounts and reported in the government-wide financial statements.

3. For proprietary and trust fund employers, the APC is reported as pension expense and a liability recorded for any underfunded portion.

GASB *Statement No. 45* on employer accounting and reporting for other post-employment benefits requires virtually the same accounting and reporting for these benefits as discussed in this section for pensions.

COMBINING TRUST AND AGENCY FUND FINANCIAL STATEMENTS

In the basic financial statements of a SLG, the fiduciary funds should be reported in the fund financial statements, as explained in Chapter 13. In addition, if an entity uses more than one each of the various types of Trust Funds, combining financial statements are required for these funds in the Comprehensive Annual Financial Report (CAFR), as discussed in Chapter 15.

A Combining Statement of Changes in Assets and Liabilities—All Agency Funds should be presented in the CAFR if a SLG has more than one Agency Fund. A Combining Statement of Changes in Assets and Liabilities—All Agency Funds

ILLUSTRATION 12-11   Combining Statement of Changes in Assets and Liabilities

Illustrative County
Combining Statement of Changes in Assets and Liabilities—Agency Funds
For the Year Ended June 30, 20X7
(in thousands)

Payroll Clearing	**Balance 06/30/X6**	**Additions**	**Deductions**	**Balance 06/30/X7**
Assets				
Cash and cash equivalents	$ 1,076	$ 403,728	$ 403,731	$ 1,073
Liabilities				
Deposits and rebates	$ 1,076	$ 403,728	$ 403,731	$ 1,073
Cooperative Facilitation				
Assets				
Cash and cash equivalents	$ 1,241	$1,479,380	$1,479,233	$ 1,388
Liabilities				
Deposits and rebates	$ 1,011	$ 434,547	$ 434,214	$ 1,344
Due to other governments	230	1,044,833	1,045,019	44
Total liabilities	$ 1,241	$1,479,380	$1,479,233	$ 1,388
School Districts				
Assets				
Cash and cash equivalents	$179,956	$6,456,993	$6,490,779	$146,170
Liabilities				
Due to other governments	$179,956	$6,456,993	$6,490,779	$146,170
Other				
Assets				
Cash and cash equivalents	$ 20,682	$ 518,912	$ 519,847	$ 19,747
Liabilities				
Due to other governments	$ 6,694	$ 200,090	$ 201,588	$ 5,196
Deposits and rebates	13,988	318,822	318,259	14,551
Total liabilities	$ 20,682	$ 518,912	$ 519,847	$ 19,747
Totals—All Agency Funds				
Assets				
Cash and cash equivalents	$202,955	$8,859,013	$8,893,590	$168,378
Liabilities				
Due to other governments	$186,880	$7,701,916	$7,737,386	$151,410
Deposits and rebates	16,075	1,157,097	1,156,204	16,968
Total liabilities	$202,955	$8,859,013	$8,893,590	$168,378

is presented in Illustration 12-11. Note that the statement is not an operating statement because, as discussed earlier, Agency Funds do not have operations per se. Rather, this statement simply discloses the changes in the unit's custodial responsibilities.

ADDITIONAL INTERFUND–GENERAL CAPITAL ASSET–GENERAL LONG-TERM LIABILITY ACCOUNTING ILLUSTRATIONS

At this point all the types of funds commonly employed in state and local government accounting have been presented and discussed, as have the General Capital Assets and General Long-Term Liabilities accounts. Also, the recording and reporting of representative types of transactions have been illustrated for each of these accounting entities. Recall that at the end of Chapter 9, accounting for representative transactions that affect more than one governmental fund and/or the General Capital Assets and General Long-Term Liabilities accounts was illustrated to crystallize the reader's understanding of the various interrelationships between and among those accounting entities. This section extends the Chapter 9 illustration by presenting entries for additional interfund–general capital assets–general long-term liabilities transactions—those that involve at least one proprietary or fiduciary fund.

Transactions and Entries

1. Seventy percent of the actuarially required contributions from the General Fund and from an Enterprise Fund was paid to the government's Pension Trust Fund. The actuarially required contribution was $800,000 for each fund. The balance of the required contributions has not been scheduled for payment in the near future.

Pension Trust Fund

Cash	$1,120,000	
Additions—Employer Contributions.............		$1,120,000
To record receipt of employer fund contributions.		

Enterprise Fund

Expenses—Pensions............................	$ 800,000	
Cash		$ 560,000
Net Pension Obligation		240,000
To record the pension expense for the year.		

General Fund

Expenditures—Pensions	$ 560,000	
Cash		$ 560,000
To record payment of budgeted pension fund contributions.		

General Capital Assets and Long-Term Liabilities accounts

Net Position...................................	$ 240,000	
Net Pension Obligation		$ 240,000
To record the long-term portion of the liability for the underfunding of the General Fund actuarially required pension contribution.		

2. A "payment in lieu of tax" of $900,000 was made from an Enterprise Fund to the General Fund. The payment was not for services.

General Fund

Cash	$ 900,000	
Transfer from Enterprise Fund		$ 900,000
To record "payment in lieu of tax" from Enterprise Fund.		

Enterprise Fund

Transfer to General Fund	$ 900,000	
Cash		$ 900,000
To record payment in lieu of taxes transfer to General Fund.		

3. Water Enterprise Fund billings to other funds for water services were as follows:

General Fund	$ 300,000
Special Revenue Fund	20,000
Internal Service Fund.................	50,000
Total	$ 370,000

Water Enterprise Fund

Due from Other Funds............................	$ 370,000	
Revenues—Charges for Services		$ 370,000
To record interfund billings for services.		

General Fund

Expenditures—Utilities..........................	$ 300,000	
Due to Enterprise Fund.........................		$ 300,000
To record billings for water used.		

Special Revenue Fund

Expenditures—Utilities..........................	$ 20,000	
Due to Enterprise Fund.........................		$ 20,000
To record billings for water used.		

Internal Service Fund

Expenses—Utilities	$ 50,000	
Due to Enterprise Fund.........................		$ 50,000
To record billings for water used.		

4. A $500,000, two-year advance was made from an Internal Service Fund to a Capital Projects Fund.

Internal Service Fund

Advance to Capital Projects Fund	$ 500,000	
Cash		$ 500,000
To record advance to Capital Projects Fund.		

Capital Projects Fund

Cash	$ 500,000	
Advance from Internal Service Fund		$ 500,000
To record advance received from Internal Service Fund.		

5. Because of insufficient Enterprise Fund revenues, debt service payments on long-term Enterprise Fund notes payable issued to finance capital asset acquisitions have been regularly paid from general government resources. The government determines that the Enterprise Fund will never be able to finance the debt service on the notes ($2,000,000) and reclassifies the notes payable to the General Long-Term Liabilities accounts. The notes will be serviced from general revenues.

Enterprise Fund

Notes Payable	$2,000,000	
Revenues—Capital Contributions*		$2,000,000
To record reclassification of Enterprise Fund notes.		

General Long-Term Liabilities accounts

Net Position..................................	$2,000,000	
Notes Payable		$2,000,000
To record reclassification of notes payable from Enterprise Fund.		

*This will be reported as a *transfer* in the *government-wide* Statement of Activities.

6. The government transferred $2,500,000 from the General Fund to provide initial financing for an Internal Service Fund.

General Fund

Transfer to Internal Service Fund.................	$2,500,000	
Cash		$2,500,000
To record transfer to Internal Service Fund.		

Internal Service Fund

Cash	$2,500,000	
Transfer from General Fund		$2,500,000
To record receipt of transfer from General Fund.		

7. Equipment with an original cost of $20,000 (fair market value, $12,000) was "transferred" from a General Fund department to an Enterprise Fund department halfway through its useful life.

General Capital Assets accounts

Net Position....................................	$ 10,000	
Accumulated Depreciation—Equipment	10,000	
Equipment....................................		$ 20,000

To record reclassification of equipment as Enterprise Fund asset.

Enterprise Fund

Equipment......................................	$ 20,000	
Accumulated Depreciation		$ 10,000
Revenues—Capital Contributions*		10,000

To record general government contribution of capital asset.

*This will be reported as a *transfer* in the *government-wide* Statement of Activities.

8. General obligation bonds were issued several years ago to provide the initial capital of an Enterprise Fund. The bonds have been serviced from general government taxes and other revenues. However, the Enterprise Fund activity has been so profitable that the governing body has decided to transfer money as a "dividend" every six months from the Enterprise Fund to the Debt Service Fund to pay the semiannual debt service on the bonds. The first dividend was paid, $70,000.

Enterprise Fund

Transfer to Debt Service Fund	$ 70,000	
Cash		$ 70,000

To record payment of dividend transfer to Debt Service Fund.

Debt Service Fund

Cash	$ 70,000	
Transfer from Enterprise Fund		$ 70,000

To record receipt of dividend transfer from Enterprise Fund.

9. Additional claims and judgment liabilities were recognized, of which 10% are considered current liabilities that are due and payable:

Enterprise Fund	$ 80,000
General government (70% General Fund, 30% Capital Projects Fund #3)	100,000

Enterprise Fund

Expenses—Claims and Judgments.................	$ 80,000	
Current Liabilities—Claims and Judgments		$ 8,000
Noncurrent Liabilities—Claims and Judgments....		72,000

To record additional estimated claims and judgments liabilities.

General Fund

Expenditures [(.1)(.7)($100,000)].................	$ 7,000	
Current Liabilities—Claims and Judgments		$ 7,000

To record additional estimated fund liabilities for claims and judgments.

Capital Projects Fund #3

Expenditures [(.1)(.3)($100,000)].................	$ 3,000	
Current Liabilities—Claims and Judgments		$ 3,000

To record additional estimated fund liabilities for claims and judgments.

General Long-Term Liabilities accounts

Net Position....................................	$ 90,000	
Noncurrent Liabilities—Claims and Judgments....		$ 90,000

To record additional estimated noncurrent liabilities
for general government claims and judgments.

10. A four-year, interest-free loan was made from the General Fund to an Enterprise Fund, $160,000.

General Fund

Advance to Enterprise Fund.....................	$160,000	
Cash		$160,000

To record four-year loan to Enterprise Fund. (Recall that
the balance sheet will present Nonspendable Fund
Balance equal to the $160,000 advance unless its
proceeds have been restricted, committed, or
assigned.)

Enterprise Fund

Cash	$160,000	
Advance from General Fund....................		$160,000

To record four-year loan from General Fund.

11. During the following year, $40,000 of the loan in transaction 10 was repaid.

Enterprise Fund

Advance from General Fund.....................	$ 40,000	
Cash		$ 40,000

To record partial repayment of loan from the
General Fund.

General Fund

Cash	$ 40,000	
Advance to Enterprise Fund....................		$ 40,000

To record partial repayment of interfund loan.
(Nonspendable Fund Balance reported
at the end of the second year will be $120,000.)

12. During the next year (after transaction 11), it became apparent that the Enterprise Fund was undercapitalized, and the governing body ordered the remaining balance of the interfund advance from the General Fund to the Enterprise Fund to be forgiven.

Enterprise Fund

Advance from General Fund.....................	$120,000	
Transfer from General Fund		$120,000

To record forgiveness of loan to provide additional
capitalization to this fund.

General Fund

Transfer to Enterprise Fund	$120,000	
Advance to Enterprise Fund...................		$120,000

To record forgiveness of loan to provide additional
capital to Enterprise Fund.

13. Analyses of the current year Operating Expenses account indicated that $19,000 charged to the Enterprise Fund should be charged to a Special Revenue Fund ($8,000) and an Internal Service Fund ($11,000).

Enterprise Fund

Due from Special Revenue Fund	$ 8,000	
Due from Internal Service Fund..................	11,000	
Operating Expenses...........................		$ 19,000

To record interfund reimbursements as indicated.

Special Revenue Fund

Expenditures	$ 8,000	
Due to Enterprise Fund		$ 8,000

To record reimbursement due to Enterprise Fund.

Internal Service Fund

Operating Expenses	$ 11,000	
Due to Enterprise Fund		$ 11,000

To record reimbursement due to Enterprise Fund.

14. The Inspection Department (financed from the General Fund) charged the Electric Department (financed from an Enterprise Fund) $7,000 for inspecting construction projects in process and $3,000 for routine semiannual inspections of electricity generation equipment.

General Fund

Due from Enterprise Fund	$ 10,000	
Revenues		$ 10,000

To record billings for inspection fees.

Enterprise Fund

Construction in Progress	$ 7,000	
Operating Expenses	3,000	
Due to General Fund		$ 10,000

To record inspection charges owed to General Fund.

Concluding Comments

Trust and Agency Funds are used to account for the fiduciary responsibilities of state and local governments to outside entities or to individuals. Agency Funds differ from other funds in that Agency Funds have no equity and thus no "operating results." Each increase in Agency Fund total assets is accompanied by a corresponding increase in its liabilities. Not all agency relationships require the use of Agency Funds; routine and minor agency relationships can be accounted for through governmental funds and proprietary funds.

Trust Funds, like Agency Funds, are used to report only assets held for individuals and for outside entities and not for the benefit of the government's own programs. Private-Purpose Trust Fund reporting requirements are relatively straightforward. However, the accounting required to maintain accountability during the year and to determine expendable earnings of nonexpendable endowments may be quite involved and subject to numerous provisions of law and trust agreements. Investment Trust Funds are reported in the same manner as Private-Purpose Trust Funds but are subject to additional disclosure requirements. Investment Trust Funds are used to report the external portion of investment pools sponsored by a government.

Pension (and Other Postemployment Benefit, or OPEB) Trust Fund reporting requirements distinguish between the need to report the current status of the plan and the plan's long-term viability. The financial statements are used to reflect the current status of the plan. The schedules presented as required supplementary information disclose a longer-term perspective. Accounting and reporting guidance for pensions and OPEB have been constant challenges for the GASB. One or the other has been on the GASB's agenda virtually since its inception. Many of the changes, like those in the expected new standards, have been significant.

This chapter completes the coverage of accounting and reporting for individual fund types. The next three chapters cover external financial reporting for state and local governments. Chapter 13 discusses and illustrates the basic financial statements. Chapter 14 discusses and illustrates deriving government-wide financial statement information from fund financial statements and selected records. Chapter 15 discusses and illustrates the requirements of a CAFR beyond the basic financial statements, as well as how to determine what to include in a government's financial reporting entity.

Questions

Q12-1 What are the three types of Trust Funds? For what is each type used?

Q12-2 Discuss various situations in which a government has fiduciary responsibilities but does not report them in fiduciary funds.

Q12-3 Trust Funds and Agency Funds, though separate fund types, are treated in the same chapter in this text and are often spoken of collectively. In what ways are they similar, and how do they differ?

Q12-4 A county Tax Agency Fund's GAAP financial statements do not report the taxes receivable for the county's various funds. Why?

Q12-5 In accounting for a Tax Agency Fund, why is it necessary to maintain records of taxes levied and collected for each taxing authority involved by year of levy?

Q12-6 When is an Investment Trust Fund to be used?

Q12-7 When should an Agency Fund be used to account for special assessments? Why?

Q12-8 According to the terms of A's will, the city is to become the owner of an apartment building. The net income from the building is to be used to provide bonus awards to public safety employees who are recognized for performing heroic service. What type of fund should be used to report the apartment and its operations?

Q12-9 The earnings of an endowment (nonexpendable as to corpus) Trust Fund are used to support the operation of a not-for-profit museum, art gallery, and park complex. Should these earnings be accounted for through the General Fund, a Special Revenue Fund, a Permanent Fund, or a Trust Fund? Why?

Q12-10 The status of a pension plan as reported in its financial statements typically differs significantly from its status as presented in the required supplementary information for the plan. (See 12-2 In Practice.) Why? Do you agree with providing this "dual presentation"?

Q12-11 Should the financial statements of Pension Trust Funds be included in the basic financial statements issued by a governmental unit? Explain.

Q12-12 What are other postemployment benefits (OPEB)? Explain how they are similar to and how they differ from traditional pension benefits.

Q12-13 What financial statements should be presented for (a) a Private-Purpose Trust Fund, (b) an Investment Trust Fund, (c) an Agency Fund, and (d) a Pension Trust Fund?

Q12-14 A trust indenture states that the principal (corpus) of the trust is to be maintained intact in perpetuity. Yet, although the governmental trustee did not violate the terms of the trust agreement—and it was not subsequently revised—the principal (corpus) had decreased to less than half its original amount 5 years after the trust was created. Why or how could this have happened?

Q12-15 Explain how the annual pension cost is used in determining employer government pension-related expenses, expenditures, and liabilities.

Exercises

E12-1 (Multiple Choice) Identify the best answer for each of the following:
1. Which of the following must be prepared for Agency Funds as part of a government's Basic Financial Statements?
   a. Statement of changes in net position
   b. Statement of revenues, expenditures, and changes in fund balances
   c. Statement of net position
   d. Statement of changes in agency fund assets and liabilities
2. Which of the following items should be accounted for in an Agency Fund when a special assessment project is financed by issuing special assessment debt for which the government is *not* obligated in any manner?
   a. The bond proceeds and construction costs
   b. The debt service transactions
   c. The long-term debt issued
   d. The capital assets constructed or acquired
3. Bonds issued in a situation like that described in question 2 should be reported by the government in
   a. an Agency Fund.
   b. a Capital Projects Fund.
   c. a Debt Service Fund.
   d. the General Long-Term Liabilities accounts.

4. Which of the following accounts typically would be used by an Agency Fund?
   a. Revenue
   b. Notes receivable
   c. Bonds payable
   d. Cash

5. When a Tax Agency Fund is used, the governmental funds in which the taxes should ultimately be accounted for should report tax revenues
   a. when levied.
   b. when received by year end or not more than 60 days thereafter.
   c. in the year for which the taxes are levied or later.
   d. when both b and c are true.

6. Employer governments must *measure* their annual pension contribution
   a. by using a standardized approach.
   b. in accordance with certain guidelines, but not in a standardized way.
   c. by using the unit credit method.
   d. as required by the FASB pension guidance.

7. Which of the following statements is *not* required to be presented for an Investment Trust Fund?
   a. Statement of net position
   b. Statement of changes in net position
   c. Statement of cash flows
   d. All of the above are required.

8. Which of the following statements about a Pension Trust Fund Statement of Plan Net Position is *not* true?
   a. Investments are reported at fair value.
   b. Capital assets are reported.
   c. The actuarial present value of future benefits payable is reported as a liability, not as an equity component.
   d. Net position is almost always positive.

9. Which of the following statements about a Private-Purpose Trust Fund is *false*?
   a. The principal in a Private-Purpose Trust Fund must be nonexpendable in nature.
   b. The principal in a Private-Purpose Trust Fund may be either expendable or nonexpendable in nature.
   c. Private-Purpose Trust Funds are not reported in the government-wide financial statements.
   d. Net position of a Private-Purpose Trust Fund is not reported using the net position classifications used in proprietary funds.

10. The accounting and financial reporting concepts are virtually the same for which of the following fund types?
    a. Private-Purpose Trust Funds and Permanent Funds
    b. Permanent Funds and Pension Trust Funds
    c. Pension Trust Funds and Investment Trust Funds
    d. Permanent Funds and Agency Funds

E12-2 (Multiple Choice) Identify the best answer to each of the following.

1. Which of the following fiduciary fund types, if any, does *not* have a measurement focus?
   a. Pension Trust Fund
   b. Private-Purpose Trust Fund
   c. Agency Fund
   d. All funds have a measurement focus.

2. Equity in Trust Funds is presented as
   a. Restricted Net Position.
   b. Net Position—Restricted for the Trust Purpose.
   c. Fund Balance Restricted for the Trust Purpose.
   d. Unrestricted Net Position.

3. All of the following would be an example of a trust arrangement properly accounted for in a city's Private-Purpose Trust Fund *except*
   a. a nonexpendable trust arrangement for the benefit of providing resources for perpetual maintenance to the city's cemetery.
   b. a nonexpendable trust arrangement established to provide scholarship opportunities for qualifying students.
   c. an expendable trust arrangement that provides resources for a local nonprofit organization.
   d. a nonexpendable trust arrangement that provides resources to a local private museum.

4. A trust fund's statement of changes in net position reports contributions
   a. as a revenue.
   b. as an addition.
   c. as they are collected.
   d. as an operating revenue.

5. Which of the following types of pension plans would be *least likely* to be reported as a Pension Trust Fund of a participating governmental entity?
   a. Single-employer plan
   b. Agent multiple-employer plan
   c. Defined contribution plan
   d. Cost-sharing multiple-employer plan

6. Trust Funds are most commonly reported in the government-wide financial statements as
   a. governmental activities.
   b. business-type activities.
   c. fiduciary activities.
   d. blended activities.

7. How would the capital assets of a Private-Purpose Trust Fund most likely be reported?
   a. As a capital asset of the fund and as a capital asset of governmental activities in the government-wide financial statements
   b. As a capital asset of the fund and as a capital asset of business-type activities in the government-wide financial statements
   c. As a capital asset of the fund
   d. As a capital asset of fiduciary-type activities in the government-wide financial statements

8. Assume that a governmental entity provides other postemployment benefits (OPEB) to its retirees. The entity commissions an actuarial valuation of the OPEB plan and contributes to a trust in accordance with the actuarial requirements. The OPEB trust should be reported in the same manner as
   a. a Pension Trust Fund.
   b. a Private-Purpose Trust Fund.
   c. a Special Revenue Fund.
   d. an Agency Fund.

9. GAAP require that certain actuarial information for pensions be reported as required supplementary information. Which of the following schedules is *not* an example of such actuarial information?
   a. Schedule of employee contributions
   b. Schedule of funding progress
   c. Schedule of employer contributions
   d. All of the above schedules are examples of required supplementary information

10. The net change amount is reduced by pension contributions due and payable on the operating statement of
   a. Business-type.
   b. Governmental activities.
   c. Governmental funds.
   d. Proprietary funds.

E12-3 (Private-Purpose Trust Fund Entries) Prepare the journal entries to record the following transactions.
1. A cash donation of $80,000 was received by James County. The donor stipulated that the resources were to be used solely for Carolyn City 4-H purposes.
2. Rent for an auditorium used for a Carolyn City 4-H conference and training session was paid, $800.
3. Travel and registration costs for Carolyn City 4-H members and county staff to attend a regional 4-H camp were incurred and paid, $2,000.
4. A computer was purchased for the use of the Carolyn City 4-H coordinator and leaders, $5,000.

E12-4 (Property Tax Agency Fund)
(a) Prepare general journal entries for the following transactions in the appropriate funds and General Capital Assets and General Long-Term Liabilities accounts of a county, the county school district, and a town within the county. The county serves as the tax collection agent for the county, the county school district, and the town.
   1. Taxes were levied and bills were sent to taxpayers. The county tax levy was for $4,000,000; the school district tax levy was for $5,000,000; the town tax levy was for $2,000,000. Two percent of the taxes are expected to be uncollectible. The county charges the school district and the town a collection fee of 1% of the taxes collected.
   2. Tax collections for the year totaled $8,960,000—$3,200,000 for the county; $4,000,000 for the school district; and $1,760,000 for the town.
   3. All amounts due to the county General Fund, the school district, and the town were paid from the Tax Agency Fund.
(b) Prepare the Statement of Net Position for the county Tax Agency Fund at year end. Assume that taxes receivable at the beginning of the year were $100,000 for the county, $125,000 for the school district, and $50,000 for the town.

E12-5 (Pension Trust Fund Financial Statements) The preclosing trial balance for the Pension Trust Fund of Almen County at December 31, 20X8, is presented here. Prepare the Statement of Plan Net Position at December 31, 20X8, and the Statement of Changes in Plan Net Position for 20X8 for this Pension Trust Fund.

Almen County
Pension Trust Fund
Preclosing Trial Balance
December 31, 20X8

Cash	$ 273,000	
Due from General Fund	45,500	
Interest Receivable.............................	28,000	
Investments (at fair value)........................	3,878,000	
Deductions—Net Increase (Decrease) in Fair Value of Investments	70,000	
Deductions—Payments to Resigned Employees	87,500	
Deductions—Annuity Benefits.....................	84,000	
Due to Resigned Employees.......................		$ 21,000
Annuity Benefits Payable		13,300
Net Position—Restricted for Pension Benefits........		3,661,700
Additions—Employer Contributions		437,500
Additions—Employee Contributions		175,000
Additions—Investment Income		157,500
	$4,466,000	$4,466,000

Problems

P12-1 (Private-Purpose Trust Funds) The following is a trial balance of the Camping Builds Character Trust Fund of the City of Slusher's Ridge as of January 1, 20X6:

Cash	$ 98,000	
Land...	70,000	
Buildings	162,000	
Accumulated Depreciation.........................		$ 65,000
Accrued Wages Payable		150
Accrued Taxes Payable		1,800
Net Position—Restricted for Camp Scholarships—Expendable		15,000
Net Position—Restricted for Endowment— Nonexpendable		248,050
	$330,000	$330,000

The endowment was in the form of an apartment building. Endowment principal is to be kept intact, and the net earnings are to be used in financing scholarships to not-for-profit organization camps designed to help instill positive character qualities in participants.

The following transactions took place during the year:

1. Expenses and accrued liabilities paid in cash were as follows:

Heat, light, and power	$ 5,200
Janitor's wages (including $150 previously accrued) ...	3,000
Painting and decorating	3,750
Repairs	1,500
Taxes (including $1,800 previously accrued)..........	3,750
Management fees	4,500
Miscellaneous expenses	1,500
	$ 23,200

2. A land improvement of $2,000 was constructed by an outside contractor who was paid in full.
3. Apartment rents for 20X6 (all collected) amounted to $45,000.
4. Camping scholarships of $13,500 were paid to finance 20X6 summer camp fees.
5. The following adjustments were made at the close of the year:

Depreciation	$ 6,000
Accrued Taxes..................................	1,900
Accrued Wages.................................	170

a. Prepare general journal entries to record these transactions in the Trust Fund.   *Required*
b. Prepare a Statement of Net Position as of December 31, 20X6, and a Statement of Changes in Net Position for the fiscal year ended December 31, 20X6.

P12-2 (Tax Agency Fund)
a. Prepare the general journal entries required to record the following transactions in the general ledgers of the state, the County General Fund, and the County Tax Agency Fund. You may omit formal entry explanations but should key the entries to the numbered items in this problem.
  1. The County Tax Agency Fund has been established to account for the county's duties of collecting the county and state property taxes. The levies for the year 20X0 were $600,000 for the County General Fund and $480,000 for the state. It is expected that uncollectible taxes will be $10,000 for the state and $15,000 for the county.
  2. Collections were $300,000 for the county and $240,000 for the state.
  3. The county is entitled to a fee of 1% of taxes collected for other governments. The amounts due to the state and to the County General Fund are paid except for the collection fee due to the County General Fund.
  4. The fee is transmitted from the Tax Agency Fund to the County General Fund.
  5. Uncollectible taxes in the amount of $5,000 for the state and $6,000 for the county are written off.
b. Prepare the GAAP-based Statement of Net Position for the Tax Agency Fund. Assume that the beginning balances of taxes receivable were county, $120,000, and state, $96,000.

P12-3 (Pension Trust Fund Journal Entries) The following is a trial balance of the Police Retirement Fund of the City of Cherrydale at January 1, 20X7:

Cash	$ 6,000	
Interest Receivable	450	
Investments......................................	52,000	
Pensions Payable		$ 150
Net Position—Restricted for Pension Benefits		58,300
	$58,450	$58,450

The following transactions took place during the year:
  1. Contributions became due from the General Fund, $38,000, and a Special Revenue Fund, $6,000. One-half of these amounts is the employees' share of contributions.
  2. Payments were received from the General Fund, $30,000, and the Special Revenue Fund, $4,000.
  3. Securities were acquired for cash as follows:

a. First Purchase:	
Par value.....................................	$20,000
Premiums.....................................	300
Interest accrued at purchase	200
b. Second Purchase:	
Par value	15,000
Discounts	150

  4. Interest received on investments amounted to $3,000, including interest receivable on January 1, 20X7, and the accrued interest purchased.
  5. An employee resigned prior to retirement and was paid $300, which is the amount of her contributions and interest thereon. Employer contributions do not vest until retirement.
  6. Retirement payments of $600 were made (which included beginning of year pensions payable); pensions payable of $200 remained at year end.

7. An actuary indicated that the actuarial deficiency at year end was $19,000.
8. The fair value of the pension plan investments was $200 more than the carrying value at year-end.

Required Prepare journal entries, including closing entries, to record the transactions in the general ledger of the Police Retirement Fund.

P12-4 Using the information in P12-3, prepare the Statement of Net Position at December 31, 20X7, and the Statement of Changes in Net Position for 20X7 for the City of Cherrydale's Policemen's Retirement Fund.

P12-5 (Pension Trust Fund Entries and Statements) The following is the December 31, 20X8, trial balance of the McCarthy County Public Employees Retirement Fund, a multiple-employer pension plan in which the cities of Mooresville and Sutherland's Gap participate, as well as the county.

	Debit	Credit
Cash	$ 76,000	
Due from Sutherland's Gap	12,000	
Interest Receivable	14,200	
Investments.......................................	1,456,000	
Due to Resigned Employees		$ 14,500
Due to Estates of Deceased Employees		3,000
Annuities Payable		1,700
Net Position—Restricted for Pension Benefits		1,539,000
	$1,558,200	$1,558,200

The employees' contributions are returned to them or to their estates upon resignation or death, respectively; vesting of *employers' matching contributions* occurs only at retirement.

During 20X9 the following transactions occurred:
1. Employee contributions (which are matched by the employer) for the year were:

Employees of	Contributions
McCarthy County	$60,000
Mooresville	35,000
Sutherland's Gap	25,000

2. All amounts due to the pension plan were collected except $20,000 each still due from the cities.
3. Interest accrued in the amount of $169,000.
4. Interest receivable of $168,400 was collected.
5. Five employees resigned; their contributions were determined to have been $24,000. Two employees died prior to retirement; their contributions were determined to have been $36,000.
6. Checks mailed to resigned employees during the year amounted to $34,500. Checks mailed to the estates of deceased employees totaled $33,000.
7. Annuities were accrued in the amount of $63,000; annuities in the amount of $62,700 were paid.
8. Additional investments were made as follows:

Bonds (at par)	$ 160,000
Accrued interest	30,000
Discounts	(8,000)
	$ 182,000

9. The fair value of investments at year end exceeded the carrying value by $3,000.

Required a. Prepare a worksheet (or journal entries and T-accounts) showing transactions, adjustments, and closing entries for the Retirement Fund for 20X9.
b. Prepare a Statement of Plan Net Position as of December 31, 20X9, and a Statement of Changes in Plan Net Position for the year ended December 31, 20X9.

P12-6 (Interfund-GCA-GLTL Entries) Prepare all journal entries that Hain Township should make to record the following transactions:
1. A "payment in lieu of tax" of $300,000—computed at 10% of its operating income—was made from the Township's Utilities Enterprise Fund to its General Fund.

2. Water Enterprise Fund billings to other funds for services were as follows:

General Fund	$600,000
Special Revenue Fund	50,000
Total	$650,000

3. The Township transferred $1,800,000 from the General Fund to provide initial financing for the township's Ray Robinson Memorial Golf Course Enterprise Fund.
4. Equipment with an original cost of $120,000 was transferred from a General Fund department to the Utilities Enterprise Fund department halfway through its useful life. Assume zero residual value.
5. Additional general government claims and judgment liabilities of $1,200,000 were recognized, of which $170,000 is due and payable.
6. A three-year, interest-free loan of $2,300,000 was made from the General Fund to the newly established Golf Course Enterprise Fund.
7. Analyses of the current year Operating Expenses account indicated that $5,000 charged to the Utilities Enterprise Fund should be charged to a Special Revenue Fund.

P12-7 (Research Problem) Obtain copies of the Trust and Agency Fund financial statements of a state or local government.

a. Study the Trust and Agency Fund financial statements and compare them with those discussed and illustrated in this chapter, noting the following: *Required*
   1. Similarities
   2. Differences
   3. Other matters that come to your attention
b. Study the authoritative literature to determine the following:
   1. What is an investment pool?
   2. What is meant by the "internal portion" of an investment pool?
   3. What is meant by the "external portion" of an investment pool?
   4. How are the assets of the investment pool reported in the financial statements of the government that operates the pool?
c. Prepare a brief report on requirements a and b.

P12-8 (Research Problem) Obtain copies of the GASB's new statement on accounting for pension plans issued in 2012.
a. Identify the key changes from current GAAP reporting requirements for pension trust funds.
b. Select a government's pension trust fund with your instructor's approval.
c. As much as possible, convert that fund's statement of net position from current GAAP to the new standards.

Cases

C12-1 (Pension Trust Fund Adjusting Entry and Financial Statements—City of Rockville, Maryland) Presented here is the Preclosing Trial Balance for the Pension Trust Fund for the City of Rockville, Maryland, as of June 30, 20X6. Assume that the fair market value of investments has increased by $5,163,179 over their original cost and that the adjustment for this increase is not reflected in the trial balance shown.

City of Rockville, Maryland
Pension Trust Fund
Preclosing Trial Balance
June 30, 20X6

	Dr.	Cr.
Cash	$ 3,737,051	
Investments	59,657,923	
Accrued liabilities		$ 25,300
Employer contributions		1,901,030
Plan member contributions		1,532,400
Interest and dividends.............................		25,226
Benefits paid	2,306,404	
Refunds to terminated employees......................	328,725	
Administrative expenses.............................	30,914	
Net position—restricted for pension benefits		62,577,061
Totals..	$66,061,017	$66,061,017

Required
1. Prepare the necessary journal entry to reflect the increase in the fair market value of the investments. Assume this is the only adjusting entry necessary.
2. Prepare a Statement of Fiduciary Net Position for the Pension Trust Fund as of June 30, 20X6.
3. Prepare a Statement of Changes in Fiduciary Net Position for the fiscal year ended June 30, 20X6.

(Derived from a recent Comprehensive Annual Financial Report for the City of Rockville, Maryland.)

C12-2 (Fiduciary Fund Financial Statement Preparation—City of Wilmington, Delaware) The City of Wilmington, Delaware, has an Other Postemployment Benefit Trust Fund and a Tax Collection Agency Fund. The Preclosing Trial Balance for each of these funds as of June 30, 20X6, is as follows:

City of Wilmington, Delaware
Other Postemployment Benefit Trust Fund
Preclosing Trial Balance
June 30, 20X6

	Dr.	Cr.
Cash and cash equivalents	$ 405,476	
Interest receivable	50,807	
Investments	2,767,043	
Employer contributions		$ 505,189
Employee contributions		167,721
Interest income		37,787
Increase in fair market value of investments		33,179
Benefits paid	362,325	
Administrative expenses	18,957	
Net position—restricted for benefits		2,860,732
Totals	$3,604,608	$3,604,608

City of Wilmington, Delaware
Tax Collection Agency Fund
Preclosing Trial Balance
June 30, 20X6

	Dr.	Cr.
Cash and cash equivalents	$ 282,630	
Due from other governments	211,613	
Due to other governments		$ 294,967
Due to other funds		199,276
Totals	$ 494,243	$ 494,243

Required Prepare a Statement of Fiduciary Net Position for the City of Wilmington as of June 30, 20X6, and a Statement of Changes in Fiduciary Net Position for the year ended June 30, 20X6.

(Derived from a recent Comprehensive Annual Financial Report for the City of Wilmington, Delaware.)

Harvey City Comprehensive Case

PENSION TRUST FUND

Harvey City has only one Trust and Agency Fund. The city maintains and administers a defined benefit pension plan for police department and fire department personnel. The plan is financed from contributions by the city and from investment income.

REQUIREMENTS

a. Prepare a worksheet for the Police and Fire Pension Trust Fund similar to the General Fund worksheet you created in Chapter 4. Enter the effects of the following transactions and events in the appropriate columns of the worksheet. (A different solution approach may be used if desired by your professor.)

b. Enter the preclosing trial balance in the appropriate worksheet columns.

c. Enter the preclosing trial balance amounts in the closing entry (operating statement data) and postclosing trial balance (balance sheet data) columns, as appropriate.

d. Prepare the 20X4 Statement of Changes in Net Position for the Police and Fire Pension Trust Fund.

e. Prepare the year-end 20X4 Statement of Net Position for the Police and Fire Pension Trust Fund.

BEGINNING 20X4 TRIAL BALANCE

The January 1, 20X4, trial balance for the Harvey City Police and Fire Pension Trust Fund is presented here:

Harvey City
Police and Fire Pension Trust Fund
Trial Balance
January 1, 20X4

	Debit	Credit
Cash..	$ 120,000	
Investments	1,271,800	
Accrued Interest Receivable	8,600	
Due to Resigned Employees		$ 400
Net Position—Restricted for Pension Benefits		1,400,000
Totals..	$1,400,400	$1,400,400

TRANSACTIONS AND EVENTS—20X4

1. Employer contributions of $60,200 were received from the General Fund by the Police and Fire Pension Trust Fund, which is administered by the city.

2. The city purchased investments costing $60,200 for the Police and Fire Pension Trust Fund with the contributions.

3. Refunds of $9,000, which included $400 accrued at the end of 20X3, were paid to terminated employees. The amounts refunded relate to contributions made by the terminated employees prior to 20X3 when the city increased its contributions and eliminated the requirement for employee contributions.

4. Administrative costs of $9,400 were incurred during the fiscal year. Of this amount, $8,700 was paid.

5. Retirement benefits of $78,000 were paid to retirees. Another $1,000 of retirement benefit payments was accrued at year end.

6. The accrued interest receivable of $8,600 from last year plus $60,000 of current year interest revenues were received.

7. Interest at year end was accrued, $65,000. The fair value of investments increased by $17,000.

CHAPTER 13

Financial Reporting

The Basic Financial Statements and Required Supplementary Information

LEARNING OBJECTIVES

After studying this chapter, you should be able to:

- Identify a government's basic financial statements.

- Understand the format and content of the fund financial statements and the government-wide financial statements.

- Understand the concept and content of required supplementary information (RSI).

- Identify a government's major funds and how to prepare its fund financial statements.

- Distinguish program revenues from general revenues.

- Understand the unique reporting provisions for infrastructure capital assets.

- Understand the required information components of Management's Discussion and Analysis (MD&A).

- Understand the types of notes to the financial statements required for governments.

- Understand the reporting requirements for special purpose governments.

The GASB *Codification* (sec. 2200) details the financial reporting requirements for state and local governments in its 13th principle. The next three chapters describe and discuss the substance of that principle.

This chapter focuses on the minimum requirements for reporting in accordance with GAAP—the basic financial statements (BFS)—and the related required supplementary information (RSI), including Management's Discussion and Analysis (MD&A). Although Principle 13 states that governments are to prepare and publish interim financial statements and reports and a comprehensive annual financial report (CAFR), the GASB only requires the basic financial statements, the MD&A, and certain other RSI to be presented to meet its minimum requirements for general purpose external financial reporting. These elements are the heart of the financial section of a CAFR, but a CAFR includes significant additional financial statement information, as well as introductory and statistical information, as discussed in Chapter 15.

Principle 13 also discusses the composition of the financial reporting entity covered by a government's financial report. The reporting entity is discussed in detail in Chapter 15. The nucleus of the reporting entity is the legal entity covered by the report and is called the *primary government*. Additional, legally separate entities that meet specified criteria also are included in the reporting entity and are known as *component units*. Some of these component units are essentially like departments of the primary government and are known as blended component units. The others are called *discretely presented component units*. Chapter 15 distinguishes these component units and how they affect a primary government's financial statements.

Many governments are required by law or other regulations or agreements to present a full CAFR. Still others choose to do so for a variety of reasons. When a CAFR is presented—either by choice or because of legal or contractual requirements—combining and individual fund financial statements, as well as the basic financial statements, must be presented in a manner that complies with GAAP for those statements.

As depicted in Illustration 13-1, GASB *Statement No. 34* establishes the following *minimum* requirements for general purpose external financial reports:

- Management's Discussion and Analysis
- Basic Financial Statements
  - Government-Wide Financial Statements
  - Fund Financial Statements
  - Notes to the Financial Statements
- Other Required Supplementary Information

ILLUSTRATION 13-1 Minimum Requirements for a General Purpose External Financial Report

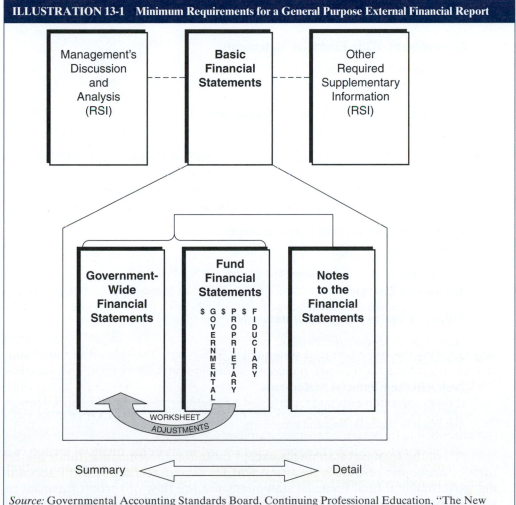

Source: Governmental Accounting Standards Board, Continuing Professional Education, "The New Financial Reporting Model—A Review of GASB *Statement 34*, 'Basic Financial Statements—and Management's Discussion and Analysis—for State and Local Governments' " (Norwalk, CT: GASB, 2000).

Portions of various GASB documents, copyright by the Governmental Accounting Standards Board, 401 Merritt, PO Box 5116, Norwalk, CT 06856-5116, are reproduced with permission. Complete copies of those documents are available from the GASB.

Each of these requirements is discussed in the following sections. We consider the financial statements and the notes to the financial statements before covering MD&A, even though governments must present their MD&A before their financial statements. This order permits you to comprehend MD&A references to the financial statements better. Chapter 14 discusses and illustrates the conversion of fund financial statement information into government-wide financial statements. As noted earlier, Chapter 15 presents an overview of the CAFR and explains how to define a government's financial reporting entity and how to incorporate component unit information into a government's financial statements.

BASIC FINANCIAL STATEMENTS OVERVIEW

The basic financial statements include two distinct types of financial statements—the government-wide financial statements and the fund financial statements—as well as the notes to the financial statements. Each set of financial statements presents the financial position and operations of the government from a different perspective. Indeed, the financial statements may be viewed as offering dual perspectives of the government. These perspectives are integrated through a required reconciliation of the information in the two sets of statements. The basic financial statements include the following:

Government-Wide Financial Statements

- Statement of Net Position
- Statement of Activities

Governmental Funds Financial Statements

- Balance Sheet
- Statement of Revenues, Expenditures, and Changes in Fund Balances (GAAP basis)
- Statement of Revenues, Expenditures, and Changes in Fund Balances—Budget and Actual (presented on the budgetary basis for the General Fund and for each major Special Revenue Fund with a legally adopted annual budget)[1]

Proprietary Funds Financial Statements

- Statement of Net Position
- Statement of Revenues, Expenses, and Changes in Net Position
- Statement of Cash Flows

Fiduciary Funds Financial Statements

- Statement of Fiduciary Net Position
- Statement of Changes in Fiduciary Net Position

Notes to the Financial Statements

The notes are an integral part of the financial statements and must be considered in any discussion of the basic financial statements.

All of the financial statements except those for governmental funds use the flow of economic resources measurement focus and accrual basis of accounting; governmental fund financial statements use the flow of current financial resources measurement focus and the [modified] accrual basis of accounting. Each of the financial statements listed is discussed and illustrated in the remainder of the chapter. After discussing the fund financial statements, we will explain the form and content of the government-wide financial statements.

---

[1]Alternatively, a government may present the budgetary comparison as required supplementary information. We consider the presentation of the budgetary comparison as a basic financial statement to be the preferable alternative. Therefore, we include it in the list of the basic financial statements.

FUND FINANCIAL STATEMENTS

Most of the previous chapters focused on accounting and financial reporting for a government's various funds. At this point, you should have acquired a reasonable level of knowledge of fund financial statements. The presentation of the financial statements for individual funds of each of the three fund categories—governmental, proprietary, and fiduciary—has been discussed and illustrated in detail in Chapters 2 to 12.

In this chapter we bring the individual fund-type statements together and report the results in fund category statements—a separate set of statements for each of the three categories of funds: governmental, proprietary, and fiduciary. The financial statements required for each category of funds are the same as the financial statements required for the fund types in that category. Hence, the financial statements for the governmental funds category, called *governmental funds financial statements*, will be virtually identical to those for the General Fund (or any other individual governmental fund). The primary difference is that the governmental funds financial statements use columns to allow reporting multiple funds in the same statement much as we saw in combining financial statements presented in some of the earlier chapters. This columnar approach permits all the governmental funds to be presented in a single statement by including

- Separate columns for each of the more important individual governmental funds (called *major funds*).
- A column for the aggregated nonmajor governmental funds.
- A total column for the governmental funds category.

Major fund reporting is used for the governmental funds and the Enterprise Funds; fund type reporting is used for the Internal Service Funds and the fiduciary funds.

Major Fund Reporting

Major funds are reported separately for certain fund types. The fund financial statements for *governmental funds* **and** for *Enterprise Funds* are required to *report each major governmental fund and each major Enterprise Fund in a separate column*. Internal Service Funds and all fiduciary funds must be reported only by *fund type* in the basic financial statements.[2]

Major Fund Statement Formats

As shown in Illustrations 13-2 and 13-3, **major fund reporting** under *Statement No. 34* means that the financial statements for **governmental funds** should present:

- A column for the General Fund
- A column for **each major** fund of the other governmental funds
- A single column for **all nonmajor** governmental funds combined
- A **total** column

Notice the reconciliations presented at the bottom of the Governmental Funds Balance Sheet (Illustration 13-2) and at the end of the Statement of Revenues, Expenditures, and Changes in Fund Balance (Illustration 13-3). These reconciliations explain why the Total Fund Balance and the Net Change in Fund Balance on the governmental funds statements differ from the total Net Position and the Change in Net Position amounts reported for governmental activities on the government-wide statements. Chapter 14 discusses and illustrates the preparation of these reconciliations. As noted earlier, budgetary comparison statements (or RSI schedules) like that in Illustration 13-4 are required for the General Fund and for each major Special Revenue Fund.

---

[2]GASB *Codification*, sec. 2200.152–153.

ILLUSTRATION 13-2 Governmental Funds Balance Sheet

Sample City
Balance Sheet
Governmental Funds
December 31, 20X6

	General	Special Revenue Fund — HUD Programs	Capital Projects Funds — Community Redevelopment	Capital Projects Funds — Route 7 Construction	Other Governmental Funds	Total Governmental Funds
ASSETS						
Cash and cash equivalents	$3,418,485	$1,236,523	$ —	$ —	$ 5,606,792	$ 10,261,800
Investments	—	—	13,262,695	10,467,037	3,485,252	27,214,984
Receivables, net	3,807,308	2,953,438	353,340	11,000	10,221	7,135,307
Due from other funds	1,370,757	—	—	—	—	1,370,757
Receivables from other governments	629,179	119,059	—	—	1,596,038	2,344,276
Liens receivable	—	3,195,745	—	—	—	3,195,745
Inventories	182,821	—	—	—	—	182,821
Total assets	$9,408,550	$7,504,765	$13,616,035	$10,478,037	$10,698,303	$ 51,705,690
LIABILITIES, DEFERRED INFLOWS OF RESOURCES, AND FUND BALANCES						
Liabilities:						
Accounts payable	$3,408,680	$ 129,975	$ 190,548	$ 1,104,632	$ 1,074,831	$ 5,908,666
Due to other funds	—	25,369	—	—	—	25,369
Payable to other governments	94,074	—	—	—	—	94,074
Unearned revenue	—	1,435,599	—	—	—	1,435,599
Total liabilities	3,502,754	1,590,943	190,548	1,104,632	1,074,831	7,463,708
Deferred Inflows of Resources:						
Deferred revenue	4,250,430	4,837,446	250,000	11,000	—	9,348,876
Fund balances:						
Nonspendable	974,747	—	—	—	—	974,747
Restricted	—	1,076,376	13,175,487	3,874,736	8,078,084	26,204,683
Committed	—	—	—	1,917,851	614,670	2,532,521
Assigned	40,292	—	—	3,569,818	930,718	4,540,828
Unassigned	640,327	—	—	—	—	640,327
Total fund balances	1,655,366	1,076,376	13,175,487	9,362,405	9,623,472	34,893,106
Total liabilities, deferred inflows of resources, and fund balance	$9,408,550	$7,504,765	$13,616,035	$10,478,037	$10,698,303	

Amounts reported for *governmental activities* in the statement of net position are different because:

Capital assets used in governmental activities are not financial resources and therefore are not reported in the funds.	161,082,708
Other long-term assets are not available to pay for current-period expenditures and therefore are deferred in the funds.	9,348,876
Internal service funds are used by management to charge the costs of certain activities, such as insurance and telecommunications, to individual funds. The assets and liabilities of certain internal service funds are included in governmental activities in the statement of net position.	3,133,459
Some liabilities, including bonds payable, are not due and payable in the current period and therefore are not reported in the funds.	(85,515,740)
Net position of governmental activities	$122,942,409

Source: Adapted for GASB *Statement No. 54* classifications and presentation of deferred inflows of resources from Governmental Accounting Standards Board, "Guide to Implementation of GASB *Statement 34* on Basic Financial Statements—and Management's Discussion and Analysis—for State and Local Governments" (Norwalk, CT: GASB, 2001), Appendix 2, Exhibit 3.
Portions of various GASB documents, copyright by the Governmental Accounting Standards Board, 401 Merritt, PO Box 5116, Norwalk, CT 06856-5116, are reproduced with permission. Complete copies of those documents are available from the GASB.

ILLUSTRATION 13-3   Governmental Funds Operating Statement

Sample City
Statement of Revenues, Expenditures, and Changes in Fund Balances
Governmental Funds
For the Year Ended December 31, 20X6

	General	Special Revenue Fund — HUD Programs	Capital Projects Funds — Community Redevelopment	Capital Projects Funds — Route 7 Construction	Other Governmental Funds	Total Governmental Funds
REVENUES						
Property taxes	$51,173,436	$ —	$ —	$ —	$ 4,680,192	$ 55,853,628
Franchise taxes	4,055,505	—	—	—	—	4,055,505
Public service taxes	8,969,887	—	—	—	—	8,969,887
Fees and fines	606,946	—	—	—	—	606,946
Licenses and permits	2,287,794	—	—	—	—	2,287,794
Intergovernmental	6,119,938	2,578,191	—	—	2,830,916	11,529,045
Charges for services	11,374,460	—	—	—	30,708	11,405,168
Investment earnings	552,325	87,106	549,489	270,161	364,330	1,823,411
Miscellaneous	881,874	66,176	—	2,939	94	951,083
Total revenues	86,022,165	2,731,473	549,489	273,100	7,906,240	97,482,467
EXPENDITURES						
Current:						
General government	8,630,835	—	417,814	16,700	121,052	9,186,401
Public safety	33,729,623	—	—	—	—	33,729,623
Public works	4,975,775	—	—	—	3,721,542	8,697,317
Engineering services	1,299,645	—	—	—	—	1,299,645
Health and sanitation	6,070,032	—	—	—	—	6,070,032
Cemetery	706,305	—	—	—	—	706,305
Culture and recreation	11,411,685	—	—	—	—	11,411,685
Community development	—	2,954,389	—	—	—	2,954,389
Education—payment to school district	21,893,273	—	—	—	—	21,893,273
Debt service:						
Principal	—	—	—	—	3,450,000	3,450,000
Interest and other charges	—	—	470,440	—	5,215,151	5,685,591
Capital outlay	—	—	2,246,671	11,281,769	3,190,209	16,718,649
Total expenditures	88,717,173	2,954,389	3,134,925	11,298,469	15,697,954	121,802,910
Excess (deficiency) of revenues over expenditures	(2,695,008)	(222,916)	(2,585,436)	(11,025,369)	(7,791,714)	(24,320,443)
OTHER FINANCING SOURCES (USES)						
Refunding bonds issued	—	—	—	—	38,045,000	38,045,000
Capital-related debt issued	—	—	18,000,000	—	1,300,000	19,300,000
Payment to bond refunding escrow agent	—	—	—	—	(37,284,144)	(37,284,144)
Transfers in	129,323	—	—	—	5,551,187	5,680,510
Transfers out	(2,163,759)	(348,046)	(2,273,187)	—	(219,076)	(5,004,068)
Total other financing sources and uses	(2,034,436)	(348,046)	15,726,813	—	7,392,967	20,737,298
SPECIAL ITEM						
Proceeds from sale of park land	3,476,488	—	—	—	—	3,476,488
Net change in fund balances	(1,252,956)	(570,962)	13,141,377	(11,025,369)	(398,747)	(106,657)
Fund balances—beginning	2,908,322	1,647,338	34,110	20,387,774	10,022,219	34,999,763
Fund balances—ending	$ 1,655,366	$1,076,376	$13,175,487	$ 9,362,405	$ 9,623,472	$ 34,893,106

> The reconciliation of the net change in fund balances of governmental funds to the change in net position in the Statement of Activities is presented on the following page.

Source: Governmental Accounting Standards Board, "Guide to Implementation of GASB *Statement 34* on Basic Financial Statements—and Management's Discussion and Analysis—for State and Local Governments" (Norwalk, CT: GASB, 2001) Appendix 2, Exhibit 4.
Portions of various GASB documents, copyright by the Governmental Accounting Standards Board, 401 Merritt, PO Box 5116, Norwalk, CT 06856-5116, are reproduced with permission. Complete copies of those documents are available from the GASB.

ILLUSTRATION 13-3 **Governmental Funds Operating Statement** (*Continued*)

Net change in fund balances—total governmental funds	$ (106,657)
Amounts reported for *governmental activities* in the Statement of Activities are different because:	
Governmental funds report capital outlays as expenditures. However, in the statement of activities the cost of those assets is allocated over their estimated useful lives and reported as depreciation expense. This is the amount by which capital outlays ($16,718,649) exceeded depreciation ($2,678,932) in the current period.	14,039,717
In the statement of activities, only the *gain* on the sale of the park land is reported, whereas in the governmental funds, the proceeds from the sale increase financial resources. Thus, the change in net position differs from the change in fund balance by the cost of the land sold.	(823,000)
Revenues in the statement of activities that do not provide current financial resources are not reported as revenues in the funds.	1,920,630
Bond proceeds provide current financial resources to governmental funds, but issuing debt increases long-term liabilities in the statement of net position. Repayment of bond principal is an expenditure in the governmental funds, but the repayment reduces long-term liabilities in the statement of net position. This is the amount by which proceeds exceeded repayments.	(16,610,856)
Some expenses reported in the statement of activities do not require the use of current financial resources and therefore are not reported as expenditures in governmental funds.	(950,084)
Internal service funds are used by management to charge the costs of certain activities, such as insurance and telecommunications, to individual funds. The net revenue (expense) of certain internal service funds is reported with governmental activities.	(620,040)
Change in net position of governmental activities (Illustration 13-12)	$(3,150,290)

> The reconciliation could be presented on the face of the statement, rather than on a separate page. However, using a separate page as a continuation of the financial statement provides more space for the preparer to explain the reconciling items. Alternatively, detailed explanations could be provided in the notes to the financial statements.

Source: Adapted from Governmental Accounting Standards Board, "Guide to Implementation of GASB *Statement 34* on Basic Financial Statements—and Management's Discussion and Analysis—for State and Local Governments" (Norwalk, CT: GASB, 2001), Appendix 2, Exhibit 5.
Portions of various GASB documents, copyright by the Governmental Accounting Standards Board, 401 Merritt, PO Box 5116, Norwalk, CT 06856-5116, are reproduced with permission. Complete copies of those documents are available from the GASB.

Likewise, as seen in Illustrations 13-5 and 13-7, each **proprietary funds** statement should present:

- A column for **each major** Enterprise Fund
- A single column for **all nonmajor** Enterprise Funds combined
- A **total** column for all Enterprise Funds
- A single column for all Internal Service Funds

The total Enterprise Funds and the Internal Service Funds amounts may be summed to present a total for all proprietary funds, but the total is not used in any other financial statement.

The fiduciary funds Statement of Fiduciary Net Position and Statement of Changes in Fiduciary Net Position are presented by *fund type* rather than by major fund. Multiple fiduciary funds of a particular type (for example, separate pension plans for police, fire, and other government employees) are reported in a single column. The Statement of Fiduciary Net Position should have one column for each type of fiduciary fund that a government has, regardless of the number of individual funds of each type. The Statement of Changes in Fiduciary Net Position should have one column for each type of Trust Fund the government has, but does *not* have an Agency Funds column because Agency Funds always have zero net position.

Identifying Major Funds

Properly identifying major funds is critical to appropriate reporting in the fund financial statements. Doing so requires professional judgment and consideration of the nature of, and financial statement user interest in, particular funds as well

ILLUSTRATION 13-4 Budgetary Comparison Statement

Sample City
General Fund
Statement of Revenues, Expenditures, and Changes
in Fund Balance—Budget and Actual
For the Year Ended December 31, 20X6

This statement uses the government's budget document format. The Statement of Revenues, Expenditures, and Changes in Fund Balances format is also acceptable.

	Budgeted Amounts		Actual Amounts (Budgetary Basis)	Variance with Final Budget-Positive (Negative)
	Original	Final		
Budgetary fund balance, January 1	$ 3,528,750	$ 2,742,799	$ 2,742,799	$ —
Resources (inflows):				
Property taxes	52,017,833	51,853,018	51,173,436	(679,582)
Franchise taxes	4,546,209	4,528,750	4,055,505	(473,245)
Public service taxes	8,295,000	8,307,274	8,969,887	662,613
Licenses and permits	2,126,600	2,126,600	2,287,794	161,194
Fines and forfeitures	718,800	718,800	606,946	(111,854)
Charges for services	12,392,972	11,202,150	11,374,460	172,310
Grants	6,905,898	6,571,360	6,119,938	(451,422)
Sale of land	1,355,250	3,500,000	3,476,488	(23,512)
Miscellaneous	3,024,292	1,220,991	881,874	(339,117)
Interest received	1,015,945	550,000	552,325	2,325
Transfers from other funds	939,525	130,000	129,323	(677)
Amounts available for appropriation	96,867,074	93,451,742	92,370,775	(1,080,967)
Charges to appropriations (outflows):				
General government:				
Legal	665,275	663,677	632,719	30,958
Mayor, legislative, city manager	3,058,750	3,192,910	2,658,264	534,646
Finance and accounting	1,932,500	1,912,702	1,852,687	60,015
City clerk and elections	345,860	354,237	341,206	13,031
Employee relations	1,315,500	1,300,498	1,234,232	66,266
Planning and economic development	1,975,600	1,784,314	1,642,575	141,739
Public safety:				
Police	19,576,820	20,367,917	20,246,496	121,421
Fire department	9,565,280	9,559,967	9,559,967	—
Emergency medical services	2,323,171	2,470,127	2,459,866	10,261
Inspections	1,585,695	1,585,695	1,533,380	52,315
Public works:				
Public works administration	388,500	385,013	383,397	1,616
Street maintenance	2,152,750	2,233,362	2,233,362	—
Street lighting	762,750	759,832	759,832	—
Traffic operations	385,945	374,945	360,509	14,436
Mechanical maintenance	1,525,685	1,272,696	1,256,087	16,609
Engineering services:				
Engineering administration	1,170,650	1,158,023	1,158,023	—
Geographical information system	125,625	138,967	138,967	—
Health and sanitation:				
Garbage pickup	5,756,250	6,174,653	6,174,653	—
Cemetery:				
Personal services	425,000	425,000	422,562	2,438
Purchases of goods and services	299,500	299,500	283,743	15,757
Culture and recreation:				
Library	985,230	1,023,465	1,022,167	1,298
Parks and beaches	9,521,560	9,786,397	9,756,618	29,779
Community communications	552,350	558,208	510,361	47,847
Nondepartmental:				
Miscellaneous	—	259,817	259,817	—
Contingency	2,544,049	—	—	—
Transfers to other funds	2,970,256	2,163,759	2,163,759	—
Funding for school district	22,000,000	22,000,000	21,893,273	106,727
Total charges to appropriations	93,910,551	92,205,681	90,938,522	1,267,159
Budgetary fund balance, December 31	$ 2,956,523	$ 1,246,061	$ 1,432,253	$ 186,192

Source: Adapted from Governmental Accounting Standards Board, ''Guide to Implementation of GASB *Statement 34* on Basic Financial Statements—and Management's Discussion and Analysis—for State and Local Governments'' (Norwalk, CT: GASB, 2001), Appendix 2, Exhibit 12.

ILLUSTRATION 13-5 Proprietary Funds Statement of Net Position

Sample City
Statement of Net Position
Proprietary Funds
December 31, 20X6

	Enterprise Funds			Internal Service Funds
	Water and Sewer	Parking Facilities	Totals	
ASSETS				
Current assets:				
Cash and cash equivalents	$ 8,416,653	$ 369,168	$ 8,785,821	$ 3,573,776
Investments	—	—	—	214,812
Receivables, net	3,564,586	3,535	3,568,121	157,804
Due from other governments	41,494	—	41,494	—
Inventories	126,674	—	126,674	139,328
Total current assets	12,149,407	372,703	12,522,110	4,085,720
Noncurrent assets:				
Restricted cash and cash equivalents	—	1,493,322	1,493,322	—
Capital assets:				
Land and improvements	813,513	3,021,637	3,835,150	—
Construction in progress	2,572,105	—	2,572,105	—
Distribution and collection systems	41,945,183	—	41,945,183	—
Buildings and equipment	101,122,561	23,029,166	124,151,727	14,721,786
Less accumulated depreciation	(15,328,911)	(5,786,503)	(21,115,414)	(5,781,734)
Total noncurrent assets	131,124,451	21,757,622	152,882,073	8,940,052
Total assets	143,273,858	22,130,325	165,404,183	13,025,772
DEFERRED OUTFLOWS OF RESOURCES:				
Deferred refunding amount	1,200,000	—	1,200,000	—
LIABILITIES				
Current liabilities:				
Accounts payable	447,427	304,003	751,430	815,982
Due to other funds	175,000	—	175,000	1,170,388
Compensated absences	112,850	8,827	121,677	237,690
Claims and judgments	—	—	—	1,687,975
Bonds, notes, and loans payable	3,944,609	360,000	4,304,609	249,306
Total current liabilities	4,679,886	672,830	5,352,716	4,161,341
Noncurrent liabilities:				
Compensated absences	451,399	35,306	486,705	—
Claims and judgments	—	—	—	5,602,900
Bonds, notes, and loans payable	55,651,549	'17,544,019	73,195,568	—
Total noncurrent liabilities	56,102,948	17,579,325	73,682,273	5,602,900
Total liabilities	60,782,834	18,252,155	79,034,989	9,764,241
DEFERRED INFLOWS OF RESOURCES				
Deferred refunding amount	—	2,000,000	2,000,000	—
NET POSITION				
Net investment in capital assets	72,728,293	360,281	73,088,574	8,690,746
Restricted for debt service	—	1,451,996	1,451,996	—
Unrestricted	10,962,731	65,893	11,028,624	(5,429,215)
Total net position	$ 83,691,024	$ 1,878,170	85,569,194	$ 3,261,531

Some amounts reported for *business-type activities* in the Statement of Net Position are different because certain Internal Service Fund assets and liabilities are included with business-type activities.   128,072

Net position of business-type activities $ 85,697,266

Source: Adapted—to present deferred outflows and deferred inflows of resources—from Governmental Accounting Standards Board, "Guide to Implementation of GASB *Statement 34* on Basic Financial Statements—and Management's Discussion and Analysis—for State and Local Governments" (Norwalk, CT: GASB, 2001), Appendix 2, Exhibit 6.

Portions of various GASB documents, copyright by the Governmental Accounting Standards Board, 401 Merritt, PO Box 5116, Norwalk, CT 06856-5116, are reproduced with permission. Complete copies of those documents are available from the GASB.

ILLUSTRATION 13-6 Proprietary Funds Operating Statement

Sample City
Statement of Revenues, Expenses, and Changes in Fund Net Position
Proprietary Funds
For the Year Ended December 31, 20X6

| | Enterprise Funds | | | Internal Service Funds |
	Water and Sewer	Parking Facilities	Totals	
OPERATING REVENUES				
Charges for services	$11,329,883	$ 1,340,261	$12,670,144	$16,735,178
Miscellaneous	—	3,826	3,826	1,066,761
Total operating revenues	11,329,883	1,344,087	12,673,970	17,801,939
OPERATING EXPENSES				
Personal services	3,400,559	762,348	4,162,907	5,349,082
Contractual services	344,422	96,032	440,454	584,396
Utilities	754,107	100,726	854,833	239,680
Repairs and maintenance	747,315	64,617	811,932	1,960,490
Other supplies and expenses	498,213	17,119	515,332	430,596
Insurance claims and expenses	—	—	—	8,004,286
Depreciation	1,163,140	542,049	1,705,189	1,707,872
Total operating expenses	6,907,756	1,582,891	8,490,647	18,276,402
Operating income (loss)	4,422,127	(238,804)	4,183,323	(474,463)
NONOPERATING REVENUES (EXPENSES)				
Interest and investment revenue	454,793	146,556	601,349	153,371
Miscellaneous revenue	—	104,925	104,925	20,855
Interest expense	(1,600,830)	(1,166,546)	(2,767,376)	(41,616)
Miscellaneous expense	—	(46,846)	(46,846)	(176,003)
Total nonoperating revenues (expenses)	(1,146,037)	(961,911)	(2,107,948)	(43,393)
Income (loss) before contributions and transfers	3,276,090	(1,200,715)	2,075,375	(517,856)
CAPITAL CONTRIBUTIONS	1,645,919	—	1,645,919	18,788
TRANSFERS IN	—	—	—	9,008
TRANSFERS OUT	(290,000)	(211,409)	(501,409)	(184,041)
Change in net position	4,632,009	(1,412,124)	3,219,885	(674,101)
Total net position—beginning	79,059,015	3,290,294		3,935,632
Total net position—ending	$83,691,024	$ 1,878,170		$ 3,261,531

Some amounts reported for *business-type activities* in the statement of activities are different because the net revenue (expense) of certain Internal Service Funds are reported with business-type activities.	(54,061)
Change in net position of business-type activities	$ 3,165,824

Source: Governmental Accounting Standards Board, "Guide to Implementation of GASB *Statement 34* on Basic Financial Statements—and Management's Discussion and Analysis—for State and Local Governments" (Norwalk, CT: GASB, 2001), Appendix 2, Exhibit 7.

Portions of various GASB documents, copyright by the Governmental Accounting Standards Board, 401 Merritt, PO Box 5116, Norwalk, CT 06856-5116, are reproduced with permission. Complete copies of those documents are available from the GASB.

ILLUSTRATION 13-7 Proprietary Funds Statement of Cash Flows

Sample City
Statement of Cash Flows
Proprietary Funds
For the Year Ended December 31, 20X6

	Enterprise Funds			Internal Service Funds
	Water and Sewer	Parking Facilities	Totals	
CASH FLOWS FROM OPERATING ACTIVITIES				
Receipts from customers	$11,400,200	$ 1,345,292	$12,745,492	$16,805,357
Payments to suppliers	(2,725,349)	(365,137)	(3,090,486)	(3,025,956)
Payments to employees	(3,360,055)	(750,828)	(4,110,883)	(4,209,688)
Internal activity—payments to other funds	(1,296,768)	—	(1,296,768)	(1,191,926)
Claims paid	—	—	—	(8,482,451)
Other receipts (payments)	(1,165,574)	—	(1,165,574)	1,061,118
Net cash provided by operating activities	2,852,454	229,327	3,081,781	956,454
CASH FLOWS FROM NONCAPITAL FINANCING ACTIVITIES				
Operating subsidies and transfers to other funds	(290,000)	(211,409)	(501,409)	(175,033)
CASH FLOWS FROM CAPITAL AND RELATED FINANCING ACTIVITIES				
Proceeds from capital debt	4,041,322	8,660,778	12,702,100	—
Capital contributions	486,010	—	486,010	—
Purchases of capital assets	(4,194,035)	(144,716)	(4,338,751)	(400,086)
Principal paid on capital debt	(2,178,491)	(8,895,000)	(11,073,491)	(954,137)
Interest paid on capital debt	(1,479,708)	(1,166,546)	(2,646,254)	(41,616)
Other receipts (payments)	—	19,174	19,174	131,416
Net cash (used) by capital and related financing activities	(3,324,902)	(1,526,310)	(4,851,212)	(1,264,423)
CASH FLOWS FROM INVESTING ACTIVITIES				
Proceeds from sales and maturities of investments	—	—	—	15,684
Interest and dividends	454,793	143,747	598,540	148,188
Net cash provided by investing activities	454,793	143,747	598,540	163,872
Net (decrease) in cash and cash equivalents	(307,655)	(1,364,645)	(1,672,300)	(319,130)
Balances—beginning of the year	8,724,308	3,227,135	11,951,443	3,892,906
Balances—end of the year	$ 8,416,653	$ 1,862,490	$10,279,143	$ 3,573,776
Reconciliation of operating income (loss) to net cash provided (used) by operating activities:				
Operating income (loss)	$ 4,422,127	$ (238,804)	$ 4,183,323	$ (474,463)
Adjustments to reconcile operating income to net cash provided by operating activities:				
Depreciation expense	1,163,140	542,049	1,705,189	1,707,872
Change in assets and liabilities:				
Receivables, net	653,264	1,205	654,469	31,941
Inventories	2,829	—	2,829	39,790
Accounts and other payables	(297,446)	(86,643)	(384,089)	40,475
Accrued expenses	(3,091,460)	11,520	(3,079,940)	(389,161)
Net cash provided by operating activities	$ 2,852,454	$ 229,327	$ 3,081,781	$ 956,454

Noncash Capital Financing Activities:

Capital assets of $1,159,909 were acquired through contributions from developers.

Source: Governmental Accounting Standards Board, "Guide to Implementation of GASB *Statement 34* on Basic Financial Statements—and Management's Discussion and Analysis—for State and Local Governments" (Norwalk, CT: GASB, 2001), Appendix 2, Exhibit 8.

as application of quantitative criteria established in GASB *Statement No. 34,* as amended by GASB *Statement No. 64.* One potential difficulty that governments must address from time to time is that, except for the General Fund, a fund can be a major fund one year but not be a major fund (or perhaps not even exist) in a subsequent year. This difficulty can be minimized in some circumstances because governments are allowed to treat funds that do not meet the quantitative major fund criteria as major funds based on professional judgment.

A government must report its General Fund as a major fund and, again, can choose to report any other governmental fund or Enterprise Fund as a major fund for any number of reasons. At a minimum, any governmental fund or Enterprise Fund that meets **both of the following quantitative criteria for a reporting period must be reported as a major fund in that reporting period**. The *quantitative* **major fund criteria** are:

a. *Total* assets and deferred outflows of resources, liabilities and deferred inflows of resources, revenues, *or* expenditures/expenses (excluding extraordinary or special items) of that individual governmental fund or Enterprise Fund are at least **10%** of the *corresponding total* (assets and deferred outflows of resources, liabilities and deferred inflows of resources, etc.) for **all** funds of that *category or type* (i.e., total governmental funds or total Enterprise Funds).

b. The *same element* that met the 10% criterion in (a) is at least 5% of the *corresponding element total* for *all* governmental funds and Enterprise Funds *combined*.

Each fund that meets these quantitative, size-based criteria *must* be treated as a major fund. However, if a fund does not meet these criteria but the government considers the fund of particular importance to financial statement users, the government has the option to treat that fund as a major fund. That is, the major fund criteria identify the *minimum* level of major fund reporting that is required by GAAP.

In Practice 13-1 illustrates the application of the major fund tests to identify the major funds of the city of Tulsa, Oklahoma, for a recent fiscal year. Note that to apply the two tests for assets and deferred outflows of resources to Tulsa's governmental funds (other than the General Fund, which is always major) requires choosing the higher of (1) 10% of all governmental funds assets and deferred outflows of resources, or (2) 5% of the sum of all governmental funds assets and deferred outflows of resources and all Enterprise Funds assets and deferred outflows of resources as the threshold for passing the test. The total assets and deferred outflows of resources of each governmental fund are compared to this threshold number to determine whether the asset and deferred outflow test makes the fund a major fund. *Each individual governmental fund with assets and deferred outflows of resources greater than or equal to the threshold number passes the test and is a major fund.* The test is applied to liabilities and deferred inflows of resources, revenues, and expenditures and expenses in the same way. Any governmental fund that passes one or more of these four tests is a major fund. Tulsa has four major governmental funds, including:

- General Fund
- Federal and State Grants Special Revenue Fund
- Bond Capital Projects Fund
- Sales Tax Capital Projects Fund

Tulsa's nine other governmental funds are considered nonmajor funds and are aggregated and reported together in a single column in the governmental funds financial statements.

The tests are applied to Tulsa's Enterprise Funds in similar fashion. Both Enterprise Funds pass one of the tests and are major funds. The Golf Course Enterprise Fund met the Liabilities and Deferred Inflows test, and the Stormwater Management Enterprise Fund met the Assets and Deferred Outflows test.

13-1 IN PRACTICE

City of Tulsa, Oklahoma
Major Fund Calculations
For the Year Ended June 30, 20X7
(in thousands)

Fund	Assets and Deferred Outflows	Liabilities and Deferred Inflows	Revenues	Expenditures and Expenses	A	L	R	E/E	
Governmental Funds									
General Fund (Major Fund by Definition)	43,631	2,625	212,168	221,003					M
Special Revenue Funds									
Convention	1,211	25	2,649	1,249	—	—	—	—	
E-911 Operating Fund	2,530	89	3,296	1,659	—	—	—	—	
Economic Development	164	40	1,656	1,737	—	—	—	—	
Federal and State Grants	9,777	3,691	24,719	24,948	—	1	—	—	M
Short-Term Capital Improvements	4,569	217	7	8,042	—	—	—	—	
Special Development	4,285	15	1,503	1,824	—	—	—	—	
Debt Service Fund	14,268	1	20,503	15,863	—	—	—	—	
Capital Projects Funds									
Bond	42,146	7,735	75	21,527	1	1	—	—	M
Capital Cost Recovery	24	—							
Enhanced 911 Construction	3,179	—	—	1,740					
Long-Range Capital Projects	550	9	3,901	3,609	—	—	—	—	
Sales Tax	98,136	2,072	63,219	48,074	1	1	1	1	M
Enterprise Funds									
Golf Course Fund	8,072	3,760	1,480	2,552	—	1	—	—	M
Stormwater Management Fund	238,873	1,021	13,276	13,062	1	—	—	—	M
Governmental Funds Total	224,470	16,519	333,696	351,275					
10% Test Amount	22,447	1,651	33,369	35,127					
Enterprise Funds Total	246,945	4,781	14,756	15,614					
10% Test Amount	24,694	478	1,475	1,561					
Grand Total	471,415	21,300	348,452	366,889					
5% Test Amount	23,570	1,065	17,422	18,344					
Threshold for Major Funds Test for:									
Governmental Funds*	23,570	1,651	33,369	35,127					
Enterprise Funds**	24,694	1,065	17,422	18,344					

1 Indicates fund passed test
— Indicates fund failed test
M Major fund by rule
MD Major fund by designation

*Larger of Governmental Funds 10% Test and Grand Total 5% Test
**Larger of Enterprise Funds 10% Test and Grand Total 5% Test

Notice that just as fiduciary funds and Internal Service Funds cannot be presented as major funds, they also do not directly affect the determination of which governmental funds or Enterprise Funds are major funds.[3]

---

[3]Reporting internal service activities in Internal Service Funds (instead of in the General Fund, for example) is often optional under both the pre-*Statement No. 34* and the *Statement No. 34* definitions of Internal Service Funds, which may cause an indirect impact. For example, whether an activity is treated as an Internal Service Fund activity or accounted for in the governmental funds affects the application of the major fund criteria and can affect the results.

One set of illustrative, fund-based financial statements from the appendix of one of the implementation guides for *Statement No. 34* is modified to include deferred outflows and deferred inflows of resources and presented in Illustrations 13-2 to 13-9 to demonstrate the application of the fund-based reporting requirements of *Statement No. 34*. Observe that, as the preceding discussion suggests, the most notable differences from the statements illustrated in previous chapters are found in the column headings.

Also, note in reviewing the fund financial statements that each of the governmental fund and proprietary fund statements except the budgetary comparison and the statement of cash flows contains, or is accompanied by, a *reconciliation of the amounts reported in the fund financial statements and those reported in the corresponding columns of the government-wide financial statements*. The fiduciary funds are not reconciled because they are not reported in the government-wide financial statements. These reconciliations are required and are included in the examples for completeness. They could be presented in separate schedules adjacent to the fund financial statements, with detailed amounts possibly presented in the notes to the financial statements. You should review these briefly now to help you understand the relationships and differences between the government-wide financial statements and the fund financial statements. However, Chapter 14 explains and illustrates the derivation of government-wide financial statements from fund financial statements, and the *reconciliation* is simply a *summary overview* of what that derivation requires.

Governmental Funds Financial Statements

The **Balance Sheet** for governmental funds is presented in Illustration 13-2. Note that:

- Each of the four major governmental funds identified for this government is presented in a separate column.

- All nonmajor governmental funds are aggregated in a single column. (Individual fund data for funds aggregated in this column are included in combining statements in the government's CAFR but are not required in the integrated set of basic financial statements.)

- A primary government total column is required by GAAP.

- Only governmental funds (no proprietary funds or fiduciary funds) are reported in this statement. Separate statements of net position are presented for the proprietary funds and for the fiduciary funds.

- General capital assets and general long-term liabilities are ***not*** reported in the governmental fund statements.

- Deferred inflows of resources are reported separate from liabilities, and deferred outflows would be reported separate from assets.

The governmental funds operating statement, the **Statement of Revenues, Expenditures, and Changes in Fund Balances,** in Illustration 13-3 demonstrates several points made in the previous section. In addition to the major fund presentation approach, notice:

- The general *format* used. This statement is presented in the format required for all governmental fund statements. (The format was discussed and illustrated in Chapters 2 through 8.) It presents revenues followed immediately by expenditures and then a subtotal reflecting the difference between the two: the excess of revenues over (under) expenditures. Other financing sources and uses, special items, and extraordinary items are presented in sections following this key subtotal.

- That *interfund transfers* are reported as *other financing sources or uses*.

- The presentation of *special items* (and extraordinary items when present).

- That the amount reported as a *special item* in Illustration 13-3 *differs* from the amount reported for it in the governmental activities column of the government-wide Statement of Activities in Illustration 13-12. This difference occurs because the two statements are using different measurement focuses and bases of accounting.

The **budgetary comparison statement** presented in Illustration 13-4 can be presented as part of the integrated set of basic financial statements, as presumed here,

13-2 IN PRACTICE

GFOA Policy Statement: Budgetary Reporting

Presenting Budget to Actual Comparisons Within the Basic Financial Statements

Background. Generally accepted accounting principles (GAAP) traditionally have required that state and local governments present as part of their basic audited financial statements a budget-to-actual comparison statement. This treatment has provided the essential link between the legal budget and GAAP financial reporting, which has served to enhance the credibility of both. During the Governmental Accounting Standards Board's (GASB) financial reporting model project, the Government Finance Officers Association (GFOA) adopted a policy statement urging the GASB to retain the budget-to-actual comparisons as a basic financial statement.

In 1999, the GASB issued *Statement No. 34*, "Basic Financial Statements—and Management's Discussion and Analysis—for State and Local Governments," which established a new financial reporting model for state and local governments. GASB *Statement No. 34* will henceforth allow governments to choose to present mandated budgetary comparisons either as part of the basic audited financial statements or as required supplementary information (RSI). By definition, RSI does *not* fall within the scope of the independent audit of the financial statements, although auditors are required to perform certain limited procedures in connection with RSI.

Adherence to the budget is of paramount importance to the majority of a government's stakeholders. Indeed, most of a government's key decisions are based in one form or another upon the budget. Given the importance attached to the budget, it is essential that stakeholders be provided reasonable assurance that a government has maintained budgetary compliance. Until GASB *Statement No. 34*, this assurance has been provided by the inclusion of the budget to actual comparison statement within the audited financial statements. Although under generally accepted auditing standards (GAAS) auditors are required to consider the effect of material instances of non-compliance, the GFOA believes that relegating budgetary information to the unaudited RSI significantly weakens this important control. As a consequence, confidence could be diminished for the public and other stakeholders in the government's budget, and even potentially in the government itself. It may also diminish the importance of the Comprehensive Annual Financial Report (CAFR) to policymakers, government managers, investors, citizens and other stakeholders.

Recommendation. The GFOA recommends that *all* state and local governments present mandated budgetary comparisons as part of their audited basic financial statements. The retention of the budget to actual comparison as a basic financial statement ensures that the strong link that has existed between the budget and financial reporting in the past will continue to enhance the credibility of both in the future.

or as required supplementary information. (The Government Finance Officers Association strongly recommends presentation as part of the basic financial statements, as do the authors of this text.) Budgetary comparisons in this statement are required for the General Fund and for each annually budgeted *major* Special Revenue Fund. Budgetary comparisons are not required for any other funds, but budgetary comparison statements or schedules may be presented as *supplemental information,* and often are. No budgetary comparisons are required in the basic financial statements for any Capital Projects Fund, Debt Service Fund, or Permanent Fund. Sample City must present a budgetary comparison for its major Special Revenue Fund—HUD Programs—in addition to the General Fund budgetary comparison illustrated here.

The GASB used the government's budget document format instead of its operating statement format in the illustration in *Statement No. 34*. However, the budgetary comparison statement may be presented by using the same format as the GAAP-basis Statement of Revenues, Expenditures, and Changes in Fund Balances. *If the budgetary basis differs from GAAP*, a *reconciliation* of the budgetary basis information presented in this statement with the GAAP-basis information presented in the governmental funds Statement of Revenue, Expenditures, and Changes in Fund Balances is required. The budgetary basis does differ from GAAP for the government reported in the illustrative budgetary comparison statement in Illustration 13-4. The budgetary-basis to GAAP-basis reconciliation is not presented here but was discussed and illustrated in Chapter 4 (see Illustration 4-9).

Proprietary Funds Financial Statements

The required proprietary funds financial statements—Statement of Net Position; Statement of Revenues, Expenses, and Changes in Net Position; and Statement of Cash Flows—are presented in Illustrations 13-5 to 13-7. Note in each statement that major fund reporting is used for Enterprise Funds but not for Internal Service Funds. Note also that only two Enterprise Funds are illustrated in this example because both are major funds. For any nonmajor Enterprise Funds, the statement would include a column labeled "Other Enterprise Funds." All Internal Service Funds are aggregated and presented in a single, fund-type column. Aside from the columnar presentation, the format and content of the proprietary fund statements are identical to those of the statements illustrated in Chapters 10 and 11 on Enterprise Funds and Internal Service Funds.

Fiduciary Funds Financial Statements

The fiduciary funds financial statements required by *Statement No. 34* as part of the integrated basic financial statements are presented in Illustrations 13-8 and 13-9. Recall that fiduciary funds, like Internal Service Funds, are reported by fund type, not by major funds.

ILLUSTRATION 13-8   Statement of Net Position—Fiduciary Funds (and Fiduciary Component Units)

Sample City
Statement of Fiduciary Net Position
Fiduciary Funds
December 31, 20X6

	Employee Retirement Plan	Private-Purpose Trusts	Agency Funds
ASSETS			
Cash and cash equivalents	$ 1,973	$ 1,250	$ 44,889
Receivables:			
Interest and dividends	508,475	760	—
Other receivables	6,826	—	183,161
Total receivables	515,301	760	183,161
Investments, at fair value:			
U.S. government obligations	13,056,037	80,000	—
Municipal bonds	6,528,019	—	—
Corporate bonds	16,320,047	—	—
Corporate stocks	26,112,075	—	—
Other investments	3,264,009	—	—
Total investments	65,280,187	80,000	—
Total assets	65,797,461	82,010	$228,050
LIABILITIES			
Accounts payable	—	1,234	—
Refunds payable and others	1,358	—	$228,050
Total liabilities	1,358	1,234	$228,050
NET POSITION			
Held in trust for pension benefits and other purposes	$65,796,103	$80,776	

> Statements of individual pension plans and external investment pools are required to be presented in the notes to the financial statements if separate GAAP statements for those individual plans or pools are not available.

Source: Governmental Accounting Standards Board, "Guide to Implementation of GASB *Statement 34* on Basic Financial Statements—and Management's Discussion and Analysis—for State and Local Governments" (Norwalk, CT: GASB, 2001), Appendix 2, Exhibit 9.

Portions of various GASB documents, copyright by the Governmental Accounting Standards Board, 401 Merritt, PO Box 5116, Norwalk, CT 06856-5116, are reproduced with permission. Complete copies of those documents are available from the GASB.

ILLUSTRATION 13-9 Statement of Changes in Net Position—Fiduciary Funds (and Fiduciary Component Units)

Sample City
Statement of Changes in Fiduciary Net Position
Fiduciary Funds
For the Year Ended December 31, 20X6

	Employee Retirement Plan	Private-Purpose Trusts
ADDITIONS		
Contributions:		
Employer	$ 2,721,341	$ —
Plan members	1,421,233	—
Total contributions	4,142,574	—
Investment income:		
Net appreciation (depreciation) in fair value of investments	(272,522)	—
Interest	2,460,871	4,560
Dividends	1,445,273	—
Total investment earnings	3,633,622	4,560
Less investment expense	216,428	—
Net investment earnings	3,417,194	4,560
Total additions	7,559,768	4,560
DEDUCTIONS		
Benefits	2,453,047	3,800
Refunds of contributions	464,691	—
Administrative expenses	87,532	678
Total deductions	3,005,270	4,478
Net increase	4,554,498	82
Net position—beginning of the year	61,241,605	80,694
Net position—end of the year	$65,796,103	$80,776

Source: Governmental Accounting Standards Board, "Guide to Implementation of GASB *Statement 34* on Basic Financial Statements—and Management's Discussion and Analysis—for State and Local Governments" (Norwalk, CT: GASB, 2001), Appendix 2, Exhibit 10.

Portions of various GASB documents, copyright by the Governmental Accounting Standards Board, 401 Merritt, PO Box 5116, Norwalk, CT 06856-5116, are reproduced with permission. Complete copies of those documents are available from the GASB.

The required statements—a **Statement of Fiduciary Net Position** and a **Statement of Changes in Fiduciary Net Position**—are the same as those illustrated for Trust Funds in Chapter 12. Finally, if a government has component units that are fiduciary in nature, they should be included in the appropriate fund type column in these statements. Fiduciary funds and component units that are fiduciary in nature are *not* included in the government-wide financial statements.

GOVERNMENT-WIDE FINANCIAL STATEMENTS

As noted earlier, the basic financial statements include two government-wide statements—the Statement of Net Position and the Statement of Activities. The data for these statements are derived from the governmental fund and proprietary fund statements already discussed in this chapter. This conversion process is described in detail in Chapter 14. As you will see in the discussion and illustrations that follow, these statements have several common features. For instance, both government-wide statements:

- Distinguish between the primary government and its discretely presented component units. (For most governments, the primary government is simply the government *legal* entity. Most separate legal entities that must be reported as part of the government's reporting entity are discretely presented in separate columns and rows in the primary government's government-wide financial statements. The reporting entity is covered in detail in Chapter 15.)
- Focus on the primary government (not the discretely presented component units).
- Distinguish between the primary government's governmental activities and its business-type activities.
- Present a total column for the primary government. (A total column for the entity as a whole that combines the primary government data and the discretely presented component unit data is permitted but is not required.)
- Apply proprietary fund accounting standards to both governmental activities and business-type activities.
- Exclude fiduciary fund and fiduciary component unit information.

Thus, the government-wide financial statements must clearly distinguish and report:

1. Governmental activities
2. Business-type activities
3. Primary government totals
4. Discretely presented component units

The goal of reporting in the government-wide financial statements is to present fairly the financial position and operating results of each of these four reporting focuses.[4] Governmental activities and business-type activities information should not be thought of as merely subclassifications of primary government information. Indeed, the GASB clearly states, in its Comprehensive Implementation Guide, that **materiality** must be judged (1) in terms of **the governmental activities column and the business-type activities column** presented *in the government-wide statements* and (2) in terms of **each major fund column** presented *in the fund financial statements*.

The distinction between governmental activities and business-type activities in the government-wide financial statements is important. Governmental activities are financed primarily through taxes, intergovernmental revenues, and other non-exchange revenues—and are generally reported in governmental funds (and perhaps in Internal Service Funds). For all but a few governments, all general capital assets and general long-term liabilities are part of governmental activities as well. Examples of governmental activities include general administration, public safety, education, streets and roads, and health and sanitation.

Business-type activities are financed in whole or in part by fees charged to external users for goods or services and are generally reported in Enterprise Funds. (Some governments have Internal Service Fund activities that are part of business-type activities, however.) Common examples include public utilities, mass transportation, landfills, airports, and certain types of recreational facilities such as golf courses and swimming pools.

---

[4]Audit standards require auditors to express (or disclaim) an opinion on whether governmental activities, business-type activities, and each major fund are fairly presented in accordance with GAAP. Materiality judgments for these opinion units must always be based on these individual opinion units, never on more aggregated amounts such as total primary governments or total governmental funds.

Statement of Net Position

The format of the government-wide **Statement of Net Position** in Illustration 13-10 is essentially the same as for the proprietary fund financial statements presented in Chapters 10 and 11 and the proprietary fund Statement of Net Position shown in Illustration 13-5. The illustration shown for the proprietary fund Statement of Net Position uses a net position format, which subtracts liabilities and deferred inflows of resources from assets and deferred outflows of resources and leaves total net position as the final number on the statement. The government-wide Statement of Net Position in Illustration 13-10 also is presented using the net position approach. As with the proprietary fund Statement of Net Position, the government-wide Statement

---

ILLUSTRATION 13-10   Government-Wide Statement of Net Position

Sample City
Statement of Net Position
December 31, 20X6

> Alternatively, the internal balances could be reported on separate lines as assets and liabilities.

	Primary Government			
	Governmental Activities	**Business-Type Activities**	**Total**	**Component Units**
ASSETS				
Cash and cash equivalents	$ 13,597,899	$ 10,516,820	$ 24,114,719	$ 303,935
Investments	27,365,221	64,575	27,429,796	7,428,952
Receivables (net)	12,833,132	3,609,615	16,442,747	4,042,290
Internal balances	313,768	(313,768)	—	—
Inventories	322,149	126,674	448,823	83,697
Capital assets, net				
Land, improvements, and construction in progress	28,435,025	6,408,150	34,843,175	751,239
Other capital assets, net of depreciation	141,587,735	144,980,601	286,568,336	36,993,547
	170,022,760	151,388,751	321,411,511	37,744,786
Total assets	224,454,929	165,392,667	389,847,596	49,603,660
DEFERRED OUTFLOWS OF RESOURCES				
Deferred refunding amount	—	1,200,000	1,200,000	—
LIABILITIES				
Accounts payable	7,538,543	786,842	8,325,385	1,803,332
Unearned revenue	1,435,599	—	1,435,599	38,911
Noncurrent liabilities:				
Due within one year	9,236,000	4,426,286	13,662,286	1,426,639
Due in more than one year	80,802,378	73,682,273	154,484,651	27,106,151
Total liabilities	99,012,520	78,895,401	177,907,921	30,375,033
DEFERRED INFLOWS OF RESOURCES				
Deferred refunding amount	2,500,000	2,000,000	4,500,000	—
NET POSITION				
Net investment in capital assets	103,711,386	73,088,574	176,799,960	15,906,392
Restricted for:				
Capital projects	11,290,079	—	11,290,079	492,445
Debt service	3,076,829	1,451,996	4,528,825	—
Community development projects	6,886,663	—	6,886,663	—
Other purposes	3,874,736	—	3,874,736	—
Unrestricted (deficit)	(5,897,284)	11,156,696	5,259,412	2,829,790
Total net position	$122,942,409	$ 85,697,266	$208,639,675	$19,228,627

Source: Adapted—to illustrate reporting deferred outflows and deferred inflows of resources—from Governmental Accounting Standards Board, Implementation Guide, "Guide to Implementation of GASB *Statement 34* on Basic Financial Statements—and Management's Discussion and Analysis—for State and Local Governments" (Norwalk, CT: GASB, 2001), Appendix 2, Exhibit 1.

Portions of various GASB documents, copyright by the Governmental Accounting Standards Board, 401 Merritt, PO Box 5116, Norwalk, CT 06856-5116, are reproduced with permission. Complete copies of those documents are available from the GASB.

of Net Position may be presented using a balance sheet format (i.e., assets and deferred outflows are totaled, liabilities, deferred inflows, and net position are totaled, and the two totals are equal). Many governments are apt to use the same format for both the fund financial statements and the government-wide statements. Also, even though a classified statement (distinguishing between current and noncurrent assets and liabilities) is required for the proprietary fund statement, it is optional for the government-wide Statement of Net Position.

The information presented in the business-type activities column of the Statement of Net Position is typically the same or virtually the same as the information presented in the total column of a government's proprietary funds Statement of Net Position for the total of its Enterprise Funds. Therefore, the most remarkable aspect of the Statement of Net Position is the "Governmental Activities" column. This column reports all assets and liabilities of general government activities on a consolidating basis using essentially the same accounting principles and standards that are required for proprietary funds. Recognize several key points:

- Assets and liabilities should be presented in the order of their relative liquidity.
- Deferred outflows of resources are reported in a separate section following assets and deferred inflows in a separate section following liabilities. (Most deferred outflows and deferred inflows of resources such as accumulated increases and decreases on hedging derivatives and deferred revenues from service concession arrangements are not illustrated because they are beyond the scope of the text.)
- Liabilities due within one year must be distinguished from those due in more than one year.
- Capital assets should be reported either (1) as a single line item, (2) differentiating between depreciable and nondepreciable assets (if nondepreciable assets are material, with major classes disclosed in the notes), or (3) by major classes of assets.
- General capital assets—including infrastructure, such as roads and bridges—less accumulated depreciation on these capital assets are reported in the "Governmental Activities" column.
- Infrastructure capital assets reported by using the modified approach (discussed later) should be reported as a separate line item.
- General long-term liabilities adjusted to reflect application of the effective interest method—that is, at their face value plus or minus any unamortized premium or discount—are reported in this column.
- Interfund payables and receivables between governmental funds have been eliminated. Likewise, interfund payables and receivables between Enterprise Funds have been eliminated.
- The internal balances reported in the governmental activities column and in the business-type activities column are the net payable and receivable amounts between governmental activities and business-type activities. (These internal balances are eliminated in deriving the primary government totals.)
- The difference between a government's assets and deferred outflows of resources and its liabilities and deferred inflows of resources—its net position—should be presented in three components:
  1. Net investment in capital assets
  2. Restricted—distinguishing between major categories of restrictions
  3. Unrestricted

Net position for governmental activities, as well as for business-type activities, the primary government, and component units, must be presented in these three classifications.

The government-wide **Statement of Activities** is presented in a unique format intended to depict the following:

Statement of Activities

1. Cost (Expense) of providing services by function
2. Related program revenues derived from that function
3. Net burden that each function places on taxpayers or other providers of general revenues
4. Sources from which the net cost of the government's activities are financed

Because this statement presents information quite differently from other statements we have studied, we discuss it extensively.

The typical format used for a Statement of Activities of a general purpose unit of government is shown in Illustration 13-11. Note that both rows and columns are used to distinguish primary government governmental activities, primary government business-type activities, the total primary government, and discretely presented component units.

Observe that the columns of the upper portion of the Statement of Activities present data by function or program, using the following equation:

$$
\begin{array}{l}
- \text{ Expenses (of a particular function)} \\
+ \text{ Program Revenues (of the function)} \\
= \text{ Net (Expense) Revenue (of the function)}
\end{array}
$$

The net expense or revenue information is presented in four columns that distinguish governmental activities, business-type activities, total primary government, and discretely presented component unit information. Alternatively, terms such as "Cost of Services" and "Net Cost of Services" may be used instead of "Expenses" and "Net (Expense) Revenue."

Each function or program classification is presented in a separate row in the upper portion of the Statement of Activities. The first set of rows reports governmental activities. The second set of rows presents the information for business-type activities. The business-type activities information is followed by a row presenting the total primary government, then by a row or rows presenting the functional classifications for the discretely presented component units. (This format is the most common, but other formats that meet the functional reporting requirements are permitted.)

For *governmental activities,* the minimum level of functional detail required for direct expenses in the upper portion of the Statement of Activities is the level of detail required in the governmental fund Statement of Revenues, Expenditures, and Changes in Fund Balances. This statement is typically presented by function. As discussed in earlier chapters, common examples of functions include general government, public safety, highways and streets, education, and so on. Governments may report more functional detail than found in the governmental fund operating statement. For example, public safety may be reported in the police, fire, and corrections subfunctions instead of the aggregated public safety function on the Statement of Activities.

Business-type activities (usually activities accounted for in Enterprise Funds) must be presented by identifiable activity. GASB *Statement No. 37,* "Basic Financial Statements—and Management's Discussion and Analysis—for State and Local Governments: Omnibus," describes a different identifiable activity as follows:

> An activity within an enterprise fund is *identifiable* if it has a specific revenue stream and related expenses and gains and losses that are accounted for separately. Determining whether an activity is *different* may require the use of professional judgment, but is generally based on the goods, services, or programs provided by an activity. For example, providing natural gas is different from supplying water or electricity, even though all three are regarded as "utility services." On the other hand, separate identifiable water districts would not be considered "different" activities, even though they may serve different parts of the government.[5]

For example, a government might report a Water and Sewer Enterprise Fund in the proprietary fund financial statements. In the Statement of Activities it would be necessary to report a Water Activity and a Sewer Activity if the government separately

---

[5]Governmental Accounting Standards Board, *Statement No. 37,* "Basic Financial Statements—and Management's Discussion and Analysis—for State and Local Governments: Omnibus" (Norwalk, CT: GASB, June 2001), par. 10, Fn. c.

ILLUSTRATION 13-11 Government-Wide Statement of Activities Format

For most governments, the following format provides the most appropriate method for displaying the information required to be reported in the Statement of Activities:

Functions	Expenses	Program Revenues			Net (Expense) Revenue and Changes in Net Position			
		Charges for Services	Operating Grants and Contributions	Capital Grants and Contributions	Primary Government			Component Units
					Governmental Activities	Business-Type Activities	Total	
Primary government								
Governmental activities								
Function #1	XXX	XX	X	X	(XX)		(XX)	
Function #2	XXX	XX	X	—	(XX)		(XX)	
Function #3	XXX	XX	X	X	(X)		(X)	
Total governmental activities	XXXX	XXX	XX	XX	(XXX)		(XX)	
Business-type activities (BTA):								
BTA #1	XXXX	XXXX	—	X		XX	XX	
BTA #2	XXXXX	XXXX	—	XX		XXX	XXX	
Total business-type activities	XXXXXX	XXXXX	—	XX		XXX	XXX	
Total primary government	XXXXXXX	XXXXX	XX	XXX	(XXX)	XXX	XX	
Component units								
CU #1	XXXX	XXXX	XX	XX				XX
General revenues—detailed					XXX	X	XXX	—
Contributions to permanent funds					XX	—	XX	—
Special items					X	X	X	—
Transfers					XX	(XX)	—	—
Total general revenues, contributions, special items, and transfers					XXX	X	XXX	—
Change in net position					X	XX	XX	XX
Net position—beginning					XXXXX	XXXXX	XXXXXX	XXXXX
Net position—ending					XXXXX	XXXXX	XXXXXX	XXXXX

Source: Governmental Accounting Standards Board, *Statement No. 34* (Norwalk, CT: GASB, 1999), par. 54, as amended

Portions of various GASB documents, copyright by the Governmental Accounting Standards Board, 401 Merritt, PO Box 5116, Norwalk, CT 06856-5116, are reproduced with permission. Complete copies of those documents are available from the GASB.

accounts for revenues, expenses, gains, and losses for each of these activities. Note that the level of detail described for both governmental activities and business-type activities is the *minimum* detail required. The GASB encourages presentation of additional detail when practicable.

General revenues (such as taxes), special items, extraordinary items, and transfers are reported in the bottom half of the statement—after the total net program expenses.

Measurement Focus Government-wide financial statements, including the Statement of Activities, are reported using the flow of economic resources measurement focus and accrual basis of accounting. The modified accrual basis of accounting is *not* used in these statements, even to report governmental activities. Revenues, expenses (not expenditures), special items, extraordinary items, and other changes such as capital contributions must be measured and reported for governmental activities in the same manner as for business-type activities. Therefore, governmental activities revenues that do not meet the availability criteria because they are not collected within the availability period (e.g., not more than 60 days after the fiscal year end for property taxes) are recognized in the current year for government-wide reporting, even though recognition must be deferred in the governmental fund financial statements. Likewise, whereas the *proceeds* from the sale of land are reported in the governmental fund financial statements, only the *gain or loss* is reported in the Statement of Activities. Indeed, the amount might be material in the fund statement and be reported as a special item but not be reported as a special item in the government-wide statement because it is immaterial.

Depreciation expense on general capital assets, including infrastructure capital assets—not capital outlay expenditures—is reported in the Statement of Activities. Retirement of GLTL is not reported in the statement because it does not change economic resources and is an expenditure, not an expense. Whereas interest expenditures in the governmental fund statements reflect cash interest due and payable during a period, interest expense, using the effective interest method, is reported in the government-wide financial statements. The interest expense measurement includes (1) amortization of discounts and premiums and of deferred interest expense adjustments associated with general government refundings and (2) changes in accrued interest payable as is true for proprietary funds.

Expenses for items—such as *compensated absences, claims and judgments, other postemployment benefits (OPEB), and pensions*—that are recognized as governmental fund expenditures when due often differ significantly from the expenditure amounts. In the fund-based statements, the "normally expected to be liquidated from available, expendable financial resources" criterion essentially means that changes in unmatured, noncurrent liabilities associated with such items are not reflected in expenditures. In measuring the expense to be reported, this criterion does not apply, and the changes in the related long-term liabilities affect the expense measurement.

To illustrate, assume that a government incurs $1,000,000 of general government compensated absence costs during a fiscal year; $600,000 of these costs are paid during the year or represent currently due and payable amounts at the end of the year. There were no fund liabilities for compensated absences at the beginning of the year. The government should report $600,000 of expenditures for compensated absences in the governmental funds Statement of Revenues, Expenditures, and Changes in Fund Balances. In its governmental activities column in the government-wide Statement of Activities, the government should include expenses (allocated by function) for compensated absences of $1,000,000.

Certain other issues affecting the Statement of Activities also require attention. In particular, the presentation of expenses and the classification of revenues as general revenues versus program revenues are of critical importance in the government-wide Statement of Activities.

The government-wide Statement of Activities reports *expenses,* not expenditures, for all functions, including those of governmental activities. Therefore, depreciation expense is included in the amounts reported as expenses. Likewise, other items that constitute expenditures but not expenses—such as general government capital outlay expenditures and general long-term debt retirement expenditures—are *not* reported in this statement.

Reporting Expenses

The minimum requirement for reporting expenses in the Statement of Activities is that **direct expenses**, including most depreciation expense, are to be **reported by function**. Governments may also **allocate indirect expenses**. Some functions, such as general government, support services, or administration, include indirect expenses of other functions. Note in the Statement of Activities in Illustration 13-12 that general government is reported as a functional category. If indirect expenses such as these are allocated, a government must present direct expenses in one column and allocated amounts of indirect expenses in a second column, labeled "Indirect Expenses." Presentation of indirect expenses in a separate column is required to enhance comparability with those governments that do not allocate these expenses. (A third column, totaling the direct and indirect expenses of each function, is permitted but not required.) In practice the reporting of a separate indirect expense column will typically be limited to governmental entities that employ significant cost allocation practices as opposed to incidental administrative allocations such as utility expenses and property insurance premiums.

Interest expense on general long-term liabilities is normally an *indirect* expense that is not to be allocated to functions. *It is to be reported as a separate line item.* However, interest on long-term debt should be included in *direct* expenses if (1) the borrowing is essential to the creation or continuing existence of a program, and (2) it would be misleading to exclude the interest from direct expenses of that program. An example would be a loan fund where the government, as an economic development incentive, provides loans for small businesses at lower interest rates than the businesses could obtain on their own. Revolving borrowing provides the ongoing resources to sustain the program indefinitely.

Depreciation expense on a capital asset that is specifically *identifiable* with a specific function should be included in the *direct* expenses of that function. Depreciation expense on capital assets used for several functions should be allocated on a ratable basis to direct expenses of the various functions served. Depreciation on *general infrastructure* capital assets should be reported in direct expenses of the function (typically public works or highways and streets) that the reporting government normally associates with capital outlays for and maintenance of the infrastructure. Alternatively, depreciation on infrastructure capital assets may be reported as a separate line item. Finally, depreciation on capital assets that essentially serve *all* the functions—such as the county courthouse or the state capitol building or most school buildings—is reported on a separate line (function) as unallocated depreciation, *not* allocated to functions.

GASB *Statement No. 34* requires program revenues to be reported in at least three classifications and deducted from the expenses of the related function. The three classifications of revenues that are program revenues are:

Program vs. General Revenues

1. Charges for services
2. Program-specific operating grants and contributions
3. Program-specific capital grants and contributions

Illustration 13-12 includes a column for each type of program revenues. Endowment and Permanent Fund investment income and other investment income that is externally restricted to a specific program may be allocated to the appropriate program-specific grant and contribution category, or a fourth column may be added to report restricted investment income. The GASB permits governments to

---

ILLUSTRATION 13-12 Government-Wide Statement of Activities

The reference to Note 1 is intended to call the reader's attention to the disclosure of the amount of depreciation expense that is included in the individual programs.

Sample City
Statement of Activities
For the Year Ended December 31, 20X6

Functions/Programs	Expenses	Program Revenues: Charges for Services	Operating Grants and Contributions	Capital Grants and Contributions	Net (Expense) Revenue and Changes in Net Position — Primary Government: Governmental Activities	Business-Type Activities	Total	Component Units
Primary government:								
Governmental activities:								
General government	$ 9,709,509	$ 3,333,265	$ 843,617	$ —	$ (5,532,627)		$ (5,532,627)	
Public safety	34,782,144	1,198,855	1,307,693	62,300	(32,213,296)		(32,213,296)	
Public works	10,131,928	850,000	—	2,252,615	(7,029,313)		(7,029,313)	
Engineering services	1,299,645	704,793	—	—	(594,852)		(594,852)	
Health and sanitation	6,705,675	5,612,267	575,000	—	(518,408)		(518,408)	
Cemetery	735,866	212,496	72,689	—	(450,681)		(450,681)	
Culture and recreation	11,534,045	3,995,199	2,450,000	—	(5,088,846)		(5,088,846)	
Community development	2,994,389	—	—	2,580,000	(414,389)		(414,389)	
Education (payment to school district)	21,893,273	—	—	—	(21,893,273)		(21,893,273)	
Interest on long-term debt	6,242,893	—	—	—	(6,242,893)		(6,242,893)	
Total governmental activities (See Note 1)	106,029,367	15,906,875	5,248,999	4,894,915	(79,978,578)		(79,978,578)	
Business-type activities:								
Water	3,643,315	4,159,350	—	1,159,909	—	$ 1,675,944	1,675,944	
Sewer	4,909,885	7,170,533	—	486,010	—	2,746,658	2,746,658	
Parking facilities	2,824,368	1,449,012	—	—	—	(1,375,356)	(1,375,356)	
Total business-type activities	11,377,568	12,778,895	—	1,645,919	—	3,047,246	3,047,246	
Total primary government	$117,406,935	$28,685,770	$5,248,999	$6,540,834	(79,978,578)	3,047,246	(76,931,332)	
Component units:								
Landfill	$ 3,382,157	$ 3,857,858	$ —	$ 11,397				$ 487,098
Public school system	31,186,498	705,765	3,937,083	—				(26,543,650)
Total component units	$ 34,568,655	$ 4,563,623	$3,937,083	$ 11,397				(26,056,552)

	Governmental Activities	Business-Type Activities	Total	Component Units
General revenues:				
Taxes:				
Property taxes, levied for general purposes	51,693,573	—	51,693,573	—
Property taxes, levied for debt service	4,726,244	—	4,726,244	—
Franchise taxes	4,055,505	—	4,055,505	—
Public service taxes	8,969,887	—	8,969,887	—
Payment from Sample City	—	—	—	21,893,273
Grants and contributions not restricted to specific programs	1,457,820	—	1,457,820	6,461,708
Investment earnings	1,885,455	619,987	2,505,442	884,277
Miscellaneous	884,907	—	884,907	19,950
Special item—gain on sale of park land	2,653,488	—	2,653,488	—
Transfers	501,409	(501,409)	—	—
Total general revenues, special items, and transfers	76,828,288	118,578	76,946,866	29,259,208
Change in net position	(3,150,290)	3,165,824	15,534	3,202,656
Net position—beginning	126,092,699	82,531,442	208,624,141	16,025,971
Net position—ending	$122,942,409	$85,697,266	$208,639,675	$19,228,627

Source: Governmental Accounting Standards Board, "Guide to Implementation of GASB *Statement 34* on Basic Financial Statements—and Management's Discussion and Analysis—for State and Local Governments" (Norwalk, CT: GASB, 2001), Appendix 2, Exhibit 2.
Portions of various GASB documents, copyright by the Governmental Accounting Standards Board, 401 Merritt, PO Box 5116, Norwalk, CT 06856-5116, are reproduced with permission. Complete copies of those documents are available from the GASB.

add additional detail that is judged to be useful. *All revenues that are not program revenues are general revenues.*

Specifically, *Statement No. 34* states:

Program revenues

Program revenues derive directly from the program itself or from parties outside the reporting government's constituency; they reduce the net cost of the function to be financed from the government's general revenues. The statement of activities should separately report three categories of program revenues: (a) charges for services; (b) program-specific operating grants and contributions; and (c) program-specific capital grants and contributions.

Charges for services is the term used for a broad category of program revenues that arise from charges to customers, applicants, or others who purchase, use, or directly benefit from the goods, services, or privileges provided or are otherwise directly affected by the services. Revenues in this category *include fees charged for specific services*, such as water use or garbage collection; *licenses and permits,* such as dog licenses, liquor licenses, and building permits; *operating special assessments,* such as for street cleaning or special street lighting; and *any other amounts charged to service recipients. Fines and forfeitures* are also included in this category because they result from direct charges to those who are otherwise directly affected by a program or service, even though they receive no benefit. *Payments from other governments that are exchange transactions*—for example, when County A reimburses County B for boarding County A's prisoners—also should be reported as charges for services.

Program-specific grants and contributions (operating and capital) include revenues arising from mandatory and voluntary nonexchange transactions with other governments, organizations, or individuals that are restricted for use in a particular program. Some grants and contributions consist of capital assets or resources that are restricted for capital purposes—to purchase, construct, or renovate capital assets associated with a specific program. These should be reported separately from grants and contributions that may be used *either* for operating expenses *or* for capital expenditures of the program at the discretion of the reporting government. These categories of program revenue are specifically attributable to a program and reduce the net expense of that program to the reporting government. For example, a state may provide an operating grant to a county sheriff's department for a drug-awareness-and-enforcement program or a capital grant to finance construction of a new jail. *Multipurpose grants* (those that provide financing for more than one program) should be *reported as program revenue if the amounts restricted to each program are specifically identified* in either the grant award or the grant application. Multipurpose grants that do not provide for specific identification of the programs and amounts should be reported as general revenue.

Earnings on endowments or permanent fund investments should be reported as program revenue if restricted to a specific program or programs. Earnings from endowments or Permanent Funds that finance "general fund programs" or "general operating expenses," for example, should not be reported as program revenue. Similarly, *earnings on investments not held by Permanent Funds may also be legally restricted to specific functions or programs.* For example, interest earnings on state grants may be required to be used to support a specific program. When earnings on the *invested accumulated resources* of a program are *legally restricted* to be used for that program, the net cost to be financed by the government's general revenues is reduced, and those investment earnings should be reported as program revenue.

General revenues

All revenues that do not qualify as program revenue are general revenues. All taxes [imposed by the reporting government], even those that are levied for a specific purpose, *are general revenues* and should be reported by type of tax—for example, sales tax, property tax, franchise tax, income tax. All other nontax revenues (including interest, grants, and contributions) that do not meet the criteria to be reported as program revenues should also be reported as general revenues. General revenues should be reported after total net expense of the government's functions.

Reporting contributions to term and permanent endowments, special and extraordinary items, and transfers

Contributions to term and permanent endowments and permanent fund principal, special and extraordinary items, and transfers between governmental and business-type activities should each be reported separately from, but in the same manner as, general revenues. That is, these sources of financing the net cost of the government's programs should be reported at the bottom of the statement of activities to arrive at the all-inclusive change in net position for the period.[6]

Charges for services result primarily from exchange transactions or from exchange-like transactions such as charges to customers or applicants who purchase, use, or directly benefit from the goods, services, or privileges provided. One clear exception is that the GASB requires fines and forfeitures to be reported in

---

[6]Governmental Accounting Standards Board, *Statement No. 34,* "Basic Financial Statements—and Management's Discussion and Analysis—for State and Local Governments" (Norwalk, CT: GASB, June 1999), pars. 48–53, as amended by *Statement No. 37,* par. 17. (Emphasis added.)

this category. Other charges for services include water use fees, garbage collection fees, and fees for licenses and permits such as driver's licenses, dog licenses, and building permits.

Charges for services are program revenues regardless of whether the use of the resources raised is unrestricted, restricted for the use of the program that generated the charge, or restricted for the use of a different program. The *other* categories of *program revenues must be restricted to a specific function or program* to be reported as program revenues. Charges for services are classified as program revenues of the function that generates the revenues—even if the revenues are restricted for use for a different function. All other program revenues are classified as revenues of the function to which their use is restricted.

Grants and contributions that are restricted to use for a single program are program revenues. Multipurpose restricted grants and contributions that specifically identify the amounts restricted to each of the multiple programs are program revenues as well. All other multipurpose grants and contributions are general revenues.

Restricted grants and contributions that are restricted for the purchase, construction, or renovation of *capital* assets associated with a specific program are reported as program-specific capital grants (or capital grants and contributions). All other restricted grants and contributions that qualify as program revenues are reported as program-specific operating grants (or grants and contributions). Earnings on investments of endowments or of Permanent Funds are reported as program revenues if the earnings are restricted to use for a specific program or function, as are restricted investment earnings from the temporary investment of program-specific grants and contributions. All other investment income is reported as general revenues.

Pass-through grants and on-behalf payments, discussed in Chapter 5, are program revenues. Likewise, if a local government receives an allocation of a tax from a state government and the resources are restricted to a specific program, it should be reported as a program revenue. For the local government, this revenue source is shared revenues (from the taxes of another government). It is not a tax of the reporting government. All of these amounts should be reported as operating grants and contributions unless a shared revenue must be used for capital asset purposes.

As stated previously, all revenues that are not program revenues are general revenues. *All taxes of the reporting government—whether restricted or unrestricted—are general revenues.* All unrestricted investment income, even if earned on restricted investments, is general revenue. All unrestricted contributions are general revenues, and all endowment and Permanent Fund contributions are reported as separate line items but in the same manner as general revenues. Illustration 13-13 indicates key examples of program revenues and general revenues. Gains from the sale of capital assets are reported as general revenues. (Losses are included in general government-type expenses.)

Two final topics should be considered before concluding our discussion of the government-wide financial statements. First is the appropriate treatment of the assets, deferred outflows of resources, liabilities, deferred inflows of resources, net position, revenues, expenses, and so on of Internal Service Funds. Second, the GASB permits governments an alternative to applying traditional capital asset reporting practices to infrastructure capital assets.

Internal Service Funds

As discussed in Chapter 11, Internal Service Funds are used to account for departments or agencies of a government that provide goods or services primarily to other departments or agencies of the government. Internal Service Funds data are incorporated into the governmental activities and business-type activities data in the government-wide financial statements. The factors that determine how and where the Internal Service Fund data are included are discussed and illustrated in Chapter 14 on deriving the government-wide financial statements.

ILLUSTRATION 13-13   Program Revenues vs. General Revenues

Program Revenues	General Revenues
Charges for services*	Tax revenues of the reporting government—
Licenses and permits*	whether unrestricted or restricted
Payments from other governments for	Unrestricted grants and contributions
services provided*	Grants and contributions restricted to
Fines and forfeitures*	multiple programs without specification
Grants and contributions *restricted* to a	of amounts to be spent on specific
specific program	individual programs
Grants and contributions *restricted* to	All other unrestricted intergovernmental
capital asset acquisition, construction, or	revenues
improvement for capital assets used *in a*	All unrestricted investment income
specific program	
Pass-through grant revenues (primary	
recipient)	
Revenues for payments made by others on	
the government's behalf	
Other intergovernmental revenues *restricted*	
to a specific program	
(or to acquire capital assets for a	
specific program)	
Earnings on endowment or Permanent	
Fund investments that are *restricted* to a	
specific program	
Earnings on unexpended grant resources if	
restricted to a specific program	

*These revenues are program revenues whether their use is unrestricted or restricted.

Recall from prior chapters that the GASB permits governments that meet certain conditions to use a modified approach to account for infrastructure. Governments that choose this alternative do not report depreciation expense on infrastructure assets such as streets and roads. Instead, all costs incurred to maintain and preserve the infrastructure assets are expensed. Only costs incurred to add to the capacity of an infrastructure asset are capitalized.

Infrastructure Capital Assets

NOTE DISCLOSURES

The notes to the basic financial statements of a governmental unit are an integral part of the statements. The notes provide information that is necessary for fair presentation of each of the various entities reported in a government's basic financial statements. The notes in a typical report are quite extensive, often as long as 25 to 50 pages, and contain significant information.

The GASB identifies numerous notes that it considers essential to fair presentation of the basic financial statements for all governments, and many other notes that should be presented when applicable. Most of these are identified in Illustration 13-14. The distinctions among the notes in each category are not clear because (1) some notes categorized as essential do not apply to all governments and thus may not be presented, and (2) all pertinent notes presented should be essential to fair presentation of the basic financial statements. Apparently, those notes listed as essential to fair presentation are thought to be applicable for the overwhelming majority of governments.

The GASB also states that the list of notes in Illustration 13-14 is not exhaustive and is not intended to replace professional judgment. Finally, the GASB emphasizes that the notes should not be "cluttered" with unnecessary disclosures.

ILLUSTRATION 13-14   Common Note Disclosures

Notes Essential to Fair Presentation of the Basic Financial Statements:

1. Summary of significant accounting policies, including
   - Description of the government-wide and major fund financial statements, including MD&A
   - Component unit(s) relationships to the primary government, including (1) criteria for inclusion and reporting method and (2) availability of separate financial statements for the component unit(s)
   - Description of the activities accounted for in each of the following columns—major funds, Internal Service Funds, and fiduciary fund types—presented in the basic financial statements
   - Measurement focus and basis of accounting used in the government-wide statements
   - Revenue recognition policies
   - Policy for eliminating internal activity in the government-wide Statement of Activities
   - Policies for capitalizing assets and for estimating useful lives of those assets for use in calculating depreciation expense (Governments that choose to use the modified approach for reporting eligible infrastructure assets should describe that approach.)
   - Description of the types of transactions included in program revenues and the policy for allocating indirect expenses to functions in the Statement of Activities
   - Policy for defining operating and nonoperating revenues of proprietary funds
   - Policy on use of FASB guidance issued after November 30, 1989, for proprietary activities
   - Cash and cash equivalents definition for cash flow statements
   - Policy for applying restricted and unrestricted resources when both are present
   - Fund balance classification policies and procedures
2. Cash deposits with financial institutions (related legal and contractual provisions and categories of risk)
3. Investments
4. Significant contingent liabilities
5. Encumbrances outstanding
6. Significant effects of subsequent events
7. Annual pension cost and net pension obligations
8. Material violations of finance-related legal and contractual provisions
9. Schedule of debt service requirements to maturity
10. Commitments under noncapitalized (operating) leases
11. Construction and other significant commitments
12. Required capital asset disclosures
13. Required long-term liabilities disclosures
14. Deficit fund balance or net position of individual funds
15. Interfund balances and transfers
16. Significant transactions between discretely presented component units and with the primary government
17. Disclosures about donor-restricted endowments

Additional Note Disclosures, If Applicable, Including:

1. Risk management activities
2. Property taxes
3. Segment information for Enterprise Funds
4. Condensed financial statements of major discretely presented component units
5. Short-term debt instruments and liquidity
6. Related party transactions
7. Nature of accountability for related organizations
8. Capital leases
9. Joint ventures and jointly governed organizations
10. Debt refundings
11. Nonexchange transactions, including grants, taxes, and contributions, that are not recognized because they are not measurable
12. Major purposes of fund balance restrictions, commitments, and assignments
13. Interfund eliminations in fund financial statements not apparent from headings
14. Postemployment benefit plans other than pensions—in both separately issued plan financial statements and employer statements
15. Pension plans—in both separately issued plan financial statements and employer statements
16. Bond, tax, or revenue anticipation notes excluded from fund or current liabilities (proprietary funds)
17. Financial statement inconsistencies associated with component units with different fiscal year ends
18. For separate component unit reports, the primary government in whose report it is included and the relationship
19. Reverse repurchase and dollar reverse repurchase agreements
20. Securities lending transactions
21. Special assessment debt and related activities
22. Demand bonds
23. Postemployment benefits other than pension benefits
24. Landfill closure and postclosure care
25. On-behalf payments for fringe benefits and salaries
26. Entity involvement in conduit debt obligations
27. Sponsoring government disclosures on external investment pools reported as investment trust funds
28. Amount of interest expense included in direct expenses in the government-wide Statement of Activities
29. Significant transactions or other events that are either unusual or infrequent but not within the control of management
30. Nature of individual elements of a particular reconciling item, if obscured in the aggregated information in the summary reconciliation of the fund financial statements to the government-wide statements
31. Discounts and allowances that reduce gross revenues, when not reported on the face of the financial statements
32. Disaggregation of receivable and payable balances
33. Impairment losses, idle impaired assets, and insurance recoveries, when otherwise not apparent from the face of the financial statements
34. Amount of the primary government's net position at the end of the reporting period that are restricted by enabling legislation
35. Termination benefits
36. Future revenues that are pledged or sold
37. Derivative instruments
38. Conditions and events causing going concern issue
39. Stabilization arrangements
40. Minimum fund balance policies
41. Information about major special revenue funds
42. Detail about individual types of deferred outflows/inflows, if not in statement
43. Significant effect of a deferred outflow/inflow on a net position classification

Source: Adapted from GASB *Codification*, secs. 2300.106–107.

Some of the notes typically presented by governments are similar, if not identical, to notes in business financial statements. Others, such as notes related to advance refunding transactions, identification of major funds, and use of the modified approach for infrastructure capital assets, are unique to governments.

REQUIRED SUPPLEMENTARY INFORMATION

Required supplementary information (RSI) is data—typically schedules, trend tables, and statistical data—that are required by GAAP to be presented *along with the basic financial statements.* However, RSI is **not** audited, and thus an opinion on its fair presentation is not rendered. The GASB has established two broad types of RSI for governmental entities—Management's Discussion and Analysis and *other* required supplementary information.

The final unique aspect of the reporting requirements of *Statement No. 34,* Management's Discussion and Analysis (MD&A), is required supplementary information that is presented *before* the financial statements. RSI normally follows the financial statements and the notes. However, the purpose of the MD&A is to *introduce* the government's basic financial statements *and* to provide an *analytical overview* of the government's activities. Given these purposes, the GASB requires the MD&A to *precede* the financial statements.

Management's Discussion and Analysis

The analysis of the government's financial activities in the MD&A is to be based on currently known facts, decisions, or conditions. It is not a forecast. Its purpose is to help users assess whether the government's financial position has improved or deteriorated during the year. *Statements No. 34* and *No. 37* identify eight specific areas to be covered in the MD&A. These areas are listed and discussed in Illustration 13-15. *The MD&A is not permitted to address additional topics.* The State of Florida, the City of Carrollton, Texas, and the State of North Carolina typically have excellent MD&A that we recommend you review by going to the electronic version of their CAFRs, which are on their websites. We also recommend that you find another CAFR of particular interest to you on a state or local government's website and review its MD&A.

The RSI is information that the GASB considers necessary to supplement the information in the basic financial statements but which is not part of those statements. The RSI, with the exception of the MD&A, is presented immediately after the notes to the basic financial statements and may consist of statements, schedules, statistical data, and other information. The most common required supplementary information, other than the MD&A, that the GASB prescribes includes:

Other RSI

- Budgetary comparison schedules not included in the basic financial statements
- Pension plan schedule of funding progress and schedule of employer contributions
- OPEB plan schedule of funding progress and schedule of employer contributions
- Certain presentations required for public entity risk pools
- Disclosures required by governments that use the modified approach to infrastructure accounting and reporting

Some governments are not required to present all of the basic financial statements required for a general purpose government such as a state or a city. Whereas some special purpose governments (e.g., school districts) typically serve several functions and may have both governmental and business-type activities, others do not. Some special purpose governments (e.g., airport authorities or a utility district) may have only enterprise operations. A government with solely business-type activities only has to present the proprietary fund financial statements. Government-wide

Special Purpose Governments

ILLUSTRATION 13-15 Requirements for Management's Discussion and Analysis

MD&A should include:

1. **A brief discussion of the basic financial statements, including:**
   - The relationships of the statements to one another
   - The differences in the information provided
   - Analyses that help readers understand why information reported in fund financial statements *either* (1) reinforces that in the government-wide (GW) statements, or (2) provides additional information

2. **Condensed financial information—derived from GW statements—comparing the current year to the prior year.** At a minimum SLGs should present information necessary to support analysis of financial position and results of operations (required in item 3), including these elements:
   - Total assets—distinguishing between capital assets and other assets
   - Total deferred outflows of resources
   - Total liabilities—distinguishing between long-term debt outstanding and other liabilities
   - Total deferred inflows of resources
   - Total net position—distinguishing among net investment in capital assets, restricted amounts, and unrestricted amounts
   - Program revenues—by major source
   - General revenues—by major source
   - Total revenues
   - Program expenses—at a minimum by function
   - Total expenses
   - Excess (deficiency) before contributions to term and permanent endowments or Permanent Fund principal, special items and extraordinary items, and transfers
   - Contributions and transfers
   - Special items and extraordinary items
   - Change in net position
   - Beginning and ending net position

3. **An analysis of the SLG's overall financial position and results of operations**—to help users assess whether financial position has improved or deteriorated as a result of the year's operations.
   - The analysis should address both governmental activities and business-type activities—as reported in the GW statements—and include reasons for significant changes from the prior year.
   - Important economic factors—such as changes in the tax or employment bases—that significantly affected the year's operating results should be discussed.
   - The analysis should include comments about the significant changes in the fund balance or fund equity of individual funds.

4. **An analysis of balances and transactions of individual funds.** The analysis should address the reasons for significant changes in fund balances or fund net position and whether restrictions, commitments, or other limitations significantly affect the availability of fund resources for future use.

5. **An analysis of significant variations between (1) original and final budget amounts and (2) final budget amounts and actual budget results for the General Fund (or its equivalent).**
   Note: The analysis should include any currently known reasons for variations that are expected to have a significant effect on future services or liquidity.

6. **A description of capital asset and long-term debt activity during the year**—including a discussion of (1) material commitments for capital expenditures, (2) any changes in credit ratings, and (3) whether debt limitations may affect the financing of planned facilities or services.

7. **Governments that use the modified approach for reporting some or all of their infrastructure assets also should discuss:**
   - Significant changes in the assessed condition of eligible infrastructure assets from previous condition assessments.
   - How the current assessed condition compares to the condition level at which the government has established and disclosed that it intends to preserve eligible infrastructure assets.
   - Any significant differences between the estimated annual amount to maintain or preserve eligible infrastructure assets and the actual amounts spent during the current period.

8. **A description of currently known facts, decisions, or conditions that are expected to have a material effect on financial position (net position) or results of operations (revenues, expenses, and other changes in net position).**

Source: Governmental Accounting Standards Board, *Codification* (Norwalk, CT: GASB, June 2012), para. 2200.109.

Portions of various GASB documents, copyright by the Governmental Accounting Standards Board, 401 Merritt, PO Box 5116, Norwalk, CT 06856-5116, are reproduced with permission. Complete copies of those documents are available from the GASB.

financial statements, governmental fund financial statements, and fiduciary fund financial statements are not required. Likewise, an entity that is solely fiduciary in nature would present only the fiduciary fund financial statements. In every case, the MD&A, notes to the financial statements, and any other appropriate RSI must be included. Similarly, if a government has only governmental activities, the government would present governmental fund financial statements and government-wide financial statements, but proprietary fund financial statements and fiduciary fund financial statements are not required.

Concluding Comments

The basic financial statements include both government-wide and fund financial statements. The previous chapters discussed and illustrated how the information presented in fund financial statements is captured and/or derived. The government-wide financial statements are derived from the fund financial statements and from additional information maintained by the government. Chapter 14 explains and illustrates how the government-wide financial statements are derived from the fund financial statements. Chapter 15 discusses the comprehensive annual financial report (CAFR) and the determination of a government's financial reporting entity.

Questions

Q13-1 What basis (bases) of accounting is used to report governmental activities in government-wide financial statements?

Q13-2 What are the required basic financial statements under *Statement No. 34*?

Q13-3 What minimum classifications must be used to report net position in the government-wide Statement of Net Position? In the proprietary funds Statement of Net Position?

Q13-4 What is meant by "major fund reporting"? How does it differ from reporting by fund type? For what fund types is major fund reporting required? For what fund types is fund type reporting required?

Q13-5 How does a government determine which governmental funds are major funds? How does a government decide which proprietary funds are major funds?

Q13-6 Distinguish between governmental activities and business-type activities. Provide examples of each.

Q13-7 Distinguish general revenues from program revenues. Provide several examples of each.

Q13-8 What are the minimum classifications into which program revenues of a particular function must be classified?

Q13-9 What determines the function in which charges for services should be reported? What determines the function in which to report restricted grants and contributions?

Q13-10 What is the minimum level of functional detail that must be presented for governmental activities in the government-wide Statement of Activities? For business-type activities?

Q13-11 What expenses should be reported as separate line items instead of being classified by function in the government-wide Statement of Activities?

Exercises

E13-1 (Multiple Choice) Identify the best answer for each of the following:
1. Which of the following is *not* considered to be part of the basic financial statements?
   a. Management's Discussion and Analysis
   b. Government-wide financial statements
   c. Fund financial statements
   d. Notes to the financial statements
2. Governmental funds financial statements typically include the following *except*
   a. a Balance Sheet.
   b. a Statement of Revenues, Expenditures, and Changes in Fund Balances.
   c. a Statement of Cash Flows.
   d. a Statement of Revenues, Expenditures, and Changes in Fund Balances—Budget and Actual.

3. Which of the following statements concerning reporting detail in the government-wide financial statements is *false*?
   a. The minimum level of detail for governmental activities is generally by function.
   b. Business-type activities must be reported by enterprise fund.
   c. Business-type activities must be reported by identifiable activity.
   d. Interest expense generally is not allocated to functions for governmental activities.

4. Which of the following types of revenues would *not* be considered a program revenue?
   a. State grant received for drug enforcement activities
   b. Occupancy tax levied by reporting government and restricted for use in tourism development activities
   c. Recreation fees charged to participate in the city's soccer league
   d. Parking fines

5. Which of the following are typically included in functional expenses for governmental activities?
   a. Depreciation
   b. Interest
   c. Departmental supplies
   d. Salaries expenses

6. Which of the following statements is *true* concerning major fund reporting?
   a. Major fund reporting is required for governmental funds and enterprise funds.
   b. The quantitative criteria for identifying major funds must be met for a fund to be reported as a major fund.
   c. Major fund reporting is required for governmental and proprietary funds.
   d. Fiduciary funds must be reported by major fund.

7. The Balance Sheet for governmental funds would potentially include all of the following items *except*
   a. liens receivable.
   b. deferred revenue.
   c. bonds payable due in five years.
   d. assigned fund balance.

8. The Statement of Revenues, Expenditures, and Changes in Fund Balance does *not* report
   a. interest on long-term debt.
   b. charges for services.
   c. transfers.
   d. depreciation.

9. The fund(s) for which budgetary comparisons would potentially be included in the basic financial statements are
   a. General Fund.
   b. General Fund and all Special Revenue Funds.
   c. General Fund and major Special Revenue Funds.
   d. General Fund and all other major governmental funds.

10. Which of the following is an accurate description of major fund reporting concepts?
    a. Fiduciary funds must be reported by fund type.
    b. Proprietary funds are subject to major fund reporting.
    c. Permanent funds are *not* subject to major fund reporting.
    d. Governmental, proprietary, and fiduciary funds are reported by major funds.

E13-2 (Multiple Choice) Identify the best answer for each of the following:

1. Both governmental funds and governmental activities include which of the following on their respective operating statements?
   a. Revenues
   b. Expenses
   c. Depreciation expense
   d. Fund balance

2. The government-wide Statement of Net Position would *not* include
   a. accounts payable.
   b. capital assets, net of accumulated depreciation.
   c. fund balance.
   d. unrestricted net position.

3. The government-wide Statement of Activities may report all of the following *except*
   a. indirect expenses.
   b. unallocated depreciation.
   c. transfers.
   d. deferred revenue.

4. Which of the following revenues would typically *not* be classified as a general revenue on the Statement of Activities?
   a. Property taxes
   b. Unrestricted grant
   c. Unrestricted parking fines
   d. Investment earnings on unrestricted investments

5. The governing board of the City of Chestnut Springs has decided to dedicate 25% of the fees generated by the city's recycling program to drug enforcement activities. This revenue would be reported on the Statement of Activities as
   a. operating grants and contributions in the public safety function.
   b. charges for services in the public safety function.
   c. operating grants and contributions in the public works function.
   d. charges for services in the public works function.
6. GAAP require fiduciary activities to be reported
   a. in the fund financial statements by fund type.
   b. in the fund financial statements by major fund and in the government-wide financial statements as governmental activities.
   c. in the fund financial statements by major fund.
   d. in the fund financial statements by fund type and in the government-wide financial statements as fiduciary activities.
7. Which of the following topics would commonly be included in the MD&A?
   a. Goals and objectives for the government's various functions for the next fiscal year
   b. A brief analysis of the local economic factors that affected the reporting period's operating results
   c. Plans for a tax increase planned for the next fiscal period
   d. All of the above
8. GAAP require primary government total columns to be reported on which of the following basic financial statements?
   a. Government-Wide Statement of Net Position if both governmental and business-type activities are reported
   b. Balance Sheet for governmental funds if multiple major funds (and potentially non-major funds) are reported
   c. Statement of Revenues, Expenditures, and Changes in Fund Balances for governmental funds if multiple major funds (and potentially nonmajor funds) are reported
   d. All fiduciary fund financial statements

Questions 9 and 10 are based on the following scenario:

Carter County, like all other counties in the state, shares in the proceeds of a state-levied sales tax. The state requires all recipient counties to use the proceeds for capital improvements to local streets and highways. Carter County's share for the current fiscal period was $105,000. Assume that the funds meet the availability criteria.

9. How would Carter County report these revenues in its government-wide financial statements?
   a. $105,000 as governmental activities general revenues
   b. $105,000 as operating grants and contributions in the public works function
   c. $105,000 as capital grants and contributions in the public works function
   d. $105,000 as governmental activities general revenues but reported separately from unrestricted grants
10. How would Carter County report these revenues in the governmental fund financial statements?
    a. $105,000 as revenues in the General Fund
    b. $105,000 as other financing sources in the General Fund
    c. $105,000 as revenues in a Permanent Fund
    d. $105,000 as other financing sources in a Permanent Fund

E13-3 (Revenue Classification) Clemens County had the following revenue sources in 20X5:

General property taxes	$8,000,000
Restricted (for education) property taxes	570,000
Meals tax (restricted for economic development and tourism)	200,000
Fines and forfeits	82,000
Federal grant restricted for police protection	132,000
Federal grant restricted for specific general government construction projects for specific functions	600,000
Unrestricted investment income	75,000

Prepare a schedule computing the amount of general revenues and of program revenues that *Required* Clemens County should report in its government-wide Statement of Activities for the 20X5 fiscal year.

E13-4 The following information was drawn from the accounts and records of Mosser Township:

Locally levied gas tax restricted to street maintenance	$1,000,000
Grant from state for widening and repaving Main Street	4,000,000
Unrestricted charges for ambulance services provided by fire department	250,000
Contributions from local businesses—restricted for youth recreation programs	75,000
Income from Permanent Fund endowment restricted to economic development purposes	120,000
Fines that are unrestricted as to use	31,000
Property taxes restricted for education purposes	720,000
Shared revenues from the state—restricted for education	1,230,000
Federal grant revenues—restricted for hiring police officers	400,000
Federal grant to replace water and sewer lines	5,000,000

Required Prepare a schedule computing the amounts to be reported in each of the three minimum program revenues classifications by Mosser Township.

E13-5 (Fund-Based Statements—Column Headings) Dorrian County's fund structure is as follows:

> General Fund
> 3 Special Revenue Funds
> 1 Capital Projects Fund
> 2 Debt Service Funds
> 4 Private-Purpose Trust Funds
> 3 Internal Service Funds
> 5 Enterprise Funds
> General Capital Assets and General Long-Term Liabilities accounts

Assume that Dorrian County determines that Special Revenue Fund A, its Capital Projects Fund, Enterprise Fund C, and Enterprise Fund D meet the major fund size criteria.

Required
a. What column headings would the county need to present in its governmental funds Statement of Revenues, Expenditures, and Changes in Fund Balances?
b. What column headings would the county need to present in its proprietary funds Statement of Revenues, Expenses, and Changes in Net Position?

Problems

P13-1 (Reporting Equity) Prepare the net position section for governmental activities in the government-wide Statement of Net Position for the City of Josiah at June 30, 20X6, given the following information as of that date.

General Fund Committed Fund Balances	$ 2,000,000
General Fund Assigned Fund Balance	3,500,000
General Fund Unassigned Fund Balance	2,500,000
Total Special Revenue Funds Restricted Fund Balances	2,000,000
Capital Projects Funds Restricted Fund Balances*	400,000
Capital Projects Funds Assigned Fund Balances	400,000
Total Debt Service Funds Restricted Fund Balances	2,000,000
General capital assets	12,000,000
Accumulated depreciation on general capital assets	5,000,000
Deferred outflows of resources:	
Deferred refunding amount (capital-asset-related)	70,000

General long-term liabilities:

Bonds payable (capital-asset-related)	3,000,000
Long-term claims and judgments payable	1,750,000
Long-term compensated absences payable	750,000

Internal Service Funds (serving only general
government departments):

Total assets (30% capital assets)	3,000,000
Total liabilities (25% capital-asset-related debt)	1,100,000
Total equity	1,900,000

*$300,000 is unexpended bond proceeds.

P13-2 (Major Fund Identification) Presented in the following table is selected information from the 20X5 financial statements of the various individual funds of Alderman City.

Fund	Assets and Deferred Outflows	Liabilities and Deferred Inflows	Revenues	Expenditures	Expenses
General	$ 23,302,450	$14,281,850	$181,338,000	$114,376,000	
Grants Special Revenue	7,636,000	6,500,000	5,700,000	5,736,000	
School Special Revenue	14,000,000	8,910,000	65,068,000	68,000,000	
Debt Service	13,934,000	800,000	545,250	9,360,000	
Capital Projects	48,090,000	1,028,000	4,135,000	21,200,000	
Transit EF	11,350,000	177,533	3,650,000		$ 5,000,000
Water & Sewer EF	165,000,000	36,300,000	25,700,000		21,250,000
Civic Center EF	10,800,000	504,000	2,800,000		3,540,000
Public Parking EF	22,100,000	9,160,000	1,800,000		1,820,000
Fleet Management ISF	9,637,000	265,000	3,200,000		3,950,000
Risk Management ISF	11,951,000	8,900,000	7,700,000		8,000,000

Identify which funds of Alderman City are, at a minimum, required to be reported as major funds.

P13-3 (Statement of Activities) Prepare a Statement of Activities for Tazewell County for calendar year 20X9, given the following:

General property tax revenues	$70,000,000
Proceeds from sale of general government land*	2,200,000
Unrestricted grant revenues	300,000
Grants restricted to education	12,000,000
Capital grants for transportation	9,000,000
Expenses (including depreciation):	
General government	10,000,000
Public safety	18,000,000
Education	34,000,000
Transportation	24,000,000
Culture and recreation	1,500,000
Interest expense on GLTL	3,000,000
GLTL principal retired	16,000,000
General government capital outlay expenditures	7,000,000
Transfers to Enterprise Funds	4,000,000
Water Enterprise Fund:	
Charges for services	13,000,000
Expenses	11,900,000
Book value of general government building destroyed in tornado (uninsured)	310,000
Net position, governmental activities, 1/1/X9	26,530,000
Net position, business-type activities, 1/1/X9	4,000,000

*The cost of the land that was sold was $350,000.

P13-4 (Statement of Activities) Prepare a Statement of Activities for the Walland County School District for the year ended December 31, 20X5, given the following information. Assume that the classifications provided for expenses are the appropriate functional classifications to be presented in the statement.

Property tax revenues.	$48,000,000
Unrestricted grants and entitlements	11,200,000
Unrestricted contributions	80,000
Unrestricted investment income.	790,000
Transfers from General Fund to Enterprise Funds.	100,000
Charges for services provided by:	
Instructional departments.	1,050,000
Support services.	440,000
Noninstructional services.	10,000
Extracurricular activities	320,000
Food service (Enterprise Fund activity).	1,500,000
Adult and community education (Enterprise	
Fund activity).	844,822
Grants and contributions revenues—restricted	
for specific operating costs of specific programs:	
Instructional departments.	800,000
Support services.	750,000
Noninstructional services.	490,000
Extracurricular activities	51,000
Food service.	365,000
Grants and contributions revenues—restricted	
for capital asset acquisitions for specific functions:	
Instructional departments.	720,000
Support services.	55,100
Expenses:	
Instructional departments.	34,000,000
Support services.	27,000,000
Noninstructional services.	575,000
Extracurricular activities	1,340,000
Food service.	1,880,000
Adult and community education	884,000
Net position, January 1, 20X5:	
Governmental activities	6,850,000
Business-type activities	1,400,000

P13-5 (Internet Research Problem) Search the Internet for the basic financial statements of several state or local governments.

Required a. Do any of the governments report negative balances of unrestricted net position for governmental activities? For business-type activities?

  b. What classifications of program revenues are presented? Do any present more than the minimum required classifications?

  c. Do any of the governments present indirect expenses in a separate column?

  d. Do the governments discuss all required topics in Management's Discussion and Analysis? Do any include additional topics?

  e. What funds are reported as major funds? How many major funds does each government present?

  f. What types of reconciling items are included in the reconciliations of fund balance and changes in fund balance in the governmental fund financial statements and net position and changes in net position for governmental activities in the government-wide financial statements?

  g. How do the statements differ from what you expected based on your study of this chapter?

P13-6 (MD&A Research Problem) Search the Internet for at least two recently published MD&As. Print the documents and perform the following:

a. Compare and contrast the content and style of the two MD&As.   ***Required***
b. Compare each MD&A to the requirements identified in Illustration 13-15. Are any requirements not met? Is there information included in the MD&A that is not required? Is it properly included?
c. Summarize your findings.

P13-7 (Research Questions) Analyze the following two scenarios. What are your recommendations?
a. A county was the recipient of a bequest. Land was donated to the county with the donor stipulating it could only be used for the new public safety facility. How would this contribution be reported in the county's Statement of Activities?
b. How would an entity report in its Statement of Activities restricted grants and contributions that qualify as program revenues but that may be used for *either* operating or capital purposes at the recipient's discretion?

Cases

C13-1 (Identifying Major Funds—City of Chattanooga, Tennessee) Presented here is information from the financial statements of the various funds of the City of Chattanooga, Tennessee, for the year ended June 30, 20X9.

Funds	Assets and Deferred Outflows	Liabilities and Deferred Inflows	Revenues	Expenditures/ Expenses
General Fund	$ 161,664,282	$105,621,572	$174,173,652	$148,252,746
Special Revenue Funds:				
Public Library Fund	1,157,754	114,128	2,635,495	5,207,192
Downtown Development Fund	17,801	—	—	16,149
Human Services Program Fund	4,002,500	301,502	12,116,912	13,707,558
Narcotics Program Fund	2,428,526	599,194	846,199	265,314
State Street Aid Fund	2,291,601	459,981	4,423,940	4,822,084
Community Development Fund	1,696,475	936,964	4,485,829	3,901,923
Hotel/Motel Tax Fund	1,696,807	734,497	3,733,796	101,890
River Pier Garage Fund	23,171	—	226,238	132,112
Capital Projects Fund	15,452,073	3,969,398	5,068,380	27,155,459
Debt Service Fund	7,139,208	—	1,652,579	14,137,674
Permanent Funds:				
Library Endowment Fund	3,277,654	2,083	204,405	61,342
Ochs-Oakes Fire and Police Medal Fund	13,244	3,148,349	562	54,427
Enterprise Funds:				
EPB Fund	398,798,000	153,030,000	•426,993,000	417,792,000
Interceptor Sewer System Fund	353,702,452	119,607,463	38,317,183	35,395,214
Solid Waste/Sanitation Fund	19,878,609	34,943,427	6,027,615	4,678,270
Storm Water Fund	45,406,196	17,082,920	5,748,844	4,475,706
Housing Management Fund	7,711,298	3,677,797	1,264,919	1,552,119
Internal Service Fund	6,349,146	4,371,741	11,516,828	9,574,499
Fiduciary Funds:				
General Pension Plan	216,459,943	215,503	32,342,661	9,004,420
Firefighters' and Police Officers'				
Insurance and Pension Fund	238,384,161	623,599	33,736,945	18,691,665
Totals	$1,487,550,901	$449,440,118	$765,515,982	$718,979,763

Prepare a schedule to apply the quantitative tests for identifying major funds. Indicate which   ***Required***
funds are major funds and why.

(Adapted from a recent Comprehensive Annual Financial Report of the City of Chattanooga, Tennessee.)

C13-2 (Net Position and Statement of Activities—City of Ashland, Oregon) Selected financial information of the City of Ashland, Oregon, is presented in the following table and narrative. The information is for the year ended June 30, 20X6.

Account	Governmental Activities	Business-Type Activities
Cash and cash equivalents—Unrestricted.....	$ 7,574,073	$12,951,933
Cash and cash equivalents—Restricted by capital grant........................	1,700,000	—
Land..	8,559,612	1,945,107
Buildings..................................	19,563,238	21,782,188
Machinery and equipment..................	12,405,182	636,103
Infrastructure............................	41,047,189	80,305,280
Construction in progress..................	798,324	2,998,341
Accumulated depreciation.................	33,506,950	28,803,335
Accrued interest payable on bonds.........	—	587,720
Bonds payable due in one year.............	590,000	1,475,373
Bonds payable due in more than one year....	5,731,134	40,366,883
Capital lease liability....................	800,000	300,000
Revenues:		
Charges for services......................	7,820,613	22,205,195
Operating grants..........................	141,500	79,665
Capital grants............................	502,153	—
Unrestricted interest earnings.............	256,648	518,138
Property taxes............................	2,970,566	86,335
Utility users tax..........................	2,323,390	—
Users tax.................................	1,784,302	1,573,251
State appropriations—unrestricted..........	1,525,220	—
Expenses:		
General government.......................	2,818,129	—
Public safety.............................	7,903,054	—
Highways and streets......................	2,419,380	—
Water....................................	—	4,974,536
Wastewater...............................	—	4,397,923
Electric..................................	—	12,831,758
Telecommunications.......................	—	4,182,956
Interest on long-term debt.................	637,146	—
Total Net Position, Beginning...............	45,144,447	57,044,003

The charges for services were earned by departments associated with the following functions:

Revenues generated by departments in the function of	Restricted for use of department that generated the revenues	Restricted for use by another department	Not restricted for use by a particular department
General government............	$ —	$2,000,000	$ —
Public safety...................	1,556,909	2,215,629	—
Highways and streets............	1,700,000	—	348,075
Water.........................	—	—	4,531,512
Wastewater....................	2,839,685	—	—
Electric.......................	7,045,360	—	5,050,003
Telecommunications............	2,738,635	—	—

Finally, the operating grants were for public safety, $141,500; water, $43,622; and electric, $36,043. The capital grants were for public safety, $299,171, and highways and streets, $202,982.

Transfers from business-type activities to governmental activities of $518,138 were made during the year to subsidize the cost of a major general government capital project.

a. Prepare a schedule to calculate the amount of Net Investment in Capital Assets, for governmental activities and for business-type activities that Ashland should report in its Government-Wide Statement of Net Position at June 30, 20X6. Assume that all bonds payable were issued to finance construction projects.   *Required*

b. Prepare the Statement of Activities for the City of Ashland, Oregon, for the year ended June 30, 20X6.

(Adapted from a recent Comprehensive Annual Financial Report of the City of Ashland, Oregon.)

Harvey City Comprehensive Case

Harvey City must now prepare its basic financial statements. In addition to the Addiction Prevention Special Revenue Fund and the Economic Development Special Revenue Fund, Harvey City has two other Special Revenue Funds. Likewise, the city has one Capital Projects Fund not presented earlier (in Chapter 7). The December 31, 20X4, preclosing trial balances for these three funds are presented here so that you can use this information in completing the requirements of Chapters 13 through 15. At this time, we will prepare the fund financial statements using the data from the trial balances and from the worksheets and financial statements that we prepared in Chapters 4 through 12.

a. Identify Harvey City's major funds, assuming that the city will not use management discretion to identify any fund as major.
b. Prepare Harvey City's governmental funds financial statements for 20X4, including any required budgetary comparison statements.
c. Prepare Harvey City's proprietary funds financial statements for 20X4.
d. Prepare Harvey City's fiduciary funds financial statements for 20X4.

Harvey City
Additional Governmental Funds
Preclosing Trial Balances
December 31, 20X4

Accounts	Tourism Development Special Revenue Fund Debit	Credit	Midtown Corridor Special Revenue Fund Debit	Credit	Veterans Memorial Park Capital Projects Fund Debit	Credit
Cash	$ 57,000		$22,000		$120,000	
Investments	16,000				250,000	
Inventory of Materials and Supplies	3,000		1,500			
Vouchers Payable		$ 8,500		$ 4,500		
Accrued Salaries and Wages Payable		1,000				
Contracts Payable—Retained Percentage						$125,000
Unreserved Fund Balance (Preclosing—All restricted)		61,200		5,500		243,500
Revenue:						
Taxes		135,000		25,000		
Investment Income		1,300				1,500
Current Operating Expenditures/Expenses:						
Economic Development	127,800					
Other			11,500			
Capital Outlay Expenditures:						
For Equipment	3,200					
Governmental Funds—Totals	$207,000	$207,000	$35,000	$35,000	$370,000	$370,000

Both the Tourism Development Special Revenue Fund and the Midtown Corridor Special Revenue Fund are financed with restricted portions of the city's hotel/motel occupancy tax. The Veterans Memorial Park Capital Projects Fund had no activity during the year because a citizens committee was addressing design issues and preparing a major campaign to raise private contributions for the park.

(*Solution Hint*) Remember that only certain types of funds are reported using major fund reporting. The fund types for which major fund reporting is not allowed are the Internal Service Funds and the fiduciary funds. Recall that the data from these funds are not used in computing the thresholds for being a major fund based on size.

CHAPTER 14

Financial Reporting

Deriving Government-Wide Financial Statements and Required Reconciliations

LEARNING OBJECTIVES

After studying this chapter, you should be able to:

- Understand and explain the types of worksheet adjustments needed to derive governmental activities data for the government-wide financial statements from governmental funds financial statement data.

- Understand and explain the types of worksheet adjustments needed to derive business-type activities data for the government-wide financial statements from Enterprise Funds financial statement data.

- Understand both the two-worksheet approach (chapter) and the one-worksheet approach (appendix) to deriving governmental activities data.

- Prepare the government-wide financial statements using information derived in the conversion worksheets.

- Prepare the required reconciliations of fund financial statements to government-wide financial statements.

The basic financial statements that state and local governments must present to comply with generally accepted accounting principles were discussed and illustrated in Chapter 13. Two broad types of statements are required: *fund financial statements* and *government-wide* financial statements. The processes used to capture and process the information presented in fund financial statements and note disclosures for the General Capital Assets and General Long-term Liabilities accounts were discussed in Chapters 3 through 9 (governmental funds), 10 and 11 (proprietary funds), and 12 (fiduciary funds). Chapter 13

- provided the key additional guidance (e.g., on major funds) required to derive the fund financial statements from information gathered and processed using fund accounting procedures explained in the prior chapters.

- explained and illustrated major fund financial reporting, how to determine which governmental funds and which Enterprise Funds to report as major funds, and the form and content of the government-wide financial statements.

Significant additional steps are required to derive much of the information presented in the government-wide financial statements. As noted previously, *deriving and reporting the government-wide financial statements* <mark>*is a fiscal year-end financial reporting event.*</mark> Governmental entities **integrate** fund accounts in their general ledger; <mark>government-wide information usually is **not** integrated into the general ledger but is derived using worksheets.</mark> Rather, the accounts and balances in the fund financial statements are the starting point from which government accounting and financial reporting practitioners derive the information to be reported in the government-wide financial statements. **This chapter discusses and illustrates deriving the government-wide financial statement information from the fund financial statements using a *two-worksheet* approach.** *Appendix 14-1* demonstrates a *one-worksheet* approach, based on the same facts used to illustrate the two-worksheet approach in the body of the chapter. Both approaches are used widely in practice and may be tested on the uniform CPA exam. Illustration 14-1 provides a brief overview of the conversion process and the relationships between the information in the fund financial statements and that in the government-wide financial statements.

Information in **government-wide** financial statements must be presented for two broad reporting units—*governmental* activities and *business-type* activities—as discussed and illustrated in Chapter 13. For most governments:

- **Governmental activities** are the general government activities, typically accounted for and reported in the governmental funds and the General Capital Assets (GCA) and General Long-Term Liabilities (GLTL) accounts.

- **Business-type activities** are the enterprise activities that are accounted for and reported in Enterprise Funds.

ILLUSTRATION 14-1   Worksheet Apiproach to Deriving Government-Wide Financial Statements

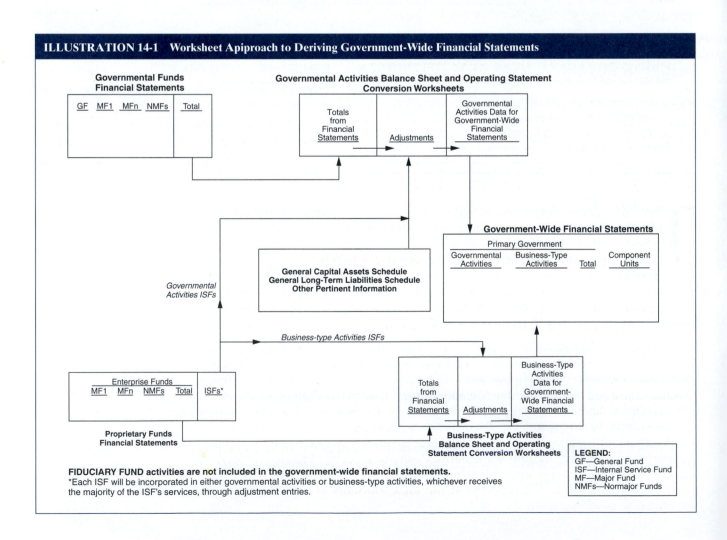

FIDUCIARY FUND activities are **not** included in the government-wide financial statements.
*Each ISF will be incorporated in either governmental activities or business-type activities, whichever receives the majority of the ISF's services, through adjustment entries.

Both the governmental activities and business-type activities are reported in the *government-wide financial statements* using the flow of *economic* resources measurement focus (MF) and the *accrual* basis of accounting (BA). Although this MFBA is consistent with the reporting of Enterprise Funds, governmental funds are reported using the flow of current financial resources measurement focus and the modified accrual basis of accounting. Hence, deriving the business-type activities data is quite simple: Enterprise Funds data are totaled after eliminating certain interfund transactions and balances. But the *conversion of governmental funds to governmental activities involves an extensive process of converting the measurement focus and basis of accounting.*

Fiduciary fund assets are held for others—not for government purposes—so fiduciary activities are *not* reported in the government-wide financial statements. Internal Service Fund activities are treated as part of business-type activities if most of the fund's services are provided to business-type (enterprise) activities and as part of governmental activities if most of the fund's services are provided to governmental activities.

The following sections discuss and illustrate the worksheet adjustments needed to derive *governmental activities* data for government-wide reporting from governmental fund financial statement data. An illustration of this process is provided, including government-wide financial statements and reconciliations of the governmental fund financial statements to the government-wide financial statements. The worksheet adjustments required to derive business-type activities data for government-wide reporting from Enterprise Fund financial statement data are also discussed and illustrated.

DERIVING GOVERNMENTAL ACTIVITIES DATA

Illustration 14-2 compares several aspects of governmental fund reporting with government-wide reporting of governmental activities. This comparison highlights key differences between reporting general government, or governmental, activities in the governmental funds financial statements and in the government-wide financial statements. Note that in both instances governmental activities are being reported. However, the reporting differs in several significant ways, including:

- Reporting governmental activities as a single entity in the government-wide financial statements rather than as multiple fund entities.
- Reporting general capital assets (GCA) and general long-term liabilities (GLTL) in the government-wide financial statements, whereas they are excluded from the governmental fund financial statements.
- Reporting using different measurement focuses and bases of accounting (MFBAs).
- Reporting appropriate Internal Service Fund (ISF) activities in governmental activities for government-wide reporting, but excluding all ISF activities from the governmental funds financial statements.

These differences require several worksheet adjustments to governmental funds financial statement data to derive the governmental activities data reported in the government-wide financial statements.

Although there are numerous differences between amounts reported under the governmental and proprietary MFBA, many assets, liabilities, and operating statement items do *not* require conversion. Cash, most receivables, inventories of materials and supplies, accounts payable, and short-term notes payable of the various governmental funds are reported at the same amounts in both the fund and government-wide statements.

ILLUSTRATION 14-2   Governmental Funds vs. Government-Wide Governmental Activities Reporting

Governmental Fund Statements	Government-Wide Statements Governmental Activities	Worksheet Adjustments Required
Report using Multiple Fund Entities	Report as a Single Entity	Eliminate the effects of transactions and relationships between governmental funds.

Accounting equation includes General Government:
   Financial Assets
   Deferred Outflows
   Related Liabilities
   Deferred Inflows
   Fund Balance
	Accounting equation includes General Government:
	   Current Assets
	   Capital Assets
	   Deferred Outflows
	   Current Liabilities
	   Long-Term Liabilities
	   Deferred Inflows
	   Net Position
		• Include general capital assets.
		• Include general long-term liabilities.
		• Convert fund balance to net position.

Current Financial Resources Measurement Focus and Modified Accrual Basis of Accounting	Economic Resources Measurement Focus and Accrual Basis of Accounting	• Convert modified accrual revenues to accrual basis measurement. • Convert modified accrual "when due" expenditures, including interest, to expenses measured on the accrual basis. • Record expenses with no expenditures counterparts. • Eliminate expenditures with no expense counterparts. • Eliminate various changes in GCA and GLTL that are reported as other financing sources or uses, or as expenditures, but do not have revenue or expense counterparts.
No Internal Service Fund activities are reported in these statements.	Internal Service Fund activities that serve primarily governmental activities are reported as part of governmental activities.	• Include Internal Service Fund assets and liabilities in governmental activities. • Report external revenues and expenses from providing services externally. • Allocate any profit or loss from interfund sales to increase or decrease appropriate functional expenses. • Record government-wide transfers that are not transfers between funds.

DERIVING GOVERNMENT-WIDE FINANCIAL STATEMENT DATA FOR GOVERNMENTAL ACTIVITIES—A WORKSHEET-BASED APPROACH

One process for deriving the government-wide, governmental activities information from the fund financial statement data is described and illustrated in the following sections. The illustration *assumes* that the government, Farley County, has no Internal Service Funds. The two key sources of data for the governmental activities conversion worksheets are

- Governmental funds financial statements. Illustration 14-3 is the December 31, 20X6, governmental funds Balance Sheet and Illustration 14-4 is the 20X6 governmental funds Statement of Revenues, Expenditures, and Changes in Fund Balances of Farley County.

- General capital assets (GCA) and general long-term liabilities (GLTL) schedules for 20X6 from the notes to the basic financial statements. These schedules are shown in Illustrations 14-5 and 14-6, respectively.

The Conversion Worksheets   The GCA and GLTL schedules, as well as other pertinent information, provide the data required for adjustments to the governmental funds financial statement

ILLUSTRATION 14-3   Farley County Governmental Funds Balance Sheet

Farley County
Governmental Funds
Balance Sheet
December 31, 20X6

	General Fund	Nonmajor Funds	Total
ASSETS			
Cash	$ 217,900	$10,885	$ 385,200
Investments	750,000	1,100	1,085,600
Due from General Fund	—	—	1,000
Due from federal government	263,665	—	1,016,000
Taxes receivable	54,000	—	54,000
Allowance of uncollectible taxes	(11,000)	—	(11,000)
Interest and penalties receivable	1,500	—	1,500
Allowance for uncollectible interest and penalties	(136)	—	(136)
Accounts receivable	13,000	—	13,000
Allowance of uncollectible accounts	(500)	—	(500)
Accrued interest receivable	37,860	150	54,800
Inventory of materials and supplies	2,400	300	4,700
Total Assets	$1,328,689	$12,435	$2,604,164
LIABILITIES, DEFERRED INFLOWS, AND FUND BALANCES			
Liabilities			
Vouchers payable	$ 178,900	$ 1,050	$ 290,400
Accrued salaries and wages payable	4,200	100	5,000
Contracts payable—retained percentage	—	—	100,000
Accrued interest payable (on current debt)	300	—	300
Unearned operating grant revenues	103,000	—	103,000
Unearned capital grant revenues	—	—	150,000
Due to Enterprise Fund	3,300	—	3,300
Due to Special Revenue Funds	1,000	—	1,000
Total Liabilities	290,700	1,150	653,000
Deferred Inflows of Resources			
Deferred tax revenues	30,800	—	30,800
Fund Balances			
Nonspendable	2,400	300	4,700
Restricted	—	10,985	810,875
Assigned	27,200	—	127,200
Unassigned	977,589	—	977,589
Total Fund Balances	1,007,189	11,285	1,920,364
Total Liabilities, Deferred Inflows, and Fund Balances	$1,328,689	$12,435	$2,604,164

Farley County's major funds other than the General Fund would be reported in individual columns but are not presented here.

information to convert that data into the data needed for the two government-wide financial statements. The adjustments groupings used in the worksheets as well as the specific adjustments required in each of the worksheets are summarized in Illustration 14-7.

ILLUSTRATION 14-4 Farley County Governmental Funds Statement of Revenues, Expenditures, and Changes in Fund Balance

Farley County
Governmental Funds
Statement of Revenues, Expenditures, and Changes in Fund Balance
For the Year Ended December 31, 20X6

	General Fund	Nonmajor Funds	Total
REVENUES			
Taxes	$ 970,000	$ —	$ 970,000
Licenses and permits	47,000	30,000	89,000
Fines and forfeitures	38,000	—	38,000
Unrestricted grants	105,000	—	105,000
Operating grants	110,000	3,000	120,000
Capital grants	—	—	2,066,000
Investment income	39,375	2,125	52,500
Other revenues	2,000	—	2,000
Total Revenues	1,311,375	35,125	3,442,500
EXPENDITURES			
Current Operating:			
General government	78,400	—	78,400
Public safety	210,000	3,000	405,000
Highways and streets	138,675	—	246,200
Health and sanitation	46,400	—	46,400
Other	6,600	12,000	18,600
Capital Outlay:			
Construction	—	—	2,540,000
Equipment	—	18,200	58,200
Debt Service:			
Bond principal retirement	—	—	200,000
Interest	—	—	101,850
Fiscal agent fees	—	—	15,000
Bond issue costs	—	—	10,000
Total Expenditures	480,075	33,200	3,719,650
Excess of Revenues over Expenditures	831,300	1,925	(277,150)
OTHER FINANCING SOURCES (USES)			
Bonds	—	—	1,800,000
Premium on bonds	—	—	12,000
Proceeds from sale of equipment	50,000	—	50,000
Transfers from General Fund	—	4,000	176,000
Transfers from Special Revenue Funds	20,000	—	20,000
Transfers from Enterprise Funds	18,000	—	18,000
Transfers to Capital Projects Funds	(16,000)	—	(16,000)
Transfers to Debt Service Funds	(160,000)	—	(160,000)
Transfers to General Fund	—	—	(20,000)
Total Other Financing Sources (Uses)	(88,000)	4,000	1,880,000
Net Changes in Fund Balances	743,300	5,925	1,602,850
Fund Balance, January 1, 20X6	263,889	5,360	317,514
Fund Balance, December 31, 20X6	$1,007,189	$ 11,285	$1,920,364

Farley County's major funds other than the General Fund would be reported in individual columns but are not presented here.

ILLUSTRATION 14-5   Farley County Capital Assets Schedule

Farley County
Capital Assets Schedule
For the Year Ended December 31, 20X6

	Balance 1/1/20X6	Additions	Deletions	Balance 12/31/20X6
Governmental Activities				
Nondepreciable Assets:				
Land	$ 125,000	$ —	$ —	$ 125,000
Construction in progress	—	2,540,000	—	2,540,000
Depreciable Assets:				
Buildings	1,250,000	—	—	1,250,000
Machinery and equipment	400,000	58,200	60,000	398,200
Infrastructure	2,000,000	—	—	2,000,000
Totals	3,775,000	2,598,200	60,000	6,313,200
Less accumulated depreciation:				
Buildings	780,000	80,000	—	860,000
Machinery and equipment	150,000	30,000	20,000	160,000
Infrastructure	1,200,000	100,000	—	1,300,000
Total Accumulated Depreciation	2,130,000	210,000	20,000	2,320,000
Governmental Activities Capital Assets, net	$1,645,000	$2,388,200	$40,000	$3,993,200
Business-Type Activities				
Nondepreciable Assets:				
Land	$1,550,000	$ —	$ —	$1,550,000
Depreciable Assets:				
Buildings	375,000	—	—	375,000
Land improvements	3,475,000	—	—	3,475,000
Machinery and equipment	1,300,000	—	—	1,300,000
Totals	6,700,000	—	—	6,700,000
Less accumulated depreciation:				
Buildings	190,000	35,000	—	225,000
Land improvements	1,340,000	255,000	—	1,595,000
Machinery and equipment	375,000	80,000	—	455,000
Total Accumulated Depreciation	1,905,000	370,000	—	2,275,000
Business-Type Activities Capital Assets, net	$4,795,000	$ (370,000)	$ —	$4,425,000

Depreciation Expense was charged to governmental activities as follows:

General government	$ 11,000
Public safety	55,000
Highways and streets	133,000
Health and sanitation	8,000
Other	3,000
Total Depreciation Expense	$ 210,000

Depreciation Expense was charged to business-type activities as follows:

Solid Waste Collection Enterprise Fund	$ 50,000
Golf Course Enterprise Fund	320,000
Total Depreciation Expense	$ 370,000

ILLUSTRATION 14-6 Farley County General Long-Term Liabilities Schedule

Farley County
General Long-Term Liabilities Schedule
For the Year Ended December 31, 20X6

	Balance 1/1/20X6	Additions	Deletions	Balance 12/31/20X6	Amounts Due Within One Year
Governmental Activities					
Bonds payable	$ 800,000	$1,800,000	$200,000	$2,400,000	$200,000
Premium on bonds	20,000	12,000	4,000	28,000	5,400
Total Bonds Payable	820,000	1,812,000	204,000	2,428,000	205,400
Other Long-Term Liabilities					
Claims and judgments payable	140,000	10,000	—	150,000	2,000
Compensated absences payable	100,000	—	8,000	92,000	3,000
Total Other Long-Term Liabilities	240,000	10,000	8,000	242,000	5,000
Total General Long-Term Liabilities	$1,060,000	$1,822,000	$212,000	$2,670,000	$210,400

ILLUSTRATION 14-7 Conversion Adjustments: Categories and Detail

Adjustments Category	Worksheet Adjustments Required for	
	Balance Sheet	**Operating Statement**
General Capital Assets	1. Add Capital Assets and Accumulated Depreciation	1a. Eliminate Capital Outlay Expenditures 1b. Add Depreciation Expense 1c. Deduct Carrying Value of Capital Assets Disposed of (leaving a balance equal to any gain or loss)
General Long-Term Liabilities	2a. Add Bonds Payable and Bond Premium (Deduct Bond Discount) 2b. Add Accrued Interest Payable	2a. Eliminate Other Financing Sources (OFS) for Bonds and Premium (or Other Financing Uses (OFU) for Discount) 2b. Eliminate Expenditures (or OFU) for Bond Retirement/Defeasance 2c. Convert Interest Expenditures to Interest Expense • Add discount amortization or deduct premium amortization • Add increase in accrued interest payable (or deduct decrease)
	3. Add other general long-term liabilities (related to "when due" expenditures such as pensions, OPEB, CJCA)*	3. Convert other "when due" type expenditures to expenses (add increases in related long-term liabilities or deduct decreases)
Other	4. Reduce Deferred Revenues to eliminate amounts earned or levied but deferred because the resources are *not* "available"(or recognition is delayed only until passage of time)	4. Convert revenue measurements from flow of current financial resources measurement focus (modified accrual) to flow of economic resources measurement focus (accrual)
	5. Eliminate or reclassify interfund payables and receivables • Eliminate interfund payables to and receivables from governmental funds • Reclassify net interfund payables to and receivables from Enterprise Funds as internal balances	5. Adjust transfers between funds to transfers between governmental and business-type activities • Eliminate transfers to or from governmental funds. • Reclassify net amount of transfers to or from Enterprise Funds as transfers to or from business-type activities. (This could be presumed and not entered on the worksheet if there is only one such amount.)

*OPEB is other postemployment benefits; CJCA is claims, judgments, and compensated absences.

The conversion process uses two separate worksheets—one for each governmental fund financial statement. The two worksheets are used to convert governmental funds:

- Balance sheet information into data required for the *governmental activities* data reported in the *government-wide* Statement of Net Position (Illustration 14-8).

- Operating statement information into the data required for the *governmental activities* data reported in the *government-wide* Statement of Activities (Illustration 14-11).

The conversion process for the balance sheet and for the operating statement each consists of three broad steps:

1. ***Enter the governmental funds financial statement total column amounts in the first column of the worksheet.***

2. ***Enter the adjustments to be made to the governmental funds financial statement information to convert it to the government-wide financial statement data.*** Data are entered in three adjustments columns, organized by topic as summarized in Illustration 14-7. *Note that the adjustments in the two worksheets parallel each another:*

   - Adjustments in the **balance sheet** worksheet add or subtract ending **balances** of GCA, GLTL, and other items such as deferred revenues to governmental funds balance sheet data to convert them to government-wide data.

   - Adjustments in the **operating statement** *worksheet add or subtract various* **changes** in GCA, GLTL, and other items such as deferred revenues to the governmental funds operating statement data to convert them to government-wide statement of activities data.

3. ***Sum the first four columns.*** This column provides the information needed to prepare the governmental activities column of the government-wide Statement of Net Position or the Statement of Activities.

The governmental funds information in the first column of each of the worksheets is copied from the total column of the corresponding governmental funds financial statement (i.e., the Balance Sheet for the Balance Sheet Conversion Worksheet and the Statement of Revenues, Expenditures, and Changes in Fund Balances for the Operating Statement Conversion Worksheet).

- Only ***total*** fund balance amounts are needed in the Balance Sheet Conversion Worksheet because the worksheet process converts Fund Balance to Net Position. The components of net position will be calculated later, so are not reflected in the worksheet.

- Much of the information for the adjustments comes from the GCA and GLTL schedules prepared for the notes to the financial statements (Illustrations 14-5 and 14-6) or from the GCA-GLTL accounts. Other sources of information might include Internal Service Funds (ISFs) financial statements and ancillary information maintained during the year or derived by year-end analyses.

Understanding the Conversion Adjustments is essential. Illustration 14-8 identifies the three categories of adjustments and a five-step adjustment sequence necessary for a basic conversion from governmental funds financial information to government-wide, governmental activities information. Every financial statement can be represented as an equation. The conversion from the governmental funds balance sheet to the government-wide statement of net position primarily requires adjusting for the differences between the two equations and some measurement focus differences that are not obvious from the equation differences. However, many of the adjustments are deduced by observing the differences in the two equations as shown below.

Balance Sheet Conversion Worksheet Adjustments

Governmental Funds Equation	Adjustments Required for	Governmental Activities Equation
Financial Assets		Current Assets
		+ Noncurrent Financial Assets
	General Capital Assets	**+ Capital Assets**
+ Deferred Outflows		+ Deferred Outflows
− Related Liabilities		− Current Liabilities
	General Long-Term Liabilities	**− Long-Term Liabilities**
− Deferred Inflows (including **deferred revenues**)	**Deferred Revenues**	− Deferred Inflows (excluding deferred revenues)
= Fund Balance	± Net effect of changes	= Net Position

ILLUSTRATION 14-8 Balance Sheet Conversion Worksheet—Governmental Funds to Governmental Activities

Governmental Funds BALANCE SHEET Conversion Worksheet

Governmental Funds Balance Sheet	Adjustments Related to			Governmental Activities Column on Statement of Net Position
	General Capital Assets Balances	General Long-Term Liabilities Balances	Other Balances and Interfund Items	
Financial Assets	(1) + GCA − Accumulated Depreciation		(5) − Due from/Advance to Other Governmental Funds	**Current Assets Internal Balances* Noncurrent Financial Assets Capital Assets (net)**
Plus **Deferred Outflows**				*Plus* **Deferred Outflows**
Less **Related Liabilities**		(2a) + Bonds Payable + Premiums (− Discounts)	(5) − Due to/Advance from Other Governmental Funds	*Less* **Current Liabilities Long-term Liabilities**
		(2b) + Interest Payable on general long-term debt		
		(3) + Other GLTL**		
Less **Deferred Inflows (Including Deferred Revenues)**			(4) − Deferred Revenues (If deferred based on availability criterion or time only)	*Less* **Deferred Inflows (Excluding Deferred Revenues— not available)**
Equals **Total Fund Balances**	+ Net Carrying Value of GCA	− Net Carrying Value of GLTL***	+ Deferred Revenues	*Equals* **Total Net Position**

*Reclassify net balance of (a) interfund receivables from Enterprise Funds (and business-type ISFs) and (b) interfund payables to those funds as *internal balances*, which typically is reported in the assets section of the government-wide Statement of Net Position.

**Each type of liability may be numbered separately, e.g., 3a for claims and judgments, 3b for compensated absences, etc.

***This column total equals the carrying value of GLTL plus accrued interest payable.

Preparing the balance sheet conversion worksheet adjustments is much like transaction analysis. Essentially, the adjustments required to convert the balances on the governmental funds financial statements to appropriate accounts and balances for government-wide reporting are shown in the worksheets as increases and decreases to various accounts. For example, to record the ending general capital assets balances, you increase general capital assets and the related accumulated depreciation (contra asset) accounts in the General Capital Assets adjustments column. The balancing effect of these changes then is added or subtracted to Total Fund Balances in converting to Total Net Position. Recognize that although we are using transaction analysis in the two-worksheet conversion, the derivation of conversion journal entries from this analysis is straightforward if preferred. (The corresponding adjustment is discussed in the Farley County conversion illustration to make the connection clear.)

Review Illustration 14-7 and Illustration 14-8 to ensure that you understand why the various adjustments are made on the balance sheet worksheet. As mentioned earlier, most are obvious if you consider the differences in the accounting equations of the governmental funds and the government-wide accounting entity. Those equations are reflected in the first and last columns of the skeleton worksheet diagram presented in Illustration 14-8.

GCA Balance Adjustments

The **first adjustments column** in the worksheet to derive government-wide Statement of Net Position data (i.e., the balance sheet worksheet) is used to **add the *ending* balances of all GCA-related accounts** to the governmental funds balance sheet information. These balances are not included in the governmental funds balance sheet but must be included in the government-wide Statement of Net Position. The adjustments in this column are the equivalent of debiting each capital asset for its ending balance, crediting accumulated depreciation for its ending balance, and crediting Net Position for the difference. Thus, the adjustment in this column increases "Total Fund Balances/Net Position" by the ending net carrying value of GCA (GCA cost less accumulated depreciation).

GLTL-Related Balance Adjustments

The **second adjustments column** is used to **add the *ending* balances of the GLTL-related accounts** to the governmental funds balance sheet information. We make this adjustment in two steps because some GLTL are related to other financing sources and debt service expenditures in the operating statement, and others are related to expenditures such as pensions; other postemployment benefits (OPEB); and claims, judgments, and compensated absences (CJCA).

Note the parallels between the conversion worksheets: This balance sheet worksheet is adjusting for *ending balances of assets, deferred outflows, liabilities, and deferred inflows*. The operating statement (or change statement) worksheet adjusts for *changes in those same accounts* during the year that affect governmental funds and the government-wide reporting differently. The "Total Fund Balances/Net Position" adjustment in this column is part of the conversion of fund balance to net position. The adjustment equals the net liability (including any related deferred outflows and deferred inflows) amount added in this column and must be subtracted from Total Fund Balances in converting to Total Net Position. The net liability amount added equals the sum of the ending carrying value of GLTL (Bonds Payable + Premiums − Discounts + Other GLTL) + Accrued Interest Payable on the bonds.

Other Balance Adjustments and Interfund Items

The **third adjustments column** relates to the ending balances of other items. The ones shown here include the deferred inflow of resources—deferred revenues—and interfund payables and receivables.

- The resource availability criterion does not apply to government-wide revenue recognition. Thus, in this case the entire **ending balance of deferred revenues** reported as deferred inflows of resources in governmental funds arose because the government did not "collect the revenues by year end or soon enough thereafter to pay current liabilities" (the resource availability criterion). This amount is not a governmental activities deferred inflow of resources. Therefore, it must be eliminated in deriving the data to report in the government-wide statement of net position. Total Fund Balance must be increased by the amount of the deferred revenues decrease to convert it to Total Net Position.

- The final adjustment in this worksheet eliminates **interfund payables and receivables** among and **between governmental funds and governmental activities ISFs**. For example, if there is an interfund liability between the General Fund and a Capital Projects Fund, both the interfund receivable balance, Due from General Fund, and the interfund payable balance, Due to Capital Projects Fund, are eliminated (deducted) from the governmental funds balance sheet information. Because this adjustment entails equal decreases of assets and liabilities, it does not impact the conversion of Total Fund Balance to Total Net Position.

Note that governmental funds interfund payables to and receivables from Enterprise Funds and business-type activities ISFs are ***not*** eliminated. The *net* amount of these interfund payables and receivables is calculated and reported as "Internal Balances" in the government-wide statement of net position. The "Total Fund Balances/Net Position" adjustment in this final column increases this total by an amount equal to the decrease in deferred revenues.

This final adjustments column may be used for additional adjustments in more complex situations or to reclassify items such as Due to and Due from Enterprise Funds as Internal Balances. Likewise, other columns could be added. For instance, a government that has a governmental activities ISF might add a column labeled "Ending ISF Asset, Deferred Outflow, Liability, and Deferred Inflow Balances" and add those account balances to the governmental funds information in this worksheet. Alternatively, the ISF amounts can be added to the third adjustments column in a worksheet set up like that in Illustration 14-8.

Farley County Balance Sheet Conversion

Illustration 14-9 demonstrates the conversion worksheet to derive government-wide Statement of Net Position information for Farley County. It follows the process outlined in Illustrations 14-7 and 14-8. The first column is copied from the total column of the Farley County Governmental Funds Balance Sheet (Illustration 14-3) except that only *total* fund balance is used.

GCA Balances

The ending balance of each general capital asset and related accumulated depreciation account from the Capital Assets Schedule (Illustration 14-5) is added in the first adjustments column. These adjustments are labeled (**1**). The adjustment in this column to convert Total Fund Balance to Total Net Position equals the ending carrying value of general capital assets, $3,993,200 for Farley County.

GLTL-Related Balances

The ending balances of all general long-term liability and related accounts are added in the GLTL-Related Balances column. This information is taken from the General Long-Term Liabilities Schedule (Illustration 14-6). The GLTL-related balances are added in two sets of adjustments.

The first set of adjustments adds general long-term liabilities such as outstanding bond and note balances, as well as related premiums and discounts (Adjustment **2a**—$2,428,000) and accrued interest payable on long-term debt (Adjustment **2b**) that was not previously accrued.

The next set of adjustments in this column (Adjustment **3**) adds the ending balances of general long-term liability accounts such as compensated absence liabilities, claims and judgments liabilities, underfunded pension obligations, and underfunded OPEB liabilities. Adjustment **3a** adds claims and judgments liabilities totaling $150,000 and adjustment **3b** adds compensated absences liabilities of $92,000. (All general long-term liabilities could have been added in a single adjustment, but this division has a logical tie to the operating statement conversion worksheet.)

The net decrease in the Net Position account from these adjustments is $2,688,750, which equals the carrying value of ending general long-term liabilities plus accrued interest payable for Farley County. This amount is deducted from "Total Fund Balances/Net Position" in the GLTL Balances column as part of the conversion from Total Fund Balances to Total Net Position.

ILLUSTRATION 14-9 Farley County Balance Sheet Conversion Worksheet

Farley County
Governmental Funds Balance Sheet Conversion Worksheet
December 31, 20X6

	Governmental Funds Balance Sheet	General Capital Assets Balance	General Long-Term Liabilities Balance	Other Balances and Interfund Items	Governmental Activities Column—Statement of Net Position
Cash	$ 385,200				$ 385,200
Investments	1,085,600				1,085,600
Due from General Fund	1,000			(5) $ (1,000)	—
Due from federal government	1,016,000				1,016,000
Taxes receivable	54,000				54,000
Allowance of uncollectible taxes	(11,000)				(11,000)
Interest and penalties receivable	1,500				1,500
Allowance for uncollectible interest & penalties	(136)				(136)
Accounts receivable	13,000				13,000
Allowance of uncollectible accounts ..	(500)				(500)
Accrued interest receivable	54,800				54,800
Inventory of materials and supplies ...	4,700				4,700
Land		(1) $ 125,000			125,000
Buildings		(1) 1,250,000			1,250,000
Accumulated depreciation—buildings ..		(1) (860,000)			(860,000)
Machinery and equipment		(1) 398,200			398,200
Accumulated depreciation— machinery and equipment		(1) (160,000)			(160,000)
Infrastructure		(1) 2,000,000			2,000,000
Accumulated depreciation— infrastructure		(1) (1,300,000)			(1,300,000)
Construction in progress		(1) 2,540,000			2,540,000
Total Assets	2,604,164	3,993,200	—	(1,000)	6,596,364
Vouchers payable	290,400				290,400
Accrued salaries and wages payable ..	5,000				5,000
Contracts payable—retained percentage	100,000				100,000
Accrued interest payable	300		(2b) 18,750		19,050
Unearned operating grant revenues .	103,000				103,000
Unearned capital grant revenues	150,000				150,000
Due to Enterprise Fund*	3,300				3,300
Due to Special Revenue Funds	1,000			(5) (1,000)	—
Bonds payable—due within 1 year			(2a) 200,000		200,000
Premium on bonds—due within 1 year			(2a) 5,400		5,400
Claims and judgments payable— due within 1 year			(3a) 2,000		2,000
Compensated absences payable— due within 1 year			(3b) 3,000		3,000
Bonds payable			(2a) 2,200,000		2,200,000
Premium on bonds			(2a) 22,600		22,600
Claims and judgments payable			(3a) 148,000		148,000
Compensated absences payable			(3b) 89,000		89,000
Total Liabilities	653,000	—	2,688,750	(1,000)	3,340,750
Deferred Inflows of Resources					
Deferred tax revenues	30,800	—	—	(4) (30,800)	—
Total Fund Balances/Net Position ...	$1,920,364	$ 3,993,200	$(2,688,750)	$ 30,800	$ 3,255,614

*Reported as Internal Balances

Other Balances and Interfund Items

The final adjustments column, the "Other Balances and Interfund Items" column, is used here to make two adjustments. In Adjustment **4**, the ending amount of Deferred Tax Revenues, $30,800, is deducted from governmental funds deferred inflows because it is not deferred in the government-wide statements. Recognition of these revenues was deferred in the governmental funds because they were not "available." However, the "available" revenue recognition criterion does not apply to government-wide revenue recognition. Eliminating this deferred inflow balance increases the "Total Fund Balances/Net Position" by $30,800.

The final adjustment in this column eliminates interfund receivables from and payables to other governmental funds (or to governmental activities ISFs). Due from General Fund of $1,000 is deducted, as is the related interfund payable, Due to Special Revenue Funds of $1,000. Because assets and liabilities are decreased by equal amounts, Adjustment **5** does not affect the "Total Fund Balances/Net Position" conversion. (Additional adjustments may be made in this column in more complex situations.)

Government-Wide Statement of Net Position Information

The government-wide information computed in the final column is the sum of the other columns. The final column amounts are used to prepare the governmental activities column of the government-wide Statement of Net Position, as demonstrated later in the chapter.

The Basic Financial Statements must include reconciliations of the governmental funds statements and the government-wide statements, including:

- Total Fund Balances of governmental funds with Total Net Position of governmental activities.
- Changes in Fund Balances of governmental funds with Changes in Net Position of governmental activities.

The worksheets provide details of the conversion process. As seen in the adjustments and in the last row of the worksheet (Illustration 14-9), they contain all the information necessary to complete these reconciliations. Therefore, the reconciliations of the governmental funds financial statements and the related government-wide financial statements can be completed at the same time as the governmental funds conversion worksheets.

Notice, for instance, that the preceding adjustments to the "Total Fund Balances/Net Position" appear in the reconciliation shown in Illustration 14-10. The descriptions of the adjustments tie to the reconciling items shown in the balance sheet conversion worksheet illustration, and the subtotals equal the column totals for the "Total Fund Balances/Net Position" line in the balance sheet conversion worksheet.

Operating Statement Conversion Worksheet Adjustments

As is clear from Illustration 14-7, conversion of the governmental funds operating statement information to government-wide financial statement information requires adjustments that parallel those required for the balance sheet worksheet. The operating statement conversion worksheet adjustments are not as intuitively obvious as the adjustments for the balance sheet conversion worksheet, but you should find it easy to relate them to the balance sheet worksheet adjustments. Every operating statement adjustment is for a *change* in some asset, deferred outflow, liability, or deferred inflow amount that was added or deducted in the balance sheet conversion worksheet. (The exception is when the balance sheet item changed to zero during the year, thereby eliminating the need for a balance adjustment.)

Illustration 14-11 provides the structure for the operating statement conversion worksheet and specifies the adjustments made. Again, it should be helpful to note that whereas the balance sheet conversion worksheet adjusted for ending balances of GCA, GLTL, and other items such as deferred revenues, the operating

ILLUSTRATION 14-10   Farley County Balance Sheet Reconciliation

Farley County
Reconciliation of Total Fund Balance to Total Net Position
December 31, 20X6

Total Fund Balances—Governmental Funds			$ 1,920,364

Amounts reported for governmental activities in the Statement of Net Position are different because:

General Capital Assets

Capital assets used in governmental activities are not financial resources and therefore are not reported in the governmental funds:

(1)	Governmental capital assets	$6,313,200		
(1)	Less accumulated depreciation	(2,320,000)	3,993,200	

General Long-Term Liabilities

Long-term debt is not due and payable in the current year and therefore is not reported in the governmental funds:

(2a)	Bonds Payable	(2,400,000)		
(2a)	Bond Premium	(28,000)		
(2b)	Interest payable of the governmental activities is not payable from current financial resources and therefore is not reported in the governmental funds	(18,750)		

Other long-term liabilities are not due and payable in the current year and therefore are not reported in the governmental fund:

(3a)	Claims and Judgments Payable	(150,000)		
(3b)	Compensated Absences	(92,000)	(2,688,750)	

Deferred Inflows of Resources

(4)	Deferred revenues reported in the governmental funds because of the financial resource availability criterion have been recognized as revenues of governmental activities		30,800
Total Net Position of Governmental Activities			$ 3,255,614

statement conversion requires adjustments for the effects of transactions that *change* the balances of GCA, GLTL, and other items. The detail of the changes made by adjustments are entered as adjustments to the body of the change statement, and the summary effect of those changes is the adjustment required to convert Net Changes in Fund Balances to Net Changes in Net Position. The summary effect is entered on the last line of each adjustments column.

GCA Changes

The **first adjustments column** of the operating statement conversion worksheet requires adjustments either to eliminate or to add changes in GCA.

- Adjustment 1a eliminates capital outlay expenditures that relate to increases in GCA through purchases, construction, or other methods of acquisition such as leases. Converting the change in fund balances to change in net position requires adding the increases in GCA to the change in fund balances. Recognize that a government will not capitalize capital outlay expenditures that do not meet its capitalization criteria. Therefore, note that this adjustment is limited to capital outlay expenditures that increase GCA, i.e., those that are capitalized.

- Adjustment 1b adds depreciation expense (which is a change in accumulated depreciation) because it must be included in expenses for governmental activities but is not an expenditure. The amount of depreciation expense must be deducted from Change in Fund Balances to convert it to Changes in Net Position. (The ending accumulated depreciation balance is recorded in the Balance Sheet Conversion Worksheet as illustrated earlier.)

- Adjustment 1c deducts the decrease in the carrying value of GCA from the Other Financing Sources—GCA Sale Proceeds to compute the gain or loss on disposal of capital assets. In effect this adjustment is eliminating the other financing source from the sale and recording

ILLUSTRATION 14-11 Operating Statement Conversion Worksheet—Governmental Funds to Governmental Activities

Governmental Funds OPERATING STATEMENT Conversion Worksheet

Governmental Funds Operating Statement	Adjustments Related to			Governmental Activities Column— Statement of Activities
	General Capital Assets Changes	General Long-Term Liabilities Changes	Other Changes and Interfund Items	
Revenues			(4) + Increase (−Decrease) in Deferred Revenues if deferred per financial resource availability criterion	**Revenues**
Less **Expenditures**				*Less* **Expenses**
Current Operating (By Function)	(1b) + Depreciation Expense	(3) + Increase (−Decrease) in GLTL related to "when due" expenditures		By Function
Capital Outlay	(1a) − Capital outlay expenditures			
Debt Service:				
Principal retirement		(2b) − Expenditures— Principal Retirement		
Interest (amount due and payable)		(2c) + Amortization of discounts − Amortization of premiums + Increase (−Decrease) in related interest payable		Interest Expense (per effective interest method)
Plus or Minus **Other Financing Sources (Uses):**				*Plus or Minus* **Gains (Losses) and Transfers**
OFS—Bonds		(2a) − OFS—Bonds		
OFS—Bond premiums		− OFS—Bond premium		
OFU—Bond discount		+ OFU—Bond discount		
OFS—GCA sale proceeds	(1c) − Carrying value of GCA sold			Gain/Loss of Sale of GCA
Transfers from (to) governmental funds			(5) − Transfers from (to) governmental funds	
Transfers from (to) Enterprise Funds				Transfers from (to) Business-Type Activities
Equals **Changes in Fund Balance***	± Net change in GCA book value	± Net change in GLTL book value and accrued interest payable (adjusted for amortization of bond issue costs)	± Change in deferred revenues balance	*Equals* **Changes in Net Position**

*Each adjustments column total equals ± changes in revenues ± changes in expenditures/expenses ± changes in other financing sources (uses).

the gain (or loss). The carrying value must also be deducted from the Change in Fund Balances to convert it to Changes in Net Position.

Note that each adjustment was related to either GCA or accumulated depreciation—the items adjusted in the GCA Balance column of the balance sheet conversion worksheet.

GLTL-Related Changes

The **second adjustments column** includes two sets of adjustments for GLTL-related changes, which parallel those in the balance sheet conversion worksheet.

- Adjustment 2a eliminates other financing sources and other financing uses amounts associated with bond issuance, while adjustment 2b eliminates expenditures for bond principal retirement. These adjustments eliminate governmental fund operating statement net financial asset inflows and outflows that are not revenues and expenses to be reported in the government-wide statement of activities.

- Adjustment 2c, on the other hand, addresses changes in the GLTL-related accounts—including premiums, discounts, and interest payable—that are not reported separately in the governmental funds statements.

Similarly, the other set of GLTL change adjustments (adjustment 3) adds or subtracts changes in GLTL related to operating expenditures recognized "when due" that are not included in the amounts reported for expenditures in the governmental funds operating statements. These adjustments convert expenditures for items such as compensated absences to expenses. (Each adjustment may be numbered separately, as in 3a, 3b, and so on).

Other Changes and Interfund Items

The **third adjustments column** serves two purposes:

1. Adjusting modified accrual basis revenues to accrual basis revenues by adding increases in or subtracting decreases in deferred revenues (deferred because of the financial resource availability criterion OR for a reason that will be satisfied solely by passage of time) to the appropriate revenue source.

2. Eliminating transfers to and transfers from governmental funds (and governmental activities ISFs). (Net transfers to and from Enterprise Funds and business-type activities ISFs are reported as transfers to or from business-type activities.)

As with the balance sheet conversion worksheet, additional adjustments may be made in the "Other" column to accommodate more complex situations and additional column(s) may be added.

Farley County Operating Statement Conversion

Illustration 14-12 demonstrates the conversion worksheet to derive government-wide Statement of Activities information for Farley County. It follows the process discussed and demonstrated in Illustration 14-11. The first column of the worksheet is copied from the total column of the Farley County Governmental Funds Statement of Revenues, Expenditures, and Changes in Fund Balance (Illustration 14-4). The next three columns present the required adjustments for GCA changes, GLTL changes, and changes in other assets, deferred outflows, liabilities, and deferred inflows.

GCA Changes

The first adjustments column of Farley County's operating statement conversion worksheet includes adjustments for three types of changes in GCA. Capital outlay expenditures are eliminated in the first adjustment (**1a**). In this example, the capital outlay expenditures ($2,598,200) equal the increase in capital assets shown on the Capital Assets Schedule (Illustration 14-5). This equality indicates that all capital expenditures met the capitalization threshold and thus should be capitalized, not reported as expenses in the government-wide financial statements.

ILLUSTRATION 14-12 Farley County Operating Statement Conversion Worksheet

Farley County
Governmental Funds Operating Statement Conversion Worksheet
For the Year Ended December 31, 20X6

	Governmental Funds Operating Statement	General Capital Assets Changes		General Long-Term Liabilities Changes		Other Changes and Interfund Items		Governmental Activities Column in Statement of Activities
Revenues								
Taxes	$ 970,000					(4) $ 10,800		$ 980,800
Licenses and permits	89,000							89,000
Fines and forfeitures	38,000							38,000
Unrestricted grants	105,000							105,000
Operating grants	120,000							120,000
Capital grants	2,066,000							2,066,000
Investment income	52,500							52,500
Other revenues	2,000							2,000
Expenditures/Expenses								
Current Operating:								
General government	78,400	(1b)	$ 11,000	(3b)	$ (2,500)			86,900
Public safety	405,000	(1b)	55,000	(3a)	10,000			467,000
				(3b)	(3,000)			
Highways and streets	246,200	(1b)	133,000	(3b)	(1,500)			377,700
Health and sanitation	46,400	(1b)	8,000	(3b)	(1,000)			53,400
Other	18,600	(1b)	3,000					21,600
Capital Outlay:								—
Construction	2,540,000	(1a)	(2,540,000)					—
Equipment	58,200	(1a)	(58,200)					—
Debt Service:								—
Bond principal retirement	200,000			(2b)	(200,000)			—
Interest	101,850			(2c)	(6,250)			91,600
				(2c)	(4,000)			
Fiscal agent fees*	15,000							15,000
Bond issue costs	10,000							10,000
Other Financing Sources (Uses)								
Bonds issued	1,800,000			(2a)	(1,800,000)			—
Premium on bonds	12,000			(2a)	(12,000)			—
Proceeds/Gain on sale of equipment	50,000	(1c)	(40,000)					10,000
Transfers from General Fund	176,000					(5)	(176,000)	—
Transfers from Special Revenue Funds	20,000					(5)	(20,000)	—
Transfers from Enterprise Funds/ Business-Type Activities	18,000							18,000
Transfers to Capital Projects Funds	(16,000)					(5)	16,000	—
Transfers to Debt Service Funds	(160,000)					(5)	160,000	—
Transfers to General Fund	(20,000)					(5)	20,000	—
Change in Fund Balances/Net Position**	$ 1,602,850		$ 2,348,200		$(1,603,750)		$ 10,800	$2,358,100

*Combined with Interest Expense for reporting on Statement of Activities.

**Each column total equals ± Changes in revenues ± Changes in Expenditures/Expenses ± Changes in Other Financing Sources (Uses).

Some governments report capital outlay expenditures by functions in the General Fund and Special Revenue Funds. If that were the case for Farley County, the capitalized amounts would be deducted from each category of functional expenditures.

The second type of GCA adjustment (**1b**) increases functional expenses for depreciation ($210,000) of general capital assets. The allocation of depreciation to governmental functions, or a more detailed allocation such as to departments, is a required part of the Capital Assets Schedule. These allocations are shown at the bottom of that schedule (Illustration 14-5) and are reflected in the adjustments on the worksheet.

The third GCA-related adjustment (**1c**) for Farley County is for the sale of GCA. The proceeds from GCA sales are reported as an Other Financing Source in the governmental funds operating statement. When preparing the government-wide statements, this amount must be converted to the gain or loss on the CGA sales. As can be seen in the Capital Assets Schedule, assets that cost $60,000 with accumulated depreciation of $20,000 were deleted from the records. Reducing the Other Financing Sources—GCA Sale Proceeds of $50,000 by the carrying value of the asset sold of $40,000 leaves a $10,000 balance, which is the gain on sale of the capital asset to be reported in the government-wide Statement of Activities.

The accumulated effect of the adjustments to various operating statements made in this column ($2,598,200 – $210,000 – $40,000, or $2,348,200) is added to the "Changes in Fund Balance/Net Position." This is needed to convert the Changes in Fund Balance to Changes in Net Position.

GLTL-Related Changes

The two sets of adjustments in the GLTL Changes column are relatively straightforward. The first set of adjustments—those not related to current operating expenditures—involve three steps:

2a. Other financing sources are not revenues or capital contributions so are not reported in the government-wide Statement of Activities. Accordingly, Farley County's other financing sources for the face amount of bonds issued ($1,800,000) during the year and for the related premiums ($12,000) must be eliminated. These changes will have a negative effect on the "Change in Fund Balance/Net Position."

2b. Expenditures for bond principal retirement ($200,000) are not expenses, so must be eliminated. The elimination increases the Change in Fund Balance/Net Position.

2c. Several adjustments are necessary to convert interest expenditures to interest expense. Two entries adjust for changes in GLTL-related accounts that do *not* affect interest *expenditures*—amortizing premium (discount) on bonds and accruing interest payable.

- The amortization of a premium ($4,000 for Farley County) is always deducted from interest expenditures to adjust to interest expenses. (Discount amortization is always added to expense.)

- The change in interest payable adjustment is an addition to interest expense if interest payable increases during the year, but is a deduction ($6,250 for Farley County) because interest payable decreased from $25,000 at the beginning of the year to $18,750 at year end.

The net effect of the interest adjustments will be to decrease interest by $10,250 and positively affect the Changes in Fund Balance/Net Position by the same amount.

The second set of adjustments in the "GLTL Changes" column addresses the remaining changes on the GLTL schedule—a $10,000 increase in the Liability for Claims and Judgments and an $8,000 decrease in the Liability for Compensated Absences. Unlike the previous adjustments in this column, additional information is required to determine which functional categories of expenditures/expenses to adjust. Some of the claims and judgments might relate to capital projects and would be capitalized. In this illustration they are assumed to relate to operations and thus operating expenditures are adjusted. *The functional assignments in this illustration are assumed amounts.* In practice, appropriate records must be maintained to support allocations to functional categories.

3a. The $10,000 increase in Claims and Judgments Payable means that this amount has not been recognized as a fund liability, so has not been recognized as expenditures. This adjustment (labeled **3a**) increases expenses for this amount because expenses are recognized in the government-wide operating statement when they are incurred rather than when the related liability matures.

3b. The decrease in the compensated absences payable of $8,000 is deducted from current year expenditures because it results from expenses of a prior year(s) being recognized as expenditures in the current year when they became due and payable. This worksheet adjustment removes the prior year expenses from the current year expenditures for the various functions and increases Changes in Fund Balances/Net Position.

The net effect of the **3a** and **3b** adjustments is to decrease the Change in Net Position that will be reported for governmental activities by $2,000. The accumulated effect of the GLTL adjustments ($1,812,000 + $200,000 + $10,250 − $2,000, or a decrease of $1,603,750) on the "Change in Fund Balance/Net Position" is entered on the last line of the worksheet.

Other Changes and Interfund Items

Adjustment 4 in the "Other Changes" operating statement adjustments column is related to adjustment 4 on the balance sheet conversion worksheet. Whereas the ending balance of deferred revenues ($30,800) was eliminated in that conversion, the adjustment in this worksheet adds the $10,800 increase in Farley County's deferred tax revenues (based on the resource availability criterion) to its modified accrual basis tax revenues. (Farley County's *beginning* of the year deferred taxes was *assumed* to be $20,000.) In government-wide reporting, taxes and other revenues are recognized when earned or levied and objectively measurable, not deferred because of the timing of collection ("availability").

The last adjustment **(5)** eliminates the interfund transfers to and from governmental funds (and governmental activities ISFs). The transfer from the Enterprise Funds is a transfer from business-type activities, so is reported in the Statement of Activities.

Reconciliation: Change in Fund Balances with Change in Net Position

As with the earlier conversion worksheet, the reconciliation of Changes in Fund Balances to Changes in Net Position would be prepared based on this conversion process. The reconciling items are tied directly to the conversion process, as shown in the reconciliation in Illustration 14-13.

DERIVING BUSINESS-TYPE ACTIVITIES DATA

Preparing the governmental activities conversion worksheets is the most complex step involved in completing the government-wide financial statements. But business-type activities information also must be derived from the related Enterprise Funds information.

The business-type activities conversion worksheets are relatively uncomplicated, even in the most complex situations. Enterprise Funds financial statements and government-wide financial statements are presented using the same MFBA. Likewise, they are based on the same accounting equation and typically aggregate data from the same funds (if there are no business-type activities ISFs).

Consequently, capital asset and long-term liability adjustments are not needed, nor are adjustments converting modified accrual revenue and expenditure measurements to accrual revenue and expense measurements. Indeed, of the adjustments illustrated for governmental activities, only those comparable to the ones labeled "5"

ILLUSTRATION 14-13   Farley County Operating Statement Reconciliation

Farley County
Governmental Funds
Reconciliation of the Changes in Fund Balances to Changes in Net Position
For the Year Ended June 30, 20X6

Change in Fund Balances of Governmental Funds			$ 1,602,850

Amounts reported for governmental activities in the government-wide Statement of Activities are different because:

General Capital Assets Changes

Governmental funds report capital outlays as expenditures. However, in the government-wide Statement of Activities, the cost of those assets is depreciated over their estimated useful lives.

(1a)	Expenditures for capital assets	$ 2,598,200	
(1b)	Less current year depreciation	(210,000)	
(1c)	When recognizing the sale of capital assets, the governmental funds report the total proceeds of the sale. Only the gain or loss on the sale is reported in the government-wide Statement of Activities	(40,000)	2,348,200

General Long-Term Liabilities Changes

Bond issues provide current financial resources to governmental funds, but issuing debt increases long-term liabilities in the government-wide Statement of Net Position. Repayment of bond principal is an expenditure in the governmental funds, but the repayment reduces long-term liabilities in the government-wide Statement of Net Position. Other costs related to debt issuance and retirement use governmental fund resources but are not expenses, so are deferred and amortized in the government-wide Statement of Activities.

(2a)	Bond principal	(1,800,000)	
(2a)	Bond premium	(12,000)	
(2b)	Principal payments	200,000	

Interest expenditures do not include the change in interest payable from the prior year to the current year. Amortization of bond premiums and discounts also affect interest expense but do not affect interest expenditures.

(2c)	Decrease in accrued interest payable on bonds	6,250	
(2c)	Amortization of bond premium	4,000	

Other changes in liabilities are not recorded as expenses in the governmental funds or were recognized as expenditures in the current period but were expenses in a prior period.

(3a)	Increase in Claims and Judgments Payable	(10,000)	
(3b)	Decrease in Compensated Absences Payable	8,000	(1,603,750)

Other Changes

(4)	Revenues in the Statement of Activities that do not provide current financial resources are not reported as revenues in the funds, and some governmental fund revenues of the current period were recognized in a prior period in the government-wide financial statements.		10,800
Change in Net Position of Governmental Activities			**$ 2,358,100**

on the governmental activities worksheets—elimination of interfund payables to and receivables from Enterprise Funds—are needed to convert Enterprise Funds financial statement data to government-wide financial statement amounts. Net interfund payables to and receivables from governmental funds will be reported as Internal Balances and will offset the equal amounts reported in governmental activities. Transfers to and from governmental funds will be netted and reported as transfers to (from) governmental activities, again offsetting the equal amounts reported in governmental activities as transfers to (from) business-type activities.

If an ISF primarily serves one or more Enterprise Funds and thus is part of business-type activities, an ISF column will be added to the balance sheet conversion worksheet for business-type activities to add the ending ISF asset and liability balances. Unless the ISF has equal revenues and expenses, a column also will be added to the business-type activities operating statement conversion worksheet to address the differences created by the profit or loss arising from ISF charges. An ISF profit or loss indicates that either governmental funds departments (governmental activities), EF departments (business-type activities), or both were charged more or less than the costs of ISF goods and services acquired. In this case, the governmental activities, business-type activities, or both are misstated by the overcharge or undercharge.

In simple situations like Farley County's, which has no ISFs and no interfund payables and receivables or interfund transfers between Enterprise Funds, business-type activities conversion worksheets are unnecessary. The business-type activities data are the same as the total Enterprise Funds data in the proprietary funds financial statements (Illustrations 14-14 and 14-16).

Statement of Net Position

Completing the government-wide Statement of Net Position (Illustration 14-15) requires the data from both the governmental activities column of Farley County's balance sheet conversion worksheet (Illustration 14-9) and the Enterprise Funds total column of the Proprietary Fund Statement of Net Position (Illustration 14-14). A few reclassifications often are necessary to report the information properly in the government-wide Statement of Net Position. As noted earlier, Farley County's interfund receivable (Due from General Fund, $3,300, in the Enterprise Funds Statement of Net Position) and its corresponding interfund liability (Due to Enterprise Fund, $3,300, in the governmental activities data) typically are reported as Internal Balances in the government-wide Statement of Net Position. Also, the amounts for (1) net investment in capital assets, (2) restricted net position, and (3) unrestricted net position for governmental activities must also be calculated using the process described in Chapter 10.

For Farley County, the Net Investment in Capital Assets is calculated as the capital assets, net ($3,993,200) less the bond liabilitiy of $2,428,000, or $1,565,200. (Contracts payable are assumed to relate to a bond-financed construction project and are not deducted.) The Restricted Net Position is assumed to equal the Restricted Fund Balance of the governmental funds. This often is not the case because there may be deferred revenues related to restricted assets in governmental funds that are not deferred in the government-wide statements or general long-term liabilities related to restricted assets that must be deducted to determine the restricted net position. The remainder of the total net position is reported as unrestricted net position.

Statement of Activities

Preparing the government-wide Statement of Activities typically requires more reclassifications than preparing the Statement of Net Position. In addition, it requires (1) proper classification of revenues between program revenues and general revenues and (2) proper allocation of operating expenses and nonoperating expenses of Enterprise Funds to departments and/or functions. This reclassification typically requires additional information beyond what is presented in the fund financial statements or developed in the conversion worksheets—such as which grant revenues are restricted and the functions to which they are restricted. Too, as noted in prior chapters, some amounts reported as capital contributions in fund financial statements are reclassified as transfers in the government-wide Statement of Activities. Transfers between governmental funds and Enterprise Funds are reclassified as transfers between governmental activities and business-type activities. Several other reclassifications and adjustments similar to these types may be needed in more complex situations.

Notice in Farley County's government-wide Statement of Activities (Illustration 14-17) that several of these reclassifications and modifications

ILLUSTRATION 14-14 Farley County Proprietary Funds Statement of Net Position

Farley County
Proprietary Funds
Statement of Net Position
December 31, 20X6

	Enterprise Funds		
	Solid Waste	Golf Course	Total
ASSETS			
Current Assets:			
Cash	$ 126,000	$ 89,000	$ 215,000
Accounts receivable (net of $3,000 allowance for uncollectible accounts)	7,000	—	7,000
Due from General Fund*	3,300	—	3,300
Due from Golf Course Enterprise Fund**	25,000	—	25,000
Materials and supplies	15,000	45,000	60,000
Prepaid rent	20,000	10,000	30,000
Total Current Assets	196,300	144,000	340,300
Noncurrent Assets:			
Land	300,000	1,250,000	1,550,000
Buildings (net)	38,000	112,000	150,000
Land improvements (net)	—	1,880,000	1,880,000
Machinery and equipment (net)	632,000	213,000	845,000
Total Noncurrent Assets	970,000	3,455,000	4,425,000
Total Assets	1,166,300	3,599,000	4,765,300
LIABILITIES			
Accounts payable	50,000	65,000	115,000
Salaries and Wages Payable	13,000	15,000	28,000
Due to Solid Waste Collection Enterprise Fund**	—	25,000	25,000
Total Liabilities	63,000	105,000	168,000
NET POSITION			
Net investment in capital assets	970,000	3,455,000	4,425,000
Unrestricted	133,300	39,000	172,300
Total Net Position	$1,103,300	$3,494,000	$4,597,300

*Reported as Internal Balances

**Both are eliminated because both are part of business-type activities.

have been made. Most of the information in the Statement of Activities came from the governmental activities operating statement conversion worksheet (Illustration 14-12) and the Proprietary Fund Statement of Revenues, Expenses, and Changes in Fund Net Position (Illustration 14-16). The governmental activities charges for services assume that Licenses and Permits Revenues of $89,000 in the worksheet were attributed partly to departments in the public safety function ($66,750) and partly to departments in the Health and Sanitation function ($22,250). The Public Safety function charges for services equals $104,750—the $66,750 that Public Safety departments are assumed to have generated in licenses and permits revenues, plus $38,000 of Fines and Forfeitures revenues. Finally, the governmental activities interest expense includes interest of $91,600, fiscal agent fees of $15,000, and bond issue expenses of $10,000 to total $116,600.

ILLUSTRATION 14-15 Farley County Government-Wide Statement of Net Position

Farley County
Statement of Net Position
December 31, 20X6

	Governmental Activities	Business-Type Activities	Total
ASSETS			
Cash	$ 385,200	$ 215,000	$ 600,200
Investments	1,085,600	—	1,085,600
Due from federal government	1,016,000	—	1,016,000
Taxes receivable (net)	43,000	7,000	50,000
Interest and penalties receivable (net)	1,364	—	1,364
Accounts receivable (net)	12,500	—	12,500
Accrued interest receivable	54,800	—	54,800
Inventory of materials and supplies	4,700	60,000	64,700
Prepaid rent	—	30,000	30,000
Internal balances	(3,300)	3,300	—
Land	125,000	1,550,000	1,675,000
Construction in progress	2,540,000	—	2,540,000
Buildings (net)	390,000	150,000	540,000
Land improvements (net)	—	1,880,000	1,880,000
Machinery and equipment (net)	238,200	845,000	1,083,200
Infrastructure	700,000	—	700,000
Total Assets	6,593,064	4,740,300	11,333,364
LIABILITIES			
Vouchers payable	290,400	115,000	405,400
Accrued salaries and wages payable	5,000	28,000	33,000
Contracts payable—retained percentage	100,000	—	100,000
Accrued interest payable	19,050	—	19,050
Deferred operating grant revenues	103,000	—	103,000
Deferred capital grant revenues	150,000	—	150,000
Long-term Liabilities			
Due within one year			
Bonds payable	200,000	—	200,000
Premium on bonds	5,400	—	5,400
Claims and judgments payable	2,000	—	2,000
Compensated absences payable	3,000	—	3,000
Due in more than 1 year			
Bonds payable	2,200,000	—	2,200,000
Premium on bonds	22,600	—	22,600
Claims and judgments payable	148,000	—	148,000
Compensated absences payable	89,000	—	89,000
Total Liabilities	3,337,450	143,000	3,480,450
NET POSITION			
Net investment in capital assets	1,565,200	4,425,000	5,990,200
Restricted	811,875	—	811,875
Unrestricted	878,539	172,300	1,050,839
Total Net Position	$3,255,614	$4,597,300	$7,852,914

ILLUSTRATION 14-16 Farley County Proprietary Funds Statement of Revenues, Expenses, and Change in Fund Net Position

Farley County
Proprietary Funds
Statement of Revenues, Expenses, and Changes in Fund Net Position
For the Year Ended December 31, 20X6

| | Enterprise Funds | | |
	Solid Waste	Golf Course	Total
OPERATING REVENUES			
Charges for Services			
Governmental	$6,230,000	$ —	$6,230,000
Residential and industrial (net of $3,000 in estimated bad debts)	147,000	—	147,000
Green fees	—	1,780,000	1,780,000
Cart rental	—	630,000	630,000
Pro shop sales	—	125,000	125,000
Total Revenues	6,377,000	2,535,000	8,912,000
OPERATING EXPENSES			
Cost of goods sold	—	50,000	50,000
Salaries and wages	338,000	390,000	728,000
Materials and supplies	4,300,000	675,000	4,975,000
Utilities	75,000	749,000	824,000
Vehicle maintenance	527,000	126,000	653,000
Rent expense	240,000	120,000	360,000
Depreciation expense	50,000	320,000	370,000
Total Operating Expenses	5,530,000	2,430,000	7,960,000
Operating Income (Loss)	847,000	105,000	952,000
Transfers to the General Fund	(18,000)	—	(18,000)
Changes in Net Position	829,000	105,000	934,000
Net Position, January 1, 20X6	274,300	3,389,000	3,663,300
Net Position, December 31, 20X6	$1,103,300	$3,494,000	$4,597,300

Reconciliations

GAAP require reconciliations (1) of the governmental activities information reported in the government-wide financial statements and the related governmental funds financial statements and (2) of the business-type activities information reported in the government-wide financial statements and the Enterprise Funds information in the related proprietary funds financial statements. Thus, as many as four reconciliations between government-wide financial statements and fund financial statements may need to be prepared and presented. The *required reconciliations* are of:

- *Total fund balances* of *governmental funds* presented in the governmental funds Balance Sheet *with total net position* of *governmental activities* presented in the government-wide Statement of Net Position.

- *Total net position* of *Enterprise Funds* presented in the proprietary funds Statement of Net Position *with total net position* of *business-type activities* presented in the government-wide Statement of Net Position.

- *Net change in total fund balances of governmental funds* presented in the governmental funds Statement of Revenues, Expenditures, and Changes in Fund Balances *with change in net position* of *governmental activities* presented in the government-wide Statement of Activities.

- *Change in net position* of *total Enterprise Funds* presented in the proprietary funds Statement of Revenues, Expenses, and Changes in Fund Net Position *with the change in net position* of *business-type activities* presented in the government-wide Statement of Activities.

ILLUSTRATION 14-17 Farley County Government-Wide Statement of Activities

576

Farley County
Statement of Activities
For the Year Ended December 31, 20X6

| | | **Program Revenues** | | | **Net (Expense) Revenue and Changes in Net Position** | | |
| | | | | | **Primary Government** | | |
	Expenses	Charges for Services	Operating Grants and Contributions	Capital Grants and Contributions	Governmental Activities	Business-Type Activities	Total
Primary Government							
Governmental Activities:							
General Government	$ 86,900	$ —	$ —	$ —	$ (86,900)	$ —	$ (86,900)
Public Safety	467,000	104,750	120,000	—	(242,250)	—	(242,250)
Highways and Streets	377,700	—	—	2,066,000	1,688,300	—	1,688,300
Health and Sanitation	53,400	22,250	—	—	(31,150)	—	(31,150)
Other	21,600	—	—	—	(21,600)	—	(21,600)
Interest on Long-term Debt	116,600	—	—	—	(116,600)	—	(116,600)
Total Governmental Activities	1,123,200	127,000	120,000	2,066,000	1,189,800	—	1,189,800
Business-Type Activities:							
Solid Waste Collection	5,530,000	6,377,000	—	—	—	847,000	847,000
Golf Course	2,430,000	2,535,000	—	—	—	105,000	105,000
Total Business-Type Activities	7,960,000	8,912,000	—	—	—	952,000	952,000
Total Primary Government	$9,083,200	$9,039,000	$120,000	$2,066,000	1,189,800	952,000	2,141,800
General Revenues							
Taxes					980,800	—	980,800
Unrestricted Grants					105,000	—	105,000
Investment Income					52,500	—	52,500
Gain on Sale of Assets					10,000	—	10,000
Other Revenues					2,000	—	2,000
Transfers					18,000	(18,000)	—
Total General Revenues and Transfers					1,168,300	(18,000)	1,150,300
Change in Net Position					2,358,100	934,000	3,292,100
Net Position—January 1					897,514	3,663,300	4,560,814
Net Position—December 31					$3,255,614	$4,597,300	$7,852,914

The reconciliations may be presented either on the face of the fund financial statements or as an accompanying schedule. In either case, detailed reconciliations may be presented, or summarized reconciliations may be presented with additional details disclosed in the notes to the financial statements.

The reconciliation of governmental funds total fund balances and governmental activities net position is presented in Illustration 14-10. The reconciliation between the changes in fund balances in the governmental funds operating statement and the changes in net position of governmental activities in the government-wide Statement of Activities is shown in Illustration 14-13. Reconciliations of the Enterprise Funds total net position and business-type activities total net position typically are not complicated. Indeed, for Farley County none was needed because the total net position reported in both statements were the same. Likewise, the reconciliation of Enterprise Funds changes in net position and the business-type activities changes in net position normally is relatively simple and was not needed for Farley County.

Concluding Comments

This chapter focuses on deriving the government-wide financial statements from the fund financial statements using *a two-worksheet conversion process. A one-worksheet approach using the same data is illustrated in the appendix.* Some professors may prefer the two-worksheet approach demonstrated in the chapter, and others prefer the one-worksheet approach demonstrated in the appendix. Many students will find it easier to understand the one-worksheet approach after studying the two-worksheet approach, so we focused initially on the two-worksheet approach.

Most conversion entries required in the one-worksheet approach combine a balance sheet conversion adjustment and the related operating statement conversion adjustment made separately in the two-worksheet approach. Regardless of the approach used, understanding the derivation of government-wide financial statement information should improve one's understanding of the nature of both the information presented in government-wide financial statements and that presented in fund financial statements.

Chapter 13 covered the basic financial statements and laid the groundwork for Chapter 14. Chapter 15 discusses and illustrates both the Comprehensive Annual Financial Report and the criteria that a government must apply to determine which related, but legally separate, entities must be included in its financial reporting entity. Finally, Chapter 15 also discusses and illustrates how to incorporate component unit information in a government's financial statements.

APPENDIX 14-1

A One-Worksheet Approach to Deriving Governmental Activities Data

Governments use various methods to derive the data needed to prepare the government-wide financial statements. This chapter demonstrated a two-worksheet approach that is intuitively appealing and relatively easy to follow. In practice, many governments use a more traditional worksheet than the ones illustrated in the chapter.

The use of a single worksheet to derive both the balance sheet and operating statement data needed to report *governmental activities* in the government-wide financial statements is discussed and illustrated in this appendix. This *one-worksheet approach* is illustrated based on the same information used for the two-worksheet approach. The business-type activities, government-wide financial statements, and reconciliations are not repeated since these discussions, and illustrations, will be identical regardless of whether a government uses a one-worksheet or two-worksheet approach to derive the governmental activities data.

The preclosing trial balance for all governmental funds of Farley County at December 31, 20X6 (after budgetary accounts have been closed), is presented in Illustration 14-18. With the exception of fund balance, the accounts and amounts in this trial balance are taken from the **total column** of Farley County's **governmental funds financial statements**. The fund balance account contains the *preclosing* amount of the total fund balances for all governmental funds. This *preclosing* amount is *not* the same as the *postclosing* ending balance reported in the governmental funds Balance Sheet.

Note that the trial balance includes expenditures (rather than expenses), other financing sources and uses, and fund balance (rather than net position). General capital assets and general long-term liabilities are omitted from the trial balance because they are not reported in governmental funds. Beginning balances of certain accounts are needed for some of the adjustment and conversion entries required to derive the governmental activities data. These balances are provided as part of the explanation of the conversion entries they affect. Remember as you study the example that the entries are *worksheet-only* entries. They are *not posted* to the fund ledgers.

The *one-worksheet approach* to derive Farley County's government-wide governmental activities data involves the following broad steps:

- Addition of the *beginning balances* of the general capital assets and general long-term liabilities to the governmental funds *preclosing* trial balance.
- Adjustments and conversions related to general capital assets.
- Adjustments and conversions related to general long-term liabilities.
- Other adjustments to convert the data from the current financial resources measurement focus and modified accrual basis to the economic resources measurement focus and accrual basis of accounting.
- Elimination of interfund activities.

GCA-GLTL ADJUSTMENTS

Our first step to adjust for general capital assets and general long-term liabilities is to *add the beginning balances of the General Capital Assets and General Long-Term Liabilities accounts to the governmental funds trial balance.* This step is accomplished in the first column of the derivation worksheet presented in Illustration 14-19. The general capital assets and general long-term liabilities accounts and balances added at this time are the amounts that were reported in the government-wide statement of net position at December 31, 20X5—the end of the prior year and the *beginning* of the current year. The credit to Net Position is the difference between the capital assets and the long-term liabilities added to the trial balance. Recall that accrued interest payable is *not* recorded in the GCA-GLTL accounts.

The remaining worksheet adjustments related to general capital assets

a. Eliminate capital outlay expenditures and record the assets acquired.

b. Eliminate the other financing source for the proceeds from the sale of capital assets, remove the carrying value of assets sold or disposed of, and recognize the gain or loss on the sale or disposal.

c. Record depreciation expense.

The remaining worksheet adjustments related to general long-term liabilities are:

d. Eliminate other financing sources (uses) from general long-term liability issuances.

e. Eliminate expenditures for retirement of general long-term liability principal.

f. Convert interest expenditures to interest expense.

ILLUSTRATION 14-18   Governmental Funds Preclosing Trial Balance

Farley County
Total Governmental Funds
Preclosing Trial Balance
December 31, 20X6

	Debit	Credit
Cash	$ 385,200	
Investments	1,085,600	
Due from General Fund	1,000	
Due from Federal Government	1,016,000	
Taxes Receivable	54,000	
Allowance for Uncollectible Taxes		$ 11,000
Interest and Penalties Receivable	1,500	
Allowance for Uncollectible Interest and Penalties		136
Accounts Receivable	13,000	
Allowance for Uncollectible Accounts		500
Accrued Interest Receivable	54,800	
Inventory of Materials and Supplies	4,700	
Vouchers Payable		290,400
Accrued Salaries and Wages Payable		5,000
Contracts Payable—Retained Percentage		100,000
Accrued Interest Payable (on Current Debt)		300
Unearned Operating Grant Revenues*		103,000
Unearned Capital Grant Revenues*		150,000
Due to Enterprise Fund		3,300
Due to Special Revenue Funds		1,000
Deferred Tax Revenues (uncollected at cut-off date)		30,800
Fund Balance (Preclosing)		317,514
Revenues:		
Taxes		970,000
Licenses and Permits		89,000
Fines and Forfeitures		38,000
Unrestricted Grants		105,000
Operating Grants		120,000
Capital Grants		2,066,000
Investment Income		52,500
Other Revenues		2,000
Current Operating Expenditures/Expenses:		
General Government	78,400	
Public Safety	405,000	
Highways and Streets	246,200	
Health and Sanitation	46,400	
Other	18,600	
Capital Outlay Expenditures:		
For Construction	2,540,000	
For Equipment	58,200	
Debt Service Expenditures:		
Bond Principal Retirement	200,000	
Interest on Bonds	101,850	
Fiscal Agent Fees	15,000	
Bond Issue Costs	10,000	
Other Financing Sources:		
Bonds		1,800,000
Bond Premiums		12,000
Proceeds from Sale of General Capital Assets		50,000
Transfers from General Fund		176,000
Transfers from Special Revenue Funds		20,000
Transfers from Enterprise Funds		18,000
Other Financing Uses:		
Transfers to Capital Projects Funds	16,000	
Transfers to Debt Service Funds	160,000	
Transfers to General Fund	20,000	
Totals	$6,531,450	$6,531,450

*These are reimbursement grants.

ILLUSTRATION 14-19 Conversion Worksheet—Governmental Activities

Farley County
Worksheet to Derive Governmental Activities
For the Year Ended December 31, 20X6

	Total Governmental Funds, General Capital Assets, General Long-Term Liabilities Trial Balance* Debit	Credit	#	Adjustments Debit	Credit	#	Preclosing Trial Balance Debit	Credit	Government-Wide Statement of Activities Debit	Credit	Statement of Net Position Debit	Credit
Governmental Funds												
Cash	$ 385,200						$ 385,200				$ 385,200	
Investments	1,085,600						1,085,600				1,085,600	
Due from General Fund	1,000				$ 1,000	(j)	—					
Due from Federal Government	1,016,000						1,016,000				1,016,000	
Taxes Receivable	54,000						54,000				54,000	
Allowance for Uncollectible Taxes		$ 11,000						11,000				$ 11,000
Interest and Penalties Receivable	1,500						1,500				1,500	
Allowance for Uncollectible Interest and Penalties		136						136				136
Accounts Receivable	13,000						13,000				13,000	
Allowance for Uncollectible Accounts		500						500				500
Accrued Interest Receivable	54,800						54,800				54,800	
Inventory of Materials and Supplies	4,700						4,700				4,700	
Vouchers Payable		290,400						290,400				290,400
Accrued Salaries and Wages Payable		5,000						5,000				5,000
Contracts Payable—Retained Percentage		100,000						100,000				100,000
Accrued Interest Payable (on Current Debt)		300						300				300
Unearned Operating Grant Revenues		103,000						103,000				103,000
Unearned Capital Grant Revenues		150,000						150,000				150,000
Due to Enterprise Fund		3,300						3,300				3,300
Due to Special Revenue Funds		1,000	(j)	1,000			—					
Deferred Tax Revenues		30,800	(i1)	$ 20,000			—					
			(i2)	10,800								
Fund Balance (Preclosing)		317,514	(l)	317,514			—					
Revenues:												
Taxes		970,000			10,800	(i2)		980,800		$ 980,800		
Licenses and Permits		89,000						89,000		89,000		
Fines and Forfeitures		38,000						38,000		38,000		
Unrestricted Grants		105,000						105,000		105,000		
Operating Grants		120,000						120,000		120,000		
Capital Grants		2,066,000						2,066,000		2,066,000		
Investment Income		52,500						52,500		52,500		
Other Revenues		2,000						2,000		2,000		
Current Operating Expenditures/Expenses:												
General Government	78,400		(c)	11,000	2,500	(h)	86,900		$ 86,900		
Public Safety	405,000		(c)	55,000	3,000	(h)	467,000		467,000		
			(g)	10,000								
Highways and Streets	246,200		(c)	133,000	1,500	(h)	377,700		377,700		
Health and Sanitation	46,400		(c)	8,000	1,000	(h)	53,400		53,400		
Other	18,600		(c)	3,000			21,600		21,600		

Conversion Worksheet — Governmental Funds to Government-Wide Statements

Account	Governmental Funds / Beginning Balances Dr	Cr	Adj. Ref (Dr)	Adjustment Dr	Adj. Ref (Cr)	Adjustment Cr	Gov-Wide Dr	Cr
Capital Outlay Expenditures:								
For Construction	2,540,000				(a)	2,540,000	—	
For Equipment	58,200				(a)	58,200	—	
Debt Service Expenditures/Expenses:								
Bond Principal Retirement	200,000				(e)	200,000	—	
Interest on Bonds	101,850				(f2) (f3)	6,250 / 4,000	91,600	
Fiscal Agent Fees	15,000						15,000	
Bond Issuance Costs	10,000						10,000	
Other Financing Sources:								
Bonds		1,800,000	(d)	1,800,000			—	
Bond Premiums		12,000	(d)	12,000			—	
Proceeds from Sale of General Capital Assets		50,000	(b)	50,000			—	
Transfers from General Fund		176,000	(k)	176,000			—	
Transfers from Special Revenue Funds		20,000	(k)	20,000			—	
Transfers from Enterprise Funds		18,000						18,000
Other Financing Uses:								
Transfers to Capital Projects Funds	16,000				(k)	16,000	—	
Transfers to Debt Service Funds	160,000				(k)	160,000	—	
Transfers to General Fund	20,000				(k)	20,000	—	
Governmental Funds—Totals	$6,531,450	$6,531,450						
General Capital Assets and General Long-Term Liabilities (*Beginning Balances*)								
Land	125,000						125,000	
Buildings	1,250,000						1,250,000	
Accumulated Depreciation—Buildings		780,000			(c)	80,000		860,000
Machinery and Equipment	400,000		(a)	58,200	(b)	60,000	398,200	
Accumulated Depreciation—Machinery and Equipment		150,000	(b)	20,000	(c)	30,000		160,000
Infrastructure (Streets and Roads)	2,000,000						2,000,000	
Accumulated Depreciation—Infrastructure		1,200,000			(c)	100,000		1,300,000
Construction in Progress			(a)	2,540,000	(e) (f3)	200,000 / 4,000	2,540,000	
Bonds Payable		800,000	(a) (e)	200,000	(d)	1,800,000		2,400,000
Premium on Bonds		20,000	(d)	4,000	(d)	12,000		28,000
Claims and Judgments Liability—Long-term		140,000			(g)	10,000		150,000
Compensated Absences Liability—Long-term		100,000	(h)	8,000				92,000
Net Position		495,000	(i1) (l)	20,000 / 317,514				897,514
	$3,775,000	$3,775,000						
Gain on Sale of General Capital Assets			(f1)	10,000	(b)	10,000		10,000
Accrued Interest Payable on Bonds			(f2)	25,000 / 6,250	(f1)	18,750		18,750
			$5,488,764	$5,488,764			$10,051,200	$10,051,200
Change in Net Position							1,123,200	
							2,358,100	
							$3,481,300	$3,481,300
							6,569,900	
							2,358,100	
							$8,928,000	$8,928,000

*The *upper portion* of this trial balance is the ***preclosing*** trial balance for all governmental funds totaled. This information is reported in the total column of the governmental funds financial statements, except for fund balance. The *lower portion* of this column contains the ***beginning balances*** of the general capital assets and general long-term liabilities accounts. These accounts and balances were added in the first step of deriving the government-wide financial statement information.

Elimination and Capitalization of Capital Outlay Expenditures

Costs incurred to acquire or construct capital assets are reported as expenditures in governmental funds. The capital assets are not reported in these funds. However, purchases of capital assets are not expenses, and general capital assets must be reported in the governmental activities column of the government-wide Statement of Net Position. Therefore, a worksheet adjustment entry must be made reducing capital outlay expenditures to zero and capitalizing the costs in the appropriate capital assets accounts. Farley County's capital outlay expenditures were $2,540,000 for partial construction of a major facility and $58,200 for equipment. The following entry is entered on the *conversion worksheet to record the general capital assets and eliminate the capital outlay expenditures:*

(a) Construction in Progress	$2,540,000	
Machinery and Equipment	58,200	
Expenditures—Capital Outlay—Construction		$2,540,000
Expenditures—Capital Outlay—Equipment......		58,200

These entries are not made except in the worksheet. They are used here for explanatory purposes. Note that this one-worksheet conversion entry (and all others except those eliminating interfund items) includes both balance sheet adjustments (increasing GCA accounts) and operating statement adjustments (reducing expenditures). Indeed, as noted in the concluding comments to the chapter, each one-worksheet approach conversion entry typically accomplishes the purposes of one adjustment on each of the worksheets in the two-worksheet approach.

For instance, in the two-worksheet approach, capital outlay expenditures are eliminated in the operating statement conversion worksheet in adjustment 1a and the ending GCA balances are added in the balance sheet conversion worksheet as part of adjustment 1 on that worksheet. In the one-worksheet approach the beginning GCA balances are added below the governmental funds preclosing trial balance, so it requires that action and entry a to accomplish the same as entry 1 in the Balance Sheet Conversion Worksheet and entry 1a in the Operating Statement Worksheet combined.

Sale of General Capital Assets

The *proceeds* of sales of general capital assets increase the fund balance of a governmental fund. These proceeds, $50,000 in our example, are reported as other financing sources in the governmental funds operating statement. Other financing sources are not reported, however, in the government-wide statements. The effect of the sale on government-wide net position is to increase them by a *gain* on the sale or to decrease them by a *loss* on the sale. Farley County sold machinery and equipment with an original cost of $60,000 and accumulated depreciation of $20,000. The sale price was equal to the $50,000 proceeds from capital asset sale in the trial balance. Therefore, the asset was sold at a gain of $10,000. The *worksheet adjustment for the capital asset sale* is:

(b) Other Financing Sources—Proceeds from Sale of General Capital Assets	$ 50,000	
Accumulated Depreciation—Machinery and Equipment..................................	20,000	
Machinery and Equipment.......................		$ 60,000
Gain on Sale of General Capital Assets...........		10,000

Again, note the connection between entry b and the adjustments under the two-worksheet approach in the chapter. The only difference between this entry and Operating Statement Conversion Worksheet adjustment 1c is that the balance sheet accounts are not adjusted because all correct asset and liability amounts are recorded in the balance sheet conversion entries. The Change in Net Position summary effect is reduced in adjustment 1c by the carrying value of the asset sold. The parallels between the two approaches are not pointed out for the remaining adjustment entries.

Depreciation Expense

Depreciation expense is not an expenditure, but must be reported in the government-wide Statement of Activities. The entry on the *conversion worksheet to record depreciation expense* (the allocations of the expenses to functional categories are *assumed*) is:

(c) Expenses—General Government	$ 11,000	
Expenses—Public Safety	55,000	
Expenses—Highways and Streets	133,000	
Expenses—Health and Sanitation.	8,000	
Expenses—Other	3,000	
Accumulated Depreciation—Buildings		$ 80,000
Accumulated Depreciation—Machinery and Equipment		30,000
Accumulated Depreciation—Infrastructure		100,000

General Long-Term Debt Issuance

Farley County's preclosing trial balance indicates that the county issued $1,800,000 of bonds at a $12,000 premium. The county incurred $10,000 of bond issue costs. Note that

- The bond proceeds and premium are reported in separate other financing sources accounts.
- The bond issue costs are reported as expenditures in the county's governmental funds financial statements and as expenses in the government-wide operating statement, so no adjustment is required for these costs.
- The bonds payable and the premium must be reported as liabilities in the government-wide financial statements.
- The premium on bonds will be amortized over the life of the bonds.

The *worksheet conversion entry for the bond issuance* is:

(d) Other Financing Sources—Bonds	$1,800,000	
Other Financing Sources—Bond Premiums	12,000	
Bonds Payable		$1,800,000
Premium on Bonds		12,000

General Long-Term Debt Principal Retirement

The governmental funds trial balance also shows that the county retired $200,000 of long-term debt—a portion of the bonds payable at the beginning of the year. This amount is reported as Expenditures—Bond Principal Retirement in the governmental funds financial statements. Bond principal retirement does not affect the government-wide Statement of Activities, but reduces the Bonds Payable balance in the Statement of Net Position. The adjustment required *to eliminate the bond principal retirement expenditures and reduce the liability* is:

(e) Bonds Payable	$ 200,000	
Expenditures—Bond Principal Retirement		$ 200,000

Converting Interest Expenditures to Interest Expenses

The interest expenditures on General Long-Term Liabilities reported in the governmental funds financial statements typically equal the interest that matured (and no doubt was paid) during the fiscal year. In the government-wide financial statements, the county must report interest expenses, not expenditures. To adjust the interest expenditures balance to an expense balance, the county must adjust for the change in accrued interest payable during the year (f1 and f2) and amortize any premium or discount (f3). The first part of the conversion entry is to establish the beginning accrued interest payable, which was *not* reported in the governmental funds financial statements. Assume the beginning amount of accrued interest payable on bonds was $25,000. This amount must be deducted from Net Position to derive its beginning balance because the payable results from amounts reported as expenses in the previous year. The *worksheet entry to establish the beginning balance of accrued interest payable* is:

(f1) Net Position....................................	$ 25,000	
Accrued Interest Payable on Bonds.............		$ 25,000

Next, assume that the accrued bond interest payable at year-end is $18,750, a $6,250 decrease. The *worksheet entry to convert the interest expenditure for a reduction of the accrued interest payable during the year* is:

(f2) Accrued Interest Payable on Bonds...............	$ 6,250	
Expenditures/Expenses—Interest on Bonds......		$ 6,250

Finally, assume that premium amortization for 20X6 is $4,000. The *worksheet entry to amortize the current year bond premium* is:

(f3) Premium on Bonds............................	$ 4,000	
Expenditures/Expenses—Interest on Bonds......		$ 4,000

BASIS OF ACCOUNTING ADJUSTMENTS

As indicated in the earlier discussions, the adjustments required to derive the governmental activities data for the government-wide financial statements result primarily from the use of the accrual basis of accounting for revenues and expenses in the government-wide statements instead of the modified accrual basis of accounting for revenues and expenditures. Some of these adjustments relate to general capital asset or general long-term liability transactions as well, and one could choose to classify them as we did with depreciation. Farley County has three such worksheet adjustments:

g. Convert claims and judgments expenditures to expenses.
h. Convert compensated absences expenditures to expenses.
i. Convert modified accrual tax revenues to accrual basis tax revenues.

Convert Claims and Judgments Expenditures to Expenses

Expenditures for items such as claims and judgments, compensated absences, and pension contributions are measured at the amount that is *both* due for payment *and* normally expected to be liquidated from available expendable financial resources of a governmental fund. When measuring and reporting expenses for these items, governments must adjust for related long-term liability changes. The beginning balance of the long-term liability for claims and judgments for Farley County was $140,000 and relates to 20X5 expenses, whereas the ending balance for 20X6 of $150,000 is for 20X6 expenses. The increase of $10,000 must be added to 20X5 expenditures to convert them to 20X6 expenses. Assuming that the claims and judgments liabilities relate to the public safety function, the **worksheet entry to convert claims and judgments from expenditures to expenses** is:

(g) Expenses—Public Safety	$ 10,000	
Claims and Judgments Liability—Long-Term		$ 10,000

Convert Compensated Absences Expenditures to Expenses

Conversion of expenditures for compensated absences to expenses follows the same logic and approach as for claims and judgments. Farley County's beginning long-term liability for compensated absences was $100,000. The December 31, 20X6, liability is $92,000. Expenses of various functions thus will be less than expenditures by the $8,000 decline in the long-term liability for compensated absences. Assume that the functional classifications of the expense reductions reflected in the following worksheet entry are appropriate. The **worksheet entry to convert compensated absences expenditures to expenses** is:

(h) Compensated Absences Liability—Long-Term	$ 8,000	
Expenses—General Government		$ 2,500
Expenses—Public Safety.....................		3,000
Expenses—Highways and Streets		1,500
Expenses—Health and Sanitation		1,000

Convert Revenues from Modified Accrual to Accrual

In the governmental funds financial statements, revenues must meet the availability criteria before they are recognized. One important part of these criteria is that in addition to being legally available for expenditure, revenues must be collected soon enough after year end to be used to pay the period's ending liabilities. Failure to meet this *collection criterion* often delays modified accrual basis recognition of some revenues for governmental funds and results in reporting *deferred revenues* in the governmental funds balance sheet. The amount of revenues recognized under the flow of economic resources measurement focus and the accrual basis of accounting required for government-wide financial reporting is *not* affected by the collection criterion. Thus, *governmental funds deferred revenues resulting solely from the collection criterion must be eliminated—and recognized as revenue—*in preparing the government-wide Statement of Net Position.

The required adjustment must eliminate the entire ending balance of the pertinent deferred revenues. *Current year tax revenues* for governmental funds must be *adjusted by the change* during the year *in the balance of deferred revenues* resulting from the availability criterion to determine the amount of accrual basis revenues. *The beginning balance of these deferred revenues must be added to beginning net position for governmental activities because the revenues associated with this beginning balance were recognized as government-wide revenues (and added to net position) in prior years.*

Farley County has deferred tax revenues of $30,800 in governmental funds at the end of 20X6. The balance at the beginning of 20X6 was $20,000. It was reported as deferred tax revenue in the governmental funds financial statements as of the end of the prior year, but included in the net assets reported in the 20X5 statement of net position. The **worksheet entry to reflect deferred revenues levied for or earned in (but not collected in) a prior year and to increase beginning net position** is:

(i1) Deferred Tax Revenues........................	$ 20,000	
Net Position................................		$ 20,000

Deferred tax revenues increased $10,800 during the *current* year (20X6), which should be reported as current year tax revenue in the government-wide financial statements. The **worksheet entry to eliminate the increase in deferred revenue that reflects revenue levied for or earned (but not collected) during the current year** is:

(i2) Deferred Tax Revenues	$ 10,800	
Revenues—Taxes		$ 10,800

ELIMINATING INTERFUND TRANSACTIONS

As discussed and illustrated in earlier chapters, various types of interfund transactions occur between a government's funds. These transactions result in interfund receivables and payables being reported in the fund balance sheets and in revenues, expenditures, or expenses, and transfers, being reported in the operating statements of the funds involved.

Transactions between governmental funds are strictly *internal* from the standpoint of governmental activities taken as a whole, which is the perspective in government-wide financial statements. For instance, a transfer from the General Fund to a Capital Projects Fund increases the fund balance of the Capital Projects Fund and decreases the fund balance of the General Fund. However, the net position of the governmental activities do not change. Likewise, $1,000 might be owed from the General Fund to a Special Revenue Fund, which may appropriately be reflected by reporting equal interfund receivables and payables in the fund financial statements. However, from the governmental activities standpoint, this approach is like owing yourself or having a receivable from yourself. No substantive receivable or payable exists under the "governmental activities as a whole" perspective. Because of the different perspective presented in government-wide financial statements, interfund transactions between funds reported as part of governmental activities should be eliminated. Farley County has both interfund transfers and interfund payables and receivables between governmental funds. The **worksheet entries to eliminate** these **interfund amounts** are:

(j) Due to Special Revenue Funds	$ 1,000	
Due from General Fund		$ 1,000
(k) Transfers from General Fund	$176,000	
Transfers from Special Revenue Funds	20,000	
Transfers to Capital Projects Funds		$ 16,000
Transfers to Debt Service Funds		160,000
Transfers to General Fund		20,000

Note that one interfund liability, Due to Enterprise Funds of $3,300, is *not* eliminated. This liability is an amount payable from governmental activities to business-type activities. This amount will be reported as "Internal Balances" in the governmental activities column and in the business-type activities column of the government-wide Statement of Net Position. The Internal Balances reported in the two columns *offset* one another, leaving a zero balance for that line item in the primary government total column.

Likewise, the interfund transfer from Enterprise Funds also is a transfer from business-type activities to governmental activities. In the government-wide Statement of Activities, the transfer will be reported as an increase in the net position of governmental activities and as a decrease in the net position of business-type activities. These changes sum to zero in the primary government total column.

COMPLETING THE WORKSHEET

The final entry on our *worksheet* is to reclassify fund balance as net position to be reported in the Statement of Net Position. This *worksheet reclassification entry* is simply:

(1) Fund Balance	$317,514	
Net Position		$317,514

Next, we add the effects of our conversion/adjustment entries to the governmental funds trial balance. This new trial balance is the preclosing trial balance for Farley County's governmental activities. Note that all expenditures have either been eliminated or converted to expenses at this point. Therefore, we have labeled some expenditures as expenditures/expenses in the worksheet. If a government does not have business-type activities, the government-wide Statement of Net Position and Statement of Activities can be prepared from the information in this worksheet alone. We extend the worksheet to include a Statement of Activities column and a Statement of Net Position column. These amounts are reported in those statements for governmental activities even if a government has business-type activities.

Questions

Q14-1 Governments present both fund financial statements and government-wide financial statements. Explain how the information reported in each type of statement is accumulated or derived.

Q14-2 What information from governmental funds financial statements is used in the worksheet(s) for deriving governmental activities data for government-wide financial statements?

Q14-3 Explain the typical relationship(s) between governmental activities and/or business-type activities and each of the following:
  a. Governmental funds.
  b. Fiduciary funds.
  c. Enterprise Funds.
  d. Internal Service Funds.
  e. General Capital Assets accounts.
  f. General Long-Term Liabilities accounts.

Q14-4 What types of worksheet adjustments for governmental activities are needed to address the absence of GCA and GLTL from governmental fund financial statements?

Q14-5 What types of reconciliations are required to be presented in the Basic Financial Statements to explain the differences between fund financial statements and government-wide financial statements?

Q14-6 Do all governmental funds financial statement items require adjustment? If not, list several accounts that are likely to be reported identically in the fund financial statement totals and in the government-wide financial statements. List several that are likely to differ.

Q14-7 What types of worksheet adjustments might have to be made to convert Enterprise Funds financial statement totals to business-type activities data?

Q14-8 Why are fiduciary activities not reported in the government-wide financial statements?

Q14-9 For what items might a government need to adjust interest expenditures amounts to convert them to interest expenses?

Q14-10 Explain the circumstances that require deferred revenues of governmental funds to be reduced or eliminated to derive the government-wide information. Why are revenues normally not increased by the total ending balance of deferred revenues?

Q14-11 Why does the conversion worksheet for governmental activities use only one net position account instead of the three net position accounts that must be reported in the financial statements?

Exercises

E14-1 (Multiple Choice) Identify the best answer for each of the following:

1. Which of the following fund types is *never* to be included as part of governmental activities?
   a. Special Revenue
   b. Private-Purpose Trust
   c. Internal Service
   d. Permanent

2. All of the following statements are true *except*
   a. Both governmental funds and proprietary funds are reported in fund financial statements using the economic resources measurement focus.
   b. Both governmental activities and business-type activities are reported in government-wide financial statements using the accrual basis of accounting.
   c. Fund balance is reported for governmental funds in the fund financial statements, but net position is reported for governmental activities in the government-wide financial statements.
   d. Depreciation expense is reported for governmental activities but not for governmental funds.

Questions 3 and 4 are based on the following scenario:

Assume that Bruderer City's General Fund had cash collections of $11,108,900 associated with property taxes as of June 30, 20X8. The levy for the fiscal year ending June 30, 20X8, net of the allowance for uncollectible accounts, was $11,925,700. Of the amount collected, $108,000 collected in November 20X7 was for past due taxes of previous fiscal years, and $25,000 collected in June 20X8 represented prepayments for the next year's levy. In addition, $975,900 was collected in July 20X8, $325,000 in August 20X8, and $100,500 in September 20X8, all associated with the tax year that ended June 30, 20X8.

3. The amount of property tax revenues reported in the *governmental activities* for the year ended June 30, 20X8, would be
   a. $11,108,900.
   b. $12,409,800.
   c. $12,384,800.
   d. $11,925,700.

4. The amount of property tax revenues reported in the General Fund for the year ended June 30, 20X8, would be
   a. $11,108,900.
   b. $12,409,800.
   c. $12,384,800.
   d. $11,925,700.

5. All of the following statements are true concerning the conversion of governmental funds to governmental activities *except*
   a. Depreciation expenditure reported in governmental funds simply becomes depreciation expense in governmental activities.
   b. A decrease in the long-term liability for compensated absences will result in expenses of various functions at the government-wide level being less than expenditures at the governmental fund level.
   c. Assuming capital outlay expenditures all reflect purchases of capital assets as per the government's capitalization threshold policy, capital outlay expenditures simply become additions to capital assets.
   d. Bonds payable are not reported in the governmental funds financial statements but will be reported in the government-wide financial statements for governmental activities.

6. Which of the following best describes the general nature of the governmental activities column?
   a. Governmental activities are simply governmental funds added together.
   b. Governmental activities are derived by adding the governmental funds together and converting the measurement focus and basis of accounting.
   c. Governmental activities include neither Permanent Funds nor any component units.
   d. Governmental activities typically include all governmental funds, with the measurement focus and basis of accounting converted, as well as all general capital assets and general long-term liabilities.

7. Business-type activities would be derived according to which of the following scenarios?
   a. All Enterprise and Internal Service Funds are added together because they use the same measurement focus and basis of accounting.
   b. Enterprise Funds are added together, with only the measurement focus converted.

    c. Enterprise Funds are added together, with only the basis of accounting converted.

    d. Enterprise Funds are added together because they have the same measurement focus and basis of accounting as the government-wide statements.

8. Assume that Nathan County sold $3,179,500 of bonds during the fiscal year at a discount of $25,000. In addition, the county incurred $22,500 of bond issue costs that were withheld from the proceeds the county received. When these events are applied to the conversion worksheet, what will be the net adjustment on the change in fund balance/net position.

    a. Net decrease of $3,179,500.

    b. Net decrease of $3,154,500.

    c. Net decrease of $3,132,000.

    d. Net decrease of $3,204,500.

9. Which of the following statements is true regarding reporting net position in the government-wide financial statements?

    a. Net position is reported for both governmental activities and business-type activities.

    b. Net investment in capital assets is calculated in the same manner for both governmental activities and business-type activities.

    c. Restricted net position in the governmental activities always equals restricted fund balance in the governmental funds.

    d. Items a and b are true.

10. When preparing the balance sheet conversion worksheet, which of the following items must be eliminated?

    a. Deferred charges for debt issuance costs

    b. Accrued interest payable

    c. Inventories and prepaid items

    d. Deferred revenue (not available)

E14-2 (Multiple Choice) Identify the best answer for each of the following:

1. Which of the following statements about the sale of general capital assets is *false*?

    a. The proceeds from the sale of general capital assets are generally reported as other financing sources in the government-wide financial statements.

    b. Gains from the sale of general capital assets are reported as general revenues in the government-wide financial statements; losses are reported as functional expenses.

    c. Gains and losses from the sale of general capital assets are *not* reported in the governmental funds.

    d. The proceeds from the sale of general capital assets increases fund balance in the governmental funds.

2. Adjustments to convert governmental funds to governmental activities would include all of the following *except*

    a. adding depreciation expense for general capital assets.

    b. adding expenses with no expenditure counterparts.

    c. adding general capital assets.

    d. eliminating inventory balances.

3. The required reconciliations of fund financial statements and government-wide financial statements include all of the following *except* the reconciliation of

    a. total net position of Enterprise Funds with total net position of business-type activities.

    b. total fund balances of governmental funds with total net position of governmental activities.

    c. change in total governmental funds fund balances with the change in net position for governmental activities.

    d. change in net position of total proprietary funds with the change in net position for business-type activities.

4. Gouge County reported $365,000 of committed fund balance in its General Fund. The commitment is for future capital improvements. How will this amount *most likely* be reflected in net position in the government-wide financial statements?

    a. Restricted net position—$365,000

    b. Included as part of unrestricted net position

    c. Included as part of net investment in capital assets

    d. Designated, unrestricted net position—$365,000

5. If Parnell Parish has two major governmental funds, two major Enterprise Funds, three fiduciary funds, and two discrete component units, what would be the minimum number of columns reported in its government-wide Statement of Net Position?

    a. Three

    b. Four

    c. Five

    d. Seven

Questions 6, 7, and 8 are based on the following scenario:

The General Fund of the village of Oxendine transferred $150,000 to a Special Revenue Fund; $35,000 to a Capital Projects Fund; and $25,000 to Enterprise Fund A. In the same reporting period, Enterprise Fund B transferred $125,000 to the General Fund and $45,000 to Enterprise Fund C.

6. The General Fund would report on its Statement of Revenues, Expenditures, and Changes in Fund Balance
   a. net transfers of ($85,000).
   b. transfers to governmental funds of $185,000, special item reduction of $25,000, and transfers from other funds $125,000.
   c. transfers in of $125,000 and transfers out of $210,000.
   d. net transfers of ($40,000).

7. What would be the amount of transfers reported for governmental activities on the Statement of Activities?
   a. Transfers in of $100,000
   b. Transfers in of $125,000 and transfers out of $185,000
   c. Transfers out of $85,000
   d. Transfers in of $85,000

8. What would be the amount of transfers reported for business-type activities on the Statement of Activities?
   a. Transfers out of $145,000
   b. Transfers in of $70,000 and transfers out of $125,000
   c. Transfers in of $145,000
   d. Transfers out of $100,000

9. Assume that Dial County issued $10 million of 5% bonds at 102 to finance a new public safety center. The debt will be serviced with general government resources. At its issuance, how will the premium be reported in the fund financial statements and the government-wide financial statements, respectively?
   a. Capital Projects Fund—$200,000 expenditure; governmental activities—$200,000 expense
   b. Capital Projects Fund—$200,000 other financing source; governmental activities—$200,000 premium on bonds (a liability)
   c. Capital Projects Fund—$200,000 revenue; governmental activities—$200,000 bonds payable
   d. Capital Projects Fund—$200,000 other financing source; governmental activities—$200,000 expense

10. Which of the following statements concerning deriving government-wide financial statements is *true*?
   a. Adjustments made to convert governmental funds to governmental activities are posted to the general ledger.
   b. The worksheet approach to deriving government-wide financial statements is required by GAAP.
   c. Net position does not reflect spendable equity.
   d. Adjustments related to interest payable on general government bonds are required.

E14-3 (Expenditures and Other Financing Sources/Uses) Listed below are four accounts from a governmental fund operating statement. Discuss how and why these accounts will be adjusted when preparing the operating statement conversion worksheet for governmental activities. If no adjustments are required, explain why.

Expenditures—Capital Outlay—Equipment	$ 500,000
Expenditures—Current—General Government	1,800,000
Other Financing Sources—Bonds	3,000,000
Other Financing Sources—Proceeds from sale of equipment	30,000

Assume the cost of the equipment sold was $185,000 and the accumulated depreciation was $170,000.
(*Alternative Requirement: Prepare the worksheet conversion entries required for this information using the one-worksheet approach in Appendix 14-1.*)

E14-4 (Interfund Receivables and Payables) Following are four accounts from a governmental fund balance sheet. Discuss how and why these accounts will be adjusted when preparing the balance sheet conversion worksheet for governmental activities. If no adjustments are required, state why.

Due from International Airport Enterprise Fund	$ 50,000
Due to Water Enterprise Fund	20,000
Due to General Fund	10,000
Due from Special Revenue Fund	10,000

(Alternative Requirement: Prepare the worksheet conversion entries required for this information using the one-worksheet approach in Appendix 14-1.)

E14-5 (Deferred Taxes) The following information is for the governmental funds (total) of Bell County for 20X6. Assume the deferred tax revenues meet the earnings criteria.

Deferred Tax Revenues (January 1)	$ 800,000
Deferred Tax Revenues (December 31)	1,300,000
Tax Revenues (20X6)	8,000,000

a. Explain the worksheet adjustments to derive the tax revenues to be reported for governmental activities in the government-wide financial statements.
b. Compute the governmental activities tax revenues to be reported in Bell County's government-wide Statement of Activities for 20X6.

(Alternative Requirement a: Prepare the worksheet conversion entries required for this information using the one-worksheet approach in Appendix 14-1.)

E14-6 (Claims and Judgments) Mosser Township's expenditures for claims and judgments for all its governmental funds totaled $5,300,000 for 20X8. Mosser's long-term liability for general government claims and judgments was $12,000,000 at January 1, 20X8, and $11,500,000 at December 31, 20X8. Explain the worksheet adjustment needed to convert Mosser's governmental funds claims and judgments expenditures to government-wide, governmental activities data. What are the total government-wide claims and judgments expenses (or losses) for governmental activities?

(Alternative Requirement: Prepare the worksheet conversion entries required for this information using the one-worksheet approach in Appendix 14-1.)

Problems

P14-1 (Worksheet Adjustments for Selected Accounts) Presented here is a partial list of accounts for the total governmental funds of the City of Bukowy. What worksheet adjustments would be required to convert this information to information that the city needs for preparing its government-wide financial statements for 20X3? The city uses the consumption method to account for materials and supplies.

Inventory of Materials and Supplies, January 1	$ 300,000
Inventory of Materials and Supplies, December 31	278,000
Expenditures—Capital Outlay—Buildings....................	4,000,000
Expenditures—Capital Outlay—Streets and Roads	8,300,000
Expenditures—Capital Outlay—Leased Equipment...........	800,000
Other Financing Sources—Bond Anticipation Notes	12,000,000
Other Financing Sources—Capital Leases	740,000
Buildings, January 1	30,000,000
Streets and Roads, January 1................................	80,000,000
Equipment, January 1......................................	10,800,000
Useful Life—All Buildings	15 years
Useful Life—Streets and Roads	30 years
Useful Life—All Equipment................................	5 years

No capital assets were sold during the year. No depreciation expense is reported on capital assets acquired in the current year. Accrued interest payable on the capital lease at December 31 was $22,000. Accrued interest payable on the bond anticipation notes was $480,000.

(Alternative Requirement: Prepare the worksheet conversion entries required for this information using the one-worksheet approach in Appendix 14-1.)

P14-2 (Conversion of Enterprise Funds Data to Business-Type Activities Information) Presented here is the preclosing trial balance information for the total of Locklear County's four Enterprise Funds for the year ended September 30, 20X7.

	Debit	Credit
Cash	$ 1,800,000	
Accounts Receivable	8,100,000	
Allowance for Uncollectible Accounts		$ 100,000
Due from Other Enterprise Funds	600,000	
Inventory	3,000,000	
Land	2,000,000	
Buildings	10,000,000	
Accumulated Depreciation—Buildings		4,500,000
Equipment	27,000,000	
Accumulated Depreciation—Equipment		18,000,000
Vouchers Payable		3,600,000
Due to General Fund		550,000
Due to Other Enterprise Funds		600,000
Unearned Grant Revenues		2,000,000
Bonds Payable		6,000,000
Discount on Bonds Payable	200,000	
Net Position		14,070,000
Charges for Services:		
Water and Sewer		8,000,000
Jacobs Ridge Golf Course		1,000,000
Transit Authority		1,500,000
Hardin-Emanuel Convention Center		4,000,000
Transfers from General Fund		3,700,000
Investment Income		100,000
Gain on Sale of Equipment		50,000
Contributions (of Capital Assets) from Locklear County		830,000
Water and Sewer Expenses	7,200,000	
Golf Course Expenses	1,100,000	
Transit Authority Expenses	2,600,000	
Convention Center Expenses	5,000,000	
Totals	$68,600,000	$68,600,000

Additional Information

1. The Contribution from Locklear County resulted from general capital assets being reassigned for use in Enterprise Fund departments.
2. Expenses of the Golf Course, Transit Authority, and Convention Center Enterprise Funds included charges for water and sewer services of $25,000, $2,000, and $8,000, respectively.

Required

a. Discuss the adjustments that are necessary to convert this information to the data to be used for the business-type activities in preparing the government-wide financial statements.
b. Prepare the business-type activities column for the government-wide Statement of Net Position and the business-type activities columns and rows of the Statement of Activities.

P14-3 (Correction of Statement of Net Position) The Finance Director of the City of Wrong Way has asked for your assistance in reviewing the Statement of Net Position that he has prepared for the year ended June 30, 20X9. The statement is shown on the next page.

Additional Information

1. The city has multiple governmental and proprietary funds. Its only fiduciary fund is a pension plan. It has four component units. All fund and component unit statements were prepared correctly.
2. All amounts disclosed for depreciable and nondepreciable capital assets in the city's Capital Assets Schedule are considered material, individually and in total.
3. Bonds for $10,000 were issued at the end of the year in a private placement (no premium, discount, or bond issue costs). All bonds have been issued for capital asset acquisition.

Required Identify the errors in the Statement of Net Position. Explain why each item you find is incorrect.

City of Wrong Way
~~Balance Sheet~~ *Stmt of Net Position* [handwritten]
~~For the Year Ended December 31, 20X9~~ *June 30, 2009* [handwritten]

	Primary Government					
	Governmental Activities	*Enterprise* ~~Enterprise Funds~~ [handwritten: Business Type Activities]	Fiduciary Activities	Total	Component Units	Reporting Entity Total
ASSETS						
Cash	$ 36,343	$ 83,147	$ 14,544	$134,034	$ 26,348	$ 160,382
Investments	67,218	82,099	844,996	994,313	78,628	1,072,941
Due from Federal Government	81,081	64,329	—	145,410	—	145,410
Taxes Receivable (net)	98,364	—	—	98,364	—	98,364
Penalties and Interest Receivable (net)	37,098	—	—	37,098	—	37,098
Capital Assets (net) [handwritten: non depreciable / depreciable]	268,448	130,977	117,243	516,668	290,115	806,783
Accounts Receivable (net)	98,581	50,720	18,048	167,349	49,587	216,936
Accrued Interest Receivable	3,215	4,517	40,005	47,737	3,621	51,358
Restricted Cash—Construction	10,000	—		10,000	—	10,000
Inventory of Materials and Supplies	71,894	16,566		88,460	1,332	89,792
Prepaid Rent	—	24,982		24,982	—	24,982
Internal Balances	13,624 [handwritten: balance]	—		13,624	—	13,624
Due from Special Revenue Fund	6,412	—		6,412	—	6,412
Due from General Fund	5,613	—		5,613	—	5,613
Due from Golf Course Enterprise Fund	—	5,217		5,217	—	5,217
Total Assets	797,891	462,554	1,034,836	2,295,281	449,631	2,744,912
LIABILITIES						
Current Liabilities						
Vouchers Payable	37,255	51,912	15,645	104,812	56,166	160,978
Accrued Salaries and Wages Payable	27,434	26,002	15,017	68,453	5,010	73,463
Contracts Payable—Retained Percentage	4,097	2,103	—	6,200	12,009	18,209
Accrued Interest Payable	4,802	5,131	—	9,933	10,051	19,984
Due to General Fund	6,412	—	—	6,412	—	6,412
Due to Capital Projects Fund	5,613	—	—	5,613	—	5,613
Due to Water Utility Enterprise Fund	—	5,217	—	5,217	—	5,217
Internal Balances	— [handwritten: balance]	14,795	—	14,795	—	14,795
Unearned Operating Grant Revenues	98,783	35,195	—	133,978	95,342	229,320
Unearned Capital Grant Revenues	60,249	55,093	—	115,342	17,106	132,448
Long-term Liabilities						
Bonds Payable	83,109	86,598	—	169,707	189,802	359,509
Bond Premium	5,817	—	—	5,817	—	5,817
Bond Discounts	—	2,993	—	2,993	—	2,993
Compensated Absences	74,033	6,250	24,728	105,011	30,463	135,474
Claims and Judgments	68,155	11,168	—	79,323	72,936	152,259
Total Liabilities	475,759	302,457	55,390	833,606	488,885	1,322,941
DEFERRED INFLOWS OF RESOURCES						
Deferred Revenue (~~Availability Criterion~~)	147,500	—	—	147,500	—	147,500
NET POSITION						
Investment in Capital Assets	179,522	47,372	117,243	344,137	100,313	444,450
Restricted for Debt Service	(15,023) [handwritten: con't be negative]	12,500	—	(2,523)	—	(2,523)
Unrestricted	10,133	100,225	862,203	972,561	(139,567)	832,994
Total Net Position	$174,632	$160,097	$979,446	$1,314,175	$ (39,254)	$1,274,921

P14-4 (Balance Sheet Conversion Worksheet—Governmental Activities) Presented here is the total column of the governmental funds balance sheet of Ravenscroft County, Iowa, for the year ended December 31, 20X9.

Ravenscroft County
Governmental Funds
Balance Sheet
December 31, 20X9

	Total
Assets	
Cash	$ 850,000
Investments	1,890,000
Due from other governments	600,000
Due from Capital Projects Fund	56,000
Taxes receivable (net)	12,000,000
Accrued interest receivable	34,000
Inventory of materials and supplies	27,200
Total Assets	15,457,200
Liabilities	
Vouchers payable	$ 324,000
Accrued salaries and wages payable	99,000
Contracts payable—retained percentage	57,000
Due to Enterprise Fund	12,000
Due to Special Revenue Funds	56,000
Total Liabilities	548,000
Deferred Inflows of Resources	
Deferred tax revenues	1,526,000
Deferred capital grant revenues	600,000
Total Deferred Inflows of Resources	2,126,000
Total Liabilities and Deferred Inflows of Resources	2,674,000
Fund Balances	
Nonspendable	27,200
Restricted	1,580,800
Assigned	200,000
Unassigned	10,975,200
Total Fund Balances	$12,783,200
Total Liabilities, Deferred Inflows or Resources, and Fund Balance	$15,457,200

Additional Information

1. Both the deferred capital grant and the deferred tax revenues were deferred because resources were not collected soon enough to be considered available.
2. Interest payable on bonds at the beginning of the fiscal year was $100,000. At year end, it was $125,000.
3. The discount on bonds (below) is amortized over a 10-year term.
4. The ending GCA balances were:

	Balance
Land	$ 2,000,000
Buildings	23,000,000
Accumulated Depreciation—Buildings	5,000,000
Equipment	11,500,000
Accumulated Depreciation—Equipment	2,500,000
Library Books	352,000
Construction in Progress	1,000,000

5. The ending GLTL balances were:

	Balance
Bonds Payable	$ 22,000,000
Discount on Bonds	3,000,000
Capital Lease Liability	2,500,000
Liability for Claims and Judgments	4,500,000

Prepare the governmental activities balance sheet conversion worksheet for Ravenscroft **Required**
County, Iowa, for December 31, 20X9.

P14-5 (One-Worksheet Conversion—Governmental Activities—Appendix)

Tierney County
Total Governmental Funds
Preclosing Trial Balance
December 31, 20X5

	Debit	Credit
Cash	$ 1,348,200	
Investments	7,355,600	
Due from General Fund	3,500	
Taxes Receivable	189,000	
Allowance for Uncollectible Taxes		$ 38,500
Interest and Penalties Receivable	5,250	
Allowance for Uncollectible Interest and Penalties		476
Accounts Receivable	45,500	
Allowance for Uncollectible Accounts		1,750
Accrued Interest Receivable	191,800	
Inventory of Materials and Supplies	16,450	
Vouchers Payable		1,016,400
Accrued Salaries and Wages Payable		17,500
Contracts Payable—Retained Percentage		350,000
Interest Payable (on Current Debt)		1,050
Unearned Operating Grant Revenues		360,500
Unearned Capital Grant Revenues		525,000
Due to Enterprise Fund		11,550
Due to Special Revenue Funds		3,500
Deferred Tax Revenues		107,800
Fund Balance (Preclosing)		695,049
Revenues:		
Taxes		3,395,000
Licenses and Permits		311,500
Fines and Forfeitures		133,000
Unrestricted Grants		367,500
Operating Grants		420,000
Capital Grants		7,231,000
Investment Income		600,000
Other Revenues		7,000
Current Operating Expenditures/Expenses:		
General Government	274,400	
Public Safety	1,417,500	
Streets and Roads	861,700	
Health and Sanitation	162,400	
Parks and Recreation	65,100	
Capital Outlay Expenditures:		
For Construction	8,890,000	
For Equipment	203,700	
Debt Service Expenditures:		
Bond Principal Retirement	700,000	
Interest on Bonds	356,475	
Fiscal Agent Fees	52,500	
Bond Issue Costs	35,000	
Other Financing Sources:		
Bonds		6,300,000
Bond Premium		42,000
Proceeds from Sale of General Capital Assets		175,000

	Debit	Credit
Transfers from General Fund		616,000
Transfers from Special Revenue Funds		70,000
Transfers from Enterprise Funds		63,000
Other Financing Uses:		
Transfers to Capital Projects Funds	56,000	
Transfers to Debt Service Funds...................	560,000	
Transfers to General Fund.......................	70,000	
Totals	$22,860,075	$22,860,075

Additional Information

1. The beginning trial balance of the general capital assets and general long-term liabilities accounts at January 1, 20X5, was:

	Debit	Credit
Land..	$ 465,500	
Buildings	4,375,000	
Accumulated Depreciation—Buildings..................		$ 2,730,000
Machinery and Equipment	1,400,000	
Accumulated Depreciation—Machinery and Equipment ...		525,000
Streets and Roads................................	7,000,000	
Accumulated Depreciation—Streets and Roads		4,200,000
Bonds Payable.................................		2,800,000
Premium on Bonds Payable		70,000
Liability for Claims and Judgments—Long-Term		490,000
Compensated Absences Liability—Long-Term		350,000
Net Position...................................		2,075,500
	$13,240,500	$13,240,500

2. The balance of the long-term claims and judgments obligation at December 31, 20X5, was $450,000. All claims and judgments of the county are related to health and sanitation.
3. The balance of the long-term liability for compensated absences at December 31, 20X5, was $425,000. Compensated absence liabilities are generated equally by the general government, public safety, streets and roads, and health and sanitation functions.
4. The bond issuance occurred at year end. The equipment purchases occurred at the beginning of the year.
5. The January 1, 20X5, balance of Accrued Salaries and Wages Payable was $25,000.
6. The January 1, 20X5, balance of Deferred Tax Revenues was $84,000.
7. The operating grants revenues were associated with Public Safety ($100,000) and Health and Sanitation. The capital grants were associated with Streets and Roads.
8. The accrued interest associated with bonds at December 31, 20X5, was $99,000. The January 1, 20X5, balance was $87,500.
9. The remaining term of the bonds payable with the premium ($70,000) is 10 years. Use straight-line amortization.
10. The county depreciates machinery and equipment over 5 years, buildings over 20 years, and streets and roads over 30 years. Assume zero salvage values.
11. Depreciation expense on the buildings and on the machinery and equipment is associated with functions as follows: General Government, 10%; Public Safety, 50%; Streets and Roads, 25%; Health and Sanitation, 10%; and Parks and Recreation, 5%.
12. The capital asset sold was equipment, which cost $500,000 and had accumulated depreciation at the January 1 sale date of $400,000.
13. The county's only Internal Service Fund provides 75% of its services to Enterprise Funds and sets its billings equal to its costs of providing services. The Internal Service Fund billings to general governmental departments during the year totaled $100,000. Billings of $25,000 were associated with each functional category of expenditures except Parks and Recreation.

Required The December 31, 20X5, total fund balance (postclosing) was $6,721,274. Prepare a balance sheet conversion worksheet to derive government-wide, governmental activities data for Tierney County.

P14-6 (Operating Statement Conversion Worksheet—Governmental Activities) Using the data from P14-5, prepare the operating statement conversion worksheet needed to derive government-wide, governmental activities data for Tierney County for 20X5.

P14-7 (One-Worksheet Conversion—Governmental Activities—Appendix)

Soucy Township
Total Governmental Funds
Preclosing Trial Balance
December 31, 20X7

	Debit	Credit
Cash	$ 1,500,000	
Investments	3,000,000	
Due from Special Revenue Funds	75,000	
Taxes Receivable	5,000,000	
Allowance for Uncollectible Taxes		$ 40,000
Interest and Penalties Receivable	300,000	
Allowance for Uncollectible Interest and Penalties		100,000
Inventory of Materials and Supplies	47,000	
Vouchers Payable		600,000
Accrued Salaries and Wages Payable		140,000
Unearned Operating Grant Revenues		90,000
Due to Internal Service Fund		33,000
Due to Enterprise Fund		80,000
Due to General Fund		75,000
Deferred Revenues (Per 60-day rule)		2,000,000
Fund Balance (Preclosing)		8,124,000
Revenues:		
Taxes		4,500,000
Licenses and Permits		68,000
Fines and Forfeitures		17,000
Investment Income		100,000
Operating Grants		20,000
Current Operating Expenditures/Expenses:		
General Government	495,000	
Public Safety	1,500,000	
Highways and Streets	1,700,000	
Health and Sanitation	1,300,000	
Capital Outlay—Equipment Purchases	750,000	
Debt Service Expenditures:		
Principal Retirement	100,000	
Interest	150,000	
Other Financing Sources:		
Transfers from General Fund		111,000
Other Financing Uses:		
Transfers to Capital Projects Funds	35,000	
Transfers to Debt Service Funds	76,000	
Transfers to Enterprise Funds	70,000	
Totals	$16,098,000	$16,098,000

Soucy Township
General Capital Assets and General Long-Term Liabilities Accounts
Trial Balance
January 1, 20X7

	Debit	Credit	
Land	$ 300,000		
Buildings	3,500,000		20-year life
Accumulated Depreciation—Buildings		$ 750,000	
Equipment	8,000,000		10-year life
Accumulated Depreciation—Equipment		5,000,000	
Bonds Payable		2,000,000	
Net Position		4,050,000	
Totals	$11,800,000	$11,800,000	

Additional Information

1. Deferred Revenues (other than for grants) at the beginning of the year were $2,200,000 — all associated with taxes.
2. The operating grants were for Health and Sanitation.
3. Accrued interest payable at January 1, 20X7, was $50,000; at December 31, it was $47,500.
4. Depreciation expense on the buildings and on the equipment is associated with functions as follows: General Government, 10%; Public Safety, 50%; Highways and Streets, 25%; and Health and Sanitation, 15%. Assume zero salvage value.
5. The county and state own all of the roads in the township, but the township is responsible for most ongoing maintenance.

Required The December 31, 20X7, total fund balance (postclosing) was $6,764,000. Prepare a balance sheet conversion worksheet to derive government-wide, governmental activities data for Soucy Township.

P14-8 (Operating Statement Conversion Worksheet—Governmental Activities) Using the data from P14-7, prepare the operating statement conversion worksheet needed to derive government-wide, governmental activities data for Soucy Township for 20X7.

Cases

C14-1 (Operating Statement Reconciliation—City of Corona, California) The City of Corona, California, Governmental Funds Statement of Revenues, Expenditures, and Changes in Fund Balances reports an increase in Fund Balances of $31,152,287.

Required Based on the following information regarding transactions and events during the period, prepare the reconciliation of the governmental funds operating statement with the government-wide operating statement.

Additional Information

1. Capital outlay expenditures from governmental funds	$14,711,035
2. Cash received on accounts receivable	4,329,777
3. Depreciation expense	9,014,913
4. Franchise fees (not due until late next year)	207,589
5. Noncurrent accrued compensated absences increase during the year	489,324
6. Cash paid on accounts payable	6,329,987
7. Repayment of bond principal	6,824,655
8. Accrued bond interest payable decrease from last year end	98,544
9. Internal Service Fund net revenue (net of expenses)	3,431,499

(Adapted from a recent Comprehensive Annual Financial Report of the City of Corona, California.)

C14-2 (Governmental Funds Balance Sheet Worksheet and Reconciliation—City of Carrollton, Texas) Following are the governmental fund financial statements of the City of Carrollton, Texas (adapted from a recent CAFR). All amounts are reported in *thousands of dollars*.

City of Carrollton, Texas
Balance Sheet
Governmental Funds
September 30, 20X1
(amounts in thousands)

	General	Debt Service	Streets and Drainage	General and Public Facilities	Other Governmental Funds	Total Governmental Funds
Assets						
Cash and cash equivalents	$24,654	$5,958	$44,310	$14,043	$21,250	$110,215
Receivables (net where applicable of allowance for doubtful accounts)						
Ad valorem taxes	572	293	—	—	—	865
Other taxes	2,453	—	—	—	—	2,453
Accrued interest	287	—	394	69	149	899
Other	22	—	—	—	—	22
Due from other governments	—	—	229	49	166	444
Prepaid items	6	—	—	—	—	6
Total assets	$27,994	$6,251	$44,933	$14,161	$21,565	$114,904

	General	Debt Service	Streets and Drainage	General and Public Facilities	Other Governmental Funds	Total Governmental Funds
Liabilities						
Accounts payable.............	$ 4,782	$ —	$ 3,042	$ 503	$ 592	$ 8,919
Accrued interest..............	—	115	—	—	—	115
Arbitrage liability.............	—	58	—	—	—	58
Unearned revenue...........	—	—	818	—	—	818
Total liabilities.............	4,782	173	3,860	503	592	9,910
Deferred Inflows of Resources						
Deferred revenue.............	568	285	229	—	—	1,082
Fund Balances						
Nonspendable.................	6	—	—	—	—	6
Restricted	—	5,793	40,444	11,435	14,968	72,640
Assigned	236	—	400	2,223	6,005	8,864
Unassigned	22,402	—	—	—	—	22,402
Total fund balances..........	$22,644	$5,793	$40,844	$13,658	$20,973	$103,912

City of Carrollton, Texas
Statement of Revenues, Expenditures, and Changes in Fund Balances
Governmental Funds
For the Year Ended September 30, 20X1
(amounts in thousands)

	General	Debt Service	Streets and Drainage	General and Public Facilities	Other Governmental Funds	Total Governmental Funds
Revenues						
Taxes						
Ad valorem..................	$29,353	$16,006	$ —	$ 2,795	$ 2,473	$ 50,627
Penalty and interest..........	342	177	—	—	—	519
Sales.......................	20,861	—	—	—	—	20,861
Occupancy..................	—	—	—	—	143	143
Franchise fees................	9,536	—	—	—	—	9,536
Assessments	—	—	215	—	118	333
Charges for services...........	4,051	—	—	—	6	4,057
Intergovernmental.............	74	—	2,290	189	1,008	3,561
Licenses and permits..........	1,751	—	—	—	—	1,751
Investment income.............	1,893	41	1,509	390	701	4,534
Fines and forfeitures..........	3,752	—	—	117	218	4,087
Miscellaneous................	454	—	63	246	105	868
Total revenues............	72,067	16,224	4,077	3,737	4,772	100,877
Expenditures						
Current						
General government and administration..........	12,693	—	—	—	—	12,693
Public safety	36,159	—	—	—	372	36,531
Development services........	9,557	—	—	—	5	9,562
Culture and recreation	10,984	—	—	—	121	11,105
Capital outlay.................	—	—	13,900	4,273	5,288	23,461
Debt service						
Principal retirement..........	—	8,960	—	—	—	8,960
Interest and fiscal charges.....	—	6,039	—	—	—	6,039
Total expenditures	69,393	14,999	13,900	4,273	5,786	108,351
Excess (deficiency) of revenues over expenditures..................	2,674	1,225	(9,823)	(536)	(1,014)	(7,474)

	General	Debt Service	Streets and Drainage	General and Public Facilities	Other Governmental Funds	Total Governmental Funds
Other financing sources (uses)						
Bonds issued..................	—	—	17,185	2,000	5,640	24,825
Premium on bonds issued.......	—	—	—	16	—	16
Sale of capital assets	20	—	—	1,600	—	1,620
Transfers in	4,816	—	337	895	—	6,048
Transfers out..................	(1,232)	(584)	—	—	—	(1,816)
Total other financing sources (uses)	3,604	(584)	17,522	4,511	5,640	30,693
Net change in fund balances.......	6,278	641	7,699	3,975	4,626	23,219
Fund balances at beginning of year	16,366	5,151	33,146	9,682	16,348	80,693
Fund balances at end of year	$22,644	$ 5,792	$40,845	$13,657	$20,974	$103,912

(Adapted from a recent Comprehensive Annual Financial Report for the City of Carrollton, Texas.)

City of Carrollton, Texas
Governmental Activities—General Capital Assets
For the Year Ended September 30, 20X1
(amounts in thousands)

	Balance October 1	Additions/ Completions	Retirements/ Adjustments	Balance September 30
Capital assets not being depreciated				
Land.......................................	$ 93,669	$ —	$ (1,083)	$ 92,586
Construction in progress.....................	—	449	—	449
Total capital assets not being depreciated.....	93,669	449	(1,083)	93,035
Capital assets being depreciated				
Buildings.................................	46,778	71	(11)	46,838
Equipment	23,224	3,266	(1,448)	25,042
Improvements.............................	29,324	1,524	(2,260)	28,588
Infrastructure	347,269	18,151	(29,665)	335,755
Total capital assets being depreciated	446,595	23,012	(33,384)	436,223
Less accumulated depreciation for				
Buildings.................................	(20,807)	(1,508)	9	(22,306)
Equipment	(12,741)	(1,921)	1,250	(13,412)
Improvements.............................	(7,459)	(1,831)	2,260	(7,030)
Infrastructure	(145,051)	(17,205)	29,665	(132,591)
Total accumulated depreciation	(186,058)	(22,465)	33,184	(175,339)
Total capital assets being depreciated, net	260,537	547	(200)	260,884
General government capital assets, net........	$ 354,206	$ 996	$ (1,283)	$ 353,919

Depreciation expense was charged as direct expense to programs of the primary government as follows:

General government and administration	$ 583
Public Safety.............................	1,763
Development services......................	17,505
Culture and recreation	2,614
	$ 22,465

(Adapted from a recent Comprehensive Annual Financial Report for the City of Carrollton, Texas.)

City of Carrollton, Texas
Governmental Activities—General Long-Term Liabilities
For the Year Ended September 30, 20X1
(amounts in thousands)

	Balance October 1	Additions	Reductions	Balance September 30	Due Within One Year
General obligation bonds	$134,732	$22,825	$ 8,467	$149,090	$10,313
Certificates of obligation	155	2,016	156	2,015	358
Notes payable	337	—	337	—	—
Compensated absences	11,288	1,384	797	11,875	674
Health claims liability..........	1,425	5,445	5,645	1,225	1,225
Long-term risk liability	2,195	1,268	1,268	2,195	—
	$150,132	$32,938	$16,670	$166,400	$12,570

Additional Information

1. Interest to be accrued on long-term debt is $948.
2. All of the deferred revenue resulted from property taxes not being collected within the 60-day availability period. Also, $564 in property tax revenue was deferred in last year's fund statements.
3. The net increase in long-term compensated absences payable, health claims liability, and long-term risk liability is allocable to the governmental functions as follows: 20%, general government; 50%, public safety; and 15% each for development services and culture and recreation.
4. The proceeds from the sales of capital assets were for all retirements that occurred in the 20X0–20X1 fiscal year.
5. Interest expenditures of $767 reported in the 20X0 fiscal year were properly accrued in the previous fiscal year.
6. The net of all transfers were from the Enterprise Funds.

Required

Prepare each of the following for the City of Carrollton as of September 30, 20X1.
 a. Governmental Funds Balance Sheet Conversion Worksheet.
 b. Total Fund Balance to Total Net Position reconciliation.
(Adapted from a recent Comprehensive Annual Financial Report of the City of Carrollton, Texas.)

C14-3 (Governmental Funds Operating Statement Worksheet and Reconciliation—City of Carrollton, Texas) Using the information provided in C14-2, prepare each of the following for the City of Carrollton, Texas, for the year ended September 30, 20X1.
 a. Governmental Funds Operating Statement Conversion Worksheet.
 b. Change in Fund Balance to Change in Net Position reconciliation.
(Adapted from a recent Comprehensive Annual Financial Report of the City of Carrollton, Texas.)

Harvey City Comprehensive Case

Harvey City's fund financial statements have been prepared (Chapter 13). To complete its basic financial statements, Harvey City must derive the information for its government-wide financial statements from the fund financial statements and other pertinent information. As you complete the worksheets to derive Harvey City's government-wide financial statements, you may find it useful at times to review transactions and trial balance information provided in previous chapters for Harvey City.

REQUIREMENTS

a.   Determine whether Harvey City's Internal Service Fund should be reported as part of governmental activities or as part of business-type activities in the government-wide financial statements.

b.   Prepare the worksheets to derive the governmental activities data for Harvey City's government-wide financial statements. (The worksheets should be similar to those in Illustrations 14-9 and 14-12.) The total column of Harvey City's governmental funds financial statements should be the starting point for your worksheet. Additional information that may be required and selected information from prior chapters (included to refresh your memory of pertinent information) are also presented.

c.   Prepare the year-end 20X4 government-wide Statement of Net Position for Harvey City.

d.   Prepare the 20X4 government-wide Statement of Activities for Harvey City.

e.   Prepare the reconciliation of the total fund balances of governmental funds to net position of governmental activities.

f.   Prepare the reconciliation of the total net change in fund balances of governmental funds to the change in net position of governmental activities.

ADDITIONAL INFORMATION

1.   Seventy-five percent of licenses and permits revenues were associated with public safety, and the remainder was associated with health and sanitation.

2.   All fines and forfeitures revenues were derived from the public safety function.

3.   General Fund deferred tax revenues at January 1, 20X4, amounted to $79,100. General Fund deferred interest and penalties revenues at January 1, 20X4, amounted to $20,900. (See General Fund transaction number 24 in Chapter 5.)

4.   General Debt Service Fund deferred tax revenues at January 1, 20X4, were $43,100. General Fund deferred interest and penalties revenues at January 1, 20X4, were $6,900. (See General Debt Service Fund transaction number 8 in Chapter 8.)

5.   All Special Revenue Fund assets are restricted except for $60,000 of unrestricted assets in the Addiction Prevention Special Revenue Fund.

6.   The lawsuit in General Fund transaction number 28 in Chapter 6 is associated with a parks and recreation employee.

7.   Investment income of $62,000 in the Economic Development Special Revenue Fund was earned from temporary investment of unexpended grant proceeds. (Transaction 3 from Chapter 6 for that fund indicates that the grant requires all investment income from the investment of grant proceeds to be used for economic development.)

8.   Except for $200,000 that is unrestricted, all of the fund balance of the Parks and Recreation Capital Projects Fund is restricted for the project.

9.   All of the assets of the General Debt Service Fund are restricted solely for debt service on general long-term debt.

10. Review the information under Additional Transactions and Events for the General Capital Assets and General Long-Term Liabilities accounts in Chapter 9 to determine the functions to which depreciation must be assigned and to which the compensated absences liabilities relate.

11. Amortization of bond premiums totaled $14,580 during the year, including amortization of $11,250 of the premium on the *original* city hall bonds before they were defeased. The accrued interest payable on bonds at the end of 20X4 was $580,000. The January 1, 20X4, balance of accrued interest payable on bonds was $480,000.

12. The equipment purchase in the Tourism Development Special Revenue Fund occurred at year end.

CHAPTER **15**

Financial Reporting

The Comprehensive Annual Financial Report and the Financial Reporting Entity

LEARNING OBJECTIVES

After studying this chapter, you should be able to:

- Explain the nature and contents of the three major sections of a Comprehensive Annual Financial Report.

- Understand the relationships between combining financial statements and the basic financial statements.

- Determine the combining statements that a government needs to present in its Comprehensive Annual Financial Report.

- Explain how to determine whether a government should treat an associated entity as a component unit.

- Understand which component units should be blended and which should be discretely presented.

- Understand the differences between blending and discrete presentation.

- Explain the differences between and among the reporting requirements for related organizations, jointly governed organizations, and joint ventures.

As discussed in Chapter 13, the Basic Financial Statements and notes—accompanied by the Management's Discussion and Analysis (MD&A) and other required supplementary information—meet the *minimum* GAAP requirements for general purpose external financial reporting. However, the GASB also *recommends* that this information be provided within the context of a Comprehensive Annual Financial Report (CAFR), which is consistent with the governmental accounting and financial reporting principles statement that a "comprehensive annual financial report should be prepared and published." This chapter explains and illustrates the presentations that comprise a CAFR.

In discussing the Basic Financial Statements in Chapters 13 and 14, we considered governments with a simple reporting entity structure. Although we pointed out where component units should be reported in the Basic Financial Statements, most of the coverage presumed that the entity being reported upon was limited to a single legal entity. This approach focused attention on the fundamental content of the Basic Financial Statements and how to derive and present that information rather than on the complexities caused by having other separate legal entities reported as part of the reporting government.

We continue this single legal entity focus in the first section of this chapter in order to emphasize the fundamental nature and content of a CAFR and the relationships between the various levels of financial statements presented in a CAFR.

The final section of the chapter discusses and illustrates the unique issues and requirements involved when governments have a complex reporting entity structure containing multiple separate legal entities. In that section, we discuss how a government determines when legally separate entities must be included in their financial report and the manner in which information about those entities should be included.

THE COMPREHENSIVE ANNUAL FINANCIAL REPORT

A government's CAFR often is referred to as its *official* annual report. The CAFR contains a variety of information in addition to its Basic Financial Statements. The CAFR includes individual fund financial statement data on each fund of the government—not just the major funds—as well as combining statements, introductory material, and statistical information. Many governments make their CAFRs (or significant portions of them) available on the Internet. You may want to review a government's CAFR as you study the remainder of this discussion.

A CAFR contains three distinct sections:

1. Introductory Section
2. Financial Section
3. Statistical Section

These CAFR sections and their contents are presented in Illustration 15-1. The Basic Financial Statements were discussed and illustrated in Chapter 13. The other CAFR sections and contents are discussed briefly here.

The Introductory Section

As noted in Illustration 15-1, the Introductory Section of the CAFR includes a table of contents, letter(s) of transmittal, and other materials deemed appropriate by management. Other materials might include, for example, the organization chart, a copy of the prior year's Certificate of Achievement for Excellence in Financial Reporting awarded by the Government Finance Officers Association (GFOA), the roster of elected officials, and a description of the government entity being reported on. Further information on the GFOA's Certificate of Achievement for Excellence in Financial Reporting program may be obtained at the organization's Web site at http://www.gfoa.org.

The *transmittal letter* from the chief financial officer is an extremely important part of the Introductory Section of a CAFR. The letter typically communicates:

- The legal requirements for the presentation of the CAFR,
- The fact that the report is management's responsibility and consists of management's representations regarding the financial position and operating results of the government, and
- The results of the audit of the financial statements.

The letter of transmittal may also contain a profile of the government and information that readers are apt to find useful in evaluating the financial condition of the government. This information may include such topics as the local economy, long-term financial planning information regarding items for which final decisions are not yet made, cash management practices, and risk management practices. Many areas that would otherwise be covered in the letter are not included because the information is included in the MD&A in the Financial Section. *The transmittal letter should not duplicate information that is presented in the MD&A, but may refer readers to the MD&A.*

Finally, because they may seem similar based on a cursory discussion or review, it is important to understand the differing nature and purposes of the transmittal letter and MD&A. First, as noted, the transmittal letter introduces and relates to the entire CAFR; the MD&A relates only to the Basic Financial Statements. Also, recall from Chapter 13 that the MD&A covers only certain GASB-specified

ILLUSTRATION 15-1 General Outline and Content of a CAFR—Simple Entity Structure

INTRODUCTORY SECTION

Components Required by the GASB	Other Items Commonly Included
1. Table of Contents 2. Letter(s) of Transmittal 3. Other materials deemed appropriate by management	1. List of Principal Officials 2. Organization Chart 3. GFOA Certificate of Achievement for Excellence in Financial Reporting (if received for the previous fiscal year)

FINANCIAL SECTION

Auditor's Report

Basic Financial Statements and Required Supplementary Information (See Chapter 13)

- Management's Discussion and Analysis
- Government-Wide Financial Statements
- Governmental Funds Financial Statements
- Proprietary Funds Financial Statements
- Fiduciary Funds Financial Statements
- Notes to the Financial Statements
- Other Required Supplementary Information

Combining Financial Statements

Funds Reported:	Combining Statement:
Nonmajor Governmental Funds	• Balance Sheet • Statement of Revenues, Expenditures, and Changes in Fund Balances
Nonmajor Enterprise Funds	• Statement of Net Position • Statement of Revenues, Expenses, and Changes in Fund Net Position • Statement of Cash Flows
Internal Service Funds	• Statement of Net Position • Statement of Revenues, Expenses, and Changes in Fund Net Position • Statement of Cash Flows
Trust Funds (for Fund Type)	• Statement of Fiduciary Net Position • Statement of Changes in Fiduciary Net Position
Agency Funds	• Statement of Changes in Agency Fund Assets and Liabilities

Individual Fund Financial Statements and Schedules

- Individual fund budgetary comparisons that are not part of the Basic Financial Statements
- Individual fund statements with prior year comparative data
- Individual fund statements with greater detail than combining or Basic Financial Statements
- Schedules necessary to demonstrate compliance with finance-related legal and contractual provisions
- Schedules to present information spread throughout the statements that can be brought together and shown in greater detail (e.g., taxes receivable, long-term debt, and investments)
- Schedules to present greater detail for information reported in the statements (e.g., additional revenue sources detail and object of expenditure data by departments)

Narrative Explanations

Notes useful in understanding combining and individual fund statements and schedules that are not included in the notes to the Basic Financial Statements. They may be presented on divider pages, directly on the statements and schedules, or in a separate section.

(Continued)

ILLUSTRATION 15-1   General Outline and Content of a CAFR—Simple Entity Structure (*Continued*)

STATISTICAL SECTION

Statistical Information Categories	Statistical Tables	Periods Reported
Financial Trends Information	Information about Net Position	Last 10 Fiscal Years
	Information about Changes in Net Position	Last 10 Fiscal Years
	Information about Governmental Funds	Last 10 Fiscal Years
Revenue Capacity Information	Information about Revenue Base	Last 10 Fiscal Years
	Information about Revenue Rates	Last 10 Fiscal Years
	Information about Principal Revenue Payers	Current Year and Ninth Year Prior
	Information about Property Tax Levies and Collections	Last 10 Fiscal Years
Debt Capacity Information	Information about Ratios of Outstanding Debt	Last 10 Fiscal Years
	Information about Ratios of General Bonded Debt	Last 10 Fiscal Years
	Information about Direct and Overlapping Debt	Current Fiscal Year
	Information about Debt Limitations:	
	Legal Debt Margin	Current Fiscal Year
	Other Debt Limitation Information	Last 10 Fiscal Years
	Information about Pledged-Revenue Coverage	Last 10 Fiscal Years
Demographic and Economic Information	Information about Demographic and Economic Indicators	Last 10 Fiscal Years
	Information about Principal Employers	Current Year and Ninth Year Prior
Operating Information	Information about Government Employees	Last 10 Fiscal Years
	Information about Operating Indicators	Last 10 Fiscal Years
	Information about Capital Assets	Last 10 Fiscal Years

topics and must be based only upon currently known facts, conditions, or decisions. The transmittal letter can cover other topics and discuss the implications of events that might happen or decisions that are not yet made—such as the potential effects of an expected major expansion of a large company within the government's jurisdiction. The possible effect of such a decision must not be included in the MD&A unless the decision has been made by the date of the auditor's report.

The Financial Section   The financial section of a CAFR for a government with a simple entity structure has several subsections:

- Auditor's Report
- Basic Financial Statements and Required Supplementary Information
- Combining and Individual Fund Financial Statements and Schedules

Narrative explanations are not a separate section but are notes to combining and individual fund financial statements.

The Auditor's Report

The auditor's report on the financial statements is the first item presented in the financial section of a government's CAFR. The auditor's report on the Guilford County, North Carolina, financial statements for a recent fiscal year appears in Illustration 15-2. Note that this report states the auditor's opinion on the Basic Financial Statements. MD&A, other required supplementary information, the combining financial statements, the introductory section, and the statistical section

ILLUSTRATION 15-2 Independent Auditor's Report

Independent Auditor's Report

The Honorable Members of the Board of
    County Commissioners
Guilford County, North Carolina

We have audited the accompanying financial statements of the governmental activities, the discretely presented component unit, each major fund, and the aggregate remaining fund information of Guilford County, North Carolina (the "County"), as of and for the year ended June 30, 20X1, which collectively comprise the County's basic financial statements as listed in the Table of Contents. These financial statements are the responsibility of the County's management. Our responsibility is to express opinions on these financial statements based on our audit.

We conducted our audit in accordance with auditing standards generally accepted in the United States of America and the standards applicable to financial audits contained in *Government Auditing Standards,* issued by the Comptroller General of the United States. Those standards require that we plan and perform the audit to obtain reasonable assurance about whether the financial statements are free of material misstatement. The financial statements of the Greensboro/Guilford County Tourism Development Authority were not audited in accordance with *Government Auditing Standards*. An audit includes examining, on a test basis, evidence supporting the amounts and disclosures in the financial statements. An audit also includes assessing the accounting principles used and significant estimates made by management, as well as evaluating the overall financial statement presentation. We believe that our audit provides a reasonable basis for our opinions.

In our opinion, based on our audit, the financial statements referred to above present fairly, in all material respects, the respective financial position of the governmental activities, the discretely presented component unit, each major fund, and the aggregate remaining fund information of the County as of June 30, 20X1, and the respective changes in financial position and cash flows, where applicable, thereof and the budgetary comparison for the General Fund for the year then ended in conformity with accounting principles generally accepted in the United States of America.

In accordance with *Government Auditing Standards*, we have also issued our report dated December 2, 20X1 on our consideration of the County's internal control over financial reporting and on our tests of its compliance with certain provisions of laws, regulations, contracts, grant agreements, and other matters. The purpose of that report is to describe the scope of our testing of internal control over financial reporting and compliance and the results of that testing, and not to provide an opinion on the internal control over financial reporting or on compliance. That report is an integral part of an audit performed in accordance with *Government Auditing Standards* and should be considered in assessing the results of our audit.

Accounting principles generally accepted in the United States of America require that the Management's Discussion and Analysis and the Required Supplementary Information as listed in the Table of Contents be presented to supplement information to the basic financial statements. Such information, although not a part of the basic financial statements, is required by the Governmental Accounting Standards Board, who considers it to be an essential part of financial reporting for placing the basic financial statements in an appropriate operational, economic, or historical context. We have applied certain limited procedures to the required supplementary information in accordance with auditing standards generally accepted in the United States of America, which consisted of inquiries of management about the methods of preparing the information and comparing the information for consistency with management's responses to our inquiries, the basic financial statements, and other knowledge we obtained during our audit of the basic financial statements. We do not express an opinion or provide any assurance on the information because the limited procedures do not provide us with sufficient evidence to express an opinion or provide any assurance.

Our audit was conducted for the purpose of forming opinions on the financial statements that collectively comprise the County's basic financial statements. The combining and individual fund statements and schedules, and the additional financial data as listed in the accompanying Table of Contents are presented for purposes of additional analysis and are not a required part of the basic financial statements. The combining and individual fund financial statements and schedules, and the additional financial data are the responsibility of management and were derived from and relate directly to the underlying accounting and other records used to prepare the financial statements. The information has been subjected to the auditing procedures applied in the audit of the basic financial statements and certain additional procedures, including comparing and reconciling such information directly to the underlying accounting and other records used to prepare the financial statements or to the financial statements themselves, and other additional procedures in accordance with auditing standards generally accepted in the United States of America. In our opinion, the information is fairly stated, in all material respects, in relation to the basic financial statements taken as a whole. The introductory and statistical sections have not been subjected to the auditing procedures applied in the audit of basic financial statements and, accordingly, we do not express an opinion or provide any assurance on them.

Cherry, Bekaert & Holland, L.L.P

Raleigh, North Carolina
December 2, 20X1

Source: Adapted from a recent Comprehensive Annual Financial Report of Guilford County, North Carolina.

are not covered by the opinion. These items are treated as *accompanying* (supplementary) data presented for purposes of additional analysis. In some financial statement audits, the auditor's report covers *both* fair presentation of the *basic financial statements and* fair presentation of the *combining and individual fund* financial statements. This "dual opinion" audit has long been recommended both by the GASB and by the Government Finance Officers Association, but is not required unless mandated by law or regulations pertaining to specific governments.

The Basic Financial Statements and Required Supplementary Information

Chapter 13 covers the *minimum* requirements for *general purpose external* financial reporting, which include:

- Management's Discussion and Analysis (Required Supplementary Information)
- Basic Financial Statements
    Government-Wide Financial Statements
    Fund Financial Statements (for each fund category)
    Notes to the Financial Statements
- Other Required Supplementary Information

These components of a CAFR should be reviewed, but the primary additional point to understand from this chapter is that the GASB recommends that this information be made available in the context of a CAFR—not solely as a separate financial report.

The Combining and Individual Fund Statements and Schedules

Both combining and individual fund financial statements have been presented in earlier chapters. Some examples were integral parts of illustrative examples; others were ancillary illustrations from actual governments. As is clear from these examples and from the diagrams in Illustration 15-3, combining statements focus on presenting information about each fund in a common group or subgroup of funds. The individual fund information in a combining statement is aggregated in a total column. As shown in Illustration 15-3, that total column articulates with a related amount in one of the Basic Financial Statements. *Combining statements are required in a CAFR to support any information in the fund financial statements that aggregates data of two or more funds.*

Note in Illustration 15-3 that **nonmajor** governmental funds are aggregated in a single column in the governmental funds financial statements—regardless of the specific fund type. Therefore, there must be a **combining financial statement** that presents the data for each of these nonmajor governmental funds and a total for all of them. This combining statement articulates with, and provides individual fund information to support, the "Other (Nonmajor) Funds" column in the governmental funds financial statements.

Likewise, combining statements must be presented for nonmajor Enterprise Funds to support the "Other (Nonmajor) Enterprise Funds" data in the proprietary funds financial statements. The information presented in the fund financial statements for each of the other fund types is aggregated by fund type. Therefore, a set of combining financial statements is required for each of the other fund types—Internal Service Funds, Pension Trust Funds, Private-Purpose Trust Funds, Investment Trust Funds, and Agency Funds. (The only combining statement for Agency Funds, however, is the Statement of Changes in Assets and Liabilities of Agency Funds, which was illustrated in Chapter 12.)

Individual fund financial statements are *not* always required by GAAP. However, they should be presented when needed to provide:

- Budgetary comparisons not included in the Basic Financial Statements.
- More detailed budgetary comparisons for the General Fund and for major Special Revenue Funds if the budgetary comparisons in the Basic Financial Statements do not contain adequate detail to demonstrate budgetary compliance.

ILLUSTRATION 15-3   Relationship of Basic Fund Financial Statements and Combining Statements

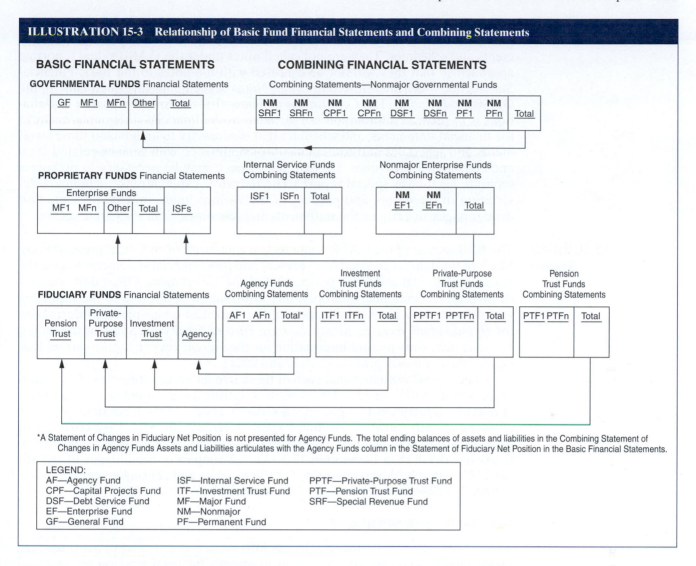

*A Statement of Changes in Fiduciary Net Position is not presented for Agency Funds. The total ending balances of assets and liabilities in the Combining Statement of Changes in Agency Funds Assets and Liabilities articulates with the Agency Funds column in the Statement of Fiduciary Net Position in the Basic Financial Statements.

LEGEND:
AF—Agency Fund   ISF—Internal Service Fund   PPTF—Private-Purpose Trust Fund
CPF—Capital Projects Fund   ITF—Investment Trust Fund   PTF—Pension Trust Fund
DSF—Debt Service Fund   MF—Major Fund   SRF—Special Revenue Fund
EF—Enterprise Fund   NM—Nonmajor
GF—General Fund   PF—Permanent Fund

- Additional classification detail beyond that included in the Basic Financial Statements or in the combining financial statements.
- Prior year comparative data for individual funds.

It should be noted that a government might choose to present individual fund financial statements for one particular fund of a fund type, but not for all funds of that type. Additional detail may be needed for that particular fund because of its importance or because of the high level of interest of a known subgroup of financial statement users.

Schedules are used primarily to:

1. Demonstrate finance-related legal and contractual compliance, such as when bond indentures require certain data to be presented in the CAFR.

2. Present more detailed data than that appearing in the financial statements, such as detailed schedules of revenues and of expenditures.

3. Present other data management deems necessary, such as cash receipts and disbursements schedules for one, some, or all funds.

Schedules are not considered to be required for fair presentation in conformity with GAAP unless they are referenced in a statement or footnote. However, the notes to the financial statements often include several schedules that are deemed essential to reporting in conformity with GAAP, and schedules are often required to demonstrate compliance with legal and contractual provisions such as budgetary statutes, bond covenants, or grant agreements and regulations.

Narrative explanations are in essence additional notes to the combining and individual fund financial statements and schedules and to the component unit statements and schedules. They are not called notes under the GASB's dual reporting approach so that they will not be confused with the notes to the Basic Financial Statements, which are referred to as *the* "Notes to the Financial Statements" in the GASB *Codification.* The *Codification* indicates that the role of narrative explanations is to provide information not included in the financial statements, notes to the financial statements, and schedules that is necessary to understand those statements and schedules and to demonstrate compliance with finance-related legal and contractual provisions. (In extreme cases, it may be necessary to prepare a separate legal-basis special report.) The narrative explanations, including a description of the nature and purpose of the various funds, may be presented on divider pages, directly on the statements and schedules, or in a separate section.

The Statistical Section

The final section of the CAFR contains five categories of statistical presentations. Much of the data is extracted from present and past financial statements to give the reader a historical and trend perspective of the government. Other data includes demographic, economic, and operating information applicable to the reporting government. As a general rule, most of the statistical tables present information for *10 individual years, including the most current fiscal year.* Some of the tables, however, may only present information for the *current year* or *for the current year and for the ninth year prior* (e.g., 2010 and 2001).

The GASB presumes that each of these five different categories of statistical presentations will be included in an entity's statistical section unless it is clearly inapplicable. Illustration 15-1 provides a broad overview of the types of information required in each category. Although space precludes an exhaustive coverage of each statistical table, this section discusses the categories of statistical information in greater detail than Illustration 15-1. Also, examples of broad types of statistical tables—that is, those presenting (1) 10-year data and (2) single-year data—are included in Illustrations 15-4 and 15-5, respectively.

Financial Trends Information

The GASB states that "financial trends information is intended to assist users in understanding and assessing how a government's financial position has changed over time."[1] To that end, four different types of information ordinarily should be reported in 10-year trend tables, as follows:

- Information about the components of ***net position*** for governmental activities, business-type activities, and the total primary government:
  - Net investment in capital assets
  - Restricted net position
  - Unrestricted net position
- Information about ***changes in net position*** for governmental and business-type activities:
  - Expenses by function, program, or other identifiable activity
  - Program revenues by category (i.e., charges for services, operating grants and contributions, capital grants and contributions)
  - Total net (expense) revenue
  - General revenues and other changes in net position by type
  - Total change in net position
- Both information about ***governmental funds*** (if applicable) fund balances and information about ***governmental funds*** (if applicable) changes in fund balances:
  - For the General Fund and all other governmental funds in the aggregate, each of the required fund balance classifications (by fund type)

---

[1]GASB *Statement No. 44,* "Economic Condition Reporting: The Statistical Section, an amendment to NCGA Statement 1," May 2004, par. 6a.

ILLUSTRATION 15-4 Statistical Table—Ten-Year Data

General Governmental Expenditures by Function 20X4–20Y3 (in thousands)

EXPENDITURES BY FUNCTION

Fiscal Year Ended Sept. 30	Total (1)	Administration	Fiscal Management	Public Safety	Public Services and Utilities	Public Health	Public Recreation and Culture		Social Services Management	Support Services	Urban Growth Management	General City Responsibilities
							Parks	Libraries				
	$	$	$	$	$	$	$	$	$	$	$	$
20X4	267,435	10,013	13,117	122,433	14,087	39,455 (2)	18,796	9,975	7,153	21,944	10,861	(399)
20X5	286,528	9,186	12,499	131,743	15,550	40,432	19,258	10,617	7,335	20,451	11,402	8,055
20X6	298,416	10,530	15,420	141,141	11,904	43,647	19,411	10,681	7,286	21,357	10,567	6,472
20X7	299,845	10,661	16,250	144,288	9,676	43,190	21,283	11,481	6,739	22,513	7,501	6,263
20X8	319,902	10,923	16,567	162,733	10,128	37,060	23,066	12,795	8,205	24,304	8,380	5,741
20X9	352,697	13,045	19,628	173,963	11,099	40,632	26,028	14,901	8,627	29,993	9,129	5,606
20Y0	373,258	15,555	21,175	191,591	6,098	41,032	27,994	16,211	9,387	30,117	10,189	3,909
20Y1	417,494	18,152	20,779	210,281	9,520	41,437	30,369	17,091	8,071	41,076	11,569	9,149
20Y2	452,487	18,750	20,115	237,590	9,191	43,655	29,563	17,133	10,448	42,613	10,882	12,547
20Y3	464,379	18,030	21,785	254,684	9,380	46,061	28,170	17,023	9,985	38,910	11,638	8,713

EXPENDITURES BY FUNCTION AS A PERCENT OF TOTAL EXPENDITURES

Fiscal Year Ended Sept. 30	Total (1)	Administration	Fiscal Management	Public Safety	Public Services and Utilities	Public Health	Public Recreation and Culture		Social Services Management	Support Services	Urban Growth Management	General City Responsibilities
							Parks	Libraries				
	%	%	%	%	%	%	%	%	%	%	%	%
20X4	100.00	3.74	4.90	45.78	5.27	14.75 (2)	7.04	3.73	2.67	8.21	4.06	-0.15
20X5	100.00	3.21	4.36	45.98	5.43	14.11	6.72	3.70	2.56	7.14	3.98	2.81
20X6	100.00	3.53	5.17	47.30	3.99	14.62	6.50	3.58	2.44	7.16	3.54	2.17
20X7	100.00	3.56	5.42	48.11	3.23	14.40	7.10	3.83	2.25	7.51	2.50	2.09
20X8	100.00	3.41	5.18	50.88	3.17	11.58	7.21	4.00	2.56	7.60	2.62	1.79
20X9	100.00	3.70	5.57	49.32	3.15	11.52	7.38	4.23	2.45	8.50	2.59	1.59
20Y0	100.00	4.17	5.67	51.34	1.63	10.99	7.50	4.34	2.51	8.07	2.73	1.05
20Y1	100.00	4.35	4.98	50.37	2.28	9.93	7.27	4.09	1.93	9.84	2.77	2.19
20Y2	100.00	4.14	4.45	52.51	2.03	9.65	6.53	3.79	2.31	9.42	2.40	2.77
20Y3	100.00	3.88	4.69	54.83	2.03	9.91	6.08	3.66	2.15	8.38	2.51	1.88

In Constant 19X4 Dollars

	20X4	20X5	20X6	20X7	20X8	20X9	20Y0	20Y1	20Y2	20Y3
Administration	$12,267	9,011	10,081	10,028	10,155	11,870	13,626	15,390	15,691	14,718
Fiscal management	16,069	12,261	14,761	15,287	15,401	17,861	18,548	17,618	16,833	17,783
Public safety	149,983	129,236	135,112	135,731	151,287	158,302	167,826	178,289	198,827	207,901
Public services and utilities	17,258	15,254	11,395	9,102	9,416	10,100	5,342	8,072	7,691	7,657
Public health	48,333 (2)	39,662	41,783	40,628	34,454	37,016	35,942	35,133	36,533	37,600
Parks	23,026	18,891	18,582	20,021	21,444	23,684	24,522	25,749	24,740	22,995
Libraries	12,219	10,415	10,225	10,800	11,895	13,560	14,200	14,491	14,338	13,896
Social services management	8,762	7,195	6,974	6,339	7,628	7,850	8,223	6,843	8,743	8,151
Support services management	26,882	20,061	20,445	21,178	22,595	27,293	26,381	34,827	35,661	31,763
Urban growth management	13,304	11,185	10,116	7,056	7,791	8,307	8,925	9,809	9,107	9,500
General city responsibilities	(489)	7,902	6,196	5,892	5,337	5,102	3,424	7,758	10,500	7,113
Total (1)	$327,614	281,073	285,670	282,062	297,403	320,945	326,959	353,979	378,664	379,077

(1) Total does not include transfers to other funds.

(2) In 20X4, the Federally Qualified Health Center was created and certain expenditures shown previously in Public Health are now reported in another fund.

Note: General governmental includes the General Fund and two Internal Service Funds, Information Systems and Support Services.

Source: Adapted from a recent City of Austin, Texas, comprehensive annual financial report.

ILLUSTRATION 15-5   Statistical Table—Single-Year Data

City of Louisville
Computation of Direct and Overlapping Bonded Debt
General Obligation Bonds
June 30, 20X6

Governmental Unit	Net General Obligation Bonded Debt Outstanding	Percentage Applicable to City of Louisville	Amount Applicable to City of Louisville
Direct debt—City of Louisville Serial Bonds	$ 6,445,000	100.00%	$ 6,445,000
Overlapping debt: Louisville and Jefferson County Board of Education	196,575,400	33.83%	66,501,458
Jefferson County	172,170,000	33.84%	58,262,328
Total direct and overlapping debt	$375,190,400		$131,208,786

Source: Adapted from a recent City of Louisville, Kentucky comprehensive annual financial report.

- For governmental funds in total
  - Revenues by source
  - Expenditures by functions
  - Other financing sources (uses) and other changes in fund balances by type
  - Total change in fund balances

Revenue Capacity Information

The GASB's objective for including revenue capacity information in the statistical section "is to help users understand and assess the factors affecting a government's ability to generate its most significant own-source revenues."[2] The primary information required (10 years of trend information unless otherwise noted) in this category of the statistical section is as follows:

- Information about the *revenue base* (e.g., real property, personal property, assessed valuation, actual value)
- Information about *revenue rates* for both direct and overlapping governments, if applicable
- Information about principal *revenue payers* (presented for the current year and the ninth year prior only and generally including the top 10 revenue payers)
- Information about *property tax levies and collections*
  - Amount levied for period
  - Amount collected prior to the period end (dollar amount and percentage of total levy)
  - Amount of levy collected in subsequent years, amount collected to date, and the percentage of the total levy collected to date

Debt Capacity Information

The GASB has concluded that debt capacity information is critical to an objective analysis of an entity's overall economic condition. Users of the financial statements need to understand and assess an entity's debt burden, as well as its ability and capacity to issue debt.

- Information about *outstanding debt ratios*
  - Presented by type of debt (e.g., general obligation bonds, loans, capital leases, revenue-backed debt)

---

[2]Ibid., par. 6b.

- Debt ratio of total outstanding debt to total personal income (or a similar denominator such as estimated actual value of taxable property)
- Per capita ratio of outstanding debt
- Information about **general bonded debt ratios**
- Information about **direct and overlapping debt,** where applicable, for the current year only
  - Total amount of debt outstanding (both direct and overlapping governments)
  - Percentage of overlap between the reported governmental entity and overlapping governments
- Information about **debt limitations**
  - Legal debt margin calculation (if applicable) for the current year only
  - Debt limit amount, total net debt applicable to the debt limit, legal debt margin amount, and the ratio of the legal debt margin to the debt limit for the last 10 fiscal years
  - Information about pledged revenue coverage, including a coverage ratio, for the last 10 fiscal years

Demographic and Economic Information

In order to understand the overall environment in which a governmental entity operates, it is important to have information concerning its demographics and local economy. This information includes not only indicators related to population, unemployment rates, and the like, but also data concerning principal employers in the jurisdiction.

- At a minimum, the following **demographic and economic information** should be included for the last 10 fiscal years:
  - Population
  - Total personal income
  - Per capita personal income
  - Unemployment rate
- Information about the jurisdiction's **10 principal employers** (presented for the current year and ninth year prior)
  - Number of employees for each principal employer
  - Percentage of total employment base each employer represents

Operating Information

The GASB states that the objective of operating information is "to provide contextual information about a government's operations and resources to assist readers in using financial statement information to understand and assess a government's economic condition."[3] Accordingly, at least three types of operating information are necessary:

- Number of reporting government employees by function, program, or other identifiable activity
- Operating indicators that provide information on the demands or level of service, such as (but not limited to)
  - Number of arrests
  - Number of fire calls
  - Tons of refuse collected
  - Recreational programs provided
- Information about the volume, utilization, or nature of capital assets, such as (but not limited to)
  - Lane miles of streets and highways
  - Miles of water and wastewater piping
  - Volume of water sold and wastewater treated

---

[3]Ibid., par. 6e.

SUPPLEMENTAL AND SPECIAL PURPOSE REPORTING

A variety of special reports has emerged in recent years. Some are necessary because a government prepares its CAFR in accordance with GAAP, but must also submit a non-GAAP report (possibly of cash receipts, disbursements, and balances) to a state agency. This type of situation is discussed in the GASB *Codification*.

Another type of report that has emerged may be called the *condensed summary* (or "*popular*") *report*. Most include highly condensed (even consolidated) financial statements, perhaps presented in short booklets or brochures highlighting the key aspects of a government's operating results and status. A form of popular reporting called *citizen-centric reporting* is being advocated by the Association of Government Accountants. Presentations of data aggregated differently than required in the Basic Financial Statements are *not* considered GAAP.

Finally, the GASB *Codification* recognizes that the standards established by the GASB and its predecessors are *minimum* standards of financial reporting, not maximum standards. Accordingly, the finance officer should assume responsibility for preparing other information needed for management, policy, and other decisions. The GASB also notes that supplementary information may be as valuable as GAAP information in meeting some information needs.

FINANCIAL REPORTING—COMPLEX ENTITY STRUCTURE

Up to this point, our financial reporting discussion typically has assumed that only data from a government's legally defined entity are included in its GAAP financial statements. (We have included component unit information in some illustrations or indicated its location for completeness but have not discussed it.) We referred to this situation as a government with a *simple* entity structure.

The GASB requires certain associated organizations to be included as component units of the government's reporting entity. A government financial report that erroneously includes or erroneously excludes a potential component unit from the government's reporting entity does *not* fairly present its financial position or results of operations.

Many SLGs have *complex* entity structures and must include other government, quasi-government, or even nongovernment organizations in their financial reports. Their reporting entities are not limited to their legally defined entity. They have varying degrees of authority over and/or responsibilities for other legally separate governmental, quasi-governmental, or other entities such as school districts, housing authorities, building authorities, fire districts, water districts, airport authorities, and transit authorities. At least one local government reporting entity includes a semiprofessional baseball team. Illustration 15-6 illustrates some of the potential interrelationships between a local government and other associated entities.

A government (such as the City of Lubburg in Illustration 15-6) that has other legally separate organizations associated with it must determine whether its reporting entity should include one or more of the associated organizations (referred to as *potential component units*) in addition to its own legal entity. The government's legal entity is called the *primary government*.

Reporting Entity Definition

According to the GASB *Codification*, each general purpose unit of government— that is, state, county, city, and so on—*is a primary government*. Special purpose governments such as school districts also are primary governments if they have (1) popularly elected governing bodies, (2) separate legal standing, and (3) fiscal independence. Any organization that is legally part of a primary government is

---

ILLUSTRATION 15-6   The Governmental Reporting Entity Issue

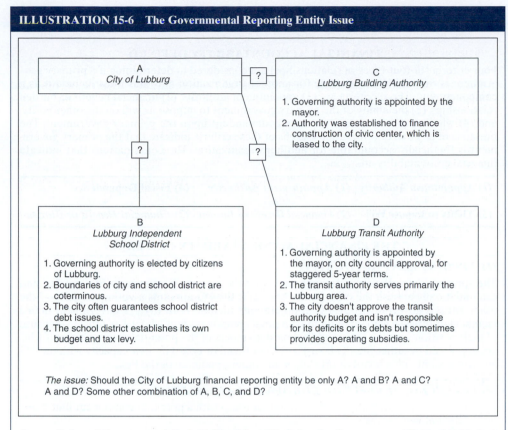

A
City of Lubburg

?

C
Lubburg Building Authority

1. Governing authority is appointed by the mayor.
2. Authority was established to finance construction of civic center, which is leased to the city.

?

?

B
Lubburg Independent School District

1. Governing authority is elected by citizens of Lubburg.
2. Boundaries of city and school district are coterminous.
3. The city often guarantees school district debt issues.
4. The school district establishes its own budget and tax levy.

D
Lubburg Transit Authority

1. Governing authority is appointed by the mayor, on city council approval, for staggered 5-year terms.
2. The transit authority serves primarily the Lubburg area.
3. The city doesn't approve the transit authority budget and isn't responsible for its deficits or its debts but sometimes provides operating subsidies.

The issue: Should the City of Lubburg financial reporting entity be only A? A and B? A and C? A and D? Some other combination of A, B, C, and D?

---

defined as part of that primary government. An entity that is a primary government can never be reported as a component unit of any other entity. Some government organizations do not meet the definition of a primary government and, though legally separate, are not in and of themselves primary governments. Some of these governments are reported as component units of other governments. However, for their own external financial reports, they define their reporting entities and incorporate component units into their CAFRs as if they were primary governments.

Component units usually are other government entities but may be not-for-profit organizations or business entities. A primary government must report legally separate organizations as component units in each of the following circumstances:

- The primary government is *financially accountable* for the other entity.
- The primary government holds *a majority equity interest* in the other entity for the purpose of facilitating the delivery of government services.
- The other entity is a *tax-exempt* organization whose ongoing *financial support* of the primary government warrants inclusion as a component unit.
- *Failure to include* the organization as a component unit would make the primary government's financial statements *misleading*.

Financial accountability is the broadest, most common basis for an organization to be a component unit. Financial accountability is explained in Illustration 15-7. As the illustration indicates, a primary government *cannot* be financially accountable for an organization *unless* it *either* (1) appoints a voting majority of the organization's governing body *or* (2) has a financial benefit or

ILLUSTRATION 15-7 Financial Accountability

FINANCIAL ACCOUNTABILITY DEFINED

Four criteria (or four types of relationships) are considered in determining if a primary government is financially accountable for another organization and thus must include it as a component unit. Those criteria are (1) appointment authority, (2) financial benefit or burden relationships, (3) the ability of the primary government to impose its will on the other entity, and (4) whether the other entity is fiscally dependent upon the primary government. The presence of any one of three combinations of these criteria indicate that the primary government is financially accountable for another organization. The combinations that indicate financial accountability are:

(1) Appointment Authority + *(3) Ability to Impose Will*	*(1) Appointment Authority* + *(2) Financial Benefit or Burden*	*(4) Fiscal Dependence* + *(2) Financial Benefit or Burden*

THE FINANCIAL ACCOUNTABILITY CRITERIA

(1) APPOINTMENT AUTHORITY:

The appointment authority criterion is met (1) if the primary government (PG) created and can unilaterally abolish the other entity OR (2) if the PG appoints a voting majority of the other entity's governing body. PG appointments include both (a) PG government board members or officials who serve on the potential component unit's board *ex officio*—because of their position with the PG—and (b) board members of the potential component unit who are appointed by either the PG board, any PG official or board in their capacity with the PG, any component unit's board or official, or any other appointee of the PG.

(2) FINANCIAL BENEFIT OR BURDEN RELATIONSHIPS:

The PG has a financial benefit or burden relationship with a potential component unit *if any one* of the following is true:

- The PG has the ability to access the resources of the entity without dissolution of the entity, *or*
- The PG is legally or otherwise obligated to finance the deficits of or provide financial support (other than in exchange or exchange-like transactions) to, the organization, *or*
- The PG is obligated in some manner for the debt of the organization

(3) ABILITY TO IMPOSE WILL RELATIONSHIPS:

A primary government has the ability to impose its will (i.e., significantly influence the types and levels of services) on a potential component unit if the primary government has the substantive authority to do any one of the following:

- Remove appointed governing board members at will, *or*
- Approve or require modification of the organization's budget, *or*
- Approve or require modification of rate or fee changes affecting the organization's revenues, *or*
- Veto, overrule, or otherwise modify other governing body decisions, *or*
- Appoint, hire, reassign, or dismiss the organization's management, *or*
- Take other actions that indicate its ability to impose its will on the organization

(4) FISCAL DEPENDENCE:

An entity is *fiscally dependent* on a PG if it requires the PG's substantive approval in order to do one (or more) of the following:

- Establish its budget
- Levy taxes or set other rates or charges
- Issue bonded debt

burden relationship with the organization. The primary government (PG) **is financially accountable** for other organizations *if* **the PG has**:

- Both *appointment authority* and a *financial benefit or burden* relationship with another entity, *or*
- *Appointment authority* over another entity upon which it has *the ability to impose its will* (see Illustration 15-7), *or*

- A *financial benefit and burden* relationship with another entity that is *fiscally dependent* on the PG (as described in the illustration).

If a PG is not financially accountable for another entity, it still may be required, or choose, to treat other entities as component units for other reasons.

Holding a majority equity interest in another entity is another important reporting entity definition criterion. Although it is unusual for a government to hold a majority equity interest in a business *for the purpose of facilitating delivery of government services*, it is very common for governments to enter into joint ventures with other governments. Airports, correctional centers, bus and rail transportation, animal shelters, and economic development activities are only a few of the types of joint ventures conducted by governments around the country. The participating governments hold equity interests in many of these joint ventures. For other joint ventures, there are no equity interests. Even if a primary government is not financially accountable for an organization, it must include it as a component unit if it holds a majority equity interest in it for the purpose of delivering government services.

Fund-raising organizations are addressed primarily in GASB *Statement No. 39*, "The Financial Reporting Entity—Affiliated Organizations." This statement requires component unit treatment for any affiliated, legally separate, *tax-exempt* entity if all of the following are true.

1. The affiliated entity's economic resources entirely (or almost entirely) *benefit directly* the primary government reporting entity or its constituency.

2. *The primary government is entitled to* (or can otherwise access) the *majority of* the organization's *resources.*

3. The accessible portion of the resources is *significant to the primary government.*

The final basis for treating an organization as a component unit is ***to avoid making the financial statements misleading*** by omission of the organization. *Statement No. 61* indicates that if an organization is closely related to or financially integrated with a primary government, the primary government should evaluate whether it is misleading to exclude the organization from its reporting entity.[4]

Extensive reporting entity disclosures—including (1) the component units of a government's reporting entity, (2) the criteria used to determine which potential component units to include, and (3) other related information—are required in the notes to the financial statements. Specifically, the following disclosures are required:

Reporting Entity Disclosures

1. The component units included in the reporting entity.

2. The rationale for including each component unit.

3. Information about whether each component unit was blended, discretely presented, or included in the fiduciary fund financial statements.

4. Availability of the separate financial statements of individual component units.

INTEGRATING COMPONENT UNITS INTO THE REPORTING ENTITY

Two approaches—blending and discrete presentation—are used to incorporate most component unit data into a primary government's CAFR. *Blending* treats component units as an integral part of the primary government and essentially

---

[4]GASB *Statement No. 61*, "The Financial Reporting Entity: Omnibus, an amendment of GASB Statements No. 14 and No. 34" (GASB, November 2010) paras. 4–5.

reports component unit funds and activities as primary government funds and activities. Blended component units are included *both* in the government-wide financial statements and in the fund financial statements. *Discrete presentation* carefully separates component unit information from primary government information. Discretely presented component units are included *only* in the government-wide financial statements. Finally, fiduciary component units are reported in the appropriate column of the fiduciary fund financial statements and are not included in the government-wide financial statements.

The approach used for each component unit depends upon whether the component unit is in substance part of the primary government. *Blending is used only if a component unit is deemed to be part of the primary government in substance.* To be considered part of the substantive primary government, a component unit must have one of the following characteristics:

- It has substantively the same governing body as the primary government's governing body and either (a) there is a financial benefit or burden relationship or (b) the PG management has day-to-day operational responsibility for the component unit. (*Substantively the same governing body* means that at least a voting majority of the primary government governing body serves on a component unit governing body and also constitutes a voting majority of that component unit's governing body.[5])

- It provides services only to, or benefits only, the primary government (meaning the government itself, not its constituency).

- The component unit's total debt outstanding, including leases, is expected to be repaid entirely or almost entirely by the primary government.

Note that, by definition, the overwhelming majority of component units will not meet either of the last two criteria. Only certain types of organizations, such as building authorities, have the potential to meet the criteria in the second bullet. Organizations such as school districts, airport authorities, civic center commissions and transit authorities can be part of the substantive primary government only if the "substantively the same governing body" criterion is met. These organizations' fundamental purpose is to serve and benefit the public and entities external to the government, not the government itself. The criterion in the third bullet is quite stringent and was designed to require blending for specific financing vehicles found almost exclusively, if not exclusively, in certain state governments.

To illustrate the *substantively the same governing body* criterion, assume that a city council has seven members and a potential component unit's governing board has five members. To meet the substantively the same governing body criterion, at least four council members must serve on the component unit governing body. If only three serve, the criterion is not met. The three council members would represent a voting majority on the component unit board but not a voting majority of the city council. *The criterion requires both.* As a further example, a state's component unit must have an extremely large governing body to meet this criterion. At least one more than half of the state legislature would have to serve on the component unit governing body!

Recall that a PG does not blend a component unit just because they have substantively the same governing body. The PG and a component unit also must share a financial benefit or burden relationship to be blended. Therefore, if a city council serves as the governing board of a public service providing component unit whose management it can hire and fire and whose services rates and budget it approves, the component unit will not be blended if there is not also a financial benefit or burden relationship.

Financial data of *component units that are part of the primary government in substance are blended* with the financial data of the primary government legal entity (as are all entities that are legally part of the primary government). *All other component*

---

[5]GASB, "Comprehensive Implementation Guide" (Norwalk, CT: GASB, October 2011), pp. 4.31.1.

15-1 IN PRACTICE

Component Units, Joint Ventures, and Related Organizations

The following are the reporting entity disclosures in the City of Tulsa, Oklahoma, Basic Financial Statements (**http://www.cityoftulsa.org**) for a recent year. Users can easily compare and contrast the criteria that defines component units, joint ventures, and other related organizations.

City of Tulsa, Oklahoma
Notes to Basic Financial Statements
June 30, 20X4

A. REPORTING ENTITY

In evaluating the City as a reporting entity, management has addressed all potential component units (traditionally separate reporting entities) for which the City may be financially accountable and, as such, should be included within the City's financial statements. The City (the primary government) is financially accountable if it appoints a voting majority of the organization's governing board and (1) it is able to impose its will on the organization or (2) there is a potential for the organization to provide specific financial burden on the City. Additionally, the primary government is required to consider other organizations for which the nature and significance of their relationship with the primary government are such that exclusion would cause the reporting entity's financial statements to be misleading or incomplete.

The financial statements are formatted to allow the user to clearly distinguish between the primary government and its discretely presented component units. Because of the closeness of their relationship with the primary government, one component unit is blended as though it is part of the primary government.

1. Blended Component Units

The Tulsa Public Facilities Authority ("TPFA")—is legally separated from the City. TPFA is reported as if it were part of the primary government because its primary purpose is to issue revenue bonds to finance major capital improvements on behalf of the City. This fund is included as an internal service fund.

2. Discretely Presented Component Units

Tulsa Metropolitan Utility Authority ("TMUA")—A public trust created to provide for a water delivery utility system and wastewater utility. Trustees of TMUA are the same as those on the City's Utility Board. The City is the sole beneficiary of the trust and will receive all trust properties and resulting revenues upon retirement of all trust indebtedness. The rates for user charges and bond issuance authorization are also approved by the City Council.

Tulsa Development Authority ("TDA")—A public authority created to finance urban renewal rehabilitation and redevelopment. Commissioners of TDA are appointed by the Mayor and approved by the City Council. The City approves urban renewal plans and the City must approve all modifications to the plan. The City provides the employees for TDA and maintains TDA's accounting records. The TDA's primary source of funding is from the Community Development Block Grant program.

Tulsa Parking Authority ("TPA")—A public trust created by the City to construct and manage various parking facilities within the City. Trustees of TPA consist of the Mayor and four trustees who are appointed by the Mayor. The City provides certain resources to TPA. The City is the sole beneficiary of TPA and will receive the remaining assets of TPA upon termination.

Tulsa Authority for Recovery of Energy ("TARE")—A public trust created to provide a system of collection, transportation, and disposal of solid waste. Trustees for TARE are appointed by the Mayor and approved by the City Council. The City participates in management decisions and acts as a collection agent by collecting TARE revenues as part of the City's utility bill.

Tulsa Airports—Tulsa Airports Improvement Trust ("TAIT") and Tulsa Airports Authority ("TAA") operate and maintain the City's two airports, Tulsa International and Richard L. Jones, Jr. Airports, and finance capital improvements. The Tulsa International and Richard L. Jones, Jr. Airports have been combined with TAIT and are included in the Airports fund. The purpose of TAIT is to fund airport improvements through the issuance of revenue bonds. All improvements are leased by TAIT to TAA and become the property of the City upon termination of the lease. The City is also designated as the sole beneficiary of the trust. TAIT and TAA trustees are appointed by the Mayor and approved by the City Council.

Tulsa Performing Arts Center Trust ("TPACT")—A public trust created to assist the City in operating the Tulsa Performing Arts Center and to sponsor events promoting the use of the Tulsa Performing Arts Center. Trustees are appointed by the Mayor and approved by the City Council. The City is the sole beneficiary of the Trust.

Metropolitan Tulsa Transit Authority ("MTTA")—A public trust created to provide public transportation systems and facilities. The Mayor appoints trustees of MTTA. The City is the sole beneficiary and finances a significant portion of annual operations and MTTA cannot incur indebtedness in excess of $100 within a year without the City's approval.

The component unit major fund statements and the nonmajor combining statements reflect these discretely presented units. Separate financial statements for the individual component units are available upon request to the City's Controller, 200 Civic Center, Suite 901, Tulsa, OK 74103.

Governmental accounting standards require reasonable separation between the Primary Government (including its blended components units) and its discretely presented component units, both in the financial statements and in the related notes and required supplementary information. Because the discretely presented component units, although legally separate, have been and are operated as if each is part of the primary government,

(continued)

(Continued)

City of Tulsa, Oklahoma
Notes to Basic Financial Statements
June 30, 20X4

there are limited instances where special note reference or separation will be required. If no separate note reference or categorization is made, the user should assume that information presented is equally applicable.

B. JOINT VENTURES AND RELATED ORGANIZATIONS

1. Joint Ventures

A joint venture is a legal entity or other organization that results from a contractual agreement and that is owned, operated, or governed by two or more participants as a separate and specific activity subject to joint control in which the participants retain (a) an ongoing financial interest or (b) an ongoing financial responsibility.

The City participates in the following joint ventures:

Emergency Medical Services Authority ("EMSA")— EMSA is a public trust created to provide emergency medical care and transportation and is governed by a ten-member board composed of five appointees from the City and five from other Oklahoma cities and towns. In accordance with the joint venture agreement, Tulsa and Oklahoma City are entitled to their respective share of annual operating income or loss. The City's net investment in EMSA is $9,630 resulting from EMSA's net income in 20X4 and previous years. Complete financial statements for EMSA can be obtained from the Executive Director of EMSA, 1417 North Lansing, Tulsa, Oklahoma 74106.

River Parks Authority ("RPA")—The City is a participant with Tulsa County in a joint venture to operate and maintain a park along the Arkansas River. RPA, a trust, was created for that purpose. The City and Tulsa County contribute to the annual operating budget of RPA. The Board of Trustees is comprised of seven members, three appointed by the City, three appointed by the County, and one by the Tulsa Metropolitan Area Planning Commission. Complete financial statements for RPA can be obtained from the Executive Director, 717 S. Houston, Suite 10, Tulsa, Oklahoma 74127. The City does not have an equity interest in this organization.

2. Related Organizations

The City's officials are also responsible for appointing the board members of other organizations; however the City's accountability for those organizations does not extend beyond the making of appointments.

The following organizations are related organizations that are excluded from the reporting entity:

Tulsa Industrial Authority ("TIA")—The Mayor of the City is an ex officio trustee and the additional six trustees are appointed by the Mayor and approved by the City Council. TIA issues industrial development bonds for private enterprises after approval by the City Council. The bonds do not constitute debt of the City and are collateralized solely by the revenues of the commercial organizations upon whose behalf the bonds are issued.

The Tulsa Metropolitan Chamber of Commerce operates TIA and the City assumes no responsibility for the operating expenses.

Tulsa Housing Authority ("THA")—Commissioners of the Authority are appointed by the Mayor; however, the City does not provide funding, has no obligation for the debt issued by THA, and cannot impose its will.

City of Tulsa/Rogers County Port Authority ("TRCPA")— The City appoints six of the nine Board members of TRCPA. The City does not provide any funding to TRCPA.

Tulsa City-County Health Department—The City appoints five of the nine City-County Health Department Board members. The City does not provide any funding to the Tulsa City-County Health Department.

Tulsa City-County Library—The Tulsa City-County Library Board is composed of eleven members, of which the City appoints six. The City does not provide any funding to the Tulsa City-County Library.

3. Jointly Governed Organizations

The following organization is a jointly governed organization that is excluded from the City's reporting entity. This organization is not a joint venture because the City does not retain an on-going financial interest or an on-going financial responsibility.

The City, in conjunction with Tulsa County and other municipalities, has created the following organization:

Tulsa County Criminal Justice Authority ("TCCJA")—The TCCJA was created for the purpose of acquiring a site and erecting, furnishing, equipping, operating, maintaining, remodeling, and repairing a county jail and other detention facilities owned or operated by Tulsa County. TCCJA is administered by a seven person Board of Trustees comprised of three Tulsa County Commissioners, the Mayor of the City of Tulsa ("Ex Officio Trustees"), and the Mayors of three additional cities situated in whole or in part within the limits of Tulsa County. The City does not provide any funding to the TCCJA.

units—those that are not part of the substantive primary government—*are discretely presented*. GASB *Statement No. 39* specifically requires discrete presentation of component units that are included in the reporting entity under its requirements. Both blending and discrete presentation are described in the following sections.

Blending incorporates the data of the blended component units into the financial statements as if the primary government legal entity and all of the blended component units were a single legal entity. Blended component units data are included in both the fund financial statements and the government-wide financial statements. Accordingly, the primary government combines the data of the various blended component units with the data of the appropriate fund types and GCA-GLTL accounts of the primary government legal entity. Some blended component units are reported as a single fund. Other blended component units are reported in several funds. In general, blended component unit funds are reported as the same types of funds in the statements of the primary government legal entity.

Blending

The single fund classification exception is that *the component unit's General Fund is treated as a Special Revenue Fund* of the primary government when blended. This classification reflects that the resources of the component unit's General Fund are to be used only for the purposes of that component unit. Hence, the General Fund of the legal entity is the General Fund of the primary government of the reporting entity.

Each blended component unit fund that is a major fund of the primary government should be presented in a separate column in the fund financial statements. The general capital assets and general long-term liabilities of a blended component unit are reported along with the other governmental activities capital assets and long-term liabilities in the government-wide financial statements.

The GASB states that the data of the blended entity—that is, the substantive primary government—are the focal point of interest for users of a government's financial reports. For many (if not most) governments, this entity will include only the legal entity; that is, it will not have any blended component units.

Discrete presentation reports component unit data along with, but separate from, primary government data in the *government-wide* financial statements. Discrete presentation is required for most component units. This reporting approach assumes that discretely presented component units are of secondary interest to financial statement users. Therefore, a broad overview of these component units' financial position and operating results supposedly will provide sufficient information for fair presentation within the reporting entity context.

Discrete Presentation

Discretely presented component units (which do not include component units that are fiduciary in nature) are included in the government-wide financial statements, as shown in Chapter 13. They are not included in fund financial statements. Fiduciary component units such as legally separate pension plans are reported in the fiduciary funds financial statements. The component unit data that are incorporated in the government-wide financial statements are based on the entity-wide total data of the component units (including data from the component units' own component units, if any).

Governments must report the data of discretely presented component units in a manner that clearly indicates that they are not part of the primary government. Thus, each government-wide financial statement presents the primary government "Governmental Activities" and "Business-Type Activities" under a "Primary Government" heading. A separate (discrete) "Component Units" column usually aggregates all of a government's discretely presented component units. At the other extreme, each discretely presented component unit may be reported in a separate column. Various degrees of aggregation of component units are permissible between these two extremes.

GASB *Statement No. 61* indicates that factors such as the importance of the services provided by the component unit, the significance of transactions with the primary government, and whether there is a significant financial benefit or burden relationship between the entities typically determine which component units a government should consider to be "major" component units. Governments must disclose certain information about *major* discretely presented component units in the Basic Financial Statements or the notes to those statements. Most governments meet this requirement by either:

- Disclosing condensed financial statements for each major component unit in the notes to the financial statements. The minimum detail to be disclosed in the condensed financial statements note is outlined in Illustration 15-8.
- Presenting combining major component unit financial statements immediately after the fund financial statements.

In most situations, discrete component units also prepare their own external financial statements. In these situations, the reporting required in the primary government's report is limited to the presentations in its government-wide financial statements, perhaps with some note disclosures as indicated previously. However, if the primary government's report is the *only* external financial reporting for the component unit, then additional component unit information is required in the fund financial statements and the note disclosures.

For example, assume that a discrete component unit has its own fund structure internally and that separate external financial statements are *not* prepared

---

ILLUSTRATION 15-8   Condensed Financial Statements Note Requirements

Major Discretely Presented Component Units
Minimum Condensed Financial Statement Disclosures

CONDENSED STATEMENT OF NET POSITION

- Total Assets—Distinguished between
    Capital assets
    Other assets, with separate reporting of amounts
    receivable from the PG or other component units
- Total Liabilities—Distinguished between
    Long-term debt outstanding
    Other liabilities, with separate reporting of amounts
    payable from the PG or other component units
- Total Net Position—Distinguished between
    Unrestricted net position
    Restricted net position
    Net investment in capital assets

CONDENSED STATEMENT OF ACTIVITIES

- Expenses (by major functions or programs and for depreciation expense, if separately reported)
- Program revenues (by type, e.g., charges for services, capital grants, and operating grants)
- Net program (expense) revenue
- Tax revenues (which are general revenues by definition)
- Other nontax general revenues
- Contributions to endowments and Permanent Fund principal
- Special items and extraordinary items
- Change in net position
- Beginning net position
- Ending net position

CONDENSED STATEMENT OF CASH FLOWS

- Net cash provided (used) by:
    Operating activities
    Noncapital financing activities
    Capital and related financing activities
    Investing activities
- Beginning cash and cash equivalent balances
- Ending cash and cash equivalent balances

Additional Required Major Component Unit Disclosures

- The nature and amount of significant transactions with the primary government
- The nature and amount of significant transactions with other component units

for the entity. The primary government would need to include, at a minimum, separate fund reporting within the financial section of the CAFR for the discrete component unit's major funds and for any of its Internal Service and fiduciary funds by type. Accordingly, certain material note disclosures for the discrete component unit would need to be incorporated into the note disclosures of the primary government, being certain that the primary government disclosures are always differentiated from any disclosures related to major component units.

Dual Reporting Entity Model

The substance of the reporting requirements for component units is that blending some component units and discretely presenting others creates a dual reporting entity definition. The blended reporting entity is called the *primary government* and is the focal point of the report. Indeed, it is to report on this focal entity that a government issues its financial statements. When the discretely presented component units (DPCUs) are added to the blended entity, it creates a second "entity perspective" that the GASB refers to as the *reporting entity*. The GASB makes it clear that this extension of the entity that is referred to as discretely presented component units is of secondary, not primary, interest.

This secondary entity component is often very significant, sometimes even larger in the aggregate than the focal entity (i.e., the primary government blended entity). Information from a recent analysis of the financial reports of the 50 states provides a perspective of how frequent and how significant component units are. It highlights the importance of ensuring that the focal entity, the primary government, is properly defined. The statistics in 15-2 In Practice provide this information. The size of the DPCUs relative to the primary government focal entity is remarkable. Eleven states had discretely presented component unit total liabilities in excess of the primary government total liabilities. On average states have 16.9 discretely presented component units and 3.5 blended component units.[6]

Other Issues

Several other issues must be addressed in combining the data of multiple component units into a single reporting entity report. These issues include:

- Transactions between the primary government and a blended component unit as well as transactions between various blended component units should be reclassified and reported as interfund activity.

- Except for interfund loans, transactions involving discretely presented component units are reported as if they were transactions with entities outside of the reporting entity. Therefore, subsidies provided by a primary government to a component unit (or vice

15-2 IN PRACTICE

State Component Unit Data

Average number of discretely presented component units (DPCU) per state	16.9
Average number of blended component units per state	3.5
Average Total DPCU Assets divided by Total Primary Government (PG) Assets	43%
Average Total DPCU Liabilities divided by Total PG Liabilities	60%
Average Total DPCU Revenues divided by Total PG Revenues	17%
Average Total DPCU Expenses divided by Total PG Expenses	16%

[6]The study was conducted by Craig D. Shoulders and was presented to the GASB as part of its board package in August 2007.

versa) and transfers between discretely presented component units must be reported as transfers, not as revenues and expenses.

- The government-wide financial statements are *permitted* to include a reporting entity total column to the right of the component units column. This *optional* column would aggregate the data in the primary government column with that in the component unit column(s).

Finally, the GASB *Codification* provides guidance for primary governments with component units that have differing fiscal years. When component units have differing fiscal years, the reporting entity financial statements are prepared for the primary government's fiscal year and include component unit data for the other component unit fiscal years ended either (1) during the primary government's fiscal year, or (2) within the first quarter after the primary government's fiscal year end if accurate component unit data are available on a timely basis.

SEPARATE ISSUANCE OF PRIMARY GOVERNMENT FINANCIAL STATEMENTS

The GASB acknowledges that in some instances a government may find it desirable to issue a financial report that covers its primary government but does not incorporate the data of discretely presented component units. However, the GASB clearly states that such financial reports do *not* conform with GAAP.

RELATED ORGANIZATIONS, JOINT VENTURES, AND JOINTLY GOVERNED ORGANIZATIONS

A final reporting entity related issue is accounting and reporting for entities that are not component units but with which an SLG participates or has certain types of relationships. Such external entities are classified into three broad categories: related organizations, joint ventures, and jointly governed organizations.

1. *Related organizations* are organizations that were excluded from the reporting entity because, although the *appointment authority criterion* was *met,* the primary government is *not financially accountable* for the organization—that is, the primary government does not have the ability to impose its will over the potential component unit and does not have a financial benefit or burden relationship with it.

2. *Jointly governed organizations* are potential component units that are subject to the *joint control* of two or more other entities, but for which the primary government has neither an ongoing financial interest nor an ongoing financial responsibility. Joint control implies that the primary government does not appoint a voting majority of the potential component unit governing body. (Another participant in the organization may appoint a voting majority of its governing body, however, and may treat it as a component unit.)

3. *Joint ventures* are like jointly governed organizations except the *primary government has either an ongoing financial interest or an ongoing financial responsibility*.

   - An *ongoing financial interest* is evidenced by the primary government having an equity interest (an explicit and measurable right to joint venture net assets that is set forth in the joint venture agreement) or another arrangement under which the primary government can access the joint venture net resources.

   - An *ongoing financial responsibility* exists if the primary government is obligated in some manner for the joint venture debts or if the joint venture cannot continue to exist without the continued financing of the primary government.

For related organizations and jointly governed organizations, a government must disclose required related party transactions information. Additionally, a government is to disclose the nature of its accountability for its related organizations.

Recall that a primary government treats joint ventures in which it has a majority equity interest for the purpose of directly enhancing delivery of government services as a component unit. A government is required to report its *joint venture* participation as follows:

- The explicit and measurable amount of any equity interest in a joint venture is reported as an asset of either governmental or business-type activities, as appropriate, in the government-wide Statement of Net Position—even if the joint venture also is reported as a discretely presented component unit.

- Changes in the government's equity interests in joint ventures are presented as a single line item in the government-wide Statement of Activities—even if the joint venture also is reported as a discretely presented component unit.

- *Proprietary fund joint venture equity interests* are reported in the investing proprietary fund using the equity method.

- *Governmental fund joint venture equity interests* are reported:

  1. As governmental fund assets (or liabilities) only if they represent financial resources receivable or payable.

  2. As governmental fund revenues and expenditures only if the governmental fund revenue and expenditure recognition criteria are met.

  3. In the notes to the extent that the equity interest of governmental fund joint venture investments exceeds the amount to be reported in the governmental funds.

- The notes to the financial statements also should provide:

  1. A general description of each joint venture, including any ongoing financial interest in or responsibility for the joint venture and information on whether the joint venture is either accumulating significant financial resources or experiencing fiscal stress. (Such conditions may give rise to an additional financial benefit or burden in the future.)

  2. Any other required related party transactions information.

Concluding Comments

This chapter focuses initially on accounting and reporting issues associated with understanding the nature and content of the Comprehensive Annual Financial Report in a simple entity context. Next, unique issues arising with more complex entity structures are considered. The recently revised criteria for determining which associated entities are component units and how component unit information must be reported are discussed and illustrated in some detail. Reporting and disclosure of other associated organizations that are not component units also are discussed briefly.

Chapters 2 through 15 focus on state and local government accounting and financial reporting. As we conclude this series of chapters we should emphasize—as presented in the top portion of Illustration 15-9—that much of the content of Chapters 2 through 15 dealt with the **Preparation Funnel**. That is:

- We dealt initially—in Chapters 3–8 and 10–12—with *individual* **fund** accounting and preparing *individual* **fund** financial statements.

- Then, in Chapter 13, our focus was on the **Basic** Financial Statements—with emphasis on the *major* **fund** financial statements, **government-wide** financial statements, and **MD&A**.

- Next, in Chapter 14, we learned how to **derive** the government-wide financial statements from the fund financial information and the general capital assets and general long-term liabilities data (Chapter 9).

We also dealt with the **Financial Reporting Pyramid**, which is summarized in the bottom portion of Illustration 15-9. Note that the financial reporting pyramid is essentially the inverse of the preparation funnel. That is:

- The *Preparation Funnel* proceeds from accounting to preparation of fund financial statements and schedules, then to preparing the major fund and government-wide financial statements and, finally, Management's Discussion and Analysis—going from the detailed to the summarized.

- The *Financial Reporting Pyramid* presents the most summarized information first, the MD&A—followed by the somewhat more detailed government-wide financial

ILLUSTRATION 15-9   The Preparation "Funnel" and the Financial Reporting "Pyramid"

–Preparation Funnel–

Accounting & Financial Statement Preparation Detailed-to-Summary Preparation Steps (1–10)

1) Transaction Data — The Accounting System

2) Individual Fund Financial Statements & Schedules

3) Nonmajor Fund Combining Financial Statements & Schedules

4) Other Supplementary Information (e.g., Compliance-Related Schedules)

5) Required Supplementary Information (RSI) — In Addition to MD&A —

6) Notes to the Financial Statements

7) Major Fund Financial Statements

8) Conversion Adjustments Worksheet

9) Government-Wide Financial Statements

10) MD&A (RSI)

–Financial Reporting Pyramid–

Financial Reporting— Summary-to-Detailed Presentations (1–9)

1) MD&A (RSI)

2) Government-Wide Financial Statements

3) Major Fund Financial Statements

4) Notes to the Financial Statements

5) Required Supplementary Information (RSI) — In Addition to MD&A —

6) Other Supplementary Information (e.g., Compliance-Related Schedules)

7) Nonmajor Fund Combining Financial Statements & Schedules

8) Individual Fund Financial Statements & Schedules

9) Special Purpose Financial Statements & Schedules

CAFR Financial Section

MEFR

BFS

CAFR = *Comprehensive* Annual Financial Report

BFS = *Basic* Financial Statements

MEFR = *Minimum* External Financial Reporting

statements, then the significantly more detailed major fund financial statements, and finally the much more detailed combining and individual fund financial statements and schedules—going from the summarized to the detailed.

Finally, in this chapter we focused on the CAFR and on identifying and incorporating component units in a government's financial statements as well as disclosing other associated entities.

This chapter concludes our coverage of financial reporting for state and local governments generally. Chapter 16 covers accounting for not-for-profit organizations that are not government entities in accordance with the Financial Accounting Standards Board's not-for-profit accounting standards. Chapters 17 and 18 discuss college and university reporting and hospital reporting, respectively, for both government and nongovernment organizations. Chapter 19 addresses financial reporting for the federal government. Chapter 20 deals with auditing in the government and not-for-profit environments.

Questions

Q15-1 Distinguish between the content and purpose(s) of the Basic Financial Statements and the Comprehensive Annual Financial Report (CAFR).

Q15-2 Distinguish between the contents and purposes of Management's Discussion and Analysis and a transmittal letter.

Q15-3 Distinguish between Basic Financial Statements and combining statements.

Q15-4 What is the purpose(s) of the notes to the financial statements? The narrative explanations?

Q15-5 What is the purpose(s) of schedules, as contrasted with statements? Are schedules necessary for reporting in conformity with GAAP?

Q15-6 What is the purpose(s) of statistical tables as contrasted with that (those) of financial statements? What are the broad categories of information included in the statistical tables?

Q15-7 Prospect resident Mickey Locklear became concerned when reviewing the City of Prospect annual report because the amount of property taxes reported for the governmental funds in the Governmental Funds Statement of Revenues, Expenditures, and Changes in Fund Balances differs significantly from the amount of property taxes reported for governmental activities in the government-wide Statement of Activities. The resident is certain an error has occurred and calls it to the attention of Mayor Carol Hunt, who immediately calls in the chief accountant, Sheila Prevatte, to explain how such an error has occurred. Can such a discrepancy exist under generally accepted accounting principles applicable to governments? Explain.

Q15-8 (a) What is a joint venture? (b) Under what circumstances must a government apply the special joint venture accounting and disclosure requirements set forth in the GASB *Codification*? (c) What are those requirements?

Q15-9 Explain the "ability to impose will" criterion. How does it affect the determination of a government's financial reporting entity?

Q15-10 What is required for a potential component unit to be fiscally dependent on a primary government? When is a fiscally dependent entity treated as a component unit?

Q15-11 What makes a government financially accountable for another entity?

Q15-12 Distinguish between blending and discrete presentation.

Q15-13 What conditions must be met for a component unit to be blended?

Q15-14 Are blended component units reported in the fund financial statements that are part of the Basic Financial Statements? Are discretely presented component units reported in those statements?

Q15-15 Under what circumstances does GASB *Statement No. 39* require a primary government to treat an affiliated, tax-exempt organization as a component unit? Would the affiliated organization be blended?

Q15-16 A county has a legally separate parks commission that it reports as a component unit because the county board of commissioners serves as the board of the parks commission and the county can impose its will on the commission. Assuming none of the other reporting entity definition criteria are met, may the county blend the parks commission data with its primary government data? Explain.

Q15-17 What do the authors mean when they suggest that governments have a dual reporting entity model? Do you agree? Justify your response.

Exercises

E15-1 (Multiple Choice) Identify the best answer for each of the following:

1. The statistical section of a comprehensive annual financial report (CAFR)
   a. is required for fair presentation of a government's financial position and operating results.
   b. is required in the CAFR.
   c. is composed solely of 10-year historical trend information.
   d. is an optional section of the CAFR.

2. A county transit authority is fiscally dependent upon the county because the transit authority—a legally separate entity—cannot set its fares without the substantive approval of the county commission. Given this scenario, in which of the following situations would the transit authority be deemed financially accountable to and thus a component unit of the county?
   1. The appointment authority criterion, but no other additional criteria, are met.
   2. The appointment authority and the ability to impose its will criteria are met.
   3. The authority has a separately elected governing board, but the financial benefit or burden criteria are met.
      a. Situation 1 only
      b. Situation 2 only
      c. Situation 3 only
      d. Two of the situations

3. In which of the following circumstances would a potential component unit *always* be fiscally dependent upon a city?
   a. The city is the sole source of revenue of the potential component unit.
   b. The city provides more than 75% of the revenues of the potential component unit.
   c. The city provides more than 50% of the revenues of the potential component unit.
   d. The city must approve the budget of the potential component unit.

4. In which of the following circumstances would a city be viewed as having appointed members of a potential component unit's governing body for the purposes of determining if the appointment criterion has been met?
   a. The mayor appoints members.
   b. The council and mayor jointly appoint members.
   c. The city finance director appoints members.
   d. All of the above.

5. If a government both created and can abolish a potential component unit, it is financially accountable for that other entity
   a. unless the potential component unit has a separately elected governing body.
   b. if it is fiscally dependent on the government.
   c. unless it is unlikely that the government would ever exercise its authority to abolish the potential component unit.
   d. if it has the ability to impose its will over the potential component unit or has a financial benefit or burden relationship with it.

6. A state college treats the university foundation as a component unit in accordance with GASB *Statement No. 39*. The college is a component unit of the state. The foundation would be included in the state reporting entity
   a. only if financially accountable to the state government.
   b. only if fiscally dependent on the state.
   c. under no circumstances.
   d. regardless of other facts.

7. Assuming that a government has some discretely presented component units that have only proprietary activities and others that have only governmental fund activities, a "Component Units" column must be presented in which of the government's Basic Financial Statements?
   a. Governmental funds financial statements
   b. Proprietary funds financial statements
   c. Government-wide financial statements
   d. Governmental funds and proprietary funds financial statements

8. In which of the following situations would blending be required under GAAP?
   a. The primary government appoints the voting majority of the component unit governing body, can impose its will on the component unit, and has financial benefit or burden relationships with it.
   b. The component unit provides services entirely or almost entirely to the primary government.
   c. The component unit provides services entirely or almost entirely to the citizenry of the primary government.
   d. The component unit has substantively the same governing body as the primary government.

9. All of the following information would be included in the financial section of a CAFR *except* the
   a. letter of transmittal.
   b. Management's Discussion and Analysis.
   c. independent auditor's report.
   d. notes to the financial statements.

10. Which of the following is *not* a required category of information included in the statistical section of a CAFR?
    a. Financial trends information
    b. Revenue capacity information
    c. Debt capacity information
    d. Receivable trends information

E15-2 (Multiple Choice) Identify the best answer for each of the following:

1. The introductory section of the CAFR would potentially include all of the following information *except*
   a. a listing of key officials.
   b. a letter of transmittal.
   c. the table of contents.
   d. Management's Discussion and Analysis.

2. A combining statement would be required to be included in a CAFR for which of the following scenarios?
   a. There are multiple major Enterprise Funds.
   b. There are multiple Internal Service Funds.
   c. There are multiple major governmental funds.
   d. There are multiple major Enterprise Funds and an Internal Service Fund.

3. Which of the following statements regarding the reporting of individual fund financial statements is *true*?
   a. Detailed budgetary information for the General Fund may be included as an individual fund financial statement even though a budgetary statement is also included in the Basic Financial Statements.
   b. A government may decide to include individual fund financial statements for one fund but not other individual funds of the same fund type.
   c. Budgetary comparisons for an Enterprise Fund may be reported as an individual fund financial schedule.
   d. All of the above statements are true.

Questions 4, 5, 6, 7, and 8 are based on the following scenario:

Chestnut County has the following:
   One General Fund
   Three major Special Revenue Funds
   One nonmajor Special Revenue Fund
   Two major Capital Projects Funds
   Two major Enterprise Funds
   One nonmajor Enterprise Fund
   Two Internal Service Funds
   One Pension Trust Fund
   One Agency Fund
   One blended component unit
   Two discretely presented component units

Further assume that the blended component unit itself has a General Fund and a Capital Projects Fund, each of which meets the criteria for a major fund.

4. How many columns *at a minimum* would be reported on the face of Chestnut County's government-wide Statement of Net Position?
   a. 2
   b. 3
   c. 4
   d. 5

5. How many *major* Special Revenue Funds would the County report in the governmental funds financial statements?
   a. 1
   b. 3
   c. 4
   d. 5

6. Assume Chestnut County prepares a CAFR. *Combining* financial statements would be required for
   a. Internal Service Funds only.
   b. Special Revenue Funds only.
   c. all governmental fund types.
   d. Enterprise Funds only.

7. How many major fund columns will be reported in the governmental funds financial statements?
   a. 4
   b. 6
   c. 7
   d. 8

8. Which of the following reporting options for Chestnut County's discretely presented component units would *not* be allowed by GAAP?
   a. Assuming the discretely presented component units are governmental in nature, each would be subject to major fund reporting in the fund financial statements.
   b. The discretely presented component units would be reported in either one or two separate columns on the Statement of Net Position.
   c. Discretely presented component units are *never* reported as part of the primary government.
   d. A total primary government column is presented *before* the presentation for the discrete component units.

9. *Potential* component units that are ultimately excluded from the reporting entity but require at least minimal disclosure in the financial statements could include all of the following *except*
   a. related organizations.
   b. jointly governed organizations.
   c. joint ventures.
   d. All of the above require at least minimal note disclosures.

10. The CAFR *must* include all of the following *except*
    a. a compliance section.
    b. a financial section.
    c. a statistical section.
    d. an introductory section.

E15-3 (Combining Financial Statements) Bowles County's fund structure is as follows:

General Fund

Three Special Revenue Funds

One Capital Projects Fund

Two Debt Service Funds

Three Internal Service Funds

Five Enterprise Funds

Assume that Special Revenue Fund #1, the Capital Projects Fund, Enterprise Fund #1, and Enterprise Fund #4 are major funds.

Required
a. List the combining financial statements required in the Bowles County CAFR.
b. List the headings of the columns that should be included in each combining statement.

E15-4 Which of the following cases meet the substantively the same governing body criterion? Is this sufficient to indicate that a component unit should be blended in a city's financial statements instead of discretely presented? Explain.
1. The city council appoints all members of the governing board of the component unit.
2. The city council also serves as the governing board of the component unit.
3. The 5 city council members all serve on the governing board of the component unit. The component unit board has 12 members.
4. The 5 city council members, the city manager, and the city finance director all serve on the governing board of the component unit on an ex officio basis. The component unit board has 12 members.
5. The component unit governing body consists of 3 of the 7 elected council members of the city.

E15-5 Which of the following sets of circumstances require a government to treat another entity as a component unit of its reporting entity? Why?
1. The government appoints 3 of the 7 members of the governing body of the other entity, guarantees substantial portions of its debt, and must approve its tax rate.
2. The government appoints 5 of the 7 members of the governing body of the other entity, guarantees a limited portion of its debt, and does not have substantive approval authority over its budget, its tax rate, or its debt issuances.

3. The government appoints 4 of the 7 members of the governing body of the other entity, annually provides in excess of 50% of its financing in nonexchange transactions, but has no direct authority over its operations or budget. Also, the other entity is a not-for-profit organization.
4. The government created the organization to perform key functions that it believed could be performed more effectively by a separate organization. The government does not appoint any board members but does have substantive approval authority over the hiring of key management personnel. If desired in the future, the government can take over the entity's operations and eliminate the other entity.

Problems

P15-1 (Notes to the Financial Statements) Obtain a recent CAFR or the Basic Financial Statements of a state or local government (SLG).

Study the Basic Financial Statements and related notes, make a copy of or prepare a table of contents to the notes, and answer the following questions from a note disclosure perspective:
1. What information can one learn about the state or local government from the notes that is not apparent from the face of the financial statements?
2. Pretend there were no notes. To what extent would the Basic Financial Statements be less useful? Why?
3. Which notes did you find the most interesting and useful? Why?
4. Which notes did you consider less useful? Why?

Required

P15-2 (CAFR Analysis) Obtain a copy of a recent CAFR of a state or local government. Evaluate the contents of the CAFR based on Illustration 15-1. Include in your brief analysis your observations with respect to:
1. *Introductory Section*
   a. Are the components required by the GASB present?
   b. What other items are included?
   c. Overall, how useful do you think this section is to the CAFR users?
2. *Financial Section*
   a. Auditor's report
      1) Compare it to the report of independent accountants in Illustration 15-2. How is it similar? How does it differ?
      2) Do any aspects of the report differ from what you expected? Explain.
   b. Basic Financial Statements
      1) Are all required Basic Financial Statements present? Do you observe any statements or statement items that differ from what you expected? Explain.
      2) Notes to the financial statements—Compare the types of notes presented to those listed in Illustration 13-14. What notes are presented that are not listed in that illustration? What notes listed in Illustration 13-14 are not presented?
   c. Combining and individual fund statements and schedules
      1) Statements—Are all of the required financial statements presented? Note the specific types of Special Revenue Funds, particularly any that differ from what you expect.
      2) Schedules—What types of schedules are presented? Were any schedules presented to demonstrate legal compliance?
3. *Statistical Section*
   a. Are all of the items listed in Illustration 15-1 present? What other informational presentations are included?
   b. What do you find most interesting in the statistical section? What do you consider most useful to one attempting to understand the government?

P15-3 (Incorporation of Component Units) Maynor County officials have concluded that several legally separate entities must be included as component units of its reporting entity in its CAFR. Three of those entities and the funds used to account for them are:

Puryear Corner School District
  General Fund
  Gymnasium Construction Fund
  Educational Buildings Improvement Fund
  Gymnasium Debt Service Fund
  Payroll Withholding Fund
  Food Services Enterprise Fund
  Central Printing Services Fund

Dalen-Fricke-Maynor Tri-County Airport Authority (Enterprise Fund)

Maynor County Public Employee Retirement System

The Maynor County board of commissioners also serves as the governing board of the Maynor County public employee retirement system, and the county appoints the voting majority of the board of the airport authority. The school board is elected.

Required   Indicate the reporting entity fund type (if any) in which each of the funds listed previously for the component units of Maynor County should be reported. Explain the reasons for your answer in detail.

P15-4 (Component Unit Identification and Reporting) The relationships between a county and several potential component units are outlined as follows.

Harrington County is organized under the county executive form of government, as provided by state law. Under this form of government, the policies concerning the financial and business affairs of the county are determined by the County Board of Supervisors. The Board is composed of eight elected members who serve four-year terms. The Board appoints a county executive who is the government's chief administrative officer and executes the Board's policies and programs. All but two of the following component units issue separately audited financial statements. The School Board and Adult Detention Center do not prepare separate financial reports at this time.

Potential Component Unit	Description of Activities and Relationship to the County
Mensah City Recreation Center	Derives revenue from a special levy on personal property and real estate within the district and user fees. Assists and advises County Board on management and planning of levy district and its recreation center. County appoints majority of board, guarantees debt.
District Home Board	Agreement between five jurisdictions. Establishes policy for operation of two district homes. Each county appoints a board member. No other formal relationships or responsibilities.
Northern Region Health Center Commission	County Board resolution created a commission for the operation of a nursing home pursuant to state code. Develops and establishes policies for the operation of a nursing home. Appoints two of the five commission board members. Another cooperating county appoints two other board members. The governor appoints the fifth member.
Maysami Regional Special Education Program	Agreement between three school districts to foster cooperation in the development and delivery of special education programs and other appropriate educational services. Each district appoints one-third of the program's board and subsidizes one-third of any operating deficiency.
Adult Detention Center (ADC)	Establishes policy for operation of regional adult detention center providing care and confinement for all County and adjoining city prisoners. Majority of Center Board is appointed by County; County hires management officials.
Park Authority	Established by County Board resolution. Acquires, develops, maintains, and operates park and recreation areas according to Authority and County Board comprehensive plans. Majority of County Board serves as the board of the authority. Financial benefit/burden relationship exists. Authority provides services to the County.
County Parkway District	Exercises the powers and duties enumerated in the state code related to the transportation improvement district. Majority of District Board is appointed by County; financial benefit/burden relationship exists.
Harrington County School Board	School Board is selected by popular election but has no taxing authority. Most resources are provided by the county, which has budget approval authority over the school board budget.

Required

a. Determine which of the potential component units the county should report as component units in its financial report. Explain the basis for your decision. If additional information is needed to make this determination for a potential component unit, state what information is needed.

b. For each component unit, indicate whether it should be blended or discretely reported. Explain. If additional information is needed to make this determination for a potential component unit, state what information is needed.

c. For each component unit, indicate whether more detail must be presented in the county's CAFR than the information in the combining component unit financial statements.

P15-5 (Identifying and Reporting Component Units) The City of Duncanville has four potential component units. The finance department staff is trying to determine which, if any, of these entities to include in the city's financial reporting entity. For each entity that is included in the city reporting entity, the staff must also determine whether it must be blended or discretely presented.

Additional Information

1. The Duncanville School District has a separately elected school board that governs the school district. By law, all school board members must reside within the Duncanville city limits. The district establishes its own budget, but its property tax levy must be approved by the Duncanville City Council. The city does not guarantee the debt of the schools or have any other authority over the school district.

2. The Greater Duncanville Natural Gas Cooperative is governed by a seven-member board. The city appoints the seven members of the utility's governing board and can remove them at will. The city approves the cooperative's budget as well as its rate structure. The utility cannot issue bonded debt without the city council's approval. The city is entitled to, and regularly receives, the operating surpluses of the utility.

3. The Duncanville Library District owns and operates all public libraries in the City of Duncanville. The members of the Duncanville City Council are designated by the District's charter as the board members of the Duncanville Library District. The district receives most of its funding from the city, and the city guarantees the district's long-term indebtedness.

4. The Duncanville Financing Authority's governing board is appointed by the city council. The Authority provides the financing for most of the city's water and wastewater projects. The Authority's resources come from lease agreements with the Water and Sewer Department of the City of Duncanville. The Authority does not provide financing arrangements for any other entities.

The funds and other accounts that each of these four entities uses for accounting and financial reporting (in its separate report) are as follows:

- Duncanville School District—General Fund, Special Revenue Fund, Capital Projects Fund, General Capital Assets and General Long-Term Liabilities accounts
- Greater Duncanville Natural Gas Cooperative—Enterprise Fund
- Duncanville Library District—General Fund, Special Revenue Fund, Permanent Fund, General Capital Assets and General Long-Term Liabilities accounts
- Duncanville Financing Authority—Enterprise Fund

Required

Evaluate each of these four legally separate entities. For each entity, determine (and explain your conclusions):

a. If it is a component unit of the City of Duncanville.

b. How each component unit identified will be reported in the government-wide financial statements.

c. How each component unit identified will be reported in the fund financial statements.

P15-6 (Blending and Discrete Presentation) Provide a brief analysis of the following and answer the related questions:

a. Describe discrete presentation in the context of the government-wide statements. Assume that a government has three discretely presented component units. The component units are a utility operation, a hospital, and a school district. What are the reporting options available on the government-wide financial statements? On the fund financial statements? What are the reporting entity note disclosure requirements? What other note disclosures may be required for each of the discrete component units?

b. Describe blending. When is it required? Is it permitted under other circumstances (i.e., is it ever optional)? How do blended component units affect the government-wide financial statements? The fund financial statements? What are the reporting entity note disclosure requirements? What other note disclosures may be required?

P15-7 (Sections of the CAFR) Indicate in which section of the CAFR the following items would appear using the following key:

(I) Introductory, (F) Financial, or (S) Statistical

_____ Computation of legal debt limit

_____ Organizational chart

_____ Required supplementary information
_____ Letter of transmittal
_____ List of principal taxpayers
_____ Independent auditor's report
_____ GFOA Certificate of Achievement for Excellence in Financial Reporting
_____ Management's Discussion and Analysis
_____ Combining financial statements
_____ Reporting entity note disclosures
_____ Fund balances for the past 10 years
_____ Budget-to-actual information for an Enterprise Fund

P15-8 (Financial Section of the CAFR) Indicate where the following financial information for the City of Green Hope would be located within the financial section of their CAFR using the following key:

(GW) Government-wide financial statements

(FF) Fund financial statements

(ND) Note disclosures

(RSI) Required supplementary information

Note: There may be more than one correct answer.

_____ Statement of Activities
_____ Balance Sheet
_____ Reporting entity description
_____ Statement of Net Position
_____ Statement of Revenues, Expenditures, and Changes in Fund Balance
_____ Subsequent events information
_____ Statement of Cash Flows
_____ Discrete component unit financial information
_____ Description of compliance violations
_____ Statement of Revenues, Expenses, and Changes in Fund Net Position

P15-9 (Research—Letter of Transmittal versus MD&A) Obtain a copy of an entity's Letter of Transmittal *and* MD&A from its CAFR. Analyze.

a. Summarize and describe the nature of the information in the Letter of Transmittal. Does it fundamentally differ from information found in the MD&A? How?

b. Who would be primarily interested in a Letter of Transmittal? MD&A? Discuss.

P15-10 (Research and Analysis—Component Units) Through an Internet search, find at least 10 different examples of reporting entity note disclosures from available CAFRs. Provide a mixture of both blended and discretely presented component units. Provide a brief analysis of your findings using the following questions as a guide:

1. How many discretely presented component units did you identify? Did the report indicate why the entity was a component unit? For what reason(s) was the component unit discretely presented?

2. How many blended component units did you identify? For what reason(s) was the component unit blended?

3. Describe the different reporting options used in the government-wide financial statements for the discretely presented component units you identified. Why do you think the reporting governments chose the reporting methods they did?

Cases

C15-1 (Defining and Reporting Component Units—City of Myrtle Beach, South Carolina) The following descriptions, modified for teaching purposes, appear in the note disclosures for the City of Myrtle Beach, South Carolina, for the year ended June 30, 20X6:

- The Myrtle Beach Downtown Redevelopment Corporation, a legally separate entity, is responsible for promoting and assisting in the development of business concerns and residential housing in the downtown area of Myrtle Beach. The City Council appoints a voting majority of the Corporation's 11-member board. The city is considered to have significant influence in the Corporation's operations. Separate financial statements are not prepared by the Corporation.

- The Myrtle Beach Public Facilities Corporation is governed by a three-member board appointed by the City Council. Although it is legally separate from the city, the corporation's sole purpose is to serve the city exclusively as a financing agent. Separate financial statements are not prepared by the corporation.

- The Myrtle Beach Convention Center Hotel Corporation, a legally separate entity, is responsible for the construction and management of a convention center hotel. The City Council appoints all members of the corporation's board. The City Council also approves the corporation's budget and debt issuances. The corporation does issue separate financial statements. The city has an equity interest in the corporation.

Answer the following questions: ***Required***

1. Are any of these entities blended component units? If so, explain which one(s) and why.
2. Are any of these entities discretely presented component units? If so, explain which one(s) and why?

(Adapted from a recent Comprehensive Annual Financial Report of the City of Myrtle Beach, South Carolina.)

C15-2 (Defining the Reporting Entity—City of St. Louis, Missouri) The following descriptions, modified for teaching purposes, appear in the note disclosures of the City of St. Louis, Missouri, financial statements for the year ended June 30, 20X5:

- The St. Louis Municipal Finance Corporation is governed by a five-member board, consisting of persons in designated city positions. The corporation's sole purpose is to provide services to finance, acquire, lease, or sublease capital property for the city. It is a separate legal entity.
- The St. Louis Development Corporation is a legally separate entity with a governing body appointed by the St. Louis City Council. Although the corporation exists to oversee development in blighted areas of the city, it may not issue debt or implement a budget for any development activities without the approval of the St. Louis City Council.
- The City Council appoints the voting majority of the St. Louis Housing Authority. The Housing Authority is legally separate, but the city does not impose its will nor is it deemed to have an ongoing financial benefit or burden relationship with the Authority.
- The St. Louis Public Library has the voting majority of its board members appointed by the St. Louis City Council. The library is considered to be a legally separate entity, and the city has no ongoing accountability for its operations.
- The St. Louis Regional Convention and Sports Complex Authority was created as a separate legal entity by the Missouri State Legislature in 199X. The Authority is governed by an 11-member board—the city appoints three members, the governing board of St. Louis County appoints three members, and the Governor of the State of Missouri appoints the remaining five members. The city, the county, and the state have each contractually agreed to provide financial assistance to the Authority for ongoing maintenance needs in equal amounts.
- The Harry S. Truman Restorative Center is a 220-bed skilled nursing facility operated as a not-for-profit separate legal entity supported by the city and located in a city-owned building. The city appoints a voting majority of the Center's board and the city's approval is required each year for the Center to finalize its budget.
- The Public Facilities Protection Corporation is governed by a five-member board of designated city positions. The Corporation, a separate legal entity, provides self-insurance for the city exclusively for claims, judgments, and other related legal matters including worker's compensation.

1. For each entity described, identify which of the following reporting entity classifications   ***Required***
   appears to be the most appropriate and explain why. Is there additional information that would be helpful? If so, specify the information.
   a. Blended component unit.
   b. Discretely presented component unit.
   c. Joint venture.
   d. Related organization.
   e. None of the above.
2. Briefly describe how each of these classifications affects the government-wide financial statements, the fund financial statements, and the note disclosures for the City of St. Louis.

(Adapted from a recent Comprehensive Annual Financial Report for the City of St. Louis, Missouri.)

Harvey City Comprehensive Case

Harvey City's basic financial statements have been prepared (Chapters 13 and 14). The financial section of the city's Comprehensive Annual Financial Report includes these basic financial statements and the notes to the financial statements as well as Harvey City's Management's Discussion and Analysis and other required supplementary information. In addition, the city must include combining financial statements in the financial section. Harvey City has only one fund of each type, except for governmental funds. Therefore, the only required combining financial statements for the city are the combining financial statements for nonmajor governmental funds.

REQUIREMENTS

a. Prepare Harvey City's combining nonmajor governmental funds year-end balance sheet for 20X4.

b. Prepare Harvey City's combining nonmajor governmental funds statement of revenues, expenditures, and changes in fund balances for 20X4.

CHAPTER 16

Non-SLG Not-for-Profit Organizations

LEARNING OBJECTIVES

After studying this chapter, you should be able to:

- Understand the sources of GAAP for nongovernment not-for-profit organizations.

- Explain the basis of accounting and the financial statements required for nongovernment not-for-profit organizations.

- Distinguish between and among the three net asset classes.

- Understand the timing of recognition and the classification of revenues and expenses of nongovernment not-for-profit organizations.

- Understand the reporting of restricted contributions and restricted investment income.

- Account for and report the satisfaction of donor-imposed temporary restrictions on the use of resources.

- Prepare journal entries for common transactions of nongovernment not-for-profit organizations.

- Prepare nongovernment not-for-profit organization financial statements.

The previous chapters of this text dealt with accounting and financial reporting for state and local government entities. This chapter explains and illustrates the basic financial reporting principles and practices that apply to all **nongovernment** not-for-profit (NFP) organizations. The GASB establishes financial reporting standards for state and local governments including *governmental* not-for-profit organizations; the FASB sets reporting standards for *nongovernment* (non-SLG) not-for-profit organizations.

Nongovernment not-for-profit accounting principles are discussed and illustrated in the context of voluntary health and welfare organizations (VHWOs) and other not-for-profit organizations (ONPOs). ONPOs are not-for-profit organizations other than health care organizations, colleges and universities, and VHWOs. The same basic principles illustrated in this chapter apply to *nongovernment* health care organizations and to *nongovernment* colleges and universities. Unique aspects of accounting for those entities are discussed in Chapters 17 and 18, as is accounting for government colleges and universities and government health care entities.

Accounting standards for VHWOs and ONPOs have evolved through several stages since the 1960s. Industry organizations took the initial steps. The AICPA began to play a central role in accounting standards for these organizations in the mid-1960s.[1] In 1979, the FASB assumed responsibility for setting accounting and reporting standards for all nonbusiness organizations except governments. The FASB accepted responsibility in its *Statement No. 32*[2] for the specialized accounting and reporting principles and practices in various AICPA Statements of Position (SOPs), audit guides, and accounting guides. The FASB's Not-for-Profit Advisory Committee (NAC) initiated its advisory activities in 2010, providing the FASB a key resource for obtaining input from the NFP sector on current and potential future guidance on issues affecting nongovernment, NFP organizations.

The primary current authoritative guidance for all nongovernment not-for-profit organizations, including VHWOs and ONPOs, was established in June 1993. At that time the FASB issued *SFAS No. 116,* "Accounting for Contributions Received and Contributions Made,"[3] and *SFAS No. 117,* "Financial Statements of Not-for-Profit Organizations."[4] These standards are the basis for most of the guidance on reporting not-for-profit organizations in Section 958 of the FASB's *Accounting Standards Codification* (ASC). They apply to all *nongovernment* not-for-profit organizations except those that operate for the direct economic benefit of their members. (Such nongovernment member benefit organizations as credit unions, rural electric cooperatives, and employee benefit plans are to be accounted for like their private-sector counterparts.) The AICPA audit and accounting guide, *Not-for-Profit Organizations,*[5] incorporates the guidance in ASC 958 and provides additional implementation guidance. This guide applies to all *nongovernment* VHWOs and ONPOs.

As noted earlier, the GASB has primary standards-setting authority for all state and local government organizations, including government VHWOs, colleges and universities, hospitals, and other not-for-profit organizations. The GASB prohibits *government* not-for-profit organizations from applying *SFAS No. 116, SFAS No. 117,* and other FASB statements issued solely for not-for-profit organizations.[6]

This chapter first discusses the requirements of the FASB standards—now in the FASB Accounting Standards Codification, section 958—for **nongovernment** VHWOs and ONPOs. The key provisions of those standards are then illustrated, and financial statements based on the guidelines are presented for the illustrative organization.

---

[1]Key documents in the progression of VHWO and ONPO accounting guidance include:

- National Health Council and National Assembly for Social Policy and Development, *Standards of Accounting and Financial Reporting for Voluntary Health and Welfare Organizations* (Washington, DC, 1964); National Health Council and National Assembly for National Voluntary Health and Social Welfare Organizations, *Standards of Accounting and Financial Reporting for Voluntary Health and Welfare Organizations,* 4th ed. (Washington, DC, 1999).
- Committee on Voluntary Health and Welfare Organizations, American Institute of Certified Public Accountants, *Audits of Voluntary Health and Welfare Organizations* (New York: AICPA, 1974).
- Accounting Standards Division, American Institute of Certified Public Accountants, *Statement of Position 78-10,* "Accounting Principles and Reporting Practices for Certain Nonprofit Organizations" (New York: AICPA, December 31, 1978).

[2]Financial Accounting Standards Board, *Statement of Financial Accounting Standards No. 32,* "Specialized Accounting and Reporting Principles and Practices in AICPA Statements of Position and Guides on Accounting and Auditing Matters" (Stamford, CT: FASB, September 1979). The FASB rescinded *SFAS No. 32* in November 1992 (*Statement of Financial Accounting Standards No. 111,* "Rescission of FASB Statement No. 32 and Technical Corrections"). The FASB considered *SFAS No. 32* unnecessary under the new GAAP hierarchy (discussed in Chapter 1) adopted by the AICPA in *Statement on Auditing Standards No. 69.*

[3]Financial Accounting Standards Board, *Statement of Financial Accounting Standards No. 116,* "Accounting for Contributions Received and Contributions Made" (Norwalk, CT: FASB, June 1993).

[4]Financial Accounting Standards Board, *Statement of Financial Accounting Standards No. 117,* "Financial Statements of Not-for-Profit Organizations" (Norwalk, CT: FASB, June 1993).

[5]Auditing Standards Board, American Institute of Certified Public Accountants, *Audit and Accounting Guide, Not-for-Profit Organizations* (New York: AICPA, 1996).

[6]Governmental Accounting Standards Board, *Statement No. 29,* "The Use of Not-for-Profit Accounting and Financial Reporting Principles by Governmental Entities" (Norwalk, CT: GASB, August 1995).

CLASSIFICATION OF ORGANIZATIONS

Properly classifying not-for-profit organizations (NPOs) as governmental or non-governmental is essential because different accounting and reporting standards apply. The definition of a government was discussed in Chapter 1 (see Illustration 1-1). GASB standards apply to all not-for-profit entities that meet the definition, and FASB standards to those that do not—which is the norm.

Likewise, properly identifying the type of not-for-profit organization—VHWO versus ONPO—is important because of the slight differences in the accounting and financial reporting principles that apply to each. The focus in this decision is typically on whether the organization is a VHWO because ONPOs are defined as all not-for-profit organizations other than hospitals (and similar health care institutions), colleges and universities, and VHWOs.

Voluntary health and welfare organizations are formed to provide various kinds of health, welfare, and community services financed primarily by voluntary contributions from the public (for no fee or a low fee) to various segments of society. VHWOs are tax exempt, organized for the public benefit, supported largely by public contributions, and operated on a not-for-profit basis. Thus, *the features that distinguish VHWOs (from ONPOs) are:*

1. Their *purpose*—to meet a community health, welfare, or other social service need.

2. Their *voluntary nature*—no fee is charged, or only a very small fee in proportion to the services provided is charged.

3. Their *relationship to resource providers*—providers of resources are *not* the primary recipients of services or benefits of a VHWO.

Some ONPOs may provide services similar to those provided by certain VHWOs, but ONPOs more often finance the services with user charges or membership fees charges to the primary recipients of the services.

The United Way—or one of the other federated community contribution solicitation and allocation organizations—is active in most cities and is perhaps the most widely recognized type of VHWO in the United States. Numerous other VHWOs such as the Boy Scouts and Girl Scouts, the American Heart Association, the YMCA and YWCA, and various mental health associations are in most cities. Many of these organizations are financed wholly or partly by allocations from the United Way or equivalent organizations. Among the many types of services provided through VHWOs are child care for working mothers, family counseling, nutritious meals and recreation for the elderly, care and treatment of persons with mental and/or physical handicaps, protection of children from abuse, halfway houses for criminal or drug offenders, and sheltered workshops for citizens who are impaired physically and/or mentally. Most VHWOs charge modest fees to those who can afford to pay them, often using a sliding fee schedule based on family size and income.

The **other** not-for-profit organizations do *not* include (1) hospitals, colleges and universities, and voluntary health and welfare organizations or (2) those not-for-profit organizations that operate essentially as business enterprises for the direct economic benefit (in the form of dividends, lower costs, etc.) of their members or stockholders. Thus, the term **other not-for-profit organizations (ONPOs)** is used for the following types of organizations and other truly not-for-profit organizations:

> Cemetery organizations
> Civic organizations
> Fraternal organizations
> Libraries
> Museums
> Other cultural institutions

Voluntary Health and Welfare Organizations

Other Not-for-Profit Organizations

Performing arts organizations
Political parties
Private and community foundations
Private elementary and secondary schools
Professional associations
Religious organizations
Research and scientific organizations
Zoological and botanical societies

Member benefit organizations such as mutual insurance companies, rural electric cooperatives, and credit unions should be accounted for in the same way as their private-sector counterparts.

CLASSES OF NET ASSETS

Not-for-profit organizations are not required to report their resources by fund. The accounting equation is Assets = Liabilities + Net Assets. Net assets (assets less liabilities) are reported in three classes (Illustration 16-1):

- **Unrestricted net assets**—the portion of net assets not temporarily or permanently restricted. (This category may include assets that previously were temporarily restricted, but the donor stipulation has been met, removing the restriction.)
- **Temporarily restricted net assets**—the portion of net assets whose use is limited by *donor-imposed* restrictions on the timing and/or purpose of use of the donated resources.
- **Permanently restricted net assets**—the portion of net assets whose use is limited by *donor-imposed* restrictions that are permanent in nature—that is, restrictions that cannot be fulfilled by either passage of time or by actions of the organization.

The restrictions reflected in the net asset classes may result from *explicitly* stated stipulations of the resource donor or grantor or explicit representations made by the organization when it solicited the resources (explicitly stating that it is raising funds for its building fund, for instance), or they may be *implied* from circumstances at the time the gift was made (i.e., the circumstances cause the donor to believe that the resources are being donated for a certain purpose). Changes in net assets must be reported separately for each net asset class.

ILLUSTRATION 16-1 Net Assets Classes			
	Net Assets Classes		
	Permanently Restricted	**Temporarily Restricted**	**Unrestricted**
Type(s) of Restrictions	Donor-imposed restrictions are permanent in nature (not capable of being satisfied or removed by the organization).	Donor-imposed (or implied) restrictions will be met (satisfied) by the passage of time or by use of resources for the required purpose.	There are *no* donor-imposed restrictions.
Examples	• Assets (less liabilities payable therefrom) that were donated as permanent endowments • Assets (less related liabilities) such as land or art that are restricted for a certain purpose for which preservation is required and sale is prohibited (or sale proceeds are required to be used to replace the assets)	• Assets restricted to a certain use (research, capital asset acquisition, etc.) • Assets restricted for use during a certain future time period • Pledges receivable due in future years (unless donor states intent to finance current year) • Assets with implied time restrictions based on the organization's policy	• All other net assets, including board-designated resources that are *not* donor-restricted—even if restricted by bond indentures or other contracts or agreements not involving donors or grantors

NON-GAAP ACCOUNTING AND REPORTING REQUIREMENTS

As with government organizations, not-for-profit organizations have numerous ongoing needs for accounting and reporting information other than for annual financial reporting on a GAAP basis. For example, not-for-profit organizations are required by the Internal Revenue Service to file Form 990, "Return of Organization Exempt from Income Tax." Donors and grantors sometimes require special reports from an organization demonstrating that restricted grants and contributions have been used in accordance with contribution or grant programs or agreements as well as with any other laws or regulations pertinent to the contribution or grant.

Although GAAP do not require use of fund accounting, many VHWOs and ONPOs that receive grants and contributions restricted for specific purposes use it to maintain and to demonstrate accountability for such restrictions. The more significant the amount of restricted financial resources held by an organization, the more useful fund accounting is for enhancing fiscal control and accountability.

Indeed, some ONPOs use fund accounting even though normally they do not have significant amounts of restricted financial resources. Fund accounting is typically used by such organizations as private schools and religious organizations, for instance, because it is a well-established practice in these fields. Some ONPOs may use fund accounting because (1) they have material amounts of property, plant, and equipment, and/or (2) capital additions are budgeted, but depreciation is not budgeted. Using fund accounting when an organization has material amounts of property, plant, and equipment, and a significant portion of its total equity results from its net investment in those assets, may permit clearer presentation of the financial resources available to finance ongoing services in the financial statements.

No specific fund structure is required for VHWOs or ONPOs that use fund accounting. *Also, reporting by funds is not permitted in place of aggregated reporting.* Thus, fund accounting and reporting are not illustrated in this chapter.

BASIS OF ACCOUNTING

Both VHWOs and ONPOs are required to report their financial statements on the economic resources measurement focus and the accrual basis of accounting—that is, accounting for revenues and expenses. It is acceptable to keep the accounts on some other basis, such as the cash basis, and make period-end adjustments to convert them to GAAP. The chapter illustration assumes a GAAP basis of accounting to enhance understanding of the GAAP reporting requirements.

FINANCIAL STATEMENTS

The financial statements required for nongovernment ONPOs are the

1. Statement of Financial Position (Balance Sheet)
2. Statement of Activities
3. Statement of Cash Flows

VHWOs must also present a Statement of Functional Expenses. Each of these financial statements is discussed and illustrated and the underlying principles are explained in the following sections.

The FASB does not prescribe a specific balance sheet format, nor does it require or prohibit reporting an organization's data disaggregated by funds or classes of net assets. *It requires aggregated totals of assets, liabilities, and net assets to be reported.* Also, net assets must be reported in the three classes described in Illustration 16-1: unrestricted, temporarily restricted, and permanently restricted. Otherwise, the aggregation and

Balance Sheet

presentation of assets and liabilities are similar to that of for-profit organizations. The AICPA audit and accounting guide, *Not-for-Profit Organizations,* provides guidance on reporting specific assets and liabilities, including those discussed here.

Investments

Investments are recorded initially at cost. (Donated securities are recorded at their fair market value at the date of the gift.) Thereafter, NPOs are to report the market value or fair value of their investments in debt securities and in equity securities with readily determinable fair values.[7] Other investments may be accounted for at cost (or lower of cost or market) or at market value. All of these other investments should be accounted for on the same basis. The net change in market value of investments is classified as unrestricted unless restricted by donor stipulation or law.

Pledges

Not-for-profit organizations should **recognize pledges** receivable **if** the pledges are **unconditional** promises to give. An *unconditional* promise to give does *not* have provisions (conditions) that release the donor from the obligation based on occurrence or nonoccurrence of a future and uncertain event. A conditional promise to give is considered unconditional if the likelihood of not meeting the condition is remote (slight). Furthermore, promises to give must be distinguished from other nonbinding statements of donors that might express donor intentions but do not constitute a promise to give.

For pledges that are to be collected within one year, the *net* expected unconditional pledge collections (gross pledges less estimated uncollectible pledges) are recognized as assets and as contributions revenue. Pledges expected to be collected over longer periods should be recorded as assets and as contributions revenue at their present value. Conditional promises to give are not reported as receivables but are disclosed in the notes. Support from conditional promises to give is recognized when the conditions are met.

Fixed Assets

Fixed (capital) assets of all NPOs are recorded at cost or, if donated, at fair market value at donation. If historical cost or fair market value data are not available, fixed asset costs may be estimated. In such cases, the valuation method(s) used should be disclosed in the notes to the financial statements.

Donated fixed assets to be used in operations are reported as unrestricted contributions unless donor restrictions or organization policies require use of the assets in a specified future period. In that case the contributions are temporarily restricted. If they are to be sold or are to be held to produce income, the fixed assets affect the net asset class that is consistent with any donor restrictions on use of the proceeds.

Depreciation expense and accumulated depreciation are recorded for exhaustible fixed assets in operating use or held to produce income. Depreciation is not recorded on fixed assets held for sale.

Collections

Some not-for-profit organizations have assets that qualify as collections. "Collections" are defined as:

> Works of art, historical treasures, or similar assets that meet all of the following criteria:
>
> (a) They are held for public exhibition, education, or research in furtherance of public service rather than financial gain.

---

[7]Financial Accounting Standards Board, Accounting Standards Codification, section 958-320. This section does not apply to investments accounted for under the equity method, to investments in consolidated subsidiaries, investments held by a financially interrelated entity, investments in derivative instruments, or short sales of securities.

(b) They are protected, kept unencumbered, cared for, and preserved.

(c) They are subject to an organizational policy that requires the proceeds of items that are sold to be used to acquire other items for collections.[8]

Not-for-profit organizations must capitalize works of art, historical treasures, and similar assets that do *not* meet the criteria for a collection. For collections, three accounting options are permitted:

1. Not capitalizing any collections.

2. Capitalizing collections acquired after adoption of *SFAS No. 116* but not those acquired prior to that date.

3. Capitalizing all collections regardless of when acquired.

Organizations that capitalize collections under either of the last two options report donated collections as assets at fair value and as contributions—increasing the appropriate net asset class. If collections are not capitalized, contributions are not reported for donated collections but are disclosed in the notes to the financial statements.

Trusts and Similar Agreements

Irrevocable trusts and similar agreements established to benefit a not-for-profit organization may be held by a third party. They should be recognized as assets and contributions unless the third party has the discretion to provide the resources or related earnings to some other entity. If the third party has such discretion, assets and contributions are recognized when the third party makes resources available to the organization. Revocable trusts and similar agreements are treated as conditional promises to give.

Irrevocable perpetual trusts established for the sole benefit of a not-for-profit organization increase permanently restricted net assets. Term endowments—in which the principal can be expended after the end of a specified term—and many similar arrangements increase temporarily restricted net assets.

The major nongovernment NPO operating statement is the Statement of Activities. Illustration 16-2 summarizes the format of the operating statement. **Revenues** and gains are reported **by source**. **Expenses**, classified between program services and supporting services, are reported **by function**. Also note in Illustration 16-2 that changes in each of the three classes of net assets are reported separately. A columnar approach—with one column for each net asset class and a total column—is acceptable as well. **Statement of Activities**

An NPO has significant flexibility as to what, if any, bottom-line measurement of operations it presents. Although some organizations may view the change in net assets or the change in unrestricted net assets to be appropriate and adequate measurements of operations, other measures may be presented. For instance, changes in unrestricted net assets may be categorized as operating activities (as defined by the organization) and nonoperating activities. This flexibility permits reporting an operating subtotal such as "changes in unrestricted net assets from operating activities." The standard even permits presentation of a separate statement of operations—but the statement must also report the total changes in unrestricted net assets for the period. Hospitals, for instance, present a statement of operations. Extraordinary items and gains or losses on discontinued operations are reported separately as the last items before the "Increase (decrease) in unrestricted net assets," regardless of the format or intermediate operating measures that are used.

Illustration 16-2 also reflects that *all expenses are reported as changes in unrestricted net assets. When restrictions on temporarily restricted net assets are met* by incurring expenses or costs for the temporarily restricted purpose or by passage of time, *the release of net assets from restrictions is reported as an addition to unrestricted net assets and as a deduction from temporarily restricted net assets.*

---

[8]Ibid., sec. 958-360-20.

ILLUSTRATION 16-2 Statement of Activities Format and Content

Not-for-Profit Organization
Statement of Activities
For Fiscal Year 20XX

Changes in unrestricted net assets:

Revenues and gains:

Contributions (unrestricted support)	xx
Other revenues (by source)	xx
Gains (may be reported net)	xx
Total unrestricted revenues and gains	xxx

Net assets released from restrictions:

Satisfaction of program restrictions	xx
Satisfaction of fixed asset acquisition restrictions	xx
Expiration of time restrictions	xx
Total net assets released from restrictions	xx
Total revenues, gains, and net assets released from restrictions	xx

Expenses and losses:

Program services (listed by function)	xx
Supporting services:	
Management and general	xx
Fund-raising	xx
Membership development	xx
Direct benefits provided to donors	xx
Losses (may be reported net)	xx
Total expenses and losses	xxx
Increase (decrease) in unrestricted net assets	xx

Changes in temporarily restricted net assets:

Restricted contributions (support)	xx
Restricted income, gain, or loss on investment of donor-restricted net assets	xx
Net assets released from restrictions	(xx)
Increase (decrease) in temporarily restricted net assets	xx

Changes in permanently restricted net assets:

Restricted contributions (support)	xx
Permanently restricted income, gain, or loss on investment of donor-restricted resources	xx
Increase (decrease) in permanently restricted net assets	xx
Increase (decrease) in net assets	xxx
Net assets, beginning of year	xxx
Net assets, end of year	xxx

Revenues and Expenses Reported at Gross Amounts

Revenues and expenses of not-for-profit organizations must be reported at gross (rather than net) amounts. Gains and losses may be reported net of related amounts. Revenues and expenses result from transactions that are part of an organization's ongoing major or central activities. Gains and losses result from transactions that are considered peripheral or incidental for the organization. Therefore, a particular type of transaction—such as a special fund-raising event—may be reported as revenue by one not-for-profit organization and as a gain by another.

Note also that revenues and gains, as well as losses, must be classified as changes in either unrestricted, temporarily restricted, or permanently restricted net assets. The classification depends on the existence and nature of donor restrictions. As noted earlier, *all expenses are reported as changes in unrestricted net assets.*

Contributions

Contributions are a significant revenue source for most NPOs. These entities often refer to contributions as public support. The FASB defines a "contribution" as follows:

> An *unconditional* transfer of cash or other assets to an entity or a settlement or cancellation of its liabilities in a *voluntary nonreciprocal transfer by another entity acting other than as owner*.[9]

Four key features that distinguish contributions from other transactions such as exchange transactions and agency transactions are that contributions are:

- Unconditional—not subject to future and uncertain event(s) that could require return of assets or reinstatement of liabilities
- Nonreciprocal—nothing of significant value is given in return for the contribution
- Voluntary
- Not an ownership investment (i.e., the contributor is not acting as an owner)

Contributions are recognized as revenues in the period they are received or unconditionally promised. Contributions are recognized at this point even if the use of the resources is restricted. Transactions such as grants, membership dues, and sponsorships should be evaluated carefully. Some of these transactions are contributions. Others are exchange transactions (or part contribution and part exchange transaction). Different revenue recognition guidance applies to exchange transactions than to contributions.

Unrestricted contributions are reported as unrestricted revenues in the "Changes in unrestricted net assets" section of the Statement of Activities. Restricted contributions are reported as revenues under "Changes in temporarily restricted net assets" if the restriction is temporary. Restricted contributions are "Changes in permanently restricted net assets" if the restriction is permanent.

Sometimes the *use restrictions* on temporarily restricted contributions or investment earnings are met in the same period the revenues are recognized. In this case, two alternative treatments of these revenues are permitted. One alternative is to report the restricted revenues as increases in temporarily restricted net assets—like any other temporarily restricted gifts. Under this alternative, the satisfaction of the restrictions is reported as both a decrease in temporarily restricted net assets and an increase in unrestricted net assets. The second alternative reports these "satisfied" portions of the current year restricted contributions or restricted investment earnings as changes in *unrestricted* net assets. Net assets released from restrictions are *not* reported. This alternative treatment must be applied consistently to both restricted contributions and restricted investment earnings, and the policy must be disclosed.

One additional issue related to contributions is how intermediary organizations that receive cash or other financial assets that they must use for or transfer to specific beneficiaries should report those transfers of assets. Contribution revenues are recognized by the intermediary organization if it is *explicitly* given the *unilateral right* to *redirect* the use of the transferred assets to parties *other than* the specified beneficiary (or the intermediary and beneficiary organizations are "financially interrelated"—meaning one of the two has the ability to influence operating and financial decisions of the other and one has an ongoing economic interest in the other). *If explicit variance power is granted,* contribution *revenues* equal to the fair value of the assets transferred should be reported. If this explicit variance power is *not* granted, the organization is an agent and typically must record a *liability* equal to the fair value of the assets transferred.

Pledges, Membership Dues, and Other Fees

As noted earlier, not-for-profit organizations record unconditional pledges receivable as assets when the pledge is made. Revenues from contributions are also recognized at this time, regardless of whether the contributions are restricted or unrestricted.

---

[9]Ibid., sec. 958-225-20. (Emphasis added.)

Conditional pledges and conditional transfers of assets (that meet the other criteria for contributions) are recognized as contributions revenue when the conditions are met. Unconditional pledges due in future years, even if not restricted as to use, are reported as restricted support unless the donor specifies that the contributions are intended to support the current year. In other words, *a time restriction (for use in subsequent periods) is implied for uncollected pledges unless explicitly contradicted by the donor(s).*

Membership dues of some organizations are exchange transactions for which benefits or services are made available by the organization. Dues of other organizations are contributions. Dues of still other organizations are part exchange transactions (to the extent benefits or services are provided) and part contributions.

Membership dues that are exchange transactions are recognized as revenue over the period(s) that the benefits are provided. Dues that are contributions should be recognized as revenue when received. Lifetime membership dues and nonrefundable initiation fees typically are reported as revenue when they are received if future fees are assessed to cover the costs of future services provided to members. If not, lifetime membership dues and nonrefundable initiation fees are unearned exchange revenues that will be recognized over future periods. The allocation of this revenue to various years is determined by such factors as the average duration of membership or other appropriate factors.

Special Fund-Raising Events

Not-for-profit organizations often hold special fund-raising events such as dinners, bazaars, telethons, and concerts to generate contributions. *Revenues* from these events should be *reported* at the *gross* amount unless the event is incidental or peripheral. If the special event is incidental or peripheral, gains, not revenues, should be reported. *Gains* from special fund-raising events *may be reported either gross or net* of direct costs of holding the event.

Direct costs of holding special fund-raising events that are reported gross may be reported as an *expense deduction from the revenues*—just as cost of goods sold is deducted from sales. Alternatively, the direct costs may be reported in the expenses section of the Statement of Activities. The cost of benefits such as meals that are provided to contributors may be reported as part of a separate line item that identifies such costs. Other direct costs such as advertising should be included in fund-raising expenses. If special event *gains* are reported net of direct costs instead of at the gross amount, the direct costs of holding the special event should be disclosed parenthetically.

Investment Income and Gains/Losses

Investment income reported and gains and losses recognized on investment transactions are determined partly by the investment valuation method(s) used. For most investments, the fair value method is used. Changes in fair value, as well as interest and dividends, are reported as changes in unrestricted net assets unless those amounts are temporarily or permanently restricted by law or by donor stipulation. Restricted income, including gains and losses, is reported as changes in temporarily or permanently restricted net assets, as appropriate.

Investment losses that would reduce the principal of permanent endowments below a stipulated amount are addressed specifically by the FASB Codification, which states:

> In the absence of donor stipulations or law to the contrary, losses on the investments of a donor-restricted endowment fund shall reduce temporarily restricted net assets to the extent that donor-imposed temporary restrictions on net appreciation of the fund have not been met before the loss occurs. Any remaining loss shall reduce unrestricted net assets. . . . If losses reduce the assets of a donor-restricted endowment fund below the level required by the donor stipulations or law, gains that restore the fair value of the assets of the endowment fund to the required level shall be classified as increases in unrestricted net assets.[10]

---

[10]FASB, *Accounting Standards Codification* 958-205-45-22 to 24.

Donated Materials, Facilities, and Services

The fair market value of significant amounts of materials donated to not-for-profit organizations should be reported as contributions when the materials are received. Expenses should be reported when the materials are used or sold. The same is true for donated (free) use of facilities and other assets.

Donated services are reported both as contributions and as assets or expenses if the services create or enhance nonfinancial assets. Donated services are also recognized if they:

1. Require specialized skills (e.g., accounting, medicine, plumbing),
2. Are provided by individuals with those skills, *and*
3. Would typically have to be purchased if they were not donated to the organization.

These criteria are rather restrictive. They prevent recording many volunteer services in fund-raising, for example, and in assisting staff members to serve agency clients.

Net Assets Released from Restrictions

Perhaps the most unique reporting feature of nongovernment, not-for-profit organizations is the reporting of "Net assets released from restrictions." *Net assets released from restrictions is reported when the NPO meets donor restrictions on resource use (whether by passage of time or by incurring costs for the restricted use).* This item is presented both as an addition to unrestricted net assets and as a deduction from temporarily restricted net assets. Though often reported with revenues, net assets released from restrictions are not considered revenue in reporting changes in unrestricted net assets. Revenues—for the temporarily restricted contributions and other temporarily restricted resources—were recognized as changes in temporarily restricted net assets when the revenue recognition criteria were met. Likewise, the deduction from temporarily restricted net assets is not an expense. (All expenses are reported as changes in unrestricted net assets.)

The increase reported in the changes in unrestricted net assets essentially communicates that temporarily restricted resources have been used to finance either current expenses—if the restriction was met by passage of time or by incurring current expenses—or future years' expenses (if the restriction was met by acquiring fixed assets or retiring debt related to fixed assets). The deduction reported as a change in temporarily restricted net assets simply reflects the reduction in those net assets. *Use restrictions are deemed to have been met to the extent that costs have been incurred during the period for the restricted use—whether or not restricted resources were actually used for payment.*

Recall from the discussion on contributions that some temporary restrictions are met in the same period that temporarily restricted contributions or investment earnings are recognized as revenues. In this case, those contributions and investment earnings—to the extent that restrictions are satisfied—may be reported as revenues in the changes in unrestricted net assets. If this policy is adopted, the organization will not report net assets released from temporary restrictions for those amounts. Reporting restricted contributions and restricted investment income under this policy is one of the examples presented in Illustration 16-3—on reporting restricted gifts, pledges, and investment income as well as net assets released from restrictions.

Expenses

Expenses of nongovernment NPOs are always reported as changes in unrestricted net assets. The expenses should be categorized appropriately between (1) **program services expenses** and (2) **supporting services expenses**. *Program* services are those that relate directly to the primary missions of the organization. *Supporting* services do not relate directly to the NPO's primary missions and include such costs as general administration, membership development, and fund-raising. Both program services and supporting services must be classified by program or function.

ILLUSTRATION 16-3	Reporting Restricted Contributions and Restricted Investment Income			

		Report in the Statement of Activities for:		
ASSUMPTIONS		**20X1**	**20X2**	**20X3**
A to D: An NPO *received $100,000 in 20X1—from* gifts, pledges, or investment income—that is *donor-restricted.*				
A. *For a specific purpose* other than capital outlay. *Incurred:* • $75,000 of qualifying expenses in **20X2** • $25,000 of qualifying expenses in **20X3**		*Changes in TRNA:* Revenues $100,000	*Changes in UNA:* Expenses $75,000 NARR $75,000 *Changes in TRNA:* NARR ($75,000)	*Changes in UNA:* Expenses $25,000 NARR $25,000 *Changes in TRNA:* NARR ($25,000)
B. *To acquire* or construct *a fixed asset** 1. $100,000 asset is acquired and *placed in service in* **20X2**		*Changes in TRNA:* Revenues $100,000	*Changes in UNA:* NARR $100,000 *Changes in TRNA:* NARR ($100,000)	
2. $75,000 of construction costs are incurred in **20X2**. $25,000 of costs are incurred in **20X3** to complete the project, which is immediately *placed in service.*		*Changes in TRNA:* Revenues $100,000		*Changes in UNA:* NARR $100,000 *Changes in TRNA:* NARR ($100,000)
C. *Per a term endowment* that *expires* in **20X3** at which time the *resources* may be used for *unrestricted* purposes.		*Changes in TRNA:* Revenues $100,000		*Changes in UNA:* NARR $100,000 *Changes in TRNA:* NARR ($100,000)
D. *To* use for a *specific purpose* other than capital outlay and NPO applies *option* of recognizing *revenues in UNA when restriction satisfied in the year of the gift.* **INCURRED:** • $30,000 of qualifying expenses in **20X1** • $45,000 of qualifying expenses in **20X2** • $25,000 of qualifying expenses in **20X3** (Note that the other option reports 20X2 temporarily restricted revenues of $100,000 and NARR of $30,000 reported as usual.)		*Changes in TRNA:* Revenues $70,000 *Changes in UNA:* Expenses $30,000 Revenues $30,000	*Changes in UNA:* Expenses $45,000 NARR $45,000 *Changes in TRNA:* NARR ($45,000)	*Changes in UNA:* Expenses $25,000 NARR $25,000 *Changes in TRNA:* NARR ($25,000)
E. Received **unrestricted pledges** of $100,000 in **20X1 which are collected in 20X2** and donor does not stipulate that the pledge is to provide financing for 20X1. Time restriction is implied.		*Changes in TRNA:* Revenues $100,000	*Changes in UNA:* NARR $100,000 *Changes in TRNA:* NARR ($100,000)	
F. *Received $100,000* gift/pledge/investment income in **20X1** *restricted to permanent endowment.*		*Changes in PRNA:* Revenues $100,000		

*Donor stipulations may require recognition of NARR over a required minimum period of use. Also, a NPO may *choose* to recognize NARR for these TRNA as depreciation expense is recognized over the period of use. (The NARR must always be reported for health care entities when the plant asset is placed in service.)

Legend
NARR Net assets released from restrictions
PRNA Permanently restricted net assets
TRNA Temporarily restricted net assets
UNA   Unrestricted net assets

Accounting for expenses during the year may center on departmental responsibility and type (object) of expense incurred rather than on functions. Furthermore, some personnel may work in more than one function, and some expenses may involve several functions. In such cases it is necessary to maintain time and activity records by functions and to maintain other records so that all expenses can be assigned, directly or by allocation, to the functions of the organization. If such records are not maintained during the year, properly classifying expenses by function at year end, as required by GAAP, may be difficult and costly, if not impossible.

Program Services Program services expenses are those that relate *directly* to the *primary* missions of the organization. Such expenses should be classified by functions, using terms that best convey the primary thrust of the programs of the organization. Program services expenses include both direct expenses that are clearly identifiable with the program or function and rational and systematic allocations of indirect costs.

Some NPOs remit a portion of their receipts to an affiliated state or national organization. When practicable, these payments should be allocated to functional classifications. If not allocable, or if some portion is not allocable, they should be reported as a separate line item under supporting services.

Supporting Services Supporting services expenses do *not* relate directly to the primary missions of the organization, including management and general, fund-raising, and other costs not associated directly with rendering program services. Analysts and regulators pay close attention to the relationship of supporting services expenses to program services expenses and total expenses. In particular, fund-raising costs are often compared among organizations and for individual organizations through time.

Management and General Costs. Management and general costs are not identifiable with a specific program or fund-raising activity but relate to the organization's existence and effectiveness. They include such costs as board meetings, business management, record keeping, budgeting, accounting, and overall direction and leadership. To the extent that some of these costs are *directly related* to the primary programs, they should be allocated to those programs in a systematic and rational manner.

Fund-Raising and Other Supporting Services. Fund-raising costs are incurred to induce contributions of money, securities, real estate or other properties, materials, or time to the organization. Fund-raising efforts and costs vary widely among the many types of not-for-profit organizations, but fund-raising costs such as the following are often incurred: mailing lists, printing, mailing, personnel, occupancy, newspaper and other media advertising, and costs of unsolicited merchandise sent to encourage contributions. Some organizations combine fund-raising efforts with educational materials or program services. Activities such as special fund-raising banquets, telethons, door-to-door canvassing, mailings, media ads, and so on, that involve both fund-raising and other functions, are referred to as *joint activities*.

Costs of joint activities must be reported as *fund-raising* expenses *unless* the activity meets three conditions related to the purpose of the activity, the audience to whom the activity is addressed, and actions the audience is asked to take. These conditions are:

1. At least one purpose of the joint activity must be to accomplish some program function that is part of the NPO's mission or to fulfill management and general responsibilities of the organization.

2. The audience for the activity must *not* be selected based on the ability or the likelihood to make contributions.

3. The activity must motivate the audience to take specific actions (other than making contributions) that support program goals or that fulfill a management and general responsibility.

When all three conditions are met, the costs of joint activities that are identifiable with specific program or management and general functions are allocated to those functions so that each is reflected appropriately in the organization's operating statement. If one of the conditions is not met, all of the costs except the costs of direct benefits to donors are reported as fund-raising expenses. Further, associating the program objective with the fund-raising appeal in an incidental way does not justify allocation of part of the costs to program costs instead of fund-raising costs.

Fund-raising costs paid directly by a contributor should be recorded by the organization as *both* a contribution and a fund-raising expense. As noted earlier, when fund-raising banquets, dinner parties, theater parties, merchandise auctions or drawings, and similar events are ongoing and major activities, the gross proceeds of such functions are reported as revenue. The direct costs of the fund-raising merchandise, meals, or other direct benefits to donors should be reported as well. These direct costs may be displayed as a deduction from the special event revenues or be reported in the expenses section of the statement. If reported in the expenses section, the direct costs of benefits (unless peripheral or incidental), such as meals provided at a fund-raising banquet, may be included in a separate line item called "Benefits provided to donors." Other direct costs such as promotional costs are included in fund-raising expenses.

Statement of Cash Flows

Nongovernment not-for-profit organization statements of cash flows closely parallel business cash flow statements. The most unique items reflected in this statement, compared to a typical business cash flow statement, are the following:

- Reporting of contributions and investment earnings that are restricted for capital-asset-related, endowment, or other long-term purposes as financing activities
- Reporting of changes in the amount of cash restricted for long-term purposes (and thus excluded from current assets and from cash and cash equivalents) as investing activities
- Reconciliation of the total changes in net assets from the statement of activities to the net cash flows from operating activities

These unique aspects are illustrated in the statement of cash flows presented for the illustrative example later in the chapter.

Statement of Functional Expenses

VHWOs are required to present a Statement of Functional Expenses (presented later in Illustration 16-9). This statement presents a detailed analysis of the expenses section of the Statement of Activities by object class or type of expense. Note that the headings correspond to the "Program Services" and "Supporting Services" expense categories of the Statement of Activities. The detailed statement of functional expenses is optional for other nongovernment NPOs.

NONGOVERNMENT VHWO AND ONPO ACCOUNTING AND REPORTING ILLUSTRATION

This section presents illustrative transactions and entries for a VHWO or ONPO. The trial balance of the Illustrative Nongovernment VHWO/ONPO at January 1, 20X1, is in Illustration 16-4.

Transactions and Entries

Transactions and entries of the illustrative entity are presented in this section. The entries illustrate most of the principles discussed thus far. Note that we record contributions revenue as support (i.e., public support) in the illustration. Support is reported as revenues. Support results from nonreciprocal transactions—it is essentially a synonym for contributions.

Transactions and Entries

1. Unrestricted gifts and pledges of prior years that donors designated for 20X1 were reclassified as unrestricted net assets because the time restriction was met.

(1) Reclassifications Out	$ 22,000	
Reclassifications In		$ 22,000
To record **reclassification** of temporarily restricted net assets as unrestricted net assets.		

"Reclassifications Out" reduces temporarily restricted net assets. "Reclassifications In" increases unrestricted net assets. This entry is made because the implied (or expressed) *time restriction* has been met. **The reclassification is reported as "Net assets released from restrictions."** (See Illustration 16-2).

ILLUSTRATION 16-4   General Ledger Trial Balance

Illustrative VHWO/ONPO
Beginning Trial Balance
January 1, 20X1

	Debit	Credit
Cash	$ 125,000	
Pledges Receivable	50,000	
Allowance for Uncollectible Pledges		$ 4,000
Accrued Interest Receivable	2,000	
Inventory of Materials	3,000	
Investments	90,000	
Cash Restricted for Plant Purposes	150,000	
Investments Restricted for Plant Purposes	120,000	
Cash Restricted for Endowment	132,000	
Investments Restricted for Endowment	313,000	
Land	50,000	
Buildings and Improvements	420,000	
Accumulated Depreciation—Buildings and Improvements		140,000
Equipment	200,000	
Accumulated Depreciation—Equipment		85,000
Vouchers Payable		28,000
Mortgage Payable		205,000
Unrestricted Net Assets		417,000
Temporarily Restricted Net Assets—Education		24,000
Temporarily Restricted Net Assets—Research		15,000
Temporarily Restricted Net Assets—Term Endowments		100,000
Temporarily Restricted Net Assets—Plant Purposes		270,000
Temporarily Restricted Net Assets—Time Restricted		22,000
Permanently Restricted Net Assets		345,000
	$1,655,000	$1,655,000

2. Unrestricted cash gifts of $5,000 available for use in 20X1 and $10,000 restricted by donors to be used to finance operations in 20X2 were received.

(2) Cash	$ 15,000	
Unrestricted Support—Contributions		$ 5,000
Temporarily Restricted Support—		
Contributions		10,000

To record cash gifts received in 20X1 for 20X1 and 20X2.

The restricted support (or restricted revenue) account is used to record temporarily restricted contribution revenues that are to be reported as changes in temporarily restricted net assets. The restriction is a *time restriction* in this case.

3. Unrestricted pledges of $250,000 were received in 20X1, of which $50,000 is restricted by donors for use during 20X2, and $200,000 is designated to support 20X1 operations. Ten percent (10%) of the pledges are expected to be uncollectible.

(3) Pledges Receivable	$250,000	
Allowance for Uncollectible Pledges		$ 25,000
Unrestricted Support—Contributions		180,000
Temporarily Restricted Support—		
Contributions		45,000

To record pledges received in 20X1 for 20X1 and 20X2 and the estimated uncollectibles.

4. Pledges receivable of $205,000 were collected in 20X1 and pledges of $18,000 were written off as uncollectible.

(4) Cash	$205,000	
Allowance for Uncollectible Pledges........	18,000	
Pledges Receivable.....................		$223,000

To record collection and write-off of pledges receivable.

5. Land and a building were donated to the organization in 20X1 and held for resale. The fair value of the land and building when donated was $150,000. There are no restrictions on the donated property or its sale proceeds.

| (5) Land and Building Held for Resale .... | $150,000 | |
| Unrestricted Support—Contributions ...... | | $150,000 |

To record donated land and building held for resale.

6. The donated land and building were sold for $150,000.

| (6) Cash .... | $150,000 | |
| Land and Building Held for Resale .... | | $150,000 |

To record sale of land and building held for resale.

7. Investment income of $20,000 on unrestricted investments and $14,000 of unrestricted investment income from endowments were received. Interest accrued at the end of 20X0 was also received, $2,000.

(7) Cash	$ 36,000	
Accrued Interest Receivable...............		$ 2,000
Unrestricted Revenues—Investment Income		34,000

To record investment income available for unrestricted purposes.

8. A fund-raising banquet was held. Banquet ticket proceeds were $75,000. Related direct costs of $25,000 for the meals and gratuities were incurred and paid.

| (8) (a) Cash .... | $ 75,000 | |
| Unrestricted Support—Special Events... | | $ 75,000 |

To record ticket sales from fund-raising dinner.

| (8) (b) Expenses—Direct Costs of Special Events.. | $ 25,000 | |
| Cash.............................. | | $ 25,000 |

To record direct costs incurred for fund-raising dinner.

9. Donated materials and contributed use of facilities that are recordable in 20X1 were:
a. Materials, $10,000 (40% unused at year end; 60% used on fund-raising projects)
b. Facilities, $8,000 (60% used for research offices; 40% used for recordkeeping)

(9) (a) Inventory of Materials...................	$ 4,000	
Expenses—Fund-Raising	6,000	
Unrestricted Support—Donated Materials.......................		$ 10,000

To record donated materials.

(9) (b) Expenses—Research	$ 4,800	
Expenses—Management and General	3,200	
Unrestricted Support—Donated Facilities..........................		$ 8,000

To record donated facilities.

10. Donated services that are recordable include the time of:
a. A CPA, who audited the agency at no cost, $6,000.
b. An attorney, who did necessary legal work at no cost, $1,000.
c. A physician, who assisted in a research project, $3,000.

(10) Expenses—Management and General . . . . $ 7,000

     Expenses—Research   3,000

        Unrestricted Support—Donated Services. . . $ 10,000

     To record donated services.

11. Annual membership dues of $17,300 were billed and collected for 20X1. The dues constitute an exchange transaction for this organization.

(11) Cash . . . . $ 17,300

     Unrestricted Revenues—Membership

        Dues. . . . . $ 17,300

     To record collection of dues.

12. Salaries and wages paid during 20X1 totaled $85,000, and $3,000 was accrued at year end. These expenses are allocated to functions as follows:

Management and General	$ 30,000
Fund-Raising	15,000
Education	27,000
Research	16,000
Total	$ 88,000

(12) Expenses—Management and General . . . . $ 30,000

     Expenses—Fund-Raising   15,000

     Expenses—Education   27,000

     Expenses—Research   16,000

        Cash. . . . . $ 85,000

        Accrued Salaries Payable   3,000

     To record salaries and wages for 20X1.

13. Other 20X1 expenses, payments, and vouchers were as follows:

	Expenses Incurred	Amounts Paid	Unpaid at Year End
Vouchers Payable, January 1, 20X1		$ 17,000	
Management and General Expenses . . .	$ 98,000	98,000	
Fund-Raising Expenses	67,000	60,000	$ 7,000
Education Expenses	85,000	80,000	5,000
Research Expenses	50,000	48,000	2,000
Materials Purchased		800	
Total	$300,000	$303,800	$ 14,000

(13) Vouchers Payable . . . . $ 17,000

     Inventory of Materials   800

     Expenses—Management and General   98,000

     Expenses—Fund-Raising   67,000

     Expenses—Education   85,000

     Expenses—Research   50,000

        Cash $303,800

        Vouchers Payable   14,000

     To record various expenses incurred during 20X1

     and payment of vouchers payable.

14. The board of directors designated $50,000 of investments to be used as an endowment. The "endowment" earnings will be used to finance research.

(14) Unrestricted Net Assets . . . . $ 50,000

     Unrestricted Net Assets—Designated

        for Endowment . . . . $ 50,000

     To record board designation of net assets.

Note that board designation of assets for a specific purpose does *not* change the classification of net assets from unrestricted to restricted.

15. Restricted gifts and pledges of prior years designated by donors for use in 20X1 to finance certain research programs have met the time restrictions imposed by donors.

(15) No entry is required at this time. Although the time restriction has been met, these assets are not reclassified as unrestricted net assets at this time because there is *another temporary restriction*—that is, the *resources must be used for certain research programs.* The resources will not be reclassified as unrestricted until this *use restriction* also is fulfilled.

16. Cash gifts of $30,000 and pledges of $100,000 (collectible over the next year), both restricted to use for certain education efforts, were received. Ten percent of the pledges are estimated to be uncollectible.

(16) Cash	$ 30,000	
Pledges Receivable	100,000	
Allowance for Uncollectible Pledges		$ 10,000
Temporarily Restricted Support—		
Contributions		120,000
To record gifts and pledges restricted to		
education.		

17. Pledges of $80,000 for restricted purposes were collected, and $7,000 of restricted pledges were written off as uncollectible.

(17) Cash	$ 80,000	
Allowance for Uncollectible Pledges	7,000	
Pledges Receivable		$ 87,000
To record collection and write-off of pledges		
receivable.		

18. Investment income of $20,500 on investments of restricted contributions was received. The income is also restricted by the donors: $10,000 is restricted to certain education efforts and $10,500 to certain research projects.

(18) Cash	$ 20,500	
Temporarily Restricted Revenues—		
Investment Income		$ 20,500
To record investment earnings restricted for		
operating uses.		

The distinction between investment income restricted for education and that restricted for research is assumed to be maintained in subsidiary ledger accounts in this illustration.

19. Education expenses of $70,000 and research expenses of $18,000—both for purposes specified by donors—were incurred and paid.

(19) (a) Expenses—Education	$ 70,000	
Expenses—Research	18,000	
Cash		$ 88,000
To record expenses for education and		
research.		

When temporarily restricted resources are available to finance a specific program, qualifying costs are presumed to be met from those resources. Indeed, net assets released from restrictions must be reported even if available restricted resources were not actually used. This requirement releases the temporarily restricted resources as early as possible. Also recall that all expenses are reported as changes in unrestricted net assets.

(19) (b) Reclassifications Out	$ 88,000	
Reclassifications In		$ 88,000
To record reclassifications of net assets upon		
satisfaction of temporary restrictions.		

20. Cash gifts of $55,000 were received to endow (permanently) one of the education programs provided by the organization.

(20) Cash Restricted for Endowment.	$ 55,000	
Permanently Restricted Support— Contributions.		$ 55,000

To record gifts received for endowment purposes.

21. Endowment Fund investment earnings that are restricted by donor stipulation to increasing the permanent endowment base were received, $10,500.

(21) Cash Restricted for Endowment.	$ 10,500	
Permanently Restricted Revenues— Investment Income		$ 10,500

To record investment income restricted to
endowment.

22. Endowment Fund investments that cost $13,000 were sold for $14,400. By donor stipulation, realized gains and losses on this endowment must be added to or deducted from permanent endowment principal.

(22) Cash Restricted for Endowment.	$ 14,400	
Investments Restricted for Endowment. . .		$ 13,000
Permanently Restricted Gain—Gain on Sale of Investments		1,400

To record sale of investments.

Again, recall that the various restrictions on the use of resources are being accounted for in subsidiary ledger accounts.

23. Cash gifts of $100,000 restricted for acquisition of fixed assets were received in 20X1.

(23) Cash Restricted for Plant Purposes.	$100,000	
Temporarily Restricted Support— Contributions.		$100,000

To record restricted contributions for capital
additions.

24. Equipment costing $140,000 was acquired using donated resources restricted for that purpose and placed in service.

(24) (a) Equipment	$140,000	
Cash Restricted for Plant Purposes. . . .		$140,000

To record purchase of equipment with
restricted resources.

(24) (b) Reclassifications Out	$140,000	
Reclassifications In		$140,000

To record reclassification of net assets upon
satisfaction of temporary restrictions.

The illustrative organization does not have a policy of implying a time restriction on fixed assets acquired with restricted resources. Likewise, the donor did not specify that the fixed assets had to be held and used for a certain minimum period of time. Hence, *the only requirement to satisfy the restriction was to purchase the fixed asset and place it in service*. That is why the reclassification entry occurs at this time. If the fixed assets were required by donors to be used a certain number of years, the reclassification would be allocated over those years.

25. Depreciation expense for 20X1 on plant assets was $30,000 ($14,000 on buildings and $16,000 on equipment), allocated as follows:

Management and General	$13,000
Research	12,000
Education	2,000
Fund-Raising	3,000

(25) Expenses—Management and General	$ 13,000	
Expenses—Research	12,000	
Expenses—Education	2,000	
Expenses—Fund-Raising	3,000	
Accumulated Depreciation—Buildings and Improvements		$ 14,000
Accumulated Depreciation—Equipment		16,000
To record depreciation of plant assets.		

As noted in Transaction 24, *explicit donor stipulations sometimes require certain depreciable fixed assets to be used for a certain period of time.* If so, reclassification of a proportional amount of those fixed assets costs from temporarily restricted to unrestricted net assets must be recorded. Likewise, *some organizations have a policy of implying a time restriction on donated or donor-financed fixed assets.* In that case, reclassification of net assets equal to the depreciation expense on those fixed assets must be recorded at this time. The illustrative organization does not imply such a time restriction.

26. Investment income of $15,000 was earned on restricted investments ($12,000 was received). The income is restricted by donors for fixed asset purchases.

(26) Cash Restricted for Plant Purposes	$ 12,000	
Interest Receivable Restricted for Plant Purposes	3,000	
Temporarily Restricted Revenues—Investment Income		$ 15,000
To record investment earnings.		

27. Mortgage payments of $60,000, including $20,000 interest, matured and were paid from resources restricted for that purpose.

(27) (a) Mortgage Payable	$ 40,000	
Expenses—Interest	20,000	
Cash Restricted for Plant Purposes		$ 60,000
To record mortgage payments.		

(27) (b) Reclassifications Out	$ 60,000	
Reclassifications In		$ 60,000
To record reclassification of net assets upon satisfaction of temporary restrictions.		

28. A $200,000 building addition was completed. The addition was paid for with $100,000 of contributions received previously for that purpose and $100,000 of unrestricted resources.

(28) (a) Buildings and Improvements	$200,000	
Cash Restricted for Plant Purposes		$100,000
Cash		100,000
To record building addition.		
(28) (b) Reclassifications Out	$100,000	
Reclassifications In		$100,000
To record reclassification of temporarily restricted net assets.		

29. Equipment that had been used in operations was sold for $40,000. The original cost of the equipment was $75,000. Accumulated depreciation on the equipment at the date of sale was $45,000. The proceeds from the sale are not restricted.

(29) Cash	$ 40,000	
Accumulated Depreciation—Equipment	45,000	
Equipment		$ 75,000
Unrestricted Gains—Gain on Sale of Equipment		10,000
To record sale of equipment.		

30. A 10-year term endowment with a balance of $100,000 expired. Of the expired term endowment, $65,000 must be used for capital outlay. The remainder is unrestricted.

(30) (a) Cash Restricted for Plant Purposes	$ 65,000	
Cash	35,000	
Cash Restricted for Endowment		$100,000

To record reclassification of assets of expired term endowment that are restricted to capital outlay.

(30) (b) Reclassifications Out	$ 35,000	
Reclassifications In		$ 35,000

To record reclassification of temporarily restricted net assets.

31. The accounts were closed at year end.

(31) (a) Unrestricted Support—Contributions	$335,000	
Unrestricted Support—Donated Materials	10,000	
Unrestricted Support—Donated Facilities	8,000	
Unrestricted Support—Donated Services	10,000	
Unrestricted Support—Special Events . . .	75,000	
Unrestricted Revenues— Membership Dues	17,300	
Unrestricted Revenues—Investment Income	34,000	
Unrestricted Gains—Gain on Sale of Equipment	10,000	
Reclassifications In	445,000	
Expenses—Education		$184,000
Expenses—Research		103,800
Expenses—Management and General .		151,200
Expenses—Fund-Raising		91,000
Expenses—Direct Costs of Special Events		25,000
Expenses—Interest		20,000
Unrestricted Net Assets		369,300

To close changes in unrestricted net assets.

(31) (b) Temporarily Restricted Support— Contributions	$275,000	
Temporarily Restricted Revenues— Investment Income	35,500	
Temporarily Restricted Net Assets	134,500	
Reclassifications Out		$445,000

To close changes in temporarily restricted net assets.

(31) (c) Permanently Restricted Support— Contributions	$ 55,000	
Permanently Restricted Revenues— Investment Income	10,500	
Permanently Restricted Gain—Gain on Sale of Investments	1,400	
Permanently Restricted Net Assets		$ 66,900

To close changes in permanently restricted net assets.

ILLUSTRATION 16-5   End of 20X1 Trial Balance

Illustrative VHWO/ONPO
Postclosing Trial Balance
December 31, 20X1

	Debit	Credit
Cash	$ 227,000	
Pledges Receivable	90,000	
Allowance for Uncollectible Pledges		$ 14,000
Inventory of Materials	7,800	
Investments	90,000	
Cash Restricted for Plant Purposes	27,000	
Cash Restricted for Endowment	111,900	
Investments Restricted for Plant Purposes	120,000	
Investments Restricted for Endowment	300,000	
Interest Receivable Restricted for Plant Purposes	3,000	
Land	50,000	
Buildings and Improvements	620,000	
Accumulated Depreciation—Buildings and Improvements		154,000
Equipment	265,000	
Accumulated Depreciation—Equipment		56,000
Vouchers Payable		25,000
Accrued Salaries Payable		3,000
Mortgage Payable		165,000
Unrestricted Net Assets		786,300
Temporarily Restricted Net Assets—Time Restricted		55,000
Temporarily Restricted Net Assets—Research		7,500
Temporarily Restricted Net Assets—Education		84,000
Temporarily Restricted Net Assets—Plant Purposes		150,000
Permanently Restricted Net Assets		411,900
	$1,911,700	$1,911,700

Illustrative Financial Statements

The financial statements for 20X1 for the illustrative nongovernment VHWO/ONPO include the **Balance Sheet, the Statement of Activities, the Statement of Cash Flows, and the Statement of Functional Expenses**. The Statement of Functional Expenses is required only if the illustrative organization is a VHWO. If the organization is an ONPO, it is optional. A postclosing trial balance is presented in Illustration 16-5. The closing entries for the illustration are useful for tracing amounts from the entries to the Statement of Activities in Illustration 16-7.

Balance Sheet

The Balance Sheet in Illustration 16-6 closely resembles that of a business organization. Two matters are worthy of special attention. First, financial resources restricted for long-term purposes are not reported as cash and cash equivalents. They should be reported as noncurrent assets if a classified Balance Sheet is presented. Therefore, for example, the beginning and ending cash balances reported in Illustration 16-6 are the sums of the unrestricted cash and the cash restricted for specific current purposes—education and research. The financial resources restricted for plant purposes in the trial balance are reported as "Assets restricted for plant purposes" in the Balance Sheet. Likewise, the financial resources restricted for endowment in the trial balance are reported as "Assets restricted for endowment" in the Balance Sheet.

ILLUSTRATION 16-6   Comparative Balance Sheet

Illustrative VHWO/ONPO
Balance Sheet
December 31, 20X1, and 20X0

	20X1	20X0
Assets		
Cash (and cash equivalents)	$ 227,000	$ 125,000
Pledges receivable* (less allowance for uncollectibles of $14,000 in 20X1 and $4,000 in 20X0)	76,000	46,000
Accrued interest receivable	—	2,000
Inventory of materials	7,800	3,000
Investments	90,000	90,000
Assets restricted for plant purposes	150,000	270,000
Land	50,000	50,000
Buildings and improvements (net of accumulated depreciation of $140,000 and $154,000)	466,000	280,000
Equipment (net of accumulated depreciation of $56,000 and $85,000)	209,000	115,000
Assets restricted for endowment	411,900	445,000
Total Assets	$1,687,700	$1,426,000
Liabilities and Net Assets		
Liabilities:		
Vouchers payable	$ 25,000	$ 28,000
Accrued salaries payable	3,000	—
Mortgage payable	165,000	205,000
Total liabilities	193,000	233,000
Net Assets:		
Permanently restricted	411,900	345,000
Temporarily restricted:		
For research	7,500	15,000
For education	84,000	24,000
For plant assets	150,000	270,000
For endowment	—	100,000
For future years	55,000	22,000
Total temporarily restricted net assets	296,500	431,000
Unrestricted:		
Designated for capital additions	—	100,000
Designated for endowment	50,000	—
Invested in fixed assets	560,000	240,000
Undesignated	176,300	77,000
Total unrestricted net assets	786,300	417,000
Total net assets	1,494,700	1,193,000
Total Liabilities and Net Assets	$1,687,700	$1,426,000

*Recall that pledges receivable are permitted to be reported at net realizable value only if they are for a period of one year or less, as in the illustration. Otherwise, these receivables should be reported at their present value.

The three classes of net assets—unrestricted, temporarily restricted, and permanently restricted—are reported as required by *SFAS No. 117*. Note that Temporarily Restricted Net Assets are classified by the nature of the restriction. Unrestricted Net Assets are subclassified to disclose amounts designated by the organization's governing board (but not donor-restricted) to certain purposes and the net cost invested in capital (fixed) assets. The subclassifications of Unrestricted Net Assets are optional.

Operating Statement

The operating statement in Illustration 16-7—the Statement of Activities— follows the format in Illustration 16-2. The amount reported for contributions under "Changes in Unrestricted Net Assets" is the sum of the balances of the Unrestricted Support accounts for contributions, donated materials, donated facilities, and donated services [closing entry (31) (a)]. Note also:

- Special events are reported as revenues, with direct costs of the event deducted immediately. Alternatively, the direct costs could have been reported under expenses.
- All expenses are reported as changes in unrestricted net assets.
- Program services and supporting services expenses are reported by function.
- "Net assets released from restrictions" are reported as an increase in unrestricted net assets and as a corresponding decrease in temporarily restricted net assets. The net effect is zero on changes in (total) net assets.

The Statement of Activities of the American Red Cross is presented in 16-1 In Practice in a columnar format, which is an equally acceptable alternative to the "pancake" format used in Illustration 16-7. Three noteworthy benefits of this format are that it

- Presents the *total* amount of *revenues* from each revenue source in addition to the detail by category of net asset changes.
- Emphasizes that expenses are reported as changes in unrestricted net assets—not as changes in temporarily restricted or permanently restricted net assets.
- Highlights the offsetting relationship between (1) the increase in *unrestricted* net assets and (2) the decrease in *temporarily* restricted net assets for net assets released from restrictions.

Statement of Cash Flows

Illustration 16-8, the Statement of Cash Flows, is quite similar to a business cash flow statement. Note the key modifications as you review the statement:

- Contributions and earnings that are restricted for plant or endowment purposes are classified as financing activities.
- The decrease in cash restricted for long-term purposes is classified as an investing activity.
- Operating cash flows are reconciled with the change in net assets instead of with net income.

This statement is prepared in accordance with FASB guidance. Unlike the GASB, the FASB allows either the direct method or the indirect method when preparing the Statement of Cash Flows. The direct method is demonstrated in this example.

Statement of Functional Expenses

The Statement of Functional Expenses in Illustration 16-9 is a basic, required financial statement of VHWOs. *This statement presents the expenses incurred for each program or function in detail by object class.* In practice, there likely will be less detailed classifications presented. Again, this statement is optional for ONPOs.

ILLUSTRATION 16-7   Operating Statement

Illustrative VHWO/ONPO
Statement of Activities
For the Year Ended December 31, 20X1

Changes in Unrestricted Net Assets:

Revenues and gains:

Contributions (net of estimated uncollectible pledges of $20,000)*		$ 363,000
Special events	$75,000	
Less: Direct costs of special events	25,000	50,000
Membership dues		17,300
Investment income**		34,000
Gain on sale of equipment		10,000
Total revenues and gains		474,300
Net assets released from restrictions		445,000
Increase in unrestricted net assets		919,300

Expenses:

Program Services:	
Research	103,800
Education	184,000
Total program services	287,800
Supporting Services:	
Management and general [includes interest]	171,200
Fund-raising	91,000
Total supporting services	262,200
Total expenses	550,000
Net increase in unrestricted net assets	369,300

Changes in Temporarily Restricted Net Assets:

Contributions	275,000
Investment income**	35,500
Net assets released from restrictions	(445,000)
Decrease in temporarily restricted net assets	(134,500)

Changes in Permanently Restricted Net Assets:

Contributions	55,000
Investment income permanently restricted by donors	10,500
Realized gains on sale of investments**	1,400
Increase in permanently restricted net assets	66,900
Increase in net assets	301,700
Net assets, January 1	1,193,000
Net assets, December 31	$1,494,700

*Contributions may be reported at the net realizable value of pledges (plus other contributions) only if pledges are to be collected within a year. Otherwise, the present value, not the net realizable value, of the pledges should be included in contributions. Donated materials, services, and facilities are included in the contributions total.

**The illustration assumes that the carrying value of investments equals their fair value at year end. If not, unrealized gains or losses on investments reported at fair value would be reported.

This statement may be presented in columnar format using one column for each class of net assets and one for the totals.

16-1 IN PRACTICE

The American National Red Cross
Consolidated Statement of Activities
Year ended June 30, 20X1
(with summarized information for the year ended June 30, 20X0)
(In thousands)

	Unrestricted	Temporarily Restricted	Permanently Restricted	Totals 20X1	20X0
Operating revenues and gains:					
Contributions:					
Corporate, foundation and individual giving	$ 227,442	$ 458,505	$ —	$ 685,947	$ 813,928
United Way and other federated	36,203	75,070	—	111,273	119,825
Legacies and bequests	51,453	8,063	22,032	81,548	92,496
Services and materials	15,174	20,098	—	35,272	34,888
Products and Services:					
Biomedical	2,189,663	—	—	2,189,663	2,200,550
Program materials	139,177	45	—	139,222	145,326
Contracts, including federal government	112,804	—	—	112,804	89,282
Investment income (Note 8)	19,339	30,245	—	49,584	48,595
Other revenues	64,429	793	—	65,222	59,545
Net assets released from restrictions	704,812	(704,812)	—	—	—
Total operating revenues and gains	3,560,496	(111,993)	22,032	3,470,535	3,604,435
Operating expenses:					
Program services:					
Services to the Armed Forces	57,403	—	—	57,403	65,300
Biomedical services (Note 12)	2,195,108	—	—	2,195,108	2,194,789
Community services	90,558	—	—	90,558	105,278
Domestic disaster services	282,974	—	—	282,974	268,864
Health and safety services	203,735	—	—	203,735	216,946
International relief and development services	340,106	—	—	340,106	250,993
Total program services	3,169,884	—	—	3,169,884	3,102,170
Supporting services:					
Fund raising	127,019	—	—	127,019	130,193
Management and general	142,682	—	—	142,682	138,472
Total supporting services	269,701	—	—	269,701	268,665
Total operating expenses	3,439,585	—	—	3,439,585	3,370,835
Change in net assets from operations	120,911	(111,993)	22,032	30,950	233,600
Nonoperating gains, net (Notes 5 and 8)	77,047	98,209	17,901	193,157	138,497
Pension-related changes other than net periodic benefit cost (Note 10)	8,929	—	—	8,929	(85,676)
Change in net assets	206,887	(13,784)	39,933	233,036	286,421
Net assets, beginning of year	448,142	884,910	625,835	1,958,887	1,672,466
Net assets, end of year	$ 655,029	$ 871,126	$ 665,768	$ 2,191,923	$ 1,958,887

See accompanying notes to the consolidated financial statements.
Source: Excerpt from AMERICAN RED CROSS FY11 FINANCIAL RESULTS A MESSAGE FROM THE CHIEF FINANCIAL OFFICER. Reprinted with permission.

ILLUSTRATION 16-8   Statement of Cash Flows

Illustrative VHWO/ONPO
Statement of Cash Flows
For the Year Ended December 31, 20X1

Cash flows from operating activities:

Cash received from contributors	$330,000
Cash received from sale of assets donated for resale	150,000
Cash received from special events	50,000
Cash received from membership dues	17,300
Interest and dividends received	56,500
Interest paid	(20,000)
Cash paid to employees and suppliers	(476,800)
Net cash provided by operating activities	107,000

Cash flows from investing activities:

Purchase of buildings and improvements	(200,000)
Purchase of equipment	(140,000)
Proceeds from sale of equipment	40,000
Proceeds from sale of investments	14,400
Decrease in cash invested in assets restricted for plant and endowment purposes*	143,100
Net cash used by investing activities	(142,500)

Cash flows from financing activities:

Proceeds from contributions restricted for:	
Investment in endowment	55,000
Investment in plant	100,000
Interest and dividends restricted to reinvestment	22,500
Payment of mortgage notes payable	(40,000)
Net cash provided by financing activities	137,500
Net increase in cash	102,000
Cash at the beginning of the year	125,000
Cash at the end of the year	$227,000

**Reconciliation of change in net assets and cash provided
by operating activities:**

Change in net assets	$301,700
Adjustments to reconcile change in net assets to net cash provided by operating activities:	
Depreciation expense	30,000
Increase in pledges receivable	(30,000)
Decrease in interest receivable	2,000
Increase in inventory	(4,800)
Decrease in vouchers payable	(3,000)
Increase in salaries payable	3,000
Gain on sale of equipment	(10,000)
Gain on sale of long-term investments	(1,400)
Contributions restricted for long-term investment	(155,000)
Interest and dividends restricted for long-term investment	(25,500)
Net cash provided by operating activities	$107,000

*In practice, this cash would probably have been invested; then the investments would have been sold. Therefore, this amount would normally have been reflected in the difference between cash used to purchase investments and cash received from sale of investments.

ILLUSTRATION 16-9 **Statement of Functional Expenses**

Illustrative VHWO/ONPO
Statement of Functional Expenses
For the Year Ended December 31, 20X1

	Program Services			Supporting Services			Total Expenses
	Research	Education	Total	Management and General	Fund-Raising	Total	
Salaries	$ 16,000	$ 27,000	$ 43,000	$ 30,000	$ 15,000	$ 45,000	$ 88,000
Employee health and retirement benefits	1,289	3,340	4,629	4,648	1,284	5,932	10,561
Payroll taxes, etc.	644	1,670	2,314	2,324	642	2,966	5,280
Total Salaries and Related Expenses	17,933	32,010	49,943	36,972	16,926	53,898	103,841
Professional fees and contract service payments	34,996	90,710	125,706	13,428	2,283	15,711	141,417
Supplies	4,852		4,852	9,296	6,000	15,296	20,148
Telephone and Internet	1,245	1,670	2,915	7,747	5,965	13,712	16,627
Postage and shipping	1,192	1,670	2,862	6,714	8,015	14,729	17,591
Occupancy	10,000	2,000	12,000	15,494	7,707	23,201	35,201
Rental of equipment	322	835	1,157	1,549	4,567	6,116	7,273
Local transportation	966	2,505	3,471	11,879	8,563	20,442	23,913
Conferences, conventions, meetings	2,577	6,680	9,257	19,626	3,711	23,337	32,594
Printing and publications	1,289	3,340	4,629	7,231	18,268	25,499	30,128
Awards and grants	16,106	39,747	55,853				55,853
Interest				20,000		20,000	20,000
Meals					25,000	25,000	25,000
Miscellaneous	322	833	1,155	8,264	5,995	14,259	15,414
Depreciation of buildings, improvements, and equipment	12,000	2,000	14,000	13,000	3,000	16,000	30,000
Total Expenses	103,800	184,000	287,800	171,200	116,000	287,200	575,000
Less: Expenses deducted directly from revenues					(25,000)	(25,000)	(25,000)
Total expenses reported by function	$103,800	$184,000	$287,800	$171,200	$ 91,000	$262,200	$550,000

Concluding Comments

VHWOs and ONPOs encompass a myriad of diverse types of not-for-profit organizations. Some of these organizations are government entities; many are not. This chapter discussed the accounting and reporting standards applicable to *nongovernment* VHWOs and ONPOs. *Government VHWOs and ONPOs are required to apply the same reporting principles and practices as all other government entities.* Significant differences also exist in the accounting and financial reporting for nongovernment and government health care organizations and colleges and universities. The key differences in accounting and financial reporting for nongovernment not-for-profit colleges and universities and health care entities compared to government organizations of these types are discussed in the following chapters.

Q16-1 What is the difference between voluntary health and welfare organizations and other not-for-profit organizations? Give common examples of each.

Q16-2 Some VHWOs and ONPOs are required to follow the FASB's not-for-profit accounting guidance. Others are not permitted to do so. Why do different standards apply? Which organizations must apply the FASB guidance? What guidance must the other organizations apply?

Q16-3 What are the basic financial statements required for nongovernment ONPOs?

Q16-4 Identify and distinguish between the three classes of net assets required by *SFAS No. 117*.

Q16-5 When should a nongovernment ONPO recognize contributions that are restricted by donors for capital asset acquisitions?

Q16-6 Inexhaustible collections of ONPOs are not required to be capitalized or depreciated, if certain criteria are met. Why is this so, and what accounting and reporting recognition, if any, is required for such inexhaustible collections?

Q16-7 Gifts, contributions, and bequests to VHWOs and ONPOs may be restricted for specified operating or capital outlay purposes. Explain how restricted contributions, gifts, and bequests are accounted for by nongovernment VHWOs (a) at receipt and (b) upon expenditure.

Q16-8 Some VHWOs and ONPOs combine educational and program brochures with their fund-raising mailings and charge part or all of the cost of the mailings to program services. Why? Also, when is this permitted by GAAP?

Q16-9 A VHWO receives pledges from donors for contributions to be received annually over the next three years. When should these contributions be recognized as revenues? As changes in which net asset class? How should the amount of revenues be measured?

Q16-10 What classificational detail must a not-for-profit organization present for expenses? What are the major classifications of expenses? Distinguish between them.

Q16-11 What is the difference between conditional and unconditional pledges? What effect does this distinction have on revenue recognition?

Q16-12 What is the difference between restricted and unrestricted contributions? What effect do restrictions have on revenue recognition?

Q16-13 What are "net assets released from restrictions"? How are they reported?

Q16-14 When are restricted contributions and restricted investment income permitted to be reported as unrestricted revenues instead of as temporarily restricted revenues?

Q16-15 Explain how each of the following transactions should be reported by a nongovernment not-for-profit organization:
a. Received a pledge for unrestricted contributions to be received in the next fiscal year, $100,000.
b. Received a pledge for $500,000, conditioned on whether the not-for-profit's clientele achieve a 10% average increase in reading scores during the next calendar year.
c. Received cash gifts of $250,000, restricted to community outreach programs—one of three broad program categories of the organization.
d. Received pledges of $800,000, restricted to purchase or construction of a headquarters building for the organization.

Q16-16 When nongovernment VHWOs and ONPOs hold fund-raising events such as banquets, auctions, and bazaars, the gross receipts must often be reported as revenues. Explain or illustrate how the direct costs of these special fund-raising events are to be reported. Also, may these nongovernment organizations report the special event using the net method?

Q16-17 Donated services are sometimes given accounting recognition—and at other times are not given accounting recognition—in the accounts and statements of VHWOs and ONPOs. Explain why some are given accounting recognition and others are not. (Do not list the criteria.)

Exercises

E16-1 (Multiple Choice) Identify the best answer for each of the following:
1. Not-for-profit reporting standards require net assets to be reported in all of the following classes *except*
   a. unrestricted net assets.
   b. invested in capital assets, net of related debt.
   c. permanently restricted net assets.
   d. temporarily restricted net assets.

2. Which of the following is *not* a common characteristic of a VHWO?
   a. Typically, no fees or only minimal fees are charged for services a VHWO provides.
   b. Resource providers are typically the primary recipients of the VHWO's services.
   c. A VHWO may be governmental or nongovernmental in nature.
   d. A VHWO's primary purpose is to meet a community health, welfare, or other social need.
3. Securities donated to a VHWO should be recorded at the
   a. donor's recorded amount.
   b. fair market value at the date of the gift.
   c. fair market value at the date of the gift or the donor's book value, whichever is lower.
   d. fair market value at the date of the gift or the donor's book value, whichever is higher.

Questions 4 and 5 are based on the following data:

The Charles Vernon Eames Community Service Center is a nongovernment VHWO financed by contributions from the general public. During 20X5, unrestricted pledges of $900,000 were received, half of which were payable in 20X5, with the other half payable in 20X6 for use in 20X6. It was estimated that 10% of these pledges would be uncollectible. In addition, Louease Jones, a social worker, contributed 800 hours of her time to the center at no charge to assist with fund-raising activities. Jones's annual social worker salary is $20,000 based on a workload of 2,000 hours.

4. How much should the center report as contributions revenue for 20X5 from the pledges?
   a. $0
   b. $405,000
   c. $810,000
   d. $413,000
5. How much should the center record in 20X5 for contributed service expense?
   a. $8,000
   b. $4,000
   c. $800
   d. $0
6. Cura Foundation, a nongovernment VHWO supported by contributions from the general public, included the following costs in its Statement of Functional Expenses for the year ended December 31, 20X6:

Fund-raising	$500,000
Administrative (including data processing)	300,000
Research	100,000

Cura's functional expenses for 20X6 program services were
   a. $900,000.
   b. $500,000.
   c. $300,000.
   d. $100,000.
7. The permanently restricted net assets of an ONPO include net assets from which of the following?

	Term Endowment Gifts	Capital Asset Restricted Gifts
a.	No	No
b.	No	Yes
c.	Yes	Yes
d.	Yes	No

8. During the years ended June 30, 20X5, and 20X6, a nongovernment ONPO conducted a cancer research project financed by a $2,000,000 restricted gift. This entire amount was pledged by the donor on July 10, 20X3, although he paid only $500,000 at that date. During the two-year research period, the ONPO-related gift receipts and research expenses were as follows:

	Year Ended June 30	
	20X5	20X6
Gift receipts	$700,000	$ 800,000
Cancer research expenses	900,000	1,100,000

How much temporarily restricted contributions revenue should the ONPO report in its Statement of Activities for the year ended June 30, 20X6?

a. $0
b. $800,000
c. $1,100,000
d. $2,000,000

9. What amount of net assets released from restrictions should the ONPO in question 8 report in its Statement of Activities for 20X6?

a. $0
b. $800,000
c. $1,100,000
d. $2,000,000

10. A nongovernment VHWO received an unconditional pledge in 20X5 from a donor specifying that the amount pledged be used in 20X7. The donor paid the pledge in cash in 20X6. The pledge should be reflected in

a. temporarily restricted net assets in the Balance Sheet at the end of 20X5, and in unrestricted net assets at the end of 20X6.
b. temporarily restricted net assets in the Balance Sheet at the end of 20X5 and 20X6, and in unrestricted net assets at the end of 20X7.
c. in unrestricted net assets at the end of 20X5.
d. net assets only after collected in 20X6.

(Questions 3–10, AICPA, adapted)

E16-2 (Multiple Choice) Identify the best answer for each of the following:
1. VHWO GAAP financial statements are prepared under which basis of accounting?

a. Cash
b. Accrual
c. Modified accrual
d. Modified cash

2. The primary financial statement(s) that must be prepared by ONPOs do *not* include a:

a. Balance Sheet.
b. Statement of Cash Flows.
c. Statement of Functional Expenses.
d. Statement of Activities.

3. On December 31, 20X7, the Greater Ottumwa (Iowa) United Fund, a VHWO, had $150,000 in pledges receivable from 20X7 pledges, all of which were receivable during 20X8. During the past five years, this nongovernment agency has collected an average of 90% of all pledges. With respect to the agency's 20X7 financial statements, what amount of contributions revenue should be recognized for the pledges?

a. $0
b. $135,000
c. $150,000
d. $135,000 or $150,000, depending on the VHWO's policy

4. Unconditional promises to give that are restricted for the purpose of acquiring fixed assets should be recognized as contributions revenue by nongovernment VHWOs and ONPOs in the period(s) that

a. the unconditional promises are made.
b. the promised amounts are received.
c. the donated resources are used to acquire the fixed assets.
d. the assets purchased with the donated resources are placed in service.

5. A nongovernment ONPO incurred expenses for its public service programs. The ONPO had resources available from prior year donations that were restricted by donors to finance expenses for these public service programs. Which of the following is (are) *true*?

a. The ONPO should recognize the expenses as decreases in temporarily restricted net assets—because they are financed from temporarily restricted net assets.
b. The ONPO should recognize contributions revenue in the current year as an increase in unrestricted net assets.
c. This transaction will reduce temporarily restricted net assets.
d. The ONPO should recognize contributions revenue in the current year as an increase in temporarily restricted net assets.

6. Which of the following would not affect a nongovernment ONPO Statement of Activities?

a. Depreciation expense
b. Expenditure of restricted contributions for the restricted purpose in the current year (but cash was received in a prior year)
c. Gain on the sale of investments
d. Proceeds from issuing bonds to finance a capital project

7. A regular contributor to a not-for-profit organization has agreed to directly pay the rental charges for a local banquet facility that will be used for the organization's annual financial campaign kick-off event. How should this transaction be reported in the financial statements of the not-for-profit organization?
   a. If material, the rental costs paid on its behalf should be disclosed in the notes.
   b. The not-for-profit organization should only report expenses for which it expended funds or incurred liabilities.
   c. The costs paid on its behalf would be reported both as a revenue and an expense of the not-for-profit organization.
   d. The transaction would not affect the financial report of the organization.

8. What characteristics distinguish not-for-profit contributions from exchange or agency transactions?
   a. They are generally unconditional (i.e., not subject to future or uncertain events that would require their return).
   b. The contributions are typically conditional and nonreciprocal in nature.
   c. They are generally unconditional and nonreciprocal in nature.
   d. An ownership interest is typically established.

9. Nongovernment not-for-profit organizations present a Statement of Cash Flows in accordance with
   a. GASB *Statement No. 9.*
   b. GASB *Statement No. 34.*
   c. The FASB *Accounting Standards Codification.*
   d. Either b or c, at management's discretion.

10. A nongovernment not-for-profit organization would present all of the following categories of cash flows *except*
    a. cash flows from financing activities.
    b. cash flows from noncapital financing activities.
    c. cash flows from investing activities.
    d. cash flows from operating activities.

E16-3 (Pledges and Gifts) Record the following transactions in the accounts of a nongovernment VHWO or ONPO.
1. Unconditional pledges made to the organization during the year total $1,000,000 unrestricted and $500,000 restricted to a specific program. All of the restricted pledges are collected during the year and 75% of the unrestricted pledges are collected; 20% of the uncollected pledges outstanding at year end are expected to be uncollectible.
2. Cash gifts of $300,000 are collected during the year. These gifts are restricted for permanent endowment purposes.
3. Qualifying costs of $222,000 are incurred for the program for which restricted pledges were received.
4. Conditional pledges made to the organization during the year total $90,000 (unrestricted). None were collected during the year.

E16-4 (Various Transactions) Record the following transactions in the accounts of a nongovernment VHWO or ONPO.
1. Purchased supplies on account, $50,000.
2. Used supplies costing $40,000.
3. Purchased equipment costing $16,000, using donor-restricted resources.
4. Issued $1,000,000 of bonds at par.
5. Sold land that had cost $33,000 for $45,000.
6. Received interest earned on investment of donor-restricted resources, $6,000. The donor did not specify that the interest income be used for the same purpose stipulated for the principal of the gift, but the organization traditionally has done so and plans to in this case.

E16-5 (Capital-Asset-Related Entries)
(a) Prepare journal entries to record the following transactions for a nongovernment not-for-profit organization.
   1. Purchased equipment from unrestricted resources at a cost of $30,000. Cash was paid.
   2. Depreciation on the equipment was $12,000 for the year.
   3. Sold the equipment for $20,000 when its book value was $18,000. Received cash (no restrictions).
(b) What are the effects of Transactions 1 through 3 on the three classes of net assets?

E16-6 (Restricted Gifts) Prepare journal entries to record the following transactions of a nongovernment not-for-profit organization.
1. Received pledges of $1,000,000; 15% are expected to be uncollectible. No collections are expected before the beginning of the next fiscal year.
2. Received cash gifts of $3,000,000, restricted for research on "killer bees."
3. Incurred $2,200,000 of costs for killer bee research.

E16-7 (Column Format Statement of Activities) Recast the Statement of Activities of the Illustrative VHWO/ONPO presented in Illustration 16-7, page 661, in a columnar format. Use one column for changes in each class of net assets and a total column.

E16-8 ("Pancake" Format Statement of Activities) Recast the Statement of Activities of the American Red Cross (16-1 In Practice, page 662) in the "pancake" format shown in Illustration 16-7.

Problems

P16-1 (Donation-Related Entries) Mr. Larry Leininger donated $3,000,000 to a nongovernment VHWO on June 17, 20X8.
1. Assume that no restrictions are placed on the use of the donated resources.
   a. Prepare the required June 17, 20X8, entry.
   b. Prepare any entries necessary in 20X9 if $400,000 of the gift is used to finance VHWO operating expenses.
2. Assume that the donation was restricted to research.
   a. Prepare the required June 17, 20X8, entry.
   b. Prepare any entries required in 20X9 as a result of spending $400,000 for research during 20X9.
3. Assume that the donation was restricted for fixed asset acquisitions.
   a. Prepare the required June 17, 20X8, entry.
   b. Prepare any entries required in 20X9 if $400,000 of the gift is used to purchase a new building. The building is placed in service at year end.
4. Explain or illustrate how each of the three preceding situations would be reported in the nongovernment VHWO's financial statements in 20X8 and in 20X9.

P16-2 Part I (Fixed-Asset-Related Entries) The Thelma Colone Society entered into the following transactions in 20X8.

April 1—Purchased equipment with donor-restricted resources for $47,300. The equipment has a 5-year useful life and no salvage value; it was used throughout the rest of the year.

July 1—Issued $10,000,000 of 10%, 20-year bonds at par to finance construction of a major building addition.

During 20X8—$800,000 of contributions to be used to service the bonds were received. Interest is due each June 30 and December 31.

October 31—Sold machinery for $19,000 halfway through its 8-year useful life. The machine originally cost $25,000 and was expected to have a $10,000 salvage value. (Assume straight-line depreciation.)

December 31—The first semiannual interest payment on the bonds was made. (Record all required adjustments as well as the interest payment.)

Prepare all entries required on the preceding dates to record these transactions, assuming that the Thelma Colone Society is a nongovernment ONPO and that December 31 is the end of the fiscal year. *Required*

P16-2 Part II (Endowment Entries) P. S. Callahan, a noted philanthropist, donated $2,000,000 to the Neuland Community Center with the stipulation that the first 10 years of earnings be used to endow specific programs of the organization. At the end of the 10-year period, half of the principal of the gift will become available for unrestricted use and half for capital additions.

(a) Assume that the Neuland Center is a nongovernment VHWO. *Required*
   1. Prepare the entry(ies) to record the gift.
   2. Prepare the entry(ies) to record the expiration of the term of the endowment.
(b) Describe how this gift should be reported in the Statement of Activities:
   1. When received.
   2. When the term expires.

P16-3 (Classification of Net Assets) A nongovernment VHWO or ONPO has the following resources:

Resources restricted for use in future years but not
   restricted to a specific purpose .... $ 1,300,000

Unrestricted resources designated for plant
   expansion 3,000,000

Undesignated, unrestricted resources 9,000,000
Resources restricted by donors for:
    Scholarships 4,000,000
    Research 10,000,000
    Plant expansion 5,000,000
    Term endowments 2,000,000
    Permanent endowments 50,000,000
Resources invested in fixed assets (net of related
    accumulated depreciation and debt) 17,000,000
Resources restricted by bond indenture
    for plant expansion 4,500,000

Required   Prepare the net assets section of the Balance Sheet for this nongovernment VHWO or ONPO.

P16-4 (ONPO Balance Sheet) The bookkeeper of the West Texas Zoological and Botanical Society, a nongovernment ONPO, prepared the following Balance Sheet:

West Texas Zoological and Botanical Society
Balance Sheet
December 31, 20X5
Assets

Cash	$ 350,000
Accounts receivable	120,000
Allowance for doubtful accounts	(20,000)
Pledges receivable	700,000
Allowance for doubtful pledges	(100,000)
Inventories	300,000
Investments	15,000,000
Land	1,000,000
Buildings and improvements	35,000,000
Equipment	2,000,000
Accumulated depreciation	(10,000,000)
Other assets	150,000
	$ 44,500,000

Liabilities and Fund Balance

Accounts payable	$ 525,000
Accrued expenses payable	100,000
Unearned revenue—unrestricted (exchange transactions) . .	75,000
Deferred support—restricted	4,500,000
Deferred capital contributions	1,200,000
Long-term debt	6,000,000
	12,400,000
Fund Balance:	
Invested in plant	22,000,000
Endowment	2,850,000
Restricted—specific programs	1,000,000
Unrestricted	6,250,000
	32,100,000
	$ 44,500,000

Additional Information

1. The Endowment Fund consists solely of investments, except for $50,000 of cash, and has no liabilities.
2. Restricted operating gifts include $115,000 cash, the pledges receivable, and $25,000 of accounts payable, in addition to investments.
3. The deferred support and deferred capital contributions relate to unconditional pledges collected.

Prepare in good form a corrected Balance Sheet for the West Texas Zoological and Botanical   ***Required***
Society, a nongovernment ONPO, at December 31, 20X5.

P16-5 (Various VHWO Entries) Prepare the general journal entries needed to record the
following transactions and events in the general ledger accounts of the Valdes Helping Hand
Institute, a nongovernment VHWO:

1. Contributions were received as follows:

a.	Cash:	$ 700,000	for general operations
		600,000	for building addition
		200,000	for aid to the elderly
		500,000	as an endowment—income restricted for aid to handicapped
		$2,000,000	
b.	Pledges:	$ 750,000	for aid to the handicapped
		950,000	for building additions
		150,000	for general operations in future years
		$1,850,000	

Experience indicates that 10% of the pledges will prove uncollectible.
2. A building addition was completed at a cost of $1,500,000. The $600,000 received in item 1
   was paid the contractor, and the balance is owed on a 5-year, 12% note.
3. Expenditures, all paid, were made as follows:

From:	*For:*	*Amount*
Unrestricted Resources	Fund-raising	$ 100,000
	General and Administrative	80,000
	Aid to Children (Program A)	320,000
		$ 500,000

From:	*For:*	*Amount*
Restricted Resources	Aid to Elderly (Program B)	$ 200,000
	Aid to Handicapped (Program C)	400,000
	1/10 of the note principal	90,000
	Six months' interest on note	54,000
	Endowment investments	450,000
		$1,194,000

4. Equipment costing $300,000 was purchased from unrestricted resources.
5. An older piece of equipment—original cost $100,000; accumulated depreciation $65,000—
   was sold for $40,000. The cash received was unrestricted.
6. A lot and building, estimated fair market value $850,000, were donated to the institute on
   the condition that they be sold and the proceeds used for Program D, which serves physically and mentally handicapped babies and children.
7. The lot and building (6) sold immediately for $850,000.
8. Investment earnings were accrued and received as follows:

Earnings on unrestricted investments	$ 40,000	accrued
Restricted earnings on program-restricted investments	60,000	accrued
Restricted earnings on endowment investments [Restricted to Aid to Handicapped]	65,000	cash
Unrestricted earnings on investments restricted for plant purposes	35,000	cash
	$200,000	

9. A fund-raising bazaar and banquet were held. All $300,000 of gross receipts were unre-
   stricted. Costs incurred—including food, gifts, kitchen help, and waiters—totaled $60,000.
   Costs would have been higher, but the hotel waived its normal charge ($10,000) and a
   local supermarket donated food and other merchandise valued at $7,500.
10. To ensure that the babies, young children, and elderly clients are receiving proper medical
    attention, a local doctor gives each a thorough physical examination annually. He refuses

to accept payment for his services, conservatively valued at $30,000. Similarly, a clinical psychologist ensures that each client is properly tested (e.g., intelligence, aptitudes, and progress) on a timely basis. His time would be conservatively valued at $15,000 if he accepted payment. Both the doctor and the psychologist have assigned duties, keep regular hours, maintain case records on each child, and call to the attention of institute staff members each child's status, potential, and psychological or medical needs. Both spend their time approximately 30% on Program A clients, 20% on Program B clients, and 25% each on Program C and D clients.

11. The family that donated the lot and building (in item 6) also donated land and a small building adjacent to the institute offices for use as an infant nursery and playground. The land and building are conservatively appraised at:

Land	$100,000
Building	250,000
	$350,000

However, there is a 6%, $50,000 mortgage note payable on the building, which the institute assumed.

P16-6 (Nongovernment VHWO Operating Statement and Balance Sheet) Following is the adjusted trial balance of the Community Association for Handicapped Children, a nongovernment voluntary health and welfare organization, at June 30, 20X6:

Community Association for Handicapped Children
Adjusted Trial Balance*
June 30, 20X6

	Dr.	Cr.
Cash	$ 49,000	
Bequest receivable	5,000	
Pledges receivable	12,000	
Accrued interest receivable	1,000	
Investments (at cost, which approximates market)	100,000	
Accounts payable and accrued expenses		$ 51,000
Unearned exchange revenue		2,000
Allowance for uncollectible pledges		3,000
Fund balances, July 1, 20X5:		
Designated		12,000
Undesignated		26,000
Restricted		3,000
Unrestricted endowment income		20,000
Contributions		315,000
Membership dues		25,000
Program service fees		30,000
Investment income		10,000
Deaf children's program	120,000	
Blind children's program	150,000	
Management and general services	49,000	
Fund-raising services	9,000	
Provision for uncollectible pledges	2,000	
	$ 497,000	$497,000

*Other information—not reflected in the trial balance:
1. Investments of permanent endowment, $500,000.
2. Equipment, $150,000.
3. Accumulated depreciation, $50,000.
4. Note payable for equipment, $12,000.
5. Current-year depreciation, management and general, $6,000.

Required   (a) Prepare the Statement of Activities for the year ended June 30, 20X6.
                (b) Prepare the Balance Sheet as of June 30, 20X6. (AICPA, adapted)

P16-7 (Nongovernment ONPO/VHWO Statement of Activities) The following information for 20X7 was derived from the records of a nongovernment ONPO or VHWO:

Unrestricted contributions	$ 5,000,000
Unrestricted contributions (intended to finance next year)	700,000
Contributions restricted for specific programs	2,300,000
Contributions restricted for permanent endowments	4,000,000
Contributions restricted for term endowments	600,000
Contributions restricted for plant assets	11,000,000
Special event revenues	3,000,000
Unrestricted investment income of permanent endowments	3,000,000
Investment income restricted for plant purposes	2,700,000
Restricted gain on sale of investments of permanent endowments	950,000
Membership dues (not contributions)	1,800,000
Expenses for research programs for which donor-restricted resources are available	3,500,000
Expenses for other research programs	1,750,000
Purchase of capital assets from donor-restricted resources	7,000,000
Expiration of term endowments (unrestricted)	1,200,000
Expenses for community service programs	3,000,000
Special events—Direct costs	2,100,000
Expenses for fund-raising	1,000,000
Expenses for administrative functions	700,000
Beginning unrestricted net assets	3,000,000
Beginning temporarily restricted net assets	9,400,000
Beginning permanently restricted net assets	22,000,000

Required Prepare a Statement of Activities for this nongovernment not-for-profit organization for the year ended December 31, 20X7. Special events are part of the major or central ongoing activities of the entity.

P16-8 (Nongovernment ONPO Statement of Activities) The following information was drawn from the accounts and records of the Kindness Cooperative, a nongovernment ONPO. The balances are as of December 31, 20X7, unless otherwise noted.

Unrestricted Support—Contributions	$335,000,000
Unrestricted Support—Donated Materials	10,000,000
Unrestricted Support—Donated Facilities	8,000,000
Unrestricted Support—Donated Services	10,000,000
Unrestricted Support—Special Events	75,000,000
Unrestricted Revenues—Membership Dues	17,300,000
Unrestricted Revenues—Investment Income	34,000,000
Unrestricted Gain—Gain on Sale of Equipment	10,000,000
Expenses—Education	184,000,000
Expenses—Research	103,800,000
Expenses—Management and General	151,200,000
Expenses—Fund-Raising	91,000,000
Expenses—Direct Costs of Special Events	25,000,000
Expenses—Interest	20,000,000
Restricted Support—Contributions	275,000,000
Restricted Revenues—Investment Income	35,500,000
Permanently Restricted Support—Contributions	55,000,000
Permanently Restricted Revenues—Investment Income	10,500,000
Permanently Restricted Gain	1,400,000
Unrestricted Net Assets, January 1, 20X7	750,000,000
Temporarily Restricted Net Assets, January 1, 20X7	250,000,000
Permanently Restricted Net Assets, January 1, 20X7	300,000,000

In addition to the unrestricted contributions of $335 million, $100 million of unrestricted pledges outstanding at the beginning of 20X7 were collected during the year. All the expenses for research were financed from resources restricted for specific research projects; $110 million of construction expenditures and equipment purchases were financed from resources restricted for those purposes.

Required   Prepare the Kindness Cooperative's Statement of Activities for 20X7 in good form.

P16-9 (Statement of Activities) Based on the following information, prepare a Statement of Activities for the year ended December 31, 20X6, for the Mark Meadows Foundation, a private, not-for-profit charity.

1. Contributions of $3,000,000 (including $250,000 of pledges not collected by year end) were received from donors during the year without restriction.
2. Contributions of $1,000,000 restricted for public presentations for education purposes were received in cash during the year.
3. The foundation received gifts of $10 million to establish a permanent endowment to be used to generate resources for the foundation's community service programs.
4. Income restricted for specific community service programs was earned on the permanent endowment, $320,000.
5. Computers were purchased from unrestricted resources, $72,000.
6. A fund-raising banquet was held. Revenues (unrestricted) were $290,500, and direct costs of the banquet totaled $97,500.
7. Contributions of $1,500,000 were received. These contributions are restricted for building an activity center for the foundation.
8. Membership dues, for which members receive no benefits, total $75,000.
9. Unrestricted investment income earned totaled $83,400.
10. Expenses incurred for mailings, brochures, and other items for the purpose of soliciting donations totaled $95,000.
11. Administrative costs incurred during the year totaled $253,000.
12. Community service program expenses payable from restricted gifts totaled $220,000. Other expenses for community service programs totaled $2,110,000. Expenses for the foundation's education programs totaled $200,000, and expenses for its public presentations program were $555,000.
13. Costs incurred on the construction of the activity center totaled $922,000.
14. Unrestricted pledges made by contributors in the prior year but collected in the current year totaled $135,000.
15. Unrestricted net assets, January 1, 20X6, were $1,400,000.
16. Temporarily restricted net assets, January 1, 20X6, were $303,000.
17. There were no permanent endowments at the beginning of the year.
18. The foundation reports restricted gifts and income as increases in temporarily restricted net assets even if the restriction is satisfied in the year the gifts or income are initially recorded.

P16-10 (General Journal Entries—Nongovernment ONPO) Prepare journal entries to record the following transactions for a nongovernment ONPO.

1. Unrestricted cash gifts that were received last year but restricted for use in the current year totaled $50,000.
2. Unrestricted pledges of $600,000 were received. Donors specified that $450,000 of this amount was intended to finance current-year operations (even though part of those donations may not be collected until early next year). Ten percent (10%) of pledges typically prove uncollectible.
3. Pledges receivable of $480,000 were collected during the year; $7,000 of pledges were written off as uncollectible.
4. Donations of materials totaled $22,000; $5,000 of the materials were on hand at year end.
5. Membership dues of $400,000 were collected during the year. Members receive only nominal or no benefits in exchange for their dues.
6. Cash gifts to finance specific community outreach projects were received, $30,000.
7. Expenses were incurred for those specific community outreach projects—salaries, $3,000; equipment rental, $15,000. Management decided to pay these costs from unrestricted (rather than restricted) resources.
8. Cash gifts restricted to finance construction of a recreation center were received, $500,000. An additional amount was pledged and is expected to be collected in full in the next fiscal year, $2,200,000. No construction costs had been incurred by year end.

CHAPTER 17

Accounting for Colleges and Universities

LEARNING OBJECTIVES

After studying this chapter, you should be able to:

- Understand why most government colleges and universities choose to report as "business-type only" special purpose governments.

- Explain unique aspects of college and university reporting such as recognition of tuition and fee revenue, operating versus nonoperating revenue classifications, expense classifications, and scholarship allowances.

- Prepare journal entries consistent with government college and university financial reporting requirements.

- Prepare government college and university financial statements.

- Understand the principal differences between reporting government and nongovernment not-for-profit colleges and universities.

- Prepare nongovernment not-for-profit college and university financial statements.

Institutions of higher education are major forces both in the government sector of the U.S. economy and in the private sector of the economy. For most of the 20th century, accounting and reporting for colleges and universities followed industry standards that required identical financial reporting for all colleges and universities—whether government or nongovernment (i.e., private). The principal contributors to the development of these standards were the National Association of College and University Business Officers (NACUBO) and the American Institute of Certified Public Accountants (AICPA). NACUBO's *Financial Accounting and Reporting Manual,* or *FARM,* provides detailed guidance for colleges and universities on implementing GASB or FASB standards, as appropriate. Also, NACUBO provides valuable input to GASB and FASB deliberations on accounting standards that affect colleges and universities.

As discussed in Chapter 16, all *nongovernment* not-for-profit organizations—including private not-for-profit colleges and universities—are required to apply the FASB's not-for-profit accounting standards for financial reporting purposes. *Government* colleges and universities, on the other hand, are required by GASB *Statement No. 35,* "Basic Financial Statements—and Management's Discussion and Analysis—for Colleges and Universities," to apply the provisions of GASB *Statement No. 34,* which were discussed and illustrated in Chapters 2 to 15.

This chapter first discusses and illustrates **government** college and university accounting and reporting. Then, the key differences between accounting and reporting for government colleges and universities and for private colleges and universities are discussed. Finally, the financial statements of our illustrative university are presented under the assumption that it is a **private,** not-for-profit college instead of a government college.

CLASSIFICATION AS "ENGAGED ONLY IN BUSINESS-TYPE ACTIVITIES"

Government colleges and universities often are special purpose governments. As discussed in Chapter 13, special purpose governments that have both governmental activities and business-type activities must present a full set of basic financial statements—both fund financial statements and government-wide financial statements. However, *special purpose governments that are engaged only in business-type activities must present only the three Enterprise Fund financial statements and the notes to the financial statements—as well as Management's Discussion and Analysis and other required supplementary information.*

If a fee is charged to external users for goods or services provided, GASB *Statement No. 34 permits* that activity to be reported as an Enterprise Fund. A government is *required* to report the activity as an Enterprise Fund if the activity is financed with debt secured solely by a pledge of the net revenues from fees charged for the activity. Likewise, an Enterprise Fund *must* be used if either law or its pricing policy requires the fees to be sufficient to cover the full cost (including capital costs such as depreciation or debt service) of providing the services.

In applying the Enterprise Fund definition, the GASB *permits* a college or university to be evaluated as a single activity in determining whether the Enterprise Fund definition applies. On that basis most government colleges and universities are at least *permitted* to be treated as Enterprise Funds. Tuition and fees are essentially user charges and are a principal source of revenues of most government colleges and universities. The GASB's expectation when it issued *Statement No. 35* was that most colleges and universities would choose to report as Enterprise Funds. For this reason, *we discuss government college and university accounting and reporting under the assumption that the college or university is to be reported as a special purpose government engaged only in business-type activities.*

Financial reporting for a college or university as an enterprise (or business-type) activity is fundamentally the same as financial reporting for any other enterprise activity. Assets, deferred outflows of resources, liabilities, deferred inflows of resources, and net position should be measured and reported in the same manner as for other typical enterprise activities of general purpose state and local governments—that is, as discussed and illustrated in Chapter 10. Likewise, no truly unique revenue and expense recognition principles apply to government colleges and universities for financial reporting purposes. Even though tuition and fee revenues are a fairly unique source of revenues, for instance, the accounting and reporting for these exchange revenues are entirely consistent with accounting and reporting for other exchange revenues of other governments.

While financial reporting for government colleges and universities is quite similar to that for other governments, it is interesting to note that for internal management purposes, colleges and universities maintain their accounts differently from the way their financial reports are presented. Indeed, most government colleges and universities, including those that report as business-type-only activities, maintain their accounts on a fund basis during the year and account for revenues and expenditures, not expenses. The fund structure that typically is used internally is unique to colleges and universities, not the fund structure established in GASB *Statement No. 34.* This fund structure, summarized in Illustration 17-1, was developed by NACUBO over many years to meet the unique information needs of colleges and universities. Prior to the issuance of GASB *Statement No. 35,* government colleges and universities presented their financial statements using this fund structure, which is now an "internal only" fund structure. Likewise, these statements presented revenue and expenditure data, not revenue and expense data. Government colleges and universities are expected to continue using the unique college and university model for internal management and internal reporting purposes even though it is no longer permitted for GAAP financial reporting purposes. Colleges and universities that continue to use this model derive the information

ILLUSTRATION 17-1 Comparison of Common Internal College and University Fund Structure to Government Fund Structure

College/University Fund Group/Subgroup	Primary Purpose of Fund Group/Subgroup	Comparable Government Fund/Accounting Entity
Unrestricted Current Fund	Finance current operations	General
Restricted Current Fund	Finance specific part of current operations	Special Revenue
Unexpended Plant Fund	Acquisition of major capital assets	Capital Projects
Plant Funds for Retirement of Indebtedness	Servicing capital-asset-related long-term debt	Debt Service
Investment in Plant Accounts	Account for capital assets and related long-term liabilities	General Capital Assets and General Long-Term Liabilities accounts
Loan Funds	Loan programs for students, faculty, and staff	Permanent
Endowment and Similar Funds, Annuity and Life Income Funds	Typically to account for term endowments, permanent endowments, or similar gifts to benefit university programs	Permanent or Special Revenue
Agency	To maintain fiduciary responsibility for assets held in agency capacity	Agency

required to report in accordance with GASB *Statement No. 35* using conversion worksheets. These worksheets are similar to those illustrated in Chapter 14 for converting governmental funds revenue and expenditure data into aggregated governmental activities revenue and expense data for government-wide financial statements.

The required financial statements for a government college or university engaged solely in business-type activities are illustrated and discussed briefly in the following sections. Then, illustrative journal entries and financial statements are presented for a hypothetical government university.

GAAP REPORTING REQUIREMENTS

Government colleges and universities engaged in *only* business-type activities present three basic financial statements—the proprietary fund financial statements discussed and illustrated in Chapter 10. These statements are:

- Statement of Net Position—Illustration 17-2
- Statement of Revenues, Expenses, and Changes in Net Position—Illustration 17-3
- Statement of Cash Flows—Illustration 17-5

In addition to the statements and the related notes, these colleges and universities must present:

- Management's Discussion and Analysis [which is required supplementary information]
- Other Required Supplementary Information

Illustration 17-2 presents a statement of net position for a government university. As mentioned earlier, none of the assets or liabilities are unique to colleges and universities. Though not found in this illustration, deferred outflows and deferred inflows of resources are reported for government colleges and universities when present. *Net position* is presented in the three broad classifications required for other proprietary activities financial statements (and for government-wide financial statements): (1) *net investment in capital assets;* (2) *restricted net position;* and (3) *unrestricted net position.*

Statement of Net Position

ILLUSTRATION 17-2 Statement of Net Position

ABC University
Statement of Net Position
June 30, 20X2

ASSETS

Current Assets:

Cash and cash equivalents	$ 4,571,218
Short-term investments	15,278,981
Accounts receivable, net	6,412,520
Inventories	585,874
Deposit with bond trustee	4,254,341
Notes and mortgages receivable, net	359,175
Other assets	432,263
Total current assets	31,894,372

Noncurrent Assets:

Restricted cash and cash equivalents	24,200
Endowment investments	21,548,723
Notes and mortgages receivable, net	2,035,323
Investments in real estate	6,426,555
Capital assets, net	158,977,329
Total noncurrent assets	189,012,130
Total assets	220,906,502

LIABILITIES

Current Liabilities:

Accounts payable and accrued liabilities	4,897,470
Deferred revenue	3,070,213
Long-term liabilities—current portion	4,082,486
Total current liabilities	12,050,169

Noncurrent Liabilities:

Deposits	1,124,128
Deferred revenue	1,500,000
Long-term liabilities	31,611,427
Total noncurrent liabilities	34,235,555
Total liabilities	46,285,724

NET POSITION

Net investment in capital assets	126,861,400
Restricted for:	
Nonexpendable:	
Scholarships and fellowships	10,839,473
Research	3,767,564
Expendable:	
Scholarships and fellowships	2,803,756
Research	5,202,732
Instructional department uses	938,571
Loans	2,417,101
Capital projects	4,952,101
Debt service	4,254,341
Other	403,632
Unrestricted	12,180,107
Total net position	$174,620,778

Source: Adapted from GASB *Statement No. 35,* Appendix D.

Compared to the statements presented in Chapter 10, two items in this university statement of net position are noteworthy. First, note that *endowment investments*—a portion of which are permanent endowments—are reported as a *separate line item in noncurrent assets.* Second, note that *restricted net position* is divided into *two required subclassifications—nonexpendable and expendable.* These subclassifications are required when a government has permanent endowments or other permanently restricted principal amounts and restricted expendable amounts. Because significant permanent endowments are common in major government universities, restricted net position will be subclassified in this manner by many government colleges and universities.

Finally, just as it is common for government colleges and universities to have significant permanent endowments, it is common for them to be one of the beneficiaries in split interest gift arrangements. A *split interest gift* is essentially a trust with two or more beneficiaries. Because of the significance of these gifts and because they are not operations-related, we discuss them separately at the end of the college and university case illustration.

Most endowment investments in financial instruments are reported at fair value under GASB *Statement No. 31.* GASB *Statement No. 52,* "Land and Other Real Estate Held as Investments by Endowments," requires governments to report land and other real estate held for investments as part of an endowment at fair value. (Changes in fair value are included in investment income.)

Several noteworthy points can be observed by reviewing the Statement of Revenues, Expenses, and Changes in Net Position in Illustration 17-3. As *Statement Nos. 34* and *35* require:

Operating Statement

a. Tuition and fee revenues are reported *net* of scholarship allowances and uncollectible amounts.

b. Operating grants (and gifts) are reported as *nonoperating* revenues. Capital gifts and grants are reported *after* nonoperating revenues (expenses). Operating revenues may include grants and contracts as a revenue source. The substance of these amounts is better reflected by the term *contract*—implying an exchange or exchange-like transaction—than by the term *grant.* Many so-called research grants fit this description because the "grantor" is receiving something of value in exchange for the resources provided.

c. Auxiliary enterprise revenues are separately identified under operating revenues. Auxiliary enterprises is a unique revenue classification. Auxiliary enterprises are activities that exist to *furnish goods or services to students, faculty, or staff that are not directly related to the university's missions of teaching, research, or public service.* Auxiliary enterprises are self-supporting activities for which a fee is charged for goods or services and for which the fee is directly related to, but not necessarily equal to, the cost of providing the goods or services. Residence halls, food services, college stores, faculty and staff parking, and intercollegiate sports (when essentially self-supporting) are common examples of auxiliary enterprises.

d. State appropriations for other than capital-asset-related purposes are reported as *nonoperating revenues.* Many government colleges and universities receive a significant portion of their financing from resources provided by state (or other general purpose) governments. These revenues are referred to as *state (or other government) appropriations,* because they result from the provider government appropriating resources for and providing resources to the college or university. These revenues are recognized when received. If restricted to capital asset purposes, the revenues are referred to as "capital appropriations."

e. Capital appropriations are reported like capital gifts and grants.

f. Additions to permanent endowments are reported after nonoperating revenues and expenses, like capital gifts and grants.

Expenses may be reported using natural classifications of expenses as in this example or by function. Typical functional classifications of expenses for colleges and universities are discussed later in the chapter.

In addition, note that special items and extraordinary items should be reported as the last items before the change in net position. These items are not included in the example in Illustration 17-3.

ILLUSTRATION 17-3 Statement of Revenues, Expenses, and Changes in Net Position

ABC University
Statement of Revenues, Expenses, and Changes in Net Position
For the Year Ended June 30, 20X2

OPERATING REVENUES:

Student tuition and fees (net of scholarship allowances of $3,214,454)	$ 36,913,194
Federal grants and contracts	10,614,660
State and local grants and contracts	3,036,953
Nongovernmental grants and contracts	873,740
Sales and services of educational departments	19,802
Auxiliary enterprises:	
Residential life (net of scholarship allowances of $428,641)	28,079,274
Bookstore (net of scholarship allowances of $166,279)	9,092,363
Other operating revenues	143,357
Total operating revenues	88,773,343

OPERATING EXPENSES:

Salaries:	
Faculty	34,829,499
Exempt staff	29,597,676
Nonexempt wages	5,913,762
Benefits	18,486,559
Scholarships and fellowships	3,809,374
Utilities	16,463,492
Supplies and other services	12,451,064
Depreciation	6,847,377
Total operating expenses	128,398,803
Operating income (loss)	(39,625,460)

NONOPERATING REVENUES (EXPENSES):

State appropriations	39,760,508
Gifts	1,822,442
Investment income	2,182,921
Interest on capital asset-related debt	(1,330,126)
Other nonoperating revenues	313,001
Net nonoperating revenues	42,748,746
Income before other revenues, expenses, gains, or losses	3,123,286
Capital appropriations	2,075,750
Capital grants and gifts	690,813
Additions to permanent endowments	85,203
Increase in net position	5,975,052

NET POSITION:

Net position—beginning of year	168,645,726
Net position—end of year	$174,620,778

Source: Adapted from GASB *Statement No. 35,* Appendix D.

Tuition and Fee Revenues

Three of the previous observations about the operating statement—on tuition and fees revenues, restricted gifts and grants, and revenue and expense classification—warrant additional explanation. As noted, tuition and fees are reported net of scholarship allowances and net of uncollectible amounts. However, as observed in the operating expenses section of Illustration 17-3, some scholarships and fellowships are reported as expenses. It is important to understand the distinction between scholarship allowances and amounts that essentially are reported as financial aid expenses or as compensation expenses. Scholarship allowances are

> ... the difference between the stated charges for goods and services provided by the institution and the amount which is paid by the student and/or third parties making payments on behalf of the student.[1]

Essentially, scholarships from general resources of the college or university, scholarships from gifts provided to the university to finance scholarships awarded to students selected by the university, and tuition and fee payments made from sources such as Pell grants (which are reported as grant revenues) and used to cover tuition and fees are "scholarship allowances."

Scholarship allowances are deducted from tuition and fee revenues. That is, *tuition and fee revenues are reported net of scholarship allowances,* which may be disclosed parenthetically or in the notes to the financial statements.[2]

Any amounts from grants or from university resources that are paid to students, (i.e., amounts that require actual expenditure of university resources rather than reduction of charges) should be reported as *"scholarship and fellowship expenses."* Tuition waivers given as a result of employment by the university—such as for staff or for graduate assistants—should be reported as part of compensation expense.

Another commonly encountered issue regarding tuition and fees revenues is the timing of recognition of tuition and fees for a term that spans two fiscal years. Summer sessions are the terms most commonly involved. Under the best current guidance, these revenues and related expenses should be recognized proportionately in the two fiscal years affected. For instance, if two weeks of a six-week summer term fall in the 20X3–X4 fiscal year and the remaining four weeks fall in the 20X4–X5 fiscal year, one-third of the tuition and fees should be reported as 20X3–X4 revenues and two-thirds as 20X4–X5 revenues.

Restricted Gifts and Grants

The second area that warrants further discussion is the recognition of restricted gifts and grants. Government universities may receive significant amounts of restricted gifts and grants from individuals, foundations, and other governments. As discussed and illustrated in previous chapters, *most restricted government grants are reimbursement grants* with detailed stipulations regarding allowability of expenditures that must be met for expenditures to qualify for reimbursement. Reimbursement grants *typically* are *recognized as revenues when qualifying expenditures are incurred.*

Gifts and grants from private foundations and individuals that are *restricted only as to use for a specific purpose(s)* typically are reported as revenues when a legally enforceable pledge or cash is received. *Purpose restrictions* cause the assets to be reported as *restricted* assets, but do not delay revenue recognition. Under GASB *Statement No. 33,* gifts and grants received for a restricted purpose should be reported as revenues in the period received *if* they are *not* subject to *either* (1) legal or contractual stipulations regarding allowable expenditures, (2) time requirements, or (3) such provisions as matching requirements. Although gifts and grants from private foundations and individuals may be subject to time requirements or matching requirements, they usually are not subject to the detailed legal and contractual stipulations regarding allowability of expenditures associated with most government grants.

Gifts and grants received as permanent endowment gifts, term endowments, and annuity and life income gifts that have *no eligibility requirements except time*

---

[1]National Association of College and University Business Officers, *Advisory Report 97-1,* "Financial Accounting and Reporting Manual for Higher Education Release 02-6," para. 331.1 (Washington, DC: NACUBO, September 2003), para. 8.

[2]Alternatively, tuition and fee revenues may be reported at gross amounts with scholarship allowances deducted immediately thereafter on the face of the statement of revenues, expenses, and changes in net position.

17-1 IN PRACTICE

Government University Financial Statement: Practice Example

The University of Minnesota's Statement of Revenues, Expenses, and Changes in Net Position shows the types and relative size of revenue sources for one major university. It also illustrates the use of functional classifications unique to this special type of entity. Finally, note the similarity of the statement to that for "ABC University" in Illustration 17-3.

University of Minnesota

Consolidated Statements of Revenues, Expenses, and Changes in Net Position
Years ended June 30, 20X3 and 20X2 (in thousands)

Revenues			20X3	20X2
Operating revenues	Student tuition and fees, net of scholarship allowances of $81,379 in 20X3; $68,314 in 20X2		$ 348,675	$ 293,127
	Federal appropriations		15,562	18,215
	Federal grants and contracts		323,467	319,825
	State and other government grants		38,368	43,866
	Nongovernmental grants and contracts		164,463	144,637
	Student loan interest income		1,719	1,851
	Sales and services of educational activities		113,746	99,440
	Auxiliary enterprises, net of scholarship allowances of $8,628 in 20X3; $7,346 in 20X2. Revenues of $2,893 in 20X3; $2,663 in 20X2 were pledged as security for various auxiliary revenue bonds		229,367	206,721
	Other operating revenues		1,991	2,982
Total operating revenues			1,237,358	1,130,664
Expenses				
Operating expenses	Education and general	Instruction	569,375	534,251
		Research	411,568	421,796
		Public service	158,913	152,237
		Academic support	271,990	244,035
		Student services	68,140	66,995
		Institutional support	118,340	103,656
		Operation and maintenance of plant	160,240	148,252
		Scholarships and fellowships	67,461	58,989
		Depreciation	129,191	119,041
	Auxiliary enterprises		161,625	150,418
	Other operating expenses		896	486
Total operating expenses			2,117,739	2,000,156
Operating Loss			(880,381)	(869,492)
Nonoperating Revenues (Expenses)				
State appropriations			633,747	643,088
Grants			120,124	114,816
Gifts			94,011	89,079
Investment income			24,472	24,880
Net decrease in the fair market value of investments			(6,749)	(81,599)
Interest on capital asset-related debt			(29,420)	(22,400)
Other nonoperating expenses, net			(1,022)	(1,432)
Net nonoperating revenues			835,163	766,432
Loss Before Other Revenues			(45,218)	(103,060)
Capital appropriations			5,502	81,711
Capital grants and gifts			29,869	21,503
Additions to permanent endowments			1,939	2,128
Total other revenues			37,310	105,342
(Decrease) Increase in Net Position			(7,908)	2,282
Net Position				
Net position at beginning of year, restated			2,171,303	2,169,021
Net position at end of year			$2,163,395	$2,171,303

requirements are recognized as revenues as soon as the institution takes the actions required of it under the gift agreement. Thus, if the university receives a permanent endowment gift, it usually should recognize revenues as soon as it begins to invest and safeguard the resources—typically immediately upon receipt. Term endowment gifts, permanent endowment gifts, annuity gifts, and life income gifts—discussed later in the chapter—usually are recognized as revenues immediately upon receipt. If explicit purpose or time restrictions are placed on the use of the resources, these gifts will be reflected in restricted net position. Private contributions for building projects will be recognized as revenues upon receipt (or when pledged if legally enforceable) if the only stipulation on their use is that they must be used for the building project.

Revenue and Expense Classifications

Colleges and universities engaged only in business-type activities are not required by *Statement No. 35* to report revenues and expenses by functional category. Revenues are reported by source, and expenses may be reported either by object (or natural) classification (as in Illustration 17-3) or by function (as in 17-1 In Practice and Illustration 17-9). *Common revenue and expense classifications identified by the NACUBO are presented in* Illustration 17-4. Further, the NACUBO recommends

---

ILLUSTRATION 17-4   Classification of Revenues and Expenses

Revenues	Expenses
Tuition and Fees	Educational and General
Appropriations	*Instruction*
Federal	*Research*
State	*Public Service,* e.g.,
Local	Cooperative Extension Service
Grants and Contracts	Public Broadcasting Service
Federal	*Academic Support,* e.g.,
State	Academic Administration
Local	Academic Advising
Private Gifts, Grants, and Contracts	Educational Media Services
Sales and Services of Educational Activities, e.g.,	Museums and Galleries
Sales of Scientific and Literary Publications	*Student Services,* e.g.,
Testing Services	Counseling and Career Guidance
Sales and Services of Auxiliary Enterprises, e.g.,	Financial Aid Administration
Residence Halls	Student Admissions
Food Services	Student Records
College Stores	Student Social and Cultural Development
Athletic Programs	*Institutional Support,* e.g.,
Sales and Services of Hospitals	Academic Senate
Investment Income	Administrative Computer Support
Other Sources	Executive Management
	Fiscal Operations—Accounting
	Public Relations
	Operation and Maintenance of Plant*
	Scholarships and Fellowships
	Auxiliary Enterprises, Hospitals, and Independent Operations

*Although this classification may be reported by government colleges and universities, others must allocate these expenses to the functional categories because this is not a functional classification. Some colleges and universities report a subtotal for total educational and general expenses, and others do not.

ILLUSTRATION 17-5   Statement of Cash Flows

ABC University
Statement of Cash Flows
For the Year Ended June 30, 20X2

CASH FLOWS FROM OPERATING ACTIVITIES

Tuition and fees	$33,628,945
Research grants and contracts	13,884,747
Payments to suppliers	(28,175,500)
Payments to employees	(87,233,881)
Loans issued to students and employees	(384,628)
Collection of loans to students and employees	291,642
Auxiliary enterprise charges:	
Residence halls	26,327,644
Bookstore	8,463,939
Other receipts (payments)	1,415,502
Net cash provided (used) by operating activities	(31,781,590)

CASH FLOWS FROM NONCAPITAL FINANCING ACTIVITIES

State appropriations	39,388,534
Gifts and grants received for other than capital purposes:	
Private gifts for endowment purposes	85,203
Net cash flows provided by noncapital financing activities	39,473,737

CASH FLOWS FROM CAPITAL AND RELATED FINANCING ACTIVITIES

Proceeds from capital debt	4,125,000
Capital appropriations	1,918,750
Capital grants and gifts received	640,813
Proceeds from sale of capital assets	22,335
Purchases of capital assets	(8,420,247)
Principal paid on capital debt and lease	(3,788,102)
Interest paid on capital debt and lease	(1,330,126)
Net cash used by capital and related financing activities	(6,831,577)

CASH FLOWS FROM INVESTING ACTIVITIES

Proceeds from sales and maturities of investments	16,741,252
Interest on investments	2,111,597
Purchase of investments	(17,680,113)
Net cash provided by investing activities	1,172,736
Net increase in cash	2,033,306
Cash—beginning of year	2,562,112
Cash—end of year	$ 4,595,418

Source: Adapted from GASB *Statement No. 35*, Appendix D. (Accompanying schedules are not presented here.)

that government colleges and universities that report expenses using the natural classifications disclose the functional classifications of expenses in the notes to the financial statements. A college might provide this disclosure by presenting the equivalent of the statement of functional expenses illustrated for nongovernment not-for-profit entities in Chapter 16. Educational and general expenses include all expenses other than auxiliary enterprises, hospitals, and independent operations and commonly are reported in the more detailed functional classifications italicized in Illustration 17-4.

Note that a college that uses the functional classifications of expenses will report both auxiliary enterprise revenues and auxiliary enterprise expenses separate from other revenues and expenses. The same will be true of university hospitals, though hospitals often are discretely presented component units. Health care organization accounting and reporting are discussed in Chapter 18.

Statement of Cash Flows

The statement of cash flows for a college or university is presented in Illustration 17-5. The statement presents cash flows from operating activities under the direct method, as required by *Statement No. 34*. Note that cash receipts from sales of auxiliary enterprises are reported distinctly in the operating activities section. The schedule reconciling operating income and cash flows from operating activities and the schedule of significant noncash financing and investing activities are required but are not shown in Illustration 17-5.

CASE ILLUSTRATION—A GOVERNMENT UNIVERSITY

This section of the chapter presents transactions and entries for a government college and university case illustration assuming that accounts are maintained on a basis consistent with government GAAP reporting requirements. Transactions associated with operations are illustrated in this section. Endowment and similar type gifts are discussed and illustrated in the two following sections; then financial statements for the illustrative university are presented. Functional classifications of expenses are used in both the journal entries and the statements. However, for simplicity only the broadest classifications are used in the journal entry illustrations. Both revenues and expenses are classified in the operations-related journal entries as either (1) educational and general or (2) auxiliary enterprises. Furthermore, *Revenues Subsidiary Ledgers and Expenses Subsidiary Ledgers are assumed to be maintained,* but are not illustrated. Only *summary* general ledger entries are presented in the example.

The beginning trial balance for A Government University at January 1, 20X3, is presented in Illustration 17-6.

ILLUSTRATION 17-6 Beginning Trial Balance		
A Government University **Trial Balance** January 1, 20X3		
	Debit	**Credit**
Cash	$ 523,000	
Cash—Restricted for Specific Programs	15,000	
Inventory of Materials and Supplies	37,000	
Investments—Endowments	330,000	
Accounts Payable		$ 15,000
Mortgage Payable		400,000
Land..	300,000	
Buildings	8,000,000	
Accumulated Depreciation		4,000,000
Equipment	1,800,000	
Accumulated Depreciation		1,010,000
Library Books...................................	200,000	
Net Position		5,780,000
	$11,205,000	$11,205,000

Transactions and entries for 20X3 are presented here.

Transactions and Entries—General Operations

1. Educational and general revenues earned during the year include tuition and fees of $1,400,000, of which $1,338,000 has been collected, and $1,200,000 of state appropriations, all of which has been received.

(1) Cash	$2,538,000	
Accounts Receivable	62,000	
Revenues—Tuition and Fees		$1,400,000
Revenues—State Appropriations		1,200,000
To record tuition and fees and state appropriations.		

2. Tuition scholarships of $12,000 were granted this year and tuition waivers of $2,000 were granted to graduate assistants.

(2) Revenue Deductions—Scholarship Allowances	$ 12,000	
Expenses—Educational and General	2,000	
Accounts Receivable		$ 14,000
To record compensation expenses for tuition deductions for employees and to record scholarship allowances.		

Tuition and fees revenues are reported *net* of uncollectible accounts and scholarship allowances.

3. Other revenues of $700,000 were collected through auxiliary enterprises.

(3) Cash	$ 700,000	
Revenues—Auxiliary Enterprises Sales		$ 700,000
To record revenues of auxiliary enterprises.		

4. Total purchases of materials and supplies for the year amounted to $600,000, of which $560,000 has been paid.

(4) Inventory of Materials and Supplies	$ 600,000	
Cash		$ 560,000
Accounts Payable		40,000
To record purchases of materials and supplies.		

5. Materials and supplies used during the year amounted to $550,000, of which $250,000 is chargeable to educational and general activities and $300,000 to auxiliary enterprises.

(5) Expenses—Educational and General	$ 250,000	
Expenses—Auxiliary Enterprises	300,000	
Inventory of Materials and Supplies		$ 550,000
To record cost of materials and supplies used.		

6. Salaries and wages paid totaled $2,200,000, of which $1,920,000 is chargeable to educational and general activities and $280,000 to auxiliary enterprises.

(6) Expenses—Educational and General	$1,920,000	
Expenses—Auxiliary Enterprises	280,000	
Cash		$2,200,000
To record salaries and wages paid.		

7. Legal fees, insurance, interest on money borrowed temporarily for operating purposes, and telephone and Internet expenses, all chargeable to educational and general activities, amounted to $100,000; all had been paid by the end of the year.

(7) Expenses—Educational and General	$ 100,000	
Cash		$ 100,000
To record legal and insurance expenses, interest on money borrowed for operating purposes, and telephone and Internet expenses.		

8. Other expenses chargeable to auxiliary enterprises and paid for totaled $10,000.

(8) Expenses—Auxiliary Enterprises..................	$ 10,000	
Cash		$ 10,000
To record expenses of auxiliary enterprises other than materials and supplies or salaries.		

9. Student aid cash grants totaled $8,000.

(9) Expenses—Educational and General	$ 8,000	
Cash		$ 8,000
To record student aid granted.		

10. Unrestricted cash, $10,000, was spent for equipment.

(10) Equipment	$ 10,000	
Cash		$ 10,000
To record cost of equipment purchases.		

11. The university borrowed $6,000 for current operations.

(11) Cash	$ 6,000	
Notes Payable		$ 6,000
To record issuance of note for current operations.		

12. A small modular building costing $12,000 was purchased for cash.

(12) Buildings	$ 12,000	
Cash		$ 12,000
To record purchase of a building.		

13. A $500,000 loan was secured to finance a building addition. The proceeds are restricted to that purpose.

(13) Cash—Construction	$500,000	
Notes Payable		$500,000
To record borrowing to finance a building addition.		

14. By year end $240,000 of capitalizable building addition expenditures had been incurred, of which $200,000 had been paid.

(14) Construction in Progress	$240,000	
Cash—Construction		$200,000
Contracts Payable		40,000
To record capitalizable construction expenditures and the related payments.		

15. A total of $25,000 was paid from unrestricted resources on an installment of the mortgage note, including $5,000 interest.

(15) Mortgage Payable.............................	$ 20,000	
Expenses—Educational and General (Interest).....	5,000	
Cash		$ 25,000
To record payment on mortgage note, including $5,000 interest.		

16. Accrued interest at year end on the note issued for current operations was $100.

(16) Expenses—Educational and General (Interest)	$ 100	
Accrued Interest Payable.....................		$ 100
To accrue interest on note.		

**Transactions and Entries—
Restricted Gifts for Operations and Plant Purposes**

17. Cash receipts during the year were as follows:

Federally Sponsored Research (grant)....	$100,000
Gifts—Library Operations.............	200,000
	$300,000

(17) Cash—Restricted for Specific Programs	$300,000	
Unearned Revenues—Federally Sponsored Research...............................		$100,000
Revenues—Private Gifts		200,000
To record resources received.		

The federal grant is a reimbursement grant. Revenues will be recognized when qualifying costs are incurred.

18. Expenses payable from restricted assets were incurred as follows, of which $7,000 remained unpaid at year end:

Sponsored Research....................	$ 40,000
Library Operations....................	130,000
Instruction and Departmental Research (Supplemental Salary Payments)	50,000
Student Aid.........................	12,000
Auxiliary Enterprises.................	2,000
	$234,000

(18a) Expenses—Educational and General	$232,000	
Expenses—Auxiliary Enterprises	2,000	
Accounts Payable..........................		$ 7,000
Cash—Restricted for Specific Programs.......		227,000
To record expenses incurred.		
(18b) Unearned Revenues—Federally Sponsored Research.................................	$ 40,000	
Revenues—Grants		$ 40,000
To recognize grant revenue upon incurring qualifying expenses.		

19. An individual donated preferred stock valued at $20,000 to finance additions to the university plant facilities.

(19) Investments—Plant Expansion	$ 20,000	
Revenues—Capital Contributions		$ 20,000
To record investments donated for the purpose of financing additions to plant.		

Note that government colleges and universities must apply the GASB *Statement No. 31* guidance on accounting for investments that all other government entities must apply.

20. A donation of $15,000 was received for the purpose of paying a $10,000 mortgage installment falling due during the current year, plus $5,000 interest.

(20) Cash—Debt Service..........................	$ 15,000	
Revenues—Private Gifts		$ 15,000
To record receipt of money to pay mortgage installment due in the current year.		

Although this donation (and that in transaction 22) is reported as *operating* grants and contributions in the Statement of Revenues, Expenses, and Changes in Net Position, it is included in cash flows from *capital and related financing* activities in the Statement of Cash Flows. This treatment is required by the GASB's implementation guide on the cash flow statement because the gift must be used for debt service on capital debt.

21. The mortgage installment was paid.

(21) Mortgage Payable	$ 10,000	
Expenses—Educational and General (Interest)	5,000	
Cash—Debt Service........................		$ 15,000
To record payment of mortgage installment: $5,000 interest and $10,000 principal.		

22. A donation of $25,000 was received for the purpose of paying a mortgage installment falling due next year.

(22) Cash—Debt Service............................	$ 25,000	
Revenues—Private Gifts.......................		$ 25,000

    To record receipt of money to pay mortgage
    installment due the following year.

23. The cash received in transaction 22 was invested.

(23) Investments—Debt Service	$ 25,000	
Cash—Debt Service		$ 25,000

    To record investing the donated cash.

24. A $200,000 gift was received with the stipulation that the resources be used to help finance construction of a new academic building.

(24) Cash—Plant Expansion	$200,000	
Revenues—Capital Contributions..............		$200,000

    To record gift to be used for financing
    construction of building.

25. New, uninsured equipment that cost $1,000 was destroyed by fire.

(25) Loss from Fire	$ 1,000	
Equipment		$ 1,000

    To remove the original cost of equipment destroyed.

26. The provision for depreciation of the university's plant assets totaled $230,000, distributed as follows:

Buildings	$175,000
Equipment...........................	55,000
	$230,000

(26) Expenses—Educational and General...............	$200,000	
Expenses—Auxiliary Enterprises	30,000	
Accumulated Depreciation—Buildings		$175,000
Accumulated Depreciation—Equipment.........		55,000

    To record the provision for depreciation for the year.

Other Resources

As mentioned earlier, colleges and universities receive gifts and grants, including many gifts in forms and for purposes not often found in cities, counties, and other governments. For instance, colleges and universities often hold resources that are required to be used for loans to students, faculty, and staff. Likewise, permanent endowment gifts are common, as are gifts in the form of split interest gift agreements that provide a stream of benefits to both the college and university and to some other individual or entity. These gifts may be held by the college or by some other entity.

This section discusses and illustrates some of these unique arrangements. Although the accounting and reporting requirements are the same for other governments that receive these types of gifts and some of them are illustrated in the earlier chapters, they are emphasized here both because of their significance in the college and university environment and because they have not been illustrated in the context of an Enterprise Fund accounting entity. The primary aspects of properly reporting these resources are (1) the timing of revenue recognition for the gifts or grants and (2) the use of restricted asset accounting to communicate in the GAAP financial statements that the use of the resources is limited to a specific purpose(s).

Loan Funds

Colleges and universities often receive assets that are restricted to use for making loans to students and, in some cases, to faculty and staff. Separate accountability must be maintained for these resources to permit the college to demonstrate that it has complied with the restrictions on their use. From a GAAP reporting perspective—for colleges that engage solely in business-type activities—the use restriction is reflected using restricted asset accounting as discussed and illustrated in Chapter 10. Recall that restricted asset accounting is often referred to as "funds within a fund" accounting. Resources restricted to use for loans, therefore, may be referred to as Loan Funds.

If only the fund's income may be loaned, the principal is part of the college's endowment, and only the income is included with the assets restricted for loans, or Loan Funds. Unrestricted resources that are set aside by the college governing board for loan purposes are not reported as part of restricted assets. Internally, the balances of Loan Funds should be classified in appropriate ways, such as by sources of resources, restricted versus unrestricted, and purposes for which loans may be made.

Loan Funds have become major activities requiring professional management at many higher education institutions. Some have raised large sums for loan purposes through gifts, and many participate in federal and state government loan programs. Both federal and state programs must be administered in accordance with many regulations, and some require the college or university to contribute a percentage of the total loan fund balance.

A simplified example of a college or university Loan Fund is presented next. In reviewing the following transactions, assume that a Loan Fund was established to make interest-free loans and that (1) income on fund investments is to be added to the principal of the fund, and (2) the total assets of the fund, both the original principal and that from earnings, may be loaned.

Transactions and Entries

1. A donation of $100,000 was received for the purpose of making loans to students.

(1) Cash—Restricted for Loans	$100,000	
Revenues—Private Gifts		$100,000
To record donation received for the purpose of setting up Loan Fund.		

2. Loans of $50,000 were made.

(2) Loans Receivable...........................	$ 50,000	
Cash—Restricted for Loans		$ 50,000
To record loans made.		

3. A total of $25,000 was invested in bonds. The bonds were purchased at par plus accrued interest of $100.

(3) Investments—Restricted for Loans	$ 25,000	
Accrued Interest Receivable—Restricted		
for Loans	100	
Cash—Restricted for Loans		$ 25,100
To record investments and accrued interest purchased.		

4. A $500 check for bond interest was received.

(4) Cash—Restricted for Loans	$ 500	
Accrued Interest Receivable—Restricted		
for Loans		$ 100
Revenues—Investment Income		400
To record receipt of interest payment.		

5. A student died and it was decided to write off his loan of $400 as uncollectible.

(5) Loss on Uncollectible Loans	$ 400	
Loans Receivable...........................		$ 400
To write off loan as uncollectible.		

Endowment and Similar Gifts

Government colleges and universities also often receive significant amounts of contributions that are to be maintained—at least for a time, if not in perpetuity— for endowment. Assets restricted for endowment (or Endowment Funds) are reported for assets that, at least at the moment, cannot be expended, although usually the income from them may be. Assets donated by outsiders fall into two categories:

1. Those that have been given in perpetuity, which are sometimes referred to as *true* or *pure* endowments.

2. Those that the donor has specified may be expended after a particular date or event, which are referred to as *term* endowments.

Revenues for both types of endowments, if under control of the college or university, are recognized under GASB *Statement No. 33* at the point that the college begins to invest them as required in the gift agreement. As noted earlier, another form of giving that is commonly found in colleges and universities is split interest gifts such as annuity and life income gifts in which the college is only one of two or more beneficiaries. These gifts are discussed and illustrated briefly after the case illustration is completed but are not included in the case illustration.

The appropriate policy-making body of an institution may also set aside (designate) unrestricted resources for the same purposes as those donated as endowments. The college may account for these similarly to endowment funds for *internal purposes,* but they are not reported as part of assets restricted for endowments because they are not either externally restricted or restricted by enabling legislation. These internally created endowments are subject to reassignment by the policy-making body that created them.

Finally, donors may choose to make the income from endowment-type funds available to a university but to leave the principal in the possession and control of a trustee other than the university. Such assets are *not* reported as assets or as revenues of government universities but should be disclosed in the financial statements by an appropriate note. Income from such trusts should be reported as gift revenues when cash is received by the university. If restricted to specific purposes, the cash received will increase restricted net position; otherwise it will add to unrestricted net position.

Determining and Reporting Income One of the most debated issues in Endowment Fund accounting is: What portion, if any, of net appreciation of Endowment Fund investments should be treated as additions to *expendable* endowment income rather than as part of the endowment principal?

Several views have found their way into practice. The alternatives range from the *classical trust or fiduciary principle*—that includes no net appreciation of Endowment Fund assets (realized or unrealized) in expendable income (or yield)—to the various *total return approaches*. Under the total return approaches, a prudent portion of the net appreciation is considered income and spent along with the dividends, rents, royalties, interest, and other realized revenues that constitute the yield under the classical trust principle.

Donors sometimes require gains and losses, whether realized or not, to be added to or deducted from endowment principal. State laws sometimes dictate the determination of expendable endowment income, where donor agreements are silent. *For financial accounting and reporting purposes, gains and losses (including most unrealized changes in fair value) must be reported as investment income.* Any portion of the appreciation that is expendable and unrestricted will increase unrestricted net position. If considered part of the endowment principal, gains will increase (and losses will decrease) nonexpendable restricted net position. If expendable, but for a restricted purpose, the gains and losses will change Restricted Net Position—Expendable.

Transactions and Entries—Endowment Gifts The following transactions and entries illustrate the GAAP reporting requirements for endowments.

Transactions and Entries

1. Cash was donated by a family during the year to establish three separate endowments, as follows:

Endowment A (for Supplemental Salary
Payments) $1,000,000
Endowment B (for Supplemental Salary
Payments) 600,000
Endowment C (for Student Aid) 400,000
$2,000,000

These endowments include a provision that any earnings in excess of $78,000 should be dedicated to the athletic program, an auxiliary enterprise of the university. Furthermore, the donor stipulates that *appreciation and depreciation of the assets comprising the endowment principal are to be added to or deducted from the principal.* They do not affect expendable earnings.

(1) Cash—Endowments.............................. $2,000,000
    Revenues—Endowment Gifts................... $2,000,000
    To record receipt of money for the purpose of
      establishing three endowments.

The college must maintain records segregating endowment assets that support different activities.

2. It was decided to invest this money in securities that were to be pooled. The following securities were acquired at the prices indicated:

Preferred stocks .... $ 500,000
Common stocks 1,000,000
Bonds:
    Par value 200,000
    Premiums......................... 10,000
Bonds:
    Par value 250,000
    Discounts......................... 5,000
Accrued interest on investments
    purchased........................ 1,000

(2) Investments in Preferred Stocks—Endowments ...... $ 500,000
    Investments in Common Stocks—Endowments 1,000,000
    Investments in Bonds—Endowments 455,000
    Accrued Interest Receivable—Endowments 1,000
      Cash—Endowments $1,956,000
    To record purchase of pooled investments.

3. Cash received on these investments for the year was as follows:

Dividends on preferred stocks .... $ 20,000
Dividends on common stocks 59,700
Interest 9,000
No material amounts of investment income were accrued at year end.

(3) Cash—Endowments.............................. $ 88,700
      Revenues—Investment Income.................. $ 87,700
      Accrued Interest Receivable—Endowments 1,000
    To record investment income received.

4. The earnings received in entry 3 are available for use for, and restricted to, specific programs and purposes of the university.

(4) Cash—Restricted for Specific Programs .... $ 87,700
      Cash—Endowments .... $ 87,700
    To reflect the availability of assets for specific purposes.

5. The fair value of the pooled investments increased by $1,500 during the year.

(5) Investments—Endowments	$ 1,500	
Revenues—Investment Income..................		$ 1,500
To record increase in fair value of investments.		

6. Common stock with a book value of $10,000 was sold for $10,500.

(6) Cash—Endowments.............................	$ 10,500	
Investments in Common Stock		$ 10,000
Revenues—Gain on Sale of Investments...........		500
To record sale of common stock at a gain.		

7. An individual donated common stock that had cost $65,000 (hereafter referred to as Endowment Fund D). At the time of the donation the stock had a fair value of $75,000. The income from these securities is unrestricted and may be used for any university purpose. An alumnus donated investments in bonds with a fair value of $850,000 as a permanent endowment gift, the income from which is to be used for student aid and for supplemental salary payments.

(7) Investment in Common Stock—Endowments	$ 75,000	
Investment in Bonds—Endowments	850,000	
Revenues—Endowment Gifts....................		$ 925,000
To record donation of common stock at its fair value.		

8. An individual set up a trust (to be administered by the Village National Bank) in the amount of $400,000, the income from which is to go to the university.

(8) No entry, or memorandum entry. The trust would be disclosed in the notes to the financial statements.

Preclosing Trial Balance and Closing Entries

The preclosing trial balance for A Government University at December 31, 20X3, is presented in Illustration 17-7.

At December 31, A Government University would close its accounts with the following entry:

Revenues—Tuition and Fees	$1,400,000	
Revenues—State Appropriations	1,200,000	
Revenues—Auxiliary Enterprise Sales...................	700,000	
Revenues—Private Gifts	340,000	
Revenues—Endowment Gifts	2,925,000	
Revenues—Federal Grants	40,000	
Revenues—Capital Contributions......................	220,000	
Revenues—Investment Income........................	89,600	
Revenues—Gain on Sale of Investments	500	
Revenue Deductions—Scholarship Allowances		$ 12,000
Expenses—Educational and General...................		2,722,100
Expenses—Auxiliary Enterprises		622,000
Loss from Fire		1,000
Loss on Uncollectible Loan		400
Net Position		3,557,600

To close the accounts.

Financial Statements

The financial statements for A Government University for 20X3 include a Statement of Net Position; a Statement of Revenues, Expenses, and Changes in Net Position; and a Statement of Cash Flows. These statements are presented in this section.

ILLUSTRATION 17-7   Preclosing Trial Balance

A Government University
Preclosing Trial Balance
December 31, 20X3

	Debit	Credit
Cash	$ 842,000	
Cash—Construction	300,000	
Cash—Restricted for Specific Programs	175,700	
Cash—Plant Expansion	200,000	
Cash—Restricted for Loans	25,400	
Cash—Endowments	55,500	
Accounts Receivable	48,000	
Inventory of Materials and Supplies	87,000	
Loans Receivable	49,600	
Investments—Debt Service	25,000	
Investments—Plant Expansion	20,000	
Investments—Restricted for Loans	25,000	
Investments—Endowments	3,201,500	
Land	300,000	
Buildings	8,012,000	
Accumulated Depreciation—Buildings		$ 4,178,000
Equipment	1,809,000	
Accumulated Depreciation—Equipment		1,062,000
Library Books	200,000	
Construction in Progress	240,000	
Accounts Payable		62,000
Unearned Grant Revenues—Federally Sponsored Research		60,000
Notes Payable		506,000
Accrued Interest Payable		100
Contracts Payable—Retained Percentage		40,000
Mortgage Payable		370,000
Net Position		5,780,000
Revenues—Tuition and Fees		1,400,000
Revenues—State Appropriations		1,200,000
Revenues—Auxiliary Enterprise Sales		700,000
Revenues—Private Gifts		340,000
Revenues—Endowment Gifts		2,925,000
Revenues—Federal Grants		40,000
Revenues—Capital Contributions		220,000
Revenues—Investment Income		89,600
Revenues—Gain on Sale of Investments		500
Revenue Deductions—Scholarship Allowances	12,000	
Expenses—Educational and General	2,722,100	
Expenses—Auxiliary Enterprises	622,000	
Loss from Fire	1,000	
Loss on Uncollectible Loan	400	
Totals	$18,973,200	$18,973,200

Statement of Net Position The Statement of Net Position for A Government University is presented in Illustration 17-8. Note in particular the amount and variety of restricted assets and the distinction between nonexpendable and expendable restricted net position, which is required for governments with permanently restricted endowments. Also, note the presentation of the three net position categories as seen previously for proprietary funds and in the government-wide statements of general purpose governments.

Net investment in capital assets equals the total capital assets, net of accumulated depreciation ($5,321,000) less the mortgage note payable ($370,000), the expended amount of the construction note payable ($200,000), and contracts payable ($40,000), or $4,711,000. Restricted net position equals the total restricted assets ($4,077,700) less the unearned grant revenues ($60,000), the portion of the construction note equal to the unexpended proceeds ($300,000), and $7,000 of accounts payable for expenses payable from restricted assets (see transaction 18), or $3,710,700. The unrestricted net position can be computed as the current assets ($977,000) less the remaining balance of the accounts payable ($55,000), the accrued interest payable on the short-term note ($100), and the short-term note payable ($6,000), or $915,900.

Statement of Revenues, Expenses, and Changes in Net Position The university's Statement of Revenues, Expenses, and Changes in Net Position is presented in Illustration 17-9. As is common in government universities, tuition and fees and other operating revenues were not sufficient to provide for all operating expenses. The university relies on significant amounts of nonoperating income and other revenues. Note the presentation of state appropriations, capital gifts and grants, and endowment gifts—all of which are significant for most government universities.

Statement of Cash Flows The Statement of Cash Flows for A Government University is presented in Illustration 17-10. The direct method is used to report operating activities as required by *Statement No. 34*. Note the classification of state appropriations, endowment gifts, and the federal grant, as well as other noncapital-asset-related gifts, as noncapital financing sources.

ANNUITY AND LIFE INCOME GIFTS

As noted earlier, in addition to endowment and similar gifts received by colleges and universities that are solely for their benefit, colleges and universities often receive split interest gifts. These gifts include another beneficiary(ies) besides the college or university. Two common examples of split interest gifts are annuity trusts and life income trusts. In annuity and life income gifts, assets are given to the institution with the stipulation that the institution make certain payments to a designated recipient(s).

- *Annuity* gifts require a fixed-dollar payment regardless of the income of the fund.
- *Life income* gifts require the amount of the payment to the beneficiary to vary based on the earnings of the trust.

Typically, annuity agreements also specify a certain number of years during which the beneficiary is to receive the annuity, but the period need not be fixed. Indeed, the period could be specified as the lifetime of the beneficiary. Similarly, a life income agreement usually requires payment of the income of the fund—or some portion of the income of the fund—until the death of the beneficiary or the donor. However, a life income agreement could specify that the earnings, or some portion of the earnings, be paid to the designated beneficiary for a specified number of years. After the specified payment period, the principal of the trust becomes available for either restricted or unrestricted use.

The Internal Revenue Code and regulations state the conditions under which an annuity trust may be accepted and must be administered from an income tax standpoint, and several states also regulate annuity trusts. The institution accepts

Annuity Gifts

ILLUSTRATION 17-8   Statement of Net Position

A Government University
Statement of Net Position
December 31, 20X3

ASSETS

Current Assets:

Cash and cash equivalents	$ 842,000
Accounts receivable, net	48,000
Inventories	87,000
Total current assets	977,000

Noncurrent Assets:

Restricted for:

Specific programs	175,700
Loans	100,000
Plant expansion and construction	520,000
Debt service	25,000
Endowment	3,257,000
Total restricted assets	4,077,700
Land	300,000
Buildings (net)	3,834,000
Equipment (net)	747,000
Library books	200,000
Construction in progress	240,000
Total capital assets (net)	5,321,000
Total noncurrent assets	9,398,700
Total assets	10,375,700

LIABILITIES

Current Liabilities:

Accounts payable and accrued liabilities	62,000
Interest payable on short-term note	100
Short-term note payable	6,000
Mortgage payable	32,000
Total current liabilities	100,100

Liabilities Payable from Restricted Assets:

Contracts payable—Retained percentage	40,000
Unearned grant revenues	60,000
Total liabilities payable from restricted assets	100,000

Noncurrent Liabilities:

Note payable	500,000
Mortgage payable	338,000
Total noncurrent liabilities	838,000
Total liabilities	1,038,100

NET POSITION

Net investment in capital assets	4,711,000

Restricted for:

Nonexpendable

Endowment	3,257,000
Loans	100,000

Expendable

Scholarships and departmental uses	108,700
Capital projects	220,000
Debt service	25,000
Unrestricted	915,900
Total net position	$ 9,337,600

Note: Some amounts are assumed for illustrative purposes.

A Government University
Statement of Revenues, Expenses, and Changes in Net Position
For the Year Ended December 31, 20X3

REVENUES

Operating Revenues

Student tuition and fees (net of scholarship allowances of $12,000) ...	$1,388,000
Auxiliary enterprises:	
Residential life (assumed amount)	500,000
Bookstore (assumed amount)	200,000
Total operating revenues	2,088,000

EXPENSES

Operating Expenses

Educational and General:	
Instruction	1,332,000
Research	140,000
Public service	75,000
Academic support	330,000
Student services	150,000
Institutional support	400,100
Operation and maintenance of plant	283,000
Scholarships and fellowships	2,000
Total educational and general	2,712,100
Auxiliary enterprises:	
Residential life	440,000
Bookstore	182,000
Total auxiliary enterprises	622,000
Total operating expenses	3,334,100
Operating income (loss)	(1,246,100)

NONOPERATING REVENUES (EXPENSES)

State appropriations* ································	1,200,000
Federal grants	40,000
Gifts	240,000
Investment income	90,100
Interest expense	(10,000)
Loan loss and fire loss	(1,400)
Net nonoperating revenues	1,558,700
Income before other revenues, expenses, gains, or losses	312,600
Capital grants and gifts	220,000
Additions to permanent endowments and loan programs	3,025,000
Total other revenues	3,245,000
Increase in net position	3,557,600

NET POSITION

Net position—beginning of year	5,780,000
Net position—end of year	$9,337,600

Note: Some amounts are assumed for illustrative purposes.

*Appropriations for capital asset construction, acquisition, or improvement are reported in the same manner as capital grants and gifts.

ILLUSTRATION 17-10   Statement of Cash Flows

A Government University
Statement of Cash Flows
For the Year Ended December 31, 20X3

CASH FLOWS FROM OPERATING ACTIVITIES

Tuition and fees	$1,338,000
Auxiliary enterprise charges:	
Residence halls	500,000
Bookstore	200,000
Payments to suppliers	(787,000)
Payments to employees	(2,200,000)
Loans issued to students and employees	(50,000)
Other receipts (payments)	(118,000)
Net cash provided (used) by operating activities	(1,117,000)

CASH FLOWS FROM NONCAPITAL FINANCING ACTIVITIES

State appropriations	1,200,000
Proceeds of noncapital debt	6,000
Gifts and grants received for other than capital purposes:	
Private gifts for programs and loans	300,000
Federal operating grant	100,000
Private gifts for endowment purposes	2,000,000
Net cash provided by noncapital financing activities	3,606,000

CASH FLOWS FROM CAPITAL AND RELATED FINANCING ACTIVITIES

Proceeds of capital debt	500,000
Capital grants and gifts received	200,000
Contributions for debt service on capital debt	40,000
Purchases and construction of capital assets	(222,000)
Principal paid on capital debt	(30,000)
Interest paid on capital debt	(10,000)
Net cash provided by capital and related financing activities	478,000

CASH FLOWS FROM INVESTING ACTIVITIES

Proceeds from sales and maturities of investments	10,500
Interest on investments	89,200
Purchase of investments	(2,006,100)
Net cash provided by investing activities	(1,906,400)
Net increase in cash	1,060,600
Cash—beginning of year	538,000
Cash—end of year	$1,598,600

Note: Some amounts are assumed for illustrative purposes. The cash balance includes both restricted cash and unrestricted cash; other required schedules have been omitted.

---

some risk by guaranteeing the beneficiary a fixed amount for a specified period, perhaps for life or even for the lifetime of two or more persons. As a result, the governing board will want assurances (1) that the assets donated should generate sufficient income to pay the specified amounts, or (2) if some of the payments must come from principal, that a significant residual balance should be available to the institution at the end of the annuity period.

When the annuity gift is received, the assets should be recorded at their fair value, together with any liabilities against the assets assumed by the institution. The liability for the annuity payments is recorded at its present value, based on the expected earnings rate and, if appropriate, life expectancy tables. Any difference between the assets and liabilities should be debited or credited, as appropriate, to the Revenues—Private Gifts account.

To illustrate annuity gifts accounting, assume that an individual donated $20,000 of cash and $180,000 of investments to Alderman University on January 2, 20X3, with the stipulation that she be paid $25,000 each December 31 for the next 10 years. Any remaining net assets should then be used to remodel the business and public administration building. The university finance officer expects to earn at least 7% on the fund's assets during each of the next 10 years. The entry to record creation of this annuity gift would be:

(a) Cash	$ 20,000	
Investments	180,000	
Annuities Payable		$175,589
Revenues—Private Gifts—Annuities		24,411

To record annuity gift. Calculation of annuity payable: $25,000 × 7.023582, the present value of an ordinary annuity of $1 for 10 periods at 7%, is $175,589.

Investment earnings and gains are credited, and annuity payments and losses are debited, to Annuities Payable. Assuming that various investment transactions already have been recorded during the year and that the annuity payments are due each December 31, the following entries would be made on December 31, 20X3, the end of the university's fiscal year:

(b) Annuities Payable	$ 25,000	
Cash (or Annuities Currently Payable)		$ 25,000

To record the annual annuity payment.

(c) Investment Income	$ 11,000	
Annuities Payable		$ 11,000

To *close* the (amounts assumed) investment earnings, gains, and losses accounts at year end.

Because the Annuities Payable account should always be carried at the present value of the future series of required payments, *the Annuities Payable account must be adjusted annually to its present value.* If actuarial assumptions such as yield estimates or life expectancies are revised, the adjustment to Annuities Payable should reflect those changes. The adjustments to Annuities Payable will be reported as revenues, or as revenue reductions, in the Statement of Revenues, Expenses, and Changes in Net Position. In this example the Annuities Payable balance at year end should be equal to the present value of the nine remaining annuity payments ($25,000 × 6.515232), or $162,881. The required adjustment to net position is the difference between the Annuities Payable balance after the preceding entries ($161,589) and the present value of the nine remaining payments. This adjustment of $1,292 is recorded as follows:

(d) Revenue Deductions—Change in Value of Annuity		
Agreement	$ 1,292	
Annuities Payable		$ 1,292

To *adjust Annuities Payable* to present value at year end.

Life Income Gifts

Life income gifts are subject to Internal Revenue Code and regulation provisions, as are annuity gifts, and may be subject to state regulations. Because only the earnings inure to the beneficiary(ies) of life income gifts, and no fixed payment is guaranteed, the college or university does not have an earnings risk as in the case of annuity gifts.

The accounting for life income gifts is not as complex as that for annuity gifts. All that is involved is:

1. **At its inception**—record the assets at fair value and record any liabilities assumed; the difference is credited to Revenues—Private Gifts. Restricted net position will be increased by the gift.

2. **During the term of the fund**—record fund revenues, expenses, gains, and losses following donor instructions or, in the absence of instructions, applicable law in determining whether gains or losses affect income or the principal, and distribute the earnings to the beneficiary(ies).

3. **At the end of the benefit period or upon the death of the beneficiary(ies)**—reclassify the resources as unrestricted if there are no purpose restrictions.

COLLEGES AND UNIVERSITIES ENGAGED IN BOTH GOVERNMENTAL AND BUSINESS-TYPE ACTIVITIES

Although most government colleges and universities are expected to report as business-type only special purpose governments, others may report as special purpose entities engaged in both governmental and business-type activities or engaged in only governmental activities. Colleges and universities engaged in both governmental and business-type activities are required to present the same financial statements as general purpose governments—that is, all the statements required by GASB *Statement No. 34*. As discussed and illustrated in Chapter 13, the required statements are:

a. *Fund-Based Statements for Governmental Funds*

1. Balance Sheet

2. Statement of Revenues, Expenditures, and Changes in Fund Balances

3. General Fund and Major Special Revenue Funds Statement of Revenues, Expenditures, and Changes in Fund Balances—Budget and Actual (This statement may be presented as required supplementary information.)

b. *Fund-Based Statements for Proprietary Funds*

1. Statement of Net Position

2. Statement of Revenues, Expenses, and Changes in Net Position

3. Statement of Cash Flows (direct method required)

c. *Fund-Based Statements for Fiduciary Funds and Fiduciary Component Units*

1. Statement of Fiduciary Net Position

2. Statement of Changes in Fiduciary Net Position

d. *Government-Wide Financial Statements*

1. Statement of Net Position

2. Statement of Activities

If a government college or university has only governmental activities, the requirements are the same as above except that proprietary and fiduciary fund financial statements are not required.

NONGOVERNMENT NOT-FOR-PROFIT UNIVERSITY REPORTING

Up to this point, our discussion of college and university reporting has focused on accounting and reporting for *government* colleges and universities. *Nongovernment* not-for-profit college and university financial reporting follows the FASB's guidance for all nongovernment not-for-profit organizations that was discussed and illustrated in detail in the previous chapter. We will depend on that guidance and on the unique college and university guidance from this chapter—regarding tuition and fees, scholarship allowances, and revenue and expense classifications, for instance—to form a basis for understanding reporting for these nongovernment colleges and universities.

There are far more similarities than differences between reporting requirements for nongovernment not-for-profit colleges and universities and government colleges and universities (that report as business-type only entities). We highlight a few of the key differences here and then present financial statements (Illustrations 17-11 to 17-13) for our illustrative university under the assumption that it is a nongovernment university. Comparing these nongovernment college and university financial statements with the government college and university statements that are based on the same information should help you see the nature and significance of both the similarities and the differences.

The key differences in reporting government colleges and universities and nongovernment not-for-profit colleges and universities are that the latter:

- Do not present the deferred outflows and deferred inflows of resources classifications in the balance sheet, which governments title a Statement of Net Position.

- Report net assets classified into the three net asset categories required by the FASB *Accounting Standards Codification*—unrestricted, temporarily restricted, and permanently restricted—instead of in the GASB's three net position classes.

ILLUSTRATION 17-11   Nongovernment Not-for-Profit University Balance Sheet

A Nongovernment Not-for-Profit University
Balance Sheet
December 31, 20X3

Assets

Cash and cash equivalents	$ 1,017,700
Accounts receivable (net)	48,000
Inventory of materials and supplies	87,000
Assets restricted for loan programs	100,000
Assets restricted for plant purposes	545,000
Assets restricted for endowment	3,257,000
Land	300,000
Buildings and improvements (net of accumulated depreciation)	3,834,000
Equipment (net of accumulated depreciation)	747,000
Library books	200,000
Construction in progress	240,000
Total assets	$10,375,700

Liabilities and Net Assets

Liabilities:	
Accounts payable	$ 62,000
Interest payable	100
Contracts payable	40,000
Mortgages and other notes payable	876,000
Total liabilities	978,100
Net Assets:	
Permanently Restricted:	
Loan funds	100,000
Endowment	3,257,000
Total permanently restricted	3,357,000
Temporarily restricted:	
Specific programs	168,700
Plant purposes	245,000
Total temporarily restricted	413,700
Unrestricted:	
Net invested in fixed assets	4,711,000
Other	915,900
Total unrestricted net assets	5,626,900
Total net assets	9,397,600
Total liabilities and net assets	$10,375,700

ILLUSTRATION 17-12   Nongovernment Not-for-Profit University Statement of Activities

A Nongovernment Not-for-Profit University
Statement of Activities
For the Year Ended December 31, 20X3

Operating revenues, gains, and net assets released from restrictions:

Revenues and gains:

Tuition and fees	$1,388,000
State appropriations	1,200,000
Sales and services of auxiliary enterprises	700,000
Total revenues and gains	3,288,000

Net assets released from restrictions for operating use by satisfying
use restrictions on:

Federal grants	40,000
Private gifts and grants	130,000
Endowment income	64,000
Total net assets released from restrictions for operations	234,000
Total operating revenues, gains, and reclassifications	3,522,000

Expenses:

Educational and general:

Instruction	1,488,000*
Research	166,000
Public service	83,000
Academic support	360,000
Student services	170,000
Institutional support	443,000
Scholarships and fellowships	2,000
Total educational and general expenses	2,712,000
Auxiliary enterprises	622,000
Total operating expenses	3,334,000
Excess of operating revenues, gains, and reclassifications over operating expenses	188,000

Nonoperating changes in unrestricted assets:

Interest expense	(10,100)
Fire loss	(1,000)
Net assets released from restrictions for plant asset-related purposes	15,000
Changes in unrestricted net assets from nonoperating activities	3,900
Net increase in unrestricted net assets	191,900

Changes in temporarily restricted net assets:

Contributions	460,000
Restricted federal grants	100,000
Endowment income	88,200
Net assets released from restrictions	(249,000)
Increase in temporarily restricted net assets	399,200

Changes in permanently restricted net assets:

Contributions	3,025,000
Realized gain on sale of investments	500
Unrealized gain on investments	1,000
Restricted interest income	400
Restricted losses of loan fund	(400)
Increase in permanently restricted net assets	3,026,500
Increase in net assets	3,617,600
Net assets, January 1, 20X3	5,780,000
Net assets, December 31, 20X3	$9,397,600

*The functional expense classifications presented here differ from those in the government illustration (Illustration 17-9) because expenses for operation and maintenance of plant must be allocated to functions in nongovernment university financial statements.

- Distinguish changes in the three categories of net assets in the operating statement—which is not done for government colleges and universities.

- Report reimbursement-type grants as revenues, which increase temporarily restricted net assets, when awarded.

- Report uncollectible accounts as expenses, not as revenue reductions.

- Report Pell grants received on behalf of individual students as collections of tuition and fees, not as a separate revenue source.

- Report net assets released from restrictions when resource restrictions are satisfied.

- Apply FASB cash flow statement guidance instead of GASB guidance.

- Classify some revenues as operating that are not operating revenues for government colleges and universities. (Nongovernment universities would be more likely to have contributions from an oversight organization such as a religious denomination than to have state appropriations.)

You should be able to observe these and other differences as you review the financial statements. Remember as you review the statements in Illustrations 17-11, 17-12, and 17-13 that they are based on the same information and transactions as the government college and university statements in Illustrations 17-8 to 17-10.

ILLUSTRATION 17-13 Nongovernment Not-for-Profit University Statement of Cash Flows

A Nongovernment Not-for-Profit University
Statement of Cash Flows
For the Year Ended December 31, 20X3

Cash flows from operating activities:	
Cash received from tuition and fees	$1,338,000
Cash received from state appropriations	1,200,000
Cash received from grants and contributions	300,000
Cash received from sales of auxiliary enterprises	700,000
Payments to suppliers and employees	(2,987,000)
Interest paid	(10,000)
Interest received	87,700
Other	(168,000)
Net cash provided by operating activities	460,700
Cash flows from investing activities:	
Purchase and construction of fixed assets	(222,000)
Purchases of investments	(2,006,100)
Proceeds from sale of investment	10,500
Increase in cash invested in assets restricted for plant, loan, or endowment purposes	(580,900)
Net cash used by investing activities	(2,798,500)
Cash flows from financing activities:	
Proceeds from contributions restricted for:	
Endowment and loan funds	2,100,000
Plant-asset-related purposes	240,000
Retirement of note principal	(30,000)
Proceeds of note issuance	506,000
Interest restricted to reinvestment	1,500
Net cash provided by financing activities	2,817,500
Net increase in cash	479,700
Cash, January 1	538,000
Cash, December 31	$1,017,700

Concluding Comments

Accounting and reporting for colleges and universities have evolved rapidly. Reporting for both government and nongovernment colleges and universities has changed dramatically in the past 10 years. Numerous major improvements in college and university accounting and reporting resulted from the joint efforts of preparers, auditors, and users of higher education financial reports.

Government college and university financial reporting was discussed and illustrated in detail in this chapter. Differences between accounting and reporting for government and for nongovernment not-for-profit institutions were highlighted as well. The next chapter addresses accounting and reporting for health care organizations, another special purpose entity with government and nongovernment counterparts that must apply differing GAAP.

Questions

Note: *Unless stated otherwise, assume the colleges and universities in the following questions are "business-type only" special purpose governments.*

Q17-1 Which standards setting body has the authority for establishing GAAP for colleges and universities?

Q17-2 What financial statements must be presented by a government university that engages in *only* business-type activities?

Q17-3 What financial statements must be presented by a government university that engages in *both* governmental and business-type activities?

Q17-4 What fund types should be used for a government university engaged in *both* governmental and business-type activities?

Q17-5 Why are some scholarships reported as revenue deductions and others as expenses?

Q17-6 A government university charges tuition (at standard rates) of $3,000,000. The university grants scholarship waivers to students of $100,000. How much tuition revenue should the university report? What if the waivers are for employees of the university in accordance with university fringe benefit policies?

Q17-7 When should permanent endowment gifts be recognized as revenues by a government university?

Q17-8 What is an auxiliary enterprise? How is it accounted for and reported by colleges and universities?

Q17-9 When are earnings of endowments reported as revenue? Might the principal of such gifts also be reported as revenue? Explain.

Q17-10 Distinguish between the key accounting aspects of *annuity* gifts and *life income* gifts.

Q17-11 How should government college and university revenues and expenses be classified for external financial reporting purposes?

Q17-12 How are uncollectible accounts for tuition and fees reported in a government university's operating statement?

Exercises

Note: *Unless stated otherwise, assume the colleges and universities in the following exercises are "business-type only" special purpose governments.*

E17-1 (Multiple Choice) Identify the best answer for each of the following:
1. GASB *Statement No. 35* requires that government colleges and universities engaged *solely* in business-type activities present
   a. a Statement of Net Position.
   b. a Statement of Cash Flows.
   c. a Statement of Revenues, Expenses, and Changes in Net Position.
   d. Management's Discussion & Analysis.
   e. all of the above.

2. Government colleges and universities solely engaged in business-type activities would present the following classes of equity *except*
   a. net investment in capital assets.
   b. restricted fund balance.
   c. restricted net position.
   d. unrestricted net position.
3. Which of the following statements about accounting for government colleges and universities is *false*?
   a. Government colleges and universities engaged in business-type activities commonly account for transactions on a fund basis unique to their environment throughout the fiscal year.
   b. Government colleges and universities engaged in business-type activities commonly account for *expenditures* instead of *expenses* throughout the fiscal year.
   c. Financial reporting for a college or university treated as an enterprise activity is basically the same as the financial reporting for *any* enterprise activity.
   d. The accounting and reporting for exchange revenues for colleges and universities is *not* consistent with the methods used for other governmental entities.
4. A government college or university's Statement of Cash Flows would potentially report all of the following categories of cash flows *except*
   a. cash flows from operating activities.
   b. cash flows from capital and related financing activities.
   c. cash flows from financing activities.
   d. cash flows from investing activities.
5. Restricted net position for a governmental college or university is commonly subclassified for
   a. designated net position.
   b. reserved net position.
   c. nonexpendable net position.
   d. net investment in capital assets.
6. How should endowment investments that are permanent in nature be reported on a university Statement of Net Position?
   a. As a noncurrent asset
   b. As a current or noncurrent asset as per the donor's specification
   c. As a current asset
   d. As part of the university's general cash and investments
7. Scholarships for students' tuition and fees that are being paid from *grants* the university received (on the students' behalf) should be reported as
   a. a reduction of tuition and fee revenues.
   b. expenses in the GAAP financial statements.
   c. expenditures in the GAAP financial statements.
   d. nonoperating expenses in the GAAP financial statements.
8. Scholarships for students' tuition and fees that are being paid from the *university's own resources* should be reported as
   a. a reduction of tuition and fee revenues.
   b. expenses in the GAAP financial statements.
   c. expenditures in the GAAP financial statements.
   d. nonoperating expenses in the GAAP financial statements.
9. Which of the following is not a common characteristic for the accounting and financial reporting of loan funds in colleges and universities that engage solely in business-type activities?
   a. Often, loan funds are major activities that require professional management.
   b. For internal purposes, loan funds are commonly accounted for within a separate fund.
   c. For GAAP reporting purposes, loan funds are reported as part of restricted assets, not as a separate fund.
   d. Changes in loan fund balances are reported as revenues and expenditures.
10. Colleges and universities that engage in *both* governmental and business-type activities are required to report which of the following external financial statements?
    a. The same financial reporting standards that apply to general purpose governments apply to these colleges and universities.
    b. Fund-based financial statements are required, but government-wide financial statements are not.
    c. Government-wide and fund financial statements are required, exclusive of fiduciary funds, which are not reported for colleges and universities.
    d. Government-wide financial statements are required, but fund financial statements are not.

[Handwritten margin notes:]

17-2

AR 3.7mil

Rev-Tution 3.7 mil

2) Allowance-scholarship 100K
Rev ded-Uncollect 12K   100K
   AR   12K
   Allowance uncollect

2) AR-Restricted 18K
   Rev ed + Gen   18K

Equip 18K

Cash-Rest 18K

17-3

1) Cash 2.4mil
   AR-tuition 600K
   Rev tuition   3mil

Rev-Red-Sch 100K
Rev-Red-unc 50K
exp-educ+Gen-edn 130K
   AR   50K
   Allowance uncollect

5) Cash-Rest 220K
   Rev-Private Gifts 220K

6) exp-ed + Gen 100K
   Cash-Rest.   100K

3mil + 100K
= 3.1 mil

E17-2 (Tuition and Fees Entries) Prepare the necessary journal entries to record each of the following transactions of Dewey County College.
1. Tuition and fees charged for the fall 20X8 semester totaled $3,700,000; $100,000 of this amount was waived as a result of scholarships and fee waivers, and $12,000 more is expected to be uncollectible.
2. For the winter 20X9 semester Dewey College levied a general student fee of $18,000. The full amount of this fee is restricted for the purchase of computer equipment and software needed to expand research labs at the college.

E17-3 (Various Transactions) Prepare the journal entries required for Rocco State University to record the following transactions.
1. Tuition and fees assessed total $3,000,000—80% is collected, scholarships are granted for $100,000; $50,000 is expected to prove uncollectible; and $20,000 of the scholarships are waivers for employees.
2. Revenues collected from sales and services of the university bookstore, an auxiliary enterprise, were $400,000.
3. Salaries and wages were paid, $1,300,000. Of this amount, $85,000 was for employees of the university bookstore.
4. Mortgage payments totaled $480,000. Of this amount, $300,000 was for interest.
5. Restricted contributions for a specific academic program were received, $220,000.
6. Expenses for the restricted program were incurred and paid, $100,000.
7. Equipment was purchased from resources previously contributed for that purpose, $22,000.

E17-4 (Grant-Related Entries) January 10, 20X8—Lumbee State College received a $100,000 government grant to be used to finance a study of the effects of the Tax Reform Act of 20X6 on the regional economy.

During 20X8—Expenditures of $72,000 were incurred and paid on the research project.

Required   a. Record these transactions in the accounts of Lumbee State College, and explain how the effects of the transactions should be reported in the college's financial statements.
b. Repeat requirement (a) under the assumption that the grant was to finance plant expansion.

E17-5 (Endowment Entries) Mr. Harvey Robinson donated $2,000,000 to the University of Aggiemania with the stipulation that earnings of the first 10 years be used to endow professorships in each of the university's colleges. At the end of the 10-year period the principal of the gift will become available for unrestricted use. The resources were used immediately to purchase investments.

Required   a. Prepare the entry(ies) needed to record the gift, assuming a government university.
b. What effect results from the expiration of the term of the endowment, assuming a government university?

E17-6 (Plant Entries) Hitech State University issued $14,000,000 of bonds to finance construction of a new computer facility on March 25, 20X8. The contractor billed the university $3,200,000 for work completed during 20X8. The university paid all but a 5% retained percentage. In 20X9 the contractor completed the facility and billed Hitech for $10,800,000. The university has paid all but a 5% retained percentage as of year end.

Required   Prepare the necessary journal entries for 20X8 and 20X9 to account for the preceding transactions.

Problems

Note: *Unless stated otherwise, assume that the colleges and universities in the following problems are "business-type only" special purpose governments.*

P17-1 (Multiple Choice—Government University) (Respond assuming a government university.) Indicate the best answer for each of the following:
1. For the spring semester of 20X4, Lane University assessed its students $3,400,000 (net of refunds) of tuition and fees for educational and general purposes. However, only $3,000,000 was expected to be realized because scholarships totaling $300,000 were granted to students, and tuition remissions of $100,000 were allowed to faculty members' children who were attending Lane. How much should Lane include in educational and general revenues from student tuition and fees?
   a. $3,400,000
   b. $3,300,000
   c. $3,100,000
   d. $3,000,000

2. During the years ended June 30, 20X6, and 20X7, Sampson University conducted a diabetes research project financed by a $2,000,000 gift from an alumnus. This entire amount was pledged by the donor on June 10, 20X4, although he paid only $500,000 at that date. The gift was restricted to the financing of this particular research project. During the two-year research period Sampson's related gift receipts and research expenditures were as follows:

	Year Ended June 30	
	20X6	20X7
Gift receipts..	$700,000	$ 800,000
Diabetes research expenditures...........................	900,000	1,100,000

How much gift revenue should Sampson report for the year ended June 30, 20X7?
   a. $0
   b. $800,000
   c. $1,100,000
   d. $2,000,000

3. On January 2, 20X6, Tim Brooks established a $500,000 trust at Wyndham National Bank, the income from which is to be paid to Mansfield University for general operating purposes. The Wyndham National Bank was appointed by Brooks as trustee of the fund. What journal entry is required on Mansfield's books?

	Dr.	Cr.
a. Memorandum entry only		
b. Cash...	$500,000	
Endowment Fund Balance		$ 500,000
c. Cash—Restricted for Endowment....................	$500,000	
Revenues—Endowment Gifts....................		$ 500,000
d. Cash—Restricted for Endowment	$500,000	
Restricted Net Position—Nonexpendable.............		$ 500,000

(AICPA, adapted)

4. The carrying value of the Annuities Payable account of a college
   a. should be adjusted to reflect changes in actuarial assumptions such as life expectancies or yield estimates.
   b. should be adjusted only for benefit payments made and investment income earned.
   c. must be adjusted annually to the present value of the required payments.
   d. a and c.

Questions 5, 6, and 7 are based on the following scenario:

Assume that a wealthy alumnus donated $1 million to Chavis University to provide loans to qualifying students. Though not required by the donor, the university's Board of Trustees voted to supplement the initial establishment of the loan fund with $500,000 of the university's own unrestricted resources. Further assume that any interest earned on the loan funds is to be added to the underlying principal of the fund and that both the original principal and that from earnings may be loaned.

5. What amount of the principal would be reported in GAAP-based financial statements as assets restricted for loans on the date of donation?
   a. $0
   b. $500,000
   c. $1,000,000
   d. $1,500,000

6. What amount of revenues would be reported in GAAP-based financial statements on the date of donation?
   a. $0
   b. $500,000
   c. $1,000,000
   d. $1,500,000

7. How would this loan fund be reported in the net position classifications?
   a. As nonexpendable restricted net position, $1,000,000, and unrestricted net position, $500,000
   b. As expendable restricted net position, $1,000,000, and unrestricted net position, $500,000
   c. As nonexpendable restricted net position
   d. As expendable restricted net position

Questions 8, 9, and 10 are based on the following scenario:
Steines College, an institution considered to be governmental in nature, had the following events occur during the year:

- Tuition scholarships of $45,000 were granted during the year and $7,500 of tuition waivers were granted.
- An alumnus donated land valued at $750,000 for the new administration building that is planned for next year.
- Student aid from unrestricted resources was paid to qualifying students in the amount of $300,750.

8. How will the tuition scholarships and waivers be reported on the college's operating statement?
   a. Expenses of $7,500 will be reported for the waivers, and $45,000 will be reported as a revenue deduction for the scholarship allowances.
   b. Expenses of $52,500 will be reported.
   c. Revenue deductions of $52,500 will be reported.
   d. Expenses of $45,000 for scholarship allowances and revenue deductions of $7,500 for tuition waivers will be reported.

9. How should the donated land be recorded in the college's general ledger?

	Dr.	Cr.
a. Capital Assets	$ 750,000	
Restricted Net Position		$ 750,000
b. Capital Assets	$ 750,000	
Net Investment in Capital Assets		$ 750,000
c. Capital Assets	$ 750,000	
Nonoperating Revenues		$ 750,000
d. Capital Assets	$ 750,000	
Capital Contributions		$ 750,000

10. How should the student aid payments be recorded in the college's general ledger?

	Dr.	Cr.
a. Expenses	$ 300,750	
Cash		$ 300,750
b. Revenue Allowance	$ 300,750	
Cash		$ 300,750
c. Tuition Revenues	$ 300,750	
Cash		$ 300,750
d. None of the above.		

P17-2 (Transactions and Entries) The trial balance of Boegner University, a government university, on September 1, 20X7, was as follows:

	Dr.	Cr.
Cash	$ 155,000	
Accounts Receivable	30,000	
Allowance for Uncollectible Accounts		$ 2,000
Inventory of Materials and Supplies	25,000	
Vouchers Payable		23,000
Capital Assets (net)	800,000	
Net Position		985,000
	$1,010,000	$1,010,000

Boegner University's dormitory and food service facilities are operated as auxiliary enterprises. The following transactions took place during the current fiscal year:

1. Collections amounted to $2,270,000, distributed as follows: tuition and fees, $1,930,000; unrestricted gifts, $170,000; sales and services of educational activities, $115,000; other sources, $25,000; accounts receivable, $30,000.
2. Receivables at year end were $29,000, consisting entirely of tuition and fees revenues.

3. It is estimated that tuition receivable of $3,000 will never be collected.
4. Revenues from auxiliary enterprises were $300,000, all collected.
5. Materials purchased during the year for cash, $500,000; on account, $50,000.
6. Materials used amounted to $510,000, distributed as follows:

Educational and general:

Institutional support	$ 30,000	
Research	5,000	
Instruction	305,000	
Academic support	7,000	
Other	53,000	$ 400,000
Auxiliary enterprises		110,000
		$ 510,000

7. Salaries and wages paid:

Educational and general:

Institutional support	$ 170,000	
Research	63,000	
Instruction	1,212,000	
Academic support	80,000	
Other	85,000	$1,610,000
Auxiliary enterprises		90,000
		$1,700,000

8. Other expenses paid:

Educational and general:

Institutional support	$ 10,000	
Research	2,000	
Instruction	53,000	
Academic support	3,000	
Other	7,000	$ 75,000
Auxiliary enterprises		20,000
		$ 95,000

9. Interest expenses chargeable to Institutional Support, $3,000, were paid.
10. Vouchers payable paid, $40,000.

Prepare journal entries for Boegner University for the 20X7–20X8 fiscal year. ***Required***

P17-3 (Restricted Gift and Grant Entries) The following transactions of Rumbaugh State College occurred during the 20X5–20X6 fiscal year:

1. Cash was received as follows for the purposes noted:

Educational and general:

Endowments—Institutional support and research	$ 75,000	
Private gifts—Research	40,000	
Federal grants—Instruction (reimbursement grant)	150,000	
State grant—Student services (reimbursement grant)	20,000	$ 285,000
Auxiliary enterprises		130,000
		$ 415,000

2. Expenses paid for the restricted purposes were:

Educational and general:

Institutional support	$ 40,000	
Research	30,000	
Instruction	125,000	
Student services	20,000	$ 215,000
Auxiliary enterprises		90,000
		$ 305,000

3. Investments of $100,000 were made.

Prepare journal entries for these transactions. ***Required***

P17-4 (Endowment Entries) Percy University, a government university, had no endowments prior to September 1, 20X7. The following transactions took place during the fiscal year ended August 31, 20X8:

1. At the beginning of the year, a cash donation of $900,000 was received to establish Endowment X, and another donation of $600,000, also in cash, was received for the purpose of establishing Endowment Y. The income from these endowments is restricted for specific purposes. It was decided to invest this money immediately; to pool the investments of both endowments; and to share earnings, including any gains or losses on sales of investments, at the end of the year based on the ratio of the original contributions of each endowment.
2. Securities with a par value of $1,000,000 were purchased at a premium of $10,000.
3. Securities with a par value of $191,500 were acquired at a discount of $2,000; accrued interest at date of purchase amounted to $500.
4. The university trustees voted to pool the investments of a new endowment, Endowment Z, with the investments of Endowments X and Y under the same conditions as applied to the latter two endowments. The investments of Endowment Z at the date it joined the pool at midyear amounted to $290,000 at book value and $300,000 at market value. (Hereafter, the investment pool earnings are to be shared 9:6:3.)
5. Cash dividends received from the pooled investments during the year amounted to $70,000, and interest receipts were $5,500.
6. Premiums of $500 and discounts of $100 were amortized.
7. Securities carried at $30,000 were sold at a gain of $2,400.
8. Each endowment was credited with its share of the investment earnings for the year (see transactions 1 and 4).
9. A provision of Endowment Y is that a minimum of $75,000 each year, whether from earnings or principal or both, is to be made available for unrestricted uses.
10. An apartment complex comprising land, buildings, and equipment valued at $800,000 was donated to the university, distributed as follows: land, $80,000; buildings, $500,000; equipment, $220,000. The donor stipulated that an endowment (designated as Endowment N) should be established and that the income therefrom should be used for a restricted operating purpose.
11. Unrestricted resources of $150,000 were set aside by the board as a quasi-endowment (or fund functioning as an endowment) and was designated Endowment O.
12. A trust fund in the amount of $350,000 (cash) was set up by a donor with the stipulation that the income was to go to the university to be used for general purposes. This fund was designated Endowment P.

Required a. Prepare the necessary journal entries for Percy University for the 20X7–20X8 fiscal year.
 b. Explain how each transaction affects the net position classifications.

P17-5 (Loan "Fund" Entries) The following transactions occurred during the 20X6 fiscal year of Pate County College.

1. A donation of $150,000 was received in cash for the purpose of making loans to students.
2. Cash in the amount of $50,000 was invested in bonds acquired at par.
3. Loans of $60,000 were made to students.
4. Interest on investments, $300, was received in cash.
5. Student loans of $1,000 were written off as uncollectible.

Required Prepare journal entries for the fiscal year.

P17-6 (Capital-Asset-Related Entries) The trial balance of Farley College, a government university, as of September 1, 20X5, includes the following:

Land	$ 200,000	
Buildings	3,300,000	
Accumulated Depreciation—Buildings		$ 900,000
Equipment	1,200,000	
Accumulated Depreciation—Equipment		300,000
Mortgage Payable		250,000
Net Investmemt in Capital Assets		3,250,000

The following transactions took place during the year:

1. A cash donation of $40,000 was received from an individual for the purpose of financing new additions to the business and public administration building.
2. The money was invested in securities acquired at par.

3. Other cash donations were received as follows:

For retiring indebtedness	$ 20,000
For plant improvements and renovations	15,000
For plant additions	15,000
	$ 50,000

4. Of the money received in entry 3, $10,000 was used to finance the acquisition of additional equipment.
5. A $1 million addition to the business and public administration building was begun. Expenditures of $600,000 were incurred (and paid) by August 31, 20X1, financed by a loan (note) of $1 million from the Last National Bank pending the receipt of more donations.
6. A total of $13,000 was spent in remodeling an art building classroom.
7. A cash donation of $75,000 was received for the purpose of paying part of the mortgage.
8. A mortgage installment of $35,000 ($10,000 principal and $25,000 interest) became due during the year and was paid from the previous donation.
9. An uninsured piece of equipment costing $5,000 was destroyed. Related accumulated depreciation was $2,000.
10. The provision for depreciation for the year was $270,000 for buildings and $120,000 for equipment.

a. Prepare journal entries for Farley College, as needed, for the 20X5–20X6 fiscal year.   ***Required***
b. Prepare a schedule computing the balance of Net Investment in Capital Assets at the end of the fiscal year.

P17-7 (Statements) Analysis of the accounts of Jonimatt State College for the fiscal year ended June 30, 20X7, provided the following information:

Revenues from:	*Unrestricted*	*Restricted*
Tuition and fees	$7,300,000	
State appropriations	5,920,000	$ 840,000
Federal grants and contracts (80% operating; 20% capital)		2,000,000
Private gifts, grants, and contracts	2,950,000	1,112,000
Sales and services of auxiliary enterprises	3,000,000	
Sales and services of educational activities	500,000	
Expenses for:		
Instruction	5,830,000	760,000
Research	1,200,000	610,000
Public service	300,000	2,000,000
Academic support	2,000,000	
Student services	925,000	
Institutional support	2,500,000	
Operation and maintenance of plant	3,125,000	
Scholarships and fellowships	200,000	155,000
Auxiliary enterprises	2,660,000	

1. Earnings of the endowments included the following: ***Additional Information***

Unrestricted	$ 100,000
Restricted for:	
Scholarships and fellowships	45,000
Plant expansion	75,000
Total	$ 220,000

2. Contributions received during fiscal year 20X7 were for these purposes:

a. Unrestricted	$2,950,000
b. Scholarships and fellowships	320,000
c. Specific academic programs	1,800,000
d. Endowment	4,300,000
e. Plant expansion	850,000
f. Debt service	40,000
g. Life income trust	160,000

3. Restricted investment income was earned for:

   a. Scholarships and fellowships $195,000
   b. Specific academic programs 250,000
   c. Plant expansion 78,000
   d. Debt service 30,000

4. Restricted federal grants and contracts of $2,230,000 received during the year were restricted for specific operating purposes. State appropriations of $340,000 restricted to specific academic programs and $500,000 restricted to expansion of the business building also were received (and are included in the account balances provided.)
5. Proceeds of equipment sales during the year, $27,000, are unrestricted. The cost of the assets sold was $140,000, and the related accumulated depreciation was $104,000.
6. Depreciation of plant facilities for the fiscal year was $800,000.
7. The university issued $4,000,000 of bonds at par to finance construction of a new chemistry building, but construction had not begun at June 30, 20X7.
8. $300,000 of long-term debt and $340,000 of interest matured and were paid in fiscal year 20X7.
9. Total net position at the beginning of the year was $27,000,000.

Required   Prepare a Statement of Revenues, Expenses, and Changes in Net Position for Jonimatt State College for the fiscal year ended June 30, 20X7.

P17-8 Prepare the journal entries for Boegner University, **P17-2**, assuming that it is a nongovernment, not-for-profit university.

CHAPTER 18

Accounting for Health Care Organizations

LEARNING OBJECTIVES

After studying this chapter, you should be able to:

- Account for unique hospital revenue sources such as patient service revenues.

- Prepare journal entries for hospital transactions.

- Prepare government hospital financial statements.

- Understand the key differences between accounting and reporting for government and nongovernment not-for-profit hospitals.

- Prepare nongovernment not-for-profit hospital financial statements.

H ealth care is a major factor in maintaining a good quality and longevity of life. Not surprisingly, it is a major industry in our economy. Health care organizations include for-profit entities of varying size and complexity, government entities, and nongovernment, not-for-profit entities.

Two industry professional associations—the American Hospital Association (AHA) and the Healthcare Financial Management Association (HFMA)—have been dominant forces in the development and improvement of health care financial management, accounting, and reporting. Accounting and statistical manuals, data processing services, symposiums and workshops, advisory services, and recognized journals are provided for the industry on a regular basis through these associations.[1] These organizations encourage their members to follow generally accepted accounting principles in reporting and to have annual audits. Additionally, HFMA's Principles and Practices Board issues Statements of Position providing guidance on certain health care accounting and financial reporting issues.

---

[1]*Hospitals and Health Networks* is the official magazine of the American Hospital Association; *hfm (Healthcare Financial Management)* is that of the Healthcare Financial Management Association.

The American Institute of Certified Public Accountants' (AICPA's) *Audit and Accounting Guide, Health Care Entities,*[2] is now recognized to constitute, together with applicable GASB pronouncements, generally accepted accounting principles for government health care providers. As with nongovernment colleges and universities, *nongovernment* not-for-profit health care organizations must report in accordance with the guidance in the FASB *Accounting Standards Codification,* including ASC 958 for not-for-profit organizations and 954 for health care entities. The AICPA audit guide provides guidance for implementing these standards in *nongovernment* not-for-profit health care organizations. Additionally, accounting and reporting standards applicable to for-profit entities vary somewhat from those for the other types.

GASB *Statement No. 29* prohibits government health care organizations from applying the "not-for-profit" SFASs. Because the FASB not-for-profit organization guidance was covered in detail in Chapter 16, *this chapter emphasizes accounting and reporting for government health care organizations in accordance with GASB standards and the health care organization audit guide.* The key differences in financial reporting for nongovernment not-for-profit hospitals are highlighted briefly at the end of this chapter, and financial statements are presented at that point in accordance with the FASB's guidance in its *Codification,* using the data from the illustrative example in this chapter.

The same accounting and reporting principles apply to the various types of government health care providers. Those principles are discussed and illustrated in the context of hospitals—the most familiar and most prominent health care provider organization. These principles, with slight variations for unique circumstances and transactions, apply also to government nursing homes and other government health care organizations.

Government hospitals are reported as enterprise activities. If they are separate legal entities—as is normally the case—they are special purpose governments engaged only in business-type activities.

Therefore, accounting for hospitals—whether government hospitals or nongovernment not-for-profit hospitals—is similar to accounting for a specialized industry in business accounting. In fact, in the absence of resources whose use is restricted by donors or grantors, the primary significant differences between hospital accounting and business accounting are certain revenue recognition practices of hospitals and the absence, in government and not-for-profit hospitals, of the distinction between contributed capital and retained earnings. Also, only governments use the deferred outflows and deferred inflows of resources as elements of their statements of financial position. When donor- or grantor-restricted assets are held, hospitals may use separate funds to account for those resources but must report them using restricted asset accounting.

FUNDS—GOVERNMENT HOSPITALS

Hospitals with significant amounts of donor- or grantor-restricted assets often use as many as three restricted fund types to account for their restricted assets. Use of these funds is optional, and they are not common in hospital financial statements. The three types of *restricted funds* used are:

1. **Specific Purpose Funds**—used to account for assets restricted by donors or grantors to specific operating purposes.
2. **Plant Replacement and Expansion Funds**—used to account for financial resources restricted by donors or grantors for capital asset purposes.

---

[2]American Institute of Certified Public Accountants, *Audit and Accounting Guide: Health Care Entities* (New York: AICPA, 2011), including Statements of Position issued by the Auditing Standards Division and the Accounting Standards Division, hereafter referred to as the *Health Care Audit Guide.*

3. **Endowment Funds**—used to account for the principal of permanent endowments, term endowments, or similar gifts.

The accounting principles that apply to government hospitals are the same as for other government enterprise activities. The accounting equation is the same as for any Enterprise Fund:

$$\begin{bmatrix} \text{Current} \\ \text{Assets} \end{bmatrix} + \begin{matrix} \text{Noncurrent} \\ \text{Assets} \end{matrix} + \begin{matrix} \text{Deferred} \\ \text{Outflows} \end{matrix} - \begin{bmatrix} \text{Current} \\ \text{Liabilities} \end{bmatrix} - \begin{matrix} \text{Long-Term} \\ \text{Liabilities} \end{matrix} - \begin{matrix} \text{Deferred} \\ \text{Inflows} \end{matrix} = \begin{matrix} \text{Net} \\ \text{Position} \end{matrix}$$

As noted earlier, this equation varies from the business accounting equation only with respect to the two financial statement elements unique to governments and the presentation of equity. Government hospital accounting differs relatively little from basic business accounting.

UNIQUE MEASUREMENT AND DISPLAY FEATURES

The predominant view is that (1) hospitals are "going concerns," even if they are not-for-profit, and (2) revenues and gains must cover all expenses and losses if the hospital's capital is to be maintained. Generally accepted accounting principles applicable to government hospitals apply the flow of economic resources measurement focus. Accounting for hospitals is similar to accounting for other entities that use Enterprise Fund accounting principles.

Hospital accounting involves several unique income determination and asset valuation features. But, for the most part, hospital assets, liabilities, revenues, expenses, gains, and losses are measured and reported the same as those of other government enterprise activities. Once again, one of the unique features is the presentation of net position in the three classifications required for government proprietary funds: net investment in capital assets, restricted net position, and unrestricted net position.

The *Health Care Audit Guide* applies the FASB Concepts *Statement No. 6* definitions of revenues, expenses, gains, and losses. *Revenues and expenses* result from "delivering or producing goods, rendering services, or other activities that constitute the entity's ongoing major or central operations."[3] *Gains and losses* occur casually or incidentally in relation to the provider's ongoing activities. GASB *Statement No. 34* requires operating and nonoperating items to be classified using similar logic, but adds the expectation of reasonable consistency with items reported as operating cash flows.

The classification of items as revenue or gain and expense or loss thus varies among health care providers. The same transaction may result in reporting revenues for one health care provider and gains for another. Donors' contributions are *revenues* for hospitals for which *fund-raising is a major, ongoing activity* through which resources are raised to finance the basic functions of the hospital. However, note that these donations still should be reported as nonoperating income in government hospitals. Hospitals that receive only occasional contributions and *have no ongoing, active fund-raising function* would report donations as *gains*.

Hospital revenues are classified broadly into three major categories:

1. **Patient service revenues** are earned in the several revenue-producing centers through *rendering inpatient and outpatient services*. Patient service revenues include revenues generated from (1) *daily patient services* such as room, board, and general nursing services; (2) *other nursing services* such as operating room, recovery room, and labor and delivery room nursing services; and (3) *other professional services* such as laboratories, radiology, anesthesiology, and physical therapy.

[3]*Health Care Audit Guide,* par. 10.2.

2. **Premium fees** (or subscriber fees) are revenues from health management organization (HMO), or other, agreements under which a hospital has agreed to provide any necessary patient services (perhaps from a contractually agreed set of services) for a specific fee—usually a per member per month (pmpm) fee. Because these fees are *earned without regard to the patient services actually provided,* they should be reported separately from patient service revenues.

3. **Other revenues** are those revenues that are derived from ongoing activities other than patient care and service. Examples are (1) student tuition and fees derived from nursing or other schools a hospital operates and (2) miscellaneous sources such as rentals of hospital plant, sales of scrap, cafeteria sales, sales of supplies to physicians and employees, and fees charged for copies of documents.

Patient service is the major source of revenues for most hospitals. Only the amount of patient service charges that someone has a responsibility to pay is reported as revenues in the hospital Statement of Revenues, Expenses, and Changes in Net Position. Government hospitals report patient service revenues *net* of charity services, uncollectible accounts, contractual adjustments arising from third-party payer agreements or regulations, policy discounts extended to patients who are members of the medical profession or clergy, administrative adjustments, and any similar amounts that neither patients nor third-party payers are deemed obligated to pay. Note that, as with all revenues of governments, revenues are reduced for estimated uncollectible amounts. An example note disclosure for patient service revenues appears in 18-1 In Practice.

Typical types of **deductions from patient service revenues** include:

- **Charity services** for patients who do not pay the established rates because they are not considered financially able to do so per the hospital's charity care criteria.

- **Policy discounts** for members of groups (doctors, clergy, employees, or employees' dependents) who receive allowances in accordance with hospital policy.

- **Contractual adjustments** for patients' bills that are paid to the hospital by third-party payers (such as insurance companies or Medicaid and Medicare programs) at lower-than-established rates in accordance with contracts between the hospital and third-party payers or with government regulations.

- **Uncollectible accounts.**

18-1 IN PRACTICE

Third-Party Payers: Significance and Accounting Policies

These accounting policies from a major government hospital's policy manual acknowledge the significance of third-party payers, reflect some of the challenges in determining the amounts of required third-party payments, and indicate the way the hospital accounts for and reports third-party payments.

Patient Service Revenue
Patient service revenue is recorded at scheduled rates when services are rendered. Allowances and provisions for uncollectible accounts and contractual adjustments are deducted to arrive at net patient service revenue.

Receivables from Third Parties and Contractual Adjustments
A significant portion of the Medical Center services are rendered to patients covered by Medicare, Medicaid, or Blue Cross. The Hospitals have entered into contractual agreements with these third parties to accept payment for services in amounts less than scheduled charges.

In accordance with the third-party payer agreements, the difference between the contractual reimbursement and the Medical Center's standard billing rates results in contractual adjustments.

Contractual adjustments are recorded as deductions from patient service revenue in the period in which the related services are rendered.

Certain annual settlements of amounts due for patient services covered by third parties are determined through cost reports that are subject to audit and retroactive adjustments by third parties. Provisions for possible adjustments of cost reports are estimated and reflected in the financial statements as considered appropriate. Because the determination of cost reimbursement settlements of amounts earned in prior years has been based on reasonable estimation, the difference in any year between the originally estimated amount and the final determination is reported in the year of determination as an adjustment of the deductions from patient service revenue.

A hospital must have established criteria to distinguish charity services from uncollectible accounts. *Charity services are not reported as revenues or as receivables* in the financial statements. Only services rendered under circumstances that meet the preestablished criteria for charity services should be treated as charity services. *Other uncollectible amounts are classified as uncollectible accounts.*

When third-party payers (usually Medicare, Medicaid, and Blue Cross) contract with hospitals to pay patients' bills, agreed reimbursement rates are likely to be based on cost or some national or regional average charge for similar hospital services. Established (standard) hospital rates typically are higher than the third-party payer rates. Hence, whereas gross revenues for services rendered to Medicare and other third-party payer patients are initially recorded at standard established rates, a contractual allowance is needed to reduce gross revenues to amounts actually receivable. This *internal accounting approach* provides information useful for management analyses of revenue patterns and certain note disclosures—for example, the amount of charity services rendered.

To illustrate, assume that a hospital's standard gross charges for services rendered in a year total $1,000,000, but the amount it ultimately expects to collect is only $850,000. The hospital rendered $40,000 of charity services and had estimated contractual adjustments of $60,000 and estimated uncollectible accounts of $50,000. The required entries are:

Accounts and Notes Receivable	$1,000,000	
Revenues—Patient Service Charges		$1,000,000
To record gross billings for services at established rates.		
Revenue Deductions—Charity Services or		
Patient Service Charges[4]	$ 40,000	
Revenue Deductions—Contractual Adjustments.	60,000	
Revenue Deductions—Provision for Uncollectible		
Accounts	50,000	
Allowance for Uncollectible Receivables and		
Third-Party Contractuals		$ 110,000
Accounts and Notes Receivable		40,000
To record deductions from gross revenues, the related allowance, and the write-off of receivables related to charity services.		

Note that when specific receivables are identified as not being collectible, the receivables should be written off against the allowance.

The appropriate reporting of the information above is:

Statement of Net Position

Accounts and notes receivable	$ 960,000	
Less: Allowance for uncollectible receivables and		
third-party contractuals.	110,000	$ 850,000

**Statement of Revenues, Expenses, and Changes in
   Net Position**

Net Patient Service Revenues	$ 850,000
($1,000,000 – $40,000 – $60,000 – $50,000)	

Note also that bad debt expenses are *not* reported by government hospitals, because they use the *net revenue* approach. Bad debt expenses will be reported by other hospitals.

---

[4]Charity services are not revenues. Hospitals may initially record the patient service charges, however, for two reasons. First, the hospital may not know initially that an account qualifies as charity service. Second, hospitals must disclose the level of charity service provided. Hospitals disclose the level of charity services by disclosing the direct and indirect costs of providing those services.

Gains As noted earlier, gains arise from activities that are *not part of a hospital's major, ongoing, or central operations.* Too, whereas revenues are reported prior to deducting related costs, gains often will be reported net of such costs, such as gains on sales of investments in securities or of capital assets. Typical nonoperating gains of hospitals result from

- Sales of investments in securities
- Sales of capital assets
- Gifts or donations (which are revenue for some hospitals)
- Investment income (which is revenue for some hospitals)

Whether items such as contributions and investment income are revenues or gains depends upon the definition of the mission of individual hospitals. The treatment is determined by whether fund-raising (for contributions) or investment income are intended to be major ongoing sources of financing for the hospital. If so, the related amounts are revenues; otherwise they are gains. In either case, these amounts should be reported as nonoperating items, not as operating income.

Donations Government hospitals receive several kinds of donations. Unrestricted gifts, grants, and bequests typically are recorded as gains. Some hospitals also receive significant amounts of restricted gifts and grants from individuals, foundations, and other governments. As discussed and illustrated in the college and university chapter, *most restricted government grants are reimbursement grants with detailed stipulations regarding allowability of expenditures that must be met for expenditures to qualify for reimbursement.* Reimbursement grants typically are recognized as revenues when qualifying expenditures are incurred. *Restricted grants and contributions received from private foundations and individuals* typically are reported as revenues when either a legally enforceable pledge or cash is received. Review the discussion of restricted gifts and grants for government colleges and universities.

Another type of donation that hospitals also may receive is *professional services.* For example, retired physicians or pharmacists may voluntarily work part-time in their professional capacities. In addition, priests and nuns who are physicians, pharmacists, or nurses may work full time for little or no pay. Contributed services were explicitly excluded from the scope of GASB *Statement No. 33* and their recognition by *government hospitals is optional.* If recognized, government hospitals must report contributed services as nonoperating revenues. (Nongovernment not-for-profit hospitals are required to report donated services as other operating revenues if the FASB criteria for recognizing donated services, discussed in Chapter 16, are met.) Gifts of *supplies and commodities* also are recorded at fair market value as other revenues or as gains.

Expense Classification The measurement and recognition criteria for expenses and losses are generally identical to those for business entities. A key exception is that the *pension expense* and other postemployment benefit expense measurements for government hospitals differ, as discussed in prior chapters. The differences in the GASB and FASB guidance on accounting for impairments of assets are also significant. Hospital expenses are typically classified by such major functions as:

- Nursing services
- Other professional services
- General services
- Fiscal services
- Administrative services
- Other services

Each of these major expense classifications may be subclassified further according to organizational unit and object classification, thus creating a multiple classification scheme not unlike the multiple classification of expenditures used in state and local government accounting. Like colleges and universities, hospitals are permitted to use natural rather than functional expense classifications in the Statement of Revenues, Expenses, and Changes in Net Position. However, if functional classifications are not reported in the statement, they must be disclosed in the notes.

Nursing services expenses include the nursing services provided in the various patient care facilities of a hospital—for example, medical and surgical, pediatrics, intensive care, operating rooms—as well as nursing administrative, educational, and various other related costs. **Other professional services expenses** is used to classify expenses incurred in providing other medical care to patients—such as laboratories, blood bank, radiology, pharmacy, anesthesiology, and social services—as well as expenses incurred for research, education, and administration in these areas. Care of the physical plant, dietary services, and other nonmedical services that are part of the ongoing physical operations of a hospital are classified as **general services expenses**. Expenses incurred for accounting, admitting, data processing, storerooms, and similar activities are grouped as **fiscal services expenses**; and expenses incurred by the executive office, personnel, purchasing, public relations, and so forth are classified as **administrative services expenses**. Depreciation, uncollectible accounts, employee benefits, interest, taxes, insurance, and similar costs may be reported under the preceding functional classifications or may be reported as separate line items in a government hospital Statement of Revenues, Expenses, and Changes in Net Position.

Restricted Assets

Government hospitals may have significant amounts of restricted cash and investments. Some of these assets are restricted by contracts such as bond indentures, externally restricted third-party (Blue Cross, Medicare, Medicaid, etc.) reimbursement agreements, or other similar arrangements. Others are restricted to specific uses by the donors or grantors. Additionally, hospitals sometimes dedicate a portion of unrestricted resources for capital acquisitions based on an internal management decision, often called board designations (shown later in the chapter in Illustration 18-3).

- All cash and investments that are designated or restricted for long-term purposes, including capital acquisitions, endowment, and research, are reported as noncurrent assets.

- Internally designated assets, assets restricted by other than donor or grantor requirements, assets restricted by donors or grantors to capital acquisition and research, and the principal of permanent endowments should each be reported separately under the Noncurrent Cash and Investments asset subcategory.

The limitations on the use of *board-designated resources* clearly are created at the board's discretion. These unrestricted resources that the board has designated (not restricted) are to be used for a specific noncurrent or nonoperating purpose. Board designations might be established, for example, for expansion of the physical plant, to retire debt, or even to serve as an endowment for the hospital. Board designation of assets for specified purposes does not change the *unrestricted* status of the related net position.

Unlike board-designated resources, *assets limited as to use by bond indentures, third-party reimbursement arrangements, and so on, are legally restricted— just as donor-restricted assets are legally restricted.* Government hospitals must apply the standard GASB guidance on restrictions in determining restricted net position.

For *nongovernment not-for profit hospitals,* the term ***restricted*** is reserved for resources that are restricted as to purpose or timing of use **by donors or grantors**. Examples of purposes for which resources may be restricted are (1) specific operating purposes, (2) additions to capital assets, and (3) endowment. As with other entities, many restrictions are temporary and are removed either (1) by meeting a specific condition—as with complying with restrictions by spending for specific purposes—or (2) by passage of time—as with term endowments. Pure endowments, in which the endowment principal can never be expended, create permanent restrictions on those net assets. Nongovernment, not-for-profit hospitals report internally designated assets and assets restricted by other than donors or grantors in a unique category called **Assets Limited as to Use**.

Property, Plant, and Equipment

Hospital capital assets should be recorded at historical cost or at fair value at donation and depreciated. Assets used by the hospital may be owned outright, leased from or made available by independent or related organizations, or provided by a governmental agency or hospital district. The nature of such relationships must be disclosed in the financial statements, and they should be accounted for and reported in conformity with GAAP.

ILLUSTRATIVE CASE

Accounting for the varied, complex, and voluminous transactions of a government hospital requires many subsidiary ledgers and other similar records. In this illustrative case we deal only with the general ledger accounts.

The case example presented here relates to Alzona Hospital, a medium-sized, government, general short-term health care facility financed from patient services fees, donations, and investment earnings. The beginning trial balance of Alzona Hospital at October 1, 20X2, the beginning of the fiscal year to which the example relates, is presented as Illustration 18-1.

Summary of Transactions and Events

1. Gross charges to patients at standard established rates were $4,400,000.

   (1) Accounts and Notes Receivable $4,400,000
         Revenues—Patient Service Charges. $4,400,000
       To record gross billings for services at established
       rates.

2. $85,000 of receivables were written off against the prior year allowance balances—$70,000 for uncollectible accounts and $15,000 for contractual adjustments.

   (2) Allowance for Uncollectible Receivables and
         Third-Party Contractuals . . . . $ 85,000
         Accounts and Notes Receivable . . . . $ 85,000
       To record write-off of receivables.

3. The hospital wrote off $265,000 of receivables established in 20X2–X3 (entry 1) associated with Medicare, Medicaid, and privately insured patients due to contractual adjustments.

   (3) Revenue Deductions—Contractual Adjustments. . . . $ 265,000
         Accounts and Notes Receivable . . . . $ 265,000
       To record contractual adjustments.

4. The hospital determined that $125,000 of the services it provided were to patients who met the hospital criteria for charity services.

   (4) Revenue Deductions—Charity Services . . . . $ 125,000
         Accounts and Notes Receivable . . . . $ 125,000
       To record charity services.

ILLUSTRATION 18-1 Beginning Trial Balance—Government Hospital

Alzona Hospital
Beginning Trial Balance
October 1, 20X2

	Debit	Credit
Cash	$ 175,000	
Cash—Restricted for Specific Programs	40,000	
Cash—Restricted for Plant Replacement and Expansion	25,000	
Cash—Endowments	5,000	
Investments	245,000	
Investments—Restricted for Specific Programs	215,000	
Investments—Restricted for Plant Replacement and Expansion	300,000	
Investments—Endowments	475,000	
Accounts and Notes Receivable	700,000	
Allowance for Uncollectible Receivables and Third-Party Contractuals		$ 85,000
Inventory of Materials and Supplies	165,000	
Land	130,000	
Land Improvements	80,000	
Accumulated Depreciation—Land Improvements		24,000
Buildings	5,000,000	
Accumulated Depreciation—Buildings		2,221,000
Equipment	690,000	
Accumulated Depreciation—Equipment		205,000
Accounts Payable		175,000
Notes Payable		150,000
Mortgage Payable		100,000
Net Position		5,285,000
Totals	$8,245,000	$8,245,000

Recall that charity services do not result in patient service revenues—gross or net—under the audit guide because the patient service provider has no expectation of receiving payment. If a hospital discloses the composition of its net patient service revenues in its notes, charity services are not part of that disclosure. The charity services may be recorded like other reductions of patient service charges, but are not reported like them. However, the level of charity services must be disclosed in a separate note and measured by the direct and indirect costs to provide the services.

5. Collections of accounts receivable totaled $3,800,000.

(5) Cash	$3,800,000	
Accounts and Notes Receivable		$3,800,000

To record collections of accounts receivable.

6. Additional accounts receivable written off as uncollectible during the year totaled $55,000.

(6) Allowance for Uncollectible Receivables and Third-Party Contractuals	$ 55,000	
Accounts and Notes Receivable		$ 55,000

To record write-off of accounts deemed uncollectible.

7. The estimated deductions for uncollectible accounts for the year totaled $120,000. Also, additional contractual adjustments related to 20X2–X3 of $25,000 are expected to result from final settlements with third-party payers of their clients' accounts.

(7) Revenue Deductions—Uncollectible Accounts	$ 120,000	
Revenue Deductions—Contractual Adjustments...	25,000	
Allowance for Uncollectible Receivables and Third-Party Contractuals		$ 145,000

To adjust deductions from gross revenues and allowance accounts to year-end balances.

8. Materials and supplies, including food purchased on account during the year, totaled $600,000. A perpetual inventory system is in use.

(8) Inventory of Materials and Supplies..............	$ 600,000	
Accounts Payable		$ 600,000

To record inventory purchases on account.

9. Materials and supplies were used as follows:

Nursing services.......................	$ 170,000
Other professional services	50,000
General services.....................	319,000
Fiscal services......................	8,000
Administrative services	3,000
	$ 550,000

(9) Expenses—Nursing Services.....................	$ 170,000	
Expenses—Other Professional Services...........	50,000	
Expenses—General Services	319,000	
Expenses—Fiscal Services	8,000	
Expenses—Administrative Services	3,000	
Inventory of Materials and Supplies		$ 550,000

To record inventory usage.

10. Accounts payable paid during the year were $725,000.

(10) Accounts Payable	$ 725,000	
Cash		$ 725,000

To record payment of accounts payable.

11. Salaries and wages paid during the year were for the following:

Nursing services......................	$1,316,000
Other professional services	828,000
General services.....................	389,000
Fiscal services......................	102,000
Administrative services	65,000
	$2,700,000

(11) Expenses—Nursing Services	$1,316,000	
Expenses—Other Professional Services.........	828,000	
Expenses—General Services	389,000	
Expenses—Fiscal Services	102,000	
Expenses—Administrative Services.............	65,000	
Cash		$2,700,000

To record salaries and wages paid.

12. Expenses, other than for salaries and materials and supplies, paid during the year were chargeable as follows:

Nursing services......................	$ 86,000
Other professional services	79,000
General services......................	221,000
Fiscal services.......................	44,000
Administrative services	327,000
	$757,000

(12) Expenses—Nursing Services	$ 86,000	
Expenses—Other Professional Services	79,000	
Expenses—General Services...................	221,000	
Expenses—Fiscal Services....................	44,000	
Expenses—Administrative Services.............	327,000	
Cash.....................................		$757,000
To record expense payments.		

13. Salaries and wages accrued at year end were for the following:

Nursing services......................	$ 35,000
Other professional services	21,000
General services......................	19,000
Fiscal services.......................	6,000
Administrative services	2,000
	$ 83,000

(13) Expenses—Nursing Services	$ 35,000	
Expenses—Other Professional Services	21,000	
Expenses—General Services...................	19,000	
Expenses—Fiscal Services....................	6,000	
Expenses—Administrative Services.............	2,000	
Accrued Salaries and Wages Payable...........		$ 83,000
To record accrued expenses at year end.		

14. Interest expense on notes payable was $8,000, of which $1,000 was accrued at year end; $20,000 of principal was retired.

(14) Notes Payable................................	$ 20,000	
Expenses—Interest	8,000	
Accrued Interest Payable.....................		$ 1,000
Cash.....................................		27,000
To record interest payment and accrual, and reduction of principal of notes payable.		

15. Interest earned during the year on unrestricted investments was $5,000, of which $2,000 was accrued at year end. The investments are exempt from the GASB fair value accounting requirements.

(15) Cash...	$ 3,000	
Accrued Interest Receivable	2,000	
Nonoperating Gains—Unrestricted Investment Income		$ 5,000
To record interest earned on unrestricted investments.		

16. Unrestricted earnings on investments restricted for specific programs, $24,000, were received.

(16) Cash...	$ 24,000	
Nonoperating Gains—Unrestricted Investment Income		$ 24,000
To record unrestricted interest earnings.		

17. Professional services donated to the hospital were objectively valued and charged as follows:

Nursing services	$17,000
Other professional services	3,000
	$20,000

(17) Expenses—Nursing Services	$ 17,000	
Expenses—Other Professional Services	3,000	
Nonoperating Revenues—Donated services		$ 20,000
To record the value of donated services received.		

18. Other revenues collected during the year were from the following:

Cafeteria sales	$45,000
Television rentals	30,000
Medical record transcript fees	15,000
Vending machine commissions	5,000
	$95,000

(18) Cash	$ 95,000	
Revenues—Cafeteria Sales		$ 45,000
Revenues—Television Rentals		30,000
Revenues—Medical Record Transcript Fees . . .		15,000
Revenues—Vending Machine Commissions		5,000
To record receipt of miscellaneous revenues.		

19. General contributions received in cash, $100,000.

(19) Cash	$ 100,000	
Nonoperating Gains—General Contributions		$ 100,000
To record receipt of unrestricted contributions.		

20. Bonds were issued at par, $3,000,000, to be used to pay for a new building wing and to retire the mortgage payable.

(20) Cash—Construction	$2,900,000	
Cash—Debt Service	100,000	
Bonds Payable		$3,000,000
To record sale of bonds at par.		

21. The mortgage notes (Illustration 18-1) were paid and the contractor billed Alzona $2,500,000 for work completed on the new wing to date. All but a 5% retained percentage was paid.

(21) Construction in Process	$2,500,000	
Mortgage Payable	100,000	
Contracts Payable—Retained Percentage—		
Construction		$ 125,000
Cash—Construction		2,375,000
Cash—Debt Service		100,000
To record payment of mortgage payable and the		
progress billings on the building, less 5% of		
contract retained pending final inspection.		

22. Equipment costing $100,000, on which there was accumulated depreciation of $60,000, was sold for $30,000.

(22) Cash	$ 30,000	
Accumulated Depreciation—Equipment	60,000	
Nonoperating Losses—Disposal of		
Capital Assets	10,000	
Equipment		$ 100,000
To record the sale of equipment at a loss.		

23. The board of directors set aside $100,000 of investments for future plant replacement and expansion.

    (23) Investments—Designated for Plant
            Replacement............................. $100,000
            Investments................................ $100,000
        To reclassify investments per board designation.

24. The charges to General Services Expenses were found to include $5,000 for equipment (which was purchased with cash). (No depreciation needs to be recorded on this equipment for the current year.)

    (24) Equipment .... $ 5,000
          Expenses—General Services................ $ 5,000
        To capitalize equipment erroneously charged to expense.

25. Depreciation expense for the year was $5,000 on land improvements, $170,000 on buildings, and $125,000 on equipment. Assume that the functional allocations shown in the entry are correct.

    (25) Expenses—Nursing Services.................. $150,000
          Expenses—Other Professional Services 80,000
          Expenses—General Services.................. 40,000
          Expenses—Fiscal Services................... 12,000
          Expenses—Administrative Services............ 18,000
            Accumulated Depreciation—Land
               Improvements .... $ 5,000
            Accumulated Depreciation—Buildings....... 170,000
            Accumulated Depreciation—Equipment 125,000
        To record depreciation expense.

26. Accrued interest on bonds payable at year end was $30,000.

    (26) Expenses—Interest .... $ 30,000
          Accrued Interest Payable................... $ 30,000
         To record interest accrued at year end on bonds outstanding.

27. A $400,000 restricted government grant to defray specific operating costs was received. Any portion not used to cover qualifying costs within the next 18 months must be refunded.

    (27) Cash—Restricted for Specific Programs $400,000
          Unearned Grant Revenues $400,000
         To record receipt of a grant to be used to pay certain operating costs.

Note that different gifts or grants may be required to be used for different operating purposes. We assume that the detail in this example is maintained in a subsidiary ledger—which is not illustrated in the example—rather than in the general ledger accounts.

28. Investments were purchased with the restricted resources from transaction 27 for $300,000.

    (28) Investments—Restricted for Specific Programs.. $300,000
          Cash—Restricted for Specific Programs $300,000
         To record investments during the period.

29. Restricted investments for specific programs maturing during the period, $150,000, had been originally purchased at par.

    (29) Cash—Restricted for Specific Programs $150,000
          Investments—Restricted for Specific
            Programs................................ $150,000
         To record the maturity of investments originally purchased at par.

30. Earnings on restricted investments, restricted to specific programs, were $15,000.

(30) Cash—Restricted for Specific Programs	$ 15,000	
Nonoperating Gains—Restricted Investment		
Income		$ 15,000
To record receipt of investment income that is		
restricted to specific purposes.		

31. The fair market value of investments restricted for use for specific purposes and on which income is restricted to the specific purposes increased by $500.

(31) Investments—Restricted for Specific Programs . .	$ 500	
Nonoperating Gains—Restricted Investment		
Income		$ 500
To record the increase in the fair market value		
of restricted investments.		

32. A benefactor gave investments in stock valued at $200,000 to the hospital. The corpus is to be maintained intact; earnings may be used for general operating purposes.

(32) Investments—Endowments	$200,000	
Contributions to Permanent Endowments		$200,000
To record a permanent endowment gift.		

33. Unrestricted income from the endowment investments was received, $45,000.

(33) Cash.	$ 45,000	
Nonoperating Gains—Unrestricted Investment		
Income		$ 45,000
To record receipt of dividends.		

34. Earnings on investments restricted for plant replacement and expansion were received, $15,400. These earnings are restricted to plant replacement and expansion.

(34) Cash—Restricted for Plant Replacement and		
Expansion	$ 15,400	
Nonoperating Gains—Restricted Investment		
Income		$ 15,400
To record earnings on investments restricted for		
plant that are restricted to use for plant		
replacement and expansion.		

35. The fair market value of investments restricted for plant replacement and expansion increased $600 during the year. Earnings are restricted for plant replacement and expansion.

(35) Investments—Restricted for Plant Replacement		
and Expansion.	$ 600	
Nonoperating Gains—Restricted Investment		
Income—Increase in Fair Value of		
Investments		$ 600
To record increase in fair value of investments		
restricted to plant replacement and expansion.		

36. Investments that cost $165,000 and that are restricted for specific programs were sold for $170,000. Gains on these investments are available for unrestricted use.

(36) Cash—Restricted for Specific Programs	$165,000	
Cash.	5,000	
Investments—Restricted for Specific		
Programs.		$165,000
Nonoperating Gains—Unrestricted Investment		
Income		5,000
To record sale of investments at a gain.		

37. Review of expenses identified $200,000 of expenses (recorded previously) that are allowable costs under the federal grant received during the year.

(37) (a) Unearned Grant Revenues.................	$ 200,000	
Revenues—Federal Grants		$ 200,000
To record grant revenue.		
(37) (b) Cash....................................	$ 200,000	
Cash—Restricted for Specific Programs...		$ 200,000
To reclassify restricted cash as unrestricted cash because of restricted expenses paid from unrestricted cash.		

38. Equipment was purchased for $18,000 from resources restricted for plant replacement and expansion.

(38) Equipment	$ 18,000	
Cash—Restricted for Plant Replacement and Expansion..............................		$ 18,000
To record purchase of equipment.		

39. Earnings restricted for specific operating purposes were received on endowment investments, $25,000.

(39) Cash—Restricted for Specific Programs	$ 25,000	
Nonoperating Gains—Restricted Investment Income...................................		$ 25,000
To record earnings restricted to specific purposes.		

The preclosing trial balance for Alzona Hospital at September 30, 20X3, is presented in Illustration 18-2.

Closing:

40. Closing entries were made at year end:

(40) Revenues—Patient Service Charges............	$4,400,000	
Revenues—Cafeteria Sales	45,000	
Revenues—Television Rentals.................	30,000	
Revenues—Medical Record Transcript Fees	15,000	
Revenues—Vending Machine Commissions.....	5,000	
Revenues—Federal Grants	200,000	
Nonoperating Revenues—Donated Services.....	20,000	
Nonoperating Gains—Unrestricted Investment Income.........................	79,000	
Nonoperating Gains—Restricted Investment Income.........................	56,500	
Contributions to Permanent Endowment	200,000	
Nonoperating Gains—General Contributions ...	100,000	
Revenue Deductions—Uncollectible Accounts..............................		$ 120,000
Revenue Deductions—Contractual Adjustments...........................		290,000
Revenue Deductions—Charity Services		125,000
Expenses—Nursing Services		1,774,000
Expenses—Other Professional Services		1,061,000
Expenses—General Services................		983,000
Expenses—Fiscal Services..................		172,000
Expenses—Administrative Services..........		415,000
Expenses—Interest		38,000
Nonoperating Losses—Disposal of Capital Assets		10,000
Net Position		162,500
To close accounts at year end.		

ILLUSTRATION 18-2 Preclosing Trial Balance—Government Hospital

Alzona Hospital
Preclosing Trial Balance
December 31, 20X3

	Debit	Credit
Cash	$ 268,000	
Cash—Restricted for Specific Programs	295,000	
Cash—Construction	525,000	
Cash—Restricted for Plant Replacement and Expansion	22,400	
Cash—Endowments	5,000	
Investments	145,000	
Investments—Designated for Plant Expansion	100,000	
Investments—Restricted for Specific Programs	200,500	
Investments—Restricted for Plant Replacement and Expansion	300,600	
Investments—Endowments	675,000	
Accounts Receivable	770,000	
Allowance for Uncollectible Receivables and Third-Party Contractuals		$ 90,000
Accrued Interest Receivable	2,000	
Inventory of Materials and Supplies	215,000	
Land	130,000	
Land Improvements	80,000	
Accumulated Depreciation—Land Improvements		29,000
Buildings	5,000,000	
Accumulated Depreciation—Buildings		2,391,000
Equipment	613,000	
Accumulated Depreciation—Equipment		270,000
Construction in Progress	2,500,000	
Accounts Payable		50,000
Accrued Salaries and Wages Payable		83,000
Notes Payable		130,000
Accrued Interest Payable		31,000
Contracts Payable—Retained Percentage		125,000
Unearned Grant Revenues (Federally Sponsored Research)		200,000
Bonds Payable		3,000,000
Net Position		5,285,000
Revenues—Patient Service Charges		4,400,000
Revenues—Cafeteria Sales		45,000
Revenues—Television Rentals		30,000
Revenues—Medical Record Transcript Fees		15,000
Revenues—Vending Machine Commissions		5,000
Nonoperating Revenues—Donated Services		20,000
Revenues—Federal Grants		200,000
Nonoperating Gains—General Contributions		100,000
Nonoperating Gains—Unrestricted Investment Income		79,000
Nonoperating Gains—Restricted Investment Income		56,500
Contributions to Permanent Endowments		200,000
Revenue Deductions—Charity Services	125,000	
Revenue Deductions—Uncollectible Accounts	120,000	
Revenue Deductions—Contractual Adjustments	290,000	
Expenses—Nursing Services	1,774,000	
Expenses—Other Professional Services	1,061,000	
Expenses—General Services	983,000	
Expenses—Fiscal Services	172,000	
Expenses—Administrative Services	415,000	
Expenses—Interest	38,000	
Nonoperating Losses—Disposal of Capital Assets	10,000	
Totals	$16,834,500	$16,834,500

FINANCIAL STATEMENTS

The financial statements that a government hospital should prepare for external use include a Statement of Net Position; a Statement of Revenues, Expenses, and Changes in Net Position; and a Statement of Cash Flows. The *Health Care Audit Guide* requires the statements to present comparative information.

Illustration 18-3 presents the year-end Statement of Net Position for the Alzona Hospital assuming that it is a government hospital. Note the similarity of this statement and the Enterprise Fund Statement of Fund Net Position discussed in Chapter 10.

Statement of Net Position

The Statement of Revenues, Expenses, and Changes in Net Position in Illustration 18-4 demonstrates some of the points made earlier. The statement should seem familiar because it is the same statement required for proprietary funds and for government colleges and universities that report as business-type-only specific purpose governments. Notice that patient service revenues are reported at the net amount that patients or third-party payees are obligated to pay—that is, net of deductions from revenues—*less* uncollectible accounts. Also note (1) the distinction between patient service revenues, other revenues, and nonoperating gains; (2) the sources of revenues and gains; and (3) the distinction between expenses and losses.

Operating Statement

The Statement of Cash Flows, Illustration 18-5, is conventional for enterprise-type organizations. Governments do not distinguish unrestricted and restricted cash and cash equivalents in reporting cash flows. Therefore, this statement reconciles total beginning and ending cash and cash equivalents. Further, it reports all cash flows for the hospital—whether affecting the unrestricted cash balance, the cash included in internally designated assets, or restricted cash. The cash balances reported in the cash flow statement are the beginning and ending balances of the sum of the balances of all of the cash accounts shown in the beginning (Illustration 18-1) and ending (Illustration 18-2) trial balances, respectively.

Statement of Cash Flows

The next section points out some of the key differences between financial reporting for a government hospital and for a nongovernment not-for-profit hospital. The latter must apply the FASB not-for-profit guidance discussed and illustrated in Chapter 16 and its health care entity guidance. Financial statements are presented for the Alzona Hospital illustration under the assumption that it is a nongovernment not-for-profit hospital.

NONGOVERNMENT NOT-FOR-PROFIT HOSPITAL REPORTING

Like colleges and universities, nongovernment not-for-profit health care organizations are required to follow the FASB not-for-profit organization accounting guidance discussed and illustrated in Chapter 16. The AICPA *Health Care Audit Guide* provides implementation guidance to assist those organizations to comply with those standards. To this point, this chapter has dealt solely with government health care organizations. This section discusses and illustrates the application of FASB not-for-profit accounting standards to nongovernment not-for-profit hospitals (hereafter, NFP hospitals).

First, note that at least as many similarities as differences exist between the accounting and reporting for government and for NFP hospitals. For instance, all of the following are accounted for and reported in much the same manner:

- Patient service revenues
- Charity services
- Deductions from revenues of various types, except uncollectible accounts
- Premium fee revenues
- Other revenues, such as cafeteria sales, medical record transcript fees, and unrestricted contributions

ILLUSTRATION 18-3 Year-End Statement of Net Position—Government Hospital

Alzona Hospital
Statement of Net Position
September 30, 20X3

Assets:

Current:

Cash	$ 268,000
Investments	145,000
Receivables (less allowance for uncollectibles of $90,000)	680,000
Accrued interest receivable	2,000
Inventory of materials and supplies	215,000
Total current assets	1,310,000

Noncurrent:

Noncurrent cash and investments:

Internally designated for capital acquisitions	100,000
Restricted by bond indenture agreement	525,000
Restricted by contributors and grantors for capital acquisition and specific programs	818,500
Principal of permanent endowments	680,000
Total noncurrent investments and special funds	2,123,500

Capital Assets:

Land	130,000
Land improvements	80,000
Buildings	5,000,000
Equipment	613,000
Construction in process	2,500,000
Total capital assets	8,323,000
Less: Accumulated depreciation	2,690,000
Net capital assets	5,633,000
Total noncurrent assets	7,756,500
Total assets	$9,066,500

Liabilities:

Current liabilities:

Notes payable	$ 130,000
Accounts payable	50,000
Accrued interest payable	31,000
Accrued salaries and wages payable	83,000
Unearned grant revenues	200,000
Contracts payable—retained percentage	125,000
Total current liabilities	619,000

Long-term debt:

Bonds payable	3,000,000
Total liabilities	3,619,000

Net Position:

Net investment in capital assets	3,033,000
Restricted for:	
Specific programs	295,500
Plant replacement and expansion	323,000
Endowment	680,000
Unrestricted	1,116,000
Total net position	$5,447,500

| ILLUSTRATION 18-4   Operating Statement—Government Hospital |

Alzona Hospital
Statement of Revenues, Expenses, and Changes in Net Position
For the Year Ended September 30, 20X3

Revenues:

Net Patient Service Revenues	$3,865,000*
Other Revenues:	
Cafeteria sales	45,000
Television rentals	30,000
Medical record transcript fees	15,000
Vending machine commissions	5,000
Total Other Operating Revenues	95,000
Total Operating Revenues	3,960,000

Expenses:

Nursing services	1,774,000
Other professional services	1,061,000
General services	983,000
Fiscal services	172,000
Administrative services	415,000
Total Expenses	4,405,000
Operating Loss	(445,000)

Nonoperating Gains and (Losses):

Federal grants	200,000
Investment income	135,500
Interest expense	(38,000)
General contributions	100,000
Donated services	20,000
Loss on disposal of assets	(10,000)
Total Nonoperating Gains (Losses)	407,500
Income before additions to endowment	(37,500)
Additions to endowment	200,000
Change in Net Position	162,500
Net Position, October 1, 20X2	5,285,000
Net Position, September 30, 20X3	$5,447,500

*Calculations: Patient service charges net of charity services ($4,275,000) less contractual adjustments ($290,000), and uncollectible accounts ($120,000).

- Most expenses
- Assets limited as to use
- Assets restricted for noncurrent purposes, such as endowment or plant purposes

The *key differences* in reporting government hospitals and NFP hospitals *are that NFP hospitals:*

- Report net assets classified into the three categories required for not-for-profit entities— unrestricted, temporarily restricted, and permanently restricted—instead of the three net position categories required by the GASB.

- Present a statement of operations and statement of changes in net assets instead of a statement of revenues, expenses, and changes in net position. (The audit guide requires NFP hospitals to present a performance measure in the operating statement that is the equivalent of net income for a business, but it is not called net income. The FASB's not-for-profit guidance requires that this statement shows total changes in unrestricted net assets in addition to the performance measurement.)

ILLUSTRATION 18-5 Statement of Cash Flows—Government Hospital

Alzona Hospital
Statement of Cash Flows
For the Year Ended September 30, 20X3

Cash flows from operating activities:

Cash received from patients	$3,800,000
Cash received from other revenues	95,000
Cash paid to suppliers of goods and services	(1,477,000)
Cash paid to employees	(2,700,000)
Net cash flows from operating activities	(282,000)

Cash flows from noncapital financing activities:

Cash paid to retire note	(20,000)
Cash paid for interest	(7,000)
Cash received from unrestricted contributions	100,000
Cash received from federal operating grants	400,000
Net cash flows from noncapital financing activities	473,000

Cash flows from capital and related financing activities:

Cash received from issuing bonds	3,000,000
Cash paid to retire mortgage	(100,000)
Cash paid to purchase capital assets	(2,398,000)
Cash received from sale of equipment	30,000
Net cash flows from capital and related financing activities	532,000

Cash flows from investing activities:

Cash paid for investments	(300,000)
Cash received from sale of investments	320,000
Cash received from investment earnings	127,400
Net cash flows from investing activities	147,400

Net increase in cash	870,400
Cash, October 1, 20X2	245,000
Cash,* September 30, 20X3	$1,115,400

Reconciliation of Net Cash Flows from Operating Activities to Loss from Operations:

Loss from operations	($ 445,000)
Adjustments to reconcile net cash flows from operating activities and operating loss:	
Depreciation	300,000
Donated services expense	20,000
Increase in inventory	(50,000)
Increase in accounts receivable	(65,000)
Increase in salaries payable	83,000
Decrease in accounts payable	(125,000)
Net cash flows from operating activities	($ 282,000)

The cash balance is comprised of all cash—both unrestricted and restricted.

- Distinguish changes in the three different categories of net assets—unrestricted, temporarily restricted, and permanently restricted—which is not done for government hospitals.
- Report the provision for bad debts as operating expenses. If the hospital includes significant amounts in patient service revenues that it has not yet determined are bad debts or charity services, the provision for bad debts is reported as shown in Illustration 18-7 instead of in operating expenses.
- Report net assets released from restrictions.
- Apply FASB cash flow statement guidance instead of GASB cash flow guidance.

ILLUSTRATION 18-6   Year-End Balance Sheet—Nongovernment Not-for-Profit Hospital

Alzona Hospital
Balance Sheet
September 30, 20X3

ASSETS

Current:

Cash	$ 563,000
Assets limited as to use—required for current liabilities	125,000
Receivables (less allowance for uncollectibles of $90,000)	680,000
Investments	345,500
Accrued interest receivable	2,000
Inventory of materials and supplies	215,000
Total current assets	1,930,500

Noncurrent:

Noncurrent investments and special funds:

Assets limited as to use by internal designation	100,000
Assets limited as to use for plant expansion by bond indenture agreement	525,000
Less assets limited as to use that are required for current liabilities	125,000
Noncurrent assets limited as to use externally	400,000
Assets restricted for plant replacement and expansion	323,000
Assets restricted for permanent endowments	680,000
Total noncurrent investments and special funds	1,503,000

Property, plant, and equipment:

Land	130,000
Land improvements	80,000
Buildings	5,000,000
Fixed equipment	500,000
Major movable equipment	113,000
Construction in progress	2,500,000
Total property, plant, and equipment	8,323,000
Less: Accumulated depreciation	2,690,000
Net property, plant, and equipment	5,633,000
Total noncurrent assets	7,136,000
Total assets	$9,066,500

LIABILITIES AND NET ASSETS

Current liabilities:

Notes payable	$ 130,000
Accounts payable	50,000
Accrued interest payable	31,000
Accrued salaries and wages payable	83,000
Contracts payable—retained percentage	125,000
Total current liabilities	419,000

Long-term debt:

Bonds payable	3,000,000
Total liabilities	3,419,000

Net assets:

Unrestricted	4,149,000
Temporarily restricted by donors or grantors	818,500
Permanently restricted by donors	680,000
Total net assets	5,647,500
Total liabilities and net assets	$9,066,500

Most of these similarities and differences are readily observable by comparing the government hospital financial statements in Illustrations 18-3 to 18-5 with the nongovernment not-for-profit hospital financial statements in Illustrations 18-6 to 18-9. The statements are based on the same transactions and assumptions.

ILLUSTRATION 18-7   Nongovernment Not-for-Profit Hospital Operating Statement

Alzona Hospital
Statement of Operations
For the Year Ended September 30, 20X3

Unrestricted revenues, gains, and other support:	
Patient service revenues (net of contractual allowances and discounts) . . .	$3,985,000
Provision for bad debts	((120,000)
Net patient service revenues less provision for bad debts	3,865,000
Other operating revenues	115,000
Unrestricted contributions	100,000
Unrestricted investment income	79,000
Total revenues	4,159,000
Net assets released from restrictions for operating use	200,000
Total revenues and net assets released from restrictions for operating use	4,359,000
Expenses and losses:	
Nursing services	1,774,000
Other professional services	1,061,000
General services	983,000
Fiscal services	172,000
Administrative services	415,000
Interest	38,000
Loss on disposal of fixed assets	10,000
Total expenses and losses	4,453,000
Excess (deficiency) of revenues, gains, and other support over expenses and losses	(94,000)
Net assets released from restrictions for plant asset purposes	18,000
Decrease in unrestricted net assets	($ 76,000)

**ILLUSTRATION 18-8   Nongovernment Not-for-Profit Hospital Statement
of Changes in Net Assets**

Alzona Hospital
Statement of Changes in Net Assets
For the Year Ended September 30, 20X3

	Unrestricted	Temporarily Restricted	Permanently Restricted	Total
Balance, October 1, 20X2	$4,225,000*	$580,000	$480,000	$5,285,000
Operating loss	(94,000)			(94,000)
Contributions and grants	—	400,000	200,000	600,000
Restricted investment income	—	56,500	—	56,500
Net assets released from restrictions	18,000	(218,000)	—	(200,000)*
Changes in net assets	(76,000)	238,500	200,000	362,500
Balance, September 30, 20X3	**$4,149,000**	**$818,500**	**$680,000**	**$5,647,500**

*$200,000 of net assets released from restrictions for operating purposes are included in the operating loss and are not shown separately in this statement.

ILLUSTRATION 18-9   Nongovernment Not-for-Profit Hospital Statement of Cash Flows*

Alzona Hospital
Statement of Cash Flows
For the Year Ended September 30, 20X3

Cash flows from operating activities:

Cash received from patients.	$3,800,000
Cash received from other revenues	95,000
Cash received from grants and contributions	500,000
Cash paid to suppliers and employees	(4,177,000)
Cash received from investment earnings	112,000
Cash paid for interest	(7,000)
Net cash flows from operating activities	323,000

Cash flows from investing activities:

Cash paid for property, plant, and equipment	(2,398,000)
Net increase in cash invested in assets limited as to use	(525,000)
Net decrease in cash invested in assets restricted for endowment and plant purposes.	2,600
Proceeds from sale of equipment	30,000
Cash paid for investments	(300,000)
Cash received from sale of investments	320,000
Net cash used in investing activities	(2,870,400)

Cash flows from financing activities:

Cash received from issuing bonds	3,000,000
Cash paid to retire debt	(120,000)
Cash received from investment earnings restricted for plant purposes and restricted endowment revenues	15,400
Net cash flows from financing activities	2,895,400

Net increase in cash	348,000
Cash balance, October 1, 20X2	215,000
Cash balance, September 30, 20X3	$ 563,000

Reconciliation of change in net assets to cash provided by operating activities:

Change in net assets	$ 362,500
Adjustments to reconcile change in net assets to net cash provided by operating activities:	
Depreciation expense	300,000
Increase in accounts receivable	(65,000)
Increase in interest receivable	(2,000)
Increase in inventory.	(50,000)
Decrease in accounts payable	(125,000)
Increase in salaries and wages payable.	83,000
Increase in interest payable	31,000
Loss on disposal of fixed assets	10,000
Gain on sale of investments.	(5,000)
Contributions restricted for permanent endowment	(200,000)
Investment income—unrealized or restricted for long-term purposes	(16,500)
Net cash provided by operating activities	$ 323,000

*Note that even though major differences distinguish this statement from Illustration 18-5, the differences would be the same for any other government versus nongovernment entity of any type. The differences are not unique to hospitals.

Concluding Comments

Health care accounting and reporting has evolved over the past 50 years to adapt to the ever-changing health care environment. Today, health care accounting and reporting is similar to accounting and reporting for business enterprises. However, because of the many unique features of the health care environment, health care financial management and accounting practices have several unique features.

The most significant unique features of government health care accounting compared to business accounting are various unique income determination features. This chapter deals primarily with reporting for *government* hospitals. Financial reporting for nongovernment not-for-profit hospitals is discussed briefly at the end of the chapter by drawing on your knowledge of government hospital accounting and of the nongovernment not-for-profit organization guidance in Chapter 16.

Chapter 19 covers accounting and reporting for the federal government. The federal government has made significant strides in improving financial accountability in recent years. Beginning to develop and present GAAP financial statements is an integral part of enhancing federal government accountability.

Questions

Q18-1 Identify the key differences between government health care accounting and commercial accounting.

Q18-2 Identify the key differences between government health care accounting and nongovernment not-for-profit health care organization accounting.

Q18-3 Identify the required financial statements for a government hospital.

Q18-4 Identify the required financial statements for a nongovernment not-for-profit hospital.

Q18-5 What is the difference between resources designated by hospital boards for specific purposes and those restricted by outside donors for specific purposes? What are the differing accounting effects?

Q18-6 Why is it important to distinguish between internal and external assets limited as to use? (Define these terms in your answer.)

Q18-7 List the principal classifications of hospital revenues.

Q18-8 Why should hospitals report only the net amount of patient service revenue in their Statement of Revenues, Expenses, and Changes in Net Position?

Q18-9 What are premium fee revenues? When should they be recognized as revenues?

Q18-10 A government hospital provides services with a standard charge of $5,000. Because of a contract with an insurance company, it only bills and collects $4,000 for the services. What amount of patient service revenues should be reported in the Statement of Revenues, Expenses, and Changes in Net Position? Why?

Q18-11 (a) Should depreciation be charged on the capital assets of a hospital if these assets have been financed from contributions but are intended to be replaced from hospital revenues? (b) Assume that the replacement of the capital assets is intended to be financed from contributions. Should depreciation be charged on such capital assets?

Q18-12 A government hospital's assets include the following:
  a. $2,000,000 set aside by the hospital board as an endowment to support research for curing the common cold
  b. $25,000,000 donated by various individuals and organizations to finance construction and equipping of a cancer treatment and research center
  c. $3,500,000 from a bond issue to finance expansion of the maternity wing
  d. $1,000,000 received from Blue Cross and Blue Shield (BCBS) as part of the hospital's reimbursement for services rendered to BCBS insurees. The reimbursement agreement with BCBS requires that this portion of the reimbursement be used for plant replacement and expansion.

How should these resources be reported in the hospital's statement of net position? How do they affect the various categories of net position?

Q18-13 (a) What is a term endowment? (b) How should a hospital account for the receipt of a term endowment? (c) How should a hospital account for the resources of a term endowment when the term of the endowment expires?

Q18-14 Following are various types of revenues, gains, and other amounts that may be received or accrued by a government hospital. For each type of revenue or gain, indicate whether it should typically be classified as:
1. Patient service revenue (P)
2. Other operating revenue (O)
3. Nonoperating gain (N)
4. None of the above (X)

_____ a. Unrestricted income on investments of endowments

_____ b. Operating room charges

_____ c. Gains from sale of land owned by the hospital

_____ d. General nursing service charges

_____ e. Harrimon Foundation grant received by hospital in recognition of outstanding past service to the community

_____ f. Room and board charges

_____ g. Cafeteria sales

_____ h. Professional services donated to the hospital

_____ i. Sales of scrap materials

_____ j. Tuition and fees from the hospital's nursing school

_____ k. Contractual Medicare allowances

_____ l. Physical therapy fees

_____ m. Interest on unrestricted investments

_____ n. Nursing salaries

_____ o. Rockefeller Foundation grant received by hospital for medical research

Exercises

E18-1 (Multiple Choice) Identify the best answer for each of the following:
1. Which of the following bodies play significant roles in establishing GAAP for government health care providers?
   a. GASB
   b. FASB
   c. Hospital Accounting Standards Board
   d. U.S. Government Accountability Office
2. Government hospitals are reported similar to
   a. enterprise activities.
   b. governmental funds.
   c. governmental not-for-profits.
   d. special revenue funds.
3. The primary differences between hospital accounting and business accounting include
   a. liability classifications.
   b. the types of equity accounts used in reporting.
   c. depreciation of capital assets.
   d. use of the effective interest method.
4. A gift to a government hospital that is restricted by the donor to use for a specific program should be credited directly to
   a. restricted net position.
   b. deferred revenue.
   c. revenue.
   d. unrestricted net position.
5. Donated medicines that normally would be purchased by a government hospital should be recorded at fair market value and should be credited directly to
   a. other operating revenue.
   b. nonoperating gain.
   c. net position.
   d. unearned revenue or gain.
6. Although their use is optional, the types of restricted funds often used in hospital financial accounting include
   a. specific purpose funds.
   b. endowment funds.
   c. plant replacement and expansion funds.
   d. All of the above.

7. Which of the following statements concerning the accounting and financial reporting practices for revenue in government hospitals is *false*?
   a. Only the amount of patient service charges that one has a responsibility to pay is reported as revenues.
   b. Patient service revenues are reported *net* of charity services and uncollectible accounts.
   c. Contractual adjustments arising from agreements with third-party payers (e.g., Medicare and Medicaid) are *not* netted with patient service revenues.
   d. Charity services are *not* reported as revenues or receivables in the financial statements.

8. Which of the following events would *not* potentially result in a gain that would be reported in a government county hospital's financial statements?
   a. Third-party reimbursements that exceed initial expectations
   b. Sales of capital assets
   c. Gifts or donations
   d. Sales of investment securities

9. Which of the following statements best describes the accounting and financial reporting for the donation of professional services?
   a. The reporting of contributed services by a government hospital is *optional*.
   b. Contributed services received by governmental hospitals should be reported as *non-operating* revenues if they are being recognized in the financial statements.
   c. Items a and b accurately reflect the reporting practices of government hospitals.
   d. Items a and b are all false statements.

10. Which of the following classifications of equity would *not* be reported on a governmental hospital's statement of net position?
    a. Net investment in capital assets
    b. Temporarily restricted net position
    c. Restricted net position
    d. Unrestricted net position

E18-2 Identify the best answer for each of the following:

1. On July 1, 20X5, Lilydale Hospital's board of trustees designated $200,000 for expansion of outpatient facilities. The $200,000 is expected to be expended in the fiscal year ending June 30, 20X8. In Lilydale's statement of net position at June 30, 20X6, this cash should be classified as
   a. assets limited as to use.
   b. a restricted noncurrent asset.
   c. an unrestricted current asset.
   d. an unrestricted noncurrent asset.

2. During the year ended December 31, 20X5, Melford Hospital received the following donations stated at their respective fair values:

Employee services from members of a religious group	$ 100,000
Medical supplies from an association of physicians	30,000

   These supplies were restricted for indigent care and were used for such purpose in 20X5.

   How much revenue or gain from donations should Melford report in its 20X5 Statement of Revenues, Expenses, and Changes in Net Position?
   a. $0
   b. $30,000
   c. $100,000
   d. $130,000

3. Glenmore County Hospital's property, plant, and equipment (net of accumulated depreciation) consists of the following:

Land.	$ 500,000
Buildings	10,000,000
Equipment (purchased from restricted resources)	2,000,000

   What portion of these assets should be reflected in restricted net position?
   a. $0
   b. $2,000,000
   c. $10,500,000
   d. $12,500,000

4. Which of the following would normally be included in other operating revenues of a government hospital?
   a. Unrestricted interest income from an endowment
   b. An unrestricted gift
   c. Donated services
   d. Both items b and c

Questions 5 and 6 are based on the following data:

Under Abbey Hospital's established rate structure, the hospital would have earned patient service revenue of $6 million for the year ended December 31, 20X5. However, Abbey did not expect to collect this amount because of charity allowances of $1 million and discounts of $500,000 to third-party payers. In May 20X5, Abbey purchased bandages from Lee Supply Co. at a cost of $1,000. However, Lee notified Abbey that the invoice was being canceled and that the bandages were being donated to Abbey.

5. For the year ended December 31, 20X5, how much should Abbey report as patient service revenue in its Statement of Revenues, Expenses, and Changes in Net Position?
   a. $6,000,000
   b. $5,500,000
   c. $5,000,000
   d. $4,500,000
6. For the year ended December 31, 20X5, Abbey should report the donation of bandages as
   a. a $1,000 reduction in operating expenses.
   b. nonoperating gain of $1,000.
   c. other operating revenue of $1,000.
   d. a memorandum entry only.
7. A government hospital is required to present all of the following financial statements *except*
   a. a Statement of Net Position.
   b. a Statement of Cash Flows.
   c. a Budgetary Operating Statement.
   d. a Statement of Revenues, Expenses, and Changes in Net Position.
8. GAAP for *nongovernment* not-for-profit hospitals are primarily established by the
   a. GASB.
   b. FASB.
   c. AICPA.
   d. American Hospital Association.
9. Equity classifications for *nongovernment* not-for-profit hospitals include all of the following *except*
   a. net investment in capital assets.
   b. unrestricted net assets.
   c. permanently restricted net assets.
   d. temporarily restricted net assets.
10. Which of the following statements about a *nongovernment* not-for-profit hospital Statement of Cash Flows is *false*?
    a. A nongovernment not-for-profit hospital Statement of Cash Flows classifies the acquisition of property as an investing activity.
    b. The Statement of Cash Flows for a nongovernment not-for-profit hospital reports only three cash flow classifications.
    c. FASB cash flow statement guidance is optional for nongovernment not-for-profit hospitals.
    d. The Statement of Cash Flows includes a reconciliation of the change in net position to cash provided by operating activities.

E18-3 (Asset Restrictions and Designations) A government hospital has the following assets, among others:
1. Investments of $2 million from a donation made specifically for the purpose of defraying part of the cost of enlarging the hospital's pediatric center.
2. Cash and investments totaling $750,000 that the hospital board has designated for use for the expansion of the pediatric center.
3. $1.5 million restricted by donors to be used to supplement the operating budget of the hospital's cancer treatment center.
4. $2 million restricted by third-party reimbursement agreements to be used to replace certain equipment.

Show how these amounts should be reported in the hospital's Statement of Net Position. *Required*

E18-4 (Restricted Gifts) A government hospital received two gifts in 20X5. The first gift, for $3,000,000, was restricted to a specific operating purpose. Costs incurred during the year that qualified for use of the resources of the gift amounted to $1,250,000. The second gift was for $8,000,000 and was restricted for a capital project; $2,000,000 of construction costs were incurred on the project in 20X5. Explain or illustrate how these transactions should be reported in the hospital's Statement of Revenues, Expenses, and Changes in Net Position for 20X5.

Problems

P18-1 (Reporting Classifications)

Government Hospital Financial Reporting Classifications

Statement of Net Position		Statement of Revenues, Expenses, and Changes in Net Position	
CA	Current Assets	PSR	Patient Service Revenues
PPE	Property, Plant, and Equipment	OOR	Other Operating Revenues
IA	Intangible Assets	NG	Nonoperating Gains
OA	Other Assets	NSE	Nursing Services Expenses
CL	Current Liabilities	OPE	Other Professional Services Expenses
LTL	Long-Term Liabilities	GSE	General Services Expenses
NP	Net Position	FSE	Fiscal Services Expenses
		ASE	Administrative Services Expenses
		OE	Other Expenses

Using the preceding abbreviations, indicate how each of the following items should be reported in these two hospital financial statements. If none of the preceding items is appropriate, explain how the item should be reported.
1. Anesthesiology expenses
2. Qualifying expenses under a restricted government grant
3. Provision for bad debts
4. Capital asset (currently in use) purchased from donor-restricted resources
5. Expiration of term endowments—restricted to use for plant expansion
6. Gain on sale of equipment
7. Admitting office expenses
8. Donated services
9. Bond sinking fund
10. Cash and investments set aside by board to finance cancer research
11. Emergency services expenses
12. Unrestricted contributions
13. Bonds payable (issued to finance construction underway)
14. Provision for depreciation
15. Gift restricted for operations
16. Intensive care expenses
17. Power plant expenses
18. Income and gain from board-designated funds
19. Dietary service expenses
20. Interest expense

P18-2 (Capital-Asset-Related Entries) Pinckney County Hospital entered into the following transactions in 20X8:

April 1—Purchased incubators for the nursery for $47,300 from unrestricted resources. (Assume straight-line depreciation on all hospital capital assets.)

July 1—Issued $10,000,000 of 10%, 20-year bonds at par to finance construction of a major hospital addition. Construction is to begin early in 20X9, but bond market conditions are expected to become much less desirable over the next few months. The proceeds are invested in securities that also yield 10% interest.

October 31—Sold a kidney dialysis machine for $19,000 halfway through its useful life. The machine originally cost $25,000 and accumulated depreciation was $12,500 when it was sold.

December 31—(a) The incubators have a five-year useful life. (b) The first semiannual interest payment on the bonds is made.

Prepare all entries required on the preceding dates for these transactions. (Assume straight- **Required**
line depreciation.)

P18-3 (Selected Revenue-Related Entries)
1. Svoboda County Regional Medical Center's gross charges for services rendered to patients in 20X8 were $82,000,000. Of this, $2,500,000 was for services rendered to individuals who were certified by the county as having no means to pay. Also, contractual adjustments granted on services rendered to insured patients and Medicare patients during 20X8 totaled $4,800,000 by December 31, 20X8, and it was estimated that another $350,000 of contractual adjustments would be made associated with those services. In addition, the hospital estimated that it will incur bad debt losses of approximately $3,200,000 associated with the services rendered in 20X8.
2. Svoboda County Regional Medical Center received $875,000 of donations in 20X8 to be used to cover the cost of charity services provided to patients who do not have sufficient means to pay for the needed medical care.

a. Prepare the general journal entries that Svoboda County Regional Medical Center should **Required**
make to record these transactions.
b. Prepare the portion(s) of the Svoboda County Regional Medical Center's Statement of Revenues, Expenses, and Changes in Net Position affected by these transactions.

P18-4 (Donation- and Grant-Related Transactions) Miss Jenny Russ donated $3,000,000 to Broadus Memorial Hospital, a county hospital, on June 17, 20X8.
1. Assume that no restrictions are placed on the use of the donated resources.
   a. Prepare the required June 17, 20X8, entry.
   b. Prepare any entries necessary in 20X9 if $400,000 of the gift is used to finance hospital operating expenses.
2. Assume that the donation was restricted to leukemia research.
   a. Prepare the required June 17, 20X8, entry.
   b. Prepare any entries required in 20X9 as a result of spending $400,000 for leukemia research during 20X9.
3. Assume that the donation was restricted for use in adding a pediatrics intensive care unit to the hospital.
   a. Prepare the required June 17, 20X8, entry.
   b. Prepare any entries required in 20X9 if $400,000 of the gift is used to begin constructing the intensive care unit.

a. Explain or illustrate how each of the three situations described previously would be **Required**
reported in Broadus Memorial Hospital's financial statements in 20X8 and in 20X9. Include the effect of each transaction on the amounts reported in the various net position categories in your explanation.
b. Repeat items 2 and 3 under the assumption that the hospital received a $3,000,000 government reimbursement-type grant instead of a donation.

P18-5 (Various Entries) The following transactions and events relate to the operation of a government hospital.
a. Prepare journal entries to record the effects of these transactions and events in the general ledger accounts of the hospital. Explanations of entries may be omitted.
1. Total billings for patient services rendered, $85,000; it was estimated that bad debt losses on these billings would be $1,000 and that contractual adjustments would amount to $6,000.
2. Expenses of $15,000 were incurred for heart research. Restricted assets that were received in prior years were used to finance this research.
3. Equipment (cost, $8,000; accumulated depreciation, $5,000) was sold for $1,000.
4. Depreciation expense on buildings was recognized, $18,000.
5. Earnings on endowment investments are restricted to use for intern education; $14,000 was earned in the current year.
6. Unrestricted income on endowment investments, $3,500, was received.
7. Of the billings for patient services rendered (see item 1), $1,000 was written off.
b. Explain how each of the preceding transactions affects the Statement of Revenues, Expenses, and Changes in Net Position.

P18-6 (Operating Statement) Based on the following information, prepare a Statement of Revenues, Expenses, and Changes in Net Position for Hudgins County (government) Hospital for the year ended December 31, 20X7:

Patient service charges (gross)	$14,000,000
Premium fees earned	5,000,000
Restricted contributions for heart research	20,000,000
Medical record transcript fees	75,000

Cafeteria sales	150,000
Restricted contributions for specialized equipment purchases	6,500,000
Unrestricted income from endowments.	1,000,000
Donated services.	330,000
Donated materials.	88,000
Unrestricted contributions.	550,000
Nursing services expenses	7,850,000
Other professional services expenses.	5,400,000
General services expenses	3,210,000
Fiscal services expenses	300,000
Administrative expenses	900,000
Interest expense.	440,000
Depreciation expense	1,200,000
Provision for uncollectibles	430,000
Charity services.	375,000
Contractual adjustments	950,000
Equipment purchases paid from donor-restricted resources	3,750,300

Also, a term endowment restricted to heart research expired during the year. The foregoing expenses include $800,000 payable from donor-restricted resources.

P18-7 (General Journal/Ledger Entries) Prepare general ledger entries to record the following transactions.

1. Patient service charges totaled $8,000,000; 1% is expected to be uncollectible and 0.5% is expected to be charity services; $880,000 of contractual adjustments are expected to be made.
2. Received premium fees for the month, $100,000. Only half of the covered patients actually received any treatments during the month.
3. Received contributions for a restricted program, $2,000,000.
4. Incurred expenses for the restricted program, $1,200,500.
5. Received contributions restricted for purchase of MRI equipment, $600,000.
6. Purchased MRI equipment, $480,000.
7. Received contribution in the form of a term endowment, $300,000.

CHAPTER 19

Federal Government Accounting

LEARNING OBJECTIVES

After studying this chapter, you should be able to:

- Understand the federal financial management environment, including the roles and responsibilities of various federal organizations.

- Identify the sources of GAAP for the federal government financial report.

- Understand the federal accounting model.

- Explain the basic budgetary process and terminology used by the federal government.

- Prepare basic budgetary accounting entries and basic proprietary accounting entries for a federal agency.

- Understand the financial statement requirements for federal agencies.

- Understand the financial statements presented for the U.S. government as a whole.

The federal government of the United States is engaged in an unparalleled number and variety of functions, programs, and activities both here and abroad. It is by far the country's biggest employer and also its biggest consumer. Federal disbursements were $591 billion during 1980, up about twelvefold from 1950, and exceeded *$3.8 trillion* during fiscal year 2011. Federal disbursements have more than doubled every 10 years since 1950 and are on track to do so during the current decade. If so, federal disbursements will approach $7 trillion by 2020.

Federal accounting, like that of state and local governments, is heavily influenced by law and regulation. It serves as a major tool of fund and appropriation control at both the central government and agency levels. But federal accounting is noticeably different. First, the agency,[1] not the fund, is generally considered the primary accounting entity. Furthermore, agency accounting provides—via dual-track systems—for both budgetary and proprietary accounting and reporting.

Thus, the accounting system of the federal government is made up of many sets of systems and subsystems. Complete financial data are to be maintained for each agency by its system; financial reports are to be prepared by the agency. Financial reports for the federal government as a whole are compiled by the Office of Management and Budget (OMB) and the Department of the Treasury from the central accounts and from agency reports or electronic data provided by the agency.

---

[1]The term *agency* is used in this chapter to refer to departments, establishments, commissions, boards, or organizational entities thereof, such as a bureau.

THE FEDERAL FINANCIAL MANAGEMENT ENVIRONMENT

The importance of budgeting, accounting, and reporting to governmental financial management and accountability was recognized by those drafting the Constitution of the United States. Thus, they included a mandate (Article I, Section 9):

> No money shall be drawn from the treasury, but in consequence of appropriations made by law; and a regular statement and account of the receipts and expenditures of all public money shall be published from time to time.

From the outset, therefore, financial management was seen as a shared function of the legislative and executive branches of the federal government. Then, as now, the "power of the purse string" was vested in Congress. But the executive branch was charged with administering the activities of the federal government and reporting on its stewardship both to the Congress and to the public.

Financial Accounting Responsibilities

Several federal organizations have significant influence on financial management directives, requirements, and trends. However, in the financial management component of accounting and financial reporting, responsibilities center primarily around (1) three oversight agencies: the Department of the Treasury, the Office of Management and Budget, and the Government Accountability Office (Comptroller General); (2) the Federal Accounting Standards Advisory Board; and (3) the individual agencies. Illustration 19-1 summarizes these responsibilities, which are discussed in the following sections.

Department of the Treasury

The Department of the Treasury, in the executive branch, is headed by the Secretary of the Treasury. The Treasury acts as both chief accountant and banker for the federal government. The Treasury's functions include the following:

- Central accounting and reporting for the federal government as a whole, including development of government-wide consolidated financial statements.

- Cash receipt and disbursement management, including supervising the federal depository system and disbursing cash for virtually all civilian agencies.

- Management of the public debt, including the scheduling of borrowing to meet current needs, repayment of debt principal, and meeting interest requirements.

ILLUSTRATION 19-1 **Federal Accounting and Financial Reporting Roles and Responsibilities—A Summary**

Central Agencies	**Department of the Treasury** Cash receipts/disbursements; central proprietary accounting and reporting; Standard General Ledger (SGL); prepare and present (with OMB coordination) audited, government-wide financial statements; debt management.	**Office of Management and Budget** Budget preparation; apportionment; central budgetary accounting and reporting; form and content of financial statements; establish audit requirements for federal financial statements.	**Government Accountability Office** Prescribe the accounting and auditing standards and audit selected agency financial statements and the government-wide statements.

Federal Accounting Standards Advisory Board
Develop and recommend accounting and financial reporting principles, standards, and related requirements.

Federal Agencies
Maintain adequate accounting systems; implement and operate the SGL; and prepare and submit proprietary and budget execution reports required by oversight agencies.

- Supervision of agency borrowing from the Treasury.
- Maintenance of the government-wide Standard General Ledger (SGL).

Numerous directives issued by the Secretary of the Treasury affect federal accounting and reporting, the most comprehensive being the *Treasury Financial Manual.* This manual includes agency proprietary reporting requirements, as well as agency requirements to implement the SGL.

Office of Management and Budget (OMB)

An agency within the Executive Office of the President, the OMB has broad financial management powers, as well as the responsibility of preparing the executive budget. Among the accounting and financial reporting duties assigned to the OMB are:

- To apportion enacted appropriations among the agencies and establish reserves in anticipation of cost savings, contingencies, and so on.
- To set forth the requirements for accounting and reporting on budget execution.
- To prescribe the form and content of financial statements consistent with applicable accounting principles, standards, and requirements.
- To provide guidance on all matters related to budget preparation and execution.

Numerous bulletins, circulars, and other directives relating to federal budgeting, accounting, and reporting that are required to be followed by agencies have been issued by the OMB.

Government Accountability Office (GAO)

A multitude of roles and responsibilities have been assigned to the GAO—headed by the comptroller general of the United States—since its inception in 1921. The primary responsibilities of the GAO are assisting the Congress in the general oversight of the executive branch and serving as the independent legislative auditor of the federal government. The GAO's two primary responsibilities related to accounting and financial reporting are:

1. **Prescribing principles and standards for federal agency accounting and financial reporting, internal control, accounting systems, and auditing.** This responsibility is carried out largely through issuance of separate publications on each subject.
2. **Auditing the financial statements of federal agencies.** The GAO audits selected federal agency financial statements and also audits the consolidated financial statements of the overall government. The GAO has rendered opinions on agency financial statements, but, to date, has disclaimed an opinion on the consolidated financial statements of the U.S. Government.

Federal Accounting Standards Advisory Board (FASAB)

The Federal Accounting Standards Advisory Board (FASAB), created by a joint agreement between the Treasury, OMB, and GAO, began operations in early 1991. This board promulgates accounting principles and standards to be followed by federal agencies.

The FASAB is a nine-member board with one representative each from the Treasury, OMB, GAO, and six representatives from outside the federal government. The chairperson is a nonfederal member. The FASAB has a staff director and dedicated full-time staff. The FASAB standards are recognized as GAAP for federal agencies under *AICPA Statement on Auditing Standards No. 91,* "Federal GAAP Hierarchy."

As of early 2010, the FASAB had issued 6 Statements of Federal Financial Accounting Concepts, 36 Statements of Federal Financial Accounting Standards, 7 Interpretations, and numerous Technical Bulletins and other documents. In addition to addressing accounting for typical items such as inventory, federal standards must address accounting and reporting for numerous assets and liabilities unique to the federal government. (To learn more about the FASAB and its work on federal accounting standards, go to the FASAB's Web site at **http://www.fasab.gov**.)

Federal Agencies

The effectiveness of federal financial management depends on the individual federal agencies. Similarly, federal budgeting, accounting, and reporting can be no better than that of the related agency systems and subsystems on which the central systems depend. Among the many accounting-related functions and activities of agencies are these:

- To prepare agency budget requests for submission to the President through the OMB.
- To establish and maintain effective systems of accounting and financial reporting and internal control, in conformity with the principles and standards prescribed by the GAO.
- To implement and operate the SGL. (The SGL Board, made up of agency representatives, maintains account definitions, transactions, and crosswalks to reports.)
- To prepare and submit proprietary reports[2] and budget execution reports in accordance with the accounting and reporting requirements of the oversight agencies.

Most federal agencies have an **Inspector General** (IG) or similar internal audit and investigation officer who continually studies and evaluates the agency's activities. Each IG must prepare a semiannual report on audit findings and forward it to appropriate congressional committees. Most IGs are involved in the audit of the financial statements of the agency.

Overview   Responsibility for accounting and financial reporting principles, standards, and related requirements in the federal sector is not as simple or clear-cut as those in the private or state and local government sectors. Congress, through legislation, has established numerous guidelines for accounting and financial reporting. As discussed throughout this chapter, responsibility for developing, promulgating, and implementing accounting and financial reporting principles, standards, and requirements within the guidelines set forth in law is shared within the federal government. The two major categories of principles, standards, and requirements are *budgetary* and *proprietary*.

Although *budgetary* accounting and financial reporting guidelines traditionally have not been labeled as principles and standards, significant requirements direct its application in the federal sector. Budgetary requirements are developed and promulgated by the OMB. Requirements for reporting certain budgetary amounts in agency financial statements and in the consolidated financial statements are in the FASAB standards. Implementation mandates are also set by the OMB, but it is the agencies that must actually implement those mandates. Also, the Treasury sets forth several requirements to help implement fiscal reporting and management in the federal government and provide support for the SGL Board.

Proprietary principles, standards, and requirements are by law the responsibility of the GAO. The GAO establishes requirements such as those for accounting systems and internal controls. The OMB is required by law to promulgate the requirements for the form and content of financial statements. The Treasury implements the principles, standards, and requirements by directing agencies to provide it with financial statements periodically and annually. (Most agencies provide trial balances to the Treasury. These trial balances provide the information needed to prepare the consolidated financial statements.) Currently, the GAO,

---

[2]*Proprietary accounting* or *proprietary reporting* is the terminology used to indicate accounting and reporting for *actual* revenues, expenses, gains, losses, assets, liabilities, and so on—as opposed to *budgetary* accountability for budgetary authority granted and the use of that budgetary authority.

the OMB, and the Treasury have agreed that FASAB should establish standards. This agreement resolves conflicts among the authorities granted to each by Congress and provides an open process for the development of principles and standards.

In October 1999, the AICPA Council passed a resolution recognizing the FASAB as the authoritative body designated to establish generally accepted accounting principles (GAAP) for federal governmental entities under Rule 203, *Accounting Principles,* of the AICPA's Code of Professional Conduct. In July 2009, the FASAB established a **hierarchy** of accounting principles for **federal governmental entities**.

The GAAP hierarchy for financial statements of federal governmental entities is:

a. Category (*a*), officially established accounting principles, consists of FASAB Statements of Federal Financial Accounting Standards (Standards) and Interpretations. FASAB Standards and Interpretations will be periodically incorporated in a publication by the FASAB.

b. Category (*b*) consists of FASAB Technical Bulletins and, if specifically made applicable to federal governmental entities by the AICPA and cleared by the FASAB, AICPA Industry Audit and Accounting Guides.

c. Category (*c*) consists of Technical Releases of the Accounting and Auditing Policy Committee of the FASAB.

d. Category (*d*) includes implementation guides published by the FASAB staff, as well as practices that are widely recognized and prevalent in the federal government.[3]

In the absence of a pronouncement covered by Rule 203 or another source of established accounting principles, the auditor of financial statements of a federal governmental entity may consider other accounting literature, depending on its relevance in the circumstances.

THE BUDGETARY PROCESS

The budgetary process in the federal government, along with the related budgetary accounting, is more complex than in a municipality. (Although the process involves many intricate steps and is multifaceted, only those major processes affecting accounting are covered here.) The following primary reasons highlight the differences and the complexity of the federal budget process:

- Agency authority to incur obligations for future disbursement is usually not directly based on estimates of revenues, either at the agency or overall federal level. (Congress can increase or decrease the legal limit on the debt ceiling to raise cash, if needed.)

- Budget authority to incur obligations is granted by Congress under three types— appropriations, contract authority, or borrowing authority; also, appropriations can be one-year, multiyear, no-year, or permanent authorizations. Contract and borrowing authority can also contain various year limitations. Additional authority may be derived from collections from performing services to other agencies and the public.

- The process of spending budget authority is divided into five clearly distinct steps, most of which are closely monitored for legal and regulatory compliance. The five steps are apportionment, allotment, commitment, obligation, and expended appropriation.

The federal budget cycle, like that of state and local governments, has four phases: (1) preparation, (2) approval, (3) execution, and (4) reporting. (Auditing is included in the fourth phase but is not discussed in this chapter.)

The Budget Cycle

---

[3]AICPA, Statement on Auditing Standards No. 91, *Federal GAAP Hierarchy* (New York: AICPA, 2000).

Preparation and Approval

Budget preparation begins in the executive branch and ends when the budget is formally presented to Congress in the form of the President's budget. Budget preparation and presentation of the budget to Congress is a presidential responsibility. Preparation requires continuous exchange of information, proposals, evaluations, and policy determinations among the President, central financial agencies, and operating agencies.

Budget approval is a congressional function. The Congressional Budget Act of 1974 created the present procedure by which Congress determines the annual federal budget. In the initial step, Congress adopts a concurrent resolution to establish target levels for overall expenditures, budget authority, budget outlays, broad functional expenditure categories, revenues, the deficit, and the public debt.

An appropriation is contained in an act passed by Congress that becomes a public law. About 13 major laws are passed through the normal congressional budget process each year, containing between 1,200 and 1,400 individual appropriations. Congressional appropriations are not based directly on expended appropriations (i.e., receipt of goods or services) but on *authority to obligate the federal government* to ultimately make disbursements. (Essentially, then, encumbrances outstanding are treated as uses of appropriations authority.)

Execution

When an appropriation bill becomes law, an appropriation warrant is prepared by the Treasury and forwarded to the agency. The agency sends a request for apportionment to the OMB. The OMB makes apportionments to the agency, reserving some appropriations for contingency, savings, timing, or policy reasons. The agency carries on its programs with the apportioned appropriations through allotments for programs and activities; committing, obligating, and expending money; and providing goods and services. It reports to the OMB on its activities and uses of budgetary authority. The agencies prepare vouchers for expended appropriations (expenditures) and submit them to the Treasury or disbursement officers for payment.

An explanation of each aspect of budget execution for basic operating appropriations follows.

Warrants A warrant is a document required by law as a means of verification of an appropriation amount contained in a public law. A warrant is signed by the Secretary of the Treasury (or by the secretary's designee). The warrant contains the amount of the appropriation and is the primary source of recognition by an agency in its accounts for the budget resources awarded to it. The Treasury or the disbursing agent maintains central control by limiting an agency to a line of credit for disbursements not to exceed the amount of the warrant.

Apportionment Apportionments are divisions, or portions, of appropriations granted to agency heads by the OMB. Apportionments are required by law to prevent obligation or use of an appropriation at a rate that might result in a deficiency or a supplemental appropriation.

Apportionments divide appropriation amounts available for use by specific time periods, activities, projects, types of uses, or combinations thereof. The most common apportionments are divisions based on time periods, usually quarterly. An agency will record its entire appropriation in its accounts when it receives a warrant from the Treasury. However, it can only use the amount of the apportionment received from the OMB. The total apportionments granted for each appropriation cannot exceed the amount of the appropriation. (Note that *apportionments by time periods are the equivalent of allotments for state and local governments (SLGs),* as discussed in Chapter 6.) Apportionment control is maintained centrally by the OMB "after the fact": It is monitored from the monthly budget execution reports submitted by agencies.

Allotment An *allotment* is budget authority in the form of *apportionments delegated by the agency head to subordinate managers* for use. *Suballotments* are further divisions of budget authority to lower management levels. The total allotments per apportionment cannot exceed the amount of the apportionment, and the total suballotments cannot exceed the total of their related *allotment amount.* (Note that *allotments in federal government terminology are like SLG allocations,* discussed in Chapter 6.)

Commitment A commitment is a preliminary, administrative reservation of budget authority (allotment or suballotment) for the order of goods and services for program purposes. It is a charge to an allotment account based on a preliminary estimate. A commitment is usually a request within an agency for the purchase of items, travel, or other related purposes. Commitment accounting is not required by law, regulation, or directive from oversight agencies. However, it is a useful planning tool that agencies employ to reserve appropriation authority prior to obligation. Indeed, *commitments* might be thought of as *pre-encumbrances.*

Obligation An obligation is a formal reservation of budget authority. It is a formal charge to an allotment or related commitment with the latest estimate of the cost of goods or services being purchased. Obligations for the purchase of goods and services are required by regulations and directives from the oversight agencies. *Obligations* represent orders for the acquisition of goods and/or services for program purposes and compare to *encumbrances* in SLG budgetary accounting.

Expended Appropriations Expended appropriations represent the amount of goods and/or services received and accepted or program costs incurred. It is the formal use of budget authority in an actual amount and either (1) it releases the related prior obligation, or (2) in cases where obligations are not required, for example, in payroll in some agencies, it is a charge to the related allotment. *Expended appropriations* are equivalent to *expenditures* in state and local government accounting. When expended appropriations are incurred for budgetary accounting, an agency also recognizes a financing source, called Appropriations Used, for proprietary accounting.

Expired Authority Expired authority represents unexpended, unobligated (i.e., unused) appropriation authority of prior years. Expended appropriations against prior year obligations that exceed the previously obligated amount are charged against this expired authority. Likewise, if the expended appropriations against prior year obligations are less than obligated, expired authority is credited for the difference. Expired authority is canceled at the end of the fifth year after the authority first became expired authority.

One aspect of the preceding description bears repetition and emphasis: Only part of an agency's annual obligational authority is available to it at any time—the apportioned part. The agency head (or designee), in turn, allots its apportioned obligation authority to subordinate managers to operate their programs and/or organizational subunits. Only allotted apportionments may be obligated by organizations within an agency.

Reporting

Budget execution is reported periodically and annually to the OMB. For each category of appropriation or other budget authority, agencies report the amount of authority, the amount of expended appropriations, the amount of obligations, the amount of apportionments unobligated (unused budget authority), and the amounts of outlays (essentially disbursements) incurred. The OMB reports centrally for the overall government on an obligation and outlay basis each year in the annual budget proposal submitted to Congress by the President. The annual budget proposal contains the current year's projected amounts, along with summary amounts of actuals (total obligations and total outlays) for preceding years. Although the OMB reports amounts related to the budget, both proposed and prior years' actuals, the Treasury reports periodic and annual amounts of actual disbursements.

Exceeding Budget Authority

Numerous laws and regulations highlight the impropriety of exceeding budget authority. Budget authority is considered exceeded when *any* of the four following events occur:

1. An apportionment exceeds an appropriation.
2. An allotment exceeds an appropriation or an apportionment.
3. An obligation exceeds an appropriation, apportionment, or allotment.
4. An expended appropriation exceeds an appropriation, an apportionment, or an allotment.

Note that *commitments* are *not* considered formal *use of budget authority.*

Laws and regulations provide for criminal penalties for those responsible (the agency head or the managers responsible for allotments and suballotments) when authority is exceeded. In addition, agency management is required to submit reports to the President and Congress when budget authority is exceeded. Congress makes the decision of whether to provide for a deficiency appropriation to make up the amounts exceeded. The administrative and judicial processes determine any punishment.

ACCOUNTING PRINCIPLES AND STANDARDS FOR FEDERAL AGENCIES

Accounting principles and standards for federal agencies set forth requirements for preparing basic financial statements. *Agencies are required to prepare six basic year-end financial statements, if applicable:*

1. Balance Sheet
2. Statement of Net Cost
3. Statement of Changes in Net Position
4. Statement of Budgetary Resources
5. Statement of Custodial Activity
6. Statement of Social Insurance

The Federal Model

The federal accounting model is different from the private or state and local government models. It contains what is referred to in this chapter as a *dual-track system,* which consists of *a complete set of self-balancing accounts for both budgetary and proprietary amounts.* Each set of self-balancing accounts reflects an accounting equation.

The *budgetary equation* is: Budgetary Resources = Status of Authority. The components of each side of the equation are:

Budgetary Resources	=	Status of Authority
Appropriations		Unapportioned Appropriations (Authority)
+ Borrowing Authority		+ Apportionments
+ Contract Authority		+ Allotments
+ Reimbursable Authority (between agencies)		+ Commitments
		+ Obligations
+ Collections from Other Sources		+ Expended Appropriations (Authority)
		+ Expired Authority

The *proprietary equation* is: Assets = Liabilities + Net Position. This equation is similar to the private-sector accounting equation. However, because of the processes in the federal government and the need to account for appropriations, several unique variations to this equation that do not exist in the private sector are used for federal accounting. The primary variations deal with the cash account and disbursements, net position accounts, and the unique nature of and interrelationships between the components of net position. These key variations are discussed in the following sections.

Cash and Disbursements

Although agencies have small balances of cash for imprest funds and in rare cases significant balances, the predominant amount is represented by a line of credit with the Treasury (or, in the case of the Department of Defense, a disbursing agent) in the amount of the warrants it has received. *This line of credit is referred to as Fund Balance with Treasury and* is handled as cash in a bank account would be handled by a business. To use this line of credit, the normal process is for an agency to complete a request for payment to the Treasury. *When the request for payment is forwarded to the Treasury, a liability account, Disbursements in Transit, is recognized.* When the agency receives the completed request back from the Treasury, indicating that checks have been written and mailed or wire transfers made (referred to as an *accomplished request*), the agency reduces the liability account Disbursements in Transit and the Fund Balance with Treasury for the same amount.

Net Position

The Net Position of the U.S. Government (or an agency) represents the net assets of the federal government or the agency and is equal to the difference between the assets and liabilities of the entity. *Net position* comprises two items:

1. Cumulative results of operations
2. Unexpended appropriations

These components of net position are illustrated in Illustration 19-2 and discussed in this chapter.

Cumulative Results of Operations The Cumulative Results of Operations is defined as the *net difference between* (1) *expenses and losses from the inception* of an agency or activity *and* (2) *financing sources* (i.e., appropriations used and revenues) *and gains from the inception* of an agency or activity (whether financed from appropriations, revenues, reimbursements, or any combination) to the reporting date. *For a revolving fund or business-type activity* (with no trust assets), this portion of net position is *essentially the same as the total equity of a business.* The Unexpended Appropriations would be zero. *If an agency is financed exclusively or almost exclusively with appropriations*, this component will be the *difference between* (1) the cumulative expended appropriations of the agency over the years and (2) the cumulative expenses and losses over the same period.

ILLUSTRATION 19-2 Components of Net Position of a Federal Agency	
Unexpended Appropriations	**Cumulative Results of Operations**
• *Some*, but not *all*, agencies report *Unexpended Appropriations*.	• *All* agencies report *Cumulative Results of Operations*.
• Represents appropriations not yet obligated or expended, including undelivered orders.	• Represents amounts accumulated over the years by the entity from its financing sources less its expenses and losses.
• Includes valid unused appropriation authority that carries over to the next fiscal year or other reporting period.	• Agrees with net assets of an agency (other than Fund Balance with Treasury and advances, which are associated with unexpended budget authority) or net assets held in trust.

The Cumulative Results of Operations is comprised of two parts: earmarked funds and non-earmarked funds. Earmarked funds are required by statute to be used for designated activities, benefits, or purposes and are required to be accounted for separately from general revenues. Non-earmarked funds is the portion of net position that is not earmarked. The total of earmarked and non-earmarked funds equals the cumulative results of operations.

Unexpended Appropriations Unexpended appropriations—the *budgetary fund balance* of an agency—represent *amounts of obligational authority* (appropriations) *that have neither been expended nor withdrawn* as of the reporting date. To the extent that unused appropriations have not been withdrawn, this portion of the net position of the agency equals the sum of the unapportioned appropriations, unallotted apportionments, unobligated allotments, obligations at the reporting date, and expired authority. If an agency is operated solely on a business-type basis and receives no appropriations, this component of net position will be zero.

Changes in Net Position

The causes of changes in each of the components of net position are highlighted in Illustration 19-3. The most significant ones are discussed in the following sections. The changes in net position are recorded in separate temporary accounts as necessary for proper reporting.

Enacting Appropriations Perhaps the most difficult feature of federal agency accounting to understand is the interrelationships among appropriations and the various components of net position. These interrelationships can be explained best in a simplified context. Assuming that an agency is financed *solely* from appropriations, how would a $1,000,000 appropriation affect the net position components of the agency?

First, when the appropriation is made, it increases the Unexpended Appropriations component of net position, as indicated in Illustration 19-4. From the perspective of the agency, appropriations increase net position (although the

---

ILLUSTRATION 19-3   Changes in Components of Net Position of a Federal Agency

Cumulative Results of Operations	Unexpended Appropriations
Increases	**Increases**
(1) Financing sources:	(1) Appropriation authority granted for the fiscal year
(a) Receipts from taxes, duties, donations, and other unearned revenue	
(b) Expended appropriations (appropriations used)	
(c) Operating revenues from business-like activities	
(d) Reimbursements from other agencies	
(2) Gains	
(3) Initial investments made to begin operations or a new activity of a revolving fund or business-like activities	
Decreases	**Decreases**
(1) Expenses	(1) Expended appropriations
(2) Losses	(2) Withdrawal of unexpended and/or unobligated appropriation authority
(3) Amounts representing initial investments in revolving funds or business-like activities are returned to investor agency or entity or otherwise transferred out	

ILLUSTRATION 19-4 Interrelationship of Net Position of U.S. Government Components (for Agency Financed Solely by Annual Appropriations)

Transaction or Event	Cumulative Results of Operations	Unexpended Appropriations
• Appropriation granted		+
• Expenditure incurred to finance operating expense	Operating Expense + Report Appropriations Used as financing source in Statement of Changes in Net Position	
• Expended appropriation incurred to acquire fixed asset, inventory, etc.	+ Report Appropriations Used as financing source in Statement of Changes in Net Position	–
• Fixed asset depreciated or other assets expensed	– Depreciation (or other) expense	
• Unfunded expenses (e.g., employees' annual leave)	–	
• Unobligated appropriations are withdrawn or expired authority is canceled		–
• Year-end balance	Equal to book values of nonmonetary assets less the liability for unfunded expenses	Equals sum of obligations outstanding (undelivered orders), unpaid expended authority (accounts payable), and expired authority

net position of the consolidated federal government entity does not change). If a portion of this appropriation authority is withdrawn by the OMB or Congress before it is used, the Unexpended Appropriations account is reduced by that amount.

Incurring Expended Appropriations When expended appropriations are incurred for goods or services received, *the proprietary accounts are affected in three ways.* First, the Unexpended Appropriations account is reduced, reflecting the decrease in unused obligational authority. At the same time, a temporary account, Appropriations Used, is increased by the same amount. The Appropriations Used account is reported in the Statement of Changes in Net Position as a financing source and is closed to cumulative results of operations. Finally, either (a) the fixed assets, inventory, or other assets acquired are capitalized, or (b) the expenses incurred are recorded in the amount of the expended appropriations.

Incurring Unfunded (or Future Funded) Expenses Not all expenses result in recognition of appropriations used in the same year. Agencies incur some *expenses that will be funded in future years for budgetary purposes.* Appropriations used will be recognized in that future year. *Examples of unfunded expenses include pension costs, contingent liabilities, and employees' annual leave earned but not taken.* Most agencies incur at least one unfunded expense, that of the annual leave benefits earned by employees. In most agencies these expenses are immaterial to the total expenses; however, in smaller, service-oriented agencies, these can be material. *Recognition of unfunded expenses in the proprietary accounts is the same as in the private sector*. An expense account is debited and a liability is credited. For agencies, the expense account that is debited is called *Future Funded Expenses*.

Illustration 19-4 points out the interrelationships between the components of net position. These relationships are explained further later in the example of accounting for a federal agency.

Standard General Ledger

The U.S. Government Standard General Ledger (USSGL or SGL) was developed in 1986 and issued as a requirement to all agencies by the three oversight agencies in 1988. The SGL has perhaps been the most effective requirement for inducing agencies to implement the dual-track federal model, which was first required in 1984. Treasury oversees an SGL Board made up of members representing the major federal agencies. The board maintains and updates the SGL.

The SGL contains more than 300 separate accounts in its chart of accounts. The principal SGL accounts, account definitions, transactions, and crosswalks to reports are organized as follows:

1000s	Asset Accounts
2000s	Liability Accounts
3000s	Net Position Accounts
4000s	Budgetary Accounts
5000s	Revenues and Other Financing Sources
6000s	Expenses
7000s	Gains and Losses

Because this chapter is a summary overview of federal accounting, we will use only 25 accounts, 11 budgetary and 14 proprietary. Also, we will assume that budgetary authority is granted only in the form of a one-year operating appropriation and will not cover subsequent year transactions involving the expired authority account. The 11 budgetary accounts are as follows.

Budgetary Resources Accounts (Normal Debit Balance):

Appropriations Realized

Total Actual Resources Collected

Status of Authority Accounts (Normal Credit Balances):

Unapportioned Authority

Apportionments

Allotments—Realized Resources

Commitments

Undelivered Orders—Paid

Undelivered Orders—Unpaid

Expended Appropriations—Paid

Expended Appropriations—Unpaid

Expired Authority

As previously discussed, federal budgetary accounting uses two types of accounts—budgetary resources accounts and status of authority accounts. The budgetary resources accounts track the resources received by an entity while the status accounts track where the resources are in the spending process. The total of all budgetary resource accounts (Total Actual Resources Collected and Appropriations Realized) must equal the total of all status accounts.

Illustration 19-5 shows the effect on the accounts when *budgetary* authority is granted, delegated, and used, as well as the closing entries involved. At the beginning of the fiscal year, the Total Actual Resources Collected account is the budgetary resource account that can have a balance. It represents cumulative prior year resources collected net of expenditures. Note that Appropriations Realized and Expended Appropriations—Paid are closed at year-end to the budgetary resources account, Total Actual Resources Collected. Undelivered Orders (encumbered amounts) and Expended Appropriations—Unpaid (accounts payable amounts) are not closed. The remaining Status accounts are closed into the Expired Authority account, making its balance equal to the unobligated, unexpended appropriation authority that has not been canceled.

Illustration 19-6 contains a graphic illustration of the *proprietary* accounts used. As with the budgetary accounts, the account titles are those required in the SGL.

Integration of both budgetary and proprietary accounts is required when implementing the SGL. Integration occurs when entries are required in both budgetary and proprietary accounts as a result of the same transaction. For example, when an agency receives a warrant as a result of the passage of an appropriation bill into law, the agency makes entries in both the budgetary and proprietary accounts, as follows:

Budgetary:	Appropriations Realized	XXX	
	Unapportioned Authority.		XXX
Proprietary:	Fund Balance with Treasury	XXX	
	Unexpended Appropriations		XXX

The case illustration at the end of this chapter shows other example entries required by both tracks as a result of the same transaction.

Federal Fund Structure

Fund structures employed in federal government accounting may be broadly classified as (1) funds derived from general taxing and revenue powers and from business operations, also known as *federal or government-owned funds,* and (2) funds held by the government in the capacity of custodian or trustee, sometimes referred to as not-government-owned, or *Trust and Agency* funds. Six types of funds are employed within these two broad categories.

Government-Owned or Federal Funds	**Trust and Agency Funds**
General Fund	Trust Funds
Special Funds	Deposit Funds
Revolving Funds	
Management Funds	

However, in the federal sector, the fund type or the specific fund does not influence accounting or financial reporting as it does in the state and local government sector. The federal entity is instead twofold. For *budgetary* purposes, the entity is each appropriation or other budget authority granted by Congress. Budget execution reports are required for each appropriation. Thus, each appropriation for each specific year has a complete SGL. The *proprietary* entity is broader, although it can also be each appropriation. The Treasury requires approximately 650 to 750 complete sets of the primary proprietary financial statements each year. These sets include many single-year appropriations that, for each agency and department, are consolidated to form agency-wide and department-wide consolidated statements. The SGL is designed to separately maintain two proprietary accounts, Fund Balance with Treasury and Unexpended Appropriations, on an appropriation basis by year in the subsidiary accounts.

Financial Reporting

Federal financial reporting includes both agency-level and government-wide statements. In 1990, Congress passed the Chief Financial Officers Act (CFO Act). Among other provisions, this act established financial statement and audit requirements for certain federal agencies. In 1994, Congress passed the Government Management Reform Act, extending the financial statement and audit requirements of the CFO Act to all major agencies and making them permanent requirements. These acts also require annual government-wide audited financial statements. Specifically, each major agency must submit agency-level financial statements covering the last fiscal year to the director of the OMB by

ILLUSTRATION 19-5   The Use of Budget Authority and Closings of Budget Accounts

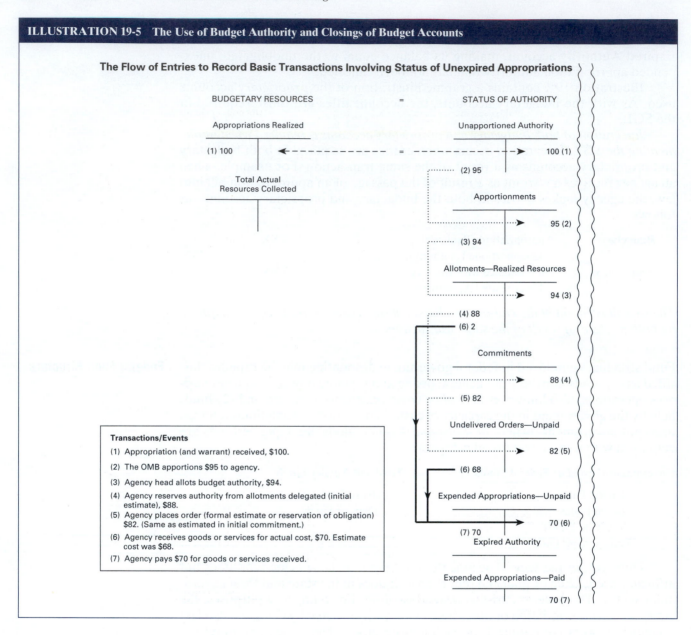

The Flow of Entries to Record Basic Transactions Involving Status of Unexpired Appropriations

Transactions/Events

(1) Appropriation (and warrant) received, $100.

(2) The OMB apportions $95 to agency.

(3) Agency head allots budget authority, $94.

(4) Agency reserves authority from allotments delegated (initial estimate), $88.

(5) Agency places order (formal estimate or reservation of obligation) $82. (Same as estimated in initial commitment.)

(6) Agency receives goods or services for actual cost, $70. Estimate cost was $68.

(7) Agency pays $70 for goods or services received.

March 1 each year. Consolidated, government-wide, audited financial statements for that fiscal year must be presented to the President and the Congress within one year thereafter. Essentially, government-wide audited financial statements for the year ended September 30, 2012, are required to be available by March 1, 2014.

Agency Level

Although agency managers determine the internal reports needed, six basic statements are required at least annually of all federal agencies (two additional proprietary statements are optional but preferred), if applicable. The statements are:

1. Balance Sheet
2. Statement of Net Cost
3. Statement of Changes in Net Position
4. Statement of Budgetary Resources
5. Statement of Custodial Activity
6. Statement of Social Insurance

ILLUSTRATION 19-5   The Use of Budget Authority and Closings of Budget Accounts (Continued)

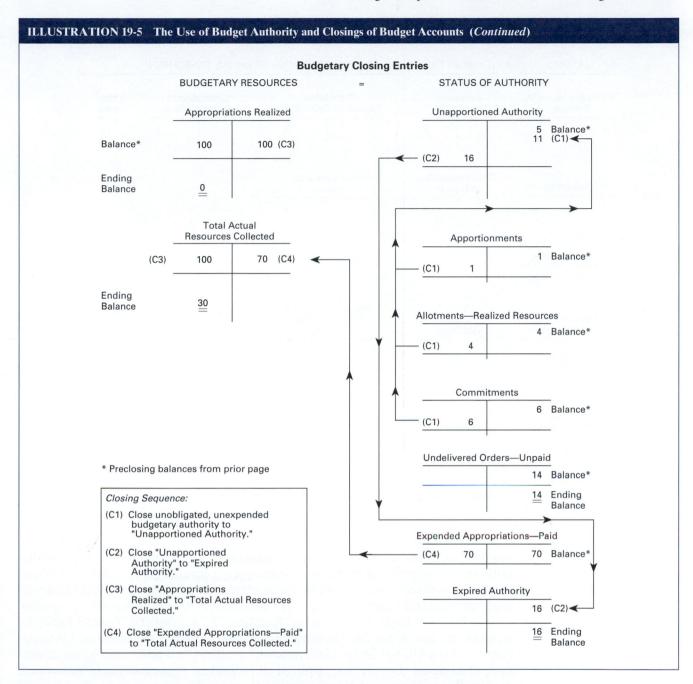

The first three statements are illustrated in the final section of this chapter. Other financial reports are required by Congress, its committees, or the central oversight agencies.

Government-Wide Statements

The first two financial statements required for each agency—the Balance Sheet and the Statement of Net Cost—are also required to be presented on a government-wide basis; however, the format and the content of the these financial statements are different for government-wide reporting. (The different formats for the Balance Sheets prepared for an agency and at the government-wide level can be seen by comparing Illustration 19-11 and Illustration 19-14. Likewise, the different formats for the Statement of Net Cost prepared for an agency and at the government-wide level can be seen by comparing Illustration 19-12 and Illustration 19-15.)

A Statement of Operations and Changes in Net Position is required at the government-wide level instead of the Statement of Changes in Net Position that is

ILLUSTRATION 19-6 Overview of the Federal Government Proprietary Accounting Equation

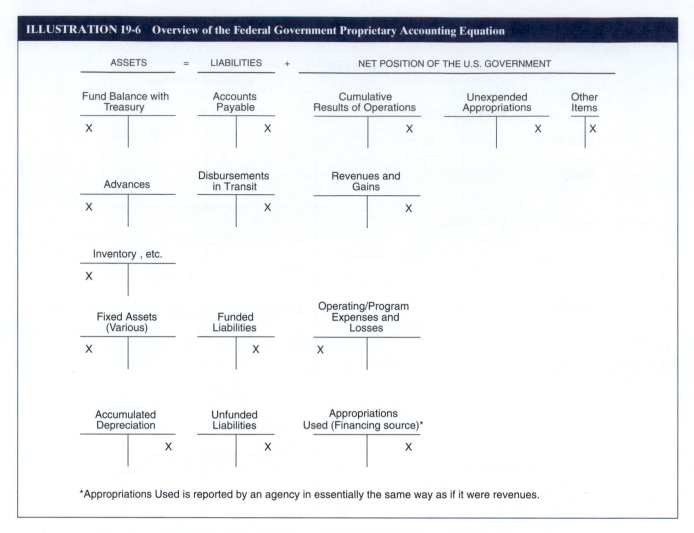

*Appropriations Used is reported by an agency in essentially the same way as if it were revenues.

required for agencies. A Statement of Social Insurance is required to be presented both for an agency and at the government-wide level. The Statement of Social Insurance provides actuarial information about the expected long-term financial contributions and expenditures for the government's social insurance programs, such as Social Security and Medicare. Additionally, *Statement of Federal Financial Accounting Standards 24,* "Selected Standards for the Consolidated Financial Report of the United States Government," requires two additional government-wide statements that are not required of individual agencies. These statements are the Reconciliation of Net Operating Revenue (or Cost) and Unified Budget Surplus (or Deficit) and the Statement of Changes in Cash Balance from Unified Budget and Other Activities. Beginning in fiscal year 2013, a new government-wide statement is required—a **Statement of Long-Term Fiscal Projections**. The objective of the statement and accompanying analysis is to allow the reader to assess the fiscal sustainability of current policies. It will provide a projection of all federal government receipts and expenditures over a period sufficient to allow such an assessment to be made (usually 75 years). The analysis will include information regarding the fiscal gap—the adjustment to receipts and/or spending needed to maintain a target debt to GDP level. The government-wide financial statements include all of the federal government's departments, agencies, and other units.

In preparing the government-wide statements, all interdepartmental and interagency balances and transactions are eliminated. Any other adjustments needed to report the consolidated entity's financial statements from the perspective of the U.S. government as a single entity also are made.

FEDERAL AGENCY ACCOUNTING AND REPORTING ILLUSTRATED

This section of the chapter contains (1) a *case* illustrating federal *agency accounting* and (2) *agency* financial *statements*. The case is designed to illustrate the major federal accounting principles and standards. Those interested in more in-depth and specific coverage of federal government accounting may wish to review the U.S. Standard General Ledger developed by the Treasury (**http://www.fms.treas .gov/ussgl**) and the prescribed financial report formats established by the OMB (**http://www.whitehouse.gov/OMB/circulars/**).

In this case illustration, we initially demonstrate how the agency would maintain budgetary accountability in its accounting system. Next, the simultaneous maintenance of proprietary information is illustrated. Then various transactions of the agency are presented, with both budgetary and proprietary entries being made as needed. The accounts are closed at year end in a manner that highlights the relationship between the budgetary accounts and the proprietary accounts. Finally, financial statements are presented for the agency.

Specific methods of accounting vary among agencies, as do their functions and financing methods. However, *the approach illustrated is typical and serves to highlight the major aspects of federal agency accounting and reporting.* Illustration 19-7 indicates which transactions affect budgetary accounts, which affect proprietary accounts, and which affect both.

A Case Illustration

To illustrate the principal aspects of federal agency accounting, assume that (1) an agency began the 20X0–20X1 fiscal year with the trial balance in Illustration 19-8, and (2) its activities are financed solely through a single-year appropriation. To simplify the illustration, we also (1) assume that general ledger control accounts similar to those in Illustrations 19-5 and 19-6 are employed; (2) limit our presentation to general ledger entries; and (3) make summary entries when similar transactions typically recur throughout the year. The agency's functions primarily entail rendering services to the public.

Maintaining Budgetary Control

Budgetary control is maintained on a *fixed-dollar* basis for operations of the federal government agencies, as is true with state and local governments. However, as indicated in Illustration 19-9, the means for implementing budgetary control in the accounting system tend to be somewhat more complex than with SLGs.

ILLUSTRATION 19-7 Effects of Transactions on Budgetary and Proprietary Accounts		
	Effects	
Transaction (Transaction Number(s))	**Budgetary Accounts**	**Proprietary Accounts**
Appropriations enacted (1)	X	X
Apportionments (2)	X	
Allotments (3)	X	
Commitments (4)	X	
Purchase order approved and placed (5, 9, and 17)	X	
Receipt of fixed assets or materials ordered (6 and 18)	X	X
Use of materials (7)		X
Treasury notifies agency that checks are issued (8, 11, 15, and 24)	X	X
Payment-related transactions (13 and 23)		X
Travel advances (10)		X
Travel costs incurred (12)	X	X
Collection of advances (14)	X	X
Unobligated funded expenses incurred (other than those resulting from use of materials or fixed assets) (16)	X	X
Salary expense incurred (19)	X	X
Request for approval of contracts for services (20)	X	
Contract approved and signed (21)	X	
Contract services received (22)	X	X
Depreciation on equipment (25)		X
Salaries and benefits accrued (26)	X	X
Increase in liability for (unfunded) accrued annual leave (27)		X

Budgetary accounting and proprietary accounting are shown simultaneously in this illustration, using the *dual-track approach*. As noted earlier, Illustration 19-7 identifies transactions that affect only budgetary accounts, those that affect only proprietary accounts, and those that affect both budgetary and proprietary accounts.

Summary of Transactions and Events/Entries

1. Congress enacted appropriations that included $225,000 for XYZ Agency. The agency received an appropriation warrant in that amount from the Treasury.

   Proprietary Entry

   (1a) Fund Balance with Treasury—20X1 . . . . $225,000

         Unexpended Appropriations—20X1 . . . . $225,000
       To record receipt of appropriation warrant.

   This proprietary entry establishes the agency's line of credit with the Treasury as an asset of the agency and the related net position increase. Recall that you may wish to think of the Fund Balance with Treasury as if it were a Cash account.

   Budgetary Entry

   (1b) Appropriations Realized $225,000

         Unapportioned Authority $225,000
       To record receipt of budgetary authority.

This budgetary-track entry establishes initial accountability for the agency's appropriation for the fiscal year.

The budgetary accounting and control mechanism appears more complex in the federal government in part because not all of the appropriations adopted by Congress serve as valid expenditure authority for the various agencies. Instead, as

ILLUSTRATION 19-8 Beginning Trial Balance

XYZ Agency
Trial Balance
October 1, 20X0

Budgetary Accounts

Appropriations Realized	—	—
Total Actual Resources Collected	$ 63,000	—
Unapportioned Authority..............................	—	—
Apportionments.....................................	—	—
Allotments—Realized Resources	—	—
Commitments.......................................	—	—
Undelivered Orders—Unpaid	—	—
Undelivered Orders—Paid	—	$ 800
Expended Appropriations—Unpaid...................	—	50,000
Expended Appropriations—Paid	—	—
Expired Authority	—	12,200
	$ 63,000	$ 63,000

Proprietary Accounts

Fund Balance with Treasury—20X0	$ 62,200	—
Advances to Others.................................	800	—
Inventory for Agency Operations	17,000	—
Equipment	20,000	—
Accumulated Depreciation on Equipment	—	$ 8,000
Disbursements in Transit............................	—	12,000
Accounts Payable	—	30,000
Accrued Funded Payroll and Benefits	—	8,000
Accrued Unfunded Annual Leave	—	50,000
Unexpended Appropriations—20X0	—	13,000
Cumulative Results of Operations	21,000	—
	$121,000	$121,000

mentioned earlier, the OMB initially apportions part of the appropriation authority to the agencies. Thus, it is necessary to distinguish between appropriations and apportionments of the federal agency, just as we distinguish between Unallotted Appropriations and Allotments in state and local governments (see Chapter 6). However, not all of the apportionments are typically available to agency field offices for any purpose because the agency head will normally make allotments of the apportionments. Therefore, a federal agency must also distinguish between available apportionments of appropriations and allotments. (The allotments account is called Allotments—Realized Resources.) Hence, only the balance in Allotments—Realized Resources provides valid budgetary authority against which field offices can obligate the agency. The next two transactions and entries illustrate the reclassification of appropriations as apportionments and allotments are made.

2. The OMB apportioned $220,000 of the congressional appropriation, reserving $5,000 for possible cost savings and contingencies. The apportionments were distributed as follows:

First quarter	$ 68,000
Second quarter	58,000
Third quarter	44,000
Fourth quarter	50,000
	$220,000

ILLUSTRATION 19-9   Maintaining Budgetary Accountability for a Federal Agency

Event	Unapportioned Authority	Apportionments	Allotments—Realized Resources	Commitments	Undelivered Orders—Unpaid*	Expended Appropriations—Unpaid	Expended Appropriations—Paid
1. Congress enacts appropriations (and related warrants are issued).	+						
2. OMB apportions appropriation authority to agencies.	−	+					
3. Agency directors allot apportionments to various purposes.		−	+				
4. Goods/services are requested for order.			−	+			
5. Goods are ordered or contracts for services are signed.				−	+		
6. Goods or services are received.					−	+	
7. Payment is made for goods or services.						−	+

*The Undelivered Orders—Unpaid account represents orders that have not been received and have not been paid. The Undelivered Orders—Paid account, which represents orders that are paid prior to receipt of goods or services, is not illustrated because the federal government seldom pays for purchases in advance.

Proprietary Entry—None
Budgetary Entry

(2a) Unapportioned Authority	$ 68,000	
Apportionments		$ 68,000

To record OMB apportionment of appropriation for the first quarter.

Note that only the $68,000 balance in Apportionments can be allotted, committed, or obligated during the first quarter. Similar entries would be made as additional apportionments are made:

Proprietary Entry—None
Budgetary Entry

(2b) Unapportioned Authority	$152,000	
Apportionments		$152,000

To record OMB apportionments of appropriation for the remaining quarters.

Entry 2b is a summary entry. In practice an entry would be made each quarter; the $152,000 is the total of the apportionments made during the last three quarters. Subsequent transactions will assume that the entire $220,000 has been apportioned.

3. Administrative allotments made by the agency head were distributed as follows:

Salaries and benefits	$135,000
Material and supplies	40,000
Fixed assets	12,000
Travel	2,000
Other	25,000
	$214,000

Proprietary Entry—None
Budgetary Entry

(3) Apportionments	$214,000	
Allotments—Realized Resources		$214,000
To record allotments of apportioned		
appropriations.		

The subsequent accounting for obligations (encumbrances) and expended appropriations incurred by a federal agency against its allotments differs from the treatment illustrated in SLG accounting. Separate encumbrance and expenditure accounts are used in SLG accounting, and their total is subtracted from allotments to determine the unencumbered balance still available for encumbrance and expenditure for a particular purpose. In federal agency accounting, however, this unencumbered balance is maintained in a single account, the Allotments—Realized Resources account, or in that account and a Commitments account, which may be used to formally capture purchase requests prior to orders being approved and placed. Too, the encumbrances of a federal agency are referred to as obligations and recorded in an account called Undelivered Orders. The recording of commitments, obligations, and expended appropriations of a federal agency is illustrated in the next three transactions.

4. Preliminary requests were made within the agency for the purchase of $37,000 of supplies and for equipment expected to cost $11,000.

Proprietary Entry—None
Budgetary Entry

(4) Allotments—Realized Resources..............	$ 48,000	
Commitments		$ 48,000
To record purchase requisitions being processed		
within the agency.		

Note that this entry reduces the Allotments—Realized Resources by the estimated cost of the purchase request, leaving the unobligated (unencumbered), uncommitted balance of the allotments (or the unused expenditure authority) in the account.

5. Purchase orders were approved and placed for materials estimated to cost $37,000—all of which had been previously committed in that amount.

Proprietary Entry—None
Budgetary Entry

(5) Commitments	$ 37,000	
Undelivered Orders—Unpaid		$ 37,000
To record purchase orders outstanding.		

Two types of Undelivered Orders accounts are used. The most commonly used account is Undelivered Orders—Unpaid (encumbrances) account, which represents orders that have not been received and have not been paid. The federal government occasionally pays for items when they are ordered or makes an advance to an employee. In that case, the Undelivered Orders—Paid account is used.

6. Materials estimated to cost $30,000 were received; the invoice was for $30,500.

Budgetary Entry

(6a) Undelivered Orders—Unpaid	$ 30,000	
Allotments—Realized Resources..............	500	
Expended Appropriations—Unpaid		$ 30,500
To record expenditure of budgetary authority.		

Note that the actual cost of the materials purchased is reflected as Expended Appropriations—Unpaid when the materials are received, whereas the estimated cost is removed from the Undelivered Orders—Unpaid (encumbrances) account.

Maintaining Proprietary Accounts

The preceding entries demonstrate how budgetary control is maintained in the agency's accounting records. However, as stated earlier, the agencies are also required to account for and report their activities in proprietary accounts. Therefore, in addition to the budgetary accounting entries illustrated earlier, the agency must record the following entries:

Proprietary Entry

(6b) Inventory for Agency Operations	$30,500	
Accounts Payable		$30,500
To record materials received.		
(6c) Unexpended Appropriations—20X1	$30,500	
Appropriations Used		$30,500
To record Appropriations Used resulting from purchase of inventory.		

The first entry records the materials purchased as inventory and the related payable. The second entry records the use of appropriations, as discussed earlier. Subsequently, the cost of materials used is recorded as an expense of the agency. No budgetary entry is necessary when the expense is recorded.

7. Materials costing $25,000 were used by the agency.

Proprietary Entry

(7) Operating/Program Expenses—Materials and Supplies	$25,000	
Inventory for Agency Operations		$25,000
To record cost of materials used.		

Budgetary Entry—None

Other Transactions and Entries

Various other transactions entered into by the agency are recorded in this section. Notice that budgetary entries and proprietary entries are often required simultaneously.

8. The Treasury notified the agency that the checks ordered but not issued in fiscal year 20X0 (Disbursements in Transit in the beginning trial balance—$12,000) were issued in 20X1.

Proprietary Entry

(8a) Disbursements in Transit	$12,000	
Fund Balance with Treasury—20X0		$12,000
To record notification of issuance of checks requested in 20X0.		

Budgetary Entry

(8b) Expended Appropriations—Unpaid	$12,000	
Expended Appropriations—Paid		$12,000
To record that expended appropriations are paid.		

The budgetary entry (8b) records the payment of a portion of the Expended Appropriations—Unpaid from the beginning trial balance. Expended Appropriations—Unpaid is increased (credited) when goods or services are received that the government has not yet paid. When payment is made, Expended Appropriations—Paid is increased (credited) and Expended Appropriations—Unpaid is reduced (debited). The Expended Appropriations—Paid account is closed at year end (see entry 28c).

9. Travel orders in the amount of $1,200 were issued.

Proprietary Entry—None

Budgetary Entry

(9) Allotments—Realized Resources	$ 1,200	
Undelivered Orders—Unpaid		$ 1,200
To record approval of travel orders.		

10. Checks for travel advances totaling $1,000 were requested from the Treasury.

Proprietary Entry

(10) Advances to Others	$1,000	
Disbursements in Transit		$1,000

To record request to the Treasury for travel
advances.

Budgetary Entry—None

11. The Treasury notified the agency that the checks for the travel advances were issued.

Proprietary Entry

(11a) Disbursements in Transit	$1,000	
Fund Balance with Treasury—20X1		$1,000

To record issuance of checks by Treasury.

Budgetary Entry

(11b) Undelivered Orders—Unpaid	$1,000	
Undelivered Orders—Paid		$1,000

To record payment in budgetary accounts.

12. Travel vouchers for $1,050 were received, including $880 to which advances were to be applied. Travel orders had not been issued (in transaction 9) for $50 of the travel costs.

Proprietary Entry

(12a) Operating/Program Expenses—Travel	$1,050	
Advances to Others		$ 880
Accounts Payable		170

To record travel expenses incurred.

(12b) Unexpended Appropriations—20X1	$1,050	
Appropriations Used		$1,050

To record financing source for unexpended
appropriations used to finance operating
expenses.

Budgetary Entry

(12c) Allotments—Realized Resources	$ 50	
Undelivered Orders—Unpaid	120	
Undelivered Orders—Paid	880	
Expended Appropriations—Unpaid		$ 170
Expended Appropriations—Paid		880

To record expenditure of budgetary authority
for travel costs.

13. Checks to pay the travel claims not previously advanced were ordered from the Treasury.

Proprietary Entry

(13) Accounts Payable	$ 170	
Disbursements in Transit		$ 170

To record order of checks from the Treasury
to settle accounts payable.

Budgetary Entry—None

14. The Advances to Others **related to the prior fiscal year** were repaid by employees, $800.

Proprietary Entry

(14a) Fund Balance with Treasury—20X0	$ 800	
Advances to Others		$ 800

To record collection of unused advances.

Budgetary Entry

(14b) Undelivered Orders—Paid	$ 800	
Expired Authority		$ 800

To record increase in expired authority for
repayment of advances applicable to
prior year.

15. The Treasury notified the agency that the checks ordered to date, $170, were issued.

Proprietary Entry

(15a) Disbursements in Transit	$ 170	
Fund Balance with Treasury—20X1		$ 170

To record issuance of checks by the Treasury.

Budgetary Entry

(15b) Expended Appropriations—Unpaid	$ 170	
Expended Appropriations—Paid		170

To record payment in budgetary accounts.

16. The agency incurred rental expenses, $13,000; utility costs, $8,200; and miscellaneous expenses totaling $3,500 during the year. These items had not been obligated previously.

Proprietary Entry

(16a) Operating/Program Expenses—Rent	$13,000	
Operating/Program Expenses—Utilities	8,200	
Operating/Program Expenses—Miscellaneous	3,500	
Accounts Payable		$ 24,700

To record various expenses incurred.

(16b) Unexpended Appropriations—20X1	$24,700	
Appropriations Used		$ 24,700

To record financing source for unexpended appropriations used to finance various operating expenses.

Budgetary Entry

(16c) Allotments—Realized Resources	$24,700	
Expended Appropriations—Unpaid		$ 24,700

To record expenditure of budgetary authority for various operating expenses.

17. Purchase orders were approved and placed for equipment estimated to cost $10,200, which had been previously committed at $10,500.

Proprietary Entry—None

Budgetary Entry

(17) Commitments	$10,500	
Allotments—Realized Resources		$ 300
Undelivered Orders—Unpaid		10,200

To record purchase orders outstanding.

18. The equipment was received, together with an invoice for $10,000.

Proprietary Entry

(18a) Equipment	$10,000	
Accounts Payable		$ 10,000

To record acquisition of equipment.

(18b) Unexpended Appropriations—20X1	$10,000	
Appropriations Used		$ 10,000

To record financing source for unexpended appropriations used to purchase equipment.

Budgetary Entry

(18c) Undelivered Orders—Unpaid	$10,200	
Allotments—Realized Resources		$ 200
Expended Appropriations—Unpaid		10,000

To record expenditure of budgetary authority.

19. Salaries and wages totaling $134,000 were paid during the year, including the agency's share of related payroll expenses. Of this amount, $8,000 was accrued at the beginning of the year. (Withholding deductions and the use of the disbursements in transit account are omitted for purposes of this illustration.)

Proprietary Entry

(19a) Accrued Funded Payroll and Benefits	$ 8,000	
Operating/Program Expenses—Salaries and Benefits	126,000	
Fund Balance with Treasury—20X0		$ 8,000
Fund Balance with Treasury—20X1		126,000
To record payment of payroll.		
(19b) Unexpended Appropriations—20X1	$126,000	
Appropriations Used		$126,000
To record financing source for unexpended appropriations used to finance payroll expenses.		

Budgetary Entry

(19c) Allotments—Realized Resources	$126,000	
Expended Appropriations—Unpaid	8,000	
Expended Appropriations—Paid		$134,000
To record expenditure of budgetary authority for payroll costs.		

20. Commitments were placed for contractual services estimated at $3,000.

Proprietary Entry—None
Budgetary Entry

(20) Allotments—Realized Resources	$ 3,000	
Commitments		$ 3,000
To record commitment for contract request.		

21. A contract was approved for the services requested in transaction (20).

Proprietary Entry—None
Budgetary Entry

(21) Commitments	$ 3,000	
Undelivered Orders—Unpaid		$ 3,000
To record approval of contract for services.		

22. The contracted services were received, $3,000.

Proprietary Entry

(22a) Operating/Program Expenses— Contractual Services	$ 3,000	
Accounts Payable		$ 3,000
To record receipt of contractual services.		
(22b) Unexpended Appropriations—20X1	$ 3,000	
Appropriations Used		$ 3,000
To record financing source for unexpended appropriations used to finance contractual services expense.		

Budgetary Entry

(22c) Undelivered Orders—Unpaid	$ 3,000	
Expended Appropriations—Unpaid		$ 3,000
To record expended appropriations for contractual services.		

23. Checks to pay all accounts payable, except for the contractual services, were requested from the Treasury, $95,200.

Proprietary Entry

(23) Accounts Payable	$ 95,200	
Disbursements in Transit		$ 95,200
To record request for the Treasury to pay accounts payable.		

Budgetary Entry—None

24. Treasury notified the agency that checks totaling $85,000 were issued, including $30,000 relating to accounts payable outstanding at the beginning of the fiscal year.

Proprietary Entry

(24a) Disbursements in Transit...................	$ 85,000	
Fund Balance with Treasury—20X0........		$30,000
Fund Balance with Treasury—20X1........		55,000
To record issuance of checks by the Treasury.		

Budgetary Entry

(24b) Expended Appropriations—Unpaid.........	$85,000	
Expended Appropriations—Paid..........		$85,000
To record expended appropriations for contractual services.		

25. Depreciation on agency equipment was $2,500.

Proprietary Entry

(25) Operating/Program Expenses—Depreciation...	$ 2,500	
Accumulated Depreciation		$ 2,500
To record depreciation of equipment.		

Budgetary Entry—None

26. Salaries and benefits (other than annual leave) amounting to $7,000 were accrued at year end.

Proprietary Entry

(26a) Operating/Program Expenses— Salaries and Benefit...................	$ 7,000	
Accrued Funded Payroll and Benefits		$ 7,000
To accrue payroll at year end.		
(26b) Unexpended Appropriations—20X1.........	$ 7,000	
Appropriations Used		$ 7,000
To accrue financing source for unexpended appropriations used to finance accrual of payroll expenses.		

Budgetary Entry

(26c) Allotments—Realized Resources............	$ 7,000	
Expended Appropriations—Unpaid		$ 7,000
To record accrual of expended appropriations against budgetary authority for payroll.		

27. The liability for accrued annual leave increased $10,000 during the year.

Proprietary Entry

(27) Future Funded Expenses....................	$10,000	
Accrued Unfunded Annual Leave		$10,000
To accrue annual leave earned in excess of leave used.		

Budgetary Entry—None

Closing Entries   The closing process for a federal agency entails closing both budgetary and proprietary accounts. The preclosing trial balance for the example agency at September 30, 20X1, Illustration 19-10, provides the information needed for the closing entries. (The temporary accounts are in italics for ease of identification.) The closing entries for the budgetary accounts and for the proprietary accounts for the example agency are presented in the following separate sections.

Budgetary Accounts

Unexpended appropriation authority is retained by law by the agency until canceled. This retention permits the following:

1. Expended appropriations resulting from prior year obligations can be charged against the Undelivered Orders balance established in the prior year.

ILLUSTRATION 19-10   Preclosing Trial Balance

XYZ Agency
Preclosing Trial Balance
September 30, 20X1

Budgetary Accounts

Appropriations Realized	$225,000	
Total Actual Resources Collected	63,000	
Unapportioned Authority		$ 5,000
Apportionments		6,000
Allotments—Realized Resources		4,050
Commitments		500
Undelivered Orders—Unpaid		7,080
Undelivered Orders—Paid		120
Expended Appropriations—Unpaid		20,200
Expended Appropriations—Paid		232,050
Expired Authority		13,000
	$288,000	$288,000

Proprietary Accounts

Fund Balance with Treasury—20X0	$ 13,000	
Fund Balance with Treasury—20X1	42,830	
Advances to Others	120	
Inventory for Agency Operations	22,500	
Equipment	30,000	
Accumulated Depreciation on Equipment		$ 10,500
Disbursements in Transit		10,200
Accounts Payable		3,000
Accrued Funded Payroll and Benefits		7,000
Accrued Unfunded Annual Leave		60,000
Unexpended Appropriations—20X0		13,000
Unexpended Appropriations—20X1		22,750
Cumulative Results of Operations	21,000	
Appropriations Used		202,250
Operating/Program Expenses—Salaries and Benefits	133,000	
Operating/Program Expenses—Materials and Supplies ...	25,000	
Operating/Program Expenses—Rent	13,000	
Operating/Program Expenses—Utilities	8,200	
Operating/Program Expenses—Depreciation	2,500	
Operating/Program Expenses—Travel	1,050	
Operating/Program Expenses—Contractual Services	3,000	
Operating/Program Expenses—Miscellaneous	3,500	
Future Funded Expenses	10,000	
	$328,700	$328,700

2. Any excess of actual over estimated cost of expended appropriations from prior year obligations can be charged against expired appropriation authority from the prior year.

Hence, note that the unobligated, unexpended appropriations are closed to an account called Expired Authority. Also note that Expended Appropriations—Paid are closed to Total Actual Resources Collected, leaving the unexpended and unpaid expended balance of appropriations in that Budgetary Resources account:

28. The budgetary accounts are closed with the following entries:

(28a) Apportionments...........................	$ 6,000	
Allotments—Realized Resources	4,050	
Commitments...........................	500	
Unapportioned Authority.................		$ 10,550
To close apportionments, allotments, and commitments.		

| (28b) Unapportioned Authority .... | $ 15,550* | |
| Expired Authority .... | | $ 15,550 |

To close expired appropriation authority.

*Note that a balance was left in Unapportioned Authority for illustrative purposes. The OMB normally apportions the full amount of an agency's appropriations.

(28c) Expended Appropriations—Paid	$232,050	
Total Actual Resources Collected		$ 7,050
Appropriations Realized		225,000

To close expended appropriations and appropriations realized.

Proprietary Accounts

Expended Appropriations and the budgetary accounts were closed separately to better emphasize the complete separation of budgetary and proprietary accounting. The proprietary accounts must also be closed.

29. The proprietary accounts are closed with the following entries:

(29) Appropriations Used	$202,250	
Cumulative Results of Operations		$ 3,000
Operating/Program Expenses—Salaries and Benefits.........................		133,000
Operating/Program Expenses—Materials and Supplies..........................		25,000
Operating/Program Expenses—Rent.......		13,000
Operating/Program Expenses—Utilities		8,200
Operating/Program Expenses— Depreciation		2,500
Operating/Program Expenses—Travel......		1,050
Operating/Program Expenses—Contractual Services.............................		3,000
Operating/Program Expenses— Miscellaneous........................		3,500
Future Funded Expenses		10,000

To close proprietary accounts to cumulative results of operations.

Reporting As noted earlier, the principal financial statements prepared for federal agencies include the following:

1. Balance Sheet (Illustration 19-11)
2. Statement of Net Cost (Illustration 19-12)
3. Statement of Changes in Net Position (Illustration 19-13)
4. Statement of Budgetary Resources
5. Statement of Custodial Activity
6. Statement of Social Insurance

The preclosing trial balance in Illustration 19-10 should facilitate your transition from the journal entries to the financial statements presented for our example agency. The Treasury consolidates the account balances from the various federal agencies, along with data from central accounting records, to prepare the consolidated financial statements of the U.S. government. The consolidated financial statements include counterparts to the first three statements—the Balance Sheet, the Statement of Net Cost, and the Statement of [Operations and] Changes in Net Position. Recent *U.S. consolidated financial statements are presented in* Illustrations 19-14 to 19-16. The Reconciliation of Net Operating Costs and Unified Budget Deficit, the Statement of Changes in Cash Balance from Unified Budget and Other Activities, and the Statement of Social Insurance are not illustrated here. The U.S. government financial statements in their entirety can be found at the Treasury Web site (**http://www.fms.treas.gov/fr/**).

ILLUSTRATION 19-11   Federal Agency Balance Sheet

XYZ Agency
Comparative Balance Sheet
September 30 of Fiscal Years 20X1 and 20X0

	September 30 of Fiscal Year 20X1		September 30 of Fiscal Year 20X0	
Assets				
Intragovernmental:				
Fund Balance with Treasury—20X0		$13,000		$ 62,200
Fund Balance with Treasury—20X1		42,830		—
Total Intragovernmental		55,830		62,200
Advance to Others		120		800
Inventory for Agency Operations		22,500		17,000
Equipment	$30,000		$20,000	
Less Accumulated Depreciation	(10,500)	19,500	(8,000)	12,000
Total Assets		$97,950		$ 92,000
Liabilities				
Intragovernmental:				
Disbursements in Transit		$10,200		$ 12,000
Accounts Payable	$ 3,000		$30,000	
Accrued Funded Payroll and Benefits	7,000	10,000	8,000	38,000
Accrued Unfunded Annual Leave		60,000		50,000
Total Liabilities		80,200		100,000
Net Position				
Unexpended Appropriations—20X0	$13,000		$13,000	
Unexpended Appropriations—20X1	22,750		—	
Cumulative Results of Operations	(18,000)		(21,000)	
Total Net Position of XYZ Agency . . .		17,750		(8,000)
Total Liabilities and Net Position		$97,950		$ 92,000

Although it is beyond the scope of this chapter to discuss the many eliminations, adjustments, and additions made in preparing the consolidated statements, some of the adjustments and eliminations are obvious when you compare the agency statements (Illustrations 19-11 to 19-13) with the consolidated statements. For example, note the absence of Unexpended Appropriations as a component of net position.

ILLUSTRATION 19-12   Federal Agency Statement of Net Cost

XYZ Agency
Statement of Net Cost
For Year Ended September 30 of Fiscal Year 20X1

Program A:	
Gross Costs	$199,250
Less Earned Revenues	—
Net Program Costs*	$199,250

*This section is repeated for each program.

ILLUSTRATION 19-13 Federal Agency Statement of Changes in Net Position

XYZ Agency*
Statement of Changes in Net Position
For Year Ended September 30 of Fiscal Year 20X1

Cumulative Results of Operations:		
Beginning Balance..........................		($21,000)
Budgetary Financing Sources:		
Appropriations Used........................	$ 202,250	
Total Budgetary Financing Sources..............	202,250	
Net Costs of Operations.....................	(199,250)	
Net Change................................		3,000
Cumulative Results of Operations		($18,000)
Unexpended Appropriations:		
Beginning Balance..........................		13,000
Budgetary Financing Sources:		
Appropriations Received.....................	225,000	
Appropriations Used	(202,250)	
Total Budgetary Financing Sources..............		22,750
Total Unexpended Appropriations...............		35,750
Net Position		$17,750

*Assumes XYZ Agency only had non-earmarked funds.

ILLUSTRATION 19-14 U.S. Government Balance Sheet

United States Government
Balance Sheets
As of September 30

(In billions of dollars)	20X1	20X0
Assets:		
Cash and other monetary assets (Note 2)	177.0	428.6
Accounts and taxes receivable, net (Note 3)	106.3	94.6
Loans receivable and mortgage-backed securities, net	772.1	688.6
TARP direct loans and equity investments, net (Note 5)	80.1	144.7
Non-TARP Investments in American International Group	10.9	20.8
Inventories and related property, net (Note 7)	296.1	286.2
Property, plant, and equipment, net (Note 8)	852.8	828.9
Debt and equity securities (Note 9)	99.7	98.9
Investments in Government-Sponsored Enterprises (Note 11)	133.0	109.2
Other assets (Notes 10 and 12).................................	179.3	183.3
Total assets	2,707.3	2,883.8
Stewardship land and heritage assets (Note 27)		
Liabilities:		
Accounts payable (Note 13)	63.4	72.9
Federal debt securities held by the public and accrued interest	10,174.1	9,060.0
Federal employee and veteran benefits payable (Note 15)	5,792.2	5,720.3
Environmental and disposal liabilities (Note 16)...................	324.1	321.3
Benefits due and payable (Note 17)	171.0	164.3
Insurance and guarantee program liabilities	161.7	175.6
Loan guarantee liabilities (Note 4)	63.0	65.8
Liabilities to Government-Sponsored Enterprises	316.2	359.9
Other liabilities (Notes 10 and 19)	427.0	416.5
Total liabilities	17,492.7	16,356.6
Contingencies (Note 22) and Commitments (Note 23)		
Net position:		
Earmarked funds (Note 24)	748.2	646.9
Non-earmarked funds	(15,533.6)	(14,119.7)
Total net position	(14,785.4)	(13,472.8)
Total liabilities and net position	2,707.3	2,883.8

ILLUSTRATION 19-15   U.S. Government Statement of Net Cost

United States Government
Statement of Net Cost
For the Years Ended September 30, 2011

(In billions of dollars)	Gross Cost	Earned Revenue	Subtotal	(Gain)/Loss from Changes in Assumptions	Net Cost
Department of Health and Human Services	943.4	66.4	877.0	0.1	877.1
Social Security Administration	782.9	0.4	782.5	—	782.5
Department of Defense	828.7	78.0	750.7	(32.0)	718.7
Interest on Treasury Securities Held by the Public ..	250.9	—	250.9	—	250.9
Department of Veterans Affairs	124.3	4.7	119.6	58.9	178.5
Department of Agriculture	154.2	9.4	144.8	—	144.8
Department of Labor	132.8	—	132.8	—	132.8
Department of the Treasury	115.2	30.6	84.6	—	84.6
Department of Transportation	77.9	0.7	77.2	—	77.2
Department of Housing and Urban Development ..	60.8	1.2	59.6	—	59.6
Department of Education	69.7	15.0	54.7	—	54.7
Department of Homeland Security	58.9	9.4	49.5	0.4	49.9
Department of Energy	52.5	7.9	44.6	—	44.6
Department of Justice	31.3	1.3	30.0	—	30.0
Office of Personnel Management	43.7	19.1	24.6	0.3	24.9
Department of State	27.0	3.4	23.6	0.4	24.0
Department of the Interior	23.8	2.7	21.1	—	21.1
National Aeronautics and Space Administration ..	18.8	0.1	18.7	—	18.7
Agency for International Development	12.1	0.7	11.4	—	11.4
Railroad Retirement Board	17.0	5.9	11.1	—	11.1
Environmental Protection Agency	11.3	0.5	10.8	—	10.8
Federal Communications Commission	9.3	0.4	8.9	—	8.9
Department of Commerce	11.3	2.5	8.8	—	8.8
National Science Foundation	7.1	—	7.1	—	7.1
Pension Benefit Guaranty Corporation	12.8	7.4	5.4	—	5.4
Small Business Administration	3.6	0.4	3.2	—	3.2
Smithsonian Institution	0.7	—	0.7	—	0.7
U.S. Nuclear Regulatory Commission	1.0	0.8	0.2	—	0.2
Farm Credit System Insurance Corporation	—	0.1	(0.1)	—	(0.1)
Export-Import Bank of the United States	0.6	0.7	(0.1)	—	(0.1)
General Services Administration	0.4	0.6	(0.2)	—	(0.2)
Tennessee Valley Authority	11.5	11.8	(0.3)	—	(0.3)
Securities and Exchange Commission	1.1	1.6	(0.5)	—	(0.5)
National Credit Union Administration	0.2	3.1	(2.9)	—	(2.9)
U.S. Postal Service	56.2	64.6	(8.4)	—	(8.4)
Federal Deposit Insurance Corporation	(2.1)	13.7	(15.8)	—	(15.8)
All other entities	47.4	0.5	46.9	—	46.9
Total	3,998.3	365.6	3,632.7	28.1	3,660.8

The comparative statement for 2010 requires a separate page and is not presented here.

ILLUSTRATION 19-16 **U.S. Government Statement of Operations and Changes in Net Position**

United States Government
Statements of Operations and Changes in Net Position
For the Years Ended September 30, 2011, and 2010

(In billions of dollars)	Non-Earmarked Funds	Earmarked Funds	Consolidated	Non-Earmarked Funds	Earmarked Funds	Consolidated
	2011			2010		
Revenue:						
Individual income tax and tax withholdings	1,092.9	772.9	1,865.8	902.6	830.3	1,732.9
Corporation income taxes	175.1		175.1	179.6		179.6
Unemployment taxes		56.1	56.1		45.2	45.2
Excise taxes	21.3	52.2	73.5	22.6	49.0	71.6
Estate and gift taxes	7.3		7.3	18.8		18.8
Customs duties	28.5		28.5	25.1		25.1
Other taxes and receipts	120.4	20.9	141.3	96.9	30.6	127.5
Miscellaneous earned revenues	11.3	4.9	16.2	11.3	4.5	15.8
Intragovernmental interest		202.0	202.0		195.0	195.0
Total revenue	1,456.8	1,109.0	2,565.8	1,256.9	1,154.6	2,411.5
Eliminations			(202.0)			(195.0)
Consolidated Revenue			2,363.8			2,216.5
Net Cost of Government Operations:						
Net cost	2,110.6	1,550.2	3,660.8	2,553.5	1,742.5	4,296.0
Intragovernmental interest	202.0		202.0	195.0		195.0
Total net cost	2,312.6	1,550.2	3,862.8	2,748.5	1,742.5	4,491.0
Eliminations			(202.0)			(195.0)
Consolidated net cost			3,660.8			4,296.0
Intragovernmental transfers	(540.5)	540.5		(482.1)	482.1	
Unmatched transactions and balances (Note 1.T)	(15.6)		(15.6)	(0.8)		(0.8)
Net operating (cost)/revenue	(1,411.9)	99.3	(1,312.6)	(1,974.5)	(105.8)	(2,080.3)
Net position, beginning of period	(14,119.7)	646.9	(13,472.8)	(12,208.6)	752.7	(11,455.9)
Prior period adjustments—changes in accounting principles (Note 21)	(2.0)	2.0	—	63.4	—	63.4
Net operating (cost)/revenue	(1,411.9)	99.3	(1,312.6)	(1,974.5)	(105.8)	(2,080.3)
Net position, end of period	(15,533.6)	748.2	(14,785.4)	(14,119.7)	646.9	(13,472.8)

Concluding Comments

The federal government is the largest, most complex entity in the United States. Accordingly, the accounting and reporting systems of the various agencies must meet the many multifaceted needs of both internal and external persons and groups. The discussion of the financial management structure of the federal government in the first part of this chapter indicates the many agencies involved in helping to meet those needs.

Federal agency accounting and reporting are the focus of the latter part of this chapter. These agencies are significant reporting entities; furthermore, the reports for the government as a whole must be derived from the accounts and reports of the various agencies. Each agency's accounting and reporting systems must provide both information needed by the agency's management and information needed to ensure and demonstrate compliance with budgetary and other legal requirements.

Federal government accounting integrates accrual basis accounting and budgetary accounting in a unique manner. Some aspects of federal agency accounting are unique to the federal government; others are somewhat similar to state and local government accounting; and other aspects are similar to business accounting. This chapter discusses and illustrates the basic principles and concepts that federal agencies are required to apply.

Questions

Q19-1 Explain the meaning of the following terms in federal accounting:
a. Apportionment
b. Allotment
c. Obligation
d. Commitment
e. Expended Appropriations

Q19-2 List the types of financial statements issued annually by federal agencies.

Q19-3 Describe the components of the net position for a federal agency.

Q19-4 Compare the manner in which budgetary accounting is accomplished in a federal agency with that of a municipality.

Q19-5 What are the principal duties of the Federal Accounting Standards Advisory Board?

Q19-6 (Research) Describe the function of a federal agency's inspector general. To whom and in what manner does the agency inspector general report?

Q19-7 What are the key functions and responsibilities of the U.S. Government Accountability Office?

Q19-8 When a federal agency purchases a fixed asset, what are the impacts on the components of net position? On the statement of changes in net position?

Q19-9 What is expired authority? What is its primary purpose?

Exercises

E19-1 (Multiple Choice) Identify the best answer for each of the following:
1. Formal notification that Congress has enacted an appropriation for an agency requires recognition by the agency in
   a. budgetary accounts only.
   b. proprietary accounts only.
   c. both budgetary and proprietary accounts.
   d. neither budgetary nor proprietary accounts. (No entry is required until apportionments are made.)
2. Primary responsibility for accounting for agency resources and expended appropriations rests with
   a. each individual agency.
   b. the Department of the Treasury.
   c. the Government Accountability Office.
   d. the Office of Management and Budget.
   e. the Federal Accounting Standards Advisory Board.
3. A federal agency's accounting system does *not* need to include information pertaining to
   a. expended appropriations.
   b. fixed assets.
   c. obligations.
   d. expenses.
   e. All of the above must be included.
4. In 20X5, the U.S. Weather Service purchased a parcel of land near Verlene, California, with $850,000 of appropriated funds, with the intention of constructing a facility there. The effect of this transaction on Cumulative Results of Operations is
   a. no change.
   b. to increase it by $850,000.
   c. no change, but Unexpended Appropriations would decrease by $850,000.
   d. None of the above.

5. An appropriation that has expired
   a. is reported by a federal agency as unapportioned authority.
   b. is reported by a federal agency as unexpended appropriations.
   c. is reported by a federal agency as unobligated allotments.
   d. is not reported by a federal agency in any of its net position accounts.

6. Direct labor costs incurred by a federal agency during a period will be reflected in the agency's budgetary accounts as
   a. a debit to Expended Appropriations and credit to Cash.
   b. a debit to Expended Appropriations and credit to Cumulative Results of Operations.
   c. a debit to Allotments—Realized Resources and credit to Expended Appropriations.
   d. a debit to Undelivered Orders and credit to Expended Appropriations.

7. On June 1, 20X7, the Department of Labor ordered $10,000 worth of stationery and office supplies from an authorized contractor. At the time of the purchase order, this transaction should be recorded by the agency as
   a. a $10,000 debit to current assets and a $10,000 credit to liabilities.
   b. a $10,000 debit to Commitments and a $10,000 credit to Undelivered Orders—Unpaid.
   c. a $10,000 debit to Expended Appropriations and a $10,000 credit to Cumulative Results of Operations.
   d. a $10,000 debit to Allotments—Realized Resources and a $10,000 credit to Expended Appropriations.
   e. a $10,000 debit to Unapportioned Authority and a $10,000 credit to Expended Appropriations.

8. Unapportioned Authority is reclassified as Apportionments when
   a. the Office of Management and Budget releases enacted appropriations to the federal agency.
   b. the appropriate agency officials assign appropriations to various departments within the agency.
   c. purchase orders are approved and sent to suppliers of goods.
   d. suppliers are paid for goods furnished to an agency.
   e. assets are returned by a federal agency to the Treasury.

9. Six proprietary financial statements have been identified for use by a federal agency. These statements are required to be prepared and presented for
   a. government-wide financial reporting, but not for federal agency reporting.
   b. both federal agency and for government-wide reporting.
   c. each federal agency, but only some are required for government-wide reporting.
   d. None of the above.

10. Which of the following financial statements is *not* required to be reported on a government-wide basis?
    a. Balance Sheet
    b. Statement of Net Cost
    c. Statement of Changes in Net Position
    d. All of the above are required.

E19-2 (Budgetary Accounting) Prepare journal entries to record the following transactions in the budgetary accounts of ABC Agency.
1. Congress enacted appropriations that included $500,000 for the ABC Agency for the year 20X9. ABC Agency received an appropriation warrant in that amount from the Treasury.
2. The OMB apportioned $240,000 of the congressional appropriation.
3. The agency head made administrative allotments for salaries of $120,000 and for supplies of $80,000.
4. Purchase requests for supplies of $62,000 were made within the agency.
5. Purchase orders were placed for supplies estimated to cost $62,000.
6. The supplies that had been estimated to cost $62,000 were received. The invoice for the supplies was for only $60,800.

E19-3 (Proprietary Accounting) Prepare necessary journal entries to record the six transactions in Exercise 19-2 in the proprietary accounts of ABC Agency. (Hint—Not all of the transactions will require a journal entry.)

E19-4 (Various Proprietary Accounting Transactions) Prepare journal entries to record the following transactions in the proprietary accounts of ABC Agency for 20X8.
1. Supplies costing $42,000 were used by ABC Agency.
2. ABC Agency incurred rental expense of $24,080 for which it had not previously been obligated.
3. ABC Agency requested a check in the amount of $24,080 from the Treasury to pay accounts payable.
4. The Treasury notified ABC Agency that a check in the amount of $24,080 was issued.

E19-5 (Net Position) The credit balance in ABC Agency's *Unexpended Appropriations* at the beginning of its current fiscal year was $42,000, and the credit balance in ABC Agency's *Cumulative Results of Operations* at the beginning of its current fiscal year was $8,000. In its year-end closing entries, ABC Agency debited *Appropriations Used* for $387,000 and credited *Appropriations Realized* for $406,000. In addition, the net costs of operations for ABC Agency for its current fiscal year were $367,000. What is the total net position for ABC Agency at the end of its current fiscal year?

Problems

P19-1 (Budgetary Accounting) Prepare the general journal entries required to record each of the following transactions.
1. The Interstate Fur Trading Commission received a warrant from the Treasury for a $2,000,000 appropriation from Congress for the fiscal year beginning October 1, 20X7.
2. The OMB apportioned to the commission $500,000 of its appropriation.
3. The commission head allotted $400,000 to specific purposes.
4. Salaries incurred and paid for the quarter totaled $120,000.
5. Purchase orders for equipment estimated to cost $50,000 were requested.
6. Equipment estimated to cost $33,000 was ordered.
7. The equipment was received along with an invoice for its cost, $32,890.

P19-2 (Expended Appropriations and Net Position) Prepare the general journal entries to adjust and close the Environmental Enhancement Agency's accounts at year end, assuming the agency is financed solely from appropriations.

Appropriations expended for operating costs	$3,700,000
Appropriations expended for inventory	400,000
Appropriations expended for property, plant, and equipment	1,200,000
Depreciation expense	250,000
Cost of inventory used during the period	420,000
Expired authority for the year	212,000
Undelivered orders at year end	185,000

P19-3 (Various Transactions) Record the following transactions and events of Able Agency, which occurred during the month of October 20X6:
1. Able Agency received a warrant for its fiscal 20X7 appropriation of $2,500,000.
2. The Office of Management and Budget apportioned $600,000 to Able Agency for the first quarter of the 20X7 fiscal year.
3. Able Agency's chief executive allotted $500,000 of the first-quarter appropriation apportionment.
4. Obligations incurred during the month for equipment, materials, and program costs amounted to $128,000.
5. Goods and services ordered during the prior year—and to be charged to obligations carried over from the 20X6 fiscal year—were received:

	Obligated For	Actual Cost
Materials	$ 20,000	$ 21,000
Program A costs	7,000	6,200
Program B costs	3,000	2,500
	$ 30,000	$ 29,700

6. Goods and services ordered during October 20X6 were received and vouchered:

	Obligated For	Actual Cost
Materials	$ 6,000	$ 5,000
Equipment	10,000	10,000
Program A costs	30,000	32,000
Program B costs	80,000	81,000
	$126,000	$128,000

7. Depreciation for the month of October was estimated at $200, chargeable to Overhead.
8. Materials issued from inventory during October were for Program A, $18,000; Program B, $7,000; and general (Overhead), $3,000.
9. Liabilities placed in line for payment by the U.S. Treasurer totaled $145,000.
10. Other accrued expenses at October 31, 20X6, not previously recorded, were Program A, $1,000; Program B, $6,000; and general (Overhead), $1,500.

P19-4 (Comprehensive—Transactions and Entries) Following is the September 30, 20X8, trial balance for ABC Agency:

ABC Agency
Postclosing Trial Balance
September 30 of Fiscal Year 20X8
(Amounts in thousands of dollars)

Budgetary Accounts:

Total Actual Resources Collected	$183	
Undelivered Orders—Paid		$ 15
Expended Appropriations—Unpaid		165
Expired Authority		3
	$183	$183

Proprietary Accounts:

Fund Balance with Treasury—20X8	$168	
Advances to Others	15	
Inventory for Agency Operations	75	
Equipment	300	
Accumulated Depreciation on Equipment		$135
Disbursements in Transit		30
Accounts Payable		60
Accrued Funded Payroll and Benefits		75
Accrued Unfunded Annual Leave		210
Unexpended Appropriations—20X8		18
Cumulative Results of Operations		30
	$558	$558

The agency applies the following accounting policies:

- Commitment accounting is used only for fixed assets, inventories for agency operations, and services.
- Salaries and benefits do not have undelivered orders placed in advance of expending the appropriation for them.
- All disbursements except for salaries, benefits, and advances to others must have accounts payable established first.

Following are transactions during fiscal year 20X9. All are in thousands of dollars.

1. The agency received an appropriation warrant from the Treasury in the amount of $30,000, notifying it that its appropriation had been enacted in that amount. The enabling legislation specified that $9,000 was for salaries and benefits, $6,000 was for travel, and $15,000 was for fixed assets, materials, and services.
2. The OMB apportioned the entire appropriation during the year.
3. The agency head allotted $8,700 for salaries and benefits, $6,000 for travel, and $14,450 for fixed assets, inventory, and supplies.
4. The Treasury notified the agency that the checks ordered but not issued in fiscal year 20X8 were issued.
5. a. Travel orders in the amount of $5,400 were issued.
   b. Checks for travel advances totaling $3,000 were requested from the Treasury.
   c. The Treasury notified the agency that the checks ordered for the travel advances were issued.
   d. Travel vouchers in the amount of $2,700 were received, including $375 for which travel orders had not been issued. Advances of $970 were to be applied.
   e. Checks to pay the travel claims not previously advanced were ordered from the Treasury.
   f. The advances related to fiscal year 20X8 were repaid by employees.
   g. The Treasury notified the agency that the checks ordered in (e) were issued.

6. a. The agency head allotted the remaining payroll budget.
   b. Payroll paid during the year, including the agency's share of expenses, amounted to $9,015. Ignore withholding deductions and omit going through the disbursements in transit account. Remember that $75 was included in year 20X8 Expended Appropriations and is accrued.
7. a. Commitments were placed for $14,450 of fixed assets, inventory, and services.
   b. The agency head allotted an additional $300 for fixed assets, inventory, and services.
   c. Orders were placed for $14,700 of fixed assets, inventory, and services. Of those, $14,250 had previously been committed in the amount of $14,400. Because of failure to follow procedures, the remaining $450 had not been previously committed.
   d. Orders in (c) were received and approved, as follows:

	Estimated	Actual
Equipment............................	$ 3,000	$ 3,300
Inventory.............................	600	540
Services Used	10,875	10,800
	$14,475	$14,640

   e. Checks for accounts payable of $14,100 were requested from the Treasury during the year, including those related to fiscal year 20X8. The Treasury notified the agency that checks amounting to $13,980 were issued during fiscal year 20X9, including those relating to fiscal year 20X8 accounts payable.
8. The following year-end information was compiled:
   a. Depreciation on equipment amounted to $45.
   b. Salaries and benefits other than annual leave to be accrued amounted to $60.
   c. According to a report from the payroll department, the annual leave liability at fiscal year end was $219.
   d. A physical count of inventory indicated that $164 of inventory had been used.

(a) Prepare the general journal entries required for ABC Agency for fiscal year 20X9.   *Required*
(b) Post the entries to T-accounts.
(c) Prepare a preclosing trial balance for September 30, 20X9.
(d) Close the accounts.

P19-5 (Financial Statement Preparation) Using the information from Problem 19-4, prepare the three financial statements illustrated in the chapter for federal agencies:
(a) Balance sheet
(b) Statement of net cost
(c) Statement of changes in net position

P19-6 (Research) Find the most recent copy of the Financial Report of the U.S. Government. Evaluate it to determine the following:
(a) Similarities and differences between the report and what you would expect after studying this chapter.
(b) The type of audit opinion received by the U.S. government.
(c) Changes in the report resulting from recent pronouncements of the FASAB.
(d) Any material weaknesses in internal controls present in the U.S. government.

CHAPTER 20

Auditing Governments and Not-for-Profit Organizations

LEARNING OBJECTIVES

After studying this chapter, you should be able to:

- Understand the different types of government and not-for-profit organization audits.

- Understand the sources of standards for governments and not-for-profit organization auditing—and the relationships between and among generally accepted auditing standards (GAAS), generally accepted government auditing standards (GAGAS), and the Single Audit standards.

- Understand the basic aspects of an audit of government or not-for-profit organization financial statements under GAAS and GAGAS—as well as compliance audits and attestations under GAAS.

- Be better acquainted with the SLG "reporting units" and "major program" approaches to judging materiality

  quantitatively as well as the major G&NP audit-related Internet sites.

- Understand the Single Audit—its purposes, required frequency, and key components.

- Determine which federal programs should be treated as major programs in a Single Audit of a government or not-for-profit organization.

- Explain the responsibilities of both the auditor and the audited government or not-for-profit organization under single audit requirements.

- Identify and understand the audit reports required by a single audit and who is to receive the audit reports.

Auditing is the process of collecting and evaluating evidence to form and support an independent, professional opinion or other judgment about assertions made by management. The auditing process should be conducted in accordance with appropriate professional standards, and the auditor's opinion or other judgment should relate to the proper established criteria, such as generally accepted accounting principles, laws and regulations, contractual agreements, or other criteria agreed upon with users of the audit report.

The typical readers of financial statements or operational reports issued by management have no opportunity to review the operations or balances in question or to assess the credibility of management's representations. Few could do a good job if given the opportunity. The auditor's examination provides an expert's independent, professional judgment on the matters covered in the audit report.

The purpose of the auditor's opinion or other report is to add credibility to those representations properly made by management and to reduce the credibility of those that the auditor does not consider appropriate. These representations may take the form of financial statements, other reports on the activities of organizations in conducting programs assigned by legislative action or financed by intergovernmental grants, or implied representations about carrying out basic managerial responsibilities. For example, management is responsible for compliance with legal requirements, for maintaining adequate internal controls, and for conducting programs economically and efficiently. The auditor may be asked to give an opinion or to present other findings on such matters even when management's representation is an implied one.

OVERVIEW

This chapter is intended to familiarize the reader with the *major unique aspects of government and not-for-profit (G&NP) organization auditing*. An overview of the nature, purpose, and scope of G&NP organization auditing is presented first. This overview is followed by a summary of *generally accepted government auditing standards (GAGAS)* established by the U.S. Government Accountability Office (GAO). Finally, the concept and framework of a *single audit* are explained.

WHAT IS AN AUDIT?

Although there are several specific types of audits, most can be generally visualized as illustrated in Illustration 20-1:

1. An **auditee** is considered accountable for certain events, activities, and transactions—and makes assertions, either directly or indirectly, about such accountability—such as whether its financial statements are presented fairly and whether it has complied with applicable regulatory and grant provisions.

2. The **auditor** compares the auditee's assertions against established criteria—following an appropriate audit process and standards—and reports an opinion or other judgment based on the result of the audit.

3. The audit report **users** are given information by both the auditee (assertions) and the auditor (opinion or other judgment) to use in making their evaluations and decisions about the auditee's accountability.

Audits may be classified as internal or external on the basis of the relationship of the auditor to the agency being examined. Management customarily uses **internal auditors**—who are employees of the agency being audited—to review the operations of the agency, including employee compliance with managerial policies, and to report to management on these matters. They may also assist the external auditors, but the internal auditor's responsibility is ordinarily to top management of the agency.

    External auditors are *independent* of the audited agency and are responsible to the legislative body, the public, and other governmental units. External auditors typically express an *opinion*—primarily for the benefit of third parties—on the

Classifications of Audits

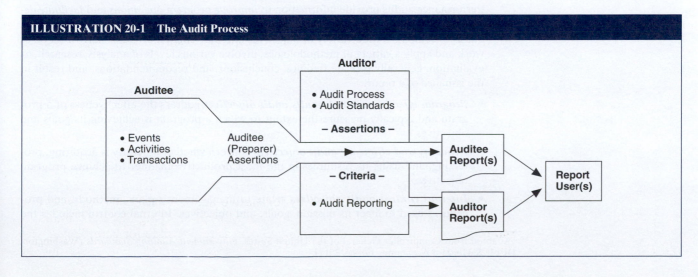

ILLUSTRATION 20-1 The Audit Process

fairness of presentation of the financial statements. However, their audit scope may extend beyond financial statements, and they may issue *nonopinion* reports on matters such as internal controls and compliance as well as a variety of *attestation* reports.

GAGAS (the GAO "Yellow Book" audit standards) further subdivide audits and attestation engagements into three categories and several subcategories:[1]

1. **Financial audits**—typically are primarily concerned with providing reasonable assurance about whether financial statements are presented fairly in all material respects in conformity with:

   • generally accepted accounting principles (GAAP), *or*

   • a comprehensive basis of accounting other than GAAP (OCBOA).

   Other objectives of financial audits—which provide for different levels of assurance and entail various scopes of work—may include (a) providing *special reports* for specified elements, accounts, or items of a financial statement; (b) reviewing *interim* financial information; (c) issuing *letters for underwriters* and certain other requesting parties; (d) reporting on the *processing* of transactions by *service organizations;* and (e) auditing *compliance* with regulations relating to federal award expenditures and other governmental financial assistance in conjunction with or as a by-product of a financial statement audit.

2. **Attestation engagements**—concern *examining, reviewing,* or *performing agreed-upon procedures* on a subject matter or assertion and *reporting* on the results. Attestation engagements can cover a broad range of financial or nonfinancial subjects, can be part of a financial audit or performance audit, and may include reports on the following:

   • An entity's *internal control* over *financial reporting*

   • An entity's *compliance* with requirements of specified laws, regulations, rules, contracts, or grants

   • The *effectiveness* of an entity's internal control over *compliance* with specified requirements, such as those governing the budgeting for, accounting for, and reporting on grants and contracts

   • Management's Discussion and Analysis (*MD&A*) presentation

   • *Prospective* financial statements or *pro-forma* financial information

   • The reliability of *performance measures*

   • Final *contract cost*

   • *Allowability* and *reasonableness* of proposed contract amounts

   • Agreed-upon procedures

3. **Performance audits**—entail both:

   • An *objective* and *systematic examination* of evidence to provide an independent assessment of program performance and management compared with objective criteria, and

   • Assessments that provide a *prospective* focus or that *synthesize* information on best practices or cross-cutting issues.

   Performance audits provide information to *improve* program *operations* and *facilitate decision making* by those who oversee programs or initiate corrective action. Performance audits encompass a wide variety of objectives and may entail a broad or narrow scope of work and apply a variety of methodologies; involve various levels of analysis, research, or evaluation; generally provide findings, conclusions, and recommendations; and result in the issuance of a report.

   • *Program effectiveness and results audit objectives* address the effectiveness of a program and typically measure the extent to which a program is achieving its goals and objectives.

   • *Economy and efficiency audit objectives* concern whether an entity is acquiring, protecting, and using its resources in the most productive manner to achieve program objectives.

   • *Internal control audit objectives* relate to management's plans, methods, and procedures used to meet its mission, goals, and objectives. Internal control includes the

---

[1]Adapted from Comptroller General of the United States, *Government Auditing Standards* (Washington, DC: U.S. General Accounting Office, 2011).

processes and procedures for planning, organizing, directing, and controlling program operations, and the system put in place for measuring, reporting, and monitoring program performance.

- *Compliance audit objectives* relate to compliance criteria established by laws, regulations, contract provisions, grant agreements, and other requirements that could affect the acquisition, protection, and use of the entity's resources and the quantity, quality, timeliness, and cost of services the entity produces and delivers.

Financial audits and attestation engagements typically are performed by independent public accountants and auditors or by state auditors, whereas performance audits typically are performed by internal audit divisions of a government or by a subunit of a state audit organization. The U.S. Government Accountability Office has published extensive guidance for conducting performance audits. The *primary focus of this chapter,* however, is on *external financial audits*—particularly *single audits.* In-depth discussions of attestation engagements and performance audits are beyond the scope of the chapter.

Management's Representations

An organization's *management* is *responsible* for recording, processing, and reporting on financial and other economic transactions, events, and balances. The reports generated by management contain various representations and assertions about the events summarized. The *auditors' responsibilities* are to collect sufficient objective data that allow them to express an opinion on the accuracy and reliability of the explicit and implicit representations and assertions contained in a given report.

Even if it does not publicly address itself to nonfinancial and other matters, *management implicitly asserts* that it has complied with applicable laws and regulations, has achieved agency and program objectives or has made reasonable progress toward them, and has operated economically and efficiently. Although these representations may not be as specific as those about finances, they can be evaluated—and the auditor's opinion may be as useful as if specific representations had been made.

External Auditor Classifications

External audits are performed by persons who are *independent* of the administrative organization of the unit audited. There are three groups of independent auditors: (1) those who are officials of the governmental unit being examined, (2) those who are officials of a government other than the one being examined, and (3) independent public accountants and auditors.

Most states and a few municipalities have an independent auditor either elected by the people or appointed by the legislative body. In such cases the auditor is directly responsible to the legislative body or to the citizenry, not to the chief executive or anyone else in the executive branch of the government. Election of the independent auditor works well in some jurisdictions, but in others only minimal qualifications are needed to seek the office and the auditor may be elected "on the coattails" of the governor. The elected auditor's independence and effectiveness may be significantly impaired in the latter situation.

The term *auditor* is sometimes applied to the principal *accounting* officer of a state or county. In such cases the auditor is not, of course, an independent external auditor.

State audit agencies in some states are responsible for auditing local governmental units, either routinely or at the request of the units or state officials. Such audit agencies do not necessarily audit any of the state agencies, though some do. Most local governmental audits are performed by independent certified public accountants, however. State audit agencies are increasingly (1) setting standards for the scope and minimum procedures of local government audits in their jurisdiction, (2) reviewing reports prepared by independent public auditors to ensure compliance with the standards, (3) performing "spot check" or test audit procedures when audit coverage appears to be insufficient, and (4) accumulating reliable and useful statewide statistics on local government finance.

Engagement Letter   The term *audit* is used in many ways in government, and the several audit categories and subcategories are not universally understood. To prevent misunderstandings about the nature, scope, or other aspects of the independent auditor's engagement, the audit agreement should be formalized in a *written* audit *contract*—often referred to as an engagement letter. Among the matters to be covered in the engagement letter are (1) the type and purposes of the audit or attestation—including a clear specification of the scope, any limitation of the scope, the parties at interest, how materiality is to be evaluated, and whether a single audit is to be performed; (2) the departments, funds, and agencies to be included and the personnel to be assigned; (3) the period covered; (4) approximate beginning and completion dates and the report delivery date; (5) the facilities, information, personnel, and other assistance the auditee will provide; (6) the means of handling unexpected problems, such as the discovery of fraud, which require a more extensive audit than was agreed upon, and how and to whom the auditor is to report any fraud, malfeasance, and so on, discovered; and (7) the engagement fees and expense reimbursements.

AUDITING STANDARDS

Audit standards should be distinguished from audit procedures. Audit *standards* are guidelines that deal with overall audit quality, whereas *procedures* are the actual work that is performed. Standards govern the auditor's judgment in deciding which procedures will be used, the way they will be used, when they will be used, and the extent to which they will be used. No listing of audit procedures is attempted here.

In conducting audits of governments, auditors must comply with *both* generally accepted auditing standards (GAAS) established by the AICPA and generally accepted government auditing standards (GAGAS)—the GAO audit standards established by the Comptroller General. GAGAS incorporate but go beyond GAAS. This section provides an overview of both GAAS and GAGAS.

 AICPA Auditing   The membership of the American Institute of Certified Public Accountants
Standards   (AICPA) has approved a set of standards of audit quality. *These ten standards apply to all audits—whether private sector or public sector*—and are the foundation of *generally accepted auditing standards (GAAS)* in the United States:

- **General Standards**
  1. The auditor must have adequate **technical training and proficiency** to perform the audit.
  2. The auditor must maintain **independence** in mental attitude in all matters relating to the audit.
  3. The auditor must exercise due **professional care** in the performance of the audit and the preparation of the report.
- **Standards of Field Work**
  1. The auditor must adequately **plan** the work **and** must properly **supervise** any assistants.
  2. The auditor must obtain a sufficient **understanding** of the entity and its environment, including its internal control, to **assess the risk of material misstatement** of the financial statements whether due to error or fraud, and to determine the nature, timing, and extent of further audit procedures.
  3. The auditor must obtain sufficient appropriate **audit evidence** by performing audit procedures to afford a reasonable basis for an opinion regarding the financial statements under audit.
- **Standards of Reporting**
  1. The auditor must **state** in the auditor's report **whether** the **financial statements** are presented in accordance with **generally accepted accounting principles**.

2. The auditor must **identify** in the auditor's report those **circumstances** in which such **principles have not been consistently observed** in the current period in relation to the preceding period.

3. When the auditor determines that **informative disclosures** are not reasonably adequate, the auditor must so state in the auditor's report.

4. The auditor must either **express an opinion** regarding the financial statements, taken as a whole, **or state that an opinion cannot be expressed**, in the auditor's report. [a] When the auditor cannot express an overall opinion, the auditor should state the reasons therefor in the auditor's report. [b] In all cases where an auditor's name is associated with financial statements, the auditor should clearly indicate the character of the auditor's work, if any, and the degree of responsibility the auditor is taking, in the auditor's report.[2]

In addition to these broad standards, auditors are given more detailed guidance in *Statements on Auditing Standards* (SASs) issued by the AICPA Auditing Standards Board (ASB). For some special types of audits, including government audits, specific recommended procedures are set forth in AICPA Audit and Accounting Guides and Statements of Position (SOPs). For example—as summarized in Illustration 20-2—the AICPA state and local government (SLG) audit guidance instructs auditors to plan, conduct, evaluate, and report upon SLG audits in manners that are consistent with the basic financial statements (Chapter 13) required by GASB. Thus, as a minimum, the following must be presented fairly in all material respects for an unqualified opinion to be rendered on a state or local government's basic financial statements:

- Each government-wide financial statement, each *major* governmental fund financial statement, and each *major* Enterprise Fund financial statement.
- Taken together, the discretely presented component units, the aggregate *nonmajor* governmental funds and Enterprise Funds, and the Internal Service Funds and Fiduciary Funds *by fund type.*

ILLUSTRATION 20-2   Overview of Reporting Units and Opinion Units

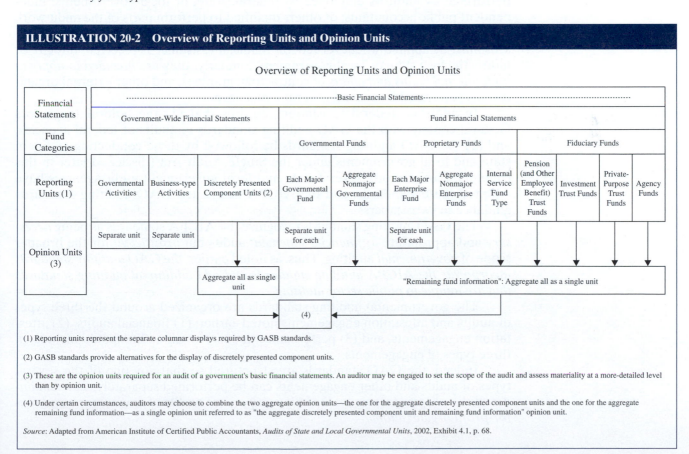

(1) Reporting units represent the separate columnar displays required by GASB standards.

(2) GASB standards provide alternatives for the display of discretely presented component units.

(3) These are the opinion units required for an audit of a government's basic financial statements. An auditor may be engaged to set the scope of the audit and assess materiality at a more-detailed level than by opinion unit.

(4) Under certain circumstances, auditors may choose to combine the two aggregate opinion units—the one for the aggregate discretely presented component units and the one for the aggregate remaining fund information—as a single opinion unit referred to as "the aggregate discretely presented component unit and remaining fund information" opinion unit.

Source: Adapted from American Institute of Certified Public Accountants, *Audits of State and Local Governmental Units*, 2002, Exhibit 4.1, p. 68.

[2]American Institute of Certified Public Accountants, *Codification of Statements on Auditing Standards* (New York: AICPA, revised annually), AU150. (Emphasis added.)

From a materiality perspective, each major fund column of the fund financial statements and the governmental activities, business-type activities, and component units columns of the government-wide statements are viewed as separate financial statements. Accordingly, the auditor's:

- *Fund financial statement* materiality evaluations must be based on *each* major governmental fund and *each* major Enterprise Fund—*not* the fund type totals.
- *Government-wide statement* materiality evaluations must be based on the Governmental Activities, Business Activities, and Component Units columns—*not* on the total Primary Government or Total Reporting Entity amounts.

In the remainder of this chapter, reference to GAAS includes all of these sources and levels of audit standards.

GAO Auditing Standards

Although there are many similarities between auditing profit-seeking and governmental organizations, there are also many differences. Furthermore, there was no comprehensive statement of generally accepted *government* auditing standards prior to issuance of the initial *Standards for Audit of Governmental Organizations, Programs, Activities & Functions*[3] by the Comptroller General of the United States. These *government* auditing standards are commonly referred to as the Government Accountability Office (GAO) standards, generally accepted *government* auditing standards (GAGAS), or the *"Yellow Book"* standards (because of its yellow cover). The several types of audit and other attestation engagements—as set forth in the most recent update of these GAO standards, or GAGAS—are summarized earlier in this chapter.

The GAO auditing standards are *intended to be applied in all audits of governmental organizations, programs, activities, and functions*—whether they are performed by auditors employed by federal, state, or local governments; independent public accountants; or others qualified to perform parts of the audit work contemplated under the standards. Indeed, these GAGAS or Yellow Book standards *must* be applied whenever federal financial assistance is received, directly or indirectly, by a state or local government. Similarly, they are *intended to apply to both internal audits and audits* of contractors, grantees, and other external organizations performed by or for a governmental agency.

In addition, federal legislation requires that (1) the federal Inspectors General comply with the GAO auditing standards in audits of federal agencies, and (2) the GAO auditing standards be followed by those conducting audits of state and local governments under the Single Audit Act (discussed later in this chapter). Furthermore, several state and local government audit agencies have adopted these standards, and the AICPA has issued GAO auditing standards guidance to its members.

The GAO auditing standards recognize the AICPA standards as being *necessary* and appropriate to *financial statement* audits but *insufficient* for the broader scope of *governmental* auditing. Thus, as noted earlier, *the GAO auditing standards incorporate the AICPA auditing standards and add additional auditing standards that are unique to public sector auditing.*

The governmental auditing standards are organized around the three types of audits and attestation engagements noted earlier: (1) financial audits, (2) attestation engagements, and (3) performance audits. Not all audits should include all three types of engagements.

Indeed, the GAO standards are structured so that any one of the several types of audits and other engagements can be performed separately. *The remainder of this chapter focuses on the unique aspects of **audits** of governments and not-for-profit organizations.*

---

[3]Comptroller General of the United States, *Standards for Audit of Governmental Organizations, Programs, Activities & Functions* (Washington, DC: U.S. General Accounting Office, 1972).

The GAO's 2011 Generally Accepted Government Auditing Standards establishes standards for audits of governments and other recipients of federal financial assistance. It incorporates the auditing standards established by the AICPA's Auditing Standards Board (ASB) by reference and also includes additional auditing standards established by the GAO.

The ASB Clarity Project to more closely align U.S. auditing standards with those of the International Auditing and Assurance Standards Board was an important consideration in revising the Yellow Book. As this alignment progresses, the GAO reviews the standards and assesses their potential impact on GAGAS. Practitioners can assume that the GAO concurs with new ASB auditing standards unless the GAO indicates its disagreement.

GAGAS includes other significant changes to further clarify and harmonize the GAO and AICPA audit standards. For example, the additional standards the GAO added to the AICPA audit standards are clearly indicated, and relevant AICPA auditing standards, including definitions such as for "material weaknesses" and "significant deficiencies," are incorporated by reference rather than repeated in the Yellow Book. The most significant change from previous editions of the Yellow Book is the incorporation of a conceptual framework for evaluating independence.

Independence

The new GAGAS "independence" *conceptual framework* closely aligns the Yellow Book and AICPA "independence" standards. This framework requires the auditor to identify threats to auditor independence and then assess the significance of the threats:

- If identified threats are deemed significant to the engagement, the auditor determines whether safeguards could be put in place to mitigate the threats to an acceptable level.
- The framework also provides guidance on the significance of certain specific threats and whether those threats can be mitigated.
- If the auditor concludes that there are no safeguards sufficient to reduce a threat to an acceptable level, then the threat is an impairment to independence.
- The auditor is required to document any independence issue requiring significant discussion or analysis.

Threats and Safeguards The GAO standards identify several categories of threats to an auditor's independence:

- **Self-review.** An auditor audits his or her own work.
- **Self-interest.** An auditor has a vested interest in the results of the audit.
- **Bias.** An auditor has a preconceived notion about an organization or program regardless of audit results.
- **Familiarity over time.** An auditor has become too close to the audited organization or program.
- **Undue influence.** Personal, political, or other pressures might impair an auditor's judgment.
- **Management participation.** An auditor makes management decisions or otherwise takes on the role of management of the audited organization or program.
- **Structural.** The location of a government auditor in the government organization structure may impact the auditor's independence or create an appearance of impairment.

If a ***nonaudit*** service is *not* expressly prohibited, the auditor should apply the conceptual framework to decide whether a potential impairment exists. The standards identify safeguards created by the profession as well as those directly related to the work environment, including:

- Professional or regulatory monitoring and disciplinary procedures, such as peer reviews.
- External reviews by third parties of reports, such as by grantor audit agencies.
- Using different management and engagement teams with separate reporting lines to provide nonaudit services to an audited entity.

- Additional review requirements for nonaudit services, such as by professional ethics committees.
- Additional oversight by the audited entity's management over nonaudit services.

In some cases, safeguards may mitigate threats to an acceptable level. However, even if properly applied, safeguards may not always be sufficient to reduce some threats.

Prohibitions within Certain Nonaudit Services Certain nonaudit services are explicitly prohibited by GAGAS. These prohibitions involve nonaudit services that have raised issues related to auditor independence (in fact or appearance) in the government environment. Specific auditor services are expressly prohibited within each of the following nonaudit categories:

- **Internal Audit Services**
  - Establishing an auditee's internal audit policies or strategic direction.
  - Selecting or implementing internal audit recommendations.
  - Designing, implementing, or maintaining internal control.
- **Internal Control Monitoring and Assessments** – Providing ongoing monitoring procedures.
- **Information Technology (IT) Services**
  - Designing or developing an information system that would be subject to an audit.
  - Modifying source code.
  - Operating or supervising an information technology (IT) service.
- **Valuation Services**
  Providing valuation services that would have a material effect (separately or in the aggregate) on the financial statements or other information that is subject to an audit, if the valuation involves a significant degree of subjectivity.
- **Financial Statement Preparation, Bookkeeping, and Client Assistance**
  Independence issues arise when the auditor provides the audited entity with assistance in bookkeeping and financial statement preparation. For example, auditors often walk a fine line between independence and impairment when converting cash basis accounts to an accrual basis, preparing financial statements, or assisting with reconciliations. The GAO and AICPA audit standards are consistent in identifying certain auditor activities that create an ***automatic impairment***, such as:
  - Determining or changing journal entries, account coding, transaction classifications, or other accounting records without obtaining client approval.
  - Authorizing or approving transactions.
  - Preparing source documents.
  - Changing source documents without client approval.

The GAO standards do not expressly prohibit an auditor from providing other bookkeeping or financial statement preparation services. However, before performing bookkeeping and financial services that are not expressly prohibited, the auditor should evaluate them within the conceptual framework to determine whether an impairment exists and, if so, whether it can be adequately mitigated.

In addition, in order for the auditor to provide bookkeeping and financial statement activities that are not expressly prohibited, management charged with overseeing the nonaudit service should possess suitable skill, knowledge, or experience to evaluate the adequacy and results of the services performed. If management does not, an impairment exists, as is true under the AICPA's Code of Professional Conduct, Rule 101, *Independence* (Interpretation 101-3, *Performance of Nonattest Services*).

Audits Subsequent to Nonaudit Services GAGAS introduces the concept of a *post-impairment period* after the auditor provides an independence-impairing service. Under the GAO standards, auditors who perform independence-impairing nonaudit services may audit in subsequent periods only after sufficient safeguards have been identified to mitigate the threat.

- One type safeguard would be that an audit has been performed by an auditor who did not provide the original nonaudit service.
- The auditor should also consider *independence in appearance* issues that may arise should an audit be performed after an impairing nonaudit service has been provided.

Continuing Professional Education (CPE) Requirements

Auditors who work under GAGAS should complete a minimum of 24 hours of governmental accounting, auditing, and related CPE every two years. Internal specialists who apply their specialized knowledge to the audit should complete 24 hours of CPE in their area of specialty. External specialists are not required to follow the CPE requirements; however, auditors are required to consider whether external specialists are qualified to serve an engagement.

THE FINANCIAL AUDIT

The usual purpose of a financial statement audit is to determine whether the fund and government-wide financial statements of the government being audited *present fairly* the financial position and operating results of the major governmental and proprietary funds (and cash flows of the major proprietary funds) and its governmental- and business-type activities in accordance with GAAP. In making this determination, the *auditor must determine whether the entity has complied with laws and regulations applicable to transactions and events for which noncompliance might have a material effect on the entity's financial statements*. Legal compliance is considered an integral part both of managerial responsibility and accountability and of the financial audit of governments.

The financial statement audit must be concerned with the possibility that noncompliance might create contingent or actual liabilities—or invalidate receivables—that are material to the entity's financial statements. The legal constraints under which governments operate and the control orientation of governmental accounting systems have been commented upon at numerous points throughout this book. Obviously, the accountability process is incomplete if the audit of the financial statements does not include the legal compliance aspects.

Auditing Standards

The AICPA standards are designed for the financial aspects of financial statement audits generally, and are adapted to government audits by being incorporated in the GAO auditing standards. *The laws, regulations, and other legal constraints under which the government operates establish the standards against which legal compliance is measured.*

Audit Procedures

Specific guidance for audits of governments, hospitals and other health care organizations, colleges and universities, voluntary health and welfare organizations, and other nonprofit organizations is available in the several AICPA audit and accounting guides for these types of organizations, cited at various points in this text. The most detailed authoritative guidance to the procedural aspects of financial audits is generally contained in the AICPA's *Audits of State and Local Governments* (*ASLGU*), the state and local government audit guide. This guide covers such topics as audit standards to be applied, audit procedures to be followed, audit reports to be prepared, planning the audit, audit workpapers, compliance with legal and regulatory requirements, study of internal control, and tests of account balances.

ASLGU notes that in preparing and auditing the basic financial statements the governmental activities, business-type activities, and major fund reporting units are presumed to be quantitatively material. In other words, both planning and reporting *materiality* usually must be evaluated *quantitatively (and qualitatively)* for *each* column of each major governmental fund, each major Enterprise Fund, and each government-wide *basic* financial statement.

Legal compliance auditing procedures vary with the circumstances. The auditor must determine the legal provisions of laws, ordinances, bond indentures, grants, and so on that are applicable in the situation. The auditor then determines the extent of compliance with these provisions and the adequacy of the related reporting and disclosure in the financial statements and notes. The auditor must also obtain reasonable assurance that the auditee has not incurred significant unrecorded liabilities through violation of pertinent laws and regulations.

The Audit Report

The auditor's report on a financial statement audit of a government is similar to an auditor's report for the audit of corporate financial statements, as is seen in Illustration 15-2, the auditor's report on the Guilford County, North Carolina, financial statements. The key differences in an auditor's report on the examination of government financial statements result from (1) the need to follow GAGAS as well as GAAS and (2) the different levels of financial statements—both government-wide and fund financial statements—as discussed in Chapter 13.

The audit report must clearly indicate the responsibility the auditor assumes for the different levels of financial statements, as well as for any accompanying information. The GASB position on the degree of responsibility that auditors should accept for different levels of financial statements is that *whereas the basic financial statements are the minimum acceptable audit scope, the GASB recommends that the audit scope also encompass the combining and individual fund financial statements and schedules in the comprehensive annual financial report.*[4] The GFOA agrees, and has a similar policy statement.

GAGAS also require the auditor to issue written reports on the auditee's *overall*

- internal control, and
- compliance with applicable laws and regulations.

These reports are *not* opinion reports. Rather, GAGAS require public reporting of the results of tests and evaluation of *overall* internal control and *overall* compliance related to the *financial* audit—both of which can be important to grantors and others who attempt to evaluate the audited entity's management style and abilities. In addition, the auditor will perform certain tests of Management's Discussion and Analysis (MD&A) and other required supplementary information (RSI).

The AICPA provides illustrative auditor's reports for GAGAS (Yellow Book) audits both:

- where internal controls over financial reporting and on compliance and other matters do *not* indicate significant internal control deficiencies, reportable instances of noncompliance, or other relevant matters, and
- where the auditors' consideration of overall internal control over financial reporting, compliance, and other matters indicate there *are* significant internal control deficiencies, reportable instances of noncompliance, or other relevant matters.

Illustration 20-3 presents a recent AICPA illustrative audit report where the auditor's procedures for the financial statement audit indicated significant internal control deficiencies and reportable compliance and other matters.

Finally, although the independent auditor is engaged primarily to render an opinion on the financial statements, one of the auditor's most valuable services can be to provide a letter to responsible officials known as the *management letter*. In the management letter the auditor provides discussions, analyses, and recommendations on operational matters such as accounting systems and procedures, including internal accounting and administrative controls; protection, utilization, and disposition of assets; types and numbers of funds; cash management; organizational arrangements; and insurance and bonding practices.

---

[4]GASB Codification, Appendix D, pars. 103–104.

ILLUSTRATION 20-3   Illustrative Auditor's Report on Internal Control Over Financial Reporting and on Compliance and Other Matters

Example 4-5

Report on Internal Control Over Financial Reporting and on Compliance and Other Matters Based on an Audit of Financial Statements Performed in Accordance With *Government Auditing Standards* (*No Material Weaknesses Identified; Significant Deficiencies and Reportable Instances of Noncompliance, and Other Matters Identified*)

[*Addressee*]

We have audited the financial statements of Example Entity as of and for the year ended June 30, 20X1, and have issued our report thereon dated August 15, 20X1. We conducted our audit in accordance with auditing standards generally accepted in the United States of America and the standards applicable to financial audits contained in *Government Auditing Standards*, issued by the Comptroller General of the United States.

Internal Control Over Financial Reporting

Management of Example Entity is responsible for establishing and maintaining effective internal control over financial reporting. In planning and performing our audit, we considered Example Entity's internal control over financial reporting as a basis for designing our auditing procedures for the purpose of expressing our opinion on the financial statements but not for the purpose of expressing an opinion on the effectiveness of Example Entity's internal control over financial reporting. Accordingly, we do not express an opinion on the effectiveness of Example Entity's internal control over financial reporting.

A *deficiency in internal control* exists when the design or operation of a control does not allow management or employees, in the normal course of performing their assigned functions, to prevent, or detect and correct misstatements on a timely basis. A *material weakness* is a deficiency, or a combination of deficiencies, in internal control such that there is a reasonable possibility that a material misstatement of the entity's financial statements will not be prevented, or detected and corrected on a timely basis.

Our consideration of internal control over financial reporting was for the limited purpose described in the first paragraph of this section and was not designed to identify all deficiencies in internal control over financial reporting that might be deficiencies, significant deficiencies or material weaknesses. We did not identify any deficiencies in internal control over financial reporting that we consider to be material weaknesses, as defined above. However, we identified certain deficiencies in internal control over financial reporting, described in the accompanying [*include the title of the schedule in which the findings are reported (e.g., schedule of findings and responses or schedule of findings and questioned costs)*] that we consider to be significant deficiencies in internal control over financial reporting. [*List the reference numbers of the related findings, for example, 20X1-1, 20X1-3, and 20X1-4*]. A *significant deficiency* is a deficiency, or a combination of deficiencies, in internal control that is less severe than a material weakness, yet important enough to merit attention by those charged with governance.

[***NOTE:*** . . . this guide recommends identifying each finding with a reference number. . . .]

Compliance and Other Matters

As part of obtaining reasonable assurance about whether Example Entity's financial statements are free of material misstatement, we performed tests of its compliance with certain provisions of laws, regulations, contracts, and grant agreements, noncompliance with which could have a direct and material effect on the determination of financial statement amounts. However, providing an opinion on compliance with those provisions was not an objective of our audit, and accordingly, we do not express such an opinion. The results of our tests disclosed instances of noncompliance or other matters that are required to be reported under *Government Auditing Standards* and which are described in the accompanying [*include the title of the schedule in which the findings are reported (e.g., schedule of findings and responses or schedule of findings and questioned costs)*] as items [*list the reference numbers of the related findings, for example, 20X1-2 and 20X1-5*].

[***NOTE:*** The referenced findings include reportable: (*a*) instances of noncompliance; and (*b*) fraud or abuse that is not the result of a significant deficiency.]

We noted certain matters that we reported to management of Example Entity in a separate letter dated August 15, 20X1.

Example Entity's response to the findings identified in our audit are described in the accompanying [*include the title of the schedule in which the findings are reported (e.g., schedule of findings and responses or schedule of findings and questioned costs) "or above" if findings and responses are included in the body of the report*]. We did not audit Example Entity's response and, accordingly, we express no opinion on it.

This report is intended solely for the information and use of management, [*identify the body or individuals charged with governance*], others within the entity, and [*identify the legislative or regulatory body*] and is not intended to be and should not be used by anyone other than these specified parties.

[Signature]

[Date]

Source: AICPA at http://www.aicpa.org. Copyright 2009 by the American Institute of Certified Public Accountants, Inc. All rights reserved. Reprinted with permission.

THE SINGLE AUDIT

The $1+ trillion of federal grants to, and contracts with, state and local governments, universities, hospitals, and other not-for-profit organizations each year has led to greater scrutiny of the use of federal financial assistance and the method of auditing entities for compliance with grant provisions and other federal requirements. These factors resulted in the development of the concept known as the **Single Audit**. Several states also require the auditor to include *state* financial aid programs in the scope of Single Audits.

The basic notion of the Single Audit is that one audit can provide both (1) the basis for an opinion on the recipient entity's financial statements and (2) a basis for determining whether federal financial assistance program resources are being managed and controlled appropriately and used in accordance with legal and contractual requirements.

Illustration 20-4 illustrates how GAGAS incorporate but add requirements beyond GAAS, and how a Single Audit incorporates GAGAS (including GAAS) and adds requirements beyond GAGAS. Indeed, *Single Audit requirements extend well beyond those for GAAS or GAGAS audits.*

One disadvantage of the Single Audit approach is that some grantor agencies do not receive as much information about their grant programs as when separate grant or grant program audits are performed. As a result, some grantor agencies require audit work that goes beyond the Single Audit requirements. *Grantor agencies have the right to require additional work when necessary to fulfill their oversight responsibilities, but they must pay the additional audit costs.* Thus, whereas most federal financial assistance is audited using the Single Audit approach discussed here,

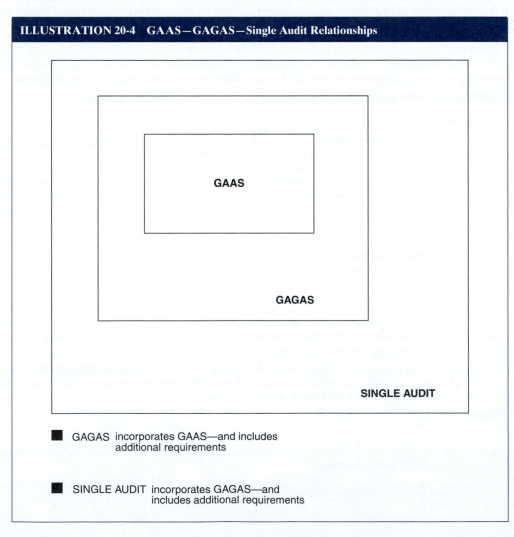

ILLUSTRATION 20-4   GAAS—GAGAS—Single Audit Relationships

GAAS

GAGAS

SINGLE AUDIT

■ GAGAS incorporates GAAS—and includes additional requirements

■ SINGLE AUDIT incorporates GAGAS—and includes additional requirements some grant-by-grant and program-by-program audits are performed either in addition to the Single Audit or instead of a Single Audit under the options and exceptions permitted by the Single Audit Act of 1984, as amended. Also some state audit agencies perform grant-by-grant audits on selected state assistance programs.

Congress stated that the purposes of the Single Audit Act are to: **Purposes**

- Improve the financial management and accountability of state and local governments (SLGs) and not-for-profit organizations (NPOs) with respect to federal financial assistance programs.
- Establish uniform requirements for audits of federal financial assistance provided to state and local governments and not-for-profit organizations.
- Promote the efficient and effective use of audit resources.
- Ensure that federal departments and agencies rely on and use audit work done pursuant to the Act to the maximum extent practicable.

The Single Audit Act of 1984 and OMB Circular A-133 require SLGs and not-for-   **Applicability**
profit organizations that *expend $500,000 or more of federal financial assistance in a fiscal year* to have a Single Audit for that fiscal year. (This $500,000 expenditure threshold may be increased by the OMB but may not be decreased.) The applicability of the Single Audit Act, as amended, and OMB Circular A-133 is summarized in Illustration 20-5.

    The Act permits some exceptions to these requirements. Specifically, a *series of audits* of the SLG's or NPO's individual departments, agencies, and establishments for the same fiscal year satisfies the audit requirements of the Act—providing all operations are included. Too, in some circumstances, the SLG or NPO may have a *program audit* of a specific federal financial assistance (FFA) program(s) rather than a Single Audit.

    Finally, SLGs and NPOs that expend less than $500,000 in federal financial assistance in any fiscal year are *exempt* from the Single Audit requirements—as well

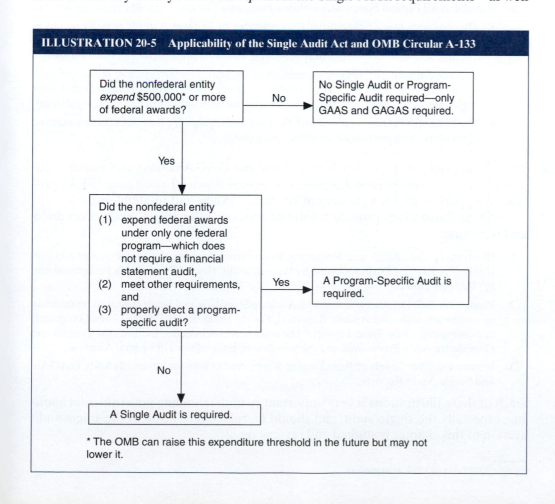

ILLUSTRATION 20-5   Applicability of the Single Audit Act and OMB Circular A-133

Did the nonfederal entity *expend* $500,000* or more of federal awards? — **No** → No Single Audit or Program-Specific Audit required—only GAAS and GAGAS required.

Yes ↓

Did the nonfederal entity
(1) expend federal awards under only one federal program—which does not require a financial statement audit,
(2) meet other requirements, and
(3) properly elect a program-specific audit? — **Yes** → A Program-Specific Audit is required.

No ↓

A Single Audit is required.

* The OMB can raise this expenditure threshold in the future but may not lower it.

as other federal audit requirements—for that year. However, these governments must keep adequate accounting records and make them available for inspection and audit upon request.

Definitions Federal financial *assistance* is assistance provided by a federal agency that nonfederal entities receive or administer. The assistance may be grants, contracts, cooperative agreements, loans, loan guarantees, property, interest subsidies, insurance, food commodities, or direct appropriations—and includes both direct federal awards received and those received indirectly (*pass through*) from other SLGs.[5] In sum, federal financial assistance is defined to include all assistance provided by federal agencies to SLGs or NPOs, even if that aid is subsequently passed on to other governments, organizations, or individuals. Federal financial *awards* are defined by OMB Circular A-133 as including both federal financial assistance (including loans) and cost-reimbursement-type contracts. A *schedule of expenditures of federal awards* is illustrated in Illustration 20-9.

Objectives Under the Act, a Single Audit should achieve several objectives:

1. **Related to the Entity as a Whole.** The audit should be designed to determine whether the basic financial statements fairly present the financial position and results of operations—for the governmental activities, business-type activities, and major funds—in accordance with GAAP (or the non-GAAP basis indicated). The audit also includes

   - Determining whether the government or other not-for-profit organization has *complied* with laws and regulations with which noncompliance may have a material effect on the *financial statements* of the entity.

   - Studying and evaluating *internal controls* of the entity to determine the nature, extent, and timing of the auditing procedures necessary to express an opinion on the entity's *financial statements*.

2. **Related to All Federal Financial Assistance Programs.** The audit should determine whether

   - The supplementary Schedule of Expenditures of Federal Awards is fairly stated *in all material respects in relation to the basic financial statements* taken as a whole. (An example schedule of expenditures of federal awards is presented in Illustration 20-10.)

   - The government or NPO has established *internal control* systems, including both accounting and administrative controls, to provide reasonable assurance that *each **major** federal program* is managed in compliance with applicable laws and regulations.

   - The SLG or NPO has *complied* with the laws and regulations that could have a *material effect* on *each **major** federal assistance program*.

Overview The Single Audit incorporates both GAAS and GAGAS—and also requires additional audit procedures and reports on federal financial assistance (FFA) programs. Appendix 20-1 is a glossary of key Single Audit and related terms.

Three illustrations provide helpful overviews of the Single Audit procedures and reporting:

1. Illustration 20-6: Audit and Reporting Requirements under the Single Audit Act and OMB Circular A-133 summarizes, by type of audit, the (1) Procedures Performed and (2) Reports Issued.

2. Illustration 20-7: GAAS, Governmental Auditing Standards, and Single Audits summarizes, in an outline schematic, the Auditor Reports (I. For the Entity and II. For the Federal Programs) in relationship to the Basic Financial Statements and Schedules, the Internal Control and Compliance Audit Procedures, and the Schedule of Expenditures of Federal Awards.

3. Illustration 20-8: Levels of Reporting in Single Audits lists the several GAAS, GAGAS, and Single Audit Reports.

Each of these illustrations is very important to understanding governmental auditing, especially the single audit, and should be referred to often as the single audit section of this chapter is studied and reviewed.

---

[5]Single Audit Act of 1984, as amended.

ILLUSTRATION 20-6   Audit and Reporting Requirements under the Single Audit Act and OMB Circular A-133

Type of Audit	Procedures Performed	Report Issued
GAAS (only)	1. Audit of the financial statements in accordance with generally accepted auditing standards	• Opinion on the financial statements
GAGAS (includes GAAS)	2. Audit of the financial statements in accordance with Government Auditing Standards	• Report on compliance with laws and regulations that may have a material effect on the financial statements • Report on internal control structure related matters based solely on an assessment of control risk performed as part of the audit of the financial statements
Single Audit (includes GAAS and GAGAS)	3. Obtain an understanding of the internal controls over major federal financial assistance programs, assess control risk, and perform tests of controls	• Report on internal controls over major federal financial assistance programs (MFAPs)
	4. Audit of supplemental Schedule of Expenditures of Federal Awards	• Opinion on supplemental Schedule of Expenditures of Federal Awards
	5. Audit of compliance with specific requirements applicable to major federal financial assistance programs as defined by the Single Audit Act or OMB Circular A-133	• Opinion on compliance with specific requirements applicable to *each* major federal financial assistance program
	6. Perform follow-up procedures related to the Summary Schedule of Prior Audit Findings	• Schedule of Findings and Questioned Costs • Report *if* Summary Schedule of Prior Audit Findings materially misrepresents the status of any prior audit finding

The audited government or not-for-profit organization is required to:

Auditee Responsibilities

1. *Identify* in its accounts all federal awards received and expended and the federal programs under which they were received.

2. *Maintain internal controls over federal programs* that provide reasonable assurance that the auditee is managing federal awards in compliance with laws, regulations, and the provisions of contracts or grant agreements that could have a material effect on *each of its federal programs*.

3. *Comply* with laws, regulations, and the provisions of contracts or grant agreements related to *each of its federal programs*.

4. Prepare appropriate financial statements, including the schedule of expenditures of federal awards. (See Illustration 20-9, Schedule of Expenditures of Federal Awards).

5. Ensure that the audits required are properly performed and the audit reports and related information are submitted when due.

6. Follow up and take corrective action on audit findings, which includes preparing a summary schedule of prior audit findings and a corrective action plan.

OMB Circular A-133 summarizes the auditor's responsibilities—and the scope of the Single Audit—in six topic areas: (1) general, (2) financial statements, (3) internal control, (4) compliance, (5) audit follow-up, and (6) data collection form. These six topic areas—cross-referenced to Illustration 20-7—include:

Auditor Responsibilities

1. **General**
   a. The audit must be conducted in accordance with GAGAS.
   b. The audit must cover the entire operations of the auditee. (At the option of the auditee, the audit may include a series of audits covering all its departments, agencies,

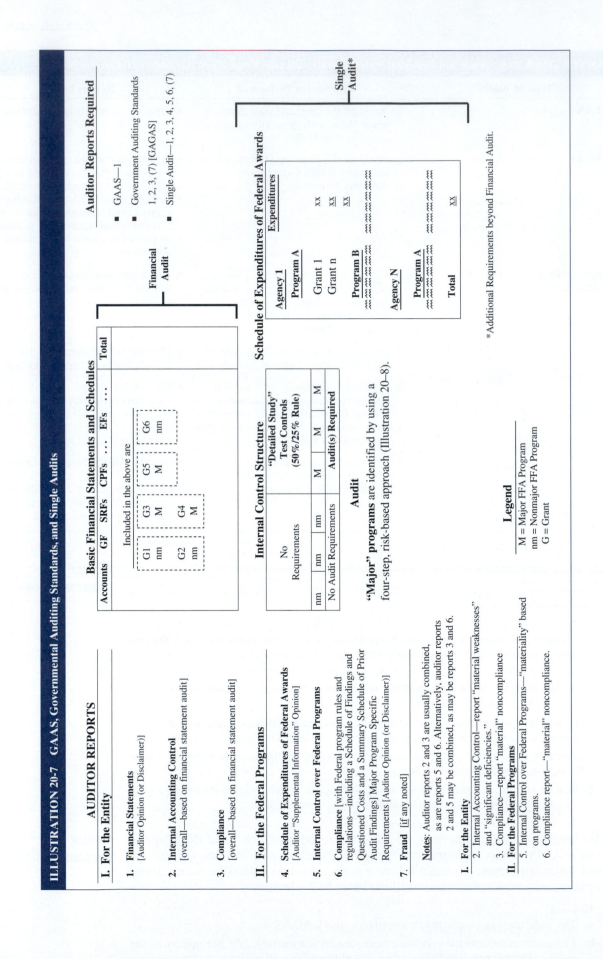

ILLUSTRATION 20-7   GAAS, Governmental Auditing Standards, and Single Audits

AUDITOR REPORTS

I. For the Entity

1. Financial Statements
[Auditor Opinion (or Disclaimer)]

2. Internal Accounting Control
[overall—based on financial statement audit]

3. Compliance
[overall—based on financial statement audit]

II. For the Federal Programs

4. Schedule of Expenditures of Federal Awards
[Auditor "Supplemental Information" Opinion]

5. Internal Control over Federal Programs

6. Compliance [with Federal program rules and regulations—including a Schedule of Findings and Questioned Costs and a Summary Schedule of Prior Audit Findings] Major Program Specific Requirements [Auditor Opinion (or Disclaimer)]

7. Fraud [if any noted]

Notes: Auditor reports 2 and 3 are usually combined, as are reports 5 and 6. Alternatively, auditor reports 2 and 5 may be combined, as may be reports 3 and 6.

I. For the Entity

2. Internal Accounting Control—report "material weaknesses" and "significant deficiencies."
3. Compliance—report "material" noncompliance

II. For the Federal Programs

5. Internal Control over Federal Programs—"materiality" based on programs.
6. Compliance report—"material" noncompliance.

Auditor Reports Required

- GAAS—1
- Government Auditing Standards
  1, 2, 3, (7) [GAGAS]
- Single Audit—1, 2, 3, 4, 5, 6, (7)

Basic Financial Statements and Schedules

Accounts	GF	SRFs	CPFs	...	EFs	...	Total
	Included in the above are						
	G1 nm	G3 M	G5 M		G6 nm		
	G2 nm	G4 M					

Internal Control Structure

No Requirements	"Detailed Study" Test Controls (50%/25% Rule)
nm	nm	M	M	M
No Audit Requirements	Audit(s) Required

Audit

"**Major" programs** are identified by using a four-step, risk-based approach (Illustration 20–8).

Legend

M = Major FFA Program
nm = Nonmajor FFA Program
G = Grant

Schedule of Expenditures of Federal Awards

	Expenditures
Agency 1	
Program A	
Grant 1	xx
Grant n	xx
Program B	xx
	~~ ~~~ ~~~ ~~~
Agency N	
Program A	
	~~ ~~~ ~~~ ~~~
Total	xx

*Additional Requirements beyond Financial Audit.

ILLUSTRATION 20-8   Levels of Reporting Single Audits

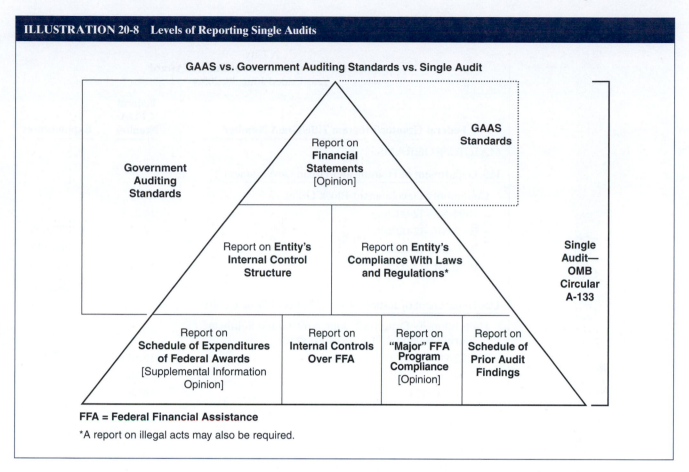

GAAS vs. Government Auditing Standards vs. Single Audit

FFA = Federal Financial Assistance

*A report on illegal acts may also be required.

and other organizational units that expended or administered federal awards during the fiscal year.)

   c. The financial statements and Schedule of Expenditures of Federal Awards must be for the same fiscal year.

2. Financial Statements. The auditor is required to determine:

   a. Whether the audited entity's financial statements are presented fairly in all material respects in conformity with generally accepted accounting principles (I, 1), and

   b. Whether the Schedule of Expenditures of Federal Awards (Illustration 20-9) is presented fairly in all material respects in relation to the auditee's financial statements taken as a whole (II, 4).

3. Internal Control. The A-133 guidance on internal control is relatively specific:

   a. In addition to the requirements of GAGAS (I, 2), the auditor must perform procedures to *obtain an understanding of the internal control over federal programs* (II, 5) *sufficient to plan the audit to support a low assessed level of control risk for major programs.*

   b. Except as provided in 3(c), the auditor must:

   (i) *Plan* the testing of internal control over *major* programs to support a low assessed level of control risk for the assertions relevant to the compliance requirements for each major program; and

   (ii) *Perform testing* of internal control as planned in paragraph 3(b)(i).

   c. When internal controls over some or all of the compliance requirements for a major program are likely to be ineffective in preventing or detecting noncompliance, the planning and performing of testing described in paragraph 3(b) are not required for those compliance requirements. However, the auditor must report a *significant deficiency* (including whether any such condition is a *material weakness*), assess the related control risk at the maximum, and consider whether additional compliance tests are required because of ineffective internal control.

ILLUSTRATION 20-9   Schedule of Expenditures of Federal Awards

A City
Schedule of Expenditures of Federal Awards
Year Ended June 30, 20X4

Federal Grantor/Program Title/Grant Number	Federal CFDA Number	Expenditures
MAJOR PROGRAMS:		
U.S. Department of Housing and Urban Development:		
Community Development Block Grant		
B-94-MC-12-0026	14.218	
B-93-MC-12-0026	14.218	$ 517,690
B-92-MC-12-0026	14.218	364,132
B-90-MC-12-0026	14.218	147,900
		1,029,722
U.S. Department of Justice/Office of National Drug Control:		
High Intensity Drug Trafficking Area Grant; Southeast Florida Regional Task Force Program		
93-HJ-H3-K042	16.580	273,117
94-HJ-I4-K005	16.580	
GE-3-M24	16.580	52,416
		325,533
Total major programs		1,355,255
NONMAJOR PROGRAM:		
U.S. Department of Agriculture:		
Pass through Florida Department of Education; Summer Food Service Program		
04-984	10.559	27,743
Total nonmajor program		27,743
Total federal financial assistance		$1,382,998

See notes to schedule of federal financial assistance.
CFDA = Catalog of Federal Domestic Assistance

4. **Compliance**

   a. In addition to the requirements of GAGAS (I, 3), the auditor must determine whether the auditee has complied with laws, regulations, and the provisions of contracts or grant agreements that may have a direct and material effect on each of its *major* programs (II, 6).

   b. The principal compliance requirements applicable to most federal programs and the compliance requirements of the largest federal programs are included in the OMB *compliance supplement.*

      • An audit of the compliance requirements related to federal programs contained in the compliance supplement will meet the requirements of A-133.

      • When changes have been made to the compliance requirements and the changes are not reflected in the compliance supplement, the auditor must determine the current compliance requirements and modify the audit procedures accordingly.

   c. For federal programs not covered in the compliance supplement, the auditor should use the types of compliance requirements contained in the compliance supplement as guidance for identifying the types of compliance requirements to test and determine the requirements governing the federal program by reviewing the provisions of contracts and grant agreements and the laws and regulations referred to in the contracts and grant agreements.

   d. The compliance testing must include tests of transactions and other auditing procedures necessary to provide the auditor sufficient evidence to support an opinion on compliance.

5. **Audit Follow-Up (II, 6).** The auditor is required to:

   a. Follow up on prior audit findings,

   b. Perform procedures to assess the reasonableness of the summary schedule of prior audit findings, and

   c. Report—as a current year audit finding—when the auditor concludes that the summary schedule of prior audit findings materially misrepresents the status of any prior audit finding. (The auditor must perform audit follow-up procedures regardless of whether a prior audit finding relates to a major program in the current year.)

6. **Data Collection Form.** The auditor must complete and sign specified sections of the data collection form (http://harvester.census.gov/sac).

These scope elements permeate the Single Audit planning, performance, and reporting processes discussed and illustrated in this chapter.

Several sources of guidance are available to those conducting a Single Audit. **Auditing Guidance** Such guidance is typically available in publications, loose-leaf services, and on the Internet. For example, much guidance is available at

- The OMB site, **http://www.whitehouse.gov/omb**
- The Federal Audit Clearinghouse site, **http://harvester.census.gov/sac**
- **http://www.gaqc.AICPA.org/(Governmental Audit Quality Center)** and **http://www .AICPA.org**
- **http://www.GAO.gov**
- **http://www.USA.gov**

As noted in Illustration 20-4, 20-7, and 20-8, the requirements of the Single Audit Act go beyond those of GAAS and GAGAS. For example, the level of compliance auditing and internal control study and evaluation is much more extensive than that required by GAGAS for a financial statement audit. Thus, auditors who conduct Single Audits must be familiar with auditee grant agreements, the Act, and related implementation guidance provided in OMB Circular A-133, as well as with GAGAS and the *OMB A-133 Compliance Supplement,* which summarizes relevant federal rules and regulations and includes suggested compliance auditing procedures. Also, the AICPA state and local government audit guide (*ASLGU*) and the OMB A-133 "questions and answers" publication provide extensive implementation guidance based on the Act, OMB Circular A-133, and extensive consultations with representatives of the OMB, the GAO, and the inspectors general.

Two other sources of implementation guidance are the Council of the Inspectors General on Integrity and Efficiency (CIGIE) and the auditee's cognizant agency or other oversight agency. The CIGIE (**http://www.ignet.gov/cigie1.html**) is composed of the federal inspectors general and is responsible for overseeing implementation of the Single Audit. The CIGIE occasionally issues Statements of Position on issues related to the Single Audit as questions and problems arise.

Federal *cognizant agencies* are assigned by the OMB to oversee implementation of the Single Audit of states and local governments that expend more than $50 million of federal financial assistance annually. (Other governments are under the general oversight of the federal agency or department from which they receive the most *direct* assistance in a particular year, referred to as the "oversight agency.") OMB Circular A-133 places the following **responsibilities** on **cognizant agencies**:

1. Provide technical audit advice and liaison to auditees and auditors.

2. Consider auditee requests for extensions to the report submission due date. (The cognizant agency for audit may grant extensions for good cause.)

3. Obtain or conduct quality control reviews of selected audits made by nonfederal auditors; and, when appropriate, provide the results to other interested organizations.

4. Promptly inform other affected federal agencies and appropriate federal law enforcement officials of any direct reporting by the auditee or its auditor of irregularities or illegal acts, as required by GAGAS or laws and regulations.

5. Advise the auditor and, where appropriate, the auditee of any deficiencies found in the audits when the deficiencies require corrective action by the auditor. (Major inadequacies or repetitive substandard performance by auditors are referred to appropriate state licensing agencies and professional bodies for disciplinary action.)

6. Coordinate audits or reviews made by or for federal agencies that are in addition to single audits and program-specific audits, so that additional audits or reviews build upon these audits.

7. Coordinate a management decision for audit findings that affect the federal programs of more than one agency.

8. Coordinate the audit work and reporting responsibilities among auditors to achieve the most cost-effective audit.

9. For biennial audits consider auditee requests to qualify as a "low-risk auditee."[6]

In view of the oversight, technical assistance, and quality control responsibilities of cognizant agencies and other oversight agencies, auditors often seek their advice or concurrence when planning and conducting a Single Audit. In addition to the federal cognizant agencies, some states assign cognizant agencies to local governments in the state—particularly to those that have no federal cognizant agency.

Major FFA Programs

The Single Audit Act does not modify the auditing procedures designed to determine whether the entity's financial statements fairly present its financial position and operating results. However, it requires that extensive work be performed by the auditor to determine:

1. *Whether the entity has complied with laws and grant provisions* that might have a material effect on *major* federal financial assistance *programs*.

2. *Whether internal control systems* have been established over *major* federal financial assistance *programs* to ensure that the resources are expended in accordance with applicable laws and grant provisions.

Because the audit focus is on *major* programs, it is important to understand the Act's definition of a *major federal financial assistance program* (MFAP) and that OMB Circular A-133 includes cost-type contracts in defining federal financial awards subject to Single Audit.

The auditor uses a four-step, **risk-based approach** to determine which federal programs are **major** programs. This approach—which includes consideration of program size, the current and prior audit experience, oversight by federal agencies and pass-through entities, and the inherent risk of the federal program—is summarized in Illustration 20-10. Determining *MFAPs* under the *risk-based* approach involves:

 Step 1: The auditor identifies the larger federal programs, which are called **Type A** programs. Type A programs are defined as federal programs with federal awards *expended* during the audit period of the *larger of:*

- $300,000 or 3% (.03) of total federal awards expended in the case of an auditee for which total federal awards expended equal or exceed $500,000 but are less than or equal to $100 million.

- $3 million or three-tenths of 1% (.003) of total federal awards expended in the case of an auditee for which total federal awards expended exceed $100 million but are less than or equal to $10 billion.

- $30 million or fifteen-hundredths of 1% (.0015) of total federal awards expended in the case of an auditee for which total federal awards expended exceed $10 billion.

---

[6]Office of Management and Budget (OMB), Circular No. A-133, "Audits of State and Local Governments," 2003. (Emphasis added.)

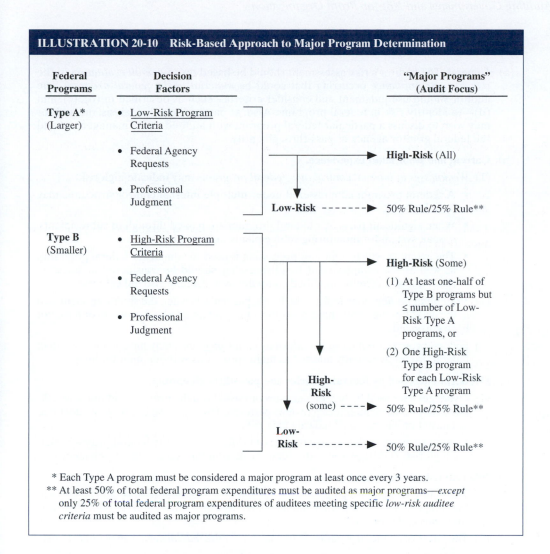

ILLUSTRATION 20-10   Risk-Based Approach to Major Program Determination

Federal Programs	Decision Factors	"Major Programs" (Audit Focus)

* Each Type A program must be considered a major program at least once every 3 years.
** At least 50% of total federal program expenditures must be audited as major programs—*except* only 25% of total federal program expenditures of auditees meeting specific *low-risk auditee criteria* must be audited as major programs.

The smaller federal programs that are not Type A programs are called **Type B** programs.

Step 2: The auditor then identifies **low-risk Type A** programs:

- *Type A* programs considered *low risk*

  1. Have been audited as a major program in at least one of the last two years audited, *and*

  2. In the most recent audit period, had no audit findings that must be reported.

- The *auditor may use judgment.* For example, most audit findings from questioned costs and audit follow-up for the summary schedule of prior audit findings do not preclude a Type A program from being considered low risk.

- The auditor also considers the *federal program risk criteria* specified in OMB Circular A-133, results of *audit follow-up,* and whether any *changes in personnel or systems* affecting a Type A program have significantly increased risk.

- Finally, the auditor considers any *federal agency requests* and applies professional judgment in determining whether a Type A program is low risk.

Regardless of the auditor's judgments, however, the OMB may approve a federal awarding agency's request that a Type A program at certain recipients not be considered low risk.

Step 3: The auditor identifies **high-risk Type B** programs by using professional judgment and the federal program risk criteria in OMB Circular A-133. These criteria are summarized in Illustration 20-11. Note also that:

- If the auditor selects Option 2 under Step 4, he or she is not required to identify more high-risk Type B programs than the number of low-risk Type A programs.

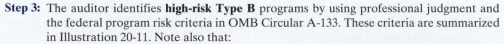

ILLUSTRATION 20-11   Criteria for Federal Program Risk

(a) **General.** The auditor's risk assessment should be based on an *overall evaluation* of the *risk of noncompliance* occurring that could be *material to the federal program*. The auditor should use judgment and consider criteria—such as described in (b), (c), and (d)—to identify risk in federal programs. Also, as part of the risk analysis, the auditor may wish to discuss a particular federal program with audited entity management and the federal grantor agency or pass-through entity.

(b) **Current and prior audit experience.**

  (1) *Weaknesses in internal control over federal programs* may indicate high risk.

   • A federal program administered under multiple internal control structures may have high risk.

   • When significant parts of a federal program are passed through to subrecipients, a weak system for monitoring subrecipients indicates high risk.

   • The extent to which computer processing is used to administer federal programs, as well as the complexity of that processing, should be considered in assessing risk. New and recently modified computer systems may also indicate risk.

  (2) *Prior audit findings* may indicate high risk, particularly when the situations identified in the audit findings could have a significant impact on a federal program or have not been corrected.

  (3) Federal programs *not recently audited as major programs* may have higher risk than federal programs recently audited as major programs without audit findings.

(c) **Oversight exercised by federal agencies and pass-through entities.**

  (1) Oversight exercised by federal agencies or pass-through entities could indicate risk. For example, recent monitoring reviews performed by an oversight entity that disclosed significant problems would indicate high risk.

  (2) Federal agencies, with the concurrence of OMB, may identify federal programs that are high risk. (OMB provides this identification in the compliance supplement.)

(d) **Inherent risk of the federal program.**

  (1) The nature of a federal program may indicate risk. Consideration should be given to the complexity of the program and the extent to which the federal program contracts for goods and services.

  (2) The *phase* of a federal program in its *life cycle* at the *federal agency* may indicate risk.

   • For example, a new federal program with new or interim regulations may have higher risk than an established program with time-tested regulations.

   • Also, significant changes in the federal programs, laws, regulations, or the provisions of contracts or grant agreements may increase risk.

  (3) The *phase* of a federal program in its *life cycle* at the *auditee* may indicate risk. For example, during the first and last years an auditee participates in a federal program, the risk may be high due to start-up or closeout of program activities and staff.

  (4) Type B programs with larger federal awards expended would be higher risk than programs with substantially smaller federal awards expended.

   • A first-year audit is the first year the entity is audited under OMB Circular A-133 or the first year of a change of auditors.

   • To ensure that a frequent change of auditors does not preclude audit of high-risk Type B programs, the OMB prohibits this first-year audit election by an audited entity more than once every three years.

• Except for known significant deficiencies in internal control or significant compliance problems, a single program risk criterion would not usually cause a Type B program to be considered high risk.

The auditor is *not* expected to perform risk assessments on *relatively small* federal programs. Thus, the auditor is only required to perform risk assessments on Type B programs that exceed the larger of:

• $100,000 or three-tenths of 1% (.003) of total federal awards expended when the auditee has less than or equal to $100 million in total federal awards expended.

- $300,000 or three-hundredths of 1% (.0003) of total federal awards expended when the auditee has more than $100 million in total federal awards expended.

Step 4: At a minimum, the ***auditor is required to audit all of the following as major programs:***

- **All Type A** programs, *except* the auditor may exclude any Type A programs identified as *low risk* under Step 2.
- **High-risk Type B** programs as identified under either of the following two options:
    1. *Option 1* — at least one-half of the Type B programs identified as high risk under Step 3, *except* the auditor is not required to audit more high-risk Type B programs than the number of low-risk Type A programs identified as low risk under Step 2.
    2. *Option 2* — one high-risk Type B program for each Type A program identified as low risk under Step 2.

    The OMB encourages auditors identifying which high-risk Type B programs to audit as major, under either Option 1 or 2, to use an approach that provides an opportunity for different high-risk Type B programs to be audited as major over a period of time.

- Such additional programs as may be necessary to comply with the *percentage of coverage rule,* which may require the auditor to audit more programs as major than the number of Type A programs.

The **percentage of coverage rule** requires that programs classified as major federal programs, in the aggregate, encompass at least **50%** of total federal awards expended. If the auditee meets the criteria for a **low-risk auditee**, the major federal programs audited must, in the aggregate, encompass at least **25%** of total federal awards expended. The low-risk auditee criteria are summarized in Illustration 20-12.

A significant **first-year audit** deviation from the use of risk criteria is permitted. For first-year audits, the auditor may elect to determine major programs as all Type A grants plus any Type B programs necessary to meet the percentage of coverage rule. Under this option, the auditor would consider the larger programs to be the major programs and would not be required to perform the risk assessment procedures discussed in Steps 2 and 3.

The auditor's report on compliance is accompanied by a *schedule of findings and questioned costs*. OMB Circular A-133 defines **questioned cost** as follows:

Findings & Questioned Costs

> **Questioned cost** means a cost that is questioned by the auditor because of an audit finding:
>
> - Which resulted from a violation or possible violation of a provision of a law, regulation, contract, grant, cooperative agreement, or other agreement or document governing the use of Federal funds, including funds used to match Federal funds;
> - Where the costs, at the time of an audit, are not supported by adequate documentation; or
> - Where the costs incurred appear unreasonable and do not reflect the actions a prudent person would take in the circumstances.[7]

In general, the **criteria** for determining and reporting **questioned costs** are as follows:

a. Unallowable costs — Certain costs specifically unallowable under the general and special award conditions or agency instructions (including, but not limited to, pre-grant and post-grant costs and costs in excess of the approved grant budget either by category or in total).

b. Undocumented costs — Costs charged to the grant for which adequate detailed documentation does not exist (for example, documentation demonstrating their relationship to the grant or the amounts involved).

---

[7]Ibid.

ILLUSTRATION 20-12 Criteria for Low-Risk Auditee

An auditee that meets **all** of the following *conditions* for *each* of the *preceding two years* (or, in the case of biennial audits, preceding two audit periods) qualifies as a **low-risk auditee**, eligible for reduced audit coverage.

(a) **Single Audits performed.** Single audits were performed on an annual basis in accordance with the provisions of OMB Circular A-133. (A nonfederal entity that has *biennial* audits does not qualify as a low-risk auditee unless agreed to in advance by the cognizant agency or the oversight agency for audit.) *And*

(b) **Auditor's opinions unqualified.** The auditor's opinions on the financial statements and the schedule of expenditures of federal awards were unqualified. (However, the cognizant or oversight agency for audit may judge that an opinion qualification does not affect the management of federal awards and may provide a waiver.) *And*

(c) **No GAGAS internal control material weaknesses.** No deficiencies in internal control were identified as material weaknesses under the requirements of GAGAS. (However, the cognizant oversight agency for audit may judge that any identified material weaknesses do not affect the management of the federal awards and may provide a waiver.) *And*

(d) **No Type A program findings.** None of the federal programs had audit findings from any of the following in either of the preceding two years (or, in the case of biennial audits, preceding two audit periods) in which they were classified as Type A programs:

   (1) Internal control deficiencies identified as material weaknesses.

   (2) Noncompliance with the provisions of laws, regulations, contracts, or grant agreements that has a material effect on the Type A programs.

   (3) Known or likely questioned costs that exceed 5% of the total federal awards expended for Type A programs during the year.

---

   c. Unapproved costs—Costs that are not provided for in the approved grant budget, or for which the grant or contract provisions or applicable cost principles require the awarding agency's approval, but for which the auditor finds no evidence of approval.

   d. Unreasonable costs—Costs incurred that may not reflect the actions a prudent person would take in the circumstances, or costs resulting from assigning an unreasonably high valuation to in-kind contributions.

More specifically, AICPA *Statement of Position 98–3* states,

> The **schedule of findings and questioned costs** should contain a summary of all reportable instances (findings) of noncompliance and should identify total amounts questioned, if any, for each federal financial assistance program. *Government Auditing Standards . . .* suggests that well-developed findings, which provide sufficient information to federal, state, and local officials to permit timely and proper corrective action, generally consist of statements of the following:
>
> • The Condition (what is)
>
> • Criteria (what should be)
>
> • Effect (the difference between what is and what should be)
>
> • Cause (why it happened)
>
> However, the auditor may not be able to fully develop all of these points, given the scope and purpose of Single Audits.[8]

 **Illegal Acts**   In addition to the internal control evaluation and compliance testing required in a Single Audit, the auditor is required to report any illegal acts discovered during the audit. *The auditor is not required to test for illegal acts.* But if the auditor becomes aware of situations or transactions that could be indicative of fraud, abuse, or illegal expenditures, additional audit steps and procedures should be applied to determine whether such irregularities have occurred. Both *ASLGU* and the GAO

---

[8] *ASLGU* (1999), Appendix M.

auditing standards contain specific guidance for the steps to be taken if such situations or transactions are discovered, which is relatively rare.

SLGs that *pass through* federal financial assistance *to a subrecipient* must:

Subrecipients

- **Identify Federal Awards.** Identify federal awards made by informing each subrecipient of the CFDA title and number, award name and number, award year, whether the award is for research and development, and the name of the federal agency. If some of this information is not available, the pass-through entity should provide the best information available to describe the federal award.

- **Advise Subrecipients.** Advise subrecipients of requirements imposed on them by federal laws, regulations, and the provisions of contracts or grant agreements, as well as any supplemental requirements imposed by the pass-through entity.

- **Monitor Subrecipient Activities.** Monitor the activities of subrecipients as necessary to ensure that federal awards are used for authorized purposes in compliance with laws, regulations, and the provisions of contracts or grant agreements and that performance goals are achieved.

- **Ensure Audit Requirements Are Met.** Ensure that subrecipients expending $500,000 or more in federal awards during the subrecipient's fiscal year have met the audit requirements of OMB Circular A-133 for that fiscal year.

- **Issue a Management Decision.** Issue a management decision on audit findings within 6 months after receipt of the subrecipient's audit report and ensure that the subrecipient takes appropriate and timely corrective action.

- **Consider Adjusting Own Records.** Consider whether subrecipient audits necessitate adjustment of the pass-through entity's records.

- **Require Access.** Require each subrecipient to permit the pass-through entity and auditors to have access to the records and financial statements as necessary for the pass-through entity to monitor the subrecipient's activities.

OMB Circular A-133 does *not* permit pass-through entities to recover *Single Audit* costs to monitor subrecipients expending less than $500,000 annually. However, it does permit pass-through entities to arrange for—and be reimbursed for—*agreed-upon procedures* attestation engagements that address specified compliance requirements of subrecipients.

The primary recipient's responsibilities to monitor subrecipients may be discharged by (1) relying on independent audits performed of the subrecipient, performed in accordance with OMB Circular A-102 or A-133 (or, in some cases, Circular A-110), (2) relying on appropriate procedures performed by the primary recipient's internal audit or program management personnel, (3) expanding the scope of the independent financial and compliance audit of the primary recipient to encompass testing of subrecipients' charges, or (4) a combination of those procedures.

The primary recipient is also responsible for (1) reviewing audit and other reports submitted by subrecipients and identifying questioned costs and other findings pertaining to the federal financial assistance passed through to the subrecipients and (2) properly accounting for and pursuing resolution of questioned costs and ensuring that prompt and appropriate corrective action is taken in instances of material noncompliance with laws and regulations.

Subrecipient noncompliance can result in questioned costs for the primary recipient. Thus, the primary recipient controls established to monitor subrecipient compliance should be studied and evaluated.

Specific instances of subrecipient noncompliance need not be included in the primary recipient's audit report. However, the auditor should consider whether reported *subrecipient* exceptions, events, or indications of material weaknesses in the primary recipient's monitoring system could materially affect any major federal financial assistance program of the *primary* recipient.

Audit reports prepared at the completion of the audit should meet the requirements of the Single Audit Act, as amended, and OMB Circular A-133. The auditor's report(s) may be in the form of either combined or separate reports, is

Auditor Reports— Single Audit

required to state that the audit was conducted in accordance with OMB Circular A-133, and includes the following:

A. Opinion on Financial Statements and on Schedule of Expenditures of Federal Awards. Two auditor opinions must be reported: (1) an opinion (or disclaimer of opinion) on whether the financial statements are presented fairly in all material respects in conformity with generally accepted accounting principles and (2) an opinion (or disclaimer of opinion) on whether the Schedule of Expenditures of Federal Awards is presented fairly in all material respects in relation to the financial statements taken as a whole.

B. Report(s) on Internal Controls. Report(s) on internal control—related to (1) the financial statements and (2) the major programs—must describe the scope of testing of internal controls and the results of the tests and, where applicable, refer to the separate Schedule of Findings and Questioned Costs.

C. Report(s) on Compliance. A report(s) must be made on compliance with laws, regulations, and the provisions of contracts or grant agreements—noncompliance with which could have a material effect on the financial statements. The report(s) must also

- Include an opinion (or disclaimer of opinion) on whether the auditee complied with laws, regulations, and the provisions of contracts or grant agreements that could have a direct and material effect on each major program.
- Where applicable, refer to the separate Schedule of Findings and Questioned Costs.

D. Schedule of Findings and Questioned Costs. A Schedule of Findings and Questioned Costs should include these three components:

1. A summary of the auditor's results, which should include

   (a) The type of report the auditor issued on the financial statements of the auditee (unqualified opinion, qualified opinion, adverse opinion, or disclaimer of opinion).

   (b) Where applicable, a statement that significant deficiencies in internal control were disclosed by the audit of the financial statements and whether any such conditions were material weaknesses.

   (c) A statement about whether the audit disclosed any noncompliance that is material to the financial statements of the auditee.

   (d) Where applicable, a statement that significant deficiencies in internal control over major programs were disclosed by the audit and whether any such conditions were material weaknesses.

   (e) The type of report the auditor issued on compliance for major programs (unqualified opinion, qualified opinion, adverse opinion, or disclaimer of opinion).

   (f) A statement about whether the audit disclosed any audit findings that the auditor is required to report under OMB Circular A-133.

   (g) An identification of major programs.

   (h) The dollar threshold used to distinguish between Type A and Type B programs.

   (i) A statement about whether the auditee qualified as a low-risk auditee.

2. Findings relating to the financial statements that are required to be reported in accordance with GAGAS.

3. Findings and questioned costs for federal awards.

Illustration 20-13 presents an AICPA illustrative example auditor's report: "Report on Compliance With Requirements Applicable to Each Major Program and on Internal Control Over Compliance in Accordance With OMB Circular A-133 (Unqualified Opinion on Compliance and Significant Deficiencies in Internal Control Over Compliance Identified)." The detail of Single Audit findings that must be reported is summarized in Illustration 20-14.

The Single Audit report must include several components that can either be bound into a single report or presented together as separate documents. The required audit report components, as well as any report needed on illegal acts, are summarized in Illustration 20-15 and *categorized in terms of whether they relate to the entity as a whole or only to its federal financial assistance programs.* Finally, note that three of the reports—those on the examination of the financial statements, the schedule of federal financial assistance, and compliance for MFAPs—require expression of an opinion by the auditor. The others do not.

ILLUSTRATION 20-13   AICPA Illustrative Auditor's Report on Compliance

Example 12-2—Report on Compliance With Requirements Applicable to Each Major Program and on Internal Control Over Compliance in Accordance With OMB Circular A-133 (Unqualified Opinion on Compliance and Significant Deficiencies in Internal Control Over Compliance Identified)

[Addressee]

Compliance

We have audited the compliance of Example Entity with the types of compliance requirements described in the OMB *Circular A-133 Compliance Supplement* that are applicable to each of its major federal programs for the year ended June 30, 20X1. Example Entity's major federal programs are identified in the summary of auditor's results section of the accompanying schedule of findings and questioned costs. Compliance with the requirements of laws, regulations, contracts, and grants applicable to each of its major federal programs is the responsibility of Example Entity's management. Our responsibility is to express an opinion on Example Entity's compliance based on our audit.

We conducted our audit of compliance in accordance with auditing standards generally accepted in the United States of America; the standards applicable to financial audits contained in *Government Auditing Standards*, issued by the Comptroller General of the United States; and OMB Circular A-133, *Audits of States, Local Governments, and Non-Profit Organizations*. Those standards and OMB Circular A-133 require that we plan and perform the audit to obtain reasonable assurance about whether noncompliance with the types of compliance requirements referred to above that could have a direct and material effect on a major federal program occurred. An audit includes examining, on a test basis, evidence about Example Entity's compliance with those requirements and performing such other procedures as we considered necessary in the circumstances. We believe that our audit provides a reasonable basis for our opinion. Our audit does not provide a legal determination of Example Entity's compliance with those requirements.

As described in item [*list the reference numbers of the related findings, for example, 20X1-10 and 20X1-4*] in the accompanying schedule of findings and questioned costs, Example Entity did not comply with requirements regarding [*identify the major federal program*]. Compliance with such requirements is necessary, in our opinion, for Example Entity to comply with the requirements applicable to that program.

In our opinion, Example Entity complied, in all material respects, with the requirements referred to above that are applicable to each of its major federal programs for the year ended June 30, 20X1. However, the results of our auditing procedures disclosed instances of noncompliance with those requirements, which are required to be reported in accordance with OMB Circular A-133 and which are described in the accompanying schedule of findings and questioned costs as items [*list the reference numbers of the related findings, for example, 20X1-3 and 20X1-6*].

Internal Control Over Compliance

The management of Example Entity is responsible for establishing and maintaining effective internal control over compliance with the requirements of laws, regulations, contracts, and grants applicable to federal programs. In planning and performing our audit, we considered Example Entity's internal control over compliance with the requirements that could have a direct and material effect on a major federal program in order to determine our auditing procedures for the purpose of expressing our opinion on compliance, but not for the purpose of expressing an opinion on the effectiveness of internal control over compliance. Accordingly, we do not express an opinion on the effectiveness of the Entity's internal control over compliance. Our consideration of internal control over compliance was for the limited purpose described in the preceding paragraph and would not necessarily identify all deficiencies in the entity's internal control that might be significant deficiencies or material weaknesses as defined below. However, as discussed below, we identified certain deficiencies in internal control over compliance that we consider to be significant deficiencies.

A *control deficiency* in an entity's internal control over compliance exists when the design or operation of a control does not allow management or employees, in the normal course of performing their assigned functions, to prevent or detect noncompliance with a type of compliance requirement of a federal program on a timely basis. A *significant deficiency* is a control deficiency, or combination of control deficiencies, that adversely affects the entity's ability to administer a federal program such that there is more than a remote likelihood that noncompliance with a type of compliance requirement of a federal program that is more than inconsequential will not be prevented or detected by the entity's internal control. We consider the deficiencies in internal control over compliance described in the accompanying schedule of findings and questioned costs as items [*list the reference number of the related findings, for example, 20X1-7, 20X1-8, and 20X1-9*] to be significant deficiencies.

A material weakness is a significant deficiency, or combination of significant deficiencies, that results in more than a remote likelihood that material noncompliance with a type of compliance requirement of a federal program will not be prevented or detected by the entity's internal control. We did not consider any of the deficiencies described in the accompanying schedule of findings and questioned costs to be material weaknesses.

Example Entity's response to the findings identified in our audit are described in the accompanying schedule of findings and questioned costs. We did not audit Example Entity's response and, accordingly, we express no opinion on it.

This report is intended solely for the information and use of management, [*identify the body or individuals charged with governance*], others within the Entity, [*identify the legislative or regulatory body*], and federal awarding agencies and pass-through entities and is not intended to be and should not be used by anyone other than these specified parties.

[Signature]

[Date]

Source: AICPA at http://www.aicpa.org. Copyright 1982–2007 by the American Institute of Certified Public Accountants, Inc. All rights reserved. Reprinted with permission.

ILLUSTRATION 20-14   Audit Findings Detail: Single Audit

OMB Circular A-133 states that audit findings must be presented in sufficient detail (1) for the **auditee** to prepare a corrective action plan and take corrective action and (2) for **federal agencies and pass-through entities** to arrive at a management decision. *The following specific information should be included, as applicable, in audit findings:*

1. *Federal program* and specific federal award identification—including the *Catalog of Federal Domestic Assistance* (CFDA) title and number, federal award number and year, name of federal agency, and name of the applicable pass-through entity.

2. The *criteria or specific requirement* upon which the audit finding is based—including statutory, regulatory, or other citation.

3. The *condition* found—including facts that support the deficiency identified in the audit finding.

4. Identification of *questioned costs* and how they were computed.

5. Information to provide *proper perspective* for judging the prevalence and consequences of the audit findings, such as whether the audit findings represent an isolated instance or a systemic problem. (When appropriate, instances identified should be related to the universe and the number of cases examined and be quantified in terms of dollar value.)

6. The possible asserted *effect*—to provide sufficient information to the auditee and federal agency, or pass-through entity in the case of a subrecipient, to permit them to determine the cause and effect to facilitate prompt and proper corrective action.

7. *Recommendations* to prevent future occurrences of the deficiency identified in the audit finding.

8. *Views of responsible auditee officials,* especially when they disagree with the audit findings (to the extent practical).

Auditee Reporting Responsibilities

The auditee is responsible for assembling a Single Audit **reporting package** that includes the:

1. Financial statements
2. Schedule of Expenditures of Federal Awards

ILLUSTRATION 20-15   Single Audit Reports

For the Organization or Other Entity:	For Its Federal Financial Assistance Programs:
A report on an examination of the *Basic Financial Statements* of the entity as a whole, or the department, agency, or establishment covered by the audit. Includes opinion on *fairness of presentation* of financial statements. (GAAS)	A report on the *supplementary schedule of expenditures* of the entity's federal financial assistance award programs, showing total expenditures for each federal assistance award program. Includes *opinion* on whether fairly stated *relative to* the Basic Financial Statements taken as a whole.
A report on *internal accounting control* based *solely* on a study and evaluation made as a *part of the audit* of the Basic Financial Statements. (GAGAS)	A report on *internal controls* related to the *major* federal award *programs*.
A report on *compliance* with laws and regulations that may have a *material effect* on the *financial statements*. (GAGAS)	A report on *compliance* with specific *program requirements* and related federal laws and regulations—including, where appropriate, reference to the schedule of findings and questioned costs. Includes auditor *opinion(s)* on whether *MFAPs* were administered in *compliance* with those specific program laws and regulations for which noncompliance could have a material effect on the allowability of program expenditures.

A report on fraud or other illegal acts, or indications of such, *when discovered* (a written report is required). Normally, such reports are issued separately and only if irregularities are discovered.

3. Summary Schedule of Prior Audit Findings
4. Auditor's report(s), including the Schedule of Findings and Questioned Costs
5. Corrective Action Plan

One copy of this **reporting package**, as well as a **uniform data collection form**—see **Appendix 20-2**—must be sent online to the Federal Audit Clearinghouse of the U.S. Census Bureau (**http://harvester.census.gov/sac**). In addition, wherever there are audit findings, copies of the reporting package must be:

- Provided to the clearinghouse for each federal agency that made findings-related awards directly to the auditee.

- Sent to each pass-through entity that made findings-related awards indirectly to the auditee.

Other Matters

Practitioners and grantors continue to raise questions about other implementation-related matters as they conduct Single Audits. In response to these questions and concerns, the AICPA, OMB, GAO, and the President's Council on Integrity and Efficiency continue to study, discuss, and interpret the Act and related guidance and to provide additional guidance on implementing the specific requirements of the Act and regulations.

Concluding Comments

Both the theory and the practice of governmental auditing are evolving rapidly. The Single Audit Act, as amended, and OMB Circular A-133 require that governmental and not-for-profit audits go significantly beyond the traditional financial audit, particularly in evaluating and reporting legal compliance and internal controls for federal financial assistance programs.

The Single Audit Act has had a significant impact on the auditing profession, including internal, external, and governmental auditors. The Act covers all 50 states, most of the 80,000 plus local governmental units, and many not-for-profit organizations. Indeed, whereas public accountants perform fewer than 5,000 audits of publicly held business corporations each year, they perform several times as many Single Audits.

OMB recently proposed to (1) increase the Single Audit threshold to entities that expend $1,000,000 or more of federal awards; (2) require entities that expend $1,000,000–$3,000,000 to have a modified Single Audit in which major program compliance audit procedures would focus on allowable/unallowable costs and one additional requirement; and (3) require entities that expend more than $3,000,000 to be subject to a complete Single Audit. The OMB "advance notice" also proposed other changes in Single Audits and allowable cost principles.

APPENDIX 20-1

Glossary

This glossary of governmental audit terminology is adapted from the "Definitions" section of OMB Circular A-133, "Audits of States, Local Governments, and Non-Profit Organizations" (2003).

Auditee: any nonfederal entity that expends federal awards that must be audited under Circular A-133.

Audit finding: deficiencies that the auditor is required to report in the schedule of findings and questioned costs.

Auditor: a public accountant or a federal, state, or local government audit organization that meets the general standards specified in generally accepted government auditing standards (GAGAS). The term *auditor* does *not* include *internal* auditors of nonprofit organizations.

CFDA number: the number assigned to a federal program in the *Catalog of Federal Domestic Assistance (CFDA)*.

Cluster of programs: a grouping of closely related programs that share common compliance requirements. The types of clusters of programs are research and development (R&D), student financial aid (SFA), and other clusters. "Other clusters" are as defined by the Office of Management and Budget (OMB) in the compliance supplement or as designated by a state for federal awards the state provides to its subrecipients that meet the definition of a cluster of programs.

Cognizant agency for audit: the federal agency designated to carry out the responsibilities described in Circular A-133.

Compliance supplement: the *Circular A-133 Compliance Supplement,* included as Appendix B to Circular A-133, or such documents as OMB or its designee may issue to replace it. (This document is available at the OMB Web site.)

Corrective action: action taken by the auditee that:

(1) Corrects identified deficiencies;

(2) *Produces recommended improvements; or*

(3) Demonstrates that audit findings are either invalid or do not warrant action by the audited entity.

Federal awarding agency: the federal agency that provides an award directly to the recipient.

Federal financial assistance (FFA): assistance that nonfederal entities receive or administer in the form of grants, loans, loan guarantees, property (including donated surplus property), cooperative agreements, interest subsidies, insurance, food commodities, direct appropriations, and other assistance; it does not include amounts received as reimbursement for services rendered to individuals.

Federal program:

(1) All federal awards to a nonfederal entity assigned a single number in the *CFDA.*

(2) *When no CFDA number is assigned, all federal awards from the same agency made for the same purpose should be combined and considered one program.*

(3) *Notwithstanding paragraphs (1) and (2) of this definition, a cluster of programs. The types of clusters of programs are*

(i) Research and development (R&D)

(ii) Student financial aid (SFA); and

(iii) "Other clusters," as described in the definition of cluster of programs in this section.

GAGAS: generally accepted government auditing standards issued by the Comptroller General of the United States, which are applicable to financial audits.

Internal control: a process, effected by an entity's management and other personnel, designed to provide reasonable assurance regarding the achievement of objectives in the following categories:

(1) Effectiveness and efficiency of operations;

(2) *Reliability of financial reporting; and*

(3) Compliance with applicable laws and regulations.

Internal control pertaining to the compliance requirements for federal programs (internal control over federal programs): a process—effected by an entity's management and other personnel—designed to provide reasonable assurance regarding the achievement of the following objectives for federal programs:

(1) Transactions are properly recorded and accounted for to

(i) Permit the preparation of reliable federal financial reports;

(ii) Maintain accountability over assets; and

(iii) Demonstrate compliance with laws, regulations, and other compliance requirements.

(2) Transactions are executed in compliance with

    (i) Laws, regulations, and the provisions of contracts or grant agreements that could have a direct and material effect on a federal program; and

    (ii) Any other laws and regulations that are identified in the compliance supplement.

(3) Funds, property, and other assets are safeguarded against loss from unauthorized use or disposition.

Major programs: a federal program determined by the auditor to be a major program in accordance with Circular A-133 guidelines or a program identified as a major program by a federal agency or pass-through entity.

Management decision: the evaluation by the federal awarding agency or pass-through entity of the audit findings and corrective action plan and the issuance of a written decision on what corrective action is necessary.

OMB: the Executive Office of the President, Office of Management and Budget.

Oversight agency for audit: the federal awarding agency that provides the predominant amount of direct funding to a recipient not assigned a cognizant agency for audit. When there is no direct funding, the federal agency with the pre-dominant indirect funding shall assume the oversight responsibilities. (A federal agency can reassign its oversight role to another federal agency that (1) provides substantial funding and (2) agrees to be the oversight agency.)

Pass-through entity: a nonfederal entity that provides a federal award to a subrecipient to carry out a federal program.

Program-specific audit: an audit of one federal program (rather than a single audit) as provided for in Circular A-133.

Questioned cost: a cost that is questioned by the auditor because of an audit finding:

(1) That resulted from a violation or possible violation of a provision of a law, regulation, contract, grant, cooperative agreement, or other agreement or document governing the use of federal funds, including funds used to match federal funds;

(2) When the costs, at the time of the audit, are not supported by adequate documentation; or

(3) When the costs incurred appear unreasonable and do not reflect the actions a prudent person would take under the circumstances.

Recipient: a nonfederal entity that expends federal awards received directly from a federal awarding agency to carry out a federal program.

Single Audit: an audit that includes both the entity's financial statements and the federal awards as described in OMB Circular A-133.

Subrecipient: a nonfederal entity that expends federal awards received from a pass-through entity to carry out a federal program but does not include an individual that is a beneficiary of such a program. A subrecipient may also be a recipient of other federal awards directly from a federal awarding agency.

Types of compliance requirements: the types of compliance requirements listed in the compliance supplement. Examples include activities allowed or unallowed; allowable costs/cost principles; cash management; eligibility; matching, level of effort, and earmarking; and reporting period.

APPENDIX 20-2

Data Collection Form for Reporting on Audits of States, Local Governments, and Nonprofit Organizations

Office of Management and Budget (OMB) Form SF-SAC, "Data Collection Form for Reporting on Audits of States, Local Governments, and Non-Profit Organizations," is reproduced on pages 812–814:

- To illustrate how the results of a Single Audit (or program-specific audit) are summarized in a brief uniform informational report, and
- To provide a succinct summary of many of the discussions and illustrations in this chapter.

OMB No. 0348-0057

FORM **SF-SAC**
(12-15-2009)

U.S. DEPT. OF COMM.– Econ. and Stat. Admin.– U.S. CENSUS BUREAU
ACTING AS COLLECTING AGENT FOR
OFFICE OF MANAGEMENT AND BUDGET

Data Collection Form for Reporting on
AUDITS OF STATES, LOCAL GOVERNMENTS, AND NON-PROFIT ORGANIZATIONS
for Fiscal Year Ending Dates in 2010, 2011, or 2012

▶ Complete this form, as required by OMB Circular A-133, "Audits of States, Local Governments, and Non-Profit Organizations."

PART I	**GENERAL INFORMATION** *(To be completed by auditee, except for Items 6, 7, and 8)*

1. Fiscal period ending date for this submission

Month Day Year
/ /

2. Type of Circular A-133 audit
1 ☐ Single audit
2 ☐ Program-specific audit

3. Audit period covered
1 ☐ Annual 3 ☐ Other – [ ] Months
2 ☐ Biennial

4. Auditee Identification Numbers

a. Primary Employer Identification Number (EIN)

[ ][ ] – [ ][ ][ ][ ][ ][ ][ ]

d. Data Universal Numbering System (DUNS) Number

[ ][ ] – [ ][ ][ ] – [ ][ ][ ][ ]

b. Are multiple EINs covered in this report? 1 ☐ Yes 2 ☐ No

e. Are multiple DUNS covered in this report? 1 ☐ Yes 2 ☐ No

c. If Part I, Item 4b = "Yes," complete Part I, Item 4c on the continuation sheet on Page 4.

f. If Part I, Item 4e = "Yes," complete Part I, Item 4f on the continuation sheet on Page 4.

5. AUDITEE INFORMATION

a. Auditee name

b. Auditee address *(Number and street)*

City

State ZIP + 4 Code [ ][ ][ ][ ][ ] – [ ][ ][ ][ ]

c. Auditee contact
Name

Title

d. Auditee contact telephone
( ) –

e. Auditee contact FAX
( )

f. Auditee contact E-mail

g. AUDITEE CERTIFICATION STATEMENT – This is to certify that, to the best of my knowledge and belief, the auditee has: (1) engaged an auditor to perform an audit in accordance with the provisions of OMB Circular A-133 for the period described in Part I, Items 1 and 3; (2) the auditor has completed such audit and presented a signed audit report which states that the audit was conducted in accordance with the provisions of the Circular; and, (3) the information included in **Parts I, II,** and **III** of this data collection form is accurate and complete. I declare that the foregoing is true and correct.

Auditee certification   Date

Name of certifying official

Title of certifying official

6. PRIMARY AUDITOR INFORMATION
(To be completed by auditor)

a. Primary auditor name

b. Primary auditor address *(Number and street)*

City

State ZIP + 4 Code [ ][ ][ ][ ][ ] – [ ][ ][ ][ ]

c. Primary auditor contact
Name

Title

d. Primary auditor contact telephone
( ) –

e. Primary auditor contact FAX
( )

f. Primary auditor contact E-mail

g. AUDITOR STATEMENT – The data elements and information included in this form are limited to those prescribed by OMB Circular A-133. The information included in Parts II and III of the form, except for Part III, Items 7, 8, and 9a-9g, was transferred from the auditor's report(s) for the period described in Part I, Items 1 and 3, and **is not a substitute** for such reports. The auditor has not performed any auditing procedures since the date of the auditor's report(s). A copy of the reporting package required by OMB Circular A-133, which includes the complete auditor's report(s), is available in its entirety from the auditee at the address provided in Part I of this form. As required by OMB Circular A-133, the information in **Parts II** and **III** of this form was entered in this form by the auditor based on information included in the reporting package. The auditor has not performed any additional auditing procedures in connection with the completion of this form.

7a. Add Secondary auditor information? (Optional)
1 ☐ Yes 2 ☐ No

b. If "Yes," complete **Part I, Item 8** on the continuation sheet on page 5.

Auditor certification   Date

Primary EIN: ☐☐ – ☐☐☐☐☐☐☐

PART II	FINANCIAL STATEMENTS *(To be completed by auditor)*

1. Type of audit report

Mark either: 1 ☐ Unqualified opinion **OR**

any combination of: 2 ☐ Qualified opinion 3 ☐ Adverse opinion 4 ☐ Disclaimer of opinion

2. Is a "going concern" explanatory paragraph included in the audit report? 1 ☐ Yes 2 ☐ No

3. Is a significant deficiency disclosed? 1 ☐ Yes 2 ☐ No – *SKIP to Item 5*

4. Is any significant deficiency reported as a material weakness? 1 ☐ Yes 2 ☐ No

5. Is a material noncompliance disclosed? 1 ☐ Yes 2 ☐ No

PART III	FEDERAL PROGRAMS *(To be completed by auditor)*

1. Does the auditor's report include a statement that the auditee's financial statements include departments, agencies, or other organizational units expending $500,000 or more in Federal awards that have separate A-133 audits which are not included in this audit? (AICPA Audit Guide, Chapter 12) 1 ☐ Yes 2 ☐ No

2. What is the dollar threshold to distinguish Type A and Type B programs? (OMB Circular A-133 §___ .520(b)) $ _____

3. Did the auditee qualify as a low-risk auditee? (§___ .530) 1 ☐ Yes 2 ☐ No

4. Is a significant deficiency disclosed for any major program? (§ ___ .510(a)(1)) 1 ☐ Yes 2 ☐ No – *SKIP to Item 6*

5. Is any significant deficiency reported for any major program as a material weakness? (§ ___ .510(a)(1)) 1 ☐ Yes 2 ☐ No

6. Are any known questioned costs reported? (§ ___ .510(a)(3) or (4)) 1 ☐ Yes 2 ☐ No

7. Were Prior Audit Findings related to **direct** funding shown in the Summary Schedule of Prior Audit Findings? (§___.315(b)) 1 ☐ Yes 2 ☐ No

8. Indicate which **Federal** agency(ies) have current year audit findings related to **direct** funding or prior audit findings shown in the Summary Schedule of Prior Audit Findings related to **direct** funding. *(Mark (X) all that apply or None)*

98 ☐ U.S. Agency for International Development

10 ☐ Agriculture

23 ☐ Appalachian Regional Commission

11 ☐ Commerce

94 ☐ Corporation for National and Community Service

12 ☐ Defense

84 ☐ Education

81 ☐ Energy

66 ☐ Environmental Protection Agency

39 ☐ General Services Administration

93 ☐ Health and Human Services

97 ☐ Homeland Security

14 ☐ Housing and Urban Development

03 ☐ Institute of Museum and Library Services

15 ☐ Interior

16 ☐ Justice

17 ☐ Labor

09 ☐ Legal Services Corporation

43 ☐ National Aeronautics and Space Administration

89 ☐ National Archives and Records Administration

05 ☐ National Endowment for the Arts

06 ☐ National Endowment for the Humanities

47 ☐ National Science Foundation

07 ☐ Office of National Drug Control Policy

59 ☐ Small Business Administration

96 ☐ Social Security Administration

19 ☐ U.S. Department of State

20 ☐ Transportation

21 ☐ Treasury

64 ☐ Veterans Affairs

00 ☐ **None**

☐ Other – *Specify:*

_____

_____

Primary EIN: ☐☐ – ☐☐☐☐☐☐☐

PART III	FEDERAL PROGRAMS – Continued

9. FEDERAL AWARDS EXPENDED DURING FISCAL YEAR

10. AUDIT FINDINGS

CFDA Number		Research and develop-ment	A R R A³	Name of Federal program	Amount expended	Direct award	Major program		Type(s) of compliance requirement(s)⁵	Audit finding reference number(s)⁶
Federal Agency Prefix¹ (a)	Extension² (b)	(c)	(d)	(e)	(f)	Direct award (g)	Major program (h)	If yes, type of audit report⁴ (i)	(a)	(b)
.	.	1☐Y 2☐N	1☐Y 2☐N		$ .00	1☐Y 2☐N	1☐Y 2☐N	1☐Y 2☐N		
.	.	1☐Y 2☐N	1☐Y 2☐N		$ .00	1☐Y 2☐N	1☐Y 2☐N	1☐Y 2☐N		
.	.	1☐Y 2☐N	1☐Y 2☐N		$ .00	1☐Y 2☐N	1☐Y 2☐N	1☐Y 2☐N		
.	.	1☐Y 2☐N	1☐Y 2☐N		$ .00	1☐Y 2☐N	1☐Y 2☐N	1☐Y 2☐N		
.	.	1☐Y 2☐N	1☐Y 2☐N		$ .00	1☐Y 2☐N	1☐Y 2☐N	1☐Y 2☐N		
.	.	1☐Y 2☐N	1☐Y 2☐N		$ .00	1☐Y 2☐N	1☐Y 2☐N	1☐Y 2☐N		
.	.	1☐Y 2☐N	1☐Y 2☐N		$ .00	1☐Y 2☐N	1☐Y 2☐N	1☐Y 2☐N		
.	.	1☐Y 2☐N	1☐Y 2☐N		$ .00	1☐Y 2☐N	1☐Y 2☐N	1☐Y 2☐N		
.	.	1☐Y 2☐N	1☐Y 2☐N		$ .00	1☐Y 2☐N	1☐Y 2☐N	1☐Y 2☐N		
.	.	1☐Y 2☐N	1☐Y 2☐N		$ .00	1☐Y 2☐N	1☐Y 2☐N	1☐Y 2☐N		

TOTAL FEDERAL AWARDS EXPENDED ⟶ $ .00

¹ See Appendix 1 of instructions for valid Federal Agency two-digit prefixes.
² Or other identifying number when the Catalog of Federal Domestic Assistance (CFDA) number is not available. (See Instructions).
³ American Recovery and Reinvestment Act of 2009 (ARRA).
⁴ If major program is marked "Yes," enter only one letter (**U** = Unqualified opinion, **Q** = Qualified opinion, **A** = Adverse opinion, **D** = Disclaimer of opinion) corresponding to the type of audit report in the adjacent box. If major program is marked "No," leave the type of audit report box blank.
⁵ Enter the letter(s) of all type(s) of compliance requirement(s) that apply to audit findings (i.e., noncompliance, significant deficiency (including material weaknesses), questioned costs, fraud, and other items reported under §___.510(a)) reported for each Federal program.

A. Activities allowed or unallowed
B. Allowable costs/cost principles
C. Cash management
D. Davis – Bacon Act
E. Eligibility
F. Equipment and real property management
G. Matching, level of effort, earmarking
H. Period of availability of Federal funds
I. Procurement and suspension and debarment
J. Program income
K. Real property acquisition and relocation assistance
L. Reporting
M. Subrecipient monitoring
N. Special tests and provisions
O. None
P. Other

⁶ N/A for NONE

Q20-1 Compare the responsibilities of a local government's officers and its independent auditor for the financial report.

Q20-2 A municipality requires auditors to submit bids of their charges for the annual audit. The audit contract is awarded to the lowest bidder. What could be wrong with this method of engaging auditors?

Q20-3 The comptroller of D City is responsible for approval of all city receipts and disbursements. The city council takes the position that, because the comptroller is auditing both receipts and disbursements for accuracy and legality, no additional audit by independent accountants is necessary. What position would you, a new council member, take?

Q20-4 What are the responsibilities of the government being audited with respect to the Single Audit report? (Hint: See text and Federal Audit Clearinghouse, http://harvester.census.gov/sac.)

Q20-5 Describe the nature of a Single Audit of a state or local government.

Q20-6 When is a state or local government required to have a Single Audit?

Q20-7 Explain how both program size and related risk factors affect the decision about which federal award programs are considered major programs.

Q20-8 What advantages accrue to the auditee and auditor if the auditee subject to Single Audit qualifies as a low-risk auditee? What criteria must be met?

Q20-9 Distinguish between major and nonmajor federal financial assistance award programs. Why is this distinction important?

Q20-10 Auditing has been defined as the process of collecting and evaluating evidence to formulate an opinion about assertions made by management. What assertions does the external auditor address in an opinion as the result of a financial audit? What assertions does the external auditor address in giving an opinion as the result of a performance audit? What assertions does the external auditor address in giving an opinion as the result of a compliance audit of a MFAP?

Q20-11 The state auditor has for years been responsible for examinations of the financial operations of all state agencies. A bill is under consideration to make the state auditor the chief accounting officer of the state as well. You are testifying before a legislative committee that is considering the bill. What is the tenor of your testimony?

Q20-12 (a) What types of reports are required to be presented as a result of a Single Audit? (b) How many are "opinion" reports? (c) How many quantitative materiality thresholds are apparent in these Single Audit reports?

Q20-13 What is a cognizant agency? What are its responsibilities? Which federal agency would be the cognizant agency for smaller governments such as the city of Providence, Kentucky, which has a population of approximately 2,500?

Q20-14 What is the OMB Compliance Supplement? What is its purpose?

Q20-15 Distinguish between the internal control evaluation required for MFAPs and for non-MFAPs. What level of internal control evaluation is required if a government has no MFAPs?

Q20-16 Distinguish the compliance audit requirements for MFAPs from those for non-MFAPs. What requirements apply if there are no MFAPs?

Q20-17 What types of audit findings could result from a single audit? Explain.

Q20-18 Briefly summarize the GAGAS "independence" conceptual framework and standards.

Q20-19 (Research & Analysis) The "Advance Notice" referred to at the end of this chapter—the Advance Notice of Proposed Guidance titled *Reform of Federal Policies Related to Grants and Cooperative Agreements; cost principles and administrative requirements (including Single Audit Act)*—may have been approved as exposed, changed considerably, or withdrawn. Conduct Internet and/or library research sufficient to write a brief 1–3 page "update" paper for your professor and classmates.

Exercises

E20-1 (Multiple Choice) Identify the best answer for each of the following:
1. A financial audit for a governmental entity may
   a. be primarily concerned with providing reasonable assurance that financial statements are in conformity with GAAP.
   b. be primarily concerned with providing reasonable assurance that financial statements are in conformity with a comprehensive basis of accounting other than GAAP.
   c. provide for differing levels of assurance and entail various scopes of work.
   d. be focused on items a, b, or c.
   e. be focused on items a and b only.

2. For which of the following functions is the management of a governmental entity *not* primarily responsible?
   a. Recording financial and other economic events
   b. Reporting financial and other economic events
   c. Asserting that management has complied with the law
   d. Ensuring that internal controls are adequate and functioning properly
   e. Management is primarily responsible for *all* of the above functions

3. Which of the following statements regarding generally accepted auditing standards is *false*?
   a. The AICPA's auditing standards apply only to private sector audits since public sector audits have their own unique standards.
   b. Generally accepted government audit standards (GAGAS) are established by the Government Accountability Office.
   c. The AICPA auditing standards are adopted and incorporated into GAGAS.
   d. If GAGAS is being applied, the audit report must include a statement that indicates the audit was conducted in accordance with GAGAS.
   e. The AICPA Audit and Accounting Guides have specific recommended procedures that are applicable to governmental audits.

4. Which of the following is *not* a characteristic of GAGAS?
   a. An auditor must make written reports on tests of compliance.
   b. Specific continuing professional educational requirements for auditors of state and local governments.
   c. Independence standards that *do not* limit nonaudit-related work.
   d. Additional supplemental standards for governmental audits.
   e. All of the above are characteristic of governmental audits.

5. The *minimum* audit scope that should be accepted by external auditors of state and local governmental entities, as per the GASB, is
   a. the government-wide financial statements.
   b. the basic financial statements.
   c. the fund financial statements.
   d. the combining and individual fund financial statements.
   e. the primary government.

6. Who is assigned by the OMB to oversee implementation of the Single Audit of states and local governments that expend more than $50 million of federal financial assistance annually?
   a. External independent auditors
   b. Federal cognizant agencies
   c. AICPA
   d. Government Accountability Office
   e. Auditor General of the United States Department of Treasury

7. Which of the following is *not* a topic area OMB Circular A-133 identifies as being a specific responsibility of the auditor?
   a. Financial statements
   b. Internal control
   c. Fraud identification
   d. Data collection form
   e. Compliance
   f. All of the above are cited as being specific auditor responsibilities.

8. The Schedule of Findings and Questioned Costs would potentially include all of the following *except*
   a. information on the type of report the auditor issued on the *financial statements* of the auditee, but only if a qualified or adverse opinion was rendered.
   b. information on the type of report the auditor issued on the *financial statements* of the auditee, regardless of the opinion rendered.
   c. the dollar threshold used to distinguish between Type A and Type B programs.
   d. a statement regarding significant deficiencies in internal control, if applicable.
   e. Items b and d.
   f. Items a and d.

9. Which of the following statements regarding an auditor's engagement is *false*?
   a. Audit agreements should be formalized in a written audit contract.
   b. GAGAS require audit services to be formally bid.
   c. The auditor engaged for the financial audit may not be the auditor engaged for the entity's single audit.
   d. Audit contracts should specify how unexpected problems, such as the discovery of fraud, will be handled.
   e. Audit contracts should specify how materiality will be evaluated.

10. Which of the following statements regarding the Single Audit approach is *true*?
    a. Grantor agencies have the right to require additional work above and beyond Single Audit requirements, but only when fraud is suspected.
    b. Grantor agencies have the right to require additional work above and beyond Single Audit requirements, but only if the grant exceeds $500,000 in a given fiscal year.

c. Grantor agencies have the right to require additional work above and beyond Single Audit requirements, but at the cost of the grantor agency.

d. Grantor agencies have the right to require additional work above and beyond the Single Audit requirements and the additional costs are borne by the grantee.

e. Grantor agencies do *not* have the right to require audit work above and beyond the Single Audit requirements.

E20-2 (Multiple Choice) Identify the best answer for each of the following:

1. Generally accepted government auditing standards are issued by the
   a. Office of Management and Budget.
   b. Government Accountability Office.
   c. Governmental Accounting Standards Board.
   d. Auditing Standards Board.
   e. Department of the Treasury.

2. In performing audits under the Single Audit Act, auditors must comply with
   a. generally accepted auditing standards (GAAS).
   b. generally accepted government auditing standards (GAGAS).
   c. both GAAS and GAGAS.
   d. neither GAAS nor GAGAS because the provisions of the Act override both.

3. Which of the following would *not* be an element of a Single Audit?
   a. Determination of whether the government's financial statements are fairly presented
   b. Determination of whether the government has established adequate internal control systems
   c. Determination of whether the government has complied with laws and regulations relating to major federal financial assistance programs
   d. Determination of whether the government has accurately listed the federal financial assistance it has expended during the period in its schedule of expenditures of federal awards
   e. None of the above

4. During the 20X9 fiscal year, the city of Metropolis Human Services Department spent $410,000 of a $450,000 federal grant. The only other Metropolis department or agency that received a federal grant during the fiscal year was its Police Department, which received a $295,000 federal grant and spent $195,000 of that grant. The city of Metropolis
   a. is exempt from all auditing requirements for the 20X9 fiscal year.
   b. is exempt from audit requirements for the 20X9 fiscal year but is required to keep adequate accounting records and to make them available for inspection and audit upon request.
   c. must either have a Single Audit or, at the grantor's option, a Program-Specific Audit for the 20X9 fiscal year.
   d. must have a Single Audit for the 20X9 fiscal year.
   e. None of the above.

5. Which of the following statements are accurate depictions of either performance audits or financial audits?
   a. Performance audits do not focus on an entity's conformity to GAAP while financial statement audits do have that primary focus.
   b. Performance audits may provide information to improve program operations.
   c. Performance audits, unlike financial audits, *do not* evaluate or address internal control issues.
   d. All of the above are accurate depictions of performance and financial audit characteristics.
   e. Items a and b only.
   f. Items b and c only.

6. Consider the following facts and events concerning the city of Tampando and its airport (reported as an enterprise fund of the city):
   - The city's fiscal year end is December 31.
   - The city was awarded a $9,000,000 construction cost-reimbursement construction grant in December 20X6.
   - The city expended $9,000,000 for the project in November 20X7.
   - The reimbursement was received in January 20X8.
   The city must have a Single Audit because of grant expenditures in
   a. 20X6.
   b. 20X7.
   c. 20X8.
   d. All of these years.

7. The state of Oklabraska spent a total of $525,000 in federal financial assistance during its 20X8 fiscal year. It passed on $60,000 of these grants to the city of Lineman to help finance a pilot police training program. The city of Lineman also spent $300,000 in financial assistance directly from federal government agencies during fiscal 20X8. Which government(s) would be required to have a Single Audit for the 20X8 fiscal year?
   a. The state of Oklabraska only
   b. The city of Lineman only
   c. Both the state of Oklabraska and the city of Lineman
   d. Neither the state of Oklabraska nor the city of Lineman

8. In fiscal year 20X8, the city of Celtics received $7,000,000 in federal financial assistance and incurred $6,000,000 in federal financial assistance program expenditures. During the same fiscal year the city of Lakers received $12,000,000 in federal financial assistance and made $11,500,000 in federal financial assistance program expenditures. Each city received $310,000 for and expended $290,000 on a driver safety education program (not risky) financed by the U.S. Department of Transportation. This program would constitute a major federal assistance program
   a. for Celtics but not for Lakers.
   b. for Lakers but not for Celtics.
   c. for both Celtics and Lakers.
   d. for neither Celtics nor Lakers.

9. Cognizant agencies are assigned to
   a. state governments.
   b. large local governments.
   c. small governments.
   d. both items a and b.
   e. both items b and c.
   f. all governments.

10. The city of Lukeville (not a low-risk auditee) has three major federal assistance programs (none high-risk) with the following expenditures in 20X7:

Program	Expenditures
A	$2,000,000
B	1,000,000
C	500,000

If the city has total federal assistance expenditures for 20X7 of $5,500,000, Lukeville's Single Audit should include a study and evaluation of internal controls of the type conducted when intending to rely on those controls to reduce substantive testing for which programs?
   a. Program A
   b. Program B
   c. Program C
   d. Both A and B
   e. All three programs

E20-3 (Matching Government Audit Terms) Place the letter of the terms at the right to the left of the numbered terms at the left. The same term at the right may be a proper match in more than one instance, and one or more of the terms may have an appropriate match:

1. AICPA	a.	ASLGU
2. Auditee	b.	Audited Nonfederal Entity
3. Data Collection Form	c.	Expend $.01 of FFA
4. FFA	d.	Expend $5.00 of FFA
5. GAGAS	e.	Expend $500,000 of FFA
6. GAO Auditing Standards	f.	Expend $1,000,000 of FFA
7. Low-Risk Auditee	g.	Federal Food Audit
8. Program-Specific Audit	h.	Federal Financial Assistance
9. Risk-Based Approach—Major Programs	i.	GAO Auditing Standards
10. Schedule of Expenditures of Federal Awards	j.	Government Auditing Standards
	k.	OMB Circular A-133
11. Single Audit Standards	l.	Receive $.01 of FFA
12. Single Audit Threshold	m.	Receive $500,000 of FFA
13. Type A	n.	Smaller FFA Programs
14. Type B	o.	Larger FFA Programs
15. Yellow Book	p.	Statements on Auditing Standards (SAS)

E20-4 (Matching Organizations and Audit Terms) Indicate the organization that is most closely associated with the terms at the left. An organization may be associated with more than one term or with none of the terms.

____ 1. ASLGU	a.	American Accounting Association (AAA)
____ 2. Data Collection Form	b.	American Institute of Certified Public Accountants (AICPA)
____ 3. Economy Audits		
____ 4. Efficiency Audits	c.	Association of Government Accountants (AGA)

_____ 5. Financial Audits
_____ 6. Low-Risk Auditee
_____ 7. Opinion on Major FFA Program Compliance
_____ 8. Opinion on Financial Statements
_____ 9. Opinion on Supplemental Schedule of Expenditures of Federal Awards
_____ 10. Opinion Units
_____ 11. Performance Audits
_____ 12. Report on Entity's Compliance with Laws and Regulations
_____ 13. Report on Entity's Control Structure
_____ 14. Report on Internal Controls over Major FFA Programs
_____ 15. Report on Prior Audit Findings
_____ 16. Report on Schedule of Prior Audit Findings
_____ 17. Reporting Units
_____ 18. Schedule of Findings and Questioned Costs

d. Government Accountability Office (GAO)
e. Government Finance Officers Association (GFOA)
f. Office of Management and Budget (OMB)
g. Electronic Municipal Market Access (EMMA)
h. Municipal Securities Rulemaking Board (MSRB)

Problems

P20-1 (Single Audit) The A City schedule of expenditures of federal awards is presented in Illustration 20-10. If A City is not a low-risk auditee and this is the first year under new auditors, what level of internal control and compliance auditing work should be performed for each of the city's programs? Justify your response.

P20-2 (Single Audit—Various) Following are the expenditures incurred in 20X5 and 20X6 by Thompson County under each of its federal assistance programs.

Federal Program	Grant	20X5 Expenditures	20X6 Expenditures
A	1	$ 380,000	$ 40,000
	2	75,000	320,000
	3	60,000	100,000
B		271,000	250,000
C		3,000,000	220,000
D		500,000	—
E	1	80,000	280,000
	2	130,000	110,000
Total		$4,496,000	$1,320,000

Required

1. Which of Thompson County's federal financial assistance programs are Type A federal assistance programs in 20X5? In 20X6?
2. If _no_ Type A programs are considered low-risk, which programs are major? What level of internal control study and evaluation must be performed for each major program in 20X5 under the single audit requirements? In 20X6?
3. What level of compliance auditing is required for each major program in 20X5 under the single audit requirements? In 20X6?

P20-3 (Major Program Determination) Sharendale County expended $7,000,000 of federal financial assistance during 20X9 in the following programs:

Federal Program	Expenditures	Risk Assessment
A	$1,100,000	Low
B	1,500,000	High
C	900,000	High

Federal Program	Expenditures	Risk Assessment
D	2,500,000	Low
E	800,000	Low
F	200,000	—
	$7,000,000	

Required

1. Assume that Sharendale County is *not* a low-risk auditee and programs A–E had been audited as major programs in one of the two previous years. Which programs will probably be selected as major programs this year?
2. Assume that Sharendale County *is* a low-risk auditee and programs A–E had been audited as major programs in one of the two previous years. Which programs will probably be selected as major programs this year?

P20-4 (Major Program Determination) A government receives and expends funds under several federal programs during 20X7. The programs and amounts expended follow:

Program A	$ 290,000
Program B	$ 500,000
Program C	$1,000,000
Program D	$ 250,000
Program E	$ 180,000
Program F	$ 700,000
Program G	$ 220,000
Program H	$ 150,000
Program I	$ 230,000
Program J	$ 475,000

Programs C and J have been audited as major programs (with no audit findings) in the past two years.

Required Which programs would you treat as major programs in a single audit for 20X7 if the government is not a low-risk auditee? Document the basis for your decision, including any risk assessments that you would conduct. (Indicate programs that you have assessed as high risk—that is, assume that some are high risk and indicate them.)

P20-5 (Research and Analysis—Single Audit) Obtain a copy of a recent single audit report and evaluate it in terms of the requirements for single audit reports discussed in this chapter. Prepare a brief report (5–10 pages) summarizing your analyses, findings, and conclusions, and attach a photocopy of any unusual or otherwise noteworthy examples.

P20-6 (Research and Analysis—GAGAS) Obtain and evaluate copies of at least three GAGAS auditor reports. Write a brief paper (3–8 pages) summarizing your research and findings, and attach copies of the most useful Web sites and selected other pages.

P20-7 (Research and Analysis—Audit Reports) Locate several recent GAGAS and single audit reports—including those from your home municipality or county—and compare them to
1. the standards and guidelines discussed and illustrated in this chapter and
2. each other.

Write a brief (6–12 pages) summary of your findings.

P20-8 (Research and Analysis—Independence Standards) Analyze the sections of the GAO Standards that deal with independence and condense the essence of these standards to an 8- to 10-page paper (or article) or one or more succinct tabular or graphical illustrations.

Cases

C20-1 (Impact of Legislation on Auditor's Report) Recent State of Texas legislation gives local governments the option of implementing, or not implementing, GASB *Statement No. 45* on Other Postemployment Benefits (OPEB). The officials of your audit client, Travail County, are concerned that implementing GASB *Statement No. 45* will lead to news media criticism of their long-standing commitments to pay substantial amounts of retiree health care insurance premiums, rating agency concerns or even bond rating downgrades, and, ultimately, recognition of large liabilities in the county's Statement of Net Assets.

The county attorney's opinion is that the county should not implement GASB *Statement No. 45*. "We're not legally required to implement GASB *Statement No. 45*," he notes, "so why should we do it, especially if it will be controversial?" One of the county commissioners is concerned, however, that the auditor may have to issue a qualified or even adverse opinion on the county's financial statements. "Nonsense," said another commissioner, a CPA who was in practice before becoming a county commissioner 14 years ago. "By state law we have the option to implement, or not implement, GASB S45. If we do implement, we comply with GAAP, and if we don't, we are in compliance with what is known as a *comprehensive basic of accounting other than GAAP, so the auditor's report should not have to be qualified or adverse.*" They then turn to you and ask, "How will our not implementing GASB S45 affect your auditor's report on our financial statements?"

Required

Based on this chapter and further research, including professional articles and Internet research (e.g., http://www.aicpa.org), draft a letter responding to these questions and concerns. Your letter should be specific with respect to the type of auditor's report (opinion) that will be appropriate should the county not implement GASB S45.

C20-2 (Evaluating Single Audit Findings and Questioned Costs) A recent single audit report for the County of Alameda, California, contains the following: "**I. Summary of Auditor's Results**." Based on the content of this chapter, information contained in the AICPA Website (www.aicpa.org) and these excerpts from the county's Single Audit Report, analyze and respond briefly to the following questions.

Part 1: Financial Statement Audit (GAGAS). **Refer to items 1–3 in the county's Schedule of Findings and Questioned Costs that follows:**

a. Which of these is based primarily on the AICPA audit standards? The GAO auditing standards?
b. What are *significant deficiencies* in internal controls? What are *material weaknesses*?
c. How could the auditor properly render an unqualified opinion on the financial statements if there are material weaknesses in internal controls over financial reporting, *significant deficiencies* and material weaknesses in internal control over major programs, and several qualified opinions on major program compliance?

Part 2: Single Audit (OMB Circular A-133). **Refer to items 4–9.**

d. Explain the focus difference(s) between the item 2 and item 4 reports on internal control.
e. Explain the focus difference(s) between item 3 and item 5.
f. How can a single auditor's report contain both qualified and unqualified opinions? Explain.
g. What does the term "cluster" mean in item 7?
h. Item 9 states that the auditee is <u>not</u> a *low-risk auditee*. Explain why the county might not qualify as a low-risk auditee.

COUNTY OF ALAMEDA, CALIFORNIA
Schedule of Findings and Questioned Costs
Year ended June 30, 20X3

I. **Summary of Auditors' Results**
1. The type of report issued on the basic financial statements: **Unqualified Opinion**.
2. Significant deficiencies in internal control over financial reporting were disclosed by the audit of the basic financial statements: **Yes**. Material weaknesses: **Yes**
3. Noncompliance that is material to the basic financial statements: **No**
4. Significant deficiencies in internal control over major programs: **Yes**. Material weaknesses: **Yes**
5. The type of report issued on compliance for major programs: **Unqualified, except for 10.551, 10.561, 84.027, 93.558, and 93.959, which were qualified**
6. Any audit findings that are required to be reported under Section 510(a) of OMB Circular A-133: **Yes**
7. Major programs:

Program	CFDA	Type of Report Issued
Food Stamps Cluster:		
Food Stamps	10.551	Qualified
State Administrative Matching Grants for Food Stamps Program	10.561	Qualified
Supportive Housing Program	14.235	Unqualified
Shelter Plus Care	14.238	Unqualified
Violent Offender Incarceration and Truth in Sentencing Incentive Grants	16.586	Unqualified
Workforce Investment Act Cluster:		
Workforce Investment Act—Adult Programs	17.258	Unqualified
Workforce Investment Act—Youth Activities	17.259	Unqualified
Workforce Investment Act—Dislocated Workers/Rapid Response—Title 1	17.260	Unqualified
Special Education Cluster—Grants to States	84.027	Qualified

Program	CFDA	Type of Report Issued
Aging Cluster:		
Special Programs for the Aging—Title III		
Part B—Grants for Supportive Services and Senior Centers	93.044	Unqualified
Special Programs for the Aging—Title III		
Part C—Nutritional Services	93.045	Unqualified
Nutrition Services Incentive Program	93.053	Unqualified
Temporary Assistance for Needy Families	93.558	Qualified
Child Support Enforcement	93.563	Unqualified
Foster Care—Title IV, Part E	93.658	Unqualified
Adoption Assistance	93.659	Unqualified
Medical Assistance Program (Medicaid)	93.778	Unqualified
HIV Emergency Relief Project Grants	93.914	Unqualified
Block Grants for Prevention and Treatment of Substance Abuse	93.959	Qualified

8. Dollar threshold used to distinguish between Type A and B programs: **$3,000,000**
9. Auditee qualified as a low-risk auditee under Section 530 of OMB Circular A-133: **No**

Index

A

G